Cooking at High Altitudes

Every increase in elevation brings a decrease in air pressure, which results in a lower boiling point. At 7,000 feet, for example—the altitude of many towns in the Southwest—water boils at 199°F. This means slower cooking times (and makes a pressure cooker a more desirable appliance). Families who have been living in the mountains for years have already discovered, though trial and error, the best ways to adjust. Newcomers to high altitudes must be patient and experiment to discover what works best, under which specific conditions. But here are some general tips for high-altitude cooking:

1. For stovetop cooking, use higher heat when practical; extend cooking times as necessary. Beans and grains will require significantly more time than at sea level.

2. Assume that batters and doughs will rise faster than at sea level.

3. Over 3,000 feet, increase baking temperatures by 25 degrees F.

4. Over 3,000 feet, reduce baking powder (or other leavening) measurements by about 10 percent; increase liquid in baked goods by the same percentage. You may want to reduce the amount of sugar slightly as well.

5. For every 2,000 foot increase in altitude above 3,000 feet, reduce leavening a few percentage points further.

Some Useful Substitutions

1 cup cake flour = $7/8$ cup all-purpose flour + $1/8$ cup cornstarch

1 tablespoon baking powder = 2 teaspoons baking soda + 1 teaspoon cream of tartar

1 cup buttermilk = 1 scant cup milk at room temperature + 1 tablespoon white vinegar

1 cup brown sugar = 1 cup white sugar + 2 tablespoons molasses

1 cup sour cream = 1 cup yogurt (preferably whole-milk)

Measurement Conversions

Note that volume (like 1 cup) measures and weight (like 1 ounce) measures convert perfectly for liquids only. Solids don't fit this formula; 1 cup of flour weighs only 4 or 5 ounces, not 8.

Dash or pinch = less than $1/4$ teaspoon
3 teaspoons = 1 tablespoon
2 tablespoons = 1 fluid ounce
4 tablespoons = $1/4$ cup = 2 fluid ounces
16 tablespoons = 1 cup = 8 fluid ounces
2 cups = 1 pint
2 pints = 1 quart
4 quarts = 1 gallon

Imperial Measurements

Theoretically, both the United Kingdom and Canada use the metric system, but older recipes rely on the imperial measurement system, which differs from standard U.S. measurements in its liquid (fluid) measurements:

$1/4$ cup = 2.5 ounces
$1/2$ cup (gill) = 5 ounces
1 cup = 10 ounces
1 pint = 20 ounces
1 quart = 40 ounces

Imperial vs. Metric

These are approximate but are fine for all uses:
1 ounce = 28 grams
1 pound = 500 grams or $1/2$ kilo
2.2 pounds = 1 kilo
1 teaspoon = 5 milliliters (ml)
1 tablespoon = 15 milliliters
1 cup = $1/4$ liter
1 quart = 1 liter

How to Cook
Everything®

COMPLETELY REVISED TENTH ANNIVERSARY EDITION

How to Cook *Everything*®

2,000 Simple Recipes for Great Food

Mark Bittman

Illustrations by Alan Witschonke

WILEY

John Wiley & Sons, Inc.

Library of Congress Cataloging-in-Publication Data:

Bittman, Mark.

How to cook everything : 2000 simple recipes for great food / Mark Bittman ; illustrations by Alan Witschonke.—2nd ed.

p. cm.

Includes bibliographical references and index.

ISBN 978-0-7645-7865-6 (cloth : alk. paper)

1. Cookery. I. Title.

TX714.B573 2008

641.5—dc22   2008018984

ISBN: 978-0-7645-7865-6

ISBN: 978-0-470-39857-9 (special edition)

Printed in the United States of America

10 9 8 7 6 5 4 3 2 1

Design by *Nick Anderson*

Layout by *North Market Street Graphics*

Contents

What do you need to know—and own—to make great meals? Not much.

Here's a guide to seasoning, made easy.

From no-cook to elaborate, here are finger foods, snacks, and knife-and-fork first courses.

These simple, fresh soups from around the world are surprisingly easy, with most ready in minutes, not hours.

Handheld food, including new fillings and toppings, in the time it takes to order take-out.

Crisp, crunchy, colorful, and simply dressed—few meals are quicker to make.

The ultimate lexicon of vegetables and fruit, a real primer with recipes.

Learn how to cook—and love—legumes, alone or in combination with vegetables, rice, meat, and seafood.

Acknowledgments

Given that I began writing the original *How to Cook Everything* in 1994, it almost feels as if a cast of thousands has been involved in making this series work; in fact it's been literally a cast of hundreds. Although much has changed in this second edition, I remain indebted to the people who helped me create the concept and its core, the very distinctive cookbook identity with which I'm happily associated. From those halcyon days I want to rethank especially Pam Hoenig, Jennifer Griffin, and Jack Bishop; I get nothing but warm glows whenever I see or think of any of them.

Likewise many members of the editorial, sales, production, art, and marketing teams that were involved then, at least some of whom remain. Two people who have expended enormous amounts of fruitful energy on *HTCE* over many, many years are Natalie Chapman and Linda Ingroia, and singling them out in no way diminishes the roles of people like Todd Fries, Rob Garber, Michael Olivo, Michael Friedberg, Gypsy Lovett, Jeff Faust, Alan Witschonke, and Nick Anderson. Once again I'm ecstatic to be able to thank Chris Benton, the ideal cookbook copyeditor.

Adam Kowit, the newest (and probably the youngest) member of this team, assumed the awesome and unenviable responsibility of editing an already successful book by an increasingly impatient and ever-aging author and did so with flair, ease, and skill that belied his years. Thank you, Mr. Kowit.

Amanda McDougall, who played a big role in the success of *How to Cook Everything Vegetarian,* worked with us in the early stages of this book. Suzanne Lenzer joined us when we were about halfway through and made daily and increasingly significant contributions.

When I say "we," I'm including Kerri Conan, who joined me as a younger if not junior partner four years ago and brought with her unparalleled cooking, analytic, and writing and editing skills, along with daily good spirits, wit, and joie de vivre. If this sounds like hyperbole, fine, but while I'm the name associated with *How to Cook Everything,* many of the improvements to this edition were the result of the true collaboration between us. (Kerri in turn would like to thank her husband, Sean Santoro, for his unwavering enthusiasm.)

Outside of the *How to Cook Everything* world, I'm once again joyful that my roster of friends and relatives hasn't changed much: These are David Paskin, Pamela Hort, Semeon Tsalbins, my darling little sister Shari and her husband, Harry, Charles L. Pinsky, John Ringwald, and my oldest friends, Mitch Orfuss, Mark Roth, and Fred Zolna. As always, Angela Miller and my dear friend John H. Willoughby give me amazing support day after day, year after year, and now decade after decade. (To those friends I haven't mentioned: I haven't forgotten you!)

My treasured daughters, Kate and Emma—who were cute kids when I first wrote *How to Cook Everything*—are now adults and of greater stature than ever (it won't be long before they're telling me what to do). I'm blessed by the ongoing love of my parents (and uber-fans), Murray and Gertrude Bittman. And it just gets better: There's my relentlessly optimistic wife, the Kellster.

Manhattan, Summer 2008

In loving memory of Sherry Slade, whose energy is infusing cooking somewhere.

Introduction

Much has changed in the world of food and cooking since *How to Cook Everything* was first published in 1998. Our reliance on restaurants, take-out food, and so-called convenience food has increased. Yet there has been a paradoxical resurgence in home cooking, thanks to an odd combination of renewed appreciation for simplicity and self-sufficiency, along with our newfound worship of super-ingredients and celebrity chefs.

Happily, there are now more good ingredients available to all of us than ever before. When I started cooking, thirty-five years ago, you sometimes had to visit a pharmacy to buy olive oil, and you could find ingredients like soy sauce and ginger only at Asian markets. Now you can buy nam pla (Thai fish sauce), shallots, fresh herbs, tofu, ginger, curry paste, and scores of other once-exotic ingredients at supermarkets all over the country.

This expands our potential repertoire enormously. Where "American" cooking once drew largely from northern European cuisines—these reflected, after all, the origins of many of our first citizens—we now routinely enjoy food from the rest of the world. This new edition of *How to Cook Everything* reflects that.

It also reflects my further disenchantment with what was once called *haute cuisine*—fancy food. This, I think, is best left to restaurants. So where in the original *How to Cook Everything* I made some attempts to address the needs of those who like to replicate restaurant food as a hobby, here I'm leaving most of that behind. Home cooking is best when it's simple, straightforward, unpretentious, and easy.

Our exposure to ultra-sophisticated cooking—whether at restaurants, in cookbooks, or on television—sometimes makes us forget how wonderful simple food can be. But each year I'm more satisfied with the staples of the world's cuisines, and happy with the food I cook, though I'm the first to admit that it's not on the same level as that of great restaurants. (It's often better, though, than that served in the vast majority of restaurants; yours can be too.)

Everyday cooking is not about striving for brilliance but about preparing good, wholesome, tasty, varied meals for the ones you love. This is a fundamentally satisfying pleasure. Your results need not be perfect to give you this gift, to which all humans are entitled.

What's Convenient?

I began the original edition of *How to Cook Everything* like this: "Anyone can cook, and most everyone should. It's a sorry sign that many people consider cooking 'from scratch' an unusual and even rare talent. In fact, it is a simple and rewarding craft, one that anyone can learn and even succeed at from the get-go."

It's even more true now. That so-called convenience foods—frozen dinners, prepared deli items, snack food, take-out and fast food of course, candy, sugary drinks, etc.—are more prominent than ever is a national (and nutritional) tragedy. Yes, I'll grab a Snickers at four in the afternoon, I relish a good pizza delivered to my door, and I've been known to stop at Burger King on long drives or even on a whim. But in general I cook.

Contemporary marketing has convinced many people that "convenience" food is not only quicker than home cooking but better and cheaper. In fact, it's worse, and more expensive, and only marginally faster. (Fully half the recipes in this book can be prepared in less than 30 minutes.)

With few exceptions, we all shop in supermarkets, purchasing ingredients that are more likely to come from 10,000 miles away than from 10. Though there's an argument that local ingredients are best, you can at least cook with ingredients from afar. But when flavor, nutrition, tradition, and enjoyment are sacrificed at the sacred altar of "convenience," that's a national tragedy.

Convenience foods supposedly attest to how busy we are: "I don't have time to cook." My job, my quest, is to demonstrate the opposite: that you *do* have time to cook and that the rewards are so great that you'll never regret the time spent doing it. Though we may gain marginal amounts of time by buying and eating prepared and take-out foods, we lose the delights of working in the kitchen, the wonders of creation, the pleasures of time spent in the honest pursuit of tradition and the nourishment of our bodies and those of our family.

We have the opportunity to create home-cooked food that is unimaginable in the take-out world, with a minimum of effort (*conveniently*, in fact) and with a variety and quality of ingredients unparalleled in history. (Do you imagine for a second that the supermarket is using extra virgin olive oil at the salad bar or real mayonnaise in the deli's potato salad? Have you ever read the list of ingredients on a frozen entrée? Can you imagine the tortured process it takes to create a Chicken McNugget?) When enough people realize this (and realize how disastrous the now-conventional style of eating in America is to our health and that of the environment), everyone will benefit.

The fact that you've read this far indicates your interest in cooking; it remains for me to convince you that the process is manageable. There are no secrets—only good guidance combined with experience. You need only begin to cook and continue. I hope *How to Cook Everything* will be a good companion.

What About Time?

Time, of course, is precious, but if you set aside one hour a day—a half hour, even—you'll find that cooking becomes rewarding, even energizing, and the people you cook for will love you for it—no small thing.

And after all, you must eat, and unless you're committed to eating at restaurants, you need to put food on the table. And, as often as not, it takes no more time to cook than it does to call for a pizza and pick it up or wait for it to be delivered. Grilling a piece of meat or fish and steaming a vegetable or preparing a salad is a 20-minute activity. So is making a simple pasta or vegetable dish. These are meals that will *never* make you feel like you made a mistake: You won't overeat, you won't feel sick, you won't feel like you "sinned"—on the contrary, you'll know exactly what you ate and how simple and (relatively) pure it was.

I can't argue that cooking is faster than microwaving a frozen dinner. Only that, even in the hands of a novice cook, it's infinitely better, cheaper, and healthier.

And there's a relaxed state that cooks experience in the kitchen, one that comes from being close to real food, peeling, chopping, browning, stirring, tasting. These routine tasks become second nature with practice. You don't have to think a tremendous amount to cook, but you do have to be in one place, calm and focused.

When you do that enough, you find yourself comfortable, the way you might on any routine task you like. Some people even use cooking as a relaxing break in their day. I guarantee that if you get into cooking, you'll love it and find it meaningful work. And then you won't question the time spent at all.

Still, there are times you'll be in a hurry—a lot of them. So every recipe in *How to Cook Everything* includes a realistic estimation of how long it takes to prepare from start to finish and notes when much of that requires no active attention. Obviously, how long it actually takes you to prepare a recipe will vary based on your experience, but you don't have to be an expert cook to meet my time estimates.

Keep in mind, too, that the timing for every recipe ever created is approximate. The rate at which food cooks depends on the moisture content and temperature of the food itself; measurements (which are rarely perfectly accurate); heat level (your medium-high heat may not be the same as mine, or your oven may be off by 25 degrees); the kind of equipment (some pans conduct heat better than others); even the air temperature. Part of learning how to cook is judging doneness. As you're learning, poke at the food, peek inside it, taste it, and learn what each ingredient looks and feels like when it's done; the best cooks use time as a rough guideline, judging doneness by touch, sight, smell, taste—and even sound.

How to Use This Book

Nearly fifteen years have passed since I started writing *How to Cook Everything*, and I've learned a lot about how people cook and how to teach them to do so. As a result I've organized the book somewhat differently and added a few new elements. This major revision should make it even easier for you to cook and to learn how to cook better. If nothing else, *How to Cook Everything* is a big book, and it won't do you any good if you can't find your way around it. Many of the changes I've made are intended to help you find what you're looking for more easily.

Chapter at a Glance are like mini-tables-of-contents that outline in brief what you're going to find in each chapter.

Essential Recipes, the first recipes given in the chapter, are exactly as they sound: *essential*. These are the recipes that I believe you should know because they're building blocks, or recipes that you'll want to know—super-easy and/or super-popular. Usually these are jumping-off points into larger sections of recipes in the same category that follow later in the chapter.

Charts now play a big role. With them, using a single technique, you can see many more ways to combine similar ingredients to create a variety of dishes. This is the way experienced cooks work: by applying what they've learned across a wide range of ingredients, substituting freely.

Variations are more numerous than ever. I've always felt it was easier for people to learn if I gave one soup recipe with a number of easy twists rather than twenty separate soup recipes. Not that I hold back on the number of recipes here, but there are even more with variations than in the original *How to Cook Everything*.

Lists and sidebars build on and anticipate variations and text. They (and the charts) offer even more ideas for combining ingredients and flavor profiles or elaborate on ideas presented in the main text. Like variations, they help transform recipes from a simple set of instructions into ways of cooking.

Lexicons, or what I call the ingredients-in-a-nutshell features of this book, which are sometimes in chart form and sometimes in text, are rundowns of key ingredients, like grains, oils, and spices. The produce chapter is made up almost exclusively of lexicons, with recipes that feature the particular vegetables and fruits.

Icons (there are four: **F** **M** **V** **✪**) may accompany recipes, in any combination. **F** means fast: the recipe takes 30 minutes or less to prepare; ⓜ indicates that the dish can be made ahead—either in full or to a certain point—and stored for finishing or serving later (these are excellent dishes for entertaining); ⓥ means vegetarian: no meat, chicken, or fish in the recipe (though there may be some options that add nonvegetarian ingredients). ✪ indicates Essential Recipes (see above).

The index is bigger, better, and more comprehensive than in the first edition. If you know what you're looking for (fried chicken, brownies, the basics of tofu), this is the fastest way to find it.

Learning to Cook—Simply

All of the recipes in this book—just about all the recipes I do—have this in common, no matter what their source: They're simple, straightforward, and (I hope) appealing. My experience, and my continued hope, is that by trying the ones that appeal most to you, you'll have instant success. With that success will come experience and increased confidence. With that confidence will come a willingness to try more of the variations and suggestions here.

As time goes on, you'll quickly recognize which recipes appeal to your style and—equally important—you'll see which variations are the most appealing to you. Furthermore, you'll be able to make the transition from "main" recipe to variation quickly and easily. Eventually, you'll begin creating your own variations.

How to Cook Everything amounts to a cooking school in a book, one that has already encouraged hundreds of thousands of beginners to get into the kitchen and has kept them there. It's the best way I know to learn simple, honest, real cooking.

Kitchen Basics

COOKING ISN'T MAGIC, AND IT SHOULDN'T be difficult either. But if you feel comfortable in the kitchen, every step of the process will be far more enjoyable. So if you're new to cooking, or if you're someone who wants to quickly and easily upgrade your abilities without spending a fortune or going to cooking school, spend a little time with this chapter.

Ingredients, equipment, and techniques—these are really the fundamentals of cooking. Here I tackle these building blocks one at a time, in sections that include basic terminology, lots of illustrations, and some guidance about what's really important and what's not.

1

What Ingredients Should I Buy?

Local, farm-raised food has become a luxury for most of us. Almost everything in the supermarket is grown or raised for its hardiness, profitability, shelf life, and ability to withstand the rigors of transit, rather than for its flavor and nutritional value. Most of it comes to us from thousands of miles away, little of it is truly fresh, and it is sold to us not by the individuals who raised it or even selected it but by anonymous corporations.

Nevertheless, supermarket food is of reasonably high quality, inexpensive, and almost uniformly safe to eat. (Don't get me wrong; it should be better, and I hope it soon will be.) With one shopping trip, you can have the makings of many meals on hand at all times, just by maintaining the right mix of staples.

To me, the ingredients that follow are the true convenience foods. Different people like to eat different ways, obviously, but certain items belong in every kitchen all the time and keep nearly indefinitely. To stock your pantry and refrigerator, make sure you have these on hand. (Note that almost every one of these ingredients is described in detail somewhere in the book; just see the index to find where.)

- Extra virgin olive oil, and some decent neutral oil, like grapeseed or corn
- Vinegar
- Soy sauce
- Rice, long-grain and short-grain
- Pasta
- Beans, dried and canned (frozen if you can find them)
- Spices and dried herbs
- Flours and cornmeal
- Canned tomatoes
- Canned—or packaged—stock
- Aromatic vegetables, like onions, garlic, shallots, celery, and carrots
- Baking soda, baking powder, and cornstarch
- Dried mushrooms
- Eggs
- Parmesan cheese
- Nuts and seeds
- Lemons and limes
- Butter
- Sugar, honey, and maybe maple syrup
- Long-lasting vegetables and fruits, like potatoes, apples, and oranges
- Standard condiments like ketchup, mustard, salsa, and mayonnaise

You would not be going overboard to stock capers, miso, dark sesame oil, bread crumbs, fresh scallions, chiles, and ginger, coconut milk, hot sauce, dried fruit, frozen vegetables (definitely better than nothing), parsley (especially) and other fresh herbs, and red and white wine (yes, you can cook without them, but if you drink wine you should cook with it).

Thus stocked, you'll be able to make scores of different meals, from pancakes to pasta. When you add the fresh ingredients that you'll likely have in the refrigerator as a result of normal shopping—vegetables, fruit, meat, fish, milk, cheese, and other perishables—you'll be able to prepare most of the recipes in this book without going out for special ingredients.

Some people become obsessed by ingredients, and this is understandable (but no, you do *not* need Himalayan salt in your pantry). In general, the better the ingredients you have, the simpler your cooking can be. An omelet made with farm-fresh eggs, a locally raised chicken roasted with wonderful olive oil, sliced tomatoes straight from the garden—these experiences cannot be duplicated with supermarket ingredients.

Of course, if you had perfect ingredients all the time, you would hardly need a cookbook. But the story of cooking is often the story of compromise; you buy the best ingredients you can lay your hands on and combine them in ways that make sense. That's the thinking behind my recipes.

What About Organic?

This is a political question, not a cooking question, and it's complicated. I can only tell you that I don't routinely buy organic food, and I rarely go out of my way to buy organic food. It's not that I'm against it; when I had a large garden, it was mostly organic. But that's small time, and that's my point: I would rather buy local vegetables from a conscientious farmer than so-called organic vegetables from a multinational corporation.

But even that is largely impractical: I don't have the time or energy to seek out local produce on a regular basis; I do most of my shopping at a supermarket, just like almost everyone else in this country. And at supermarkets, organic food doesn't have much of an advantage over conventional food. For the most part, they're both industrially produced in faraway places. And I'm not convinced that industrially produced "organic" food is any healthier or more sustainable than industrially produced "conventional" food.

It's an evolving issue. My quick advice, for what it's worth, is: Buy local when you can. Buy the best food you can find when you can't find local. Be flexible; there may be times when the best vegetable you can find is not only not local and not organic but might even be frozen.

The Basics of Food Safety

Most food-borne illnesses can be prevented, and since food sickens millions of Americans each year it's worth taking precautions. Begin by keeping your hands and all food preparation surfaces and utensils clean; soap and hot water are fine. Wash cutting boards after using them, and don't prepare food directly on your counters unless you wash them as well. Never put cooked food on a plate that previously held raw food. Change sponges frequently (or wash them in hot water). Change your kitchen towel frequently also—at least once a day.

Make sure your refrigerator is at about 35°F (40°F is too warm), and your freezer at 0°F or lower. Thaw foods in the refrigerator or under cold running water. Don't leave cooked foods at room temperature forever; the government recommends no longer than two hours, though in all honesty I often stretch that rule.

Those are the easy parts; everything else requires judgment. Let me say from the outset that I do not obey many of the following rules, because there's little you can do about ingredients containing disease-causing bacteria except cook everything to well-done, and that's not a desirable cooking technique, since it often results in food you don't want to eat.

Of common foods, cooked vegetables and grains are the safest; next comes cooked fish; then comes cooked meat other than hamburger; then come cooked chicken, eggs, hamburger, and raw vegetables, with which most concerns are associated.

To be as safe as possible, you should never eat raw meat or fish. And cook all foods, especially hamburger, eggs, and chicken, until well done.

With the exception of cooking chicken to absolute doneness, these rules run counter to the spirit of good cooking and good eating. To most of us, a well-done hamburger is a hamburger better left uneaten; but the decision is yours.

As for me, I keep a spotlessly clean kitchen, wash my hands about twenty times a day, and cook food so that it tastes as good as it can; that's how the recipes in this book are designed.

If you or someone in your family is at greater risk of serious food-borne illness—this includes infants, pregnant women, the elderly, and people with compromised immune systems—you should take every precaution possible. But this is a cookbook; if you have any questions at all about your personal food safety, I suggest you speak with a doctor and a nutritionist.

For the rest of us, it boils down to common sense: Don't let your kitchen be a breeding ground. Many experienced cooks and chefs are fanatical about cleanliness, and it works; that's the best way to avoid food-related illness.

What Equipment Do I Need?

You can spend tens of thousands of dollars on kitchen equipment, or you can spend a couple hundred bucks, then let your cooking style dictate how to expand your collection. (If you inherit or are given cookware, start with that.)

Good cookware need not be expensive: There are real bargains to be had, even with first-rate products, especially at a restaurant supply house. Upscale "culinary" stores are more for show than for function, and big-box stores sell mostly junk. Look for tools—and tableware—at tag sales and thrift stores; some of the most useful utensils are old-school anyway.

When you do buy new equipment, hold hand tools to get a feel for them, check the movement on electric appliances (and ideally turn them on in the store so you can check out the noise and vibration levels), and compare the weights of different pans. Since the ultimate goal is to buy pieces you will actually use, make sure you'll be comfortable with your equipment before taking it home.

I recommend that you cook with minimal equipment for a while so that you can discover your preferences and therefore your priorities. Perhaps you need a couple of skillets, a huge stockpot, and a springform pan but have no use for cookie cutters or a pizza peel; it depends on what you want to eat. Here, then, is a list—with highly personal comments—about what you ought to start with and what you might want to wait for.

The Basics of Knives

A good knife is worth the investment, but it need not be a big investment: There are now so many good knives sold in so many places that there's really no excuse for buying junk. Go to a kitchen supply store and look at those with high carbon-steel alloy blades, which is what everyone—from chefs to experienced home cooks—uses now. The handle may be wood or plastic, although plastic handles are somewhat more durable and dishwasher-safe.

A chef's knife, essentially an all-purpose blade that you will use daily, should set you back no more than $30 and could be less. Make sure the handle feels good when you hold it; the grip is almost as important as the blade, and only you can judge whether it's a comfortable fit.

The Three Knives You Must Have

1. **Chef's knife:** An 8-inch blade is what most home cooks like; go to 10 inches if you have especially big hands and like the feel or 6 inches if your hands are smaller. You'll use this for almost all kitchen tasks.
2. **Paring knife:** You can buy expensive paring knives or pretty good ones that are so cheap you can almost consider them disposable. It's nice to have a couple of slightly varying styles. Use for peeling, trimming, and other precise tasks.
3. **Long serrated knife or bread knife:** A must for bread and other baked foods, for splitting cakes into layers, for ripe tomatoes, and for large fruits or vegetables like melons and squash.

Sharpening Knives

Dull knives may slip off the food you're cutting and onto the closest surface—your finger, for instance. Although you must be extremely careful with sharp knives—casual contact will lead to a real cut—at least they go where you want them to. Respect your knives: Start with good ones, keep them sharp—you'll know when it's time to sharpen them—and they will become your friends.

An electric sharpener is the best, easiest, and most expensive way to keep knife blades sharp; even moderately serious cooks should consider this a worthwhile investment. The alternatives are to learn to use a whetstone (not that difficult, and very effective, but time-consuming) or to take them to a hardware store to have them sharpened professionally.

A steel is a handy tool for maintaining the edge of knives between sharpenings. (You should use it every few days, at least.) It's nothing more than a sturdy rod stuck in a handle, but it takes some practice to get the hang of it; follow the illustrations on the next page, repeating the motions a few times on each side of the blade.

Washing and Storing Knives

Though you can put plastic-handled knives in the dishwasher, it's easy for them to get nicked there, so it's better to wash by hand. It's also a good idea to keep knives out of dish racks and other places where they might hurt someone.

Kitchen drawers are fine for knives if you buy inexpensive plastic guards to prevent the blades from chipping and to protect their edges—and your hands. Wood blocks with slots that sit on the countertop and magnetic racks that hang on the wall or cabinet and suspend your knives from the blades are slightly better.

USING A STEEL

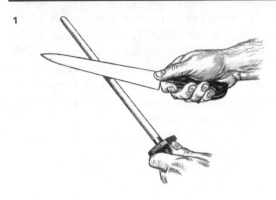

1

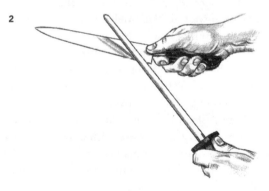

2

Using a steel is easy and effective at keeping knives sharp. The important thing is the angle, which should be between 15 and 20 degrees. **(STEP 1)** Pull one side of the knife toward you across the top of the steel, simultaneously sliding it from base to tip (your pulling hand will move in a diagonal motion); then **(STEP 2)** repeat with the other side across the bottom of the steel, always pulling toward you and trying to maintain a consistent angle.

The Basics of Pots and Pans

It's tempting to buy a full set of shiny new pots and pans. But your choices should be dictated by how you cook, not what a manufacturer can fit into a box.

Copper pots and pans are the ideal: They conduct heat perfectly, last forever, and look incredible. But they're prohibitively expensive and difficult to maintain; most people shouldn't even consider them.

There are other good choices. Cast iron conducts heat nearly as well at a fraction of the cost and is pretty much nonstick to boot. With the growing concerns about nonstick coatings (see next page), I now cook almost everything in well-seasoned cast iron. But cast iron is heavy (make sure large pots and pans have handles on both sides), and the iron itself can react with some foods and discolor them. (Enamel-coated cast iron takes care of this problem, though at a cost.)

Durable and attractive, stainless steel is a "neutral" metal, meaning you can cook anything in it without worrying about pitting or reacting. (This is what is meant by the term *nonreactive*.) It's great for stockpots and saucepans, where you're working with mostly liquids and where cast iron can cause discoloration or even adversely affect flavor. Sauté pans and skillets are fine too, as long as you accept the fact that food will stick to their surfaces unless you use at least a thin coating of butter or oil and properly heat the pan (see page 18).

Stainless should be high quality; the cheap stuff is usually too thin to conduct heat properly. The best have bottoms made by wrapping relatively thick stainless steel around a core of aluminum and/or copper; the combination conducts heat evenly, prevents warping, and minimizes burning. These pans should be fairly heavy. If not, keep looking.

Aluminum is another popular material for cookware, provided it has been anodized, a process that hardens the metal and makes it more durable and less reactive. Even though various cookware lines might look similar, quality and prices can range wildly, so be sure the metal is thick, especially on the bottom.

Ceramic cookware is fine for oven-braising, gratins,

and baking, but with rare exceptions, you can't use it on the stove. Don't even bother with glass pots and pans. They break when you least expect it, and they're worthless for anything but boiling water.

A word about nonstick coatings: Like most people, I've become convinced that concerns about their safety at high temperatures are warranted. So I don't buy them anymore; cast iron, believe it or not, really does just about as good a job of preventing sticking.

Handles and Lids

Good pots and pans have their handles attached by rivets, and those handles are made of metal; wood and plastic are functional enough as long as you know the pan will never *ever* go in the oven or broiler. But how would you know that? Stick with metal handles.

The more pans you have with lids, the better. And though the material isn't that important, once again metal is best.

Using, Cleaning, and Storing Pots and Pans

You can improve the performance and nonstick capabilities of virtually all cookware by doing two simple things before frying or sautéing: Heat the empty pan slowly to the desired temperature. (Don't start the stove on heat that's too high only to knock it back down and don't do this with nonstick pans, which should always be heated with something in them.)

You can use metal cooking utensils with stainless-steel, cast-iron, or most other all-metal pans, but you might cause some scratching, especially when deglazing the pan and scraping up browned bits. So as a general rule, I favor wooden spoons and spatulas. With nonstick or enamel coatings or you must use nonmetal utensils.

You can use the dishwasher for all but cast iron, but it's easy enough to use regular dish soap, a nonabrasive sponge or nylon scrubbie, and a little elbow grease. For stubborn messes, soak; for really hard stuff, boil some water in the pan while scraping the bottom with a wooden spoon. Some pans can even take a sprinkle of mildly abrasive cleanser. (For really burned-on stuff, put some ammonia in the pan and let it sit overnight, in a place where the smell won't drive you out of the house.)

Caring for Cast Iron

Cast iron is porous and rough, and until the pan is used and "seasoned" with a combination of heat and fat, food will stick to it. You can now buy preseasoned cast iron, but you can also just use it carefully—for sautéing or frying only—for a while, following the washing directions that follow.

If you'd rather season right away, wash and dry the new pan; heat the oven to 350°F and use a brush or paper towel to spread a tablespoon or so of oil around the inside of the pan, sides and all. There should be no excess, but the entire surface should be shiny. Put the pan in the oven and bake for about an hour, then turn off the oven and leave it inside to cool.

To maintain newly seasoned cast iron, it helps if you use the pan for sautéing or frying the first few times you cook in it. That way the pan is guaranteed to absorb more oil and seal its surfaces.

Once it's seasoned, you can use a mildly abrasive scouring pad to wash it. You might hear that soap will tear off the seasoning, but I've never found that to be true; a little mild soap and hot water is fine. (The pan must be dried, though, or it will rust.) Every few uses—especially after braising in liquids that break down the seasoning, like tomato sauce or wine—I dry my cast-iron skillet over low heat. When the water begins to evaporate, I wipe it out with a towel and use a paper towel to smear around a little oil, let it sit over the heat for a few more minutes, then wipe it out again.

Besides the rare instance of cracking (which will render the pot or pan useless), the worst that can happen to cast iron is that the pan will lose its seasoning or rust; both can be fixed by reseasoning. In the case of rust, scour the pan out well with steel wool or a wire brush before heating and oiling. As the pan ages with use (assuming you care for it properly), it will darken and become increasingly smooth, beautiful, and nonstick.

5 Crucial Pots and Pans

This pretty much covers everything you need for basic stovetop cooking:

1. **Large, deep skillet, 12 inches across and 2 to 3 inches deep, with a lid:** You need a fair amount of surface area to sauté, stir-fry, and pan-roast food properly without crowding. Curved sides are better than straight for most uses. Make this cast iron or stainless steel.

2. **Large stockpot with a lid:** At least 2 gallons, preferably stainless steel or aluminum. For making stock; shocking, parboiling, or steaming vegetables; braising big cuts of meat; and boiling pasta, noodles, or dumplings. If you can find one with a steamer basket, all the better, though it's easy enough to improvise (see page 20).

3. **Medium skillet, 8 to 10 inches (eventually you'll probably have both), preferably with a lid (the lid from your stockpot may fit this):** For small-batch sautéing, frying, cooking eggs, and the like. Cast iron or stainless steel.

4. **Large Dutch oven or saucepan with a lid:** Sometimes this is referred to as a "casserole," though it should be both flameproof and ovenproof, and hold at least 3 quarts. For soups, stews, sauces, grains and beans, and deep frying. I like enameled cast-iron or some other nonreactive interior. For braising, it's important that the lid fit well.

5. **Small or medium saucepan with a lid:** Something in the 1- to 2-quart range. Use this for boiling eggs and warming, cooking, and reheating small amounts of food.

The Basics of Ovenware

You have three dependable ways to go for ovenware: metal (including metal pans coated in enamel), glass, and ceramic. There's nothing glamorous about taking metal pans to the table, but if you're new to cooking, that's where I suggest you start, since they will be the most versatile and economical. You can always add to your collection.

Any metal pans except uncoated aluminum are fine for baking. These days you can find good, heavy, professional-style metal pans, even in discount stores, and they're virtually indestructible. You can even heat them on top of the stove to deglaze the bottom or melt butter. When you're using glass or ceramic ovenware, be careful not to change temperature too rapidly or they'll crack; you can't add cold liquid to a hot baking dish, nor use them on the stove. And of course these pans can both chip and break.

4 Essential Pans for the Oven

These are pans you'll always use; they'll last for the rest of your life. Start with these, then move on to the next list when you're ready.

1. **Rectangular roasting pan, preferably metal:** The standard measurement is 9 × 13 inches. Make sure it's at least 2 inches deep so it holds at least 12 cups of food or liquid. The large surface area makes it perfect for roasts of all kinds, baked potatoes, roast vegetables, and all sorts of sweet and savory baking.

2. **Large rimmed baking sheet:** You might as well buy two. Also known as *jelly-roll pans,* these are more versatile than rimless baking sheets and work great for cookies, as well as crisp-roasting meat or vegetables and baking and warming things like burgers, fritters, and savory cakes.

3. **Square pan, 8 or 9 inches:** Universally useful, but essential for quick breads, brownies, cobblers, cakes, and the like.

4. **Large gratin dish:** Not quite as big or as deep as your main roasting pan. It can be oval, round, or rectangular and made of glass, ceramic, or metal. Ideally it will hold about 8 cups of food. With it, you can make virtually all of the gratins in this book.

10 More Pans for the Oven

Not everyone will want all of these, but devoted cooks will. Get 'em as you need 'em.

1. **Standard loaf pan:** These measure $8^1/_2 \times 4^1/_2 \times 3$ inches; avoid glass loaf pans—bread may not rise or bake as evenly in them. Also good for meat loaf of course.

2. **Pie plate, 9 inches:** For pies, tarts, and quiches. Plus, almost anything you can make in an 8-inch square

pan you can make in a pie plate; just cut it into wedges instead of squares. (I prefer a standard size to a deep-dish plate, and most of my recipes are designed for that size.) This is the one place where glass is really nice.

3. **Springform pan, 9 inches:** This is the one where the bottom drops out and the sides are held together with a big clip. It's essential for cheesecake. Good quality is important here to prevent leaking.

4. **Custard cups or ramekins:** The 6-ounce size is standard, and you'll probably want eight of them. Beyond their intended purpose for making individual custards, gratins, gelées, cobblers, and so on, they're great for holding small amounts of ingredients while you cook.

5. **Two 9-inch cake pans:** For when you want to bake a layer cake. Otherwise, one will do. Nonstick is nice here.

6. **Muffin tins:** To some people these are more important than cake pans. Remember, though, every muffin can be baked as a quick bread. Buy nonstick or cast iron.

7. **Tube or bundt pan:** For cake enthusiasts. The tube pan is deep and flat sided, while the bundt is rounder and indented for a more decorative effect. One or the other generally does it. You can bake any recipe for a two-layer cake in one of these pans; increase the cooking time by 10 to 15 minutes.

8. **Soufflé dish:** 2-quart is the standard size, and ceramic is the standard material. You can use it for more than soufflés of course (it's essentially a bowl), but you can't make a soufflé without one.

9. **Cookie sheets:** If you bake a lot of cookies, rimless baking sheets are more convenient than rimmed pans. And you'll be able to keep them cleaner.

10. **Fluted tart pan, 9 inches:** Metal ones have removable bottoms, but ceramic ones are easier to clean and look great on the table.

The Basics of Kitchen Tools

A variety of manual tools can make kitchen tasks easier. Eventually you'll probably acquire as much kitchen stuff as your cabinets can hold. Here are three lists to help you prioritize a bit.

12 Must-Have Kitchen Tools

These are the ones you can't do without. They're in no particular order because you really do need them all.

1. **Mixing bowls:** Small, medium, and large to start, preferably stainless steel—the most basic and functional—and this is one thing that's practical to buy in a set. (Stainless even looks okay on the table, but if you want nice-looking serving bowls, buy them separately.)

2. **Cutting boards:** One is enough if it's a big one, but I prefer having a few of different sizes so at least one is always dry. Wood or plastic, your choice. Wooden ones can be sanded clean; plastic can go in the dishwasher. To keep cutting boards from sliding around on the countertop while you work, lay a damp towel underneath them.

3. **Wooden and stainless spoons and spatulas:** Keep these in a pottery crock or an old coffee can right by the stove: a few wooden spoons, a couple of wide and narrow spatulas (one flexible metal if possible), a ladle, and at least one slotted spoon. If you have nonstick pans, you may need some plastic or silicone utensils; otherwise wood and stainless steel will do.

4. **Tongs:** The single best item for turning most foods. Get spring-loaded rather than scissorlike or tension kinds.

5. **Pot holders (or mitts) and kitchen towels:** It doesn't matter what they look like; what's important is that they protect your hands from heat.

6. **Measuring cups—liquid and dry measure—and measuring spoons:** It sounds silly, but you really shouldn't use liquid and dry measuring utensils interchangeably. The first you pour from (it looks like a pitcher with writing on it), and the second you level off with the back of a knife (see page 16). A 2-cup glass liquid measuring cup is a good place to start; buy a 4-cup as the second if possible. Dry-measure cups and measuring spoons generally come in sets.

They're relatively inexpensive, so if you can, get two of everything so one is always likely to be clean.

7. **Colanders and strainers:** The family of bowl- or basket-like devices with holes in them for draining. You need a colander immediately, and soon you will want at least one fine-mesh strainer to strain fine foods or use for pressing and mashing purées.

8. **Cheese grater:** An old-fashioned box grater is fine, but get stainless steel if you can afford it or be willing to throw out cheaper models at the first sign of rust. The new ultra-sharp hand-held Microplanes are very good and easy to use.

9. **Timer:** You probably have one on your microwave or oven, in which case you just saved ten bucks!

10. **Vegetable peeler:** The easiest way to deal with carrots, potatoes, and more. Sharpness and the handle grip are more important than the shape, though I lean toward the U-shaped ones. Those with a ceramic blade are relatively expensive ($12 or so) but work perfectly.

11. **Instant-read thermometer:** Very handy for making sure foods are done. I absolutely depend on one when baking bread. It's also the foolproof way to check for doneness in large cuts of meat and whole chickens. (I give a temperature range for doneness in my recipes for these meats.)

12. **Salad spinner:** Not only the best way to wash greens, but a good vessel for storing washed greens in the fridge, which prolongs their life by days. (See "The Basics of Preparing Salad Greens" on page 193.)

14 More Kitchen Tools You'll Probably Want
You might call these necessary luxuries.

1. **Balloon whisk:** Especially if you don't have any other rotary or electric mixer. Start with a medium to large one that feels comfortable in your hand.

2. **Rolling pin:** Get a straight wooden pin without ball bearings (you can save money by buying a piece of dowel); you'll have more control, and it won't break.

3. **Wire racks:** Mostly for cooling baked foods, but also for roasting. Get at least a couple and make sure one fits into your main roasting pan. (Round ones are handy too.)

4. **Funnel:** It's a shame and also usually a big mess not to have one when you need one. Plastic is fine.

5. **Citrus reamer:** Or some sort of tool to easily extract citrus juice from its fruit.

6. **Skewers:** Use metal, which are permanent and don't need to be soaked before grilling; I prefer nonround ones because they grip the food better.

7. **Wooden salad bowl and servers:** The most convenient way to assemble, dress, toss, and serve salads. Easiest to clean up too.

8. **Grilling utensils:** Their long handles make grilling simpler.

9. **Mandoline:** You might think you're pretty good with a knife, but once you see the pile of paper-thin potatoes you just cut in about 5 seconds flat with a mandoline, you'll be hooked. And the very good plastic mandolines are now all over the place for less than 40 bucks. (Be extra-careful around this tool; use the guard and, if you like a little wine when you cook, be sure to tackle the mandoline while you're still on your first glass.)

10. **Zester:** Easier than peeling and mincing with a paring knife and the only way to get long strands.

11. **Asian skimmers and "spiders":** These look like baskets on wooden sticks, come in all different sizes, and are more useful than slotted spoons for deep frying.

12. **A huge mixing bowl:** For shocking vegetables, icing down wine and drinks at a party, or serving punch. You can use a stockpot for some of these tasks, but it's not the most attractive serving piece.

13. **Brushes:** For spreading melted butter, oil, or water in an even layer. The new silicone ones are cool because they don't leave nylon bristles behind.

14. **Kitchen scissors:** Snipping is often easier—and safer—than chopping, especially for herbs, dried fruit, roast chicken, bean threads and other long noodles, cutting string, and opening packages.

8 Nice-to-Have Kitchen Tools
Cherry-pick from this list, depending on where your cooking enthusiasms lie. But remember this rule of thumb to

distinguish want from need: If you make something more than once a year—and think you might tackle it more often with the right tools—a gadget is probably worth the money and space.

1. **Steaming basket:** These expand to fit different-sized pots. You can use an inverted plate or shallow bowl (see page 20), but these are more convenient and not expensive.

2. **Melon baller:** Sure, you can cube melon or use a spoon, but this tool makes all sorts of stuff look so cool. Good for coring pears too.

3. **Offset spatula:** For frosting cakes and lifting things directly up from the bottom without disturbing them much.

4. **Manual pasta machine:** If you have any interest at all in making pasta, or have tried and failed to roll it out by hand, this simple machine is worth the money.

5. **Food mill:** Basically a strainer on steroids, with a hand-crank paddle wheel to push foods through the holes. Essential if you make a lot of tomato or apple sauce.

6. **Baking stone, peel, and pizza cutter:** If you're going to bake pizza (and you should), these are nearly essential.

7. **Ricer:** A ricer improves mashed potatoes, and anything you make with them, like gnocchi (see page 550).

8. **Silicone mat:** A flexible rubbery mat used for lining baking sheets in place of butter and flour; it helps insulate heat so whatever you're baking doesn't burn or stick. Good for delicate cookies.

The Basics of Appliances and Electric Gadgets

Let's assume you have neither the desire nor the space nor the money to buy every kitchen appliance on the market. Here is a roundup of the electric gadgets that might make your kitchen life a little easier. (Note that if something isn't here, I don't think it's even worth considering, though I'm assuming you have a fridge and a toaster, for example.)

Food processor: It can grate massive amounts of almost anything in seconds; it can make bread dough, pie dough, and even some cookie batters in a minute; it can purée vegetables, slice potatoes, grind meat and fish, and whip up spreads and dips. If you don't have one, make the investment when you can; there are very good ones available for less than $60, and if you cook a lot, you will use it daily. Get a large one, a model that can handle at least eight 8 (and preferably 12) cups of batter or dough.

One tip on using a food processor: Don't overprocess. If you want a purée, turn the machine on and walk away. But if you want to mince, use the "pulse" button, turning the machine on and off as many times as is necessary to get the texture you need. These are very powerful machines, capable of puréeing almost anything within seconds.

Electric mixer: If you bake a lot, you will probably want both a powerful standing mixer and a small, hand-held mixer. If you bake occasionally, you will want one or the other. If you never bake, you might be perfectly happy with a whisk.

Blender: Crucial if you want creamy soups. An immersion blender—which you stick into a pot or a bowl and work with your hands (page 123)—is helpful, but not as versatile or powerful. A blender is also good for perfect vinaigrettes, blended drinks, smoothies, and super-smooth dips and sauces.

Coffee/spice grinder: An electric coffee grinder (a spice grinder is essentially the same thing) is the best tool for grinding whole spices. Coffee drinkers probably already have one, but it's nice to have a separate one for spices.

Ice cream maker: You might want to start with an inexpensive manual model with a container you freeze. At the other end of the spectrum are the top-end electric models with self-contained refrigeration and a price tag of at least $200 and often much more. If you're going to make that kind of investment, do your homework and make sure you get one with a powerful compressor and motor for reliability and ease.

Pressure cooker: Pressure cookers can help you make soups and stews fast. If you have one, try it. If you don't, first try some of the make-ahead techniques in these recipes. Or get in the habit of making extra and setting some aside, because then you'll probably never miss a pressure cooker. If you do want one, buy it new—they're safer and easier to use than they were even ten years ago.

Microwave: The microwave is good for reheating, melting butter, and taking the chill off foods; and it's not bad at "steaming" vegetables and fish. I wouldn't rush out and buy one, but you probably have one already.

Techniques

Your cooking can be plenty good while you are learning proper technique, and there are some techniques you can ignore altogether. You can cut up an onion efficiently and effectively without knowing the "correct" way to slice or dice it. (My grandmother had terrible technique, but she was a great cook.) And while it may take you 10 seconds longer to do it as a result, and the pieces won't be exactly uniform, it won't affect the flavor (or in most cases even the appearance) of finished dishes.

Fortunately, you can become proficient at most kinds of everyday cooking with only a handful of techniques and a little practice. I'm trying to cultivate your enthusiasm in the kitchen, not only by offering great recipes but also by showing you that executing them is not nearly as intimidating as TV chefs might lead you to believe.

And the process of learning to cook is hardly painful. Once in a while you might make a blunder that renders something inedible; every cook I know, from my colleagues in the press to the world's great chefs, flubs a dish now and then. But one of the joys of working in the kitchen is that not only do you learn from your mistakes, they never last long enough to haunt you. (And you can usually eat them anyway.)

Preparing Food for Cooking

First things first: The way you prepare food has a direct impact on how it cooks. So here's an overview of the tasks required before you subject anything to heat—roughly in order of how you might tackle them.

Washing, Peeling, and Trimming

Most food should be washed just before being cooked. Wash away visible dirt and, we hope, pesticide residue, bacteria, fungi, and the by-products of handling.

Fish and meat generally need not be washed, but it doesn't do any harm. Mollusks (clams, mussels, oysters) must be scrubbed really clean; shellfish can be peeled or not. Some seafood (squid, for example) have special cleaning techniques that are detailed in the appropriate chapter; the same is true for any vegetables that might not be obvious. And some people wash their eggs before cracking.

You can trim and peel produce before or after washing; do what makes sense to you. (Even if you're peeling, do give a rinse to remove any bacteria or dirt on the outside.) Use a paring knife to remove stems, blossom ends, cores, and any blemishes or bruises. A peeler or a paring knife will handle thin and medium skins (carrots, potatoes, apples, turnips, and the like). For tough, thick skins, you'll need to work (cutting away from you, please) on a cutting board, usually with a chef's knife (see page 4). A spoon works best for scooping out seeds and other interior fibers.

For meat, poultry, or fish, trim excess fat (generally, not *all* fat, just excess) and any inedible parts. Again, see the chapters for specific info.

The Basics of Cutting

Cut food is easier to handle, cooks faster, and is convenient to serve and eat. So a few simple knife skills will make your food both tastier and more attractive.

Hold your knives however you feel most comfortable and secure. Some people "shake hands" with their chef's knife, but the way to hold one for maximum stability and flexibility is to grip the handle as close to the blade as is comfortable and put your thumb on the inside, against the hilt, with your other fingers wrapped around the other side. You can even stretch your forefinger up the blade a little bit for more control.

When you work with a chef's knife, use your other hand to hold the food on the cutting board, curling the fingers and thumb a bit so your knuckles act as a bumper or guide, keeping the tips of your fingers out of harm's way. Almost all cutting skills with a chef's knife are basically variations on a rocking motion, with the tip held steady on the cutting board while you maneuver the handle up and down—the way a paper cutter works. If this is new to you, try practicing without any food first and hold your curled fingers against the blade so you feel how they work as a guide.

Whether you're chopping an onion, mincing a clove of garlic, or cutting slices from a pork tenderloin to throw on the grill, you want all pieces to be approximately the same size and thickness. My recipes tell you how big to cut things only when it's important (which I don't think is very often), but it's okay if the measurement isn't spot on as long as you cut everything in pretty much the same way.

Here are the specific cuts:

Chopping

This most basic cut results in three sizes: roughly chopped, chopped, and minced. For all of these, you can forget super-even cutting; truly equal size is unimportant; you're just trying to get the job done. You generally chop foods that play a supporting role in the dish—like onions or other aromatics—or things that are going to cook so long they almost melt away.

Roughly chopped: Chunks that are somewhat uneven, bite-sized or even bigger; you're just passing the food under the knife blade, without worrying much about where. Use this cut before puréeing or mashing or when the texture of the dish is intended to be rustic and chunky. Pieces can be as big as an inch in any dimension.

USING A CHEF'S KNIFE

1 **2** **3**

(STEP 1) You can choose to hold a knife with your hand completely on the handle or with your first finger or two wrapping around the blade. In either case, the position should be comfortable. (STEP 2) To finely chop herbs or small vegetables, put the tip of the blade on the cutting surface and rock the knife up and down; use your hand to hold the food on the cutting board, curling your fingers and thumb a bit so your knuckles act as a bumper or guide, keeping the tips of your fingers out of harm's way. (STEP 3) When the pieces become very small and stable, you won't have to hold them anymore, so you can put your free hand over the point of the blade for greater stability; use a rocking motion to finely chop or mince the food further.

Chopped: Pieces from $1/2$ to $1/4$ inch in size. Onions, bell peppers, and celery are the most common vegetables to get this treatment. In recipes where I don't specify size and just say "chopped," this is what I mean.

Minced: The tiniest bits you can manage: Once you get things finely chopped, it's just a final burst of short, quick chops to get food to this stage. (Sometimes it helps to steady the tip of the knife blade while you mince, to keep it anchored to the cutting board.) Mince when you want an almost invisible, textureless result with foods like garlic, ginger, shallots, or chiles.

Slicing

To slice with a chef's knife, you still press down, just with a little more precision, and cut into thick or thin slices of fairly uniform size. (Raw meat and poultry are almost always easier to slice if you freeze them for about 30 minutes first.) You can slice crosswise, lengthwise, or on the diagonal. The diagonal slice is probably most attractive and gives you the largest surface area for crisping (it's nice to use in stir-fries). To slice with a serrated knife—for bread, cake, and the like—grip the handle comfortably and use a gentle sawing motion to work your way through the food.

A mandoline (see page 9) is handy for getting even slices and for other tasks too; I can't recommend one highly enough.

Julienne

Translation: Cut into sticks. They can be big like French fries or small like matchsticks. I don't call for julienne often, but it's an impressive cut and really not that tough (especially if you use a food processor or mandoline, both of which have attachments to make it a breeze). By hand, first make round foods—think of zucchini as an example—stable on the cutting board by slicing off one side. Slice the food crosswise into whatever length you want the final julienne, then slice the food lengthwise. Stack the pieces into piles of three or so layers, then slice them through lengthwise into the same thickness as your first slices.

CHOPPING

1

2

3

Cutting vegetables—or any food—into small pieces is best done in a series of steps. **(STEP 1)** First, cut the food into manageable and somewhat even-sized chunks. **(STEP 2)** Then chop it into smaller pieces. **(STEP 3)** Finally, if necessary, mince, using a rocking motion; the knife must be sharp.

Dicing

Dice means "perfect cube," but stray geometry isn't going to wreck a dish. Dice can be larger, like chopped (say, $1/2$-inch cubes), or teeny (called *brunoise*), as if you cut julienne sticks crosswise at $1/8$- or $1/4$-inch intervals.

Roll Cut (Oblique Cut)

These look sort of like round triangles or diagonally cut chunks. (You've seen vegetables cut like this in stir-fries.) The roll cut works best on round, narrow vegetables like zucchini, carrots, and Japanese eggplant. Here's how: Slice one end diagonally, then roll the rest of the vegetable a quarter turn and slice on the same angle. Your knife never changes position; you just keep rolling the vegetable. Try it; you'll like it.

Chiffonade

Another translation: Cut into strands or ribbons. Use the chiffonade cut on big leafy vegetables like kale or small leaves like basil; the technique is the same regardless of the size: Make a pile (not too high) of washed leaves, roll them from end to end, and slice the roll as thickly or thinly as you like.

Paring, Coring, Peeling, and Other Special Tasks

Here you hold manageable pieces of food in one hand, a small paring knife in the other, and work in a controlled way without a cutting board; you might be coring and peeling an apple, for example, or trimming the eyes from a potato. Often these jobs involve pulling the paring knife toward you. If you're not confident working this way, stick to putting the food on a board and cutting away from you.

SLICING

There are many ways of slicing, though they all require you to keep your nonknife fingers out of the way (some people call this position "the claw"). (1) For round vegetables like cucumbers or zucchini, you can just cut across. (2) Or you can cut into long strips or (3) on an angle, for attractive ovals. (4) To slice bread, use a serrated knife (a "bread knife") and a sawing motion.

MAKING JULIENNE

1

2

MAKING CHIFFONADE

1

2

(STEP 1) The easiest way to cut even strips from a vegetable with rounded sides is to square it off first by removing thin slices. (STEP 2) Then it will sit flat so you can first it cut crosswise to the desired length and then stack and slice into strips.

This works for large leaves, such as kale, as well as smaller ones, like basil. (STEP 1) Roll the leaf up from bottom to top. (STEP 2) Cut off slices of the leaf from top to bottom.

MAKING DICE

USING A PARING KNIFE

To make dicing easier, first square off the vegetable by removing thin slices, then cut into even-sized sticks (see "Making Julienne," above). Then cut the sticks crosswise into dice.

Before there were vegetable peelers, there were paring knives; as long as you're careful—peel toward you, using your thumb to counter the pressure of the knife—they work perfectly.

The Basics of Measuring

All of the recipes in this book can be measured with cups and spoons, though I sometimes offer weights when it might be easier. Many experienced cooks eyeball everything (except when baking), and though I wouldn't advocate ignoring the recipes, with practice you'll get there. Think about this for starters: Does it matter whether your stir-fry has a heaping cup or a shy cup of chopped carrots?

Sometimes measurement really matters, however, so you should learn the right way to do it. Whenever you bake breads, make desserts, or work with eggs in custards, soufflés, and the like, you must measure carefully.

To measure liquids, set the cup on the counter and fill it to where you think the correct marking is. Then get down at eye level to the cup and double-check. Surface tension causes the liquid to look a little like a concave bubble, and the bottom "line" of that bubble should be even with the line on the cup. Add or pour off some liquid until it is. This may sound obsessive, but it's easy enough.

For dry ingredients, scoop them up or use a spoon to put them in the cup, heaping them a bit over the top. Then rest the flat side of a knife or spatula on the rim and

MEASURING DRY INGREDIENTS

To measure flour accurately, scoop up ingredients or use a spoon to overfill the measuring cup, then sweep the top evenly with the flat side of a knife.

swipe the excess off the top. For measuring spoons, either fill them to capacity with liquid or fill them with dry ingredients and use the same swiping technique to level them off.

The Importance of Heat

Much of cooking is about heat. Whatever your instincts tell you, high heat does not automatically lead to burned food. Quite the opposite: Often, unless the pan, oven, water, or grill is hot enough, the food won't cook properly. Though a few beginning cooks veer toward the other extreme, most are understandably too timid with heat.

Food responds best when it comes into sudden contact with something hot. Whether you're plunging spaghetti into boiling water or a steak into a hot skillet, this heat impact is what will get you tender (not mushy) pasta and a crisp brown crust on your steak. You almost never want to start with cold ingredients in a cold pan or a cold oven or a cold pot of water (there are exceptions).

Whether you cook with gas or electric barely matters. Electric stoves do take longer to heat up and cool down, so you need to accommodate this, usually by working on two burners at the same time (one set lower than the other), or by making adjustments a little before they're needed; it's no big deal. When the heat gets too high for your food, shift the pan; if it gets too low, shift it again. Chefs do this all they time, even though they use gas; they're constantly moving things off burners because they know that the pan retains heat and it's faster and easier than reaching down and fiddling with the knobs.

What counts most when working with heat is your ability to trust your senses, especially smell. Heat has its own aroma (try putting your nose over a dry skillet that's heating), as does food as it's cooking—and burning. Learn to listen for the sound of food cooking vigorously, and learn to visually recognize signs of doneness, like crisping around the edges, dryness, and releasing from the pan or grill. Being observant puts you in control and gives you the confidence to use heat more assertively.

The Eleven Essential Cooking Techniques

All of these are described in more detail within the recipe chapters, but here's an elementary overview of cooking techniques.

Grilling

Cooking over an open flame was our ancestors' original method and is still one of our favorites. There's direct-heat grilling, where you put the food on a grate set right over a hot gas flame or charcoal to crisp, darken, and cook quickly. And there's indirect-heat grilling, with the food off to the side of the fire and the lid on, so the grill works like an oven and cooks foods more slowly. Thick foods are better off with indirect grilling: The outsides don't burn before the insides are done. Anything that's an inch or less thick is a good candidate for direct-heat grilling. (Barbecuing isn't grilling but actually slow cooking with smoke or liquid—a kind of grill-braising. You can also call anything *barbecue* if it's been treated with a barbecue sauce.)

If you've got a gas grill, all you have to do is turn it on and wait for the grates to heat up. If you want to use indirect heat on a gas grill, simply turn a burner or two off and use that side for the food.

For charcoal grills, I like to use lump charcoal and a chimney starter to get the fire going, but you can use briquettes if you like or an electric starter. Stay away from lighter fluid, which you can taste even if you grill after it burns off. Once the charcoal is going, spread it out for direct grilling or pile it on one side for indirect grilling. To build a two-tiered fire—one that has both hot and low heat sources—spread a thin layer of charcoal on one side of the grill and a thicker layer of coals on the other side.

Generally, you want to wait until the coals are covered with ash before you start grilling. You're ready to sear when you can hold your hand right above the rack for only a couple of seconds. For less intense grilling, you want to be able to hold your hand above the heat for 4 seconds or so. So adjust the distance of the rack from the fire if you can or spread out the coals a bit. Or just wait. You don't want the flames lapping up to kiss the grill grates periodically, unless you like the flavor of burned food. (For the record, unless you use a wood fire or add soaked wood chips right before cooking, you're not getting much more flavor by grilling than you would out of a broiler.)

Broiling

Broiling is essentially upside-down grilling: You get the same browning and even charring, though without grill marks. It's less work and, unless you use wood or wood chips, the flavor is about the same.

Broil food from 2 to 6 inches away from the heat source. Use the greater distance with thicker foods or toppings that burn easily. When the food browns and cooks on one side, take the food out and flip it over. Adjust the distance to the broiler as needed; as with grilling, you want browned, crisp outsides and moist, tender insides.

Some electric broilers require that the door be open during use: Check your manufacturer's instructions. If that's the case, try heating the oven to its highest setting with the door closed, then switch to broil and open the door a crack.

Roasting

Roasting takes dry heat, in a confined environment, and uses it to crust food on the outside while cooking it through. All you need is a big shallow pan and maybe a little oil or butter to coat the food. Two crucial points: The oven must be very hot, almost always over 400°F. The roasting pan can't be too crowded either; the hot air must be able to circulate so moisture in the food can evaporate easily. Otherwise, you're really just steaming, and you can forget about browning or crispness. You can use seasonings and even a little extra liquid, usually after the food is finished roasting, to make a pan sauce (see page 45).

Baking

Like roasting, but usually with moisture and at lower heat. Most food that's baked is either a semiliquid or a fairly wet solid when it goes in the oven; think of cake batter, custard, or bread dough. There may be sauce, water, or other liquid surrounding solids, as in gratins, casseroles, or lasagne. As the dry heat from the oven warms whatever's in the pan, it causes the moisture to steam and jump-starts all the other chemical reactions needed to raise the dough, melt the cheese, brown the crust, and so on. Delicate items like cakes are usually baked at a lower temperature, like 325°F or 350°F. Breads, pizza, and other sturdy dishes can take higher heat. It's a good idea to have an oven thermometer, because even a glitch of 10 or 15 degrees can make a big difference when you bake.

Braising

This is the most common combined cooking method: You first sear the ingredients, as if you were sautéing, then add liquid to the pot or skillet, cover, and simmer. (You can do this in the oven, with low heat—300°F or lower—or on top of the stove.) As the dish cooks, both the cooking liquid and the solid ingredients develop lots of flavor and a luxurious texture. Since the results are often called *stews*, sometimes people call braising *stewing*, though you don't necessarily sear the food first when you stew.

Braising is used frequently to slow-cook tough pieces of meat—short ribs, brisket, veal shank, and so on—but you can make delicious braised fish, chicken, and vegetables; the cooking time is shorter than for meat braises, but there's nothing wrong with that.

Sautéing

Sautéing (it means "jump") is the method for cooking food in oil or butter: Put a large skillet on the stove and add the butter or oil. Turn the heat to medium-high. When the butter bubbles or the oil shimmers, add the food you want to sauté. You can dredge the pieces of food in flour, bread crumbs, or seasonings before adding them, but it isn't necessary. (What *is* necessary is some fat; otherwise you're "pan-grilling," a technique that's useful only if the food you're cooking has some fat in it to begin with; see Pan-Grilled Steak, page 717.)

The idea is to sizzle the food (some say you "surprise" it) to create a crust around it, so that it's lightly browned (caramelized, therefore tasty) outside and tender and moist inside. You must follow a few rules to get there: Make sure the fat is hot, almost smoking, before you add the food. And don't crowd the pan or else the food will steam and never brown. (An inch or so between big pieces is fine; smaller pieces require less elbow room.) Once everything starts cooking, don't mess with anything until the pieces start to brown and release easily from the pan. You should be able to hear the food sputtering as it cooks and see the fat bubbling around the edges as they brown. You can adjust the heat and gently swirl the fat around if you like, but let the food itself be.

Panfrying

The related panfrying, also called *shallow frying,* is sautéing but with more fat, halfway between sautéing and deep frying. You put about $1/2$ inch of oil in a large, deep skillet over medium-high heat. When it's hot, you add the food; since the food isn't submerged, you've got to turn it to cook the other side, but because there's more fat than with sautéing, the crust develops better, similar to deep frying.

Panfrying works best for cooking thin slices (veal, chicken, or eggplant cutlets, sole fillets, etc.), small pieces (meat chunks, scallops and shrimp, thick-cut vegetables or fruits), and battered foods and fritters—whenever you want some serious crisping but don't want to deep-fry. As with sautéing, you can dredge the food in a topping or even batter it or do nothing to it before panfrying; it depends on whether you want a coating.

Stir-Frying

Stir-frying is a lot like sautéing, except you keep things moving. Though woks are marketed as the ideal pans for stir-frying, this is only the case if you have a special stovetop burner for accommodating a wok, which almost no one does. Better, for the vast majority of us, is a regular old skillet, preferably large and cast iron. Start by putting the pan on the stove over medium-high or in this case even high heat, add some fat—for stir-frying it's always oil—and let it get very hot, almost smoking. Then you add the food and stir. For more details about the different ways to precook, add, or remove ingredients, see "6 Tips for Successful Stir-Fried Vegetables" on page 242.

Deep Frying

Like sautéing and stir-frying, deep frying uses hot oil to cook and brown food. You just use a lot more of it, so the oil surrounds the food. When it's done right, the result is crisp, moist, hot, and ethereal (I'm sure I don't have to sell you on how good fried food can be). Mostly, success depends on having enough good oil at the right temperature, usually 350°F or a bit higher.

Though deep frying is easy, it's a bit of a production, so I consider it special-occasion cooking, though there is nothing like a spontaneous bit of it on a weeknight. In any case, the rewards are worth the work, especially when you control the ingredients and everyone can eat the results crisp and piping hot.

Countertop electric deep-fryers make things easy but are really worth the expense and space only if you deep-fry a lot. Assuming you're not going that route, use a Dutch oven or a large, deep saucepan (a medium saucepan is fine if you want to use less oil and don't mind working in batches). The best oils are grapeseed (neutral and clean), peanut (best for Asian-type frying), and olive (best for European-type frying). Plain supermarket vegetable oil—corn, soy, canola, or a blend—is okay, too.

Put at least 2 inches of oil into the pot; there should be several inches of room left to allow the food and the oil to rise without overflowing. Turn the heat on the burner to medium and wait several minutes before you check the temperature; a candy or frying thermometer is ideal for this (all deep-frying recipes give you a specific temperature, or should). If you don't have one, put a piece of plain bread in the oil. It should bubble, float immediately to the top, and turn golden brown within 30 to 60 seconds. If it sinks and soaks up oil, jack up the heat a notch. If it doesn't sink and turns brown quickly,

lower the heat a bit; give the oil a few minutes to adjust, then test again.

It's very important not to overheat the oil because it can spontaneously catch fire (though this has never happened to me or anyone I've ever known, so don't get freaked out here). If you see the oil start to smoke, turn off the heat or carefully move it to a cool burner. If the oil catches fire, don't put water on it or try to move it. If you can, slip a lid over the pan and turn off the heat. Or use a fire extinguisher or smother it with a cup or two of baking soda, flour, or sand.

Add the food to the oil with metal tongs or a slotted spoon, allowing plenty of room. (Crowding will lower the temperature and prevent proper browning; work in batches if necessary.) Gently turn the food as it cooks so it browns evenly. Then, if you're new to deep frying, you might want to take a piece out when it looks done and cut it open. There should be a nice crisp crust surrounding a tender, just-done interior. Remove the cooked food to drain and you're ready to fry another batch. If you need to add more oil to the pot, be sure to let it heat thoroughly before proceeding.

Boiling

Few things are more straightforward than this most fundamental of moist-heat cooking methods. Put water in a pot (usually to about two-thirds full) and turn the heat to high. When the bubbles start to vigorously break the surface, the water has reached a rolling boil. (This is what I refer to when I say to bring a pot of water to a boil.) Usually, you'll add salt.

Boiling works well for most food but is used most frequently for dried ingredients like pasta, rice, or legumes, where the food must absorb water as it cooks. And boiling is necessary for stocks and soups, where the water is part of the final dish. Many fresh vegetables are also great boiled, and plain boiled meat or fish can be good too (we usually call this *poaching*).

Boiling can leave some foods bland and leached of nutrients, especially if you overcook, so check the food frequently to prevent it from turning to mush.

Parboiling would be better described as preboiling, and it refers to a brief boiling before draining and using another technique to finish the cooking. I frequently use this method in conjunction with shocking (see page 240) to prepare vegetables for stir-frying, but it's handy any time you want to partially prepare ingredients in advance.

Simmering is when liquids bubble gently, just below the point of a rolling boil. *Poaching* is also another word for simmering.

Steaming

Steaming is an excellent moist-heat method for cooking vegetables, fish, dumplings, tofu, and custards. The idea is to suspend food above, not in, boiling water. The pot should be large enough to hold the food comfortably and allow the steam to circulate freely.

I often choose steaming over boiling because it's almost as fast (faster, in a way, because you don't have to bring a big pot of water to a boil) and the color and texture can be better. To steam, place your steamer in a pot, fill with water to just below the steamer base, add your food, cover, and turn the heat to high. Once the water starts boiling, lower the heat so that it bubbles steadily. As with boiling, check the food frequently so it doesn't overcook and check the pot to make sure it doesn't run dry, adding more water if necessary.

You can steam with an inexpensive folding metal basket, though most have an annoying metal rod in the center, which you have to work around. Bamboo steamers can be fun, but they're not always easy to use. To me, the best solution is to rig your own steamer: Turn an ovenproof plate, shallow bowl, two or three ramekins, or a pie plate upside down in a large pot with a tight-fitting lid and put a plate right-side up on top; make sure it's stable.

Microwaving in a covered, moist environment—a piece of fish or broccoli on a plate with a tablespoon or two of water, for example—is very similar to steaming, and a good alternative.

WAYS TO RIG A STEAMER

1

2

There are many ways to make a steamer. (1) You can just buy a collapsible metal steaming insert, which will work in any pot. (2) Or you can use a heatproof plate, slightly smaller than the pot; to raise it off the bottom of the pot, put it on an upside-down plate, a couple of small ramekins, a "raft" of sticks, or whatever else is heatproof and stable.

Sauces, Condiments, Herbs, and Spices

IN THE LAST TEN YEARS, NOTHING IN

cooking has changed as much as the way we season and accompany our food. This explains, in large part, why this chapter now appears here, in the front of *How to Cook Everything*. Sauces and seasonings have become easy, international, and omnipresent; they're much more important in everyday cooking than they used to be.

Until relatively recently, most popular sauces were French and downright intimidating. Often thickened, usually fat laden and stock based, almost always complicated, these old standbys now seem staid and tame.

In the last ten or twenty years, though, we've adopted a more straightforward approach to adding flavor, most of it decidedly un-French. From salsas to pesto to vinaigrette (yes, it's French—but it's raw) all the way to chutneys, cooked vegetable and fruit sauces, yogurt sauces, and the huge variety of chile pastes and spice pastes and blends, we have at our disposal a host of easy-to-make, easy-to-understand, and incredibly useful preparations.

The result is that you can take the blandest recipes you can find—steamed chicken or fish, plain rice or pasta, even a slice of toast—and find fifty different accompaniments for each, creating a powerfully flavorful dish every time.

Spice blends are crucial to this new approach to seasoning, especially if you're interested in exploring global cuisines. Easily assembled, with a long shelf life, they're perhaps the ultimate convenience food, whether used on their own or in a sauce or condiment. Some store-bought sauces and spice blends are bound to be staples in your kitchen. (There's a good recipe for ketchup here, but the reality is you're not likely to rely on it exclusively.) Even though there are decent bottled condiments, most homemade sauces and spice blends—from curry and chile powder to simple salsa—are far superior and, because they are customized, far more likable than anything you can buy.

ESSENTIAL RECIPES

Here is a handful of super-fast and almost ridiculously easy sauces based on ingredients you probably have on hand. Some are served cold or at room temperature. Most you can make ahead and store in the fridge for a bit. And all can be varied to go with virtually anything you make, at any time of year.

Five-Minute Drizzle Sauce

MAKES: 4 servings (1/2 cup)
TIME: 5 minutes

F **V**

Nothing could be easier or more versatile. All you have to do is boil some pasta or rice or broil a piece of chicken or fish, then get this going while it cooks. I'll start you off with the base recipe—a kind of warm vinaigrette—and a handful of variations, but no doubt you'll soon come up with even more ideas.

4 tablespoons extra virgin olive oil or butter

1 tablespoon minced onion, garlic, ginger, shallot, scallion, or lemongrass

2 tablespoons freshly squeezed lemon juice or mild vinegar, like balsamic

Salt and freshly ground black pepper

1 Put the oil or butter in a small saucepan over medium heat. When the oil is warm or the butter is melted, add the onion and cook, stirring occasionally, until it softens (turn the heat down if it starts to color), a minute or two.

2 Stir in 2 tablespoons water and the lemon juice and sprinkle with some salt and pepper; maintain the heat so it bubbles gently for a minute or two. Taste, adjust the seasoning, and serve.

Spiced Five-Minute Drizzle Sauce. Along with the onion or other aromatic, add a pinch of any spice (such as ground cumin, coriander, or saffron) or spice blend like chili powder or curry powder (to make your own, see pages 65–69), or a small cinnamon stick or piece of vanilla bean.

Herbed Five-Minute Drizzle Sauce. Just before serving, stir in some chopped fresh herbs: 2 tablespoons of milder herbs like parsley, basil, chives, cilantro, or mint or 2 teaspoons of more potent herbs like rosemary, tarragon, sage, or oregano.

 Fast   Make Ahead   **V** Vegetarian

Fiery Five-Minute Drizzle Sauce. Along with the onion or other aromatic, add 1 tablespoon minced fresh chile (like jalapeño or Thai) or a whole dried chile (chipotle is wonderful; whatever you use, remove it before serving) or a sprinkle of hot red pepper flakes or cayenne.

Sesame-Soy Five-Minute Drizzle Sauce. Replace the olive oil with 2 tablespoons each of dark sesame and peanut oil; replace the lemon juice with soy sauce. Along with the onion or other aromatic, add 1 tablespoon sesame seeds or finely chopped peanuts if you like. Finish by adding 2 tablespoons chopped fresh cilantro leaves just before using if desired.

Miso Five-Minute Drizzle Sauce. Scrap the whole main recipe and do this: Combine $^1/_2$ cup miso, $^1/_4$ cup sugar, and $^1/_4$ cup mirin (or 2 tablespoons honey mixed with 2 tablespoons water) or sake (white wine or even water is okay too) in a small saucepan. Bring almost to a boil to dissolve the sugar, then just keep warm until ready to serve.

Ten-Minute Juicy Drizzle Sauce. Almost any high-quality juice works here—try carrot, tomato, orange, or pomegranate, for example. Omit the lemon juice and water. In Step 2, stir in 1 cup fruit or vegetable juice instead. Bring the mixture to a boil and adjust the heat so it bubbles steadily. Cook, stirring occasionally, until the juice reduces by half and thickens almost to a syrup, about 5 minutes. Add herbs (see the first variation) if you like and serve.

5 Other Super-Fast Sauces or Condiments

1. Compound Butter (page 32)
2. Tahini Sauce or Dressing (page 35)
3. Raw Onion Chutney (page 36)
4. Thai Chile Sauce (page 39)
5. Homemade Mayonnaise (page 41)

✪ Fresh Tomato or Fruit Salsa

Salsa Fresca or Pico de Gallo

MAKES: About 2 cups
TIME: 15 minutes

Salsa fresca (also known as *pico de gallo* or, in Mexico, *salsa mexicana*) is fast, tasty, useful, and simple. It's fantastic with chips or grilled meat or fish but also simply cooked grains, eggs, and veggies. And if you double the recipe, you can serve this like a chunky gazpacho and eat it with a spoon.

To take this in an unusual direction, replace the tomatoes with a couple cups of fruit: Apples (especially tart green ones), peaches, pears, and plums are the obvious choices, but seeded grapes, pineapple, orange or grapefruit segments, and even cherries or berries are all wonderful.

2 large ripe fresh tomatoes, cored and chopped (about 1$^1/_2$ cups)

$^1/_2$ large white onion or 3 or 4 scallions, chopped

1 teaspoon minced garlic, or to taste

Minced fresh chile (like jalapeño, Thai, or less of habanero) or hot red pepper flakes or cayenne, to taste

$^1/_2$ cup chopped fresh cilantro or parsley leaves

2 tablespoons freshly squeezed lime juice or 1 tablespoon red wine vinegar

Salt and freshly ground black pepper

❶ Combine everything but the salt and pepper in a medium bowl. Sprinkle with salt and pepper, then taste and adjust the seasoning.

❷ If possible, let the flavors develop for 15 minutes or so before serving, but by all means serve within a couple of hours.

Puréed Tomato or Fruit Salsa. For a less chunky version: Toss the salsa into a food processor and blend as smooth as you like.

Chilean Salsa. A little more assertive but less acidic: Increase the minced garlic to 1 tablespoon; add 1 teaspoon chopped fresh oregano leaves and 1 to 2 tablespoons olive oil; omit the lime juice.

Salsa Cruda. This makes a good pasta sauce: Eliminate the onion and chile; substitute basil leaves for cilantro and balsamic vinegar for the lime juice. Add a tablespoon or more of good extra virgin olive oil.

Avocado–Red Pepper Salsa. Add a chopped avocado and chopped Roasted Red Peppers (page 330).

Bean Salsa. Black beans are most traditional, but pintos or even chickpeas work well here too: Add a cup of your favorite cooked beans; substitute red onion for the white and add 1 teaspoon ground cumin. Let sit for about 30 minutes to develop the flavors.

Mexican Cheese Salsa. Add $1/2$ cup or more crumbled queso fresco and replace the garlic with $1/2$ English cucumber, peeled and chopped.

✪ Simplest Yogurt Sauce

MAKES: 1 cup
TIME: 3 minutes
F **M** **V**

Good yogurt is sour and rich, practically a sauce itself; add a little salt and you're set. The recipe and variations here build on that idea, adding various seasonings or chopped vegetables in the traditions of (mostly) India—where yogurt sauces are called *raitas*—and the Middle East.

You can make your own yogurt (see page 823), but good yogurt is sold in stores too; just avoid those containing gelatin or pectin or lacking live cultures. Good yogurt may be thick or thin, it may have a hard, almost cream cheese layer on top, or it may not, but it always has a fresh, sweet-sour smell and delicious flavor. If you want a slightly thicker sauce, drain the yogurt for 15 minutes or so before starting (see page 824).

1 cup yogurt, preferably whole milk
1 teaspoon minced garlic

Salt and freshly ground black pepper
Freshly squeezed lemon juice if necessary

❶ Combine the yogurt with the garlic, a pinch of salt, and a grinding or two of pepper. Taste and adjust the seasoning, adding some lemon juice if necessary.

❷ Serve immediately or refrigerate for up to a few hours; bring back to near room temperature before serving.

Herbed Yogurt Sauce. Add $1/4$ cup chopped fresh herbs or to taste. Use mint leaves, parsley, dill, cilantro, or any other tender herb. A teaspoon of dried mint or dill is also acceptable (other dried herbs are not as good).

Onion Yogurt Sauce. Add a tablespoon or more minced onion, shallot, or scallion; you can omit the garlic or not, as you like.

Richer Yogurt Sauce. Top with a tablespoon or so of good extra virgin olive oil, along with a sprinkling of paprika or cumin if you like.

Avocado Yogurt Sauce. Stir in (or purée in a food processor) $1/2$ ripe avocado or more, along with a little extra lemon juice.

Raita (Cucumber Yogurt Sauce). The classic Indian yogurt sauce: Add about 1 cup cucumber, peeled if you like, seeded, and chopped (and salted if necessary, see page 207); or peeled, seeded, cored, and diced tomato; or any mixture of vegetables, like those you'd use in Chopped Salad, Five Ways (page 204).

Ginger Yogurt Sauce. Stir in a tablespoon or so of minced fresh ginger.

Fiery Yogurt Sauce. Add hot red pepper flakes, chili powder (to make your own, see page 66), or minced fresh chile to taste.

Spicy Yogurt Sauce. Add a pinch or more of cumin, paprika, cayenne, dry mustard, saffron (let the sauce stand for a while before using it or use turmeric for the same color if less flavor), or ground ginger.

Nutty Yogurt Sauce. Or Seedy Yogurt Sauce: Stir in up to $1/2$ cup finely chopped nuts or seeds. Shredded unsweetened coconut is an Indian classic, but anything is fair game. (Poppy seeds look gorgeous.)

Yogurt Sauce with Beans. Add 1 cup drained cooked (or canned) beans, especially chickpeas.

Sweet Yogurt Sauce. A spoonful of honey—either alone or in combination with any of the above—goes well with heavily seasoned food, and the sweetness helps round out yogurt's natural acidity.

Blue Cheese Dressing. Good with sour cream or mayonnaise too: Add about $^1/_2$ cup crumbled blue cheese (Roquefort, for example) along with a bit of freshly squeezed lemon juice. Omit the garlic.

Vinaigrette: The Ultimate Sauce

You could make the argument that vinaigrette—basically, oil and vinegar with seasonings—is not only the mother of all salad dressings, but also of sauces, and marinades for that matter. (See pages 198–202 for a master recipe and tons of flavoring options.) Here's a handful of ideas for using vinaigrette beyond salads:

1. Toss with finely chopped fruit or vegetables (or both) for an instant salsa.
2. Serve as a dipping sauce for crudités, dumplings, or other finger foods.
3. Use as a base for building other dips by adding yogurt or sour cream.
4. Drizzle on plain roasted, broiled, grilled, or steamed meat or vegetables toward the end of cooking.
5. Use to marinate fish, meat, or poultry before broiling, grilling, or roasting. Just be sure to blot the food dry before cooking; often I'll also cover it with a fresh coat of oil to promote browning. If you want to use the leftover marinade as a sauce, be sure to boil it for several minutes first.
6. Brush on thickly sliced bread before grilling or broiling or use as a condiment to drizzle on sandwiches.

7 Uses for Simplest Yogurt Sauce

Any of the previous yogurt sauces can be used in myriad different ways. Some ideas:

1. As a salad dressing (thin with a little lemon juice or sherry vinegar and olive oil)
2. Alongside any simply grilled, broiled, roasted, steamed, or sautéed meat, fish, or poultry
3. Atop grilled or steamed vegetables or baked potatoes
4. As a dip for raw veggies or chips or any sort of fritter or other fried snack
5. Stirred into cooked rice or other grains for extra creaminess, body, flavor, and protein
6. Cooked on top of roasted vegetables, poultry, or meat as you might cheese (do not overcook, but add during the last 5 or 10 minutes of cooking)
7. Stirred into chopped raw fruit and/or nuts for a more complex fruit salad

✪ Soy Dipping Sauce and Marinade

MAKES: About 1$^1/_2$ cups
TIME: 15 minutes

Ⓕ Ⓜ Ⓥ

This is an ideal dipping sauce for simply prepared (even steamed) fish, shrimp, chicken, or pork, and of course Fried Wontons or Egg Rolls (page 102); it's also perfect for drizzling over Sushi Bowls (page 473) or tossing with hot or cold Chinese egg noodles. And you can make it even easier by skipping any or all of the garlic, ginger, or scallion. You also might try substituting $^1/_4$ cup ketchup for the sugar (don't knock it until you try it) or, in Korean style, adding $^1/_4$ cup toasted sesame seeds to the sauce.

If you don't have rice vinegar or sake, use fruity white wine or a tablespoon of cider or white vinegar mixed with a tablespoon of water.

$^1/_2$ cup soy sauce

2 tablespoons rice vinegar or sake

2 tablespoons dark sesame oil

1 tablespoon sugar

2 large cloves garlic, minced

1 tablespoon minced or grated fresh ginger

¼ cup minced scallion

Combine all the ingredients and stir until the sugar is dissolved. Use immediately or refrigerate for up to 2 days.

Tahini Soy Sauce. Thicker and richer and terrific with anything grilled: Omit the ginger and scallion. Substitute ¼ cup honey for the vinegar and add 2 tablespoons tahini; sprinkle with hot red pepper flakes if you like.

Sweet-and-Sour Sauce. Omit the sesame oil. Increase the sugar to 2 tablespoons; increase the vinegar to 3 tablespoons. Cook briefly over low heat, stirring, to dissolve the sugar. Taste and add more vinegar or sugar if necessary. Cool before serving or use warm as a basting sauce for roasted, grilled, or broiled vegetables, fish, poultry, or meat. You can make this hot-and-sour sauce by adding cayenne to taste.

The Basics of Flavored Oils

By taking an herb, spice, or aromatic and infusing its essence into oil, you create something delicious, akin to Compound Butter (page 32).

The first thing to consider is the oil itself: Do you want olive oil, another flavorful oil like peanut or dark sesame oil, or a neutral oil like grapeseed or corn? This is a judgment call you make on a case-by-case basis, but it's mostly common sense. You're likely to pair rosemary with olive oil, for example, because both are most often used in Mediterranean cooking; you're likely to pair star anise with peanut oil because both are likely to be used in Asian cooking. But whenever you're in doubt, reach for your neutral oil; you can't go wrong here. (In any case, do not use your best olive oil for infused oils; it will not make the final product any better.)

Infused oils can go bad and even cause illness, but you need not worry about this if you make small—½ cup—batches, enough to store comfortably in the refrigerator and use in a week or two. You don't want it sitting around much longer than that.

Refrigerating many oils causes them to solidify, but this isn't a problem: Solidified oils will melt as soon as they come back to room temperature (or you can use them as a spread).

One last word: Don't bother to make infused oils with ground spices or herbs. These flavor oil (or anything else) so quickly that infusion contributes nothing further. And they're too easy to burn.

Flavored Oil

MAKES: ½ cup

TIME: 20 minutes, plus time to cool

It's almost impossible to use too much of the flavoring ingredients in this preparation, but if you do—if your oil becomes too strong—simply dilute it with a little fresh oil. You can certainly mix or match among the "OR" options here, but remember that combinations will limit the range of the oil's usefulness.

¼ cup washed and dried fresh herb leaves: rosemary, thyme, bay leaf (dried will do), tarragon, marjoram, oregano, etc.

OR

1 tablespoon whole spice: star anise, peppercorns, cloves, allspice, nutmeg, dried chiles (or less if they're very hot), etc.

OR

Aromatics: 2 cloves garlic, lightly crushed; or 2 tablespoons fresh ginger slices, roughly chopped shallot or scallion, celery leaves, or a combination

Pinch salt

½ cup extra virgin olive oil or neutral oil, like grapeseed or corn

1 Combine the ingredients in a saucepan over low heat. Warm gently until the mixture sizzles, then continue to cook until the oil is very fragrant, another minute or two.

2 Cool, then strain into a clean bottle or other container. Refrigerate and use within a month or, at the most, two.

Pesto, Herb Purées, and Herb Sauces

Herb pastes and purées give as much bang for the buck as any sauce preparation I know. The herb is always the dominant flavor (just look at the quantities), even when it's combined with spices or garlic. Use the best oil you can find and—more important—make sure it tastes fresh.

Traditional Pesto

Pesto Genovese

MAKES: About 1 cup

TIME: 10 minutes

The best pesto is made with a mortar and pestle, and in Genoa, where pesto originated, few people will admit to using a food processor. But when you get into their kitchens, that's just what they do. And so do I.

If you have a garden filled with basil, by all means make as much pesto as you can and throw it in the freezer. It keeps fairly well, but to help retain its bright green color, drizzle a layer of olive oil over the top once it's in a container and don't add Parmesan until you're ready to use the sauce.

If you're using store-bought basil, you might as well just make it in the quantities given here and enjoy it fresh. And although it's not traditional, you can substitute parsley for all or some of the basil, with fine results.

2 loosely packed cups fresh basil leaves, rinsed and dried

Salt

1/2 clove garlic, peeled, or more to taste

2 tablespoons pine nuts or chopped walnuts

1/2 cup extra virgin olive oil, or more as desired

1/2 cup freshly grated Parmesan, pecorino Romano, or other hard cheese (optional)

1 Combine the basil with a pinch of salt, the garlic, the nuts, and about half the oil in a food processor or blender. Process, stopping to scrape down the sides of the container if necessary and adding the rest of the oil gradually. Add more oil if you prefer a thinner mixture.

2 Store in the refrigerator for a week or two or in the freezer for several months. Stir in the cheese by hand just before serving.

Pesto with Butter. Toss this with pasta or rice or use it as you would Compound Butter (page 32); it's really quite special: Blend in 2 tablespoons softened butter along with the last bit of oil (do not store this version).

Mint or Dill "Pesto." Super on pasta or grilled fish, chicken, or vegetables: Substitute mint or dill for the basil; the garlic is optional. Use a neutral oil, like grapeseed or corn, instead of olive oil and omit the cheese. Finish, if you like, with a squeeze of lemon juice. Use within a day.

Arugula "Pesto." Terrific with grilled steak or vegetables or plain rice: Substitute arugula—tough stems removed—for the basil. Omit the cheese. Use within a day.

Parsley (or Other Herb) Purée

MAKES: About 1 cup

TIME: 10 minutes

Simpler, purer, less complex than traditional pesto, parsley purée is also even more of a standby. For one thing, you can find decent parsley year-round. For another, it's a brighter, fresher purée and therefore less specific in its uses. And, as you can see from the variations, it's equally effective with different herbs.

2 cups fresh parsley leaves (thin stems are okay), rinsed and dried

Salt

½ clove garlic, peeled, or more to taste

½ cup extra virgin olive oil, or more as desired

1 tablespoon sherry vinegar or freshly squeezed lemon juice

❶ Combine the parsley with a pinch of salt, the garlic, and about half the oil in a food processor or blender. Process, stopping to scrape down the sides of the container if necessary, and adding the rest of the oil gradually. Add the vinegar, then a little more oil or some water if you prefer a thinner mixture.

❷ Taste and adjust the seasoning, then serve or cover and refrigerate for up to a couple of days.

Cilantro, Dill, Basil, or Mint Purée. These are good for their straight herbaceous flavors; cilantro purée is terrific with grilled chicken, mint with lamb, and so on: Substitute any of these herbs (leaves only or leaves and very thin stems) for the parsley.

Chimichurri. Very strong stuff: Use 3 or more cloves garlic, 2 tablespoons vinegar or freshly squeezed lemon juice, and at least 1 teaspoon of hot red pepper flakes. Do not refrigerate.

Green Olive Mojo. Caribbean and intense: Reduce the olive oil to ¼ cup; use ¼ cup freshly squeezed lime juice, or to taste, in place of the vinegar or lemon juice. After puréeing, use the food processor to pulse in 1 cup pitted green olives; or chop the olives by hand and add them. In any case, do not purée them.

Cilantro (or Other Herb) Sauce

MAKES: About 1 cup

TIME: 10 minutes

  Ⓥ

Here just enough oil is added to thicken the mixture a bit; it doesn't become creamy like pesto, but it retains a vibrant herb flavor. Wonderful drizzled over fish or vegetables or stirred into soups. You can also make this with parsley, basil, dill, mint, or a combination.

2 cups loosely packed fresh cilantro leaves

Salt

1 clove garlic, peeled

3 tablespoons peanut oil or neutral oil, like grapeseed or corn

1 tablespoon freshly squeezed lime juice

❶ Combine the cilantro, a pinch of salt, the garlic, and the oil in a food processor or blender. Process, stopping to scrape down the sides of the container if necessary. Add the lime juice and blend for a second; add a little water if necessary to thin the mixture, then purée.

❷ Taste and adjust the seasoning, then serve or cover and refrigerate for up to a couple of days.

Cilantro "Pesto" with Ginger and Chile. Serious kick here and a must for chile lovers: Double the garlic and add about 1 tablespoon roughly chopped fresh ginger and hot fresh chile (like habanero or jalapeño, seeded) or hot red pepper flakes to taste.

REMOVING LEAVES FROM THYME

To remove the leaves from thyme or other fresh herbs, hold the top of the stem tightly with one hand and run your fingers downward to strip off the leaves.

The Herb Lexicon

Literally thousands of plants are used as herbs. The ones used in this book are in the following charts, which are pretty self-explanatory. The first lists the most frequently

Ⓕ Fast **Ⓜ** Make Ahead **Ⓥ** Vegetarian

EVERYDAY HERBS

HERB	DESCRIPTION	USES
Basil *Basilico*	The most familiar varieties (like Genovese) have flavors of licorice and cloves; the more exotic, like Thai, may be peppery and minty. Sold everywhere and easy to grow in warm weather.	Best raw or cooked only briefly. Use the leaves whole or tear them; or chop them if you don't mind the leaves turning black. The edible flowers look great in salads.
Bay Leaves *Sweet Bay, Sweet Laurel, Bay Laurel*	Glossy, green, and leathery when fresh; grayed and brittle when dried. The flavor is subtle but complex; fresh are much stronger than dried, though both are good; whole dried leaves are far better than ground. Turkish (small, round leaves) are superior to Californian (long, narrow leaves). Easy to grow in Mediterranean climates.	In stocks, soups, sauces, poaching liquids, to flavor vinegars; with roasts of all kinds (throw in a few leaves the next time you're roasting vegetables).
Chervil	Looks similar to parsley but smaller, with lacy leaves and an anise-basil flavor. Fresh only; dried is useless. Easy to grow in not-too-hot climates, but so delicate it's not easy to find in supermarkets.	So delicate it's best used raw or added at the end of cooking. Delicious in omelets, creamy or light sauces, salads, and with vegetables.
Chives	Bright green, hollow, and grasslike, with mild onion flavor. Garlic chives have wider and flatter leaves and a more garlicky taste but aren't as common. Fresh are far preferable, sold everywhere, and easy to grow.	Best raw or cooked only briefly. An assertive addition to soft cheese spreads and compound butter.
Cilantro *Coriander, Chinese Parsley, Mexican Parsley*	Tender and parsleylike in appearance, but distinctive in aroma and flavor (those who don't like it, and they're not insignificant in number, say it tastes soapy). Useless dried, though the seeds are the spice coriander, see page 61.) Sold everywhere and easy to grow.	Like basil and many other herbs, best added at the last minute. Widely associated with the flavors of Mexican, Thai, and Indian cooking. Use the roots in stews or other long-cooked dishes.
Dill *Dill Weed*	Stalks with blue-green feathery, tender leaves, with familiar flavor. Fresh is superior to dried, which has less flavor but at least retains some character. Sold in most supermarkets and easy to grow in not-too-hot weather. Dill seed is used as a spice.	Use at the end of cooking, as its flavor is diminished by hot temperatures (though tying stems in a bundle and cooking with stews gives a nice flavor). Super in dishes made with sour cream, yogurt, or mustard or tossed into a green salad.
Marjoram *Sweet Marjoram, Knotted Marjoram, Wild Marjoram*	Short, square stems with light green, fuzzy, oval leaves. Often confused with oregano, but superior. Dried marjoram isn't too bad, though far more pungent than fresh. Sold in most supermarkets and an easy-to-grow perennial in most climates.	Add fresh toward the end of cooking; crumble dried leaves between your fingers. Wonderful with green salads, vinaigrettes, eggs, beans, all sorts of vegetables, and especially tomato sauces.
Mint	Square stems with bright green, wrinkled leaves (spearmint) or smooth ones (peppermint and other varieties). Best fresh, though dried is sometimes a decent substitute. Sold in most supermarkets and easy to grow (invasive, in fact).	Chop or crush fresh leaves to release their flavor. Traditional with peas or potatoes, goes well with many vegetables and fruits; perfect in yogurt-based sauces, chutneys, and many Southeast Asian dishes. Ideal in herbal teas and cocktails.

HERB	DESCRIPTION	USES
Oregano *Greek Oregano, Mexican Oregano, sometimes Wild Marjoram*	Square stems with dark green, fuzzy, spade-shaped leaves. Stronger and spicier than marjoram. Fresh is infinitely better, but dried is acceptable. Sold in most supermarkets, and an easy-to-grow perennial in most climates.	Fresh and dried can be cooked or used as a garnish in small amounts. Good with tomatoes, cheeses, pizza, vegetables, beans, and vinaigrettes.
Parsley	Crisp stems with bunches of dark leaves with fresh flavor. There are two varieties: curly and flat-leaf (Italian) parsley; the latter is somewhat better, but it's not worth making a big deal about. Sold everywhere; dried is useless.	Impossible to overstate its importance; used in just about everything from soups to salads, vinaigrettes, sauces, vegetables, eggs, and pasta and as a garnish. Especially valuable in winter for its freshness.
Rosemary	Grayish green needles on woody branches, with crisp, piney aroma and flavor. Fresh rosemary is sold increasingly in supermarkets and is easy to grow as a perennial (warmer climates) or an annual. Dried leaves are also flavorful.	Wonderful with beans and roast meats, also with most vegetables, egg dishes, pasta, and breads. The woody branches make perfect skewers for broiling or grilling too.
Sage	Soft, woolly, oval grayish green or multicolored leaves. Sharply flavored, slightly bitter, and very aromatic. Fresh leaves are best; dried are stronger and somewhat mustier, but not bad. Increasingly sold in supermarkets or can be grown as a perennial almost anywhere.	Use fresh leaves whole or chopped. Crumble dried leaves with your fingers. One of the most important herbs of Italy; wonderful with beans, stuffings, breads, biscuits, and pasta.
Tarragon	Narrow, lance-shaped, bright to dark green leaves, with strong, complex flavor and aroma, faintly licoricelike. Fresh is always best; dried is less flavorful but usable. Often sold in supermarkets and easily grown as a perennial in most climates. (If you have a choice, grow French tarragon.)	Whole or chopped fresh leaves can be cooked; flavor is not at all tamed by heat, so use it sparingly. Good with seafood, chicken, or eggs. Crumble dried tarragon between your fingers to release essential oils.
Thyme	A small shrub with tiny green or grayish green leaves. Minty, lemony, and earthy. Fresh is more pungent and aromatic than dried, though dried is useful. Often sold in supermarkets and easily grown as a perennial in most climates.	The classic French cooking herb, often used in long-simmering or braising recipes. Use fresh leaves and tips as a garnish, but very sparingly—its strong flavor easily overwhelms everything else. Perfect teamed with olive oil and garlic at the beginning of many sautés.

used herbs, in alphabetical order. The second includes several others that are a little more unusual and are sometimes but not always found in supermarkets.

Though no herb is a direct substitute for any other, there are many situations in which you're not necessarily looking for a specific flavor but rather the freshness that herbs provide. In these cases you can substitute parsley for basil, cilantro for mint, and so on. Just don't expect the end product to taste the same.

Fresh herbs keep best when stored in the refrigerator. Most should simply be wrapped in damp paper towels and slipped into a plastic bag. Set those with fragile leaves—like basil, chervil, dill, mint, and parsley—stem down in a jar of water with a plastic bag over the leaves; change the water every day (and try not to upset the glass!).

Store dried herbs in sealed lightproof jars (or in a dark place) for up to a year. Taste before using them and you'll know when it's time for a new batch.

Before using, it's usually best to strip herb leaves from

SPECIALTY HERBS

HERB	DESCRIPTION	USES
Epazote *Mexican Tea, Worm-seed, Pigweed*	Bright green, jagged, and pointed leaves with green stems, usually sold in bunches when fresh. Its aroma is unusual and its taste powerful, but it adds a valuable flavor to Mexican dishes. Fresh leaves are better, but dried are more common. Sold in Mexican and Latin American markets; easily grown as an annual.	Use chopped or whole fresh or dried leaves in small quantities. Traditionally used with beans and some moles; also good with corn and other summer vegetables, in quesadillas, and in scrambled eggs.
Lavender	Narrow gray-green leaves with long purple or pink flower spikes. The scent and flavor is minty and floral—you'll recognize it immediately. Can be grown as a perennial in any moderate climate.	Fresh leaves and flowers can be minced and tossed into salads and fruit dishes or cooked in sauces, candies, and pastries. Great with roasted or grilled meat, especially lamb. Works well in infusions (see page 962).
Lemongrass *Citronella Root, Sereh*	A stiff, narrow stalk that could be mistaken for a scallion. Strong citrus flavor and aroma; think citronella candles. Best fresh; dried is acceptable. Sold in supermarkets and Asian markets (especially Vietnamese and Thai). Easy to grow in warm climates or as an annual in temperate zones.	Cut off woody tops and peel off tough outer layers (see illustration below); mince or pound the pieces to release their flavor and aroma. Soak dried lemongrass in hot water for at least 30 minutes before using.
Lime Leaves *Kaffir Lime Leaves*	Tough, shiny green leaves; very aromatic, with unusually floral and limy flavor. Fresh is best, but dried are good. Sold in most Asian markets and can be grown wherever citrus will grow.	In Southeast Asian dishes of all types. Mince or toss in the whole leaves during cooking; use double the amount of dried leaves for fresh. Or use a teaspoon of grated or minced lime zest for each leaf.
Shiso *Perilla, Japanese Basil or Mint, Beefsteak Plant*	Flat bright green or reddish purple leaves with a jagged edge. Combination of basil, mint, and cinnamon flavors. Dried is less flavorful but somewhat useful. Sold in many Asian (especially Japanese) and some Mexican markets; easy to grow inside or out (like mint, it is invasive and will spread like mad).	As you would use basil or mint. Traditionally served with sashimi and sushi, cucumbers, pickles, tempura; in salads, soups; when dried, sprinkled over rice.

PREPARING LEMONGRASS

To prepare lemongrass, cut off the woody tops and peel off tough outer layers.

Make a couple lengthwise cuts, then slice crosswise to mince.

their tougher, more bitter stems (this is especially true of the strongest herbs like rosemary and oregano). Just hold the top of the stem tightly with one hand and run your fingers downward to strip off the leaves.

The Basics of Compound Butters

Compound butter is nothing more than butter mixed with a flavorful ingredient: anything from an herb or spice to a bit of fruit, like lemon, or a condiment like mustard or soy sauce. It's best used as a finishing ingredient in sauces and also on grilled or broiled meats and vegetables.

To make it, you just combine butter and your chosen ingredient(s); there is no exact ratio. But use good-quality unsalted butter and certainly avoid margarine. (If you want to avoid butter, see Flavored Oil, page 26.)

You can refrigerate compound butter for days or freeze it for a month or so. Roll it into a log and wrap in two or

ROLLING COMPOUND BUTTER INTO A LOG

For an elegant presentation, you can roll compond butter into a log; using wax or parchment paper is the easiest, though foil works in a pinch. A rubber spatula can help form smooth sides, though rolling with your hands is fine, too. Once the butter is firm, remove the wrapper and cut crosswise into pats as thick or thin as you like.

three layers of plastic before freezing. When you need some, slice a piece off and return the rest to the freezer.

Compound Butter

MAKES: 4 to 8 servings
TIME: 10 minutes

Ⓕ Ⓜ Ⓥ

Herb butters are the most basic and traditional compound butters; variations follow. Bear in mind that some herbs are stronger than others—and spices are stronger still—so adjust the amount based on taste.

2 tablespoons chopped parsley, chervil, cilantro, chives, dill, or sage, or smaller amounts of tarragon, rosemary, or thyme leaves, or a combination

4 tablespoons (1/2 stick) butter, at room temperature

Salt

Freshly ground black pepper (optional)

Juice of 1/2 lemon (optional)

❶ Use a fork to cream the herbs with the butter; add salt as needed and pepper and lemon juice if you like.

❷ Use or wrap and refrigerate or freeze for later.

15 Easy Flavorings for Compound Butter

These can be used in conjunction with the herb or not, as you prefer (same with the lemon juice) or combined with one another. Amounts are approximate; adjust to taste.

1. 2 tablespoons chopped scallion

2. 1 tablespoon minced fresh ginger

3. For a sweet butter: 1 to 2 tablespoons honey or minced crystallized ginger

4. 1 teaspoon grated lemon or lime zest, along with 1 tablespoon freshly squeezed lemon or lime juice

5. 1 tablespoon capers, rinsed and mashed, with 1 teaspoon minced lemon zest

6. 1 tablespoon balsamic vinegar, with 1 tablespoon minced shallot if you like

7. 1 tablespoon Dijon mustard or horseradish or 1 teaspoon wasabi powder

8. 2 teaspoons Spanish paprika
9. 2 tablespoons minced pitted green or black olives
10. 1 teaspoon minced garlic
11. Mashed flesh of ¹/₂ peach, plum, or pear
12. 1 or 2 teaspoons soy sauce
13. 1 or 2 (or more if you're a fanatic) mashed anchovies
14. 2 or 3 tablespoons finely chopped dried shrimp
15. 1 or 2 tablespoons minced fresh or dried chiles, or to taste

6 Almost-as-Easy Flavorings for Compound Butter

Cooking takes the edge off garlic, onions, and other foods, so you'll have a milder-tasting compound butter. Let the flavoring cool before adding them.

1. 2 or more cloves Roasted Garlic (page 303).
2. 1 teaspoon minced garlic cooked in 1 tablespoon butter for 2 to 3 minutes, or until soft. Enhance it with 1 teaspoon minced fresh ginger (add for the last minute of cooking) and a little soy sauce.
3. 2 finely chopped scallions or shallots, sautéed with 1 or 2 tablespoons butter in a pan over medium-low heat.
4. About 3 tablespoons chopped cashews or other nuts, sautéed with a tablespoon or two of butter in a pan over medium-low heat until light golden.
5. About 2 tablespoons chopped carrot, cooked over medium-low heat in a tablespoon or two of butter until very soft. Nice with parsley.
6. 2 pieces crisply cooked bacon, crumbled.

Fresh (Uncooked) Sauces

A classically trained French chef would scoff at calling a bunch of chopped tomatoes, onions, chiles, and seasonings a "sauce," yet salsa is most Americans' favorite condiment, and if it's not a sauce, I don't know what is.

Salsa isn't the only uncooked sauce: Here too are chutneys, American classics like horseradish sauce and relishes, and Asian-style dipping sauces. (For the simplest uncooked sauces, see pages 22 to 26 in the Essential Recipes section.)

Generally the building blocks are simple and vegetable based, but fruits and nuts can also be excellent. Season with herbs, aromatics, or chiles (or all three) and balance with acidity or sweetness as needed.

Fresh Tomatillo Salsa

MAKES: About 2 cups
TIME: 10 minutes

Super-fresh and perfect in summer. Look for firm unshriveled tomatillos still covered with tight husks (after husking, be sure to rinse off the tacky residue). If fresh tomatillos are not available, canned are okay, though the results will be less crunchy.

Poblanos and some other fresh chiles have tough skins that are best removed. The easiest way to peel them is to char the skin, which has the added benefit of giving the salsa a light smoky flavor. You can, however, skip this step if you're rushed.

> 2 medium poblano or other mild fresh green chiles
>
> 2 cups chopped husked tomatillos (about 1 pound)
>
> 3 scallions, chopped
>
> 2 teaspoons minced garlic, or to taste
>
> ¹/₄ cup chopped fresh cilantro leaves
>
> 3 tablespoons freshly squeezed lime juice, or to taste
>
> Salt and freshly ground black pepper

1 If you like, roast the chiles according to the directions on page 330. Or leave raw. Either way, remove the stems and seeds from the chiles and either mince them or pulse them a few times in a food processor.

2 Put the remaining ingredients into a medium bowl with the chiles and stir to combine. Taste, adjust the seasoning, and serve or refrigerate for up to 2 days (bring back to room temperature and adjust the seasoning again before serving).

Green Tomato Salsa. Good in fall, when green tomatoes are plentiful and cheap: Substitute green tomatoes for the tomatillos.

Green Chile Salsa. Stronger: Replace the tomatillos with 2 cups chopped fresh mild green chiles, like more poblano or New Mexican; increase the minced garlic to 2 tablespoons; substitute parsley for the cilantro and lemon for the lime juice.

Pepita Salsa. Easily made from the pantry: Replace half of the tomatillos with toasted pepitas (see page 317). Serve immediately.

Corn Salsa. Distinctive and delicious: Substitute 2 cups corn kernels from Corn on the Cob, Grilled or Roasted (page 289) for the tomatillos.

Jícama Salsa. Very crunchy: Replace the tomatillos with chopped peeled jícama and substitute minced fresh ginger for the garlic. Add 2 tablespoons chopped fresh mint leaves. Let sit for about 30 minutes before serving.

Papaya Salsa

MAKES: About 2 cups
TIME: 20 minutes

This fruit salsa is a natural with fish and seafood, and you can make any fruit the star here: mango, melon, and nectarine are some of my favorites. Just be sure to taste while you're assembling, balancing the sweetness (which, of course, varies with every fruit) with the acidity of the citrus juice and the heat of the chiles.

2 cups firm but ripe papaya, cut into ¹/₂-inch chunks

¹/₂ cup diced red onion

¹/₂ cup diced red, yellow, or green bell pepper or a combination

2 tablespoons minced fresh chile (like jalapeño or Thai), to taste, or hot red pepper flakes or cayenne, to taste

¹/₄ cup or more chopped fresh cilantro leaves

1 tablespoon olive oil

3 tablespoons freshly squeezed lime juice, or more to taste

Salt and freshly ground black pepper

1 Put all the ingredients in a medium bowl and stir to combine. Let sit for about 5 minutes, then taste and adjust the seasoning, adding more chile, lime, or salt as needed.

2 Serve immediately or refrigerate for up to a couple of hours. (Bring back to room temperature before serving.)

Citrus Salsa. Lovely in winter: Make this salsa just before serving it. Substitute a combination of orange, grapefruit, and lemon segments (see page 398) for the papaya. Omit the olive oil.

Peach-Melon-Tomato Salsa. Perfect in summer: Use 1 medium ripe tomato, 2 medium peaches, and ¹/₄ small cantaloupe (you should still have about 2 cups of fruit). Use basil or mint instead of cilantro if you like. Serve within 30 minutes.

Chipotle-Cherry Salsa. Unusual and wonderful: Replace the papaya with pitted cherries (fresh or frozen); omit the peppers and chile and instead add 1 tablespoon chopped canned chipotle chiles in adobo sauce. Serve at room temperature or cover and refrigerate for up to 2 days.

Radish Salsa

MAKES: About 2 cups
TIME: 30 minutes

Radishes are a classic salsa ingredient in Mexico, and the technique—mixing a vegetable (or fruit) with onion, an acid, chiles, and fresh herbs—is downright common. Serve with any Grilled Steak (page 717) or Cheese Quesadilla (page 109), Shredded Pork (page 759), or just a big bowl of tortilla chips.

 Fast Make Ahead Vegetarian

2 cups chopped radishes, like daikon, red, or a combination (about 1 pound)

$^1/_2$ English cucumber, peeled and diced

$^1/_2$ small red onion, chopped

1 scallion, thinly sliced

1 teaspoon minced garlic

1 tablespoon minced fresh chile (like jalapeño or Thai), or to taste, or hot red pepper flakes or cayenne, to taste

2 tablespoons freshly squeezed lemon juice, or more to taste

$^1/_4$ cup chopped fresh cilantro leaves

Salt and freshly ground black pepper

❶ Put all the ingredients in a medium bowl and mix thoroughly.

❷ Taste and adjust the seasoning, adding more chile, lemon, or salt as needed. Serve immediately or cover and refrigerate for up to a day.

Cucumber Salsa, Thai Style. Replace the radishes with additional diced cucumber and carrot (about 1 medium of each); red onion with shallots; and lemon with lime juice. Add a tablespoon of rice vinegar. Omit the garlic.

Green Papaya Salsa, Thai Style. Sort of a mini papaya salad: Substitute peeled, seeded, and shredded green papaya for the radishes, use lime instead of lemon juice, and replace the scallion and red onion with a thinly sliced shallot. Add a tablespoon or so of rice vinegar.

Tahini Sauce

MAKES: About 1 cup
TIME: 10 minutes

  Ⓥ

Ground sesame paste is the base for one of the fastest, easiest, richest sauces on the planet. You don't even need a food processor, though it makes the sauce much smoother and the variations easier.

The most common way to eat tahini sauce is on Falafel (page 439) or on a salad of cucumbers, tomatoes, and onions. But you can use it to dress all sorts of salads or drizzle on any not-too-heavy grilled fish, meat, or vegetable.

$^1/_2$ cup tahini, with a tablespoon or two of its oil

Juice of 1 lemon, or more to taste

1 clove garlic, peeled, or more to taste

$^1/_2$ teaspoon ground cumin (optional)

Salt and freshly ground black pepper

❶ Put the tahini, $^1/_2$ cup water, the lemon juice, garlic, and the cumin if you're using it in a food processor, sprinkle with salt and pepper, and process until smooth. Or whisk the ingredients in a bowl (mince the garlic first).

❷ Taste and adjust the seasoning, adding more lemon juice, oil, water, or garlic as you like. Serve immediately or cover tightly and use within a day or so.

Yogurt Tahini Sauce. Richer: Instead of water, use $^1/_2$ cup yogurt (whole milk, low-fat, or nonfat).

Coconut Tahini Sauce. Perfect with grilled or broiled chicken or pork: Instead of water, use $^1/_2$ cup coconut milk (to make your own, see page 389; use slightly less than $^1/_2$ cup canned with a little water).

Roasted Pepper Tahini Sauce. Use either the main recipe or either of the preceding variations and add a Roasted Red Pepper (page 330) to the food processor.

Roasted Garlic Tahini Sauce. Instead of the raw garlic, use the soft flesh from 1 head Roasted Garlic (page 303).

Minty Tahini Sauce. Add 1 cup fresh mint leaves to the food processor.

Curry Tahini Sauce. Omit the cumin and add up to 2 tablespoons curry powder (to make your own, see pages 66–67).

Anchovy Tahini Sauce. Lovely on Grilled or Broiled Eggplant (page 294) or steamed asparagus (see page 239): Omit the salt. Add 1 or 2 anchovies (if whisking, mash them first in the bottom of the bowl).

Homemade Horseradish

MAKES: About 1 cup
TIME: 10 minutes, plus time to rest

Thanks to the food processor, horseradish is easy to prepare. But it really clears out the sinuses, so be careful. If you're planning to process large quantities, consider goggles and gloves—really.

> One 1-foot-long horseradish root (about 1 pound)
> About ½ cup white or rice wine vinegar
> Salt

❶ Peel the horseradish with a sturdy vegetable peeler or paring knife and cut it into chunks. Put in a food processor with about half the vinegar. Process, stopping the machine and scraping the mixture down as needed, until finely minced. (Do not try this with a blender; it will not work. The only alternative is to grate the horseradish by hand.)

❷ Taste and add more vinegar as needed and salt to taste. Store in the refrigerator. Horseradish will keep almost indefinitely, but will become increasingly mild.

Cranberry Relish with Orange and Ginger

MAKES: About 4 cups
TIME: 10 minutes

 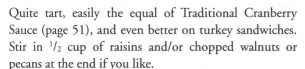

Quite tart, easily the equal of Traditional Cranberry Sauce (page 51), and even better on turkey sandwiches. Stir in ½ cup of raisins and/or chopped walnuts or pecans at the end if you like.

> 1 large navel or other orange
> 4 cups fresh cranberries (about 1 pound), picked over and rinsed, or frozen cranberries
> ½ cup sugar, or more to taste
> 1 teaspoon minced or grated fresh ginger, or to taste

❶ Use a vegetable peeler or paring knife to remove the entire zest of the orange; set aside. Remove and discard the thick white pith. Separate the orange into sections.

❷ Combine the orange flesh, zest, cranberries, and sugar in a food processor. Process until the mixture is chunky. Stir in the ginger and more sugar if needed. Serve right away, but it's best if it sits for at least 30 minutes to allow the flavors to marry. It keeps well, refrigerated, for a few days.

Red Pepper Relish

MAKES: 4 servings
TIME: 1 hour

Use this on almost anything grilled, but especially chicken or fish. Add a pinch or two of ground cumin if you like.

> 4 Roasted Red Peppers (page 330)
> 1 tablespoon olive oil
> 1 teaspoon balsamic vinegar
> ¼ teaspoon minced garlic
> Salt and freshly ground black pepper

Roughly chop the peeled roasted peppers and mix with the oil, vinegar, and garlic. Sprinkle with salt and pepper. Stir, then taste and adjust the seasoning. Serve immediately or refrigerate for a day or two (bring back to room temperature to serve).

Raw Onion Chutney

MAKES: About ¾ cup
TIME: 1 hour, largely unattended

There's nothing shy about this classic condiment from India, and that's why it's perfect with the subtle flavors of beans or the smokiness of grilled meats. A dab on a sandwich isn't half bad either.

  Fast   Make Ahead   V Vegetarian

2 small to medium or 1 large red or Vidalia onions, quartered and thinly sliced or chopped

1 teaspoon salt, or more to taste

1/2 teaspoon coarsely cracked black peppercorns

1/4 cup red wine vinegar

1 teaspoon paprika, or more to taste

Pinch cayenne, or to taste (optional)

Pinch chaat masala (to make your own, see page 68), to taste (optional)

❶ Separate the layers of the onion and combine with the salt, black peppercorns, vinegar, and paprika in a small dish. Let sit for an hour.

❷ Stir in the cayenne and chaat masala if you're using them and serve immediately or refrigerate for a day or two (bring back to room temperature to serve).

Hot or Mild Pepper Chutney. Not necessarily fiery: Replace the onions with 4 to 5 fresh, hot red chiles (or use 1 medium red bell pepper or a combination for a milder version). Substitute 2 cloves garlic for the black peppercorns. Pulse everything in a food processor until coarsely chopped, but do not purée. (At this point, you may refrigerate the chutney for about 2 weeks; bring back to room temperature before serving.)

Cilantro-Mint Chutney

MAKES: 1 1/2 cups
TIME: 15 minutes

  Ⓥ

Cilantro and mint have a wonderful affinity, with sweet grassy flavors that are assertive but food friendly. That said, you can certainly make a respectable version of this with one herb or the other; or use Thai or regular basil as a substitute for either.

1 1/2 cups firmly packed chopped fresh cilantro leaves

1/2 cup firmly packed fresh mint leaves

1 to 2 Thai or other hot fresh green chiles, seeded if you like, or to taste, or hot red pepper flakes, to taste

2 inches fresh ginger, cut into chunks

1/2 red onion, quartered

2 cloves garlic, peeled

1/4 cup freshly squeezed lime juice

1/2 teaspoon salt, or more to taste

❶ Combine the herbs, chiles, ginger, onion, and garlic in a food processor and pulse until finely ground.

❷ Add the lime juice and salt and process until nearly smooth (you may need to add up to 1/4 cup water to help the food processor get going); taste and adjust the seasoning. Refrigerate for up to a day; serve at room temperature.

Creamy Cilantro-Mint Chutney. This cools the whole thing down a bit and makes it closer to a Raita (page 24): Add 1/2 cup or more good yogurt, then adjust the seasoning again and serve.

Long-Lasting Cilantro-Mint Chutney. Increase the garlic to 5 cloves and use 1/2 cup white wine vinegar instead of lime juice. (At this point, you may cover and refrigerate the chutney for several weeks.)

Coconut Chutney

MAKES: About 1 cup
TIME: 10 minutes

This fresh, chewy—and very easy—chutney goes well with Chicken Biryani (page 654) and many other Indian dishes and can be made with ingredients from the pantry. In fact, if you don't have coconut, it's just as delicious (and certainly more colorful) made with chopped carrots or beets.

1/2 cup shredded coconut

1 inch fresh ginger, chopped, or 1 teaspoon ground ginger

1 small hot fresh green or red chile (like jalapeño or Thai), or hot red pepper flakes, to taste

1/2 bunch fresh cilantro, leaves only

¼ teaspoon ground cumin

2 tablespoons freshly squeezed lime juice

Pinch salt

1 Put the coconut, ginger, chile, cilantro, and cumin in a food processor or blender and pulse until finely ground.

2 Add the lime juice and salt and pulse again, until nearly but not quite smooth. Taste, adjust the seasoning, and serve at room temperature or refrigerate for up to a few hours.

Crunchy Nut Chutney

MAKES: About 1 cup
TIME: 15 minutes

A chunky, well-seasoned chutney to stir into sauces or soups, toss with noodles or rice, or serve alongside roasted vegetables, chicken, or meat. Peanuts and cashews are the most common choices, but any nut or seed will work here, as long as you taste and adjust the seasonings accordingly. Remember that nuts vary widely in flavor, so be prepared to add more salt or garlic or even a little brown sugar or oil if the mixture seems too bitter or dry.

1 teaspoon cumin seeds

1 teaspoon coriander seeds

1 dried Thai or other small red chile, or to taste

1 cup roasted unsalted peanuts or cashews

½ teaspoon salt, or more to taste

½ teaspoon freshly ground black pepper, or more to taste

1 clove garlic, peeled

1 Toast the seeds and chile in a small dry skillet over medium heat, shaking the pan frequently until the seeds color slightly, about 5 minutes. (If the nuts are raw, you can toast them the same way.)

2 Process all the ingredients together in a blender or food processor, stopping the machine to scrape down the sides if necessary, until coarsely ground (not as smooth as peanut butter). Serve immediately or refrigerate for up to a week (bring back to room temperature before serving).

Dried Fruit and Nut Chutney. With the other ingredients, add ¾ cup dried fruit, like dates, apricots, raisins, cranberries, or cherries. Again, go for a coarse grind, not a purée.

Real Garlicky Nut Chutney. If you want a chunky chutney, roughly chop the nuts and garlic (and coconut if you're using it) by hand: In Step 2, add 2 to 3 cloves garlic with or without ½ cup shredded coconut and a tablespoon or so of freshly squeezed lime juice.

Walnut and Yogurt Chutney. Use walnuts for the nuts and a fresh green chile, like jalapeño or Thai, instead of the dried chile. Proceed with the recipe and then stir in ½ cup or more yogurt at the end.

Basil-Soy Dipping Sauce

MAKES: About ½ cup
TIME: 15 minutes

This dead-easy sauce is even better than it might seem, because you can completely change the main flavor by replacing the basil with cilantro, mint, lemongrass, lime leaves, or even a different type of basil. This makes a fantastic dipping sauce for Vietnamese Summer Rolls (page 107).

1 clove garlic, minced

2 tablespoons soy sauce

2 tablespoons rice wine vinegar

1 tablespoon sugar

1 or 2 fresh Thai chiles, seeded and thinly sliced

¼ cup thinly sliced fresh basil leaves, preferably Thai

Whisk together all the ingredients plus 2 tablespoons water until the sugar is dissolved. Let sit for 5 minutes so the flavors meld.

 Fast   Make Ahead   Vegetarian

Thai Chile Sauce

Nam Prik

MAKES: About ½ cup
TIME: 5 minutes

An essential, slightly sweet Thai sauce (the Vietnamese *nuoc cham* is almost identical), used as a dressing for vegetables, noodles, meats, and fish and as a dipping sauce for almost any tidbits of food. Addictive, if you ask me. (Try it with plain grilled shrimp and you'll see.) Many people make this blazingly hot; though my version is much tamer, if you add five, or even ten, small Thai chiles you won't be breaking with tradition.

2 tablespoons freshly squeezed lime juice

2 tablespoons nam pla (Thai fish sauce)

1 teaspoon minced garlic

¼ teaspoon minced hot fresh chile (like Thai or jalapeño), cayenne, or hot red pepper flakes, or to taste

2 teaspoons sugar

1 tablespoon minced dried shrimp (optional)

1 tablespoon finely shredded carrot (optional)

❶ Combine all the ingredients and stir until the sugar dissolves.

❷ Taste and adjust the seasonings as necessary (I often add more nam pla). Let rest for a few minutes before serving or refrigerate for up to a day (bring back to room temperature before using).

Ginger-Scallion Sauce

MAKES: About 1 cup
TIME: 15 minutes

The combination of ginger and scallions is the traditional accompaniment to Steamed Dumplings (page 106). It's also a fabulous addition to soups; finally (well, probably not finally—you'll think of other uses), it's terrific on top of plain thin Chinese egg noodles (see page 552).

To cut way down on the chopping: Throw the ginger, scallions, and garlic into a food processor (a mini food processor works too) and pulse until chopped thoroughly and evenly—but do not purée.

¼ cup minced fresh ginger

½ cup chopped scallion

1 clove garlic, minced

1 teaspoon salt, or more to taste

½ cup peanut oil or neutral oil, like grapeseed or corn

❶ Mix the ginger, scallion, garlic, and salt together thoroughly in a heatproof bowl.

❷ Put the oil in a small saucepan or skillet over high heat until smoking. Carefully pour the oil over the ginger-scallion mixture, mix well, and serve or refrigerate for up to 3 days (bring back to room temperature before serving).

Garlic-Scallion Sauce. Less complex but more powerful: Increase the garlic to ¼ cup and eliminate the ginger.

Chile-Scallion Sauce. A little heat: Add 3 tablespoons (or to taste) of your favorite finely chopped fresh chile (see the chart on page 71). Increase the garlic to 2 large cloves and reduce the ginger to 1 tablespoon or omit it entirely.

Simple Miso Dipping Sauce

MAKES: About 1 cup (4 servings)
TIME: 15 minutes

Serve this as a dipping sauce, in individual small bowls, or as a dressing or finishing sauce for Grilled or Broiled Potatoes (page 342), whole wheat pasta, Grilled or Broiled Boneless Chicken (page 641) or Grilled or Broiled Tofu (page 445). The type of miso you choose will make this sauce lighter or heavier.

6 tablespoons miso

3/4 cup warm water or sake or a mixture

1 teaspoon sugar

1 tablespoon mirin or white wine

1 tablespoon rice vinegar, or more to taste

Salt

❶ Put everything except the salt in a small bowl and whisk together. Taste and add more vinegar and salt if needed.

❷ Serve immediately. To use warm, heat gently but do not boil. Or refrigerate for up to a week (and serve warm or cold).

Simple Miso Herb Dipping Sauce. Lots of bang for your buck: Add 1/2 cup chopped fresh cilantro, basil, Thai basil, shiso, or mint (or a combination.) For a smooth green sauce, combine everything in the blender.

Simple Miso Citrus Dipping Sauce. Brighter and fresher: Instead of the rice vinegar, add a tablespoon or two of freshly squeezed lemon, lime, orange, or tangerine juice. If you like, grate some of the skin into a fine zest (page 393) and float a sprinkle on top of each little bowl.

Simple Miso Soy Dipping Sauce. A no-brainer and good: Add a tablespoon or two of soy sauce to the main recipe or either of the preceding variations.

Miso Carrot Sauce with Ginger

MAKES: About 1 1/4 cup
TIME: 15 minutes

A high-quality version of the goopy orange stuff put on salads in many Japanese restaurants. Try it on warm or chilled chickpeas or edamame (see page 411 or 424) or over any plain cooked whole grain (see page 451) or Grilled Fish Fillets or Steaks (page 564).

1/4 cup peanut oil or neutral oil, like grapeseed or corn

1/4 cup rice vinegar

3 tablespoons mild or sweet miso, like yellow or white

1 tablespoon dark sesame oil

2 medium carrots, roughly chopped

1 inch fresh ginger, cut into coins

Salt and freshly ground black pepper

❶ Put all the ingredients except the salt and pepper into a food processor and pulse a few times to mince the carrots. Then let the machine run for a minute or so, until the mixture is chunky-smooth. (If you want it smoother, use a blender.)

❷ Taste and adjust the seasoning, then serve immediately or cover tightly and refrigerate for up to several days.

Ponzu Sauce

MAKES: About 2 cups
TIME: Overnight, completely unattended

The famous Japanese dipping sauce usually made with dried bonito (a relative of tuna), yuzu (a Japanese citrus), and mirin, but the substitutions here all work fine.

1 cup freshly squeezed yuzu juice or 1/2 cup each freshly squeezed lemon and lime juices

1 cup soy sauce

1/3 cup mirin (or 3 tablespoons honey mixed with 3 tablespoons water)

1 tablespoon sugar

1/2 cup dried bonito flakes or a 4-inch piece kombu

❶ Whisk together all the ingredients in a mixing bowl, cover, and refrigerate overnight.

❷ Strain into an airtight container and refrigerate until ready to use (it will keep for several days).

Lemongrass Ponzu. Omit the yuzu juice. Increase the mirin to 3/4 cup, reduce the soy sauce to 1/4 cup, add

❶ Fast   ❶ Make Ahead   ❶ Vegetarian

¹/₂ cup water (or Dashi, page 160) and a stalk of lemongrass, peeled, trimmed and crushed, in the pot with the bonito. Simmer for 15 minutes, strain, and serve warm or at room temperature.

The Basics of Mayonnaise

Most beginning cooks find the whole idea of making mayonnaise from scratch daunting, but it's really not difficult at all. And when you get it right—which is likely to happen on your first try—you'll have a sauce that is a zillion times better than anything you'll ever eat out of a jar.

As for the fear of raw eggs: If you you're worried about this (and I'm not going to argue with you), you can try making mayonnaise with pasteurized eggs (though it's not my first choice), or try the eggless Skordalia on page 94. Or buy the best mayo you can find and doctor it up with some of the suggestions in this section.

Demystifying Mayo

Mayonnaise is an emulsion, in which oil is dispersed into eggs through vigorous stirring to produce a thick pale yellow cream; a few basic seasonings balance the flavors. Homemade mayos go south when you add the oil too quickly or (less often) you add too much oil. You might also make sure your eggs aren't too cold and your oil is at room temperature, because temperature fluctuations can cause some instability, though this is a really minor point. And if you've heard that the direction in which you whisk matters, forget it.

To help you add the oil in a slow steady stream, you could put it in a squeeze bottle or a liquid measuring cup with a spout. Or use a teaspoon to start with literally drops at a time. If you're using a food processor, note that many have a feed tube with a small hole in it, put there specifically for this purpose; you put the oil in the tube and it drips out. (I have drilled holes in feed tubes without them, which also works.)

For general purposes, I like grapeseed oil best because of its neutral flavor, especially if you're planning on adding ingredients; corn oil delivers slightly more flavor and golden color. Use olive oil if you want a particularly Mediterranean taste, which is often the case, especially with the Aïoli variation. Asian ingredients go better with a mayonnaise made from grapeseed, corn, or—for a more pronounced flavor—peanut oil. For vinegar, I like sherry or white wine vinegar, but try lemon or even lime juice for a brighter flavor. All of these decisions should be based on how you plan to use the mayo.

Homemade Mayonnaise

MAKES: 1 cup
TIME: 10 minutes

I have made mayonnaise countless times with blender, food processor, and whisk, and though the machines make things marginally easier, all techniques are foolproof if you follow the preceding suggestions (see "Demystifying Mayo") along with this recipe.

What will change is the texture of the mayonnaise when you make additions. By hand, there will always be bits and pieces of the stir-ins for a more rustic sauce. By machine, the mayonnaise will be smooth and evenly colored.

1 egg yolk

2 teaspoons Dijon mustard

1 cup neutral oil, like grapeseed or corn, or extra virgin olive oil

Salt and freshly ground black pepper

1 tablespoon sherry vinegar, white wine vinegar, or freshly squeezed lemon juice

❶ To make by hand: Put the yolk and mustard in a medium bowl. Beat together with a wire whisk. Begin to add the oil in dribbles as you beat, adding more as each amount is incorporated. You'll notice when a thick emulsion forms, then you can add the remaining oil a little faster. Depending on how fast you beat, the whole process will take about 5 minutes.

To make by machine: Put the yolk and mustard in a blender or food processor and turn the machine on. While it's running, add the oil in a slow, steady stream. When an emulsion forms, you can add it a little faster, until all the oil is incorporated.

2 Add salt and pepper, then stir in the vinegar. Taste and adjust the seasoning. Use immediately or refrigerate for about a week (less if using fresh herbs or aromatics).

Garlic Mayonnaise (Aïoli). A Mediterranean classic, strong stuff, but addictive: Peel 3 to 8 cloves garlic, to taste. If mixing by hand, mince; if using a machine, roughly chop. Use at least half olive oil (you can go all the way if you like) and proceed with the recipe, adding the garlic in Step 2.

Chile Mayonnaise. Use mild chiles, like ancho, or hot like Thai or dried chipotle: Soak one or two dried chiles in warm water until soft (see page 70). Drain and pat dry. Or use 1 canned chipotle and a little of its adobo sauce. If mixing by hand, mince the chiles; if using a machine, roughly chop. Add the chile in Step 2.

Roasted Pepper Mayonnaise. Pretty and complex: Add 1 Roasted Red Pepper (page 330) or use yellow or orange. If mixing by hand, mince; if using a machine, roughly chop. Add the pepper in Step 2.

Green Sauce, French Style. Easier by machine: After the mayonnaise is made in Step 2, add to the blender or processor 1 sprig fresh tarragon, about 10 sprigs watercress (thick stems removed), 10 chives, and the leaves from 5 parsley stems. Process until not quite puréed but definitely green.

Cold Mustard Sauce. Fabulous sandwich spread: Add 1 heaping tablespoon Dijon or whole grain mustard along with the other ingredients in Step 2. Thin with a tablespoon or two of cream—fresh, fraîche, or sour— to the desired consistency.

12 Easy Ways to Flavor Mayonnaise

After the mayo is done, stir, blend, or process in any of the following ingredients, alone or in combination. If working by hand, be sure to mince the ingredients well. (And of course you can use any of these—and the preceding variations—to flavor store-bought mayo too.)

1. **Saffron Mayonnaise:** A pinch of saffron threads
2. **Herbed Mayonnaise:** Up to 1 tablespoon chopped strong fresh herb leaves like rosemary, oregano, tarragon, marjoram, epazote, or thyme or up to $1/4$ cup chopped mild fresh herb leaves like parsley, cilantro, chives, chervil, or basil
3. **Tartar Sauce:** Up to $1/4$ cup chopped sweet pickles or capers and a spoonful of mustard
4. **Soy Mayonnaise:** 2 tablespoons soy sauce, or to taste
5. **Wasabi Mayonnaise:** 1 teaspoon wasabi powder, or to taste
6. **Citrus Mayonnaise:** 1 teaspoon (or more) grated citrus zest
7. **Horseradish Mayonnaise:** At least a teaspoon of prepared horseradish
8. **Seasoned Mayonnaise:** A few dashes of Tabasco, Worcestershire, or other prepared sauce
9. **Nutty Mayonnaise:** Up to $1/2$ cup toasted chopped almonds, walnuts, or pecans (see page 317)
10. **Ginger Mayonnaise:** 1 tablespoon minced fresh ginger
11. **Spiced Mayonnaise:** Up to 2 tablespoons of any spice blend, like curry or chili powder (to make your own, see pages 65–69)
12. **Anchovy Mayonnaise:** 2 or 3 anchovies, blended in at the very end (omit the salt)

Real Ranch Dressing

MAKES: 2 cups
TIME: 10 minutes

The secret to ranch dressing is buttermilk powder, which is probably in the baking section of your supermarket.

Nothing else delivers that characteristic tang, and it works as a thickener to boot.

1 cup mayonnaise (to make your own, which is preferable, see page 41)

1 cup buttermilk

$1/4$ cup buttermilk powder

Salt and freshly ground black pepper

$1/4$ cup chopped fresh chives or parsley leaves (optional)

❶ Put the mayonnaise, buttermilk, and buttermilk powder in a medium jar with a tight-fitting lid. Sprinkle with a little salt and lots of freshly ground black pepper. Add the chives or parsley if you like, put on the lid, and shake vigorously for 30 seconds or so.

❷ Taste and adjust the seasoning. Use immediately or refrigerate for a few days. (It will keep longer if you don't add the fresh herbs.)

5 Ways to Spin Real Ranch Dressing

1. **Chili Ranch Dressing:** Add 2 teaspoons chili powder (to make your own, see page 66) to the mixture.

2. **Curry Ranch Dressing:** Add 1 tablespoon curry powder (to make your own Fragrant Curry Powder, see page 67) to the mixture.

3. **Parmesan Ranch Dressing:** Add 2 tablespoons freshly grated Parmesan to the mixture and cut back on the salt.

4. **Bacon Ranch Dressing:** Add $1/4$ cup or so of crisply fried and crumbled bacon to the jar.

5. **"Bleu" Ranch Dressing:** Add $1/4$ cup finely crumbled blue cheese to the jar.

The Basics of Mustard

The pungent mustard plant belongs to the same family as broccoli, cabbage, and turnips. We eat the greens, at least sometimes (see page 315), but it's the seeds—ground into a paste we call *mustard*—with which we're most familiar.

Yellow and White Mustard Seeds: The largest of the mustard seeds and the mildest. Their tart flavor makes them good for everyday ground and prepared mustards, though when used alone, the flavor is one-dimensional.

Brown Mustard Seeds: The most pungent mustard, ranging from reddish to brown. The sharpest Chinese-, German-, and English-style mustards are all based on these.

Black Mustard Seeds: Indian cooking often features these slightly oblong seeds, which are sharp. In ground mustards they help add another dimension and deepen the color.

Dry (Powdered) Mustard: When seeds are ground very finely, the result is a powder or "flour." The simplest mustard is made from this powder: Just mix about $1/4$ cup with a sprinkle of salt and a teaspoon or two of sugar. Then stir in water, wine, or beer a little at a time until you get the desired consistency. The paste will be very strong, though the sugar rounds it out a bit. Chinese Mustard Dipping Sauce, below, is a little more sophisticated.

Dijon-Style Mustard: The name given to the smooth, pleasantly hot, wine-based mustards modeled after those from Dijon, France. Since getting such a smooth grind with everyday kitchen equipment is impossible, you've simply got to buy it. American-made Grey Poupon is the most familiar brand; Maille (from France) is another good choice. Use Dijon mustard for salad dressings, sauces, and all-purpose smearing.

Coarsely Ground, Whole Grain, or Stone-Ground Mustard: If bits of the seeds remain intact, the mustard has a slight crunch with an almost nutty flavor. (See the recipe on page 44.) Perfect for hearty dishes, next to a slab of corned beef, or whenever you want a more assertive flavor combined with texture.

Chinese Mustard: You can find this saucelike mustard in Asian markets, well-stocked grocery stores, and of course Chinese restaurants; it's on the thin side and quite sharp. To make your own, just make a thinner version of the powdered mustard recipe above. To make delicious Chinese Mustard Dipping Sauce, add a little dark sesame oil and a splash of soy sauce; serve it with any dumplings (page 104), Fried Wontons or Egg Rolls (page 102) or deep-fried vegetables, like those on page 247.

Flavored Mustards: "Gourmet" mustards, mostly made by small companies, are spiked with all sorts of things, from tarragon to beer to roasted shallots to fruit. Some are better than others, but you can also make your own (see below).

Prepared Yellow Mustard: There's no reason to bother with old-fashioned neon-yellow mustards. About the only thing they have going for them is their mildness, which isn't really a plus, and most contain extra ingredients you don't want anyway.

Wasabi: Natural, fresh wasabi is a rhizome (a stem that grows underground like ginger). It's bright green, with a heat that will clear your sinuses. But mustard is the main ingredient of the prepared "wasabi" we use most often.

Grainy Mustard

MAKES: 1¹⁄₂ cups

TIME: 15 minutes, plus a day or two to soak the seeds

You'll be amazed at how easy, cheap, and good homemade mustard is. Plus, you can customize the flavor many ways with minor adjustments; see the list that follows. Make sure, though, to mix yellow mustard seeds with brown or black, or the results will be too harsh.

To make a faster—though undeniably sharper and less subtle—mustard, use a spice grinder or coffee mill to grind the mustard seeds into a coarse powder, then slowly stir in the liquids until you get the consistency you want (you might have to add a little more). Sprinkle with salt and serve immediately or keep as you would any mustard.

¹⁄₄ cup yellow mustard seeds (about 1¹⁄₂ ounces)

¹⁄₄ cup brown or black mustard seeds
  (about 1¹⁄₂ ounces)

¹⁄₂ cup red wine or water

¹⁄₂ cup sherry vinegar or malt vinegar (or any vinegar with at least 5 percent acidity; see page 197)

Pinch salt

❶ Put all the ingredients in a jar with a tight-fitting lid or other sealed glass or ceramic container. (Don't use metal; it will corrode.) Shake or stir, then set aside to soak for a day or two.

❷ Put the mixture in a blender and purée for several minutes to grind, adding a little extra water as needed to keep the machine running. Stop and scrape the sides down once or twice and repeat. You'll never get the mustard as smooth as Dijon, but you can control the coarseness by how long you blend. Taste and add more salt if you like.

❸ Return the mustard to the container and cover tightly. Store in a cool, dark place (or refrigerate) for up to several months. The mustard will be quite sharp at first, but it will thicken and mellow with time.

16 Ways to Flavor Grainy Mustard

Start with ¹⁄₂ cup mustard, then stir in the following ingredients. Note that using fresh herbs, fruit, or vegetables will reduce the mustard's storage time to a week.

1. **Mustard Relish:** Add ¹⁄₂ cup chopped sweet pickle and ¹⁄₄ cup each chopped red onion and red bell pepper.
2. **Tarragon Mustard:** Add 1 tablespoon chopped tarragon leaves.
3. **Rosemary Mustard:** Add 1 teaspoon minced fresh rosemary leaves.
4. **Tomato Mustard:** Add 1 tablespoon tomato paste.
5. **Honey Mustard:** Add 2 tablespoons honey.
6. **Horseradish Mustard:** Add 1 teaspoon freshly grated or prepared horseradish (see page 306), or more to taste.
7. **Molasses Mustard:** Add 1 tablespoon molasses.
8. **Balsamic Mustard:** Add 1 to 2 tablespoons balsamic vinegar, to taste.
9. **Creole Mustard:** Add ¹⁄₄ teaspoon cayenne, or more to taste.

 Fast   Make Ahead   Vegetarian

10. Roasted Garlic Mustard: Add 2 to 3 cloves Roasted Garlic (page 303), mashed with a fork.

11. Chile Mustard: Add 1 teaspoon minced fresh chile (like jalapeño or Thai), or to taste, or hot red pepper flakes or cayenne to taste.

12. Peach Mustard: Add ¼ cup fresh peach purée (1 medium peach, peeled, pitted, sliced, and puréed or mashed with a fork).

13. Mango Mustard: Add ¼ cup fresh mango purée (½ medium mango, peeled, pitted, cubed, and puréed or mashed with a fork).

14. Nori Soy Mustard: Add 1 sheet toasted and crumbled nori (see page 350), plus 1 tablespoon soy sauce.

15. Port Wine Mustard: Instead of the red wine or water, use ½ cup ruby or tawny port.

16. Brewhouse Mustard: Instead of the red wine or water, use ½ cup strong-flavored beer, like stout, porter, bock, or dark or amber ale.

Cooked Sauces

This section ranges from near-spontaneous reductions to make-ahead sauces that keep for ages, like ketchup and barbecue sauce. Some, like Dashi Dipping Sauce (page 56), weren't everyday sauces when I first wrote *How to Cook Everything,* but they certainly are now. And others, like the handful of classic French sauces, never seem to go out of style. For Fast Tomato Sauce (and tons of variations) see pages 502–504.

The Basics of Reduction Sauces

A reduction sauce is nothing more than simple pan sauce that builds on the drippings and cooked bits left after you roast or sauté something. Add some liquid—like stock, wine, cream, or water—then reduce its volume and thicken it by boiling. Sometimes the reduction is finished with butter or cream. The result is a flavorful sauce that naturally relates to the food instead of being added as a separate component.

The process is straightforward and foolproof:

1. Once the meat, chicken, fish, or vegetables are cooked, remove them from your roasting or sauté pan. Then add about twice as much liquid as you would like sauce.

2. Turn the heat to high (if you're working with a large roasting pan, set it over two burners) and deglaze the pan: Stir, scraping the bottom of the pan to release any solids left from cooking.

3. Keep the liquid bubbling vigorously until it is reduced by about half. (If you'd like a smooth sauce, you can strain the solids out before proceeding.)

4. To finish the sauce, stir in some softened butter (or Compound Butter, page 32, or Flavored Oil, page 26), extra virgin olive oil, or cream. Taste and sprinkle with a little salt and pepper and, if necessary (it might not be), some chopped herbs. To serve, you can pool the sauce underneath your food, pour a little on top, or pass it at the table.

Every reduction sauce is a variation on these simple steps. Some are thickened by adding flour before the liquid or a cornstarch mixture after reducing; most are more heavily seasoned. You change reduction sauces by manipulating the various stages. For example, when you heat the pan before deglazing, you might sauté a little garlic, shallot, or other aromatic. But basically, that's about it.

Here are the two basic reductions—one thickened, one not—with plenty of ideas for more.

Simple Pan Sauce

MAKES: ½ cup
TIME: 10 minutes

Here's a sauce made in the same pan you just used to cook meat or vegetables. Keep your food warm in a low oven if necessary while you prepare the sauce. Or just add the food back to the pan with the finished sauce and heat through for a minute or so.

> 1 tablespoon minced shallot or onion
>
> $1/2$ cup dry white (for fish, poultry, or vegetables) or red wine (for red meat)
>
> $1/2$ cup chicken, beef, or vegetable stock (to make your own, see pages 157–159) or water, warmed
>
> 2 tablespoons softened butter (optional)
>
> Salt and freshly ground black pepper
>
> A few drops freshly squeezed lemon juice or vinegar (optional)
>
> Chopped fresh parsley leaves for garnish

1 Pour off all but 1 or 2 tablespoons of the cooking fat (if there are dark, nonfatty juices in the skillet or roasting pan, leave them in there). Turn the heat under the skillet or pan to medium-high and add the shallot and the wine. Cook, stirring and scraping, until most of the wine has evaporated, the shallot is soft, and the bottom of the pan is clean.

2 Add the stock and cook, stirring, until there is just under $1/2$ cup of liquid, then turn off the heat. Add the butter, a little at a time, stirring well after each addition to incorporate it. Taste and sprinkle with salt, pepper and/or lemon juice or vinegar if necessary. Sauce the meat or vegetables however you like. Garnish with parsley right before serving.

Lemon-Caper Sauce. Add 1 tablespoon or more minced capers along with the shallot and wine. Finish with at least 1 tablespoon freshly squeezed lemon juice to taste.

Asian-Style Reduction Sauce. Cook 1 tablespoon each minced garlic, ginger, and scallion (in place of shallot) until soft before adding the wine. Omit the butter. Stir in 1 tablespoon soy or nam pla (Thai fish sauce) or Worcestershire sauce and finish with a few drops of freshly squeezed lime juice. Garnish with minced fresh cilantro leaves.

Mushroom Sauce. Before adding the wine, cook $1/2$ cup chopped wild or domestic mushrooms along with 2 tablespoons minced shallot, until soft. Best with $1/4$ cup or more heavy cream added at the last minute.

13 Ways to Flavor Simple Pan Sauce

1. Aromatic Pan Sauce: Add $1/2$ cup or more chopped aromatic vegetables—onion, shallots, mushrooms, celery, carrot, or a combination—to the fat remaining in the pan before adding the wine. Cook, stirring, until soft, then add the liquid.

2. Creamy Pan Sauce: Substitute heavy cream for half or all of the stock.

3. Boozy Pan Sauce: Substitute sherry, Madeira, port, vodka, bourbon, or vermouth for the wine.

4. Seasoned Pan Sauce: Add chopped fresh herb leaves or ground spices at the beginning or the end. Those added at the beginning will become better incorporated; those added at the end will retain more of their flavor. Add them twice if you like.

5. Piquant Pan Sauce: Add chopped anchovies, dried tomatoes, or olives along with the shallot.

6. Tart Pan Sauce: Add 1 tablespoon or more of freshly squeezed lemon juice or any vinegar at the end of cooking, tasting as you add.

7. Tomato Pan Sauce: Add chopped or crushed tomatoes or tomato sauce in place of or in addition to some of the stock.

8. Jammy Pan Sauce: Add 1 tablespoon or more of marmalade or jam, whisked in at the end of cooking; especially good with broiled meats.

9. Mushroom Pan Sauce: Add reconstituted dried mushrooms (see page 314) along with the shallot or onion. Use the mushroom-soaking liquid to replace some of the broth.

10. Juicy Pan Sauce: Use fruit juice—especially orange or tomato or anything freshly juiced—in place of some of the stock or water.

11. Mustardy Pan Sauce: Add prepared Dijon or grainy mustard, along with some cream if you like, in place of or in addition to the optional butter.

12. Sauce-Spiked Pan Sauce: Stir in a spoonful or two of any salsa or chutney in place of or in addition to the optional butter.

13. Spicy Pan Sauce: After you pour off the excess fat in Step 1—but before you add the wine—stir in a tablespoon or so of any spice mixture, like curry powder,

F Fast   **M** Make Ahead   **V** Vegetarian

4 Ways to Thicken a Sauce

I've got the same attitude about thickening sauces as I do about thickening soups: If you want them thicker—and sometimes you do—use less liquid or cook them a little longer. Here are some other ways you can add body and sheen to many of the cooked sauces.

1. **Puréeing:** Chunky sauces turn smooth and luxurious when puréed. An upright blender will give you the best results (always cool food to a safe temperature before putting it in a blender); an immersion blender is easier but not as powerful. A food processor or food mill will give you a little rougher texture.

2. **Enriching:** Adding cream, sour cream, yogurt, egg yolks, or small bits of very cold butter will add body to cooked sauces. But beware of excess heat: Cream and butter are relatively stable even if the sauce bubbles a bit, but boiling will curdle sauces made with yogurt or eggs. (Eggs are best tempered before being added to sauces: Stir a bit of the hot sauce into beaten eggs to warm them, then stir that mixture back into the sauce.)

3. **Starting with a Roux:** To make a roux, cook butter or oil and flour together in equal proportion, constantly stirring over medium heat, until the flour begins to toast. (The darker you cook the roux, the deeper and nuttier the flavor; just be careful not to let it burn.) You can cook the roux first and then whisk in a liquid like stock or milk (this is the technique used in Béchamel, page 57); or you may add the cooked roux to an already simmering sauce. Either way, let the mixture cook for a few minutes to thicken fully.

4. **Adding Cornstarch:** When you dissolve cornstarch (you can use other starches, but this is the most common) in water, or a bit of the sauce you want to thicken, the result is a cloudy mixture known as a *slurry*, and it works brilliantly. A general formula is 1 tablespoon cornstarch dissolved in 1/2 cup of liquid to thicken 2 to 4 cups of sauce. Whisk it smooth with a fork or spoon, then incorporate into the sauce, which will thicken and get shiny as it is gently heated.

chili powder, or garam masala (to make your own, see pages 65–69) or any single ground spice. (You can stir in 2 or 3 tablespoons finely chopped or ground nuts at this point if you like.) Cook and stir for about a minute, until just toasted. Then add the liquid.

Thickened Pan Sauce

Gravy

MAKES: 2 cups
TIME: 20 minutes

This is the standard gravy for turkey or meat loaf, again starting with the browned bits left in your pan from cooking meat. This version is easy, fast, and lump-free. Stir in 1/4 cup or more of heavy cream just before serving if you want a creamier, richer-tasting sauce. For more about ways to thicken any cooked sauce, see "4 Ways to Thicken a Sauce," which follows.

1 cup dry white wine

1/2 cup chopped onion

3 cups plus 3 or 4 tablespoons chicken, beef, or vegetable stock (to make your own, see pages 157–159) or water

1/2 cup minced giblets or other meat, or more to taste (optional)

2 tablespoons cornstarch, or a bit more as needed

Salt and freshly ground black pepper

1 Spoon off all but 1 or 2 tablespoons of the cooking fat (if there are dark, nonfatty juices in the skillet or roasting pan, leave them in there). Add the wine and onion and turn the heat under the pan to high. Cook, stirring and scraping, until most of the wine has evaporated, the onion is soft, and the bottom of the pan is clean, about 5 minutes.

2 Add 3 cups stock and continue to cook, stirring, until reduced by about half, 5 to 10 minutes. If you have any solids—like giblets—add them and turn the heat down to low. Combine the remaining stock with the cornstarch and stir it into the liquid; it will begin to thicken almost immediately.

❸ Cook, stirring, for about 5 minutes; season with salt and pepper to taste. If the sauce is not as thick as you'd like, combine another tablespoon of cornstarch with 1 tablespoon water or stock and add to the mixture. Cook for another 5 minutes and serve.

Salsa Roja

Cooked Tomato Salsa

MAKES: About 2 cups
TIME: 45 to 50 minutes

This classic cooked tomato and chile sauce can be served chunky or puréed and used for enchiladas, tacos, or whatever you like. The guajillo chiles called for here lend a complex, smoky flavor, and moderate heat. If you want a milder salsa, substitute ancho or other mild chiles.

2 large guajillos or other medium-hot dried chiles, toasted, soaked, and cleaned (see page 70), soaking water reserved

¼ cup neutral oil, like grapeseed or corn

2 large onions, chopped

4 cloves garlic, minced

2 pounds tomatoes, peeled, seeded, cored, and chopped, with their liquid (about 3 cups; canned are fine)

1 tablespoon sugar

Salt and freshly ground black pepper

¼ cup chopped fresh cilantro leaves

3 tablespoons freshly squeezed lime juice

❶ Mince the chiles. Put the oil in a medium saucepan or deep skillet with a lid over medium-high heat. When hot, add the chiles, onions, and garlic and cook, stir-

ring occasionally, until the onions soften, about 5 minutes. Add the tomatoes, sugar, some salt, and plenty of pepper.

❷ Adjust the heat so the mixture bubbles gently and cook, stirring occasionally, until the mixture has thickened and come together, about 20 minutes. If the salsa gets too thick, thin it with some of the reserved chile-soaking water or plain water.

❸ Stir in the cilantro and lime juice. Taste and adjust the seasoning if necessary. Serve hot or at room temperature or refrigerate for up to 2 days.

Red Enchilada Sauce. Essential on Cheese Enchiladas (page 826): Use an immersion blender to purée the sauce in the pan. Or cool the mixture slightly, pour into a blender or food processor, and purée carefully.

Salsa Borracha. Translates as "drunk salsa" because it's cooked with beer and finished with tequila: In Step 1, add a bottle of beer with the tomatoes. (It might take a little longer to thicken.) Use an immersion blender to purée the finished sauce in the pan. Or cool the mixture slightly, pour into a blender or food processor, and purée carefully. Finish with 2 tablespoons (about a shot) of tequila if you like.

Charred Salsa Roja. Cut the tomatoes and onions into thick slices and grill on both sides until charred, about 10 minutes total. Proceed with the recipe; add 2 tablespoons or so of chopped fresh mint along with the cilantro, if you like, in Step 3.

Chipotle Salsa Roja. Toast, soak, and clean a chipotle chile along with the others. Or add a canned chipotle chile with its adobo along with the tomatoes.

Salsa Sofrito. Substitute Roasted Red (or yellow) Peppers (page 330) for the guajillos; replace the cilantro with a tablespoon or so of chopped fresh oregano leaves, and use red wine vinegar instead of the lime juice.

Ⓕ Fast   Ⓜ Make Ahead   Ⓥ Vegetarian

Salsa Verde

Cooked Tomatillo Salsa

MAKES: About 2 cups

TIME: 30 minutes

Green salsa goes especially well with pork and egg dishes, though you can use it anywhere you would Salsa Roja (preceding recipe). To keep this on the mild side, substitute another poblano for the hot fresh chile. If in-your-face heat is what you're looking for, add even more hot chiles or some of their seeds.

10 to 12 tomatillos, husked and rinsed

2 medium poblano or other mild fresh green chiles, roasted and cleaned (see page 330)

1 or 2 serrano or other hot fresh green chiles, (optional), roasted and cleaned (page 330)

3 tablespoons neutral oil, like grapeseed or corn

2 large onions, diced

5 cloves garlic, minced

1 teaspoon Mexican or other oregano

1 cup vegetable stock (to make your own, see page 157) or water

Salt and freshly ground black pepper

$^{1}/_{2}$ cup chopped fresh cilantro leaves

$^{1}/_{4}$ cup freshly squeezed lime juice

1 Heat the oven to 400°F. Put the tomatillos on a baking sheet and roast until the skins are lightly browned and blistered, about 20 minutes. Remove the tomatillos; when they're cool enough to handle, chop them finely, along with the chiles, saving their juices.

2 While the tomatillos are roasting, put the oil in a large deep skillet over medium heat. Add the onions and garlic and cook, stirring occasionally, until they are very soft and lightly browned, about 10 minutes. Add the tomatillos, chiles, oregano, stock, and a large pinch of salt and pepper; stir and bring to a low simmer. Cook, stirring occasionally, until the mixture thickens slightly, 10 to 15 minutes.

3 Stir in the cilantro and lime juice, taste, and adjust the seasoning. Serve at room temperature or refrigerate for up to 2 days.

Green Enchilada Salsa. Use an immersion blender to purée the finished sauce in the pan. Or cool the mixture slightly, pour into a blender or food processor, and purée carefully.

Green Chile Salsa. Milder and simpler: Increase the chiles to 5 poblanos; omit the tomatillos and serranos. Decrease the stock to $^{1}/_{4}$ cup, more or less, as needed. Proceed with Steps 1 and 2; then use an immersion blender to purée the salsa. Or cool the mixture slightly, pour into a blender or food processor, and purée carefully. Proceed with Step 3.

Pumpkin Seed Sauce. Thick and with a toasted nut flavor like green mole, only much easier: Toast or roast 1 cup green pumpkin seeds (pepitas; see page 317) and pulse them several times in a food processor until finely chopped. Add them to the onion-garlic mixture in Step 2, along with 1 tablespoon chopped fresh epazote if you like. Proceed with the recipe.

Super-Hot Chile-Garlic Salsa. Substitute 3 to 5 habaneros for the poblanos and serranos; omit the tomatillos, onion, oregano, and stock. Put the habaneros and garlic in a small skillet over medium heat. Cook, shaking the skillet occasionally, until the garlic and chiles are brown (or partially wrap the garlic and chiles in foil and roast in a 400°F oven for about 30 minutes). Stem and seed the chiles (wear gloves, if you have them, or wash your hands thoroughly). Put the chiles, garlic, cilantro, and lime juice in a food processor or blender and purée until pasty.

Corn and Tomato Relish

MAKES: About 1 cup

TIME: 10 minutes

A quintessential summer sauce with a bit of bite. Pass it at the table with red meat, chicken, or flavorful fish.

1 teaspoon olive oil

4 ears corn, husked and stripped of their kernels

2 large luscious red tomatoes, cored and roughly chopped

1 teaspoon ground cumin, or to taste

¼ teaspoon cayenne, or to taste

Salt and freshly ground black pepper

❶ Place the oil in a medium nonstick skillet over high heat and heat for 2 minutes. Add the corn and sauté until lightly browned, a minute or two.

❷ Turn the heat down to medium, add the tomatoes, cumin, and cayenne, and cook for 30 seconds more; turn off the heat.

❸ Sprinkle with salt and pepper. Serve immediately or refrigerate for a day or two and serve at room temperature.

Grilled Pineapple and Onion Salsa

MAKES: About 2½ cups

TIME: 20 minutes

Grilled fruit makes a fabulous base for salsa; its caramelized sweetness is offset perfectly by the tang of lime juice and the heat of chiles. Use this to dress a green salad, as a dip for tacos, or alongside Grilled or Broiled Boneless Chicken (page 641) or Huevos Rancheros (page 800).

1 pineapple, peeled, cored, and cut into thick rings (see page 402; canned rings, drained of excess juices, are also okay)

1 large red onion, cut into thick slices

3 tablespoons olive oil

1 tablespoon minced fresh hot chile (like jalapeño or Thai), or to taste, or hot red pepper flakes or cayenne, to taste

1 stalk lemongrass, peeled, trimmed, and minced

2 tablespoons chopped fresh Thai basil or mint leaves

2 tablespoons freshly squeezed lime juice

Salt and freshly ground black pepper

❶ Heat a charcoal or gas grill fire to fairly low heat, and put the rack about 4 inches from the heat source. Brush the pineapple and onion slices with the olive oil; if you're worried about the slices falling through the grate, thread them on soaked wooden skewers. Cook, turning once or twice, until soft and slightly charred, about 8 minutes total. Remove the slices as they finish cooking. When cool enough to handle, discard the skewers and chop into bite-sized chunks, saving as much of the juices as possible.

❷ Put the pineapple and onions in a medium bowl with the chile, lemongrass, basil, and lime juice. Sprinkle with salt and pepper and stir to combine. Let sit for about 5 minutes, then taste and adjust the seasoning, adding more chile, lime, or salt as needed. Serve immediately or refrigerate for up to an hour.

Grilled Apricot and Onion Salsa. If you can get good apricots—and that's a big if—this is terrific; but it's not bad with good dried apricots, soaked in water or wine to cover until soft: Substitute about 8 halved fresh or dried apricots for the pineapple, a tablespoon of minced fresh ginger for the lemongrass, and lemon for the lime juice.

Grilled Peach and Corn Salsa. A nice midsummer salsa: Replace the pineapple with 3 or 4 ripe peaches, halved, and use a tablespoon of minced fresh ginger instead of the lemongrass; add 1 or 2 cobs' worth of

Corn on the Cob, Grilled or Roasted (page 289) and 2 chopped scallions. Use lemon or lime juice.

Traditional Cranberry Sauce

MAKES: About 1 quart
TIME: 20 minutes, plus time to chill

If cranberry sauce generally tastes too sweet to you, know that the sugar is what helps it gel. So go ahead and use less sugar if you want, but expect the sauce to be runnier. (A better solution for you might be to make Cranberry Relish with Orange and Ginger, page 36). If you want a very firm sauce, make the variation.

4 cups (about 1 pound) fresh cranberries, picked over and rinsed, or frozen cranberries

1¹/₂ cups sugar

❶ Combine the cranberries and sugar with 2 cups water in a medium saucepan over medium-low heat. Cover and cook, stirring occasionally, until the berries are broken, 10 to 15 minutes.

❷ Transfer to a bowl; cool, then chill until ready to serve. The sauce can be refrigerated, covered, for up to a week.

Firm Cranberry Sauce or Cranberry Jelly. Increase the sugar to 2 cups. For sauce, proceed as directed. For jelly, cook for 5 minutes longer, stirring frequently. Pass through a strainer into a mold, bowl, or jelly jars and cool, then chill until firm. Slice to serve.

Balsamic Syrup

MAKES: ¹/₄ cup
TIME: About 15 minutes

A good use for inexpensive balsamic vinegar, which is both sweet (it usually contains sugar) and sour, so the rich syrup naturally works well drizzled over both savory and sweet foods like grilled chicken, watermelon, or strawberries. This keeps in the refrigerator almost indefinitely.

1 cup balsamic vinegar

❶ Put the balsamic vinegar in a small nonreactive pan over medium-low heat. Bring to a boil, then immediately lower the heat so it bubbles gently.

❷ Cook until reduced to ¹/₄ cup, about 20 minutes; it should be thickened and syrupy. (It will thicken a little more as it cools.) Serve warm or refrigerate for several months.

8 Great Ways to Flavor Balsamic Syrup

For more flavor, slip any of the following ingredients into the pan while the vinegar is reducing. When you're done, strain the syrup if needed (or if you want).

1. Raw or Roasted Garlic (page 303), to taste
2. Caramelized Onions (page 325) or shallots (¹/₂ cup)
3. A sprig of a strong herb like rosemary, tarragon, or thyme; or a few sprigs of milder ones like parsley, mint, or basil
4. ¹/₄ cup fresh, fruity red wine
5. ¹/₂ cup fresh chopped fruit or berries, like raspberries, apples, figs, strawberries, blackberries, pears, grapes, or cherries
6. ¹/₃ cup chopped dried fruits, like dates, apricots, pears, cherries, strawberries, figs
7. 2 tablespoons molasses, maple syrup, or honey
8. ¹/₂ cup freshly squeezed orange juice

Homemade Ketchup

MAKES: About 1 quart
TIME: About 2 hours

Though it's unquestionably easier to buy ketchup, this is infinitely better, and it's not loaded with high-fructose corn syrup like most bottled ketchup (in fact, it has just a bit of sugar). If you're a gardener, you must try the Green Ketchup variation.

3/4 cup cider vinegar

2 tablespoons Pickling Spice (to make your own, see page 67)

2 tablespoons neutral oil, like grapeseed or corn

1 red or yellow bell pepper, cored, seeded, and roughly chopped

1 large onion, roughly chopped

1 celery stalk, roughly chopped

2 cloves garlic, crushed

2 tablespoons tomato paste

6 cups chopped ripe tomato (about 3 pounds tomatoes—canned are fine; don't bother to drain)

1/4 cup brown sugar

Salt

Cayenne, to taste

1 Heat the cider vinegar and Pickling Spice in a small pot until just beginning to boil; turn off the heat and let the spices steep until ready to use, at least 45 minutes.

2 Meanwhile, put the oil in a large pot over medium-high heat. When hot, add the bell pepper, onion, celery, and garlic. Cook, stirring occasionally, until the onion is soft, about 10 minutes. Stir in the tomato paste until it is evenly distributed and begins to color, another minute or two. Add the tomato and stir well, scraping the bottom of the pot to prevent sticking. Adjust the heat so the mixture bubbles gently and cook, stirring occasionally, until slightly thickened, about 45 minutes, being careful not to let the tomato stick to the bottom and burn.

3 Strain the spiced vinegar and stir it into the tomato mixture along with the brown sugar, salt, and cayenne; cook until just a little thinner than bottled ketchup, about 45 minutes. Taste, adjust the seasonings, and

remove from the heat. Use an immersion blender to purée the ketchup in the pot or pass it through a food mill. Or let the mixture cool slightly, pour it into a blender or food processor, and purée carefully. Cool and serve or refrigerate for up to 2 weeks.

Green Ketchup. Very useful for gardeners: Replace the red or yellow pepper with a green one and use 2 pounds green tomatoes and 1 pound peeled and cored tart apples instead of red tomatoes (you should have about 6 cups total). Substitute a seeded jalapeño for the garlic if you like. Omit the tomato paste and increase the brown sugar to 1/2 cup. Add a cup or so of water when you add the green tomatoes in Step 2.

Tomatoless Ketchup. Blurring the lines between ketchup and chutney: Replace the tomatoes with 3 pounds chopped carrots and 2 pounds peeled and chopped beets. Add 2 cups water and 1/2 cup freshly squeezed lemon juice along with the carrots and beets in Step 2. Omit the tomato paste if you like.

Basic Barbecue Sauce

MAKES: About 2 cups
TIME: 20 minutes

One of my standard barbecue sauces, which simply builds more flavor into ketchup. If you want to baste with this sauce when grilling or roasting, add it toward the end of the cooking to prevent burning. If you want to add some heat, use more chili powder or add some cayenne, or Tabasco or other hot sauce.

2 cups ketchup (to make your own, see the preceding recipe)

1/2 cup dry red wine or water

1/4 cup wine vinegar or rice vinegar

1 tablespoon Worcestershire sauce or soy sauce

1 tablespoon chili powder (to make your own, see page 66), or to taste

1 tablespoon minced onion

1 clove garlic, minced or crushed

Salt and freshly ground black pepper

1 Combine all the ingredients except the salt and pepper in a small saucepan over medium-low heat. Cook, stirring occasionally, until the flavors have a chance to blend, about 10 minutes.

2 Taste and add salt and pepper if necessary. Use immediately or cool, cover, and refrigerate for up to a week.

Curry Barbecue Sauce. More fragrant: Add a teaspoon or more of curry powder (to make your own, see pages 66–67) along with the other ingredients.

Horseradish Barbecue Sauce. Add up to ¼ cup freshly grated horseradish or up to 2 tablespoons prepared horseradish to taste. Add it up front for a milder kick or at the end for a big kick.

Mustardy Barbecue Sauce. Reduce the vinegar to 2 tablespoons. Add ¼ cup Dijon or stone-ground mustard.

Chipotle Barbecue Sauce. Serious heat: In a small bowl, use a fork to mash 1 or 2 canned and minced chipotle chiles along with some of their adobo sauce into a paste. Add to the sauce with the rest of the ingredients.

Bourbon Barbecue Sauce. There's some woody complexity in this one: Instead of wine, use ½ cup bourbon.

Beer Barbecue Sauce. More down-home: Instead of wine, use ½ cup beer (the darker the better—use stout or porter if you can).

Light Barbecue Sauce. A tad more elegant: Replace 1 cup of the ketchup with vegetable stock (to make your own, see page 157).

Asian Barbecue Sauce. Replace 1 cup of the ketchup with 1 cup hoisin sauce. Use plum wine instead of the red wine if you like and use rice vinegar and soy sauce. Add 1 tablespoon minced fresh ginger and 1 tablespoon Chinese mustard (see page 43) if you like.

Indian-Style Tomato Sauce

Makhani

MAKES: 2 cups
TIME: 30 minutes

A decidedly un-Italian tomato sauce. The spices are toasted in butter, resulting in a sauce that is rich, almost sweet, a little hot. It turns grilled lamb and plain rice (and everything else it touches for that matter) into something remarkable, and I really love it with Hard-Boiled Eggs (page 791).

4 tablespoons butter or neutral oil, like grapeseed or corn

1 medium onion, chopped

2 cloves garlic, minced

1 inch fresh ginger, minced

1 tablespoon minced fresh chile (like jalapeño or Thai), or to taste, or hot red pepper flakes or cayenne, to taste

2 teaspoons garam masala or any curry powder (to make your own, see pages 66–67)

½ teaspoon chili powder (to make your own, see page 66)

Large pinch sugar

Salt and freshly ground black pepper

2 cups chopped ripe tomato (about 1 pound), preferably peeled and seeded (drained canned is okay)

½ cup cream or coconut milk (to make your own, see page 389)

½ cup chopped fresh cilantro leaves

1 teaspoon cumin seeds

1 teaspoon mustard seeds

1 Put 3 tablespoons of the butter or oil in a deep skillet over medium-high heat. When the butter is melted or the oil is hot, add the onion, garlic, ginger, and chile. Cook, stirring occasionally, until the onion is soft, about 5 minutes. Stir in the garam masala, chili powder, and sugar and sprinkle with salt and pepper; cook and stir until the spices become fragrant, a minute or two more.

2 Add the tomato and cook, stirring frequently, until it starts to release its liquid, about 3 minutes. Add the cream and the cilantro and keep cooking and stirring until the mixture comes to a boil.

3 Turn the heat down so that the sauce bubbles gently and cook, stirring occasionally, until the tomato breaks up and the mixture comes together and thickens, about 30 minutes. Taste and adjust the seasoning. (At this point, you may cool, cover, and refrigerate the sauce for up to 3 days. Reheat gently before proceeding.)

4 Put the remaining butter or oil in a small pan over medium-high heat. When the butter is melted or the oil is hot, add the cumin and mustard seeds and toast them until they begin to pop, less than a minute. Spoon over the sauce just before serving.

Smooth Green Chile Sauce, Indian Style

MAKES: 4 to 6 servings

TIME: 20 minutes

 F **M** **V**

Nothing about this chile sauce is subtle; the color is deep green, the aroma is mouthwatering, and the flavors are intense (you can increase the heat, if you like, by adding some serrano or other hot fresh chiles). It's delicious with Paratha (page 849) and Dry-Pan Eggplant (page 294). Add some yogurt (see the Chile-Yogurt Sauce variation) to mellow it a bit.

6 poblano or other mild fresh green chiles, roasted and cleaned (see page 330), or canned

1 tablespoon minced fresh ginger

2 teaspoons cumin seeds

¼ cup chopped fresh cilantro

Pinch asafetida (optional)

¼ cup neutral oil, like grapeseed or corn

Salt and freshly ground black pepper

3 tablespoons freshly squeezed lime juice

1 Put the chiles, ginger, cumin, cilantro, and asafetida if you're using it in a blender or food processor; purée until smooth, adding a tablespoon or so of water if necessary to keep things moving.

2 Heat the oil in a medium saucepan over medium-high heat. When hot, add the chile purée and cook, stirring frequently, for about 2 minutes. (Be careful when adding the chile purée—it will splatter when it hits the hot oil.) Reduce the heat and cook, stirring occasionally, until thickened, another 2 to 3 minutes.

3 Sprinkle with salt and pepper to taste and stir in the lime juice. Serve hot or refrigerate for up to 3 days.

Red Chile Sauce, Indian Style. Lovely color, spectacular flavor: Replace the poblanos with 6 New Mexico or other mild fresh red chiles, roasted and cleaned (see page 330).

Red Chile Sauce, North African Style. Replace the poblanos with 6 New Mexico or other mild fresh red chiles. Substitute 2 cloves garlic for the ginger; add ½ teaspoon each caraway, coriander, and fennel seeds; omit the asafetida.

Chile-Yogurt Sauce. A wonderful combo of cool and hot, especially with samosas (see page 106) or as a dip: Let the chile sauce cool and then add ½ cup or more yogurt. Serve at room temperature.

Chile and Coconut Sauce. Rich, spicy, creamy, and delicious: In Step 2, stir about 2 cups coconut milk (to make your own, see page 389) into the simmering chile purée.

F Fast   **M** Make Ahead   **V** Vegetarian

Peanut Sauce

MAKES: 2 cups
TIME: 35 minutes

Toss this Thai-style sauce with Chinese egg noodles or pool some on the bottom of a plate and top with broiled or grilled shrimp, chicken, pork, vegetables, or tofu. Or use it as a dip for celery, red bell pepper, cherry tomatoes, and rice crackers. If you want a smooth sauce, use peanut butter instead of chopped peanuts; for a sweeter one, add about 1/4 cup of ketchup (to make your own, see page 51) along with the coconut milk; for lightness, substitute stock or water for the coconut milk.

- 3 small dried red chiles (like Thai or piquin), seeded, or cayenne or hot red pepper flakes, to taste
- 3 garlic cloves
- 2 shallots, peeled
- 1 stalk lemongrass, white part only, peeled, trimmed, and thinly sliced (optional)
- 2 teaspoons ground turmeric
- 1 tablespoon peanut oil or neutral oil, like grapeseed or corn
- 1 cup coconut milk (to make your own, see page 389)
- 1 tablespoon brown sugar
- 2 tablespoons soy sauce, or more to taste
- 2 tablespoons freshly squeezed lime juice
- 1/2 cup chopped roasted peanuts or crunchy peanut butter
- Salt

❶ Combine the chiles, garlic, shallots, lemongrass, and turmeric in a food processor and grind and until fairly smooth; scrape down the sides of the machine once or twice if necessary.

❷ Put the oil in a medium saucepan or skillet over medium heat. When hot, add the chile-garlic mixture and cook until fragrant, about 1 minute. Add the remaining ingredients and whisk until smooth. Simmer, stirring occasionally, until the sauce thickens, about 15 minutes. Taste and add a sprinkle of salt or a little more soy sauce if necessary. Serve immediately or refrigerate for up to a week (warm gently over very low heat or in a microwave before using).

Curry Peanut Sauce. Another layer of flavor: Omit the chiles, lemongrass, and turmeric. Instead, put one 2-inch piece of fresh ginger and 2 tablespoons of curry powder or curry paste (to make your own, see pages 66–67 or 75–76) in the food processor along with the shallots.

Simpler Peanut Sauce. More peanutty (and makes less): Omit everything except the chiles, sugar, soy sauce, and peanuts. Use the food processor to blend, adding a little water or more soy sauce to get the consistency you like. Then gently heat the sauce in a small saucepan over low heat or in the microwave. Finish with 1/4 cup each sliced scallion and minced fresh cilantro.

Southern-Style Peanut Sauce. Peanut sauce, down-home style: Omit the chiles, lemongrass, turmeric, and soy sauce. You can hand-mince the shallots and garlic if you like, instead of using the food processor. Proceed with the recipe, but use cream instead of coconut milk and lemon juice instead of lime juice.

Teriyaki Sauce

MAKES: About 1 cup
TIME: 15 minutes

Familiar and always popular, teriyaki sauce is also fast and simple. You can slather it on virtually any grilled or broiled seafood, poultry, or meat or add it at the last minute to stir-fried vegetables.

- 1/2 cup soy sauce
- 1/2 cup mirin (or 1/4 cup honey mixed with 1/4 cup water)
- 1 tablespoon minced or grated fresh ginger

1 clove garlic, minced

¹/₄ cup chopped scallion

Combine the soy sauce and mirin in a small saucepan over medium-low heat. Cook until bubbling, about 2 minutes. Turn off the heat, stir in the ginger, garlic, and scallion, and use immediately or refrigerate for up to a day.

Mushroom Teriyaki Sauce. Add ¹/₂ cup finely chopped mushrooms—shiitake, cremini, and button are all fine—before cooking.

Caramelized Onion Teriyaki Sauce. Put about ¹/₂ thinly sliced onion in a small saucepan over medium heat. Cover and cook, stirring occasionally, until the onion is dry and almost sticking to the pan, 10 to 15 minutes. Add 1 tablespoon neutral oil, like grapeseed or corn, and cook, stirring occasionally, until the onion browns, another 10 minutes or so. Proceed with the recipe, adding the ingredients to the pan with the caramelized onion.

Roasted Garlic Teriyaki Sauce. Increase the garlic to 2 cloves. Leave them whole and don't bother to peel. Wrap them in foil and roast in a 375°F oven until soft, about 20 minutes. Remove the skin from the garlic, mash it into a paste, and add it to the soy sauce and mirin.

Dashi Dipping Sauce

MAKES: About 1 cup

TIME: 5 minutes, plus time to cool

F **M** **V**

A useful sauce that's especially fast if you make the dashi in advance. It's wonderful with Tempura (page 101), Pot Stickers (page 104), and Asian-style noodles (see page 552).

1 cup Dashi (page 160)

¹/₄ cup mirin (or 2 tablespoons honey or sugar mixed with 2 tablespoons water)

2 tablespoons soy sauce

In a small pot, combine the ingredients and bring to a boil. Turn off the heat and let cool. Use or cover and refrigerate for up to 3 days.

7 Quick Additions to Dashi Dipping Sauce

This stuff is so easy to spice you won't believe it—once it's cooked, you can stir in almost anything. Use the amounts here as guidelines; you can really just add to taste.

1. Ginger: About 1 tablespoon grated fresh or 1 teaspoon ground
2. Daikon: About ¹/₄ cup grated
3. Wasabi: About 1 tablespoon paste
4. Sesame: About 1 tablespoon toasted seeds (see page 317) or tahini
5. Garlic: About 1 teaspoon raw or 1 tablespoon roasted (see page 303)
6. Scallion or shallot: About ¹/₄ cup minced
7. Chile (see pages 71–73): About 1 teaspoon minced fresh or dried

Butter Sauces

Though these classics based on butter are not as popular as they once were, there's a great deal to be said for their richness and creaminess, which are both satisfying and elegant. And as we conquer our fear of butter they may once again become more common.

Brown Butter

Beurre Noisette

MAKES: ¹/₄ cup

TIME: 15 minutes

F **V**

Cooking butter till it browns gives it not just color but also a range of complex flavors. Try this anywhere you might use a pat of butter. It takes only a few minutes to make, even with the additions in the variation and the following list.

4 tablespoons (½ stick) unsalted butter

1 Put the butter in a small saucepan over medium heat. Stir, scraping down the sides with a rubber spatula, until the butter foam subsides and the butter turns nut brown.

2 Turn off the heat and keep warm until you're ready to use it, but use it as quickly as you can, certainly within 15 minutes.

Black Butter Sauce (Beurre Noir). One step further and more dramatic: Cook the brown butter until black flecks start to form, another 2 or 3 minutes. Immediately drizzle the butter over whatever food you are serving, then turn the heat to medium and rinse the pan with 2 tablespoons sherry or white wine vinegar, shaking and letting about half the vinegar evaporate. Add 1 tablespoon drained capers if you like and ¼ cup chopped fresh parsley. Sprinkle with salt and pepper and drizzle this mixture over the food. Toss if necessary and serve.

4 Simple Additions to Brown Butter

Stir in any of these during the last minute of cooking, when the butter is just about ready (this point is easy to recognize once you've made brown butter a couple of times). If you want to use them in combination, increase the quantity of butter by 2 tablespoons for each additional ingredient.

1. Finely ground nuts (¼ to ½ cup): The usual ones like hazelnuts, cashews, pistachios, walnuts, or almonds, but also macadamia nuts or sunflower or pumpkin seeds; also whole pine nuts
2. Chopped fresh herbs: A tablespoon or so of oregano, rosemary, sage, thyme, or tarragon or up to ¼ cup milder herbs like parsley, cilantro, mint, dill, or basil
3. Mustard: Up to a tablespoon of either Dijon or whole grain, to taste, whisked in a bit
4. Vinegar: About a tablespoon of sherry or balsamic, which will make a "broken" sauce rather than emulsifying into the butter

Béchamel and 12 Other Creamy Sauces

MAKES: About 1½ cup
TIME: 10 to 20 minutes

These all begin with flour and butter (or oil), cooked together to make a roux (see page 47). To guarantee success, cook the fat-and-flour mixture long enough to rid the flour of its raw taste; this takes just a couple of minutes but requires nearly constant stirring. Then add the milk slowly, so no lumps form. (You can always beat or blend them out, but that's more work.)

2 tablespoons butter or extra virgin olive oil

2 tablespoons all-purpose flour

1 to 1½ cups milk

Salt and freshly ground black pepper

1 Put the butter or oil in a small saucepan over medium-low heat. When the butter melts or the oil is hot, use a wire whisk to incorporate the flour. Turn the heat to low and cook, whisking almost constantly, until the mixture turns tan, about 3 minutes.

2 Stir in the milk a little bit at a time, whisking constantly. When about a cup of the liquid has been stirred in, the mixture will be fairly thick. Add more milk a little at a time until the consistency is just a little thinner than you like, then cook, still over low heat, until the mixture thickens again.

3 Sprinkle with salt and pepper and serve immediately or keep warm over gently simmering water or in a double boiler for up to an hour, stirring occasionally.

Brown Sauce. A pinch of thyme is good here: In Step 1, cook the flour-fat mixture until brown, 3 to 5 minutes. Use beef, chicken, or vegetable stock (to make your own, see pages 157–159) in place of the milk.

Velouté (White) Sauce. Use chicken, fish, or lobster stock in place of the milk.

10 Simple Additions to Butter Sauces

Not every addition here is appropriate for every variation in the section, so I give some guidance. But please experiment.

1. Cook 1 tablespoon minced shallot in the butter until softened before adding the flour. Especially good with Brown Sauce.
2. Cook 1 or 2 tablespoons pine nuts or other chopped nuts in the butter until lightly browned before adding the flour. Good with Brown, Velouté, Old-Fashioned, and Curry Sauces.
3. Whisk in 1 tablespoon or more mustard during the last minute of cooking. Always appropriate.
4. Season to taste with lemon or vinegar during the last minute of cooking. Always appropriate.
5. Stir in 1 tablespoon or more capers during the last minute of cooking. Best with Brown and Velouté Sauces (see above).
6. Use mushroom-soaking liquid for part of the stock and add 1 or 2 tablespoons minced reconstituted dried mushrooms during the last minute of cooking. Always appropriate.
7. Stir in any minced fresh or dried herbs you like during the last minute of cooking. Always appropriate.
8. Stir in 1 tablespoon or more prepared horseradish during the last minute of cooking. Always appropriate.
9. Add Worcestershire, soy, or fish sauce (nuoc mam or nam pla, available at Asian markets) to taste during the last minute of cooking. Use your judgment.
10. Add about 1 tablespoon tomato paste about a minute before removing the sauce from the heat. Best with Béchamel or Velouté Sauce.

Shallot Sauce. Cook $1/4$ cup minced shallot, onion, or scallion (or 1 tablespoon minced garlic) in the butter until softened before adding the flour.

Nut Sauce. Cook 1 or 2 tablespoons pine nuts or other chopped nuts in the butter until lightly browned before adding the flour.

Mustard and/or Caper Sauce. Whisk in 1 tablespoon or more prepared mustard, capers, or both during the last minute of cooking.

Lemon Sauce. Season to taste with lemon juice (at least a tablespoon) or vinegar during the last minute of cooking.

Beurre Noisette Sauce. Cook the butter until it's brown before adding the flour. This adds a distinctively nutty flavor.

Mushroom Sauce. Use mushroom-soaking liquid for part of the stock and add 1 or 2 tablespoons minced reconstituted dried mushrooms during the last minute of cooking.

Herb Sauce. Stir in any minced fresh or dried herbs you like during the last minute of cooking.

Light Tomato Sauce. Add about 1 tablespoon tomato paste about a minute before removing the sauce from the heat.

Mornay (Cheese) Sauce. Add $1/2$ to 1 cup grated Emmental (Swiss), Gruyère, or other good cheese to the mixture after it has thickened.

Old-Fashioned Curry Sauce. Add 1 tablespoon curry powder (to make your own, see pages 66–67) or to taste, along with the flour.

Béarnaise Sauce

MAKES: About 1 cup
TIME: 20 minutes

Ⓕ Ⓥ

Béarnaise is overkill, but it does such wonderful things to grilled meat and fish that it deserves to be made every now and then, and it's not at all difficult. In addition to the variation, you can spike the completed béarnaise with a dollop of Dijon mustard or horseradish, $1/2$ teaspoon or so of minced garlic, a tablespoon of chopped capers, or

 Fast   Ⓜ Make Ahead   Vegetarian

chopped fresh herbs—especially tarragon, chervil, or parsley—to taste. See "10 Simple Additions to Butter Sauces" (left) for more ideas.

1 tablespoon minced shallot

2 teaspoons chopped fresh tarragon leaves or
    $^{1}/_{2}$ teaspoon dried tarragon

Salt and freshly ground black pepper

3 tablespoons white wine or other vinegar

2 egg yolks

8 tablespoons (1 stick) butter, cut into bits

Freshly squeezed lemon juice if needed

1 In a small saucepan over medium-low heat, combine the shallot, most of the tarragon, a sprinkle of salt and pepper, and the vinegar. Cook until all but about 2 tablespoons of the vinegar has evaporated, just a minute or two. Let cool.

2 Beat the egg yolks with 1 tablespoon water and stir into the vinegar mixture. Return to the stove over low heat and beat continuously with a wire whisk until thick, about 5 minutes.

3 With the heat as low as possible, use a wooden spoon to stir in the butter $^{1}/_{2}$ teaspoon or so at a time. Add the remaining tarragon and taste; add salt and pepper if necessary and, if the taste is not quite sharp enough, a bit of lemon juice. If the sauce is too thick, stir in hot water, a teaspoon at a time. Serve immediately.

Béarnaise Sauce with Tomato (Choron Sauce). Stir $^{1}/_{2}$ cup or more puréed tomato sauce (like Fast Tomato Sauce, page 502) into the finished béarnaise. Or combine $^{1}/_{4}$ cup tomato paste with $^{1}/_{4}$ cup cream and stir that in.

Beurre Blanc

MAKES: About $^{1}/_{2}$ cup
TIME: 10 minutes

Light and easy, beurre blanc is essentially béarnaise without egg and is brilliant over any simply cooked fish or vegetable. Make sure the butter is cold.

2 tablespoons minced shallot

$^{1}/_{3}$ cup white wine vinegar or rice vinegar

$^{1}/_{3}$ cup dry white wine

Salt and freshly ground black pepper

8 tablespoons (1 stick) cold butter, cut into bits

1 Combine the shallot, vinegar, and wine in a small saucepan over medium heat. Sprinkle with salt and pepper and cook, stirring occasionally, until reduced to a couple of tablespoons, about 5 minutes. Cool for 2 minutes.

2 Turn the heat as low as possible and whisk in the butter a bit at a time. As each piece is incorporated, add the next. When the sauce is creamy and smooth, and all the butter is incorporated, you're done. Serve immediately; this sauce will not keep.

Hollandaise Sauce

MAKES: About 1 cup
TIME: 10 minutes

You can make hollandaise in a blender (see the variation), but the stovetop version is perhaps a little finer, a bit more fun, and pretty much foolproof. Hollandaise takes well to fresh herbs added at the end; try tarragon (a teaspoon), dill or chervil (a tablespoon), or another herb, depending on how you're using the sauce.

3 egg yolks

Salt

6 tablespoons ($^{3}/_{4}$ stick) butter, softened

1 teaspoon freshly squeezed lemon juice

Pinch cayenne (optional)

1 Put the egg yolks, 2 tablespoons water, and a pinch of salt in a small saucepan over very low heat. Cook, whisking constantly, until light, foamy, and slightly thickened, 3 to 5 minutes. (If at any point during this process the yolks begin to curdle, immediately remove from the heat and continue to whisk for a minute before returning the pan to the stove.)

2 Remove from the heat and stir in the butter a tablespoon or two at a time. Return to the heat and continue to whisk until the mixture is thick and bright yellow. Add the lemon juice, then taste, adjust the seasoning (add the cayenne now if you're using it), and serve. (If you like, you can keep the finished sauce warm over extremely low heat or—better—over very hot water for 15 or even 30 minutes, whisking occasionally.)

Blender Hollandaise. Melt the butter in a small saucepan over low heat or in the microwave; do not let it brown. Combine all the other ingredients in the blender and turn on the machine. Slowly drizzle in the butter; the mixture will thicken. Taste and add more lemon juice or other seasonings if necessary.

The Basics of Spices

When I first wrote *How to Cook Everything,* many of the seasonings I used were a bit obscure; now most of them are mainstream. Still, you won't find all of these in your local supermarket, especially whole. And I wouldn't suggest you buy them there even if they were.

Rather, I encourage you to buy spices from somewhere that specializes in them or at least sells them in bulk. That generally means Asian or Indian markets, gourmet shops, on-line, or by mail (see Sources). Most whole spices keep so well, for so long, you won't need to stock up more than once or twice a year.

Whole spices have huge advantages over ground. Not only do they tend to be of higher quality to begin with, but they keep much better, and you can toast and grind them at the last minute, for maximum flavor.

That said, everyone uses preground spices, because they're so convenient. So toast and grind whole spices when you can—even if that means every fifth time or every tenth time.

Whole spices stay potent for months, up to a year, sometimes even longer. Sunlight, moisture, and heat are their only enemies. So just keep them in a tightly covered opaque container or in a jar in a dark place. The cooler, the better, though the refrigerator is too humid.

Toasting and Grinding Spices

It doesn't matter whether the spice is a seed, a flower, a piece of bark, or a dehydrated version of something fresh (like amchoor and ginger). Gentle warming activates and releases their essential oils and makes them aromatic. But too much direct heat burns them, resulting in a bitter taste.

When I can, I toast whole spices just before grinding. If they're big, like cinnamon sticks or nutmeg, break them up or crush into pieces—with your fingers, the back of a knife, a hammer, the bottom of a pan, whatever. If they're encased in pods, like cardamom, lightly crush the pods and remove the seeds (discard the husks). Then set a dry skillet over medium-high heat. Add the spices and cook, swirling the pan or stirring constantly with a wooden spoon, until they smell really good, for just a minute or two. Immediately remove them from the pan.

Whir the spice or spices in a coffee grinder or spice grinder. (You can use a cheap one, which costs ten bucks; purists use a mortar and pestle.) Unplug it, then wipe it out as best you can. (If you're feeling really energetic, grind a little rice to a powder after removing the spices; the rice powder will remove the seasonings when you dump it out.) Store the ground spices in a tightly covered container, preferably an opaque one (or at least away from light). They'll stay potent as long as any other ground spices, which is to say a few weeks.

The Spice Lexicon

In the first chart that follows are the spices most people use to cook and bake. It's not a comprehensive list—"Specialty Spices" contains many others—but you can certainly get by, and cook well, with the everyday spices alone. These are, however, judgment calls; if you were going to cook a lot of North African or Middle Eastern dishes, you'd put sumac in the first list instead of the second; similarly, if you

F Fast   **M** Make Ahead   **V** Vegetarian

EVERYDAY SPICES

SPICE	DESCRIPTION	USES
Allspice *Jamaica Pepper, Myrtle Pepper, Newspice, Pimento*	Berries that come from the aromatic evergreen pimento trees (not to be confused with pimientos, the peppers; see page 73). Small and shriveled, they look like large peppercorns, smell a bit like a combination of cloves and nutmeg, and taste slightly peppery. Available as whole berries and ground.	By the pinch; a little goes a long way. Particularly delicious with grains like bulgur, couscous, rice, and polenta and vegetables like beets, carrots, parsnips, winter squashes, and sweet potatoes. Extremely useful in pies, puddings, gingerbread, and some chocolate desserts.
Cardamom	Whole pods may be green, brown-black, or whitish. Each contains about 10 brown-black slightly sticky seeds with a rich spicy scent, a bit like ginger mixed with pine and lemon. You may find whole pods, "hulled" (just the seeds), and ground. Ground is the most common but the least potent. I buy whole pods (most often white).	A staple in Middle Eastern and Indian (it's a key ingredient in many spice mixtures) cooking; also used in some pastries, especially in Scandinavia. Sometimes pods are cooked whole, especially in braised dishes, where they soften (I like to eat them this way). Otherwise, gently crush the pods with the flat side of a knife, remove the seeds, and grind or crush as required.
Celery Seeds	Tiny tan whole seeds, usually from lovage, a relative of celery that has an intense celery flavor.	A little goes a long way. Often used in pickling brines, cheese spreads, and salad dressings.
Cinnamon *Canela, Ceylon or Sri Lanka Cinnamon*	The aromatic bark of a tropical laurel tree. Cassia—cinnamon's less expensive cousin—is often sold as cinnamon; it's the bark from a laurel tree native to China. Cinnamon or cassia bark dries into long, slender, curled sticks, reddish brown in color. Ground cinnamon is useful, though it's easy enough to grind sticks when necessary. Cassia is redder and usually comes in chip form; its flavor is more biting and bitter, making it better suited to savory dishes than sweet ones.	Use whole cinnamon sticks or pieces of cassia in soups, stews, chiles, and curries or add to rice or other grains. True cinnamon is excellent in pastries, as well as in rice puddings and other concoctions that feature sweet cream. It's delicious paired with apples or in mulled cider or cold fruit soups.
Cloves	The unripe flower buds of a tall evergreen native to Southeast Asia. Pink when picked, they are dried to reddish brown, separated from their husks, then dried again. Whole cloves should be dark brown, oily, and fat, not shriveled. They have a sweet and warm aroma and a piercing flavor. Both whole and ground forms are common, and both are useful.	Use cloves sparingly—their flavor can be overwhelming—and try to remove whole cloves before serving (or at least warn people to look out for them!). To make this easier, you can stud an onion with cloves and then remove the onion or wrap them in cheesecloth. A pinch of ground cloves is good in spice blends, batters and doughs, fruit pie fillings, and stewed fruit.
Coriander	Seeds of the cilantro plant (page 29), these are small, round, and vary in color from pale green when fresh to light or dark brown when dried. The lemony flavor is somewhat like cilantro leaves, but the overall taste is much more complex, with hints of cumin, fennel, and even cloves. Both whole seeds and ground are common.	Coriander seeds can be cooked whole into dishes (and are quite pleasant to eat) or ground first. Coriander is most often used in conjunction with other spices, especially cumin and cardamom, and is an important part of many spice mixtures or alone in Asian- and Latin American–style stews and soups.

SPICE	DESCRIPTION	USES
Cumin *Comino*	The highly aromatic dried fruit of the cumin plant, a relative of parsley. Because they look similar, cumin and caraway are often confused, though they don't taste alike at all. If you find cumin bitter, seek out the black seeds, which are more peppery and sweet. Whole seeds and ground are available in brown (the most common), black, and white varieties. (Black and white cumin can usually be found in Indian markets.)	Lightly toasting the seeds before using enhances their flavor. Like coriander, it's frequently included in spice mixtures, like garam masala, kebsa, and chili powder. But it's also used solo a great deal, especially in Latin American and Middle Eastern cooking.
Dill Seed	The seeds are light brown, oval, and flat. They have a stronger taste than the fresh or dried herb and a good one. Seeds and leaves are both common, though the leaves are considered an herb (see page 29).	Often used whole, though occasionally ground. Excellent with cucumbers, radishes, potatoes, and sauces made with sour cream, yogurt, or mustard. They are also featured in Pickling Spice (page 67).
Fennel Seed *Sweet Cumin*	From bulbless fennel, these seeds are small, pale greenish brown ovals with tiny ridges and an aromatic, warm, sweet taste reminiscent of licorice. Not as strong as anise and a bit more useful. Whole seeds are most common.	Delicious in salad dressings, yogurt sauces, and pilafs; one of the five ingredients in Five-Spice Powder (page 68) and some curry powders and a popular flavor in India, Italy (think sausages), and southern France. Whole or ground fennel seed makes an interesting addition to spice cookies, shortbread, and quick breads.
Ginger	Yellowish tan and powdery, with the distinctive aroma of ginger, dried ginger is inferior to fresh (see page 304) but useful nevertheless. Crystallized (candied) ginger is delicious out of hand and can be used in cooking.	Ground ginger is often used in sweets, like cakes, cookies, quick breads; it's very convenient for spice mixtures.
Nutmeg	The egg-shaped kernel inside the seed of the fruit of a tropical evergreen tree, dark brown and about 1 inch long. (Its covering is called mace; see the following chart.) It is sometimes a whitish color, the result of being dusted with lime to discourage insects (wash this off before grating or grinding). Available whole or ground; since the whole keeps nearly forever and is easily grated, there's no reason to buy ground.	Strong and slightly bitter, so use sparingly, by grating it directly (just put the unused portion back in the jar or bag) or by breaking into pieces first (use a hammer). A sweet and warm spice, it's lovely with fruit dishes, custards, cakes, and other sweets, as well as vegetables, especially spinach. It also works well with cream and cheese sauces for pasta.
Paprika *Pimentón*	Bright red-orange powder with a spicy-sweet aroma; anything turning brown is too old. Varying in heat from mild (sweet) to hot; peppery to smoky (usually Spanish). The best paprika comes from Spain (pimentón, which may be smoked and is really good) or Hungary (*Szegedi* is a good word to look for). California paprika is usually quite mild and not as good. (See "The Basics of Chiles and Peppers," page 69.)	As you would any ground dried chile (that's what it is). Delicious with grains, eggs, cheese, and many vegetables and in soups, stews, sauces, rice, and potato dishes. You can substitute ground mild chile (like ancho) for paprika with no problem.

SPICE	DESCRIPTION	USES
Saffron *Zafran, Asafran*	Even at $40 or so an ounce, worth having around; really. (Buying in smaller quantities can mean that instead of $600 a pound you pay more like $4,000 a pound. And if it's much cheaper than that, it's probably not saffron at all, but marigold or another imitation.) The threads should be strong, long, and a brilliant orange-red color. It's highly aromatic, warm, and spicy, with a slightly bitter taste and gives food a distinctive and lovely yellow color and an exotic, wonderful flavor. To approximate its color you can use annatto or turmeric, but nothing tastes like saffron. Buy only threads; ground is useless.	Use saffron sparingly (a good pinch is about right); too much can give food a medicinal taste. Add threads directly to the dish or steep them in some of the cooking liquid or oil for a few minutes first. Used in many traditional breads and cakes, as well as in rice (like Yellow Rice, the Best Way, page 463), pasta, and cheese dishes.
Sesame Seeds *Benne Seeds*	Small, flat, and oval with a pointed tip and a nice nutty, somewhat sweet, flavor, especially when toasted. Available whole, as paste (tahini, page 196), or as sesame oil (see page 196). White (most common), red, and black varieties; also unhulled white seeds, which are slightly bitter and harder to digest. (You can also buy pretoasted sesame seeds, but they sometimes have an off flavor.)	With their rich natural oils and nutty flavor, sesame seeds are an important flavoring in the cooking of China, Korea, Japan, India, and the Middle East; they are also used in Europe and are often lightly toasted (see page 317) before use. They are delicious as a coating for fried foods or as a garnish, sprinkled into sauces, dressings, on salads. Store in the refrigerator or freezer to prevent rancidity.
Star Anise *Chinese Anise*	The fruit of an evergreen tree native to China; pods are a dark brown, eight-pointed star, about 1 inch in diameter, with seeds in each point, perhaps the strangest-looking spice you'll ever buy and quite lovely. Although it has a licoricelike flavor, it is botanically unrelated to anise. Available whole.	Whole stars make an attractive garnish. If less than a whole star is required, break the star into individual points. You may want to wrap the points in cheesecloth and remove them before serving. Use in soups, marinades, and spice mixtures; part of Five-Spice Powder (page 68).
Vanilla Beans	From the seed pod of a climbing orchid, grown in tropical forests. Good pods are 4 to 5 inches long, dark chocolate brown, tough but pliant, and sometimes covered with white crystals, called *givre* ("frost") in French. Inside, they have hundreds of tiny black seeds. Good vanilla is expensive, so be suspicious of cheap beans. Wrap tightly in foil or seal them in a glass jar and store them in a cool place or the refrigerator. Available in whole pods (superior) and extract (convenient).	You can steep pods whole in sauces or syrups, but it's usually best to split the pod lengthwise and scrape the seeds into the liquid. Make vanilla sugar by burying a couple of whole beans in a jar of sugar, which will absorb their aroma after a few days (replenish the sugar in the jar as you use it). Exceptional with chocolate and coffee; used to flavor all kinds of desserts. Good with fruits: try poaching pears, apples, figs, or pineapple in a syrup flavored with vanilla.

SPECIALTY SPICES

SPICE	DESCRIPTION	USES
Amchoor *Amchur, Green Mango Powder*	Made from unripe green mangoes that are peeled, sliced, dried, and ground, amchoor has a tangy sour taste. Used much like lemon juice, primarily in Indian cooking. Available powdered or in dried slices.	Sift if necessary to remove lumps before using. Best with curries, chutneys, and pickles and especially in the blend Chaat Masala (page 68).
Anise Seeds *Aniseed, Sweet Cumin*	Tiny crescent-shaped greenish brown seeds with a sweet licorice flavor. Star anise or fennel can usually fill in for these and vice versa. Available whole or ground.	Although most common in desserts, anise works well in both sweet and savory dishes that include apples, cucumbers, carrots, turnips, or cabbages, or in fruit salads, salad dressings, pickles, stuffings, and sauerkraut.
Annatto *Achiote*	Triangular brick-colored seeds that smell earthy or musky and taste slightly peppery but subtle. Traditionally used in Latin American dishes. Available whole, ground, or less frequently as a prepared paste.	The seeds are too hard to crush easily and must be soaked for 10 minutes in boiling water first. Once drained, grind them with a mortar and pestle or in a clean spice mill or coffee grinder. More often, whole seeds are used to color and flavor oil as a first step in cooking dishes; just be sure to fish them out before adding the other ingredients.
Asafetida *Hing, Devil's Dung, Stinking Gum*	Made from the dried sap of giant fennel. The lumps are a waxy brownish black, and the powder is a beige color. Its unfortunate high-sulfur odor—like rotten garlic—can overcome your kitchen. But with a bit of cooking, it's transformed into a haunting flavor that smells a bit like onion. The powder is undeniably easier to use, but it's generally less pure, so go for the lump form if you can find it.	Indian cuisine primarily, especially vegetables, beans, potatoes, and in chutney, pickles, and sauces, usually in spice mixtures, like sambar powder. It is very potent, so use it only by the pinch. Try adding a tiny amount to plain boiled rice. To minimize the smell, double-pack powdered asafetida in a jar inside another jar, or it will stink up your pantry. A lump will keep indefinitely and should be pulverized just before use.
Caraway	Slender, ridged, whole brown seeds from a parsley-related plant, with an anise-cumin flavor	Traditionally used in rye bread, caraway is delicious with a variety of cabbage and potato dishes and other hearty soups and stews.
Capers *Caper Berries*	The flower buds of a shrub that grows in the Mediterranean, Southeast Asia, and California. Dried and then salted or soaked in brine. The tiniest (usually from France) are the most prized, though the biggest—which are the size of small grapes—are attractive and tasty too.	Whether brined or salted, rinse capers before using. Their tart, piquant flavor makes them perfect with rich, oily foods and sauces like sautéed meats or buttery pilafs. Add them to simple sauces or mayonnaise as a last-minute flavor boost.
Fenugreek *Methi*	Distinctive rectangular seeds; small, brownish yellow, and very hard. They have a pungent, almost acrid aroma and an earthy, somewhat bitter taste that is found in many Indian dishes. Available whole and ground.	Used mainly in the cuisines of India and northern Africa, in chutneys, dals (lentils), and curries. It goes especially well with eggplant and potatoes. An essential ingredient in many curry powders.

SPICE	DESCRIPTION	USES
Juniper Berries	The berrylike cones from the evergreen tree of the same name; the size of dried peas, blue-black in color. They taste like a mix of pine, fruit, and lemon peel and are the dominant flavor in gin. Delicious, but limited in use.	Very pungent, so use in moderation. Toasting brings out their aroma, and crushing releases their flavor. You can also use whole, in a cheesecloth bag or tea ball, and then remove before serving. Classic in stuffings, sauerkraut, sauces, and pickling.
Mace	The hard, lacy coating—or aril—that covers the pod that contains the nutmeg kernel. When the fruit first opens, mace is bright red. After drying and pressing, it becomes a dried yellow-brown color. Its flavor is very similar to that of nutmeg, though more bitter. Usually available ground; called blades when whole.	Add ground mace directly to savory dishes toward the end of cooking. Whole blades can be used as is in soups or stews and then removed before eating. Commonly used in cakes and other sweets, traditional in doughnuts and pumpkin pie. Nutmeg is almost always an adequate substitute.
Poppy Seeds	From the same plant as opium; the teeny seeds, which are about the size of a pinhead, come from inside the flower's pods. Most of the seeds we use in the U.S. are slate blue, but those used in India are usually smaller and a yellow-white color. They add a nutty flavor and a subtle crunch to foods. Available whole or crushed into a paste.	Used in Europe and the Middle East in or on sweets and baked goods. Good in salad dressings, fruit salads, and with Eastern European–style noodle dishes. In India, poppy seeds are toasted, ground, and used to flavor and thicken curries. The paste is used as a filling for strudel-type pastries and in other baked foods. Very finely ground almonds or almond paste is a good substitute.
Sumac *Summaq*	Dried, ground fruit, used as a souring agent—much like lemon—in the Middle East. The brick-red berries also lend a bit of color. Available in whole dried berries or ground, which is more common.	Toast and grind dried berries or use whole: Crack them and soak in water for 15 to 20 minutes, then wrap in cheesecloth and squeeze to extract the juice, which can be used like lemon juice. Powder is usually added during the last few minutes of cooking. Use with grilled items, on salads, or in dips like hummus or baba ghanoush.
Turmeric *Indian Saffron*	Darker skinned than ginger (like ginger, it's a rhizome), with thin fingers; its flesh is bright orange-red and difficult to grind. Available ground (most common) or in dried pieces.	Turmeric is most frequently used dried in spice blends (if you see some fresh, try mincing some in pickles; see page 229. But use sparingly; too much tastes bitter. Typical in Indian vegetarian cooking, especially in dal; also good with rice and other grain dishes, like couscous.

weren't interested in Chinese cooking, you'd forget about star anise (and Sichuan peppercorns, which are described along with other peppercorns on page 78). For real Indian cooking, you must have asafetida. And so on.

A note about garlic powder, which is probably conspicuous by its absence: I simply see no reason to use anything but fresh garlic, which is cheap and easy to use, keeps for a long time, and is one of the most important flavors in cooking.

For mustard seeds, see "The Basics of Mustard" (page 43); for chiles, see the charts on pages 71 to 73. For peppercorns, see the lexicon on page 78.

Spice Mixtures

Spice mixtures may be the ultimate convenience foods; with a few tucked away in your pantry the world of flavor is at your fingertips. If you have any doubt, sprinkle one piece of boiled potato with chili powder and another with curry and then taste.

As with single spices, there are several ways to use mixtures: Try them as a last-minute dusting of flavor on already cooked foods. Or put them in at the beginning as flavor foundations, cooking them in the butter or oil before building in other ingredients. They also make terrific rubs to season seafood, poultry, meats, tofu, or vegetables before grilling, broiling, or roasting—just sprinkle the blend on when you season with salt and pepper and use your hands to spread it evenly.

The blends in my spice cabinet are based on seasonings used around the world, though there are very few unusual ingredients among them. I've arranged them loosely in the order of how frequently I use them in this book.

With all of these, you can of course combine preground spices; but if you start (as the recipes do) with whole spices whenever practical, and toast and grind them yourself before blending, your spice mixtures will really sing.

Chili Powder

MAKES: About 1/4 cup
TIME: 5 minutes

Do yourself and everyone you cook for a favor and toss out any taco seasoning or jarred chili powder tucked away in your spice rack. Not only will this mixture blow anything you can buy out of the water, but it's also easy to make.

2 tablespoons ground ancho, New Mexico, or other mild dried chile (see page 72)

1/2 teaspoon cayenne, or to taste

1/2 teaspoon black peppercorns

2 teaspoons cumin seeds

2 teaspoons coriander seeds

1 tablespoon dried Mexican oregano

❶ Put all the ingredients in a small skillet over medium heat. Toast, shaking the pan occasionally, until the mixture is fragrant, 3 to 5 minutes.

❷ Grind in a spice or coffee grinder until powdery. Store in a tightly covered container for up to several weeks.

Hot Curry Powder

MAKES: About 1/4 cup
TIME: 10 minutes

Curry powder is a generic term for what we think of as an Indian blend of spices. These mixtures can be quite personal, so adjust this recipe to your taste. If it sounds too hot for you (the black peppercorns alone pack quite a punch), try the others that follow or just reduce the amount of chiles.

2 small dried Thai or other hot chiles

1 tablespoon black peppercorns

1 tablespoon coriander seeds

1 teaspoon cumin seeds

1 teaspoon fennel seeds

1 teaspoon ground fenugreek

1 tablespoon ground turmeric

1 tablespoon ground ginger

Cayenne, to taste (optional)

❶ Put the chiles, peppercorns, and seeds in a medium skillet over medium heat. Cook, shaking the pan occasionally, until lightly browned and fragrant, just a few minutes; for the last minute of cooking, add the ground spices.

❷ Cool, then grind to a fine powder in a spice or coffee grinder; add cayenne to taste at this stage if you're using it. Store in a tightly covered opaque container for up to several months.

❶ Fast   ❶ Make Ahead   ❶ Vegetarian

Fragrant Curry Powder

MAKES: About ¼ cup
TIME: 10 minutes

A mild and complex spice mix, perfect when you're looking for loads of flavor without heat.

> ¼ teaspoon nutmeg pieces
>
> Seeds from 5 white cardamom pods
>
> 3 cloves
>
> One 3-inch cinnamon stick
>
> 1 teaspoon black peppercorns
>
> 2 tablespoons cumin seeds
>
> ¼ cup coriander seeds
>
> 2 bay leaves
>
> 2 dried curry leaves (optional)
>
> 1 teaspoon ground fenugreek

❶ Put all the ingredients except the fenugreek in a medium skillet over medium heat. Cook, shaking the pan occasionally, until lightly browned and fragrant, just a few minutes; for the last minute of cooking, add the fenugreek.

❷ Cool, then grind to a fine powder in a spice or coffee grinder. Store in a tightly covered opaque container for up to several months.

Garam Masala

MAKES: About ¼ cup
TIME: 15 minutes

Literally meaning "warm mixture," this North Indian spice blend should be made in small quantities and used quickly so it's as fresh as possible. Like the preceding mixtures, it can be customized to your taste and used wherever a recipe calls for curry powder.

> Seeds from 10 cardamom pods
>
> One 3-inch cinnamon stick

> 1 teaspoon whole cloves
>
> ½ teaspoon nutmeg pieces
>
> 1 tablespoon cumin seeds
>
> 1 tablespoon fennel seeds

❶ Put all the ingredients in a medium skillet over medium heat. Cook, shaking the pan occasionally, until lightly browned and fragrant, just a few minutes.

❷ Cool, then grind to a fine powder in a spice or coffee grinder. Store in a tightly covered opaque container for up to several months.

Pickling Spice

MAKES: About 1 cup
TIME: 10 minutes

A traditional spice blend that gives a pickled flavor to virtually anything; see Three-Day Pickles (page 231), or for a more unusual use, try some on Grilled or Broiled Boneless Chicken (page 641) or Mashed Potatoes (page 339).

> Two 3-inch cinnamon sticks
>
> 10 bay leaves
>
> 2 small dried hot red chiles (like Thai) or 1 tablespoon hot red pepper flakes, or to taste
>
> ¼ cup mustard seeds
>
> 2 tablespoons allspice berries
>
> 2 teaspoons cloves
>
> 2 tablespoons black peppercorns
>
> 2 tablespoons coriander seeds
>
> 2 teaspoons cardamom seeds
>
> 2 tablespoons dill seeds

❶ Break the cinnamon sticks, bay leaves, and chiles into pieces.

❷ Roughly chop (or crush by pressing on the spices with a heavy skillet) all the other ingredients, leaving most of the seeds whole.

3 Stir to combine the spices and store in a tightly sealed container for up to several months.

Jerk Seasoning

MAKES: About ¹⁄₄ cup
TIME: 5 minutes

F **M** **V**

In Jamaica, jerk seasoning is typically used as a rub or marinade for grilled chicken or pork.

1 tablespoon allspice berries

¹⁄₄ teaspoon nutmeg pieces

1 teaspoon black peppercorns

2 teaspoons dried thyme

1 teaspoon cayenne, or to taste

1 tablespoon paprika

1 tablespoon sugar

2 tablespoons salt

2 teaspoons minced garlic

2 teaspoons minced fresh ginger or 2 teaspoons ground ginger

1 Put the allspice, nutmeg, peppercorns, and thyme in a spice or coffee grinder and grind to a fine powder.

2 Mix in the remaining ingredients and use immediately. Or leave out the garlic and fresh ginger and store in a tightly covered container for up to several weeks, adding the ginger and garlic as you use the seasoning.

Chaat Masala

MAKES: About ¹⁄₂ cup
TIME: 5 minutes

F **M** **V**

Chaat masala is among my favorite spice blends, with an intense sourness that comes from amchoor, a powder made from dried mangoes that's available in Indian markets (where you'll find the other unusual ingredient, hing, or asafetida). Traditionally used as a seasoning for raw or cooked vegetables or fruit, it's good on plain rice, salads, beans, fresh cheeses like feta, and even chicken or fish.

¹⁄₄ cup amchoor

2 teaspoons ground cumin

2 teaspoons freshly ground black pepper

2 teaspoons ground coriander

2 teaspoon ground ginger

¹⁄₄ teaspoon asafetida

¹⁄₄ teaspoon cayenne

Pinch salt

Put all the ingredients in a tightly covered opaque container and shake or stir to combine. Use immediately or store for up to several months.

Five-Spice Powder

MAKES: About ¹⁄₄ cup
TIME: 5 minutes

F **M** **V**

Sichuan peppercorns make this spice blend unusual and unforgettable. This tiny fruit pod (it's not really a peppercorn; see page 78) has an unusual smoky, citrusy flavor. Use this in stir-fries, for spiced nuts, and even sprinkled on desserts, like Butter Cookies (page 892) and Old-Fashioned Baked Custard (page 885).

1 tablespoon Sichuan peppercorns or black peppercorns

6 star anise

1¹⁄₂ teaspoons cloves

One 3-inch stick cinnamon

2 tablespoons fennel seeds

F Fast   **M** Make Ahead   **V** Vegetarian

Put all the ingredients in a spice or coffee grinder and grind to a fine powder. Store in a tightly covered opaque container for up to several months.

Seaweed "Shake"

MAKES: About ¼ cup
TIME: 20 minutes

This "shake" is not a green smoothie, but an American translation for the ubiquitous family of Japanese seasonings that you sprinkle on food as a last-minute condiment—using either your fingers, a spoon, or some kind of big-holed shaker (thus the name). Sushi Rice (page 474) and Sushi Bowls (page 473) are good places to use it; so are bowls of broth with soba or udon noodles and fish, meat, or vegetables.

Make this in small batches, because it stays fresh for only a little while; if you think you'll use it all within a week or so, double or triple the recipe.

2 sheets nori or ¼ cup crumbled dulse

1 tablespoon sesame seeds

1 teaspoon salt, preferably sea salt

Cayenne, to taste (optional)

❶ Set a large dry skillet (preferably cast iron) over medium heat. When it's hot, put a nori sheet in the pan and toast until it turns slightly green, which will take only a few seconds. Turn and quickly toast on the other side. Set aside to cool and repeat with the other nori sheet.

❷ While the pan is still hot, toast the sesame seeds, stirring or swirling the pan constantly to keep them from burning. When they are fragrant and beginning to turn golden, after about a minute, put them in a small bowl, sprinkle with salt, and stir.

❸ Crumble the nori into the bowl with the sesame seeds and salt. Or if you want a finer shake, whir the nori in a spice grinder for a few pulses, then add. Stir in the cayenne if you like. Store, tightly covered, in a dark place for up to a week.

The Basics of Chiles and Peppers

One of the most frequently used ingredients in this chapter is the chile: dried, fresh, chopped, whole, with seeds, without, processed, in paste—it's everywhere. This isn't surprising, since we've become a nation of hot heads, gobbling down more chiles than ever before. Maybe we've caught on to the fact that chiles have something extra going for them: Capsaicin, the thing that gives peppers their heat, releases "feel good" endorphins in the brain. On top of that, they're high in vitamin C and contain some antioxidants (especially the red ones, which contain beta-carotene). But really, the taste's the thing.

The Chile/Pepper Lexicon

All chiles and peppers are in the same botanical family, capsicum. There are literally thousands of varieties, ranging from fingernail size to foot-long, from sunset orange to purplish green. They vary in terms of heat (some, like bell peppers, are not hot at all) and complexity of flavor, sometimes as much from pepper to pepper as from variety to variety. That variability can make things a bit unpredictable. That's why the way I cook with chiles is to take a few home, slice a tiny piece out of one before I prepare a dish, and taste. Then I decide how much to use. Really, it's the only foolproof method. Habaneros are hot, poblanos are mild, but "hot" and "mild" vary wildly. You gotta taste.

When I use chiles, sometimes I'm looking for just a little heat, in which case hot red pepper flakes will do. Sometimes, though, I want the complex flavors chiles can bring, and then I pay attention to the type I'm using. When it really matters to the flavor of a dish, I will call for a specific variety, though this is rare (and usually limited to milder chiles, or to chipotle, which has a distinctively smoky taste). The entries in the following charts include a list of substitutions. Where you live has a lot to do with the kinds you will find, as does your proximity to

Latin or Asian stores, which offer larger selections. But really, if you go to the store and they've got only one type of chile, you might as well buy it. Even if it's the super-hot habanero (unlikely), you can buy a few, take them home for a taste test, and then use as you like.

Keep in mind that you can always substitute dried chiles (which obviously stores better, so you can always have some around) for fresh, and usually vice versa. The bottom line, though, is this: Use what you like, what you can find, and as much as you think tastes good.

The chiles in the following charts are divided into three groups: fresh, dried, and mild and sweet. They're organized from hottest to mildest and, within that order, by how frequently I use them.

Buying and Storing Chiles

Look for firm, smooth fresh chiles, with shiny skins and fresh-looking stems. Keep them in the fridge, wrapped loosely in a plastic bag for a week to two, maybe even longer.

Dried chiles that are still pliable are ideal—there's no need for them to be bone-dry—and they should never be dusty, dank, or moldy. When you get them home, put them in an airtight container and tuck them away in a dark corner of your pantry or spice shelf. Soak, grind, or crumble as needed.

For the sake of measurements, here are two general rules. Every square inch of chile flesh—not including seeds, pith, or the core—will yield about 1 tablespoon when minced. One medium bell pepper—cored, seeded, and chopped—will yield about a cup.

Working with Fresh Chiles

Unless they're stuffed (see page 333), fresh chiles are almost always cut up before using, the hotter ones minced, the medium and mild ones (like poblanos or bell peppers) chopped. Cook them along with aromatic vegetables like onions, garlic, and ginger before adding them to other ingredients, use them raw as a last-minute garnish, or add them anywhere in between.

Working with Dried Chiles

The simplest way to use dried chiles is to add them whole. The only problem with this is that you have no idea what kind of heat level they will contribute to the dish, and I've gotten some intense surprises this way.

Making Chile Powder: Next easiest is to remove the stem—and the seeds and veins too, if you want less heat—then toss them into a spice grinder and pulse until you get the desired texture. (Be careful when you open the lid; the aroma could be powerful.) Stored tightly covered in a dark place, this ground chile—it's real chile powder—will remain potent for months.

Toasting Dried Chiles: Toasting dried chiles in a dry skillet set over medium heat before using them is the best way to bring out their smoky flavor. It takes only a couple minutes on each side, though I usually bother with it only when the chile will be featured prominently.

Soaking Dried Chiles: Especially for use in soups and stews, dried chiles are often soaked. Cover the chiles in boiling water and soak until they're soft and pliable, which may take as little as 15 minutes or up to 30, depending on the age of the chiles. Then remove the seeds and veins. Some of the larger chiles will separate from their tough skins, so remove those too. Strain and save the soaking water (which can be very potent) if you want. Now you can chop and use the chiles, or purée them, either in a soup or stew or with a little of the soaking water and served as a straight chile sauce.

Working with Mild or Sweet Peppers

Chiles are actually fruit, so maybe it's not surprising that some of the milder ones can be quite sweet. Minced, chopped, or sliced, they are versatile both cooked and raw. The only thing you don't want to do is simmer them in liquid for too long; they'll turn bitter.

The Heat Factor

There are ways to measure a particular chile's heat or give a range within specific varieties. Scoville units are the most

EVERYDAY FRESH CHILES

CHILE	DESCRIPTION	HEAT	OTHER FORMS	SUBSTITUTIONS
Habanero *Scotch Bonnet (not technically the same, but virtually interchangeable)*	Round and fairly small, like teeny bell peppers, ranging in color from neon green to yellow, gold, and orange, depending on maturity and variety. The flavor is slightly fruity and bright once you get past the fire.	Very hot	Dried	Nothing has the same complex flavor (or packs quite the same wallop)
Cayenne *Finger Chile*	Long, slightly gnarled, and slender; green to red when mature	Very hot	Also available dried whole and ground	Thai, or use ground cayenne (see previous page)
Thai *Thai Bird*	Pinky size or smaller; green to red when mature	Very hot	Dried (see the following chart) and sometimes pickled	Cayenne
Giant Thai	Basically a bigger Thai pepper (see above)	Hot	Usually fresh only	Thai or jalapeño (use more jalapeño)
Chile de Arbol *Red Chile*	Finger length and slender; green to red when mature	Hot	Dried (more common)	Jalapeño
Serrano	Finger size or smaller, thin skinned; sold either red (mature) or green	Hot	Dried	Cayenne or Thai (use less); jalapeño (use more)
Jalapeño	Sold green mostly, though sometimes red; the flavor is slightly herbaceous and grassy	Hot to medium	Smoked and dried (see Chipotle in the following chart)	Serrano or chile de arbol
Fresno	Like jalapeños, only with thinner flesh; usually red (mature), but sometimes available green	Hot to medium	Usually only fresh	Serrano or jalapeño
Poblano	Like a smaller, flatter bell pepper; usually very dark green or purple or sometimes red (mature). Super for stuffing (you should peel first; see pages 330–333), grilling, and roasting.	Medium to mild	Dried (see Ancho in the following chart)	Anaheim or New Mexico
Anaheim *Chile Colorado (when red)*	Long and wide, somewhat flat; available both green and red (mature). Used for stuffing, grilling, roasting; egg dishes, mild salsas, sauces and dressings.	Medium to mild	Dried (see California in the following chart)	Poblano or New Mexico
New Mexico *Green Chiles or Red Chiles, depending on maturity*	Similar to Anaheim, only pointed on both ends, available both green and red (mature). Used for stuffing, grilling, roasting, puréeing into sauces and chilies.	Medium to mild	Both available dried	Anaheim

EVERYDAY DRIED CHILES

CHILE	DESCRIPTION	HEAT	OTHER FORMS	SUBSTITUTIONS
Dried Habanero	Small, roundish, reddish brown, very wrinkled. Use judiciously in chiles, soups, broths.	Very hot	Fresh (see the preceding chart), and sometimes smoked and dried	Dried chipotle
Chipotle *Chile Seco; Smoked Jalapeño*	Dried: light to reddish brown; canned: quite dark, almost purple. Because they're smoked, the flavor is incomparable—smoky, hot, and complex. These give a rich smokiness to chilies, stews, cooked salsas. If using dried, grind and use judiciously as you would cayenne. Minced or puréed, canned chipotles—with a little of their adobo—add body along with the heat.	Very hot to hot	(Fresh, they're jalapeños; see the preceding chart)	Nothing, really
Piquin *Piquín*	Fingernail size and shape, bright red; somewhat shiny skins; very complex flavors	Very hot to hot	Fresh (rare)	Dried Thai chiles
Chile de Arbol *Red Chile (see Thai in the preceding chart)*	Unlike many dried chiles, these retain a bright reddish brown to almost orange color; narrow and a couple inches long; nice heat and depth of flavor.	Very hot to hot	Fresh (less common; see the preceding chart)	Guajillo (which is milder, too)
Thai *Red Chile (not the same as other small Asian or American varieties, but virtually interchangeable)*	Small, narrow, brownish red	Hot	Fresh (see the preceding chart)	
Hot Red Pepper Flakes *Crushed Red Pepper; Dried Red Pepper; Ground Red Pepper*	The ubiquitous combination of seeds and bits of pepper, sometimes suspended in oil, always red. With supermarket kinds, assume that a variety of peppers are used to achieve a level of heat specified by the manufacturer. Use whenever you want to add plain old heat. For more character, make your own (see page 70).	Hot to medium	None	Crumble or grind any whole dried red pepper like Thai or Serrano; or for a milder flavor, use California
Cascabel *Chile Bola or Rattle Chile (because the seeds shake around inside)*	Smooth skinned and puffy—kind of like brown Ping-Pong balls, only smaller, with deep, smoky flavor	Hot to medium	Fresh (rare)	Chile de arbol

EVERYDAY DRIED CHILES (CONTINUED)

CHILE	DESCRIPTION	HEAT	OTHER FORMS	SUBSTITUTIONS
Guajillo	Dark reddish brown with shiny, thick skin; flat and about an inch wide and a couple inches long	Medium	Fresh guajillo (rare)	New Mexico or ancho
New Mexico—Red and Green	Long, somewhat wide, and flat; red or green	Medium	Fresh (see the preceding chart)	California or ancho
Ancho	Almost purple or black; compact, squarish; medium size. The classic in mild chili powder and an excellent mild dried chile.	Medium to mild	Fresh (and called poblano; see the preceding chart)	Pasilla or California
Pasilla *Chile Negro*	Almost black, very wrinkled, long, and narrow	Ranges from hot to mild, depending on the variety	Fresh (less common)	New Mexico
California	Longish and narrow, slightly flat, with rusty red color	Medium to mild	Fresh (see Anaheim in the preceding chart)	Ancho
Paprika *Hungarian Paprika or Spanish Paprika*	Usually found ground in cans or jars in sweet or smoked varieties (especially Spanish)	Mild	Rarely found fresh	none

MILD OR SWEET PEPPERS

PEPPER	DESCRIPTION	FORMS
Bell Peppers *Sweet Peppers; Holland Peppers; also called by their color—red, yellow, orange, or green*	The familiar large bell pepper, thick walled and moister than hot peppers; crisp, with a grassy or sweet flavor, depending on maturity. They range in color from shades of green (usually bitter, because immature) to yellow, orange, or red (or even purple).	Fresh
Shishito *Guernika, or Padrone*	Of Japanese or Spanish origin; finger sized, slightly gnarled, pale green. Delicious grilled or fried, served with salt.	Only fresh
Pimiento	Narrower and slightly smaller than a bell pepper, with a pointed end; more intense, sweet flavor, and red only	More commonly found in jars, but sometimes you see fresh.
Banana Peppers	Slightly larger than a jalapeño, yellowish green in color; don't confuse them with the hot Hungarian wax peppers.	Fresh

common, but there are others. I don't find any of them useful since each chile is different. There are, however, a few generalizations that are useful to know about: Small peppers tend to be hotter than large ones (with a few notable exceptions), while mature (red or orange) peppers pack a bigger wallop than green ones. And the seeds and veins (the pith) are the hottest parts of the chile. Any chile can be tamed (relatively) by removing the seeds and pith. Simply include some seeds if you want to pump up the heat.

Please remember that chiles can burn, literally. If you've got rubber gloves, think about using them. If not, every time you touch a chile, wash your hands with warm soapy water—twice is better than once—and be careful not to touch your eyes or any other tender areas for a while. If your hands are chapped or cut, chiles will irritate them.

And if your mouth is on fire, don't reach for that margarita—at least not to tame the heat. You'll get more relief from a glass of milk, strange as that may sound. Plain bread and crackers are also good options.

Chile Pastes

Like spice blends and rubs (see pages 65–69), chile pastes are not exactly sauces but cooking ingredients that are useful in dressings, sauces, and marinades and to smear on foods before grilling or roasting.

Chile Paste, Eight Ways

MAKES: About ¹/₂ cup

TIME: 45 minutes, largely unattended

Ⓜ   Ⓥ

Pure dried chiles, reconstituted and puréed, make a terrific paste. Use relatively mild ones like ancho, dried Anaheim, or New Mexico green (which will make the paste green). Guajillo or chipotle will be much hotter. Better yet, use a combination of mild and hot, which gives you both heat and complexity (my favorite is mostly ancho with a hit of chipotle).

The variations simply build additional flavors into the all-chile base. Whichever kind you make, if fresh herbs or aromatics are involved, use within a day or so for maximum freshness and oomph. Chile paste made with only dried seasonings will last for a couple of weeks.

> 2 ounces (6 to 12, depending on size) any dried whole chiles
>
> Salt
>
> 2 tablespoons neutral oil, like grapeseed or corn

❶ Toast the chiles in a dry skillet over medium heat for a minute or two on each side, then soak them in boiling water until soft, 15 to 30 minutes. Drain the chiles, saving the soaking liquid, and remove and discard the seeds and veins (for a hotter paste, save some of the seeds).

❷ Put the chiles, any seeds you're using, and a pinch of salt in a blender or food processor. Purée until smooth, adding a spoonful of soaking water at a time until you reach the desired consistency.

❸ Put the oil in a small skillet and over medium-high heat. Cook the chile paste, stirring constantly, until deeply colored and fragrant, about 2 minutes. Use immediately or refrigerate for up to 2 days. Just before serving, taste and adjust the seasoning.

Mexican-Style Chile Paste. Use all guajillo or other dark chiles: To the blender or processor, add 2 cloves garlic, 1 teaspoon ground cumin, and 2 tablespoons fresh epazote, Mexican oregano, or oregano leaves (or 2 teaspoons dried herbs). Use corn oil if you like instead of grapeseed and proceed with the recipe.

Chipotle Paste. Hot. Hot. Hot: Use some or all dried chipotles. Or skip Step 1 and use 1 small can of chipotles, with their adobo sauce (about ¹/₃ cup).

Thai-Style Chile Paste. Quite complex: Use 2 or 3 Thai chiles along with the mild chiles. To the blender or processor, add 1 inch lemongrass, peeled, trimmed, and chopped and ¹/₄ cup fresh cilantro or Thai basil leaves. Use peanut oil if you like instead of grapeseed.

Ⓕ Fast   Ⓜ Make Ahead   Ⓥ Vegetarian

Vietnamese-Style Chile Paste. Use 2 or 3 Thai chiles along with the mild chiles. To the blender or processor, add 3 or 4 cloves garlic and 2 tablespoons nam pla (Thai fish sauce), 2 tablespoons sugar, and 1/4 cup fresh mint leaves. Use peanut oil if you like instead of grapeseed. After cooking, squeeze in the juice of 1 lime.

Indian-Style Chile Paste. Useful if you want to add heat to Indian dishes: To the blender or processor, add 1 tablespoon garam masala (to make your own, see page 67), or more to taste. Use peanut oil if you like instead of grapeseed.

Harissa. The flavor is quite complex: To the blender or processor, add 1 tablespoon ground coriander seeds, 2 teaspoons ground cumin, and 1 or 2 cloves garlic. Use extra virgin olive oil instead of grapeseed.

How to Use Chile Pastes

Some uses of chile pastes are obvious. Others take a bit of thought. Some of each:

- Rub pastes directly onto fish, poultry, or meat before cooking—any kind of cooking, not just grilling.
- Toss a spoonful or two of any chile paste with simply cooked vegetables, pasta, or grains (along with a little butter or oil if you like).
- To turn chile paste into a "real" sauce, heat a batch with 1/4 cup or so of oil, butter, cream, stock, tomato sauce, or even water, then use.
- Stir chile paste directly into yogurt, sour cream, or mayonnaise for a quick chilled sauce.
- Mix with a little extra virgin olive or neutral oil, like grapeseed or corn, and brush on fish, chicken, meat, vegetables, or tofu as they come off the grill.
- Stir a little into nut pastes for a spicy spread for toasted bread.
- Smear a little on sandwiches (especially grilled cheese!).

Chile and Black Bean Paste. To the blender or processor, add 2 tablespoons fermented black beans and eliminate the salt until you taste for seasoning. Use peanut oil if you like instead of grapeseed.

Chile-Garlic Paste

MAKES: About 2 cups
TIME: 10 minutes

Among the most ubiquitous and versatile of Asian sauces, used in hundreds of dishes and other sauces. Like the previous recipe, you can learn to make this instinctually, and you can customize the heat level by using milder chiles (like New Mexico) or hotter ones (Thai, chile de arbol, piquin, or habanero). You can also reduce the heat level some by removing the seeds from the chiles before crushing them.

1 cup dried red chiles, like red Thai, chile de arbol, piquin, or red New Mexico

1/4 cup chopped garlic

1/4 cup hot water, or more if needed

1/4 cup white wine vinegar or distilled vinegar

2 teaspoons sugar

1 teaspoon salt, or to taste

1 Combine all the ingredients in a blender or food processor and purée to a smooth paste. Add more hot water by the tablespoon if the paste is too thick.

2 Use immediately or refrigerate for up to 3 months.

Red Curry Paste

MAKES: About 3/4 cup
TIME: 25 minutes

Cilantro roots—the roots of the cilantro plant, often attached to the bunch of cilantro you buy at the supermarket—lend that bright cilantro flavor without your having to use the entire bunch. Just be sure to rinse them very well to get all the sand and dirt off before using. To use the leaves, see Cilantro-Mint Chutney (page 37) and Cilantro "Pesto" with Ginger and Chile (page 28).

10 Thai or other medium to hot dried red chiles, seeded, or to taste

4 dried lime leaves or fresh lime leaves, finely chopped, or 1 tablespoon grated lime zest

1 teaspoon coriander seeds

1 teaspoon cumin seeds

2 stalks lemongrass, peeled, trimmed, and roughly chopped

2 shallots, roughly chopped

4 cloves garlic, smashed

$1/2$ to 1 inch fresh ginger, roughly chopped

2 tablespoons cilantro roots, rinsed well, or 3 tablespoons chopped cilantro stems

3 tablespoons peanut oil

1 Soak the chiles and lime leaves in warm water for about 15 minutes.

2 Put the coriander and cumin seeds in a small skillet over medium heat. Cook, shaking the pan occasionally, until lightly browned and fragrant, about 3 minutes. Cool, then grind to a powder in a spice or coffee grinder.

3 Drain the chiles and lime leaves and, along with all the remaining ingredients except the oil, transfer to a blender or food processor; grind to a paste, stopping the machine to scrape down the sides as necessary. Gradually add the oil while blending; you are looking for a fairly smooth, thick paste. Store in a tightly covered container and refrigerate for up to 2 weeks.

Green Curry Paste. Substitute fresh green chiles for the red chiles and add 1 tablespoon ground turmeric to Step 3.

Red or Green Curry Sauce. Put 2 tablespoons neutral oil, like grapeseed or corn, into a deep skillet over medium heat. Add $1/4$ cup Red or Green Curry Paste and cook, stirring constantly, until it becomes fragrant and the color deepens, about 2 minutes. Stir in $1^1/2$ cups coconut milk (to make your own, see page

389) and just bring to a boil, reduce the heat a bit, and let it bubble gently until thickened, about 5 minutes. Stir in $1/2$ cup chopped fresh Thai basil, mint, or cilantro if you like.

The Basics of Salt

All salts are created naturally—in rock and bodies of water—but they're not all the same. Common table salt is mined, milled, refined, and "enhanced" with iodine and other ingredients into small, free-flowing grains. But consistency has a downside: the flavor of table salt is harsh, with iodine the predominant mineral taste.

At the other end of the spectrum is an array of specialty salts, pulled from both oceans and clay, with nuances of flavor and color you may or may not think are worth the expense. In between is a handful of everyday salts—either coarsely milled from deposits in rock or made by evaporating ocean water. Either way the result is an additive-free "coarse salt." These are the ones I use both in the kitchen and on the table.

Salt gets its name and primary flavor from sodium chloride, the major compound present in all types in varying degrees. The subtle flavors of sea salts (which may be described as "briny," "metallic," or "earthy") come from traces of minerals. The more trace minerals, the less sodium chloride, which is why many sea salts taste less "salty" than table and kosher salts.

Storing Salt

Even the wettest sea salts are extremely long-lived and stable. But because salts can have a corrosive effect, you should keep them in glass, ceramic, crockery, or wood containers—definitely not metal. Plastic is okay for short periods of time.

Grinding Salt

Some very coarse salts require additional grinding. Use a special salt mill designed for this purpose or crush small amounts in a mortar and pestle. Again, the idea is to avoid metal parts, which will only corrode and rust.

 Fast   Make Ahead   **V** Vegetarian

Seasoning Salt

It's easy enough to season your own salt with herbs and spices. For example, try putting a sprig of fresh rosemary, lavender, oregano, or thyme into a small shaker bottle of salt for a few days (then remove). Or toast a spoonful of coriander, cardamom, or cumin seeds or even a dried chile and stir into the salt, either whole or ground. Use these during cooking or as a last-minute finish.

Salt in My Recipes

I primarily use either kosher salt or sea salt. Salting food is a matter of personal taste, so I rarely specify quantities. But I won't totally leave you in the dark. The instructions suggest when to season with salt—usually more than once during the process and almost always at the end—and I always encourage you to taste.

I do specify exact measurements in rare dishes where a precise amount of salt really makes a difference and of course in baking recipes, where I almost always use kosher salt; sea salt is less uniform and might have overpowering mineral flavors.

The Salt Lexicon

Kosher and sea salts are common in supermarkets. Less common salts like Maldon (from England), fleur de sel (Brittany), and smoked salts are usually available in gourmet shops and definitely by mail order (see Sources).

Kosher Salt

This usually comes in big boxes, either flaked or coarsely ground. I like the flaked best, but both are fine. It's as white as table salt, but the flavor is clean and slightly mineral, with no lingering aftertaste.

Uses: This is my all-purpose salt for baking, salting cooking water, and last-minute seasoning.

Generic Sea Salt

Made by either heating saltwater in pipes and tubs or open-air evaporation; the most complex generally start with the most complex saltwaters. That said, connoisseurs will argue that heating the water destroys some flavor. Try a few different ones and see what you think; your palate may be more sensitive than mine, because I can't really find that much difference among them.

Uses: Because these tend to be more expensive than other kinds of salt, I generally reserve them for cooking and final seasoning rather than add them to pasta water and the like. And I never use it in sweet baking recipes.

Fleur de Sel

Literally "flower of the sea," this prized sea salt from the coast of France (Brittany) is fine, grayish white, and slightly damp.

Uses: After cooking, as the final seasoning. It's so good you can use it to "dress" fresh salad greens, either alone or with a light squeeze of lemon.

Maldon Sea Salt

Made by a special process in England, this salt is rolled flat and flaky. The result melts on your tongue and on hot food unlike any other salt, leaving behind a pleasant flavor that builds slowly. It can be tough to find (though easy by mail order), but when you do it's usually relatively inexpensive.

Uses: Absolutely the best on piping-hot fried foods, roasted potatoes, and scrambled eggs.

Table Salt

As mentioned above, this is the common salt of shakers and paper packets across America. Iodine was added several decades ago and remains in the mix today, frequently along with other noncaking ingredients. The fine grains dissolve faster than most coarse salts, which can be an advantage.

Uses: Anywhere—but it's quite "salty," so use less.

Rock Salt

This less pure salt is commonly used in roasting and ice cream making to conduct heat or cold. A small bit probably wouldn't kill you, but you definitely don't want to eat it.

Salts for Enthusiasts

If you feel like getting carried away, there's a rainbow of colors and flavors to try: Look for the ivory Ravidà from Sicily, bright red Alae salt from Hawaii, black salts from India, and Celtic gray sea salt from France. Some may be tough to find, but each is renowned—sometimes even justifiably—for conveying the distinct flavors of its earth and sea.

The Basics of Pepper

Native to India and now cultivated throughout the hot and humid regions of the world, this vine-growing fruit has been fought over and for throughout history, with good reason. The flavor is deep, sharp, smoky, slightly acidic, and pleasantly hot, a balance that cannot be duplicated with anything else. It's become ubiquitous, and its value can't be overstated. But it's easy to lose sight of this if you use packaged ground pepper.

A Word About Grinding Pepper

What you grind at the moment doesn't taste at all like the same spice you shake out of a can or jar, and it barely resembles its home-ground kin that's a few hours old. That said, if you really can't bear to grind as you go, do it every few weeks in small batches and keep the ground pepper in a tightly sealed container.

There are many types of peppermills for table and kitchen grinding. Ideally you want a sturdy metal or wooden mill with a screw at the top or bottom to adjust the grind. Of course you can also grind pepper in a spice or coffee grinder (see "Toasting and Grinding Spices," page 60). Or simply crack pepper into large chunks with the flat side of a big knife or put peppercorns into a plastic bag and take a hammer to them.

The Peppercorn Lexicon

Don't confuse pepper with chiles (see page 69). Peppercorns are technically fruit—not seeds—that grow in clusters on long "spikes." They are harvested ripe as they begin to mature from green to red or yellow-green fruit. After curing in the sun, they shrivel and turn black.

Black Peppercorns

There are many varieties, known mostly by the region in which they were raised, but what you will usually find is a blend simply labeled *black pepper*. Take a whiff if possible to make sure the aroma is complex and sharp without being acrid. Store these and other dried peppercorns whole, in tightly sealed containers in a cool, dark place.

White Peppercorns

Because the skins have been removed, white pepper is milder than black. It's perfect for everything from cream sauces to fruit desserts, anytime you're looking for the range of pepper flavors with a little less punch. But if you're going to use it, commit to buying another pepper mill and grind your own.

Green Peppercorns

These are best—but rare—fresh, where their mild fruity and grassy flavor is at its peak. They're also packed in brine (refrigerate after opening) or dried (you must reconstitute these in hot water like dried chiles or mushrooms).

Pink Peppercorns

Though they are not from the same plant as pepper, the flavor is very similar to black pepper, only slightly sweet.

Sichuan Peppercorns

Also called *Chinese peppercorns, anise pepper, gagara, flower pepper,* and *sansho,* Sichuan peppercorns aren't from the pepper vine at all but are the flowers of a small tree. Sichuan pepper's flavor is unique and essential to Sichuan cooking; a flowery, slightly smoky aroma combines with a somewhat lemony-medicinal flavor, and a tongue-numbing, unhot "spiciness" that feels almost like local anesthesia. (This is how Sichuan food can contain so many chiles without being overwhelmingly hot.)

Appetizers

EVERYONE LIKES WHAT WE NOW CALL

"small plates" so much that they commonly become whole meals. Really, more than half the recipes in this book can be served as starters, as snacks, or as part of an array of dishes. Pasta, of course, is always served before the main course in Italy; salads are wonderful starters and one of the truly American traditions when served that way; and soups are eaten before other foods more often than not.

But increasingly, in the Spanish style of tapas, cooked meats, poultry, fish, and vegetables are served

How Many Appetizers to Cook?

Serving sizes always depend on appetite and the amount of other food being served. That's particularly true for appetizers: A hungry television watcher can eat a couple cups of nuts in thirty minutes with no problem; put the same nuts out at a party with five other finger foods and they'll be enough for ten people to nibble on. So use the serving sizes here as guidelines rather than absolutes.

in appetizer-size portions before a main course, with or without a fork. Think of skewered grilled food (like kebabs), pizza and its relatives, and many egg dishes, especially quiches and frittate. Furthermore, many vegetable, bean, and meat dishes can serve as dips. (Throughout this chapter you'll find lists of ideal small-plate dishes that appear elsewhere in the book.)

What, then, is left to cover in a chapter devoted to appetizers? Dishes specifically intended to be served as finger food, foods that are not filling enough or "serious" enough to be served as a main course—or are in fact too rich to eat a plateful—or that are traditional starters or snacks. These range from simple spiced nuts to slightly more complicated bruschette and fritters, to the relatively complex egg rolls, empanadas, and samosas.

We think of most of these as dishes for entertaining, and rightfully so. Few meals are ready the moment guests walk in the door; even if you're serving buffet style, some time passes between the arrival of the first and usually somewhat early guest to the arrival of the latecomers. During that time, it's essential to have a few things to nibble on: At the minimum, you might make a bowl of nuts or marinated olives, either of which can be done well in advance. At the maximum, you can make the greeting food as impressive as the meal. The options for these kinds of dishes are literally endless.

3 Ways to Serve Appetizers

To minimize the pressure of entertaining, try to plan as many room-temperature dishes as possible.

1. For a buffet: Set foods right next to the accompanying condiments or sauces. Put plenty of napkins, plates, toothpicks, and other necessary eating utensils among the dishes where they will be most handy. There's no law that says they all have to be at one end of the table or the other.

2. When passing appetizers: Offer the sauce on the same plate and carry some extra napkins. If toothpicks are needed, put them in the food or carry them in a shot glass or small cup.

3. For individual portions: Set all the serving plates out on a workspace and assemble them as a group. For example, put all the main items on the plates, then follow with the sauce—instead of finishing one plate before turning to the next.

ESSENTIAL RECIPES

Serve these as casual snacks for family and friends or set them out as part of a larger assortment of finger foods for a larger party. All can be made well in advance.

✪ Roasted Nuts with Oil or Butter

MAKES: 4 to 6 servings
TIME: 15 minutes

These are a revelation, so far from canned mixed nuts that you may have trouble believing it; and they're almost no work at all. I suggest relying heavily on pecans or walnuts, almonds, pistachios, and cashews, with a sprinkling of anything else handy. See page 318 for "The Nut and Seed Lexicon" for more options.

2 cups (about 1 pound) mixed unsalted shelled nuts

2 tablespoons peanut oil or melted butter

Salt and freshly ground black pepper

Heat the oven to 450°F. Toss the nuts in a bowl with the oil or butter and some salt and pepper. Put on a baking sheet and roast, shaking occasionally, until lightly browned, about 10 minutes. Cool before serving; they will crisp as they cool.

Sautéed Buttered Nuts. Even better tasting: Put 4 tablespoons butter or peanut oil in a large skillet over medium-low heat. When the butter melts or the oil is hot, add the nuts and cook, stirring, until lightly browned, about 10 minutes. Be patient; high heat will burn the nuts. As they cook, season with salt and pepper. Cool before serving.

Spiced Buttered Nuts. Real bar food: Add 1 teaspoon to 1 tablespoon of any spice mixture (pages 65–69), like chili or curry powder, to the mix. If roasting, toss the nuts with the spice at the beginning. If sautéing, add it to the butter or oil as it heats.

Roasted Nuts with No Added Fat. Not exactly a compromise, because these are still infinitely better than nuts straight from a jar or can: Heat the oven to 350°F. Run cold water over the nuts and put them, still wet, in one layer on a baking sheet. Sprinkle with coarse salt and put in the oven. Bake, without stirring, until they are light brown and fragrant, 10 to 15 minutes. Remove from the oven, cool slightly, and serve or hold at room temperature for up to a few hours.

Roasted Pumpkin, Squash, or Sunflower Seeds. You can also use fresh pumpkin or squash seeds; see page 319: Use the main recipe or any of the variations, baking at 350°F for about 30 minutes, tossing occasionally, or until tan. Like nuts, they will crisp as they cool.

Caramelized Spiced Nuts

MAKES: 4 to 6 servings
TIME: 15 minutes

A crisp sugar shell and bit of spice make these not too sweet and not too spicy, and they're only slightly more involved than the roasted nuts in the preceding recipe.

Serve a bowl of them with cocktails or other appetizers; they will go quickly, so have backup ready.

Add seeds to the mix as well; sunflower, pumpkin, and sesame seeds all add flavor and texture.

> 2 tablespoons peanut or neutral oil, like grapeseed or corn
>
> 2 cups sugar
>
> 2 teaspoons garam masala (to make your own, see page 67)
>
> ½ teaspoon cayenne
>
> 1 teaspoon salt
>
> 2 cups (about 1 pound) mixed unsalted shelled nuts

❶ Heat the oven to 450°F. Grease a baking sheet with the oil. Put a wide pot or deep skillet over high heat and add 2 cups water and the sugar. Bring to a boil and stir in the spices, salt, and nuts. Reduce the heat to medium and cook, stirring frequently, until the liquid is reduced to a syrup, 5 to 10 minutes.

❷ Turn the heat to low and remove the nuts with a slotted spoon, letting the excess syrup drain off a bit and then spreading the nuts on the baking sheet (be sure to turn off the burner when you've finished).

❸ Roast the nuts for 10 minutes, tossing once or twice with a spatula. Remove from the oven and let cool (the sugar coating will be very hot, so resist sampling for a few minutes!); the sugar coating will harden as the nuts cool. Serve or store in an airtight container at room temperature for 2 or 3 days.

Fiery Caramelized Nuts. Substitute a tablespoon or more finely minced canned chipotle chile with the adobo sauce for the garam masala.

Real Popcorn

MAKES: 4 to 6 servings
TIME: About 10 minutes

Unless you're at work, please forget about microwave popcorn. It doesn't compare to the real thing (especially if you don't store the kernels forever), which takes at most twice as long. And popcorn takes brilliantly to real butter (instead of that artificially butter-flavored oil), cheese, and many other seasonings; see "9 Flavor Boosters for Popcorn or Roasted Nuts," below.

> 2 tablespoons neutral oil, like grapeseed or corn
>
> 1/2 cup popping corn
>
> 4 tablespoons (1/2 stick) butter or extra virgin olive oil (optional)
>
> Salt

1 Put the oil in a large, deep saucepan (6 quarts or so) with a lid. Turn the heat to medium, add 3 kernels of corn, and cover.

2 When the 3 kernels pop, remove the lid and add the remaining corn. Cover and shake the pot, holding the lid on. Cook, shaking the pot occasionally, until the popping sound stops, after about 5 minutes. Meanwhile, melt the butter (or gently warm the oil) if you're using it.

3 Turn the popcorn into a large bowl; drizzle with the butter and sprinkle with salt while tossing the popcorn. Serve immediately if possible; popcorn is best hot.

9 Flavor Boosters for Popcorn or Roasted Nuts

Just toss any of these thoroughly into the cooked popcorn or nuts. Some are more potent than others, so be careful (you don't want to use a tablespoon of cayenne, for example).

1. Chopped fresh herbs
2. Freshly ground black pepper
3. Chili powder (to make your own, see page 66)
4. Chaat masala (to make your own, see page 68)
5. Five-spice powder (to make your own, see page 68)
6. Ground sumac
7. Cayenne or hot red pepper flakes
8. Hot or Fragrant Curry Powder (page 66 or 67)
9. Finely ground nuts

Salty-Sweet Popcorn. Serve with or without the butter: Sprinkle the popcorn with salt and superfine sugar as soon as it's done, tossing to coat evenly. Taste and add more seasoning if needed.

Parmesan Popcorn. You can use whatever cheese you like here, but Parmesan is the best; grate it as finely as possible: Add 1/4 cup finely grated Parmesan and toss with the hot popcorn.

✪ Marinated Olives

MAKES: 8 or more servings

TIME: 5 minutes, plus time to marinate

Marinated olives are so much better than those straight from the jar or barrel that most people assume there is some trick to them. There isn't, other than to start with good olives (a few different kinds if possible; see page 322). I don't use red pepper flakes when I marinate olives, but many people like a little bit of heat here; suit yourself. Other good additions are a tiny bit of vinegar (start with a teaspoon) or some bits of lemon, segmented as you would a grapefruit. For a slightly more involved version of this dish, see Sautéed Olives (page 323).

> 1 pound olives, green, black, or a mixture, preferably imported from Greece, Italy, or Spain
>
> 2 tablespoons extra virgin olive oil, or to taste
>
> 4 cloves garlic, crushed
>
> Several sprigs fresh thyme or rosemary, 1 teaspoon fresh thyme or rosemary leaves, or 1/2 teaspoon dried thyme
>
> 2 bay leaves (optional)
>
> 1 teaspoon hot red pepper flakes (optional)

Mix all the ingredients and transfer to a jar or serving bowl. You can serve these immediately, although they are better if they sit, covered and refrigerated, for a day or two. They will keep, improving in flavor, for several weeks, but bring to room temperature before serving.

 Fast   Make Ahead   **V** Vegetarian

Marinated Mozzarella

MAKES: 8 servings
TIME: 20 minutes, plus time to rest

Ⓕ Ⓜ Ⓥ

If you can find small mozzarella balls, by all means use them. Otherwise, cut a chunk of mozzarella into bite-sized pieces. In either case, use fresh mozzarella if at all possible for the best flavor.

Other cheeses you can use: cubes of feta, queso fresco (try it with cilantro), or ricotta salata.

¼ cup extra virgin olive oil

¼ cup chopped fresh basil, parsley, or oregano leaves or any combination

1 pound mozzarella, drained if packed in water and cut into bite-sized pieces if necessary

Salt and freshly ground black pepper

Hot red pepper flakes, to taste

❶ Combine the oil and the herb; toss in a bowl with the mozzarella.

❷ Taste and add salt and both peppers to taste. If possible, let stand for at least 30 minutes before serving.

Edamame in Their Shells

MAKES: 4 servings
TIME: 5 minutes

Ⓕ Ⓜ Ⓥ

A staple at Japanese restaurants, edamame are immature soybeans either in their pods or shelled. In their pods, they make terrific finger food for appetizers. To eat edamame from the pod the traditional way, hold the far end of the pod between your teeth and pull, using your teeth to squeeze the beans into your mouth. It's also easy to shell them like peanuts or peas and pluck them from the pods.

Salt

1 pound fresh or frozen edamame in their pods

Bring a large pot of water to a boil and salt it. Add the edamame, return to a boil, and cook until bright green, 3 to 5 minutes; drain. Or put them in a dish with a couple tablespoons of water, partially cover, and microwave for 3 to 5 minutes, depending on your microwave power. Sprinkle with salt and any of the garnishes in the following list if you like. Serve hot, warm, or chilled. (Serve with an extra bowl for the empty pods.)

Spicy Stir-Fried Edamame. Flash-cooking in a skillet with chiles gives the edamame a nice kick: Use either shelled or unshelled edamame. Put 1 tablespoon neutral oil, like grapeseed or corn, 1 teaspoon dark sesame oil, the edamame, 2 tablespoons water, 3 or more Thai or other small hot fresh or dried chiles, 1 teaspoon Sichuan peppercorns (optional), and 1 teaspoon minced garlic into a large skillet over high heat. Cover and cook, shaking the pan often, for about a minute. Remove the lid and stir-fry until softened, about 3 minutes longer. Sprinkle with salt and serve.

7 Simple Garnishes to Sprinkle on Edamame
1. Toasted sesame seeds
2. Dark sesame oil
3. Togarashi seasoning
4. Soy sauce
5. Chile oil
6. Rice vinegar
7. Finely minced garlic or ginger

Bruschetta and Crostini

MAKES: 4 servings
TIME: About 20 minutes

Ⓕ Ⓥ

Grilled bread, doused with olive oil, scented with raw garlic, finished with coarse salt—what can be better than bruschetta (or crostini)? Add toppings and you have a classic starter. Use thick slices of Italian-style bread—or one of the home-baked European-style breads on pages 856 to 859—so that the outside gets crunchy while the inside stays moist.

8 thick slices rustic bread

Extra virgin olive oil as needed

1 to 4 cloves garlic, halved or crushed

Salt and freshly ground black pepper

1 Heat a gas or charcoal grill or a broiler to medium-high heat and put the rack about 4 inches from the heat source. Brush both sides of the bread lightly with oil, then grill or broil until lightly browned on both sides.

2 Rub one or both sides of the bread with garlic. Put the bread on a plate, then drizzle it with olive oil (a tablespoon or so per slice is not too much); sprinkle with salt and, if you like, pepper. Serve warm.

Crostini. Until recently, these Italian-style croutons were known in America as "toast points": Cut the bread into thinner, smaller slices so you have 16 to 24. Brush them with oil and crisp them on a grill, under a broiler, or in a 400°F oven until golden on all sides. Rub them with garlic if you like and top them in any of the ways that follow.

Bruschetta or Crostini with Parmesan. For the broiler instead of the grill, this offers lots of bang for the buck: Omit the garlic, drizzle the bread with oil, and then sprinkle it with grated Parmesan; run under the broiler until the Parmesan just melts and serve immediately.

Bruschetta or Crostini with Tomatoes and Basil. With good tomatoes, there's nothing better: Core about a pound of ripe tomatoes, squeeze most of the seeds out, and coarsely chop them. If you have time, put them in a strainer for a few minutes to drain the excess water. When the bread is ready to cook, toss the tomatoes, about a cup of torn basil leaves, a drizzle of olive oil, and a sprinkle of salt together in a bowl. Top the bread with the mixture after rubbing the garlic on the bread in Step 2, sprinkle with pepper, and serve.

25 Toppings for Bruschetta and Crostini

1. Fresh Tomato or Fruit Salsa (page 23)
2. Traditional Pesto (page 27)
3. Any of the spreads in this chapter (see pages 89–97)
4. Corn Salad with Avocado (page 207)
5. Any bean salad (pages 215–218)
6. Chicken Salad with Olive Oil and Fresh Herbs (page 222)
7. Crab Salad (page 225)
8. Seafood Salad, Mediterranean Style (page 226)
9. Virtually any puréed vegetable (see pages 242–244)
10. Sautéed Eggplant with Basil (page 295)
11. Braised Endive, Escarole, or Radicchio with Prosciutto (page 298)
12. Garlic Braised in Olive Oil (page 303)
13. Sautéed Mushrooms (page 313)
14. Caramelized Onions (page 325)
15. Spinach with Currants and Nuts (page 352)
16. Grilled or Broiled Tomatoes with Basil (page 362)
17. Oven-Baked Ratatouille (page 373)
18. White Bean Purée (page 413)
19. Beans and Tomatoes (page 414)
20. White Beans, Tuscan Style (page 427)
21. Beans and Greens (page 427)
22. Lentils, Six Ways (page 431)
23. Salt Cod in Tomato Sauce (page 630)
24. Salt Cod Mousse (page 631)
25. Shredded Pork (page 759)

More Finger and Toothpick Foods

These are not quite as straightforward as the preceding recipes, but they're still easy to pull together quickly.

Deviled or Stuffed Eggs

MAKES: 4 servings

TIME: 5 minutes with precooked eggs

A wonderful old standard that can be varied in dozens of ways. For lower-fat deviled eggs, replace the mayonnaise with yogurt.

F Fast   **M** Make Ahead   **V** Vegetarian

4 Hard-Boiled Eggs (page 791)

Salt

2 tablespoons mayonnaise, preferably homemade
(page 41)

1 teaspoon Dijon mustard, or to taste

1/4 teaspoon cayenne, or to taste

Paprika or fresh parsley leaves for garnish

1 Cool the eggs, peel them, cut them in half length-wise, and carefully remove the yolks.

2 Mash the yolks with some salt and the mayonnaise, mustard, and cayenne. Taste and adjust the seasoning. Spoon the filling back into the whites. (If you are making a lot of deviled eggs and want them to be especially attractive, use a pastry bag to pipe them back into the whites.)

3 Sprinkle with paprika and serve or cover and chill, well wrapped, for up to 1 day before serving.

Deviled Eggs with Anchovies. As with anything containing anchovies, about half the people in the room will love these: In Step 2, substitute 1 tablespoon olive oil for the mayonnaise; mash 2 or more anchovies with the yolks. Garnish with a piece of anchovy fillet and a couple of capers.

Herb-Stuffed Eggs. Fresh looking and tasting: In Step 2, substitute 1 tablespoon olive oil for the mayonnaise. Add 1/4 teaspoon minced garlic, 2 tablespoons minced fresh parsley leaves, 1 tablespoon drained and chopped capers (optional), and 1 teaspoon minced fresh tarragon leaves or 1 tablespoon minced fresh basil leaves. Garnish with parsley sprigs or small basil leaves.

Curried Deviled Eggs. Subtly spiced: Substitute yogurt for the mayonnaise if you like and Fragrant Curry Powder (page 67) or other spice mix for the mustard. Garnish with cilantro leaves.

Jalapeño Deviled Eggs. Make these as spicy as you like: Substitute sour cream for the mayonnaise, 2 teaspoons or more minced jalapeño for the mustard, and 1/8 teaspoon ground cumin for the cayenne. Garnish with cilantro leaves.

Spring Vegetable–Stuffed Eggs. A little more work, because you have to mince the vegetables: Add a tablespoon each minced radish or cucumber (seeded; see page 293); snow peas, peas, or green beans; and scallions, shallots, or onion. Garnish with a piece of parsley or a bit of any vegetable.

14 Tasty Additions to Deviled Eggs

Add a touch of mayonnaise, sour cream, yogurt, or olive oil as necessary to help bind the filling and keep it moist.

1. Chopped cooked shrimp, lobster, or crabmeat (excellent with chopped tarragon)
2. Finely crumbled chorizo or other spicy sausage
3. Crumbled bacon
4. Avocado bits
5. Bits of dried tomato
6. Finely chopped olives, capers, or gherkins
7. Lightly cooked spinach or watercress, squeezed dry and finely chopped
8. Finely grated or crumbled cheese—the stronger the better—like Parmesan, feta, or manchego
9. Horseradish or wasabi
10. Any miso
11. Any pesto (pages 27–28) or salsa (pages 33–35 and 48–50)
12. Grainy Mustard (page 44) or any grainy mustard
13. Cooked corn kernels (especially pan-grilled, see page 289)
14. Finely chopped red bell pepper (raw or roasted and peeled, see page 330)

Marinated Celery and Carrots, Chinese Style

MAKES: 4 appetizer or side-dish servings

TIME: 10 minutes, plus time to marinate

An easy and surprising little nibble, crunchy and ultra-savory. Substitute any vegetable you can eat raw or try this marinade with parboiled and shocked vegetables (see page 240) like broccoli or snow peas.

½ pound celery stalks

½ pound carrots

1 teaspoon salt

1 tablespoon sugar

2 tablespoons dark sesame oil

2 tablespoons soy sauce

2 teaspoons vinegar, preferably rice or cider

1 clove garlic, minced

Pinch cayenne (optional)

1 Cut the celery and carrots into 2-inch lengths, then into rough matchsticks. Mix with the salt and set aside for at least 10 minutes and up to an hour while you whisk together the remaining ingredients.

2 Rinse, drain, and pat the vegetables dry, then toss with the dressing. Serve or marinate in the refrigerator for up to a day and serve chilled or at room temperature.

Quick Marinated Mushrooms

MAKES: 4 servings

TIME: 5 minutes

F **V**

Arguably the best use for white button mushrooms, which have more flavor raw than cooked.

½ pound mushrooms, trimmed and cut into chunks

Juice of 1 lemon

About 1 tablespoon extra virgin olive oil

Salt and freshly ground black pepper

¼ pound Parmesan cheese in 1 chunk

1 Gently toss the mushrooms with the lemon juice, olive oil, and some salt and pepper. Taste and adjust the seasonings.

2 Break the Parmesan into small chunks. Use a toothpick to skewer a mushroom and a piece of cheese, repeating until all the mushrooms and cheese are used up. Serve immediately or refrigerate for up to an hour.

18 Other Ideas for Finger or Toothpick Foods

These can be picked up reasonably neatly with fingers or served on a toothpick and are easy to produce in quantity.

1. Virtually any hot or cold sandwich (see pages 166–171)
2. Any focaccia, pizza, or calzone (see pages 164 and 178–184)
3. Quick-Pickled Vegetables (page 229)
4. Spicy Pickles, Asian Style (page 229)
5. Kosher Pickles, the Right Way (page 230)
6. Three-Day Pickles (page 231)
7. Grilled Vegetables, especially on skewers (page 249)
8. Beet Rösti with Rosemary (page 264)
9. Boiled, Grilled, or Roasted Chestnuts (page 287)
10. Corn Fritters (page 291)
11. Corn Pancakes, Thai Style (page 292)
12. Sautéed Olives (page 323)
13. French Fries (page 346)
14. Broiled Figs with Cream Cheese (page 391)
15. Roasted Chickpeas (page 416)
16. Indian-Style Split Pea Fritters, (see pages 100–101)
17. Aloo Paratha (Potato-Stuffed Flatbread (page 850)
18. Any frittata, cut into small pieces (see pages 804–806)

Marinated Vegetables

MAKES: About 8 servings

TIME: About 45 minutes

M **V**

These fall somewhere between a quick pickle and a salad, perfect at a party served with toothpicks or on a buffet table with a spoon. For a more substantial salad, toss

 Fast   Make Ahead   Vegetarian

them with cooked greens, grains, or pasta and use some of the brine as a dressing.

2 cup red wine vinegar

2 tablespoons salt

2 sprigs fresh oregano or 2 teaspoons dried

2 bay leaves

2 cloves garlic, peeled

1 cup extra virgin olive oil

1 head broccoli, cut into florets

1 small head cauliflower, cut into florets

2 medium zucchini or summer squash, sliced crosswise

2 medium carrots, cut into $1/2$-inch-thick slices or sticks

1 red bell pepper, cored, seeded, and sliced

1 onion, cut into eighths

$1/2$ cup green or black olives (optional), pitted if you like

Freshly ground black pepper

❶ Put the vinegar, salt, oregano, bay leaves, garlic, olive oil, and 1 quart water in a large pot and bring to a boil. Add the broccoli and cauliflower and cook for a minute, then add the zucchini, carrots, bell pepper, onion, and olives; cover and turn off the heat.

❷ Let cool to room temperature in the pot. Serve at room temperature or chilled, drizzled with some of the liquid and olive oil and sprinkled with lots of black pepper. Keep it in its liquid in a covered plastic or glass container in the refrigerator for a month or more.

Marinated Fennel with Preserved Lemons. Artichoke hearts also work well here: Substitute white wine vinegar for the red wine, 1 tablespoon each coriander and cumin seeds for the oregano, and 4 large fennel bulbs, trimmed and cut into $1/4$-inch-thick slices, for the vegetables. Add $1/2$ cup Preserved Lemon slices (page 393). Add the fennel to the boiling liquid in Step 1, then add the preserved lemon and turn off the heat. Proceed with the recipe.

Shrimp Cocktail

MAKES: 4 servings

TIME: 20 minutes

Some might say this is a retro appetizer, now hip again. But I don't remember it ever going out of style. You can also serve boiled crawfish with this sauce, though peeling them is trickier. I prefer very large shrimp here, but use whatever size you can find.

1 pound jumbo shrimp (16 to 20)

$1/2$ cup ketchup

1 teaspoon chili powder (to make your own, see page 66)

3 tablespoons freshly squeezed lemon juice

Salt and freshly ground black pepper

1 tablespoon Worcestershire sauce, or to taste

Several drops Tabasco or other hot sauce

1 tablespoon prepared horseradish, or to taste

1 tablespoon minced onion (optional)

Iceberg lettuce (optional)

❶ Put the shrimp a large pot over high heat with water to cover. Salt the water, and when it boils, reduce the heat to medium-low and cook just until the shrimp are pink all over, 3 to 5 minutes. Drain the shrimp and rinse them immediately in cold water. Peel the shrimp.

❷ Combine all the other ingredients except the lettuce; taste and adjust the seasoning. If time allows, chill both the shrimp and the sauce.

❸ Serve individual portions of shrimp, on a bed of lettuce if you like, with a small bowl of sauce.

3 Ways to Spin Shrimp Cocktail

1. Skip the ketchup sauce and serve it with a fresh fruit, tomato, or tomatillo salsa (see pages 33–35 and 48–50).

2. Add a couple tablespoons of mayo, cream, or crème fraîche to the cocktail sauce or serve the shrimp instead with a flavored mayonnaise (see pages 42–43).

3. Serve the shrimp and sauce with slices of crisp raw vegetables, like jícama, carrots, radishes, daikon, or chayote.

Cheese Straws

MAKES: At least 10 servings

TIME: 20 minutes

Our beloved Cheez-Its were originally—of course—based on a real pastry-and-cheese cracker, commonly called *cheese straws*. Homemade, these have become my default finger food for guests, not quite as easy as marinated olives or spiced nuts but far more unusual and impressive. To make them you basically dump everything in the food processor; you have to cut out the straws by hand, but that doesn't take long either.

$1/2$ pound cheddar or other flavorful hard cheese

$1/3$ pound Parmesan cheese

2 cups (about 9 ounces) all-purpose flour

Pinch cayenne

8 tablespoons (1 stick) chilled butter, cut into chunks, plus a little more for greasing the baking sheet

Few drops ice water, if necessary

Coarse salt (optional)

❶ Heat the oven to 450°F. Grate the cheese in a food processor, then remove from the bowl. Add the flour and cayenne to the processor and pulse. Add the butter and process to combine the butter and flour; pulse in the cheese. To mix by hand, pinch the butter with flour mixture between your fingers (or use a pastry blender or two forks) until it resembles cornmeal. Then blend in the cheese the same way.

❷ Knead by hand until the dough comes together, adding a few drops of ice water if necessary. (At this point, you may wrap the dough well in plastic and refrigerate for up to 2 days.)

❸ Roll the dough out into a rectangle about $1/4$ inch thick, using flour as necessary (or roll between 2 sheets

of plastic wrap), then cut into strips as long as you like and about $1/2$ inch wide. Put on a lightly greased baking sheet and sprinkle with the salt if you like. Bake until golden brown, 5 to 8 minutes. Serve hot, warm, or at room temperature.

Suzanne Goin's Bacon-Wrapped Dates

MAKES: 24 pieces

TIME: 35 minutes

Ⓜ

My friend, the Los Angeles chef Suzanne Goin, serves these at her trendsetting wine bar, A.O.C. They're perfect finger food for parties—sweet, savory, and salty, with a soft, chewy texture—and can be made ahead.

1 tablespoon fresh thyme leaves

24 pitted dates

12 slices bacon

Heat the oven to 350°F. Put a few thyme leaves in the cavity of each date. Cut the bacon in half lengthwise. Roll each date in a piece of bacon and secure it with a toothpick or two. Put the dates on a baking sheet and roast, turning once or twice, until the bacon is crisp and cooked, 20 to 25 minutes, depending on the thickness of the bacon. Transfer to a serving dish and serve hot or wrap and refrigerate for up to 3 days or freeze in resealable plastic bags (thaw before roasting).

Stuffed Bacon-Wrapped Dates. Before wrapping in bacon, stuff a chunk of manchego, Gouda, or Parmesan into each date.

Prosciutto-Wrapped Dates. You definitely want soft, plump dates for this; the overdried hard ones just won't cut it: Substitute prosciutto for the bacon and skip the roasting.

Dates with Goat Cheese. Omit the bacon. Stuff the dates with soft goat cheese (use a pastry bag to make it eas-

 Fast   Make Ahead   Ⓥ Vegetarian

ier; see page 901), flavored with minced fresh herbs, like thyme, rosemary, sage, chives, chervil, and/or parsley, or sweetened with honey to serve as a dessert. Roast in the oven until the cheese softens; let sit for a minute before serving.

Almond-Stuffed Dates. Good with any of the preceding: Slip an almond into each date cavity before proceeding.

Dips and Spreads

You start with something creamy—mayo, sour cream, puréed beans or vegetables, softened cheese—and then flavor it, simply or with something a little more complex. Presto: You have a dip for crackers, toasted pita, or raw vegetables.

Generally, dips are served in bowls and spreads are smeared on crackers or bread (when topped with a little garnish, they make canapés) or into the natural troughs of celery or endive. But almost any spread can be made into a dip by thinning it slightly with sour cream, yogurt, cream, milk, or mayonnaise. And nearly any dip can be converted to a spread by adding more cream cheese or replacing some of the sour cream with butter or cream cheese. Refrigeration also stiffens most of these combinations.

Remember that Vinaigrette (page 199)—in all its various forms—also makes a splendid, tasty, and easy dip, especially with crudités (raw vegetables, see page 90). And many of the sauces and salsas in the "Sauces, Condiments, Herbs, and Spices" chapter can be used as dips or spreads, too.

Sour Cream or Yogurt Dip, Five Ways

MAKES: 6 to 8 servings
TIME: 10 minutes

Perhaps the easiest dip to make, but a revelation if the only version you've had is onion dip made with dried soup mix.

A couple of pointers and ideas: If your yogurt is thin, drain it in a cloth-lined strainer for 15 to 30 minutes (see page 824) before using it. You can chop the vegetables in a food processor, but be careful not to purée them. If you prefer a slightly more textured dip, add $1/4$ cup or so of creamy cottage cheese to the mix. For a stiffer and more flavorful dip, substitute mayonnaise (preferably homemade, see page 41) for half the sour cream or yogurt.

1 cup chopped mixed raw vegetables, like seeded cucumber (see page 293), red or green bell pepper, carrot, and/or peas

1 scallion, finely chopped

2 tablespoons chopped fresh dill or parsley leaves or 1 teaspoon dried dill

2 cups sour cream or yogurt

Salt and freshly ground black pepper

Freshly squeezed lemon juice, to taste (optional)

Mix the vegetables with the scallion, herb, sour cream, and some salt and pepper. Taste and adjust the seasoning, then add a little lemon juice if necessary. Cover and refrigerate for up to a day. Serve with vegetables, crackers, or thin slices of toast.

Onion Dip. Easy and amazing: Use a food processor to mince the onion, but stop the machine before it gets too watery (if you go too far, just drain the onion a bit before mixing it with the sour cream). Use 1 cup onion and $1/2$ cup parsley leaves; you won't need lemon juice.

Horseradish Dip. Add Dijon mustard to taste to give this dip even more kick: Add 1 tablespoon or more prepared horseradish.

Smoked Salmon or Trout Dip. Also good with salmon or trout roe: Omit or include the vegetables as you like; add $1/2$ cup flaked smoked trout or minced smoked salmon. Lemon juice is a must here.

Watercress or Arugula Dip. The pepperiness of these greens is fabulous in a dip: Omit or include the vegetables as you like; add 1 cup trimmed, washed, dried (drying is essential), and chopped watercress or arugula.

Crudités

Crudités—essentially cut-up raw vegetables—are quick and easy to throw together, though there are more interesting and attractive vegetables you can use than the most common (and most staid) carrot and celery sticks.

The best vegetables are, of course, the freshest you can find, but there are a couple of other criteria to consider: If they're not somewhat mild in flavor when raw, they should be cooked lightly. And they must be "dippable." Onions and spinach do not work for obvious reasons, but barely cooked asparagus spears are perfect, as are raw Belgian endive leaves.

Cutting vegetables for crudités is pretty simple: Keep the pieces large enough to pick up easily and dip without dipping your fingers (very small pieces are annoying) or breaking the vegetable, but small or slender enough to pop into your mouth or bite easily; usually about 1/2-inch wide is just right. Broccoli and cauliflower florets work best with about an inch or so of stem to hold on to; core and seed bell peppers and slice them into roughly 1/2-inch-wide sticks, cutting the curved ends off (chop them and use in a rice salad, with pasta, stir-fried vegetables, or fried rice) if you like.

You can prepare all the components of a crudité platter, including the dip, in advance. Just store raw vegetables in ice water to keep them crisp and lightly cooked vegetables in airtight containers; both will hold for a day or so. Drain the raw vegetables well and put them on a kitchen towel or a few layers of paper towels to dry (dip doesn't stick to wet vegetables); bring the cooked vegetables to room temperature.

9 Interesting Vegetables to Use as Crudités

1. Baby carrots (not the nubby kind sold in bags) with the green tops, tops trimmed to 1 inch and carrots peeled
2. Asparagus spears, trimmed and very lightly steamed (still crunchy and bright green)
3. Green or wax beans, steamed or boiled until crisp-tender
4. Sugar snap peas, raw if very fresh or very lightly steamed
5. Belgian endive leaves
6. Jícama, peeled and cut into sticks
7. Purple potatoes, steamed until just tender and cut into long wedges
8. Small "new" potatoes, steamed whole
9. Red or white radishes, whole or cut in half

15 Dips to Serve with Crudités

1. Simplest Yogurt Sauce (page 24)
2. Blue Cheese Dressing (page 25)
3. Parsley (or Other Herb) Purée (page 27)
4. Traditional Pesto (page 27)
5. Tahini Sauce (page 35)
6. Creamy Cilantro-Mint Chutney (page 37)
7. Ginger-Scallion Sauce (page 39)
8. Simple Miso Dipping Sauce (page 39)
9. Real Ranch Dressing (page 42)
10. Garlic Mayonnaise or any flavored mayonnaise (page 42)
11. Peanut Sauce (page 55)
12. Any bean dip (see pages 92–93)
13. Hummus (page 93)
14. Nearly any salad dressing works fine, especially Vinaigrette (page 199)
15. Any well-seasoned vegetable purée (see page 242)

 Fast   Make Ahead   Vegetarian

Flavorful Cream Cheese Spread

MAKES: 6 to 8 servings

TIME: 10 minutes

Here's a stiff cream cheese–based spread that can be thinned with sour cream, yogurt, mayonnaise, or cream to make a dip. You can substitute virtually anything sharp and salty for the blue cheese or simply use more cream cheese.

1/2 pound cream cheese

1/4 pound Roquefort, Maytag blue, or other good blue cheese

Sour cream or yogurt as needed

Cayenne or Tabasco or other hot sauce, to taste

❶ In a bowl, cream the cheeses together with a fork.

❷ Stir in enough sour cream or yogurt to thin the mixture to a spreading consistency or use more to make a dip. Add cayenne to taste and refrigerate until ready to use.

Cream Cheese Spread with Fruit and Nuts. Also makes a terrific companion for Poached Pears with Vanilla (page 401): Omit the hot sauce. After the cheeses are well combined, stir in 1/2 cup each of minced dried fruit (prunes, apricots, cherries, apples, or cranberries), and chopped nuts (hazelnuts, walnuts, almonds, pecans, or pistachios).

Roasted Pepper and Garlic Spread. This is good with some chopped cooked bacon (what isn't?). Omit the blue cheese. Add 1/2 cup chopped Roasted Red Peppers (page 330; or use jarred pimientos) and about 1/2 head Roasted Garlic (page 303) to the cream cheese. Thin with extra virgin olive oil instead of sour cream. Mash well and proceed as directed. Add salt, pepper, and lemon juice in place of the cayenne.

Anchovy Spread. Omit the blue cheese. Add 4 mashed anchovy fillets, or more to taste, and 1/4 teaspoon minced garlic to the cream cheese. Mash well, using olive oil, sour cream, or yogurt to thin the spread if necessary. Add black pepper and lemon juice in place of the cayenne.

Crab or Shrimp Spread. Omit the blue cheese. Add about 1 cup shredded or minced cooked crabmeat or shrimp, 1 tablespoon mayonnaise, and a few dashes of Worcestershire or soy sauce to the cream cheese. Thin with lemon juice, if necessary, in place of sour cream. Mash well and proceed as directed. Add salt and cayenne.

Cheese-and-Herb Dip or Spread. If you like a very smooth dip, use a blender or food processor to combine the ingredients and thin with a little milk or cream as needed. Add about 2 tablespoons minced fresh parsley leaves, 1/2 teaspoon minced garlic, and 1 teaspoon minced fresh marjoram, oregano, sage, or thyme leaves.

Herbed Goat Cheese

MAKES: 6 to 8 servings

TIME: 10 minutes

Easy to make quickly, you can use this as a spread or a dip; its consistency is somewhere in between. Start with fresh, mild, unflavored goat cheese.

Other cheeses you can use: fresh ricotta or feta (you'll need to use a food processor).

1/2 pound fresh goat cheese

2 tablespoons cream, sour cream, yogurt, or milk, or as needed

1/4 teaspoon finely minced garlic, or to taste

1/2 cup chopped mixed fresh mild herbs, like basil, parsley, chervil, dill, and/or chives

1 teaspoon minced fresh tarragon or thyme

Salt and freshly ground black pepper

1 tablespoon extra virgin olive oil, or as needed

1 Thin the goat cheese with enough of the cream to make it spreadable or usable as a dip. You may need more or less depending on the thickness of the cheese and the consistency you prefer.

2 Stir in the garlic and herbs. Taste and add salt if necessary (some goat cheese is quite salty) and pepper to taste. Drizzle with the olive oil and serve, or refrigerate for up to several hours—then add the olive oil and serve.

Herbed Feta Cheese. Briny and with a pleasantly gritty texture: Use feta cheese instead of the goat cheese.

Rosemary-Honey Goat Cheese. Slightly sweet and lovely with any fresh or dried fruit: Omit the garlic and salt and pepper; use 2 tablespoons minced fresh rosemary and as much honey as you like instead of oil.

Goat Cheese–Stuffed Figs. Terrific grilled: Cut 8 ripe fresh figs in half. Thin the cheese as directed, using only $^1/_2$ pound; omit the garlic and herbs; taste the mixture and add salt if necessary. Spread about 1 tablespoon of the cheese onto the top of each fig half, pressing just enough so that it adheres. Drizzle with a little olive oil, sprinkle with some freshly ground black pepper, and serve or refrigerate for up to an hour before garnishing and serving. To grill, just pop onto a not-too-hot grill, cheese side up, until the figs are warm.

Refried Bean Dip

MAKES: At least 8 servings

TIME: 10 minutes with precooked beans

Ⓕ　Ⓜ　Ⓥ

A basic bean dip that's made for tortilla chips, though you could serve it with almost anything: raw sliced vegetables; grilled, broiled, or fried tofu cubes; pita or toast or crackers—you name it.

Use 3 cups cooked—and lightly mashed—pinto or other beans if you don't have Real Refried Beans on hand, but be sure to increase the seasoning (see the chart that follows for ideas).

1 recipe Real Refried Beans (page 418)

About 1 cup bean-cooking liquid or vegetable stock (to make your own, see page 157), or as needed

$^1/_2$ cup minced red bell pepper

$^1/_2$ cup minced onion

$^1/_2$ cup peeled, seeded, and diced tomato (optional)

1 tablespoon minced fresh chile (like jalapeño or Thai), or to taste, or cayenne or hot sauce, to taste

1 teaspoon red wine or other vinegar

Salt and freshly ground black pepper

1 Put all but 1 cup of the beans in a food processor or blender. Add enough liquid to start the purée.

2 Combine the remaining mashed beans with the puréed beans. Stir in the bell pepper, onion, tomato if you're using it, chile, vinegar, and some salt and pepper. Taste and adjust the seasoning if necessary; thin with more liquid if necessary. Serve immediately or cover and refrigerate for up to 2 days; bring to room temperature or reheat gently before serving.

Fast Bean Dip. Save a few minutes and some chopping by using prepared salsa: Substitute $1^1/_2$ cups Fresh Tomato or Fruit Salsa (page 23) or Fresh Tomatillo Salsa (page 33) for the bell pepper, onion, tomato, chile, and vinegar.

Creamy Bean Dip. Use sour cream for a richer dip, yogurt for a tangy and lower-fat dip: Substitute sour cream or yogurt for the bean-cooking liquid or stock.

Cheesy Bean Dip. Easy-melting cheeses work best here; harder cheeses must be grated more finely: Add about $^3/_4$ cup grated cheese, like cotija, cheddar, or Monterey Jack. After Step 1, gently heat the beans over low heat; stir in the cheese until it's melted. Serve hot or warm.

Ⓕ　Fast　　Ⓜ　Make Ahead　　Ⓥ　Vegetarian

6 MORE BEAN DIPS

Here are some combinations that work well for particular types of beans. The technique remains the same as for the Refried Bean Dip recipe (and its variations), only you should mash the beans a little before starting. Use the bean-cooking liquid, stock, or water to thin the purée when a liquid isn't listed. The flavorings, like the roasted red peppers or caramelized onions, can be puréed with the beans if you like.

BEANS (3 CUPS COOKED AND DRAINED)	FLAVORINGS	SEASONINGS (ALONG WITH SALT AND FRESHLY GROUND BLACK PEPPER)
Black Beans	1 1/2 cups chopped Roasted Red Peppers (page 330) or dried tomatoes; 2 teaspoons minced garlic	1 tablespoon ground coriander
Pink Beans	1 cup chopped Caramelized Onions (page 325); 1/2 cup diced tomato	2 teaspoons smoked paprika
Red Lentils or Yellow Split Peas (no need to drain)	1 tablespoon each minced ginger and garlic; 1 cup yogurt	1 or 2 tablespoons chaat masala (to make your own, see page 68); 1/4 cup chopped fresh cilantro
Lima Beans	1/2 cup toasted pine nuts; 1/2 cup grated Parmesan; 2 teaspoons minced garlic	1 cup chopped fresh basil leaves
Soybeans	1/2 cup white or yellow miso; 1/2 cup chopped scallion; 1 tablespoon minced ginger	2 tablespoons rice vinegar
Fava Beans	1 tablespoon minced garlic; 1/2 cup fruity extra virgin olive oil	2 teaspoons grated lemon zest; 2 tablespoons lemon juice; lots of freshly ground black pepper

Hummus

MAKES: 6 to 8 servings

TIME: 15 minutes with precooked chickpeas

The Middle Eastern classic has become daily fare for many Americans, whether as a dip or a sandwich spread. Make it as garlicky, lemony, or spicy as you like (try it with smoked pimentón (see page 62) or Aleppo or other mild Middle Eastern pepper); I love it with lots of lemon juice.

If you're serving it as a dip, you may need to add more bean-cooking liquid, water, olive oil, or lemon juice to thin it.

2 cups drained well-cooked or canned chickpeas, cooking liquid reserved if possible

1/2 cup tahini, with some of its oil if you like

1/4 cup extra virgin olive oil, plus oil for garnish

2 cloves garlic, peeled, or to taste

Juice of 1 lemon, plus more as needed

Salt and freshly ground black pepper

1 tablespoon ground cumin or paprika, or to taste, plus a sprinkling for garnish

Chopped fresh parsley leaves for garnish

❶ Put the chickpeas, tahini, oil, garlic, and lemon juice in a food processor (or a blender for even smoother hummus), sprinkle with salt and pepper, and begin to process; add chickpea-cooking liquid or water as needed to produce a smooth purée.

❷ Taste and adjust seasoning, adding more salt, pepper, or lemon juice as needed. Serve, drizzled with some olive oil and sprinkled with a bit of cumin or paprika and some parsley.

Roasted Red Pepper Hummus. Tangy and rose colored: Add 2 Roasted Red Peppers (page 330) to the processor before puréeing.

Skordalia

MAKES: 6 to 8 servings
TIME: 10 minutes

A wonderful dip, sauce, and (eggless) mayonnaise substitute from Greece (in Turkey it's called *tarator*) that can be used on cooked meats (combine it with leftover chicken to make a fine chicken salad) and vegetables. Try any nut you like here: hazelnuts, pine nuts, and blanched almonds are all good.

    1 thick slice day-old bread

    About 1¹/₂ cups stock (pages 157–159), milk,
        or water

    2 tablespoons extra virgin olive oil, plus more
        if needed

    1 cup walnuts

    2 cloves garlic, peeled, or to taste

    ¹/₄ teaspoon cayenne or 1 teaspoon not-too-hot
        ground dried chile (see page 70), or to taste

    1 tablespoon freshly squeezed lemon juice,
        or to taste

    Salt and freshly ground black pepper

❶ Put the bread in a bowl and saturate it with some of the liquid. Squeeze bread to drain off excess, then put it in a food processor with the oil, nuts, garlic, and

cayenne. Process the mixture until the walnuts are ground, then, with the machine running, pour in enough of the remaining liquid and more olive oil to form a creamy sauce.

❷ Add the lemon juice and some salt and pepper and serve immediately or cover and refrigerate for up to 2 days.

Taramasalata. The classic fish roe purée from Greece: In Step 2, add a 7- or 8-ounce jar of tarama (salted mullet, cod, or salmon roe); mash lightly; you will probably need more lemon juice to cut the richness.

Artichoke Dip. With fresh artichoke hearts, just brilliant, but pretty good with frozen (thawed, of course) as well: If you like, reduce the garlic and omit the cayenne from Step 1. In Step 2, leave the mixture in the food processor and add 1 cup cooked artichoke hearts; pulse the machine until they are well integrated and chopped but not puréed. Proceed with the recipe.

Olive Dip. If you have Tapenade (page 96), just stir that into the Skordalia, to taste. Or use 1 teaspoon fresh thyme or sage leaves in place of the cayenne. In Step 2, leave the mixture in the food processor and add 1 cup pitted black olives, preferably a mixture of oil cured and kalamata (see page 322); pulse the machine until they are well integrated and chopped.

Guacamole

MAKES: 6 to 8 servings
TIME: 10 minutes

At its core a combination of mashed avocado with a couple of crunchy, strong-tasting ingredients and some acidity, guacamole takes well to all sorts of variations and is justifiably popular today as a sandwich ingredient. It's obviously a natural in tacos and burritos. Add ¹/₂ cup peeled, seeded, and diced tomato if you like.

 Fast   Make Ahead   Vegetarian

2 large or 3 medium avocados

1/4 cup minced onion or shallot

1/2 teaspoon minced garlic, or to taste

1 serrano or jalapeño chile (optional), seeded and minced or cayenne, to taste

1 teaspoon chili powder (to make your own, see page 66) or any mild pure chile powder, or to taste

Salt and freshly ground black pepper

1 tablespoon freshly squeezed lime juice, or to taste

Chopped fresh cilantro leaves for garnish

1 Cut the avocados in half. Peel, then mash the pulp in a bowl with a fork or potato masher, along with the onion, garlic (if you are using it), chile, chili powder, some salt and pepper, and lime juice. Taste and adjust the seasoning as necessary.

2 Garnish and serve or cover with plastic wrap, pressing down on the dip so there is no air trapped between the guacamole and the wrap, and refrigerate for up to 4 hours before garnishing and serving.

Crunchy Corn Guacamole. A nice twist: Add 1 cup corn, preferably just stripped from the cobs (see page 288), but thawed frozen is acceptable; garnish, if you like, with about 1/4 cup roughly chopped toasted pumpkin seeds (see page 317).

"Guacasalsa." For salsa lovers, and very fast if you have salsa on hand: Add about 1 cup Fresh Tomato or Fruit Salsa (page 23), Fresh Tomatillo Salsa (page 33), or bottled salsa; add all the other seasonings judiciously.

Avocado and Goat Cheese Spread or Dip. Not traditional, but fantastic: Omit the garlic, chile, and cilantro. Substitute lemon for the lime and add 3/4 cup soft fresh goat cheese. Put everything in a food processor if you want a smooth spread; for a chunkier spread, just use a potato masher or fork.

Avocado Crab Spread or Dip. Chopped cooked shrimp also works here, or lobster for an even more luxurious treat: Omit the garlic, chile, and cilantro; substitute lemon juice for the lime juice. In Step 1, stir in 1 cup lump crabmeat. Use 1/4 cup chopped fresh parsley for garnish, along with a tablespoon of minced fresh tarragon if you like.

Grilled or Roasted Eggplant Dip

MAKES: 6 to 8 servings

TIME: About 1 hour, largely unattended

There is nothing like grilled eggplant, and its smoky flavor makes for a sensational dip; if you grill or roast a red pepper at the same time, so much the better.

2 medium or 4 small eggplant (about 1 pound)

1 red bell pepper (optional)

1/4 cup freshly squeezed lemon juice

1/4 cup extra virgin olive oil

1/2 teaspoon minced garlic, or to taste

Salt and freshly ground black pepper

Chopped fresh parsley leaves for garnish

1 Heat a charcoal or gas grill to medium-high heat or heat the oven to 500°F. Pierce the eggplant in several places with a thin knife or skewer. Grill or roast it, along with the pepper if you're using one, turning occasionally, until the eggplant and pepper collapse and their skins blacken, 15 to 30 minutes, depending on size. Remove and cool.

2 When the eggplant is cool enough to handle, part the skin (if it hasn't split on its own), scoop out the flesh, and mince it. Peel and core the pepper if you're using it (see page 330), then chop it. Mix both with the lemon juice, oil, garlic, and some salt and pepper. Taste and adjust the seasonings (adding more lemon juice, too, if needed), then garnish with parsley and serve with bread or crackers.

Baba Ghanoush. A little more elaborate: Omit the oil and bell pepper. While the eggplant is grilling or roasting, toast ¹/₂ cup pine nuts in a dry skillet over medium heat, shaking occasionally, just until they begin to brown. When the eggplant is cool, put it in a food processor with the pine nuts, lemon juice, garlic, pepper, and ¹/₃ cup tahini. Process until very smooth, adding a few teaspoons of water or olive oil if necessary. Taste and add salt and/or more lemon juice or garlic to taste. Garnish with chopped parsley leaves and serve.

Mushroom-Egg Spread

MAKES: 6 to 8 servings

TIME: 20 minutes

A classic tapa of mushrooms bound with egg, usually served on toast. The dried porcini are optional but really add a lot.

¹/₄ cup extra virgin olive oil

About ¹/₂ pound fresh mushrooms, preferably a mixture of different types, trimmed and roughly chopped

¹/₄ cup dried porcini, reconstituted (see page 314) and chopped (optional)

Salt and freshly ground black pepper

1 tablespoon minced shallot

1 tablespoon minced garlic

3 eggs, lightly beaten

❶ Put the olive oil in a large, deep skillet over medium heat. When hot, add the mushrooms. Sprinkle with salt and pepper. Cook, stirring, until quite soft but not yet brown, about 15 minutes.

❷ Stir in the shallot and garlic and cook for another 2 or 3 minutes. Stir in the eggs and cook, stirring, just until the mixture holds together, another 2 or 3 minutes. Serve immediately on toast.

7 Ways to Use Any Dip or Spread

1. On sandwiches or wraps, either alone or in combination with other ingredients
2. Tossed with hot pasta for a quick sauce, thinned with a little of the pasta-cooking water if necessary
3. As a topping for baked potatoes
4. Served alongside simply grilled or roasted meat, fish, or chicken
5. As a topping for Bruschetta and Crostini (page 83)
6. Spread on pizza instead of a sauce or crumbled or dolloped on top
7. As an accompaniment for Corn Bread (page 831) or other quick or yeasted breads (see pages 829–877)

Tapenade

MAKES: 6 to 8 servings

TIME: 20 minutes

This Mediterranean paste is probably as old as olive oil, which makes it about as ancient as "cuisine." It can be used not only as a spread but also as a dip, and it's terrific stirred into Vinaigrette (page 199) or Fast Tomato Sauce (page 502) and used as a spread for meat, poultry, or fish that you're going to roast, grill, or broil.

1 pound good black olives, preferably oil cured, pitted

3 tablespoons capers, rinsed if salted, drained if brined

6 or 8 anchovies with some of their oil

1 or 2 cloves garlic, smashed

About ¹/₂ cup extra virgin olive oil, plus more if desired

1 teaspoon fresh thyme leaves (optional)

Chopped fresh parsley leaves for garnish (optional)

 Fast   Make Ahead   Vegetarian

❶ Combine the olives, capers, anchovies and their oil, and garlic in a food processor, along with a bit of the olive oil. Pulse the machine once or twice, then turn it on and add the remaining olive oil rather quickly; you don't want this purée too uniform but rather rough, as it would be if you had the energy to use a mortar and pestle (which you can use if you prefer).

❷ Stir in the thyme if you're using it, thin with more olive oil if necessary, garnish with parsley, and serve or refrigerate for up to at least a month.

Green Olive Tapenade. A wedge or two of Preserved Lemon (page 393) is a nice addition here too: Substitute green olives for black. Add 1 teaspoon toasted and ground cumin seeds or ground cumin, or to taste.

Dried Tomato Tapenade. Replace half if not all of the olives with roughly chopped Oven-Dried Tomatoes (pages 362) or store-bought dried tomatoes. Add 2 teaspoons chopped fresh thyme leaves or 1 teaspoon dried.

Crispy Starters

Most of these are fried—though there are instances when baking works well—and frying is undeniably work. But it's a lot of fun too, especially if friends are on hand to keep you company. Once you get a rhythm going (see "Deep Frying," page 19), things proceed smoothly. And the results are almost always worth the work: Because we rarely use oil more than once or twice and we can use first-rate oil and other ingredients, fried food is often better at home than elsewhere, a pleasant surprise for newbie cooks.

Tortilla Chips and Plantain Chips might be a good place to start. They require less than 2 minutes in the oil and never spatter, meaning you can produce a significant amount in 10 or 15 minutes. With a little practice you can easily work your way up to Tempura and the like. Meanwhile, if you want a starter that resembles fried food but is easier, try Gougères or—of course—good old Nachos.

Fried Tortilla Chips

MAKES: 50 large or 100 small chips, enough for about 10 people
TIME: 15 to 30 minutes

No matter how good store-bought tortilla chips are (and they're considerably better than they used to be), freshly made ones are special. They're easy and really delicious, especially if you use lard. (Sadly, commercial chips are rarely made with lard, which is no worse for you than most oils; and these don't absorb much fat anyway.) Sprinkle them with any spice mixture or seasoned salt when they're done or use them to make Nachos in the recipe on page 98.

Lard or neutral oil, like grapeseed or corn,
    for deep-frying
12 corn tortillas, 6 or 8 inches in diameter
Salt

❶ Put at least 1 inch of oil in a deep pan on the stove and turn the heat to medium-high; bring to 350°F (see "Deep Frying," page 19). The broader the vessel, the more of these you can cook at once, but the more oil you will use. (They cook very quickly, so don't worry if your pan is narrow.)

❷ Stack the tortillas and cut them, pielike, into 4 to 8 wedges. Fry as many at once as will fit without crowding, turning if necessary. Total cooking time will be about 2 minutes; the chips should not brown but just begin to darken in color. Remove with tongs or a slotted spoon and drain on paper towels or paper bags. Sprinkle with salt or any of the suggestions in the list that follows and serve hot or at room temperature.

Baked Tortilla Chips. Heat the oven to 400°F. Lightly brush or spray each tortilla on both sides with peanut oil or neutral oil, like grapeseed or corn. Stack and cut as directed. Bake on ungreased baking sheets, shaking once or twice, until just beginning to color, 6 to 10 minutes. Sprinkle with salt or anything in the following list and serve hot or at room temperature.

5 Sprinkles for Chips

Season chips when they're piping hot, tossing gently with a spatula. Even if it all doesn't stick, it will lend a little extra flavor.

1. Any good coarse sea salt
2. Chile powder (to make your own, see page 66)
3. Any curry powder (to make your own, see pages 66–67)
4. Hot red pepper flakes
5. Grated lemon, lime, or orange zest

Nachos

MAKES: 6 to 8 servings

TIME: 30 minutes with premade tortilla chips

A guilty pleasure, I suppose, but arguably more nutritious than straight chips. And, of course, irresistible. Since overloading the chips quickly makes them soggy, I often pass the toppings at the table.

> 8 to 12 ounces tortilla chips (1 big bag or about the amount of chips from the preceding recipe)
>
> 2 cups grated cheddar, Jack, or other mild cheese
>
> 1½ cups well-seasoned cooked red, pink, or kidney beans, like Black Beans with Orange (page 419) optional
>
> Chopped scallions (optional)
>
> Chopped jalapeño chiles (optional)
>
> 1 cup Fresh Tomato or Fruit Salsa (page 23) or Salsa Roja (page 48)

❶ Heat the oven to 375°F. Meanwhile, warm the beans if you're using them. Spread the chips in one layer in a shallow pan with a rim, such as a pizza pan or a baking sheet. Top with the beans if using, then the cheese, and bake until the cheese melts, about 10 minutes.

❷ Sprinkle with the scallion and/or jalapeño if you're using them and serve immediately with a bowl of salsa on the side.

10 Ideas for Topping Nachos

Use any of these alone or in combination.

1. Chopped cilantro
2. Sour cream
3. Chopped tomato
4. Minced fresh jalapeño or serrano chile
5. Chopped black olives
6. Chopped red onion or scallion
7. Cooked ground beef, seasoned with chili powder (to make your own, see page 66)
8. Spicy Grilled or Broiled Shrimp (page 574)
9. Strips of Grilled or Broiled Boneless Chicken (page 641)
10. Shredded Pork (page 759)

Plantain, Yam, Beet, and Other Vegetable Chips

MAKES: 4 servings

TIME: 15 minutes

Easier to fry than potatoes, plantains and several different root vegetables make for a flavorful and lovely basket of chips, especially when combined and especially when fried in the traditional lard. In addition to the ones mentioned in the title and variations, try carrots, parsnips, turnips, taro, or other tropical tubers (see page 363). Best served hot, simply sprinkled with salt, but not at all bad a few hours later.

> Lard or neutral oil, like grapeseed or corn, for deep-frying
>
> 2 medium-ripe plantains (yellow-green, not green, yellow, or yellow-black), peeled (see page 334)
>
> Salt
>
> Cayenne, to taste (optional)
>
> Lime wedges (optional)

❶ Put at least 2 inches of oil in a deep pan on the stove over medium-high heat; bring to 350°F (see "Deep

Frying," page 19). The broader the vessel, the more of these you can cook at once, but the more oil you will use. (They cook very quickly, so don't worry if your pan is narrow.)

 While the oil is heating, use a mandolin set to just about the thinnest setting to shave the plantains; or slice as thinly as you can by hand. Traditionally, they're cut the long way, but you can make round chips if you find it easier. Combine some salt with a bit of cayenne if you want a spicy mixture for sprinkling.

❸ Fry as many slices at once as will fit without crowding, turning if necessary. Total cooking time will be about 2 minutes; the chips should not brown but turn a deeper yellow. Remove with tongs or a slotted spoon and drain on paper towels or paper bags. Sprinkle with salt and lime juice if you like and serve as soon as you can, though they will remain crisp and delicious for several hours.

Beet or Yam (Sweet Potato) Chips. Gorgeous and sweet; be careful not to overcook, or their sugars will burn: Peel, then slice thinly. Cook as directed.

Gougères

MAKES: 6 to 8 servings
TIME: About 30 minutes

Ⓥ

Take a cream puff–like pastry, add cheese, and bake or fry: The result is crisp, light, rich, and cheesy, an almost perfect finger food and among the best fritters you can produce. Gougère dough can support any number of ingredients; so, for example, try substituting up to 1 cup minced cooked shrimp or other shellfish or sautéed mushrooms for the cheese stirred into the dough.

4 tablespoons (½ stick) butter

½ teaspoon salt

1½ cups (about 7 ounces) all-purpose flour

3 eggs

1 cup freshly grated Emmental, Gruyère, Cantal, or cheddar cheese

1 cup freshly grated Parmesan or other hard cheese

❶ Heat the oven to 425°F. Combine 1 cup water with the butter and salt in a medium saucepan over medium-high heat. Bring to a boil and cook, stirring, until the butter melts, a minute or two. Add the flour all at once and cook, stirring constantly, until the dough holds together in a ball, 5 minutes or less.

❷ Add the eggs one at a time, beating hard after each addition (this is a little bit of work; use an electric mixer or plan for a little upper-body workout). Stop beating when the mixture is glossy. Stir in the cheeses.

❸ To bake the gougères, drop teaspoonfuls onto the baking sheet and bake until light brown, 10 to 15 minutes.

Fried Gougères. These will come out pretty much perfect on your first try: Put at least 2 inches of oil in a deep pan on the stove over medium-high heat; bring to 350°F (see "Deep Frying," page 19). The broader the vessel, the more of these you can cook at once, but the more oil you will use. (They cook very quickly, so don't worry if your pan is narrow.) Drop teaspoonfuls of the batter into the hot oil and cook, turning once if necessary, until lightly brown, just 3 or 4 minutes. Don't crowd; you'll probably need to cook in batches. Drain on paper towels or paper bags and serve at once or keep warm in a low oven for up to 30 minutes.

Vegetable Fritters

MAKES: 4 to 6 servings
TIME: 30 minutes without salting

Ⓕ   Ⓥ

You can make these Italian-style fritters with virtually any raw vegetable (though broccoli or cauliflower, greens, and eggplant must be cooked first; see the variations). Salting the raw vegetable usually improves texture, but it isn't essential. But always take a moment to squeeze the raw vegetables dry.

Other vegetables you can use: grated sweet potatoes, carrots or parsnips, winter squash, celeriac, chayote, beets, turnips, rutabaga, or kohlrabi; sliced or chopped okra, celery (use the leaves too), rhubarb, chiles or bell peppers, mushrooms, bean sprouts, green beans, or sugar snap or snow peas; or use whole shell peas.

About 1½ pounds zucchini, trimmed and grated or chopped

Salt and freshly ground black pepper

1 egg

½ cup fresh chopped parsley leaves

½ cup freshly grated or roughly chopped Parmesan cheese

1 clove garlic, peeled

Pinch cayenne

½ cup bread crumbs, preferably fresh (page 876), or all-purpose flour

Neutral oil, like grapeseed or corn, for deep-frying

Lemon wedges for serving

❶ If you like, put the zucchini in a colander, sprinkle with a large pinch of salt and let sit for at least 30 minutes, preferably an hour; rinse.

❷ Put the zucchini in a towel and wring to remove the excess moisture. Beat the egg in a large bowl and add the zucchini, parsley, cheese, garlic, cayenne, and bread crumbs. Toss with a fork to combine thoroughly. If you didn't salt the vegetables in Step 1, add a pinch of salt to the mixture.

❸ Put at least 2 inches of oil in a deep pan on the stove over medium-high heat; bring to 350°F (see "Deep Frying," page 19). If you're going to serve all the fritters at once, heat the oven to 200°F. Drop the fritters by the ¼ cup or large spoonful into the hot oil; you'll probably need to raise the heat to maintain the temperature. Cook the fritters in batches, turning once, until nicely browned on all sides, a total of 4 to 6 minutes per batch. Drain the fritters on paper towels, then eat them as they are done or keep them warm in the oven until they are all done.

Sprinkle with additional salt if you like and serve with lemon wedges.

Broccoli or Cauliflower Fritters. Boil and shock the broccoli or cauliflower heads (see page 240); drain well and chop roughly. Proceed with the recipe from Step 2.

Greens Fritters. Use chard, collards, spinach, watercress, Asian greens, or cabbage: Boil and shock the greens (see page 240); squeeze all the water out of them and chop roughly. Proceed with the recipe from Step 2.

Eggplant Fritters. Trim and peel the eggplant, cut it into chunks, and then blanch it in boiling water until just tender, 5 minutes or so. Drain well, pressing down in the colander to make sure it's dry. Or cook the eggplant according to Dry-Pan Eggplant (page 294) or Grilled or Broiled Eggplant (page 294) and leave the skin on. Pulse in the food processor until finely chopped and add to the egg along with the remaining ingredients in Step 2.

Indian-Style Split Pea Fritters

MAKES: 4 to 8 servings
TIME: 3 to 4 hours, mostly soaking time

A recipe I learned from Julie Sahni (author of *Classic Indian Cooking*) over 20 years ago and still love. If you remember to soak the split peas (you can do it before you leave for work—longer soaking times, within reason, are not a problem), these are fast to make and incredibly delicious. Their outside is crisp, but the interior flavors remain fresh and bright.

1 cup yellow or green split peas, washed and picked over, soaked if you have time (see page 412)

Peanut or other oil as needed

1 jalapeño or other hot fresh or dried chile, seeded and minced, or to taste

1½ inches fresh ginger, roughly chopped

1 small clove garlic, peeled

❶ Fast   ⓜ Make Ahead   Ⓥ Vegetarian

½ cup fresh cilantro (some stems are okay)

1 teaspoon ground coriander

1 teaspoon ground cumin

½ teaspoon ground fenugreek

½ cup chopped onion

Salt and freshly ground black pepper

1 to 2 tablespoons all-purpose flour, if necessary

Lime wedges for serving

1 Soak the split peas in water to cover for at least 3 hours if you have time. Drain but leave them wet. Put at least 3 inches of oil in a large, deep saucepan over medium-high heat. Let it heat while you prepare the fritters; it should reach a temperature of 365–375°F. Heat the oven to 200°F.

2 Put the drained peas in a food processor with the chile, ginger, garlic, cilantro, coriander, cumin, and fenugreek. Process until the mixture is a coarse purée—not perfectly smooth, but with no whole peas remaining. Add a couple tablespoons of water if necessary to help the machine with its work.

3 Stir in the onion and some salt and pepper. Taste the mixture and adjust the seasoning if necessary. The mixture should be fairly loose; add a little water if it is quite thick or a tablespoon or two of flour if soupy.

4 Drop the mixture by the heaping tablespoon into the oil; do not crowd. Cook until lightly browned and crisp, turning if necessary; total cooking time will be 3 or 4 minutes. Drain on paper towels and keep warm in the oven while you finish cooking. Serve hot or at room temperature, with lime wedges.

Tempura

MAKES: 6 to 8 servings
TIME: About 40 minutes

Where do you draw the line between appetizer and "real" dish? I don't know, but tempura works either way. If you're serving only a couple of people, it's easy to deep-fry enough food. It's when you have a crowd that it gets difficult. But if you want to deep-fry a few tidbits of fish, shrimp, chicken, and/or vegetables for a number of people, tempura is among the lightest and easiest of the batter-fried foods. Serve immediately; like many fried foods, it's best eaten standing up, around the stove. But it will hold in a low oven for a few minutes.

Peanut oil or neutral oil, like grapeseed or corn, for deep-frying

1½ to 2 pounds assorted vegetables: zucchini, eggplant, winter squash or sweet potatoes, mushrooms, bell pepper, green beans, broccoli or cauliflower, leeks, onions

½ pound seafood or chicken: firm white fish, like cod or haddock, cut into chunks; 6 to 8 large shrimp, peeled and sliced in half lengthwise; or chicken tenders, cut into thin strips

1½ cups all-purpose flour, plus 1 cup for dredging

3 egg yolks

Soy Dipping Sauce and Marinade (page 25) or lemon wedges

1 Put at least 2 inches of oil in a deep pan on the stove over medium-high heat; bring to 350°F (see "Deep Frying," page 19). The broader the vessel, the more of these you can cook at once, but the more oil you will use. While the oil is heating, prepare the vegetables, the meat, and the sauce.

2 When you're ready to cook, combine 2 cups water and 2 cups ice; let sit for a minute, then measure 2 cups water from this. Beat lightly with 1½ cups of the flour and the egg yolks; the batter should be lumpy and quite thin.

3 One piece at a time, dredge the vegetables and shrimp in the remaining flour, then dip in the batter. Fry each piece until golden, turning once if necessary, less than 5 minutes total. Drain on paper towels and serve immediately, with the dipping sauce or lemon wedges.

Eggless Vegetable Tempura. Club soda adds airiness to this two-ingredient batter and makes a nice light coating for delicate vegetables like thinly sliced eggplant or even leaves of spinach or chard: Omit the egg yolks and substitute well-chilled sparkling water for the ice water. Use rice flour if you prefer.

Pakoras. The batter-fried vegetables of India, good served with any dipping sauce or wedges of lime. Make a thick batter by mixing together 2 cups all-purpose flour, 1 teaspoon baking powder, 1 teaspoon salt, 1 egg, 1 tablespoon peanut or neutral oil, and about 1 cup water (or milk). Season the batter with 1 tablespoon curry powder (to make your own, see pages 66–67). Dip (you need not predredge in flour) and fry as directed. Serve with Cilantro-Mint Chutney (page 37), any of the recipes under Chile Paste, Eight Ways (page 74), any hot sauce, or lime wedges.

10 Excellent Dipping Sauces for Tempura and Pakoras

For Tempura:

1. A mixture of soy sauce and rice vinegar
2. Basil-Soy Dipping Sauce (page 38)
3. Simple Miso Dipping Sauce (page 39)
4. Homemade Mayonnaise with wasabi (page 42)
5. Dashi Dipping Sauce (page 56)

For Pakoras:

1. Simplest Yogurt Sauce (page 24) or any of its variations
2. Coconut Chutney (page 37)
3. Cilantro-Mint Chutney (page 37)
4. Curry Ranch Dressing (page 43)
5. Smooth Green Chile Sauce, Indian Style (page 54)

Dumplings and Other Wrapped Finger Foods

We've come a long way from pigs-in-a-blanket: Finger foods in wrappers are now more likely to be samosas, pot stickers, gyozas, quesadillas, wontons, phyllo cigars, and a variety of other dumplinglike creations made with the premade doughs available at just about every supermarket. Once you begin to experiment, you'll realize that you can fill these traditional finger foods with nearly anything you like.

These are the dumplings and wraps that (I think) are best eaten with the fingers. There are many more in the pasta chapter.

Fried Wontons or Egg Rolls

MAKES: At least 36 wontons or 6 egg rolls (6 to 12 servings)
TIME: About 30 minutes

These are the simplest and most basic dumplings. They're deep-fried, but they don't spatter (as long as the package is sealed well enough to contain the filling), they take almost no time to cook, and they're virtually foolproof. If you prefer, switch the proportions of pork and cabbage, using $1/2$ cup of the former and 1 cup of the latter.

Peanut oil or neutral oil, like grapeseed or corn, for deep-frying

1 cup ground or minced pork or shrimp or a combination

$1/4$ cup minced scallion

$1/2$ cup finely shredded cabbage, preferably Napa

1 teaspoon minced garlic

1 teaspoon minced or grated fresh ginger

$1/4$ cup cored, seeded, and minced red bell pepper

Salt and freshly ground black pepper

1 teaspoon soy sauce

1 teaspoon dark sesame oil

1 egg

36 to 48 wonton skins or at least 6 egg roll skins (to make your own, see right)

Soy Dipping Sauce or Marinade (page 25)

 Fast   Make Ahead   Vegetarian

1 Put at least 2 inches of oil in a deep pan on the stove over medium-high heat; bring to 350°F (see "Deep Frying," page 19). The broader the vessel, the more of these you can cook at once, but the more oil you will use. (They cook very quickly, so don't worry if your pan is narrow.)

2 Combine all remaining ingredients except the wonton skins and dipping sauce. To fill the skins, put 1 or 2 rounded teaspoons of filling in the center of each skin (use more for egg rolls); fold over to make a triangle and seal carefully with a few drops of water. Let rest on wax paper until you've filled all the skins.

3 Put the wontons in the oil two or more at a time, raising the heat to maintain the temperature. Cook, turning once, until nicely browned, a total of 3 or 4 min-utes. Drain on paper towels and serve immediately, with the dipping sauce on the side.

Vegetarian Wontons or Egg Rolls. Omit the pork or shrimp. Add 1 cored, seeded, and minced sliced red bell pepper; 1 shredded carrot; and 4 or 5 minced fresh (or reconstituted dried) shiitake (black) mushrooms.

Lighter, Steamed Wontons. In Step 1, set up a steamer (to improvise, see page 20) in a covered pot. In Step 2, use minced shrimp or boneless chicken breast instead of the pork or shrimp. Fill and seal the wontons as directed; keep them moist by covering them with a damp towel until you're ready to cook. Steam the wontons in one or two batches, for about 10 minutes per batch. Serve hot with the dipping sauce.

MAKING DUMPLINGS AND EGG ROLL WRAPPERS OR WONTON SKINS

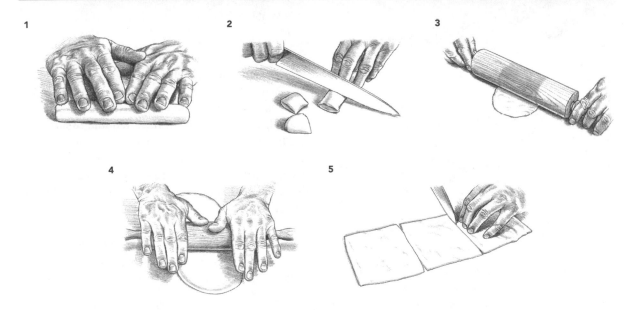

Make Asian-Style Dumpling Wrappers (page 542). Roll each piece of dough out on a lightly floured surface. **(STEP 1)** First roll into a log about 1 inch wide. **(STEP 2)** Then cut into 1-inch pieces. **(STEP 3)** Roll each one out from the center to form a thin 4-inch circle or square, adding a bit of flour if necessary. **(STEP 4)** To make larger egg roll wrappers, roll each log into a thin, roughly rectangu-lar shape, then **(STEP 5)** cut into squares.

1

2

3

(STEP 1) To make half-moon pot stickers (or ravioli), put a small amount of filling in the middle of your wrapper. Brush the seam lightly (you can use you fingertip) with water or beaten egg yolk, (STEP 2) then bring one edge of the wrapper over the filling to meet the other. (STEP 3) Secure the dumpling with the thumb of one hand, then press the edges closed.

To make wontons, put a small amount of filling on a square dumpling wrapper; brush the seam lightly (you can use your fingertip) with water or beaten egg yolk, then press closed.

Pot Stickers

MAKES: At least 24 dumplings (4 to 8 servings)
TIME: 30 to 45 minutes

Make these with round wonton or gyoza wrappers, 3 or 4 inches in diameter. Panfried until crisp on the bottom and then cooked through by steaming, they are just as easily simply steamed. Either way they are wonderful, and either way they should be served immediately. You can fill and dust them with flour and then refrigerate them, covered, for a couple of hours or freeze them for a few days before cooking (you can cook them frozen or thawed), but they're really best when cooked right after filling.

Gyoza is the Japanese version of this type of dumpling; mandoo is the Korean version. They may be filled with pork, shrimp or other shellfish, vegetables, or—in the Korean model—a mixture of kimchi and other food.

$1/2$ pound ground pork, chicken, or other meat

$1/4$ cup minced scallion

1 cup washed and chopped leek, Napa cabbage, or bok choy

🅕 Fast   🅜 Make Ahead   🅥 Vegetarian

1 teaspoon minced fresh ginger

1 teaspoon rice wine or dry sherry

1 teaspoon sugar

1 tablespoon soy sauce

1 tablespoon dark sesame oil

1 egg, lightly beaten

1 teaspoon freshly ground black pepper

Large pinch salt

24 round dumpling skins (to make your own, see page 103)

Peanut oil or neutral oil, like grapeseed or corn, as needed

Ginger-Scallion Sauce (page 39)

1 Combine the first eleven ingredients and mix gently but thoroughly. Put about 2 teaspoons of the filling in the center of a wrapper, then moisten the edge of the wrapper with water and fold over to form a semicircle. Press the seam tightly to seal; it's best if there is no air trapped between the filling and wrapper. Set on a lightly floured plate or wax paper. (At this point, you may cover tightly and refrigerate for up to a day or freeze for a couple of weeks.)

2 Coat a large, deep skillet with a thin layer of oil and turn the heat to medium-high. Put the dumplings, one at a time, into the skillet, seam side up, leaving space between them (you will probably have to cook in 2 batches). Turn the heat down to medium, then cover and

SHAPING SPRING ROLLS AND EGG ROLLS

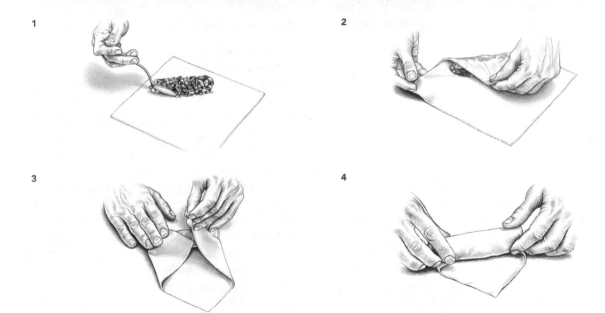

1

2

3

4

(STEP 1) Lay the wrapper with one point facing you and put a large spoonful of filling about one-third of the way up, leaving a border on either side. (STEP 2) Fold up the bottom point. (STEPS 3–4) Fold in the sides and roll up. Seal with a few drops of water or beaten egg.

cook for about 5 minutes. Add $1/2$ cup water to the skillet, then cover and cook for another 2 minutes. Remove the lid, turn the heat to high, and cook until the water has evaporated, about 3 minutes. Remove the dumplings and serve with the dipping sauce.

Steamed Dumplings. Set up a steamer (to improvise, see page 20) in a covered pot. Lightly oil the steamer or plate to prevent sticking. Steam the dumplings in one or two batches for about 10 minutes per batch. Serve immediately with Soy Dipping Sauce and Marinade (page 25).

Vegetarian Pot Stickers or Gyoza. Substitute $1/2$ pound drained and mashed soft tofu for the meat. Cut the amount of leeks in half and add $1/4$ cup shredded Napa cabbage, $1/4$ cup chopped fresh mushrooms, $1/4$ cup shredded carrot, and $1/4$ cup chopped walnuts to the filling. Use the thinner gyoza wrappers if you can find them. Fill and cook as directed. (Note that if you use gyoza, the cooking time at each stage will be a little bit shorter.)

Potato-Filled Samosas

MAKES: 20 to 30 dumplings (5 to 10 servings)
TIME: At least 1 hour

A classic dumpling of India and one of the best because the dough, which contains butter and yogurt, is rich and tangy. Traditionally, it is made by cutting the cold butter into bits and rubbing it and the flour very quickly between your fingers: Pick it up, rub it, and drop it. (If the mixture begins to feel greasy, refrigerate it for a few minutes before proceeding.) The food processor may not be as charming, but it's much easier. Take your pick.

Samosas are usually deep-fried, but you can bake them: Just put them on a lightly greased baking sheet and bake at 350°F until golden brown, 20 to 30 minutes. Don't think of this as a compromise; baked samosas are terrific.

About $11/4$ pounds starchy potatoes (1 large or 2 medium)

2 cups all-purpose flour, plus a little more as needed

Salt and freshly ground black pepper

8 tablespoons (1 stick) butter

2 tablespoons yogurt, sour cream, or buttermilk

1 tablespoon ice water, plus more as necessary

1 cup chopped onion

1 fresh chile, like jalapeño or serrano, seeded and minced, or cayenne, to taste

1 tablespoon minced garlic

2 teaspoons minced or grated fresh ginger

1 tablespoon any curry powder (to make your own, see pages 66–67)

$1/2$ cup green peas (frozen are fine; defrost them in water to cover while you prepare the other ingredients)

Neutral oil, like grapeseed or corn, as needed

1 Peel the potatoes and dice them into $1/2$-inch cubes. Put them in a pot and add water to cover. Turn the heat to high and boil them until soft, 5 to 10 minutes. Drain.

2 Meanwhile, make the dough: Put the flour and 1 teaspoon salt in a food processor; pulse for a couple of seconds to blend. Cut half the butter into bits, add it to the flour, and turn on the machine; let it run until the butter and flour are combined. Add the yogurt and pulse a few times. Then, with the machine running, add ice water 1 tablespoon at a time through the feed tube. The instant the dough forms a ball, stop adding water. Knead the dough for a minute by hand, then cover with plastic wrap or a damp towel and set aside.

3 Put the remaining butter in a large skillet, preferably nonstick, and turn the heat to medium. Add the onion and the chile and cook, stirring, until the onion softens, about 5 minutes; add the garlic, ginger, and curry powder. Add salt and pepper to taste and cook, stirring, for about 2 minutes. Add the cooked potatoes

 Fast   Make Ahead   V Vegetarian

and the peas (drained if they've been sitting in water), raise the heat a little, and cook, stirring frequently, until the potatoes begin to brown, about 10 minutes. Taste and adjust the seasoning if necessary; the mixture should be spicy but not fiery. Cool while you roll out the dough.

④ Knead the dough for a few seconds, sprinkling it with a little flour if necessary. Break off a small piece of the dough (you'll want to make 20 to 30 samosas, so judge accordingly) and roll it out on a lightly floured surface until it is a circle at least 3 inches in diameter. Make 5 or 6 circles, then fill them: Put 1 tablespoon or so of filling in the center, then fold over and seal with a few drops of water. Keep covered with a damp towel. Repeat until all the dough and filling are used up.

⑤ When you're about halfway through making the samosas, put enough oil to come to a depth of at least 2 inches in a large, deep pan. The broader the saucepan, the more samosas you can cook at once, but the more oil you will use. Turn the heat to medium-high; you want the temperature to be at about 375°F when you start cooking.

⑥ Fry the samosas a few at a time, turning if necessary, until they are golden brown. Drain on paper towels or paper bags and serve immediately, or keep warm in a low oven, or serve at room temperature (but within 1 hour or so).

Beef-Filled Samosas. To make the filling, heat 2 tablespoons butter or oil in a large skillet over medium heat. Add the onion, chile, garlic, ginger, and curry as directed in Step 3. Add $3/4$ pound ground beef or lamb and cook, stirring, until the meat loses its color, about 5 minutes. Remove from the skillet with a slotted spoon, leaving all fat and other liquid in the pan. Stir $1/4$ cup minced fresh cilantro into the mixture and proceed to Step 4.

Lentil-Filled Samosas. For the filling, use half of the recipe for Split Peas, Mung Beans, or Lentils and Potatoes with Curry (Dal) on page 415. Drain the peas, beans, or lentils very well before proceeding to Step 4.

(STEP 1) Put a small amount of filling on one side of the rolled samosa dough. (STEP 2) Fold over and pinch closed.

Vietnamese Summer Rolls

MAKES: 2 to 4 servings
TIME: About 30 minutes

These no-cook rolls are made with wonderfully pliable rice paper. If you have leftover shrimp (or chicken or pork), you can make them in no time flat, especially once you've practiced on a batch or two.

1 small fresh chile, minced, or $1/2$ teaspoon hot red pepper flakes

1 tablespoon rice or other mild vinegar

1 tablespoon nam pla (Thai fish sauce) or soy sauce

1 teaspoon sugar

1 tablespoon freshly squeezed lime juice

1 teaspoon minced garlic

8 medium to large shrimp, cooked, peeled, and cut in half lengthwise, or an equivalent amount of cooked pork, beef, or chicken

1 cup grated, shredded, or julienned carrot

1 cup bean sprouts

2 scallions, cut into lengthwise slivers

2 tablespoons roughly chopped fresh mint leaves

2 tablespoons roughly chopped fresh cilantro leaves

2 tablespoons roughly chopped peanuts (salted are okay)

4 sheets rice paper, 8 to 10 inches in diameter

① Combine the first six ingredients and set aside as a dipping sauce.

② Prepare the other ingredients and set them out on your work surface. Set out a bowl of hot water (110–120°F) and a clean kitchen towel.

③ Put a sheet of rice paper into the water for about 10 seconds, just until soft (don't let it become too soft; it will continue to soften as you work). Lay it on the towel.

④ In the middle of the rice paper, lay 4 shrimp pieces and about a quarter each of the carrot, bean sprouts, scallions, mint, cilantro, and peanuts. Roll up the rice paper, keeping it fairly tight and folding in the ends to seal. Repeat this process until all the ingredients are used up. Serve, with the dipping sauce.

Lettuce Cups and Wraps

Several types of fresh raw leaves work as wrappers that turn other dishes into something you can eat with your hands, making perfect party food or appetizers. Iceberg, Bibb or Boston, endive, and radicchio are ideal, since they're naturally cupped like spoons to hold fillings; broad and sturdy green and red leaf lettuces are better for folding and wrapping like burritos (see page 173).

The preparation is a snap: Cut the core out of head lettuce and pull the leaves off; be careful not to tear them. If you're preparing the lettuce in advance, keep it crisp by stacking the leaves, wrapping in damp paper towels, and then wrapping in plastic or closing in a plastic bag. They can be stored this way for a day or two.

I usually let guests wrap their own lettuce cups, so I serve a plate piled high next to a bowl of whatever goes inside. If you're doing the assembly, save this task for the last minute so the lettuce cups or wraps stay fresh. Keep in mind that small diced or chopped foods make the best fillings (large pieces can crush or tear the lettuce; besides, they're unwieldy) and warm, hot, or heavily sauced food will wilt the lettuce.

Don't neglect the possible garnishes: chopped scallions, fresh herbs, olives, capers, or nuts; seeds; crumbled or grated cheese; a dollop of sour cream, yogurt, Guacamole (page 94), or any salsa or chutney (see pages 23, 33–38, and 48–50).

16 Dishes to Spoon into Lettuce Cups and Wraps

Use at room temperature or lightly chilled and chop into small pieces if necessary.

1. Stir-Fried Tofu with Scallions (pages 417–418)
2. Deep-Fried Seafood (page 568)
3. Poached Fish Steaks or Fillets with Vegetables (pages 569–570)
4. Any stir-fried shrimp dish (see pages 575–577)
5. Squid with Chiles and Greens (page 626)
6. Any stir-fried chicken dish (see pages 674–677)
7. Any stir-fried beef dish (see pages 731–732)
8. Any stir-fried pork dish (see pages 748–749)
9. Stir-Fried Lamb with Green Peppers (page 769)
10. Any Stir-Fried Vegetables (pages 241–245)
11. Roasted Cauliflower with Raisins and Vinaigrette (page 281)
12. Twice-Fried Green Beans (page 306)
13. Roasted Vegetables (page 241)
14. Kimchi Rice (page 461)
15. Any Fried Rice (pages 468–470)
16. Four-Grain Pilaf (page 497)

 Fast   Make Ahead   Vegetarian

Cheese Quesadillas

MAKES: 8 to 16 servings

TIME: 15 minutes

As with many stuffed wrappers, the key to successful quesadillas is to resist overfilling them. Too much cheese makes them ooze all over the place; too many other ingredients, and the cheese never melds the two tortillas together.

That said, few hot dishes make better (or easier) use of little bits of leftovers. (See the chart in "The Basics of Tacos and Burritos" on page 174 for ideas.) Any shredded or thinly sliced cooked meat is a fine addition to quesadillas, too.

You can assemble all four quesadillas at once, then wrap and refrigerate them until you're ready to cook. (The cooking itself takes almost no time at all.) If you prefer, cook these without oil, in a nonstick or well-seasoned cast-iron skillet.

  $^{1}/_{2}$ cup neutral oil, like grapeseed or corn (optional)

  Eight 8-inch flour tortillas

  2 cups grated cheese—cheddar, Jack, other cheese, or a combination

  $^{1}/_{2}$ cup minced scallion

  $^{1}/_{4}$ cup minced canned green chiles

  $^{1}/_{4}$ cup salsa (pages 23, 33–35, and 48–50; optional)

❶ The easiest way to make these is to build them in the skillet: Put 1 tablespoon of oil, if you're using it, in a medium skillet over medium heat. When hot, put a tortilla in the skillet. Top with a quarter of the cheese, scallion, chiles, and the salsa if you're using it, then with another tortilla.

❷ Cook until the cheese begins to melt, about 2 minutes. Turn and cook until the cheese is melted and both sides are toasted, another 2 to 3 minutes. Drain if necessary, then cut into wedges and serve or keep warm until the remaining quesadillas are done.

Grilled Quesadillas. Crisp, slightly smoky, and delicious: Heat a gas or charcoal grill to medium-high heat and put the rack about 4 inches from the heat source. Brush one side of a tortilla with oil and set on the grill. Build the quesadilla as instructed in Step 1 and brush oil on the top tortilla.

Chile-Bean Quesadillas. Nearly any type of bean or chile works here: Substitute 3 or 4 jalapeño, poblano, or serrano chiles, seeded and chopped, for the green chiles, if you like, and add 1 tablespoon minced garlic and 1 cup well-drained cooked or canned pinto beans. Cook the chiles and garlic in a tablespoon or so of the oil and set aside. Proceed with the recipe.

Quesadilla for One. Great for snacking: Scale the quesadilla ingredients back to a drizzle or two of oil, 2 tortillas, about $^{1}/_{4}$ cup cheese, 2 tablespoons minced scallion, 1 tablespoon minced green chile, and a dollop of salsa.

Stuffed Grape Leaves

MAKES: About 30 (10 to 15 servings)

TIME: At least 11/2 hours

This is a project, but a memorable one, especially if you begin with a visit to a grape arbor, as I did the first time I made these over thirty years ago. Unless you can get fresh grape leaves (which are not that hard to find in most parts of the country), you might prefer making these with cabbage or chard leaves; bottled grape leaves have little flavor.

  Around 40 large grape leaves (you need extra because some will be imperfect)

  2 tablespoons extra virgin olive oil, plus oil for garnish

  1 cup chopped onion

  $^{1}/_{4}$ cup pine nuts

  1 cup long-grain rice

  $^{1}/_{2}$ teaspoon ground allspice

Salt and freshly ground black pepper

1½ cups chicken, beef, or vegetable stock (to make your own, see pages 157–158) or water

2 tablespoons minced fresh mint or dill leaves

¼ cup freshly squeezed lemon juice

① Bring a large pot of water to a boil. Parboil the grape leaves, a few at a time, until they are tender and pliable, just a couple of minutes. Drain, then cut off the stems and remove any hard veins near the base of the leaves. Pat dry with paper towels.

② Meanwhile, put the olive oil in a large, deep skillet over medium-high heat. When hot, add the onion and cook, stirring, until tender, about 5 minutes. Add the pine nuts, rice, allspice, 1 teaspoon salt, and the stock. Cover, turn the heat down to medium-low, and cook until the rice is somewhat tender but still quite firm, about 10 to 12 minutes. Cool in a large bowl, check for salt, and add lots of pepper, the mint, and half of the lemon juice.

③ One at a time, put the grape leaves, shiny side down, on a work surface and put 1 tablespoon or so of the rice mixture in the middle of the leaf. Fold over the stem end, then the sides, then roll toward the tip, making a neat little package. Don't roll too tightly, as the rice will continue to expand during subsequent cooking.

④ Put the packages side by side in a roasting pan or skillet (you can layer them if you like), add water (or, even better, more stock) to come about halfway up the rolls, and weight with a heatproof plate. Cover the pan or skillet and cook over low heat for 30 minutes or so, until most of the liquid is absorbed. Drain; serve at room temperature, sprinkled with the remaining lemon juice and a bit of olive oil.

Spinach-Cheese Triangles

MAKES: About 40 pieces (20 to 40 servings)
TIME: About 1 hour

Typically made with cheese, these can be made with spinach only or cheese only; see the variations. Working with phyllo dough (sold in supermarkets, usually in the freezer compartment) is not at all difficult. There's more about handling phyllo on page 946. But here are a couple of handy rules: Defrost phyllo dough overnight in the refrigerator. If you change your mind, or use only half a box, don't worry; it will keep for weeks in the fridge (and for months in the freezer). Allow yourself plenty of room and keep a damp towel handy to cover those sheets of phyllo that you aren't working on; it dries out quickly. Brush the layers lightly with butter or oil; don't glob it on.

1½ pounds fresh spinach, trimmed and well washed

2 tablespoons olive oil

1 cup chopped onion

½ cup chopped scallion

Salt and freshly ground black pepper

⅛ teaspoon freshly grated nutmeg

3 eggs

½ pound feta cheese, crumbled

½ pound cottage cheese or ricotta, drained

¼ cup minced fresh dill leaves or 1 tablespoon dried dill

¼ cup chopped fresh parsley leaves

½ pound phyllo dough (about 15 sheets)

8 tablespoons (1 stick) butter, melted, or extra virgin olive oil

1 cup bread crumbs, preferably fresh (page 876)

① Steam or parboil the spinach until it wilts (see Just-Tender Boiled or Steamed Vegetables, page 239). Drain, squeeze dry, and chop.

② Put the olive oil in a medium skillet over medium heat. When hot, add the onion and scallion and cook, stirring, until softened, about 5 minutes. Add the spinach, salt, pepper, and nutmeg and stir.

③ Beat the eggs with the cheeses. Stir in the spinach mixture, dill, and parsley. Heat the oven to 350°F.

④ Unroll the phyllo sheets and cut them into thirds lengthwise. Working with one piece at a time, brush lightly with butter or oil, then sprinkle lightly with bread crumbs. Put 1 heaping teaspoon of spinach filling in one corner of

F Fast   **M** Make Ahead   **V** Vegetarian

the dough and fold the corner over to make a triangle. Continue to fold the phyllo, making triangles—as you learned to do with a flag. As each piece is finished, brush the top with melted butter and put on a baking sheet.

❺ When all the triangles are done, bake until nicely browned, about 20 minutes. Let rest for 5 to 10 minutes before serving.

Phyllo Triangles with Greens. This is also good with about 1 cup mushrooms cooked with the onion: In Step 1, steam or parboil any mixture of about 3 pounds of greens—spinach, kale, dandelions, escarole, etc.—until very tender. Drain and chop. In Step 2, add ½ cup crumbled walnuts to the onion; season the greens and onion with 2 tablespoons freshly squeezed lemon juice. Let cool for a few minutes, then stir in 2 beaten eggs; omit the cheese. Proceed as directed.

Phyllo Triangles with Cheese. Omit the spinach and everything in Step 2. In Step 3, add 1 cup grated Parmesan, pecorino, or other hard cheese (hard Greek sheep's milk cheese would be ideal) to the mix along with nutmeg and black pepper to taste; omit the dill and parsley.

Fried Rice Balls

Suppli

MAKES: 6 to 8 servings
TIME: 30 minutes with cooked rice

A Roman treat, and a fine use for leftover rice (especially risotto). Formally called *suppli al telefono* because the stringy mozzarella center stretches when you bite through the center and is reminiscent of telephone wires. If you use packaged bread crumbs, they should be unseasoned. This is a snack or a very informal starter.

  3 eggs
  2 cups cold cooked rice, preferably Risotto alla Milanese (page 466)
  3 ounces fresh mozzarella, chopped
  2 ounces prosciutto, minced (optional)

2 cups fresh bread crumbs, preferably homemade (to make your own, see page 876)

Neutral oil, like grapeseed or corn, for deep-frying

❶ Break one of the eggs into the rice and mix well. Form the rice into 2-inch balls. With your thumb, make a small indentation in the center of each ball, fill with a little mozzarella and prosciutto (if you're using it), and reseal the ball with the risotto around it.

❷ Lightly beat the remaining 2 eggs. Dip each ball into the egg mixture and then the bread crumbs. Set the finished balls on wax paper; they can be refrigerated for up to a couple of hours or cooked right away.

❸ Put at least 3 inches of oil in a deep pan on the stove and turn the heat to medium-high; bring to 350°F (see "Deep Frying," page 19). Gently slide the balls into the oil and fry until golden brown, turning once if necessary, about 4 minutes.

❹ Drain on paper towels and serve hot or at room temperature.

More-Formal Appetizers

These versatile dishes work as first courses, on buffets, as snacks, or even as light meals by themselves. Though they're usually eaten at a table, there are alternatives for parties: Some you can eat standing up but with a fork. Others, like Prosciutto and Melon (page 112), can be cut into bite-sized pieces and served with toothpicks. Still others, like Carpaccio (page 120), can be served on toasted bread or crackers. Finally, there are those you can skewer for easy handling.

Cheese Fondue

MAKES: 8 to 10 servings
TIME: 25 minutes

Cheese and wine are a natural combination in Switzerland, the home of fondue. Using Swiss cheeses—like

Gruyère, Emmental (the original "Swiss"), Appenzeller, Fribourg, or vacherin, for example—is traditional, but any good melting cheese works equally well (cheddar, Jack, Comté, or fontina, to name just a few). Dry and acidic white wines are good for balancing the heaviness of the cheese, but beer, dry cider, and red wine are also nice.

If you don't have a fondue pot, use any enamel or ceramic-lined pot; or start the process in any pot at all, then transfer the finished fondue to an ovenproof ceramic dish that you can set over a tea light.

Serve with cubes of crusty bread, cooked meat, and cut-up fruits and vegetables. Many vegetables can be used raw, but some—potatoes, eggplant, and artichokes, for example—should be cooked first. Other vegetables, like green beans, asparagus, broccoli, and cauliflower, are best when cooked lightly, until barely tender. In any case, be sure the vegetables are completely dry, or the fondue will not stick to them.

> 2 cups dry white wine, or a little more
>
> 1 large clove garlic, peeled and crushed (optional)
>
> 2 tablespoons cornstarch
>
> 1 pound Gruyère cheese, shredded (about 4 cups)
>
> 1 pound Emmental cheese, shredded (about 4 cups)

1 Combine the wine and garlic, if you're using it, in a large saucepan over medium heat and bring to a slow bubble. Whisk together the cornstarch and 1 tablespoon cold water; set aside.

2 Lower the heat, then gradually stir in the cheese until it's melted and creamy; do not let the fondue boil. Whisk the cornstarch slurry again and then add to the fondue while stirring; cook until thick and creamy, another 5 minutes. If the fondue is too thick, add a little more wine and cook for another 3 minutes or so. Serve immediately.

Mustard-Cheese Fondue. Perfect with hearty, dark bread, like pumpernickel or seedy whole grain: Substitute dry cider for the wine. Add ¼ cup any Dijon-style or grainy mustard or 2 to 3 tablespoons yellow mustard seeds with the cheese in Step 2.

Fontina and Porcini Fondue. An Italian-style fondue; the mild fontina cheese really lets the porcini flavor shine: Use 2 pounds grated fontina and 1 cup dried porcini. Soak the porcini in hot water until soft, squeeze out the excess water, chop finely, and stir in with the cheese in Step 2; substitute the porcini-soaking water (strain it first if it's sandy) for some or all of the wine.

12 Ways to Add More Flavor to Fondue

It's easy to add subtle—or not so subtle—flavors to your fondue. Some ideas:

1. 2 to 3 ounces dried mushrooms (or 1 cup finely chopped fresh)
2. 1 cup peeled, seeded, and chopped tomato
3. 1 cup finely chopped Caramelized Onions (page 325)
4. 4 to 8 cloves Roasted Garlic (page 303)
5. 1 tablespoon minced chipotles in adobo sauce, or to taste
6. 1 tablespoon minced jalapeño
7. 1 or 2 tablespoons horseradish
8. ¼ cup or so prepared mustard or 2 to 3 tablespoons mustard seeds
9. Pinch cayenne
10. Large pinch smoked paprika
11. Splash or two of Worcestershire sauce
12. ¼ cup Traditional Pesto (page 27; stirred in at the last minute)

Prosciutto and Melon

MAKES: 8 servings

TIME: 10 minutes

F **M**

Good dry-cured ham, like Prosciutto di Parma, and a good melon are all you need for this classic combination. If you have ripe figs or fresh dates, the results will be equally fine. The combination of sweet, juicy fruit and dry, salty ham is incomparable.

1 ripe cantaloupe or other melon

About 10 thin slices prosciutto

① Cut the melon into eighths, scrape out the seeds, and remove the rind. Cut the slices into chunks. Cut the prosciutto into pieces roughly the same size as the melon.

② Use a toothpick to skewer a piece of ham and a chunk of melon and repeat until all the ham and melon are used up. Serve immediately or refrigerate, covered, for up to 2 hours. Serve cool but not ice cold.

Grilled or Broiled Mushroom and Bacon Skewers

MAKES: 4 servings

TIME: 20 minutes

For a three-ingredient dish, it's hard to do any better. To make this vegetarian, skewer just mushrooms or mushrooms with other vegetables—like red peppers and zucchini. The vinaigrette will jazz up their flavor considerably.

12 medium button mushrooms, trimmed

6 slices thick bacon, cut into 12 pieces

Any Vinaigrette (page 199) or Garlic Mayonnaise (page 42)

① If you're using wooden skewers, soak them in water before beginning. Heat a charcoal or gas grill or a broiler to medium-high heat and put the rack at least 4 inches from the heat source. Make 4 small skewers, alternating mushrooms and bacon. (If you are using sliced bacon, cut the slices in half, then fold each over onto itself as you skewer it.)

② Grill, turning frequently, until the bacon is crisp on the outside and the mushrooms tender, 10 to 15

minutes. Serve, offering vinaigrette or aïoli as a dipping sauce.

Pan-Cooked Mushrooms and Bacon. Half of an English breakfast: Put 1 tablespoon extra virgin olive oil in a skillet over medium-high heat. A minute later, add the mushrooms and bacon and cook, stirring occasionally, until the bacon is crisp and the mushrooms browned and tender, about 10 minutes. Skewer if you like (it's a nicer presentation) and serve.

Stuffed Mushrooms

MAKES: At least 6 servings

TIME: 30 minutes

Another good use for button mushrooms, which have a fine shape for stuffing.

1 pound large button mushrooms

1 egg

1/2 cup fresh bread crumbs, preferably homemade (page 876)

1/2 cup freshly grated Parmesan cheese

1/2 cup chopped fresh parsley leaves

Salt and freshly ground black pepper

1 teaspoon minced garlic

Extra virgin olive oil as needed, plus oil for greasing the baking sheet

① Heat the oven to 400°F. Clean the mushrooms, trim off the bottoms of the stems, and remove the stems, taking care to leave the caps intact. Chop the stems and combine them in a bowl with the egg, bread crumbs, cheese, parsley, salt and pepper to taste, and garlic.

② Stir enough olive oil into the mixture to make it shine—a tablespoon or two. Lightly grease a baking sheet with more oil. Stuff the mushroom caps with the stem mixture and bake, stuffed side up, until lightly browned on top, about 15 minutes. Let cool a little, then serve, hot or at room temperature, on toothpicks or with napkins.

10 More Stuffings for Button Mushrooms

Fill the mushroom caps with any of these stuffings or add them to the stuffing in the recipe.

1. Flavorful Cream Cheese Spread or any of its variations (page 91)
2. Herbed Goat Cheese (page 91)
3. Crumbled blue, goat, or feta cheese (with nuts and/or fresh herbs if you like)
4. Skordalia or any of its variations (page 94)
5. Tapenade (page 96)
6. Simple Risotto (any kind, pages 466–467)
7. The raw meat stuffing from Fried Wontons or Egg Rolls (page 102) or Pot Stickers (page 104)
8. Meatballs, Three Ways (page 114; fill the caps with the raw meat mixture and bake until done)
9. Cooked crumbled sausage or chorizo (alone or added to the main recipe ingredients)
10. Minced raw or cooked shrimp, lobster, or crabmeat (alone or added to the main recipe ingredients)

Meatballs, Three Ways

MAKES: 6 to 8 servings

TIME: About 40 minutes

Here meatballs get three cocktail-party treatments, none of them Swedish. The main recipe—an Italian version called *polpette,* at least in Rome—are made with a load of fresh Parmesan, lightened with parsley, and bound with bread instead of egg. The second adds almonds, for a popular tapas meatball. The third is Vietnamese influenced, with rice and pork. All three can be mixed and rolled in advance, then simmered, baked, pan-roasted, or grilled, and take just minutes to cook.

Other meat you can use: ground pork, lamb, veal, turkey, chicken, or duck (or a combination).

1 thick slice or 2 thin slices white bread

$^{1}/_{2}$ cup milk

1 pound ground sirloin or your own ground beef (see page 722)

$^{1}/_{2}$ cup chopped onion

$^{1}/_{2}$ cup freshly grated Parmesan cheese

$^{1}/_{4}$ cup chopped fresh parsley leaves

Salt and freshly ground black pepper

1 Soak the bread in the milk until soggy, about 5 minutes. Squeeze the milk from the bread and combine the bread gently with the meat, onion, Parmesan, parsley, and some salt and pepper. Shape into 1-inch meatballs, pressing no more than is necessary.

2 Cook the meatballs one of three ways: gently drop into a large pot of simmering stock or water for 10 minutes; put on a lightly greased baking sheet and bake in a 350°F oven for 7 to 8 minutes; or sauté in a tablespoon of olive oil (working in batches) in a pan for about 8 minutes, turning every couple of minutes. Serve immediately or warm with Aïoli (page 42) or Fast Tomato Sauce (page 502) as a dip, if you like.

Spanish-Style Almond Meatballs. Serve with Saffron Mayonnaise (page 42) or Fast Tomato Sauce (page 502): Omit the bread and the milk. Substitute bread crumbs for the Parmesan. In Step 1, whisk together $^{1}/_{4}$ cup roughly chopped almonds and 1 egg in a large bowl, then proceed with the recipe.

Meatballs, Vietnamese Style. Serve with Thai Chile Sauce (page 39) or Basil-Soy Dipping Sauce (page 38): Omit the bread and the milk. Use ground pork instead of beef; scallion instead of onion; cooked white rice (preferably short-grain or sticky) instead of the Parmesan, and cilantro instead of parsley. In Step 1, beat 1 egg in a large bowl and stir in the rice. Carefully combine the remaining ingredients along with 1 tablespoon minced ginger or garlic if you like.

Skewered and Grilled Meatballs, Three Ways. Add other vegetables or shrimp to the skewers too: Heat a gas or charcoal grill to medium-high heat and put the rack about 4 inches from the heat source. Put 1 to 3 meatballs on a skewer, depending on whether you're add-

 Fast   Make Ahead   **V** Vegetarian

ing anything else to the skewer, brush with oil, and set on the grill. Cook, rotating carefully to cook and brown all sides, about 4 minutes.

Chicken Wings, Six Ways

MAKES: 6 to 8 servings

TIME: About 1½ hours, largely unattended

Wings are perfect party food, even at room temperature. Real buffalo chicken wings, credited to the Anchor Bar in—where else?—Buffalo, are a deep-fried, two-pan, stove-to-oven affair (with margarine as the secret ingredient no less). This roasting technique (which is essentially oven-frying) skips the oleo and is virtually foolproof, with many opportunities for variation.

You can also grill the wings over a moderately hot fire, starting them with indirect heat and finishing them over the flames. (See "The Basics of Grilled or Broiled Chicken Parts," page 658). Or cook them over indirect heat for 20 minutes or so; then, when they're crisp and just cooked through, pull them off and toss them in a bowl with the sauce (this gives the fire a chance to die down a bit). Return them to the grill for a final browning and crisping directly over the heat.

¼ cup relatively mild hot sauce like Durkee, Crystal, Cholula, or Louisiana (Tabasco will be very hot, but you might want to add a dash)

4 tablespoons (½ stick) butter, melted

2 tablespoons sherry vinegar or white wine vinegar

1 tablespoon minced garlic

3 pounds chicken wings, rinsed and patted dry with paper towels, cut into 3 pieces each (see page 648), wing tips saved for stock

2 tablespoons neutral oil, like grapeseed or corn

Salt and freshly ground black pepper

8 to 12 celery stalks, cut into sticks (optional)

1 cup Blue Cheese Dressing (page 25; optional)

1 Heat the oven to 375°F. Combine the hot sauce, butter, vinegar, and garlic in a small bowl.

2 Put the chicken wings in a large roasting pan, drizzle with the oil, and sprinkle liberally with salt and pepper. Toss to coat, then spread the wings out in a single layer. (It's okay if they're a little crowded; they'll shrink.) Put the wings in the oven and roast, undisturbed, until the bottom of the pan is coated with fat and the wings are beginning to brown, about 30 minutes. Use a spoon to baste the wings with the drippings, then carefully pour them out of the pan. If the wings are still sticking to the bottom of the pan, return them to the oven until they release easily, another 5 or 10 minutes.

3 Turn the wings over, baste again, then carefully pour off any more fat. Return them to the oven until nicely browned, another 20 minutes or so (again, they'll release easily from the pan when they're ready).

4 Raise the oven temperature to 450°F. Carefully pour off any accumulated fat, then drizzle the wings with the hot sauce mixture and toss to coat. Spread them back out into a single layer and return them to the oven. Cook, tossing once or twice, until crisp all over, about 10 more minutes. Serve hot or at room temperature, with the celery and blue cheese dressing for dipping if you like.

Honey Mustard Chicken Wings. Omit the hot sauce, vinegar, and garlic and combine the butter with ¼ cup Dijon mustard and 2 tablespoons honey. Proceed with the recipe, using this sauce to coat the wings in Step 3. Serve with Balsamic Syrup (page 51) for dipping if you like or simply lemon wedges.

Chicken Wings with Ginger Soy Glaze. Omit the hot sauce and melted butter. Replace the vinegar with rice vinegar and the garlic with 2 tablespoons minced fresh ginger, then add ¼ cup soy sauce and 2 tablespoons dark sesame oil. Proceed with the recipe, using this sauce to coat the wings in Step 3. You really don't need a sauce with this, but if you must, try Ginger-Scallion Sauce (page 39).

Beer-and-Butter Chicken Wings. Omit the hot sauce, vinegar, and garlic. In Step 1, combine the butter with

1 cup strong beer (a stout or an ale is excellent) in a small saucepan. Once the wings are in the oven, bring the sauce mixture to a boil. Lower the heat to a simmer and cook, stirring occasionally, until it's thickened and reduced by about half. Use this sauce to coat the wings in Step 3. No dipping sauce needed.

Smoky Chile Lime Chicken Wings. Omit the hot sauce, vinegar, and garlic and replace the butter and the neutral oil with extra virgin olive oil. Make the tossing sauce by combining the olive oil with 2 tablespoons freshly squeezed lime juice, 2 tablespoons chili powder (to make your own, see page 66), and 1 tablespoon smoked paprika. Proceed with the recipe, using this sauce to coat the wings in Step 3. Garnish with lime wedges and cilantro and serve with Avocado Yogurt Sauce (page 24).

Spicy Peanut Chicken Wings. Omit the hot sauce and vinegar and replace the butter with coconut milk (to make your own, see page 389). Make the tossing sauce by combining the coconut milk and garlic with 2 tablespoons peanut butter and 1 tablespoon hot curry powder (to make your own, see page 66). Proceed with the recipe, using this sauce to coat the wings in Step 3. Serve with Raita (page 24) for dipping.

Roasted Peppers and Anchovies

MAKES: 4 servings

TIME: 30 minutes with raw peppers, 5 minutes if they're already roasted

F **M**

Best with your own roasted peppers, this is still good with canned or jarred red peppers (pimientos).

4 Roasted Red Peppers (page 330)

Salt and freshly ground black pepper

8 anchovy fillets, rinsed if salted

Extra virgin olive oil, to taste

Several drops of freshly squeezed lemon juice or balsamic vinegar (optional)

About 1 teaspoon capers (optional)

1 Cut the peppers in half and sprinkle them with a little bit of salt and pepper. Top each half with an anchovy fillet.

2 Drizzle with olive oil and lemon juice if you like. Serve on rounds of bread or toast, sprinkling a few capers on top if you like, or skewer with toothpicks.

Socca or Farinata

Chickpea Pancake

MAKES: 4 to 6 servings

TIME: 1 hour, plus time for the batter to rest

M **V**

Large chickpea pancakes are a classic throughout Provence and Liguria, where they are called *socca* and *farinata,* respectively, and have been made for hundreds of years. Traditionally cooked in wood- or coal-burning ovens—in France on disk-shaped copper plates called *plaques*—they are simple, rustic, everyday dishes that are sold piping hot, wrapped in paper as snacks in shops and by vendors on the streets. (I'm drooling just writing about it.)

Wonderful plain or dressed up with anything from onions to cheese to rosemary, this is one of those dishes you can whip up in the morning and forget about until dinner. The onions and rosemary are strictly optional; most soccas contain no more than chickpea flour, water, oil, salt, and pepper.

1½ cups lukewarm water

1 cup chickpea flour

1 teaspoon salt

1 teaspoon freshly ground black pepper, or more to taste

4 tablespoons extra virgin olive oil, plus more as needed

 Fast   Make Ahead   Vegetarian

¹/₂ small yellow onion, thinly sliced (¹/₄ to ¹/₂ cup, loosely packed, to taste; optional)

1 tablespoon fresh rosemary leaves (optional)

1 Pour the warm water into a mixing bowl and sift the chickpea flour into it. (You can do this with a sifter or just by shaking the chickpea flour through a fine-mesh strainer; the goal is to eliminate any lumps of chickpea flour, which are ubiquitous.) Whisk the chickpea flour, water, salt, pepper, and 2 tablespoons of the olive oil together, cover the bowl with a towel, and let the batter sit on the kitchen counter for at least a few minutes and as long as 12 hours.

2 Heat the oven to 450°F. Put another 2 tablespoons of the olive oil in a well-seasoned or nonstick 12-inch pizza pan or skillet. Stir the sliced onion and rosemary leaves into the batter—it will still be a little thicker than it was originally—then pour the batter into the greased pan. Bake for about 15 minutes, or until the pancake is firm and the edges set. Heat the broiler and brush the top of the socca with a little more oil if you like.

3 Set the socca a few inches away from the broiler for a minute or two, just long enough to brown it spottily, but not long enough that it would color evenly or burn. Cut it into wedges and serve hot or at least warm.

Chicken or Pork Satay

MAKES: 10 skewers (5 to 10 servings)
TIME: 30 minutes to 24 hours, depending on marinating time

Especially when thinly sliced for satays, boneless chicken thighs produce much juicier results than do breasts.

4 boneless, skinless chicken thighs or about ³/₄ pound boneless pork shoulder or loin

¹/₄ cup soy sauce

¹/₄ cup nam pla (Thai fish sauce) or more soy sauce

1 teaspoon ground cumin

1 teaspoon ground coriander

1 tablespoon natural peanut butter or tahini

1 teaspoon minced fresh ginger

1 tablespoon minced garlic

1 tablespoon sugar

1 tablespoon freshly squeezed lime or lemon juice or vinegar

1 Slice the chicken about 1/8 inch thick (it's easier if you freeze it for 15 to 30 minutes first). Mix together the remaining ingredients plus ¹/₂ cup water and stir in the meat slices. Let sit until the grill or broiler is ready or marinate, refrigerated, for up to 24 hours. If you're going to use wooden skewers, soak them in water to cover for a few minutes while the chicken is marinating.

2 When you're ready to cook, heat a charcoal or gas grill or a broiler until quite hot and put the rack as close to the heat source as possible. Thread the meat onto skewers without crowding. Grill or broil until browned all over, a total of 5 to 8 minutes. While the meat is cooking, bring the marinade to a boil and reduce it slightly. Serve the skewers hot, using the marinade as a dipping sauce.

Ceviche

Marinated Scallops

MAKES: 4 to 8 servings
TIME: 30 minutes

Essentially a raw dish, these scallops are "cooked" by the acid in the lime juice. A combination of scallops, shrimp, conch, and octopus—the latter two usually precooked to the point of tenderness—is also good. If you can find spanking-fresh fillets of your local white fish, you can use that here too, although scallops alone are easy and fabulous. (They're also the safest shellfish to eat raw, but if the whole thing makes you nervous, see the following recipe for Mock Ceviche.)

1 pound perfectly fresh sea scallops, tendons removed if you like and cut into $1/4$ -inch dice, or a mixture of fish (see the headnote)

$1/2$ cup chopped bell pepper

1 teaspoon grated lime zest

$1/4$ cup freshly squeezed lime juice

Salt

Cayenne, to taste

Chopped fresh cilantro leaves for garnish

1 Toss together everything but the cilantro and let sit at room temperature for 15 minutes.

2 Taste, adjust the seasoning, and serve, garnished with the cilantro.

15 Other Fish, Poultry, or Meat Dishes That Work as Appetizers

1. Spicy Grilled or Broiled Shrimp (page 574)
2. Gravlax (page 585)
3. Grilled or Broiled Scallops with Basil Stuffing (page 600)
4. Grilled or Broiled Fish Skewers, Basted with Herbs (page 603)
5. Spicy Grilled or Broiled Chicken Kebabs (page 670)
6. Baked Clams with Wasabi Bread Crumbs (page 621)
7. Marinated Mackerel (page 623)
8. Salt Cod Mousse (page 631)
9. Crab Cakes (page 633)
10. Shrimp Burgers, made small (page 633)
11. Fish Fritters (page 634)
12. Salmon Croquettes (page 635)
13. Chicken MarkNuggets (page 646)
14. West Indian Crispy Pork Bits or its variations (page 749)
15. Grilled or Broiled Lamb Ribs (with plenty of napkins) (page 778)

Mock Ceviche

MAKES: 6 or more servings

TIME: 30 minutes or less

There are a couple of reasons to cook "ceviche" (you can't rightly call cooked fish *ceviche*, any more than you can serve cooked steak tartare). It makes the fish more tender, and it's a good a form of reassurance: No one will worry about eating raw fish.

Salt and freshly ground black pepper

$1/2$ pound shrimp (any size)

$1/2$ pound sea scallops, tendons removed if you like

$1/2$ pound cleaned squid, cut into rings (tentacles left whole)

2 tablespoons olive oil

1 small chile, like Thai or jalapeño, seeded and minced, or to taste (or use hot red pepper flakes or cayenne)

$1/2$ cup diced red onion

1 small clove garlic, minced (optional)

$1/4$ cup diced red or yellow bell pepper (optional)

$1/4$ cup diced tomato (optional)

$1/4$ cup diced avocado (optional)

$1/4$ cup freshly squeezed lime juice

$1/2$ cup fresh cilantro leaves, roughly chopped

1 Bring about 2 quarts of water to a boil and salt it. Add the shrimp, reduce the heat to medium, and cook for about 4 minutes, or until they are pink and firm. Remove with a slotted spoon and run under cold water to chill. Peel and set aside.

2 Cook the scallops and squid together in the same water until the scallops are firm and not quite cooked through and the squid is fairly tender, about 2 minutes. Remove with a slotted spoon (reserve the cooking water) and run under cold water to chill, then combine with the shrimp.

3 Toss the seafood with the olive oil and, if you like, cover and refrigerate until ready to serve, for up to 24 hours.

F Fast   **M** Make Ahead   **V** Vegetarian

4 Toss with all the remaining ingredients except the cilantro, then taste and adjust the seasoning; if the mixture is dry, add a little more olive oil or lime juice or some of the cooking water. Stir in most of the cilantro, then garnish with the rest and serve.

Gefilte Fish

MAKES: 8 to 12 servings

TIME: About 2$^1/_2$ hours, largely unattended, plus time to chill

Any white freshwater or saltwater fish is good here, though carp, whitefish, and pike are most traditional. Horseradish is the nearly mandatory accompaniment. Don't skimp on the carrots, which turn out mushily delicious.

Make this a day before you want to serve it.

3 pounds scraps of white fish—skeletons, heads (gills removed), and skin

2 large onions

2 celery stalks, roughly chopped

2 bay leaves

1 tablespoon peppercorns

3 pounds fillets of assorted white fish, preferably freshwater, like carp, whitefish, and pike, rinsed and patted dry

3 eggs, lightly beaten

3 tablespoons matzo or cracker meal

Salt and freshly ground white or black pepper

About 3 cups carrot chunks

About $^1/_2$ cup horseradish (to make your own, see page 36), thinned with a little cream if you like

1 Put the fish scraps in a large pot with 1 onion, the celery, bay leaves, peppercorns, and water to cover; bring to a boil, then reduce the heat to low.

28 Other Dishes You Can Serve as Sit-Down Appetizers

Obviously, you can make small portions of almost any savory dish and call it an appetizer; and virtually any pasta or soup qualifies as well. These are some of my personal favorites to serve before a meal.

1. Shrimp Cocktail or really any shrimp dish (pages 87 or 573–578)
2. Any artichoke recipe (see pages 253–257)
3. Beet Rösti with Rosemary (page 264)
4. Any leek recipe (see pages 311–312)
5. Grilled or Broiled Mushrooms (page 315)
6. Chiles Rellenos (page 333)
7. Crisp Panfried Potatoes, Spanish Style (page 342)
8. Potato Rösti (page 345)
9. Rich Spinach Pie (page 353)
10. Spinach Croquettes (page 354)
11. Zucchini Pancakes (page 355)
12. Panfried Green and/or Red Tomatoes (page 363)
13. Falafel (page 439)
14. Any polenta (see pages 485–488)
15. Any risotto (see pages 466–468)
16. Lamb and Bulgur Patties (pages 499–500)
17. Deep-Fried Seafood (page 568)
18. Steamed Clams or Mussels, Unleashed (page 619)
19. Grilled Octopus (page 627)
20. Slow-Grilled Sardines (page 629)
21. Fresh Sea Snails with Garlic Butter (page 631)
22. Salmon Croquettes (page 635)
23. Grilled or Broiled Squab, Vietnamese Style (page 710)
24. Grilled Quail, Tuscan Style (page 712)
25. Roast Quail with Honey, Cumin, and Orange Juice (pages 712–713)
26. Sesame Spareribs (page 762)
27. Cheese Soufflé (page 807)
28. Any quiche or baked custard (see pages 808–810)

2 Peel the other onion, quarter it, and combine it with the fish fillets in a food processor; pulse until coarsely chopped; do not overprocess. (You may have to do this in batches.) Add the eggs, one at a time, pulsing after each addition. Add the matzo meal and about 1/2 cup water and process for a few seconds; the mixture should be light, smooth, and almost fluffy. Add a little more water if it seems too dry. Sprinkle with salt and pepper.

3 Drop the carrots into the simmering stock. With wet hands, shape the fish mixture into small ovals, about the size of eggs. Lower each one of them into the simmering stock; don't worry about crowding. Cover and adjust the heat so the mixture simmers; cook for about 1 1/2 hours, then turn off the heat and let the fish cool in the liquid.

4 Use a slotted spoon to transfer the fish balls and the carrots to a platter. Raise the heat to high and reduce the stock, if necessary, to about 2 cups. Strain it over the fish balls, cover the platter, and refrigerate. Remove the fish from the refrigerator about 30 minutes before serving. Serve with a bit of the jelly, a few carrot pieces, and plenty of horseradish.

Carpaccio

MAKES: 4 to 8 servings
TIME: About 1 1/2 hours, largely unattended

The now-classic appetizer of the 1980s, which can be made with beef, tuna, or salmon. (Skip the Parmesan if you're using fish; grated lemon or lime zest or just a drizzle of soy sauce and lemon juice is fantastic.) Needless to say, use only the highest-quality beef (or fish), from a completely trustworthy source.

1/2 pound beef tenderloin (filet mignon) or skinless tuna or salmon loin, in 1 piece

1 tablespoon extra virgin olive oil, or a little less

2 teaspoons freshly squeezed lemon juice

Coarse salt and freshly ground black pepper

1/4 pound Parmesan cheese, in 1 chunk

1 Cover the beef well with plastic wrap and freeze it for an hour or so, until very firm. Slice it as thinly as possible (a slicing machine is ideal; alternatively, use a very sharp carving knife).

2 Toss the beef with the oil, lemon juice, and some salt and pepper. Break the Parmesan into small chunks. Use a toothpick to skewer a piece of beef and a piece of cheese and repeat until all the beef and cheese are used up. Serve immediately or refrigerate for up to an hour.

F Fast   **M** Make Ahead   **V** Vegetarian

Soups

MAKING SOUP IS NOT ONLY INCREDIBLY

satisfying, it's also ridiculously easy. At its most basic, you start with water, add some means of making it taste better—usually meat, poultry, fish, or aromatic vegetables, along with seasonings—and finish with a few (or a slew of) vegetables and/or grains. Really, it's almost impossible to make "bad" soup. If you start with good ingredients—and you should—the results are likely to be great, because every bit of flavor remains in the part you eat. When you're done, you have an ideal first course for entertaining or weeknight suppers or an easy course to build a meal around.

121

The process need not be elaborate or time consuming, and it rarely requires precision. There's little measuring and a lot of room for improvisation; even the timing is flexible. In fact, most soups are simple and forgiving, and many take less than thirty minutes to prepare; if one takes longer, most of the cooking time is unattended. And almost every stock and soup can be made ahead.

It's worth noting here that every soup is best when it begins with stock, so when you can, start with one of the stocks toward the end of the chapter (see pages 155–160); the body and extra flavor will improve any soup. If you cannot, though, see the sidebar "Why Not Use Water?"

The Basics of Making Soup

There are a few issues to consider in soup making:

Preparing foods for soup: Cutting vegetables or other ingredients to about the same size allows them to all cook at pretty much the same rate; you don't want your carrots tender while your potatoes are still hard. And using small pieces allows you to eat soup elegantly, without cutting in the bowl or cramming too-large pieces of food into your mouth.

Using leftovers in soup: One of my first cooking teachers made cream-of-something-or-other almost every night with leftover vegetables. She rinsed the left-overs with boiling water, combined the vegetables with stock and seasonings, puréed, and reheated, sometimes with cream, sometimes with milk or yogurt, sometimes with nothing. Almost any leftover whose flavor does not conflict with the basic seasonings of your soup is fair game: pasta, rice, bread, meat, fish, poultry, vegetables—even mashed potatoes, which can blend in nicely.

Heating stock for use in soup: Most soups begin by cooking some meat or vegetables, then adding stock or water. If you heat the stock or water while you prepare the solid ingredients, you will cut your cooking time by as much as ten or fifteen minutes.

Puréeing soup: Upright and immersion blenders can purée almost any soup in an instant. (A hand-cranked food mill is not a ton of work, but it's not nearly as fast.) If the purée is too thick, stir in some water or half-and-half, which will add flavor, enhance texture, and thin the soup all at the same time. If your purée is too thin, see "Giving Soups More Body" (page 132).

Incidentally, guilt factor aside, heavy cream is a sensational thickener, adding wonderful flavor and silken texture. And you don't need much—$^1/_2$ cup or even less is usually enough for 6 cups of soup.

Adding pasta or rice to soup: Rice or pasta add body, flavor, and variety to soups, but they're best cooked in separate water, because they absorb so much water and give off so much starch that cooking them directly in the soup changes the character entirely. (There is nothing wrong with this, of course, but you should be aware of it.)

Storing soup: Many soups can be made in advance, or at least partly so (I've noted the best time to interrupt cooking when there is one), and freeze brilliantly for a month or more, so there's rarely a reason not to double or even quadruple a given recipe to reserve some for another time. Generally, it's best not to freeze or even refrigerate a soup once you've added starches like rice and pasta. Since they continue to absorb water even during storage, they break down, becoming soft and thickening the soup unnecessarily (of course if you like these qualities, go right ahead). Nor should you freeze soups made with dairy, which are likely to curdle when reheated.

Why Not Use Water?

Stock is flavoring for soups and sauces that you can make in advance. But it is not the only way of flavoring them. All stocks are basically a combination of water and solids. So it stands to reason that you can begin any soup with water instead of stock, as long as you add sufficient vegetables and other flavorings—wine, extra vegetables, soy sauce, or herbs, for example—and cook the mixture long enough for a flavorful liquid to develop.

F Fast   **M** Make Ahead   **V** Vegetarian

An immersion blender lets you purée soup right in the pot. Remove the pot from the heat. Hold the blender upright and make sure the blade is immersed to prevent splattering.

ESSENTIAL RECIPES

These are not necessarily the "easiest" soups in this chapter (though few of my soup recipes are what you'd call difficult), but rather the most basic, like "Boiled Water" and Puréed Vegetable Soup Without Cream, or those that have become emblematic, like Chicken Soup, Many Ways.

"Boiled Water"

MAKES: 4 servings
TIME: 20 minutes

F　**V**

This Mediterranean classic, as ancient and almost as simple as boiling, is the quintessential beginner's or just-plain-basic soup. It's one you'll cook forever.

- 6 to 10 cloves garlic, lightly crushed
- 1 bay leaf
- Salt and freshly ground black pepper
- ¼ cup extra virgin olive oil
- 4 thick slices French or Italian bread (slightly stale bread is fine)

¹/₂ cup freshly grated Parmesan or pecorino Romano cheese

Chopped fresh parsley leaves for garnish

1 Combine 4 cups water with the garlic, bay leaf, and some salt and pepper in a saucepan or stockpot. Bring to a boil, cover partially, and turn the heat to very low. Let the liquid bubble gently for 15 minutes.

2 Meanwhile, put the olive oil in a large skillet over medium heat. When hot, brown the slices of bread in the oil, turning once, for a total of about 5 minutes.

3 Put the bread in bowls and top with the grated cheese. Strain the soup into the bowls, garnish with parsley, and serve.

Roasted Garlic Soup. Substitute 10 or more cloves Roasted Garlic (page 303) for the crushed garlic. Or put the crushed garlic in the skillet with the olive oil and cook over medium-low heat until fragrant and just starting to color, about 4 minutes. Fish out the garlic, chop it finely, and add it to the pot in Step 1.

Tomato-Garlic Soup. Add 2 cups chopped tomato (canned is okay; don't drain) in Step 1. Don't strain the soup.

Lime-Garlic-Coconut Soup. Omit the olive oil, bread, and cheese. Juice and zest 2 limes. In Step 1, use 1 can of coconut milk (to make your own, see page 389 and use about 1¹/₂ cups) and 3 cups of water, along with the lime zest. Omit Step 2. In Step 3, add the lime juice to the soup right before straining. If you like, ladle the soup over a small mound of plain white rice, bean threads, or rice vermicelli. Garnish with cilantro instead of parsley.

Chunky Vegetable Soup

Minestrone

MAKES: 4 to 6 servings
TIME: 45 to 60 minutes

M　**V**

Think of this as a what-have-you soup with infinite and easy variations. You're looking for a mix of vegetables, always with tomato, though combining "hard" and "soft" vegetables improves the results. If you have an old piece of Parmesan lying around, cut the rind into small pieces and add it along with the first batch of vegetables; it'll become chewy during cooking and is not only edible but (not surprisingly) delicious.

1/4 cup extra virgin olive oil

1 medium onion, diced

1 carrot, diced

1 celery stalk, peeled (see page 283) and diced

1/2 cup chopped prosciutto or other ham (optional)

1 1/2 to 2 cups hard vegetables, like potatoes, winter squash, parsnips, or turnips, peeled if necessary and cut into smaller than 1/2-inch dice

Salt and freshly ground black pepper

6 cups chicken, beef, or vegetable stock (to make your own, see pages 157–159) or water

1 cup peeled, seeded, and chopped tomato (canned is fine; include the juices)

1 1/2 to 2 cups soft vegetables, like green beans, cooked dried beans, zucchini or summer squash, or dark, leafy greens like kale or collards, cut into smaller than 1/2-inch dice

1/2 cup chopped fresh parsley leaves

Freshly grated Parmesan cheese for garnish

1 Put 3 tablespoons of the oil into a large, deep pot over medium heat. When hot, add the onion, carrot, and celery. Cook, stirring, until the onion softens, about 5 minutes. Add the ham if you're using it and cook, stirring, for another 3 minutes.

2 Add the hard vegetables and sprinkle with salt and pepper. Cook, stirring, for a minute or two, then add the stock and the tomato; bring to a boil, then lower the heat so the mixture bubbles gently. Cook, stirring every now and then, until the vegetables are fairly soft and the tomato is broken up, about 15 minutes. (At this point, you may refrigerate the soup, covered, for up to 2 days; reheat before proceeding.)

3 Add the soft vegetables and the parsley and adjust the heat once again so the mixture simmers. Cook until all the vegetables are very tender, about 15 minutes. Taste and adjust the seasoning, add the remaining tablespoon of olive oil, and serve, passing the cheese at the table if you like.

Pistou. Traditionally you'd use pesto with a whole lot of garlic here: Stir in 1/2 cup or more of freshly made Traditional Pesto or any of its variations (page 27).

Pasta e Fagioli (Pasta and Bean Soup). Use about half as much of the vegetables and add 2 cups cooked beans—kidney, white, borlotti, chickpeas, cannellini, or a mixture—with the soft vegetables. With them, add 1/2 to 1 cup small uncooked pasta, like tubetti, or larger pasta broken into bits. About 5 minutes before serving, stir in a teaspoon (or more, to taste) of minced garlic.

Ribolitta (White Bean and Bread Soup). Purée 1 cup of cooked cannellini beans (canned are fine) with some of their liquid into a thick paste. For each bowl, toast a thick slice of rustic Tuscan or Italian bread and set in the bottom of the bowls. In Step 3, add the beans to the simmering soup. Thin with a little more water or stock if necessary. To serve, pour the bubbling soup over the bread and drizzle with a little extra virgin olive oil if you like.

Mulligatawny (Spicy Indian Vegetable Soup). Leave this chunky and brothy or purée it: Substitute neutral oil, like grapeseed or corn, for the olive oil. Skip the ham. Add 1 teaspoon each ground cumin and turmeric and cook with the onion in Step 1. Add 2 tablespoons curry powder (to make your own, see pages 66–67) along with the soft vegetables. Substitute cilantro for the parsley and omit the Parmesan.

4 Creative Takes on Minestrone

The tomato is a given, but other vegetables are completely flexible.

1. Summer Minestrone: Use fresh corn kernels, zucchini or summer squash, and garnish with chopped fresh basil, mint, or thyme.

2. Autumn Minestrone: Use mostly cubes of butternut

or other winter squash and garnish with chopped fresh sage and bits of toasted hazelnuts.

3. Green Minestrone: Use peas, asparagus, green beans, and $^3/_4$ cup mixed chopped fresh herbs, like parsley, basil, dill, mint, chervil, and chives.

4. Spicy Chile Minestrone: Use roasted, cleaned, and chopped poblanos (see page 330); minced jalapeño; a mix of potato, corn, chayote, or any summer squash; and cilantro.

How to Improvise a Soup

Soup is the most flexible and forgiving thing you can cook. Just follow these five steps and you'll be improvising soup in no time:

1. Start with a little fat and a lot of flavor. Cooking one or two aromatic vegetables, like garlic, ginger, onions, or shallots, in a little olive oil or butter takes only a few minutes and gives a soup backbone.

2. Add seasonings. This can be as basic as salt and freshly ground black pepper or as complex as spice blends or citrus zest or as simple as a dried bay leaf. (In general, add fresh herbs at the last minute for the most impact.) Lightly heat them until you can smell their fragrance.

3. Stir in the liquid. Stock, water, juice, wine, beer, or whatever combination you think best complements the other ingredients.

4. Add your main ingredients in order of the longest cooking time to the shortest. Two examples: first dried beans, then uncooked rice, then tomatoes, finally spinach; or first mushrooms, then carrots, then bok choy, finally cooked rice noodles. If you want vegetables to melt away into the soup, add them early; for a fresh, crisp taste, add them at the last minute. When using cooked leftovers, add them at the very end.

5. Taste as you go along. Dip your spoon into the pot frequently. Rethink your ingredients and adjust the seasonings. It's only soup.

Puréed Vegetable Soup without Cream

MAKES: 4 servings
TIME: 45 minutes

Puréeing makes any vegetable soup velvety smooth and elegant. All sorts of vegetables can be used, but the best have some body, like winter squash or potatoes, and aren't overly fibrous (celery, for example, can be tough to purée without straining first).

You can use various tools to purée your soup; some yield smoother results than others. The smoothest purées are done in a blender, in the pot with an immersion blender, or with a food mill; a food processor or ricer does a good job but doesn't get the soup velvety smooth; and a potato masher or fork, of course, gives you the chunkiest results. After pureeing, passing the soup through a fine-meshed strainer, though laborious, will guarantee the ultimate in smoothness and is especially worthwhile if the vegetable is fibrous.

Other vegetables you can use: peeled and chopped winter squash, like butternut, pumpkin, or acorn; sweet potatoes; chopped cauliflower, broccoli, or sunchokes; green peas.

2 tablespoons butter

2 shallots or 1 small onion, chopped

1$^1/_2$ pounds carrots, sliced

6 cups chicken or vegetable stock (to make your own, see page 157) or water

Salt and freshly ground black pepper

2 tablespoons chopped fresh chervil or parsley for garnish

❶ Put the butter in a large, deep pot over medium-high heat. When the butter is melted, add the vegetables and cook until they start to soften, about 5 minutes.

❷ Add the stock and bring it to a boil. Lower the heat so that the stock bubbles gently and cook, stirring occasionally, until it thickens slightly and the vegetables become fully tender, 10 to 15 minutes more.

❸ Use an immersion blender to purée the soup in the pan or cool the mixture slightly, pour into a blender, and purée carefully. Cool and refrigerate, covered (it will keep for a day or so), to serve it cold. Or reheat over low heat to serve hot. Taste and adjust the seasoning. Serve garnished with chervil or parsley.

Puréed Turnip or Celery Root Soup. A bit of potato mellows out the flavor so it's not overpowering: Substitute 1 pound peeled and chopped turnips or celery root and 1 medium peeled and chopped potato for the carrots.

7 Terrific Combinations for Puréed Soups

Although a simple vegetable purée is delicious for its purity of flavor, there are plenty of tantalizing flavors to add to give the soup a bit of kick. Follow the recipe for Puréed Vegetable Soup Without Cream (page 125) with these combinations:

1. Puréed Broccoli-Basil Soup: Use chopped broccoli instead of the carrots. Add $1/2$ cup chopped fresh basil leaves when it's puréed. Garnish with a drizzle of good extra virgin olive oil and some shaved or grated Parmesan.

2. Puréed Butternut Squash–Coconut Soup: Use peeled and chopped butternut squash instead of carrots and substitute 2 cups coconut milk (to make your own, see page 389) for 2 cups of the stock. Add 2 tablespoons chopped garlic and $1 1/2$ tablespoons curry powder (to make your own, see pages 66–67) in Step 1. Garnish with fried sliced shallots or garlic and chopped fresh cilantro leaves.

3. Puréed Roasted Red Pepper Soup: Use 5 or 6 Roasted Red Peppers (page 330) and 1 large peeled and chopped potato for the carrots. Add 2 teaspoons smoked paprika and 1 tablespoon chopped garlic to Step 1. Garnish with chopped fresh parsley or cilantro.

4. Puréed Eggplant-Sesame Soup: Use the Puréed Eggplant Soup variation and add $1/4$ cup tahini when it's puréed. Garnish with a dollop of yogurt and chopped fresh cilantro or mint.

5. Puréed Sweet-and-Sour Beet Soup: Use 12 ounces trimmed, peeled, and chopped beets and 12 ounces peeled and chopped potato instead of the carrot. Add 3 tablespoons good red wine vinegar, or to taste, when it's puréed. Garnish with some crumbled goat cheese or a dollop of sour cream and chopped fresh chives.

6. Puréed Carrot-Ginger Soup: Add 1 tablespoon minced fresh ginger in Step 1. Season with soy sauce and dark sesame oil or drizzle a bit of cream or yogurt into each bowl before serving.

7. Puréed Cauliflower-Saffron Soup: Use chopped cauliflower instead of the carrot. Add $1/4$ teaspoon saffron threads to Step 1 and 1 cup cream when it's puréed. Garnish with chervil.

✪ Noodle Soup

MAKES: 4 servings
TIME: 30 minutes

Straight water really doesn't work in this soup, but water with a big splash of soy sauce works surprisingly well in the second variation or anytime you spin it with Asian flavors. For more ideas, see the variations and the following list.

8 ounces small pasta, like shells, pastini, orzo, or broken angel hair

1 tablespoon neutral oil, like grapeseed or corn

1 medium onion, halved and thinly sliced

1 carrot, diced

1 celery stalk, diced

6 cups chicken, beef, or vegetable stock (to make your own, see pages 157–159)

Salt and freshly ground black pepper

$1/4$ cup chopped fresh parsley leaves for garnish

Freshly grated Parmesan cheese for garnish (optional)

SUPER-EASY 3-INGREDIENT SOUPS

Many soups are little more than a couple of ingredients combined with water or stock; this chart demonstrates that beautifully and gives you options for making things a bit heartier and more flavorful.

Many of these soups have more complicated cousins in the surrounding pages, but for fast and easy planning, start here.

SOUP	1	2	3	OPTIONAL ADD-INS
Miso Soup	4 cups Dashi (page 160) or water, hot but not boiling	$1/3$ cup any miso	$1/4$ cup chopped scallion	4 ounces diced soft or silken tofu; 1 cup reconstituted wakame or other sea greens (see page 348); 1 cup cooked and chopped greens, like collards or spinach; or 1 cup sliced fresh or dried (and reconstituted; see page 314) shiitake mushroom caps
Egg Drop Soup	4 cups any stock at a slow bubble	4 beaten eggs, slowly poured in while stirring so the eggs "scramble" in the stock	$1/4$ cup chopped cilantro or scallion	1 tablespoon soy sauce, or more to taste; 1 tablespoon dark sesame oil; or 1 cup freshly grated Parmesan cheese (omit the soy sauce and cilantro)
Poached Eggs and Greens Soup	4 cups any stock at a slow bubble	4 eggs, cracked and ladled into the stock (see Poached Eggs, page 793)	2 cups tender spinach or arugula or 1 cup cooked chopped kale, collards, or other greens	3 cloves garlic, smashed; grated Parmesan and hot red pepper flakes to taste; or 1 tablespoon each dark sesame oil and soy sauce, to taste
Wonton Soup	4 cups any stock, boiling	12 to 24 wontons or gyoza (to make your own, see page 102) cooked in the stock	$1/4$ cup chopped cilantro or scallion	1 tablespoon soy sauce, or more to taste; 1 cup sliced carrot; 2 cups sliced tender spinach, cabbage, or bok choy; or 1 cup sliced fresh or dried (and reconstituted; see page 314) shiitake mushroom caps
Shrimp and Tomato Soup	4 cups any stock, boiling	$1/2$ pound large (21–30) shrimp, peeled	2 cups chopped tomato	Fish sauce and freshly squeezed lime juice to taste; or $1/2$ cup chopped fresh basil and Garlic Croutons (page 877)
Chicken Noodle Soup	4 cups chicken stock (to make your own, see page 157)	2 cups or more cooked egg noodles	2 cups or more shredded or diced cooked chicken meat	$1/2$ cup each diced or sliced carrot, celery, and onion; 1 cup peas; $1/4$ cup chopped fresh dill, parsley, or cilantro
Beef and Barley Soup	4 cups beef or veal stock (to make your own, see page 158)	2 cups or more cooked barley	2 cups or more shredded or diced cooked beef	1 cup chopped tomato; 1 cup diced potato, carrot, or parsnip; Worcestershire sauce, to taste; or 1 tablespoon chopped garlic

1 Bring a large pot of water to a boil and salt it. Add the pasta and cook it until it's just about done—there should still be a light chew to it. Drain it and rinse in cold water until cool; set aside. (If you're cooking the pasta in advance by more than 30 minutes, hold the pasta in a bowl of cold water or toss with a couple tablespoons neutral oil.)

2 Put the oil in a deep saucepan or casserole over medium-high heat. When hot, add the onion, carrot, and celery and cook until the onion is translucent, about 5 minutes. Add the stock, sprinkle with salt and pepper, and bring to a boil.

3 Stir in the cooked pasta and heat until the pasta is hot and cooked through. Taste and adjust the seasoning. Garnish with the parsley and the Parmesan if you're using it and serve.

Chicken Noodle Soup. In Step 2, add $^1/_2$ to $^3/_4$ pound cut-up boneless chicken meat (thighs are the most flavorful) to the pan before adding the stock; then proceed, simmering until just cooked through. Or add $^1/_2$ pound cooked and cut-up boneless chicken meat in Step 3 when you add the pasta.

Pasta and Pesto Soup. Skip the onion, carrot, and celery if you want. Stir in $^1/_2$ cup Traditional Pesto (page 27) just after the pasta.

Pasta and Chickpea Soup. Add 1 tablespoon chopped garlic, 2 teaspoons cumin seeds or 1 tablespoon chopped fresh rosemary (or 1 teaspoon dried), and about 2 cups drained cooked or canned chickpeas. Add the garlic and cumin, if you're using it, in the last minute of cooking the onion; add the chickpeas and rosemary, if you're using it, with the stock. Garnish with fresh cilantro (if you used cumin) or parsley (if you used rosemary).

Fusilli and Roasted Garlic Soup. Use fusilli or really any pasta. Add a head of Roasted Garlic (page 303) and remove the garlic cloves from the skins; mash them into a paste with the side of a wide knife blade or using a fork. Add to the onion mixture and stir just before adding the stock.

Orzo and Fresh Herb Soup. Use orzo or similar pasta. Add $^1/_2$ cup each finely chopped fresh parsley, cilantro, chives, and mint leaves; stir in just before serving, along with 1 cup yogurt if you like.

Chinese Noodle Soup with Cabbage and Ginger. Use fresh or dried thin Chinese egg noodles. Add 1 tablespoon each minced fresh ginger and garlic and 3 cups each chopped or shredded Napa or green cabbage and bok choy; cook in the oil. Garnish with chopped scallion.

12 Simple Additions to Noodle Soup

Add any of these to your noodle soup for extra flavor and texture. Keep in mind that you still want the noodles to be the main event, so limit additions to 2 cups or so. Also, add the ingredients according to how long they take to cook: Hard vegetables like winter squash, fennel, and tough collards or kale will take longer than tender or soft vegetables, like spinach, peas, or bean sprouts.

1. Shredded cooked chicken, pork, or beef
2. Shrimp, squid, scallops, clams, or mussels
3. Tofu, cubed, or cooked just about any way (see pages 443–448)
4. Sliced or chopped fennel
5. Shredded cabbage or bok choy
6. Sliced or chopped spinach, kale, collard, or other greens
7. Diced summer or peeled button squash
8. Sliced shiitake, cremini, or button mushrooms
9. Chopped tomato
10. Snow, snap, or green peas
11. Bean sprouts
12. Chopped scallion

Chicken Soup, Many Ways

MAKES: 4 servings
TIME: 30 minutes

F **M**

This not-too-thick soup makes a warming but not super-filling first course, with the rice, meat, and vegetables

 Fast   Make Ahead   Vegetarian

supporting actors rather than major players. For Chicken Noodle Soup, see the preceding recipe.

> 6 cups chicken stock (to make your own, see page 157)
>
> $^1/_2$ cup white rice
>
> 1 carrot, thinly sliced
>
> 1 celery stalk, thinly sliced
>
> 1 cup raw or cooked chopped boneless, skinless chicken, or more
>
> Salt and freshly ground black pepper
>
> Chopped fresh parsley, dill, or cilantro leaves for garnish

❶ Put the stock in a large, deep pot over medium-high heat. When it is just about boiling, turn the heat down so that it bubbles, but not too vigorously. Stir in the rice, carrot, and celery and cook, stirring occasionally, until they are all tender, about 20 minutes.

❷ Stir in the chicken. If it is raw, cook until it is cooked through, another 5 to 8 minutes. If it is cooked, cook 2 or 3 minutes, until it is hot. Taste and adjust the seasoning. Garnish with the herbs and serve.

Chicken Soup with Vegetables. Omit the rice, if you like, and add up to $1^1/_2$ cups mixed $^1/_4$-inch diced vegetables, like carrots, celery, onion, turnip, parsnip, zucchini or yellow squash, or potato; sliced mushrooms; peas or corn kernels; thinly shredded cabbage, bok choy, or greens. Add the vegetables to the stock by cooking times, starting with the harder, longer-cooking vegetables like carrots or potato.

Chicken Soup with Rice, Mexican Style. Omit the carrot and celery, if you like. Add 1 cup diced tomatoes along with the chicken. Then add $^1/_2$ cup minced raw white onion, $^1/_4$ cup freshly squeezed lime juice, or to taste, $^1/_2$ cup roughly chopped cilantro, or more to taste, and minced fresh jalapeños or other chiles to taste (optional) just before serving. Taste and adjust the seasoning.

Chicken Soup with Rice, Chinese Style. Add 1 teaspoon each minced fresh ginger and garlic with the chicken.

A cup or so green peas (frozen are fine; add at the last minute) or chopped mushrooms are a nice addition (added during the last few minutes of cooking). Season with a couple tablespoons soy sauce and a lot of black pepper and stir in 2 teaspoons dark sesame oil if you like.

Chipotle Chicken Soup. Add 4 to 6 dried chipotle chiles, 2 cloves garlic, 2 tablespoons tomato paste, and 1 teaspoon dried oregano. Soak the chiles in just-boiled water to cover until soft, about 20 minutes; drain and use a knife to slice open and scrape out all the seeds and remove the stems. Put the chiles, garlic, tomato paste, and oregano in a blender or food processor and purée; add only enough chicken stock from the soup to get the purée going. Add the chipotle paste to taste to the soup or pass it with the soup servings.

9 Simple Additions to Chicken Soup

When it comes to chicken soup, the question is not "What can you add?" but "What can't you add?" Here are some ideas:

1. Fresh herbs, especially dill, parsley, or chervil, but almost anything else, including tender sprigs of watercress or arugula, added at the last minute
2. Spices, especially ginger, chiles, garlic, or other strong spices, added with the rice
3. Any croutons (see page 877) for garnish
4. Any cooked grain, like rice (white, brown, or wild), wheat berries, barley, quinoa, or others
5. Leftover chicken, grilled fresh chicken, small cubes of raw boneless chicken (which will cook in 2 minutes), or any other poultry, added when described in Step 2
6. Small pieces of rind from Parmesan cheese (along with the stock) or grated cheese for garnish
7. Precooked vegetables of any type, as long as the flavor does not conflict with that of the soup; onions, carrots, and celery are almost always appropriate, added at the last minute and just warmed through
8. Cooked tortellini or other small stuffed pasta, added at the last minute and just warmed through
9. Poached Eggs (page 793); after dividing into bowls

⭐ Essential Recipe

Vegetable Soups

This huge category includes soups that are completely vegetarian by nature and those that do not suffer by being made with water instead of stock. (Many of them contain meat or meat stocks as optional ingredients, and some contain dairy, but most can be made vegetarian or even vegan with little trouble.)

Cream of Mushroom (or Any Vegetable) Soup

MAKES: 4 servings
TIME: 30 minutes

There are thousands of recipes for true cream of vegetable soup, but the differences among them are small. Basically, you cook the vegetable you want with good flavorings until it's done. Then you purée it and reheat it with cream.

The addition of rice or potato makes soup thick and creamy, but if you prefer a thinner consistency, skip these. Even $1/4$ cup of cream is enough to lighten the color and smooth the texture; a full cup lends an incomparable richness. (You can replace cream with milk or yogurt, but it won't be the same.) To intensify the mushroom flavor, add $1/2$ cup or so of reconstituted porcini mushrooms, along with their soaking water.

> About 1 pound button mushrooms, trimmed and chopped
>
> $1/2$ cup white rice or 1 medium baking potato, peeled and cut into quarters
>
> 4 cups chicken, beef, or vegetable stock (to make your own, see pages 157–159) or water
>
> Salt and freshly ground black pepper
>
> $1/4$ to 1 cup cream or half-and-half
>
> Chopped fresh parsley leaves or chives for garnish

1 Combine the mushrooms, rice, and stock in a large, deep pot over medium-high heat. Bring to a boil, then lower the heat to medium and cook until the vegetables are very tender, about 15 minutes.

2 Cool slightly, then purée through a food mill or in a blender. (At this point, you may refrigerate the soup, covered, for up to 2 days; reheat before proceeding.)

3 Return the soup to the pot and reheat over medium-low heat. Sprinkle with salt and pepper, then add the cream. Heat through again, garnish, and serve.

Cream of Asparagus Soup. Nice and light without the rice or potato: Substitute asparagus, trimmed and stalks peeled, for the mushrooms. Omit the rice or potato or reduce the amount by half. Use vegetable stock or water. Strain the soup after puréeing if the texture isn't completely smooth.

Cream of Fennel or Celery Soup. Substitute fennel or celery, trimmed and chopped, for the mushrooms and start with a light stock. Strain after puréeing.

Cream of Watercress, Spinach, or Sorrel Soup. Substitute 4 cups chopped watercress, spinach, or sorrel, well washed and trimmed of thick stems, for the mushrooms and 2 cups cream for half the stock. Omit the rice or potatoes if you like. Cook just until the greens are tender.

Cream of Cauliflower or Broccoli Soup. Substitute 4 cups cauliflower or broccoli florets for the mushrooms and up to 2 cups cream for the same amount of stock if you like.

Tomato Soup

MAKES: 4 servings
TIME: 30 minutes

Most tomato soups are simply not tomatoey enough. One solution is tomato paste; it adds the depth that even good fresh tomatoes sometimes lack. If good tomatoes aren't around—about nine months of the year—use good-quality canned tomatoes.

2 tablespoons extra virgin olive oil

2 tablespoons tomato paste

1 large onion, sliced

1 carrot, diced

Salt and freshly ground black pepper

3 cups peeled, seeded, and chopped tomato (canned is fine; include the juices)

1 teaspoon fresh thyme leaves or ¹/₂ teaspoon dried thyme or 1 tablespoon chopped fresh basil leaves

2 to 3 cups chicken, beef, or vegetable stock (to make your own, see pages 157–159) or water

1 teaspoon sugar (optional)

Chopped fresh parsley or basil leaves for garnish (optional)

1 Put the oil in a large, deep pot over medium heat. When hot, add the tomato paste and let it cook for a minute, then add the onion and carrot. Sprinkle with salt and pepper and cook, stirring, until the onion begins to soften, about 5 minutes.

2 Add the tomato and the herb and cook, stirring occasionally, until the tomato breaks up, 10 to 15 minutes. Add the stock, stir, and cook until hot, then adjust the heat and simmer until the flavors meld, about 5 minutes. (At this point, you may refrigerate the soup, covered, for up to 2 days; reheat before proceeding.) Taste and adjust the seasoning; if the soup tastes flat, stir in the sugar. If the mixture is too thick, add a little more stock or water. Garnish with the herbs and serve.

Puréed Tomato Soup. Increase the tomato to 4 cups and reduce the stock to 1 cup. When the soup is done, purée it carefully in a blender, with an immersion blender, or through a food mill. Reheat, garnish, and serve, preferably with Real Croutons (page 877).

Cream of Tomato Soup. Substitute butter for the olive oil and use the proportions in the preceding variation, substituting 1 cup cream or half-and-half for the stock, added just before puréeing.

Wintertime Tomato Soup. Substitute 1 cup (loosely packed; about 2 ounces) dried tomatoes (preferably the kind not packed in oil) and 1 large can (28 ounces) whole peeled tomatoes for the fresh tomatoes. Soak the dried tomatoes in 1 cup boiling water until softened. Remove the canned tomatoes from their juice and chop them. Add the reserved tomato juice with the tomato paste and cook until reduced by half, stirring frequently. Proceed with the recipe, adding the dried tomato water along with the stock.

Tomato and Bread Soup. Brush both sides of 4 thick slices Italian or French bread (slightly stale is fine) with extra virgin olive oil; broil or grill until nicely browned and crisp. Rub a large clove garlic on each slice of bread if you like. Break or cut the bread into pieces and pour the finished soup over the top. Garnish with freshly grated Parmesan.

Tomato-Garlic Soup. Add 2 tablespoons chopped garlic along with the onion or 8 to 10 cloves Roasted Garlic (page 303).

Potato and Leek Soup

MAKES: 4 servings
TIME: 30 minutes

  Ⓥ

Here's the simplest potato and leek soup, a recipe that strikes me as medieval. It can warm you on a cold winter day or—if you make it in advance—cool you down in the middle of summer. Use a large sliced onion if you don't have leeks or if you want potato soup.

2 tablespoons butter or extra virgin olive oil

3 medium potatoes, any type, peeled and cut into small cubes

3 leeks, white and light green parts only, washed and sliced into thin rings

Salt and freshly ground black pepper

4 cups chicken, beef or vegetable stock (to make your own, see pages 157–159) or water

① Put the butter or oil in a large, deep pot over medium heat. When the butter melts or the oil is hot, add the vegetables. Sprinkle with salt and pepper and cook, stirring, until starting to soften, 2 or 3 minutes.

② Add the stock, adjust the heat so it gently bubbles, and cook until the vegetables are very tender, about 20 minutes. (At this point, you may refrigerate the soup, covered, for up to 2 days; reheat before proceeding.) Taste and adjust the seasoning and serve.

Puréed Potato and Leek Soup. Carefully purée the above soup in a blender or with an immersion blender, then return it to the pot you cooked in. Stir

Giving Soups More Body

A soup doesn't have to be thick to be good; I'd rather eat a bowl of fresh-tasting soup than one thickened gratuitously with flour or cornstarch. But for those times when you want something a little heartier and maybe even more luxurious, here are the basic rules for making a good soup thicker:

Potato: The starch in an all-purpose or russet ("baking") potato adds heft and a little flavor. (Waxy potatoes, like "new" potatoes, don't break down in the same way.) If you're going to purée the soup after cooking, just peel and dice a potato and add it at the same time as the stock or water. To thicken a chunky bean or vegetable soup, mash cooked potatoes a bit with a fork first (a spoonful or two of leftover mashed potatoes will do the trick). A few minutes before serving, stir them into the pot until completely dissolved and heat through.

Pasta: Cooking small amounts of noodles in soup releases thickening starches. Be sure you have a little extra liquid and room in the pot to accommodate the noodles as they swell and serve the soup immediately: All noodles have a short window of time before they turn to mush.

Grains: Adding a scoop of cooked grains to nearly finished soup thickens slightly and adds heft, but if you want to increase body and richness, add a small quantity of grain at the beginning of the recipe; cook until it's falling apart, then purée.

Legumes: Beans are among the most flavorful soup thickeners. White beans are the most versatile, lending a creaminess rivaled only by butter or cream, especially when puréed. Like grains, cooked legumes can be added to already-made soups as an afterthought or cooked along with the other ingredients until tender, then puréed or mashed.

Bread: If possible, use stale bread, which absorbs broth without disintegrating. Croutons are the most obvious way to enhance soup with bread, but bread crumbs work well, too. And few things are simpler or more satisfying than slipping a piece of good toast into a bowl and pouring a ladleful of soup over it.

Butter: For unsurpassed velvety texture and heightened flavor, cut up a tablespoon or two of cold butter. When the soup is ready to serve, turn off the heat, add to the pot, and stir until melted.

Dairy and Nondairy Creams and Milks: All of these—cream, half-and-half, sour cream, milk, yogurt, Mexican crema, crème fraîche, as well as nondairy milks, like coconut and soy—have some thickening power, though most separate when boiled. Cream is the most stable, but all work well added to puréed soups, where they easily combine with other ingredients.

Eggs: A convenient way to add both creaminess and richness to soup. You have two choices: Stir beaten eggs into simmering stock or soup and you'll get egg drop soup. The eggs scramble softly and remain visible, adding a distinct meatiness to many soups, especially brothy ones. Or use eggs strictly as a thickener: First beat a couple of yolks, then whisk about a cup of the hot soup into the yolks, then gradually stir the yolk mixture back into the soup. Treated this way, the eggs add body to the soup with a smooth texture.

 F Fast   **M** Make Ahead   **V** Vegetarian

in $1/2$ to 1 cup cream, sour cream, or yogurt and reheat gently; do not let it boil if you use yogurt. Add more salt and pepper as needed, garnish with minced chives, and serve.

Vichyssoise. Make the preceding variation, but do not reheat. Instead, chill thoroughly and serve garnished with minced chives.

Cabbage-and-Something Soup, Three Ways

MAKES: 4 servings

TIME: 40 minutes

A perfectly light first-course soup in three guises, much different from most heavy cabbage soups.

1 tablespoon extra virgin olive oil

3 tablespoons butter

1 large onion, sliced

1 small head cabbage, just over a pound, preferably Savoy, cored and shredded

10 sprigs fresh thyme

Salt and freshly ground black pepper

6 cups beef, chicken, or vegetable stock (to make your own, see pages 157–159) or water

3 Golden Delicious or other good apples, peeled and cubed, for garnish

❶ Combine the oil and 1 tablespoon of the butter in a large, deep pot over medium-high heat. When the butter melts, add the onion and cabbage and cook, stirring occasionally, until the onions and cabbage wilt and begin to brown, about 3 minutes. Add 8 of the thyme sprigs and cook for a few minutes more. Sprinkle with salt and pepper.

❷ Add the stock and lower the heat to medium; stir occasionally as it heats. Put the remaining 2 tablespoons butter in a skillet over medium-high heat. When the butter foam subsides, add the apple pieces; cook, stirring occa-

sionally, until they brown and become tender, about 10 minutes. Strip the leaves from the remaining thyme sprigs and sprinkle them over the apples along with a bit of salt.

❸ Taste the soup and adjust the seasoning; remove the thyme sprigs. Serve the soup hot, garnished with the apple.

Cabbage Soup with Potatoes and Caraway. Substitute 2 thick slices bacon, diced, for the olive oil, if you like,

Not all vegetable soups can be treated the same; I would not, for example, add croutons to miso soup. Having said that, as long as you exercise good judgment, this is a useful list:

1. Real Croutons (page 877)
2. Grains—rice (white, brown, or wild), wheat berries, barley, or quinoa—cooked in the soup or left over (rinse first to remove unwanted seasonings)
3. Any vegetable that will not greatly change the character of the soup
4. Small pieces of rind from Parmesan cheese or some grated cheese
5. Leftover bits of meat
6. Freshly chopped herbs or quick-cooking greens
7. Any spice you like, from jalapeños or other chiles to lots of black pepper to curry powder or other spice mixtures (to make your own, see pages 65–69), added to the oil and aromatics about a minute before adding the other ingredients and liquid
8. A drizzle of extra virgin olive oil (or, for soups with Asian seasonings, dark sesame oil)
9. A swirl of Traditional Pesto (page 27), especially in Italian soups, or any of the herb pastes or flavored oils you'll find in the same chapter
10. Cooked aromatics, like Roasted Garlic (page 303), Caramelized Onions (page 325), or Leeks Braised in Oil or Butter (page 311)

and 1 tablespoon caraway seeds, lightly crushed, for the thyme. Add 2 medium potatoes, peeled and cut into 1/2-inch dice. Omit the apples. In Step 1, cook the bacon, then the onions and cabbage in its fat, or use the olive oil as directed. Add the potatoes with the stock and cook until the potatoes are very tender. Proceed with the recipe.

Cabbage Soup with Mushrooms and Ginger. Substitute dark sesame oil for the olive oil, peanut or other neutral oil (like grapeseed or corn), for the butter, and 2 tablespoons minced fresh ginger for the thyme. Instead of the apples use 2 cups sliced shiitake mushroom caps (stems discarded or reserved for stock) or button mushrooms. In Step 1, use 2 tablespoons of the peanut oil for the onion and cabbage; add the ginger when you would the thyme. Sauté the mushrooms in the remaining oils for garnish.

Onion Soup

MAKES: 4 servings

TIME: About 1 hour

Many American "French" restaurants seem to believe that onion soup should look like pizza, gobbed with cheese. The real thing—and this is it—is something else entirely: robust, flavorful, and elegant. This is as compelling a reason as there is to make your own beef stock.

4 tablespoons (1/2 stick) butter

4 large onions, thinly sliced (about 6 cups)

5 cups beef, chicken, or vegetable stock (to make your own, see pages 157–159) or water

2 or 3 sprigs fresh thyme or a pinch dried thyme

2 or 3 sprigs fresh parsley

1 bay leaf

Salt and freshly ground black pepper

2 tablespoons cognac or other brandy (optional)

4 Real Croutons (page 877), made with bread slices and butter (optional)

1 cup freshly grated Parmesan, Gruyère, or Emmental cheese (optional)

 Put the butter in a large, deep pot over medium heat. When melted, add the onions and cook, stirring occasionally, until very soft and beginning to brown, 30 to 45 minutes. Adjust the heat so they do not brown too fast but slowly turn into a melting mass. Don't rush.

 Heat the oven to 400°F if you're using the croutons and cheese. Add the stock, raise the heat to medium-high, and bring just about to a boil. Lower the heat so the mixture sends up a few bubbles at a time. Add the herbs, some salt and pepper, and the cognac and cook for 15 minutes. Fish out the bay leaf and herb sprigs. (At this point, you may refrigerate the soup, covered, for up to 2 days; reheat before proceeding.)

❸ If you're using the croutons and cheese, put a crouton in each of 4 ovenproof bowls. Add a portion of soup and top with cheese. Put the bowls in a roasting pan or on a sturdy cookie sheet and bake for 5 to 10 minutes, just long enough to melt the cheese. Serve immediately.

Corn Chowder

MAKES: 4 servings

TIME: About 1 hour

This chowder celebrates the bounty of a single summertime crop: corn. And since you will probably make it only once or twice a year, I would opt for the richer, half-and-half option, though the leaner version has a purity of flavor I also love.

6 ears fresh corn

Salt and freshly ground black pepper

4 tablespoons butter or neutral oil, like grapeseed or corn

1/2 cup chopped scallion

1/2 teaspoon sugar

$^1/_4$ cup all-purpose flour

4 cups milk or half-and-half

Corn Bread Croutons (page 877) for garnish (optional)

1 Shuck the corn. Stand each ear up in a bowl and use a knife to scrape off the kernels (see page 288). Put the corncobs and 2 cups water in a large pot with a tight-fitting lid over medium-high heat. Sprinkle with salt and pepper. Bring to a boil, then lower the heat so the water bubbles gently, cover, and cook, checking occasionally, for about 30 minutes. Leave the cobs in the pot until you are ready to make the soup, then discard them and save the corncob broth.

2 Put the butter or oil in a large, deep pot over medium-high heat. When the butter is melted or the oil is hot, add the scallion and sugar and cook, stirring occasionally, until soft, about 1 minute. Lower the heat to medium and stir in the flour. Cook, stirring constantly with a whisk or a wooden spoon, until the mixture starts to turn golden and the flour no longer smells raw, just a couple of minutes. Add the milk and the reserved corncob broth and raise the heat to medium-high. Stir or whisk constantly until the flour is dissolved and the soup starts to thicken, about 2 minutes.

3 Stir in the corn kernels and bring to a boil, then lower the heat so that the soup bubbles gently. Cook, stirring occasionally, until the corn is tender and the soup has thickened, 10 to 15 minutes. Taste, adjust the seasoning, garnish with croutons if you like, and serve.

Thicker Corn Chowder. Peel 1 large baking potato and cut into $^1/_2$-inch dice. Add the potato to the pot along with the corn in Step 3. After bringing the soup to a boil, cook covered instead of uncovered, stirring occasionally.

Roasted Corn Chowder. Heat the oven to 400°F. Rub the shucked corn with a little extra virgin olive oil. Sprinkle with salt and pepper and put on a rimmed baking sheet. Roast the corn, turning frequently, until the kernels start to brown, 15 to 25 minutes. When the corn is cool enough to handle, scrape off the kernels and proceed with the recipe.

Frozen Vegetables in Soup

There are frozen vegetables I would almost never eat solo or as the main ingredient in a dish—broccoli or spinach, for example—that can work quite well in soups. Others, like corn and peas, are soup staples. Stock a few bags in your freezer, complement them with fresh vegetables if possible, and you can put together something brilliant with little time and effort.

The rules for buying frozen vegetables in general are described on page 236. There are two good ways to use them in soup. If you're in a hurry, just dump 'em in, straight from the bag. Just remember this will cool off your soup fast, so it's going to take longer to cook.

The second method—and it's better if you have the time—is to brown the vegetables lightly in oil to defrost them. This will add flavor to both the vegetable and the broth.

Cheesy Corn Chowder. Prepare either the main soup or one of the variations through Step 2. In Step 3, along with the corn, add $^1/_2$ cup grated cheese, like Parmesan, sharp cheddar, or hard goat cheese.

Bean Soups

If there was ever a category of soups that can be made successfully from water and one other ingredient, this is it. Legumes work as a thickener, add distinct textures and tastes, and are filling. Some soups call for cooking raw beans in the soup pot, so their broth is integral to the soup; this is the most nutritious and flavorful option. Other recipes add already-cooked beans. Most recipes and variations explain how to make the soup using either method.

I'm not a fan of super-thick bean soups, in which the texture overrides the flavor and of which a cup leaves you too full for the rest of your meal. But if it's thick soup you're after, either decrease the amount of stock or water in these recipes by $1/2$ cup or so or toss in another handful or two of beans.

Basic Bean Soup

MAKES: 4 servings

TIME: 1 to 2 hours, depending on the bean

You can make any legume a soup with this recipe. Some will take longer to cook than others (and will need more stock or water), but the recipe is universal.

$1^1/2$ cups dried beans, washed, picked over, and soaked if time allows (see page 411)

6 cups vegetable, chicken, or beef stock (to make your own, see pages 157–159) or water, or more as needed

1 medium onion, chopped

1 medium to large carrot, chopped

1 celery stalk, chopped

2 bay leaves

1 teaspoon fresh thyme leaves or pinch dried thyme

Salt and freshly ground black pepper

Chopped fresh parsley leaves for garnish (optional)

1 Drain the beans if you've soaked them, then put them in a large, deep pot over medium-high heat. Add the stock, onion, carrot, celery, bay leaves, and thyme. Bring to a boil, then turn the heat down so the mixture simmers steadily. Cook, stirring occasionally, until the beans are very soft, at least 1 hour; add more liquid as necessary so the mixture remains soupy.

2 When the beans are very tender, season to taste with salt and pepper. If you like, you can purée the soup with an immersion blender or in a blender. (At this point, you may refrigerate the soup, covered, for up to 2 days; reheat before proceeding.) Serve, garnished with the parsley.

10 Ideas for Bean Soup

As good as basic bean soup is, it can be made gloriously delicious with a few simple additions. Try any of these, alone or in combination:

1. About $1/4$ cup tomato paste or a cup or two of canned (or, of course, fresh) tomatoes, added at the beginning of cooking

2. 1 or 2 mild chiles, like anchos, stemmed and seeded, added at the beginning of cooking

3. A ham bone or 2 or 3 ham hocks or about $1/4$ pound chopped bacon or pancetta, added at the beginning of cooking

4. 1 to 2 cups chopped fresh vegetables—carrots, celery, potatoes, shallots, turnips, whatever you like—added about 20 minutes before the end of cooking

5. Any whole grain, like brown rice, barley, or peeled wheat ($1/2$ cup or so, with the beans reduced by the same amount) added at the beginning of cooking; or quick-cooking grains, like white rice, pearled barley, or bulgur, added during the last 15 to 20 minutes of cooking

6. At least 1 teaspoon minced garlic, added about 5 minutes before the end of cooking

7. Chopped greens, like kale or collards (1 to 2 cups), added during the last 5 minutes of cooking

8. About 2 tablespoons butter, stirred in at the end of cooking

9. Extra virgin olive oil, about 1 tablespoon per serving, added at the last minute

10. 4 to 8 Garlic Croutons (page 877), 1 or 2 added to the bottom of each soup bowl before serving

White Bean and Collard Green Soup

MAKES: 8 or more servings

TIME: At least $1^1/2$ hours

Smoky, hammy, and rich: Soup doesn't get much better than this. An ideal place for roasted stock (see "How to Make Any Stock Darker and Richer," page 158).

 Fast   Make Ahead   Vegetarian

Other beans you can use in this recipe: split peas, black-eyed peas, pinto or any pink bean, or black beans.

3 cups any dried white beans, washed, picked over, and soaked if time allows (see page 411)

1 ham bone or 2 or 3 smoked ham hocks

12 cups chicken, beef, or vegetable stock (to make your own, see pages 157–159) or water

2 medium onions, chopped

Salt and freshly ground black pepper

1 1/2 pounds collard greens or kale, thick stems removed, washed, and chopped

2 tablespoons chopped garlic (optional)

❶ Drain the beans if you soaked them, then put them in a large, deep pot over medium-high heat. Add the ham bone, stock, and onions. Bring to a boil, then lower the heat so the mixture bubbles steadily and cover partially. Cook, stirring occasionally, until the beans are very soft and any meat is falling off the bone, at least 1 hour; add more liquid as necessary so the mixture remains soupy.

❷ Turn off the heat; remove the bone from the pot and let cool slightly. Take all the meat off the bone, chop it, and set it aside. Mash or purée the beans, then return them to the pot along with the ham; reheat over medium heat until almost boiling.

❸ Add the collards, along with the garlic if you're using it, and cook until the greens are tender, about 10 minutes. Taste, adjust the seasoning, and serve.

White Bean and Mushroom Soup. Omit the ham, if you like. Substitute trimmed and sliced mushrooms for the collards.

Smoky Black Bean Soup

MAKES: 4 servings

TIME: 30 minutes with cooked beans

  Ⓥ

This works best when you purée some of the sturdy black beans and stir them back in for a smooth-chunky effect.

But in many Latin American versions, the beans are left whole, with chunks of sweet potato, squash, or even mango added toward the end of cooking.

2 tablespoons neutral oil, like grapeseed or corn

1 large or 2 medium onions, chopped

1 tablespoon minced garlic

1 tablespoon chili powder (to make your own, see page 66)

1 chipotle chile, dried or canned in adobo (if using canned, use just a little bit of the adobo)

3 cups cooked black beans, drained

4 cups vegetable, chicken, or beef stock (to make your own, see pages 157–159) or water

Salt and freshly ground black pepper

2 teaspoons freshly squeezed lime juice, or to taste

Sour cream or yogurt for garnish

Chopped fresh cilantro leaves for garnish

❶ Put the oil in a large, deep pot over medium heat. When hot, add the onions and cook, stirring, until softened, about 5 minutes. Stir in the garlic and chili powder and cook, stirring, for another minute.

❷ Add the chipotle chile, beans, stock, and some salt and pepper. Raise the heat to medium-high and bring the soup to a boil, then lower the heat to medium-low and cook, stirring occasionally, for about 10 minutes. Turn off the heat.

❸ Purée some of the soup with an immersion blender or in a blender. (At this point, you may cool and refrigerate the soup, covered, for up to 2 days; reheat gently before proceeding.)

❹ Add the lime juice and stir; taste and adjust the seasoning. Serve, garnished with the sour cream and cilantro.

Black Bean and Beer Soup. Substitute 2 teaspoons ground cumin for the chili powder and 1 bottle or can beer for a cup of the stock or water. Omit the chipotles and sour cream. Add 1 cup grated cheddar or Jack cheese if you like.

Simplest Split Pea Soup

MAKES: 4 servings

TIME: About 1½ hours

Pea soup requires split peas and water (or stock, of course). Everything else is a luxury. Some of those luxuries are detailed in "10 Ideas for Bean Soup, page 136," but you can combine them as you like.

Split peas fall apart quickly, and it's easy to inadvertently make this soup too thick, so watch it (you can always stir in more water to thin it out).

> 2 cups green split peas, washed and picked over
>
> 6 cups chicken, beef, or vegetable stock (to make your own, see pages 157–159) or water
>
> Salt and freshly ground black pepper
>
> Real or Cubed Croutons (page 877) for garnish (optional)

❶ Put the split peas and the stock in a large, deep pot over medium-high heat. Bring to a boil, then turn the heat to low, cover partially, and cook, stirring occasionally, until the peas are very soft, 45 to 60 minutes.

❷ Mash the mixture with a fork or potato masher. (For an ultra-smooth soup, purée with an immersion blender or in a blender.) Reheat the soup, adding more stock or water if it's too thick. Taste, add salt and pepper, and serve, garnished with croutons if you like.

Red Lentil Soup with Curried Drizzle. Use red lentils (or yellow split peas) instead of the green split peas. Replace up to 2 cups of the liquid with coconut milk if you like (to make your own, see page 389). While the soup is cooking, heat 4 tablespoons butter or neutral oil, like grapeseed or corn, over low heat. Stir in 2 tablespoons Fragrant Curry Powder (to make your own, see page 67) and a pinch of salt; keep stirring until it darkens and becomes, well, fragrant. Keep warm. Serve with a spoonful of the flavored butter or oil drizzled on top of each bowl.

Lentil Soup, Seven Ways

MAKES: 4 servings

TIME: About 45 minutes

Lentils make soup making easy—they cook quickly and are incredibly tasty. And unlike many lentil soups, which are so thick they put people off completely, this one is nicely balanced with some simple vegetables. The lentils break down a bit during the cooking to give the soup a hearty consistency, but you can purée it if you prefer.

> 2 tablespoons extra virgin olive oil
>
> 1 onion, chopped
>
> 1 carrot, cut into ½-inch dice
>
> 1 celery stalk, cut into ½-inch dice
>
> 1 cup lentils, washed and picked over
>
> 1 bay leaf
>
> 6 cups chicken, beef, or vegetable stock (to make your own, see pages 157–159) or water
>
> Freshly ground black pepper
>
> Salt

❶ Put the oil in a large, deep pot over medium heat. When hot, add the onion and cook, stirring frequently, until soft, just a minute or two. Add the carrot and celery and keep cooking and stirring until brightly colored and hot, about 2 minutes.

❷ Add the lentils, bay leaf, and stock; sprinkle with freshly ground black pepper. Bring to a boil, then turn the heat to low and cook, stirring occasionally, until the lentils are tender, about 30 minutes. (At this point, you may cool and refrigerate the soup, covered, for up to 2 days; reheat gently.) Add more stock if the soup is too thick. Just before serving, taste, sprinkle with salt and more pepper if needed, and serve.

Lentil Soup with Lemon and Dill. About a minute before serving, stir in 3 tablespoons freshly squeezed lemon juice and ½ cup chopped fresh dill, or to taste.

 Fast   Make Ahead   Ⓥ Vegetarian

Lentil Soup with Cumin. Add $1\frac{1}{2}$ teaspoons ground cumin along with the bay leaf. Add a squeeze of lime or orange juice, if you like, and garnish with a dollop of yogurt and chopped fresh cilantro.

Lentil Soup with Smoked Paprika. Add 1 teaspoon smoked paprika along with the bay leaf. Garnish with chopped fresh parsley or chives if you like.

Lentil Soup with Sausage or Bacon. Start with about $\frac{1}{4}$ pound chopped sausage, bacon, or pancetta and cook it in the soup pot until slightly crisp before adding the other ingredients in Step 1. Drain the fat if you like or use it and omit the olive oil.

Lentil Soup with Roasted Garlic. Omit the onion, carrot, and celery. Prepare and peel 1 or 2 heads of Roasted Garlic (page 303). In Step 1, cook the garlic in the olive oil for a minute or two, mashing and stirring until fragrant.

Lentil Soup with Dried Tomatoes. Omit the onion, carrot, and celery. Prepare and peel 1 or 2 heads of Roasted Garlic (page 303). In Step 1, cook the garlic in the olive oil for a minute or two, mashing and stirring until fragrant.

Grain Soups

Whole grains work brilliantly as supporting actors in soup, contributing flavor—usually subtly—and body. Here, though, they're featured in leading roles, which is unusual.

Mushroom-Barley Soup

MAKES: 4 servings

TIME: 45 minutes

Barley and mushrooms are a wonderfully earthy combination, especially in winter. If you have some dried mushrooms on hand, reconstitute a small handful and add them to the fresh mushrooms about halfway through cooking. (Strain and use their soaking liquid to replace some of the water or stock.) You can also make this soup even heartier by stirring in chopped parsnips, sweet potatoes, or potatoes after cooking the carrots and mushrooms.

> 2 tablespoons extra virgin olive oil
>
> 10 to 16 ounces fresh shiitake or button mushrooms, stemmed (shiitakes only) and roughly chopped
>
> 2 medium carrots, sliced
>
> $\frac{3}{4}$ cup pearled barley
>
> Salt and freshly ground black pepper
>
> 1 bay leaf

1 Put the olive oil in a large, deep pot over medium-high heat. When hot, add the mushrooms and carrots and cook, stirring occasionally, until they begin to brown, about 10 minutes. Add the barley and continue to cook, stirring frequently, until it begins to brown, about 5 minutes; sprinkle with a little salt and pepper.

2 Add the bay leaf and 6 cups water (or stock if you prefer). Bring to a boil, then lower the heat to a simmer; cook until the barley is very tender, 20 to 30 minutes.

3 Taste and add more salt if necessary and plenty of pepper. (At this point, you may refrigerate the soup, covered, for up to a day; reheat before serving, adding a little more water to thin the soup if necessary.)

Jook

Congee or Rice Porridge

MAKES: 6 servings

TIME: About $2\frac{1}{2}$ hours

Like many dishes of really impoverished people, the basic jook or congee—a bit of rice cooked in water until it's soupy—is not super-appealing on its own. But when made a little fancier, it's wonderful stuff.

10 fresh (stemmed) or dried shiitake mushrooms

1 cup short-grain rice, rinsed

1 teaspoon salt, or to taste

2 inches fresh ginger

Soy sauce, to taste (optional)

Dark sesame oil, to taste (optional)

$1/2$ cup chopped scallion for garnish (optional)

$1/2$ cup fresh cilantro leaves for garnish (optional)

$1/2$ cup chopped roasted peanuts or cashews for garnish (optional)

❶ If you're using dried shiitakes, cover them with boiling water and soak until pliable, about 15 minutes, changing the water if necessary; drain. Put the rice in a large pot with 6 cups water and the salt. Bring to a boil over high heat, then turn the heat to low; the mixture should simmer, but only gently. Slice half the ginger and add it to the pot; mince the remaining ginger and set aside. Slice the mushrooms and add them to the pot.

❷ Partially cover the pot and simmer for about 2 hours, stirring occasionally to make sure the rice is not sticking to the bottom. The jook should have a porridge-like consistency, so if it becomes very thick too quickly, turn down the heat and stir in more water. When it is done, the jook will be soupy and creamy. Add the minced ginger and, if you're using them, soy sauce and/or sesame oil, along with more salt if necessary. Serve with whatever garnishes you choose.

Jook with Vegetables. During the last 30 minutes of cooking, add 2 cups chopped Savoy, Napa, or other cabbage, iceberg or romaine lettuce, or spinach; 1 cup chopped carrot; 1 cup fresh or frozen peas; or any combination of these. Be sure to add more water to keep the mixture soupy.

Jook with Meat. In Step 2, cut all the ginger into thin slivers. Add it, along with $1/2$ pound sliced sirloin, sliced Chinese-style sausage, chicken breast, or lean pork, during the last 15 minutes of simmering.

Jook with Seafood. In Step 2, during the last 30 minutes of simmering, add $1/4$ pound sliced squid; during the last 5 minutes of simmering, add $1/4$ pound peeled shrimp and $1/4$ pound firm white fish, skinned and sliced.

Wheat, Whole Barley, or Farro Soup

MAKES: 4 to 6 servings
TIME: $1^1/2$ hours or more, largely unattended

A hearty, slow-to-make soup based on any whole grain. Very Italian—Tuscan in particular—and so good with extra virgin olive oil or grated Parmesan to finish.

$1/4$ cup extra virgin olive oil

1 large onion, sliced

2 celery stalks, chopped

2 carrots, chopped

Salt and freshly ground black pepper

1 tablespoon minced garlic

1 cup whole wheat berries, hulled barley, or farro

1 cup dried white beans, washed, picked over, and soaked if time allows (see page 411)

2 cups chopped tomato (canned is fine; include the juices)

6 cups water or vegetable, chicken, or beef stock (to make your own, see pages 157–159)

$1/4$ cup chopped fresh parsley leaves

$1/4$ cup chopped fresh basil leaves (optional)

Freshly grated Parmesan cheese or more oil for garnish

❶ Put the oil in a large, deep pot over medium heat. When hot, add the onion, celery, carrots, a large pinch of salt, and some pepper. Cook until the vegetables are glossy and the onion is softened, 5 to 10 minutes. Add the garlic and stir; add the grain, beans, tomato, and water and stir.

F Fast   **M** Make Ahead   **V** Vegetarian

2 Bring to a boil, then adjust the heat so the mixture simmers steadily. Cook until the grain and beans are tender, at least an hour, adding stock or water as necessary if the mixture becomes too thick. (At this point, you may refrigerate the soup, covered, for up to 2 days; reheat before proceeding. If the beans and farro soak up all the liquid in the soup, add water to thin it out, simmer for 5 minutes, and season to taste with salt before proceeding.)

3 Stir in the parsley and the basil if you're using it, then cook for another 5 minutes. Taste and adjust the seasoning, then serve, sprinkled with lots of Parmesan or drizzled with extra virgin olive oil.

Noodle Soups

Usually the best way to make noodle soup is to add cooked noodles to cooked soup just before serving. This way each element maintains its integrity and you don't end up with an undifferentiated starchy mess. Cook the noodles as usual, but undercook them slightly so they don't turn to mush in the hot soup. (You can even cook them ahead if you like, then rinse them in cold water to stop the cooking and set them aside in a bowl of water; or use leftovers.) Then add to the soup during the last couple minutes of cooking.

Several recipes in this section ignore this principle and cook the noodles right in the soup. While it's true that noodles cooked this way have only a narrow window of time before they start to break down, I've tried to leave that window open as long possible by using the sturdiest noodles or frying them first to make them a little less soluble.

Garlic Fideo Soup

MAKES: 4 servings
TIME: 30 minutes

Browned noodles are a real treat. Fideo noodles form the basis of a robust soup typical of Spain.

1 pound fideo, capellini, or other very thin pasta

¼ cup extra virgin olive oil

1 small head garlic, peeled and minced (about ¼ cup)

Salt and freshly ground black pepper

2 teaspoons sweet paprika (preferably pimentón; see page 62)

1/4 cup chopped fresh parsley, cilantro, or epazote leaves, plus 2 tablespoons for garnish

6 1/2 cups chicken, beef, or vegetable stock (to make your own, see pages 157–159) or water

1/2 cup bread crumbs, preferably fresh (page 876)

1 Put the noodles in a sturdy bag and whack them with a rolling pin or the back of a knife, breaking them into 1- to 2-inch pieces.

2 Put the olive oil in a large, deep pot over medium-low heat. When hot, add the garlic and cook, stirring frequently, until soft and beginning to color, 5 to 8 minutes.

3 Raise the heat to medium-high. Add the noodles, sprinkle with salt and pepper, and cook, stirring almost constantly, until they darken, a minute or two. They will probably not cook perfectly evenly—some will become darker than others—but try to avoid letting more than a few pieces blacken.

4 Add the paprika and 1/4 cup herbs and stir for a minute to coat the noodles. Add the stock, taking care to loosen any noodles or garlic that might have stuck to the bottom of the pan. Cook, stirring occasionally, until the pasta is just tender, 8 to 10 minutes. Taste, adjust the seasoning if necessary, and serve, garnished with a sprinkle of the remaining herbs and the bread crumbs.

Udon Noodle and Miso Soup with Shiitake Mushrooms

MAKES: 4 servings
TIME: About 30 minutes

F **V**

Udon noodles are the long, thick, now-familiar Japanese wheat noodle that can be treated pretty much like Italian pasta. Make this soup with any stock—dashi, meat, poultry, seafood, or vegetable.

8 ounces dried, frozen, or fresh udon noodles

1 1/2 quarts Dashi (page 160) or water

1/3 cup any miso

2 cups thinly sliced shiitake mushrooms or a handful dried

1/2 cup chopped scallion

1 Bring a large pot of water to a boil and salt it. Add the udon and cook it until it's just about done—there should still be a light chew to it—about 5 minutes. Drain it and rinse in cold water until cool; set aside. (If you're cooking the pasta in advance by more than 30 minutes, hold the pasta in a bowl of cold water or drizzle or toss with a couple tablespoons neutral oil.) If you're using dried mushrooms, pour some of the boiling noodle water over them to cover; soak until soft, about 30 minutes.

2 Heat the dashi in a large, deep pot over medium heat until bubbles rise from the sides. Put the miso in a bowl, add a cup or so of the hot dashi, and whisk until smooth. Pour the miso mixture into the rest of the dashi and mix.

3 Slice the reconstituted mushrooms, if you're using them; strain their soaking liquid and add it to the dashi. Add the mushrooms to the dashi and cook gently (do not boil) for about 5 minutes. Add the udon and heat though, garnish with the scallion, and serve.

Udon Noodles with Miso, Tofu, and Nori. Toast 4 sheets of nori (see page 350); cut a 1-pound brick of firm tofu into 1/2-inch cubes. (Or use a 12-ounce box of soft silken tofu and break it into large pieces.) In Step 3, stir in the tofu and heat with the noodles. After garnishing with scallion, crumble the toasted nori on top of each bowl.

Udon Noodle and Mixed Seafood Soup. Add 1 pound mixed peeled shrimp, chopped small squid, and scallops; simmer gently (do not boil) in the dashi-miso broth until the shrimp is pink, about 5 minutes.

Soba or Somen Noodle Soup. In the main recipe of any of the variations, use dried or fresh soba or somen noodles instead of the udon; they won't take quite as long to cook, just 5 minutes or so.

F Fast   **M** Make Ahead   **V** Vegetarian

Hanoi Noodle Soup

MAKES: 4 main-course servings
TIME: About 1 hour

Akin to the Vietnamese soups known as *pho* and usually made with beef, this anise- and cinnamon-scented soup is equally good with chicken or with no meat at all. Rice noodles are sold in Asian markets and many supermarkets, and can be softened by soaking in hot water.

- 8 cups beef, chicken, or vegetable stock (to make your own, see pages 157–159)
- 4 star anise
- One 3-inch cinnamon stick
- 1 inch fresh ginger
- 1 onion, quartered (don't bother to peel)
- 4 cloves
- 1 pound rice vermicelli
- 1/2 pound boneless, skinless chicken or beef (preferably sirloin, tenderloin, or round), cut into thin slices
- 2 tablespoons nam pla (Thai fish sauce) or soy sauce
- Freshly ground black pepper
- Salt
- Chopped fresh cilantro leaves for garnish
- Lime wedges
- 1 fresh jalapeño chile, seeded and minced

❶ Combine the stock, star anise, cinnamon, ginger, onion, and cloves in a large, deep saucepan or casserole over high heat. When it boils, reduce the heat to an occasional bubble and cover. Cook, undisturbed, for as little as 20 and as long as 60 minutes, depending on your available time. Strain and return to the saucepan.

❷ Soak the rice noodles in hot water to cover until soft, 15 to 30 minutes. Rinse under cold water for a minute or so; drain.

❸ Bring the soup to a steady bubble; put the chicken or the beef in the pot and cook for 2 minutes, stirring occasionally. Divide the noodles among 4 large bowls.

Add the nam pla and plenty of pepper to the soup. Taste and add salt or more seasoning.

❹ Top the noodles with broth and meat, then garnish with cilantro. Serve, passing the lime wedges and minced chile at the table.

Quick Asian Noodle Soup with Pork. Season the broth and soak the noodles as directed; cook the broth for only 20 minutes. Instead of the uncooked chicken or beef, add to the broth 1/2 recipe Braised Pork with Spicy Soy Sauce (page 758), along with some of its liquid. Omit the nam pla. Season and proceed with the recipe.

Fish Soups

If you have fish stock, you're literally three-quarters of the way home when it comes to making fish soup—you just add a couple of potatoes and some fish, for example, and you have chowder. But it's rarely essential; I've designed most of these recipes so that you can make them not only with fish stock but also with chicken stock or, if necessary, water. (What is essential, as with all dishes containing fish, is freshness; see page 560 for a discussion of this.)

Unlike most soups, fish soups are usually best prepared at the last minute, because many fish—especially finfish—overcook in the heat of a soup. You can often make the base one day and add the fish the next, but as a group these are so quick and easy that there isn't much point in that.

Lightning-Quick Fish Soup

MAKES: 4 servings
TIME: 20 minutes

The bright fish flavor in this simple soup is a perfect base for adding more vegetables, rice, or even pasta. If you have fish stock and fish scraps in the freezer, use them as the base here. If not, use chicken stock or water and fresh fish.

- 5 cups fish, chicken, or shrimp stock (to make your own, see pages 157–159) or water
- 1 large onion, chopped
- 1 tablespoon minced garlic
- 1 teaspoon paprika
- Pinch saffron (optional)
- 1 tablespoon extra virgin olive oil
- 1 cup peeled, seeded, and chopped tomato (canned is fine; include the juices)
- Salt and freshly ground black pepper
- 1½ pounds any white fish, cut into small chunks, or fish mixed with shelled seafood, like clams, shrimp, or scallops
- Chopped fresh parsley leaves for garnish

1 Put all the ingredients except for the fish and parsley in a large, deep pot and bring to a boil; reduce the heat to a steady bubble and cook for 5 minutes, stirring occasionally.

2 Add the fish and cook, stirring, until it cooks through, about 5 minutes. Garnish with the parsley and serve.

Lightning-Quick Fish Soup, Chinese Style. Substitute 3 tablespoons soy sauce for the paprika, 2 teaspoons dark sesame oil for the olive oil, and green peas (frozen are fine) for the tomato. Omit the saffron. (Be sure to taste before adding salt.) Garnish with lots of cilantro and/or chopped scallion.

Lightning-Quick Fish Soup, French Style. Substitute ½ cup dry white wine and ½ cup cream for 1 cup of the stock; be sure to use the saffron and substitute ¼ teaspoon cayenne, or to taste, for the paprika. Add the cream when you add the fish in Step 2 and don't let the soup come to a rolling boil. Use 2 tablespoons minced fresh tarragon leaves instead of parsley.

Lightning-Quick Fish Soup, Latin Style. Omit the paprika and saffron and add a minced jalapeño or other fresh chile, or to taste, along with the tomato. Use cilantro instead of parsley and add 3 tablespoons freshly squeezed lime juice, or to taste.

Lightning-Quick Fish Soup with Coconut Milk. Omit the paprika and saffron, and add 1 tablespoon minced or grated fresh ginger. Add either 1 tablespoon minced lemongrass for a Southeast Asian flavor or 1 tablespoon curry powder for an Indian flare. Use cilantro instead of parsley.

Hot and Sour Shrimp Soup

Tom Yum

MAKES: 4 servings
TIME: 40 minutes

With a citrusy broth, this Thai favorite is deliciously hot and spicy and sour. Shrimp is traditional, but substitute chicken, tofu, or squid if you like.

- 1 tablespoon neutral oil, like grapeseed or corn
- 2 cloves garlic, sliced
- 1 pound shrimp, peeled, shells reserved
- 6 cups fish or chicken stock (to make your own, see page 159 or 157) or water
- 3 stalks lemongrass, trimmed, smashed, and cut into 2-inch lengths
- 3 inches fresh ginger, sliced and smashed
- 4 fresh chiles, preferably Thai, or to taste, seeded and chopped, or hot red pepper flakes, to taste
- 1 tablespoon grated lime zest
- 1 cup sliced fresh or canned bamboo shoots, drained if canned
- 2 tablespoons nam pla (Thai fish sauce)
- 1 tablespoon freshly squeezed lime juice
- 2 teaspoons sugar
- Chopped fresh cilantro leaves or scallion for garnish
- Lime wedges

 Fast   Make Ahead   **V** Vegetarian

❶ Put the oil in a large, deep pot over medium heat. When hot, add the garlic and cook for about a minute; add the reserved shrimp shells and cook, stirring occasionally, until they turn pink, about 2 minutes.

❷ Add the stock, lemongrass, ginger, chiles, and lime zest; raise the heat to high and bring to a boil. Lower the heat and simmer, uncovered, for about 20 minutes.

❸ Carefully strain the stock; return it to the pot and bring to a boil. Add the shrimp and turn the heat to low; cook until the shrimp turn pink, 3 to 5 minutes. Remove from the heat and stir in the nam pla, lime juice, and sugar. Stir, taste, and adjust the seasoning, adding more fish sauce, lime juice, or sugar. Garnish and serve with the lime wedges.

Hot and Sour Shrimp Soup, Mexican Style. Omit the lemongrass, ginger, and nam pla. Add about 1 cup corn kernels (frozen are fine) along with the shrimp.

Hot and Sour Shrimp Soup, Indian Style. Omit the lemongrass and nam pla. Add 1 teaspoon each ground cumin, coriander, and turmeric along with the ginger. Add 1 cup green peas (frozen are fine) along with the shrimp.

No-Holds-Barred Clam or Fish Chowder

MAKES: 4 servings
TIME: 30 minutes

A top-notch New-England–style chowder (for Manhattan style, see the variations), even better with a cup or so of fresh corn kernels added along with the fish.

> 4 to 6 slices good bacon (about ¼ pound), chopped
>
> 1 cup chopped onion
>
> 2 cups peeled and roughly chopped waxy or all-purpose potatoes

> 1 teaspoon fresh thyme leaves or ½ teaspoon dried thyme
>
> 2 cups fish or chicken stock (to make your own, see page 159 or 157), augmented by as much juice as you can salvage when shucking the clams
>
> Salt and freshly ground black pepper
>
> 1 cup milk
>
> 1 cup cream or half-and-half or more milk
>
> 24 littleneck or other hard-shell clams, shucked; about 1 pint shucked clams, cut up if very large, with their juice; or about 2 cups diced or chunked fresh delicate white fish, like cod
>
> 1 tablespoon butter (optional)
>
> Chopped fresh parsley leaves for garnish

❶ Cook the bacon in a large, deep pot over medium-high heat until crisp. Remove with a slotted spoon and cook the onion, potatoes, and thyme in the bacon fat until the onion softens, 10 minutes. Add the stock and cook until the potatoes are tender, about 10 minutes. (At this point, you may refrigerate the soup, covered, for up to 2 days; reheat before proceeding.)

❷ Sprinkle with some salt and pepper, then add the milk and cream. Add the clams or fish and bring barely to a simmer over low heat, taking care not to let the soup boil. If you're using the butter, float it on top of the chowder; simmer for another 5 minutes or so, then garnish and serve.

Lower-Fat Clam Chowder. Substitute 2 tablespoons extra virgin olive oil for the bacon. Add another cup chopped potatoes and use 4 cups fish or chicken stock. Add 2 cups corn kernels, preferably fresh, with the clams. Use 1 cup low-fat milk and omit the cream. For Step 1, cook the onion and potato in the olive oil.

Manhattan Clam Chowder. Substitute 1 cup each chopped carrot and celery for the potatoes and one 28-ounce can peeled tomatoes (you can use fresh, of course—3 cups or so), chopped, for the milk and cream. Add the tomatoes with the stock.

Bouillabaisse

MAKES: 8 servings
TIME: 1 hour

Every seaside culture has its own fish stew, but bouillabaisse is probably the best known; it's no more (or less) than a highly seasoned soup made with the day's catch. So vary this recipe according to what you find at the store—or what you bring home from a day's fishing.

1 tablespoon extra virgin olive oil

2 medium onions, roughly chopped

1 navel or other orange

1 tablespoon fennel seeds

Big pinch saffron threads (optional)

1 dried chile (like Thai) or a pinch cayenne, or to taste

2 cups chopped tomato (canned is fine; include the juices)

1 to 1½ pounds monkfish, catfish, or other firm white fish, cut into 1-inch cubes

3 pounds clams, cockles, or mussels, scrubbed

1 to 1½ pounds scallops or peeled shrimp, cut into bite-sized pieces if necessary

1 to 1½ pounds cod or other delicate white fish, cut into 6 large chunks

1 tablespoon minced garlic

½ cup roughly chopped parsley leaves for garnish

Sliced crusty bread for serving

½ cup Garlic or Saffron Mayonnaise (optional; page 42)

1 Put the olive oil in a large, deep saucepan over medium heat. When hot, add the onions and cook, stirring occasionally, until softened, about 5 minutes. Meanwhile, use a vegetable peeler to strip the zest from the orange (save the orange itself for another use). Add the zest, fennel, saffron, and chile and cook for about a minute.

2 Add the tomato and 3 cups water and raise the heat to medium-high. When the mixture boils, reduce the heat to medium and cook, stirring occasionally, until the mixture becomes saucelike, 10 to 15 minutes. (At this point, you can cover the soup and set it aside for several hours.)

3 Add the monkfish and raise the heat to medium-high. When the mixture begins to boil, reduce the heat to medium-low and cook, stirring occasionally, until it is just about tender, 10 minutes or so.

4 Add the clams, raise the heat to high, and stir; when the mixture boils, reduce the heat to low, cover, and cook until the clams begin to open, 5 to 10 minutes. Add the scallops and cod, stir, and cover; cook, stirring gently once or twice, until the cod is just about done (a thin-bladed knife will pierce it with little resistance), about 5 minutes. If the mixture is very thick—there should be some broth—add a cup or so of hot water.

5 Stir in the garlic and cook for 1 minute more. Stir in the parsley and serve, with crusty bread and a dollop of the aïoli if you're using it.

Lobster Bisque

MAKES: 4 servings
TIME: 1 hour

This is a relatively simple and quick lobster bisque, one that retains two critical qualities: big-time lobster flavor and a luxurious creaminess. There are two good ways to obtain lobster bodies. One is to save them from a lobster feast. The other is to beg them from an old-fashioned fishmonger, who will either give them away free or charge you only minimally.

4 tablespoons (½ stick) butter

1 medium onion, chopped

1 teaspoon minced garlic

1 medium carrot, chopped

1 bay leaf

3 sprigs fresh thyme or $^1/_2$ teaspoon dried thyme

4 to 8 whole lobsters, cooked or uncooked, with as many other lobster shells or bodies as you can scavenge, plus coral, tomalley, and any stray bits of meat you might find

1 cup dry white wine

1 cup peeled, seeded, and chopped tomato (canned is fine; include the juices)

6 cups lobster, chicken, or fish stock (to make your own, see pages 157–160) or strained liquid reserved from boiling lobsters

1 cup heavy cream

Salt and freshly ground black pepper

Chopped fresh parsley leaves for garnish

❶ Put 2 tablespoons of the butter in a large, deep pot over medium heat. When it melts, add the onion, garlic, carrot, bay leaf, and thyme and cook, stirring, until the onion softens, 5 to 10 minutes.

❷ Add the whole lobsters and, if they are uncooked, cook, stirring, until they turn red, about 10 minutes; if they're already cooked, cook, stirring, for about 5 minutes.

❸ Add the wine and tomato and raise the heat to medium-high. Bring to a boil, then turn the heat to low, cover, and cook for 10 minutes.

❹ Add the stock, raise the heat to high, and bring back to a boil. Once again, turn the heat to low and cover; cook for 20 minutes. Remove the lobsters and shells, crack them if necessary, and pick off any meat you find. Return the bits of meat to the soup (reserve any large pieces of meat you may have for the final addition).

❺ Pass the soup through a food mill or purée it in a blender. (At this point, you may refrigerate the soup, covered, for up to 2 days; reheat before proceeding.) Return the soup to the pot and bring to a boil, then lower the heat so it bubbles gently. Add the remaining butter, in bits, until it melts. Add the cream and any bits of lobster meat and heat through. Season with salt and pepper, garnish with parsley, and serve.

Chicken Soups

Ironically, few chicken soups contain much chicken, because if the stock is good enough, there's no reason for it—the flavor is right there. But if you like to have something meaty to chew on, by all means add chicken to your chicken soup.

Chicken Soup with Matzo Balls

MAKES: 6 servings

TIME: At least 2 hours

Traditionally, matzo balls are served in broth, with only carrots (thick cut instead of sliced), but you can add other vegetables, rice or noodles (thin egg noodles are good), and chicken meat. And don't let tradition stop you from using stocks other than chicken; beef, vegetable, and mushroom stocks are equally delicious, especially for the passatelli and butter dumpling variations, where tradition is less of an issue.

3 eggs

6 to 9 cups chicken stock (to make your own, see page 157)

$^1/_4$ cup minced or grated onion (optional)

$^1/_4$ cup melted rendered chicken fat or neutral oil, like grapeseed or corn

$^1/_2$ teaspoon salt

$^1/_2$ teaspoon freshly ground black pepper

About 1 cup matzo meal

4 carrots, cut into chunks

❶ Beat together the eggs and $^1/_2$ cup of the stock. (If you prefer light matzo balls, separate the eggs and beat the yolks with the stock. Beat the whites until stiff and fold them in after adding the matzo meal.)

❷ Stir in the onion if you're using it, the fat, the salt, and the pepper. Add the matzo meal; the dough should be quite moist, barely stiff enough to make into balls. If it's too moist, add a little more meal.

3 Cover the mixture and refrigerate for an hour or overnight. When you're ready to cook, bring a large pot of water to a boil and salt it. (You can also cook the matzo balls directly in your stock, but use the larger quantity of stock.) Using wet hands, shape the mixture into balls about 1 inch in diameter. Meanwhile, simmer the carrots in 5½ cups of the stock until just tender, about 20 minutes.

4 Turn the heat under the boiling water to medium-low, so that it bubbles gently, and cook the balls until expanded and set, about 30 minutes. Set them in soup bowls and ladle the stock and carrots over them.

Chicken Soup with Passatelli. A wonderful fresh "noodle" made from bread crumbs and cheese: Reduce the stock to 4 cups and bring to a steady bubble. Make the passatelli by mixing together ⅓ cup Fresh Bread Crumbs (page 876), ¾ cup grated Parmesan, ⅛ teaspoon freshly grated nutmeg, ¼ cup minced fresh parsley leaves, and 2 eggs; it will form a soft, granular dough. Press the dough into the bubbling stock through a ricer, a food mill fit with large holes, or a colander (using a large spoon); cook until the passatelli is tender but firm, about 2 minutes. Serve immediately with more grated Parmesan.

Chicken Soup with Butter Dumplings. Use 6 cups of stock and bring to a steady bubble. Make the

---

MAKING PASSATELLI OR SPAETZLE

Use the back of a spoon or a ladle to press the dough through the holes of a colander (or use a ricer or food mill with large holes), letting the dough fall right into the bubbling liquid.

---

dumplings by whipping 4 tablespoons (½ stick) softened butter, then beating in 2 eggs. Stir in ½ cup all-purpose flour, ¼ cup minced fresh parsley leaves, ¼ cup minced or grated onion, and a large pinch salt and pepper. Add heated stock 1 tablespoon at a time, just until the batter is soft—not too loose or the dumplings will fall apart. Drop the batter by the teaspoonful into the bubbling stock. Cook until set, about 10 minutes, removing them as they are done. Serve immediately in the soup.

Chicken Tortilla Soup

MAKES: 4 to 6 servings
TIME: 1 hour

Whoever thought you'd make soup in the broiler? Turns out that it's an excellent tool for classic tortilla soup.

2 fresh chiles, like serrano, Fresno, or jalapeño

1½ pounds tomatoes, each halved

2 tablespoons neutral oil, like grapeseed or corn

3 cloves garlic, sliced

1 large onion, sliced

Salt and freshly ground black pepper

Pinch dried oregano

4 cups chicken stock (to make your own, see page 157) or water

2 cups sliced or shredded cooked chicken

1 to 2 cups tortilla chips, plus more for garnish

2 limes, 1 juiced, 1 cut into wedges

1 cup chopped fresh cilantro leaves for garnish (optional)

1 ripe avocado, pitted, peeled, and sliced, for garnish (optional)

1 or 2 radishes, thinly sliced, for garnish (optional)

1 Heat the broiler. Arrange the chiles and tomatoes in a single layer on a rimmed baking sheet and put a few inches away from the heat. Cook until charred on one side, then flip them with tongs and char the other side, 5 to 8 minutes total. When cool, peel and seed the chiles, then chop them.

2 Put the oil in a large, deep pot over medium heat. When hot, add the garlic and onion and cook, stirring occasionally, until golden and softened, about 10 minutes. Add the tomatoes and chiles, crushing the tomatoes with the back of a wooden spoon. Season with salt, pepper, and oregano; add the stock and adjust the heat so the mixture simmers gently. Cook for 20 to 30 minutes, crushing the tomatoes from time to time. (At this point, you may let the soup sit for a few hours or refrigerate, covered, for up to a day before reheating and finishing.)

3 Stir in the chicken and tortilla chips and simmer for another 3 to 5 minutes. Season to taste with lime juice, sprinkle with salt and pepper, then garnish with any of the optional ingredients if desired and serve with lime wedges.

Thai Coconut Soup with Chicken

MAKES: 4 servings
TIME: 40 minutes

A Thai restaurant favorite, easily re-created at home.

- 4 cups coconut milk (to make your own, see page 389)
- 1 cup chicken stock (to make your own, see page 157) or water
- 1 pound boneless, skinless chicken, breast or thigh, cut into 1-inch strips
- 3 stalks lemongrass, trimmed, smashed, and cut into 2-inch lengths
- 10 nickel-sized slices fresh ginger
- 2 fresh chiles, preferably Thai, seeded and minced, or hot red pepper flakes, to taste
- 1 cup sliced shiitake mushroom caps (discard the stems or reserve them for stock) or button mushrooms

- 3 tablespoons nam pla (Thai fish sauce)
- 3 tablespoons freshly squeezed lime juice
- 1 teaspoon sugar
- Salt and freshly ground black pepper
- 1/4 cup chopped fresh cilantro leaves

1 Combine the coconut milk and stock in a large, deep pot over medium-high heat and bring to a boil. Lower the heat a bit, add the chicken, and simmer until cooked through, about 10 minutes. Remove the chicken with a slotted spoon and set aside.

2 Add the lemongrass, ginger, and chiles; simmer for 15 minutes. Remove the larger pieces of spices. Return the chicken to the pot along with the mushrooms and heat about 3 minutes. (At this point, you can let the soup sit for a few hours or refrigerate, covered, for up to a day before reheating and proceeding.)

3 Turn off the heat and stir in the nam pla, lime juice, and sugar. Sprinkle with salt and pepper, taste, and adjust the seasonings, adding more nam pla, lime juice, or sugar. Garnish with the cilantro and serve.

Meat Soups

Most meat soups are more like stews—see the meat chapter for those—but these are lighter, more soupy than stewy. Of all the soups, these are the ones where you're safest using water instead of stock, because the long simmering times and the presence of meat guarantee that you'll wind up with a flavorful broth.

Beef and Vegetable Soup

MAKES: 4 to 6 servings
TIME: 1 1/2 hours

All sorts of vegetables work in this soup, so use whatever is fresh. Here are a few to get you thinking: tomatoes, pearl onions, potatoes, rutabaga or turnips, winter squash, or green beans. To make this soup a thick stew, just reduce the stock by 2 cups—or increase the meat and vegetables.

2 tablespoons neutral oil, like grapeseed or corn

1 pound beef chuck or round, trimmed of surface fat and cut into ¹/₂-inch cubes

1 onion, chopped

6 cups beef or other stock (to make your own, see pages 157–159) or water

2 parsnips or carrots, peeled and diced

¹/₂ celeriac or 1 celery stalk, peeled and diced

¹/₂ small butternut squash, peeled and diced (about 1 cup)

2 sprigs fresh thyme or rosemary

1 bay leaf

¹/₂ cup green peas (frozen are fine)

Salt and freshly ground black pepper

Chopped fresh parsley leaves or chives for garnish

❶ Put the oil in a large, deep pot over medium-high heat. When hot, add the beef and brown it on one side before stirring it; cook until deeply browned on all sides, about 8 minutes total. Work in batches if the meat starts to get crowded in the pan and remove pieces when they are done. Pour off all but 2 tablespoons of the fat from the pan. Add the onion and cook until translucent, about 5 minutes.

❷ Add the stock and bring to a near boil; reduce the heat to a steady bubble, cover, and cook for 30 minutes. Add the parsnips, celeriac, squash, herb sprigs, and bay leaf and stir; cook until the meat and vegetables are tender, another 30 to 40 minutes. (At this point, you may refrigerate the soup, covered, for 2 days; reheat gently before proceeding.)

❸ Remove the herb sprigs and bay leaf, stir in the peas, and sprinkle with salt and pepper; taste and adjust the seasoning. Garnish with the parsley and serve.

Spicy Beef and Vegetable Soup. Add 1 tablespoon chopped garlic and 2 dried cascabel, guajillo, or pasilla chiles. Soak the chiles in just-boiled water to cover; drain and use a knife to scrape out the seeds

22 Whole-Meal Soups

Some of these chunky soups can become stews just by being cooked a little longer, thereby reducing the ratio of liquid to solid. Or you can just add more vegetables, meat, grains, noodles, or what have you. But that's not necessary; each is filling and interesting enough to serve as a main course.

1. Chunky Vegetable Soup (page 123)
2. Chinese Noodle Soup with Cabbage and Ginger (page 128)
3. Potato and Leek Soup (page 131)
4. Cabbage Soup with Potatoes and Caraway (page 133)
5. Basic Bean Soup (page 136)
6. White Bean and Collard Green Soup (page 136)
7. Smoky Black Bean Soup (page 137)
8. Simplest Split Pea Soup (page 138)
9. Lentil Soup with Lemon and Dill (page 138)
10. Mushroom-Barley Soup (page 139)
11. Jook (page 139)
12. Wheat, Whole Barley, or Farro Soup (page 140)
13. Udon Noodle and Miso Soup with Shiitake Mushrooms (page 142)
14. Hanoi Noodle Soup (page 143)
15. Lightning-Quick Fish Soup (page 143)
16. Hot and Sour Shrimp Soup (page 144)
17. No-Holds-Barred Clam or Fish Chowder (page 145)
18. Bouillabaisse (page 146)
19. Chicken Tortilla Soup (page 148)
20. Beef and Vegetable Soup (page 149)
21. Scotch Broth (page 151)
22. Three-Pork Soup (page 152)

 Fast   Make Ahead   **V** Vegetarian

and remove the stems; chop and add along with the garlic to the cooked onion. Strain and add the chile-soaking liquid (and reduce the stock) for more kick.

Beef and Mushroom Soup. Add 1 ounce dried porcini or other mushrooms or 4 cups chopped fresh mushrooms. Soak the dried mushrooms in 3 cups just-boiled water until soft, about 30 minutes. Don't discard the soaking liquid; strain it and add it to the soup, reducing the stock by 3 cups. If you're using fresh mushrooms, cook them along with the onion in Step 1 (it will take a few minutes longer.)

Hot and Sour Soup

MAKES: 4 servings
TIME: 30 minutes

To Americans, one of the best-known Chinese soups and much better made at home than at most restaurants. It gets its heat from freshly ground pepper (use a lot of it) and its sourness from rice vinegar. Don't be put off by the long ingredient list: This doesn't take much time to prepare. Normally, I think thickening with cornstarch is unnecessary, but here it feels appropriate to give the soup its signature thickness; you can eliminate it if you like.

1 tablespoon dark sesame oil

3 tablespoons soy sauce

3 tablespoons cornstarch

$^1/_2$ pound lean pork loin, chicken breast, or flank steak, cut into thin shreds against the grain (optional)

6 cups chicken stock (to make your own, see page 157) or water

1 teaspoon minced garlic

1 tablespoon minced fresh ginger

5 dried shiitake (black) mushrooms, soaked in hot water for at least 10 minutes

5 Chinese wood ear mushrooms, soaked in hot water for at least 10 minutes

$^1/_2$ pound extra-firm tofu, cut into $^1/_2$-inch cubes

$^1/_4$ cup rice vinegar, or to taste

3 teaspoons freshly ground black pepper, or to taste

2 eggs, lightly beaten

$^1/_4$ cup chopped fresh cilantro leaves

$^1/_2$ cup chopped scallion

❶ Whisk together 1 teaspoon of the sesame oil with 1 tablespoon each of the soy sauce and cornstarch. If you're using them, marinate the meat shreds in this mixture. Meanwhile, combine the stock with the garlic and ginger in a large, deep pot and bring to a boil over medium-high heat. Drain the mushrooms, trim off all the hard spots, cut into thin slices, and add to the stock. Reduce the heat to low and cook at a steady bubble for 5 minutes.

❷ Bring the stock back to a boil over medium heat and add the meat. Stir to make sure the pieces do not stick together and cook until the meat loses its pinkness, about 3 minutes. Then add the tofu, vinegar, pepper, and remaining soy sauce. Reduce the heat to low again and simmer for 5 minutes.

❸ Mix the remaining cornstarch with 1/4 cup cold water and stir that mixture into the soup until it thickens, about 1 minute. Continue to stir and pour in the eggs in a slow stream. The eggs should form thin, almost transparent ribbons. Remove from the heat and season with the remaining sesame oil and more vinegar or pepper to taste. Garnish with the cilantro and scallion and serve.

Vegetarian Hot and Sour Soup. Omit the meat and add $^1/_2$ pound more tofu and $^1/_2$ pound shredded bamboo shoots. Substitute good vegetable stock (to make your own, see page 157) for the chicken stock.

Scotch Broth

MAKES: 6 to 8 servings
TIME: About 2 hours

Scotch broth has two essential ingredients: lamb (you don't see many lamb soups) and barley. You can make it

even more typical by simmering some lamb bones for a couple of hours with aromatic vegetables and using that for the stock.

 10 cups lamb, beef, or chicken stock (to make your own, see pages 157–159), or water, or a combination

 1/2 cup pearled barley

 1 1/2 to 2 pounds boneless lamb, preferably from the shoulder or leg, trimmed of excess fat and cut into 1-inch cubes

 1 large or 2 medium leeks, washed and chopped

 2 or 3 carrots, cut into 1-inch chunks

 3 medium turnips, potatoes, or a combination, peeled and cut into 1-inch chunks

 2 celery stalks, chopped

 Salt and freshly ground black pepper

 Chopped fresh parsley leaves for garnish

❶ Put the stock, barley, lamb, and leeks in a large, deep saucepan or casserole over high heat. When it boils, reduce the heat so the mixture bubbles gently. Skim any foam that rises to the top and cook, stirring occasionally, until the lamb and barley are very tender, at least 45 minutes.

❷ Add the remaining vegetables and cook, stirring occasionally, for 20 minutes. Add salt and pepper to taste and stir. Cook until everything is very tender, another 10 to 20 minutes. Taste and adjust the seasoning, garnish with parsley, and serve.

Lamb Soup, North African Style. Substitute 2 cups cooked and drained chickpeas or uncooked lentils for the barley. Omit the turnips and celery. Add 1 cup each chopped parsley and cilantro, 1 teaspoon each ground cinnamon and turmeric, and about 2 cups chopped seeded tomato. Brown the lamb in a tablespoon of olive oil, then add the leeks (or use onion) and herbs, spices, and finally the tomatoes, beans, and stock; cook until the lamb is tender. Add a squeeze of lemon juice just before serving if you like.

Three-Pork Soup

MAKES: 4 main-dish or 6 starter servings
TIME: 1 1/2 hours, largely unattended

A light version of Spain's famous caldo gallego, this still makes a terrific one-pot meal. You can prepare the soup entirely in advance, but don't let it sit for more than a few hours or the potatoes will begin to disintegrate.

 2 tablespoons extra virgin olive oil

 1/4 pound salt pork or bacon, diced

 1/4 pound ham, preferably Serrano or prosciutto, with some of its fat, diced

 1/2 pound potatoes (any kind), peeled and cubed

 1 onion, sliced

 1/4 pound turnips, peeled and diced

 6 cups beef or chicken stock (to make your own, see page 158 or 157) or water

 1/2 pound smoked chorizo sausage, peeled and sliced

 1 small head cabbage, preferably Savoy, cored and shredded

 1 cup cooked and drained large white beans, like cannellini, lima, or gigante if you can find them

 Salt and freshly ground black pepper

❶ Put the oil in a large, deep pot over medium-high heat. When hot, add the pork and ham and cook until brown, about 5 minutes.

❷ Add the potatoes, onion, turnips, and stock; simmer until the potatoes are tender, about 20 minutes. Then add the chorizo, cabbage, and beans and cook just until the chorizo is heated through and the greens are soft, 10 to 20 minutes more. Season to taste with salt and pepper and serve.

Three Pork Soup, Southern Style. Substitute 2 ham hocks for the ham, mild smoked sausage for the chorizo, and 1 pound collard or kale greens for the cabbage. After cooking the potatoes in Step 2, fish out the ham hocks, take all the meat off the bones, chop it, and return it to the pot. For the greens, remove and discard any stems over $^1/_4$ inch thick; chop the stems and the leaves; add with the sausage in Step 2.

Cold Soups

Most cold soups—which may be savory, as in borscht or gazpacho, or sweet and fruity, like smoothies in a bowl—are best when cool but not ice cold, because extreme cold dulls flavor. (For this reason, you should oversalt savory soups slightly; with sweet dessert soups, add a little more sugar than you think necessary.) In either case, remove the soup from the refrigerator for at least fifteen minutes before serving, to take the edge off its iciness.

Obviously, summer is the best time to enjoy cold soups, when vegetables like tomatoes, cucumbers, and radishes are in season. But there are options here designed for year-round eating too. And to open up even more possibilities, you can consider chilling hot soups; see the list at right.

Fast Avocado Soup

MAKES: 4 servings

TIME: 10 minutes, plus time to chill

Creamy, with a gorgeous color, this soup couldn't be simpler. If you like, dress it up with chopped cherry tomatoes, sliced scallion, chopped chervil or mint, or a dollop of crème fraîche (or any of those in combination). Or see the variation for some seafood additions.

3 or 4 ripe avocados, pitted, peeled, and chopped (about 2 cups)

3 cups milk, preferably whole milk

Salt and cayenne

2 tablespoons freshly squeezed orange or lime juice, or to taste (optional)

❶ Put the chopped avocado in a blender. Add half the milk, a large pinch of salt, and a small pinch of

cayenne and process to a purée. Beat in the remaining milk, then chill for up to 6 hours if you have time (press a piece of plastic wrap onto the surface of the soup so it doesn't discolor).

❷ Taste and adjust the seasoning if necessary, add the citrus juice if you're using it, and serve—in chilled bowls if you want to be precise.

Fast Avocado and Seafood Soup. Before preparing the soup, chop some boiled shrimp (or if you have any leftover grilled, use that) or cooked crabmeat. If you like, toss it in a little Vinaigrette (page 199), but a little salt and pepper and a squeeze of citrus is just fine. Chill while you prepare the soup. Serve a spoonful of seafood on top of each bowlful.

10 Soups You Can Also Serve Cold

Chilled soups make a perfect start to a spicy meal in any season. They're ideal for entertaining, of course, because they're always made ahead and usually served straight from the refrigerator.

In every case, when you make the soup, let it cool a bit, then transfer it to a covered container and put it in the fridge until cold. This usually takes at least a couple of hours.

1. Summer Minestrone (page 124)
2. Green Minestrone (page 125)
3. Puréed Vegetable Soup Without Cream (page 125)
4. Puréed Carrot-Ginger Soup (page 126)
5. Puréed Sweet-and-Sour Beet Soup (page 126)
6. Cream of Asparagus Soup (page 130)
7. Cream of Fennel or Celery Soup (page 130)
8. Cream of Watercress, Spinach, or Sorrel Soup (page 130)
9. Puréed Tomato Soup (page 131)
10. Vichyssoise (page 133)

Gazpacho, Fast and Simple

MAKES: 4 servings
TIME: About 20 minutes

No one can definitively say what "gazpacho" is—you see it with grapes, with almonds, even with melon—and you can indeed make delicious gazpacho with all those things. This basic recipe is what you probably expect when you hear the word *gazpacho,* but with this formula you can replace the tomatoes and cucumber with fruits of similar texture and change the soup in infinite ways.

2 pounds tomatoes, roughly chopped, or one 28-ounce can (include the juices)

1 medium cucumber, peeled, seeded if you like (see page 293), and chopped

2 or 3 slices bread, a day or two old, crusts removed, torn into small pieces

¼ cup extra virgin olive oil, plus more for garnish

2 tablespoons sherry vinegar or red wine vinegar, or more to taste

1 teaspoon minced garlic

Salt and freshly ground black pepper

1 Combine the tomatoes, cucumber, bread, oil, vinegar, and garlic with 1 cup water in a blender; process until smooth. If the gazpacho seems too thick, thin with additional water.

2 Taste and adjust the seasoning. Serve immediately (or refrigerate and serve within a couple of hours), garnished with a drizzle of olive oil.

Spicy Gazpacho. Omit the vinegar. Garnish the finished soup with ½ red or yellow bell pepper, seeded and chopped; 2 scallions or shallots or ½ red onion, minced; and ½ fresh jalapeño or serrano chile (or to taste), seeded and minced. Add fresh lemon or lime juice to taste and serve.

Chunky Gazpacho. Finely chop the tomatoes, cucumber, and bread, collecting all of the juices you can as you work. Toss together in a large bowl with the remaining ingredients and 1 cup water or dry white wine and stir for a minute or two to combine thoroughly.

Red Onion Borscht

MAKES: 4 servings
TIME: About 1 hour

A borscht that combines the sweetness of red onion with the earthiness of beets for a more approachable version of the all-beet classic; even people who don't like beets will like it. You can serve this soup hot or cold, and either way it's best with a dollop of sour cream. To make it heartier, pass the optional garnishes at the table.

4 tablespoons butter or extra virgin olive oil

4 large red onions, thinly sliced (about 6 cups)

1 medium to large beet, peeled and grated

Salt and freshly ground black pepper

1 bay leaf

¼ cup ruby port, red wine, or freshly squeezed orange juice

5 cups vegetable stock (to make your own, see page 157) or water

½ cup sour cream, or more to taste, for garnish

Snipped chives or thinly sliced scallion greens for garnish (optional)

4 hard-cooked eggs, cut into wedges (optional)

12 small waxy potatoes, like red or fingerling, halved and boiled or steamed (optional)

1 Put the butter or oil in a large, deep pot over medium heat. When the butter is melted or the oil is hot, add the onions and grated beet and cook, stirring occasionally, until the onions are very soft and have taken on the color of the beet, 30 to 45 minutes.

2 Sprinkle the onion-beet mixture with salt and pepper, turn the heat to high, and add the bay leaf and port.

 F Fast   **M** Make Ahead   **V** Vegetarian

Add the stock a minute later and bring to a boil. Lower the heat and cook the soup for 15 minutes at a low simmer, with bubbles breaking the surface only occasionally. (At this point, you may refrigerate the soup, covered, for up to 2 days; reheat before proceeding.)

❸ Divide the soup among bowls, finish each with a dollop of sour cream, scatter with snipped chives if you're using them, and serve at once. Pass the optional garnishes at the table if you like.

The Basics of Stock

Stock is the liquid that results from simmering foods in water, then straining them out. The solids may be vegetables, meat, fish, poultry, herbs, spices, or any combination. Stock is only rarely served clear, as a consommé or broth (which, essentially, is stock with nothing, or very little, added to it). Far more often it's combined with fresh vegetables or other ingredients—noodles, rice, eggs, cheese, and so on—to make a flavorful soup or become the basis of sauce.

Is stock essential for every soup? No. Will it improve almost any soup? Yes. Even the simplest vegetable stock—an onion, a carrot, a celery stalk, a few other scraps, simmered together for 20 minutes—will make a difference in most soups. And a grand, full-flavored chicken, meat, or fish stock is good enough to serve on its own.

Stock Ingredients

Stock need not be expensive: It's easy enough to start with bits of vegetables that you've frozen and saved over the course of weeks, the trimmings and ends from celery, carrots, and onions (onion peels, especially, add color), and other vegetables, bearing in mind that trimmings from strong-tasting vegetables like broccoli and asparagus will lend a distinct flavor to the stock, one you probably don't want.

Save, too, just about every scrap (except for fat, chicken skin, and fish gills and innards) from trimming chicken, meat, or fish. Stock making gives you yet another incentive for buying whole chicken and cutting it up; the meaty raw bones of a single chicken, combined with a few vegetables, provide enough flavor for a quart or two of stock. Same thing with seafood in the shell, whole fish, or any other meat on the bone.

Of course, it's easier and arguably better, if more expensive, to begin with fresh, whole ingredients. Take a carrot, an onion, a celery stalk, a chicken, some seasoning, at a total cost of a few dollars, and you can make three quarts of stock, enough for two or three batches of soup, or a batch of soup and a fantastic risotto. Keep the simmering time short and you can even make the soup and still have a chicken worth eating.

Onion, carrot, and celery should find their way into most stockpots, but almost anything can substitute for anything else: turkey for chicken, cooked meat for raw, varying amounts of ingredients.

Bones are an integral part of many stocks, lending body to long-simmering stocks. But a stock made only of bones tastes like bones rather than meat. Most raw bones are quite meaty, so that isn't so much of a problem. But if you are making a stock with leftovers and are using bones that have been completely stripped of meat, buy a few chicken wings, backs, or necks and add them along with the bones; you'll improve the flavor significantly.

There are other ingredients you might or might not add according to taste and circumstance: a mild or hot chile, fresh or dried; a few cloves of garlic, which will become quite mellow; some dried mushrooms (almost always appropriate). You'll soon find out what you favor.

Stock-Making Techniques

Removing Fat: There are two considerations about fat and stock. First, don't allow stocks (or, for that matter, soups) to boil vigorously: Rapid boiling can so thoroughly disperse fat that it becomes difficult to remove it. This makes for a fattier stock (obviously), one that can taste greasy. To cook stock, bring it just about to a boil, skim any foam that rises to the top, and then turn the heat down to about medium-low, so it simmers gently.

On some stoves it helps to turn the heat down and partially cover the pan at the same time or move the pot partially off the heat.

Removing the fat, however, is simple enough, as long as you make your stock a day or two in advance. After cooking, strain the stock (see below) and refrigerate it. (If the weather is cold—say 40°F or lower—just set the strained stock outside, covered of course.) When the fat rises to the top and solidifies—as long as a day later, depending on the quantity of stock and the temperature of the storage place—just skim it off with a spoon and discard it (or save it for cooking, especially if it is from chicken). If you can't wait that long, you can pour the strained stock into a degreasing pitcher or simply spoon off the fat that rises to the top of the stockpot.

Browning: If you roast stock ingredients before simmering, you get a darker, more complex stock, though not necessarily a better one; stocks that don't begin with browning are brighter and cleaner in flavor. The choice is yours; see "How to Make Any Stock Darker and Richer" (page 158).

Straining: When you strain a stock—usually through a sieve, lined with cheesecloth if you like—you have two options. If you press on the vegetables and other ingredients, you intensify flavors; if you do not, your stock will be clearer. I almost always opt for flavor, because to make a stock perfectly clear requires extreme measures that I'm rarely willing to take.

Reducing: The less water a stock contains, the more intense the flavor and the less room it takes to store. Concentrated stock, undiluted, makes a wonderful, low-fat flavor addition to stir-fries, sauces, and plain steamed vegetables. Remember, though, salt doesn't reduce, so if you're planning to reduce a stock by more than half, wait to season it until you've boiled off the extra water.

To reduce stock, begin by straining and defatting the stock, then boil it down, stirring now and then and watching to prevent burning, which can occur when the liquid becomes very thick. And be aware that reducing takes a while; reducing a gallon to a quart can take a half hour or longer. To speed the process, use the broadest pot you have or divide the stock between two or more pots so more of the liquid is exposed to the air, where it will evaporate more quickly.

On Storing Stock

The problem with homemade stock is it's so good that you eventually run out and have to make it again. This argues for cooking larger quantities at once, and—fortunately—making big batches isn't much more difficult than making small ones. Then it just becomes a question of storing.

If you store it in the refrigerator and bring it back to a boil every second or third day, it will keep more or less indefinitely. Freezing, of course, is more efficient. Here you have a couple of options: One is to simply ladle or pour the stock into convenient-sized containers—4-cup ones are usually good. (You can recycle yogurt or similar containers.) Cover and freeze.

If you want to save space, boil the strained stock down to about half its original volume to make concentrate. You can even store the equivalent of 12 cups of stock in an ice cube tray. To use, just pop out a cube (it's actually best to pop them all out once they're frozen, then freeze the cubes in a tightly sealed container or plastic bag) and thaw it in a cup of boiling water. With any stock concentrate, just remember to add water when you start cooking.

Frozen stock will keep for weeks or months, though it does deteriorate somewhat in flavor over time. If you remember you have it, however, it's unlikely to last that long. And the cycle will begin again.

Canned Stock and Bouillon Cubes

Canned stock, whether chicken, beef, or vegetable, is usually worse than starting with water and simmering it for 10 minutes with a few vegetables. Really. If you find

F Fast   **M** Make Ahead   **V** Vegetarian

a good canned stock (I'm not saying it's impossible, just difficult), lay in a supply, because the recipe is rarely consistent. If you must buy canned stock, however, here are some pointers:

- Low-salt canned stock sometimes has more flavor than regular varieties. (Sometimes, however, it tastes like water.)
- Stock containing MSG should be avoided at all costs.
- Brand names are no guarantee of quality. The best stock I purchased last year was an off-brand that cost $0.25 a can (which, incidentally, meant that a gallon cost about $3, still more expensive than making decent stock from scratch).
- Any canned stock will benefit from the treatment described on page 160.

As for bouillon cubes, forget them. You're always better off with water and a few vegetables.

Vegetable Stock

MAKES: About 12 cups
TIME: About 1 hour, somewhat unattended

Making good vegetable stock takes a little work: You really should cut the vegetables into small pieces and brown them at least a bit. You can do without these steps, but the flavor won't be the same. I also add mushrooms and soy sauce, which make a big difference. Despite all of this, preparation and cooking take less than an hour.

    4 large carrots, sliced
    2 large onions, chopped (don't bother to peel)
    1 large potato, sliced
    2 celery stalks, chopped
    5 or 6 cloves garlic (don't bother to peel)
    10 to 20 medium button mushrooms, trimmed and
        halved or sliced

    2 medium tomatoes, chopped
    10 or 20 fresh parsley stems or stems and leaves
    Freshly ground black pepper

❶ Combine all the ingredients and add 14 cups water and some pepper. Bring to a boil and adjust the heat so the mixture simmers steadily but gently and cook for about 30 minutes, or until the vegetables are very tender. (Longer is better if you have the time.)

❷ Cool slightly, then strain, pressing on the vegetables to extract as much juice as possible. Use immediately or refrigerate for up to 5 days or freeze for up to 3 months.

Clear Vegetable Stock. Substitute 3 medium parsnips, peeled and chopped, for the potato.

Mushroom Stock. Use 1 carrot, 2 pounds mushrooms, and add 2 ounces dried shiitake, porcini, or a combination.

Quickest Chicken Stock

MAKES: 12 cups
TIME: 40 to 60 minutes

This stock takes less than an hour to make, has clear, clean flavor, and gives you a whole cooked (*not* overcooked) chicken, for salad or any other use.

    One 3- to 4-pound chicken
    1 large onion, roughly chopped (don't bother to peel)
    1 large carrot, roughly chopped
    1 celery stalk, roughly chopped
    1 bay leaf
    Several sprigs fresh parsley (optional)
    Salt and freshly ground black pepper

❶ Cut the chicken up if you like (see page 648); it will speed cooking. Combine all the ingredients in a large pot with 14 cups water and turn the heat to high.

How to Make Any Stock Darker and Richer

Roasting ingredients—whether meat, poultry, or vegetables—before adding water yields a darker, more deeply flavored stock that's ideal for hearty soups, stews, braises, and rich gravies or sauces.

The technique is simple and universal: Put at least 2 tablespoons neutral oil, like grapeseed or corn, into a wide pot or roasting pan. It's best to use the pot you'll cook the stock in, but if all the ingredients don't fit in one layer (it's likely that beef or veal bones won't), then use a large roasting pan. Add bones or meaty parts and brown on all sides; then add the vegetables and continue cooking until the vegetables are browned. Keep in mind that the larger the bones or parts, the longer they take to brown; beef and veal bones will take the longest, up to 20 or 30 minutes, while thinly cut vegetables may take as little as 5 minutes.

Some other ingredients that will darken stock and make it more complete:

Tomato paste: Mix it with the browned ingredients, cooking and stirring until it turns a deep rust color.

Red wine: Add after removing the browned ingredients (you can also use it in combination with tomato paste, after cooking the paste a bit); stir it into the pan, scraping up the bits on the bottom (this is called *deglazing*; see page 45). Once that's done, add the water as you normally would.

Garlic: Sometimes I put a whole head of garlic right into my simmering stock, but once it's in you can't take it out, so I do it only when I'm making a relatively small amount of stock and know that the garlic will be a welcome flavor regardless of how I use the stock.

Dried mushrooms: The distinctive flavor of mushrooms is almost always a fine addition, and I usually throw some directly into the stock as it's simmering. In fact, there's almost no reason not to do this. Use dried porcini (expensive) or dried shiitakes (cheap, especially when bought as black mushrooms in Chinese markets). The trimmings from fresh mushrooms are also good, of course.

---

② Bring just about to a boil, then lower the heat so the mixture sends up a few bubbles at a time. Cook, skimming any foam that accumulates, until the chicken is done, 30 to 60 minutes (depending on the size of the chicken and whether it's cut up).

③ Cool slightly, then strain, pressing on the meat and solids to extract more juice. Remove the chicken from the solids and use in another recipe; discard the remaining solids. Sprinkle with a little salt and pepper. Use the stock immediately or refrigerate (skim off any hardened fat from the surface) and use within 3 days or freeze for up to 3 months.

Full-Flavored Chicken, Turkey, or Duck Stock. Turkey or duck can be substituted for some or all of the chicken: Substitute 3 to 4 pounds chicken parts, preferably wings, thighs, and legs. Cook for at least 1 hour but no more than 2 hours. Discard all the solids.

Beef, Veal, Lamb, or Pork Stock

MAKES: About 14 cups
TIME: At least 3 hours, largely unattended

Primarily used for beef or veal, but lamb and pork stocks are good in limited roles also. In any case, a fine use for scraps, inexpensive cuts (shin, neck, and so on make terrific stock), and bones, meaty or not.

You can use chicken stock in a recipe if you don't have beef stock, but I'd rather use water than canned beef stock, which is essentially useless.

3 to 4 pounds meaty beef or veal bones, like shank, shin, tail, or short ribs

2 medium onions, chopped (don't bother to peel)

 Fast   Make Ahead   Vegetarian

2 medium carrots, chopped

2 celery stalks, chopped

1 bay leaf

At least 10 sprigs fresh parsley (optional)

1 teaspoon salt, plus more to taste

3 cloves

10 peppercorns

① Rinse the bones well under cold running water, then transfer to a large stockpot and add the remaining ingredients. Add about 16 cups water, enough to cover by a couple of inches.

② Bring just about to a boil, then partially cover and adjust the heat so the mixture sends up a few bubbles at a time. Cook, skimming off any foam that accumulates at the top, until the meat falls from the bones and the bones separate from one another, 2 to 3 hours.

③ Cool slightly, then strain, pressing on the vegetables and meat to extract as much juice as possible. Taste and add salt if necessary. Use immediately or refrigerate (skim off any hardened fat from the surface) and use within 4 or 5 days or freeze for up to 3 months.

Fish Stock

MAKES: About 4 cups
TIME: 40 minutes

Fish yields its flavor almost instantly; 15 to 30 minutes is plenty of time to simmer fish for a stock. And though the fish industry is more factory oriented than ever, you can still grab a few heads and racks (skeletons) from fishmongers for free, even at supermarkets. All you have to know is that usually you want white-fleshed fish, without their guts (which are strong tasting) or gills (which are bitter). Once you have those, you can make good fish stock in less than an hour.

1 medium onion, chopped (don't bother to peel)

1 carrot, roughly chopped

1 celery stalk, roughly chopped

$^1/_2$ cup dry white wine

1 pound bones and/or cleaned heads from white fish

1 bay leaf

① Combine all the ingredients and add 4 cups water. Bring just about to a boil, then adjust the heat so the mixture sends up a few bubbles at a time and cook for about 30 minutes.

② Cool slightly, then strain, pressing on the vegetables and fish to extract as much juice as possible. Use immediately or refrigerate for up to 3 days or freeze for up to a few weeks.

Full-Flavored Fish Stock. Add 1 tomato, chopped (canned is fine), 1 smashed clove garlic, a few sprigs fresh parsley, 2 slices lemon, and 3 or 4 whole black peppercorns.

Shrimp Stock

MAKES: About 4 cups
TIME: 20 minutes

The easiest, best-tasting, most useful stock you can make from something you normally throw away, perfect for risotto, pasta sauces, and as a substitute for fish and even light chicken stock. Make a small batch every time you peel shrimp, or freeze shrimp shells as you accumulate them and make a large batch at once.

Shells from 1 to 2 pounds shrimp (about 4 loosely packed cups)

$^1/_2$ onion, sliced (optional)

$^1/_2$ carrot, sliced (optional)

$^1/_2$ celery stalk, sliced (optional)

① Combine all the ingredients and add $4^1/_2$ cups of water. Bring to a boil, then turn the heat to very low, cover, and cook for 15 minutes.

7 Stock Variations

You can easily enhance pretty much any stock—even canned stock. Here's how:

1. **Vastly Improved Canned Stock:** For every can of stock, add a sliced carrot, a thinly sliced onion, a smashed garlic clove, a bay leaf, 5 whole peppercorns, and several fresh parsley stems, if you have them; cook the ingredients in the canned stock at a slow bubble for 15 minutes. Strain and use.

2. **Garlicky Stock:** Add 1 whole head garlic (unpeeled) to the pot along with the other ingredients.

3. **Asian-Style Stock:** Add five ⅛-inch-thick slices unpeeled ginger, 4 trimmed and roughly chopped scallions, ¼ cup soy sauce, 2 tablespoons dark sesame oil, and 1 star anise (optional) with the other ingredients.

4. **French-Style Stock:** Add 2 or 3 sprigs fresh thyme, 2 or 3 cloves, 5 to 10 peppercorns (less for lighter stocks, more for richer stocks), and ½ cup dry white wine (optional) with the other ingredients.

5. **Southern-Style Stock:** Best with chicken, beef, or veal, especially when roasted: Add a ham hock along with the bones.

6. **Southeast Asian–Style Stock:** Add 1 stalk chopped lemongrass, four ⅛-inch-thick slices unpeeled ginger, 3 smashed cloves garlic, a few sprigs fresh cilantro instead of parsley. Omit the bay leaf.

7. **Indian-Style Stock:** Add 4 or 5 smashed cloves garlic, two ⅛-inch-thick slices unpeeled ginger, 1 tablespoon curry powder or garam masala (to make your own, see pages 66–67), and a few sprigs fresh cilantro instead of parsley.

 Cool slightly, then strain, pressing on the shells to extract as much juice as possible. Use immediately or refrigerate for up to 3 days or freeze for up to a few weeks.

Lobster Stock. Substitute lobster shells and legs, preferably uncooked, for the shrimp.

Dashi

MAKES: 8 cups
TIME: 15 minutes

F **M**

Dashi is a quickly made stock that gives all kinds of foods—mostly Japanese—a good, distinctive flavor. The two main ingredients—kelp (also called *kombu;* see page 349) and dried bonito flakes (bonito is a type of tuna) are esoteric, but they're sold in every Japanese market, many other Asian markets, and even some major supermarkets. The process is simple, the results reliable; try it.

1 piece dried kelp (kombu), 4 to 6 inches long
½ to 1 cup dried bonito flakes

1 Combine the kelp and 8 cups water in a medium saucepan over medium heat. Do not allow the mixture to come to a boil; as soon as it is about to, turn off the heat and remove the kelp (you can use it as a vegetable in stir-fries or salads if you like).

2 Immediately add the bonito flakes and stir; let sit for a couple of minutes, then strain. Use the dashi immediately or refrigerate for up to 2 days.

Vegetarian Dashi. Omit the bonito flakes and add 2 or 3 nickel-sized pieces of ginger (don't bother to peel).

 Fast   Make Ahead   Vegetarian

Sandwiches and Pizza

LIKE SO MUCH ELSE IN THE AMERICAN

kitchen, the sandwich has changed dramatically over the course of the last generation. Not too long ago, the quintessential American sandwich was a couple of slices of bologna on mushy white bread with bad mustard; about the best you could hope for was ham and cheese or meatballs on a decent roll. Now you're equally likely to see hot pressed Cuban sandwiches and Italian panini in the supermarket, along with wraps or other filled tortillas, freshly baked stuffed dough, or mozzarella and arugula on ciabatta.

Even pizza has changed: no longer solely the domain of the pizza parlor, it's become something anyone can make quickly and easily at home, whether by making dough or simply buying fresh dough from a local pizza maker or frozen dough at the supermarket. Similarly, pita bread and flour tortillas are sold almost everywhere, and they also take well to a variety of fillings.

ESSENTIAL RECIPES

When it comes to sandwiches, tacos, pizza, and the like, everyone has favorites—and most people have personal specialties. This is my list, the handful of dishes that I can't live without.

Most are pretty straightforward and super-fast. Don't let the fact that focaccia is a yeast dough keep you from trying it—it's a virtually foolproof pizza and a terrific introduction to working with raised doughs.

Tuna Salad with Lemon and Olive Oil

MAKES: 4 sandwiches
TIME: 10 minutes

This low-fat alternative to the traditional tuna sandwich (try it with pita) has loads of bright flavor from the lemon zest and capers. If you use water-packed tuna, drain well and add another tablespoon or two of extra virgin olive oil.

Two 6-ounce cans tuna, preferably packed in olive oil, drained

Grated zest and juice of 1 lemon

1 small shallot or 3 scallions, minced

1 or 2 tablespoons capers, rinsed, drained, and chopped

1/2 cup chopped fresh parsley leaves

3 tablespoons extra virgin olive oil

Salt and freshly ground black pepper

4 leaves romaine lettuce, washed and dried

8 slices any bread

1 Mix the tuna with the lemon zest and juice, shallots, capers, parsley, and olive oil and sprinkle with some salt and pepper.

2 Make sandwiches with the tuna mixture and lettuce. Serve immediately.

Tuna Salad with Lime and Cilantro. Substitute the juice of 2 limes for the lemon and cilantro for the parsley; use the scallions and omit the capers and olive oil.

Tuna Salad with Olives. Substitute 1/4 cup Tapenade (page 96) or finely chopped olives for the capers and use less lemon juice—to taste, at the end (you may decide to use none).

Tuna Salad with Mayo. Substitute 1/4 cup or more mayonnaise for the olive oil; omit the lemon zest and juice if you like and try chopped pickles instead of the capers.

Egg Salad with Mayo. Instead of the tuna in the preceding variation, use 6 Hard-Boiled Eggs (page 791). Chop them as finely or coarsely as you like before combining with the mayonnaise. Add a tablespoon of mustard (or more to taste) and add either pickles, capers, or minced celery or scallion—or a combination.

Welsh Rarebit

MAKES: At least 4 servings
TIME: About 20 minutes, plus time to cool

A fancy (but easy), old-fashioned, and entirely wonderful take on grilled cheese. The intensely flavored topping—basically seasoned Mornay (Cheese) Sauce (page 58)—can be made in advance and has the added advantage of being ideal for breakfast, lunch, or late-night snacking. One word of advice: Don't shortcut the second toasting

 F Fast   **M** Make Ahead   **V** Vegetarian

under the broiler, which will keep the bread from becoming soggy.

2 tablespoons butter

2 tablespoons all-purpose flour

1 tablespoon dry mustard, or to taste

$1/2$ teaspoon cayenne, or to taste

$3/4$ cup strong dark beer, like Guinness stout

2 tablespoons Worcestershire sauce, or to taste

1 pound cheddar or other English cheese (or other good semihard cheese, like Comté or Gruyère, or a mixture), grated

4 to 8 slices lightly toasted bread

1 Put the butter in a saucepan over medium heat and, as it melts, stir in the flour. Cook, stirring occasionally, until golden brown and very fragrant, 3 to 5 minutes. Stir in the mustard and cayenne, then whisk in the beer and Worcestershire sauce.

2 When the mixture is uniform, turn the heat down to low and stir in the cheese, again whisking until smooth. Remove from the heat and pour into a baking dish or deep, wide bowl to set (at this point, you can refrigerate the cheese mixture for up to a day).

3 Heat the broiler and put the bread on a large baking sheet. Toast on one side, moving the slices as needed to brown them evenly. Flip the slices and return them to the broiler just long enough to dry them out a bit. Then spread the mixture thickly on the toast and put under the broiler one last time until bubbly and crisp. Serve immediately.

✪ Fish Tacos, Four Ways

MAKES: 4 servings
TIME: 20 minutes

F

This is a case where you can cook the fish in the microwave with good results. As with any tacos, resist the urge to overfill; they'll just fall apart. (For a more involved taco, see the variations. And for more about tacos in general, see page 172.)

Other protein you can use: shrimp or scallops, salmon (fillets or steaks), split whole lobster, boneless white or dark meat chicken or turkey, or pork loin (the poultry and pork will take a little longer to cook than the seafood).

1 large onion, roughly chopped

2 jalapeño chiles, roughly chopped

About $1 1/2$ pounds thick white fish fillets, like cod, red snapper, sea bass, grouper, or halibut

Salt and freshly ground black pepper

Twelve to sixteen 6-inch corn tortillas

Fresh salsa (to make your own, see pages 23 and 33–35)

Hot sauce or Chile Paste (page 74; optional)

Sour cream or crumbled queso fresco or other grated cheese (optional)

Shredded cabbage, chopped tomato and cucumber, and cilantro sprigs (optional)

Lime wedges

1 Put the onion and jalapeños in a large skillet with a tight-fitting lid (or microwavable casserole). Add 1 tablespoon water and the fish; sprinkle with salt and pepper. Cover and put over medium heat (or in the microwave). Cook for about 6 minutes (3 in the microwave), or until the fish is done.

2 While the fish cooks, heat the tortillas. Either toast them in a skillet, one at a time, over medium heat, flipping once or twice until hot, a minute or so, or heat in a microwave, half a dozen at a time, wrapped in a slightly damp towel, for about a minute.

3 To serve, put a small portion of fish along with a bit of the onion and jalapeño in a warm tortilla. Top with salsa and, if you like, hot sauce, sour cream, and/or vegetables. Squeeze lime juice over all. Repeat with the remaining tortillas.

Grilled Fish Tacos. Omit the onion and jalapeño (or chop them up as another garnish.) Brush the fish with some extra virgin olive oil and sprinkle with salt and pepper and, if you like, rub with chili powder (to make your own, see page 66). Let it rest for a bit while you follow the instructions for Grilled Fish Fillets or Steaks on page 564.

Broiled Fish Tacos. Prepare the fish as described in the preceding variation, then follow the instructions for Broiled Thick Fillets or Steaks on page 563.

Fried Fish Tacos. You have a few choices, depending on whether you want deep-, shallow-, or oven-fried fish; substitute cornmeal for the flour in any of them if you like: Prepare the fish as described in the preceding variation, then follow the instructions for either Deep-Fried Seafood (page 568), Pan-Cooked Thick Fish Fillets (page 565), or Oven-"Fried" Fish Fillets (page 568).

✪ Clayuda

Tortilla with Black Bean Purée

MAKES: 4 to 8 servings
TIME: 30 minutes

🅕 🅥

This Mexican specialty from Oaxaca combines the best of pizza, quesadilla, and an open-face taco or burrito. Skip the meat and finish with a sprinkling of chopped cilantro and onion and a squeeze of lime if you like. Just make sure whatever goes into the oven is chopped into fairly small pieces, since the baking time is short.

> 2 cups cooked or canned black beans, drained and liquid reserved
>
> Salt and freshly ground black pepper
>
> 1 tablespoon minced garlic
>
> 1 small onion, chopped
>
> 1 teaspoon ground or crumbled mild dried chiles, like New Mexico or ancho, or to taste
>
> 1 tablespoon ground cumin, or to taste
>
> Two 12-inch tortillas, preferably corn

> 1 cup chopped quesillo (Mexican string cheese) or mozzarella or a crumbly cheese like queso fresco, slightly dried goat cheese, or feta
>
> 4 ounces Spanish chorizo or other smoked or cooked sausage or pork (optional)
>
> 1 cup chopped green cabbage

① Heat the oven to 450°F. Heat the beans with a small amount of their liquid in a small pot with some salt and pepper, the garlic, onion, chiles, and cumin; stir and cook just long enough to take the edge off the garlic and onion, about 5 minutes.

② Drain and reserve the liquid. Carefully place the mixture in a blender or food processor with enough bean liquid to allow the machine to do its work and roughly purée, leaving the mixture a bit chunky.

③ Put 1 tortilla on a pizza peel or baking sheet and spread half the bean mixture on it; top with half the cheese and half the meat, if you're using it. Bake (on a pizza stone if you're not using a baking sheet) for about 5 minutes, then sprinkle with half the cabbage. Bake for another 5 minutes or so, until the topping is hot and the tortilla crisp on the edges. Cut into wedges and serve. Repeat with the other tortilla.

✪ Rosemary Focaccia

MAKES: 1 focaccia
TIME: About 3 hours, largely unattended

🅜 🅥

Focaccia is like pizza, but a little easier to make, since it's just pressed into the pan. You generally top it more minimally too, unless you're making deep-dish pizza (see the variation).

> 1 recipe Pizza Dough (page 178), made with an extra tablespoon olive oil, mixed, and risen (Steps 1–3)
>
> 3 tablespoons extra virgin olive oil
>
> 1 tablespoon chopped fresh rosemary leaves, plus more to taste
>
> Coarse kosher or sea salt

 Fast   Make Ahead   Vegetarian

1 Lightly knead the dough, form it into a ball, and put it on a lightly floured surface. Sprinkle with a little more flour, cover with plastic wrap or a towel, and let it rest for 20 minutes.

2 Use 1 tablespoon of the oil to grease an 11 × 17-inch jelly-roll pan. Press the dough into a small rectangle and put it in the pan; let it relax there for a few minutes. Press and stretch the dough to the edges of the pan. If it resists, let it rest for a few minutes, then stretch it some more. Sometimes this takes a while, because the dough is so elastic. Don't fight it; just stretch, rest, then stretch again. Try not to tear the dough. Cover the dough and let it rise for at least 30 minutes or until somewhat puffy.

3 Heat the oven to 425°F. Uncover the dough and dimple the surface all over with your fingertips. Drizzle with the remaining olive oil and sprinkle with the rosemary and plenty of salt.

4 Put the focaccia in the oven, lower the temperature to 375°F, and bake for about 30 minutes, or until the focaccia is golden. Remove and cool on a rack before serving. Cut the focaccia into squares and serve with meals or as a snack. Or cut squares in half horizontally and use to make sandwiches. Focaccia, well wrapped (first in plastic, then in foil), freezes fairly well for 2 weeks or so. Reheat, straight from the freezer (unwrap, remove the plastic, and then rewrap in foil), in a 350°F oven for 10 to 15 minutes.

Deep-Dish Pizza, Chicago Style. Like focaccia, this is pressed right into the pan. Bake the dough partially, for about 10 minutes. Grate 2 cups of mozzarella cheese and $1/2$ cup of Parmesan; heat about $1^1/2$ cups of Fast Tomato Sauce (page 502). Smear the pizza with a thin layer of sauce, sprinkle with the cheeses (and any other ingredients you like), and bake for 20 to 25 minutes more, until hot and bubbly and browned on the bottom. For more toppings, see Pizza with Tomato Sauce and Mozzarella (page 181) and "18 Ideas for Pizza Toppings" (page 181).

7 Other Ingredients for Topping Focaccia

1. Any other minced fresh herbs or chiles
2. Thinly sliced tomatoes, patted dry
3. Caramelized Onions (page 325)
4. Pitted black or green olives, or Tapenade (page 96)
5. Grated Parmesan or other sharp cheese
6. Thin slices of prosciutto
7. Thin slices of peeled fruit, like peaches, nectarines, apples, or plums, or halved grapes or cherries

The Basics of Sandwiches

Two pieces of bread—or a roll or loaf cut in half—with some kind of filling. The sandwich has been around for a few hundred years, supposedly named after its accidental inventor, the Earl of Sandwich (though who really believes that?). Sandwiches run the gamut from PB&J to something as deluxe as sliced steak with caramelized onions and Gorgonzola (first rate, by the way).

Sandwiches are lunch staples but especially when hot make regular appearances at the dinner table, where more elaborate sandwiches make excellent main courses, using a large loaf of ciabatta or thick focaccia and cut into individual pieces. Alternatively, downsize a sandwich to make finger food or canapés by using thin slices of bread (with the crusts cut off if you like) and cutting the sandwich into 2-inch squares. Bottom line: There is a sandwich for every occasion.

Sandwich Breads

Bread's role in a sandwich goes beyond its function as a holder and transporter of a filling. You want to be able to taste it, which means store-bought white is not the best choice. In fact, it might be the worst.

Yeast breads or flatbreads and rolls are usually the best sandwich breads because they have the structure to support the filling and a nice chewy texture. But some yeast breads simply aren't cut out for sandwiches; those with very hard or thick crusts can make sandwiches nearly impossible to eat, and breads with large holes just can't hold the filling. Crumbly quick breads can work but are best as open-face sandwiches with simple and small amounts of topping. (The cold and hot sandwiches charts, see pages 170–171, give bread pairing suggestions for all sorts of sandwiches.) Beyond the type of bread you use, there's what you do with it: Toasting, grilling, and broiling make bread crisp and tastier. (You can also toast most sandwiches after filling.)

Fillings and Spreads

There are few rules for fillings and even fewer for spreads. Obviously you don't want a filling that's so moist that it sogs up the bread or so dry that you need a gulp of water with every bite. And you want the food sliced thin (or cut small) enough to bite into the sandwich easily but not so small that the filling falls out of the bread. (When in doubt, just stuff a pita pocket or roll the fillings up in a big tortilla.)

Spreads should be full of flavor and provide some moisture and/or creaminess, so cheese spreads, soft cheeses, and vegetable and bean purées are ideal. Many spreads can become the filling as well, like hummus; they make simple but tasty sandwiches that can easily be transformed into bite-sized hors d'oeuvres.

Grilled Cheese, Simple and Complex

MAKES: 1 sandwich
TIME: 10 minutes

You may have grown up with grilled cheese, but the concept of griddling a sandwich isn't exclusive to one cuisine. And you don't need a fancy press to make a beautifully crisp and browned sandwich; the plate technique here does the job perfectly. Improve simple grilled cheese by adding your favorite dressing or using more filling—see the following chart.

1 tablespoon butter, extra virgin olive oil, or neutral oil, like grapeseed or corn

Top 8 Things to Have Handy for Filling and Spreading on Sandwiches

The classic sandwich spreads are mustard and mayonnaise (there are recipes in this book for both). But consider the items on this list:

1. The old standbys: thinly sliced roast beef, turkey or chicken, ham or other cured meat. Think, too, of firm tofu (baked, fried, grilled, etc.) and leftovers like meat loaf.
2. Hard-Boiled Eggs (page 791), sliced or in egg salad, or scrambled or fried eggs.
3. Hummus (page 93) or any bean spread or purée.
4. Cheese spread (see page 91) or slices.
5. Tomato or onion slices.
6. Greens like lettuce, arugula, watercress, or spinach, including cooked greens (pressed dry).
7. Vinaigrette and other salad dressings ("Russian" dressing, ranch dressing, and so on).
8. Condiments: mustard, mayo, ketchup, and relish, of course, but don't forget the dozens of other options from the sauces chapter: Traditional Pesto or other herb sauces (pages 27–29), Basic Barbecue Sauce (page 52), any chutney, or cooked or fresh salsas.

2 slices any bread

Several slices (2 to 3 ounces) good melting cheese: Emmental, Gruyère, Jarlsberg, cheddar, etc.

1 Put a small skillet over medium heat and add the butter or oil. Make a sandwich of the bread and cheese.

2 When the butter melts or the oil is hot, put the sandwich in the skillet. Cover it with a plate and weight the plate with whatever is at hand—a couple of cans of soup or a small but heavy pot cover, for example.

3 Cook until the bottom of the bread is browned lightly, 2 or 3 minutes. Turn and repeat. Eat immediately.

 Fast   Make Ahead   Vegetarian

7 OTHER GRILLED SANDWICHES

For any of the griddled sandwiches below, use the technique in Grilled Cheese (page 166), smearing one slice of bread with the spread, filling as described, and cooking long enough to brown the bread and melt the cheese.

SANDWICH	BREAD	SPREAD	FILLING
Grilled Cheese and Onions	Any bread, but whole wheat or multigrain is best	None	Several slices smoked cheddar or other smoked cheese, up to $1/4$ cup Caramelized Onions (page 325)
Tuna Melt	Any bread; try a sourdough	None	$1/4$ to $1/2$ cup Tuna Salad (page 162); several slices good melting cheese: Emmental, Gruyère, Jarlsberg, cheddar, etc.
Reuben	Rye bread	Russian dressing (an equal mix of ketchup and mayonnaise) or mustard	2 or 3 ounces sliced pastrami or corned beef, $1/4$ cup drained sauerkraut, several slices of any Swiss melting cheese
Cuban Sandwich	6- to 10-inch section of long French loaf or baguette	Yellow mustard	3 ounces sliced roast pork, ham, and/or mortadella if you like, several slices good melting cheese, thinly sliced dill pickle
Chicken-Pesto Panino	Ciabatta or similar crusty Italian-style bread	Traditional Pesto (page 27)	2 to 3 ounces sliced cooked chicken breast, several slices mozzarella cheese (preferably fresh), 2 or 3 thin slices ripe tomato
Croque Monsieur or Madame	Sandwich Bread (page 859), challah, or brioche; for Monsieur, soak the bread in an egg beaten with a little milk as in French toast	None	Several slices Gruyère cheese, 2 ounces or so sliced country ham; for Madame, add a fried or poached egg on top
Grilled Nut Butter and Banana Sandwich	Fast French Bread (page 857) or Sandwich Bread (page 859)	Almond or any nut butter (spread on both pieces of bread)	$1/4$ cup banana slices, chocolate chips or marshmallows (optional)

Pan Bagnat with Chicken Breast

MAKES: 4 servings

TIME: 1 hour, plus time to rest overnight

Pan bagnat—which translates as "bathed bread" because of the way the bread is dressed—is not only one of the most beautiful sandwiches you've ever seen but also ideal for picnics: The longer it sits (within reason), the better it gets. View this recipe as a general guideline; you can make the sandwich with whatever cooked food you have on hand, including leftover grilled fish or meat and leftover vegetables.

1 medium zucchini, summer squash, or eggplant

Salt and freshly ground black pepper

$1/2$ pound boneless, skinless chicken breast

2 tablespoons extra virgin olive oil, plus oil for brushing the vegetables

1 or 2 red bell peppers (or use whole pimientos from cans or jars)

One 8- to 10-inch round crusty loaf of bread

1 teaspoon drained capers, or more to taste

6 or 8 black or green olives, pitted

4 to 6 anchovy fillets, or more to taste

4 marinated artichoke hearts, quartered

2 or 3 slices ripe tomato

Chopped fresh parsley or basil leaves

Juice of ¹/₂ lemon

1 Cut the zucchini lengthwise into ¹/₄-inch slices. If time allows, put it in a colander and salt liberally; let sit for 30 to 45 minutes, then rinse and dry thoroughly, pressing to extract excess moisture. Meanwhile, heat a charcoal or gas grill or a broiler to moderate heat and put the rack 4 inches or so from the heat source.

2 Sprinkle the chicken with salt and pepper and grill until just cooked through, 2 to 4 minutes per side, depending on thickness. At the same time, brush the zucchini with some olive oil and grill until lightly browned on both sides, 5 to 7 minutes total. Grill the red peppers until the skin blackens and blisters all around, about 5 minutes total. When the peppers are cool enough to handle, peel, core, and seed them; cut into strips.

3 Cut the bread in half horizontally. Remove some of the white crumbs from each half to make the bread somewhat hollow. Then build the sandwich, layering on the chicken, bell pepper, zucchini, capers, olives, anchovies, artichoke hearts, tomato, and herb. Sprinkle with some salt and pepper, drizzle with 2 tablespoons olive oil (or a little more), and sprinkle with lemon juice.

4 Close the sandwich; wrap well in aluminum foil. Put it on a plate, with another plate on top, and weight the second plate with rocks, bricks, a gallon jug of water—whatever is handy. Use a lot of weight—5 pounds or more. Refrigerate overnight or for up to 24 hours. Unwrap, cut into wedges, and serve.

6 Tips for Preventing Soggy Sandwiches

Aside from the obvious—eating it immediately—here's how to keep a packed sandwich fresh:

1. Use cold or room-temperature ingredients; heat will create steam and condensation, which the bread will absorb.

2. For picnics and traveling, wrap the components separately and assemble the sandwich just before eating.

3. Omit the tomato; substitute Roasted Red Pepper (page 330) pieces, blotted dry with paper towels.

4. Use a somewhat dry filling or blot a moist filling with paper towels.

5. Use dry, dense, crusty breads; they are far more resilient than very soft, fluffy breads and will soften up after a few hours of being wrapped with the fillings.

6. Make a wrap using a large flour tortilla (see "Wraps," page 170); tortillas don't absorb moisture as readily as bread.

Mixed Veggie Sandwich with Tahini Dressing

MAKES: 4 sandwiches

TIME: 20 minutes

The basic technique for turning a salad into a sandwich—the pita pockets hold the filling nicely, or you can wrap the mixture up in a big flour tortilla. Follow this method to make the classic Mediterranean sandwich filled with Falafel (page 439).

2 carrots, grated

1 cup alfalfa or other sprouts

¹/₄ head red or other cabbage, shredded

1 cup sliced cooked or drained canned beets, cut into strips

¹/₄ cup raisins

¹/₄ cup roughly chopped pecans, walnuts, or almonds

1 cup tahini

1 clove garlic, peeled

1/4 cup freshly squeezed lemon juice

Salt and freshly ground black pepper

2 ripe tomatoes, cored and cut into 8 wedges

4 pita breads, cut in half, 4 flour tortillas (8- or 10-inch), 8 slices bread, or 4 rolls, split in half

4 leaves romaine lettuce

1 Mix together the carrots, sprouts, cabbage, beets, raisins, and pecans.

2 Put the tahini in a blender or food processor with the garlic and lemon juice and process until smooth; gradually add 1/4 cup water, processing until creamy, then add salt and pepper to taste. Thin with a little more water if necessary.

3 Toss the vegetable mixture with the tomatoes and dressing, then make sandwiches with the vegetables and the lettuce. Serve immediately.

Gert's Pepper, Onion, and Sausage Sandwich

MAKES: 2 large or 4 small sandwiches

TIME: 30 minutes

My mother's favorite, best with red or yellow peppers, but not bad with green either. This sandwich can be made vegetarian, of course, by omitting the sausage.

2 tablespoons butter or olive oil, plus more for the rolls if desired

2 large Italian sausages (about 1/2 pound), split lengthwise

2 bell peppers, preferably red or yellow, roasted and peeled (see page 330), seeded, and cut into strips

2 medium to large onions, cut in half and thinly sliced

Salt and freshly ground black pepper

2 to 4 long hard rolls

1 Put the butter or oil in a large, deep skillet over medium heat. When the butter melts or the oil is hot, add the sausages and cook until lightly browned on both sides, about 5 minutes total. Add the peppers and onions. Season with salt and pepper and cook, stirring occasionally, until very tender, about 20 minutes. Taste and adjust the seasoning.

2 Butter the rolls or drizzle them with olive oil if you like. Spread the sausage into the rolls and pile the pepper-and-onion mixture on top. Serve hot.

Fish Sandwich with Chili-Lime Mayo

MAKES: 4 sandwiches

TIME: 30 minutes

I love fried fish sandwiches, but you can always broil or grill the fish if you prefer (see pages 562–564).

1/4 cup mayonnaise (to make your own, see page 41)

2 tablespoons freshly squeezed lime juice

1 tablespoon chili powder (to make your own, see page 66)

1 teaspoon minced garlic

Salt and freshly ground black pepper

1/4 cup neutral oil, like grapeseed or corn, plus more as needed

Four 4-ounce fillets of firm white fish, like cod, halibut, or catfish, salmon, or mahi-mahi

1/4 cup all-purpose flour

1 egg, beaten with 2 tablespoons water

3/4 cup bread crumbs, preferably fresh (page 876)

4 rolls or 8 slices bread, toasted if you like

8 slices ripe tomato

2 cups shredded Napa cabbage or iceberg lettuce

1/4 cup chopped fresh cilantro leaves (optional)

① Mix together the mayonnaise, lime juice, chili powder, garlic, and some salt and pepper; taste, adjust the seasoning, and set aside.

② Put the oil in a large skillet over medium-high heat. Sprinkle the fish with salt and pepper, then dredge both sides of the fillets in the flour; dip in the egg, and coat in the bread crumbs. When the oil is hot, add the fillets and cook until golden brown on both sides, about 8 minutes total.

③ To assemble the sandwiches, smear the rolls with the chili-lime mayo, add the fillets (cut in half to fit on the bun as necessary), and top with tomato slices, cabbage, and cilantro if you're using it. Serve immediately.

Fried Chicken Sandwich with Ranch Dressing. You can stick with straight mayo if you like: Substitute Real Ranch Dressing (page 42) for the chili-lime mayo, torn mixed greens for the cabbage, four 4-ounce boneless chicken tenders (or half-breasts) for the fillets, and cornmeal for the bread crumbs.

WRAPS

The sandwich/burrito hybrid has become a standard. Because wraps are folded and rolled like a burrito, they can hold items that would otherwise fall out of two pieces of bread or make a soggy mess of sandwich bread (like beans and rice).

Any large, flat, flexible bread will work as a wrapping; flour tortillas and lavash are the most common, though you can also use pita.

Lavash comes both soft (basically freshly baked) and as a hard cracker. Both can be used for wraps. To soften the cracker (large Ak-Maks, widely available, work here), run it under water on both sides, put it in a plastic bag, seal it, and let it sit in a cool place or refrigerator until it's completely soft, about 3 hours.

You can load up a wrap with a dressed salad, sliced or ground meat, cooked fish or shellfish, grains, legumes, stir-fried vegetables, or chopped raw vegetables and any condiment you can think of. Roll it up, tucking the ends in like a burrito (see the illustration on page 173). Eat whole, cut in half (it looks nice cut on a slight diagonal), or get multiple servings by slicing crosswise into thick rounds. This chart will give you plenty of ideas.

WRAP	WRAPPER	SPREAD AND/OR CONDIMENTS	FILLING
Caesar Wrap	Plain tortilla	Shaved or finely grated Parmesan	Caesar Salad (page 203), sliced grilled chicken or shrimp
Asian-Style Wrap	Plain or flavored tortilla	Chile-Garlic Paste (page 75) or Peanut Sauce (page 55); chopped scallion, fresh cilantro (optional)	Stir-Fried Vegetables (page 241) with or without meat or tofu
Curry Wrap	Lavash or Ak-Mak	Raita (page 24) or plain yogurt, any chutney (pages 36–38), fresh cilantro	Chicken with Yogurt and Indian Spices (page 650) or chickpeas
Steak-and-Pepper Wrap	Lavash, Ak-Mak, or plain tortilla	Roasted Pepper and Garlic Spread (page 91) or Horseradish Dip (page 89)	Steak slices, My Mom's Pan-Cooked Peppers and Onions (page 331)

 Fast   Make Ahead   **V** Vegetarian

IMPROVISING HOT SANDWICHES

Some of these are assembled from leftovers and heated; others begin with raw ingredients that are then cooked together in the sandwich (like grilled cheese). Again, mix up these combos as you like, drawing inspiration rather than rules from this chart.

SANDWICH	BREAD	SPREAD AND/OR CONDIMENTS	FILLING	COOKING
Broiled Roast Beef and Avocado Sandwich	Sandwich or Anadama Bread (page 859)	Guacamole (page 94) or mashed or sliced avocado or Garlic Mayonnaise (page 42)	Roast beef slices, Roasted Red Peppers or poblanos (page 330), cheddar or Jack cheese	Toast the bread, layer the spread and fillings on one slice of bread and broil until the cheese melts, then add the second piece of bread.
Pita Sandwich Stuffed with Spicy Lamb and Onions	Pita bread (page 872)	Simplest Yogurt Sauce (page 24)	Ground lamb; chopped onion, chopped garlic, and a pinch of cinnamon; thinly sliced zucchini; tomato slices	Sauté the lamb in a little extra virgin olive oil with the onion, garlic, and cinnamon until done; warm the pita in the oven; assemble the sandwich.
Ratatouille Sandwich with Melted Mozzarella	Sourdough Bread (page 858), Semolina Bread (page 865), or any Italian-style bread	Fresh basil leaves, a drizzle of extra virgin olive oil (optional)	Grilled or Broiled Eggplant (page 294) or Eggplant Slices with Garlic and Parsley (page 297); Roasted Red Peppers (page 330) or tomato slices; sliced mozzarella	Cook the eggplant as directed; grill or toast the bread if you like. Layer the vegetables on both sides of the bread, top with mozzarella, and melt the cheese under the broiler. Garnish with the basil and eat open face.
Grilled Chicken Breast Sandwich with Roasted Garlic and Mustard	Rich Golden Sandwich Bread (page 862) or Sandwich Bread (page 859)	Mashed Roasted Garlic (page 303) and grainy mustard	Grilled or roasted boneless chicken breast, Muenster or provolone cheese, arugula or spinach	Melt the cheese on the chicken in the last couple minutes of cooking; grill or broil the bread and spread the garlic and mustard on each slice; assemble.
North Carolina BBQ Sandwich	Fast French Rolls (page 856), Rich Golden Rolls (page 862), or other rolls	Basic Barbecue Sauce (page 52)	No-Work Smoked Pork Shoulder or Spareribs (page 759), Spicy No-Mayo Coleslaw (page 206)	Wrap the rolls in foil and warm in the oven; heat the pork if necessary, then shred using two forks. Assemble the sandwich, adding the slaw last.
Fruit-and-Brie Sandwich	Brioche loaf, Challah (page 866), or Rich Golden Sandwich Bread (page 862)	Applesauce (page 383) or apple butter; honey mustard or Dijon	Brie slices; apple or pear, cored and sliced; frisée (optional)	Toast the bread; smear one piece with applesauce; layer on the apple or pear, then the Brie, and broil until the cheese is soft; assemble.
Warm Goat Cheese Sandwich with Toasted Nuts	50 Percent Whole Wheat Sandwich Bread (page 861) or any multigrain bread	Plain goat cheese	Toasted chopped almonds, Roasted Red Peppers (page 330), arugula or spinach leaves	Spread the goat cheese on both pieces of bread and broil until bubbly; sprinkle with almonds and finish with peppers and arugula or spinach.

28 Perfect Dishes for (Mostly) Hot Sandwiches

In general, rolls, buns, pita, or whole loaves stuffed and cut into wedges are the best breads for fillings like the following. Use these hot or at room temperature.

1. Tomato, Mozzarella, and Basil Salad (page 187)
2. Any chicken, meat, or seafood salad on pages 222–228
3. Crab Salad (page 225)
4. Fried Chile-Spiced Clam Salad (page 225)
5. Eggplant Parmesan (page 297)
6. Seafood prepared by any of the Essential Recipes on pages 563–572
7. Chile Shrimp (page 577)
8. Gravlax (page 585)
9. Grilled or Broiled Soft-Shell Crab or Lobster (page 614)
10. Crab Cakes (page 633)
11. Grilled or Broiled Boneless Chicken (page 641)
12. Chicken MarkNuggets (page 646)
13. Broiled or Grilled Boneless Chicken Escabeche (page 669)
14. Herb-Roasted Chicken Cutlets (page 672)
15. Any Poached Chicken (page 682)
16. Grilled, Pan-Grilled, or Broiled Steak, Many Ways (page 717)
17. Any of the Burgers on pages 721–723 and page 764
18. Meat Loaf (page 723)
19. Roast Tenderloin with Herbs (page 735)
20. Braised Beef Brisket (page 743)
21. Corned Beef (page 744)
22. West Indian Crispy Pork Bits (page 749)
23. Grilled or Broiled Pork Tenderloin with Mustard Curry (page 752)
24. Any of the roast pork recipes on pages 754–756
25. Shredded Pork (page 759)
26. Baked Country Ham (page 765)
27. Roast Leg of Lamb, Four Ways (page 770)
28. Veal Cutlets, 1950s Style (page 781)

The Basics of Tacos and Burritos

Tacos and burritos—which are really just sandwiches—have a lot in common: They use tortillas (corn or flour for tacos, only flour for burritos); can be filled with meat, chicken, fish, beans, rice, vegetables, salsas, etc.; and are eaten with your hands. They don't share the same origins (burritos are a north-of-the-border Tex-Mex invention), but they're both quick and convenient to make and eat. Both serve brilliantly at a do-it-yourself buffet.

Most supermarkets sell a half dozen varieties of tortillas these days, varying in type (corn or flour), size, and flavor. (If you live near a Mexican or Latin market, it's worth the trip to buy really good tortillas.) Flour tortillas are soft and subtle, almost neutral in flavor; when fresh, they are delicious and almost fluffy (too often they're dull and rubbery). You'll find plain (the most useful), whole wheat, and flavored (and colored) ones, like spinach or tomato. Flour tortillas are almost always served and used soft but are occasionally fried crisp.

Corn tortillas—white, yellow, and sometimes blue—offer more texture and flavor. I always buy raw corn tortillas and cook them myself. Like flour, the fresh ones are completely different from those that sit on the supermarket shelves for weeks at a time. The best have a fresh corn taste and are soft and pliable. Cooked corn tortillas can be either soft or crisp, depending on your taste or the freshness of the tortilla. Serve them soft if they're fresh; fry them if they're stale.

Preparing Tortillas

Soft flour or corn tortillas should be served hot or warm. Warm them over direct heat, like a grill or the flame of a gas stove, turning them every few seconds, or in a dry skillet, turning once; or wrap them in a damp kitchen towel and microwave for about 30 seconds. Keep them hot in a tortilla holder (a shallow round container with a lid) or wrapped in a towel or two.

Corn tortillas are more commonly served crisp, but both fry up nicely. There are two methods: Panfry in a skillet with shallow or deep hot oil, turning when the edges brown (you can mold it into a taco shape when it's still slightly soft and flexible); or stuff with filling, secure with toothpicks, and panfry in $1/4$ inch or so hot oil until both sides are golden. (Drain the tortillas on paper towels for several seconds before serving.)

Filling Tortillas

Don't overfill. For tacos, a couple of tablespoons of filling does the trick and leaves room for garnishes. Burritos hold more, especially if you use those huge tortillas. Just make sure your first fold comfortably encloses the ingredients (see the illustrations at right).

Seasoned meat, chicken, and fish are the most common taco fillings. Grilled fillings are most common, though broiled, pan-fried, and deep-fried fillings are all standard. I generally like things chopped up a bit. Beans and rice are an excellent filling, either on their own or with meat or vegetables; be sure the beans are well seasoned and not too soupy; partially mash whole beans to thicken them if there's too much liquid. Add more texture by using firmer grains, like wheat berries, instead of rice.

Vegetables are another option, especially when grilled or breaded and fried. You can use just about any vegetable that works with your cooking method (see Roasted Vegetables, page 241; Breaded Fried Eggplant, page 245; or Grilled Vegetables, page 249).

The Toppings

Homemade salsa can improve tacos and burritos immeasurably; see pages 23, 33–35, and 48–50 and don't forget Crunchy Corn Guacamole (page 95), which adds creamy richness, especially valuable when you're using a vegetable filling.

Shredded lettuce or cabbage, chopped tomatoes,

ROLLING BURRITOS

1

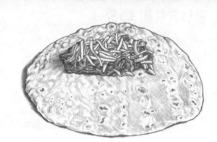

2

3

Rolling a burrito doesn't take too much skill as long as you don't overstuff. The solution: Fill it with less stuff or use a larger tortilla. **(STEP 1)** Put the filling in the middle of the tortilla, slightly off center toward the edge closest to you. **(STEP 2)** Fold in the sides a little bit and **(STEP 3)** roll up from the edge closest to you, tucking in the sides and the top edge to form a tight roll. Put the burrito seam side down on the plate or wrap the bottom half in foil or wax paper to help keep it together.

10 UNUSUAL IDEAS FOR FILLING TACOS AND BURRITOS

Mix and match as you like, but remember not to overfill. For tacos, use crisp or soft flour or corn tortillas; for burritos, warm any size flour tortilla until pliable, then fill and roll.

FILLINGS	SALSAS, TOPPINGS, AND EXTRAS
Black Beans and White Rice, Spanish Style (page 435)	Avocado-Red Pepper Salsa (page 24), shredded iceberg or romaine lettuce
Roasted Chickpeas (page 416) and Yellow Rice, the Fast Way (page 463)	Radish Salsa (page 34) and sour cream
Crisp Panfried Potatoes (Home Fries; page 341) with crisp-fried slices of Spanish chorizo	Oven-Roasted Plum Tomatoes (page 361) and Chili Ranch Dressing (page 43); garnish with chopped fresh cilantro
Garlic Shrimp with Tomatoes and Cilantro (page 574)	Chopped green cabbage, sliced avocado, and a squeeze of lime
Crispy-Skin Salmon, Grilled or Broiled, with Gingery Greens (page 583)	Citrus Salsa (page 34)
Arroz con Pollo (page 653; remove the bones)	Shredded romaine lettuce and Chipotle-Cherry Salsa (page 34)
Grilled Smoky Whole Chicken (page 689; remove the bones)	Shredded red cabbage, Fresh Tomatillo Salsa (page 33), crumbled queso fresco
Marinated and Grilled Flank Steak (page 729)	Broiled Cherry Tomatoes with Herbs (page 362), Cilantro "Pesto" with Ginger and Chile
Carnitas (page 759) or Shredded Pork (page 759)	Shredded cabbage, Papaya Salsa (page 34)

grated cheese (or the more authentic crumbled queso fresco), sour cream (or yogurt), avocados or guacamole, and hot sauces are givens; serve them in bowls on the table for everyone to add as desired.

Fajitas

MAKES: 4 to 6 servings
TIME: 30 minutes

Fajita has come to mean any assemble-it-yourself assortment of meat, chicken, or even fish (usually shrimp) and grilled vegetables. Here's the basic formula:

- 1 pound Grilled or Broiled Boneless Chicken (page 641) or any variation, 1 pound Marinated and Grilled Flank Steak (page 729), or 1 pound Spicy Grilled Shrimp (page 574)
- 1 pound grilled or broiled mixed vegetables (see page 249)
- 1 cup sour cream
- 1 cup Guacamole (page 94)
- 1 cup Fresh Tomato Salsa (page 23), Fresh Tomatillo Salsa (page 33), or other salsa
- 2 cups shredded lettuce
- 2 cups seeded and diced tomato
- 8 to 12 flour tortillas

1 Heat the chicken, meat, or shrimp and vegetables if needed and keep them warm. Meanwhile, put the sour cream, guacamole, salsa, lettuce, and tomato in serving bowls.

2 Heat the tortillas on a grill for about 15 seconds per side, in a medium skillet over medium-high heat for about 15 seconds per side, or all together in a 250°F oven, wrapped in a towel, just until warm. Serve the tortillas with all the fixings.

Bean and Cheese Empanadas

MAKES: 12 (4 to 12 servings)
TIME: About 1 hour with cooked beans

Beans, cheese, and sturdy vegetables are traditional, but you can fill these turnovers with anything you like; see

 Fast   Make Ahead   Vegetarian

the variations. Serve them hot or at room temperature, with any cooked or raw salsa.

1½ cups all-purpose flour, plus a little more

½ cup masa harina, finely ground cornmeal, or more all-purpose flour

1½ teaspoons baking powder

1 teaspoon salt

½ cup plus 2 tablespoons lard or vegetable oil

2½ cups well-seasoned cooked beans, like Real Refried Beans (page 418)

2 cups grated or crumbled queso fresco, Monterey Jack, or cotija cheese

½ cup milk

❶ Mix the flour, masa harina, baking powder, and salt together in a food processor; process for about 5 seconds. With the machine running, add ½ cup of the shortening and process for 10 seconds. Then, with the machine running, add just enough water for the dough to form a ball, about ½ cup. Don't add more water than necessary; the dough should be fairly dry. Knead by hand until smooth, just a minute or so.

Tostadas

Tostada = "toasted." So a tostada is an open-face taco on a fried or oven-toasted tortilla. Generally, corn tortillas are preferable: They have more flavor than flour tortillas and are easy and quick to toast. See "Preparing Tortillas" (page 172) for specific techniques.

The other main difference between a taco and a tostada is that for a tostada you want something to help the toppings stick to the tortilla. Refried or just mashed beans are traditional, as are not-too-soupy braised meats. Top the base with shredded cabbage or lettuce, grated or crumbled cheese, salsa, and guacamole or sour cream and you're done. Serve tostadas within 10 minutes or so to prevent sogginess.

❷ Divide into 12 pieces, roll into balls, and wrap in plastic or cover with a damp towel and let rest for at least 20 minutes. (You can refrigerate the dough overnight; be sure to let it come to room temperature before proceeding.) On a well-floured surface, roll each piece into a 6-inch circle, adding flour as necessary.

❸ Heat the oven to 450°F. Put a couple of tablespoons of the beans on a dough circle, followed by a sprinkling of cheese, then fold each circle over; seal the seam with a few drops of water and press with the tines of a fork to close. Put on an ungreased baking sheet and brush lightly with milk. Bake until the dough is golden brown and hot, about 20 minutes. Serve immediately or at room temperature.

Chorizo and Cheese Empanadas. Substitute 1 pound crumbled or chopped chorizo for the beans.

Roasted Pepper and Cheese Empanadas. Instead of the beans, use 2½ cups Roasted Red Peppers or poblanos (page 330); large pieces are nice.

Shredded Pork Empanadas. Instead of the beans and cheese, use about 3 cups Shredded Pork (page 759) to fill the empanadas. Proceed with the recipe.

The Basics of Pizza

Home-baked pizza is different in just about every way from calling the delivery guy: At home, you have complete control over ingredients, and—once you get good at it—you'll be in love with the results.

But you have to plan ahead.

Pizza dough is a simple bread dough, made with flour, yeast, salt, and water, usually with olive oil for a little extra crunch and flavor. The toppings are also simple: tomatoes, cheese, mushrooms, olives, meat, a variety of vegetables . . . just what you'd expect. But at home you have the option of using better ingredients than the ones they use at a pizza shop, and that makes a huge difference.

The biggest challenge in making pizza is shaping the dough, which can be intimidating. But if you let go of the idea that the pie has to be perfectly round, that hurdle is soon cleared. Baking also has a bit of a learning curve, but you'll get the hang of it quickly.

Preparing Pizza Dough

A food processor makes pizza dough in a minute. Literally. You can also use a standing mixer (see "Making Bread Dough with a Standing Mixer," page 863) or mix and knead the dough by hand, first in a big bowl, then on a floured board. In any case, start to finish, you can have pizza dough ready in about an hour, but to develop more flavor—and make this a do-ahead dish—let it rise and ferment in the refrigerator for 6 to 8 hours, even overnight.

The Shaping

The romantic image of pizza makers spinning, stretching, and tossing the dough into a perfect circle is hard to shake. No denying that kind of treatment yields a gorgeous crust, but it's neither practical nor necessary. With even modest experience you'll get equally good results laying the dough on a work surface and gently pressing it with opened fingertips until it dimples and slowly stretches into shape. (This is how professionals make focaccia, which is just another form of pizza.) Equally easy is to flatten the dough a bit, then roll it.

In either case, patience is key; your goal is to coax the dough into shape, and this is easiest if you allow the dough to rest between steps as you shape it. You can plow right

SHAPING DOUGH FOR PIZZA AND CALZONES

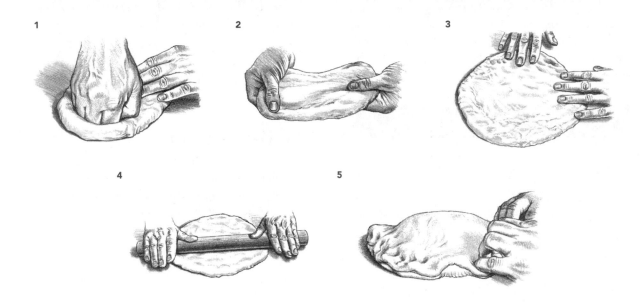

(STEP 1) Punch the dough down and (STEP 2) stretch it with your hands. If at any point the dough becomes very resistant, cover and let it rest for a few minutes. (STEPS 3–4) You can press the dough out with your hands or roll it with a pin; either is effective. Use a little flour or olive oil to keep it from sticking. (STEP 5) To make a calzone; add your filling, fold the dough over onto itself, and pinch the seams closed.

through from start to finish, but whenever you handle the dough it becomes more elastic and more difficult to work (that's the gluten doing its thing). The rest periods let it relax, which in turn makes it easier for you to shape.

Thick or Thin?

You can make any size or thickness of pizza using the same recipe and technique. It all depends on how you divide and shape the dough. Large, thin pizzas are the hardest to handle because they are more likely to tear during rolling. I usually divide the dough into at least two pies; three or four if they're going on the grill (see page 178).

No matter how thin you roll the crust, it will just about double in thickness as it bakes. (The temperature of your kitchen, the toppings, and even how you shaped the dough will affect this.) You can increase the thickness of the crust somewhat by letting the dough rise for a few extra minutes after you shape it and before topping it, but don't let it puff up too much or your pizza will have big bubbles and sunken valleys.

The Toppings

Topping pizza is much like saucing pasta; distinct, clean flavors are better than a mishmash of ingredients. You can stick to classic combinations: tomatoes, basil, and Parmesan; tomato sauce and mozzarella; or a little mozzarella with some crumbled sausage or sliced pepperoni. You can, of course, play around with different meats, seafood, poultry, vegetables, and cheeses, like grilled eggplant and feta or caramelized onions and Gorgonzola or White Pizza (page 179) with clams and garlic added.

But "house special" territory is trouble; too many ingredients taste muddled on a pizza, and they do no favors to your crust, which really deserves equal billing with whatever you put on it. If you smother the dough with toppings, it will steam as it bakes, turning a potentially crisp and light crust into a soggy mess.

Baking

Pizza must be baked in a very hot oven, 500°F or even higher (professional pizza ovens are around 700°F). The best way to cook pizza is directly on a pizza stone, which crisps up the bottom of the crust and dries it out perfectly. (But pizza is also just fine baked on a flat baking sheet or one with a small lip. And of course there's always pizza on the grill; see page 178.) You want the oven—and the stone—thoroughly heated, so wait a good half hour after turning the oven on before baking.

The ideal pizza stone is a large rectangle; it should be unglazed and relatively thick. Once you've got the stone, you really need a peel—the board with a handle that looks like a large Ping-Pong paddle—to simplify the process. Sprinkle flour or cornmeal on it and you can shape and top the dough directly on the peel, then just

4 Tips for Foolproof Pizza Toppings

Whether you bake or grill, the trick is for the toppings and the dough to cook in sync. Keep these points in mind:

1. Cook meat and veggies before topping: Pizza just doesn't bake long enough for most raw meat and vegetables to become tender. Better to use slices or crumbles than chunks, which will just burn on top. Just about any meat or vegetable is fair game.

2. Pick the right time to add toppings to oven-baked pizzas: Delicate ingredients may overcook if left in the oven for the full baking time. It may be better to add them about halfway through cooking.

3. Cover the grill after adding moist toppings (like cheese or tomatoes) to grilled pizzas, or they may not cook through.

4. Don't overload grilled pizzas: You risk losing part of the topping. Use the oven instead.

slide it right onto the stone. Wooden peels are more attractive than metal ones but can get a little dingy looking after a while (you can sand yours if it gets too stained); metal peels are much easier to clean.

One more thing to remember about equipment: If you use a baking sheet to bake the pizza, grease it with a little olive oil to keep the dough from sticking, rather than dusting the surface with flour or cornmeal as you would with a peel. Once you do that, just press the dough right onto the pan to shape it.

Cutting and Serving

Pizzas with little or no cheese—or other rich ingredients that might congeal when cooled—are also good served at room temperature, like bread. You can cut pizza into wedges like pie or into smaller squares, which are good if you're feeding a crowd or just prefer smaller pieces.

Pizza Dough

MAKES: Enough for 1 large or 2 or more small pies
TIME: 1 hour or more

You won't believe how simple it is to make pizza dough at home. And because the dough freezes very well (at least

---

4 Alternative Crusts for Making "Pizzas"

You can make a pizza without making pizza dough. Try any of these:

1. Flour tortillas
2. Pita bread
3. Polenta (see Polenta "Pizza," page 488)
4. Lightly toasted English muffins

---

for a couple of weeks), it's even practical to whip up a batch for one or two people and tuck the rest away for another day.

To make pizza dough by hand or with a standing mixer, follow the directions, but use a bowl and a heavy wooden spoon or the mixer's bowl and the paddle attachment instead of the food processor. When the dough becomes too heavy to stir, use your hands or exchange the mixer's paddle for the dough hook and proceed with the recipe.

> 3 cups all-purpose or bread flour, plus more as needed
>
> 2 teaspoons instant yeast
>
> 2 teaspoons coarse kosher or sea salt, plus extra for sprinkling
>
> 2 tablespoons extra virgin olive oil

1 Combine the flour, yeast, and salt in a food processor. Turn the machine on and add 1 cup water and the oil through the feed tube.

2 Process for about 30 seconds, adding more water, a little at a time, until the mixture forms a ball and is slightly sticky to the touch. If it is still dry, add another tablespoon or two of water and process for another 10 seconds. (In the unlikely event that the mixture is too sticky, add flour a tablespoon at a time.)

3 Turn the dough onto a floured work surface and knead by hand for a few seconds to form a smooth, round dough ball. Put the dough in a bowl and cover with plastic wrap; let rise until the dough doubles in size, 1 to 2 hours. (You can cut this rising time short if you're in a hurry, or you can let the dough rise more slowly, in the refrigerator, for up to 6 or 8 hours.) Proceed to Step 4 or wrap the dough tightly in plastic wrap or a zipper bag and freeze for up to a month. (Defrost in the bag or a covered bowl in the refrigerator or at room temperature; bring to room temperature before shaping.)

4 When the dough is ready, form it into a ball and divide it into 2 or more pieces if you like; roll each piece into a round ball. Put each ball on a lightly floured surface, sprinkle with flour, and cover with plastic wrap or a

 Fast   Make Ahead   **V** Vegetarian

towel. Let rest until they puff slightly, about 20 minutes. Proceed with any of the pizza recipes that follow.

Whole Wheat Pizza Dough. With a nutty flavor and a little fiber: Use $1^1/_2$ cups each whole wheat and white flour (all-purpose or bread flour). You'll probably need to add closer to $1^1/_2$ cups water or maybe even a little more.

Crunchier Pizza Dough. This dough may be a little more difficult to handle, but it has superior flavor and a pleasant crunch: Substitute $^1/_2$ cup cornmeal for $^1/_2$ cup of the flour.

7 Quick Ideas for More Flavorful Pizza Dough

You can mix and match a bit as long as you don't overdo it and overpower the natural flavor of the crust or make it soggy. Before adding the water to the dough, try the following, alone or in combination:

1. Add $^1/_2$ to 1 teaspoon freshly ground black pepper.
2. Add 1 teaspoon to 1 tablespoon fresh herbs.
3. Add $^1/_4$ to $^1/_3$ cup chopped prosciutto, ham, or cooked bacon.
4. Substitute $^1/_2$ to 1 cup rice, semolina, or other alternative flour for the white flour (see "The Basics of Flour," page 835).
5. Add 1 tablespoon Roasted Garlic (page 303) or $^1/_2$ teaspoon minced raw garlic, or to taste.
6. Use Flavored Oil (page 26), like garlic or rosemary oil, in place of regular olive oil.
7. Add $^1/_4$ to $^1/_3$ cup chopped nuts or seeds.

Pizza on the Grill

Grilled pizza is fun to make, and easier than you'd think, especially if your grill has a cover. Wood fires are the trickiest fuel to control, but impart a great flavor to the crust; gas grills are naturally the easiest, and charcoal lies somewhere in between.

You want a fire that is hot enough to brown the dough, but not so hot that it scorches it before the interior cooks; you should be able to hold your hand a few inches above the fire for 3 or 4 seconds. An ideal setup is one where part of the grill is hot and part of it cool. On a gas grill, this means setting one side to "high" and the other to "low," or some similar arrangement. With a charcoal grill, just build your fire on one side; use the hot side for the initial browning of the dough, the cool side to heat the toppings.

The process is straightforward: Grill the dough on one side, just enough to firm it up and brown it a bit, then flip it (for small pizzas, use tongs; otherwise a spatula aided by your fingers does the trick) and add toppings. If you want the toppings to become very hot, cover the grill. If you don't care whether they actually cook, but just warm up a bit, you can leave the grill open.

It's especially important when grilling to keep pizza toppings to a minimum. Fully loaded grilled pizzas won't cook properly and will be impossible to handle. One way around this is to grill pizzas with one or two ingredients, then add more when you remove them from the fire.

White Pizza

MAKES: 1 large or 2 or more small pies
TIME: About 1 hour with premade dough

Pizza bianca—white pizza, pizza without sauce—is the mother of all pizzas. This may seem spare, but I urge you to try it and experiment with some of the possible additions and tweaks that follow, because it's among the best pizzas you'll ever eat.

1 recipe Pizza Dough (page 178), mixed and risen (Steps 1–3)

All-purpose flour for stretching or rolling the dough

Extra virgin olive oil as needed

Coarse kosher or sea salt

1 tablespoon or more roughly chopped fresh rosemary leaves

Several fresh rosemary sprigs (optional)

1 When the dough is ready, knead it lightly, form it into a ball, and divide it into 2 or more pieces if you like; roll each piece into a round ball and put each ball on a lightly floured surface. Sprinkle with flour, cover with plastic wrap or a towel, and let rest for about 30 minutes while you heat the oven.

2 Put a baking stone on a lower rack if you're using one and heat the oven to 500°F, or higher. Roll or lightly press each dough ball into a flat round, lightly flouring the work surface and the dough as necessary (use only as much flour as you need to). Let the rounds sit for a few minutes; this will relax the dough and make it easier to roll out. If you have a peel and baking stone, roll or pat out the dough on the peel, as thinly as you like, turning occasionally and sprinkling it with flour as necessary. If you're using baking sheets, oil them, then press each dough ball into a flat round directly on the oiled sheets.

3 Sprinkle the top with some salt and the rosemary, drizzle with olive oil, and slide the baking sheet into the oven on a rack set in the middle (or the pizza itself onto the stone, which should be set on a lower rack). Bake from 6 to 12 minutes, depending on the oven heat, until nicely browned. Serve immediately or at room temperature (these will keep for a few hours).

Margherita Pizza. The classic Neapolitan pizza: Top the pie(s) with sliced fresh tomato, extra virgin olive oil, a little mozzarella, preferably fresh, and some fresh basil leaves, salt, and Parmesan.

Marinara Pizza. All tomatoes, no cheese: Top the pies with sliced fresh tomato, thinly sliced garlic (or Fast Tomato Sauce, page 502), extra virgin olive oil, and, if you like, a few chopped black olives or whole capers.

White Pizza with Prosciutto and Parmesan. Omit the salt and rosemary. Top each pizza with a few very thin slices of prosciutto, a drizzling of olive oil, and a grating of Parmesan cheese. Add the toppings about halfway through the baking time.

White Pizza with Clams. Also good with diced peeled lightly cooked shrimp or shelled lightly steamed mussels. Omit the rosemary. Top each pizza with a few freshly shucked littleneck clams (and some of their juice, if you have it), a few very thin slivers of garlic, a little coarse salt, and some minced fresh parsley leaves.

White Pizza with Mushrooms. Omit the rosemary. Top each pizza with some Sautéed Mushrooms (page 313). Use plenty of minced fresh parsley leaves; sage is also good. Add the toppings about halfway through cooking.

White Pizza with Caramelized Onions and Vinegar. This takes some work in advance: Omit the rosemary. Make 1 recipe Caramelized Onions (page 325), cooked fairly dark. Season to taste with salt and pepper, then stir in about 1 tablespoon balsamic vinegar, or to taste. Top each pizza with a portion of these onions and some minced fresh basil, thyme, or sage leaves. A sprinkling of plain bread crumbs is also good. Add the toppings about halfway through cooking.

Versatile Flatbread. Tear or cut off pieces to eat with everything from Simplest Dal (page 433) to stir-fries, or dips and spreads like Hummus (page 93), any yogurt sauce (see pages 24–25), or any chutney (pages 36–38): For a neutral flavor, make the Pizza Dough recipe—or any of its variations—with a neutral oil, like grapeseed or corn. In the main recipe, omit the olive oil, coarse salt, and rosemary. Shape the dough into 1 or 2 large flatbreads or several small ones; irregular shapes have a great rustic appeal. Proceed with the recipe.

F Fast   **M** Make Ahead   **V** Vegetarian

18 Ideas for Pizza Toppings

Use the following ingredients, alone or in combination, on any of the pizzas in this section.

1. Lightly cooked sausage, bacon, or other meat.
2. Sliced salami, prosciutto, Spanish chorizo, or other cured meat.
3. Small amounts of Gorgonzola or other blue cheese or fontina or other semisoft cheese; gratings of Parmesan are almost always welcome.
4. Soft goat cheese or ricotta.
5. Minced raw or mashed roasted garlic.
6. Minced fresh chile (like jalapeño or Thai) or hot red pepper flakes to taste.
7. Pitted black olives, especially the oil-cured kind (good in combination with caramelized onions and vinegar, above). Green olives are good too.
8. Canned anchovy fillets, with some of their oil.
9. Reconstituted dried tomatoes (or Oven-Dried Tomatoes, page 362).
10. Thinly sliced tomatoes and basil, with olive oil and/or grated Parmesan. Or peeled, seeded, and chopped tomatoes tossed with basil.
11. Traditional Pesto or other herb paste or sauce (pages 27–28).
12. Sliced boiled potatoes—waxy or all-purpose kinds work best (great added to White Pizza, page 179).
13. Well-washed and dried tender greens, especially spicy ones, like arugula and watercress. Add greens when pizzas are finished baking or grilling and let the heat from the crust wilt them, which will take about a minute.
14. Sautéed spinach.
15. Roasted Red Peppers (page 330).
16. Grilled or Broiled Eggplant (page 294) or the pan-cooked eggplant slices from Eggplant Parmesan (page 297).
17. Slices of grilled zucchini (see "How to Grill Vegetables," page 250).
18. Any lightly cooked seafood, canned clams, or shredded canned tuna.

Pizza with Tomato Sauce and Mozzarella

MAKES: 1 large or 2 or more small pies

TIME: About 1½ hours with premade dough

Your basic American-style pizza. It's a little too loaded to grill as is (see the last variation for that), but the good news is that the cheese helps unwieldy toppings—like broccoli, bell peppers, or olives—stick to the pie. For more variations, see "18 Ideas for Pizza Toppings," left.

1 recipe Pizza Dough (page 178), mixed and risen (Steps 1–3)

All-purpose flour for stretching or rolling the dough

2 tablespoons extra virgin olive oil, or more as needed

2 cups Fast Tomato Sauce (page 502) or any other tomato sauce

2 cups grated mozzarella cheese

Salt and freshly ground black pepper

1 When the dough is ready, knead it lightly, form it into a ball, and divide it into 2 pieces if you like; roll each piece into a round ball and put each ball on a lightly floured surface. Sprinkle with a little more flour, cover with plastic wrap or a towel, and let rest while you heat the oven.

2 Heat the oven to 500°F or higher. Roll or lightly press each dough ball into a flat round, lightly flouring the work surface and the dough as necessary (use only as much flour as you need to). Let the rounds sit for a few minutes; this will relax the dough and make it easier to roll out. If you have a peel and baking stone, roll or pat out the dough on the peel, as thinly as you like, turning occasionally and sprinkling it with flour as necessary. If you're using baking sheets, oil them, then press each dough ball into a flat round directly on the oiled sheets.

3 Drizzle the rounds with the olive oil, then top them with the sauce and cheese; sprinkle with salt and pepper. Put the baking sheet in the oven or slide the pizza directly onto the stone and bake until the crust is crisp and the cheese melted, usually 8 to 12 minutes. Let stand for several minutes before slicing to set up the cheese.

Pizza with Tomato Sauce and Fresh Mozzarella. Since fresh mozz doesn't melt the same way as the commercial stuff, and because it's moist, slice it, don't grate it: Use less than $^1/_2$ pound fresh mozzarella—usually 1 medium ball packed in water. Drain well and slice thinly. After you top with the oil and cheese, spread the slices on top of the pizza (you will have gaps in between so the pizza can breathe and crisp up). Proceed with the recipe. When it comes out of the oven, sprinkle with chopped fresh basil or oregano if you like and some grated Parmesan.

Pizza with Tomato Sauce, Mozzarella, and Sausage or Pepperoni. Scatter 4 ounces or so crumbled and lightly cooked sausage (or thinly sliced pepperoni) over the cheese.

Pizza with Tomato Sauce, Mozzarella, and Broccoli. Best with broccoli rabe: Sauté about $^1/_2$ pound broccoli florets (or broccoli raab spears), with a little garlic if you like, making sure you stop cooking them as soon as they're just tender. In Step 3, after you put the cheese on the pizza, distribute the broccoli around the top and press gently into the cheese. Proceed with the recipe.

Grilled Pizza with Tomato Sauce and Mozzarella. Great on the grill as long as you pare down the toppings: Reduce the sauce to 1 cup and the grated mozzarella to 1 cup. Follow the directions for cooking, flipping, topping, and finishing grilled pizzas on page 178, drizzling a little extra olive oil onto the pizza before grilling if you like.

Pissaladière

MAKES: 1 thick-crust pizza (4 main-dish or 8 appetizer servings)

TIME: About 1 hour with premade dough

M **V**

The classic Niçoise pizza, loaded with sweet, soft-cooked onions; salty olives and anchovies add contrast. Be sure to simmer the onions very, very slowly.

$^1/_2$ recipe Pizza Dough (page 178) made with extra virgin olive oil

All-purpose flour for stretching or rolling the dough

3 tablespoons extra virgin olive oil

1$^1/_2$ pounds onions, thinly sliced

Salt and freshly ground black pepper

1 teaspoon fresh thyme leaves or $^1/_2$ teaspoon dried thyme

6 to 10 anchovies (optional)

About 12 black olives, pitted and halved (optional)

6 to 8 thin slices tomato (optional)

1 Heat the oven to 450°F. Knead the dough lightly. Put it on a lightly floured surface, sprinkle it with a little flour, and cover it with plastic wrap or a towel. Let it rest while you cook the onions.

2 Put the olive oil in large skillet over medium-high heat. When hot, add the onions along with some salt and pepper and cook, stirring frequently, until the onions give up their liquid and become quite soft, at least 15 minutes; don't let them brown. When they are cooked, turn off the heat and stir in the thyme.

3 Pat or roll out the dough to a diameter of 12 inches, using more flour as necessary. The process will be easier if you allow the dough to rest occasionally between rollings. If you have a peel and baking stone, roll or pat out the dough on the peel, as thinly as you like, turning occasionally and sprinkling it with flour as necessary. If you're using baking sheets, oil them, then press each dough ball into a flat round directly on the oiled sheets. Let the dough rest for 15 to 30 minutes, or until it begins to puff ever so slightly.

4 Spread the dough with onions and then decorate, if you like, with anchovies, olives, and tomato. Bake until nicely crisp, 15 minutes or more; if the pizza is browning unevenly, rotate it back to front about halfway through the cooking time. Serve hot or at room temperature.

Sicilian Onion Pizza. Omit the tomatoes and olives. In Step 1, stir the anchovies into the cooked onions and

F Fast   **M** Make Ahead   **V** Vegetarian

cook for 5 minutes more. Stir a 6-ounce can of tomato paste into the onions and cook for a few more minutes over low heat. Sprinkle with salt and pepper. Drizzle the rolled-out dough with 2 tablespoons olive oil and bake for 10 to 12 minutes, or until the bottom begins to turn pale golden. Spread the partially baked dough with 1 cup plain bread crumbs, preferably fresh (see page 876), then spread with the onion mixture. Return to the oven and bake for 15 to 20 minutes more, until the bottom is dark golden but not burned and the top is a richly colored caramel. Remove and cool for a few minutes before cutting; best served hot or warm.

Alsatian "Pizza" (Tarte Flambé). Finely chop half the amount of onions and substitute $1/2$ cup finely chopped bacon for the anchovies. Omit the olives and tomato. In Step 2, cook the onions and bacon until the onions are soft, about 5 minutes. Proceed with the recipe. In Step 4, spread the dough with 1 cup fromage blanc or crème fraîche or $3/4$ cup sour cream thinned with $1/3$ cup milk. Top with the onion mixture, then bake as directed.

Calzone

MAKES: 2 calzones (4 main-dish servings)
TIME: About 1 hour with premade dough

One day I messed up on sliding a pizza into the oven; part of it folded onto itself on the baking stone. I couldn't take it back out, and I couldn't bake it the way it was. So I finished the job, folded it over (and not too neatly), encasing the filling entirely in the dough. Thus, by making the best of a bad situation, I "discovered" homemade calzone.

Intentionally made calzone is better than that, since the filling is neatly enclosed in the dough. While you can fill a calzone with any pizza toppings (see "18 Ideas for Pizza Toppings," page 181), it's best with cheese and something else, rather than all cheese. The filling should be substantial and fairly dry; very wet fillings will leak or make the dough soggy; that's why drained ricotta is an ideal base.

Serve calzone with Fresh Tomato Sauce (page 502) or any other tomato sauce for dipping or topping. Or naked, as they usually do in Naples, where it's from.

1 recipe Pizza Dough (page 178), mixed and risen (Steps 1–3)

All-purpose flour for stretching or rolling the dough

2 cups ricotta cheese

1 cup crumbled cooked Italian sausage or chopped ham or finely chopped cooked spinach or other greens, like chard or broccoli raab, squeezed dry

1 cup chopped or grated mozzarella cheese

1 cup grated Parmesan cheese

Salt and freshly ground black pepper

1 Knead the dough lightly and cut it into 2 pieces. Form 2 balls and put them on a lightly floured surface. Sprinkle with a little more flour and cover with plastic wrap or a towel; let them rest for 20 minutes. If the ricotta is very moist, drain it in a fine-meshed strainer for 10 minutes or so.

2 Combine the sausage, ricotta, mozzarella, and Parmesan. Taste and add salt, if necessary, and pepper. Heat the oven to 350°F.

3 Roll or lightly press each dough ball into a flat round, lightly flouring the work surface and the dough as necessary (use only as much flour as you need to). Let the rounds sit for a few minutes; this will relax the dough and make it easier to roll out. Roll or pat the dough into an 8- to 10-inch round on a floured pizza peel or lightly oiled baking sheet.

4 Put half the filling into the middle of each dough round. Moisten the edges with a little water. Fold one edge over onto the other and press closed with your fingertips (see the illustration on page 176).

5 Bake the calzones on a baking sheet or directly on a baking stone for 30 to 40 minutes, or until nicely browned. Serve hot or warm.

5 Totally Untraditional Pizzas

Thanks to Wolfgang Puck and a slew of imitators, it's become acceptable (in this country at least) to put virtually anything on pizza dough. Again the key—and I can't stress this strongly enough—is to avoid overloading and overmixing: If you wouldn't eat the combination on a plate, don't put it on a pizza. Some "new" combos:

1. Crumbled goat cheese, sliced fresh figs or blackberries, and, when it comes out of the oven, a layer of arugula leaves (add the arugula just after the pizza is done so it wilts in the heat of the crust).

2. Roughly shredded roasted or grilled chicken or duck, chopped scallion, and a drizzle of hoisin sauce or barbecue sauce (to make your own, see page 52).

3. Lightly cooked shrimp, feta cheese, dried tomatoes, black olives, and a chiffonade of basil when it comes out of the oven.

4. Any saucy chutney (see pages 36–38) or Indian-Style Tomato Sauce (page 53) smeared on the crust, sliced Tandoori Chicken (page 694) or thinly sliced cooked potato; chopped fresh cilantro and Raita (page 24) for dipping.

5. Real Refried Beans (page 418) smeared on the crust, followed by a layer of grated cheddar and Jack cheese and cooked crumbled ground beef or turkey; when it comes out of the oven, top with shredded iceberg lettuce and minced red onions; serve with Salsa Roja (page 48), Guacamole (page 94), and sour cream on the side.

Salads

SALADS ARE EASY, FAST, WIDELY ADORED,

and everywhere a staple. If you can imagine a salad, you can probably create it, especially once you can prepare a vinaigrette, the basic dressing that can turn almost any food, cooked or raw, into a salad.

Perhaps even more than with most other foods, it's critical to start with the best ingredients, particularly since they're often served raw. It's tough to beat a few slices of fresh-from-the-garden tomato drizzled with oil and sprinkled with salt.

But unless you're a fanatic, you're going to have to compromise from time to time. Fortunately, even at a salad's most basic level, you can take ordinary supermarket ingredients—iceberg lettuce, packaged carrots and celery, a few radishes—and, with the help of a little extra virgin olive oil and lemon juice or decent vinegar, turn them into something delicious, not to mention healthy.

Although there's undoubtedly something to be said for including uncooked foods in our diets, a salad can include cooked vegetables as well, and the salad bowl is a perfect place for leftovers or vegetables you cook in advance, knowing that you're going to serve them at room temperature or cold (which sometimes is all that distinguishes a salad from a cooked vegetable dish).

Salads are among the quickest dishes to prepare, especially if you take advantage of the fact that many of the ingredients can be prepared in advance and leftovers can readily be thrown into the mix. Furthermore, most salad dressings keep for at least a few days and often longer.

ESSENTIAL RECIPES

If you never made any salads other than these, you'd still be pretty well set in the salad department. From a few leaves tossed with oil and vinegar (or lemon juice) to a bowl of cut-up fruit, these are the super-simple, ultrabasic salads upon which most others are built. Most of them are on the table as fast as you can wash and chop; the dressing is just an ingredient or two tossed together in the bowl or right on the salad. (For information on vinaigrettes, see page 198.)

✪ Simple Green Salad

MAKES: 4 servings
TIME: 10 minutes

The basic green salad remains a staple because it's fresh, quick, easy, and even healthy; it doesn't even really require whisking up vinaigrette, though of course using one instead of the oil, vinegar, and seasonings listed here won't hurt.

> 6 cups torn assorted greens, like mesclun or any lettuce
>
> About $1/3$ cup extra virgin olive oil
>
> About 2 tablespoons sherry vinegar, balsamic vinegar, or freshly squeezed lemon juice
>
> Salt and freshly ground black pepper

Put the greens in a bowl and toss them with oil, vinegar, a pinch of salt, and some pepper. Toss and taste. Adjust the seasoning and serve immediately.

Green Salad with Fresh Herbs. Use 5 cups assorted greens (mesclun or the like) and add a cup (more or less) of fresh parsley, dill, mint, or basil leaves or any combination. Substitute lemon juice for the vinegar or use Lemon Vinaigrette (page 201) if you like.

Watercress and Sesame Salad. Use watercress for the greens; substitute Soy Vinaigrette (page 201) for the olive oil and vinegar. Sprinkle with toasted sesame seeds for garnish.

Endive Salad with Nut Oil Vinaigrette. Substitute roughly chopped Belgian endive leaves for the assorted greens; add radicchio, watercress, and other strong-flavored greens if you like. Toss in about $1/2$ cup toasted walnuts or hazelnuts (see page 317) and use Nut Oil Vinaigrette (page 201).

Greek Salad, Simplified. Add about $1/4$ cup chopped fresh mint or parsley leaves (or both), about $1/3$ cup crumbled feta cheese, and about $1/4$ cup pitted and roughly chopped black olives. Use lemon juice in place of vinegar.

Mesclun with Goat Cheese and Croutons. Add 4 ounces soft goat cheese and 4 Real Croutons (page 877).

F Fast   **M** Make Ahead   **V** Vegetarian

Spread the goat cheese on the croutons; top each serving with a crouton.

15 Ideas for Simple Green Salad

1. Omit the oil or minimize the vinegar (either way, it'll still be good).
2. Substitute any good but flavorful oil, like walnut, hazelnut, or dark sesame. (Use less at first, because these are stronger than olive oil.)
3. Add tomatoes, in quarters or eighths; you might want to remove their seeds first (see page 361), but it isn't essential. Or use cherry or grape tomatoes. Best with balsamic vinegar.
4. Add freshly grated or shaved Parmesan. This is probably the easiest upgrade you can make to many salads.
5. Add chopped vegetables (see Chopped Salad, Five Ways page 204).
6. Add chopped (pitted) olives.
7. Add chopped shallot, onion, scallion, or leek or minced garlic (just a little bit).
8. Add chopped or sliced Hard-Boiled Egg (page 791) or top with one or more Poached Eggs (page 793) or peeled Soft-Boiled Eggs (page 790).
9. Add crumbled blue or any other cheese.
10. Add any nuts or seeds, crumbled or chopped if necessary.
11. Add sliced pears, apples, oranges, or other fruit.
12. Add sea greens, about a quarter the amount in Sesame Seaweed Salad (page 212), soaked and drained as in that recipe. Or add nori (laver), toasted briefly over a hot flame and crumbled as on page 350.
13. Add diced Roasted Red (or yellow) Peppers (page 330),or capers or anchovies.
14. Use more intensely flavored greens: arugula, watercress, endive, radicchio, frisée, escarole, etc.
15. Sprinkle with crumbled cooked bacon or top with anchovy fillets.

Tomato, Mozzarella, and Basil Salad

MAKES: 4 servings
TIME: 5 to 15 minutes

Ⓕ　Ⓥ

This is barely more than the three ingredients listed in the title, so all three must be of excellent quality. I like to salt the tomatoes a little bit before assembling the salad—it removes a little of their liquid—but it isn't necessary.

> 4 perfectly ripe medium tomatoes
>
> Salt
>
> Eight ¹/₄-inch-thick slices fresh mozzarella cheese, plus more if desired
>
> 8 large fresh basil leaves
>
> Freshly ground black pepper
>
> Extra virgin olive oil for drizzling

❶ Core and cut the tomatoes into about ¹/₄-inch-thick slices. If you like, lay them on a board and sprinkle them lightly with salt. Set the board at an angle so the liquid can drain into the sink (or a bowl; it makes a refreshing drink).

❷ Layer the tomatoes, mozzarella, and basil on a platter or 4 individual plates. Sprinkle with salt and pepper, drizzle with olive oil, and serve.

Cherry Tomato Salad with Soy Sauce

MAKES: 4 servings
TIME: 15 to 30 minutes

Ⓕ　Ⓥ

The combination of soy sauce and tomatoes is amazingly good, and because cherry and grape tomatoes are among the few supermarket fruits that are actually worth eating in winter, this can help satisfy your cravings until the summertime slicers are back in full swing. If you have the time, let this salad sit at room temperature for up to 15 minutes to release some of the juice from the tomatoes. The dressing tints them with a deeply flavored mahogany glaze.

    2 tablespoons soy sauce, plus more to taste

    Pinch sugar

    2 teaspoons dark sesame oil

    4 cups cherry or grape tomatoes, stemmed and
      halved crosswise

    $1/2$ cup whole basil leaves, preferably Thai basil

    Freshly ground black pepper

1 Combine the soy sauce, sugar, and oil in a large bowl. Add the tomatoes and basil and sprinkle liberally with pepper. Stir gently to coat the tomatoes with dressing.

2 Let stand at room temperature for up to 15 minutes, stirring once or twice. Taste and add more soy sauce and black pepper if you like and serve.

Carrot Salad with Cumin

MAKES: 4 servings

TIME: 15 minutes

Here's a simple salad in a typically North African style that features the sweetness of fresh oranges offset nicely by the tang of ground cumin. You can also combine carrot and celeriac, jícama, or sunchokes using the same dressing.

    $1^1/2$ pounds carrots, grated

    Juice of 2 oranges

    Juice of 1 lemon

    2 tablespoons extra virgin olive oil

    1 teaspoon ground cumin, or more to taste

    Salt and freshly ground black pepper

1 Use the julienne disk of a food processor to cut the carrots into fine shreds or cut into $1/8$-inch-thick slices.

2 Whisk together the juices, olive oil, and cumin; sprinkle with salt and pepper and pour the dressing over the carrots. Toss, taste and adjust the seasoning, and serve.

Beet Salad with Cumin. Cook the beets (see Beets Done Simply, page 263), peel, and slice. Substitute 1 clove garlic, minced, for the orange juice.

Whole Baby Carrot Salad with Cumin. Substitute $1^1/2$ pounds whole baby carrots for the grated carrots. Skip Step 1. Trim the green tops and halve the carrots if they are on the big side (longer than 4 inches); steam or boil the carrots until barely tender (you want a bit of crunch here), then shock and pat dry (see page 240). Proceed with the recipe.

Cold Cooked Greens, Greek Style

Horta

MAKES: 4 servings

TIME: 20 minutes

This is a wonderful use for cooked greens (including leftovers), but it's so good that you may buy dark greens just to cook and serve them this way. It's also great with broccoli, broccoli raab, or gai lan.

    Salt

    1 to 2 pounds dark leafy greens, like kale, collards,
      chard, or spinach

    Several tablespoons extra virgin olive oil

    Freshly ground black pepper

    2 lemons, halved

1 Bring a large pot of water to a boil and salt it. Trim the greens of any stems thicker than $1/4$ inch; discard them. Wash the greens well.

2 Simmer the greens until tender, just a minute or two for spinach, up to 10 minutes or even longer for

 Fast   Make Ahead   Vegetarian

older, tougher greens. Drain them well and cool them quickly by running them under cold water.

③ Squeeze the greens dry and chop them. (At this point, you may refrigerate the salad, covered, for up to a day, then bring to room temperature before proceeding.) Sprinkle with olive oil, salt, pepper, and a squeeze of lemon juice; serve with the remaining lemon halves.

Cold Asian Greens and Ginger Salad. Light on oil and heavy on ginger: Use bok choy or one of the other greens listed on page 192. Substitute 2 tablespoons grated fresh ginger, $^1/_4$ cup rice vinegar, and 1 teaspoon dark sesame oil for the olive oil and lemons.

Cold Escarole, Garlic, and Parmesan Salad. Use escarole for the greens. Add 2 tablespoons chopped garlic. In Step 3, put $^1/_4$ cup olive oil in a large skillet over medium heat. When hot, add the garlic and cook until fragrant (do not brown), about 30 seconds. Remove from the heat and stir in 3 tablespoons freshly squeezed lemon juice and a sprinkling of grated zest if you like. Toss the greens with the garlic-lemon vinaigrette and $^1/_2$ cup shaved or grated Parmesan cheese and sprinkle on salt and lots of black pepper.

✪ Potato Salad with Mustard Vinaigrette

MAKES: 4 servings

TIME: 30 minutes, plus time to cool

To me, the best and simplest potato salad is made of just-boiled potatoes dressed in a freshly made vinaigrette. If you're in a hurry, whisk together the vinaigrette ingredients in a bowl, then just add the potatoes. Parsley and chopped onion are easy, flavorful additions. After that, you can add any of the suggestions from the following list.

If it's classic potato salad (with mayonnaise) you're after, see the variation and be sure to check out the chart that follows.

> 1$^1/_2$ pounds waxy potatoes, like red new potatoes or fingerling; or all-purpose, like Yukon Gold (or even starchy baking potatoes are fine)
>
> Salt
>
> $^1/_2$ cup minced fresh parsley leaves
>
> $^1/_4$ cup chopped scallions or red or yellow onion
>
> $^1/_2$ cup Mustard Vinaigrette (page 201), or any other vinaigrette (pages 199–202), plus more to taste
>
> Freshly ground black pepper

① Peel the potatoes if you like (or wash and scrub them well), then cut them into bite-sized pieces. Put them in a pot with enough water to cover them and add a large pinch of salt. Bring to a boil, then lower the heat so the water bubbles gently. Cook the potatoes until tender but still firm and not all mushy, 15 minutes or so, depending on the potato. Drain, rinse in cold water for a minute, then drain again.

② Toss the still-warm potatoes with the parsley and scallion. Add the vinaigrette until the mixture is as dressed as you like. Taste and adjust the seasoning, adding black pepper. Serve as is or refrigerate for an hour or so to chill the salad. (At this point, you may refrigerate the salad, covered, for up to a day.)

Classic Potato Salad. Omit the vinaigrette. Whisk together $^1/_2$ cup mayonnaise (to make your own, see page 41) with 3 tablespoons sherry vinegar or white wine vinegar. (Mayonnaise flavored with herbs, garlic, mustard, or virtually any seasoning is fine here.) Taste and make sure there's enough salt. Proceed with the recipe, using the mayonnaise mixture as the dressing.

Grilled Potato Salad. Also good with sweet potatoes: Instead of boiling the potatoes, grill them according to the directions on page 342. While they are still warm, proceed with the recipe from Step 2.

15 Simple Additions to Potato Salad

You will probably need to add more dressing, depending on the ingredient.

1. Chopped fresh herbs, like chives, chervil, dill, oregano, rosemary, or sage, to taste
2. Chopped sweet pickle
3. Chopped celery or fennel
4. Chopped red bell pepper, raw or roasted (page 330), or use canned pimientos
5. Capers or roughly chopped olives
6. Chopped shallots, raw or lightly cooked in olive oil
7. Cooked fresh peas (or thawed frozen)
8. Chopped Hard-Boiled Egg (page 791)
9. Cayenne or minced fresh chile (jalapeño, Thai, serrano, or habanero)
10. Curry powder (to make your own, see pages 66–67) or other spice mixtures (start with a teaspoon)
11. Chopped or mashed anchovies
12. Crumbled cooked bacon or bits of ham or prosciutto
13. Grated hard cheese, like Parmesan, cheddar, or manchego, or crumbled feta, queso fresco, or ricotta salata
14. Sliced or grated radishes
15. Cooked and chopped greens, like escarole or kale, or raw tender greens like spinach, arugula, or watercress

Which Potato for Salads?

In most instances, you want low-starch "waxy" potatoes for salad, which keep their shape even after boiling. Waxy potatoes, often referred to as "new"—even when they're not freshly dug—have thin skins and may be red or tan (tans ones are called "white," though they're not even close). You might even see purple ones, which make stunning salads.

But you might also like to try using starchy ("baking") potatoes, like Idaho or other russets. The breakdown of their starches gives the salad a little creaminess—if you were thinking negatively, you might call it gumminess, but it's all a matter of taste. In addition, their mealy texture is not a bad attribute in salads.

Or you can use a so-called all-purpose potato, like Yukon Gold, which will give you a firm potato whose exterior disintegrates just a little.

My personal preference is a waxy potato, but yours may differ.

For much more about potatoes, see page 336.

Mixed Fruit Salad

MAKES: 4 servings
TIME: About 30 minutes

Any combination of fruit will work here. Choose what's ripe and fresh; there's no point in using fruit that has no flavor. Lemon zest adds a lovely element.

½ small cantaloupe or papaya, seeded, peeled, and cut into chunks

¼ small honeydew or 2 mangoes, seeded, peeled, and cut into chunks

½ pineapple, peeled, cored, and cut into chunks

Zest and juice of 1 lemon

1 tablespoon sugar, or to taste

1 pint strawberries, hulled and halved

1 pint blueberries

1 pint blackberries

2 oranges, peeled and segmented

Put the melons, pineapple, lemon zest and juice, and sugar in a bowl and toss; add the remaining ingredients and toss gently (taking care not to crush the berries). Serve within a few hours of mixing.

Mixed Fruit Salad with Mint. Add ¼ cup Sugar Syrup (page 921) and 5 sprigs fresh mint. Pick the leaves

 Fast   Make Ahead   Vegetarian

from the mint sprigs and set aside. Combine the sugar syrup and stems in a small pot; bring to a boil, then turn off the heat and steep until cool; discard the stems. Chop the mint leaves. Toss the fruit in the mint syrup along with the mint leaves.

Mixed Fruit Salad with Coconut. Great with tropical fruits like papaya, mango, and pineapple: Add 2 tablespoons Sugar Syrup (page 921), 2 tablespoons coconut milk (to make your own, see page 389), and $^1/_4$ cup shredded coconut. Toss with the fruit as in the main recipe.

The Basics of Salad Greens

In some ways, the simple green salad is more challenging than salads containing other vegetables or grains, beans, meat, or seafood. Although quality ingredients are always important, the difference between an average green salad and a great one is determined by just three things: the greens, the oil, and the vinegar. Even if you have good oil and vinegar, drizzle them on some tasteless old lettuce and all you have is terrible lettuce with good dressing. Luckily, these days, even average supermarkets have a good assortment of greens, and it is always more interesting to combine at least two or three—preferably more—with varying flavors and textures.

This is easy enough, because there are literally hundreds of edible green, leafy vegetables, each with its own personality. They range from mustard greens, which can be searing hot, to chard, which is beet sweet. In between is a spectrum of flavors as varied as that of the animal kingdom. (In addition, many greens are high in basic nutrients, important trace elements, and the micronutrients shown to be potent disease fighters.)

Even in small supermarkets, even in winter, you can find more than a dozen greens for sale, from the standards—iceberg, green leaf, red leaf, romaine, and Boston lettuces—to radicchio, dandelion, mustard, turnip, arugula, kale, chard (red and white), collards, bok choy, watercress, endive, chicory, escarole, and frisée, as well as mesclun and a slew of prepacked salad mixes.

Here's a brief primer on the salad greens you're most likely to encounter. Some other greens are detailed in the produce chapter (see pages 233–404).

Lettuces

There are four basic types:

- **Iceberg:** the familiar light green ball of crisp, super-moist leaves.
- **Romaine:** long, crunchy leaves, still moist but with some bitterness.
- **Boston** (or *butterhead*): soft but well-defined heads with tender, only slightly bitter leaves.
- **Loose-leaf,** bunching, or cutting lettuce, like green and red leaf: the biggest category of lettuces and the one whose greens tend to be the most bitter.

Buying and Storing: Look for firm leaves without discoloration or wilting, especially toward the center. Iceberg and romaine keep literally for weeks, because their tight heads keep the inner leaves moist. Boston and loose-leaf lettuces don't keep for more than a few days.

Using: Romaine and Boston lettuces are fine by themselves, though better in mixes because they're mild tasting. Iceberg needs more help, though it's good in combination with other vegetables, as in a Chopped Salad (page 204), or broken into big wedges and used as a vehicle to show off dressing, like Real Ranch or Blue Cheese Dressing (page 42 or 25). Loose-leaf lettuce varies so much in taste and quality that it's hard to generalize. Lettuce can also be braised (see page 298) or thrown into soups.

This variety of texture and flavors is exactly why lettuces are almost always better in combination than they are singly. The bland tenderness of Boston-style lettuce, for example, mingles nicely with some bitter loose-leaf or radicchio and a few pieces of super-crisp romaine. But don't sacrifice quality just because you want a specific mixture; buy what looks best.

Chicory and Endive

The flavor, texture, color, and versatility of this huge group of greens—which includes radicchio, Belgian endive, curly endive, escarole, frisée, and more obscure greens like treviso and puntarella—is unmatched (see page 298 for more detail on these greens).

They're all sharp, crunchy vegetables that vary wildly in appearance but less so in taste and texture. Tight-headed bright red radicchio; long, leafy radicchio; thick-ribbed lettuce-looking escarole and chicory; the smooth oval Belgian endive; and lacy, frilly frisée all feature a stark bitterness that is readily tamed by cooking or smoothed by olive oil. All are bitter, most are super-crunchy, and some are very expensive.

Storing: Keep in plastic, in the vegetable bin, and count on at least a few days before you see browning or wilting. Still, the sooner you eat them the better.

Using: Many people find these too bitter to use alone in salads, but they're all fine when mixed with other greens. Belgian endive can be served like celery, drizzled with olive oil or spread with cream cheese. All of these greens are delicious braised (see page 237), stir-fried as described in Stir-Fried Vegetables (page 241), or brushed with olive oil, sprinkled with salt, and grilled (see Grilled or Broiled Radicchio with Balsamic Glaze, page 299).

Arugula, Watercress, and Dandelion Greens

The only way these greens are related is that they're all dark green and intensely flavorful. Dandelion greens—among the most vitamin-packed foods on the planet—are mild flavored when young, incomparably bitter when mature. Arugula (also called *rocket* or *rucola*) is the most strangely flavored green, possessing a distinctive hot muddiness that may be an acquired taste but is an easily acquired one. (The now widely available baby arugula is much milder, bordering on insipid.) And the super-peppery cresses are unjustly used more as a garnish than as a food. These are best in spring and fall but like almost everything else are now available year-round.

Storing: These greens are fairly fragile: Buy and use quickly or risk rotting. If you're desperate to store one for more than a couple of days, dunk the stem end in a glass half-full of water and wrap the whole thing, glass and all, in a plastic bag. Store this cool tropical mini-environment in the refrigerator.

Using: Arugula, lightly dressed with extra virgin olive oil and lemon juice, is a real treat and also a fine bed for anything grilled (this is true for many greens, of course). Watercress makes a fine addition to salads but is also good on sandwiches and in soups. Dandelion greens can be eaten in salads when young but quickly become too bitter to eat raw and are then best when steamed or stir-fried with soy sauce or garlic and lemon. For this and other recipes for cooking these greens, see pages 315–316.

Mesclun

Mesclun, from the Niçoise dialect for "mixture," is a word used to describe a mixture of greens, herbs, even edible flowers. Supermarket mesclun may not be as interesting as mesclun you make yourself (especially if you're a gardener), but it sure is easy to use, and it's become a year-round staple, thanks to a special process called *modified atmosphere packaging* that keeps them fresh for a week or longer. (The same is true of other prepackaged salads.) Once opened, however—or if you buy your mesclun in bulk—use within a couple of days, before it starts to turn even the slightest bit funky. (All such packing contains greens that are at least theoretically pre-washed, but I wash them anyway, and I recommend you do too.)

The Other Greens

These are the leafy salad greens that don't easily fall into any of the categories described so far. Some, like spinach (see page 352), are available everywhere in many forms.

Some, like mizuna and tatsoi (a small-leafed member of the bok choy family) are traditional Asian greens now going mainstream in America. Others, like mâche, lamb's tongue, and their relatives, are quite tender and fragile, with a small window of freshness.

If you frequent farmers' markets or specialty grocers, you'll run into all of these and more. I encourage you to experiment. It's no big deal; just treat them as you would any other lettuces or salad greens. And they may be swapped out for "any mixed salad greens" in the recipes here. Almost all may also be lightly cooked—steamed, boiled, and shocked or stir-fried—though when they're young, fresh, and tender, the best way to eat them is raw.

The Basics of Preparing Salad Greens

To Trim: For head and whole loose-leaf lettuces, first scoop or cut out the core. (If the head is tight, you'll probably have to use a knife.) Trim away the outer round of leaves and any browned or wilted stems. Tear or cut into smaller pieces if you like and wash.

To Wash: A fast and easy process: Put the greens into a salad spinner or in a colander inside a large pot. Fill the container with water and swirl the greens around. Now lift the colander or salad spinner insert out of the water. Pour out the water and repeat as necessary until the water contains no traces of sand. Then spin the greens or pat them dry with towels.

Storing: Washed, dried salad greens are good to have on hand and keep pretty well. If you have a salad spinner, pour the water out of it after spinning and pop it into the fridge, greens and all. The remaining moisture and ventilated basket provide a good environment for keeping greens fresh for a couple days or more. If you don't have a salad spinner, line a small plastic bag with clean cloth or paper towels, put the washed greens inside (taking care not to pack them too tightly), loosely tie the top, and refrigerate.

1

2

3

You can wash salad greens up to a day or two in advance. **(STEP 1)** Plunge them into a salad spinner filled with water (or a colander set in a large pot or bowl); swirl the greens around, then lift the insert or colander and change the water, repeating as many times as necessary to remove all traces of grit. **(STEP 2)** If you have a salad spinner, spin the greens dry; otherwise, dry them in a towel. **(STEP 3)** Store, wrapped loosely in cloth or paper towels, in a semiclosed resealable plastic bag.

The Basics of Oil and Vinegar

A decade ago, America had nearly abandoned butter and was gradually making the move away from trans fats to more healthy oils; olive oil was making serious inroads on Wesson. Today we have a completely different mind-set about oils; we use them not only for cooking and salad dressings, but for "drizzling," a concept that barely existed ten years ago. And olive oil is dominant.

Not surprising: Olive oil is easy to make; it's ancient, natural, and traditional; it's supremely useful; it's among the best tasting, and—calories aside (all fats have plenty of those!)—it's good for you.

Some other oils are almost as good, whether used in cooking or raw. But before I run down my favorite oils and how to use them, here's an overview of how they're made, what they contain, and how to store them, all useful information in choosing which to buy.

The Oil-Extracting Process

There are a number of ways to coax oil from fruit (like olives), vegetables (corn), seeds (grapes, or rapeseed, which produces canola), nuts (peanuts), or legumes (soy). Most "oil seeds" are first crushed, washed in a solvent called *hexane,* then heated. These chemically extracted oils are common and cheap.

Cold-pressed oils, in which the seeds are put under intense pressure, are better; no hexane is used, and temperatures remain below 180°F. The result is oil with a distinct flavor that reminds you of its source. These oils are less stable, less tolerant of heat, and quicker to turn rancid, but you can easily deal with all these factors.

The term *extra virgin,* by the way—associated only with olive oil—refers to the first cold pressing of the fruit. This was once done by pressing the olives between mats, using a large screw, but is now done by machine. Still, it's a much simpler process than chemical extraction.

Expeller-pressed oils fall somewhere in between chemical extraction and cold pressing. They too are pressed, not chemically extracted, though the process involves high heat. These retain some flavor and are generally more stable for cooking and storage; they're a good compromise.

After oils are extracted, they may be refined further—by heating or filtering—to remove impurities and improve their shelf life. Refined oils can handle higher heat than their unrefined counterparts, but they don't have as much flavor.

Oils, Fats, and Health

Oils contain saturated, monounsaturated, or polyunsaturated fats, usually in combination. Olive oil, for example, is the best known for being high in monounsaturated fats. Soy, seed, and vegetable oils tend to be high in polyunsaturated fats. Coconut oil is a mostly saturated fat, like animal fats.

There is debate about the right balance among these types of fats, but for most people it's enough to know that you should not overeat saturated fat and should even watch your consumption of polyunsaturates.

Trans fats are made when liquid vegetable oil, usually from soybeans or cottonseed, is turned into a semisolid form with the addition of hydrogen (hydrogenation). Solid shortening is the most common source of trans fatty acids or trans fat in our diets, but there is so much concern about the negative health effects of trans fat that it is now identified on the "Nutrition Facts" label of every food product and seems to be disappearing from many of them. I never use solid shortening or margarine, and I see no reason for anyone else to either, since butter and even lard are better-tasting and even healthier alternatives.

Storing Oils

When oil starts to turn rancid, it oxidizes, a process that converts some of its components into free radicals, which can be harmful and at least ruins flavor. Since cold-pressed oils spoil fastest, you have to watch out for this. It's easy enough: Keep your oil in a dark, cool place, preferably not stored in clear glass containers. If you buy large quantities, put a pint or so in a bottle and keep the rest in a dark place

EVERYDAY OILS

Listed in order of preference and usefulness, though not too strictly because many oils are interchangeable.

OIL	TYPE OF FATS	DESCRIPTION	USES	SUBSTITUTES
Extra Virgin Olive Oil	Mostly monounsaturated	Good extra virgin olive oil is readily available at a good price. The best balance the flavor of olives with a little acidity. They range from pale gold to radiant green, and you can spend a fortune on them, but need not. Buy extra virgin olive oil in 1-liter bottles or 3-liter cans; it's a commodity, so it tastes different each time, but it's almost always good. The expensive stuff has the equivalent of "vintages" too—some years are better than others. You can also buy more refined olive oils, sometimes labeled *pure*, sometimes just *olive oil*, but the flavor is not nearly as intense as that of extra virgin, and the price differential has grown so small that I don't bother now. ("Lite" olive oil is further processed and almost tasteless. It's not worth bothering with; use grapeseed oil instead.)	Dressings and cold sauces, Flavored Oil (page 26), drizzling, low-heat cooking, or warming	Nothing. Nada. Niente. You gotta have it.
Grapeseed Oil	Mostly polyunsaturated	My go-to oil for high-heat cooking or when I want almost no flavor, grapeseed oil is both neutral and versatile, with a velvety smoothness that reminds me of olive oil. (They both come from fruit, after all.) These can vary a bit; darker, greener ones have a pleasant but mild flavor.	Sautéing, panfrying, grilling, roasting	Corn oil
Peanut Oil	Almost balanced, with slightly more polyunsaturated than monoun-saturated and a teeny bit of saturated fat	I love peanut oil for deep-frying because it can withstand high heat, a characteristic that also makes it ideal for stir-fry cooking. It also has a distinctively peanutty flavor that is perfect for many Asian dishes. As with other oil, cold pressed is best.	Deep-frying, panfrying, grilling, roasting, some baking	Grapeseed or corn oil
Corn Oil	Mostly polyunsaturated	A good oil for all-purpose cooking. It's mild, full bodied, and nicely colored. It works especially well in Mexican, Caribbean, and Latin American dishes. As with other oil, cold pressed is best.	Sautéing, panfrying, grilling, roasting, deep-frying	Grapeseed oil

OIL	TYPE OF FATS	DESCRIPTION	USES	SUBSTITUTES
Dark Sesame Oil	Almost 50/50 mono- and polyunsaturated, with a little saturated fat	The quintessential Asian condiment, full flavored, with a distinctive sesame taste and aroma. A little goes a long way. You might see this seasoned with chile ("hot oil"), though I prefer to flavor it myself, while I'm cooking (or by making Flavored Oil, page 26). If you're cooking with it—which is sometimes quite nice—watch it well; it has a low smoke point.	Salads, dipping sauces, drizzling, seasoning	There are none, though toasted nut oils (below) come close.
(Light) Sesame Oil	Almost 50/50 mono- and polyunsaturated, with a little saturated fat	Untoasted, a good neutral oil that withstands cooking well. It's both milder and lighter in color than its roasted cousin.	Salads, stir-frying, and baking	Neutral oils, like grapeseed or corn
Nut Oils	This varies: Almond and hazelnut contain predominantly monounsaturated fats, while walnut is mostly polyunsaturated.	Nut oils are super-flavorful, which makes them so much fun to use, especially on salads. Almond, walnut, and hazelnut are the most common; all are delicious. There are also roasted nut oils (check out pistachio oil if you see it), but their strong flavors limit their use.	Salads and drizzling; more refined nut oils work well for low-heat cooking and baking.	They are fairly interchangeable within this category but otherwise utterly distinctive.
Not-So-Everyday Oils: Apricot Kernel, Coconut, and Avocado Oils	Varies, depending on the oil, so read the labels.	Coconut oil has become a darling of the health crowd, because it has the potential to raise metabolism despite the fact that it's nearly all saturated fat. (Don't ask me how this works. And don't expect this infatuation to last; in fact, it'll probably be over by the time you read this.) It's solid at room temperature, though, so you can't use it for salads. Nothing beats apricot kernel oil for high-heat roasting and cooking. Avocado oil is tasty on salads.	Varies, depending on the oil	These are one-of a kind, special-occasion oils.
Not-Recommended oils: Soybean, "Vegetable," Sunflower, Safflower, and Canola	Varying combinations of mono- and polyunsaturated fats	These are the most common supermarket oils; if the bottle just says *vegetable oil*, there's an excellent chance it's all soybean oil, but check the fine print on the label: it could be cottonseed, sunflower, or safflower oil (or a combination). Of these, I like safflower oil for its high heat tolerance (it also has the lowest amount of saturated fat of the three). Canola is made from rapeseeds, which are not edible, and I often find its flavor off-putting.	All-purpose, though I prefer other oils for everything	Grapeseed or corn oil or extra virgin olive oil.

EVERYDAY VINEGARS

The order in which these vinegars is listed is a combination of personal preference and availability; I think sherry vinegar is the best value in vinegar, and it's now sold in most supermar-kets. Near the bottom of the list are vinegars that are inter-esting and good but whose uses are limited, hard to find or, in the case of ordinary white vinegar, without flavor.

VINEGAR (ACIDITY)	DESCRIPTION	USES	SUBSTITUTES
Sherry Vinegar (8%)	The best and most flavorful vinegar for the money and increasingly available (the bottle must say *vinaigre de Jerez* for it to be genuine). It is very acidic, so start by using less than you'd use of other vinegars or cut it with a little water.	Wherever you'd reach for balsamic, this will work, from salads to cooked dishes.	White wine or champagne vinegar
Rice Vinegar (4.5%)	A must-have for Japanese and other East Asian cooking as well as all sorts of good light vinaigrettes. Note that it is very low in acid, which has its advantages.	Virtually any Asian salad, cooked dish, or sauce; or anytime you want to use less oil (and therefore more vinegar) in a salad	No good ones, but in a pinch, white vinegar diluted with water; or lemon juice
Balsamic Vinegar (about 6%)	Most sold in this country is distilled vinegar flavored with caramel syrup. But some inexpensive balsamic has a pleasant flavor, is fine in salads, and is perfect for Balsamic Syrup (page 51). *Aceto Balsamico Tradizionale di Modena*—real balsamic vinegar—is expensive. If you like the flavor of balsamic and use it frequently, look for one made from wine vinegar and aged at least a little while in wood barrels.	Vinaigrette (page 201), though some of the more traditional Italian ways (like Balsamic Syrup, page 51) are wonderful	Sherry vinegar or Chinese black vinegar
Red Wine Vinegar (6% to 7%)	Unless you're going to spend the money ($8 to $30) for a good one—the best (and most expensive) come from Spain and California—go with sherry vinegar.	Salads and cooked dishes (though remember it turns brown when cooked)	Sherry vinegar
White Wine Vinegar; Champagne Vinegar (5% to 7%)	Like white wine, white wine vinegar can be dull or delightful. Some is sold as "champagne vinegar," but few are actually made from Champagne (when they are, they're among the best). Buy neither the cheapest nor the most expensive.	Vinaigrettes and refrigerator (not preserved) pickles	Rice vinegar or fresh citrus juice
Malt Vinegar (4% to 8%)	Made from malted grain, malt vinegar actually tastes malty. Get real brewed malt vinegar—not a "nonbrewed condiment," which is, like industrial balsamic vinegar, nothing more than water, acetic acid, and caramel coloring.	Pickling, splashing on fried or roasted foods	Cider vinegar

VINEGAR (ACIDITY)	DESCRIPTION	USES	SUBSTITUTES
Chinese Black Vinegar *Zhenjiang or Zhejiang* (usually about 5% but may vary)	An unusual condiment made from glutinous rice with a delicious, almost haunting flavor. Look for one with a short list of ingredients and the word *Chinkiang* (or something similar) on the label; that's the province in which it's traditionally made.	In stir-fries and cooked dishes like Simplest Fried Rice (page 453) and as a dipping sauce or dressing by itself	A mixture of rice vinegar, soy sauce, and brown sugar—but it just won't be the same
Cider Vinegar (5%)	Made from apple cider, juice, or by-products of cider making, and it can have a distinct fruity flavor. The quality varies from fllavored white vinegar to small-batch, imported, and domestic vinegars worthy of the best salads and vegetables.	The complex ones make rich dressings and sauces; others are good for pickling, chutneys, and glazes.	White or malt vinegar
Raspberry Vinegar (4% to 6%)	This peaked in popularity in the nineties, though it still has its fans and its uses. Spinach salad (either with or without fresh raspberries for garnish) is one of them. Light, fruity, and very pink, it's got a distinct fruity flavor balanced by acidity.	Dressing cucumbers, radishes, and spinach; fruit salsas, especially those with cantaloupe or watermelon; a few drops on fresh cheese, like cottage or ricotta; or on cooked fish or chicken	Rice vinegar and lightly crushed raspberries
White Vinegar *Distilled Vinegar* (5%)	Acetic acid and water. Used primarily for or in cooked dishes when you just want straight acidity, with no added flavor. Very, very inexpensive.	Pickling, acidulated water	No reason to, really; most other vinegars have more flavor.

or, even better, in the refrigerator. (If you do store your oil at room temperature, smell it before using it. You'll know when it's become rancid; if it has, toss it.)

Vinegar

All vinegar provides acidity, which is valuable for balance and brightness. But only good vinegar—usually made from wine or fruit—adds flavor, depth, and complexity. Like wine or spirits, vinegar can be fermented from just about any fruit, vegetable, or grain.

Always keep vinegar in nonreactive glass or ceramic containers, preferably with corks, or glass or lined-metal lids. Kept in a cool, dark place and used regularly, it will be gone before it ever goes bad.

The Mother of All Dressings: Vinaigrette

Vinaigrette is arguably one of the true foundations of modern cuisine. It's all-purpose, simple, and as delicious as you care to make it. And even the most complicated vinaigrettes are five-minute affairs. The keys are good oil and vinegar (or citrus juice) and seasonings.

Vinaigrette is more than the sum of its parts, and within each of these three essential components you have endless options. When you combine good extra virgin olive oil, vinegar, salt and pepper, and a piece of garlic or shallot, an herb or a little good mustard, you create something astonishingly delicious, the kind of thing chefs amaze people with, something you can make every day, serve with pride, and vary for the rest of your life. You can drizzle this mixture on everything from salad to grilled vegetables to cold grilled chicken or fish—almost anything, really.

The Components: Oil, Acid, Seasonings

I discuss oils and vinegars on the preceding pages, but it's enough to say here that most vinaigrettes start with good extra virgin olive oil and whatever vinegar you happen to like. Variations can employ more flavorful oils, like those made from nuts, or less flavorful ones, like those made from corn or grapeseed. Vinegar may be sherry, balsamic, rice (which is milder than most), red or white wine. Or you can skip the vinegar entirely and use citrus juice or even wine or sake. Spices, herbs, solid ingredients like tomatoes or chopped pickles, creamy ones like mustard or egg or roasted garlic—all of these are good options.

Demystifying Emulsifying: Novices may wonder how to turn these components into a creamy, cohesive dressing. The process itself is called *emulsification* (many vinaigrettes are emulsions, as is mayonnaise)—think of it as forcing oil and water to combine—and it takes some energy. Of course this need not be your energy; it can be electrical energy powering a blender, which can produce a vinaigrette so stable that it can be prepared hours before serving.

Try this little experiment: Put vegetable oil and water together in a blender and turn it on. The mixture will turn white and creamy; add salt, pepper, and a few other flavorings, and you have something you can sell for $3 a cup, as long as you're a multinational food company. Bottled dressing—trust me or read the long list of ingredients yourself—is not much better than this: an emulsion of inferior oil (usually soy or "vegetable") and liquid (often water, with some vinegar, especially in "low-fat" or "lite" dressings), seasonings (often artificial, or at least far from fresh), and preservatives.

I emphasize this because I'm trying to convince you to make your own vinaigrette rather than buying bottled dressing. Do it in a blender, by shaking the ingredients in a jar, by beating them with a fork or whisk, or with an immersion blender. Hand tools—like forks—won't emulsify much, though there's nothing wrong with that (or with a "broken" vinaigrette, in which the oil and vinegar are barely combined), but for a creamy, rich emulsion, just use a blender, which also has the advantages of puréeing whatever solids you're adding and producing a vinaigrette that will keep nicely.

The Right Proportion: The standard ratio is three parts oil to one part vinegar, but many people prefer more oil; a ratio of four to one can be quite delicious. If you use mild vinegar and strong-tasting olive oil, you may prefer two parts oil to one part vinegar or something even a little stronger. Somewhere in that range, between four to one and one to one, you're going to find a home for your own taste. But that's the key: Taste your vinaigrette, then taste it some more. Eventually your palate will find a home that it loves.

Vinaigrette

MAKES: About ¾ cup
TIME: 5 minutes

From here grow all other vinaigrettes. To vary the flavors, use your instincts or any of the suggestions in the list and chart that follow. My everyday dressing almost always includes a bit of mustard, which helps emulsify the dressing while adding tang. You can add a touch of honey or sugar to balance the acid if you find it too strong.

½ cup extra virgin olive oil

3 tablespoons or more good wine vinegar

Salt and freshly ground black pepper

1 large shallot (about 1 ounce), cut into chunks (optional)

❶ Combine all the ingredients except the shallot in a blender and turn the machine on; a creamy emulsion will form within 30 seconds. Taste and add vinegar a teaspoon or two at a time until the balance tastes right to you.

❷ Add the shallot and turn the machine on and off a few times until the shallot is minced within the dressing. Taste, adjust the seasoning, and serve. (This is best made fresh but will keep, refrigerated, for a few days; bring it back to room temperature and whisk briefly before using.)

20 Simple Additions to Vinaigrette

1. Any dried herb or spice: The specific quantities will vary, but start with as little as a pinch—$1/8$ teaspoon or so—and work your way up from there. Be careful not to blow away the vinaigrette; dried herbs and spices can be quite strong.
2. Minced fresh garlic: Start with a small clove. For milder garlic flavor, let a crushed clove sit in the vinaigrette for a few minutes, then fish it out. Or wipe your salad bowl with a crushed clove of garlic and discard. Roasted Garlic (page 303) makes a great addition and emulsifies like crazy; because it's mild, you can use 5 cloves or more.
3. Minced red onion, scallion, shallot, mild white onion, leek, etc.: Start with a tablespoon or so.
4. Mustard, soy sauce, Worcestershire sauce, or nam pla (Thai fish sauce): as much as a tablespoon.
5. Honey, maple syrup, or other sweeteners, within reason: no more than a tablespoon or so.
6. Freshly grated Parmesan (or other hard cheese or crumbled blue cheese, feta, or goat cheese: from a tablespoon to $1/4$ cup.
7. Minced crunchy vegetables, such as red or yellow bell pepper, cucumber, celery, carrot, or fennel: a couple tablespoons.
8. Minced pickles, preferably cornichons: from a tablespoon to $1/4$ cup.
9. An egg or a couple of tablespoons fresh or sour cream or yogurt, or puréed soft tofu, any of which will add incredible creaminess to your vinaigrette.
10. Prepared or freshly grated horseradish: at least 1 teaspoon.
11. Minced tomato, seeded and, preferably, peeled, or bits of reconstituted dried tomato.
12. A tablespoon or two of any stock (to make your own, see pages 157–159), juice, wine, beer, or booze.
13. A small handful of seeds, like sesame, poppy, sunflower, or minced pumpkin seeds.
14. Canned chipotle: 1 pepper is plenty, with just a tiny bit of its adobo.
15. A $1/2$ cup soaked and softened sea vegetable, like arame, hijiki, or wakame.
16. 1 small slice of day-old bread (crust removed).
17. 1 small peach, pear, or apple, peeled, seeded, and cut into chunks.
18. $1/4$ cup salsa or chutney.
19. Up to $1/4$ cup dried fruit, like blueberries, cherries, raisins, apricots, pineapple, or mango.
20. Any pitted black or green olives, $1/4$ cup or even more if you like (do this before you salt the vinaigrette).

Salad Dressings Beyond Vinaigrette

Generally these dressings are creamier, thicker, and richer than vinaigrette, so to prevent sogginess I suggest using them to top mixed greens right before serving, rather than tossing the whole salad. Alternatively, you can thin them to make them more dressinglike than diplike: Use a little oil or some sour cream, cream, milk, or yogurt; or lemon juice or a little vinegar; or just water.

Here's where you'll find them:

1. Simplest Yogurt Sauce (page 24)
2. Blue Cheese Dressing (page 25)
3. Green Sauce, French Style (page 42)
4. Real Ranch Dressing (page 42)
5. Peanut Sauce (page 55)

 Fast   Make Ahead   Vegetarian

18 VARIATIONS ON VINAIGRETTE

Beyond simple additions, you can vary vinaigrette easily by swapping out some ingredients. Use this chart to get you started with the most familiar, then mix and match oils, vinegars, and flavorings from around the chart, with the preceding list of additions and your own ideas. For all, the method in the Vinaigrette recipe remains exactly the same.

VINAIGRETTE	OIL(S)	VINEGAR OR ACID	FLAVORINGS AND SEASONINGS (IN ADDITION TO SALT AND FRESHLY GROUND BLACK PEPPER)
Mustard or Honey Mustard Vinaigrette	$1/2$ cup extra virgin olive oil	3 tablespoons or more good wine vinegar	1 heaping teaspoon any good mustard or $1/2$ teaspoon or so dry mustard, 1 to 2 tablespoons honey (optional)
Herb Vinaigrette	$1/2$ cup extra virgin olive oil	3 tablespoons or more freshly squeezed lemon juice or good wine vinegar	$1/4$ cup tender, milder herbs like parsley, basil, or dill; 1 teaspoon stronger, tougher herbs like rosemary, tarragon, or thyme
Creamy Vinaigrette	$1/3$ cup extra virgin olive oil	3 tablespoons or more good white wine vinegar	3 tablespoons fresh or sour cream, yogurt, mayonnaise, or puréed soft tofu; 1 teaspoon Dijon mustard, or to taste; and 1 small shallot, chopped
Lemon or Lime Vinaigrette	$1/2$ cup extra virgin olive oil	$1/4$ cup or so freshly squeezed lemon or lime juice, plus 1 tablespoon warm water	Zest of 1 lemon or lime, grated or minced (optional); lots of black pepper
Soy Vinaigrette	$1/2$ cup neutral oil, like grapeseed or corn; 1 teaspoon dark sesame oil, or to taste	3 tablespoons or more vinegar, lemon, or lime juice	1 tablespoon soy sauce
Roasted Garlic Vinaigrette	$1/2$ cup extra virgin olive oil	3 tablespoons or more balsamic vinegar	1 clove garlic, 1 tablespoon honey
Bacon Vinaigrette	$1/4$ cup extra virgin olive oil; 2 tablespoons rendered bacon fat	3 tablespoons sherry or balsamic vinegar	1 large shallot, chopped; $1/4$ cup finely chopped cooked bacon (stirred in just before using)
Ginger Vinaigrette	$1/2$ cup neutral oil, like grapeseed or corn	1 tablespoon sherry vinegar, 1 tablespoon lime juice, about 1 tablespoon warm water	1 inch fresh ginger, peeled and roughly chopped; lots of black pepper
Tomato-Basil Vinaigrette	$1/2$ cup extra virgin olive oil	2 tablespoons or more good wine vinegar	$1/4$ cup seeded and chopped tomato, 3 tablespoons chopped fresh basil leaves
Nut Oil Vinaigrette	$1/2$ cup walnut, hazelnut, or other nut oil	3 tablespoons sherry vinegar	1 large shallot (about 1 ounce), chopped (optional)
Nutty Vinaigrette	$1/2$ cup extra virgin olive oil	3 tablespoons sherry, balsamic, or good wine vinegar	$1/4$ cup almonds, hazelnuts, pine nuts, pecans, or walnuts, ground in a food processor; 1 clove garlic

VINAIGRETTE	OIL(S)	VINEGAR OR ACID	FLAVORINGS AND SEASONINGS (IN ADDITION TO SALT AND FRESHLY GROUND BLACK PEPPER)
Maple Vinaigrette	½ cup extra virgin olive oil	2 tablespoons cider, sherry, or white wine vinegar	1 tablespoon maple syrup, or to taste
Avocado Vinaigrette (this is delicious but discolors after an hour or so)	None	¼ cup or more freshly squeezed lime or lemon juice	½ avocado, 1 teaspoon minced garlic or 2 tablespoons chopped onion (optional)
Roasted Pepper Vinaigrette	⅓ cup extra virgin olive oil	3 or more tablespoons good wine or balsamic vinegar	½ Roasted Red Pepper (page 330)
Anchovy-Caper Vinaigrette	½ cup extra virgin olive oil	3 tablespoons good wine vinegar	4 anchovy fillets with a bit of their oil, 1 teaspoon capers with a bit of their brine, 2 tablespoons chopped fresh parsley leaves
Coconut Curry Vinaigrette	½ cup coconut milk (to make your own, see page 389)	3 tablespoons or more rice vinegar	1 tablespoon curry powder (to make your own, see pages 66–67)
Miso Vinaigrette	3 tablespoons neutral oil, like grapeseed or corn	3 tablespoons rice vinegar, 2 tablespoons warm water	3 tablespoons white or light miso, 1 tablespoon soy sauce
Pomegranate Molasses Vinaigrette	½ cup extra virgin olive oil	1 tablespoon pomegranate molasses, 2 tablespoons or more warm water	1 or 2 teaspoons honey

Citrus or Vinegar?

Freshly squeezed citrus juice is often a terrific substitute for vinegar. Lemon juice is most common, though limes, tangerines, oranges, blood oranges, and even grapefruits have their place, especially in salad dressings. Of course the flavor isn't at all like vinegar, and the acidity is considerably lower (usually about 3 percent versus 5 percent or higher). But that makes citrus juice a good choice when you want lower acidity or just a different flavor.

Green Salads

The basic green salad is one or more greens, drizzled with oil and a little lemon juice or vinegar and sprinkled with some salt and pepper (see Simple Green Salad, page 186). As detailed on page 191, the greens may vary considerably, as may the dressing. But there are plenty of other directions in which you can go, and I offer some of them here. To shortcut the recipes, be sure to see the list on page 187, "15 Ideas for Simple Green Salad." A couple of advance hints: Jazz up your dressing with mustard, Roasted Garlic (page 303), or a fresh herb (but don't overdo it); or toss in leftover cooked vegetables (rinsed

 Fast   Make Ahead   **V** Vegetarian

with hot water if any of last night's dressing is clinging to them).

Greens with Fruit, Cheese, and Nuts

MAKES: 4 servings
TIME: 20 to 30 minutes

The now-classic combination of pears, Gorgonzola, and walnuts can be easily varied; see the list that follows. Generally, for this I like the strong flavor of blues and other aged cheeses like Parmesan, but feta and goat cheese are also good choices. When it comes to the nuts, the differences are subtle, so go with your favorites. Of course a crumble of bacon on top never hurts.

About 1 pound fresh fruit or 1 cup dried fruit

1 tablespoon freshly squeezed lemon juice

1/4 pound Gorgonzola or other blue cheese

3/4 cup shelled walnuts or any other nut you like

6 cups mixed greens, like mesclun,
    torn into bite-sized pieces

About 1/2 cup Vinaigrette (page 201)

❶ Peel and core the fresh fruit if necessary and remove any seeds or pits. If large, cut them into 1/2-inch chunks or thinly slice. Toss the fruit with the lemon juice. If you're using dried fruit, toss it with the vinaigrette. In either case, cover and refrigerate until needed, up to 2 hours.

❷ Crumble the cheese into small bits; cover and refrigerate until needed. Put the nuts in a dry skillet over medium heat and toast, shaking the pan frequently until they are aromatic and beginning to darken in color, 3 to 5 minutes.

❸ When you're ready to serve, toss the fruit, cheese, and greens together with as much of the dressing as you like. Chop the nuts coarsely, sprinkle them over all, and serve.

5 Good Fruit, Cheese, and Nut Combinations

1. Grapes, Parmesan, pine nuts
2. Fresh or dried apples, blue cheese, walnuts
3. Fresh or dried figs or apricots, goat cheese, pecans
4. Oranges or dried cherries, manchego, almonds
5. Melon (cantaloupe, honeydew, or watermelon), feta, hazelnuts

Caesar Salad

MAKES: 4 servings
TIME: 20 minutes

All kinds of junk passes for Caesar salad, but this is the real thing. The essentials in a great Caesar salad are garlic, egg, lemon juice, anchovies, and real Parmesan. Compromise on any of these and you'll still have a good salad, but you won't have a great Caesar.

Take a page from casual restaurants if you like and top the salad with grilled or broiled chicken cutlets or shrimp (peeled) to make it far more substantial; it makes a great lunch.

1 clove garlic, halved

2 eggs or 1/2 cup pasteurized egg product

2 tablespoons freshly squeezed lemon juice

6 tablespoons extra virgin olive oil

2 tablespoons minced anchovies, or to taste

Dash Worcestershire sauce

Salt and freshly ground black pepper

1 large head romaine lettuce, torn into pieces

Garlic or other Croutons (page 877)

1/2 to 1 cup freshly grated Parmesan cheese

❶ Rub the inside of your salad bowl with the garlic clove; discard it.

❷ Bring a small pot of water to a boil. Pierce a tiny hole in the broad end of each of the eggs with a pin or a needle and boil them for 60 to 90 seconds; they will just begin to firm up. Crack them into the salad bowl, being sure to scoop out the white that clings to the shell.

❸ Beat the eggs with a fork, gradually adding the lemon juice and then the olive oil, beating all the while.

❹ Stir in the anchovies and the Worcestershire. Taste and add salt if needed and plenty of pepper. Toss well with the lettuce; top with the croutons and Parmesan, then toss again at the table. Serve immediately.

Chicken, Shrimp, or Scallop Caesar Salad. Top the salad with slices of Grilled or Broiled Boneless Chicken (page 641) or grilled or broiled shrimp or scallops (see page 563 or 564).

Chopped Salad, Five Ways

MAKES: 6 servings
TIME: 30 minutes

The most popular nonrecipe in the salad world, chopped salad is no more than a mix of whatever crunchy fresh vegetables you have on hand, tossed with some lettuce and dressed with whatever vinaigrette you like. It can be so big, hearty, and flavorful that you need nothing else for dinner. This recipe will get you started, but the accompanying list will show you the real possibilities.

2 celery stalks (preferably from the heart), chopped

2 carrots, chopped

1 small to medium red onion, minced

1 cucumber, peeled if necessary and seeded (see page 293), chopped

1 red or yellow bell pepper, cored, seeded, and chopped

1 cup diced ham or chicken (optional)

1 medium head romaine lettuce, torn into pieces (about 4 cups)

Salt and freshly ground black pepper

½ cup or more Vinaigrette (made with a small clove garlic instead of shallot) or one of the variations (pages 201–202)

❶ Combine the vegetables, the meat if you're using it, and the lettuce in a bowl; sprinkle lightly with salt and pepper and toss.

❷ Drizzle with the vinaigrette, taste and adjust the seasoning, and serve immediately.

Chopped Salad, Asian Style. Use carrots, scallions, cabbage (shredded), and snow or snap peas for the vegetables and Soy or Ginger Vinaigrette (page 201) for the dressing. Add diced chicken or shrimp if you like.

Chopped Salad, Mexican Style. Use avocado, jícama, tomatoes (seeded), and red or yellow bell pepper for the vegetables, and orange, red onion, or Avocado Vinaigrette (page 202) for the dressing. Proceed with the recipe. Add diced ham, chicken, or shrimp if you like. Garnish with crumbled tortilla chips.

Chopped Salad, Indian Style. Use seeded tomatoes, steamed new potatoes, carrots, and chickpeas (rinsed and drained) for the vegetables, and Coconut Curry Vinaigrette (page 202) or Creamy Cilantro-Mint Chutney (page 37) for the dressing. Garnish with fresh cilantro leaves.

Chopped Salad with Peanut Dressing. Use Peanut Sauce, (page 55), thinned with soy sauce, freshly squeezed lime juice, and/or water for the dressing. Add diced chicken if you like.

14 Other Ingredients for Chopped Salad

1. Fennel, ½ bulb or so, trimmed and chopped

2. Avocado (not too ripe) pitted, peeled, and chopped

3. Cabbage, shredded or chopped, about a cup

4. Haricots verts or green or wax beans, about a cup, cooked briefly and shocked (see page 240)

5. Fresh peas, snow peas, or snap peas, about a cup, very lightly cooked and shocked (see page 240)

6. ½ cup grated or crumbled cheese, like Parmesan, blue, or feta

7. $^1/_2$ cup chopped radish

8. Steamed waxy potatoes, cut into small chunks, about a cup

9. Tomato, seeded and chopped, about a cup

10. Beets, cooked, peeled, and chopped, about a cup

11. Corn kernels, about a cup, cooked any way (grilled is excellent)

12. Jícama, peeled and chopped, about a cup

13. Cooked or canned chickpeas, $^1/_2$ cup or more, lightly rinsed

14. Nuts, like almonds, pistachios, or peanuts, $^1/_2$ cup, chopped into large pieces

Warm Spicy Greens with Bacon and Eggs

MAKES: 4 servings
TIME: About 30 minutes

The salad for meat-eaters.

2 tablespoons extra virgin olive oil

About $^1/_2$ pound of the best slab bacon you can find or pancetta, cut into $^1/_2$-inch cubes

1 small shallot, chopped

4 cups torn dandelion or other bitter greens, like mustard or turnip greens, watercress, or frisée

About $^1/_4$ cup top-quality red wine vinegar

1 teaspoon Dijon mustard

Salt and freshly ground black pepper

4 Poached Eggs (page 793), or peeled Medium-Boiled Eggs (page 791)

❶ Put the olive oil in a skillet over medium heat. When hot, add the bacon and cook slowly until it's crisp all over, 10 minutes or more. Add the shallot and cook until softened, another minute or two. Keep the bacon warm in the skillet.

❷ Warm a salad bowl by filling it with hot water and letting it sit for a minute. Dry it and toss in the greens.

Add the vinegar and mustard to the skillet and bring just to a boil, stirring. Pour the liquid and the bacon over the greens, toss, and season to taste (it shouldn't need much salt). Top each portion with an egg and serve immediately.

Warm Spinach Salad with Bacon and Eggs. Substitute tender spinach leaves for the dandelion greens.

Salade Lyonnaise. The French classic: Use frisée for the greens. Skip warming the salad bowl and boiling the vinaigrette in Step 2. Toss the greens in the vinaigrette and serve immediately.

BLT Salad. Omit the shallots, if you like, and the eggs. Substitute any lettuce or salad greens for the dandelion; add 2 large ripe tomatoes, cored, seeded, and chopped, and $^1/_2$ cup crumbled blue cheese. Let the bacon cool in the pan after it's cooked. For Step 2, stir the vinegar and mustard in with the bacon, then pour over the lettuce, tomatoes, and blue cheese in an unheated bowl; serve immediately.

Vegetable Salads

In their raw state some vegetables—beets, carrots, artichokes, celery and celeriac, mushrooms, and others—make fantastic salads. With many, the crunch is unsurpassed, while others are sublimely tender. The flavors are sometimes subtle, sometimes stark; they can stand up to a range of bold dressings, which provide contrast and emphasis. So from beet salad with vinaigrette to new versions of coleslaw, from old favorites to newer creations, the recipes here are quick and interesting.

Simple Radish or Jícama Salad

MAKES: 4 servings
TIME: 15 to 30 minutes

Radishes are usually eaten out of hand from a crudité or relish assortment and sometimes tossed into green salads.

But they make a nifty crisp, picklelike salad on their own. The combination of lime and lemon juice here mimics the juice of sour orange, which is often used in Mexico but is tough to find in the United States.

About 16 radishes, sliced, 1 medium daikon, peeled and chopped, or 1 small to medium jícama, peeled and chopped

1 small white onion, chopped

1 tablespoon salt

$^1/_4$ teaspoon freshly ground black pepper

2 tablespoons freshly squeezed lime juice, or to taste

2 teaspoons freshly squeezed lemon juice (optional)

2 tablespoons chopped fresh parsley or cilantro leaves

1 If time allows, toss the radishes or jícama and onion with the salt in a strainer and let sit for 15 minutes; rinse and drain.

2 Toss the radishes and onion with the salt, pepper, citrus juices, and parsley. Taste, adjust the seasoning, and serve immediately or refrigerate for up to an hour.

Radish-Celery-Mint Salad. Nice and bright: Substitute $^1/_2$ cup chopped celery for the onion, extra virgin olive oil for the lime juice, and orange juice for the lemon juice. Toss the radishes with $^1/_2$ cup finely chopped fresh mint leaves instead of the parsley and sprinkle with salt (if you haven't already salted them) and pepper. Drizzle with the oil and orange juice, toss again, and serve.

Spicy No-Mayo Coleslaw

MAKES: 8 servings

TIME: 30 minutes

F **M** **V**

If you want restaurant-style coleslaw, you take shredded cabbage and combine it with mayo and maybe a little lemon juice. This version is far more flavorful with far less fat. I like cabbage salad (which is what coleslaw

amounts to) on the spicy side, so I use plenty of Dijon, along with a little garlic and chile (you could substitute cayenne for the chile or just omit it if you prefer), and scallions.

2 tablespoons Dijon mustard, or to taste

2 tablespoons sherry vinegar, red wine vinegar, or freshly squeezed lemon juice

1 small clove garlic, minced

1 tablespoon minced fresh chile, like jalapeño, Thai, serrano, or habanero, or to taste (optional)

$^1/_4$ cup peanut oil or extra virgin olive oil

6 cups cored and shredded Napa, Savoy, green, and/or red cabbage

1 large red or yellow bell pepper, cored, seeded, and diced or shredded

$^1/_3$ cup chopped scallion, more or less

Salt and freshly ground black pepper

$^1/_4$ cup chopped fresh parsley leaves

1 To make the dressing, whisk together the mustard and vinegar in a small bowl, along with the garlic and chile. Add the oil a little at a time, whisking all the while.

2 Combine the cabbage, bell pepper, and scallion and toss with the dressing. Sprinkle with salt and pepper and refrigerate until ready to serve. (It's best to let the slaw rest for an hour or so to allow the flavors to mellow; the cabbage will also soften a bit and exude some juice. You can let it sit longer, up to 24 hours, if you like. Drain the slaw before continuing.) Just before serving, toss with the parsley.

Cabbage and Carrot Slaw, Mexican Style. Grate 2 medium carrots and use them instead of the bell pepper. Use freshly squeezed lime juice in place of the vinegar. Finish with cilantro if you like instead of the parsley.

Apple Slaw. Use carrots instead of bell pepper, as in the preceding variation. Use 1 medium onion, grated, in place of the scallion. Shred or grate 2 medium or 1 large Granny Smith apples (or use any tart, crisp, apple) and include them in the mix. Lemon juice or cider vinegar is the best choice of acid here.

Corn Salad with Avocado

MAKES: 4 servings

TIME: 30 minutes

Here you have three choices for preparing the corn: If it's truly fresh and really good, leave it raw; just shave the kernels from the ears and toss them with the rest of the ingredients.

That's not usually the case, though, and almost as good is to roast the kernels from good corn in a skillet with a little oil. Or use the kernels from already steamed corn, which—if the corn was good in the first place—is an excellent way to take care of the leftovers.

2 tablespoons corn oil

4 to 6 ears corn, stripped of their kernels (2 to 3 cups; see page 288)

1 small red onion, chopped

1/2 red bell pepper, cored, seeded, and chopped

1 teaspoon mild chile powder, like ancho

Salt and freshly ground black pepper

1 medium tomato, peeled if you like, seeded, and chopped

1 medium ripe avocado, pitted, peeled, and chopped

Juice of 2 limes, or more to taste

1/2 cup chopped fresh cilantro leaves, more or less

To Salt or Not to Salt

The word *salad* comes from the ancient word for "salt," so it's no surprise that the two concepts go hand in hand: salting vegetables, even briefly, can maximize their crispness and flavor by causing them to release their water. (This is exactly why you don't want to salt greens or dress salads in advance—it dilutes the dressing and prevents the greens from absorbing its flavors.)

Salting can remove some of the water from many vegetables beforehand and make them firmer, crisper, and more flavorful. Specifically:

Cabbage: When slaws are made with salted cabbage, they are noticeably less watery and stay crisp and fresh a few days longer. Just put sliced cabbage in a colander, sprinkle with salt (about a tablespoon for 6 cups of cabbage), and set aside to drain. After about an hour, rinse, gently squeeze dry, and drain.

Cucumbers: Ordinary cukes benefit greatly from salting. First peel, seed, and slice them (see page 293). Then use the same procedure as for cabbage. For extra crispness, rinse, then wring dry in a towel after salting; if that's not your goal, just pat them dry after rinsing.

Radishes: Sliced radishes may be salted like cabbage and cucumbers—they become milder and crisper—but only for an absolute maximum of 45 minutes, or they will become limp.

Tomatoes: Lightly salting tomatoes always improves their flavor and tightens their flesh, but they are fragile. Use less salt (about 1 teaspoon per pound of tomatoes) and leave them for only 15 minutes or so. Put salted chopped tomatoes in a colander (and set a bowl under it if you want to trap the tomato water for another use, like that on pages 130–131). Salted, sliced, and wedged tomatoes work best put directly on towels or spread out on wire racks or even a plate.

Onions: You can make onions milder and crisper by salting them, either directly or in a saltwater bath (about 1 tablespoon salt per 4 cups of water). Let sit for a half hour or longer, then rinse and dry before using.

① Put the oil in a large skillet (cast iron is good here, but anything will do) and turn the heat to high. When the oil is very hot but not yet smoking, toss in the corn. Let it sit for a minute or so, then stir or shake the pan; brown the corn a bit, 5 minutes or less, then turn off the heat and stir in the onion, pepper, chile powder, salt, and pepper.

② Cool for a few minutes, then toss with the remaining ingredients. Taste, adjust the seasoning, and serve hot, warm, or at room temperature.

Corn Salad with Arugula. Omit the chile powder and cilantro and substitute 3 cups torn arugula leaves for the avocado and 2 tablespoons white wine vinegar for the lime juice.

Corn Salad with Tarragon. Omit the chile powder and avocado and substitute 2 tablespoons rice vinegar for the lime juice and 1 tablespoon chopped tarragon leaves for the cilantro.

Corn Salad with Feta and Mint. Omit the chile powder and lime juice and substitute 1 cup crumbled feta cheese for the avocado and mint for the cilantro. Add a sprinkle of any Vinaigrette (pages 199–202).

Fennel and Orange Salad

MAKES: 4 servings
TIME: 15 minutes

F **V**

Among the most underrated vegetables, fennel has celery-like crunch and a widely appealing anise flavor. Combined with orange, it really shines.

1 pound fennel (1 large or two small bulbs)

3 small sweet oranges or tangerines

Salt

1 tablespoon freshly squeezed lime
 or lemon juice

2 tablespoons chopped fresh cilantro, basil,
 or chervil leaves

① Trim and core the fennel and cut it into small cubes, $1/4$ inch or so, or into thin slices (or shave it super-thinly on a mandoline).

② Squeeze the juice from one of the oranges, pour it over the fennel, add salt and lime juice, and let it sit (for up to several hours) while you prepare the other oranges.

③ Peel the remaining oranges and slice into wheels (see page 398); then slice in half again, removing any pits and tough, fibrous material. Add the oranges and cilantro to the fennel, toss, taste and adjust the seasoning, and serve.

Red Onion and Orange Salad. Substitute 1 small red onion, thinly sliced, for the fennel and 1 teaspoon fresh rosemary leaves or $1/2$ teaspoon dried for the cilantro. Use 4 navel or Valencia oranges, but do not juice any of them; peel and chop them all. Omit the lime juice.

Jícama and Orange Salad. Substitute shaved or julienned jícama for the fennel. Use cilantro.

Shaved Artichoke Salad

MAKES: 4 servings
TIME: 30 minutes

F **V**

Adding artichoke hearts, cooked or marinated, is an easy way to kick any salad up a notch since they're available already prepared in supermarkets. But for a real treat, one that is four-star-restaurant delicious, you must try cleaning artichokes, shaving them, and layering them with Parmesan. Unbelievable. With baby artichokes (see the variation) it's even better.

 Fast   **M** Make Ahead   Vegetarian

Almost as good, considerably easier and cheaper, is virtually the same salad made with button mushrooms or barely cooked sunchokes (Jerusalem artichokes); see the variations.

1 lemon, plus 1 for garnish (optional)

4 artichokes, trimmed and cleaned (see page 253)

Parmesan as needed

3 tablespoons extra virgin olive oil, or more as necessary

Salt and freshly ground black pepper

Chopped fresh parsley or basil leaves for garnish

❶ Squeeze the juice of a lemon into a bowl of ice water. Prepare the artichokes, then slice the hearts (and bottoms, if they're tender enough) as thinly as possible; use a mandoline if you like. As you slice them, drop them into the water to keep them from browning.

❷ Thinly slice the Parmesan; you want about as many pieces, about the same size, as you have artichoke slices. Mince or grate the zest of the second lemon if you're using it. Remove the artichoke slices from the water and dry, then toss with the olive oil and 1 tablespoon juice from the remaining lemon. Sprinkle with a little salt and a fair amount of pepper, then layer with the Parmesan. Taste and add more olive oil, lemon juice, salt,

Composed Salads

Composed salad is a fussy name for putting all the ingredients on a plate, then drizzling dressing on top; you might think of them as modern chef salads. You can make individual composed salads or one big serving. Give yourself some room to reduce overcrowding. Start with the greens, either piled up in the middle of the plate or off to one side, then choose at least three components that provide contrasting—yet complementary—textures and flavors. These can be cooked or raw, leftovers or specially prepared. Arrange them around the greens without fuss, then garnish with croutons, toasted nuts, or other crunchy tidbits. You can do all this a little in advance, but don't pour the dressing on top until right before serving.

5 Different Directions for Composed Salads

The pile of greens in composed salads can always be mesclun or simply lettuce, but don't shy away from more assertively flavored greens like arugula, watercress, or any of the chicories, which you can combine with some mild greens to take the edge off. Any of the Greens with Fruit, Cheese, and Nuts (page 202) salads also make lovely composed salads.

1. Sliced grilled chicken breast, ripe tomato slices or wedges, diced red pepper, super-thin red onion slices, toasted pumpkin seeds, and Roasted Pepper Vinaigrette (page 202)

2. Seared sea scallops (see page 598), thinly sliced radishes and scallions, orange or tangerine segments, toasted sesame seeds, Soy or Ginger Vinaigrette (page 201)

3. Cooked and lightly seasoned lentils, crisp bacon slices, steamed or roasted waxy potatoes (cut into wedges), chopped fresh chives, Honey Mustard Vinaigrette (page 201)

4. Thinly sliced prosciutto, cooked peas, fava, or lima beans, shaved pecorino or Parmesan cheese, extra virgin olive oil stirred with a little Balsamic Syrup (page 51).

5. Battered and Fried Vegetables (zucchini, summer squash, or squash blossoms, see page 247), slices of goat cheese, whole tender basil leaves, 3 to 4 kalamata olives, Tomato-Basil or Herb Vinaigrette (page 201)

or pepper as needed, then garnish with herbs and zest if you like and serve immediately.

Shaved Baby Artichoke Salad. Use 8 baby artichokes instead of the large ones. In Step 1, trim and slice the whole artichoke (see page 253).

Shaved Sunchoke (Jerusalem Artichoke) Salad. Tougher sunchokes must be parboiled: Scrub and trim about a pound of sunchokes (see page 357), then put in a small pan with salted water to cover; bring to a boil and cook just until barely tender, 7 to 10 minutes (they turn mushy fast). Plunge into a bowl of ice water with the juice of a lemon in it, then cut into thin slices and treat them exactly as you would the artichoke hearts.

Shaved Mushroom Salad. Instead of using raw artichokes, use 1 pound button mushrooms and slice them as thinly as possible (no need to drop the mushroom slices into lemony water).

Shaved Fennel Salad. Substitute 1 fennel bulb, thinly shaved, for the artichoke. Omit the Parmesan and use orange or grapefruit juice instead of lemon.

Raw Beet Salad

MAKES: 4 servings
TIME: 20 minutes

Beets, like carrots, can be eaten raw. And they're delicious that way, crunchy and sweet. So sweet, in fact, that they need a strongly acidic dressing like this one for balance.

1 to 1¹/₂ pounds beets, preferably small

2 large shallots

Salt and freshly ground black pepper

2 teaspoons Dijon mustard, or to taste

1 tablespoon extra virgin olive oil

2 tablespoons sherry vinegar or other good strong vinegar

1 sprig fresh tarragon, minced (optional)

¹/₄ cup chopped fresh parsley leaves

❶ Peel the beets and the shallot. Combine them in a food processor fitted with the metal blade and pulse carefully until the beets are shredded; do not purée. (Or grate the beets by hand and mince the shallots; combine.) Scrape into a bowl.

❷ Sprinkle with salt and pepper, then add the mustard, oil, and vinegar and toss. Taste and adjust the seasoning. Toss in the herbs and serve.

Raw Beet Salad with Cabbage and Orange. Use equal parts beet and cabbage, about ¹/₂ pound of each. Shred the beets (with the shallot) as directed, then shred the cabbage by hand or by using the slicing disk of the food processor. Add 1 navel orange (including its juice), peeled and roughly chopped, to the rest of the ingredients.

Raw Beet Salad with Fennel. Use equal parts beet and fennel, about ¹/₂ pound of each. Shred the beets (with the shallot) as directed, then shave the fennel very thinly. Omit the Dijon and substitute lemon juice for the sherry vinegar.

Raw Beet Salad with Carrot and Ginger. Use equal parts beet and carrot, about ¹/₂ pound of each. Treat the carrots like the beets (you can process them together) and add about a tablespoon of minced ginger to the mix; omit the tarragon. Substitute peanut for olive oil, lime juice for sherry vinegar, and cilantro for the parsley.

Celery Rémoulade. Replace the beets with 1 medium celery root or 1 bunch celery (1 to 1¹/₂ pounds). Peel the celery root and cut it into matchsticks or trim the celery and slice thinly. Mince the shallot. In Step 2, replace the olive oil with 2 tablespoons mayonnaise if you like.

Cauliflower Salad with Olives and Bread Crumbs

MAKES: 4 servings

TIME: 45 minutes

Since it's better after it marinates for a day, this is perfect for entertaining. Cook the cauliflower until just tender enough to bite without a crunch; you want the florets to hold together and not fall apart when tossed. For more flavor and only a bit more work, separate the cauliflower into florets and roast at 400°F until just starting to soften, about 15 minutes.

1 medium cauliflower (about 1¹/₂ pounds), trimmed

¹/₂ small red onion, very thinly sliced

¹/₂ cup oil-cured or other good black olives, pitted and coarsely chopped

2 tablespoons extra virgin olive oil

2 tablespoons red wine vinegar

Salt and freshly ground black pepper

1 cup bread crumbs, preferably fresh (page 876)

¹/₄ cup chopped fresh parsley leaves

❶ Rig a steamer (see page 20) and set it over an inch or so of water. Put in the cauliflower, cover, and bring to a boil. Cook the cauliflower until just barely tender, 10 to 20 minutes, depending on how dense it is. Check by sticking the tip of a knife into the core; there should still be some resistance. When done, immediately transfer the cauliflower to a bowl of ice water.

❷ Drain the cauliflower well and break into relatively small florets; put them in a medium bowl along with the onion and olives. Drizzle with the olive oil and vinegar and sprinkle with just a little salt and lots of pepper. Toss and set aside. (At this point, you may refrigerate the salad, covered, for up to a day. Return it to room temperature before proceeding, tossing occasionally to coat well with dressing.)

❸ Put the bread crumbs in a dry skillet over medium heat. Swirl the pan to keep them moving while they toast

a little. When golden and fragrant, toss them with the cauliflower; sprinkle with the parsley and toss again. Taste, adjust the seasoning, and serve.

Cauliflower Salad with Capers. Instead of the olives, use ¹/₄ cup capers, preferably salt-cured, rinsed.

Cauliflower Salad with Roasted Red Peppers. Substitute 2 Roasted Red Peppers (page 330), chopped, for the olives. Add ¹/₂ cup toasted pine nuts (see page 317). Proceed with the recipe.

Roasted Eggplant and Tomato Salad

MAKES: 4 servings

TIME: About 1 hour

An easy and straightforward salad with loads of flavor, which you can further intensify by grilling or broiling both the eggplant and tomatoes; adding cubes of mozzarella or ricotta salata; using a mixture of fresh herbs, like chives, parsley, and dill; or adding a splash of balsamic or good red wine vinegar.

About 1 pound eggplant

Salt

¹/₄ cup extra virgin olive oil, or more as needed

Freshly ground black pepper

8 ripe plum tomatoes, quartered and seeded, or 24 or so small cherry or grape tomatoes

2 teaspoons minced garlic

¹/₂ cup chopped fresh basil leaves

❶ Peel the eggplant if the skin is thick or the eggplant is less than perfectly firm; cut it into ¹/₂-inch-thick slices and salt it if time allows (see page 293).

❷ Heat the oven to 400°F. Smear 2 baking sheets generously with some olive oil. Divide the eggplant slices between the sheets, leaving some space in between; put the tomato pieces in the empty spaces. Drizzle the vegetables with the remaining oil and sprinkle with salt and pepper. Roast without turning until the eggplant is soft and the tomatoes are a bit shriveled, about 25 minutes. (At this point, you may refrigerate the vegetables, covered, for up to a day. Return it to room temperature before proceeding.)

❸ Roughly chop the eggplant slices, then toss them with the tomatoes, garlic, and basil; taste, adjust the seasoning, and serve within 20 minutes or so.

Eggplant-Sesame Salad. Omit the tomatoes, garlic, and basil. Replace the olive oil with a neutral oil, like grapeseed or corn. Add 1 bunch scallions, trimmed, and roast along with the eggplant. In Step 3, chop the scallions and toss the vegetables with 2 tablespoons each toasted sesame seeds (see page 317) and soy sauce and 1 tablespoon freshly squeezed lemon juice. Taste, adjust the seasoning, and serve.

Eggplant and Tomato Salad with Yogurt. Excellent with Grilled Eggplant (page 294): Add ¼ cup or more yogurt and substitute fresh mint or cilantro leaves (or a mixture) for the basil. Add ½ teaspoon toasted cumin seeds (see page 317) if you like. Toss the cooled eggplant with the yogurt and herbs and serve.

Spiced Eggplant and Tomato Salad. Substitute neutral oil, like grapeseed or corn, for the olive oil. Sprinkle the eggplant and tomatoes with 1 tablespoon garam masala or Fragrant Curry Powder (page 67) before roasting. Substitute cilantro for the basil.

Mixed Vegetables with Peanut Sauce

MAKES: 4 servings

TIME: About 40 minutes

You can use any mixture of cooked and raw vegetables you like in this salad, which is based on the Indonesian gado gado.

Other vegetables you can use: cooked cauliflower, broccoli, asparagus, or peas (green, snow, or snap peas) or raw jícama, bean sprouts, celery, bell peppers, or radishes.

1 large waxy potato, boiled, peeled, and cubed

4 ounces green beans, trimmed, cooked briefly, and shocked (see page 240)

2 medium carrots, sliced or julienned (raw or lightly cooked)

1 cup shredded green or red cabbage

½ cup Simpler Peanut Sauce (page 55), thinned to vinaigrette consistency and at room temperature

1 small head romaine or iceberg lettuce, torn into pieces

1 cucumber, peeled if necessary and seeded (see page 293), sliced

2 Hard-Boiled Eggs (page 791), sliced

½ cup chopped scallion

Put the cooled potato, green beans, carrots, and cabbage in a bowl and toss with the peanut sauce. Arrange the lettuce and cucumbers on the plate(s) and top with the dressed vegetables; garnish with the egg slices and scallion. Serve immediately.

Sesame Seaweed Salad

MAKES: 4 servings

TIME: 20 minutes

The easiest way to produce this salad is to buy a small package of mixed seaweeds (available at many natural food stores and most Japanese food stores), but once you get more familiar with seaweed, you can use wakame, kelp, hijiki, or others, alone or in any combination you like.

1 ounce assorted dried seaweeds or all wakame

¼ cup chopped shallot, scallion, or red onion

2 tablespoons soy sauce, or to taste

1 tablespoon rice wine or other light vinegar, or to taste

1 tablespoon mirin or 1 teaspoon sugar, or to taste

$^{1}/_{2}$ tablespoon dark sesame oil, or to taste

Pinch cayenne, or to taste

Salt, if necessary

1 tablespoon toasted sesame seeds (see page 317) (optional)

❶ Rinse the seaweed once and soak it in at least 10 times its volume of water. When it is tender, about 5 minutes later, drain and gently squeeze the mixture to remove excess water. Pick through the seaweed to sort out any hard bits (there may be none) and chop or cut up (you may find it easier to use scissors than a knife) if the pieces are large. Put in a bowl.

❷ Toss with the remaining ingredients except the sesame seeds; refrigerate for up to a day before serving. When you're ready, taste and add salt or other seasonings as necessary and serve, garnished with the sesame seeds.

10 Additions to Sesame Seaweed Salad
You can add these singly or in combination. I love radishes and cucumber combined here, for example.

1. $^{1}/_{2}$ to 1 pound cucumber, peeled and seeded if necessary (see page 293), thinly sliced, then salted and squeezed to remove excess water (see page 207)
2. Several radishes or a piece of daikon, peeled if necessary, thinly sliced, then salted and squeezed to remove excess water (page 207)
3. A tablespoon or two of Dashi or Vegetarian Dashi (page 160) for extra juiciness and flavor
4. About 1 tablespoon grated fresh ginger, to taste
5. 1 medium tomato, seeded, peeled, and chopped
6. $^{1}/_{2}$ to 1 cup peeled and chopped Granny Smith apple or Asian pear
7. $^{1}/_{2}$ cups chopped nuts, like walnuts, almonds, cashews, or pecans
8. $^{1}/_{2}$ to 1 cup julienned or chopped carrot
9. $^{1}/_{2}$ to 1 cup peeled and julienned or chopped jícama
10. A 2-ounce bundle of thin (vermicelli) rice noodles, cooked (see page 553)

Fruit Salads
Mixed Fruit Salad (page 190) is the most familiar and versatile option. But some single-fruit or specific combinations of fruits turn the expected into something much more distinctive. As the recipes in this section prove, they aren't limited to breakfast or dessert, nor do they need to be sweet. In fact, savory fruit salads have some of the most interesting contrasts of flavor and work beautifully alongside grilled and roasted fish, meat, or poultry.

Green Papaya Salad

Som Tum

> **MAKES:** 4 servings
> **TIME:** 20 minutes

This fiery northern Thai specialty (if it's made correctly, you will really reek after eating it, but it's worth it) is one of the most popular dishes in Thailand and in Thai restaurants elsewhere. You can usually find green, or unripe, papayas and yard-long beans in Asian or Latin groceries, but you can also substitute Granny Smith apples for the papaya and Napa cabbage for the beans.

1 green, unripe papaya, peeled and seeded

2 garlic cloves, lightly smashed

1 shallot, minced

2 fresh chiles, preferably Thai, seeded and minced

2 tablespoons nam pla (Thai fish sauce)

3 tablespoons freshly squeezed lime juice

2 teaspoons sugar

2 or 3 yard-long beans or about a dozen green beans, trimmed and cut into 1-inch lengths

1 small tomato, cored and cut into eighths

2 tablespoons finely chopped dry-roasted peanuts

$^{1}/_{2}$ cup chopped fresh cilantro leaves for garnish

❶ Use a knife or the julienne disk of a food processor to cut the papaya into fine shreds.

❷ Combine the garlic, shallot, and chiles on a cutting board and mince and press with the side of the knife until pasty (or, as is traditional, use a mortar and pestle). Combine in a bowl with the papaya, nam pla, lime juice, sugar, beans, and tomato and stir to combine.

❸ Taste and adjust the seasoning; the mixture will be hot but may need more fish sauce, lime juice, and/or sugar. Garnish with peanuts and cilantro and serve.

Watermelon and Tomato Salad

MAKES: 4 servings

TIME: 15 minutes

A quintessential summer dish; beautifully ripe tomatoes and sweet, juicy watermelon are musts for this salad. Use variously colored heirloom tomatoes for an outrageous presentation.

3 large ripe tomatoes, cored, peeled if you like, and thickly sliced

¹/₄ watermelon, seeded, peeled, and cut similarly to the tomato slices

Salt and freshly ground black pepper

4 ounces fresh goat or feta cheese, crumbled

Extra virgin olive oil as needed

Alternately stack the tomato and watermelon slices on a large plate or platter, sprinkling each layer with a tiny bit of salt and pepper. Crumble the goat cheese over the top and drizzle with olive oil. Serve immediately.

Cantaloupe and Tomato Salad with Rosemary. Replace the watermelon with 1 medium cantaloupe, honeydew, or cassava melon. Omit the cheese and sprinkle with a teaspoon or two of minced fresh rosemary leaves. Drizzle with olive oil and serve.

Peach and Tomato Salad. Substitute 3 large ripe peaches, pitted, peeled if you like, and thickly sliced, for the

watermelon. Use blue cheese instead of goat cheese if you like or omit the cheese and sprinkle with chopped fresh basil leaves.

Peach, Tomato, Melon, and Bacon Salad. Add 1 large ripe peach, pitted, peeled if you like, and thickly sliced, and ¹/₂ cup chopped cooked bacon. Use any kind of melon you like. Substitute blue cheese for the goat cheese. Layer the melon, tomato, and peaches, then sprinkle with the blue cheese and bacon.

Balsamic Strawberries with Arugula

MAKES: 4 to 6 servings

TIME: 15 minutes

In the original *How to Cook Everything*, I featured these strawberries as a peppery, slightly sweet compote. In Italy, where balsamic vinegar originated, strawberries and balsamic are served as a dessert. The combination is equally fantastic in a savory salad.

3 cups strawberries, hulled and halved or quartered

1 tablespoon excellent balsamic vinegar, or more to taste

Freshly ground black pepper

4 cups arugula leaves

Salt

1 tablespoon extra virgin olive oil

❶ Toss the strawberries with the vinegar and black pepper in a large salad bowl and let sit for 10 minutes.

❷ Add the arugula, sprinkle with salt, and toss again. Drizzle with olive oil and toss gently one last time. Taste, adjust the seasoning, and serve.

Balsamic Strawberries with Arugula and Goat Cheese. Before the final toss in Step 2, crumble 4 ounces of goat cheese over the salad.

Balsamic Red Grapes with Radicchio. Substitute seedless red grapes for the strawberries and chopped radicchio for the arugula.

Bean Salads

Unlike most salads, these benefit from being made ahead and soaking in their juices, so you might get in the habit of doubling the ingredients to have a bean salad in your fridge that you can then pull out whenever you like.

Undercooking the beans—just slightly, so they are barely tender inside and their skins remain intact—is the key to good texture here; that and dressing them while still warm so they absorb the flavors around them.

Bean Salad

MAKES: 6 to 8 servings

TIME: 1½ to 3 hours, depending on the bean, largely unattended

You can rely on this master recipe forever, because the idea of "marinating" warm beans will be the same whether you use small lentils, big white gigante beans, or anything in between. What changes are your choice of seasonings and the cooking time.

Note that I say "cooking time" and not "opening-the-can time." Though you can certainly use canned beans, if you try this recipe once from scratch you will favor it always. It doesn't mean you'll never use canned beans again, but you'll know your own cooked beans are better.

The amount in this recipe is big enough to woo a small crowd or to keep some in the fridge to eat over the course of several days (it's best to add the parsley just before eating). You can also cook a whole batch of beans and freeze half for another use, or cut the recipe in half.

1 tablespoon red wine vinegar, other good vinegar, or freshly squeezed lemon juice, or to taste

2 to 4 tablespoons chopped red onion or shallot

Salt and freshly ground black pepper

2 cups dried beans, split peas, or lentils, picked through, sorted, cooked by any method (see pages 411–413), and drained, or 4 to 5 cups cooked or canned

¼ cup extra virgin olive oil, plus more to taste

¼ to ½ cup chopped fresh parsley leaves

❶ Stir the vinegar and onion together in a large bowl. Sprinkle with salt and pepper. Stir in the olive oil.

❷ If you've just cooked the beans, add them to the bowl with the dressing while they are still hot. Toss gently until the beans are coated with dressing, adding more olive oil if you like.

❸ Let cool to room temperature (or refrigerate), stirring once or twice to distribute the dressing. Stir in the parsley just before serving, then taste and adjust the seasoning.

7 Simple Last-Minute Additions to Bean Salads

Depending on what you add, you may need more dressing: For every tablespoon of extra oil, add a teaspoon or so of vinegar or freshly squeezed lemon juice. You will also probably want to add a dash more salt or soy sauce, pepper, and fresh herbs.

1. Chopped fresh, dried, or oven-roasted (page 361) tomatoes
2. Raw or roasted (page 330) chopped peppers or chiles
3. Chopped or torn salad greens, like romaine, mesclun, arugula, spinach, radicchio, or frisée
4. Cooked greens, like kale, chard, spinach, broccoli, broccoli raab, bok choy, or green beans
5. Chopped cooked mushrooms
6. Grated, shaved, or cubed cheese, like Parmesan, blue, feta, queso fresco, Jack, or cheddar
7. Crumbled or chopped crisp bacon or pancetta, chorizo or other sausage, or chunk tuna

8 VARIATIONS ON BEAN SALAD

To make any of these salads, use the quantities and instructions in Bean Salad (page 215); only the ingredients change. And feel free to use whatever dried or canned beans you like in these variations, not just the ones listed in the variation column.

VARIATION	FLAVORINGS AND OTHER INGREDIENTS	VINAIGRETTE OR OTHER DRESSING	GARNISH
Lentil Salad with Herbs	2 to 4 tablespoons minced red onion or shallot; ½ cup chopped fresh parsley; ½ cup mixed chopped fresh chives, dill, basil, chervil; 1 tablespoon chopped fresh thyme, tarragon, or rosemary	Good wine vinegar or freshly squeezed lemon juice, extra virgin olive oil	Thin slices of lemon
Chickpea Salad with Salsa or Chutney	Any fresh or cooked salsa (pages 23, 33–35, and 48–50); ½ cup or more as needed to moisten beans	None necessary	Any appropriate crunchy topping, like crumbled tortilla chips or fried wontons, bread crumbs, or toasted coconut
Garlicky Fava or Kidney Bean Salad	2 tablespoons minced garlic and 2 tablespoons minced red onion, shallot, or chives; or 1 head Roasted Garlic (page 303)	White wine vinegar, extra virgin olive oil	1 teaspoon minced fresh rosemary or ¼ cup chopped fresh basil leaves
White Bean Salad, Mediterranean Style	1 cup chopped tomato; 1 cup peeled, seeded, and chopped cucumber (see page 293); 3 tablespoons finely chopped red onion	Freshly squeezed lemon juice, extra virgin olive oil	¼ to ½ cup chopped fresh parsley leaves
Spicy Black Bean Salad	2 teaspoons chopped garlic; ½ cup chopped red bell pepper; 1 cup Pan-Roasted Corn kernels (page 290) or plain fresh or frozen corn; 1 or 2 canned chipotle chiles, minced with some of its adobo sauce	Red wine vinegar, extra virgin olive oil	¼ cup each finely chopped fresh cilantro leaves and scallion
Lemony Green Lentil Salad	1 lemon, peeled, chopped, and seeded; 1 tablespoon capers	Freshly squeezed lemon juice, extra virgin olive oil	¼ cup minced fresh chives, shallot, or red onion
Curried Chickpea or Lentil Salad	2 teaspoons each minced fresh ginger and garlic; 3 tablespoons finely chopped red onion; 1 tablespoon curry powder (to make your own, see pages 66–67)	Rice vinegar or freshly squeezed lemon juice, peanut oil	¼ cup or so chopped fresh cilantro leaves
Three-Bean Salad (use 1 cup kidney beans or black-eyed peas)	1½ cups cooked edamame or chickpeas; 1½ cups green or wax beans, trimmed, chopped into ½-inch pieces, cooked, and shocked (see page 240); 2 to 4 tablespoons minced red onion or shallot	Red or white wine vinegar or freshly squeezed lemon juice, extra virgin olive oil	¼ cup or more minced fresh chives or parsley leaves

 Fast   Make Ahead   **V** Vegetarian

Warm Chickpea Salad with Arugula

MAKES: 4 side- or 2 main-dish servings
TIME: 20 minutes with cooked beans

Chickpeas are found in salads throughout the Mediterranean and Middle East. My version is a panorama of these recipes that includes ginger, garlic, and cumin. After cooking the seasonings and warming the beans, you finish the dressing in the pan and toss it with the arugula leaves, which wilts them slightly. Serve small portions as a side salad or an appetizer or add the hard-cooked egg and make this into a light meal.

> 3 tablespoons extra virgin olive oil
> 1 tablespoon minced fresh ginger
> 1 tablespoon minced garlic
> 1/2 teaspoon cumin seeds
> Salt and freshly ground black pepper
> 1 1/2 cups cooked or drained canned chickpeas
> 1 tablespoon rice wine vinegar
> 1 teaspoon honey
> 1 small red onion, halved and thinly sliced
> 4 cups arugula leaves
> 4 Hard-Boiled Eggs (page 791), quartered (optional)

1 Put the olive oil in a deep skillet over medium heat. When hot, add the garlic, ginger, and cumin and cook, stirring constantly, until fragrant and the ginger and garlic are soft, 1 to 2 minutes. Sprinkle with salt and pepper, add the chickpeas, and stir until hot and coated in the oil and seasonings, about 3 minutes more.

2 Remove from the heat and, with a fork, stir in the vinegar, honey, and 1 tablespoon water. Mash a few of the chickpeas as you stir to add texture to the dressing. Put the arugula and red onion in a large bowl and toss with the warm chickpea dressing. Taste and adjust the seasoning if necessary. Serve immediately, garnished with hard-cooked eggs if you like.

White Bean Salad with Tuna. Use cannellini beans instead of the chickpeas. Substitute grated lemon zest for the ginger, mustard seeds for the cumin, and lemon juice for the vinegar; omit the honey. Add one 7-ounce can of tuna, preferably packed in olive oil, drained, to the bowl along with the arugula (with or without the eggs).

Fava Bean and Mint Salad with Pecorino

MAKES: 4 servings
TIME: About 1 hour with unshucked beans

Fava beans and mint are a quintessential springtime combination found throughout Europe; they're often combined with artichokes or asparagus, which you can easily add to this dish (just use a little more oil and lemon juice). And though this salad is at its best when these key ingredients are fresh and in season, if you swap out any or all of them, this can become a year-round dish. Try fresh or frozen edamame or peas instead of the fava beans (they're a *lot* faster to prepare); parsley or basil in place of mint; green beans instead of adding artichokes or asparagus.

> 2 tablespoons extra virgin olive oil
> 2 teaspoons freshly squeezed lemon juice
> 1/2 teaspoon sugar
> 3 pounds fresh fava beans, shucked, blanched, and shelled (see page 426), about 3 cups cleaned, or frozen edamame, peas, or lima beans
> 1 cup fresh mint leaves
> Salt and freshly ground black pepper
> 1 cup crumbled or shaved pecorino or Parmesan cheese
> 1 tablespoon grated lemon zest for garnish (optional)

Whisk together the olive oil, lemon juice, and sugar in a large bowl until the sugar is dissolved. Add the fava beans and mint and toss to coat. Taste and add more salt if needed and a sprinkle of pepper. Sprinkle with the pecorino and serve, garnished with lemon zest if you like.

Grain Salads

You can eat grain salads, which are delicious, filling, and quite healthy, by themselves or piled onto greens or with many of the other salads in this chapter for satisfying and complete meals. They are unbeatable as side dishes, as daily fare or for entertaining, because just about all of them can be made way ahead of time.

I discuss the different cooking techniques for grains in the Grains chapter (page 449). But for salads, I rely mostly on Cooking Grains, the Easy Way (page 451), rinsing after cooking to remove some of the starch and keep the grains separate.

In an ideal world, you would have time to prepare the grains right before using, undercook them slightly, and dress them warm so they become tender and absorb flavor as they cool. But you and I both know that won't happen very often. So here's a real-life approach: Whenever you cook grains, make extra and keep some in the fridge. It's not a bad habit to get into; if you think ahead, you will always have the ingredients for big-time last-minute salads at your fingertips.

Rice Salad with Tomatoes

MAKES: 4 servings
TIME: About 30 minutes

Ⓕ   Ⓜ   Ⓥ

Arborio rice isn't essential here, but it really can make this salad stand out. The anchovies are not essential if you want to make this dish vegetarian.

Other grains you can use: any medium- or long-grain white rice, short- or medium-grain brown rice, pearl couscous, or pearled barley.

1 recipe cooked rice (see page 451), preferably
 Arborio or other good short-grain, cooled

1 tablespoon minced garlic

¼ cup thinly sliced red onion

2 to 4 anchovy fillets, chopped (optional)

1 cup halved cherry or grape tomatoes or seeded and
 chopped plum tomatoes

¼ to ½ cup Vinaigrette (page 201)

1 teaspoon minced fresh rosemary leaves or
 ½ teaspoon dried

½ cup grated Parmesan cheese

Salt and freshly ground black pepper

❶   Put the rice, garlic, red onion, anchovies if you're using them, and tomatoes in a large bowl. Drizzle with vinaigrette and sprinkle with the rosemary; use two big forks to combine, fluffing the rice and tossing gently to separate the grains.

❷   Stir in the Parmesan, taste, and adjust the seasoning or moisten with a little more dressing. Serve at room temperature or refrigerate for up to a day; bring back to room temperature before serving.

Rice Salad with Peas. Substitute fresh or frozen peas, cooked for a minute or two and drained, for the tomatoes.

Rice Salad with Pesto. Omit the garlic and red onion if you like. Substitute Traditional Pesto (page 27) for the vinaigrette. Proceed with the recipe, adding more olive oil or water if the salad is too thick.

Rice Salad with Olives. Omit the tomatoes and rosemary if you like. Add ¾ cup chopped pitted good black olives and 2 tablespoons roughly chopped capers if you like.

Rice Salad with Dried Apricots

MAKES: 4 servings
TIME: About 30 minutes

Ⓕ   Ⓜ   Ⓥ

This isn't your traditional rice salad, but its sweet and savory flavor will make it a household favorite. Basmati rice is wonderful, but only if you use freshly cooked (and cooled) rice—it doesn't fare well when refrigerated. Otherwise, any medium-grain rice is fine, and brown rice is wonderful here.

Other grains you can use: wild rice, wheat berries, pearl barley, couscous, or quinoa.

3 to 4 cups cooked rice (see page 451), cooled

1 cup chopped dried apricots

$1/2$ cup slivered almonds, toasted (see page 317)

$1/4$ cup chopped scallion

$1/4$ to $1/2$ cup Vinaigrette (page 201), made with white wine vinegar

1 tablespoon ground coriander

2 teaspoons ground ginger

$1^1/2$ teaspoons cayenne

Salt and freshly ground black pepper

$1/2$ cup chopped fresh cilantro leaves

1 Put the rice, apricots, nuts, and scallion in a large bowl. Drizzle with vinaigrette and sprinkle with the spices and salt and pepper; use two big forks to combine, fluffing the rice and tossing gently to separate the grains.

2 Stir in the cilantro, taste, and adjust the seasoning or moisten with a little more dressing. Serve at room temperature or refrigerate for up to a day, bringing back to room temperature before serving.

Rice Salad with Grapefruit and Pistachios. Substitute grapefruit segments for the dried apricots and pistachios for the almonds.

Wild Rice Salad with Dried Fruit and Pecans. Use wild rice and substitute mixed dried cherries, cranberries, and/or blueberries for the dried apricots and pecans for the almonds. Use parsley instead of cilantro.

Wheat Berry Salad with Apples and Walnuts. Use wheat berries instead of rice and Maple Vinaigrette (page 202) as the dressing. Substitute chopped or thinly sliced Granny Smith or Pink Lady apples for the dried

apricots and walnuts for the almonds. Omit the scallion and cilantro.

Tabbouleh

MAKES: 4 servings

TIME: 40 minutes

The best tabbouleh is all about herbs. The grain may be the traditional bulgur, couscous, quinoa, millet, or even rice (which, because it is starchier, may require a bit more dressing). But you must include fresh herbs, and lots of them, to make good tabbouleh, which is why it's a perfect midsummer dish and exceptional with grilled food.

Other grains you can use: cooked cracked wheat or (totally untraditional but great) quinoa, millet, rice, or couscous.

$1/2$ cup fine-grind or medium-grind bulgur

$1/3$ cup extra virgin olive oil, or more as needed

$1/4$ cup freshly squeezed lemon juice, or to taste

Salt and freshly ground black pepper

2 cups roughly chopped fresh parsley leaves with small stems only

1 cup roughly chopped fresh mint leaves

$1/2$ cup chopped scallion

4 medium tomatoes, cored, seeded, and chopped (optional)

1 Soak the bulgur in hot water to cover until tender, 15 to 30 minutes. Drain well, squeezing out as much of the water as possible. Toss the bulgur with the oil and lemon juice and season to taste.

2 Just before you're ready to eat, add all the remaining ingredients and toss gently. Taste, adjust the seasoning, and serve.

Tabbouleh with Lots of Tomatoes. Reduce the parsley and mint by half and add 6 medium tomatoes, cored, seeded, and chopped.

Barley Salad with Cucumber and Yogurt-Dill Dressing

MAKES: 4 servings

TIME: 40 minutes

Cool, crunchy, and chewy, this is a perfect summer salad, and quickly made with pearled barley, which cooks relatively fast.

Other grains you can use: brown rice, wheat berries, cracked wheat, pearl couscous, or wild rice.

1 cup pearled barley

Salt

1 English (long) cucumber, 6 Kirby (pickling) cucumbers, or 2 or 3 medium cucumbers

3 or 4 scallions, chopped

Freshly ground black pepper

2 tablespoons freshly squeezed lemon juice, or more to taste

2 tablespoons extra virgin olive oil

1 cup yogurt

1/2 cup fresh dill, mint, or parsley leaves or a combination

❶ Rinse the barley and put it in a saucepan with water to cover by at least 2 inches. Add a large pinch of salt and cook over medium-high heat, stirring occasionally, until the barley is tender, about 20 minutes from the time the water boils. Drain and spread on a plate to cool (if you're in a hurry, you can rinse under cold water for a minute or so).

❷ Meanwhile, if you're using an English cucumber (or other virtually seedless cucumber), simply cut it into bite-sized chunks. If you're using a cucumber with lots of big seeds, peel it, cut it in half lengthwise, and scoop out the seeds. Cut it into chunks, put in a colander or strainer, and sprinkle with about a tablespoon of salt. Let sit for 20 minutes or so, then rinse and drain well.

❸ Toss together the barley, cucumber, and scallions in a salad bowl; sprinkle with pepper. Whisk together the

lemon juice, oil, and yogurt. Toss this dressing with the cucumber mixture, then taste and adjust the seasoning. Add the herb(s), toss all together, and serve.

Barley and Cress Salad. Omit the scallions and yogurt. Add 3 cups trimmed watercress and use the dill. Proceed with the recipe, adding the cress along with the herbs.

Barley Salad with Peas and Yogurt-Dill Dressing. Instead of the cucumber, use 1 1/2 cups cooked and shocked fresh or frozen peas (see page 240). Fresh sugar snap peas are a rare seasonal treat that work great in this salad too.

Barley Salad with Cucumber and Smoked Salmon. In Step 3, add 1 cup smoked salmon pieces to the salad bowl and toss with the other ingredients.

Wheat Berry Salad with Roasted Peppers

MAKES: 4 servings

TIME: 20 minutes with cooked grains and roasted peppers

This mild, rich salad is not only delicious but also gorgeous, especially if you use red and yellow peppers you've roasted yourself. Store-bought peppers, piquillo peppers, or even bottled pimientos are fine substitutes.

Admittedly, there's a lot of precooking to do here—the peppers, the grain, and the garlic—but it's actually a snap to put together. And you'll find plenty of other uses for the peppers and garlic.

Other grains you can use: cracked wheat, coarse-grind bulgur, brown rice, or quinoa.

1/4 cup pine nuts

2 or 3 roasted or grilled bell peppers (see page 330 or 250), preferably a mix of red and yellow, peeled, seeded, and torn or cut into strips

2 cups cooked wheat berries

1 head Roasted Garlic (page 303), the flesh squeezed
  from the skins

1 cup julienned fresh basil leaves

¼ cup extra virgin olive oil, or as needed

3 tablespoons red wine or other vinegar

Salt and freshly ground black pepper

❶ Toast the pine nuts in a small, dry skillet over
medium heat, shaking the pan occasionally, until they are
lightly browned. Set aside.

❷ Toss together the pepper strips, wheat berries, garlic, and about half the basil in a salad bowl. Whisk
together the oil and vinegar, along with some salt and
pepper. Toss the dressing with the salad, then taste and
adjust the seasoning (this can sit at room temperature for
an hour or so). Just before serving, garnish with the pine
nuts and remaining basil.

Wheat Berry Salad with Zucchini. If you're grilling the
peppers for this (or another dish), halve 2 or 3 small
to medium zucchini lengthwise and grill them at the
same time (see page 251 for more specific directions).
Cut the zucchini into chunks or slices and toss with
the other ingredients in Step 2.

Wheat Berry Salad with Fennel. Omit the pine nuts and
roasted garlic if you like. Substitute 1 fennel bulb,
sliced and roasted or grilled (see page 241) for the
peppers, and 3 tablespoons chopped fresh tarragon
leaves or ¼ cup chopped fresh chervil for the basil.
Use white wine vinegar.

Wheat Berry Salad with Mushrooms. Substitute sesame
seeds for the pine nuts, 2 to 3 cups chopped mushrooms for the peppers, ½ cup chopped scallion for
the basil, and Soy or Ginger Vinaigrette (page 201)
for the olive oil and vinegar.

Wheat Berry Salad with Mustard. Substitute ½ cup
chopped walnuts for the pine nuts, 2 cups finely
shredded or chopped radicchio, frisée, or cabbage for
the peppers, and ½ cup chopped fresh parsley for the
basil leaves. Add 2 tablespoons coarse mustard (like

22 Picnic-Perfect Salads

Few greens can be tossed with dressing before traveling, although you can, of course, pack them and the
dressing separately and toss on the spot. But most of
the following salads can be finished and packed to
travel—carefully, of course—then served with little or no
loss of quality. Some of these have greens as a base;
pack the greens separately and assemble at the last
minute.

Moutarde de Meaux), or to taste, and reduce the vinegar to 2 tablespoons.

Fattoush

Lebanese Bread Salad

MAKES: 4 servings
TIME: 30 minutes

The trick to fattoush is to toast the pita nice and crisp. To turn the salad into a meal, just spread a layer of Lentils, Moroccan Style (page 431) on a plate and put a mound of Fattoush on top; crumbled feta cheese makes a nice garnish. Or serve the fattoush alone or tossed with greens.

Four 6-inch pita breads

$^1/_2$ cup chopped fresh mint, parsley, or basil leaves

$^1/_4$ cup chopped fresh parsley leaves

1 large or 2 medium ripe tomatoes, cored and roughly chopped

1 medium cucumber, peeled, seeded if you like (see page 293), and roughly chopped

1 red or yellow bell pepper, cored, seeded, and roughly chopped

About $^1/_2$ cup Vinaigrette (page 201) or extra virgin olive oil and freshly squeezed lemon juice

❶ Heat the oven to 350°F. Cut the pitas like pies into 8 wedges each, put the pieces on a baking sheet, and toast in the oven, turning once or twice, until both sides are crisp and golden, about 15 minutes. Let cool. (You can store the pita croutons, tightly covered, for up to 2 days.)

❷ While the bread is toasting, combine all the other ingredients in a large salad bowl, adding either vinaigrette or olive oil and lemon juice to taste. Toss several times to coat. Add the pita wedges and toss gently again. Taste, adjust the seasoning, and serve.

Crouton Salad. Substitute about 8 ounces crusty bread (stale is fine) or 8 ounces Dry-Baked Croutons (page 877) for the pita and 1 small red onion, halved and thinly sliced into half-rings, for the bell pepper. Reduce the herbs to no more than $^1/_2$ cup roughly chopped fresh basil and/or parsley leaves and add 1 clove garlic, minced. Cut the bread into 1-inch cubes and toast just like the pita. Proceed with the recipe.

Grilled Bread Salad. Make the preceding variation, but grill the bread on both sides on a charcoal or gas grill at medium-high heat, with the rack 4 inches from the heat source, 3 to 5 minutes total. Let cool a bit, cut roughly into large cubes, and add to the salad.

Corn Bread Salad. Use about 8 ounces cubed Corn Bread (page 831) instead of pita. Reduce the herbs to $^1/_2$ cup chopped fresh cilantro leaves and add 1 teaspoon chili powder (to make your own, see page 66) and $^1/_2$ cup chopped scallion to the tomato mixture.

Salads with Chicken, Meat, or Fish

When you add animal protein to a salad, you take it to another level; there is no longer any way the salad is a side dish. It may be lunch, it may be a hearty or elegant first course, or it may be a meal in itself. And, of course, salads are an ideal place to use leftover meat, poultry, or fish.

Chicken Salad with Olive Oil and Fresh Herbs

MAKES: 4 to 6 servings
TIME: 45 minutes; 20 minutes with cooked chicken

This is a highly versatile salad in terms of the meat you use: Make it with breast or thigh meat or a mixture; left-

    Fast   Make Ahead   Ⓥ Vegetarian

over chicken is perfectly acceptable (and indeed may give the salad deeper flavor). So you need to cook up a batch only if you don't have enough handy. (For this recipe, start with about 1¹/₂ pounds raw, bone-in meat.) Or forget the chicken and use salmon, tuna, or shrimp instead. Serve this solo, on top of greens, on cooked pasta or grains, or use it in sandwiches.

1 pound shredded or cubed roasted, grilled, or poached chicken meat

3 tablespoons chopped shallot or red onion

¹/₄ cup chopped pitted black olives

1 tablespoon grated lemon zest

3 tablespoons freshly squeezed lemon juice, plus more to taste

¹/₄ cup extra virgin olive oil, plus more to taste

¹/₂ cup chopped mixed fresh herbs, like chives, parsley, chervil, dill, and/or basil

Salt and freshly ground black pepper

4 to 6 cups torn assorted greens (optional)

1 Put the chicken, shallot, olives, and zest in a bowl and mix. (At this point, you may refrigerate the salad, covered, for a day; take out of the fridge 15 minutes or so before proceeding to take the chill off).

2 Drizzle on the lemon juice and olive oil and sprinkle on the herbs and salt and pepper; mix again. Taste and adjust the seasoning. Use as is or arrange the greens on the plate(s) and top with the chicken salad.

Traditional Chicken Salad. With mayo: Instead of the olives, use Dijon mustard and substitute mayonnaise (to make your own, see page 41) for the olive oil. Keep the herbs if you like or replace them with 1 cup chopped celery. Add sliced almonds or chopped walnuts or pecans if you like.

Lobster Salad. Especially good with a pinch of saffron stirred into the mayonnaise: Omit the olives; substitute mayonnaise (to make your own, see page 41) for the olive oil. Reduce the quantity of herbs to 1 table-

14 Poultry Dishes That Go Great on Greens

Almost any leftover (or even just-cooked) poultry, without sauce, turns a salad into a meal. If you put the poultry on the greens while it is hot, the greens will wilt and mingle with the juices, a nice touch.

1. Chicken or Pork Satay (page 117)
2. Roast Chicken Parts with Herbs and Olive Oil (page 640)
3. Grilled or Broiled Boneless Chicken or its variations (pages 641–643)
4. Broiled or Grilled Boneless Chicken Thighs, whole or in kebabs (page 643)
5. Simplest Whole Roast Chicken, Six Ways (page 644)
6. Chicken MarkNuggets (page 646)
7. Herb-Roasted Chicken Cutlets (page 672)
8. Chicken Under a Brick (page 692)
9. Grilled or Broiled Split Chicken (page 693)
10. Turkey Thighs Braised in Red Wine (pages 701–702)
11. Roast Duck (page 706)
12. Fast "Roast" Duck, Chinese Style (pages 707–708)
13. Steamed and Roasted Duck (page 706)
14. Grilled or Broiled Squab, Vietnamese Style (page 710)

spoon and chop them as finely as you can. (Try tarragon, which has an affinity for lobster.)

Grilled Beef Salad with Mint

MAKES: 3 to 4 servings
TIME: 25 minutes

A simple, bright, and light salad with tons of flavor. One of the best possible lunch dishes.

Other protein you can use: chicken, pork, shrimp.

12 ounces beef tenderloin or sirloin

4 cups torn Boston or romaine lettuce leaves, mesclun, or any salad greens mixture

1 cup torn fresh mint leaves

$^1/_4$ cup chopped red onion

1 medium cucumber, peeled, seeded if necessary (see page 293), and diced

Juice of 2 limes

1 tablespoon nam pla (Thai fish sauce) or soy sauce

$^1/_8$ teaspoon cayenne, or to taste

$^1/_2$ teaspoon sugar

1 Heat a charcoal or gas grill or a broiler to medium-high; the rack should be about 4 inches from the heat source. Grill or broil the beef until medium-rare, 5 to 10 minutes; set it aside to cool.

2 Toss the lettuce with the mint, onion, and cucumber. Combine all remaining ingredients with 1 tablespoon of water—the mixture will be thin—and toss the greens with this dressing. Transfer the greens to a platter, reserving the dressing.

3 Thinly slice the beef, reserving its juice; combine the juice with the remaining dressing. Lay the slices of beef over the salad, drizzle the dressing over all, and serve.

Grilled Chicken Salad with Lemongrass. Substitute boneless chicken breast or thighs for the beef. If you have time, marinate the raw chicken in the juice of 1 lime, 1 tablespoon soy sauce, $^1/_2$ teaspoon sugar, and 2 tablespoons minced lemongrass for up to 30 minutes. Grill or broil until cooked through, about 5 minutes. Proceed with the recipe, omitting the mint and adding 2 tablespoons minced lemongrass to the dressing.

Grilled Shrimp Salad with Chile and Basil. Substitute peeled large shrimp for the beef. If you have time, marinate the shrimp in 2 tablespoons soy sauce, 1 tablespoon or more Chile-Garlic Paste (page 75), and 1 tablespoon minced fresh Thai basil leaves for up to 15 minutes. Grill or broil until pink, about 3 minutes. Proceed with the recipe, substituting torn Thai

basil leaves for the mint and 1 tablespoon Thai Chile Sauce (page 39) for the cayenne.

11 Meat Dishes to Serve on Greens

As with poultry, you can use any unsauced meat dish—either hot or cold—to top a bed of greens.

1. Grilled Steak or its variations (pages 717–719)
2. Marinated and Grilled or Broiled Flank Steak (page 729)
3. Beef (or Other Meat or Seafood) Kebabs or its variation (page 732)
4. Boneless Prime Rib, leftovers only (page 735)
5. Grilled or Broiled Pork Chops (page 747)
6. West Indian Crispy Pork Bits or its variations (page 749)
7. Grilled Pork Tenderloin with Mustard Curry (page 752)
8. Baked Country Ham or Baked Wet-Cured Ham, leftovers only (page 765)
9. Roast Leg of Lamb, Four Ways leftovers only (page 770)
10. Grilled or Broiled Butterflied Leg of Lamb (page 771)
11. Veal Cutlets, 1950s Style (page 781)

Salade Niçoise

MAKES: 4 servings

TIME: 15 minutes

The Niçoise is a country salad, with ingredients that depend on what's in season. The basics are lettuce, hard-cooked eggs, anchovy fillets, black olives, tomatoes, and garlic in the dressing. Most people add tuna too, but consider it optional. Among the myriad other possible addi-

F Fast   **M** Make Ahead   **V** Vegetarian

tions are cooked green beans, potatoes, artichoke hearts, raw or roasted bell pepper, capers, and basil.

- 6 cups torn assorted lettuces and other salad greens
- 2 Hard-Boiled Eggs (page 791), sliced
- 1 cup good black olives, preferably Niçoise or any oil-cured
- 3 ripe tomatoes, cored, seeded, and cut into quarters or eighths
- 6 anchovies
- One or two 7-ounce cans tuna, preferably packed in olive oil, or 12 ounces grilled fresh tuna, cut into chunks
- $^1/_8$ cup red wine vinegar, plus a little more if needed
- $^1/_2$ cup extra virgin olive oil, more or less
- Salt and freshly ground black pepper
- 1 garlic clove, minced
- 1 small shallot, minced
- 1 teaspoon Dijon mustard

❶ Arrange all the salad ingredients nicely on a platter—greens on the bottom, topped with egg slices, olives, tomatoes, anchovies, and tuna. Or—less attractive but easier to serve—toss all the ingredients together.

❷ Make the vinaigrette by adding the vinegar to the oil, along with some salt and pepper, the garlic, shallot, and mustard. Stir and taste. Add more vinegar if necessary and adjust the seasoning. Stir or shake vigorously, pour over the salad, and serve.

Crab Salad

MAKES: 2 servings

TIME: 1 hour, with cooked defrosted crab

Dungeness crab is my first choice here, but unless you live in the Northwest, you'll be buying your Dungeness crab cooked and possibly frozen, in which case fresh lump crabmeat is a better option. Add sliced celery or onions here if you like.

- About $^1/_2$ pound cooked crabmeat
- $^3/_4$ cup any vinaigrette (see pages 199–202) or flavored mayonnaise (see page 42)
- Salt and freshly ground black pepper
- About 4 cups torn mixed greens (washed and dried)

❶ Pick through the meat to remove all remaining shell, being careful not to shred it too finely. Gently toss the crab with the vinaigrette or mayonnaise and refrigerate for an hour or so before eating, stirring occasionally.

❷ Taste and adjust the seasoning if necessary. Serve the crab over the greens, and pour any remaining juices from the bowl over all.

Fried Chile-Spiced Clam Salad

MAKES: 4 servings

TIME: 30 minutes

This combination contains the elements that almost everyone loves: It's spicy, it's crunchy, it's cool, and it's moist. A winner that can also be made with oysters or chunks of boneless chicken (see the first variation).

- 6 tablespoons extra virgin olive oil
- 2 tablespoons balsamic vinegar
- 2 teaspoons Dijon mustard
- $^1/_2$ cup cornmeal
- 2 tablespoons chili powder (to make your own, see page 66)
- Salt and freshly ground black pepper
- 3 tablespoons peanut or neutral oil, like grapeseed or corn
- 20 to 25 fresh littleneck or other hard-shell clams, shucked
- 6 cups torn assorted salad greens

❶ Mix together the olive oil, vinegar, and mustard; set aside.

2 Season the cornmeal with chili powder, salt, and pepper. Put the peanut oil in a large nonstick skillet over medium-high heat. When hot—a pinch of cornmeal will sizzle—dredge the clams in the cornmeal and add them, a few at a time, to the skillet. Raise the heat to high and cook until golden, turning once, about 2 minutes total.

3 Drain the clams on paper towels and toss the greens with the dressing. Divide the greens among 4 plates and top each with a portion of clams. Serve immediately.

Fried Chile-Spiced Chicken Salad. Substitute 8 ounces boneless, skinless chicken breast or thigh meat, cut into bite-sized cubes, for the clams.

13 Fish and Shellfish Dishes That Are Perfect on Greens

For a great light meal, grill some fish, toss it on some greens, and dress with vinaigrette. Here are some possibilities:

1. Broiled Fish Fillets (page 562)
2. Basic Grilled or Broiled Salmon Steaks (pages 563–565)
3. Grilled Fish Fillets or Steaks (page 564)
4. Deep-Fried Seafood (pages 568–569)
5. The Simplest and Best Shrimp Dish (pages 573–574)
6. Spicy Grilled or Broiled Shrimp (page 574)
7. Grilled or Broiled Scallops with Basil Stuffing (page 600)
8. Grilled Marinated Swordfish, Tuna, or Other Fish Steaks (page 603)
9. Grilled or Broiled Fish Skewers, Basted with Herbs (page 603)
10. Monkfish or Other Steaks Roasted with Herbs (page 603)
11. Shad Roe (page 632)
12. Slow-Grilled Sardines (page 629)
13. Grilled or Broiled Salmon Kebabs (page 732)

Steamed Chile-Spiced Clam Salad. Omit the cornmeal and peanut oil. Put a cup of water or white wine in a pot and bring to a boil. Add the unshucked clams, cover, and steam until they open (discard those that stay closed), about 3 minutes. Remove the clams from their shells and put in a bowl with some of their liquid. Sprinkle with $^1/_2$ teaspoon chili powder, or to taste, and some salt and pepper. Proceed with Step 3; no need to drain the clams.

Seafood Salad, Mediterranean Style

MAKES: 4 servings

TIME: 30 minutes, plus time to chill

In most parts of the world, and certainly throughout the Mediterranean, seafood salad is as simple as this: You take some poached fish and dress it with olive oil and loads of lemon. (Actually, vinegar is traditional in many places, but I use lemon if I have it.) If you want to make it more elaborate, you add parboiled (and shocked, see page 240) vegetables or serve it on a bed of greens.

So see this simple recipe as a guideline, not as dogma; use whatever fish you have, a variety or something as simple and common as shrimp or squid. Add vegetables and vary the seasonings if you like. It will be fine any way you do it.

$^1/_2$ pound firm white fish (see page 585), skinned and cut into $^1/_2$-inch chunks

$^1/_2$ pound shrimp, peeled

$^1/_2$ pound sea scallops, cut in half if large

$^1/_2$ cup chopped fresh parsley leaves

1 tablespoon brined capers with a little of their liquid, or to taste

1 shallot, minced

$^1/_4$ cup extra virgin olive oil

Salt and freshly ground black pepper

Freshly squeezed lemon juice

 Fast   Make Ahead   **V** Vegetarian

10 MORE FISH, CHICKEN, OR MEAT SALADS

Your choice: Toss the ingredients together, then serve the salad alone (with crackers or toasted bread) or on a bed of greens. Or deconstruct the ingredients and present as a composed salad (see page 209). Any of these also make delicious sandwich or wrap fillings (see "The Basics of Sandwiches," page 165, and "Wraps," page 170).

SALAD	MEAT	VEGETABLES AND SEASONINGS	DRESSING AND GARNISHES
Chicken and Cucumber Salad	12 ounces shredded chicken breast	8 ounces peeled, seeded (see page 293), and finely julienned cucumber (use a mandoline)	Ginger Vinaigrette (page 201), 2 teaspoons each black and white sesame seeds, toasted
Pulled Pork and Mango Salad	12 ounces No-Work Smoked Pork Shoulder or Spareribs (page 759)	1 not-too-ripe mango, peeled and chopped; 1/2 small red onion, thinly sliced	Lime Vinaigrette (page 201), 1/2 cup or more chopped fresh cilantro leaves
Steak and Roasted Pepper Salad	12 ounces grilled or broiled steak (see page 717), thinly sliced	2 to 3 Roasted Red Peppers (page 330), cored, seeded, and chopped; 3 cups chopped radicchio; 1 cup crumbled Gorgonzola (optional)	Vinaigrette (page 201) made with balsamic vinegar, 1/2 cup chopped fresh chives or parsley leaves
Pesto Shrimp Salad	1 pound peeled large (21–30) shrimp, grilled (see page 564) or steamed (see page 570)	1 cup cored, seeded, and chopped ripe tomatoes	1/4 cup Traditional Pesto (page 27), thinned with olive oil or water
Curried Chicken Salad	12 ounces diced or shredded chicken breast	1/2 cup peeled and diced apple, 1/2 cup chopped cashews	3 tablespoons mayonnaise (to make your own, see page 41) or yogurt, or to taste; 1 tablespoon curry powder (to make your own, see pages 66–67); 1/4 cup chopped fresh cilantro leaves (optional)
Duck Salad with Dried Cherries	12 ounces diced or shredded leg meat	1/2 cup dried cherries, 1/2 cup toasted hazelnuts (see page 317), 3 cups chopped frisée (optional)	Vinaigrette (page 201), made with sherry vinegar; 1/4 cup chopped fresh chives or parsley leaves
Beef and Avocado Salad	12 ounces beef tenderloin, grilled or broiled to medium rare and cubed	1 avocado, peeled and cubed; 1 cup seeded and chopped tomatoes; 1 red bell pepper, cored, seeded, and chopped	Avocado Vinaigrette (page 202) or Lime Vinaigrette (page 201), 1/2 cup chopped scallions
Buttermilk Chicken Salad with Corn Bread	12 ounces diced or shredded chicken breast	1 cup crumbled Corn Bread (page 831) or Corn Bread Croutons (page 877), 1/2 cup dried cranberries	1/4 cup Real Ranch Dressing (page 42) with 2 teaspoons minced garlic; 1/2 cup toasted pumpkin seeds
Miso-Salmon Salad with Peas	12 ounces cooked salmon	1 cup green peas or sliced snow peas or snap peas	1/2 cup Miso Vinaigrette (page 202), 1/4 cup chopped scallion
Spicy Pork Salad with Green Beans	12 ounces cooked pork tenderloin, diced	1 cup cooked chopped green beans (see page 239), 1 cup shredded Napa cabbage, 1 tablespoon chopped jalapeño or other hot fresh chile	1/4 cup Soy Vinaigrette (page 201), 1/4 cup chopped scallion, 1 tablespoon toasted sesame seeds (see page 317; optional)

1 Bring a saucepan of water to a boil and salt it. (If you have Fish Stock, page 159, use it; when you're done, strain it and save it for reuse.) Turn the heat to medium-low and add the fish; 30 seconds later, add the shrimp and scallops. Cover and turn off the heat; let the fish sit in the liquid for about 10 minutes. Drain and cool, then chill. (At this point, you may refrigerate the fish for up to 24 hours.)

2 Toss the fish with the parsley, capers, shallot, olive oil, and some salt and pepper. Add lemon juice to taste, then taste, adjust the seasoning, and serve.

Mussel and Potato Salad

MAKES: 4 servings

TIME: 1 hour

Ⓜ

You can easily make this with leftover mussels, should you have any, but it's worth starting it from scratch.

> 3 or 4 pounds mussels, prepared according to the recipe on page 570
>
> 1¹/₂ pounds waxy red or white potatoes, peeled and cut into 1-inch cubes
>
> ¹/₄ cup grainy or Dijon mustard, or to taste
>
> ¹/₃ cup extra virgin olive oil
>
> 1 tablespoon balsamic or sherry vinegar, or to taste
>
> 3 tablespoons chopped fresh basil leaves
>
> Salt and freshly ground black pepper

1 Shell the mussels and set aside. Strain the broth, then put it in a large covered saucepan over high heat. Add the potatoes to the mussel broth—don't worry if it doesn't completely cover the potatoes—cover, and bring to a boil. Turn the heat to medium-low and cook until the potatoes are tender but not mushy, about 15 minutes. Drain.

2 Mix the mustard, oil, vinegar, and basil together. Toss with the mussels and potatoes while the potatoes are

still warm. Sprinkle with salt and pepper, taste, and adjust the seasoning, and serve within an hour.

The Basics of Pickling Fruits and Vegetables

Pickles have been around for thousands of years, sustaining people through winters, expeditions, wars, and famine. Every cuisine has at least a handful of pickled things, and pickling isn't simply a means of food preservation; with its variety of salty, sour, sweet, and hot flavors, pickled food is almost universally appealing. We're most familiar with cucumbers, specifically the small and nubby Kirby cucumbers, as pickles, so much so that the word almost inherently means a pickled cucumber. But almost anything—from cabbage to peppers to watermelon rind to hard-cooked eggs—can be pickled.

Simply put, pickling is the introduction of acid to a food that prevents the growth of harmful microbes. There are two basic methods for getting this acid into foods: by using vinegar (an acid) or by salting (using straight salt or a saltwater brine). Vinegar penetrates by replacing the natural water in the food. Salting is a less direct and more complex process where the salt draws out the food's natural water and allows just enough bacterial growth to produce lactic acid, which then ferments or pickles the food. Salt is also used when pickling with vinegar, to draw out water to crisp the vegetables and to keep the vinegar that seeps into the vegetable or fruit undiluted.

Though vinegar and salt help flavor pickles, extra seasonings—spices, herbs, garlic, onions, and other aromatics—are often added as well. Dill is a favorite seasoning for cucumber pickles in the United States, as are garlic, mustard, black peppercorns, and chiles or hot red pepper flakes. But you can use any spice or herb you like; create an Asian-flavored pickle with ginger, Sichuan peppercorns, or five-spice powder (to make your own, see page 68); a Caribbean flavor by using jerk seasoning (to make your own, see page 68), and so on.

Ⓕ Fast   **Ⓜ** Make Ahead   **Ⓥ** Vegetarian

There are a few guidelines to keep in mind: Use the freshest foods for pickling; food that has blemishes or soft spots will start with more of the harmful microbes you want to avoid. Also, consider the size and density of the fruit or vegetable; smaller and softer pieces pickle more quickly than larger pieces. You also want to think about timing; the pickle recipes here can take anywhere from 20 minutes to several days to cure. If you want your pickles right away, go with the Quick-Pickled Vegetables (below) or Spicy Pickles, Asian Style (below). The Kosher and Three-Day Pickles (pages 230 and 231) take two to three days.

Quick-Pickled Vegetables

MAKES: 4 servings
TIME: 1 hour or less

Salting vegetables, even for just 15 minutes, really changes their texture and flavor; they become both pliable and crunchy (see page 207). Of course, the thinner you slice the vegetables, the more quickly they will pickle. Shredding is also a good option to shave off a few minutes of salting and pickling time.

Other vegetables you can use: shredded or sliced carrots, radish, jícama, or kohlrabi; thinly sliced celery, fennel, cabbage, or onion.

1 pound cucumber, zucchini, summer squash, or eggplant

1 tablespoon salt

$^1/_2$ teaspoon sugar

1 tablespoon minced fresh dill or 1 teaspoon dried

2 teaspoons vinegar

❶ Wash the vegetables well, peel them if you like, and slice them as thinly as possible (a mandoline is perfect for this). Put the vegetables in a colander and sprinkle them with the salt; toss well. Gently rub the salt into the vegetables with your hands for a minute.

❷ Let sit in the sink or in a bowl for 15 to 30 minutes (cucumbers take less time than eggplant), tossing and squeezing every few minutes. When little or no more liquid comes out of the vegetable, rinse well in cold water. Put in a bowl.

❸ Toss with the sugar, dill, and vinegar and serve immediately (this does not keep well).

Quick-Pickled Vegetables, Mexican Style. This makes a spicy garnish for tacos, rice, beans, and more: Use an assortment of thinly sliced radishes, jícama, cucumber, and red onion. Substitute cilantro for the dill; add a thinly sliced jalapeño if you like (or habanero if you like it mouth searing); and use red wine vinegar.

Quick-Pickled Mango or Papaya. A perfect use for under-ripe mangoes or papaya, and it easily moves between Indian, Southeast Asian, Latin, and Caribbean cuisines: Substitute thinly sliced or julienned still-firm mango or papaya for the vegetables and cilantro, mint, or ginger for the dill.

Spicy Pickles, Asian Style

MAKES: 4 servings
TIME: At least 1 hour

Spicy East Asian pickles are traditionally served in small portions with an assortment of other pickled or fermented items along with meals. I love them for their hot, salty, and slightly sweet flavors.

Other vegetables you can use: radish, jícama, celery, cabbage, kohlrabi, cauliflower, turnips, or summer squash.

1 pound Kirby cucumbers

1 tablespoon salt

3 to 4 tablespoons Chile-Garlic Paste (page 75)

1 teaspoon sugar

2 tablespoons dark sesame oil

2 tablespoons soy sauce

① Wash the cucumbers well, scrub them if they're spiny, and cut into ¹/₄-inch-thick slices. Put them in a colander and sprinkle with the salt; toss well. Gently rub the salt into the cucumbers with your hands for a minute.

② Lay a plate over the vegetable mixture while it is in the colander and weight the plate with whatever is handy: a few cans, your teakettle filled with water, or a brick, for example. Let rest for about 30 minutes (1 hour is fine). Rinse the cucumbers, pat dry, and put in a bowl.

③ Toss them with the chile-garlic paste, sugar, sesame oil, and soy sauce and let sit for at least 30 minutes. Serve immediately or transfer to an airtight container, packing the cucumbers so the liquid covers them, cover, and refrigerate for up to 3 weeks.

Salted Cabbage with Sichuan Peppercorns. A sweet and hot quick pickling: Substitute 6 cups shredded green, Savoy, or Napa cabbage for the cucumbers and use 1 tablespoon each salt, mirin (or 1¹/₂ teaspoons honey mixed with 1¹/₂ teaspoons water), soy sauce, and Sichuan peppercorns, reducing the sesame oil to 1 teaspoon. Skip Step 1. Instead mix all the ingredients together in a bowl (toss very well), then press in the bowl with a weighted plate (see Steps 2 and 3); do not rinse. Remove the plate, toss again, and serve or refrigerate for up to 5 days or so.

Kimchi

MAKES: 12 servings

TIME: About 2 hours, largely unattended

The best-known pickled cabbage in this country is sauerkraut, but rapidly gaining in popularity is kimchi, the super-spicy Korean version. You can buy kimchi in jars at many Asian (especially Korean) markets, but making it yourself is neither difficult nor especially time-consuming and gives you far more control over the level of spiciness.

Other vegetables you can use: all scallions (use about 50, total, halved lengthwise) or 2 to 3 pounds daikon, black radish, or turnip, peeled and shredded.

1 medium head green, Savoy, or Napa cabbage (about 2 pounds), separated into leaves

¹/₂ cup salt, more or less

20 scallions, including most of the green, roughly chopped

1 tablespoon hot red pepper flakes, or to taste

¹/₄ cup soy sauce

¹/₄ cup minced garlic

3 tablespoons minced fresh ginger

¹/₄ cup sugar

① Layer the cabbage leaves in a colander, sprinkling each layer with a little salt. Let sit over a bowl for at least 2 hours. When the cabbage is wilted, rinse and dry.

② In a bowl, mix together the scallions, red pepper flakes, soy sauce, garlic, and sugar. Roughly chop the cabbage and toss with the spice mixture. Serve immediately or refrigerate for up to a week; it will become stronger every day.

Kosher Pickles, the Right Way

MAKES: About 60 pickle quarters or 30 halves

TIME: 1 to 2 days

Ⓜ Ⓥ

No vinegar here, so these don't keep for very long (about a week), but they'll be eaten quickly enough that you'll never see one go bad. These are my favorite pickles and those of everyone for whom I've made them too.

¹/₃ cup kosher salt

1 cup boiling water

2 pounds Kirby cucumbers, washed (scrub if spiny) and halved or quartered lengthwise

At least 5 cloves garlic, crushed

1 large bunch fresh dill, preferably with flowers, or
  2 tablespoons dried dill and 1 teaspoon dill seeds,
  or 1 tablespoon coriander seeds

1 Combine the salt and boiling water in a large bowl; stir to dissolve the salt. Add a handful of ice cubes to cool the mixture, then add all the remaining ingredients.

2 Add cold water to cover. Use a plate slightly smaller than the diameter of the bowl and a small weight to keep the cucumbers immersed. Set aside at room temperature.

3 Begin sampling the cucumbers after 4 hours if you've quartered them, 8 hours if you've halved them. In either case, it will probably take from 12 to 24 or even 48 hours for them to taste pickly enough to suit your taste.

4 When they are ready, refrigerate them, still in the brine. The pickles will continue to ferment as they sit, more quickly at room temperature, more slowly in the refrigerator. They will keep well for up to a week.

Three-Day Pickles

MAKES: About 60 pickle quarters or 30 halves

TIME: 3 days

These sweet-and-sour pickles are certainly not the usual dill or bread-and-butter pickle. Technically a "refrigerator pickle" (since the curing must be done in the refrigerator), this recipe uses salt, sugar, and vinegar to add sweet-and-sour flavor. And the pickling spice adds layers of flavors that are warm (hot even, if you add more chiles) and quite exotic.

Other vegetables and fruit you can use: carrots, radishes, celery, fennel, kohlrabi, pearl onions, cauliflower, peppers, turnips, summer squash, eggplant, peaches, watermelon rind, spaghetti squash, or beets.

2 pounds Kirby cucumbers

6 tablespoons kosher salt

2 cups white or white wine vinegar

$^1/_4$ cup sugar

$^1/_4$ cup pickling spice (to make your own, see
  page 67)

1 Wash the cucumbers well, scrub them if they're spiny, and halve or quarter them lengthwise or slice them. Put the cucumbers in a colander and sprinkle them with 2 tablespoons of the salt; toss well.

2 Let sit in the sink or in a bowl for about 2 hours. Rinse the cucumbers and then pat dry with paper towels; put in a nonmetal bowl.

3 Put the remaining $^1/_4$ cup salt, the vinegar, sugar, and pickling spice, along with 2 cups water, in a pot over high heat. Bring to a boil, then let cool for about 5 minutes. Pour the mixture over the cucumbers and let cool to room temperature. (Add more vinegar or water if the cucumbers are not covered.)

4 Transfer the cucumbers and pickling liquid to airtight jars or containers; store in the refrigerator for at least 3 days or longer for stronger pickles. They will keep in their pickling liquid for up to 3 weeks.

Pickled Peaches, Afghan Style (Tershi). Used like a condiment (great with rice dishes), these potent tangy-sweet pickles can be made with anything from peaches to tomatoes to eggplant: Substitute peeled, pitted, and sliced peaches for the cucumbers. Reduce the salt and sugar by half and use just cider vinegar (no water) to cover. Substitute 4 crushed cloves garlic, 2 teaspoons dried mint, 2 teaspoons coriander seeds, and 1 tablespoon hot red pepper flakes for the pickling spice. Skip Steps 1 and 2. These pickles will keep indefinitely.

Vegetables and Fruit

THE WONDERFUL THING ABOUT VEGETABLES

and fruits is that although they are very, very distinctive—it would be much easier to mistake beef for lamb than it would be to mistake zucchini for broccoli—most of them can be handled in very similar ways. Few vegetables cannot be simmered or steamed to tenderness and then dressed lightly with something as simple as lemon juice, vinaigrette, or that old standby, butter. And few vegetables cannot be cooked in a little olive oil, either over high heat so that they become crisp or with some liquid, covered, over lower heat, so that they become meltingly tender.

233

In this chapter I've divided vegetables and fruits according to the ways we usually think of them, even though the tomato, eggplant, winter and summer squashes, cucumber, and even corn are technically fruits. Similarly, rhubarb, though a vegetable, is usually cooked like a fruit, so you'll find it in that section.

I don't want to put too fine a point on such distinctions, though. It's worth knowing how to cook fruit in ways that are usually reserved for vegetables, like frying and sautéing, so you'll find instructions for those cooking methods in both the vegetable and fruit sections. Out-of-season or unripe fruit almost always benefits from cooking, and certain fruits—apples and bananas, for example—are so ubiquitous that there comes a point when grilling, roasting, or cooking them in some other unexpected way is a welcome change.

Savory recipes like Grilled Watermelon Steak (page 397) and Coconut-Fried Plantains (page 246), combined with "The Basics of Cooking Fruit" (page 377), should get you thinking about how to enjoy fruit throughout the meal rather than just for dessert (or breakfast). You'll find many sweet fruit recipes in the dessert chapter, of course.

Here, then, is information about shopping, storing, and basic cooking of vegetables, followed by a complete lexicon of vegetables, then fruits—a couple of hundred (slightly) more advanced recipes in total. The chapter is a primer for dealing with the most important building blocks of daily eating.

The Basics of Buying and Handling Fresh Produce

These days it's a mistake to think "fresh or nothing." Some frozen vegetables and even fruits are not only good enough to eat but sometimes better than what passes for fresh (see "Don't Freeze Out Frozen," page 236), especially, of course, in winter.

Be picky when you buy produce. You probably know the drill: Most vegetables should be slightly firm and most fruits slightly soft. Check for damage or rotten spots and make sure the color is close to ideal. Pay attention to the little stickers to see where the produce came from, keeping in mind that miles traveled are a good indication of how long ago fruits and vegetables were harvested. (Unless it was flown, that broccoli that traveled three thousand miles is at least a week old.) After a while, you'll naturally gravitate to what's seasonal, since that's what's both freshest and grown closer to home. This is easy enough in the summer or if you live in the South. But elsewhere it means turning more frequently to root vegetables in the winter months, as many of our ancestors did.

Be flexible. Virtually all fresh produce is available year-round, but seasonal selections mean better quality. Because of the many climates in the United States, we don't have a nationwide growing season. So throughout the year, try to tune in to what's being grown in your region. If you go to the store, and something you'd planned on doesn't look too fresh, reach for an alternative or head to the freezer case. In almost every recipe in this chapter I offer substitutions to help make your choices easier.

If you're concerned about the impact of mainstream farming methods on your health and the environment, you might think about buying organic fruits and vegetables (see "What About Organic?" on page 2). But my feeling is that it's even more important to seek out locally or regionally grown fresh produce—if it's organic, so much the better—because you'll be getting the best fruits and vegetables available and supporting the people who raise them.

Storing and Preparing Fresh Produce

Once home, wait until you're ready to use your vegetables or fruits before washing them, because washing removes not only pesticide residues but also natural defenses against rotting, and storing moist produce can promote growth of mold or bacteria. Remember, too, that not all fruits and vegetables benefit from refrigeration; check the individual entries in this chapter for more details.

I like to wash almost all fresh vegetables and fruits before cooking or eating. Even when the peel is inedible, it's a good idea to give it a rinse, because if there are any bacteria or dirt on the outside, they'll spread to the inside with handling. A soft scrubbing brush is perfect for potatoes you don't want to peel, cucumbers with little spines, and other, more rigorous jobs. (You can also use a mildly abrasive dishwashing pad.) Washing greens and other vegetables couldn't be easier:

1. Put them in a salad spinner (or a colander inside a large pot).
2. Fill it with water.
3. Swish the veggies around.
4. Lift the colander out of the water.
5. Drain.

The Basics of Cooking Vegetables

The main reason to cook a vegetable (the main reason to cook any food, really) is to make it tender and tastier and to release nutrients that aren't available in raw food. But the way you cook a particular vegetable can completely change its taste and texture and, for that matter, its nutritional profile. Some cooking methods deepen flavor by caramelizing the natural sugar or starches—usually with some fat—while others brighten both taste and color with moisture.

Virtually all vegetables can be cooked according to any of the general methods explained here, though there are exceptions. My goal is to help you grow more comfortable cooking vegetables spontaneously and experimenting with your own favorite flavors and techniques. The recipes here provide a starting place for beginners and a reference for more experienced cooks.

Keeping the Nutrients in Vegetables

Despite what enthusiasts of raw diets contend, cooking generally increases the bioavailability of the nutrients.

For example, the starch in potatoes is not absorbed by the stomach (and can cause gastric distress) unless the potatoes are cooked until just about soft. And anything with even a moderate amount of fiber or protein requires at least some heat (or juicing, which also breaks down the fibers) for the body to digest it properly.

At the same time, most vitamins, minerals, and other nutrients migrate out of the vegetables and into the surrounding liquid during cooking. Submerging vegetables for a long time in boiling water is the least nutritious way to cook them; steaming is a slightly better alternative, especially if the vegetables remain above the steaming liquid or if you incorporate the steaming liquid into the dish.

To get the most out of your vegetables, cook them just enough to unlock the nutrients but not long enough to allow the bulk of them to escape. If you want the vegetables cooked beyond al dente, for puréeing, mashing, or blending into soups or sauces, you might consider cooking them in a way that uses little or no water—like roasting, stir-frying, or microwaving—or include the cooking liquid in the finished dish. And if you really love boiled vegetables, consider saving the cooking water and using it for soups or beverages. Or—and this is a very real alternative—don't worry too much about the nutrition profile.

Recognizing Doneness in Vegetables

Once your veggies are prepared, try bending a piece to get an idea of how long it might take to cook. Harder, starchier vegetables take longer to cook. (That time can always be decreased by cutting the vegetable into smaller pieces, of course.) Spinach requires virtually no heat to wilt; likewise thin asparagus tips or matchsticks of carrots. But thick asparagus stalks or chunks of carrots will take much longer. Things you can't bend at all—like potatoes and other root vegetables—are going to take quite a bit longer.

The preceding discussion implies that there's only a small window of ideal doneness. It's true that it doesn't take more than a few minutes for many vegetables to turn from raw to mushy. Though mushy vegetables can offer their own pleasures, here are a handful of ways to recognize when vegetables reach their ideal window of doneness:

- Watch for the color to brighten. Vegetables cooked al dente are even more vibrant than they are when raw. But they quickly peak and begin to look washed out as they start to soften.

Don't Freeze Out Frozen

In the winter, when you freak out about the quality and price of the red peppers and green beans sitting in the supermarket's vegetables bins, you might be pleasantly surprised shopping in the frozen vegetable case. Not that you're going to have a mind-blowing experience with plain steamed frozen vegetables. But even frozen cut corn emptied straight from the package into a hot pan of olive oil, cooked until browned, and then served with a sprinkle of salt and a squeeze of lemon, provides a pleasant flashback to summer.

There are times when frozen vegetables—fruits too—are "fresher" (meaning brighter in color, more distinctive in flavor, and more consistently pleasing in texture) than much of what you can buy in the "fresh" produce bins. For example, frozen Brussels sprouts, bell pepper strips, spinach leaves, kale and collards, chunks of winter squash and turnips—these are all pretty good.

They can also be more convenient and are often less expensive, and these issues matter unless you're a bit of a food snob. And since the quality of vegetables is pretty much preserved at the stage they're frozen, the nutritional value may be superior.

I'm not crazy about frozen broccoli or cauliflower (and you can get these year-round anyway), but just about everything else is good, including berries and peaches, provided you're using the produce for cooking or the fruit for smoothies.

- Check them frequently. Since most vegetables don't take long to cook, the color change will happen in an instant. There's no shame in poking around with a knife tip, toothpick, or skewer or even tasting. Every once in a while, grab a piece and taste. It's the only way you'll ever know for sure. Eventually you'll be able to do this by sight, smell, and a poke of your finger.
- Remember that vegetables—like other foods—continue to cook as they cool down. Remove them from the heat just before they reach the stage of doneness you want. (This will come easily with practice, trust me.)
- Take control of doneness by learning to "shock" vegetables. This technique gets them ready ahead of time for finishing to perfect doneness at the last minute. (See "Shocking Vegetables," page 240.)

Vegetable Cooking Techniques

Here is a rundown of the common ways to cook vegetables and control their doneness.

Microwaving Vegetables

The microwave is good for steaming veggies with hardly any water at all, provided you know your machine well enough to yank them out before they overcook. Put vegetables on a plate or in a shallow bowl and sprinkle them with a few drops of water, then cover them loosely with a vented microwave cooking lid, a paper towel, or a heavy fitted lid (be careful when you open it; the steam will be very hot). Set the timer and press the button.

Steaming Vegetables

Cooking vegetables above a small amount of simmering water—not in it—is fast and efficient and preserves much of the vitamin content. This method is ideal for plain vegetables you want to eat right away or marinate in a vinaigrette as they cool. (For a specific example, see

 Fast   Make Ahead   Vegetarian

Basic Steamed Cauliflower on page 279.) You can buy a fancy vegetable steamer, but a fold-up basket that you put in the bottom of a covered pot works fine, as does a metal colander or even, in a pinch, a bowl (see "Ways to Rig a Steamer," page 20). Fill the steamer with vegetables, set it over an inch or so of water (see "Steaming," page 20), cover, and turn the heat to medium-high. Check frequently to prevent overcooking and to make sure there's still water in the bottom of the pot. To keep the steamed vegetables perfectly crisp-tender (good if you will finish them by some other method), shock them immediately in ice water (see page 240).

Boiling and Parboiling Vegetables

Simple and straightforward: Bring a large pot of water to a boil, salt it generously, and toss in whole or cut vegetables. (For an example, see Just-Tender Boiled or Steamed Vegetables, page 239.) When the vegetables begin to get tender, drain them, either by fishing them out with a strainer or slotted spoon or by pouring the water and the vegetables through a colander. The term *parboiling* really means nothing more than "preboiling," where vegetables are intentionally left underdone because they'll be cooked again by another method. Because fully boiled vegetables tend to leave both color and nutrients behind in the water, I often boil tender vegetables only briefly (sturdier ones a bit longer), shock them afterward (see page 240), and reheat just before serving.

Boiling or parboiling is handy if you have different vegetables and each requires a different cooking time; you simply keep the water rolling and work in batches. Since the goal is for all of them to finish cooking at the same time—on the grill or in a stir-fry, for example—try to parboil each to the point where it is just getting tender. (Again, remember to keep checking as they cook.)

Blanching Vegetables

When you want to make a sharp-tasting vegetable—like garlic, onions, or shallots—milder before further cook-

ing, you can blanch it in a pot of bubbling liquid for a few minutes. (For a specific example, see Creamed Onions on page 326.) Water is the simplest, though you can also use milk, stock, wine, beer, or juice. The idea is not to make them soft but just to cook them long enough to take the bite out. Three to 5 minutes will do. It's worth noting that the same technique, with the time reduced to 30 seconds or less, makes almost all fruits and vegetables—from peaches to tomatoes to garlic—easy to peel.

Sautéing Vegetables

I wish there were another word for this technique, since it sounds much more intimidating than it is—nothing more than cooking food quickly in hot fat. (Stir-frying, see page 18, is a subset of sautéing.) Start with a deep, broad skillet, set it over medium to medium-high heat, and add some oil or butter—1 or 2 tablespoons per pound (you can use more, of course). When the oil gets hot or the butter is melted, stir or toss the vegetables around in the pan until they're cooked, seasoning as needed. (For a specific example, see Sautéed Mushrooms on page 313.)

The only downside is that sautéing raw vegetables takes a little practice to keep them from burning before they're cooked through; you must check them frequently. A good alternative is to use the basic techniques of parboiling and shocking (see left), then proceed to Precooked Vegetables in Butter or Oil (page 240). This combination is excellent.

Braising Vegetables

A combination of sautéing and simmering, braising allows you to cook vegetables until they're fully tender and take advantage of all their flavor. Root vegetables, cabbages, sturdy winter greens, and alliums (garlic, shallots, leeks, and onions) are all good for braising. (For a specific example, see Braised Potatoes, Ten Ways, on page 343.)

Begin with sautéing, described above. After the vegetables have been softened a little and coated in hot oil (or begun to turn golden and caramelize if you like), add enough liquid—stock, milk, juice, wine, or water—to come about halfway up the vegetables. Bring to a boil, then lower the heat so the mixture bubbles gently or put the pot in a moderate oven. You can cover vegetables during braising or leave them uncovered, adding more liquid as needed to keep everything from drying out.

Braising and Glazing Vegetables

This valuable technique is less straightforward than the others, but you can master it easily. The idea is to combine the benefits of steaming, namely speed and moisture, with the power of sautéing—caramelization and crispness—all in one pot. As an added benefit, when you braise and glaze vegetables, their nutrients don't get left behind in a pot of water. (For a specific example, see Braised and Glazed Brussels Sprouts on page 270.)

Here's how it works: Put some oil or butter in a deep skillet and turn the heat to medium. Sauté some chopped or sliced garlic, onion, shallot, and/or ginger or other aromatics if you like, just for 30 seconds or so; then add your vegetable (like carrots, broccoli, cauliflower, asparagus, or any root vegetable, sliced or chopped as you will)

What Does *Crisp-Tender* Mean?

Applied to asparagus, green beans, broccoli, and more, *crisp-tender* describes a state where vegetables retain a subtle, pleasant crunch but are tender and moist enough to be pierced easily with a skewer or thin-bladed knife (or your teeth). When crisp-tender, vegetables like asparagus and broccoli will be flexible but not flopping over, and their color will be bright. You'll learn to assess crisp-tender doneness by sight after a while, but start by just taking a bite of the vegetable as it cooks.

with a little water and a sprinkle of salt. The longer the vegetables need to cook, the more water you'll need, but generally $^1/_4$ to $^1/_2$ cup will do.

Now cover the pan. Cook, uncovering only to stir occasionally and check the water level, until the vegetables are just tender, 5 to 15 minutes depending on the vegetable and how large the pieces are. The goal is to keep just enough water in the pan to steam the vegetables until they're cooked without letting the pan go dry. To glaze, uncover and raise the heat to cook out virtually all the remaining water; the combination of the fat and the starches and sugars from the vegetables will create a glossy coating.

Frying Vegetables

Messy, with a lot of added fat, but our favorite, right? When it comes to frying vegetables, you've got a few choices, starting with the decision to coat or not coat; see Breaded Fried Eggplant (or Any Other Vegetable) on page 245 and Battered and Fried Vegetables on page 247. Whether you coat the vegetables or not, you can either panfry in shallow oil ($^1/_2$ inch deep or so) or deep-fry in enough oil to submerge them (2 or 3 inches of oil in a deep pot).

To panfry: Set a deep skillet over medium to medium-high heat and pour in the oil. It should be hot but not smoking before you add the vegetables (test a small piece first; the vegetable should sizzle immediately and vigorously).

To deep-fry: The oil should maintain a temperature between 350°F and 375°F, depending on the recipe. (See "Deep Frying," page 19, and Battered and Fried Vegetables, page 247.) Be careful to allow enough room at the top of the pot for the vegetables to displace the oil and cause it to rise. And be careful not to overload the pot or the vegetables will get soggy.

Roasting Vegetables

The dry heat of roasting in a relatively hot oven intensifies the flavor of vegetables by driving out their internal water. Depending on the vegetable, the results range

 Fast   Make Ahead   Vegetarian

from slightly chewy to completely tender on the inside and crisped on the outside, with good color. Roasting is a fine method for entertaining, because the results can be served right out of the oven or at room temperature. For a specific example, see Roasted Vegetables (or Fruits) on page 241.

Grilling or Broiling Vegetables

Ideal for large pieces or slices. It might sound obvious, but when you expose the surface of vegetables to intense heat, the outsides will cook much faster than the insides. So ideally you get browning (or charring) outside and tenderness inside, with the added bonus of a smoky flavor. (For a specific example, see Grilled or Broiled Eggplant on page 294.)

Sturdier vegetables—eggplant, onions, mushrooms, squash, corn on the cob, and potatoes—are the most obvious candidates to grill or boil, though tomatoes, green beans, and asparagus work great too. You can thread smaller pieces on skewers or use a grilling basket. Coat everything lightly with a little oil—or a marinade—and grill or broil about 4 inches away from the heat source. You don't even need to parboil really hard vegetables, like squash or potatoes; either slice them fairly thinly or grill them part of the time over indirect heat with the lid of the grill closed.

ESSENTIAL RECIPES

I can provide you with hundreds of specific vegetable recipes (and this chapter comes close to doing that), but as a veteran home cook I know as well as anyone that the basics are the most important. If you know how to handle a vegetable simply and quickly and make it taste good, you're likely to cook it and eat it more often, and those are the recipes you're going to turn to most.

Here they are: the basics of steaming, boiling, stir-frying, reheating, saucing, puréeing, and more—the fast, easy, everyday ways to make vegetable dishes a standard part of life.

✪ Just-Tender Boiled or Steamed Vegetables

MAKES: 4 servings
TIME: 10 to 30 minutes
 F **M** **V**

This is the basic method for cooking just about any vegetable at all. Boiling gives you a little more control; steaming is faster. Both work just fine. Read "The Basics of Cooking Vegetables" (page 235) for more detail, and see Precooked Vegetables in Butter or Oil (page 240) for the best ways to make this simple preparation more elaborate.

Salt

1 to 2 pounds of the vegetable of your choice, peeled, stemmed, seeded, and/or chopped as needed

Freshly squeezed lemon juice, extra virgin olive oil, butter, or any of the toppings from "11 Ways to Jazz Up Simply Cooked Vegetables" (page 242)

Rig a steamer (see page 20) or bring a pot of water to a boil and salt it. Add the vegetables as specified as follows and cook until either crisp-tender or tender. Drain, then serve, drizzled with lemon juice, oil, butter, or whatever you like. Or shock in ice or cold water (see page 240), drain again, and set aside.

For greens: Trim and wash the greens. If the leaves and stems are pliable and can be eaten raw—like spinach, arugula, or watercress—that's a tender green. If the stems are as crisp as celery (over $1/8$ inch or so) and the leaves a little tough—like bok choy, chard, kale, or collards—it's best to separate the leaves from the stems (see the illustration on page 308) and give the stems a little head start. Add the stems or the stems and leaves to the pot and cook until bright green and tender, from 3 minutes (for spinach) to 10 (for kale and collards). (If you held back the leaves, add them when the stems are just about tender.)

For tender vegetables: This will work for broccoli, cauliflower, green beans, asparagus, peas of any type, bok choy, corn, even eggplant (be careful not to overcook). Keep in

Shocking Vegetables

With just a little effort, a bowl, and some ice, you can guarantee that many vegetables will be perfectly done and beautifully colored. The technique is called *shocking*, because after a brief boil (often called *parboiling*), you "shock" the vegetables by immediately plunging them into a bath of ice water. The idea is to cook the vegetables just enough to tenderize them, then rapidly stop the cooking process.

Shocking works brilliantly for most green vegetables, like asparagus and green beans, and also for carrots, cauliflower, turnips, and many others. And it's a fine method when you're cooking vegetables for a crowd, leaving only a quick warming in butter or oil for the last minute (see Precooked Vegetables in Butter or Oil, below). It's also the best way to prepare multiple vegetables of differing cooking times for stir-fries, salads, or other dishes where some lingering crispness is desirable. And shocking cooked greens—spinach, kale, escarole, and the like—gives you both vivid color and the opportunity to squeeze out extra moisture.

Here's what to do: Bring a large pot of water to a rolling boil and salt it well. Set up a large bowl of water with lots of ice cubes. Drop the vegetable into the boiling water. After about 30 seconds (shorter for spinach, longer for most other things; of course the size of your pieces will affect matters greatly), start testing—you can poke with a thin-bladed knife, or taste; you're looking for the vegetable to be just about tender, but not quite. When that happens, immediately fish the vegetables out with a large strainer, tongs, or a slotted spoon and put them in the bowl of ice water for a minute or two. When they've cooled down, remove from the ice bath and drain in a colander. (You can shock small amounts of boiled vegetables under or in a bowl of cold tap water, which will slow but not dramatically halt cooking. This works best, of course, if your tap water is really cold, which is not always the case.)

Squeeze drained greens tightly to remove as much water as possible, then chop, slice, or cook according to the recipe. Work in batches if you're shocking more than one type of vegetable, simply moving them through the process until you're done; there's no need to change the water. (If you are doing a lot of vegetables, the cooking water effectively becomes vegetable stock.)

You can store shocked and drained vegetables—covered tightly and refrigerated—for a day or two before proceeding. Or use them immediately.

---

mind that the smaller the pieces, the quicker they will cook. Cook until the vegetable is just tender, which will vary from about 3 minutes (peas) to 7 (broccoli florets) to 10 or 12 (broccoli stems, some green beans) and up to 25 minutes for a whole large head of cauliflower.

For root vegetables or tubers: Not quite so simple; in many ways it's best to follow individual recipes as given in this chapter, especially for potatoes and sweet potatoes. But as a general rule, this will work; use for beets, turnips, radishes, winter squash, and so on: Peel the vegetable or not, as you prefer; leave whole if possible to prevent waterlogging. Proceed with the recipe, but cook until the vegetable is quite tender and can be pierced easily with a thin-bladed knife, from 10 minutes (radishes, for example) to nearly an hour (larger potatoes).

Precooked Vegetables in Butter or Oil

MAKES: 4 servings
TIME: 5 minutes

This is the one indispensable vegetable technique. It will work for just about every vegetable and can be taken to the

table within 5 minutes—*and* it can be brought to that point as long as a day or two in advance. This means that you can start and finish the vegetable as you're taking other dishes to the table or just before. It's also useful with left-over simmered or steamed vegetables (rinse them first with boiling water to remove any prior seasoning if necessary).

But the process could not be much simpler.

Butter or olive oil

Just-Tender Boiled or Steamed Vegetables (preceding recipe), cooked until just *beginning* to get tender

Salt and freshly ground black pepper

Additional seasonings, like fresh chopped herbs or spice blends (optional)

❶ Put enough butter or olive oil—usually a tablespoon or two—into a skillet over medium heat to cover the bottom of the skillet.

❷ When the butter is melted or the oil is hot, add the vegetables to the pan, turn the heat up to medium-high, and cook, stirring, until hot, just a couple of minutes. Sprinkle with salt and pepper (alone or with other seasonings) and serve.

Roasted Vegetables (or Fruits)

MAKES: 4 servings

TIME: About 1 hour

 ⓜ ⓥ

Something truly magical happens when vegetables are roasted; their flavors concentrate, the texture becomes soft and a bit chewy, and the outside turns a beautiful golden brown. All this and a nearly hassle-free cooking method too. Just remember not to overcrowd the pan. Ideally you want a little breathing room between pieces (though the pieces will shrink, so you can cheat a little bit); if necessary, divide the vegetables between two or more pans or roast in batches.

Vegetables and fruits you can use: apples, artichoke hearts (precooked, see page 253), asparagus, Brussels sprouts, carrots, cauliflower, celery root, eggplant (use more oil), fennel, grapes, leeks, onions, parsnips, potatoes, radishes, shallots (leave whole), summer or winter squash, sweet potatoes, yams, turnips, or rutabaga.

3 tablespoons extra virgin olive oil, melted butter, or a mixture, plus more as needed

1½ to 2 pounds vegetables, one kind or a combination, peeled, stemmed, seeded, and chopped or sliced as needed

Salt and freshly ground black pepper

❶ Heat the oven to 425°F while you prepare the vegetables. Drizzle half the oil or butter on the bottom of a roasting pan or baking sheet. Add the vegetables and drizzle on the remaining oil or butter; sprinkle with salt and pepper and stir (for items that will fall apart with stirring—like fennel, leeks, or onion slices—use a pastry brush to coat them with the oil or butter).

❷ Roast the vegetables, stirring once or twice, until they are tender and beginning to brown, 15 to 60 minutes (depending on the type of vegetable; tender ones will cook relatively fast). If they are browning too fast, lower the temperature to 400°F and stir more frequently. Taste and adjust the seasoning. Serve hot or warm.

Stir-Fried Vegetables

MAKES: 4 servings

TIME: 15 minutes

ⓕ ⓥ

Stir-fries are among the best ways to use those single carrots, celery stalks, and other vegetables sitting in your fridge. One key to a fast stir-fry is the size of the cut vegetables: The smaller you cut them, the more quickly they will cook.

2 tablespoons neutral oil, like grapeseed or corn

1 tablespoon minced garlic

1 tablespoon minced fresh ginger

½ cup chopped scallion or onion

1 large carrot, cut into pieces, sliced, or julienned

2 celery stalks, cut into pieces, sliced, or julienned

1 pound snow or snap peas, trimmed (thawed frozen are fine)

$1/4$ cup stock (to make your own, see pages 157–160) or water, or a little more

2 tablespoons soy sauce

1 teaspoon dark sesame oil

1 Heat a large, deep skillet over medium-high heat for 3 or 4 minutes. Add the oil and, almost immediately, the garlic, ginger, and scallion. Cook, stirring, for about 15 seconds, then add the carrot, celery, snow peas, and stock and turn the heat to high.

2 Cook, stirring frequently, until the vegetables are tender, about 7 minutes. If the mixture is completely dry, add a couple tablespoons more stock, then the soy sauce and sesame oil; stir and turn off the heat. Serve or store, covered, in the refrigerator for up to a day.

Shrimp, Chicken, or Any Meat and Vegetable Stir-Fry. Add 1 pound peeled shrimp, boneless chicken, pork (preferably shoulder), or beef (preferably sirloin), cut into thin shreds and patted dry. In Step 1, make sure the skillet is very hot; add the oil and then the meat, stir once or twice, and cook until it begins to brown, about a minute. Stir and cook until just done, another minute or so; remove from the pan. Proceed with the recipe, adding more oil or liquid as needed. During the last couple of minutes of cooking, return the shrimp, chicken, or meat to the pan to heat through.

Tofu and Vegetable Stir-Fry. Add 1 pound extra-firm tofu, cubed and dried on paper towels. In Step 1, make sure the skillet is very hot; add the oil, then the tofu, and cook, turning the pieces, until golden brown on all (or most) sides, about 5 minutes; remove from the pan. Proceed with the recipe, adding more oil or liquid as needed. During the last couple of minutes of cooking, return the tofu to the pan to heat through.

11 Ways to Jazz Up Simply Cooked Vegetables

No matter how you cook vegetables, there are some quick, last-minute additions that make a big difference. Just toss gently to coat—along with a little butter or oil if you like—and serve. (Saucing is always an excellent way to finish vegetables; browse through the sauces and condiments chapter for dozens of ideas.)

1. Freshly squeezed lemon or lime juice
2. Chopped fresh herbs
3. Grated citrus zest
4. Chopped nuts
5. Toasted bread crumbs
6. Nut or seed oil, like sesame, walnut, hazelnut, or pumpkin seed oil
7. Flavored Oil (page 26)
8. Compound Butter (page 32)
9. Spice blends, especially za'atar and chaat masala (to make your own, see page 68), or Seaweed "Shake" (page 69)
10. Vinaigrette (pages 199–202)
11. Any croutons (see page 877)

6 Tips for Successful Stir-Fried Vegetables

Stir-frying is one of the best, easiest, and fastest ways to get an entire meal on the table, and you can stir-fry just about any vegetable. The procedure is this: You chop your ingredients into more-or-less bite-sized pieces. You start rice, if you want it, and set the table, because the stir-frying itself is usually the last thing you do. In the last 10 minutes you'll be as busy as a chef, but up to that point it's all completely relaxed.

You'll find more detail on stir-frying in general on page 18, but here are the basics:

1. The smaller you cut the food, the faster it will cook.
2. There are many options, as you can see from the list

F Fast   **M** Make Ahead   **V** Vegetarian

that follows, but too many ingredients will slow you down and muddy the flavor.

3. Use the largest flat-bottomed skillet you have; nonstick or well-seasoned cast iron is best, and high heat is essential.

4. Stir almost constantly unless you want to promote searing and browning, in which case stir less frequently.

5. You may need to parboil and shock vegetables that won't become tender through direct stir-frying even if you cut them small: broccoli stems, thick asparagus, and turnips, for example. If you don't have time for that, cut them small and stir-fry them first. (For the most control this way, remove them from the pan when they're almost done, cook the other vegetables, and return the first batch to the mix for final warming.)

6. You need a little liquid in stir-fries. That liquid can be water or something with more flavor, like wine or stock. Add a little with the vegetables to encourage them to cook more quickly and a little at the end, if necessary, to keep ingredients from burning and create a sauce.

16 Additions to Stir-Fried Vegetables

Generally you can add a total of 1 to 2 cups of any of the following vegetables to the basic recipe. If you keep the scallion, carrot, and celery, you can substitute for the snow or snap peas or reduce that amount and compensate with any of the following. Or you can build a bigger stir-fry by using one or more of these in combination with what's already in the basic recipe; all you'll need to do is add a bit more liquid.

1. Bamboo shoots, added at the last minute
2. Water chestnuts, added at the last minute
3. Green beans, preferably parboiled and shocked (see page 240), added with the peas
4. Spinach, washed, dried, and added with about a minute to go
5. Watercress, washed, dried, and added at the last minute
6. Leeks, rinsed and chopped, instead of the scallion or onion but in greater quantity if you like

7. Mushrooms, fresh or dried and reconstituted (Chinese black mushrooms, a form of shiitakes, are especially good), trimmed and sliced or chopped, added with the peas
8. Daikon, trimmed and julienned or shredded, added with about a minute to go
9. Corn kernels, added with about a minute to go
10. Cabbage or bok choy, trimmed and shredded, added with the scallion
11. Asparagus, blanched (see page 237) and added with the peas
12. Zucchini or summer squash, cut into slices or chunks and added with the scallion
13. Any color bell pepper, cored, seeded, and sliced, added with the scallion
14. Soy or mung bean sprouts, added at the last minute
15. Broccoli or cauliflower, blanched (see page 237) and added with the peas
16. 1 medium to large tomato, halved and seeded, then chopped, added with the scallion

✪ Puréed Vegetables

MAKES: 4 servings
TIME: 40 minutes

Puréed vegetables are luxurious, delicious, and simple. The best vegetables for puréeing are root vegetables, like carrots, broccoli and cauliflower, spinach, winter squash, and starchy potatoes. I use extra virgin olive oil or butter to bind and enrich basic purées, but cream or milk, or even bread crumbs or other starch, also help to enrich the purée, keep it from leaching water, and give it a velvety texture. See the chart that follows for many more ideas.

Warm vegetable purées make an elegant bed for simply cooked fish, poultry, or meat. And at room temperature or chilled, they are excellent impromptu dips and spreads.

MORE IDEAS FOR VEGETABLE PURÉES

VEGETABLE 2 POUNDS RAW WILL GIVE YOU 3 TO 4 CUPS COOKED AND CHOPPED	FAT (FOR BINDER) 2 TO 3 TABLESPOONS	ENRICHMENT USE AS YOU LIKE OR AS NEEDED TO REACH DESIRED CONSISTENCY; USUALLY ABOUT ½ CUP	SEASONING 1 TO 2 TABLESPOONS, IN ADDITION TO SALT AND FRESHLY GROUND BLACK PEPPER TO TASTE	GARNISH AS MUCH OR AS LITTLE AS YOU LIKE
Broccoli or cauliflower	Extra virgin olive oil	Ricotta cheese	A pinch of nutmeg	Grated Parmesan
Butternut squash	Neutral oil, like grapeseed or corn	Coconut milk	Curry powder (to make your own, see pages 66–67)	Toasted shredded coconut
Carrots	Extra virgin olive oil	Orange juice	Minced fresh ginger	Grated orange zest
Chestnuts	Butter	Cream or crème fraîche	Honey or maple syrup	Chopped roasted chestnuts (see page 287)
Corn	Butter or extra virgin olive oil	Sour cream	2 teaspoons chili powder (to make your own, see page 66)	Queso fresco, chopped fresh tomato, and minced cilantro
Eggplant	Extra virgin olive oil	None needed, but add 1 head Roasted Garlic (page 303) if you like.	Any Middle Eastern spice blend or a large pinch of saffron	Chopped fresh parsley or mint leaves
Peas	Melted butter	Cream or half-and-half	Minced fresh tarragon leaves	Stir in a spoonful of Dijon mustard.
Pumpkin, other winter squash, or cassava	Extra virgin olive oil	Some of the boiling liquid	Lots of garlic, either fried or roasted (see page 303)	Paprika or lots of freshly ground black pepper and a squeeze of lime juice
Red bell pepper or mild green or red chiles	Extra virgin olive oil	Usually none needed	None needed	Chopped fresh cilantro or red onion
Parsnips, turnips, or rutabagas	Melted butter or extra virgin olive oil	A dab of sour cream	Minced red onions	Chopped parsley and chopped toasted nuts

About 1½ pounds vegetables, one kind or a
   combination (see the chart, above)

Salt

2 tablespoons extra virgin olive oil or butter

Freshly ground black pepper

Chopped fresh parsley leaves for garnish
   (optional)

❶ Peel and trim the vegetables as necessary; cut them into roughly equal-sized pieces, 1 to 2 inches in diameter. Put the vegetables in a pot with water to cover and add a large pinch of salt; or rig a steamer (see page 20) and put the vegetables in it above water. Bring to a boil and cook until the vegetable is tender, usually 5 to 15 minutes. You want the vegetables fully tender but not mushy.

 F Fast   **M** Make Ahead   **V** Vegetarian

❷ Drain the vegetables well, reserving some of the cooking liquid. (At this point, you may refrigerate the vegetables, well wrapped or in a covered container, for up to 2 days before proceeding.) Put the vegetables through a food mill placed over the pot or cool slightly and put them in a blender or food processor with as much of the cooking liquid as you need to get the machine going. (You can also mash the vegetables with a large fork or potato masher, adding the cooking liquid as needed.)

❸ Add the olive oil or butter and stir, then taste and season with more salt if necessary and sprinkle with pepper. Serve, keep warm, or allow to cool for reheating later. Garnish with parsley before serving.

Rich Vegetable Purée. Add up to $1/2$ cup cream, sour cream, half-and-half, or milk.

✪ Breaded Fried Eggplant (or Any Other Vegetable)

MAKES: 4 servings
TIME: 1 hour

This is a model for shallow-frying vegetables so they're crunchy and tender—like the zucchini sticks you get in chain restaurants, only better. The variety of toppings and dipping sauces you can use is huge, though I always seem to come back to lemon juice, maybe with a little hot sauce.

Frying vegetables without breading or battering is certainly an option. But be aware that you'll never achieve the same crispness as you do when a coating provides a barrier to seal in moisture and keep out the fat. Another cooking option: Substitute half the oil for butter if you like.

Fried food is crispest immediately after cooking. When done, drain the pieces briefly on paper towels and serve. If you must hold fried vegetables for a bit—no longer than 10 or 15 minutes, please—drain them briefly, then immediately transfer them to a warm oven

(see below). A wire rack set over a rimmed baking pan is the ideal, but any ovenproof platter will work.

Vegetables you can use: any winter or summer squash, mushrooms, cauliflower, broccoli.

> 4 or 5 small eggplant or 2 large (about 2 pounds), trimmed
>
> Salt
>
> 1 cup all-purpose flour for dredging
>
> 3 cups bread crumbs, preferably fresh (page 876), for dredging
>
> 3 eggs, beaten
>
> Freshly ground black pepper
>
> Extra virgin olive oil or neutral oil, like grapeseed or corn, as needed
>
> Chopped fresh parsley leaves for garnish
>
> Lemon wedges for serving

❶ Cut the eggplant into $1/2$-inch-thick slices; salt the slices if you're using large eggplant and time allows (see page 293). Heat the oven to 200°F. Set out the flour, bread crumbs, and beaten eggs on plates or shallow bowls next to each other on your counter and have a baking sheet and stack of wax or parchment paper ready; add salt and pepper to the eggs.

❷ Rinse and dry the eggplant. Dredge the slices, one at a time, in the flour, then dip in the egg, then dredge in the bread crumbs. Stack the eggplant on the baking sheet between layers of wax paper and, when it's all breaded, transfer the stack to chill in the refrigerator for at least 10 minutes and up to 3 hours.

❸ Put about $1/2$ inch of oil in a large skillet over medium-high heat. When hot, put in a few of the eggplant slices; cook in batches as necessary, making sure not to crowd the pan and adding additional oil as needed. Use a spatula, tongs, or a slotted spoon to turn the eggplant slices as soon as they're browned, then cook the other side; total cooking time will be 5 minutes or so. As each piece is done, remove it to drain on paper towels. Transfer completed batches to an ovenproof platter and put the platter in the oven.

④ Serve as soon as all the pieces are cooked, garnished with the parsley and with the lemon wedges on the side.

Sesame-Fried Eggplant. Great with any soy-based dipping sauce (pages 25, 38, and 40): Use 2 cups bread crumbs and 1 cup sesame seeds for the final dredging. Replace 2 tablespoons of the oil or butter with dark sesame oil.

Coconut-Fried Plantains. Substitute 4 or 5 yellow to yellow-black plantains for the eggplant; peel and cut straight or diagonal into about $1/4$-inch-thick slices. Use $1^1/_2$ cups bread crumbs and $1^1/_2$ cups shredded coconut for the final dredging.

Grain-Fried Butternut Squash. Replacing part or all of the bread crumbs with ground grains adds a nutty flavor: Substitute about 2 pounds peeled, seeded, and sliced butternut squash for the eggplant. Coarsely grind about 3 cups oats or barley in a food processor and use that instead of the bread crumbs for the final dredging.

Fried Onion Rings, Streamlined. Substitute 2 thinly sliced large onions (any kind but the sweet varieties like Vidalia or Walla Walla) for the eggplant. Omit the bread crumbs and eggs; dredge the onion rings in just flour and fry until golden brown.

Breaded Fried Cauliflower. Substitute 1 pound cauliflower (about 1 medium head), trimmed, broken into florets of any size, parboiled, shocked (see page 240), and dried, for the eggplant. Proceed with the recipe. When still piping hot, toss with lemon juice, a couple tablespoons capers, and chopped fresh parsley if you like.

3 Ways to Vary Any Breaded Fried Vegetable

1. Change the breading: For the bread crumbs, try using panko; shredded coconut; finely chopped nuts or seeds; pulverized raw whole grains, like rice, rolled oats or barley, or kasha (pulse in a food processor to

grind any of these); or grated Parmesan (mixed with bread crumbs).

2. Streamline the process: Omit the eggs and bread crumbs and simply dredge the vegetables in flour before frying. Note that this works best for vegetables

---

How to Add Meat, Fish, or Poultry to Almost Any Vegetable Dish

Adding animal protein to vegetables can make your vegetable dish the main course or even a one-pot meal, and it cuts down on the number of pans you use. Nearly any animal protein can be sautéed, stir-fried, braised, or roasted; steaming is best for fish, shellfish, and boneless chicken breasts. (Boiling meat and vegetables is desirable only when you plan on eating the cooking liquid too.) The easiest way is to simply add cooked (and, if necessary, cut-up or shredded) pieces of meat, fish, or poultry as the vegetables finish cooking—long enough for them to heat through. This is obviously an excellent use for leftovers.

The other way is to cook the animal protein first, then remove it from the pan. See the variation for Stir-Fried Vegetables (page 241) for an example of how this works.

Tips for Adding Protein to Vegetable Dishes:

- Add about 1 tablespoon oil for each pound of lean protein added to sautés, stir-fries, braising and glazing, and roasting (not necessary for fatty meat).
- More liquid may be required for braised or simmered dishes.
- Put the protein on the bottom when steaming.
- If you want all your ingredients to get browned nicely, but the pan isn't large enough to accommodate everything, cook in batches and remove; then return all the ingredients to the pan at the end just to heat them through.
- Consider meat as a seasoning for the vegetables; in this chapter at least, they should still be the star.

 Fast   Make Ahead   Vegetarian

with a decent amount of moisture for the flour to stick to; hard vegetables like carrots or winter squash won't take to flour coating as well as onions or zucchini.

3. Go eggless: Instead of the egg, use milk or buttermilk.

Battered and Fried Vegetables

MAKES: 4 servings
TIME: 30 minutes

There are infinite ways to batter and deep-fry vegetables, but this is the most basic. Accompanying sauces can be anything from a squeeze of lemon or lime juice to a soy sauce dip to a chutney (see the list that follows for some ideas).

Usually the best way to serve battered and fried vegetables is as a casual kitchen appetizer, the moment you pull them from the oil and drain them, though in a pinch you can keep them warm for a few minutes on a rack in a low oven. Just don't expect them to be exactly the same. Nearly any vegetable can be battered and fried, but especially zucchini, eggplant, winter squash, sweet potatoes, mushrooms, bell peppers, green beans, broccoli, cauliflower, asparagus tips, onion rings, fennel, beets, and carrots. Hard vegetables should be sliced ¼ inch thick or thinner; tender ones, like zucchini and eggplant, can be cut up to ½ inch thick or so. Smaller vegetables like mushrooms or green beans can be left whole.

As always, cook in batches to avoid overcrowding (see "Deep Frying," page 19). You want the pieces to be able to swim around in the oil and not stick together. Generally, use a neutral oil, like grapeseed or corn, for deep-frying, but olive oil and peanut oil are good options too.

Oil for frying

1 cup all-purpose flour, plus 1 cup for dredging

1 teaspoon baking powder

Salt and freshly ground black pepper

1 egg

¾ cup beer or sparkling water

Coarse salt for finishing

❶ Put at least 2 inches oil in a deep pan over medium-high heat; bring to 350°F (see "Deep Frying," page 19). While the oil is heating, prepare the vegetables and the dipping sauce, if you're using one.

❷ Mix 1 cup of the flour with the baking powder and sprinkle with salt and pepper. Whisk in the egg and the beer until just combined and the consistency of pancake batter. It's okay to have some lumps in the batter (you don't want to overmix).

❸ Dredge each piece of food lightly in the remaining cup of flour, then dip into the batter and add to the oil. Do not crowd the vegetables; you will have to cook in batches. Cook, turning once if needed, until golden all over, just a few minutes. Drain on a rack or paper towels, sprinkle with coarse salt and additional pepper if you like, and serve immediately, with a dipping sauce or lemon wedges.

Battered Apple "Fries." For a savory version, use the recipe as is. For a sweet version, use sparkling water instead of beer and add a sprinkle of confectioners' sugar to the batter and as a final dusting: Use 2 or 3 apples, like Golden Delicious, Granny Smith, or any all-purpose apple (see page 382). Peel the apple if you like. Slice the apple away from the core from top to bottom, then cut the slices into sticks (resembling fries). Or core first and cut crosswise into rings.

5 Dipping Sauces for Battered and Fried Vegetables

There are dozens of sauces that go well with this batter, but here are some that really stand out.

1. Salsa Cruda (page 24)
2. Traditional Pesto (page 27) or any herb purée (see pages 27–28)
3. Garlic Mayonnaise (page 42)
4. Real Ranch Dressing (page 42)
5. Fast Tomato Sauce (page 502)

MORE IDEAS FOR VEGETABLE GRATINS

Make impromptu gratins by using the following combos in the preceding recipe—or mix and match from each column.

VEGETABLES	TOP WITH . . . THEN BROIL	GARNISH WITH . . .
Asparagus or green beans, whole	1 cup grated Gruyère or Swiss cheese 1/2 cup fresh bread crumbs (see page 876)	A sprinkle of paprika
Winter squash, sliced or cut into wedges or chunks	1 cup fresh bread crumbs (see page 876) 1/2 cup chopped nuts, like walnuts, almonds, or pecans	1 teaspoon minced fresh sage leaves
Spinach or other greens, whole leaves, ribbons, or sliced	1/2 recipe Béchamel or Mornay (Cheese) Sauce (page 57) 1/4 cup fresh bread crumbs (see page 876) (optional)	Lots of freshly ground black pepper
Ripe tomatoes, sliced (preferably peeled and seeded)	1 cup grated melting cheese	2 tablespoons chopped fresh basil, dill, chives, or cilantro or 1 tablespoon chopped fresh rosemary, thyme, or tarragon
Mushroom caps or slices	1 cup crumbled blue cheese 1/4 cup fresh bread crumbs (see page 876)	Crumbled crisp cooked bacon
Potatoes, sliced or cut into wedges	1 cup shredded manchego cheese 1/4 cup fresh bread crumbs (see page 876; optional)	Smoked paprika
Beets, sliced	1/2 cup or more crumbled goat cheese 1/2 cup chopped walnuts (optional)	1 tablespoon chopped fresh thyme
Broccoli or cauliflower, florets or roughly chopped	1 cup or so Traditional Pesto (page 27) 1/4 cup grated Parmesan	Hot red pepper flakes
Sweet potatoes, sliced or cut into wedges	1/2 cup soft cream cheese, dotted on 1/4 cup brown sugar (optional)	1/4 cup chopped nuts
Sautéed or Caramelized Onions (page 325)	Dabs of butter 1/4 cup fresh bread crumbs (see page 876) 2 tablespoons or more chopped cooked bacon (optional)	1 tablespoon chopped fresh rosemary, thyme, or tarragon or 1/4 cup chopped fresh dill or chives

Vegetable Gratin

MAKES: 4 servings

TIME: 15 minutes with cooked vegetables

Browned vegetables essentially, often with cheese or bread crumbs. Nearly any cooked vegetable can be used in a gratin; start with boiled, steamed, roasted, grilled, or even sautéed vegetables; then slice, cut into wedges, or chop. Add some sauce (any you like, though Béchamel, page 57, is the most traditional) or some crunch—or a little of both—and run the whole thing under the broiler. If you like, season with a dusting of spices or a handful of chopped fresh herbs right before serving.

 Fast   Make Ahead   Vegetarian

In short, put some cooked vegetables—just about any will work—in a dish, add a topping, then brown the topping. That's a gratin.

2 tablespoons extra virgin olive oil or butter, plus more for the pan

1½ to 2 pounds any cooked vegetable (4 to 6 cups)

1½ to 2 cups grated cheese, sauce like Traditional Pesto (page 27), bread crumbs (preferably fresh, page 876), finely chopped nuts, or a combination

Salt and freshly ground black pepper

Spices, seasonings, or fresh herbs for sprinkling (optional)

❶ Heat the broiler and put the rack about 4 inches from the heat source. Grease a broad, shallow baking dish, an ovenproof platter, or a rimmed baking sheet. Put the vegetables in the prepared dish, spreading them out a bit into an even layer. Distribute the topping over all. Drizzle with oil or dot with bits of butter; sprinkle with salt and pepper.

❷ Put the vegetables under the broiler and cook until the topping is golden brown, hot, and bubbly—which could be as little as 2 minutes but certainly fewer than 10. (Keep a close watch so it doesn't burn.) Sprinkle with additional seasoning if you like and serve.

✪ Grilled Vegetables

MAKES: 4 servings
TIME: 10 to 30 minutes

Ⓕ　Ⓜ　Ⓥ

Almost any vegetable can be grilled, though some—like potatoes, sweet potatoes, and winter squash—will burn before they cook through if left over direct heat. So as a general rule, keep a portion of the grill free of coals or gas to move things over to indirect heat if needed.

You can serve grilled vegetables with almost anything, though it makes most sense to cook them along with other grilled foods once you've got the fire going. (You can even get in the habit of putting a load of vegetables on whenever you light the grill, since they're nice to have around to incorporate into other dishes, like pasta, pizza, sandwiches, and pilafs.) They're fine hot off the grill or at room temperature; in either case, drizzle with extra virgin olive oil just before serving. And they keep in the fridge for several days. Just plan to use 2 to 3 tablespoons of oil for every pound of vegetables.

Vegetables you can use: virtually everything except for leafy greens, though whole heads of romaine, radicchio, endive, escarole, or chicory are terrific (see the recipe on page 299). For specific ideas, see the chart on page 250.

About 1 pound any vegetable, like eggplant, squash, peppers, onions, mushrooms, or a combination

2 to 3 tablespoons extra virgin olive oil

Salt and freshly ground black pepper

Barbecue or other prepared sauce (see pages 52–56) for basting (optional)

Lemon wedges for serving (optional)

❶ If you're using wood skewers, soak them in water to cover while you prepare the vegetables. (If you can get it, use a rosemary branch as a skewer; it will flavor the vegetables nicely, and as long as it's fresh, no soaking is necessary.) Heat a charcoal or gas grill to medium-high heat and put the rack about 4 inches from the heat source. Clean the grill grate; your vegetables will be less likely to stick.

❷ Cut the vegetable into large pieces so they won't fall into the fire. For many items, like potatoes, squash, or eggplant, slices are fine; they should be between ¼ and ½ inch thick (lengthwise or on the diagonal for smaller items like zucchini); generally you want the slices thin enough so that they cook through without burning on the outside but thick (and large) enough so they don't fall through the grill. Skewer or use a grilling basket for very small items and cut all fragile items into larger pieces. Brush or drizzle them with oil until coated and sprinkle with salt and pepper.

HOW TO GRILL VEGETABLES

This chart walks you through the basics for grilling all sorts of vegetables, including some tips on how to punch up the flavor before serving.

VEGETABLE	PREPARATION	HOW TO GRILL	HOW TO SAUCE, SEASON, OR SERVE
Artichokes	Use whole (halved and chokes removed), baby, or hearts (see page 254); parboil in salted water until just tender and shock (see page 240); skewer baby and hearts; brush with oil.	Cook over direct heat, turning occasionally, until browned and tender when pierced with a skewer or knife tip, about 10 minutes.	Use Garlic (or any other flavored) Mayonnaise (page 42) for dipping or Traditional (or any other) Pesto (page 27) for topping.
Asparagus	Trim but leave whole; brush or toss in oil.	Cook over direct heat, turning occasionally, just until the thick part of the stalks can be pierced with a skewer or knife tip, 6 to 12 minutes, depending on thickness.	Top with Compound Butter (page 32) or 5-Minute Drizzle Sauce (page 22) or sprinkle with grated Parmesan.
Chiles and peppers	Core and seed; halve or cut into squares and skewer; oil is optional.	Cook over direct heat, turning occasionally, until the skin is blistered, dark brown, and tender, 10 to 15 minutes.	Top with Mint or Dill "Pesto" (page 27), Simplest (or nearly any) Yogurt Sauce (page 24), or Creamy Cilantro-Mint Chutney (page 37).
Corn	Remove silks; keep in husks or remove them; oil is optional when husks are removed.	Cook over direct heat, turning occasionally, until some of the kernels char a bit and others are lightly browned, 15 to 20 minutes with husks on, less than half that with husks off.	Top with nearly any Compound Butter (page 32) or Ginger-Scallion Sauce (page 39) or sprinkle with sumac.
Eggplant	Peel the skin if you like; cut into 1/4- to 1/2-inch-thick slices or 1 1/2-inch cubes and skewer; brush with oil.	Cook over direct heat, turning occasionally, until browned and tender, 5 to 20 minutes, depending on thickness.	Top with Peanut Sauce (page 55) or Thai Chile Sauce (page 39) or sprinkle with Seaweed "Shake" (page 69).
Mushrooms	Remove stems from portobellos or shiitakes; trim small mushrooms; grill whole, slice thickly, or cut into cubes. If small, skewer. Brush with oil.	Cook over direct heat, turning occasionally, until browned, juicy, and tender, 15 to 20 minutes.	Use Simple Miso Dipping Sauce (page 39) for dipping or marinate in any vinaigrette after grilling.
Onions	Unpeeled and halved through the root end or peeled and cut into wedges or 1/2-inch slices; brush with oil.	Cook over direct heat, turning once (use a spatula to keep together), until nicely browned and tender, about 15 minutes.	Top with almost any raw or cooked salsa (see pages 23, 33–35, and 48–50) or Teriyaki Sauce (page 55).

 F Fast   **M** Make Ahead   **V** Vegetarian

VEGETABLE	PREPARATION	HOW TO GRILL	HOW TO SAUCE, SEASON, OR SERVE
Potatoes and sweet potatoes	Use waxy red or white potatoes; parboil in salted water until just tender; sweet potatoes don't need parboiling; cut into long wedges or ¹/₂-inch slices; brush with oil.	Cook over direct heat, turning occasionally, until browned and tender, 15 to 20 minutes. Cook over indirect heat, turning occasionally, until the flesh is very tender all the way through and the outsides are golden, 20 to 25 minutes.	Top with nearly any Compound Butter (page 32), Basic Barbecue Sauce (page 52), or Simple Miso Dipping Sauce (page 39).
Squash and zucchini	Trim; cut into ¹/₂-inch lengthwise slices or long diagonal slices; brush with oil.	Cook over direct heat, turning occasionally, until browned and tender, 10 to 15 minutes.	Top with Cilantro, Dill, Basil, or Mint Purée (page 28) or Herbed 5-Minute Drizzle Sauce (page 22).
Tomatoes	Use slightly green or not fully ripe tomatoes; halve, cut into ¹/₂-inch slices, or leave whole if small and skewer; brush with oil if cut.	Cook over direct heat, turning once, until browned but not falling apart, 5 to 10 minutes.	Top with Traditional (or any other) Pesto (page 27) or Miso 5-Minute Drizzle Sauce (page 23).
Winter squash	Use butternut, acorn, or pumpkin; peel and seed; cut into ¹/₂-inch slices or 1¹/₂-inch cubes and skewer; brush with oil.	Cook over indirect heat, turning occasionally, until the flesh is very tender all the way through, 20 to 25 minutes; finish by browning over direct heat if you like.	Top with Brown Butter (page 56) or Spiced 5-Minute Drizzle Sauce (page 22).

❸ For the most part, use direct heat to cook the vegetables, but wait a bit if the fire is too hot or the vegetables will char. Move the vegetables around as needed and use indirect heat for large or dense items like a whole sweet potato or winter squash; this allows the interior to cook without drying too much or the exterior charring. Until you get the hang of grilling, watch them and move them to a cooler part of the grill if necessary. If you're grilling a variety of vegetables, be sure to start with the ones that take the longest to cook and add them incrementally, saving the quickest-cooking ones for last. But don't be overly concerned about the timing; because grilled vegetables are also delicious at room temperature, it's okay to pull them off as they are done while the rest catch up. (That said, to ensure perfect doneness you can always parboil the vegetables that take longest to cook—potatoes or winter squash, for example—and finish them on the grill with shorter-cooking vegetables.)

❹ Apply barbecue or other sweet sauce or coating toward the end of cooking so it has time to glaze but not burn. Serve the vegetables hot, at room temperature, or chilled, with lemon wedges if you like.

The Vegetable Lexicon

Here, arranged alphabetically, are the basics on the most common vegetables. In each entry, the basic information points you to the preferred cooking method and is then followed by slightly more elaborate recipes. The entire section is designed to foster flexibility, with a line in each recipe and vegetable entry offering possible substitutions. The Fruit Lexicon begins on page 381.

Artichokes and Cardoons

Artichokes are the unopened flower buds of a domesticated thistle. The petals (we call them "leaves") are tough and spiked and surround the choke. The prized heart is at the base of the bud and is attached to the thick stem, which is also edible.

Round, bulbous globe artichokes are the most common. So-called baby artichokes have more tender leaves and no chokes, so they can be eaten whole. But not all small artichokes are baby artichokes. The best are fully mature artichokes that grow at the base of the plant; unless you shop close to the source or they're marked accurately, what you see most often are small artichokes that grow on side branches and are labeled *baby*. These are not as tender and have a semideveloped choke that must still be removed. They're really good; but they're not the same thing.

You can boil whole artichokes, but I prefer steaming because they don't become as waterlogged (make sure not to burn the pot dry during the long cooking time). Eating the leaves is fun: Scrape off the flavorful meat using your front teeth. The closer you get to the center, the more tender the leaves; the soft inner leaves can be eaten in bunches, but avoid the furry needlelike choke (it got its name for a reason!) and any spiky tips. To cut to the chase, trim away the leaves and scrape away the choke with a spoon to get the delicious heart. Hearts and baby artichokes can be sautéed, braised, fried, roasted, or grilled whole, halved, or sliced. Canned, jarred, and frozen artichokes are usable but really don't taste much like fresh ones.

Cardoons, a relative of artichokes, are hard to find here in the United States outside of farmers' markets (they're easy to grow, though). To cook them, strip the dark green leaves from the white to pale green ribbed stalks, then cook and eat the stalks; the flavor is a cross between artichokes and celery.

Buying and storing: Artichokes are available throughout the year but are abundant and cheaper in spring and fall. They come in an array of sizes, but you're looking for those that are heavy for their size, don't look withered or dried out (the outer leaves should snap off), and squeak when you squeeze them. Refrigerate, wrapped loosely in plastic.

Cardoons should have firm stems and dark green leaves. Store wrapped loosely in plastic in the refrigerator.

Preparing: For whole artichokes: Cut off the pointed tips of the leaves with scissors or cut off the whole top third or so; a large serrated knife is best, but any heavy knife will do. Use a paring knife to peel around the base and cut off the bottom $1/4$ inch; pull off the toughest exterior leaves. To remove the choke before cooking, cut in half or into quarters and scrape it out or cut off the tops of the leaves, pry open the central petals, and pull and then scrape out the choke with a spoon.

For artichoke hearts: Cut off as much of the tops of the leaves as possible or halve the artichoke lengthwise. Use a paring knife to trim and peel the base; scrape out the choke with a spoon.

For small or baby artichokes: If tender enough, they can be eaten whole, but sometimes they benefit from the tops of the leaves and the exterior leaves being trimmed. Otherwise, halve, quarter, or slice lengthwise. Remove the choke if necessary.

Most canned and jarred artichokes are already cooked and can be added whole or chopped or sliced in the last few minutes of cooking; heavily marinated or brined ones can be rinsed to wash away some of the liquids' flavor. Thaw frozen artichokes and use as you would fresh, but cut the cooking time roughly in half; they're already partially cooked.

For cardoons, strip the stems of leaves and discard them; use a knife to remove the tough fibers that run down the vegetable lengthwise (like celery) and then chop into 2-inch pieces.

F Fast   **M** Make Ahead   **V** Vegetarian

Raw artichokes and cardoons discolor very quickly when cut and darken quite a bit when cooked; rub with half a lemon or dip in water with a couple tablespoons of lemon juice or vinegar immediately after cutting to minimize darkening.

Best cooking methods: Steaming (for whole, hearts, or cardoons), sautéing (only for baby artichokes and hearts), and braising (only for baby artichokes and hearts or cardoons).

When are they done? For whole artichokes: when the outer leaves pull off easily. Taste one: If the meat comes off easily and is tender, the artichoke is done. For artichoke hearts: When very tender; pierce with a skewer or thin-bladed knife to check, then taste to be sure. For cardoons: when tender enough to be pierced easily with a skewer or thin-bladed knife.

Other vegetables to substitute: In terms of flavor, artichokes and cardoons are somewhat interchangeable. There is no real substitute for artichoke hearts in recipes.

Steamed Artichokes

MAKES: 4 servings
TIME: 45 minutes

The best way to cook artichokes simply is to steam them, because you don't have to wait for a big pot of water to boil and, more important, they don't become soggy. You can add some gentle seasonings to the pot if you like: Tarragon or thyme, onion or garlic, lemon juice or vinegar

QUARTERING ARTICHOKES

1

2

3

4

(STEP 1) Use scissors or a sharp knife to cut the pointed tips from the tops and outer leaves of the artichokes. (STEP 2) Cut the artichokes in half. (STEP 3) Then cut it into quarters. (STEP 4) Scrape the fuzzy choke out of each quarter.

are all good. Serve the artichokes hot, warm, at room temperature, or cold.

> 4 large or 12 small artichokes
>
> Melted butter, Vinaigrette (page 199), mayonnaise (to make your own, see page 41), or lemon wedges, olive oil, and salt for serving

❶ Follow the illustrations below for preparing whole artichokes.

❷ Rig a steamer (see page 20) and put the artichokes bottom up in it. Cover and cook for 20 to 40 minutes. Sample an outer leaf; when it pulls away easily and its meat is tender, they're done.

❸ Drain them upside down for a minute or two longer before serving hot; store upside down if you plan to serve them later. Serve hot with melted butter, at room temperature with vinaigrette, cold with mayonnaise, or at any temperature with lemon and/or olive oil and salt.

Sautéed Artichoke Hearts

MAKES: 4 servings
TIME: 40 minutes

If you have very small ("baby") artichokes, you need not remove the choke. But cleaning four large artichokes won't take you more than 10 minutes. Dredging in flour makes the hearts crisp, but it's optional.

You can use canned or jarred artichoke hearts, but the flavor will not be the same; rinse them gently first.

PREPARING WHOLE ARTICHOKES

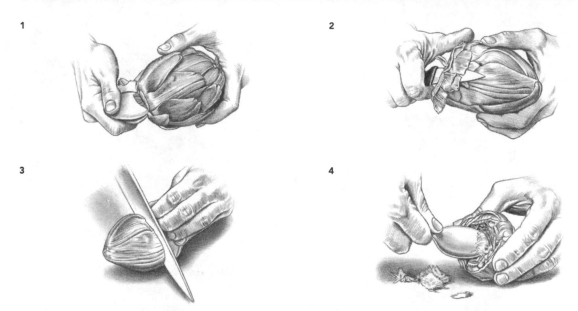

(STEP 1) Peel off tough outer leaves. (STEP 2) Trim around the bottom of the artichoke. (STEP 3) If you want to cook only the bottom, cut off the top half of the leaves. (STEP 4) Then scoop out the choke. If you want to leave the artichoke whole but remove the choke, trim the leaves somewhat less, force them open, then use a long spoon to scrape out the choke. (This will take a little while to do completely but isn't difficult.)

F Fast   **M** Make Ahead   **V** Vegetarian

4 large or 12 very small artichokes

4 tablespoons butter or extra virgin olive oil

1 clove garlic, lightly smashed (optional)

All-purpose flour for dredging

Salt and freshly ground black pepper

Chopped fresh parsley leaves for garnish

Lemon wedges for serving

❶ If you're using large artichokes, cut them into halves or quarters; remove the leaves and the choke and trim the bottom. If the artichokes are very small, simply peel off all the leaves and trim the bottom; you can ignore the choke. (Either way, reserve the leaves for another use if you like.) Drop them into boiling salted water to cover, lower the heat, and simmer just until tender, from as little as 6 minutes for little ones to as long as 20 for larger ones. Plunge immediately into ice water.

❷ Drain and dry the hearts. (At this point, you may refrigerate the artichokes in a covered container for up to 2 days.) Put the butter or oil in a large, deep skillet over medium-high heat. When the butter foam subsides or the oil is hot, add the garlic if you're using it, then dredge each heart lightly in flour. Shake off the excess; put in the skillet. Sprinkle with salt and pepper and cook, turning once or twice, until nicely browned all over, about 10 minutes.

❸ Serve hot, garnished with parsley and accompanied by lemon wedges.

Sautéed Artichoke Hearts with Mustard Seeds. Add 1 tablespoon mustard seeds with the artichokes.

Braised Artichoke Hearts

MAKES: 4 servings
TIME: 45 minutes

This dish is just as good at room temperature as it is hot. If you double it, you'll have leftovers for tossing with pasta or rice, topping pizzas, or mixing into frittatas.

Other vegetables you can use: true baby artichokes (just trimmed) or small artichokes (trimmed and with the choke removed); any winter squash, which will make things easier (and probably less expensive); cardoons, chopped into 1- to 2-inch pieces and started at Step 2.

$1/2$ cup freshly squeezed lemon juice (from 3 or 4 lemons)

Salt and freshly ground black pepper

6 large artichokes or about 3 cups frozen artichoke hearts (no need to thaw them first)

3 tablespoons extra virgin olive oil

1 tablespoon minced garlic

Chopped fresh parsley leaves for garnish

❶ Put the lemon juice in a bowl with $1/2$ cup water and sprinkle with a little salt and pepper.

❷ If you're using whole artichokes, trim down to the hearts as described in Step 1 of Sautéed Artichoke Hearts (previous recipe). As you finish each artichoke, cut the heart into thick slices and toss them with the lemon water.

❸ Put the oil in a large, deep skillet over medium heat. Add the garlic and cook, stirring frequently, until it softens, about a minute. Use a slotted spoon or tongs to transfer the artichokes to the pan, saving the liquid in the bowl. Cook, stirring occasionally, until the slices begin to soften a bit, about 5 minutes. Add the reserved liquid, bring to a boil, and cover; turn the heat down to medium-low. Cook until tender, about 10 minutes, shaking the pan every now and then to toss the artichokes.

❹ Taste and adjust the seasoning and serve hot or at room temperature, garnishing just before serving.

Roasted Artichoke Hearts. Heat the oven to 425°F. In Step 3, increase the oil to $1/4$ cup, put it in a large ovenproof skillet or roasting pan, and set it in the oven. When the oil gets hot, transfer the artichoke slices and garlic to the pan and toss to coat in the oil. (Save the lemon water.) Roast until the slices release from the pan, 10 minutes or so, then turn them and continue roasting until tender, another 10 minutes. Transfer the artichokes from the pan to a serving platter and set the pan over medium-high heat. Add about a cup of the lemon water and stir up any brown bits from the bottom of the pan. Cook until the mixture thickens a bit; after a few minutes, stir in the parsley, then taste and adjust the seasoning. Pour the sauce over the artichokes and serve immediately or at room temperature.

Vinegar-Braised Artichoke Hearts. I like this best with sherry vinegar, but you can also use white wine or even balsamic vinegar: Simply use vinegar instead of the lemon juice in either the main recipe or any of the variations.

Braised Artichoke Hearts with Potatoes. The potatoes will soak up most of the liquid, leaving you with a thick vegetable stew: Peel and steam or boil 2 large waxy potatoes (or use leftovers). Cut them into large chunks. Increase the extra virgin olive oil to $1/4$ cup and the minced garlic to 2 tablespoons. In Step 3, when you lift the lid to check the artichokes, fold in the potatoes. Cover the pan and proceed with the recipe, cooking just long enough for the potatoes to reheat.

Braised Artichoke Hearts with Lots of Roasted Garlic. Roast and peel 2 or 3 heads of garlic (see page 303). In Step 3, when you lift the lid to check the artichokes, fold in the garlic. Cover the pan and proceed with the recipe.

Braised Artichoke Hearts with Ham, Wine, and Lemon. Substitute white wine for the $1/2$ cup water in Step 1. Add 3 tablespoons finely chopped smoked ham, pancetta, or prosciutto; reduce the olive oil to 1 tablespoon. In Step 3, cook the ham until the fat is rendered and the bits are beginning to crisp, then proceed with the recipe.

11 Terrific Stir-Ins for Braised Artichoke Hearts

1. Pitted green or black olives
2. Dried fruit: especially golden raisins, currants, cherries, or apricots
3. Nuts: especially walnuts, almonds, or hazelnuts
4. Different herbs: especially chives, basil, tarragon, mint, or chervil
5. Arugula or spinach leaves
6. Oven-Dried or Oven-Roasted Plum Tomato (page 362 or 361) slices or bits
7. Chopped fresh tomato
8. Crumbled cooked bacon or sausage
9. Virtually any Crouton (page 877)
10. Grated or crumbled cheese: especially Parmesan, feta, blue, or Fresh Cheese, the Easy Way (page 824)
11. Anchovies

Baby Artichokes with Potatoes, Garlic, Olives, and Shrimp

MAKES: 4 servings
TIME: About 45 minutes

Artichokes and potatoes go well together and cook up at about the same time, whether you boil, steam, sauté, or braise them. The only trick is to keep the pieces about the same size. If you can't find baby artichokes, use artichoke hearts.

Other vegetables you can use: cardoons, fennel, or cabbage.

At least 10 baby artichokes, 1 to $1/2$ pounds

5 tablespoons extra virgin olive oil

1 pound waxy potatoes, peeled and cut, if necessary, into 1-inch chunks

Salt and freshly ground black pepper

Several sprigs fresh thyme

$1/2$ cup dry white wine, stock (to make your own, see pages 157–159), or water

1 cup small black olives, like Niçoise, pitted if you like

1 pound shrimp, peeled

1 tablespoon minced garlic

  F Fast   **M** Make Ahead   **V** Vegetarian

Chopped fresh parsley leaves for garnish

Lemon wedges for serving

1 Prepare the artichokes by trimming the stem, cutting off the pointed tips, removing the tough leaves, and cutting in half; remove the choke if necessary. As each is finished, drop into a bowl of cold water with about 10 percent vinegar or lemon juice.

2 Put 4 tablespoons of the olive oil in a large skillet over medium heat. Drain the artichokes and add them along with the potatoes. Cook until they're glossy and beginning to soften; do not brown.

3 Sprinkle with salt and pepper, then add the thyme and liquid. Bring to a boil, cover, and adjust the heat so the mixture simmers. Cook just until the potatoes are tender, about 15 minutes, then uncover and raise the heat again. Stir in the remaining olive oil, olives, shrimp, and garlic and cook, stirring occasionally, until the shrimp are pink, 3 to 5 minutes. Taste and adjust the seasoning, then garnish with parsley and serve hot or warm, with the lemon wedges.

Asparagus

Asparagus is a member of the lily family whose (usually) green spears can be delicate and thin to thick and stubby. Once a springtime favorite that's now available year-round at supermarkets, the best remains local; check out farmers' markets from as early as February in the South through May or June in the North. There are also white and purple varieties, more common in Europe but occasionally seen here. White asparagus is grown underground or under cover to prevent greening; it's more delicate in texture and has a subtle nutty flavor. (It's rare, though, that it's grown well enough here to justify its high price.)

Easy to prepare and quick cooking, asparagus is most often steamed but is also wonderful roasted or grilled; don't overcook it in any case. Serve hot, at room temperature, or cold; add leftovers to eggs or salads.

PREPARING ASPARAGUS

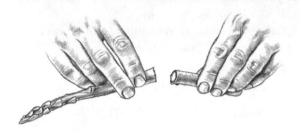

Snap off the bottom of each stalk; they will usually separate naturally right where the woody part ends.

All but the thinnest asparagus are best when peeled.

Buying and storing: Any color and size of asparagus can be good; look for plump, unshriveled spears with undamaged tips and avoid spears that look woody. Often markets store them stem down in cold water, which is fine but not entirely necessary. Store wrapped loosely in plastic in the refrigerator; use as soon as possible.

Preparing: Snap off the bottom of each spear; it will naturally break in the right place. I recommend peeling asparagus (use a vegetable peeler) to remove the fibrous skin from just below the tip to the base; this step isn't necessary if the spears are pencil thin.

Best cooking methods: Steaming, sautéing, roasting, and grilling are all fine.

When is it done? Asparagus is done when you can easily insert a skewer or thin-bladed knife into the thickest part of the stalk. Undercooked asparagus is crisp; overcooked asparagus is mushy.

Other vegetables to substitute: green or wax beans, sugar snap peas, or broccoli raab.

Asparagus Done Simply

MAKES: 4 servings

TIME: 15 minutes

F **M** **V**

You can cook asparagus almost any way you like; the simplest ways are boiling (or simmering or poaching; you can call it whatever you like), steaming, or microwaving. This recipe includes all three.

To prepare asparagus ahead of time, cook it by one of the methods below, then shock it (see page 240); drain well, cover, and refrigerate for up to 2 days. Finish by heating the asparagus through with a little butter or olive oil, or try one of the ideas on page 242.

If the asparagus are pencil thin, you don't need to peel them, and they will cook fast, really fast—like a couple of minutes. If they're thicker, peeling from the base of the flower to the end of the stalk is worth it; they'll be much more tender and less fibrous. This isn't essential, but I do think it's worth the effort.

1½ to 2 pounds asparagus, trimmed and peeled

Salt

To boil: Lay them down in a skillet that can hold the spears without crowding, cover with salted water, cover the skillet, and turn the heat to high. Cook just until the thick part of the stalks can be pierced with a knife.

To steam: Stand them in a pot with an inch of salted water on the bottom (it's nice, but hardly essential, to tie them in a bundle first), or just lay them flat or at an angle. Cover and turn the heat to high, then cook just

until the thick part of the stalks can be pierced with a knife.

To microwave: Lay them in a microwave-safe plate or shallow bowl with about 2 tablespoons of salted water; cover with a lid. Microwave on high for 3 minutes, shake the container, and continue to microwave at 1-minute intervals just until the thick part of the stalks can be pierced with a knife.

Roasted, Broiled, or Grilled Asparagus

MAKES: 4 servings

TIME: 30 minutes

F **M** **V**

Asparagus are terrific when blasted with high heat; if you haven't had them browned, you're in for a treat. If you have a grill going, try grilling them; thick spears, especially, are wonderful this way (thin ones are good too, but you have to be careful not to let them fall through the grill grates). If the grill is not fired up, roast or broil them.

Other vegetables you can use: green beans or broccoli raab (parboiled; see page 237) or snow peas.

1½ to 2 pounds asparagus, trimmed and peeled

1 to 2 tablespoons extra virgin olive oil or butter (melted if you're grilling)

Salt

Lemon wedges for serving

1 Heat the oven to 450°F or heat a charcoal or gas grill or a broiler to medium-high heat and put the rack 4 to 6 inches from the heat source. If you're roasting or broiling, put the asparagus in a shallow roasting pan and drizzle with a tablespoon or two of oil or dot with butter; sprinkle with salt. If you're grilling, brush the asparagus with oil or butter and sprinkle with salt. Put

 Fast   Make Ahead   **V** Vegetarian

the asparagus in the oven or broiler or on the grill (you might want to skewer thin asparagus in little bunches to make turning easier and keep them from falling through the grates or just be sure to lay them crosswise).

2 Cook, turning the spears once or twice, just until the thick part of the stalks can be pierced with a knife, 10 to 15 minutes. Broiling time will be shorter, 5 to 10 minutes total. Serve hot or warm, with lemon.

10 Classic Ways to Serve Any Simply Cooked Asparagus

Once you have simply cooked asparagus—by any of the techniques described in the two preceding recipes—drain it if necessary and serve in any of these ways. Many are good in combination, as you'll quickly discover.

1. Drizzle with extra virgin olive oil or melted butter (Brown Butter, page 56, is super). Any Compound Butter (page 32) or Flavored Oil (page 26) is also good.
2. Squeeze lemon or lime juice over it or drizzle with vinegar.
3. Douse with any Vinaigrette (pages 199–202).
4. Put a dollop of mayonnaise (to make your own, see page 41) or Hollandaise Sauce (page 59) alongside.
5. Top with minced or finely crumbled Hard-Boiled Eggs (page 791).
6. Serve with a hefty topping of Sautéed Mushrooms (page 313).
7. Garnish with minced Hard-Boiled Egg (page 791), toasted bread crumbs (see page 876), or minced Roasted Red Peppers (page 330).
8. Fresh herbs, especially tarragon and chervil. Or try reheating asparagus in butter or oil to which some curry powder has been added and cooked for 30 seconds or so.
9. Wrap cooked room-temperature or cold spears in thinly sliced prosciutto or other good ham.
10. Top with shaved Parmesan cheese and bake as a gratin (see page 248) if you like.

Stir-Fried Asparagus

MAKES: 4 servings
TIME: 20 minutes

Among the simplest and most straightforward of stir-fries and one of the best made with only one vegetable. Other vegetables you can use: green beans, snow peas, or chopped broccoli.

1½ to 2 pounds asparagus, trimmed, peeled, and cut into 2-inch lengths

2 tablespoons peanut oil or neutral oil, like grapeseed or corn

1 tablespoon minced garlic

2 small dried red chiles (optional)

1 tablespoon soy sauce

1 teaspoon dark sesame oil (optional)

Salt if necessary

1 If the asparagus is thick, follow the directions for Asparagus Done Simply (page 258), undercooking the asparagus a bit and shocking them (see page 240), then draining and drying. If they're thin, no precooking is necessary.

2 When you're ready to cook, heat a large skillet over high heat for 3 or 4 minutes. Add the oil, wait a few seconds, then add the asparagus. Cook, stirring, for a minute, then stir in the garlic and the chiles if you're using them. Cook until the asparagus is dry, hot, and beginning to brown, 5 to 10 minutes.

3 Add 2 tablespoons water and the soy sauce and continue to cook until the asparagus is tender. Add the sesame oil if you're using it and salt if necessary (the soy may have been salty enough) and serve.

Stir-Fried Asparagus with Squid or Shrimp. Increase the oil to 3 tablespoons. In Step 2, start with 2 tablespoons of oil; when it's hot, add 8 ounces cleaned and sliced squid or peeled shrimp. Cook, stirring frequently, until just opaque, 3 to 5 minutes, depending on their size. Remove with a slotted spoon. Add the remaining oil to the pan and proceed with the recipe, stirring in the squid or shrimp just as the asparagus begins to brown.

7 Ideas for Stir-Fried Asparagus

As with any stir-fry, this one has infinite variations. Some of my favorites:

1. Add 1 tablespoon fermented black beans, soaked for a few minutes in dry sherry, rice wine, or water to cover, along with the soy sauce.
2. At the last minute, add up to 8 ounces of cooked meat, fish, or poultry, like roast chicken or pork or grilled shrimp.
3. Add 2 tablespoons minced fresh ginger along with the garlic.
4. Cook the asparagus with about $^1/_2$ cup chopped onion and/or sliced red or yellow bell pepper.
5. Cook the asparagus with 4 to 6 halved shallots.
6. During the final minute of stir-frying, sprinkle with about $^1/_4$ cup chopped nuts, like peanuts, hazelnuts, cashews, or almonds.
7. Sprinkle with nam pla (Thai fish sauce) just before serving.

Avocados

Technically a fruit, the avocado is almost always used in a savory manner, though almost never cooked. And while it is loaded with fat, that fat is mostly monounsaturated, which is good. At its best, avocado flesh is a pretty light green, ultra-smooth, and creamy, with a rich and subtle flavor. It's perfectly complemented by acid in citrus fruit or a mild vinegar but easily overwhelmed by stronger flavors.

There are many varieties—from tiny to melon size—but we see mostly Hass and Fuerte. Hass are pear shaped, with dark green to black leathery, wrinkled skin; they're great for eating straight, spreading, or mashing. Fuerte are usually larger and have smoother green skin; generally, they're not as rich, but they're decent.

PREPARING AVOCADOS

1

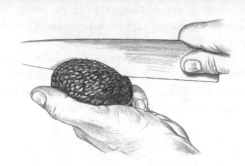

2

3

Pitting and peeling an avocado is easy. **(STEP 1)** Cut through the skin and flesh lengthwise to the pit, then rotate the avocado to cut all the way around it. Twist the halves apart. **(STEP 2)** A careful, swift, and not-too-forceful strike of the knife will implant it in the pit, which will then lift out easily. **(STEP 3)** Finally, scoop out the flesh with a spoon.

F Fast   **M** Make Ahead   **V** Vegetarian

Buying and storing: Avocados ripen nicely at room temperature, so they are often sold nearly rock hard. Give them a gentle squeeze before buying: You don't want mushy spots or bruises; when one is ripe, it will yield to pressure. To ripen avocados more quickly, put them in a paper bag at room temperature. Store ripe avocados in the refrigerator for up to a week.

Preparing: Slice avocados in half from pole to pole around the seed; peel off the skin or scoop out the flesh with a spoon. If you want to store half, wrap it with the pit intact and refrigerate—the pit helps keep it from turning brown.

Avocados discolor quickly when cut; sprinkle with lemon or lime juice immediately after cutting to minimize darkening.

Best cooking method: Best eaten raw (sliced, mashed, or puréed, especially in Fast Avocado Soup, page 153). Delicious simply spread on bread and sprinkled with lemon or lime juice or a mild vinegar and salt.

When is it done? Avocado needs no cooking, though you can halve or slice and grill it until lightly browned.

Other fruits or vegetables to substitute: None.

Bean Sprouts

Just about every bean, seed, or grain can be sprouted, but we most commonly see mung and soybean sprouts. Mung bean sprouts have pale yellow or green heads with fairly long, semitranslucent, plump tails. They are available fresh in bags or bulk (also canned, but these aren't worth the tin they're in).

Soybean sprouts—also sold in bags or loose—are larger; their heads are a yellow split soybean, and the white crunchy tails are about 2 inches long. Soybean sprouts are often used in Korean dishes and offer a more substantial crunch than mung bean sprouts.

Buying and storing: Look for bean sprouts at Asian markets if they're not at your supermarket; they should be plump, crisp, and fresh-smelling sprouts (avoid those that are slimy or off-smelling). Store loosely wrapped in

plastic or in the store's packaging in the refrigerator; use as soon as possible.

Preparing: Some people like to trim the tails, but it's hardly necessary. Rinse and drain the sprouts well.

Best cooking method: Stir-frying, added at the last minute.

When are they done? When just heated through and still crunchy.

Other vegetables to substitute: There is no substitute for bean sprouts, but if it's bland crunch you're after, try bamboo shoots or water chestnuts.

Stir-Fried Bean Sprouts

MAKES: 4 servings
TIME: 10 minutes

One of the quickest things you can get on the table and endlessly versatile too. Serve it with Steamed Sticky Rice, Thai Style (page 459) or crisp outer leaves of romaine or iceberg lettuce for wrapping the beans into crunchy little bundles.

Other vegetables you can use: shredded or julienned zucchini; kale or collards cut into ribbons.

2 tablespoons peanut or neutral oil, like grapeseed or corn

1 pound bean sprouts (about 4 cups), trimmed if you like

1 tablespoon minced fresh ginger or garlic

2 tablespoons any spice blend, like five-spice powder or any curry powder (to make your own, see pages 66–68)

Salt and freshly ground black pepper

❶ Put the oil in a deep skillet over medium-high heat. When it's hot, add the bean sprouts and the ginger, turn the heat up to high, and toss to coat.

❷ Let the vegetables cook until they begin to sputter, after a couple minutes, then stir them around a bit.

Sprinkle with the spice blend and salt and pepper and stir again, adding a few drops of water if they're starting to stick to the pan. Stir once or twice more. The bean sprouts are ready when barely tender and the spices are fragrant, which takes just a couple minutes. Taste and adjust the seasoning and serve hot or at room temperature.

Chile-Sesame Stir-Fried Bean Sprouts. Substitute 1 tablespoon dark sesame oil for half the peanut oil, and Chipotle Paste (page 74) for the spice blend.

Beet Greens

The leafy greens attached to the beetroot, these are closely related to chard and often mistaken for it; you can treat them identically. Both the stems and the leaves are edible; young and very tender ones can be tossed into salads, while tougher leaves and stems must be cooked.

Buying and storing: Most often beet greens are available only when attached to the root (it's two vegetables in one!). Look for greens that are fresh looking, vibrantly colored, and unwilted. Remove the greens from the root and store wrapped loosely in plastic in the refrigerator; use as soon as possible.

Preparing: Wash the greens well. Leave small leaves whole and chop or tear larger ones into strips or pieces.

Best cooking methods: Steaming and braising. See Chard (page 284) for ways to use them.

When are they done? When wilted and tender.

Other vegetables to substitute: Chard (often called *Swiss chard*) or turnip greens.

Beets

Beets come in a beautiful array of colors—from dark red to golden yellow to striped—sizes, and shapes, from the familiar round to long and thin to tiny. They're all wonderful, and the beet's sweet and earthy flavor is just as good served cold or room temperature as it is hot. Additionally, raw beets keep for weeks in the fridge and for several days once cooked.

If staining from the vibrantly colored juices is the only thing keeping you from cooking beets, check out the preparation tips that follow and Beets Baked in Foil (below) for a nearly stain-free beet experience.

Buying and storing: Unlike most root vegetables, size doesn't matter when it comes to beets; large ones are almost always just as good as small, and they're easier to handle. One sure sign of freshness is the presence of the greens (which are edible and lovely); if they're fresh looking, the roots are fresh too. Beets should be nearly rock hard when you buy them; avoid any that are soft. Remove all but an inch of the greens (cook the greens as soon as you can) and store the roots wrapped loosely in plastic in the refrigerator. They keep for weeks.

Preparing: Scrub well; leave on an inch or so of the greens to minimize bleeding. (Peel the beets after they've cooked.)

Best cooking methods: Baking in foil, roasting, and braising and glazing.

When are they done? When tender all the way through; pierce with a skewer or thin-bladed knife to check. Slight overcooking is usually preferable to undercooking.

Other vegetables to substitute: Turnips, rutabagas, carrots, or parsnips.

Beets Baked in Foil

MAKES: 4 servings
TIME: About 1 hour

This is the single best method for cooking beets. It produces beets that are firm and not at all waterlogged. And

F Fast   **M** Make Ahead   **V** Vegetarian

it's easy, neat, and convenient: Once the beets are cooked, you can eat them or store them as is. When you're ready, unwrap and peel them, then slice them and heat in butter or oil, eat them cold, or proceed with any other beet recipes.

Since large beets take longer to cook than small ones, try to buy beets that are roughly equal in size. And you don't have to roast them individually wrapped. If you're planning to use them all at once, right away, just put in a roasting pan or heavy skillet, cover, and proceed as directed.

Other vegetables you can use: turnips or rutabagas or other root vegetables.

4 large or 8 medium beets, about 1¹/₂ to 2 pounds

❶ Heat the oven to 400°F. Wash the beets well. Wrap them individually in foil and put them on a cookie sheet or roasting pan.

❷ Bake, undisturbed, for 45 to 90 minutes, until a thin-bladed knife pierces one with little resistance (they may cook at different rates; remove each one when it is done). Use in Precooked Vegetables in Butter or Oil (page 240) or any of the variations on Beets Done Simply or other recipes that call for cooked beets; or store, refrigerated, for a couple of days before using.

Beets Done Simply

MAKES: 4 servings
TIME: About 45 minutes

Faster than the preceding recipe, and almost as convenient, but a little messier, or at least potentially so. Use these in Precooked Vegetables in Butter or Oil (page 240) or any other recipe that calls for cooked beets; or store, refrigerated, for a couple of days before using in any recipe for cooked beets. For a nice salad, cool a bit and toss with Vinaigrette (page 199).

Other vegetables you can use: turnips, rutabagas, daikon, or parsnips.

Salt

4 large or 8 medium beets, 1¹/₂ to 2 pounds, with about 1 inch of their tops

To boil: Bring a large pot of water to a boil; salt it. Put the beets in the water, cover the pot, and turn the heat to medium-low. Simmer until the beets can be pierced with a thin-bladed knife, 30 to 45 minutes. Drain and drop into ice water; drain again and peel.

To steam: Rig a steamer (see page 20) and put the beets in the steamer above an inch or two of salted water. Cover and cook for 30 to 45 minutes, until they can be pierced with a thin-bladed knife. Drain and drop into ice water; drain and peel.

To microwave: Put the beets in a microwave-safe plate or shallow bowl with about 2 tablespoons salted water; cover with a lid. Microwave on high for 6 minutes, shake, and continue to microwave at 2-minute intervals, just until they can be pierced with a thin-bladed knife. Drain and drop into ice water; drain and peel.

Beets with Nut Butter. Especially good with pistachios, but walnuts are also good: While the beets cook, put ¹/₄ cup extra virgin olive oil in a skillet over medium heat. Add 4 cloves garlic, smashed and peeled, and cook for about a minute, then add 1 cup shelled pistachios or walnuts; cook, stirring often, for about 3 minutes. Cool for a bit, then purée in a blender or food processor until smooth, adding more oil as necessary; the consistency should be thinner than that of peanut butter, just pourable. Chop the beets into bite-sized pieces and drizzle with the nut butter.

Beets with Sour Cream and Chives. Slice the beets and arrange on a platter; top with dollops of sour cream and sprinkle with chopped chives. Serve at room temperature or warm.

Beet Rösti with Rosemary

MAKES: 4 servings
TIME: 20 minutes

An almost unbelievably sweet and wonderful side dish. The sugar in the beets caramelizes, and the flavors of the rosemary, beets, and butter meld beautifully. With thanks to Michael Romano, who shared this recipe with me 20 years ago. If you like, dust with any spice blend (to make your own, see pages 65–69) just before serving.

Other vegetables you can use: carrots, parsnips, rutabagas, kohlrabi, sweet potatoes, or turnips.

About 1¹⁄₂ pounds beets

1 teaspoon coarsely chopped fresh rosemary

1 teaspoon salt

¹⁄₄ cup all-purpose flour

2 tablespoons butter

1 Trim the beets and peel them as you would potatoes; grate them in a food processor or by hand. Put a medium to large nonstick skillet over medium heat.

2 Toss the grated beets in a bowl with the rosemary and salt, then add about half the flour; toss well, add the rest of the flour, then toss again.

3 Put the butter in the skillet and heat until it begins to turn nut brown. Scrape the beet mixture into the skillet and press it down with a spatula so it fills the pan. Adjust the heat so that the pancake sizzles without burning and cook, shaking the pan occasionally, until the bottom of the beet cake is nicely crisped, 6 to 8 minutes. Slide the cake out onto a plate, top with another plate, invert the two plates, and slide the cake back into the pan. Continue to cook, adjusting the heat if necessary, until the second side is browned, another 6 to 8 minutes. Cut into wedges, sprinkle with more salt if you like, and serve.

Beet Rösti with Parmesan. Omit the rosemary if you like and add 1 cup grated Parmesan.

Carrot and Onion Rösti. Substitute carrots for the beets and add 1 large onion. Grate the onion and squeeze out the excess liquid.

Bok Choy and Other Asian Greens

The Cantonese word *choy* can be translated loosely as "cooking greens," and there's a slew of choy to choose from, especially at Asian markets. To keep things simple, only the most common are included here, but don't let that stop you from trying more; almost all can be prepared and cooked the same way.

Bok choy (also called *pak choi* or *Chinese white cabbage*) is sold everywhere now. It grows in large, loose heads with wide, crisp white stalks and flat dark green leaves. Its flavor is mildly cabbagey and fresh, and the stalks take on a marvelous, almost creamy texture once cooked. The miniature jade-green variety—called *Shanghai* or *baby bok choy*—is equally delicious and tender, plus it's cute.

Gai lan (aka *Chinese broccoli, kale,* or *mustard greens*) is not often found at supermarkets but is abundant at Asian markets. It's similar to broccoli raab, with long, narrow stalks, smooth, thick, and green with dark green leaves and small clusters of flower buds. The flavor is a cross between broccoli and mustard greens but milder than either. (Choy sum, aka *white flowering cabbage,* and yao choy, aka *green flowering cabbage,* look and cook very much like gai lan.)

Tatsoi (also called *spoon cabbage*) is often found in various spring or mesclun lettuce mixes and is good both raw and quickly cooked. The leaves are small (about 2 inches across), dark green, and round, with a delicate light green stem—looking rather like a spoon. The flavor is mild with a hint of mustard.

Buying and storing: The leaves and stems should be fresh looking and crisp; avoid any with yellowing leaves. Bok choy's stems should be unbroken and bright white.

Look for unopened flowers on gai lan, choy sum, and yao choy, though a few open buds are okay. Store wrapped loosely in plastic in the refrigerator.

Preparing: Wash and remove any damaged or yellowing leaves.

Bok choy: Cut off the root end and the inch or so above it and slice or chop it as you like. If the stems are thick, separate them from the leaves and start by cooking them for a couple minutes before the leaves. Shanghai bok choy can remain whole.

Gai lan: Trim any dried-out or tough stems and separate the leaves from the stems (the stems take longer to cook).

Tatsoi: Cut the stems from the root end if they are still attached.

Best cooking methods: Steaming and sautéing or stir-frying.

When is it done? When the stems are tender but still crisp (especially for gai lan) and the leaves are wilted.

Other vegetables to substitute: Cabbage, kale, or broccoli can replace any of the Asian greens.

Quick-Cooked Bok Choy

MAKES: 4 servings
TIME: 30 minutes

Bok choy is, dare I say it, unique. Not the greens; they're about the same as those of many other cabbages. But its fat, thick stems become creamy and tender during cooking in a way that you cannot duplicate with other greens. This makes even this simple treatment for bok choy just wonderful; the slightly more complicated variations are even better.

Other vegetables you can use: Napa or other Chinese cabbages, white chard (probably the closest in texture but with different flavor), broccoli raab, or gai lan.

1 head bok choy, about 1½ pounds

3 tablespoons peanut or neutral oil, like grapeseed or corn

Salt and freshly ground black pepper

½ cup chicken, beef, or vegetable stock (see pages 157–158) or water

1 Cut the leaves from the stems of the bok choy (see the illustration on page 308). Trim the stems as necessary, then cut them into pieces 1 inch or so long and, if you like, the greens into pieces or ribbons; rinse everything well. Put the oil in a large skillet over medium-high heat; a minute later, add the stems and cook, stirring occasionally, until they just lose their crunch, about 3 minutes. Add the greens, a sprinkling of salt and pepper, and about ½ cup water or stock.

2 Cook, stirring occasionally, until the liquid evaporates and the stems are very tender, about 10 minutes more; add a little more water if necessary. Serve immediately.

Bok Choy, Mediterranean Style. In Step 1, use extra virgin olive oil. In Step 2, when the greens are tender, stir in 2 tablespoons capers, ¼ to ½ cup chopped pitted olives (preferably oil-cured), and 1 tablespoon minced garlic. Cook for another minute or so, stirring, then add freshly squeezed lemon juice or balsamic vinegar to taste (start with 1 tablespoon). Cook for another 5 seconds and serve.

Bok Choy with Black Beans. While cooking the stems in Step 1, soak 1 tablespoon fermented black beans in 2 tablespoons sherry, rice wine, or water. In Step 2, when the greens are tender, stir in the beans and their liquid, along with 2 teaspoons minced garlic and 1 teaspoon minced fresh ginger. Cook for another minute or so, stirring, then add 1 tablespoon soy sauce, or to taste. Cook for another 5 seconds and serve.

Seared Baby Bok Choy with Bacon Vinaigrette

MAKES: 4 servings
TIME: 25 minutes

An unusual side dish that's lovely with a nice piece of salmon or other full-flavored fatty fish. You can grill the bok choy instead of sear it if you like.

Other vegetables you can use: bok choy, Napa cabbage (cut lengthwise into long spears), endive (halved lengthwise), or radicchio (quartered).

1½ to 2 pounds Shanghai or (baby) bok choy, parboiled and shocked (see page 240)

6 ounces bacon, finely chopped

3 tablespoons sherry vinegar or white wine vinegar

Salt and freshly ground black pepper

5 tablespoons neutral oil, like grapeseed or corn

1 Cut the bok choy in half lengthwise and put the cut side down on paper towels to drain. Meanwhile, put the bacon in a small pan over medium-high heat. When it starts to sizzle, reduce the heat to medium and cook until crisp and the fat is rendered, about 10 minutes. Turn off the heat, add the vinegar, sprinkle with salt and a good amount of pepper, and then whisk in 3 tablespoons of the oil (it won't fully emulsify). Set aside.

2 Put a large, wide skillet over high heat. When it's very hot, add the remaining neutral oil and put a few pieces of bok choy, cut side down, in the pan (it will spatter, so be careful). Do not overcrowd the pan; you want at least an inch on all sides between the pieces. Cook the bok choy without moving it until the cut side is dark brown and slightly charred. Continue cooking the bok choy in batches.

3 Pile the seared bok choy on a platter in a serving bowl; give the bacon vinaigrette a stir and drizzle it over the bok choy. Serve warm or at room temperature.

Seared Baby Bok Choy with Chile Vinaigrette. Substitute 1 or 2 tablespoons minced fresh chiles (like jalapeño or Thai) or hot red pepper flakes for the bacon and rice vinegar for the sherry vinegar. Instead of Step 2, mix the chiles, vinegar, ¼ cup neutral oil, and 1 teaspoon each minced garlic and sugar to make the vinaigrette.

Seared Baby Bok Choy with Black Vinegar. Sweet and smoky, Chinese black vinegar is available at most Asian markets: Substitute 1 tablespoon each minced fresh ginger and garlic for the bacon and black vinegar for the sherry vinegar. For Step 2, cook the ginger and garlic in the 3 tablespoons oil for a minute (don't brown it), then drizzle in the black vinegar and a couple teaspoons soy sauce.

Asian Greens, Chinese Restaurant Style

MAKES: 4 servings
TIME: 15 minutes

The common bright green stir-fry of Chinese restaurants, usually made with gai lan; it doesn't get much simpler.

Other vegetables you can use: broccoli raab, any other Asian green, collard greens, kale, or broccoli.

1½ pounds gai lan

2 tablespoons peanut oil

1 tablespoon minced garlic (optional)

¼ cup oyster sauce

1 Separate the leaves and stems of the gai lan; cut the stems into 2-inch lengths.

2 Heat a large skillet over high heat for 3 or 4 minutes. Add the oil, wait a few seconds, then add the leaves of the greens and toss until they wilt, about 3 minutes; put on a platter. Add the stems, the garlic if you're using it, and about ¼ cup water. Toss until the stems are crisp-tender, 3 to 5 minutes. Remove them and put on top of the greens. Top with oyster sauce and serve.

 Fast   Make Ahead   **V** Vegetarian

Asian Greens with Thickened Soy Sauce. Instead of the oyster sauce, make a slurry by whisking 2 teaspoons cornstarch into $1/4$ cup soy sauce; substitute this mixture for the oyster sauce.

Broccoli and Broccoli Raab

Broccoli Rape, Rabe, or Rapini

A longtime regular in Italian cuisine, broccoli was barely known in the United States until the 1920s. Now, of course, it's available year-round at every supermarket (there's no reason to buy frozen), and with good reason: It's easy to grow and ship, inexpensive and flavorful, a snap to cook, delicious, and nutritious. It also can be prepared in a variety of ways, which makes it a great standby vegetable to keep in the fridge. Serve it raw, lightly cooked, or completely cooked.

The related broccoli raab is one terrific vegetable: strong, bitter, unusually delicious, and easy to prepare and cook. It has elongated stems with small flower heads surrounded by variously sized spiky leaves.

Buying and storing: For broccoli, look for tightly packed florets with no yellowing, on top of a crisp stem. For broccoli raab, look for bright green color, crisp stems, and unwilted leaves. Avoid those with more than a few tiny yellow flowers blooming; they'll be too bitter. Store wrapped loosely in plastic in the refrigerator; broccoli will keep for several days, but use broccoli raab as soon as possible.

Preparing: For broccoli: Strip the stalk of leaves, if any (these are perfectly edible; cook along with the tops if you like). Cut off the dried-out end of the stalk and use a vegetable peeler or paring knife to peel the tough outer skin as best you can without going crazy. (To peel with a paring knife, hold the broccoli upside down; grasp a bit of the skin right at the bottom between the paring knife and your thumb. Pull down to remove a strip of the skin.) Cut the stalk into equal-length pieces and break the head into florets.

For broccoli raab: Trim the dry ends of the stems and pull off any yellowing or wilted leaves. Parboil and shock (see page 240) to preserve the green color or for quicker final cooking.

Best cooking methods: Steaming, microwaving, boiling, braising, braising and glazing, sautéing, and stir-frying are all good. For broccoli, regardless of the method, it often makes sense to cook the stalks longer than the florets; just start them a minute or two earlier.

When is it done? For broccoli: It's a matter of taste. When bright green, it's still crisp and quite chewy, and some people like it that way. Cook it another couple of minutes and it becomes tender; overcook it and it becomes mushy and begins to fall apart. Try cooking until a skewer or thin-bladed knife can easily pierce the stalk. For broccoli raab: It's done when you can insert a skewer or thin-bladed knife into the thickest part of the stalk. Undercooked broccoli raab is too crisp; overcooked broccoli raab is mushy.

Other vegetables to substitute: Broccoli and cauliflower are almost always interchangeable; or use broccoflower, Romanesco, or broccoli raab in place of broccoli. For broccoli raab: broccoli, asparagus, gai lan, or turnip or mustard greens.

Stir-Fried Broccoli

MAKES: 4 servings
TIME: 30 minutes

Broccoli is ideal for stir-fries: You get crunch from the stems (cut them fairly thin so they'll cook quickly) and tenderness from the florets. And you can use broccoli as a main ingredient in just about any stir-fry recipe in this book. If you have leftover cooked broccoli, by all means use it, but stir-fry no longer than it takes to heat the broccoli through.

Other vegetables you can use: cauliflower, broccoflower, Romanesco, or broccoli raab.

2 tablespoons peanut or neutral oil, like grapeseed or corn

About 1½ pounds broccoli, trimmed, the stems cut into pieces no more than ⅛ inch thick

Salt

1 teaspoon sugar

1 cup stock (to make your own, see pages 157–160) or water

2 tablespoons soy sauce

1 Put the oil in a large, deep skillet over medium-high heat. When it's hot, add the broccoli, raise the heat to high, and cook, stirring, until it's bright green and glossy and beginning to brown, about 5 minutes.

2 Sprinkle with salt and add the sugar and stock. Stir and continue to cook until almost all the liquid evaporates and the broccoli is tender, about 5 minutes more. Stir in the soy sauce, taste and adjust the seasoning, and serve.

Stir-Fried Broccoli with Dried Shiitakes. Soak about ¼ cup dried black (shiitake) mushrooms in 1 cup very hot water until tender, changing the water if it cools off before they're tender. Drain them, reserving the liquid, trim them, and cut them up. In Step 1, add the mushrooms along with the broccoli. In Step 2, add 1 teaspoon minced garlic and 1 teaspoon minced fresh ginger along with the salt and sugar. Stir for 15 seconds before adding the strained mushroom-soaking liquid in place of the stock.

Breaded Sautéed Broccoli or Cauliflower

MAKES: 4 servings
TIME: 30 minutes

There are many ways to sauté vegetables with bread crumbs (or nuts; see the variations) for a little added crunch, and they're all good. Whether the bread crumbs stick to the vegetable is not all that important, because you'll get the crunch no matter where the bread crumbs wind up, but for the prettiest presentation, use the egg.

Other vegetables you can use: green beans or Brussels sprouts.

1 pound broccoli or cauliflower (about 1 medium head), trimmed, broken into florets of any size, parboiled, shocked (see page 240), and patted dry

All-purpose flour for dredging (optional)

2 or 3 eggs, lightly beaten (optional)

1 cup bread crumbs, preferably fresh (page 876), for dredging

4 tablespoons butter or extra virgin olive oil

Salt and freshly ground black pepper

Chopped fresh parsley leaves for garnish

Lemon wedges for serving (optional)

1 If you're using the egg, roll each piece of broccoli or cauliflower in the flour, then dip in the egg, then in the bread crumbs. If you're not using the egg, just roll the pieces in the bread crumbs, patting to help them adhere.

2 Put the butter or oil in a large skillet over medium heat. When the butter melts or the oil is hot, begin to add the broccoli or cauliflower. Cook the pieces, adjusting the heat so the bread crumbs brown without burning on all sides and sprinkling with salt and pepper as they cook.

3 When the broccoli or cauliflower is browned and tender, anywhere from 8 to 12 minutes, garnish with parsley and serve, with lemon wedges if you like.

Breaded Sautéed Broccoli or Cauliflower with Onion and Olives. Use olive oil; before cooking the broccoli or cauliflower, add 1 cup chopped onion (red is nice); cook, stirring occasionally, until the onion softens, 3 to 5 minutes. Proceed as directed, adding ½ to 1 cup pitted black olives (oil-cured are good here, though you can use whatever you like) and ½ teaspoon hot red pepper flakes, or to taste.

Breaded Sautéed Broccoli or Cauliflower with Garlic, Vinegar, and Capers. Use olive oil; add 1 tablespoon

F Fast   **M** Make Ahead   **V** Vegetarian

chopped garlic along with the broccoli or cauliflower. Just before it's done, add 1 tablespoon red wine, sherry, or other vinegar and about a tablespoon of capers.

Breaded Sautéed Broccoli or Cauliflower with Feta and Mint. Instead of the parsley, chop about $1/2$ cup fresh mint leaves. In Step 3, when the broccoli or cauliflower is ready, stir in $1/2$ cup finely crumbled feta cheese and the mint.

Breaded Sautéed Broccoli or Cauliflower with Almonds, Raisins, and Saffron. Golden raisins look particularly nice here: In Step 3, when the broccoli or cauliflower is just beginning to turn golden, stir in a pinch of saffron, $1/4$ cup chopped almonds, and $1/4$ cup raisins. Proceed with the recipe, cooking and stirring until everything is browned.

Roasted Broccoli Gratin with Blue Cheese

MAKES: 4 servings
TIME: About 30 minutes

Roasting broccoli isn't typical, but the tops brown nicely while the stems remain somewhat crisp and the flavor is wonderful. Feel free to switch out the cheese if blue isn't your favorite; Emmental, Gruyère, goat cheese, Gouda, or any good melting cheese works fine.

Other vegetables you can use: cauliflower, broccoflower, Romanesco, asparagus, or broccoli raab.

$1^1/2$ to 2 pounds broccoli, trimmed, the stems cut into pieces no more than $1/8$ inch thick

3 tablespoons extra virgin olive oil

Salt and freshly ground black pepper

2 cloves garlic, smashed in the skins

1 cup crumbled blue cheese

$1/2$ cup bread crumbs, preferably fresh (page 876)

① Heat the oven to 425°F. Put the broccoli in a bowl, drizzle on the olive oil, and sprinkle with salt and pepper while tossing to coat; transfer to a gratin dish or any ovenproof dish. Nestle the garlic in the broccoli and cook until the tops are browning and the stems are crisp-tender, 10 to 15 minutes.

② Remove the dish from the oven and fish out the garlic. Sprinkle the top of the broccoli with the blue cheese and then the bread crumbs. Return to the oven and cook until the cheese is bubbling and the bread crumbs are golden brown, about 10 minutes. Serve hot or warm.

Roasted Broccoli Gratin with Creamy Cheese Sauce. Omit the blue cheese. Add 1 recipe Mornay (Cheese) Sauce (page 58). For Step 2, mince the garlic and mix it into the cheese sauce if you like, then pour it over the broccoli.

Roasted Broccoli Gratin with Hollandaise Sauce. Omit the blue cheese. Add 1 recipe Hollandaise Sauce (page 59). For Step 2, pour the sauce over the broccoli, sprinkle on the bread crumbs, and run under the broiler until the bread crumbs are browned. Serve immediately.

Broccoli Raab with Sausage and Grapes

MAKES: 4 servings
TIME: About 30 minutes

This is more of a main course than a side dish, a simple Italian classic and one of my favorites. Without the grapes, and thinned with a little water or stock, it can serve as a sauce for pasta. Substitute regular broccoli if you like.

Other vegetables you can use: broccoli, gai lan, turnip or mustard greens, asparagus, kale, or collards.

About 1½ pounds broccoli raab, trimmed and cut up

About 1 pound sweet, garlicky sausage

2 cloves garlic, slivered

About ½ pound seedless grapes

Salt and freshly ground black pepper

❶ Boil or steam the broccoli raab for about 3 minutes, until it is bright green and beginning to get tender. Drain and plunge it into ice water for a few moments and drain again. (At this point, you may refrigerate the broccoli raab, wrapped well or in a covered container, for up to 2 days.)

❷ Cook the sausage over medium heat in a large, deep skillet, pricking it with a fork or thin-bladed knife a few times and turning from time to time, until it is nicely browned, 10 to 15 minutes.

❸ Remove the sausage from the skillet (don't worry about it being done) and cut it into bite-sized pieces. Return it to the skillet over medium heat; cook, turning occasionally, until all sides of the sausage are nicely browned, about 5 more minutes.

❹ Squeeze the excess liquid from the broccoli raab and chop it coarsely. Add it to the skillet along with the garlic and cook, stirring occasionally, for 3 or 4 minutes. Add the grapes and heat through. Check for salt and sprinkle liberally with pepper. Serve immediately.

Broccoli Raab with Garlic and Pecorino. Omit the sausage, increase the garlic to 4 cloves, and substitute 1 cup grated pecorino cheese for the grapes. Skip Steps 2 and 3; toss with pecorino just before serving.

Broccoli Raab with Anchovies. Omit the sausage and substitute 8 anchovies (rinsed if salt packed) for the grapes. Put 3 tablespoons extra virgin olive oil in a wide skillet over medium heat. When hot, add the garlic and anchovies and cook for about 2 minutes. Skip Steps 2 and 3 and proceed with the recipe.

Brussels Sprouts

Believed to have been developed in Belgium (hence the name), these miniature cabbages are super when cooked properly. The tiny heads grow in vertical rows on long, thick stalks; occasionally they're sold still on the stalk, which isn't necessarily a sign of freshness, though it looks nice.

Buying and storing: Brussels sprouts are a winter vegetable, best from early fall through early spring. Smaller is better; reject any with yellow or loose leaves or those that are soft or not tightly packed. Store wrapped loosely in plastic in the refrigerator.

Preparing: Trim the hard edge of the stem and remove any loose leaves. Cut, slice, or leave whole.

Best cooking methods: Roasting, sautéing, and simmering.

When are they done? When just tender enough to pierce easily with a skewer or a thin-bladed knife. Do not overcook.

Other vegetables to substitute: Any cabbage.

Braised and Glazed Brussels Sprouts

MAKES: 4 servings
TIME: 30 minutes

Sometimes I like to brown Brussels sprouts a bit, which is why this braise-and-glaze technique is a little different from the general description on page 238 and deserves a special recipe. Leave the Brussels sprouts whole—they'll look beautiful and be less likely to overcook.

Other vegetables you can use: shredded green or red cabbage, broccoli, or cauliflower.

3 tablespoons butter or extra virgin olive oil

1 pound Brussels sprouts, trimmed

¹/₂ cup or more stock (to make your own, see pages 157–159), white wine, or water

Salt and freshly ground black pepper

1 Combine the butter, Brussels sprouts, and stock in a deep skillet with a tight-fitting lid, sprinkle with salt and pepper, and bring to a boil. Cover and adjust the heat so the mixture simmers; cook until the sprouts are just tender, 5 to 10 minutes, checking once or twice and adding liquid as needed.

2 Uncover and raise the heat to boil off all the liquid so that the vegetables become glazed and eventually browned. Resist the urge to stir them frequently; just let them sizzle until golden and crisp, then shake the pan and loosen them to roll them over. It's okay if some sides are more well done than others. Taste and adjust the seasoning and serve hot or at room temperature.

Sautéed Brussels Sprouts with Bacon

MAKES: 4 servings
TIME: 30 minutes

Perhaps the most delicious way to cook Brussels sprouts; their affinity for bacon is legendary.

Other vegetables you can use: cabbage (shredded), green or wax beans, chicory or its relatives (see page 298).

6 ounces bacon, chopped

1 pound Brussels sprouts

Salt and freshly ground black pepper

1 tablespoon balsamic vinegar or freshly squeezed lemon juice

1 tablespoon chopped fresh thyme (optional)

1 Put the bacon in a large skillet over medium-high heat. When it starts to sizzle, reduce the heat to medium

and cook until crisp and the fat is rendered, 5 to 10 minutes. Meanwhile, trim the hard edge of the stem from the Brussels sprouts, then cut each one into thin slices or shreds; you can do this on a mandoline, with the blade side of a box grater, or with a knife. Or cut them into quarters.

2 Add the sprouts and ¹/₄ cup water to the pan with the bacon; sprinkle with salt and pepper, turn the heat to medium, and cover. Cook, undisturbed, until nearly tender, about 5 minutes.

3 When the sprouts are ready, uncover and raise the heat back to medium-high. Cook, stirring occasionally, until any remaining water evaporates and the sprouts are fully tender, another 5 to 10 minutes. Stir in the vinegar and the thyme if you like and serve.

Sautéed Brussels Sprouts with Hazelnuts. Omit the bacon, add ¹/₂ cup chopped toasted hazelnuts (see page 317), and substitute ¹/₄ cup chopped fresh mint or dill for the thyme. In Step 2, heat 3 tablespoons extra virgin olive oil and then add the sprouts. Proceed with the recipe. Sprinkle on the hazelnuts and herbs with the vinegar or lemon juice in Step 3.

Sautéed Brussels Sprouts with Caramelized Onions. Substitute 1 large onion, thinly sliced, for the bacon. Start cooking the onion in 2 tablespoons butter or extra virgin olive oil while you prepare the sprouts. Cook the onion until browned, then proceed with the recipe.

Roasted Brussels Sprouts with Garlic

MAKES: 4 servings
TIME: 45 minutes

Brussels sprouts must be cooked thoroughly, but not until they're mushy; they're best when the insides are tender but not soft. And they're ideal, I think, when the exterior is crisp. This combination of sautéing and roasting does the trick nicely, and these sprouts are good when very, very dark brown, almost burned.

Other vegetables you can use: red cabbage (I like it cut into wide ribbons) or wedges of radicchio.

1/4 cup extra virgin olive oil

1 pound Brussels sprouts, trimmed and halved

5 cloves garlic, peeled, or more to taste

Salt and freshly ground black pepper

1 tablespoon balsamic vinegar

1 Heat the oven to 450°F. Put the oil in a large ovenproof skillet over medium-high heat. When it shimmers, arrange the sprouts in one layer, cut side down. Toss in the garlic and sprinkle with salt and pepper.

2 Cook, undisturbed, until the sprouts begin to brown, 3–5 minutes, then transfer to the oven. Cook, shaking the pan occasionally, until the sprouts are quite brown and tender, about 30 minutes.

3 Taste and adjust the seasoning. Drizzle with the vinegar, stir, and serve hot or warm.

Creamed Brussels Sprouts, Two Ways

MAKES: 4 servings
TIME: About 30 minutes

The first of these two Brussels sprouts dishes is based on a more traditional European dish, while the second—bolder and spicier—features Indian flavors.

2 tablespoons butter

2 shallots, finely chopped

1 bay leaf

1 sprig fresh thyme

1 cup cream or half-and-half

Salt and freshly ground black pepper

1 pound Brussels sprouts, trimmed and halved

Pinch freshly grated nutmeg

1 Put the butter in a medium pot over medium heat. When the butter is melted, add the shallots and cook until translucent, about 2 minutes. Add the bay leaf, thyme, cream, and a good sprinkling of salt and pepper; bring to a bubble and add the sprouts. Cover and cook until the sprouts are tender, about 20 minutes.

2 Stir in the nutmeg and check the seasoning, adding more salt and pepper as necessary, and serve.

Brussels Sprouts in Coconut Milk. Substitute 3 tablespoons neutral oil, like grapeseed or corn, for the butter; 1 tablespoon yellow or black mustard seeds for the shallots; 1 tablespoon Hot Curry Powder (page 66), or any similar spice blend, for the bay leaf and thyme; and coconut milk for the cream. Proceed with the recipe, toasting the mustard seeds in the oil for 20 seconds or so before adding the other ingredients. Omit the nutmeg.

Burdock

Gobo

The root of a thistle plant (and related to artichokes), burdock is sweet and earthy; in Japan, where it's most popular, it's often braised with carrots or other vegetables. The long, slender, and fibrous roots are often sold still covered in dirt—most often at Asian markets and health food stores—and are anywhere from 1 to 3 feet long.

Buying and storing: Look for dirt-coated pieces (it helps keep them fresh) that are firm and no more than an inch or so thick. Store (with the dirt on) wrapped loosely in plastic in the refrigerator; use as soon as possible.

Preparing: Scrub the dirt off the root just before using; peeling is not necessary. Trim the ends and crush and/or chop, slice, or shred as you like.

Raw burdock discolors very quickly when cut; rub with half a lemon or dip in water with a couple table-

F Fast   **M** Make Ahead   **V** Vegetarian

spoons of lemon juice or vinegar immediately after cutting to minimize darkening.

Best cooking methods: Braising and stir-frying.

When is it done? When it's tender but still crisp.

Other vegetables to substitute: Artichoke hearts and cardoons are similar in flavor; carrots and celery are similar in texture.

Quick-Braised Burdock and Carrots

Kinpira Gobo

MAKES: 4 servings
TIME: 15 minutes

If you've never tried burdock, this traditional Japanese dish is a nice introduction. Serve with plain white or brown rice or, for a less authentic—though delicious—approach, try tossing the finished dish with warm soba noodles.

Other vegetables you can use: in virtually any combination, potatoes, kohlrabi, parsnips, turnips, beets, or winter squash.

About 8 ounces burdock, peeled and julienned

2 teaspoons dark sesame oil

1 medium carrot, julienned

2 tablespoons soy sauce

1¹/₂ tablespoons mirin (or 2¹/₄ teaspoons honey mixed with 2¹/₄ teaspoons water)

1¹/₂ tablespoons sake

2 teaspoons sugar

2 teaspoons toasted sesame seeds (see page 317)

❶ Immerse the burdock in a bowl of water with a squeeze of lemon juice or a splash of vinegar so it doesn't turn dark. Drain just before adding it to the pan.

❷ Put the sesame oil in a small pan over medium-high heat. Add the burdock and cook for about 2 minutes. Add the carrot and cook until the burdock and carrot are just

tender. Add the soy sauce, mirin, sake, sugar, and sesame seeds and cook until about half the liquid remains, about 2 minutes. Turn off the heat and cool to room temperature or store, covered, in the refrigerator for up to 2 days.

Cabbage

Green Cabbage, Red Cabbage, Savoy Cabbage, and Napa Cabbage (for Chinese Cabbage, see Bok Choy)

When it comes to head cabbage, the best of the lot is Savoy, which has tender, crinkly, light green leaves. The elongated, mostly white, and ruffled Napa is also tender and lovely used raw. The smooth-leaf green and red varieties are decent, the red offering distinctive color, but they're tougher and often more strongly flavored. If you think you hate cabbage, try it raw or quickly cooked, like in a stir-fry or very lightly poached, before making a final judgment; you will be pleasantly surprised, especially if you've always been served overcooked cabbage.

Buying and storing: Look for tightly packed heads that are heavy for their size; avoid any with yellowing or loose leaves. Size is irrelevant in terms of flavor. (But how much will you actually use? Rare is the occasion that you'll need a 4-pound head.) Cabbage is available year-round (it thrives in cold weather), so there's no reason to buy canned or frozen. Store fresh in the refrigerator; it'll last for a couple of weeks.

Preparing: Remove the first layer or two of exterior leaves. Then use a thin-bladed knife to remove the core: Cut a cone-shaped section out of the stem end wider than the area of the core and pull it out. To shred the head, cut the cabbage into quarters (or eighths, depending on size) and cut crosswise into thin strips or use a mandoline. Napa cabbage can be cut crosswise whole to shred it.

Best cooking methods: Sautéing, stir-frying, and braising. Also, see Kimchi (page 230).

When is it done? When crisp-tender to soft but not mushy.

Other vegetables to substitute: Brussels sprouts, collards, bok choy (especially for stir-frying).

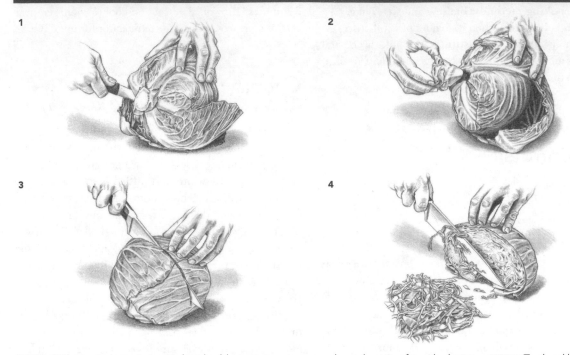

(STEPS 1–2) The easiest way to core a head cabbage is to cut a cone-shaped section from the bottom. **(STEP 3)** To shred head cabbage, first cut it into manageable pieces. **(STEP 4)** Cut thin sections across the head; they'll naturally fall into shreds. (You can also use a mandoline for this; see page 347.) If the shreds are too long, just cut across them.

Buttered Cabbage

MAKES: 4 servings

TIME: 20 minutes

Pretty great for a two-ingredient vegetable dish, especially when you consider that everyone pooh-poohs cabbage. Start with Savoy, don't overcook, and it'll be simply delicious. For extra flavor, melt the butter with a clove of garlic, some minced shallot, or a little good paprika. Serve with other relatively plain dishes, like Boiled Potatoes (page 337), Simplest Whole Roast Chicken, Six Ways (page 644), or Chickpeas in Their Own Broth (page 430).

Other vegetables you can use: Of course this is a basic vegetable preparation, but to keep it in the same spirit, think collards, kale, bok choy, and the like.

Salt and freshly ground black pepper

2 to 4 tablespoons butter, to taste

About 20 cabbage leaves (any kind)

1 Set a medium to large pot of water to boil and salt it well. Put the butter in a small saucepan over medium-

F Fast　**M** Make Ahead　**V** Vegetarian

low heat and melt it; if you let it brown a little bit, so much the better, but don't burn it.

② When the water boils, add the cabbage and cook, stirring every now and then, until it becomes tender, about 5 minutes. Remove with tongs or a slotted spoon and drain well; toss gently with the melted butter and serve.

Sautéed Cabbage with Balsamic Vinegar

MAKES: 4 servings

TIME: 20 minutes

Thin shreds of cabbage and minimal ingredients let you cook this dish in a flash. Tuck a small pile under any simply cooked meat, poultry, or fish for a silky and slightly acidic counterpoint.

Other vegetables you can use: any cabbage type, sliced Brussels sprouts, endive, or radicchio.

3 tablespoons extra virgin olive oil

6 cups shredded cabbage, preferably Savoy (about 1 small head)

1 tablespoon garlic slivers (optional)

Salt and freshly ground black pepper

2 tablespoons balsamic vinegar

Toasted pine nuts (see page 317) for garnish (optional)

Put the oil in a large, deep skillet over medium-high heat. When it's hot, add the cabbage and garlic; cook, stirring occasionally, until the cabbage softens and is only lightly browned, about 10 minutes. Sprinkle with salt, lots of pepper, and the balsamic vinegar; cook until the liquid has thickened a bit. Garnish with pine nuts if you are using them and serve hot.

Gingered Cabbage. Use Napa cabbage if possible. Substitute a neutral oil, like grapeseed or corn, for the olive oil and soy sauce for the balsamic vinegar. Add 1

tablespoon minced fresh ginger. Proceed with the recipe, garnishing with chopped fresh cilantro.

Cabbage Braised with Onions

MAKES: 4 servings

TIME: About 1 hour

Slow-cooked onions add sweetness to this dish, and the touch of cayenne makes it wonderfully spicy.

Other vegetables you can use: any cabbage, kale, chard, or collards.

2 cups sliced onion

3 tablespoons butter or olive oil

3 tablespoons tomato paste

$^1/_4$ teaspoon cayenne, or to taste

$1^1/_2$ to 2 pounds Savoy or other white cabbage, cored and shredded (see previous page)

Salt and freshly ground black pepper

① Put the onion in a large, deep skillet or casserole over medium-low heat. Cover and cook, stirring every 5 minutes, until the onion has given up its liquid and is almost sticking to the pan. Add the butter or oil, raise the heat to medium-high, and cook until the onion browns nicely, 5 to 10 minutes.

② Add the tomato paste, cayenne, $^1/_2$ cup water, and the cabbage and sprinkle with salt and pepper. Stir, then cover. Cook until the cabbage is tender but not mushy, about 30 minutes, stirring occasionally. Serve hot or warm.

Cabbage Braised with Wine and Nutmeg. Omit the onion, tomato paste, and cayenne. In Step 1, cook the cabbage in the oil until it starts to brown. Substitute white wine for the water and add it to the cabbage; then add 1 teaspoon brown sugar and $^1/_4$ teaspoon freshly grated nutmeg. Proceed with the recipe, cooking for another 15 minutes.

Cabbage Braised with Apples. Substitute 1 pound sweet apples, peeled, cored, and roughly chopped, for the onion; cook the apples, cabbage, and 3 cloves in butter until the cabbage is glossy, about 3 minutes. In Step 2, substitute stock or cider for the water if you like; omit the tomato paste and cayenne. Stir in 2 tablespoons apricot or raspberry jam and a few drops of lemon juice or cider vinegar to taste just before serving.

Cabbage Braised with Beer and Kielbasa. Substitute 1 pound sliced kielbasa sausages for the onion. In Step 1, turn the heat to medium-high and add the oil; cook the sausage until it's browned. In Step 2, omit the tomato paste and cayenne and substitute 1 bottle of beer for the water.

Sauerkraut with Juniper Berries

MAKES: 4 to 6 servings
TIME: 40 minutes

If possible, use prepared sauerkraut without preservatives (or homemade if you're lucky enough to have access to some); it's sold in bulk in specialty stores or in jars at some natural food stores. Substitute caraway seeds for the juniper berries if you like.

Other vegetables you can use: shredded fresh cabbage.

2 tablespoons butter or neutral oil, like grapeseed or corn

1 onion, sliced

1¹/₂ to 2 pounds sauerkraut, rinsed

1 bay leaf

1 tablespoon juniper berries, crushed lightly with the side of a knife, or caraway seeds

1 cup chicken, beef, or vegetable stock (to make your own, see pages 157–159), or not-too-dry white wine

❶ Put the butter or oil in a large, deep skillet over medium heat. When the butter melts or the oil is hot, add the onion and toss until it begins to wilt, about 3 minutes.

❷ Add the remaining ingredients, stir, and cook until some of the liquid bubbles away, 1 to 2 minutes. Cover, lower the heat, and cook until the sauerkraut is tender, about 30 minutes. Serve hot or warm (this can also be reheated successfully).

Sauerkraut with Juniper Berries and Ham. Add 8 ounces chopped thinly sliced cooked ham in Step 2 about halfway through the cooking.

Carrots

The most common of all root vegetables, carrots are cheap, versatile, and available year-round. And though we take them for granted, they taste good and they're sweet; you can eat them raw, of course, or cook them almost any way you like.

Buying and storing: Bagged carrots are a no-brainer—as long as they're hard and crisp. If the carrots have tops, the greens should be bright and unwilted; remove the tops before storing the carrots, as they draw out moisture and nutrients from the root. Avoid any carrot that is soft, flabby, cracked, or growing new leaves. Store wrapped loosely in plastic in the refrigerator; they keep for at least a couple of weeks.

So-called baby carrots are actually cut and peeled regular carrots; they're undeniably convenient, though they dry out more quickly than whole carrots.

Preparing: Peel with a vegetable peeler, then trim off both ends. Chop, slice, or grate as you like.

Best cooking methods: Steaming, braising, braising and glazing, and roasting.

When are they done? When tender but not soft. Taste and you'll know.

Other vegetables to substitute: Parsnips, beets, turnips, or celery root.

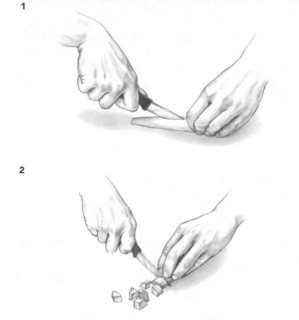

1

2

(STEP 1) To dice a carrot, cut it in half lengthwise, then into quarters or, if necessary, smaller sections. (STEP 2) Cut across the sections, as small as you like.

Quick-Glazed Carrots

MAKES: 4 servings

TIME: 30 minutes

 F **M** **V**

One of the most useful recipes ever and, sadly, one that is often overlooked. Carrots cooked this way are terrific hot, warm, or at room temperature (use oil instead of butter if you plan to serve them less than hot) and take to a wide variety of herbs and other simple treatments. If you can find real baby carrots—the very thin ones—just trim them quickly (don't even bother to peel them); they'll be super.

Other vegetables you can use: parsnips or turnips.

1 pound carrots, more or less, cut into coins or sticks

2 tablespoons butter or extra virgin olive oil

Salt and freshly ground black pepper

1 teaspoon freshly squeezed lemon juice (optional)

Chopped fresh parsley, dill, mint, basil, or chervil leaves for garnish (optional)

1 Combine the carrots with the butter or oil in a saucepan with a bottom no more than 6 inches in diameter. Sprinkle with salt and pepper. Add about $^1/_3$ cup water (or white wine or stock if you prefer). Bring to a boil, then cover and adjust the heat so the mixture simmers. Cook, more or less undisturbed, until the carrots are tender and the liquid is pretty much gone, 10 to 20 minutes.

2 Uncover and boil off the remaining liquid, then add the lemon juice if you're using it. Taste and adjust the seasoning; serve hot, or within an hour or two, garnished with the herb if you like.

Quick-Glazed Carrots with Orange and Ginger. Add 1 tablespoon minced or grated fresh ginger to the initial mix; use freshly squeezed orange juice in place of water. Garnish with a teaspoon or more of grated orange and/or lemon zest.

Quick-Glazed Carrots with Walnuts. Or pistachios: Add 1 tablespoon packed brown sugar, 1 teaspoon minced garlic (optional), and 1 cup walnut halves.

Balsamic-Glazed Carrots with Garlic. Use balsamic vinegar in place of the water and add 5 to 10 whole cloves garlic along with the carrots. Proceed with the recipe, adding water if the mixture dries out before the carrots are done.

Maple-Glazed Carrots. Add 3 tablespoons maple syrup and 2 tablespoons water to the mixture in Step 1. Add up to 1 cup pecans if you like.

6 More Ways to Jazz Up Quick-Glazed Carrots

1. Add $^1/_2$ cup or so chopped onion, shallot, scallion, or leeks.

2. Add ¹/₂ cup or so chopped pitted dates or raisins, dried currants, or dried tomatoes.

3. Whisk together 1 tablespoon soy sauce and 1 tablespoon miso, then stir this into the carrots just as they're done. (Use sake as the glazing liquid instead of the water if you have it.)

4. Add 1 cup or so peas, snow peas, or snap peas along with the carrots (thawed frozen are fine).

5. Add a tablespoon or so of any mild Chile Paste (pages 74–75); one made with ancho chiles would be ideal.

6. Add up to 1 cup whole or chopped nuts or seeds, like peanuts, pistachios, hazelnuts, cashews, sesame seeds, or sunflower seeds.

Shredded Carrots with Chiles and Chives

MAKES: 4 servings

TIME: 10 minutes

Fast and fiery hot, this stir-fry is perfect next to or even piled on top of a piece of grilled meat, poultry, fish, or tofu.

Other vegetables you can use: potatoes, parsnips, turnips, daikon radish, or jícama.

1 tablespoon peanut or neutral oil, like grapeseed or corn

1 tablespoon dark sesame oil

1 pound carrots, shredded

1 tablespoon minced fresh chile (like jalapeño or Thai), or hot red pepper flakes or cayenne to taste

20 chives, preferably Chinese ("garlic") chives, cut into 2-inch pieces

Soy sauce

❶ Heat a large skillet over high heat for 3 or 4 minutes. Add the oils, wait a few seconds, then add the carrots. Cook, stirring, for a minute.

❷ Stir in the chile and cook until the carrots are dry, hot, and beginning to brown, about 10 minutes. Add the chives and a dash of soy sauce; stir quickly to mix and serve.

Shredded Curried Carrots. Use all peanut or neutral oil. Add a tablespoon curry powder (to make your own Fragrant Curry Powder, see page 67) along with the chiles. Substitute ¹/₄ cup shredded coconut for the chives and salt for the soy sauce.

Roasted Carrots with Cumin

MAKES: 4 servings

TIME: 35 minutes

Sweet and totally delicious, with many wonderful variations possible.

Other vegetables you can use: parsnips, turnips, sweet potatoes, or winter squash.

1 to 1¹/₂ pounds baby carrots, green tops trimmed, or full-sized carrots, cut into sticks

3 tablespoons extra virgin olive oil

2 teaspoons cumin seeds

Salt and freshly ground black pepper

Heat the oven to 425°F. Put the carrots on a baking sheet and drizzle with the olive oil; sprinkle with the cumin and salt and pepper. Roast until the carrots are tender and browning, about 25 minutes. Serve hot, warm, or at room temperature.

Roasted Carrots with Fennel Seeds. Substitute fennel for the cumin.

Roasted Carrots with Pine Nuts. Omit the cumin. Add ¹/₄ cup pine nuts in the last 3 or 4 minutes of roasting.

Roasted Carrots with Sesame. Substitute 2 tablespoons peanut or neutral oil, like grapeseed or corn, and 1 tablespoon dark sesame oil for the olive oil. Substitute up to 2 tablespoons black and white sesame seeds for the cumin; add them in the last 3 or 4 minutes of roasting.

Roasted Carrots with Dates and Raisins. Omit the cumin. Add ¼ cup each golden raisins and chopped dates in the last 10 minutes of roasting. Garnish with chopped nuts, like pistachios, almonds, or walnuts, and a couple tablespoons chopped fresh mint leaves.

Cauliflower

Even normal white cauliflower is striking looking, and cooler still are the chartreuse-colored broccoflower and the outlandishly spiky, lime green Romanesco, both of which are hard to identify as either cauliflower or broccoli. A more recently developed type (read: genetically modified) is a peachy-colored, vitamin A–rich (like twenty-five times the amount of white) orange cauliflower. Whatever the type, all cauliflowers can be prepared in a variety of ways; serve them raw, lightly cooked, or completely cooked; steamed, boiled, roasted, sautéed, stir-fried, fried, or braised.

Buying and storing: Cauliflower should be heavy, beautifully white with no gray or brown spots, and crisp. Ideally, the leaves will still be wrapped around the flower. Store wrapped loosely in plastic in the refrigerator and use within a week or so.

Preparing: Remove the outer leaves and, if necessary, scrape off any gray or brown spots. You can cook it whole or separate it into florets before cooking. To separate into florets, begin at the base of the head and cut florets from the core, one after the other. The florets may in turn be broken or cut into smaller pieces if you like.

Best cooking methods: Steaming, braising and glazing, and roasting.

When is it done? When just tender enough to pierce with a skewer or thin-bladed knife. Overcooking is not as disastrous as it is with other members of the cabbage family, but naturally it's not desirable.

Other vegetables to substitute: Broccoli and cauliflower are almost always interchangeable.

First remove all the outer leaves.

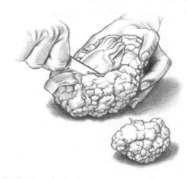

You can cook the head whole or cut it into florets.

Basic Steamed Cauliflower

MAKES: 4 servings
TIME: About 30 minutes

With cauliflower, steaming is better than simmering, not only because it's faster but because the cauliflower won't become waterlogged. (If you're in a hurry, cut the cauliflower up first.)

When you're done, you have several choices: Serve hot with butter, extra virgin olive oil, and/or lemon juice and garnish with parsley. Or shock (see page 240), put in a covered container, and either refrigerate for up to 2 days or break the cauliflower into florets and follow the directions for Precooked Vegetables in Butter or Oil (page 240) or use in other recipes. Or try any of the ideas in "11 Ways to Jazz Up Simply Cooked Vegetables" (page 242).

1 head cauliflower, about 1½ pounds, trimmed

① Put the cauliflower in a steamer above an inch or two of salted water.

② Turn the heat to high, cover and cook until the cauliflower is just tender enough to be pierced with a thin-bladed knife. (Because it's large, whole cauliflower will retain quite a bit of heat after cooking, so it should still be ever-so-slightly underdone when you remove it from the steamer.) Total cooking time will be 12 to 25 minutes, depending on the size of the head.

Cauliflower with Garlic and Anchovies

MAKES: 4 servings
TIME: 15 minutes

① **④**

Though the garlic and anchovies mellow here, this is still a highly flavorful sauce, a truly wonderful classic.

Other vegetables you can use: broccoli, broccoli raab, gai lan, chard, or kale.

1 recipe Basic Steamed Cauliflower (preceding recipe), slightly underdone

¼ cup extra virgin olive oil

2 to 10 anchovy fillets, chopped, to taste

1 tablespoon minced garlic

1 teaspoon hot red pepper flakes, or to taste (optional)

Minced fresh parsley leaves for garnish

① Break or cut the cauliflower into florets 1½ inches across or less.

② Combine the oil, anchovies, garlic, and red pepper if you're using it in a large, deep skillet over medium-low heat. Cook, stirring occasionally, until the anchovies begin to break up and the garlic begins to color, about 5 minutes.

③ Add the cauliflower and raise the heat to medium-high. Continue to cook, stirring, for about 5 minutes, until the cauliflower is coated with oil and heated through. Garnish with parsley and serve hot, warm, or at room temperature.

Cauliflower, Roman Style. Omit the anchovies. Add the grated zest and juice of a lemon along with the parsley just before serving.

Cauliflower with Warm Spices. Omit the anchovies. Add 1 tablespoon mustard seeds and 1 teaspoon cumin seeds along with the garlic and red pepper. Garnish with a sprinkle of lemon juice and chopped fresh cilantro.

Roasted Cauliflower with Roasted Red Peppers and Balsamic Vinegar

MAKES: 4 servings
TIME: 45 minutes, largely unattended

④ **♥**

Roasting toughens cauliflower and dries it out a bit. With many foods this result might not sound that desirable, but because cauliflower is often mushy and watery, these are good things. I like to get it nice and brown, and a bit of vinegar deepens its flavor.

Other vegetables you can use: broccoli spears or any root vegetable, cut into cubes and roasted.

1 large cauliflower, trimmed and separated into florets

3 tablespoons extra virgin olive oil

Salt and freshly ground black pepper

 Fast   Make Ahead   **♥** Vegetarian

2 Roasted Red Peppers (page 330), chopped

2 tablespoons balsamic or sherry vinegar, or to taste

Toasted pine nuts (see page 317) for garnish

1 Heat the oven to 400°F. Put the cauliflower in a roasting pan, drizzle with the oil, sprinkle with salt and pepper, and toss to distribute. Roast until it is just starting to soften and brown, about 15 minutes.

2 Add the roasted peppers and stir; continue roasting, stirring once or twice, until the cauliflower is tender and nicely browned, about 10 minutes more. (At this point, you may cool the cauliflower, cover it tightly, and refrigerate for up to 2 days. Return to room temperature before proceeding.)

3 When you're ready to serve, put the cauliflower in a large bowl, drizzle with the vinegar, sprinkle with the pine nuts, and toss. Taste and sprinkle with more salt if needed and lots of pepper, then serve hot, warm, or at room temperature.

Roasted Cauliflower with Raisins and Vinaigrette. Substitute $^1/_2$ cup raisins for the red peppers and $^1/_2$ cup Vinaigrette (page 199) made with balsamic or sherry vinegar for the balsamic vinegar. Omit the pine nuts and add chopped fresh parsley leaves. Proceed with the recipe, adding the raisins and vinaigrette in Step 3.

Mashed Cauliflower with Cheese

MAKES: 4 servings
TIME: 30 minutes

This is one dish that came out of the low-carb diet craze that is actually worth making. The diet set touted this dish as a mashed potato substitute, because of the fluffy, creamy texture. Whatever: It makes a good main or side dish. Use any good melting cheese you like here or all Parmesan for a less creamy, fluffier version.

Other vegetables you can use: broccoli.

1 large cauliflower, trimmed and separated into florets

1 cup milk or cream, plus more as needed

2 tablespoons butter

2 cups grated white melting cheese, like cheddar, Asiago, or Gruyère

Salt and freshly ground black pepper

$^1/_4$ teaspoon freshly grated nutmeg

Chopped fresh parsley leaves for garnish

1 Bring a large pot of water to a boil and salt it. Boil the cauliflower until very tender, about 15 minutes. Drain, reserving about a cup of the cooking water. Wipe the pot dry.

2 Put the milk, butter, and cheese in the pot; sprinkle with salt, pepper, and nutmeg. Turn the heat to medium-low and cook, stirring occasionally to keep the mixture from sticking, until the cheese and butter start to melt, 3 to 5 minutes. Stir in the cauliflower and mash with a fork or potato masher; stir well to combine. The mixture should be the consistency you like mashed potatoes. If it's not creamy enough, add a little of the cauliflower-cooking water or more milk or cream until it is. Taste and adjust the seasoning, garnish, and serve.

Manchurian-Style Cauliflower

MAKES: 4 to 6 servings
TIME: 30 minutes

This recipe—which inspired Stir-Fried Chicken with Ketchup (page 677)—comes courtesy of my friend Suvir Saran, one of this country's best and most consistent Indian chefs; he reports it's a dish that's closely associated with the Chinatown in Calcutta, where it's sold on the street, to be eaten off toothpicks. But whatever the case, it drives people nuts—it's just that good. It's a bit of work, a two-step process that includes deep-frying, but the work goes quickly and the dish will be the centerpiece of any table on which you put it.

Other vegetables you can use: broccoli.

Neutral oil, like grapeseed or corn, for deep-frying

3 eggs

²/₃ cup cornstarch

1 teaspoon freshly ground black pepper

Salt

1 large or 2 small heads cauliflower, trimmed and separated into florets

2 teaspoons finely minced garlic

1 cup ketchup, preferably homemade (page 51)

¹/₂ teaspoon cayenne, or to taste

❶ Put at least 2 inches of oil in a deep pan on the stove and turn the heat to medium-high; bring to 350°F (see "Deep Frying," page 19).

❷ Beat the eggs and cornstarch together until well blended in a bowl large enough to accommodate the cauliflower. Sprinkle the batter with 1 teaspoon salt and pepper, then add the cauliflower. Use your hands to toss until the florets are coated evenly.

❸ Fry the cauliflower in batches small enough not to crowd your pan or fryer and make sure to let the oil return to 350°F between batches. Fry until the florets take on a pale, sandy color, with a little brown mottling, about 5 minutes; transfer to paper towels to drain.

❹ Warm 1 tablespoon oil in a large nonstick pan over medium heat and immediately add the garlic. Cook the garlic for a minute or two, until fragrant but not colored, then add the ketchup. Cook, stirring, for about 5 minutes, until the sauce bubbles, thickens, and starts to caramelize around the edges of the pan. Add the cayenne; taste and add salt as necessary. Toss the cauliflower in the sauce until coated evenly and serve.

Roasted Cauliflower, Manchurian Style. Easier: Reduce the amount of oil to 3 tablespoons. Omit the eggs and cornstarch. Heat the oven to 400°F. Put the cauli-flower in a large baking pan or rimmed baking sheet, drizzle with 2 tablespoons of the oil, and sprinkle with 1 teaspoon each of the pepper and salt. Toss until well coated. Roast for about 30 minutes, stirring once or twice, until the cauliflower is tender and golden. During the last 5 minutes or so of roasting, prepare the sauce as described in Step 4 and proceed with the recipe.

Celery and Celeriac
Celery Root, Celery Knob

Celery is rarely cooked alone, which is a shame because it can be wonderful: Its flavor and texture are mellow, making it mild but still unusually flavored.

Celeriac is the large, often oddly shaped, bulbous and knotty root of a type of celery grown only for its root; its flavor is familiar but mellower when cooked. Celeriac is often used raw in salads (like in Celery Rémoulade, page 210), but it's also delicious boiled, sautéed, or roasted, and especially puréed and blended with mashed potatoes.

Buying and storing: Celery should be crisp, bright pale green, and tightly packed—I like celery with its leaves, which are terrific used like an herb. Avoid rubbery, wilted, or yellow celery. Store loosely wrapped in plastic in the refrigerator; celery keeps for about 2 weeks. For celeriac: Look for firm, heavy specimens with no soft spots; the smoother the skin, the easier it will be to peel. Don't mind the dirt that often covers them. As with most root vegetables, celery root keeps for a long time, but its flavor is most intense when it is firm and crisp; don't wait until it becomes flabby to eat it. Store wrapped loosely in plastic in the refrigerator.

Preparing: Trim the leaves from the celery (and reserve them for use as a garnish if you like) and cut off the bottom core or remove as many stalks as you need. String the celery if it's tough and very fibrous (see next page) or just cut it into whatever size pieces you need. For

F Fast   **M** Make Ahead   **V** Vegetarian

celeriac: It must be peeled; use a sharp knife rather than a vegetable peeler and acknowledge from the outset that you will lose a good portion of the flesh. If more than a few minutes will pass between peeling the celery root and using it, you might drop it into acidulated water (1 tablespoon lemon juice or vinegar per cup of water) to keep it from discoloring.

Best cooking methods: For celery: Braising, hands down. For celeriac: Boiling, sautéing, braising and glazing, and roasting.

When is it done? For celery: When good and tender; taste a piece. For celeriac: When it's soft.

Other vegetables to substitute: Celery and fennel are almost always interchangeable. For celeriac: Parsnips or turnips.

PREPARING CELERY

Celery is usually best when its "strings" are removed. Simply grasp the end of the stalk between your thumb and a paring knife and pull the strings down the length of the stalk.

Oven-Braised Celery

MAKES: 4 servings
TIME: 30 minutes

You can cook celery using the basic braise-and-glaze method (see page 328) but, because it's more fibrous than most other vegetables, it benefits from slightly longer cooking in somewhat more liquid. Cooked this way, celery becomes downright tender and mild.

Other vegetables you can use: fennel, which takes quite well to this treatment, and celeriac.

1½ pounds celery, more or less, trimmed

2 tablespoons extra virgin olive oil or butter

Salt and freshly ground black pepper

1 cup any stock (to make your own, see pages 157–160) or water

Chopped fresh parsley or dill leaves for garnish

❶ Heat the oven to 375°F. Cut the celery into pieces about 2 inches long. Put the oil or butter in a large, deep ovenproof skillet or flameproof gratin dish over medium heat. When the oil is hot or the butter is melted, add the celery and cook, stirring occasionally, for about 2 minutes. Sprinkle with salt and pepper and add the stock; bring to a boil and put in the oven.

❷ Cook until the celery is very tender, about 15 minutes. If much liquid remains, cook a little longer (in the unlikely event that it dries out before the celery becomes tender, add a little more liquid). Garnish with the herb and serve hot or warm.

Braised Celery with Tomato, Olives, and Capers. In Step 1, add 2 tablespoons minced onion or shallot along with the celery. In the last 5 minutes of cooking, stir in 1 tablespoon drained capers, ½ cup pitted and chopped black olives, and 1 cup seeded and chopped tomato (drained canned is fine). Garnish with the herb and serve.

Braised Celery with Buttered Almonds. Use butter for the celery. While the celery is cooking, lightly brown 1/2 cup blanched, slivered almonds in 2 tablespoons additional butter. Proceed with the recipe, and when the celery is done, toss it with the buttered almonds and serve.

Pan-Roasted Celeriac with Rosemary Butter

MAKES: 4 servings

TIME: 40 minutes

This recipe is simple but full of flavor; if you use bacon or pancetta and its rendered fat instead of butter, it's even richer. Note the variation, which can double as a delicious dressing for turkey or any poultry.

Other vegetables you can use: parsnips, rutabaga, turnips, potatoes, or carrots.

 4 tablespoons (1/2 stick) unsalted butter

 2 sprigs fresh rosemary, sage, or thyme

 2 cloves garlic, peeled

 2 pounds celeriac, trimmed, peeled, and cubed

 Salt and freshly ground black pepper

 1 teaspoon minced fresh rosemary leaves

1 Put the butter in a large skillet over medium heat. When melted, add the rosemary and garlic and let sizzle gently until fragrant, about 2 minutes. Don't let the rosemary brown; adjust the heat as needed.

2 Add the celeriac; it should be in a single layer on the bottom of the skillet with some space between pieces (work in batches if necessary). Cook, turning the celeriac a few times, until it's soft and golden brown on all (or most) sides, about 30 minutes. (Remove the rosemary and garlic when it gets browned.)

3 Sprinkle with salt and pepper and the minced rosemary; stir and serve.

Pan-Roasted Celeriac and Croutons. Add 1 recipe Real Croutons or Garlic Croutons (page 877) along with the rosemary in Step 3. Serve immediately.

Chard

Swiss Chard

Chard is beautiful, with dark green and sometimes ruffled leaves and stems that may be brightly colored crimson red, orange, yellow, or stark white. It's related to the beet, whose greens (see page 262) can be used just like chard.

Chard's strong flavor comes from the presence of oxalic acid, which is in spinach and rhubarb; here it's offset by sweetness. Young and very tender stems and leaves can be used raw in salads, while tougher ones must be cooked (they're classic in both omelets and quiches).

Buying and storing: Chard is usually named by the color of its stem; those with white stems are called simply *chard, Swiss chard,* or sometimes *green chard;* there's also red chard and rainbow chard (most if not all of the color disappears when cooked). All can be either thick or thin stemmed. Look for undamaged stems and deeply colored, unwilted leaves. Store wrapped loosely in plastic in the refrigerator; it will keep for several days.

Preparing: Wash it well and tear or chop the leaves. If the stems are very thick, strip the leaves from them before proceeding so you can cook the stems a couple minutes longer.

Best cooking methods: Steaming, braising, and sautéing. Regardless of the method, it often makes sense to cook thick stems longer than the leaves; just start them a minute or two earlier.

When is it done? When wilted and tender.

Other vegetables to substitute: Chard and beet greens are almost always interchangeable; or substitute dandelion, turnip greens, or spinach.

 Fast   Make Ahead   **V** Vegetarian

Chard with Oranges and Shallots

MAKES: 4 servings

TIME: 25 minutes

A perfect winter dish, this warm salad has vibrant color and tangy sweet-sour flavor. The skin of the orange or tangerine becomes almost candied and provides a nice chew, but if you'd rather not eat it, simply peel before chopping.

Other vegetables you can use: any chard, bok choy, kale, or any cabbage. For the citrus, use kumquats (quartered) if available.

1 pound chard, washed and trimmed

2 tablespoons extra virgin olive oil

2 shallots, thinly sliced

2 tablespoons sugar

1 small orange or tangerine, seeded and coarsely chopped

2 tablespoons sherry vinegar

Salt and freshly ground black pepper

❶ Cut the stems out of the chard leaves. Cut the leaves into wide ribbons and slice the stems (on the diagonal if you like); keep the leaves and stems separate.

❷ Put the oil in a large skillet with a lid over medium heat. Add the shallots and sugar and cook for a minute, then stir in the orange or tangerine bits and reduce the heat to low. Cook, stirring frequently, until everything is caramelized, about 10 minutes. Stir in the vinegar.

❸ Return the heat to medium and stir in the chard stems. Cook, stirring occasionally, until they soften a bit, just a minute or two. Add the chard ribbons, cover, and turn off the heat. Let the chard steam for 2 or 3 minutes, then stir and re-cover the pan for another couple of minutes. Sprinkle with salt and lots of pepper and serve immediately or within an hour or two at room temperature.

Chard with Olives and Feta. Omit the sugar and orange. Substitute $^{1}/_{4}$ cup or so pitted olives for the sherry vinegar. Add up to 1 cup feta cheese in Step 3 when you add the chard ribbons.

Braised Chard with Olive Oil and Rice

MAKES: 4 servings

TIME: 50 minutes, largely unattended

A simple little thing but delicious. The sweetness of the carrots really comes through, and the reserved olive oil adds a nice touch. Good with sautéed or roast poultry or meats.

Other vegetables you can use: kale, Belgian endive (cut in half the long way), bok choy, or leeks.

1 pound chard, washed and trimmed

$^{1}/_{3}$ cup extra virgin olive oil

2 small carrots, roughly chopped

Salt and freshly ground black pepper

$^{1}/_{4}$ cup white rice

Juice of $^{1}/_{2}$ lemon

❶ Cut the stems out of the chard leaves. Cut the leaves into wide ribbons and slice the stems; keep the leaves and stems separate.

❷ Put all but a tablespoon of the oil in a large skillet over medium heat. When hot, add the chard stems and carrots, along with a sprinkling of salt and pepper, and cook, stirring occasionally, until the chard is tender, about 15 minutes.

❸ Add the chard leaves, some salt and pepper, the rice, and $1^{1}/_{2}$ cups water. Cover, adjust the heat so the mixture simmers, and cook for about 30 minutes, or until the water is absorbed; the mixture should be moist but not soupy. Serve hot, at room temperature, or cold. (At this point, you may cover and refrigerate the dish for a day, and then reheat it.) Just before serving, drizzle with the remaining olive oil and the lemon juice.

Baked Chard in Béchamel

MAKES: 4 servings
TIME: About 40 minutes

This is probably the ideal recipe if your chard is mostly stems; use the leaves as you would spinach, in a different recipe, or toss them in a salad.

Other vegetables you can use: beet greens, kale, or spinach.

> ¹/₂ recipe Béchamel Sauce (page 57)
>
> Pinch freshly grated nutmeg
>
> ¹/₄ teaspoon cayenne
>
> Stalks from 2 pounds very stemmy white chard, cooked as in Just-Tender Boiled or Steamed Vegetables (page 239), drained well and roughly chopped
>
> ¹/₂ cup bread crumbs, preferably fresh (page 876)

1 Heat the oven to 375°F.

2 Gently heat the béchamel if it's not already hot; add the nutmeg and cayenne. Add more milk to the sauce if it's too thick to pour. Put the chard in a small ovenproof dish and pour the sauce over it. Top with bread crumbs and bake until the mixture is hot and the bread crumbs are lightly browned, 12 to 15 minutes. Serve immediately.

Baked Chard with Gruyère and Bacon. Melt ¹/₂ cup grated Gruyère or any Swiss or cheddar cheese into the warm béchamel. Add ¹/₂ cup or more crumbled cooked bacon. Proceed with the recipe.

Chestnuts

Native to southern Europe and the eastern United States, chestnuts were once an abundant American crop until about a hundred years ago, when a blight wiped out nearly all the chestnut trees. Now we get most of our chestnuts from Europe and China.

Sweet, starchy, and mealy, chestnuts have smooth shells, dark brown and rounded with a flattened side, and are sold fresh in their shells (the best way to get them) in the fall and early winter. Frozen chestnuts are a good substitute out of season, but canned or jarred ones are usually soggy and break apart easily; they're fine for puréeing or mashing but not much else.

Buying and storing: Fresh and in-season are the best. Look for heavy, big, full, unblemished nuts; they dry out as they age and begin to rattle around in their shells. Store wrapped in damp paper towels in a plastic bag in the refrigerator for up to 2 weeks, but use as quickly as you can.

Preparing: Chestnuts must be precooked and their shells and skins removed. The easiest way to precook and peel is to make a shallow cut (or an X) on the flat end,

PREPARING CHESTNUTS

Before cooking a chestnut, score the flat side with a sharp knife, making an X.

After cooking, remove both outer shell and inner skin. If the peeling becomes difficult, reheat.

F Fast   **M** Make Ahead   **V** Vegetarian

using a sharp paring knife. Then simmer in water to cover or bake at about 350°F until the shells curl and can be peeled off. (You can also roast or deep-fry to take off the shells, always making the shallow cut first.) Remove the inner skin as well, using a paring knife. If the process becomes difficult, reheat the chestnuts.

Best cooking methods: Boiling is best if you're going to mash or purée; roasting or grilling is ideal for eating out of hand or sautéing.

When are they done? They're ready to eat when the shell is easily removed, or they can be cooked a little longer if you want to purée them.

Other vegetables to substitute: None, really.

Boiled, Grilled, or Roasted Chestnuts

MAKES: 1 pound (4 to 6 servings)
TIME: About 30 minutes

Boiled chestnuts are best for puréeing, mashing, or using in recipes. For eating out of hand or sautéing, grilling or roasting is better.

You must peel chestnuts when they're hot, so there's a certain amount of "ooh" and "aah" as your tender fingers come in contact with the just-cooked chestnuts (use a thin towel to protect them as much as you can). They need not be sizzling hot for the skins to slip off, but as you'll see, the hotter the better. If they start to cool, and the skins start to stick a bit, reheat and start again.

1 pound chestnuts, flat side cut (see previous page)

To boil: Put in a pot with lightly salted water to cover and bring to a boil. Turn off the heat after 3 or 4 minutes. Remove a few chestnuts from the water at a time and use a sharp knife to cut off the outer and inner skins. Purée, mash, or use in other recipes.

To grill or roast: Heat a charcoal or gas grill to medium-high heat or turn the oven to 450°F. Put the chestnuts directly on the grill or on a sheet of aluminum foil with holes poked in it or on a baking sheet. Grill (preferably with the cover down) or roast, turning occasionally, until you can remove the shells easily, after about 15 minutes. Eat warm out of hand, sauté in olive oil or butter, or use in other recipes.

Glazed Chestnuts

MAKES: 4 servings
TIME: 25 minutes with prepared chestnuts

A really wonderful way to prepare whole chestnuts— they'll have a beautiful glaze over them from the butter or oil and reduced stock. And the richer the stock, the better the dish.

4 tablespoons butter or extra virgin olive oil

2 shallots or 1 small onion, minced

1/2 cup dry white wine (optional)

1 pound chestnuts, grilled or roasted and peeled (see previous recipe)

1 cup any stock (to make your own, see pages 157–159)

2 sprigs fresh thyme

Salt and freshly ground black pepper

❶ Put half the butter or oil in a large skillet with a lid over medium-high heat. When the butter is melted or the oil is hot, add the shallots and cook until translucent, 3 to 5 minutes. Add the wine if you're using it and cook until almost gone, about 3 minutes. Add the chestnuts, stock, and thyme and sprinkle with a bit of salt and pepper. Turn the heat down to medium, cover, and cook, undisturbed, until the chestnuts are nearly tender, about 5 minutes.

❷ Uncover the skillet, raise the heat back to medium-high, and add the remaining butter or oil.

Cook, stirring occasionally, until any remaining liquid evaporates and the chestnuts are fully tender, another 5 to 10 minutes. Discard the thyme sprigs, adjust the seasoning, and serve.

Port-Glazed Chestnuts. Tawny and ruby port are both delicious; ruby port will yield sweeter and more ruby-colored results: Substitute 1 cup port for the wine and half of the stock.

Balsamic-Glazed Chestnuts. Substitute 1 cup balsamic vinegar for the wine and half of the stock.

Creamy Glazed Chestnuts. Add ¹/₂ cup cream once the liquid has evaporated; let it boil for a couple of minutes and thicken slightly. Proceed with the recipe.

Corn

Maize

One of America's favorite vegetables, as it should be—it's indigenous to the Americas and has been cultivated for thousands of years. When fresh it's used as a vegetable; dried, it acts more like a grain (see "Dried Corn," page 487). Though "the fresher the better" still holds true for fresh corn, the new breeds of corn retain their sweetness for several days.

Buying and storing: Still best purchased at a farmers' market or farmstand, just picked. Look for ears that are tightly wrapped in their husks, which should be green and fresh looking, not overly dried out; the silks should be supple, the kernels tightly packed, plump, and reaching the tip of the cob. Store corn, still in its husk, in the refrigerator; it will not go bad, but it will decline in sweetness. Frozen corn is fine to cook with but isn't nearly as good; canned corn is a different creature altogether, practically a novelty item.

Preparing: Shuck the corn just before cooking it. Always remove the silk from cobs before cooking it, even if you're cooking in the husk: Just peel back the husk, remove the silk, and fold the husk back over the corn. If you want kernels only, cut or scrape them from the cob with a knife.

Best cooking methods: Steaming, roasting, and grilling. Stir-fried is also nice, and salsa made with corn is delicious (see Corn Salsa, page 34).

When is it done? When it's hot; there's no point in cooking it any further.

Other vegetables to substitute: Really, there is no substitute for corn on the cob. For corn kernels, green peas or green or wax beans; for raw corn kernels, diced jícama.

PREPARING CORN

To shuck corn, you can remove the husk or simply peel it back and take out the silk, then fold the husk back over the corn. This works well for grilling; for steaming or boiling, remove the husk entirely.

When you want kernels only, use a sharp knife to scrape them from the cob.

F Fast   **M** Make Ahead   **V** Vegetarian

Steamed Corn on the Cob

MAKES: 4 servings

TIME: 20 minutes or less

There is no reason at all to boil corn: Steaming does a perfect job, and you avoid the hassle of bringing a huge quantity of water to a boil. You can keep corn warm over the boiling water for a while without a problem; this is not to say you should overcook it, or cook it in advance, but that you can eat four ears while holding the other four in the pot.

8 ears fresh corn, shucked

Salt and freshly ground black pepper

Butter (optional)

1 Put the corn in a pot with an inch or two of salted water; it's okay if some of the corn sits in the water and some above it. Cover and cook over high heat until it is just hot, 10 minutes or less (if the water is already boiling when you add the corn, and/or the corn is very fresh, and your stove is powerful enough to keep the water boiling, the cooking time could be as little as 3 minutes).

2 Serve the corn with salt, pepper, and, if you like, butter.

Milk Steamed Corn on the Cob. Tender and sweet, especially good with less-than-ideal corn: Use milk instead of water to steam the corn.

10 Flavorings for Hot Corn

Add either alone or in combination:

1. Grated Parmesan or pecorino cheese
2. Freshly squeezed lemon or lime juice (especially with a few dashes of hot sauce)
3. Hot red pepper flakes or cayenne
4. Finely chopped pumpkin, sunflower, or sesame seeds
5. Finely chopped nuts, like hazelnuts, almonds, cashews, or peanuts
6. Minced fresh herbs, like parsley, mint, chervil, or chives
7. Any Compound Butter (page 32) or simply more butter!
8. Any spice blend (to make your own, see pages 65–69), especially chaat masala or chili powder
9. Seaweed "Shake" (page 69)
10. Mashed Roasted Garlic (page 303)

Corn on the Cob, Grilled or Roasted

MAKES: 4 servings

TIME: 20 minutes

Grilled corn is unbeatable; I like to prepare it this way, but you can also peel down the husk, remove the inner silks (see previous page), and smooth the husks back in place; this will give you bright yellow corn with attractive, nicely charred husks. But I like to blacken the kernels a bit.

Grilled corn is nice sprinkled with a little chili powder (to make your own, see page 66) too.

Other vegetables you can use: None are quite the same, but you can grill whole zucchini.

8 ears fresh corn, shucked

Salt and freshly ground black pepper

Butter (optional)

Heat a charcoal or gas grill to medium-high heat and put the rack about 4 inches from the heat source. Or turn the oven to 500°F. Grill or roast the corn, turning occasionally, for 10 to 20 minutes, or until some of the kernels char a bit and others are lightly browned. Serve with salt, pepper, and, if you like, butter.

Grilled Corn, Central and South American Style. Peel back the husk without removing it and remove the silk. Smooth the husk back into place, but don't worry about making it completely cover the kernels. Proceed with the grilling for 10 to 15 minutes. As the ears start to brown, carefully pull back the husk. Coat the corn with butter and return to the grill with the husk back in place. Grill, turning occasionally, until nicely browned—some of the kernels will blacken, and that's fine—another 5 to 10 minutes. Squeeze the juice of 1 lime on the corn, sprinkle with 1 tablespoon high-quality chili powder (to make your own, see page 66), plus more to taste, and serve immediately.

Grilled Corn with Cream and Cheese. Use the preceding variation if you like (omit the lime juice) or the main recipe: When the corn is done, sprinkle with chili powder to taste, then coat with Mexican crema, or thinned sour cream, about 1 tablespoon per ear, and sprinkle with grated cotija or Monterey Jack cheese, about 2 tablespoons per ear.

Pan-Roasted Corn with Cherry Tomatoes

MAKES: 4 servings
TIME: 20 minutes

At some point in the summer, you may get sick of plain corn on the cob or even grilled corn; here's the recipe to turn to then. Its fast, it's easy, and it's completely different; when browned like this, corn takes on a brand-new flavor. This is also lovely in Corn Salad with Avocado and its variations (page 207).

Other vegetables you can use in this recipe: shell peas.

6 ears fresh corn, shucked

1 tablespoon neutral oil, like grapeseed or corn

1 pint cherry or grape tomatoes

1 tablespoon minced shallot or white or red onion

Salt and freshly ground black pepper

Chopped fresh tarragon leaves for garnish

1 Use a knife to strip the kernels from the corn. It's easiest if you stand the corn up in a shallow bowl and just cut down the length of each ear as many times as is necessary; you'll quickly get the hang of it.

2 Put the oil in a large skillet over high heat. When hot, add the corn, tomatoes, and shallot; let sit for a moment. As the corn browns, shake the pan to distribute it so each kernel is deeply browned on at least one surface.

3 Sprinkle with salt and pepper, then stir in the tarragon; serve hot or at room temperature.

Pan-Roasted Corn with Stewed Tomatoes. In Step 2, cook only the corn. When it browns, add 2 more tablespoons oil and 1 chopped large onion; cook until the onion softens, 5 to 10 minutes. Add 2 cups chopped tomato (preferably, way preferably, fresh and good, but canned will do in a pinch) and cook, stirring occasionally, until the tomato breaks down. Proceed to Step 3; garnish with fresh basil, dill, or mint if you like.

Pan-Roasted Corn with Poblano Chiles. Substitute 4 medium poblano or other mild fresh chiles or Roasted Red Peppers (page 330), chopped, for the cherry tomatoes. Garnish with cilantro and a sprinkling of freshly squeezed lime juice.

Creamed Corn

MAKES: 4 servings
TIME: 20 minutes

All I can say is, if you've never made this with freshly shucked corn, you may pass out with pleasure. The cornstarch, which will thicken the mixture and make it more like the canned creamed corn some of us grew up with, is entirely optional.

This recipe will get you started on some ideas for additions, though the possibilities are endless. Shrimp, chunks of firm fish, mussels, shucked oysters, and bits of smoked salmon are all surprisingly good. Add them as you would the clams in the last variation.

6 ears fresh corn or 3 cups frozen corn kernels (no need to thaw)

3 tablespoons butter

1¹/₂ to 2 cups cream or half-and-half

Salt and freshly ground black pepper

Cayenne, to taste (optional)

Sugar, if necessary

1 tablespoon cornstarch (optional)

Chopped fresh parsley leaves for garnish

1 Shuck the corn and strip the kernels from it into a bowl (see page 288) to save the liquid. Put the butter in a skillet or broad saucepan over medium heat. When the butter foams, add the corn and cook, stirring, for a minute or two. Add 1¹/₂ cups cream and bring to a gentle simmer; add a good pinch of salt, some pepper, and a pinch of cayenne if you like. Simmer for about 10 minutes, or until the corn is tender.

2 Taste and add a little sugar if you like. Continue to cook until the mixture is thick, another few minutes, adding a little more cream if necessary. If you'd like it thicker, combine the cornstarch with a tablespoon of cold water and stir it into the corn; the mixture will thicken almost immediately. Taste and adjust the seasoning, garnish with parsley, and serve.

Creamed Corn with Onion. Before adding the corn to the butter, cook about ¹/₂ cup chopped onion, stirring frequently, until quite tender but not browned, about 10 minutes.

Creamed Corn with Cheese. Instead of cornstarch, thicken with about a cup of grated semihard cheese, like cheddar. If you like, finish this with a sprinkling of Parmesan and run under the broiler for a minute or two.

Creamed Corn with Pesto. Stir in 3 tablespoons Traditional Pesto (page 27) just before serving.

Creamed Corn with Clams. In Step 1, when you add the corn, stir in a pound or so of well-scrubbed clams in the shell. Cover the pan and cook as directed, until the clams open and the corn gets tender, about 10 minutes. Proceed with the recipe.

Corn Fritters

MAKES: 4 servings
TIME: 30 minutes

These are mostly corn, lightly bound and deep-fried. They're super-crisp, really good, and among the easiest things to fry. You can eat them as a side dish or serve them as an appetizer. For more fritters, see pages 99–101.

Other vegetables you can use: fresh or frozen peas.

Neutral oil, like grapeseed or corn, as needed

³/₄ cup cornmeal, the fresher the better

¹/₂ cup all-purpose flour

2 teaspoons baking powder

Salt and freshly ground black pepper

³/₄ cup milk, plus more if needed

1 large egg

2 cups corn kernels, preferably just stripped from the cobs (see page 288), but thawed frozen is acceptable

1 Put at least 2 inches of oil in a deep pan on the stove over medium-high heat; bring to 350°F (see "Deep Frying," page 19).

2 Combine the cornmeal, flour, baking powder, and some salt and pepper in a large bowl. Beat the milk and egg together, then pour the mixture into the dry ingredients, adding a few tablespoons more milk if necessary to make a thick but smooth batter. Stir in the corn.

3 Drop the fritters by the ¹/₄ cup or large spoonful into the hot oil; you'll probably need to raise the heat to maintain the temperature. Cook the fritters in batches, turning once, until nicely browned on all sides, a total of 4 or 5 minutes per batch. Drain the fritters on paper towels, then eat them as they are done or keep them warm in the oven until they are all done.

Arepas. A South American staple, made with cheese: Omit the baking powder. Add 1 cup grated cheese—like cheddar—to the mix, along with the milk and egg. Add a little more milk to make a slightly thinner, pancakelike batter and cook in a shallow skillet with just a few tablespoons of butter or oil, as you would pancakes.

Corn Pancakes, Thai Style

MAKES: 4 servings

TIME: 30 minutes

I have made fried corn tidbits twenty different ways over the years, and I do think these are the best: fresh corn barely bound by eggs, seasoned with soy and chile, cooked in butter. Serve naked, with Basil-Soy Dipping Sauce (page 38), or with a bit of lime and perhaps some minced chile and chopped basil on top.

Other vegetables you can use: peas, preferably fresh.

2 eggs, separated

Salt and freshly ground black pepper

$^1/_2$ cup chopped scallion

1 teaspoon minced fresh chile (like jalapeño or Thai), or to taste, or hot red pepper flakes or cayenne to taste

2 cups corn kernels, preferably just stripped from the cobs (see page 288), but thawed frozen is acceptable

1 tablespoon soy sauce

$^1/_4$ cup all-purpose flour

3 to 4 tablespoons butter, peanut oil, or neutral oil, like grapeseed or corn

❶ In a large bowl, combine the egg yolks, a pinch of salt, a good $^1/_2$ teaspoon or more black pepper, the scallion, chile, corn, soy sauce, and flour; mix well.

❷ Beat the egg whites until stiff (see page 901). Put 3 tablespoons butter or oil in a large skillet (cast-iron or nonstick is best) over medium-high heat. Fold the egg whites into the corn mixture. When the butter foam subsides or the oil is hot, spoon pancake-sized dollops into the pan, 4 to 6 at a time.

❸ Cook until nicely browned on one side, 3 to 5 minutes, then turn and brown the other side. Keep warm in a low oven if necessary while you cook the remaining pancakes, adding the remaining butter or oil as necessary. Serve immediately.

Corn Pancakes, Korean Style. Add 1 tablespoon each minced fresh ginger and garlic; the chile is optional. Proceed with the recipe; use half neutral oil and half dark sesame oil to cook the pancakes.

Hot Curry Corn Pancakes. Increase the chiles to 2 teaspoons or more and substitute Hot Curry Powder (page 66) for the soy sauce. Serve with Raita (page 24) to cool off some of the heat.

Cucumbers

Ubiquitous in salads and often pickled, cucumbers—actually a fruit—come in three familiar varieties: the common cucumber with dark green, often waxed skin that we see in every grocery store; the long, slender, and almost always plastic-wrapped hothouse or English cucumber; and the small, striped, nubby-skinned Kirby, most often used to make pickles (see page 228).

Buying and storing: Look for firm, unshriveled, and preferably unwaxed cucumbers. Generally, more narrow specimens have fewer and less bitter seeds. Store unwrapped in the refrigerator for up to a week, but use as soon as possible.

F Fast   **M** Make Ahead   **V** Vegetarian

1

2

Thick cucumbers should almost always be seeded. It takes almost no time at all. **(STEP 1)** First cut the cucumber in half the long way. **(STEP 2)** Then scrape out the seeds with a spoon.

Preparing: Always peel waxed cucumbers; otherwise peeling is optional. Cut the cucumber in half lengthwise and use a spoon to remove the seeds if there are a lot of them. And consider salting (see page 207) to remove excess water if you're looking for extra crispness or less bitterness or if you're cooking it.

Best cooking methods: Best raw or for pickling (see page 228).

When is it done? Cucumbers are rarely cooked, though a quick sauté in butter or oil can be a nice change.

Other vegetables to substitute: Celery, jícama, or water chestnuts.

Eggplant

There are literally dozens of varieties of eggplant, though we most commonly see the large, oblong, dark purple ones. Reliably better is the slender lavender variety, usually sold at Asian markets but sometimes at Italian ones as well. Other varieties are green, white, striped, or speckled; long and skinny, round and fat, oblong, or oval; and they range in length from 2 inches to a foot. The long and slender types slice up nicely for stir-fries, while the large type is good when you want large chunks or slices for grilling. If you have the option of choosing different types, by all means do so, but if the usual large dark purple variety is all you can get, don't worry about it.

Buying and storing: In general, smaller eggplant contain fewer seeds and are less likely to be bitter (I love the golf ball–sized ones, which do not require any trimming or cleaning). But firmness is the most important aspect when buying an eggplant. Look for the hardest specimens, undamaged, with no brown spots. The color of the stems also indicates freshness; the greener and fresher looking they are, the fresher the eggplant. Store in the refrigerator and use it as soon as possible; although the outside will not look much different, the inside will become soft and bitter within a few days.

Preparing: Trim the stem end; peel if you like (if the eggplant is good, the skin is sometimes the best part). Slice it crosswise or lengthwise between $1/2$ inch and 1 inch thick or cube it any size. Salting eggplant to remove bitterness is optional. If the eggplant isn't fresh and firm, to remove bitterness sprinkle it liberally with salt and let it rest in a colander for up to an hour or so; then rinse, pat dry, and proceed with the recipe.

Best cooking methods: Roasting, grilling, broiling, sautéing, and stir-frying.

When is it done? When it's tender—almost creamy—and there are no dry spots.

Other vegetables to substitute: None.

Dry-Pan Eggplant

MAKES: 4 servings

TIME: 30 minutes

If you want to cook eggplant for later use, especially stir-fries or stuffed eggplant (see page 371), this is the technique. It uses no fat, it turns the skin into a thin, crunchy, smoky delight, and it makes the flesh creamy and tasty. A real winner and easy to boot.

> 3 or 4 small to medium eggplant, preferably slender ones (1¼ to 1½ pounds total)
>
> Salt and freshly ground black pepper (optional)
>
> Extra virgin olive oil (optional)
>
> Freshly squeezed lemon juice (optional)

❶ Put the eggplant in a dry, heavy skillet, preferably cast iron, over medium heat.

❷ Cook, turning the eggplant as they blacken on each side and adjusting the heat so the skin darkens without burning, until the skin is blistered and black all over and the flesh collapses (you'll know when it happens), about 15 minutes.

❸ Transfer (the stems won't be hot, so you can just pick them up that way) to a cutting board and slit them lengthwise. Let cool until you can handle them, then chop or purée for other recipes or season with salt and pepper, drizzle with olive oil and lemon juice if you like, and serve.

Grilled or Broiled Eggplant

MAKES: 4 servings

TIME: 30 minutes without salting

Among the fastest, easiest ways to prepare eggplant and super at room temperature. It's so reliably good it almost makes sense to prepare it whenever you've got the grill going.

> 2 medium or 1 large eggplant (1½ to 2 pounds)
>
> 1 teaspoon minced garlic (optional)
>
> 4 to 6 tablespoons extra virgin olive oil
>
> Salt and freshly ground black pepper
>
> Chopped. fresh parsley leaves for garnish

❶ Peel the eggplant if the skin is thick or the eggplant is less than perfectly firm; cut it into ½-inch-thick slices; if time allows, salt it (see page 293). Heat a charcoal or gas grill to medium-high heat and put the rack about 4 inches from the heat source. Or heat the broiler and put the rack 4 to 6 inches from the heat source.

❷ If you like, stir the garlic into the olive oil, then brush one side of the eggplant slices with the oil. Put, oiled side down, on a baking sheet or directly on the grill. Sprinkle with salt (if you salted the eggplant, hold off) and pepper, then brush with more oil.

❸ Grill or broil until browned on both sides, about 10 minutes total, turning once or twice, brushing with more oil if the eggplant looks dry, and adjusting the heat or position as necessary to keep the eggplant cooking steadily without burning. Serve hot or at room temperature, garnished with parsley.

Grilled or Broiled Eggplant with Miso. In the last minute of cooking, brush the slices with Miso Five-Minute Drizzle Sauce (page 23).

Grilled or Broiled Eggplant with Soy or Sesame Glaze. In the last few minutes of cooking, brush the slices with Sesame-Soy Five-Minute Drizzle Sauce (page 23) or Tahini Soy Sauce (page 26).

Grilled or Broiled Eggplant Salad with Yogurt. While the eggplant cooks, mix together 1½ cups yogurt, 2 teaspoons minced garlic, ¼ cup chopped scallion, ¼ cup chopped fresh mint or cilantro leaves, and a couple teaspoons freshly squeezed lemon juice. Chop the eggplant and mix it into the yogurt dressing, sprinkling with salt and pepper. Serve at room temperature or chilled, with pita if you like.

Sautéed Eggplant with Basil

MAKES: 4 servings

TIME: About 30 minutes without salting

It takes a while to cook eggplant on top of the stove, and it usually takes a fair amount of oil, but the results are worth it: creamy and flavorful, like no other vegetable.

Other vegetables you can use: zucchini or summer squash, though the results will not be as satisfying.

1½ to 2 pounds eggplant, preferably small

Salt

⅓ cup extra virgin olive oil, more or less

1 tablespoon minced garlic

Freshly ground black pepper

¼ cup or more chopped or torn fresh basil leaves

❶ Peel the eggplant if the skin is thick or the eggplant is less than perfectly firm; cut it into ½-inch cubes and salt them if the eggplant are large and time allows (see page 293).

❷ Put the olive oil and all but 1 teaspoon of the garlic in a large, deep skillet, preferably nonstick or cast iron, over medium heat. Two minutes later, add the eggplant. Stir and toss almost constantly until the eggplant begins to release some of the oil it has absorbed, after 5 or 10 minutes.

❸ Continue cooking, stirring frequently, until the eggplant is very tender, about 30 minutes (this can vary greatly). About 5 minutes before it is done, add the remaining garlic.

❹ Sprinkle with pepper and additional salt if necessary, stir in the basil, and serve.

Sautéed Eggplant with Basil and Chiles. Substitute neutral oil, like grapeseed or corn, for the olive oil. Add 1 tablespoon or more chopped fresh chile (like jalapeño or Thai) or hot red pepper flakes along with the garlic in Step 2. Sprinkle with nam pla (Thai fish sauce) if you like and serve.

Sautéed Eggplant with Tomatoes. A simple ratatouille: Step 1 remains the same. In Step 2, add 1 medium or ½ large onion, chopped, along with the garlic. In Step 3, as the eggplant become tender, stir in about 2 cups chopped tomato (ripe fresh tomatoes are best, but canned are acceptable). Cook for about 10 more minutes, stirring occasionally, until the tomato breaks up, then add the garlic and proceed with the recipe.

Sautéed Eggplant with Greens. Use about a pound of spinach, arugula, kale, collards, or any other fresh green: If you've got greens with sturdy stems, separate them from the leaves and chop everything roughly. You want 3 to 4 cups total. In Step 3, add the greens to the pan toward the end of cooking. Stems (if you've got them) should go in after the eggplant has cooked for about 15 minutes; sturdy leaves after about 20 minutes. Tender greens like spinach should go in during the last 5 minutes of cooking the eggplant. Add enough olive oil to keep the mixture moist but not greasy. When everything is tender, stir in ½ cup freshly grated Parmesan if you like. Taste and adjust the seasoning, then serve hot or at room temperature.

Sautéed Eggplant with Walnuts. Use butter instead of the olive oil if you like; omit the garlic and basil. Grind ½ cup of walnuts in the food processor or chop finely by hand. In Step 3, stir in the walnuts instead of the garlic and ½ cup cream if you like. Proceed with the recipe. Garnish with chopped fresh parsley and serve.

5 Additions to Sautéed Eggplant

Eggplant is so distinctive it can stand up to many different flavors. And a lot of these can be used in combination.

1. Make the dish creamy with the addition of yogurt, which goes especially well with spices.
2. Make it more substantial by adding sliced bell peppers, lots of onions, zucchini or other summer squash, cubed potato (which will take at least as long

as the eggplant to cook), cauliflower, whole shallots, and so on.

3. Make the dish crunchy by adding, near the end of cooking, some Fresh Bread Crumbs (page 876) or a handful of toasted pine nuts, sunflower seeds, or any toasted nuts.

4. Make it more fragrant with the addition of basil, mint, cilantro, or other strong fresh herbs.

5. Make it sharper by increasing the amount of garlic; adding chiles, chili powder (to make your own, see page 66), or Chile Paste (page 74); capers or olives; or chopped scallion, shallot, or onion toward the end of cooking.

Curried Coconut Eggplant with Potatoes

MAKES: 6 to 8 servings

TIME: About 1 hour without salting

Serve this over basmati rice for a fantastic vegetarian meal or add some protein to the curry (see "How to Add Meat, Fish, or Poultry to Almost Any Vegetable Dish," page 246). Otherwise, feel free to add more vegetables to the mix.

Other vegetables you can use: green beans, summer squash, winter squash, okra, cauliflower, or mushrooms.

2 medium to large eggplant (2 to 3 pounds total)

Salt

1 tablespoon neutral oil, like grapeseed or corn

1 teaspoon mustard seeds

1/2 teaspoon cayenne

1/2 teaspoon ground turmeric

2 teaspoons ground coriander

1 teaspoon ground cumin

1 tablespoon minced fresh ginger

2 tablespoons sliced garlic

3 large tomatoes, cored, peeled, seeded, and chopped (canned are fine; include the juices)

3 large potatoes, any kind, peeled and cut into 1/2-inch cubes

1 1/2 cups coconut milk (to make your own, see page 389), stock (to make your own, see pages 157–159), or water, or more if needed

Freshly ground black pepper

2 tablespoons freshly squeezed lime juice

Minced fresh cilantro leaves for garnish

❶ Peel the eggplant if the skin is thick or the eggplant is less than perfectly firm. Cut it into 1/2-inch cubes and salt it if you like and time allows (see page 293).

❷ Put the oil and mustard seeds in a large, deep skillet with a lid over medium heat; cook until the seeds begin to pop, about 2 minutes. Add the remaining spices, the ginger, and the garlic and cook, stirring occasionally, until the ginger and garlic soften, about 5 minutes.

❸ Add the tomatoes, potatoes, eggplant, coconut milk, and a sprinkling of salt and pepper. Turn the heat down to medium-low and cover; cook, stirring once or twice, for about 30 minutes, until the potatoes are just about tender.

❹ Uncover and turn the heat back up to medium; add more coconut milk or water if the mixture is dry. Cook, stirring occasionally, until both the eggplant and potatoes are very tender, about 15 minutes longer. Stir in the lime juice, adjust the seasoning, garnish with cilantro, and serve.

Curried Eggplant, Southeast Asian Style. Substitute 2 to 3 tablespoons red or green curry paste (to make your own, see pages 75–76) for all the ingredients starting with the mustard seeds to the garlic. If you like, use 8 ounces trimmed green beans and a sliced red bell pepper instead of the potatoes.

Eggplant Slices with Garlic and Parsley

MAKES: 4 servings

TIME: About 45 minutes without salting

Ⓜ Ⓥ

Generally speaking, large eggplant are less desirable than small ones: They have more seeds, the skin is tougher, and they are usually more bitter. But sometimes they're all you can get, and this recipe makes their size an attribute. (It does help to salt them first.) The results are beautifully creamy and savory.

> 2 medium or 1 large eggplant (1¹/₂ to 2 pounds total)
>
> Salt
>
> ¹/₄ cup extra virgin olive oil
>
> 1 tablespoon minced garlic
>
> ¹/₂ cup minced fresh parsley leaves, plus more for garnish
>
> Freshly ground black pepper

❶ Peel the eggplant if the skin is thick or the eggplant is less than perfectly firm; cut it into 1-inch-thick slices and salt it if time allows (see page 293).

❷ Heat the oven to 400°F. Smear a baking sheet with half the oil. Cut several slits on one side of each of the eggplant slices and lay them on the baking sheet. Mix together the remaining oil, the garlic, and the ¹/₂ cup minced parsley and sprinkle with salt (if you did not salt the eggplant) and pepper. Spread this mixture on the eggplant slices, pushing it into the slits.

❸ Bake without turning until the eggplant is soft, 40 minutes or more. Garnish with parsley and serve hot or at room temperature.

Eggplant Slices with Garlic and Scallions. Substitute neutral oil, like grapeseed or corn, for the olive oil and chopped scallion for the parsley. Add 2 tablespoons soy sauce and a tablespoon dark sesame oil to the garlic mixture in Step 2.

Mashed Eggplant with Garlic and Mint. Great at room temperature as a side dish or served like a thick sauce: Proceed with the recipe through Step 3. Make sure the eggplant is roasted until very tender, then put the slices in a large bowl and mash with a fork or a potato masher (it's fine to leave the skin on; it will break into small bits). Stir in 2 tablespoons freshly squeezed lemon juice, a pinch of hot red pepper flakes, and ¹/₄ cup chopped fresh mint leaves. Taste and adjust the seasoning and serve, drizzled with additional olive oil if you like.

Eggplant Parmesan

MAKES: 6 servings

TIME: About 1 hour without salting

Ⓜ Ⓥ

Though this is really a dish in which the eggplant loses some of its identity, it's as rich and filling as lasagne (and equally good without the mozz) and more flavorful. If you use Grilled or Broiled Eggplant (page 294) in this dish, you can skip sautéing the eggplant.

Other vegetables you can use: zucchini (cut lengthwise).

> 2 medium to large eggplant (2 to 3 pounds total)
>
> Salt
>
> Extra virgin olive oil as needed
>
> All-purpose flour for dredging
>
> Freshly ground black pepper
>
> 2 cups Fast Tomato Sauce (page 502)
>
> 8 ounces mozzarella cheese, grated (about 2 cups; optional)
>
> 1 cup freshly grated Parmesan cheese, plus more if you omit the mozzarella
>
> About 30 fresh basil leaves

❶ Peel the eggplant if the skin is thick or the eggplant is less than perfectly firm. Cut it into ¹/₂-inch-thick slices and salt it if you like and time allows (see page 293).

2 When you're ready to cook, heat the oven to 350°F. Put about 3 tablespoons of olive oil in a large skillet over medium heat. When the oil is hot (a pinch of flour will sizzle), dredge the eggplant slices, one at a time, in the flour, shaking off the excess. Put in the pan, but do not crowd; you will have to cook in batches. Cook for 3 or 4 minutes on each side, until nicely browned, then drain on paper towels. Add some pepper to the slices as they cook, as well as some salt if you did not salt the eggplant. Add more oil to the skillet as needed.

3 Lightly oil a baking dish, then spoon a little of the tomato sauce into it. Top with a layer of eggplant, then a thin layer of each of the cheeses, and finally a few basil leaves. Repeat until all the ingredients are used up, reserving some of the basil for garnish. End with a sprinkling of Parmesan.

4 Bake until the dish is bubbling hot, 20 to 30 minutes. Mince the remaining basil and sprinkle over the top. Serve hot or at room temperature.

Eggplant Layered with Vegetables. More in the style of Eastern European dishes: Steps 1 and 2 remain the same. When you remove the eggplant from the oil, sauté 1 carrot, diced; 2 red bell peppers, cored, seeded, and diced; 20 cloves garlic, peeled; 2 celery stalks, chopped; and 1 large onion, diced—all until fairly soft, about 10 minutes. In Step 3, omit the cheese and basil and layer the eggplant and tomato sauce with the cooked vegetables and a liberal amount of chopped parsley. Bake as directed.

Endive, Escarole, Radicchio, and Chicory

This group of bitter plants can be quite confusing. Though they're all members of the same family, chicory and endive are different species.

Chicory has a solidly green, narrow leaf and grows in a loose head. Related to chicory is the red and white radicchio. There are three types of endive: the pale, torpedo-shaped Belgian endive (aka *witloof*), the open and frilly curly endive (often called *frisée*), and the broad-leafed lettucelike escarole. Nomenclature aside, all endives and chicories are bitter, leafy, and crisp but firm; they add good texture and structure to salads and are also good cooked.

Buying and storing: Look for crisp, unwilted leaves. Belgian endive and all but the very exterior leaves of curly endive should be white to pale yellow in color; green indicates the leaves were exposed to sunlight (a negative for these vegetables) and will be more bitter. Store wrapped loosely in plastic in the refrigerator; chicory and endive keep longer than most salad greens.

Preparing: Trim and wash as you would any lettuce.

Best cooking methods: Sautéing, braising (for Belgian endive, chicory, and escarole), and grilling (for endive and radicchio).

When are they done? When sautéing or grilling: crisp-tender; when braising: soft but not mushy.

Other vegetables to substitute: Dandelion, turnip, or mustard greens when cooked or any lettuce, arugula, or watercress when raw.

Braised Endive, Escarole, or Radicchio with Prosciutto

MAKES: 4 servings
TIME: About 1 hour

Belgian endive, with its neat little shape, is perfect for braising whole, but escarole and radicchio taste just as good; I usually chop them up a bit first.

Other vegetables you can use: Brussels sprouts, cabbage, kale, chard, or beet greens.

2 tablespoons extra virgin olive oil

4 Belgian endives, trimmed and damaged leaves removed, or about 1 pound escarole or radicchio, roughly chopped

F Fast **M** Make Ahead **V** Vegetarian

1/4 cup chopped prosciutto or other
  dry-cured ham

1/2 cup chicken, beef, or vegetable stock
  (to make your own, see pages 157–159)
  or water

Salt and freshly ground black pepper

1 teaspoon freshly squeezed lemon juice or white
  wine vinegar

① Put the olive oil in a medium to large nonstick skillet with a lid over medium heat. When hot, add the endives and cook, turning once or twice, until they begin to brown.

② Add the ham, stock, and some salt and pepper. Cover and cook over the lowest possible heat, turning occasionally, until very tender, about 45 minutes. Uncover and turn the heat up a bit to evaporate any remaining liquid.

③ Drizzle with lemon juice or vinegar and serve.

Braised Endive with Orange Juice. Substitute butter for the olive oil if you like and orange juice for the stock. Omit the prosciutto. Add 2 tablespoons brown sugar and omit the lemon juice or vinegar. Proceed with the recipe, adding the brown sugar with the orange juice.

Grilled or Broiled Radicchio with Balsamic Glaze

MAKES: 4 servings
TIME: About 15 minutes

Ⓕ **Ⓜ** **Ⓥ**

With its odd combination of sweet-and-sour, balsamic vinegar works miraculously to balance the bitterness of radicchio. This makes a fine alternative to a salad and goes especially well with rich, creamy dishes like gratins or braised meat or poultry. It's also a useful ingredient: Chop it coarsely and stir it into risotto toward the end of cooking or toss it with freshly

cooked pasta along with some olive oil and Parmesan. Or stir it into Crouton Salad (page 222) or combine it with sliced steamed green beans or cooked cannellini beans.

Other vegetables you can use: endive, chicory, escarole, or romaine lettuce.

4 small or 2 large heads radicchio (about 1 pound)

2 tablespoons extra virgin olive oil

1/4 cup balsamic vinegar

1 tablespoon brown sugar or honey

Salt and freshly ground black pepper

① Heat a charcoal or gas grill or a broiler to medium-high heat and put the rack about 4 inches from the heat source.

② Core the radicchio and cut the heads into halves or quarters, depending on their size. Rub or brush the radicchio with the olive oil, taking care to keep the wedges intact. Combine the vinegar and sugar in a small bowl until dissolved and keep handy.

③ Put the radicchio wedges on the grill or on a broiler pan, cut sides toward the heat source. Grill or broil for a minute or two, then carefully turn and brush (or drizzle) with the balsamic mixture. Cook until just starting to crisp and char around the edges, another couple of minutes. Transfer to a plate or platter and sprinkle with salt and a lot of black pepper. Serve hot or at room temperature.

Grilled Radicchio with Bacon. Cut the radicchio into quarters; wrap each piece with 2 to 3 slices bacon, securing the ends with toothpicks. Omit the vinegar and sugar.

Grilled Radicchio with Bacon and Balsamic Glaze. Follow the preceding variation, but keep the balsamic vinegar and sugar to brush on the radicchio.

Mediterranean Slaw. Just cool down the radicchio and chop the leaves. Then toss with 1/2 cup or so each of chopped fresh parsley and red onion and dress with a little olive oil or mayonnaise.

Escarole Braised in Olive Oil

MAKES: 4 servings

TIME: 30 minutes

Do not skimp on the olive oil here; its flavor is integral. You can omit the anchovies if you like or add pine nuts (about $^1/_4$ cup), raisins ($^1/_4$ cup), pitted black or green olives (about $^1/_2$ cup), or chopped tomato (about $^1/_2$ cup). You can also use wine or stock in place of the water for a richer taste.

Other vegetables you can use: dandelion or mustard greens, beet greens, chard, kale, spinach, broccoli raab, gai lan, broccoli, or cauliflower. Cooking times will vary.

> $^1/_2$ cup extra virgin olive oil
>
> 1 tablespoon minced garlic
>
> 6 anchovy fillets
>
> 2 to 4 small dried red chiles or 1 teaspoon hot red pepper flakes, or to taste
>
> 1 pound escarole, radicchio, endive, or other bitter green or vegetable, trimmed
>
> Salt and freshly ground black pepper

1 Put all but a tablespoon of the oil in a large, deep skillet with a lid over medium heat. When hot, set aside a teaspoon of the garlic and put the rest in the oil, along with the anchovies and chiles. Cook, stirring occasionally, until the garlic begins to color, a minute or two.

2 Add the escarole leaves, along with $^1/_2$ cup water, and adjust the heat so the mixture simmers steadily. Cover and cook for about 20 minutes, checking and stirring occasionally and adding water if the mixture threatens to dry out. When the escarole is tender, remove the lid and raise the heat if necessary to cook off excess liquid. Stir in the reserved garlic and cook for another minute. Taste and adjust the seasoning, then serve hot or at room temperature, drizzling with the reserved olive oil just before serving.

Escarole with Olive Oil and Red Peppers. Substitute 1 red or yellow bell pepper, cored, seeded, and cut into strips, for the anchovies; add along with the chiles in Step 1.

Fennel

Anise

Like celery, fennel is used raw and cooked, and—like celery—its flavor and texture are mellowed by cooking. It can be used interchangeably with celery, as long as you understand that the flavors are not at all alike. Shaved and used in salads, or sliced and sautéed, it has a pronounced anise flavor. The bulbs range from nearly grapefruit size with celery stalk–sized fronds to petite and dainty.

Buying and storing: Fennel bulbs should be clean, white (some green is fine), and tightly packed; avoid those with soft spots or browning. Store wrapped loosely in plastic in the refrigerator; it keeps for about a week.

Preparing: Trim off the fronds and stalks (and reserve them for garnish if you like); cut off the hard bottom and slice the bulb vertically or into quarters. Or after trimming, cut the bulb in half, then slice lengthwise or crosswise.

Best cooking methods: Braising, roasting, and sautéing.

When is it done? When tender enough to pierce easily with a skewer or thin-bladed knife.

Other vegetables to substitute: Celery and fennel are almost always interchangeable.

Fennel Baked in Stock

MAKES: 4 servings

TIME: About 1 hour, largely unattended

Literally something that you throw together, put in the oven, and forget about while you make the rest of the meal. It's hard to mess up.

 Fast   Make Ahead   **V** Vegetarian

1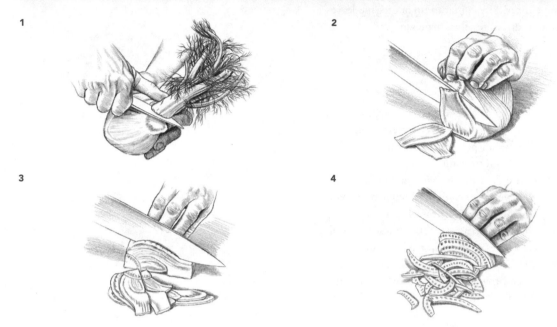

2

3

4

(STEP 1) Trim the hard, hollow stalks from the top of the bulb and cut off the hard bottom. Save the feathery fronds for garnish if you like. (STEP 2) Slice the bulb vertically or into quarters. (STEPS 3–4) Or cut the bulb in half, then slice lengthwise or crosswise.

Other vegetables you can use: celery, leeks, or onions.

1 large or 2 small fennel bulbs, trimmed and sliced (see above)

2 cups any stock (to make your own, see pages 157–159), more or less

2 tablespoons extra virgin olive oil

Salt and freshly ground black pepper

1 cup bread crumbs, preferably fresh (page 876)

1/2 cup freshly grated Parmesan cheese (optional)

Chopped fresh parsley for garnish

❶ Heat the oven to 375°F. Put the fennel slices in a gratin or similar ovenproof dish. Pour in enough stock to come to a depth of about 1/2 inch. Drizzle with the olive oil and sprinkle with salt and pepper. Top with the bread crumbs and the Parmesan if you're using it.

❷ Put in the oven and bake, undisturbed, until the fennel is tender (a thin-bladed knife will pierce it with little or no resistance) and the top is nicely browned, 45 to 50 minutes. Add more liquid during baking if the dish gets dry. Serve immediately or keep warm in the oven for up to 30 minutes. Garnish with parsley before serving.

Fennel Baked in Orange Juice. Substitute 1 cup freshly squeezed orange juice for half the stock. Omit the Parmesan and add 1 tablespoon fresh thyme leaves and/or 1/2 cup chopped almonds, hazelnuts, or pecans.

Fennel with Onions and Vinegar. Add 1 medium onion, sliced, 1 tablespoon chopped garlic, and 2 tablespoons sherry, balsamic, or other flavorful vinegar. Omit the bread crumbs if you like and substitute 1 tablespoon chopped fresh marjoram or oregano leaves (or 1 teaspoon dried) for the Parmesan.

Garlic

Garlic is probably the most important vegetable in recorded history (really) because of its universal value as a seasoning. When raw, it's pungent, hot, and even rank. Cooked, its aroma is alluring and its flavor ranges from assertively strong and delicious to sweet and mild. Roasting whole cloves or even the entire head is one of the best ways to bring out the rich sweetness of garlic. Sautéing garlic in oil or butter to season a dish is also magical: Chop or slice the cloves, add to hot oil or butter, and sauté over medium heat just until softened, usually just a minute or two. Even browned garlic, which is strong and bitter, has a role in certain sauces (see Spicy Tomato Sauce, page 503).

Dehydrated garlic, garlic salt, and garlic powder are no substitute for the real thing; nor is the chopped garlic in oil found at some markets. But the whole peeled garlic in jars or vacuum-sealed bags, as long as it's fresh, is pretty good.

To remove the garlic scent from your fingers, rinse your fingers in water and rub them on any stainless-steel surface (your sink or faucet will do); this works like a charm.

Buying and storing: Loose heads of garlic are best (avoid the boxed type) because you can select the best; look for hard, unshriveled bulbs that have not sprouted. The color and size of garlic is not especially important, though larger cloves are easier to handle and require less peeling. Store in a dark, cool, dry spot; discard when soft.

Preparing: Don't bother to peel garlic when you're roasting it whole; the cloves will slip easily from their skins when they're done. For raw garlic, peeling is easiest when the clove is half-smashed with the flat side of a knife blade. For larger quantities, simmer the garlic in

CRUSHING AND PEELING GARLIC

1

2

(STEP 1) If you're peeling more than a few cloves, drop them into boiling water for a few seconds and the skin will slip right off. To peel without parboiling, crush the cloves lightly with the side of a large knife. (STEP 2) The skin will come off easily.

water to cover for 30 seconds or toast it in a dry pan over medium heat, shaking the pan frequently, for about 5 minutes; either of these treatments will loosen the skin and make it easy to slip out the cloves. To chop large quantities, add whole cloves to a food processor with a bit of oil; this will keep well for a few days. You can crush garlic through a press if you insist, but chopping is no more difficult.

Best cooking methods: Roasting and simmering in oil.

When is it done? When roasted: very, very tender, almost mushy. The cloves will squeeze easily out of their skins. When sautéed or fried: It's up to you but generally the more you cook it the milder it becomes. Don't let it get darker than golden brown or it will be bitter.

F Fast   **M** Make Ahead   **V** Vegetarian

Other vegetables to substitute: Shallots can sometimes fill in, as can onions, but they just aren't the same.

Roasted Garlic

MAKES: 2 heads
TIME: About 1 hour, largely unattended

Mellow and invaluable, roasted garlic is a fabulous side dish, condiment, or ingredient in sauces and other dishes. And it's pretty much brainless to make. I like to use more olive oil than I need, because the oil itself—as long as it's stored in the fridge and used within a few days—is another terrific ingredient.

6 Ways to Use Roasted Garlic or Garlic Braised in Olive Oil

You could start and end like this: Spread it on bread and eat. But Roasted Garlic is so useful there's no reason to stop there:

1. Stir into any cooked sauce or soup in which you'd use garlic, usually toward the end of cooking.
2. Spread on any pizza (see pages 179–182) before adding other ingredients.
3. Add to any vegetable purée (see pages 242–244) or to Mashed Potatoes (page 339).
4. Add to Vinaigrette (page 199), mayonnaise (to make your own, see page 41), Traditional Pesto (page 27), gravy, or almost any other sauce.
5. Add to cooked grain or legume dishes or toss with cooked vegetables.
6. Mash with some olive oil or soft butter and spread on cooked meat, poultry, or full-flavored fish.

2 whole heads garlic
2 tablespoons or more extra virgin olive oil
Salt

1 Heat the oven to 375°F. Without getting too fussy or breaking the head apart, remove as much of the papery coating from the garlic as you can. Cut the top pointy part off the head to expose a bit of each clove. Drizzle with olive oil and sprinkle with salt.

2 Film a small baking dish with a little more oil and add the garlic. Cover with aluminum foil and bake until the garlic is soft (you'll be able to pierce it easily with a thin-bladed knife), 40 minutes or longer.

Faster Roasted Garlic. If you're in a hurry: Break the heads into individual cloves, but do not peel them. Spread them in a pan, sprinkle with salt, and drizzle with oil. Bake, shaking the pan occasionally, until tender, 20 to 30 minutes.

Garlic Braised in Olive Oil

MAKES: 40 or more cloves
TIME: 45 minutes or less

This is my favorite way to soften garlic for use in sauces or to serve as a vegetable. Especially when you begin with peeled garlic, it's incredibly easy. Just keep the heat low and take your time. The oil, too, can be used in sauces or for sautéing.

Other vegetables you can use: shallots (use about half as many since they're bigger).

½ cup good extra virgin olive oil
40 or more cloves garlic, peeled
Salt

1 Put the oil in a skillet large enough to fit the garlic in one layer, over medium-low heat. When hot, add the garlic. Sprinkle with salt. Adjust the heat so the garlic just sizzles.

❷ Cook, turning occasionally so the garlic browns evenly, until it gradually turns golden, then begins to brown. The garlic is done when perfectly tender; it should take 15 to 20 minutes. Store, refrigerated, in the oil and use within a few days.

Garlic Braised in Oil and Vinegar. Add ¼ cup balsamic, sherry, or other full-flavored vinegar with the garlic. Proceed with the recipe. When the vinegar is no longer visible in the skillet (it evaporates and is absorbed by the garlic), it's done.

Ginger

Spicy, aromatic, and essential in cuisines all over the world, this gnarled tropical plant is often called a root but is actually a rhizome—an underground stem. Used fresh, dried, ground, candied, and preserved, it's tan colored with a papery skin that is usually peeled; the flesh is off-yellow, pungent in flavor and fragrance, and has fibers running the length of it. Typically, the younger the ginger, the less fibrous, pungent, and spicy (and the more translucent the skin); more mature ginger can be downright hot—it contains a substance related to capsaicin, which makes chiles hot.

Buying and storing: Look for an unwithered, plump piece that is heavy for its size and not too fibrous. Break off a piece from a large branch; if it doesn't make a clean break, move on to a fresher piece if that's an option. Store wrapped loosely in plastic in the refrigerator for as long as 2 weeks; use it before it shrivels.

Preparing: Scrape off the papery skin with the blunt side of a knife, the edge of a spoon, or a vegetable peeler or peel it with a paring knife, which is faster if less economical. If the skin is thin enough, you don't even need to peel it. Grate the ginger, julienne and mince it, or cut it into coins.

Best cooking methods: In stir-fries and other sautés, soups, and braises; raw in salads.

Other vegetables to substitute: Only galangal comes close, but that's hard to find. Dried ground ginger is useful in many sweet and savory dishes, including gingerbread and curries.

Pickled Ginger

MAKES: 4 servings
TIME: At least a day, largely unattended

Homemade pickled ginger is easy, keeps in the fridge for a couple of weeks, and is far better than the pink-tinted stuff served at most Japanese restaurants, especially if you start with young, thin-skinned ginger. Use as a condiment with Sushi Bowls (page 473), Sushi Rolls (page 474), and sandwiches of all kinds.

1 large piece fresh ginger (about 4 ounces)

1 tablespoon salt

Rice vinegar as needed

2 tablespoons sugar, or more to taste

❶ Peel and thinly slice the ginger, using a mandoline if you have one. Toss it with the salt and let stand for an hour. Rinse thoroughly, drain, and put in a 1-pint glass or ceramic container with a tight-fitting lid.

❷ Combine about ¼ cup rice vinegar with an equal amount of water and the sugar in a small saucepan. Stir over low heat until the sugar dissolves. Taste and add more sugar if you like. Cool slightly and add to the ginger. If the liquid does not cover the ginger, add more vinegar and water in equal parts. Cover and refrigerate.

❸ You can begin eating the ginger within a day, though it will improve for several days and keep for up to a couple of weeks.

Citrus-Pickled Ginger. Add the zest from 1 orange, lemon, or tangerine; 2 limes; or ½ grapefruit to the rice vinegar and sugar mixture.

 F Fast   **M** Make Ahead   **V** Vegetarian

Green Beans

String Beans, Wax Beans, Long Beans, and Haricots Verts

Slender beans with edible pods are the common link here, though not all are green. We're familiar with the common green bean; wax beans are identical except for their yellow color; long beans are originally Chinese (though now grown here too) and are anywhere from a foot to a yard long; then there are the skinny, tender French haricots verts. Long beans, especially, take longer to cook, and haricots verts are more delicate, but otherwise they're interchangeable.

All can be eaten raw (best when they're fresh off the vine), barely cooked so they're still crunchy, or completely cooked and melt-in-your-mouth soft. Summer is the best season for green beans, though most are available year-round.

Buying and storing: Green and wax beans should be crisp, unshriveled, and snap when bent in half. Long beans and haricots verts are more tender and flexible but should still be crisp and unshriveled. Store wrapped loosely in plastic in the refrigerator; use soon—they lose their fresh flavor quickly.

Preparing: Snap or cut off the stem end and leave whole or cut into any length you like. To "French cut" larger beans, slice them in half lengthwise. It's a lot of work but results in an appealing look and texture.

Best cooking methods: Steaming, boiling, microwaving, stir-frying, sautéing, roasting, and braising.

When is it done? A matter of personal preference: crisp-tender, just tender, or meltingly soft.

Other vegetables to substitute: Asparagus, peas, or broccoli.

Slow-Cooked Green Beans

MAKES: 4 servings
TIME: About 1 hour

An adaptation of a Greek recipe I learned from the great cookbook author Paula Wolfert. Although "overcooking"

vegetables is out of favor, these are meltingly tender and delicious.

Other vegetables you can use: wax beans.

About 1½ pounds green beans, the smaller the better, trimmed

¼ cup extra virgin olive oil, plus oil for sprinkling

1 cup chopped onion

1 cup peeled, seeded, and chopped tomato (drained canned is fine)

½ cup water, plus more if needed

Salt and freshly ground black pepper

Freshly squeezed lemon juice to taste, plus a few drops for sprinkling

1 Combine all the ingredients in a large saucepan and bring to a boil. Cover tightly and cook over medium-low heat for 1 hour, checking every 15 minutes and adding a few tablespoons of water if necessary. Longer cooking, up to 1 hour longer, will not hurt a bit.

2 When the beans are very tender and all the liquid is absorbed, they are ready. (At this point, you may refrigerate the beans, well wrapped or in a covered container, for up to 2 days.) Serve hot or at room temperature, sprinkled with a little more oil and a few more drops of lemon juice.

Slow-Cooked Green Beans with Bacon. Add 1 strip chopped bacon to the pot along with the beans.

Green Beans, Pears, and Ham. Substitute 2 somewhat ripe pears, preferably Bosc, peeled and cut into 1-inch chunks, for the onion and 8 ounces ham, cut into ½-inch chunks, for the tomato. For Step 1, put a couple tablespoons olive oil in the hot pan, add the ham, and brown it a bit. Add the pears, green beans, and 1 cup chicken stock (to make your own, see page 157) or water; cook at a constant bubble until the green beans are crisp-tender and the liquid is reduced to a sauce (this will take only 15 to 20 minutes). Sprinkle with a bit of salt (remember the ham will add a good amount of salt too) and a good dose of pepper. Serve hot.

Green Beans with Yogurt and Dill. Omit the tomato. Add 1 cup yogurt and $^1/_2$ cup snipped fresh dill. Proceed with the recipe, adding half the dill; cook for 30 minutes (you want the beans to be tender but not meltingly so). Boil off the excess cooking liquid. Remove from the heat, stir in the yogurt and lemon juice, and sprinkle with salt and pepper. Serve warm or at room temperature.

Twice-Fried Green Beans

MAKES: 4 servings

TIME: About 30 minutes

A Chinese classic, often made with pork; substitute chicken, turkey, or beef if you prefer, or see the variations.

Other vegetables you can use: long beans, cut into 2-inch lengths.

Neutral oil, like grapeseed or corn, for deep-frying

$1^1/_2$ pounds green beans, trimmed

Salt

4 to 5 ounces minced or ground pork or extra-firm tofu

1 tablespoon chopped garlic

$^1/_2$ cup chopped scallion

1 teaspoon minced fresh chile (like jalapeño or Thai), or to taste, or hot red pepper flakes or cayenne to taste

1 tablespoon sugar

2 tablespoons soy sauce

❶ While you prepare the ingredients, put about 2 inches of oil in a countertop deep-fryer or in a deep pan on the stove over medium-high heat; bring to 350°F (see "Deep Frying," page 19). Add the beans all at once and cook, stirring occasionally, until they begin to brown, 5 to 10 minutes. Remove them with a slotted spoon and drain; sprinkle with salt.

❷ Wait a few minutes for the oil to cool a bit, then pour off all but 2 tablespoons of it (refrigerate and reserve it for making this dish again or for other stir-fries). Turn the heat up to high and add the pork; cook, stirring almost constantly, until the lumps break up and the color turns from pink to gray.

❸ Add the garlic, scallion, and chile and cook for 30 seconds, stirring. Add the beans and cook, stirring, for about 2 minutes. Add the sugar and soy sauce, stir, and turn off the heat. Taste and add more salt, chile, or soy sauce if you like and serve.

Twice-Fried Green Beans with Sausage. Substitute chopped Chinese sausage or Spanish chorizo for the pork. Cook the sausage in Step 2 until it just starts to brown.

Twice-Fried Green Beans with Cashews. Substitute $^1/_2$ cup cashews for the pork or add the cashews. After frying the beans in Step 1, fry the cashews until golden brown; drain and sprinkle with salt. Sprinkle the dish with the cashews just before serving.

Horseradish

Though it's most often sold in a jar, fresh horseradish is quite wonderful—and surprisingly mild and delicious when cooked. The tan root has a narrow branch that ends with a rounded and bulging bulb and is often sold still covered in dirt.

Buying and storing: Look for firm, crisp, unshriveled specimens. Refrigerate.

Preparing: Peel before using, with a sharp paring knife, not a vegetable peeler, and acknowledge from the outset that you will lose some of the flesh (it's hard to peel). Grate it for use as a condiment, or chop or slice it as needed. Beware: This will make you cry.

Best cooking methods: Boiling, braising, and baking, usually in combination with other vegetables.

When is it done? When it's soft.

Other vegetables to substitute: Radish, parsnips, and celery root all lend their unique flavors to a dish.

 Fast   Make Ahead   **V** Vegetarian

Likewise, fresh horseradish can be cooked in any recipe calling for those vegetables, though it will almost always be spicier.

Jícama
Mexican Potato or Turnip

The tan root of a tropical vine, jícama is native to Central America and can grow to 5 pounds, though we never see any that large here. It has a turniplike shape and light tan skin that must be peeled; the flesh is white, delicately sweet, and crisp, like raw potato or a crunchy pear, making it excellent for eating raw in salads or simply sliced and eaten as a snack.

Buying and storing: Look for firm, unshriveled specimens that are somewhat heavy for their size. Store in a cool, dry spot (the fridge is fine); it will keep for as long as a month.

Preparing: Peel using a vegetable peeler or paring knife, then chop, slice, or shred.

Best cooking methods: It's best raw; broiling, sautéing or stir-frying is also nice.

When is it done? When just heated through and still crunchy.

Other vegetables to substitute: Radish, cucumber, or water chestnuts.

Broiled Jícama with Chile-Lime Glaze

MAKES: 4 servings
TIME: 15 minutes

Serve with grilled meat, poultry, or fish or toss in a green salad.

Other vegetables and fruits you can use: daikon radish, scallions, pineapple, celeriac, or water chestnuts.

1 tablespoon neutral oil, like grapeseed or corn

Juice and zest of 1 lime

1 teaspoon chili powder (to make your own, see page 66)

1 teaspoon sugar (optional)

Salt

1 pound jícama, peeled and cut into sticks (like French fries)

❶ Mix the oil, juice, zest, chili powder, sugar, and a pinch of salt in a large bowl. Add the jícama and toss until well coated. Heat the broiler and adjust the rack to 4 inches away from the heat source.

❷ Put the jícama on a piece of foil on a baking sheet (cleanup is much easier with foil); make a single layer and leave a bit of space between the sticks. Broil the jícama until it's starting to brown, about 4 minutes. Serve hot or at room temperature.

Broiled Jícama with Ponzu Glaze. Substitute Ponzu Sauce (page 40) for the oil, lime, chili powder, sugar, and salt.

Kale and Collard Greens

Kale and collards are the prototypical dark, leafy cooking greens—healthy, delicious, and varied. Kale has been cultivated in Europe for thousands of years, and collards are an essential in southern cooking. Both have leathery, dark green leaves with thick, sometimes chalky-looking stems. (Some varieties of kale, like red Russian, are reddish or purplish, and some—like lacinato, a Tuscan variety—are nearly black.)

Kale and collards are often confused, but collards' leaves are flat and can be quite big (as much as 8 inches across), whereas kale leaves are definitely ruffled and sometimes quite narrow. The peak season for both is midwinter through early spring, but they're available year-round.

Buying and storing: Look for firm, dark leaves with no yellowing or wilting. Young leaves with stems no thicker than a pencil will be easier to clean and less wasteful and will cook more quickly. They will also have a better texture when cooked. Store wrapped loosely in plastic in the refrigerator for a few days; use before they start to turn yellow.

Preparing: If the stems are thick, strip the leaves, chop the stems, and start cooking them a couple of minutes before the leaves. To cut the leaves easily, roll them up, then cut across the roll (see below).

Best cooking methods: Boiling, steaming, stir-frying, and braising. A fine addition to soups and stews as well.

When are they done? When the stems are tender enough to pierce easily with a skewer or a thin-bladed

PREPARING LEAFY GREENS WITH THICK RIBS

You may remove the stems if they are very thick (or just cook them a little longer than the leaves). Cut on either side of them, at an angle.

The easiest way to chop large leaves is to roll them up and cut across the log.

knife. Unless—and this is sometimes the case—you want the stems on the crunchy side.

Other vegetables to substitute: Cabbage, chard, or beet greens.

Flash-Cooked Kale or Collards with Lemon Juice

MAKES: 4 servings

TIME: 15 minutes

  Ⓥ

Regardless of what green you choose, make sure the stems are $^1/_8$ inch thick or less (strip away and discard thicker stems; see left).

Other vegetables you can use: any dark greens, like turnip, mustard, or dandelion, or shredded cabbage of any type.

> 1 to 1$^1/_2$ pounds kale or collards, washed and well dried
>
> 3 tablespoons peanut oil or extra virgin olive oil
>
> Salt and freshly ground black pepper
>
> $^1/_3$ to $^1/_2$ cup freshly squeezed lemon juice, wine vinegar, or sherry vinegar

❶ Separate the leaves from the stems of the kale or collards. Chop the stems into 1-inch sections; stack the leaves, roll them up like a cigar, and cut into thin strips (see left).

❷ Put the oil in a well-seasoned or nonstick large skillet over high heat. When the oil smokes, toss in the stems. Cook, stirring almost constantly, until they begin to brown, 3 to 5 minutes.

❸ Add the leaves and continue to cook, stirring, until they wilt and begin to brown. Turn off the heat, season with salt and pepper, and add about $^1/_3$ cup lemon juice or vinegar. Taste, adjust the seasoning, and serve immediately or at room temperature.

Ⓕ Fast   Ⓜ Make Ahead   Ⓥ Vegetarian

Flash-Cooked Kale or Collards with Feta and Tomato. Add 1 cup seeded and chopped tomato (canned is fine; drain them first) along with the kale or collard leaves in Step 3. Substitute up to 1 cup crumbled feta cheese for the lemon juice.

Flash-Cooked Kale or Collards with Fermented Black Beans. Add 1 tablespoon sliced garlic and ¼ cup fermented black beans along with the kale or collard leaves in Step 3. Substitute 2 tablespoons soy sauce for the lemon juice.

Collards or Kale with Tahini

MAKES: 4 servings

TIME: 20 minutes

This rich and filling dish is wonderful spooned over rice (especially basmati).

Other vegetables you can use: broccoli raab, gai lan, beet greens, dandelion or turnip greens, chard, bok choy, tatsoi, cabbage, or spinach.

- 2 tablespoons extra virgin olive oil
- 1 tablespoon chopped garlic
- 1 pound collards or kale with stems under ¼ inch thick, well washed and roughly chopped
- ¼ cup chicken stock (to make your own, see page 157) or water
- 3 tablespoons tahini
- Salt and freshly ground black pepper
- 2 tablespoons freshly squeezed lemon juice
- Chopped fresh tomato for garnish (optional)

1 Put the oil in a large, deep skillet or pot with a lid over medium heat. When hot, add the garlic and cook until golden but not brown, about 3 minutes. Add the collards or kale, stock, tahini, and a good sprinkling of salt and pepper. Cover and cook until the greens are wilted and tender, about 5 minutes.

2 Uncover and continue to cook at a low bubble, stirring frequently, until the collards are very tender, at least 5 minutes more. Add more stock if the pot looks dry; you want some sauce, but not soup. Remove from the heat and stir in the lemon juice. Taste, adjust the seasoning, and serve hot, warm, or at room temperature, garnished with the tomato if you like.

Collards or Kale with Peanut Butter. Substitute peanut butter for the tahini. Add 1 tablespoon minced fresh ginger with the greens if you like and substitute lime juice for the lemon.

Collards or Kale with Yogurt. Add or substitute ½ cup yogurt for the tahini, but add it with the lemon juice. Garnish with fresh dill or mint.

Kohlrabi

Cabbage Turnip

A bizarre-looking vegetable that's treated like a turnip. The whole plant is edible, cooked or raw, but it's the bulbous stem base that's prized for its sweet, slightly piquant flavor and crisp texture. Usually it's sold without its stems and leaves, so you get irregular spheres with arched ridges (that's where the stems were attached). The skin is like that of broccoli stems and can be white, light green, or vibrant purple.

Buying and storing. Look for specimens that are firm, crisp, and about the size of a golf ball (larger ones can be woody and tough). Store wrapped loosely in plastic in the refrigerator.

Preparing: Peeling is optional for small kohlrabi and recommended for large ones. Slice or chop as necessary.

Best cooking methods: Steaming, sautéing, and roasting.

When is it done? For steaming or sautéing, when tender but still crisp; for roasting, when soft.

Other vegetables to substitute: Turnips.

Leeks

The leek looks like an enormous scallion, which it kind of is—like scallions, it's a member of the allium genus, along with onions and garlic. Mild and sweet, silky when cooked, leeks have only one downside: their cost. If you're paying by the pound, make sure there is plenty of white on the stalk; you'll trim off most of the green.

Buying and storing: Generally, the smaller the leek, the more tender; but big, plump leeks are wonderful too. Avoid those that are slimy, dried out, browning, or mostly green. Store loosely wrapped in plastic in the refrigerator; they will keep for weeks.

Preparing: Wash well; leeks usually contain sand between layers. The traditional process: Trim off the root end and any hard green leaves. Make a long vertical slit through the center of the leek, starting about 1 inch from the root end and cutting all the way to the green end (leaving the root end intact helps keep the leek from falling into pieces when you wash it.) Wash well, being sure to get the sand out from between the layers.

The easy way, which works only if you don't want the leeks whole: Trim, chop, and wash in a salad spinner, as you would greens.

Best cooking methods: Sautéing, braising, roasting, and grilling.

When is it done? When soft—almost melting.

Other vegetables to substitute: Onions, shallots, or scallions.

PREPARING LEEKS

(STEP 1) Always remove the tough green leaves from leeks. (STEP 2) Cut off the root end. (STEP 3) Slice the leek almost in half, just about to the root end. (STEPS 4–5) Fan out the leaves and rinse either under cold running water or in a bowl.

F Fast   M Make Ahead   V Vegetarian

Leeks Braised in Oil or Butter

MAKES: 4 servings
TIME: 30 minutes

Serve as a side dish or first course and note all the possibilities in the variations. You can also use this as a starting point for mixed vegetable dishes or sauces.

Other vegetables you can use: onions or shallots.

4 tablespoons extra virgin olive oil or butter

3 or 4 leeks (about 1½ pounds), trimmed and cleaned

Salt and freshly ground black pepper

½ cup any stock (to make your own, see pages 157–159) or water

Freshly squeezed lemon juice

Chopped fresh parsley leaves for garnish

❶ Put the oil or butter in a skillet or saucepan that will hold the leeks in one layer and has a lid. Turn the heat to medium. When the oil is hot or the butter is melted, add the leeks; sprinkle them with salt and pepper and cook, turning once or twice, until they're just beginning to brown, about 5 minutes.

❷ Add the stock and bring to a boil. Turn the heat to low, cover, and cook until the leeks are tender, about 20 minutes. If the leeks are still swimming in liquid, uncover, raise the heat, and boil some of it away, but allow the dish to remain moist.

❸ Sprinkle about 1 tablespoon of lemon juice over the leeks, then taste and adjust the seasoning. Serve hot, at room temperature, or cold, sprinkled with a little more lemon juice and garnished with parsley.

Leeks Braised in Red Wine. Substitute red wine for the stock; add a sprig of fresh thyme and a bay leaf along with the wine.

Braised Leeks with Tomato. Step 1 remains the same, but be sure to use oil. In Step 2, use 1 cup chopped tomato, preferably fresh, in place of the stock. Proceed with the recipe, finishing with either lemon juice or vinaigrette.

Braised Leeks with Olives. Use olive oil. In Step 2, after the liquid comes to a boil, add about 1 cup black olives; best are oil cured (you can leave the pits in), but any will do and all are good. (You'll need less salt.)

Braised Leeks with Mustard. In Step 2, before adding the stock or water, whisk into it 1 tablespoon Dijon mustard, or to taste.

Braised Leeks au Gratin. Cook the leeks as directed, using an ovenproof skillet. In Step 3, omit the lemon juice; sprinkle the leeks with about 1 cup of grated Emmental (Swiss) or Parmesan cheese and run under the broiler until brown, just 3 or 4 minutes.

Grilled Leeks Vinaigrette

MAKES: 4 servings
TIME: 30 minutes

If the leeks are very thin, skewer them or sandwich them in a grilling basket so they don't fall through the grill and you can turn them all at once. You can serve these with any Vinaigrette (page 199) or Flavored Oil (page 26).

Other vegetables you can use: scallions, shallots, pearl onions, onions, or garlic.

3 or 4 leeks (about 1½ pounds), trimmed and cleaned

¼ cup extra virgin olive oil

Salt and freshly ground black pepper

1½ tablespoons sherry vinegar or other wine vinegar

1 teaspoon Dijon mustard

1 teaspoon minced shallot

❶ Heat a charcoal or gas grill to high heat and put the rack about 4 inches from the heat source. Brush the leeks lightly with olive oil and sprinkle with salt and pepper.

② Grill, turning occasionally, until nicely browned all over and very tender, 5 to 15 minutes depending on their thickness. Meanwhile, mix the vinegar, mustard, shallot, and remaining olive oil. Drizzle the vinaigrette over the leeks just before serving. Serve hot, warm, or at room temperature.

Grilled Leeks, Asian Style. Substitute dark sesame oil for the olive oil. When the leeks are done, brush them with soy sauce.

Crisp Sautéed Leeks

MAKES: 4 servings

TIME: 30 minutes

These leeks make a nice jumble on top of any fillet of fish or chicken breast, and they're easy. But you must work quickly to get them to brown and crisp properly. The most common mistake is overcrowding the pan, which will result in the leeks steaming rather than sautéing; work in batches if you must. If you want to season these after frying, dust them with a little five-spice powder, chaat masala, gram masala, or other fragrant spice blend (to make your own, see pages 65–69).

Other vegetables you can use: thinly sliced shallot or red onion rings.

3 or 4 leeks (about 1¹/₂ pounds), trimmed and cleaned

3 tablespoons neutral oil, like grapeseed or corn

2 tablespoons thinly sliced garlic (optional)

Salt and freshly ground black pepper

① Cut the leeks into 3-inch lengths and then slice lengthwise into thin shreds (basically a julienne; see page 15). Pat dry thoroughly with paper towels.

② Put a large, wide skillet over medium-high heat. When hot, add the oil and the garlic if you're using it. Cook for just a few seconds until fragrant, then throw in the leeks, turn the heat up to high, and sprinkle on some salt and pepper.

③ Use a spatula to turn the leeks over as they cook; they will cook quickly, and you want them to brown and crisp rather than steam. Cook in batches if you have a small skillet, transferring the crisp leeks to paper towels to drain. (Now is the time to sprinkle with spices if you like.) Serve immediately.

Mushrooms

Countless varieties of our favorite fungus are grown and hunted worldwide—they range from large to small, white to black, bland to mind-blowingly delicious. Not many can be cultivated, which is why truly wild mushrooms are expensive. Fortunately, mushrooms are highly interchangeable (except for the fragile enoki, which is essentially a garnish), and mixing domestic mushrooms with wild is a smart way to add flavor to a dish and stretch your dollar.

Here is a brief primer on the mushrooms—both domestic and wild—you're most likely to encounter in the supermarket:

Button or white: The most common and most bland cultivated variety; white to tan in color; thick caps and stems with gray to dark brown gills; tender and brown when cooked.

Chanterelle: Wild; delicious and usually expensive. Light to golden yellow in color, shaped like fat trumpets with ruffle-edged caps. The flavor is earthy and nutty.

Cremini (baby bella or portabella): Immature (cultivated) portobello mushrooms. Tan, with dark brown gills; shaped like white mushrooms and more robust in flavor.

Enoki: A delicate Asian mushroom often used as garnish; white with toothpick-sized stems and tiny round caps; very mild in flavor and best used raw or barely cooked.

 F Fast **M** Make Ahead **V** Vegetarian

Morel: One of the treasures of cooking, this wild-only mushroom is available fresh in the spring and fall. White or brown, cone shaped with a honeycomb-textured cap and hollow center; wonderful, earthy flavor, both fresh and dried (you should have dried morels in your pantry). Make sure you rinse thoroughly, as they're usually sandy.

Oyster: Available wild and cultivated in some supermarkets. White to dark gray in color, they grow in clusters with thick stems and a round or oval leaflike "cap"; mild mushroom flavor and slightly chewy texture.

Porcini: Dried porcini should be in every pantry (fresh are seasonal, common only in the Northwest and parts of the upper Midwest and pretty pricey). It has the most robust and earthy flavor and the meatiest texture of all mushrooms; very plump, tan to dark brown caps and fat, off-white stems when fresh. Buy dried porcini from a reputable dealer (see Sources, page 982) in quantities of at least 4 ounces at a time (the ⅛-ounce packages often sold are rip-offs).

Portobello: A supermarket staple, these are tan to brown, with giant flat caps, thick stems, and dense, dark brown gills that darken whatever dish they're cooked with unless they're scraped out first. The flavor is earthy, and they're excellent grilled.

Shiitake: The most flavorful cultivated mushroom. Available fresh and dried; the latter (sold inexpensively in Chinese markets, where they're called *black mushrooms*) are excellent for stock but have a rubbery though not unpleasant texture when reconstituted and cooked. Flat tan caps with off-white gills and tough stems when fresh; brown with fatter-looking caps when dried (usually whole); texture is meaty with a hearty, earthy flavor. Always remove stems before eating (they're good in stock).

Buying and storing: Fresh mushrooms should be unbroken, plump, spongy yet firm, and fresh smelling; avoid any that are slimy, bruised, dried out, or foul smelling (especially if wrapped in plastic). True fresh wild mushrooms are in season briefly in the fall and spring. White mushrooms should have closed caps that cover the gills. Store wrapped loosely in wax paper or in a brown paper bag with a moist paper towel in the refrigerator; use wild mushrooms almost immediately, within 24 hours (they're too expensive to let rot).

Preparing: Rinse fresh mushrooms as lightly as you can (they absorb water like a sponge if they sit in it), but make sure you get any dirt out of hidden crevices; with some mushrooms it's easier to trim them first (morels are easiest to clean if you cut them in half lengthwise, but they don't look as nice afterward). Cut off any hard or dried-out spots—usually just the end of the stem. The stems of most mushrooms are perfectly edible. Clean the stems well, cut them in half if they're large (like portobello stems), and cook them with the caps.

To reconstitute dried mushrooms: See page 314.

Best cooking methods: Sautéing or stir-frying, roasting, and grilling.

When are they done? When tender, though you can cook them until they're crisp too.

Other vegetables to substitute: Mushrooms are largely interchangeable, including reconstituted dried mushrooms. Otherwise there is no substitute.

Sautéed Mushrooms

MAKES: 4 servings
TIME: About 20 minutes

You can make almost any mushroom dish better if you can find mushrooms other than button mushrooms. But it also helps to combine a portion of reconstituted dried mushrooms—preferably porcini—with button (or any) fresh mushrooms. The more exotic dried mushrooms make the tamer varieties ten times more flavorful.

Then, once you get the hang of it, you'll be in a position to create a world of delicious mushroom dishes like the ones here. Start with the basic recipe, then try the additions.

> 1/4 cup extra virgin olive oil, or a mixture of oil and butter
>
> About 1 pound mushrooms, preferably an assortment, cleaned, trimmed, and sliced
>
> A handful of dried porcini, reconstituted (optional; see right)
>
> Salt and freshly ground black pepper
>
> 1/4 cup dry white wine or water
>
> 1 teaspoon minced garlic
>
> 1/4 cup chopped fresh parsley leaves

1 Put the oil in a large skillet over medium heat. When hot, add the mushrooms, then sprinkle with salt and pepper. Cook, stirring occasionally, until tender, 10 to 15 minutes.

2 Add the wine and let it bubble away for a minute, then turn the heat down to medium-low. Add the garlic and parsley, stir, and cook for 1 minute. Taste and adjust the seasoning, then serve hot, warm, or at room temperature.

Sautéed Mushrooms with Asian Flavors. In Step 1, use peanut oil, use shiitake mushrooms if possible, add a dried chile or two to the skillet along with the mushrooms, and use lots of black pepper. In Step 2, use water; add 1 tablespoon soy sauce, or to taste, along with the garlic. Finish with cilantro instead of parsley.

Sautéed Mushrooms, Dry Style. Reduce the oil to 2 tablespoons; omit the white wine, garlic, and parsley. In Step 1, use a large skillet with a tight-fitting lid; cover with the lid after adding the mushrooms and turn the heat to medium-low. Cook, undisturbed, for 5 minutes; let the liquid from the mushrooms evaporate completely, then remove the cover and continue to cook, stirring occasionally, until they're dry, shrunken, and as crisp as you like them, 5 to 10 minutes more. Remove from the heat, taste and adjust the seasoning, and serve hot or at room temperature.

7 Additions to Sautéed Mushrooms

1. Any fresh herb you like, but especially chives (a handful), chervil (a handful), tarragon (a few leaves fresh or a pinch dried), or thyme (a teaspoon or so fresh), along with the garlic and parsley.
2. Finish with a teaspoon or more of lemon juice or any vinegar.
3. Substitute chopped shallot (1/4 cup or so), scallion (1/2 cup or so), or onion (1/2 cup or so) for the garlic, cooking for 2 or 3 minutes longer after adding.
4. Instead of oil, cook chopped bacon or pancetta until the fat is rendered and then cook the mushrooms in the bacon fat.
5. Finish the dish with 1/2 to 1 cup of cream (or sour cream), simmering gently. This is best if you cook the mushrooms in butter from the start and use scallions in place of the garlic.

Reconstituting Dried Mushrooms

A quick soak in hot liquid and dried mushrooms are ready to use, leaving you with a flavorful liquid as a bonus. Soak the mushrooms in the hot water until they are soft, anywhere from 5 to 30 minutes (for very tough or thick mushrooms you'll need to change the water).

When they're tender, lift the mushrooms out of the water, leaving sand behind—use your hands or a slotted spoon—and save the soaking liquid (strain it if necessary), and use it as a stock in soups, stews, and sauces; it has intense mushroom flavor. Trim away any hard spots on the mushrooms and use just as you would fresh.

Chinese dried shiitakes are a slightly different story; they must be soaked in boiling hot water, you'll likely have to change the water once to get them soft, and they need to be trimmed assiduously. One way to deal with all of this is to cook them in stock (or Dashi, page 160), then cool, trim, and use them; the process will enhance both stock and mushrooms.

 Fast   Make Ahead   **V** Vegetarian

6. In the Asian Flavors variation, stir in 1 tablespoon Chile Paste (page 74) or curry paste (to make your own, see pages 74–75), or to taste, along with the garlic.

7. In the Asian Flavors variation, stir in 1 tablespoon toasted sesame seeds (see page 317) with the garlic and finish with a teaspoon or more dark sesame oil.

Grilled or Broiled Mushrooms

MAKES: 4 servings

TIME: About 20 minutes

There's a big difference in how various mushrooms take to the heat of a broiler or—even more so—a grill: Ordinary button mushrooms are okay but, well, ordinary. Many wild mushrooms are simply too delicate (though the absolute best grilled mushrooms are fresh porcini if you can find them). The three best of the widely available mushrooms for grilling are shiitake, cremini, and portobello. Portobello are the most striking looking, but big shiitakes can look pretty good too, and they are delicious.

Other vegetables you can use: see "Grilling or Broiling Vegetables" (page 238).

⅓ cup extra virgin olive oil

1 tablespoon minced shallot, scallion, onion, or garlic

1 teaspoon fresh thyme leaves (optional)

Salt and freshly ground black pepper

4 large portobello mushrooms, trimmed (page 313) and cut in half right down the middle; 12 to 16 cremini, trimmed and cut in half or left whole; or 12 to 16 shiitakes, stems removed (reserve for stock), caps left whole or cut in half

Chopped fresh parsley leaves for garnish

❶ Heat a charcoal or gas grill or a broiler to until quite hot and put the rack about 4 inches from the heat source. Mix together the olive oil, shallot, thyme if you have it, salt, and pepper. Brush the mushrooms all over with about half of this mixture.

❷ Grill or broil the mushrooms with the tops of their caps away from the heat until they begin to brown, 5 to 8 minutes. Brush with the remaining oil and turn. Grill until tender and nicely browned all over, 5 to 10 minutes more. Garnish and serve hot, warm, or at room temperature.

Mustard, Turnip, and Dandelion Greens

The spicy greens of the mustard and turnip plants are tender, peppery, and really delicious when young but can become strong, bitter, and tough when mature. So, when young they're great raw; when old you gotta cook 'em.

Dandelion greens, the leaves of the pretty yellow weed, are loaded with protein, fiber, calcium, potassium (more than any other green), and beta-carotene. They're used widely in Europe and are becoming increasingly popular here, sold in many supermarkets. Early spring is the time to pick wild dandelions, from a place where no sprays have been used. Like mustard and turnip greens, these are tender when young, tougher when older.

Buying and storing: For mustard and turnip greens: Look for tender, dark green leaves; avoid those with tough, fibrous stems and any yellowing. For dandelion greens: In the early spring or even fall in some places, look for small (less than 6 inches in length) unwilted green leaves; larger leaves are bitter, which may be fine with you. The crown—the white part at the base of the leaves—is prized for its tenderness and flavor. If you're picking your own, the unopened, embryonic flowers are incredibly delicious; you'll know them when you see them. Store wrapped loosely in plastic in the refrigerator.

Preparing: Wash well; they're often sandy. Remove the stems if they're tough. Tear or chop the leaves.

Best cooking methods: Steaming, braising, and sautéing.

When is it done? When wilted and tender.

Other vegetables to substitute: Mustard, turnip, and dandelion greens are almost always interchangeable, as are broccoli raab, kale, collards, and spinach. Beet greens and chard will work as well.

Dandelion Greens with Double Garlic

MAKES: 4 servings

TIME: 15 minutes

The first measure of garlic mellows as it cooks with the greens; it's the second that adds a real kick. Substitute minced ginger for the second addition of garlic if you like.

Other vegetables you can use: broccoli raab, gai lan, beet greens, turnip greens, chard, bok choy, tatsoi, kale or collards (separate thick stems as needed), cabbage, or spinach.

¹/₄ cup extra virgin olive oil

¹/₄ cup thinly sliced garlic (5 or 6 cloves), plus 1 teaspoon minced garlic, or more to taste

¹/₂ teaspoon hot red pepper flakes, or to taste

Salt and freshly ground black pepper

1 pound dandelion greens with stems, well washed and roughly chopped

¹/₂ cup chicken, beef, or vegetable stock (to make your own, see pages 157–159) or water

Lemon wedges for serving

1 Put the olive oil in a large, deep saucepan with a lid over medium-high heat. When hot, add the sliced garlic, pepper flakes, and some salt and black pepper and cook for about 1 minute.

2 Add the greens and stock. Cover and cook until the greens are wilted and just tender but still a little firm, about 5 minutes.

3 Uncover the pan and continue to cook, stirring, until the liquid has all but evaporated and the greens are quite tender, at least 5 minutes more. Taste for seasoning and add red or black pepper and salt as needed; add the minced garlic, cook for 1 minute more, and serve hot, warm, or at room temperature, with lemon wedges.

Dandelion Greens with Capers. Reduce the sliced garlic by half and eliminate the pepper flakes and minced garlic. In Step 2, after the greens wilt, stir in 2 tablespoons drained capers. Drizzle with red or white wine vinegar and omit the lemon wedges.

Dandelion Greens or Collards with Pot Liquor. Substitute 4 or more cloves mashed Roasted Garlic (page 303) for the sliced and minced garlic. Add 2 ham hocks, ¹/₂ cup white vinegar, 1 cup maple syrup, and 2 tablespoons sherry vinegar or other vinegar. Remove the skin, fat, and meat from the ham hocks and chop it; add it with the pepper flakes in Step 1. In Step 2, add the white vinegar and maple syrup with the greens. Proceed with the recipe. Add the roasted garlic and sherry vinegar in the last few minutes of cooking; reduce the cooking liquid to a rich sauce. Serve hot, drizzled with sauce.

Nuts and Seeds

It would be a mistake to think of nuts and seeds as merely salty snacks. Of course they are that, but they're also a super way to add texture, flavor, and nutrients to many dishes. You can sprinkle them into anything from salads to grains to oatmeal and pancake batters; grind them up into flours to use in batters and doughs; grind them further to make nut butters to spread on toast or add to sauces or dips. They can also play a more prominent role, like in Traditional Pesto (page 27).

Nuts and seeds are among the most ancient of human food sources: There's evidence that humans were already cultivating nuts around 10,000 B.C.E., and certainly we were foraging for them before that. For a wild food that grows on trees, they can hardly be beaten: Almost all are

F Fast   **M** Make Ahead   **V** Vegetarian

packed with protein, fiber, minerals, vitamins, potassium, and iron; walnuts and flax seeds have omega-3s; and almonds, Brazil nuts, and hazelnuts contain significant amounts of calcium. Although they also contain large amounts of fat, the majority of that fat is unsaturated. (Brazils, macadamias, and cashews contain more saturated fat, but oh well.)

Buying and storing: Unshelled nuts will keep for a year; they should have hard, sound shells; the nuts shouldn't rattle when shaken, and they should feel heavy for their size. Shelled nuts have a shorter shelf life—as little as 3 to 4 months—so you definitely want to purchase them at a store or market that has a high turnover. Look for plump nuts that smell fresh, not rancid.

Most nuts, shelled or unshelled, and seeds should be stored in an airtight container in a cool, dark, dry place for 3 to 4 months or in the refrigerator for a few months or in the freezer for up to a year. Hazelnuts, brazil nuts, pine nuts, and sesame seeds keep for only a few weeks unless you refrigerate or freeze them.

Shelling nuts: There's no mystery to shelling nuts; having a nutcracker certainly makes things easier, but a hammer or mallet works too. (To minimize the noise and mess of hammering open nuts, cover them with a towel before smashing.) Pistachios and peanuts can be shelled with your hands (so can pecans, walnuts, and almonds if you're really tough); sunflower or pumpkin seeds between your teeth; and chestnuts must be cooked before peeling. Brazil nut shells are notoriously hard to crack, though somewhat easier after roasting.

Roasting and toasting nuts and seeds: Roasting (in the oven) and toasting (on the stovetop) nuts and seeds enhances flavor. But it takes a bit of patience: The most common mistake is trying to do it too quickly with heat that's too high.

You can roast dry or with oil. Naturally, oil roasting adds fat and calories, but it also adds flavor, especially if you use peanut or dark sesame oil or butter; extra virgin olive oil isn't bad either. Dry-roasting is done with nothing added. See Caramelized Spiced Nuts (page 81) for specific recipes.

To roast: Heat the oven to 350°F and put the nuts or seeds in an even layer on a baking sheet. Roast them until they are just starting to turn golden brown, 10 to 15 minutes, stirring every so often. Toasting in a pan on the stovetop is better suited for the smallest seeds (like sesame, poppy, or pepitas); heat a pan over medium heat and add the seeds. Toast the seeds, shaking the pan and stirring often, until they are just starting to turn golden brown (pepitas will puff up slightly), 5 to 10 minutes. Whether roasting or toasting, immediately remove the nuts or seeds from the pan and let cool; they will continue to cook for a bit afterward and will crisp up as they cool.

Blanching nuts: Blanched nuts have the (sometimes bitter) skins removed. Typically this is done by soaking or boiling them (that's why they're called *blanched*), but you can also do it by roasting or toasting. Almonds and hazelnuts are the nuts you'll most likely blanch; walnuts, with their uneven surface, are simply not worth it.

To blanch: Roast or toast as above or bring a pot of water to a boil, add the nuts, and turn off the heat; let soak until you see the skins start to loosen, typically a

4 Tips for Using Nuts and Seeds

1. Use like a seasoning: Chop and cook along with aromatics, spices, or herbs in sautéed and braised dishes, soups, or sauces.

2. Toast coarsely chopped nuts or whole seeds and use as a final garnish; they're especially delicious on salads, pasta, grain, or rice dishes.

3. Add to baked foods: Finely chop or grind and combine with dry ingredients in pie or tart crusts, cakes, or cookies; or fold big pieces into doughs, batters, or fillings just before baking.

4. Make a nut crust for coating roasted, sautéed, or fried food: Finely chop or grind and use alone or with bread crumbs, flour, or other ingredients.

THE NUT AND SEED LEXICON

Some of the following so-called nuts are technically seeds or legumes; peanuts and soy nuts, for example, are really legumes. Here, however, I'm defining nuts and seeds by their culinary and common uses, not by botanical properties.

Nuts, of course, are widely interchangeable. Often choosing which one to use is more a matter of what you have on hand than what's "right." Seeds are also fairly interchangeable, though size may also be a factor. I usually keep almonds, peanuts, pine nuts, pumpkin seeds (pepitas), sesame seeds, and walnuts or pecans in my freezer, which more than covers the basics; I buy other nuts and seeds in small quantities as I need them for specific uses. Chestnuts appear in their own section on page 286.

NUT	DESCRIPTION	FORMS
Almonds *Sweet Almonds*	Originally Middle Eastern, almonds are sweet and delicate (young, fresh almonds, which you see occasionally in spring, are incredible). Terrific in desserts and sweets, also for adding texture, richness, and a light flavor to savory dishes. (So-called Chinese almonds are actually apricot seeds that resemble almonds in look and taste; they're always roasted or blanched, because they're slightly toxic when raw.)	Shelled and unshelled, blanched, sliced, slivered, roasted and sometimes salted, made into a paste (almond paste or marzipan), ground into flour or meal or butter, pressed into oil, made into "milk," and sometimes sold "green" in their fuzzy, light green shells, which can be eaten whole if young and tender enough, or cracked open for just the tender nut
Brazil Nuts *Para Nut, Cream Nut*	Large, oblong, odd-shaped nut in a very hard dark brown shell, with meat that is more tender than crunchy. The majority are harvested in Amazon rainforests.	Shelled and unshelled, roasted and sometimes salted
Cashews	Originally South American, now grown primarily in India. Shaped like fat commas; the shells are toxic (they are related to poison ivy, if you can believe that!) so always sold shelled. Super-rich and slightly sweet; when cooked they soften a bit and acquire a somewhat meaty texture.	Shelled, roasted and sometimes salted; ground into butter
Flax Seeds *Linseed*	Recently "discovered" in the United States for their incredible nutritional properties; packed with protein, fiber, and omega-3 fatty acids. Small, shiny, flat, and nutty-flavored seeds that range in color from tan to dark brown.	Whole, ground into meal or flour, and pressed into oil
Hazelnuts *Filberts*	Often used in European pastries, small round nuts that are often found shelled; in their shells they resemble chestnuts but are smaller and lighter brown. Crunchy, with a mild nutty flavor (perfect with chocolate); lower in fat than most nuts. The slightly bitter skins can be removed by rubbing the nuts between towels or your bare hands while still warm after roasting.	Shelled or unshelled, blanched, roasted and sometimes salted, ground into flour or meal or butter, pressed into oil, and made into milk
Macadamia Nuts *Queensland Nut, Maroochi Nut*	A rich, calorie-laden, high-fat nut native to Australia. Medium in size, round, and creamy white in color, they are always sold shelled because the shells are so hard.	Shelled, roasted and sometimes salted, and pressed into oil

NUT	DESCRIPTION	FORMS
Peanuts *Goober, Groundnut, Ground Pea*	A native South American legume eaten like a nut. Virginia and Spanish are the two most common varieties; Spanish are smaller with a reddish brown papery skin.	Whole and shelled, typically dry-roasted and often salted, boiled, ground into butter, and pressed into oil. Occasionally raw (in natural food stores) and fresh (at farmers' markets, Chinese groceries, and on-line).
Pecans	Native to North America and used extensively in southern cooking, like pecan pie. Similar to walnuts but flatter, with dark brown skins and a milder and sweeter buttery flavor.	Sometimes unshelled, more commonly shelled, in pieces, roasted and sometimes salted
Pine Nuts *Pine Kernel, Indian Nut, Pignoli*	The seeds of various types of pine trees. These days China produces the most, though Native Americans have used pine nuts since ancient times. They're a slightly golden color, long and slender in shape, with a delicate flavor. Commonly used in cooking both sweet and savory dishes, like Traditional Pesto (page 27).	Shelled, raw, or roasted
Pistachios	A pretty green nut often sold in its split tan-colored shell, which cracks naturally as the nuts ripen. Originated in the Middle East; now California is the largest producer, but Middle Eastern (usually Iranian) pistachios are markedly superior and worth looking for.	Shelled and unshelled, roasted and sometimes salted, and pressed into a gorgeous deep green oil
Pumpkin and Squash Seeds *Pepitas*	The seeds of pumpkins or nearly any hard winter squash; medium in size, oval with a point, flat, and ranging in color from green to tan to white. The flavor is like a cross between peanuts and sesame seeds. Sometimes ground and used as a thickening and flavoring agent, or as a coating (like bread crumbs), tossed into salads, breads, muffins, or eaten out of hand.	Fresh (get them right out of a pumpkin or squash), dried, roasted and sometimes salted, and hulled (often called *pepitas*—Spanish for "little seed"), or roasted and pressed into oil.
Soy Nuts	Dried and roasted soybeans; small tan oval "nuts" that are quite crunchy and loaded with protein. Often eaten as a snack or tossed into salads, granola, or trail mix. (For more on soybeans, see page 409.)	Roasted and sometimes salted
Sunflower Seeds	From the gigantic sunflower plant, native to North America and used in everything from breads and muffins to salads and as a crunchy and flavorful garnish for just about anything	Shelled and unshelled, roasted and often salted, and pressed into oil
Walnuts	One of the most common and oldest known nuts, used almost everywhere. Shells are round with a point, tan, and ridged; nuts are fairly large and brain shaped. Their rich flavor and crisp texture is a nice addition to desserts and savory dishes alike. Black walnuts are less common, have harder shells, and are more flavorful.	Shelled and unshelled, in pieces, ground into meal or flour, and pressed into oil

couple minutes. Drain and pick out the skins. If the skins are stubborn, rub them in a towel until they loosen.

Grinding nuts into meal, flour, or butter: Nut butter or meal is easy to make. (Nut flour, finer than meal, requires special equipment.) All you need are nuts and a food processor or spice or coffee grinder.

When grinding nuts into meal, don't overdo it, or it will quickly turn into nut butter. Pulse the nuts in a food processor until they are finely ground and look like moist flour; if there are still larger bits of nut, either leave them in for texture or sift them out. If you see any bit of the meal clumping, stop processing; it's about to turn into butter. Combine the meal with wheat flour in breads.

Making nut butter is even easier, and about ten times better than your average supermarket peanut butter, which is loaded with salt, sugar, and even added fat. Just push the "on" button and stop it at the consistency you like; less puréeing for chunky butter, more for smooth butter. Most nut butters are made from roasted nuts—the flavor is richer—but raw nuts are good too. You can also add salt, sweetener, or spices to enhance or punch up the flavor (see the following list).

8 Ways to Season Nut Butters

Here are some ideas to add a lot or a little kick to your nut butter. Keep in mind that adding liquids, like maple syrup or coconut milk, will thin the nut butter; also, adding fresh ingredients like garlic or chiles will make the nut butter more perishable; keep it in the fridge. The following quantities are guidelines for about a cup of butter; but really, add to taste.

1. Salt: $1/4$ teaspoon
2. Sweetener: 2 tablespoons sugar, brown sugar, honey, molasses, or maple syrup
3. Spices: $1/4$ teaspoon ground cinnamon, nutmeg, cloves, allspice, cardamom, coriander, cumin, or asafetida (to name a few) or any spice mixture (to make your own, see pages 65–69), or more to taste
4. Chile: cayenne, crushed red chile flakes, or any dried or fresh chiles (see pages 70 and 330 for how to prepare), including chipotle chiles in adobo sauce; start with $1/4$ teaspoon

5. Garlic: 1 clove raw or 1 head roasted (page 303)
6. Ginger: about 1 tablespoon fresh or crystallized
7. Coconut: milk or shredded, a couple tablespoons of either
8. Tamarind paste, a teaspoon or two to start

Okra

Well-loved in the South and underappreciated elsewhere, okra is a green (or sometimes purple), slightly fuzzy, oblong tapered pod. It can range in size from 1 to well over 6 inches in length; smaller is better. Okra becomes slimy when cooked for a long time, which makes it useful for thickening stews, like the gumbo in this section, but it's exactly this quality that is often unappealing to those who didn't grow up with okra. Fried Okra (below) creates converts.

Buying and storing: Available year-round in the South and in the summer in the North. Look for unblemished, plump, firm green pods under 3 or so inches in length. Store wrapped loosely in plastic in the refrigerator for up to a few days.

Preparing: Rinse and cut off the stems; you can chop or sliver before cooking if you like. Larger pods must be cut into $1/2$-inch-or-so rounds or smaller.

Best cooking methods: Frying and stewing gently.

When is it done? When tender; overcooking makes okra slimy.

Other vegetables to substitute: Green or wax beans, asparagus.

Fried Okra

MAKES: 4 servings
TIME: 30 minutes

A quick soak in buttermilk works wonders on okra. It streamlines the breading process; the results are super-crunchy okra with silky insides. If you don't work in batches, the slices may clump up, but that can work in your favor (see the variation). This fried okra needs nothing but a final sprinkling with salt, though Homemade Ketchup (page 51) or Real Ranch Dressing (page 42) turns it into party food.

Other vegetables you can use: any winter or summer squash.

Peanut or neutral oil, like grapeseed or corn, for deep-frying

1 cup cornmeal

1 cup all-purpose flour

Salt and freshly ground black pepper

Pinch cayenne (optional)

2 cups buttermilk

1½ pounds okra, trimmed

❶ Put at least 2 inches oil in a deep pan on the stove over medium-high heat; bring to 350°F (see "Deep Frying, page 19). Combine the cornmeal and flour in a shallow bowl or pie plate; sprinkle with a little salt and pepper, along with a pinch of cayenne if you like, and stir well. Pour the buttermilk into a large bowl, sprinkle with a little salt, and stir.

❷ If the okra is small, cut it in half lengthwise; cut larger okra into thick slices, on a slight diagonal to reveal more of the interior. Working in batches, put a handful of okra into the buttermilk, then fish out the slices one by one, roll them around in the cornmeal mixture, and drop them into the hot oil, being careful not to overcrowd the pan.

❸ Cook the okra, stirring gently to cook them evenly, until they are browned all over, 3 to 5 minutes, depending on their size. Remove with a slotted spoon to drain on paper towels. Repeat until all the okra are done. Sprinkle with salt and pepper if you like and serve immediately.

Okra Hush Puppies. Cut the okra crosswise into slices ½ inch thick or less. In Step 2, add the okra to the buttermilk all at once and stir well to coat and release some slime. Use 2 soupspoons to scoop up a clump of buttermilk-coated okra slices (trust me; they will be both clumpy and coated) and roll it around in the cornmeal mixture to coat evenly. Drop the clumps—now called hush puppies—in the hot oil and fry as described in Step 3 (they might take a minute or two more to cook).

Okra Gumbo with Spicy Sausage

MAKES: 4 servings
TIME: About an hour, largely unattended

I love slow-cooked okra, especially with sausage and tomatoes. For the best texture, you've got to sear the okra first. But after that, there's little to do but let the pot bubble away. To serve this New Orleans style, pour a ladleful into a shallow soup bowl and nestle a scoop of plain white rice into the center. And if you're looking for that traditional rich flavor and texture, try the variation with roux.

Other vegetables you can use: any green (string) beans.

2 tablespoons extra virgin olive oil

1 pound spicy smoked sausage or kielbasa

1 large onion, halved and cut into thick slices

Salt and freshly ground black pepper

1 pound okra, trimmed

2 tablespoons chopped garlic

4 cups chopped tomato (canned is fine; no need to drain)

1 tablespoon chopped fresh oregano leaves (optional)

Chopped fresh parsley leaves for garnish

❶ Put 1 tablespoon of the oil in a deep skillet or large pot over medium-high heat. When hot, add the sausage, prick it with a fork a couple times, and cook until it's golden brown on all or most sides. Transfer the sausage to a cutting board.

2 Add the onion to the hot pan, sprinkle with salt and pepper, and cook, stirring frequently, until soft and turning golden, 2 to 3 minutes. Meanwhile, slice the sausage crosswise into rounds. Remove the cooked onions with a slotted spoon.

3 Add the remaining oil to the pot and stir in the okra. Cook, stirring occasionally, until it begins to brown a little, then add the garlic and cook for another minute or so, stirring once or twice. Return the sausage and onion to the skillet and add the tomato, along with a cup of water. Sprinkle with salt and pepper.

4 Bring the mixture to a boil, then lower the heat so it bubbles gently. Cook, uncovered, stirring every once in a while, until the okra are very tender and the sauce has thickened, about 45 minutes. Stir in the oregano if you like, taste and adjust the seasoning, and serve, garnished with parsley.

Vegetarian Okra Gumbo. Simply omit the sausage. Heat the oil in the pan, then skip directly to Step 2.

Okra Gumbo with Roux. Use butter instead of oil if you like and increase the quantity to 5 tablespoons. Have ¹/₄ cup of flour ready. Follow the recipe through Step 2. In Step 3 add all of the remaining oil or butter (¹/₄ cup) and turn the heat down to medium-low. Add the flour and cook, stirring almost constantly, until the mixture—called the roux—darkens to the color of iced tea and becomes quite fragrant. This can take up to 15 minutes; lower the heat if it's sticking or cooking too fast. Add the okra and continue cooking and stirring until the okra starts to soften, another 3 to 5 minutes. Proceed with the recipe.

Okra Gumbo with Seafood. Use the main recipe or the preceding roux variation: Use peeled shrimp, scallops, oysters, clams, or squid (alone or in combination) instead of the sausage. Skip Step 1 and don't add until the okra is just about done in Step 4. Then add the seafood to the pot, cover, raise the heat to keep it bubbling, and cook for another 5 minutes or so, until the seafood is opaque but not overcooked.

Okra Stew with Curry. Omit the sausage or substitute 2 boneless chicken breasts if you like and sear and slice them as directed in Steps 1 and 2. Substitute curry powder (to make your own, see pages 66–67) for the oregano and cilantro for the parsley.

Olives

Cultivated for thousands of years—its image decorates the walls of Ancient Egyptian tombs—the olive has been inestimably important to the development of cuisine and even civilization. Originally from the Mediterranean, which is still the world's major producer, olives are now grown in California, Arizona, New Mexico, and much of the rest of the world.

There are dozens of varieties; multiply that by the number of different curing processes (a half dozen or so), and you've got yourself a vast assortment to choose from. What we see in the United States is just a small fraction of what's available in all the different countries and regions that produce and cure olives. Go to any Mediterranean market (that's Greek, Italian, Spanish, North African, or Middle Eastern, to name just a few) for a far more comprehensive and regional selection.

Olives are green when immature and darken, eventually turning black, as they ripen. Most olives are picked green for curing; those intended for olive oil are allowed to ripen further; and some are picked quite dark.

As anyone who's ever eaten an olive straight from the tree knows, curing olives is essential to making them edible; they contain an extremely bitter-tasting chemical called *oleuropin,* which is minimized or eliminated by curing. Olives are most often cured in oil, saltwater, lye, or salt; the method will determine the fruit's ultimate flavor, texture, and final color. Often herbs or spices are added to further enhance flavor.

Following are brief descriptions of the most common olives:

Black or Mission: Most often pitted and canned and nearly tasteless; picked when unripe or green;

F Fast   **M** Make Ahead   **V** Vegetarian

cured in lye and then oxygenated, which turns them black.

Kalamata: Widely available, salty, and sometimes mushy, though not unpleasantly so; dark brown, purple, or black. Picked when ripe or almost ripe, then cured in saltwater or red wine vinegar. Decent standby.

Manzanilla or Spanish: Big, green, rather crisp, and often stuffed with pimientos or garlic cloves. Usually picked young; cured in lye, then brined for 6 months to a year. Can be delicious.

Niçoise: From Nice, France; dark red or brown, small but plump, with a slightly sour flavor. Picked ripe, then cured in saltwater. Flavorful, but a lot of pit for a small bite.

Moroccan: Also called *oil-* or *dry-cured*; shriveled, shiny, and jet black. Picked ripe, then cured in oil or salt, sometimes with herbs. Excellent staple, as they keep forever and can be plumped up by marinating in oil.

Picholine: From France; green, almond shaped, and crisp. Picked green, then cured in saltwater or lime and wood ashes, then brined, sometimes with citric acid, giving them a tart flavor. Delicious.

Buying and storing: There's no guesswork in canned or jarred olives. Loose olives should be firm and not dried out (unless oil- or dry-cured, in which case they are shriveled and not stored in any liquid). Taste one before buying. Keep in mind when paying by the pound that any liquid you include is adding weight (olives in a liquid will keep longer, however). Generally, don't buy more than you'll use in a week or two, though they'll keep longer (dry-cured olives, which are sold without liquid, keep well for weeks). Refrigerate.

Preparing: Remove the pit by slicing the flesh lengthwise and digging it out with your fingers; or crush with the side of a knife and pick out the pit; or use a pitter. If you like, you can reduce the saltiness by rinsing or soaking in water for 20 minutes or so or boiling for 30 seconds beforehand.

Other vegetables to substitute: Caper berries or capers.

Sautéed Olives

MAKES: 4 servings
TIME: 10 minutes

A quick and straightforward sauce, topping, appetizer, or side dish with loads of flavor. Olives don't need cooking, of course, but sautéing them with garlic and herbs adds layers of flavor that make them memorable.

3 tablespoons extra virgin olive oil

2 cloves garlic, smashed

1 pound olives, preferably a combination of black and green, rinsed and pitted

2 sprigs fresh rosemary or marjoram or 4 sprigs fresh thyme

1 tablespoon red wine vinegar

Salt and freshly ground black pepper

Put the oil in a deep skillet over medium heat. When hot, add the garlic and cook for a minute, then add the olives and herbs; cook, stirring occasionally, for 4 or 5 minutes. Sprinkle with the vinegar and pepper; taste and add salt if necessary. Serve hot, warm, or at room temperature.

Sautéed Tomatoes with Olives. Just after adding the garlic, add 3 cups chopped tomato (canned is fine; drain first). Cook, stirring occasionally, until the tomato breaks up and the mixture comes together and thickens, about 10 minutes. Add the remaining ingredients and cook for another few minutes.

Sautéed Olives with Croutons. Add 2 cups diced day-old bread and another tablespoon olive oil. Add the bread to the pan along with the garlic and cook, stirring often, until the bread browns and crisps, about 5 minutes.

Onions

Yellow (Spanish), White, and Red Onions, Pearl Onions, Scallions (Green Onions), and Cipolline

There are fresh onions with long green stems ("spring" onions); and scallions (often called *green onions*) are obviously fresh as well. But most onions are dried before sale and may be white, yellow, or red; pungent, mild, or sweet—the variety is astonishing. The onion is the bulb of a plant related to the lily, so the fact that it and other alliums (even garlic) are quite attractive in bloom is not surprising.

Dry onions are essentially interchangeable, though red and white onions are milder, and I've come to believe

PREPARING ONIONS

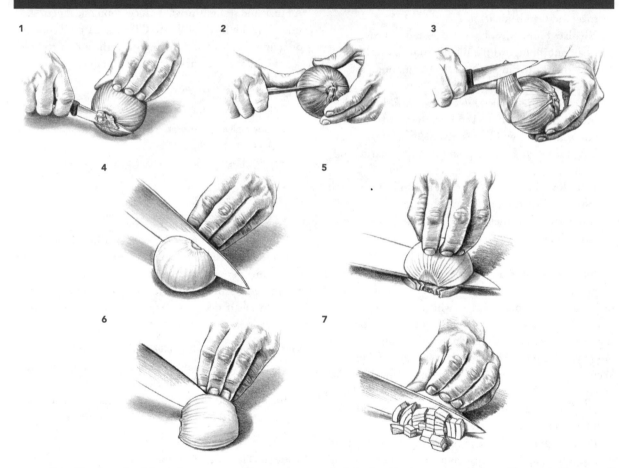

(STEP 1) Cut off both ends of the onion. (STEPS 2–3) Then make a small slit in the skin, just one layer down. The peel will come off easily, along with the outer layer of flesh. (STEP 4) Cut the onion in half. (STEP 5) Make two or three cuts parallel to the cutting board into the vegetable; don't cut all the way through. (STEP 6) Now make several cuts down through the top of the vegetable. Again leave the vegetable intact at one end. (STEP 7) Cut across the vegetable to create a dice.

F Fast   **M** Make Ahead   **V** Vegetarian

that white onions are really the best for all-purpose use, though it's not a position I could defend readily.

Sweet onions, including Maui, Vidalia, and Walla Walla, have a less pungent flavor, are juicy and sweet, and usually have a flatter spherical shape than other dry onions. They are the best onions for eating raw, though they're fine for cooking too.

On the smaller side are pearl (or boiling) and cipollini onions. Pearl onions are about the diameter of a quarter and are ideal for boiling, braising, and stewing; their small size allows them to cook through whole. Cipolline can be used the same way as pearl onions, and their completely flattened shape adds an interesting look to any dish.

Scallions and small bulb onions with green stems attached are "fresh" or "spring" onions; they are generally milder in flavor and softer in texture. Scallions in particular are often used raw as a flavorful oniony garnish for salads, soups, dips, and other dishes. Their small size makes them extremely valuable as a garnish.

Buying and storing: Fresh onions should have vibrant green, fresh-looking, crisp stems and unblemished white bulbs. Dry onions should be firm and covered tightly in at least one layer of shiny, tan to yellow or deep red skin (the outer skin of white onions is more papery). A strong onion aroma is an indication of damaged or rotting onions and should be avoided; also avoid sprouting onions. Store fresh onions in the refrigerator and dry onions in a cool, dark, airy spot or in the refrigerator, for weeks.

Preparing: If you have a lot of onions to peel, drop them into boiling water for 30 seconds to 1 minute, then rinse in cold water. Slice off the stem end and the skins will slip off easily. For just a couple of onions, cut a thin slice off the stem end, then make a small shallow cut, just through the skin and top layer of flesh; peel off both together. Then slice or chop as needed.

If you're peeling and chopping a lot of onions, you might consider wearing goggles; but a properly sharpened knife also mitigates the amount of tear-inducing chemical released into the air. (This substance, called *lachrymator*, combines with the moisture in your eyes to form a weak solution of sulfuric acid. No wonder it burns!)

Leave the root end on onions you will cook whole; they'll stay together better.

Best cooking methods: Caramelizing (see page 325), roasting, and grilling.

When is it done? When very tender but not quite falling apart.

Other vegetables to substitute: Shallots or leeks.

Caramelized Onions

MAKES: 4 servings
TIME: 25 to 60 minutes

Because onions are made primarily of water, they shrink a lot as they cook. But their flavor changes as they concentrate and caramelize, from sharp and pungent to complex and sweet. And if there ever was a dish that you "cook until it's done" this is it, because you want a deeply colored "jam" that doesn't look—or taste—anything like the raw vegetable. Let the time you have available and the desired result help you decide; see the following chart for some guidelines. Finally, you might as well make as much as your pan will hold; onion jam keeps for weeks in the fridge.

Other vegetables you can use: peel, but keep whole: pearl or cipollini onions, shallots, or garlic. (They're easiest to peel after trimming and shocking; see page 240.)

1¹/₂ to 2 pounds onions (6 to 8 medium), halved and thinly sliced or chopped (5 to 6 cups)

2 tablespoons extra virgin olive oil or butter, plus more as needed

Salt and freshly ground black pepper

❶ Put the onions in a large skillet over medium heat. Cover and cook, stirring infrequently, until the onions are dry and almost sticking to the pan, about 20 minutes.

2 Stir in the oil or butter and a large pinch of salt and turn the heat down to medium-low. Cook, stirring occasionally, until the onions are done as you like them, adding just enough oil or butter to keep them from sticking without getting greasy. The onions will be ready immediately or after 40 minutes or more later, depending on how you want them. Taste and adjust the seasoning and serve hot or at room temperature.

Caramelized Onions with Bacon or Pancetta. Substitute 4 ounces chopped bacon or pancetta for the olive oil, adding when you would the oil.

Sweeter Caramelized Onions. Good with hot, sour, or well-seasoned dishes: In Step 2, add 1 to 2 tablespoons of brown sugar with the oil or butter and salt. Proceed with the recipe, lowering the heat as necessary to prevent sticking and burning.

Sweet and Sour Caramelized Onions. In Step 2, add $^1\!/_2$ cup white wine with the oil or butter and salt; boil for a minute, then add $^1\!/_2$ cup water, 3 tablespoons red or white wine vinegar, a bay leaf, and 2 teaspoons sugar. Cook at a steady bubble until the onions are very tender and the liquid is reduced significantly, about 30 minutes. Sprinkle with salt and pepper, garnish with parsley, and serve hot or room temperature.

COOKING ONIONS

TIME	WHAT TO EXPECT
20 minutes	Ivory, softened, and still oniony tasting
25 to 30 minutes	Golden, wilted, and sweet, with a slight onion sharpness
40 to 45 minutes	Browned and starting to melt; onion flavor replaced with sweetness
60 minutes	The color of maple syrup, with a jamlike texture and flavor

10 Uses for Caramelized Onions

1. Thicken soups and sauces
2. Garnish grilled meats, poultry, seafood, or other savory foods
3. Fill omelets, sandwiches, and burritos
4. Stir into dips and spreads (or use as a spread by itself)
5. Top pizza, bread, or rolls before baking
6. Toss with pasta or add to pasta sauce
7. Fold into bread doughs and batters
8. Use to flavor meat loaf, meatballs, or burgers
9. Make Pissaladière (page 182)
10. Eat as a side dish

Creamed Onions

MAKES: 4 servings
TIME: 30 minutes

You can use these as a gravy or sauce for Mashed Potatoes (page 339) or pool a big spoonful on a plate and serve Roast Chicken Parts with Olive Oil or Butter (page 640) or Roast Pork with Garlic and Rosemary (page 754) on top. They're also classic at Thanksgiving.

Other vegetables you can use: trimmed pearl onions, whole shallots or garlic (you'll need lots, or cut the recipe in half).

Salt

6 medium onions (about 1$^1\!/_2$ pounds), trimmed

1 cup cream

2 tablespoons butter

Pinch freshly grated nutmeg (optional)

Freshly ground black pepper

1 Bring a large pot of water to a boil and salt it. Cut the onions crosswise into thick slices; there's no need to separate them into rings. Plunge the onions into the boiling water and cook for about a minute; drain well.

F Fast   **M** Make Ahead   **V** Vegetarian

2 Put the cream and butter in a deep skillet or broad saucepan over medium heat. Add the onions and bring to a boil; cook, stirring occasionally, until the onions have absorbed a lot of the cream and the sauce is thick. Add a tiny bit of nutmeg if you like and sprinkle with pepper. Taste, adjust the seasoning, and serve hot.

Creamed Spinach. Instead of the onions, use 1¹/₂ pounds trimmed spinach. In Step 1, after draining the spinach, cool it a bit or shock (see page 240), then chop it roughly. Proceed with the recipe.

Creamed Cardoons. Instead of the onions, start with 2 pounds cardoons and trim and hold them according to the directions on page 253. Proceed with the recipe.

Roasted Onion Halves

MAKES: 4 servings, plus extra for later
TIME: About 1 hour, largely unattended

Roasted onions are delicious and easy to make; to keep them intact, try not to fuss with them as they roast. Serve hot, warm, or at room temperature, garnished, if you like, with chopped herbs, toasted bread crumbs, or nuts. As a bonus, you can use the leftovers instead of raw onions in virtually any dish.

Other vegetables you can use: large shallots, peeled.

2 tablespoons extra virgin olive oil, plus more for greasing the pan

4 onions, peeled and cut in half around the equator

Salt and freshly ground black pepper

2 or 3 fresh thyme sprigs (optional)

1 Heat the oven to 400°F. Grease a small baking or roasting pan with a little olive oil or line it with parchment paper. Rub the onions with 2 tablespoons olive oil and sprinkle them with salt and pepper on all sides.

2 Put the onions in the prepared pan, cut side down. Roast, undisturbed, until they start to brown, about 20 minutes. Use a spatula to turn them over. Top with the thyme if you like, then return them to the oven for another 15 to 25 minutes, depending on how tender you want them. Check for doneness by sticking a sharp-tipped knife or skewer into the side of one. Serve hot or at room temperature.

Cream-Roasted Onion Halves. Heat the oven to 350°F. Instead of the olive oil, put ¹/₄ cup cream in a large shallow bowl and roll the onions around in it to coat them all over. Let sit for 30 minutes or so, turning every so often. Proceed with the recipe.

Balsamic-Roasted Onion Halves. Follow the preceding variation, only instead of cream, use balsamic vinegar.

Grilled Scallions

MAKES: 4 servings
TIME: 15 minutes

A Tex-Mex restaurant staple across the Southwest, these make a remarkably mild side dish, garnish, or ingredient anywhere you'd use raw or cooked onions. They're equally good, maybe even better, with spring onions, if you can find them. Cook them fast over a relatively hot fire or slowly after you've taken other foods off the grill.

Other vegetables you can use: shallots (on skewers), red or other onions (cut in half around their equator).

2 bunches scallions or spring onions, trimmed, with a lot of the greens remaining

2 tablespoons extra virgin olive oil

Salt and freshly ground black pepper

2 limes, 1 halved, 1 quartered

Chopped fresh cilantro leaves for garnish

❶ Heat a charcoal or gas grill to moderately high heat and put the rack about 4 inches from the heat source.

❷ Brush or rub the scallions with the oil until well coated. Grill, turning once or twice, until deeply colored and tender, 5 to 10 minutes. Transfer to a plate or platter, sprinkle with salt and pepper, and squeeze the juice of the lime halves over all. Garnish with cilantro leaves and serve with the lime quarters, hot or at room temperature.

Roasted Scallions. Best with Mediterranean dishes: Instead of lighting the grill, heat the oven to 400°F. Use lemons instead of limes and parsley instead of cilantro. After rubbing the scallions with oil in Step 2, spread them out on a rimmed baking sheet and roast, turning once or twice, until lightly browned and tender, about 20 minutes.

Roasted Scallions, Asian Style. Excellent with Sushi Bowls (page 473) or as a garnish for all sorts of noodle and rice dishes: Instead of lighting the grill, heat the oven to 400°F. Instead of the olive oil, use a combination of 1 tablespoon peanut oil and 1 tablespoon dark sesame oil; use 2 tablespoons rice vinegar instead of the limes. After rubbing the scallions with oil in Step 2, spread them out on a rimmed baking sheet and roast, turning once or twice, until lightly browned and tender, about 20 minutes. Proceed with the recipe. Drizzle with a little soy sauce if you like.

Parsnips

A longtime favorite in Europe (it was once as ubiquitous as the potato is now), this root vegetable looks just like a carrot in all ways but its off-white color. It's a shame that they're not more popular, because parsnips are sweeter than carrots, with a nice earthy flavor.

Buying and storing: Parsnips are available year-round, can be cooked in any number of ways, and keep for weeks. Smaller specimens (six to eight per pound) are best; larger ones can be woody and tough. They should

be firm and crisp when you buy them. Wrapped loosely in plastic in the refrigerator, they'll keep for weeks.

Preparing: Generally, treat as you would carrots. If large (more than 1 inch thick at the broad end), it's best—though not essential—to remove the woody core: Cut the thinner portion off and set it aside. Cut the thick portion in half and dig out the core with the end of a vegetable peeler, a paring knife, or a sharp spoon; the procedure is neither difficult nor time consuming (which doesn't mean I always do it!).

Best cooking methods: Steaming, braising, braising and glazing, and roasting. Cooked parsnips make an incredible purée.

When is it done? When tender enough to pierce easily with a thin-bladed knife or skewer but not mushy.

Other vegetables to substitute: Carrots.

Peas

Shell Peas, Snow Peas (Mange-Touts), Sugar Snap Peas

Peas, which are legumes, come in a variety of forms: shell peas (aka *green* or *English peas*), which must be removed from their inedible shells or pods; pod peas, which are entirely edible (pods and all); and field peas, which are nearly always shelled and dried (think black-eyed peas and chickpeas—see page 407).

Nothing compares to the flavor of fresh shelled peas, but there's rarely time for shelling these days. And snow and sugar snap peas, with their edible pods, have made shelling even less appealing, since these offer wonderful pea flavor with a lot less work (though their strings should—not must, but should—be removed before eating; see the illustration for specifics).

Buying and storing: Fresh shell peas arrive in spring and should be firm, moderately plump, unshriveled, and full of medium-size peas. (Very large peas are likely to be tough and starchy.) To be sure, open one up and taste a couple peas; if you want to keep eating, buy them. Snow and snap peas should be crisp, green, and unshriveled. Again, taste one. Store peas wrapped loosely in plastic in

F Fast   **M** Make Ahead   **V** Vegetarian

the refrigerator; use as soon as possible—their sweetness is fleeting. (Frozen peas are a decent substitute in most dishes, and you almost never need to defrost them first.)

Preparing: Open the pods of shell peas at the seam and run your finger down the inside to release the peas. For snow and snap peas, pinch the flower end of the pea pod and pull the string down toward the other end to remove it.

Best cooking methods: Steaming (and shocking if you like; see page 240), quick-braising in butter, and stir-frying. Peas are almost always a welcome addition to risotto and stir-fries (see pages 466 and 241).

When is it done? As soon as they are hot and bright green, usually less than 5 minutes.

Other vegetables to substitute: Green or wax beans, asparagus, or edamame.

STRINGING A PEA

For snow and snap peas, pinch the flower end of the pea pod and pull the string down toward the other end to remove it.

Anything-Scented Peas

MAKES: 4 servings
TIME: 20 minutes

  V

Peas have a delicate flavor that can be enhanced a variety of ways with just a touch of another ingredient, though subtlety is the key. A pinch of sugar makes the flavor even more intense.

Other vegetables you can use: about 1¹/₂ pounds of snow or sugar snap peas.

2 tablespoons butter or extra virgin olive oil

1 tablespoon of any seasoning from the list that follows

2 cups peas (frozen are fine; thaw first and drain well)

Salt to taste

Pinch sugar (optional)

1 Put the butter or oil in a large skillet over medium heat. When the butter is melted or the oil is hot, add the seasoning and cook, stirring constantly, until fragrant, just a minute or so.

2 Add the peas and cook for a couple minutes more, swirling the pan a bit to coat them in the pan juices and soften them a bit. Taste, sprinkle with salt and a bit of sugar if you like, and serve hot or at room temperature.

Peas with Bacon, Lettuce, and Mint. Substitute 4 ounces chopped bacon for the butter or oil and add 1 small finely chopped onion, 2 cups chopped hearts of romaine lettuce, and ¹/₂ cup chopped fresh mint leaves. Render the fat from the bacon and remove it from the pan with a slotted spoon (reserve the bacon). Cook the onion in the pan until soft and translucent. Add the peas and lettuce and proceed with the recipe, sprinkling the reserved bacon and mint on before serving.

11 Possibilities for Anything-Scented Peas

1. Grated lemon, orange, or tangerine zest
2. Chopped light herbs, like mint, tarragon, parsley, basil, or chervil
3. Grated fresh ginger or minced crystallized ginger
4. Sesame seeds (white or black)
5. Minced garlic
6. Fermented black beans
7. Grated coconut
8. Minced shallot
9. White wine or sake

10. Any miso paste
11. Minced flowers, like lavender, rose petals, or anise hyssop

Pea Shoots

The tender shoots and leaves of the pea plant are a sure sign of spring, the vine's new growth, vibrant green in color, with a taste between that of fresh peas and spinach. Pea shoots cook in no time and are delightful stir-fried, stirred into risotto at the last minute, or added raw to salads.

Buying and storing: Check Chinese and farmers' markets. You want tender, fresh-looking, bright green shoots. Store wrapped loosely in plastic in the refrigerator; use as quickly as possible, as they lose their sweetness fast.

Preparing: Wash well; trim away any dried-out stems or yellowing leaves.

Best cooking methods: Quick stir-frying and sautéing.

When is it done? When just wilted—no more—usually just a couple of minutes.

Other vegetables to substitute: Spinach or snow, sugar, or green peas.

Peppers and Chiles

For loads of info about both sweet peppers and hot chiles, see the section dealing with spices on pages 69–74.

Roasted Red Peppers

MAKES: 4 to 8 servings
TIME: 20 to 60 minutes

Any pepper can be roasted, though red (and yellow and orange) are sweeter than green, which are unripe. This

1

2

3
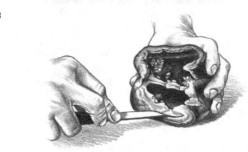

(STEP 1) To core a pepper, first cut around the stem. (STEP 2) Then pull out the core; rinse to remove remaining seeds. (STEP 3) Alternatively, cut the pepper in half, break out the core, and scrape out the seeds.

can be done in the oven, over a grill, or in the broiler. Some people even do it over an open stovetop flame. You can roast as many peppers at once as you like, and the only real work is peeling (which isn't, unfortunately, insignificant). But they'll keep for quite a while in the fridge.

F Fast   **M** Make Ahead   **V** Vegetarian

8 red or other bell peppers

Salt

Extra virgin olive oil as needed

1 To roast or broil: Heat the oven to 450°F or turn on the broiler and put the rack about 4 inches from the heat source. Put the peppers in a foil-lined roasting pan. Roast or broil, turning the peppers as each side browns, until they have darkened and collapsed, 15 or 20 minutes in the broiler, up to an hour in the oven.

To grill: Heat a charcoal or gas grill to moderately high heat and put the rack about 4 inches from the heat source. When the fire is hot, put the peppers directly over the heat. Grill, turning as each side blackens, until they collapse, about 15 minutes.

2 Wrap the cooked peppers in foil (if you roasted the peppers, you can use the same foil that lined the pan) and cool until you can handle them, then remove the skin, seeds, and stems (do this under running water to make it a little easier if you like). Don't worry if the peppers fall apart.

3 Serve the peppers immediately or store in the refrigerator for up to a few days; bring back to room temperature before serving. When you're ready to serve, sprinkle with a bit of salt and drizzle with olive oil.

9 Things to Do with Roasted Red Peppers
1. Toss with minced fresh or roasted garlic.
2. Splash with balsamic vinegar.
3. Sprinkle with lots of minced fresh herbs like parsley, mint, basil, or chervil or a little bit of oregano, thyme or rosemary.
4. Sprinkle with grated Parmesan, Asiago, Romano, or manchego cheese.
5. Use to fill sandwiches or top bruschetta, pizza, and salads.
6. Scramble with eggs.
7. Purée to make a sauce or spread or to mix with other sauces and spreads.
8. Coarsely chop and use to flavor meat loaf, meatballs, or burgers.

9 Toss with sautéed onions and serve with grilled sausages.

My Mom's Pan-Cooked Peppers and Onions

MAKES: 4 servings
TIME: 40 minutes

When I was growing up, once a week my mother would make us a sandwich of sautéed peppers and onions, loads of each. It's a wonderful combination and even better if you add some mushrooms and herbs. For a classic sausage-pepper-onion dish, see page 763.

Other vegetables you can use: about $^1/_2$ pound of any fresh chiles, mostly mild with a bit of hot.

4 tablespoonsextra virgin extra olive oil, butter, or a combination

2 or 3 bell peppers, preferably red or yellow, seeded and cut into strips

2 medium to large onions, cut in half and thinly sliced

1 cup trimmed and sliced shiitake or button mushrooms

Salt and freshly ground black pepper

1 teaspoon fresh thyme or marjoram leaves, or any fresh herb to taste (optional), plus more for garnish if you like

1 Put the oil or butter in a large deep skillet over medium heat. When the oil is hot or the butter is melted, add the peppers, onions, and mushrooms. Sprinkle with salt and pepper, stir in the thyme or other herb, and cook, stirring occasionally and adjusting the heat so the mixture cooks without browning (at least not much), until very tender, at least 20 minutes.

2 Taste and adjust the seasoning, garnish with a bit more herb if you like, and serve as a side dish or piled into rolls or baguettes.

Pan-Cooked Peppers with Vinegar. Use just bell peppers if you like. Add a couple tablespoons balsamic or good-quality red or white wine vinegar in the last couple minutes of cooking.

Pan-Cooked Peppers and Onions, Asian Style. Instead of the olive oil or butter, use peanut or a neutral oil, like grapeseed or corn. Go easy on the salt and use 1 tablespoon minced fresh ginger instead of the other herbs. In Step 2, use a dash of soy sauce and plenty of black pepper for the final seasoning and stir in ¹/₂ cup chopped fresh cilantro. Serve over Steamed Sticky Rice, Thai Style (page 459), or other plain-cooked rice dish, or toss with Chinese-style egg noodles. Garnish with the cilantro.

Pan-Cooked Peppers with Paprika. Substitute chopped tomato for the mushrooms. Start the cooking with just the onions; sprinkle with 2 tablespoons sweet paprika (or 1 tablespoon smoked); cover and cook for 5 minutes. Then add the peppers; cover and cook for another 5 minutes. Finally, add the tomatoes and cook for another 5 minutes. Sprinkle with freshly squeezed lemon juice and omit the herbs if you like; serve hot or at room temperature.

Chile Cheese Gratin

MAKES: 4 to 6 servings
TIME: 30 minutes

Cheese plays the starring role here, and tortilla chips provide the crunch; it's a far simpler form of chiles rellenos, not as elegant but with equally good flavor.

Other vegetables you can use: chayote, zucchini, summer squash, shucked corn kernels (especially Corn on the Cob, Grilled or Roasted, page 289), or green beans.

1 tablespoon neutral oil, like grapeseed or corn

12 medium poblano or other mild fresh chiles or bell peppers, roasted and cleaned (see page 330)

2 cups peeled, seeded, and chopped tomato with its liquid (canned is fine)

3 cups grated cheddar, Monterey Jack, or cotija cheese or crumbled queso fresco

Salt and freshly ground black pepper

¹/₄ cup chopped fresh cilantro leaves

¹/₂ cup crushed tortillas chips

Sour cream for garnish (optional)

❶ Heat the oven to 375°F. Grease a large gratin or similar ovenproof dish with the oil.

❷ Cut the chiles in half (large pieces are fine). Layer the chiles, tomato, and cheese (be sure to end with cheese), sprinkling every now and then with a bit of salt, pepper, and cilantro. Top with the tortilla chips.

❸ Put in the oven and cook until the cheese is melted, bubbling, and browned, about 25 minutes. Serve immediately with a dollop of sour cream or lower the heat to 250°F and keep warm for up to 30 minutes.

Chile Cheese Gratin with Chorizo. Add up to 1 pound crumbled cooked Mexican chorizo and layer with the chiles and cheese.

Hot and Smoky Corn Gratin. Substitute 4 cups corn kernels (grilled, roasted, or steamed; see page 289) for the chiles. Add 2 to 4 tablespoons chopped canned chipotle chile with its adobo along with the tomatoes.

Summer Squash and Salsa Gratin. For the chiles, substitute 3 or 4 medium zucchini or yellow squash, cut into lengthwise slices (about ¹/₄ inch thick) and cooked any way you like: grilled, roasted, steamed, or parboiled and shocked (see page 240). Use Fresh Tomatillo Salsa (page 33) instead of the tomato. Add ¹/₂ cup of so chopped or whole pumpkin seeds (pepitas) with the tortillas.

 Fast   Make Ahead   Vegetarian

Chiles Rellenos

MAKES: 4 servings
TIME: 1 hour

The classic Mexican stuffed chile: The crisp coating is light, the chiles soft and yielding, and the cheese oozing. If time is an issue, make the chiles through Step 1, cover, and refrigerate until ready to batter and cook.

For a lighter, smokier twist, you can forgo the roasting and battering and grill the stuffed chiles. The papery skin blisters a bit and can either be eaten or removed. Here's how: Cut a slit in one side of each chile, remove the seeds, and stuff. Brush with extra virgin olive oil and grill or pan-grill the chiles, turning once or twice, until the skins are blistered and the flesh is tender.

4 large or 8 small poblano or other mild green fresh chiles

3 cups grated or shredded Chihuahua or Monterey Jack cheese

Neutral oil, like grapeseed or corn, for deep-frying

2 egg whites

1/2 cup all-purpose flour

1/2 teaspoon salt

1 cup beer or water

Green Enchilada Salsa or Salsa Borracha (page 49 or 48)

Crumbled queso fresco for garnish

1 Roast the chiles as directed on pages 330–331; peel the skins but leave the stems on. Cut a slit in one side and remove the seeds. Stuff the chiles with the cheese and use toothpicks or a long bamboo skewer to "sew" them shut; set aside.

2 Put the oil in a large, deep saucepan to a depth of at least 3 inches (more is better); the narrower the saucepan, the less oil you need, but the more oil you use, the more chiles you can cook at the same time. Turn the heat to medium-high and heat the oil to about 365°F (a pinch of the batter will sizzle immediately).

3 Whip the egg whites until they hold soft peaks. Whisk the flour, salt, and beer together in a medium bowl. It should be the consistency of thin pancake batter; adjust the consistency with more flour or beer as necessary. Gently fold the egg whites into the batter; some white streaks remaining are okay.

4 Dip the stuffed chiles into the batter to coat and immediately fry until crisp and golden brown. Use the long skewers to help rotate and remove the chiles or use a spatula; drain on paper towels. Remove the picks or skewers and serve immediately with the salsa, sprinkled with the queso fresco.

Chiles Rellenos with Meat or Poultry Stuffing. Substitute 12 ounces cooked ground beef, pork, or turkey for 1 1/2 cups of the cheese; season as you like with salt, pepper, and a little chili powder (to make your own, see page 66). Or use chopped Spicy Braised Beef with Lime (page 725), Roast Chicken with Cumin, Honey, and Orange Juice (page 645), or Shredded Pork (page 759).

Chiles Rellenos with Corn and Pumpkin Seeds. Substitute equal parts corn kernels and pumpkin seeds (pepitas) for half of the cheese. Proceed with the recipe.

CHILES RELLENOS

It helps to skewer the chiles closed after stuffing; break a wooden skewer in half if necessary.

Plantains

The plantain is a type of banana, large, with thick, leathery skin. It's used much like a potato when starchy and green or sautéed for a sweet side dish when fully ripe. It's always cooked (and is often called "the cooking banana")—sautéed, fried, or used in stews and soups.

Like all bananas, plantains ripen nicely off the plant. Leave at room temperature for anywhere from a day to a couple of weeks; the longer they ripen, the softer and sweeter they become. When fully ripe, plantains are deliciously sweet and completely black—the uninitiated would almost certainly toss them in the trash—but hold together well when cooked.

Buying and storing: Plantains are sold at various stages of ripeness; they may take as long as 2 weeks to ripen fully. They have different uses for different stages of ripeness: used to thicken stews when hard and green; flattened and fried into thick chips called *tostones* when just starting to turn yellow and spot; and sautéed or fried when yellow to black. Plantains can be stored in the refrigerator to retard further ripening (the skins may turn black, but the flesh remains the same) for weeks.

Preparing: Plantains require a special peeling technique; begin by cutting off both tips of the plantain; then cut the plantain into several sections. Make three vertical slits in the skin of each section, then peel off each piece of the skin (see below). Trim any remaining skin from the plantain with a paring knife.

Best cooking methods: Sautéing and frying are the best for green plantains; braising and stewing are best

PREPARING PLANTAINS

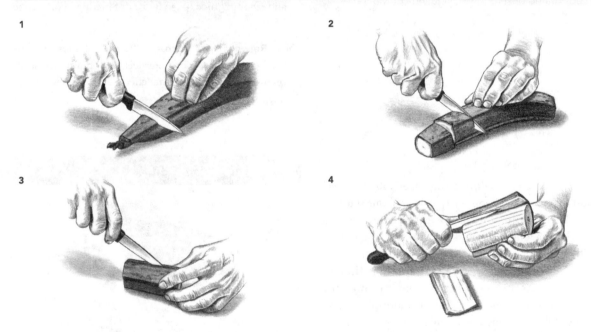

1

2

3

4

(STEP 1) Plantains are unusual and must be peeled this way. First, cut off both ends and discard. (STEP 2) Cut the plantain into several chunks. (STEP 3) Make three shallow, vertical slits in each chunk. (STEP 4) Remove the peel in pieces. If any parts of the peel cling to the flesh, remove them with a paring knife.

 Fast   Make Ahead   **V** Vegetarian

for ripe plantains. But you can really cook either any way.

When are they done? Green plantains are done when they're golden brown and slightly tender; ripe are done when they are caramelized and very soft.

Other fruits or vegetables to substitute: When starchy and green, replace with potato, yucca, boniato, or taro root; when sweeter and riper, with sweet potato or yam. Green to green-yellow bananas can often fill in for plantains in recipes; they cook up quite similarly as long as they're not too ripe.

Sautéed Ripe Plantains

Platanos Maduros

> **MAKES:** 4 servings
> **TIME:** 20 minutes
>

Sweet, but somehow appropriately so, these are the perfect side dish for Black Beans and White Rice, Spanish Style (page 435). Often, fully ripe plantains can be peeled like bananas, but if you have any trouble, peel them as you would unripe plantains; see the illustrations on the previous page.

Other vegetables you can use: just-ripe (yellow, but with only a few black spots) bananas.

> 3 or 4 yellow-black or black plantains, peeled
> Neutral oil, like grapeseed or corn, as needed
> Salt and freshly ground black pepper
> Lime wedges

Cut the plantains into about 1-inch pieces. Put the oil in a large skillet over medium heat. When hot, add the plantains. Cook, turning as necessary and adjusting the heat so the plantains brown slowly without burning. Be especially careful as they near doneness; there is so much sugar in the plantains that they burn easily. The process will take 10 to 15 minutes. Serve hot or warm, sprinkled with salt, pepper, and lime juice.

Garlicky Sautéed Ripe Plantains. In the last 3 or so minutes of cooking, add 2 tablespoons minced garlic and stir the plantains.

Tostones

> **MAKES:** 4 servings
> **TIME:** 30 minutes
>

This wonderful side dish is easy to make and as good warm (or at room temperature, as long as it's not made too far in advance) as hot. To me, this needs nothing more than salt and maybe a little lime, but some people like it with hot sauce, Chile Paste (page 74), Fresh Tomato or Fruit Salsa (page 23), or another salsa.

> 2 green-to-yellow plantains or green bananas
> Neutral oil, like grapeseed or corn, as needed
> Salt
> Lime wedges

❶ Peel the plantains as described and illustrated on the previous page. Cut into ¹/₂-inch rounds. Film the bottom of a large skillet with oil and turn the heat to medium. When hot, add the rounds (you'll probably be able to do this in one batch) and sprinkle with salt. Brown lightly, then turn and brown the other side. Transfer to a plate as they brown. (At this point, you may set the plantains aside for an hour or two before proceeding with the recipe.)

❷ When the plantain rounds have cooled a bit, put each between 2 pieces of wax paper and pound with the side of your fist or the palm of your hand until they spread out and just about double in diameter; they will look squashed and might split a little around the edges, which is right. (At this point, you may set the plantains aside for another hour or two.)

❸ Again, film the bottom of the skillet with oil, turn the heat to medium, and again, brown the rounds on each side (this time you'll probably have to cook in batches). Serve hot or warm, sprinkled with salt and lime juice.

Potatoes

One of the most abundant and ubiquitous of all vegetables, the humble potato was cultivated in Peru at least seven thousand years ago. But it didn't take root, pardon the pun, in Europe and North America until the eighteenth and nineteenth centuries. Now more than three hundred million tons are produced each year.

All potatoes fall into three basic categories: starchy, waxy, and all-purpose.

Starchy potatoes cook to a dry, fluffy, and mealy texture that's ideal for baking, frying, and mashing. They crumble and break easily when cooked, which is why they are inferior when boiled (unless you want to exploit their crumbly quality in stews and soups, where their starch thickens and adds body). Russet potatoes, which include Idaho, are the archetypal starchy potato and are often called "baking potatoes." They are large and oval-shaped with a sandy-feeling, light brown "russeted" skin and off-white flesh.

Waxy potatoes, sometimes called "new" or "boiling" potatoes, have a low starch content; their texture is moister, creamier, and firmer. They are typified by their smooth, thin skin, which is most often a rosy red or yellowish white color depending on variety. They hold their shape well during cooking and are ideal for boiling, steaming, and roasting.

All-purpose potatoes are in between starchy and waxy potatoes; they're good mashed, fried, and baked, whenever you want potatoes that don't fall apart easily with some fluffiness (they contain too much starch to make them ideal for boiling). Yukon Gold potatoes are the model all-purpose potato.

Buying and storing: Potatoes should be firm, unshriveled, and without soft spots, sprouts, or greening, which is caused by exposure to sun and produces an alkaloid called *solanine,* which is mildly toxic; just cut off that part—the rest of the potato is perfectly edible. Store in a dark, cool, dry spot for weeks.

Preparing: Wash and peel if you like; remove any eyes, dark spots, or greening. If the potato is largely green or has rot, discard it.

Best cooking methods: Any, depending on type (see the chart at right).

When is it done? When a skewer or sharp knife inserted into one meets almost no resistance.

Other vegetables to substitute: Sweet potato, taro, cassava, boniato, or malanga.

Baked Potatoes

MAKES: 4 servings
TIME: About 1 hour

Dry, fluffy, and wonderfully mealy, baked potatoes are easy. Forget wrapping them in foil or using the microwave, because both techniques basically steam the potatoes, and the results are inferior. Second, keep the oven at 425°F, which is the optimum temperature. You can crank it up to 450°F to gain a little speed, though you'll sacrifice some texture.

Other vegetables you can use: any whole, thick-skinned root vegetable, like rutabaga, turnip, or beet, though none will be as starchy and fluffy as the potato.

4 large starchy potatoes, like Idaho or other russets
Salt and freshly ground black pepper

1 Heat the oven to 425°F. Scrub the potatoes well, especially if you plan to eat the skins. Use a skewer or a thin-bladed knife to poke a hole or two in each potato.

2 Put the potatoes in the oven, right on the rack if you like, or on a rimmed baking sheet. The potatoes are done when a skewer or sharp knife inserted into one meets almost no resistance. (You can turn them once during baking, though it's not necessary.)

3 The potatoes will stay hot for a few minutes. To serve, cut a slit lengthwise into each about halfway into the flesh and pinch the ends toward the middle to fluff, sprinkle with salt and pepper, then top (see the list at right for some ideas).

Salted Baked Potatoes. After scrubbing, rub each potato with about a teaspoon of extra virgin olive oil

USING POTATOES IN RECIPES

Here is a quick rundown of what type of potato is best in various recipes. Keep in mind that sometimes it comes down to personal preference: If you like the mealy and crumbly texture of starchy potatoes in your potato salad, or the moist and creamy texture of mashed potatoes made from waxy potatoes, then by all means use them.

STARCHY POTATOES	WAXY POTATOES	ALL-PURPOSE POTATOES
Potato and Leek Soup (pages 131–133)	Potato and Leek Soup (page 131)	Potato and Leek Soup (page 131)
Baked Potatoes (page 336)	Potato Salad (page 189)	Potato Salad (page 189)
Mashed Potatoes (page 339)	Boiled or Steamed Potatoes (page 337)	Boiled or Steamed Potatoes (page 337)
Potato Gratin (page 346)	Crisp Panfried Potatoes (page 341)	Braised Potatoes (page 343)
French Fries (page 346)	Oven-Roasted Potatoes (page 341)	Potato Rösti (page 345)
	Grilled or Broiled Potatoes (page 342)	Potato Gratin (page 346)
	Braised Potatoes (page 343)	
	Potato Gratin (page 346)	

or butter. Then rub each all over with a fair amount of salt.

Bay- or Rosemary-Scented Baked Potatoes. After scrubbing the potatoes, cut a deep slit lengthwise into each and sprinkle with salt and pepper. Put a couple of bay leaves or a sprig of fresh rosemary in each slit and drizzle with extra virgin olive oil, then close them up and set them on a baking sheet. Smear some olive oil around their skins and sprinkle with more salt and pepper.

15 Toppings for Baked Potatoes

1. Any cooked or raw salsa or chutney (pages 23, 33–38, and 48–50)
2. Soy sauce or Soy Dipping Sauce and Marinade (page 25)
3. Extra virgin olive oil or Flavored Oil (page 26)
4. Garlic or other flavored mayonnaise (page 42)
5. Ketchup (to make your own, see page 51)
6. Barbecue sauce (to make your own, see page 52)
7. Any vinaigrette (pages 199–202), especially Mustard Vinaigrette
8. The classic: butter, sour cream, and/or minced chives
9. Crumbled cooked bacon, sausage, or chorizo
10. Cottage cheese
11. A few dashes of hot sauce
12. Worcestershire sauce
13. Goat or cream cheese
14. Grated cheese, like cheddar, Parmesan, Asiago, or Jack
15. Whipped cream (unsweetened and lightly salted or seasoned)

Boiled Potatoes

MAKES: 4 servings

TIME: About 30 minutes

Many potato dishes start with partially or even fully cooked potatoes; boiling or steaming is the simplest way to get the job done. You can use these techniques for starchy, waxy, and all-purpose potatoes, though the

Twice-Baked Potatoes

Not only do people love these, but almost all the work is up front, which makes them perfect for entertaining. They're also ideal for single dining, and for using up all sorts of leftovers.

Bake the potatoes, cool them a bit, and scoop their flesh into a large bowl, leaving their skins intact, like a shell. Mash the flesh, adding other ingredients to jazz them up (see the list below), then pile the works back into the skins. Wrap them up in foil (or not, as I generally prefer, so you get a nice crust), refrigerate them for up to a few hours if you like, and pop them back into the oven shortly before you're ready to eat. At 400°F, most will take only 20 to 30 minutes to reheat.

16 Fillings for Twice-Baked Potatoes

Figure a total of about ½ cup of extra ingredients for each large potato; they won't hold much more. Mix and match as you like.

1. Chopped fresh herbs
2. Chopped olives, hot red pepper flakes, chopped parsley, and olive oil
3. Grated hard cheese or soft cheese like Brie, goat, or cream cheese
4. Crumbled cooked bacon or sausage
5. Puréed or finely chopped cooked vegetables, like eggplant, carrots, broccoli, or spinach, with lots of butter or extra virgin olive oil
6. Minced shrimp with any pesto or herb purée (pages 27–28)
7. Any pesto or herb purée (pages 27–28)
8. Compound Butter (page 32)
9. Any chutney (pages 36–38)
10. Cold Mustard Sauce (page 42)
11. Salsa Roja (page 48)
12. Smooth Green Chile Sauce, Indian Style (page 54)
13. Hollandaise Sauce (page 59)
14. Any spice blend or Chile Paste (pages 66–69 or 74–75) except pickling spice; best with a little butter, flavorful oil, or dairy or nondairy milk
15. Coconut milk and curry powder, garam masala, or chaat masala (to make your own, see pages 389 and 66–68)
16. Fast Tomato Sauce (page 502)

results will vary; consult the chart on page 337 to match the right potato with the dish you plan to make. (If boiled potatoes are your ultimate goal, use any red- or thin-skinned waxy variety.) In general, it's fine to peel and/or cut potatoes before boiling or steaming, and obviously that speeds things up. The results will also be a bit waterlogged (less so if you steam), so if time is not an issue, cook your spuds whole; it's easiest to peel them when they're still hot.

2 pounds potatoes

Salt

❶ Peel the potatoes before cooking if you like. If you're in a hurry, cut the larger ones into halves or quarters. Cut or whole, the idea is to have all the pieces about the same size. Put them in a large, deep pot and cover with cold water. Add a large pinch of salt and bring to a boil.

❷ Keep the water rolling until the potatoes are done, anywhere from 15 to 30 minutes, depending on the size of the pieces and how tender you want them. The potatoes are done when a skewer or sharp knife inserted into one meets almost no resistance.

❸ Drain the potatoes well and let them dry out a bit. If peeling, give them an extra few minutes to cool enough to handle. See "The Many Ways to Flavor Mashed Potatoes" on page 340 for serving ideas (simply toss the ingredients with the warm potatoes). Or refrigerate, tightly covered, for up to 3 days. Reheat in the microwave or use in any recipe that calls for cooked potatoes.

 Fast   Make Ahead   Vegetarian

Steamed Potatoes. These don't get waterlogged, and they retain more nutrients: Set up a steamer in a large pot (see page 20). Put water in the bottom and the potatoes above them. Sprinkle with a little salt if you like. Bring the water to a boil and steam for 15 to 30 minutes.

Mashed Potatoes

MAKES: 4 servings

TIME: About 40 minutes

Starchy potatoes make the fluffiest mash, but Yukon Gold or other all-purpose potatoes do well too. If you like mashed potatoes with the peel, make sure you scrub them well before cooking. If you like them lumpy, mash with a fork or potato masher; if you like them smooth and light, use a food mill or ricer. Just keep them away from mixers, food processors, or blenders, which makes them gummy.

Other keys to keeping mashed potatoes fluffy: Cook them whole if possible; cook them with the peel on if possible (the peels will slip off easily after cooking, or you can eat them of course); and refrain from poking them. All of these steps reduce the tendency of the spuds to absorb water, which makes them heavier.

Once the potatoes are mashed and combined with the milk and butter, they will keep for a little while in a double boiler. For even better control over them for timing a full meal, it's easier to boil the potatoes a little ahead of time and let them sit for an hour or so (see Step 1).

Other vegetables you can use: any vegetable can be mashed; see "More Ideas for Vegetable Purées" (page 243).

2 pounds starchy or all-purpose potatoes

1 cup milk, plus more if needed

4 tablespoons (½ stick) butter

Salt and freshly ground black pepper

❶ Boil the potatoes according to the recipe on page 337. (The potatoes can be prepared to this point up to an hour in advance; just leave them in a colander to drain and dry out a bit.)

❷ While the potatoes are draining, wipe the pot dry and put it back on the stove over medium-low heat. Add the milk and the butter and sprinkle with salt and pepper.

❸ When the butter is almost melted, remove the pot from the heat. Rice the potatoes or run them through a food mill set over the pot or add them directly to the milk mixture and mash with a fork or potato masher. Return the pot to the heat and stir constantly with a wooden spoon to reach the desired consistency, adding more milk if necessary. Taste, adjust the seasoning, and serve.

Mashed Baked Potatoes. The drier texture means they'll soak up more milk and butter: Bake potatoes according to the recipe on page 336. Peel or not and cut into cubes. Proceed with the recipe from Step 2, adding more milk and butter if you like.

"Smashed" Potatoes. Omit the milk. In Step 3, add the potatoes directly to the melted butter in the pan and mash roughly with a fork or masher, leaving lots of lumps. Stir a few times, adding more butter if you like.

Garlicky Mashed Potatoes. Peel 1 or 2 heads of garlic (or even 3 if you're a fanatic) and boil them along with the potatoes. If you want stronger garlic mash, add a teaspoon or a tablespoon of minced garlic along with the milk and butter.

Buttermilk Mashed Potatoes. Tangy and fresh tasting: Instead of milk, use buttermilk.

Joël Robuchon Mashed Potatoes. Only a famous French chef could get away with suggesting so much butter (if you really want to go overboard, replace some or all of the milk with cream): In Step 2, after you drain the potatoes, put ½ pound (2 sticks) of butter in the pot and set it over medium-low heat to melt, taking care not to let it turn brown. Whisk in the milk or cream. Then proceed with the recipe from Step 3.

The Many Ways to Flavor Mashed Potatoes

Beyond milk and butter, there are infinite ways to customize mashed potatoes (or any plain-cooked potato for that matter). Some involve simply adding ingredients to the finished mash, while others require incorporating seasonings earlier in the process. You can mix and match as you like of course, but be careful not to fuse too many strong flavors:

Add to the butter as it melts (Step 2):

- Chopped fresh onion: up to ¹/₂ cup of any kind
- Minced fresh shallots: up to ¹/₄ cup
- Minced garlic: 2 or more teaspoons (but up to 2 tablespoons)
- Roasted Garlic (page 303): 1 or more heads, peeled
- Minced or grated fresh ginger: 1 or 2 tablespoons
- Minced fresh chile (like jalapeño or Thai), or to taste, or hot red pepper flakes or cayenne to taste
- Curry powder (to make your own, see pages 66–67): 1 tablespoon or more
- Other spice blend (to make your own, see pages 65–69): 1 to 2 tablespoons practically any kind
- Horseradish, grated fresh or prepared: 2 tablespoons or more to taste
- Chile Paste (page 74): to taste

Stir into the mashed potatoes as they heat (Step 3; reduce the milk to ¹/₂ cup; you can always add more later):

- Chopped fresh light herbs, like parsley, mint, chives, basil, or cilantro: up to 1 cup

- Grated cheese, virtually any that will melt, like Parmesan, Gruyère, cheddar, Jack, or Gouda: up to 1 cup
- Fresh goat cheese: up to 1 cup
- Cream cheese: up to 1 cup
- Sour cream: up to 1 cup
- Traditional Pesto or any herb purée (pages 27–28): up to 1 cup
- Miso: up to ¹/₂ cup of any kind
- Chopped nuts: up to ¹/₂ cup of any kind
- Chopped pitted olives: up to ¹/₂ cup
- Soy sauce: up to ¹/₄ cup
- Ketchup (sounds crazy but it's delicious; to make your own, see page 51): ¹/₂ cup or so
- Barbecue sauce (to make your own, see page 52): ¹/₂ cup or so
- Mustard: up to ¹/₄ cup
- Crumbled bacon or sausage: up to 1 cup of any kind

Use to top mashed potatoes at the table:

- Any Five-Minute Drizzle Sauce (page 22)
- A dollop of sour cream and a sprinkling of minced chives or other fresh herbs
- A drizzle of Flavored Oil (page 26) or Balsamic Syrup (page 51)
- A spoonful of Traditional Pesto or any herb purée or sauce (pages 27–28)
- A ladleful of any Simple Pan Sauce (page 45)

7 Other Vegetables to Mash Along with Potatoes

Replace up to half of the potatoes with any of the following vegetables. Add them to the potatoes while they boil if you like or cook them separately (roasted vegetables are especially nice) and mash them in later.

1. Cabbage, cut into ribbons or chopped
2. Brussels sprouts, quartered
3. Celeriac, turnips, or rutabagas, peeled and cubed
4. Carrots or parsnips, peeled and sliced
5. Peas (frozen are fine; no need to thaw them first), added during the last 3 minutes of cooking

 F Fast   **M** Make Ahead   **V** Vegetarian

6. Winter squash, like butternut or pumpkin, peeled, seeded, and cubed

7. Beets, peeled and cubed (they'll turn the mash fuchsia but taste delicious)

Oven-Roasted Potatoes

MAKES: 4 servings

TIME: About 1 hour

You can oven-roast any kind of potato, with slightly different but always desirable results. Waxy potatoes will form a crisp brown crust and, as long as you cook them long enough, a creamy interior; starchy varieties will darken more easily and turn very, very soft, without crisping as much. Either way, they're fine either hot from the oven or served at room temperature.

Other vegetables you can use: any root vegetable, winter squash, or tropical tuber.

2 tablespoons extra virgin olive oil or melted butter, plus more as needed

2 pounds potatoes

Salt and freshly ground black pepper

1 Heat the oven to 400°F. Smear a large roasting pan or rimmed baking sheet with a little of the oil. It should be large enough to hold all the potatoes in a single layer without overcrowding.

2 Scrub the potatoes and peel them if you like. Make sure they're fairly dry and cut them into chunks of equal size, anywhere from 1 to 2 inches wide. Put them in the pan, drizzle with 2 tablespoons of the oil, and toss gently to coat. Sprinkle with salt and pepper.

3 Roast, undisturbed, for 20 minutes before checking for the first time. If the potatoes release easily from the pan, stir them up a bit or turn the pieces over with tongs. If they look too dry and are sticking, drizzle with a little more oil and toss. Continue roasting, turning every 10 minutes or so, until crisp on the outside and tender inside, another 20 to 40 minutes, depending on the type of potato and how large the chunks are. The potatoes are done when a skewer or sharp knife inserted into one meets almost no resistance.

4 Remove from the oven, taste, and adjust the seasoning or toss with one of the toppings from "The Many Ways to Flavor Mashed Potatoes" (previous page). Serve hot, warm, or at room temperature.

Oven-Roasted "Fries." Not as crisp as French Fries (page 346): Heat the oven and wash the potatoes according to Step 1. Peel the potatoes or not, then cut them into French fry–style batons. Grease 2 baking sheets or line them with parchment paper. Brush the potatoes with the oil and spread out on the baking sheets without crowding. Proceed with the recipe.

Oven-Roasted Hash Browns. Increase the oil to 3 tablespoons. Heat the oven and wash the potatoes according to Step 1. Peel the potatoes, then grate them on the largest holes of a box grater or food processor attachment. Proceed with the recipe, resisting the urge to mess with the potatoes frequently. When they're crisp on the bottom, use a spatula to turn large portions over and press them down a bit like diner hash browns. Serve immediately.

Crisp Panfried Potatoes (Home Fries)

MAKES: 4 servings

TIME: About 45 minutes

This technique produces excellent restaurant-style results, but you need waxy potatoes, because starchy ones will fall apart before they get crisp, and patience. If you're short on time, make the first variation. And for a more decadent version, substitute butter for half the oil.

Other vegetables you can use: beets, rutabagas, parsnips, or carrots, though they won't get quite as crisp.

About 2 pounds waxy potatoes

¹/₄ cup peanut oil, extra virgin olive oil, or neutral oil, like grapeseed or corn

Salt and freshly ground black pepper

1 Peel the potatoes if you like—it isn't at all necessary, since waxy potatoes have thin, delicious skins—and cut them into 1-inch chunks. Put the oil in a large skillet, preferably nonstick or cast iron, over medium heat. When hot, add the potatoes. Cook, undisturbed, until they begin to brown around the edges and release from the pan, about 10 minutes.

2 Continue cooking, turning to brown all the sides without stirring too often. (This is the part that takes the most patience.) Add more oil if needed to prevent the potatoes from sticking. And if they are browning too fast, turn the heat down just a tad. They'll take up to 20 more minutes to cook.

3 When the potatoes are tender and golden, turn the heat up a bit to crisp them up. Sprinkle with salt and pepper and toss to coat. Taste, adjust the seasoning, and serve hot or at room temperature.

Last-Minute Crisp Panfried Potatoes. These are make-ahead and take less oil to cook; you can also make them from leftover boiled, steamed, or baked potatoes (pages 336–339): After cutting the potatoes, boil them in salted water to cover until tender, 10 to 15 minutes. Drain, cool, cover, and refrigerate for up to 2 days. In Step 2, cook the potatoes over medium-high heat in 2 tablespoons of oil instead of ¹/₄ cup. Proceed with the recipe, watching the potatoes more closely. They will crisp and turn brown in about half the time.

Crisp Panfried Potatoes, Spanish Style (Patatas Bravas). Serve the finished potatoes with a drizzle of Garlic Mayonnaise (page 42) and a bottle of hot sauce on the side.

Grilled or Broiled Potatoes

MAKES: 4 servings
TIME: About 40 minutes

The key to grilling or broiling potatoes is to use moderate heat at first so they don't char. To get more control over the process, try the variation; they won't be quite as crisp, though the interior will be creamier, so it's sort of a trade-off.

Other vegetables you can use: any tropical tuber or root vegetable; cooking times will vary a bit, depending on size and density.

2 pounds waxy potatoes

2 tablespoons extra virgin olive oil, plus more as needed

Salt and freshly ground black pepper

1 Heat a charcoal or gas grill to moderate heat and put the rack about 4 inches from the heat source. Or heat the broiler and move the rack 6 to 8 inches away from the heat source.

2 Scrub the potatoes and peel if you like. Cut them lengthwise into halves or thirds so the pieces are about ¹/₂ inch thick. Toss them in 2 tablespoons of olive oil, adding more as needed to coat; sprinkle with salt and pepper and toss again.

3 Put the potatoes on the grill rack or broiler pan. Grill or broil, undisturbed, for about 10 minutes, then check; they should look blistery but not yet browned. Keep cooking until they start to turn golden, then flip and repeat with the other side, brushing with more oil if needed to keep them from sticking. The potatoes are done when a skewer or sharp knife inserted into one meets almost no resistance. If they aren't yet crisp enough for you, move them closer to the fire and make the fire hotter on the grill or move the rack closer to the broiler. Taste, adjust the seasoning, and serve immediately or at room temperature.

Last-Minute Grilled or Broiled Potatoes. Great for skewering on kebabs with vegetables or other ingredients

F Fast   **M** Make Ahead   **V** Vegetarian

that cook fast because everything will be ready at the same time: After preparing the potatoes in Step 2, boil them (see page 337) until they begin to become tender, about 5 minutes at a steady boil. (At this point, you may leave the potatoes on the counter for an hour or so or refrigerate them for up to 2 days.) Grill over moderate heat or broil about 4 inches away from the heat source. The potatoes will take about half the time to crisp up as they do in the main recipe.

Braised Potatoes, Ten Ways

MAKES: 4 servings
TIME: About 40 minutes

If you sear potatoes, then simmer them in liquid with aromatic vegetables—just as you would meat—the result is a simple stew with a texture that's tough to beat. Try this recipe with small heirloom potatoes like fingerlings.

Other vegetables or fruits you can use: any root vegetable or winter squash or even apples.

2 pounds all-purpose or waxy potatoes

3 tablespoons extra virgin olive oil

Salt and freshly ground black pepper

1 small onion, minced

2 cups stock (to make your own, see pages 157–159) or water

1/4 cup chopped fresh parsley leaves for garnish

1 Peel the potatoes and cut them into large chunks, in half if they're midsized, and leave them whole if they're small.

2 Put the oil in a large pot over medium-high heat. When hot, add the potatoes and sprinkle with salt and pepper. Cook, stirring occasionally, until coated in oil and beginning to turn golden. Add the onion and stir a few times until it softens, a minute or two.

3 Add the stock and enough water so that the potatoes are barely covered. Bring to a boil, stirring once in a while to make sure the potatoes aren't sticking, then turn the heat to medium-low so that the mixture bubbles gently. Cook, stirring occasionally, until the potatoes get tender, 20 to 25 minutes. Add more liquid if they start to stick. The potatoes are done when a skewer or sharp knife inserted into one meets almost no resistance. Taste and adjust the seasoning, garnish with parsley, and serve hot or at room temperature.

Braised Potatoes and Garlic. Omit the onion. Peel 1 or 2 heads of garlic and add them along with the potatoes in Step 2. Proceed with the recipe, garnishing with grated Parmesan if you like.

Wine-Braised Potatoes with Bacon. Add 4 ounces chopped bacon. Substitute white wine for half the stock. Omit the oil, along with the onions too if you like. In Step 1, start cooking the bacon, and when some of the fat has rendered, add the potatoes. Proceed with the recipe.

Cream-Braised Potatoes. Use butter instead of olive oil. Instead of the stock or water, use cream, and use milk to finish covering the potatoes in Step 3. When the potatoes are done, stir in 1 tablespoon minced fresh tarragon or chervil if you like, instead of the parsley garnish, and serve hot.

Braised Potatoes with Kielbasa. Make this with beer as in the following variation if you like: Add 1 pound sliced kielbasa along with the onion in Step 2.

Beer-Braised Potatoes with Horseradish and Cheddar. Toss 1 cup grated cheddar cheese with 1 tablespoon of cornstarch. Instead of the stock, use beer or milk. When the potatoes are almost done, stir in the cheese mixture and a tablespoon or more of grated fresh or prepared horseradish. Add more beer or milk if the potatoes look too dry; they should be a little saucy. Stir until the cheese melts. Garnish and serve hot.

Braised Potatoes with Mustard. When you add the stock in Step 3, stir in 1/4 cup of any mustard, coarse-ground or Dijon.

Braised Curried Potatoes in Coconut Milk. Replace the olive oil with a neutral oil, like grapeseed or corn. Add 1 tablespoon each finely chopped fresh ginger and garlic and 2 teaspoons curry powder or garam masala (to make your own, see pages 66–67). Instead of the stock, use coconut milk (to make your own, see page 389). Proceed with the recipe, stirring in a cup or so fresh or frozen green peas if you like; they need only about 3 minutes to cook. Garnish with chopped fresh cilantro instead of the parsley and minced fresh Thai chile if you like.

Soy-Braised Potatoes. Instead of the olive oil, use 1 tablespoon dark sesame oil and 2 tablespoons neutral oil, like grapeseed or corn. Instead of the stock, use a mixture of $1/4$ cup soy sauce and $1^3/4$ cups water. Trim and chop a bunch of scallions and use that instead of the onion. Proceed with the recipe (don't add salt until the potatoes are just about done and taste first, using salt or more soy). Garnish with cilantro instead of parsley and sprinkle with sesame seeds and minced fresh chile.

Braised Potatoes with Miso. Use neutral oil, like grapeseed or corn, instead of olive oil. Omit the onion, and instead of the parsley, use sliced scallion for garnish. Proceed with the recipe through Step 3, taking care not to oversalt. When the potatoes are done, remove from the heat. Whisk together $1/2$ cup warm stock or water and stir in $1/4$ cup any miso; add this mixture to the potatoes and stir well to combine and warm through. Taste, adjust the seasoning, garnish, and serve.

Curried Stir-Fried Potatoes

MAKES: 4 servings

TIME: 20 minutes

If you cut potatoes small enough, they'll become tender quickly, but in this dish—inspired by similar creations popular in Sichuan and throughout India—they remain slightly crunchy. Best with homemade curry powder or garam masala. The cumin seeds add a nice bit of crunch, and the cilantro adds a fresh note at the end, but neither is essential.

Other vegetables you can use: cauliflower, broccoli, carrots, turnips, radishes, celeriac.

> 3 tablespoons neutral oil, like corn or canola
>
> 1 tablespoon cumin seeds (optional)
>
> 1 small red onion, finely chopped
>
> $1^1/2$ pounds all-purpose potatoes, peeled and shredded or minced
>
> 1 tablespoon garam masala or curry powder (to make your own, see pages 66–67), or to taste
>
> Salt and freshly ground black pepper
>
> Pinch cayenne
>
> $1/4$ cup chopped fresh cilantro leaves

1 Put the oil in a large nonstick or well-seasoned cast-iron skillet over medium-high heat. When hot, add the cumin seeds if you're using them, fry them for 30 seconds, then add half the onion and the potatoes. Add the spice blend, salt, pepper, and cayenne. Cook, stirring or tossing, until the onion has caramelized and the potatoes are lightly browned, about 10 minutes; the potatoes need not be fully tender.

2 Add the cilantro to the pan, toss once, and transfer to a serving platter. Garnish with the raw onion and serve immediately.

Stir-Fried Potatoes, Korean Style. Omit the cumin, onion, spice blend, and cilantro; use scallion instead of red onion. In Step 1, add 1 teaspoon garlic to the oil (you're going to need 2 teaspoons in all), then half the scallion and the potatoes about 30 seconds later, along with about a tablespoon minced fresh chile (like jalapeño or Thai), or to taste, or hot red pepper flakes or cayenne to taste. In Step 2, add the remaining garlic, along with a teaspoon of minced ginger, and cook for 30 seconds or so. Garnish with a tablespoon or two toasted sesame seeds (page 317) and serve.

F Fast   **M** Make Ahead   **V** Vegetarian

Potato Rösti

MAKES: 4 servings
TIME: 20 minutes

The simplest skillet potato cake—you don't even have to peel the potatoes. And it's delicious warm or at room temperature, which buys you a few minutes for getting the rest of dinner on the table.

Other vegetables you can use: beets or any other root vegetable or any winter squash.

2 pounds all-purpose potatoes

Salt and freshly ground black pepper

2 tablespoons extra virgin olive oil or butter, plus more as needed

① Scrub the potatoes and peel them if you like. Grate them in a food processor or by hand; drain well in a colander or strainer. Heat a large skillet, preferably non-stick or cast iron, over medium heat.

② Toss the potatoes in a bowl with a generous sprinkling of salt and pepper; put 2 tablespoons of the oil or butter in the skillet and heat until it begins to turn nut brown. Put the potato mixture into the skillet, shape it into a nice circle, and press it down with a spatula. Turn the heat to medium-high and cook, shaking the pan occasionally, until the bottom of the potato cake is nicely crisp, 6 to 8 minutes.

③ Slide the cake out onto a plate, top with another plate, and invert the plates. Add a little more oil or butter to the pan and slide the cake back in (see the illustration at right). Continue to cook, adjusting the heat if necessary, until the second side is browned, 5 to 10 minutes. Cut into wedges and serve.

Latkes. Small patties are traditional, but if you're short on time, make one big pancake: Use starchy potatoes and add a medium onion, 2 lightly beaten eggs, and 2 tablespoons plain bread crumbs or matzo meal. Grate the onion along with the potatoes and then mix in the eggs and bread crumbs and sprinkle well with salt and pepper. Use a neutral oil, like grapeseed or corn, for cooking. Proceed with the recipe, forming pancakes by spooning the mixture into the hot oil or butter and adding more fat as necessary.

Potato Pancakes with Scallions and Kimchi. Add 2 chopped scallions, $1/2$ cup drained and chopped Kimchi (page 230), and 1 egg. Mix the grated potatoes with the scallions, kimchi, egg, and some salt and pepper. Proceed with the recipe, making one big pancake or whatever size you like. Serve with Soy Dipping Sauce and Marinade (page 25).

FLIPPING POTATO RÖSTI OR ANY LARGE VEGETABLE PANCAKE

1

2

(**STEP 1**) To turn this or any large pancake, slide the half-cooked cake onto a plate. (**STEP 2**) Cover with another plate, invert, and slide back into the pan.

7 Garnishes for Potato Rösti or Latkes

1. Sour cream or crème fraîche
2. Applesauce (to make your own, see page 383)
3. Minced chives or other fresh herbs, like parsley, mint, dill, or chervil
4. Real Ranch Dressing (page 42)—outrageous, but excellent
5. Traditional Pesto or other herb sauce (pages 27–29)
6. Homemade Mayonnaise or any of the variations (page 41)
7. Salsa Roja (page 48) or Salsa Verde (page 49)

Potato Gratin

MAKES: 4 servings
TIME: About 1 hour

Based on raw potatoes (or other vegetables), cream, and cheese, this can be assembled and even baked up to 2 days in advance and either baked or reheated before serving. A mandoline makes slicing a breeze and gives you slices of consistent thickness with little work, which is the key to even cooking.

Other cooked vegetables you can use: alone or in combination—sweet potatoes, parsnips, celery root, sunchokes, cauliflower, rutabagas, any winter squash, burdock, celery, celeriac, carrots, or horseradish, which will mellow while cooking.

> 2 to 3 cups cream, half-and-half, milk, or a combination
>
> 1 pound potatoes, peeled and thinly sliced
>
> ¹/₂ cups grated Gruyère or Swiss cheese
>
> Salt and freshly ground black pepper
>
> 1 tablespoon fresh thyme leaves

1 Heat the oven to 375°F. Put the cream in a pot and heat until it's hot.

2 Layer the potatoes and cheese (be sure to end with cheese) in a large gratin or similar ovenproof dish; sprin-

kle every potato layer with a bit of salt, pepper, and thyme. Pour in enough hot cream to come about three-quarters of the way up the potato layers.

3 Put in the oven and cook, undisturbed, until the potatoes are tender (a thin-bladed knife will pierce them with little or no resistance) and the top is nicely browned, 45 to 50 minutes. Serve immediately or keep warm in the oven for up to 30 minutes.

Potato Gratin with Crème Fraîche or Sour Cream. Substitute crème fraîche or sour cream for the cheese. (Spread it between the layers with a spatula or knife.)

Scalloped Potatoes. Omit the cheese; you'll need closer to 3 cups cream. Sprinkle ¹/₂ cup bread crumbs, preferably fresh (page 876), over the top after pouring on the cream in Step 2.

Baked Curried Potatoes. Substitute coconut milk (to make your own, see page 389) for the cream and omit the cheese. Add ¹/₂ small onion, thinly sliced, and 2 teaspoons curry powder (to make your own, see pages 66–67). Sprinkle the top with shredded coconut and chopped cashews just before baking.

French Fries

MAKES: 4 servings
TIME: 30 minutes

It only seems like a hassle to double-fry French fries, which is the classic and, I dare say, correct technique; in reality it's a double blessing. Your fries will not only stay crisp longer, but the first step can be done well in advance, leaving you only a quick final frying right before serving. Starchy potatoes are the only option here; waxy potatoes never quite crisp up right. Purists like to salt the fries and leave it at that, but you can dust them with virtually any spice blend (to make your own, see pages 65–69).

 Fast   Make Ahead   **V** Vegetarian

Other vegetables you can use: sweet potatoes, parsnips, or celery root.

    Peanut oil or neutral oil, like grapeseed or corn, for
      deep-frying
    2 pounds starchy potatoes
    Salt and freshly ground black pepper

1 Put at least 3 inches oil in a deep pan on the stove and turn the heat to medium-high; bring to 300°F to 325°F (see "Deep Frying," page 19).

2 Scrub the potatoes and peel them if you like. Cut them any way you like—from shoestrings to big batons—and make sure they're fairly dry. Drop them, a handful at a time, into the oil, adjusting the heat as needed to maintain the temperature. Fry the potatoes in one batch, stirring occasionally, for 5 to 10 minutes, depending on the cut. The goal of this first frying is to cook them until just tender and beginning to color slightly. Drain batches on paper towels or a wire rack. (At this point, you may set the potatoes aside on the counter for an hour or so before proceeding. Be sure to take the oil off the heat.)

3 Heat the oil again, this time to around 350°F. Fry and drain the potatoes the same way, until crisp and deeply colored, just a couple of minutes. Sprinkle with salt and pepper while still hot and serve immediately.

Potato Chips. No prefrying necessary. You'll need a deeper, larger pot or deep fryer; be prepared for the potatoes to absorb more oil. Use a mandoline or a sharp knife to cut the potatoes lengthwise. You want them pretty thin, but not too wispy. Heat the oil to about 350°F. Work in batches, using a slotted spoon or strainer to fish them out of the hot oil as they turn golden. Drain on paper towels or brown bags. Season while hot and serve.

USING A MANDOLINE

Japanese mandolines are inexpensive and incredibly useful. You can make perfectly thin slices of almost any vegetable in seconds—just watch your fingers.

Radishes
Red, White, Black, and Daikon

The more common round or oblong radishes come in an array of colors—bright pink to crimson red, purple, and white. We mostly eat them raw, but they are also quite delicious cooked.

    Daikon, an Asian radish, can be as big as your arm and is often sold cut into pieces. It's ivory white, mild, and especially common in Japanese and Korean cuisines.

    Black radishes are a spicy-hot type of radish with black skin and white flesh; shred and use as garnish or eat with buttered bread.

    Buying and storing: Radishes with their greens are best (when really fresh, the leaves make a spicy addition to salads). The root should be firm, crisp, and smooth. Large specimens of naturally small radishes can be woody, so watch out for that. Store wrapped loosely in plastic in the refrigerator.

    Preparing: Trim and peel if you like (black radishes should always be peeled); slice or chop as necessary.

    Best cooking methods: Sautéing (in butter) and braising and glazing.

    When is it done? When crisp-tender to fully tender but not mushy.

    Other vegetables to substitute: Jícama or water chestnuts if raw; turnips if cooked.

Braised and Glazed Radishes, Turnips, or Other Root Vegetable

MAKES: 4 servings

TIME: 30 minutes

A basic and wonderful way to prepare all kinds of root vegetables. Jazz this up with a few sprigs of fresh thyme or a teaspoon of curry powder or other spice mix (to make your own, see pages 65–69) or a couple cloves of garlic.

Other vegetables you can use: anything hard and fibrous, really—carrots, jícama, parsnips, celeriac, carrots, waxy potatoes (but not vegetables that easily become mushy, like starchy potatoes or sweet potatoes).

2 tablespoons butter or extra virgin olive oil

1 pound radishes, trimmed, or daikon, turnips, or
    rutabaga, peeled and cut into chunks

1/2 cup stock (to make your own, see pages 157–159),
    white wine, or water, or more as needed

Salt and freshly ground black pepper

Freshly squeezed lemon juice (optional)

Chopped fresh parsley leaves for garnish

1 Combine the butter or oil, radishes, and stock in a saucepan, sprinkle with salt and pepper, and bring to a boil. Cover and adjust the heat so the mixture simmers; cook until the radishes are tender, 15 to 20 minutes, checking once or twice and adding liquid as needed.

2 Uncover and raise the heat to boil off almost all the liquid, so that the vegetable becomes glazed in the combination of butter or oil and pan juices. Taste and adjust the seasoning, add a little lemon juice if you like, garnish with parsley, and serve.

Braised and Glazed Radishes or Other Root Vegetable with Miso. Try this with daikon: In Step 1, add a tablespoon of soy sauce. In Step 2, as the mixture becomes glazed, whisk together 2 tablespoons any miso (white is mildest) and an equal amount of stock or water; turn the heat under the radishes to a minimum, add the miso mixture, stir, and heat very gently for a minute or so before serving. (Omit the lemon juice and parsley garnish.)

Sea Greens

Sea Vegetables, Seaweed

Sea greens are flavorful, nicely textured, diverse, and incredibly nutritious; they're almost always sold dry, which makes them ultra-convenient as well. For the most part, they're wild, which makes them organic. The supply is huge, and they're not expensive.

None of this explains their lack of popularity—a lack of tradition and the word *weed* is to blame for most of that—which I'm trying to do my part to rectify.

Buying and storing: The best selection is at Asian markets, natural food stores, and on-line (see Sources, page 982). Store in a cool, dry spot, where it will keep indefinitely. Fresh sea beans should be crisp, bright green, and smell like the ocean. Store in the refrigerator and use as quickly as possible.

Preparing:

Arame, hijiki, kombu, wakame, and alaria: Use a damp paper towel to wipe kombu, but don't rinse. For all of these, soak in warm water until tender, about 5 to 10 minutes. (Save the water for another use.) Chop or slice as you like.

Dulse: Use straight out of the package or just give it a rinse in cold water.

Nori: Requires no soaking; cut it with scissors as needed. It's often toasted before use (see page 350).

Sea beans: Rinse and chop only if necessary.

Best cooking methods:

Arame, hijiki, alaria, and wakame: Boiling and sautéing or stir-frying with other ingredients.

Dulse: Quickly sautéing or stir-frying.

Kombu: Boiling and braising.

Sea beans: 30 seconds in boiling water, a quick stir-fry, or in a frittata; but they're just as good raw.

When is it done? When tender.

Other vegetables to substitute: Most sea greens, with the exception of sea beans and kombu, are interchangeable. Substitute French-cut green beans (see page 305) for sea beans.

The Sea Green Lexicon

Below is a primer of the various types of sea greens you're likely to find at some supermarkets, natural food stores, and, of course, Asian markets.

Arame and Hijiki

Different varieties but similar in look and use; both are slender, almost hairy strands. Arame is finer, milder, and lighter in color, hijiki is black, briny, and expands massively when rehydrated. Use in salads, soups, and stews or add to sautés or stir-fries.

Dulse

Dark red, crumpled-looking, and relatively soft. It can be eaten straight out of the package or added to salads, sandwiches, or soups.

Kombu

Kelp

A main ingredient in Dashi (page 160), kelp contains a substance similar to MSG that enhances flavors. Best cooked with slow-simmered foods like beans, grains, soups, and stews. Sold in large, thick, hard, dark green pieces. Occasionally sold fresh on the West Coast.

Nori

Laver

The familiar thin, shiny sheets that are used to wrap sushi. Deep greenish purple, almost black, brittle when dry, and chewy when moistened. Nori dissolves in liquid and has a mild, nutty flavor; it's excellent toasted (see Nori Chips, page 350).

Sea Beans

Samphire, Glasswort

These small, delicate, thin green branches with nubby ends are lovely in salads and egg dishes or used as a garnish. They can also be poached for about 30 seconds, which enhances their flavor slightly. That flavor is as fresh and "sealike" as you can imagine, and the texture is crisp and delightful. If you see it fresh, buy it; when sold pickled, in jars, it's less exciting.

Wakame and Alaria

Used interchangeably; the former is harvested in Japan, the latter in North America. Both are dark green when dried and nearly transparent; they turn emerald green when rehydrated. Their flavor is mild, and they're nice in soups and stews or with grains or added to salads.

Sea Green and Celery Stir-Fry

MAKES: 4 servings
TIME: 25 minutes

Among the most nutrient-rich stir-fries you can make; serve it over a whole grain and you've got yourself a powerhouse of a vegetarian meal. Or you can always start by stir-frying some shrimp or sliced chicken or pork, removing it from the pan, and then beginning the recipe; simply add the cooked protein during the last minute or so of cooking.

Use any combination of arame, hijiki, dulse, kombu, wakame, and alaria. But note that kombu should be simmered or soaked first and sliced very finely, and dulse should be added at the last minute.

> 2 tablespoons neutral oil, like grapeseed or corn
>
> 1 tablespoon minced garlic
>
> 1 tablespoon minced fresh ginger
>
> 1/2 cup chopped scallion or onion
>
> 1/2 cup thinly sliced kombu, soaked or simmered in water for 15 minutes

2 celery stalks, thinly sliced lengthwise or julienned

2 cups soaked and thinly sliced (if necessary) sea greens, like arame, hijiki, dulse, wakame, and alaria

¼ cup vegetable stock or dashi (to make your own, see pages 157 and 160) or water, or a little more

2 tablespoons soy sauce

1 teaspoon dark sesame oil

1 Heat a large, deep skillet over medium-high heat for 3 or 4 minutes. Add the oil and, almost immediately, the garlic, ginger, and scallion. Cook, stirring, for about 15 seconds.

2 Add the kombu, celery, sea greens, and stock and turn the heat to high. Cook, stirring constantly, until the vegetables are tender, about 7 minutes. If the mixture is completely dry, add a couple more tablespoons of liquid, then the soy sauce and sesame oil; stir and turn off the heat. Serve or store, covered, in the refrigerator for up to a day.

Sea Green and Mushroom Stir-Fry. Shiitake are best; they add another layer of flavor: Add 1 cup or so sliced mushrooms with the kombu.

Sea Green and Noodle Stir-Fry. Add about 8 ounces fresh Chinese egg noodles or dried Chinese wheat noodles or spaghetti. Bring a large pot of water to a boil and salt it. Cook the noodles until they are tender but not mushy, about 4 minutes for fresh noodles, longer for dried, then drain and rinse; toss with a tablespoon or so of oil to prevent sticking and set aside. Proceed with the recipe; add the noodles and cook, stirring often, until the noodles are hot.

Nori Chips

MAKES: 2 to 4 servings
TIME: 5 minutes

These delicate and crisp "chips," sometimes made as an after-school snack for kids in Japan, are completely addicting. Eat them straight, as a snack, or mix with potato chips, popcorn (cooled, not hot), and Japanese rice crackers—or simply with a bowl of steamed rice.

6 sheets nori

2 tablespoons dark sesame oil

Salt

1 Put a skillet over medium-high heat. Brush one side of the nori with the sesame oil and sprinkle with salt. Put a single nori sheet in the pan and toast it until it shrinks up, about 15 seconds; turn it over and toast the other side for 15 seconds.

2 Use scissors to cut the sheets into rectangular "chips." Serve within a few hours.

Shallots

A member of the allium family (which contains not only onions and garlic but also lilies), shallots have a mild but complex flavor, making them the queen of the category. They come in individual cloves, not unlike garlic but bigger, with the flesh and flavor of a mild onion. They have a tan, papery dried outer skin that tightly covers each clove, and the inside flesh is semitranslucent white with a tinge of purple or green.

Buying and storing: Shallots should be firm and have a pretty, shiny tan outer skin. Their shape is distinctive; usually two cloves held together at the root end to make an oval shape with tapered ends. Don't be fooled by small, round, tan-skinned onions often labeled as shallots. Store in a cool, dry place or in the refrigerator for weeks.

Preparing: Break the cloves apart and remove the dry skins; trim the stem end and slice or chop as you would an onion (see page 324).

Best cooking methods: Sautéing and roasting.

When is it done? When tender and translucent.

F Fast   **M** Make Ahead   **V** Vegetarian

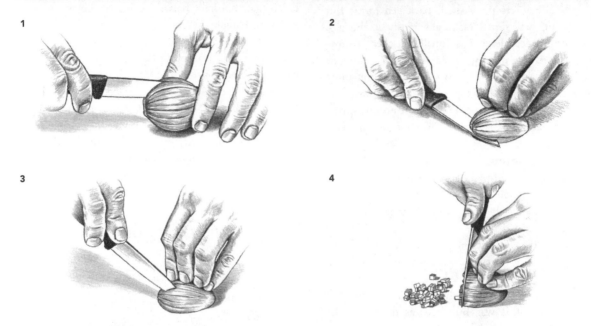

(STEP 1) First peel the shallot, then cut it in half from top to bottom. (STEP 2) Place one half, cut side down, on your cutting board. Make two or three cuts parallel to the cutting board into the vegetable; don't cut all the way through. (STEP 3) Now make as many cuts as practical down through the top. Again, leave the shallot intact at one end. (STEP 4) Cut across to mince.

Other vegetables to substitute: Scallions are closest; onions (especially red or white) and leeks are also good.

Sorrel

These oblong and arrow-shaped green leaves can be anywhere from a couple of inches to a foot in length and are a cross between an herb and a delicate cooking green. The flavor of sorrel is acidic and lemony (it's sometimes called *sourgrass*), which can be mild or intense, depending on the variety and maturity of the plant. Traditionally, sorrel is used in cream soup and to flavor cream sauces, but young, tender leaves can be tossed into salads or omelets or cooked with spinach and other greens and vegetables.

Buying and storing: Check the herb sections of supermarkets, but it's best in the spring at farmers' markets. Store wrapped loosely in plastic in the refrigerator for up to 3 days.

Preparing: Wash well and trim any tough stems; no need to chop it unless you're using it raw.

Best cooking methods: Cooked into soups, stews, and braises or sautéed for omelets. Puréed and stirred with butter, cream, yogurt, or milk, it makes a nice sauce.

When is it done? When the leaves are melted and grayish green in color.

Other vegetables to substitute: Spinach, arugula, and watercress (with a squeeze of lemon juice just before serving).

Spinach

Spinach is among the most convenient vegetables to prepare, especially in its prewashed, packaged form. But bagged or bunched, spinach is finally getting its due as a lovely-tasting vegetable that is equally wonderful slow-cooked, flashed in a pan, or tossed as a green salad. The tender flat-leaf variety is slightly better than the more common large, crinkly leaf type, but more important is where it's grown: Local is better. It's in season in spring and fall—spinach likes cool weather—but supermarkets carry it year-round.

Buying and storing: Buy vibrantly colored green, crisp leaves; those with the pink-hued stem bases are even better (rinse them well and cook them with the leaves). Store wrapped loosely in plastic in the refrigerator; use it before it turns slimy or wilts.

Preparing: If it's in a bunch, either chop off all the stems (if you're in a hurry) or untie the bunch and pick off only the tough stems, leaving the tender ones attached. Wash very thoroughly in several changes of water, especially if it was bunched, as there may be clumps of mud or sand in between the leaves. Chop or slice it after cooking.

Best cooking methods: Steaming and sautéing.

When is it done? As soon as it wilts, though you can cook it longer if you like for extra tenderness (long-and-slow-cooked spinach in butter is dreamy).

Other vegetables to substitute: Arugula, beet greens, or chard.

14 Quick Toppings for Simply Cooked Spinach

Spinach is so flavorful that it doesn't need much. But there are flavorings beyond butter. Start by steaming or boiling (and shocking if you like) a pound of spinach according to the recipe on page 239. Then toss the cooked spinach in a large skillet over low heat with any of the following, alone or in combination:

1. Extra virgin olive oil
2. Freshly squeezed lemon or lime juice
3. Soy sauce
4. Worcestershire sauce
5. Crumbled feta cheese or grated Parmesan
6. Vinegar, especially balsamic, rice, or sherry
7. A sprinkling of dark sesame oil
8. Bonito flakes
9. A pat of any Compound Butter (page 32)
10. Ponzu Sauce (page 40)
11. Balsamic Syrup (page 51)
12. Any Vinaigrette (pages 199–202) or Flavored Oil (page 26)
13. Toasted sesame seeds (see page 317) or chopped nuts
14. Toasted bread crumbs, preferably fresh (page 876)

Spinach with Currants and Nuts

MAKES: 4 servings
TIME: 20 minutes

A Mediterranean classic, sweet from the currants (or raisins), crunchy with nuts, and equally good hot or at room temperature.

Other vegetables you can use: almost any greens, chopped, though most will take a little longer time to cook than spinach, and broccoli, cooked until quite tender.

$^1\!/_4$ cup currants or raisins

1 pound spinach, trimmed of thick stems and well washed

$^1\!/_4$ cup extra virgin olive oil

1 teaspoon minced garlic (optional)

$^1\!/_4$ cup broken walnuts or pine nuts, briefly toasted in a dry skillet (see page 317)

Salt and freshly ground black pepper

❶ Soak the currants in warm water for about 10 minutes while you clean and cook the spinach. Steam or parboil the spinach (see page 239) until tender, less than 5 minutes.

 Fast   Make Ahead   Vegetarian

② When the spinach is cool enough to handle, squeeze all the excess moisture from it; chop it roughly. Put the olive oil in a large skillet over medium heat. When hot, add the garlic if you're using it and cook, stirring occasionally, until golden, about 3 minutes. Add the spinach and raise the heat to medium-high. Cook, stirring occasionally, for about 2 minutes.

③ Drain the currants and add them along with the nuts. Reduce the heat to medium. Cook, stirring occasionally, for another 3 or 4 minutes, until everything glistens. Sprinkle with salt and pepper and serve hot or at room temperature.

Spinach with Oven-Roasted Tomatoes. Omit the currants and nuts. Substitute 4 or so Oven-Roasted Plum Tomatoes (page 361) or Broiled Cherry Tomatoes with Herbs (page 362); slice or chop the plum tomatoes as you like. Add the tomatoes when you would the currants in Step 2; add a handful of chopped pitted black olives if you like, too.

Sushi-Style Spinach. Omit the currants, garlic, and nuts; skip Step 2 entirely. Cool the cooked spinach; squeeze excess moisture from it and chop it. Sprinkle the spinach with a little salt and 1 tablespoon soy sauce. Shape it into a 1-inch-thick log (if you have a bamboo sushi-rolling mat, use this to achieve a perfect shape). Cut the log into 1-inch-long slices; dip both ends of each slice into some toasted sesame seeds (see page 317) and arrange on a plate. Drizzle with a few drops of dark sesame oil; top with a tangle of bonito flakes if you like. Serve immediately or refrigerate.

Rich Spinach Pie

MAKES: 4 servings
TIME: 45 minutes

This is a wonderful, nearly decadent side dish for an elegant dinner or a fancy luncheon or brunch. You can make it even more substantial by adding up to a cup of cooked meat or seafood to the custard: Shredded chicken, chopped shrimp or bacon, and crumbled sausage or ground beef are all good. To make a faster version, skip the crust and just bake the custard in a shallow baking dish or pie plate.

1 recipe Savory Piecrust (page 929), prebaked (see page 928)

Salt

2 pounds spinach, trimmed of thick stems and well washed

1 medium onion, roughly chopped

1 teaspoon minced garlic

3 eggs, lightly beaten

$1/2$ cup cream, half-and-half, or milk

1 cup freshly grated Parmesan cheese

Freshly ground black pepper

$1/2$ cup bread crumbs, preferably fresh (page 876)

2 tablespoons butter or extra virgin olive oil

① Heat the oven to 375°F. Bring a large pot of water to a boil and salt it. Add the spinach and onion and cook for just about a minute, until the spinach wilts. Drain thoroughly and cool a bit, then squeeze out as much of the water as you can and chop it.

② Put the spinach and onion in a bowl with the garlic, eggs, cream, and about half the Parmesan. Mix well, then add salt and pepper to taste.

③ Pour the spinach mixture into the prepared piecrust, then top with more Parmesan, and then the bread crumbs. Dot with butter or drizzle with oil. Bake until the mixture is hot and set and the top is brown, about 20 minutes (if the top threatens to scorch before the mixture is set, lower the heat a bit). Serve hot, warm, or at room temperature.

Spinach-Feta Pie. Substitute crumbled feta cheese for the Parmesan; mix all the feta into the spinach mixture in Step 2.

Spinach Croquettes

MAKES: 4 servings

TIME: 30 minutes

Ⓕ Ⓜ Ⓥ

Quick and crunchy, these lightly thickened spinach patties are cooked in a pan until crisp on the outside but still soft on the inside.

Other vegetables you can use: chard or tender kale (best), collards, arugula, or watercress.

Salt

2 pounds spinach, trimmed of thick stems and well washed

1 medium onion, roughly chopped

2 eggs, lightly beaten

1/2 cup grated Gruyère, Cantal, or other fairly strong cow's milk cheese

1/2 cup bread crumbs, preferably fresh (page 876)

Freshly ground black pepper

2 tablespoons extra virgin olive oil

2 tablespoons butter (or use more oil)

❶ Bring a large pot of water to a boil and salt it. Add the spinach and onion and cook for just about a minute, until the spinach wilts. Drain thoroughly and cool a bit. Chop the spinach and put it and the onion in a bowl, along with the eggs, cheese, and bread crumbs. Mix well, then add salt and pepper to taste. If the mixture is too loose to form into cakes, add some more bread crumbs; if it's too dry, add a little milk or another egg.

❷ Put half the oil and butter into a large skillet, preferably nonstick, over medium heat. Form the spinach mixture into small cakes (this amount will make 8 to 12) and cook, without crowding—you will have to cook in batches—until nicely browned, adjusting the heat so the cakes brown evenly without burning, about 5 minutes. Turn once, then brown the other side, again about 5 minutes. Continue until all the spinach mixture is used up. Serve hot or at room temperature.

Summer Squash

Zucchini, Yellow Squash, Pattypan (Scalloped), and Chayote (Mirliton)

A quintessential summer vegetable (technically a fruit), summer squashes are tender and deliciously mild. You can steam, boil, sauté, stir-fry, braise, bread and fry, roast, or grill them, and often all they need is a pat of butter or a drizzle of olive oil and some salt.

Beyond the commonplace yellow squash and zucchini, there is the flying saucer–shaped pattypan with its cute scalloped edge and vivid greens and yellows.

There's also the chayote, called *mirliton* in the South. This pear-shaped gourd (it looks like an avocado) has bright green, wrinkled skin (sometimes covered with spines) and pale yellow to white semitranslucent flesh. Its texture is somewhat like that of a melon; the flavor is so mild it picks up the taste of whatever you cook it with. Use it raw in salads or cooked like any summer squash.

Buying and storing: Look for plump, firm, and unblemished specimens. Store wrapped loosely in plastic in the refrigerator; use as quickly as possible, especially if they are fresh from the garden or farm.

Yellow squash and zucchini: Usually the smaller and more uniformly shaped ones have better flavor and smaller seeds.

Pattypans: Go for small and tender specimens; larger than 3 or 4 inches across and the exterior skin becomes tough.

Chayote: Heavy wrinkles are a sign of being left on the vine too long, so it's best to go with less wrinkled ones.

Preparing: For yellow squash and zucchini: Trim the ends and slice or chop as you like. If the squash is flabby, salt it as you would cucumber (see page 207).

Pattypans: Leave whole if tender enough or halve.

Chayote: Peeling is optional. Cut in half through the stem end and remove the seed. Leave as halves or chop or slice as you like.

Best cooking methods: Steaming, sautéing, braising (for chayote), roasting, frying, and grilling. The blossoms can be battered and deep-fried (see page 247).

When is it done? When tender but not falling apart; pierce with a skewer or thin-bladed knife to check.

Other vegetables to substitute: Summer squashes are fairly interchangeable.

Sautéed Zucchini

MAKES: 4 servings

TIME: 20 minutes

Perhaps the fastest and most familiar vegetable dish, not only in summer, but year-round. See the list that follows for ways to vary the preparation and seasonings.

Other vegetables you can use: any summer squash or chayote (which must be seeded first).

3 tablespoons butter or extra virgin olive oil

1 tablespoon minced garlic

1½ pounds zucchini, sliced crosswise

Salt and freshly ground black pepper

2 teaspoons freshly squeezed lemon juice, or to taste

Chopped fresh parsley leaves for garnish

1 Put the butter or oil in a skillet over medium heat and add the garlic. When it sizzles, add the zucchini, sprinkle with salt and pepper, and cook, turning occasionally, until the pieces are as tender as you like, anywhere from 5 to 15 minutes.

2 Just before serving, sprinkle with the lemon juice, then taste and adjust the seasoning; garnish and serve.

5 Ways to Vary Sautéed Zucchini

1. Grate the zucchini or chop it into dice; it will take less time to soften.

2. Turn the heat up to medium-high and sear the zucchini until golden before stirring.

3. Use minced red onion, ginger, or shallot instead of garlic.

4. Substitute a mixture of 2 tablespoons dark sesame oil and 1 tablespoon neutral oil, like grapeseed or corn, instead of the butter or olive oil; garnish with chopped fresh cilantro or sliced scallion instead of the parsley.

5. Use other herbs in place of the parsley: Fresh mint, dill, and basil are all good choices.

Zucchini Pancakes

MAKES: 4 servings

TIME: At least 30 minutes

Zucchini is the main feature here; the batter just serves to hold the thing together.

Other vegetables you can use: turnips, winter squash, sweet potatoes, carrots, parsnips, beets, or celery root (all peeled if necessary); sliced scallions; or cooked, squeezed, and chopped spinach or other greens.

About 2 pounds zucchini or yellow squash

½ onion, grated

1 egg, lightly beaten

¼ cup all-purpose flour or plain bread crumbs, preferably fresh (page 876), more or less, plus more for dredging

½ cup freshly grated Parmesan cheese

Salt and freshly ground black pepper

4 tablespoons butter or extra virgin olive oil

1 Grate the squash by hand or with the grating disk of a food processor. Mix together all the ingredients but the butter or oil. Shape into 4 to 8 burger-shaped patties. (Add more flour or bread crumbs if necessary to make a mixture capable of holding its shape.) If time allows, refrigerate for 1 hour to firm them up.

2 When you're ready to cook, put the butter or oil in a large skillet over medium-high heat. When the butter is melted or the oil is hot, dredge the cakes in flour or bread crumbs and put in the skillet (if you've made 8, do this in 2 batches). Cook, turning once, until nicely browned on both sides, 10 to 15 minutes depending on the thickness. Serve hot or room temperature.

Zucchini-Pesto Pancakes. Makes a nice sandwich filler too: Substitute Traditional Pesto (page 27) for the Parmesan.

Zucchini Pancakes, Asian Style. Add 1 tablespoon each minced garlic and fresh ginger and $^1/_4$ cup chopped scallion. Omit the Parmesan and use neutral oil, like grapeseed or corn, instead of butter.

Summer Squash and Herbs in Parchment

MAKES: 4 servings
TIME: 30 minutes

Parchment packages are a great way to use less fat in cooking and still end up with a really flavorful dish. The parchment seals in the moisture so the vegetables both steam and simmer in their juices and lose no flavor. You can use foil too, though it's not nearly as pretty. Or just use a covered casserole for very similar results.

Other vegetables you can use: chayote, mushrooms, broccoli, cauliflower, asparagus, sugar and snow peas, spinach, arugula, or watercress.

$^1/_2$ small onion, thinly sliced

2 sprigs fresh tarragon or basil

$^3/_4$ pound summer squash, sliced $^1/_4$ inch thick

$^3/_4$ pound zucchini, sliced $^1/_4$ inch thick

1 tablespoon extra virgin olive oil or butter (optional)

Salt and freshly ground black pepper

Lemon wedges

1 Heat the oven to 375°F. Cut the parchment paper into 4 rectangles of about 6 × 10 inches, fold in half crosswise to crease, then open again. On one half of each rectangle, layer portions of the onion, herb, and squash, keeping the vegetables close to the center; then drizzle with the olive oil or dot with the butter and sprinkle with salt and pepper.

2 Seal the packages by rolling together the open edges and put them on a baking sheet; bake until the squash is tender, about 20 minutes. Immediately serve the squash in the packages with lemon wedges; be careful of the steam when opening them.

Summer Squash and Shrimp in Parchment. Add 3 or 4 large peeled shrimp to each package.

Shiitakes in Parchment. Any fresh mushroom will work here: Substitute 5 or 6 fresh shiso leaves for the tarragon if you like, sliced shiitake caps for the squash, and 2 teaspoons dark sesame oil for the olive oil. Add 1 teaspoon minced fresh ginger or garlic if you like too.

FOLDING SUMMER SQUASH IN PARCHMENT

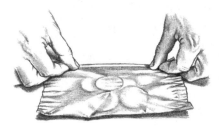

Whether you use parchment paper or foil, crimp the edges of the package tightly to keep as much moisture inside as possible.

 Fast   Make Ahead   Vegetarian

5 MORE IDEAS FOR VEGETABLES IN PARCHMENT

Keep the flavors simple and don't overload the packages.

VEGETABLES	AROMATICS	SEASONINGS
1¹/₂ pounds fennel, shaved	1 small onion, thinly sliced	2 teaspoons minced orange zest
1¹/₂ pounds tomatoes, thickly sliced	1 leek, sliced	2 teaspoons chopped fresh marjoram leaves; 3 tablespoons roughly chopped olives
1¹/₂ pounds sliced mixed bell peppers (red, orange, yellow, and green)	1 small onion, thinly sliced; 2 teaspoons minced garlic	3 sprigs fresh cilantro; 1 teaspoon chili powder (to make your own, see page 66)
1¹/₂ pounds artichoke hearts, sliced	1 teaspoon minced garlic (optional)	2 or 3 sprigs fresh basil or mint
1¹/₂ pounds peeled and sliced butternut squash	2 tablespoons minced fresh ginger	1 tablespoon any curry powder (to make your own, see pages 66–67), garam masala (to make your own, see page 67), or ground cumin or a pinch saffron

Sunchokes

Jerusalem Artichokes

Not artichokes and not from Jerusalem, these are actually tubers from a sunflower native to North America. *Sunchoke* and *sunroot* are arguably more accurate names and are becoming the preferred terms. No matter what you call them, they look like nubby little potatoes, with thin tan skin and firm, crisp, off-white flesh reminiscent of jícama. The flavor is not unlike that of artichoke, and they can be eaten raw, though I like them better cooked. (Note that sunchokes contain a type of sugar, inulin, that can cause quite severe flatulence in people with sensitivity to this; you'll know soon enough whether you're among them.)

Buying and storing: Look for firm, unshriveled specimens; the smoother, the easier to peel or wash. Store wrapped tightly in plastic in the refrigerator; they'll keep for weeks.

Preparing: Peeling is optional; I prefer just to wash and scrub well. Chop or slice as needed.

Best cooking methods: Sautéing (preferably after a brief simmering) and braising and glazing.

When is it done? When quite tender; taste one.

Other vegetables to substitute: Radish or jícama when raw or cooked; parsnip, turnip, or potato when cooked.

Crisp-Cooked Sunchokes

MAKES: 4 servings
TIME: About 30 minutes

 F **V**

Like pan-cooked potatoes, only with more flavor. Some people peel sunchokes, but I never bother; not only is it a total hassle, but you lose about half the flesh in the process. Just scrub them well before cooking.

Other vegetables you can use: waxy potatoes.

About 1¹/₂ pounds sunchokes

3 or 4 tablespoons extra virgin olive oil

Salt and freshly ground black pepper

1 tablespoon minced garlic or shallot or ¹/₄ cup chopped onion

Chopped fresh parsley leaves for garnish

Lemon wedges for serving

1 Scrub the sunchokes well, then trim off any hard or discolored spots. Slice about ⅛ inch thick.

2 Put the oil in a large deep skillet over medium heat. When hot, add the sunchokes a few slices at a time, spreading them out around the pan; season with salt and pepper. Cook, stirring and turning occasionally and adjusting the heat so they sizzle without burning, until tender and just about brown, about 20 minutes. Add the garlic and continue to cook until nicely browned and tender, about 5 minutes. Taste and adjust the seasoning, then garnish with parsley and serve with lemon wedges.

Sweet Potatoes and Yams

A yam is not a sweet potato—they're different species—though both are tubers and they can look very similar. The names *yams* and *sweet potatoes* are used interchangeably in the South, and canned "yams" are really sweet potatoes.

Sweet potatoes are common and sold year-round in every supermarket. There are two basic varieties: One has a light tan skin, yellow flesh, and a drier, less sweet texture and flavor; the other type has a reddish brown skin and bright orange flesh and is soft and sweet when cooked. Other specialty varieties of sweet potato range in flesh color from purple to rose to white.

Yams, on the other hand, are seldom grown in the United States, nor are they widely available here. When small they're hard to distinguish from a sweet potato, but they can grow to enormous proportions (like over a hundred pounds) and are often sold cut into chunks and wrapped in plastic (look for them at Latin markets, where they might be called *name*). When cooked their texture ranges from sweet and moist to dry and mealy, depending on type.

Buying and storing: Sweet potatoes should be plump and unshriveled. Avoid any with sprouts. Do not refrigerate; they are best in a cool, dark, dry place. They're fairly perishable for a tuber; use within a couple of weeks, sooner if you can.

Preparing: Peel if necessary; slice and chop as you like.

Best cooking methods: Baking, braising, and roasting.

When is it done? When very tender.

Other vegetables to substitute: Potatoes, carrots, parsnips, winter squash, or any tropical tuber.

Sweet Potatoes, Simply Cooked

MAKES: 4 servings

TIME: 1 hour or less

For basic use, sweet potatoes can be baked, boiled (or steamed), or microwaved. Baked is the best way if you're just going to eat them plain or with butter, but for mashing or use in other recipes, boiling and microwaving are easier.

2 large or 4 medium sweet potatoes (1½ to 2 pounds total)

Salt and freshly ground black pepper

To bake: Heat the oven to 425°F. Wash the sweet potatoes and poke each with a thin-bladed knife in a few places. Put them in a foil-lined baking pan and bake, turning once, until very tender, about an hour. Serve immediately, with salt and pepper and, if you like butter.

To boil or steam: Peel the potatoes, cut into large chunks, and cook according to Just-Tender Boiled or Steamed Root Vegetables or Tubers (pages 239–240). They'll probably take 20 minutes or less; don't overcook or they'll fall apart.

To microwave: Peel the potatoes, cut into large chunks, and put on a plate or in a glass baking dish with a couple tablespoons of water (and a little butter if you like). Cover and microwave on high for at least 10 minutes, or until soft.

 Fast   Make Ahead   **V** Vegetarian

Mashed Sweet Potato Gratin

MAKES: 4 to 6 servings

TIME: 25 minutes with cooked sweet potatoes

A slightly refined—and lower in fat and calories—version of candied yams, which are really sweet potatoes. Mix in some peeled and minced fresh ginger for added kick.

Other vegetables you can use: apples or pears (sliced, not mashed) or any winter squash.

4 tablespoons (¹/₂ stick) butter

1¹/₂ to 2 pounds sweet potatoes, cooked in any manner (preceding recipe)

Salt and freshly ground black pepper

Freshly grated nutmeg (optional)

¹/₂ cup chopped pecans, walnuts, almonds, or hazelnuts (optional)

① Heat the oven to 400°F. Grease a gratin dish with some of the butter. Heat the potatoes if necessary and mash them with the butter, a sprinkle of salt and pepper, and a dash of nutmeg if you're using it. Taste and adjust the seasoning. Put the sweet potatoes in the gratin dish, smoothing the surface or leaving it rustic looking.

② Sprinkle the top with the nuts. Bake until the dish is hot and golden on top, 15 to 20 minutes, and serve hot or warm.

Mashed Sweet Potato Brûlée. You can also prepare this in individual ramekins for a fancier presentation: In Step 2, after baking, sprinkle the top with ³/₄ cup brown sugar. Turn on the broiler and adjust the rack to about 4 inches from the heat source. Broil, watching carefully and turning the dish as necessary. When the sugar bubbles and browns, it's ready. Let sit for a few minutes before serving.

Maple-Glazed Mashed Sweet Potato. Follow the preceding variation, but substitute ¹/₂ cup maple syrup for the brown sugar; it won't develop a crisp top like the sugar but will thicken and create a rich glaze.

Tomatillos

Mexican Green Tomatoes

A relative of the tomato, this green, usually Ping-Pong-ball-sized fruit that looks like a tomato has a papery light brown husk. It's widely used in Mexican cooking, almost always when firm, green, tangy, and herbaceous (it turns yellow and softer when ripe). The zingy flavor makes excellent raw and cooked green salsas (see Fresh Tomatillo Salsa on page 33 and Salsa Verde on page 49). Although available year-round, you can always find them in Latin markets. Canned tomatillos are a decent substitute for fresh.

Buying and storing: Look for tightly wrapped husks covering firm, unshriveled, green fruit. Store in a paper bag in the refrigerator; they'll keep for a couple of weeks.

Preparing: Tear off the husks and rinse off the sticky resin. No need to core. Slice, chop, purée, or leave whole.

Best cooking methods: Raw or any way you'd cook tomatoes.

When is it done? From raw to cooked down into a pulp and everywhere in between.

Other fruits to substitute: Green tomatoes and, in a pinch, ripe tomatoes.

Stewed Tomatillos and Tomatoes

MAKES: 6 to 8 servings

TIME: About 1 hour, largely unattended

Green and tart tomatillos play the starring role in this stew, mellowed a bit by the sweetness of fresh tomatoes. The texture is silky and slightly thick. Serve over rice, grits or polenta, or cooked hominy (see page 451).

Other vegetables you can use: all green or not-quite-ripe tomatoes.

2 tablespoons extra virgin olive oil, plus more for drizzling

1 large onion, chopped

1 bell pepper or 2 poblano chiles, cored, seeded, and chopped (page 330)

2 cloves garlic, crushed

Salt and freshly ground black pepper

1^1/$_2$ pounds tomatillos, husked and rinsed

1 cup stock (to make your own, see pages 157–159), white wine, or water

1^1/$_2$ pounds ripe tomatoes, cut into large chunks

^{1}/$_2$ cup chopped fresh cilantro leaves

❶ Put the oil in a large pot or deep skillet over medium-high heat. When hot, cook the onion, pepper, and garlic until the onion is soft and translucent, 5 to 10 minutes. Sprinkle with salt and pepper.

❷ Add the tomatillos; cook until the skins start to break open, 10 to 15 minutes. Pour in the stock and stir. Bring to a boil, then reduce the heat to produce a slow bubble and cover; cook until the tomatillos are mostly dissolved, about 30 minutes. (At this point, you may cover and refrigerate for a day or two before proceeding.)

❸ Return the heat to medium-high, and when the mixture starts to bubble, stir in the tomatoes. Cook, stirring occasionally, until the tomatoes wilt but their skins remain intact. Stir in the cilantro, taste, and adjust the seasoning. Serve hot or at room temperature, drizzled with additional olive oil.

Tomatoes

Usually when we think of tomatoes, we picture big, fat red specimens, but tomatoes come in a wide array of colors, shapes, and sizes. Red is the most common color, but tomatoes can be anything from burgundy to white to yellow or orange to brown or striped green. Then there's the unripe green tomato, with its tangy flavor and firm flesh, wonderful fried or broiled.

Tomatoes fall into three basic categories: cherry, plum, and slicing. Cherry tomatoes are small, sweet, and tender, ideal for snacking, tossing whole into salads, and quickly sautéing or roasting with a sprinkle of fresh herbs; they make a nice fresh sauce too. Plum (or Roma) tomatoes are medium in size, oval in shape, and meaty in texture. They are available year-round (that doesn't mean they taste good year-round, though in the off-season they're usually your best choice) and are good for sauces, braising, oven-drying, or stewing. Slicing tomatoes are a broad category that are typically large and spherical (some flattened, some round); they're best raw.

Being a rather delicate fruit that's sensitive to heat and cold, ripe tomatoes do not travel well. The vast majority of supermarket varieties these days—in season or not—are either picked green and ripened off the vine or grown in hothouses; either way, the end result is the same: they don't taste real good. So, in the off-season, I usually reach for canned tomatoes.

Buying and storing: The best fresh tomatoes are undamaged, soft—yielding to light pressure but not mushy—and deeply colored. Store all tomatoes at room temperature (do not refrigerate). Canned tomatoes (whole plum are best, though prechopped are undeniably convenient for sauces) are fine substitutes in many recipes that call for cooking.

Preparing: To core tomatoes, cut a cone right around the core and remove it. To seed, cut the tomato in half through its equator and squeeze and shake out the seeds (you may want to do this over a strainer to save the liquid). To peel, cut a small "X" in the flower (smooth, nonstem) end of the tomato and drop into boiling water for 10 to 30 seconds, until the skin loosens. Plunge into ice water and peel off the skin.

Best cooking methods: Roasting, grilling or broiling, and panfrying. And, of course, making sauce and salsa.

When are they done? Whenever you want them to be: They're good from raw to cooked to a mushy sauce.

Other fruits to substitute: Tomatillos (beware: they're tangy!), pineapple, peaches, nectarines, or watermelon (for raw tomatoes).

❺ Fast   ⓜ Make Ahead   ⓥ Vegetarian

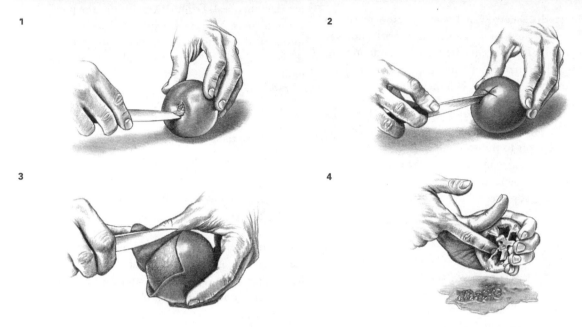

(STEP 1) First core the tomato. Cut a wedge right around the core and remove it. (STEP 2) Then peel the tomato. Cut a small "X" in the flower (nonstem) end. Drop the tomato into boiling water and leave it until the skin begins to loosen, usually less than 30 seconds; then plunge into a bowl of ice water. (STEP 3) Remove the skin with a paring knife. (STEP 4) Finish by seeding the tomato. The easiest way to remove seeds is simply to cut the tomato in half through its equator, then squeeze and shake out the seeds or pop them out with your finger. Do this over a bowl if you want to strain and reserve the juice.

Oven-Roasted Plum Tomatoes

MAKES: 4 servings

TIME: About 1 hour, largely unattended

It's tough to find good plum tomatoes at supermarkets even in season, but roasting helps make the most of them, because the process concentrates the flavor and eliminates mealiness. The results are gorgeous, and you can use them immediately in sauces, as a garnish, in pilafs or soups, or in other vegetable dishes. Or store them, tightly covered, in the fridge for up to several days. (You can also freeze them more or less indefinitely.)

Other fruits or vegetables you can use: peaches and nectarines.

2 tablespoons extra virgin olive oil, plus a little for the pan

2 pounds plum tomatoes (about a dozen), cored and cut in half lengthwise

Salt and freshly ground black pepper

❶ Heat the oven to 325°F. Grease a large baking sheet or roasting pan with a little of the olive oil.

❷ Scoop the seeds out of the tomatoes if you like and put them on the pan, cut side down. Drizzle or brush with the remaining 2 tablespoons of olive oil. Roast until they start to char a bit and shrivel (there's no need to turn), 30 minutes.

Oven-Roasted Canned Plum Tomatoes. How to turn a convenience food into something special and way more useful: Instead of the fresh tomatoes, drain a 28- or 35-ounce can of plum tomatoes, reserving the juice for another use. Proceed with the recipe.

Oven-Roasted Everyday Tomatoes. Works for heirloom, beefsteak, or hothouse tomatoes, especially when you want to improve imperfect ones: Core the tomatoes and halve them around the equator instead of lengthwise. Squeeze out the seeds (see page 361). Cut the largest pieces in half again and proceed with the recipe.

Oven-Dried Tomatoes. Omit the olive oil and salt and pepper. Heat the oven to 225°F. Set 2 wire racks on top of 2 (preferably rimmed) baking sheets. Put the tomatoes on the racks, cut side down. Put in the oven and forget about them for 2 hours. Rotate the baking sheets and continue to cook to desired doneness. If you just want to intensify the tomato flavor and use them immediately, they're done when still soft but somewhat shriveled, 2 to 3 hours total. If you want to keep them for a few days, they're done when shriveled and mostly dry, at least 4 hours total (wrap and refrigerate). If you want to keep them for weeks, they're done when dark, shriveled, and dry, 6 or more hours total (wrap and refrigerate or store in a jar in the pantry, or freeze).

Grilled or Broiled Tomatoes with Basil

MAKES: 4 servings
TIME: 30 minutes

When you grill a tomato, the high heat not only softens the flesh but caramelizes some of the fruit's sugars while driving out a bit of its liquid—all in just 5 or 10 minutes (and all, if you prefer, hours before you intend to use the tomatoes). From that point on, the possibilities are numerous. You can integrate the cooked tomatoes into a salad or a risotto, toss them with pasta, or serve them as is, drizzled with olive oil and sprinkled with basil.

Other fruits or vegetables you can use: eggplant (it will take about twice as long to cook on the grill).

3 or 4 ripe tomatoes

Extra virgin olive oil as needed

Salt and freshly ground black pepper

1/3 cup or more torn or chopped fresh basil

Freshly grated Parmesan cheese to taste (optional)

❶ Heat a charcoal or gas grill or a broiler to moderately high heat and put the rack about 4 inches from the heat source. Core the tomatoes and cut each into 3 or 4 thick slices. Brush them with olive oil and sprinkle with salt and pepper.

❷ Grill the tomatoes, turning once, until they are soft but not mushy; you should be able to lift them from the grill with a spatula without having them falling apart, but only barely. If you're broiling, put them on a rimmed baking sheet or in a gratin dish; cook until browned and bubbling (do not flip). As they cook, use tongs to remove and discard their skins. Transfer them to a platter or plates and sprinkle with basil and a grating of the cheese if you like.

Broiled Cherry Tomatoes with Herbs. Use 1 pound cherry tomatoes and 2 or 3 sprigs fresh oregano, thyme, rosemary, tarragon, or basil. Toss the tomatoes with the herbs, 2 tablespoons oil, and salt and pepper and put on a rimmed baking sheet or in a gratin dish. Broil until the skins brown, blister, and crack, 3 to 5 minutes; check the tomatoes often and shake the pan every so often to roll them around a bit; they can burn quickly. Serve straight from the broiler or warm.

F Fast   **M** Make Ahead   **V** Vegetarian

They're the darlings of restaurants and farmers' markets across America: brightly colored, often misshapen, usually intensely flavored fruits and vegetables known collectively as *heirlooms*.

As the name implies, heirloom varieties of fruits and vegetables—and other plants for that matter—were passed down from generation to generation by home gardeners who saved seeds or clippings. When supermarkets became the most common place to purchase fresh and processed produce, these varieties lost favor to hybrids that were easier to pick, ship, store, and sell. Over time the name has evolved to mean virtually any fruit or vegetable variety that is unusual, delicious, and sometimes ugly—like most homegrown vegetables, heirlooms are raised for flavor, not appearance.

Even though heirlooms are back in style, they can still be tough to find and expensive to buy. Generally, though, they do taste better—often much, much better—than their mass-market cousins. Some supermarkets and specialty grocers now sell alternative varieties of tomatoes, but for heirloom potatoes, melons, corn, cucumbers, peppers, and other produce, you'll have to shop at farmers' markets, grow them yourself (see seedsavers.com), or cozy up to someone with a green thumb.

Panfried Green and/or Red Tomatoes

MAKES: 4 servings
TIME: 20 minutes

Here's one place you want a not-too-ripe tomato: Though they make a wonderful side dish when cooked, ultra-ripe ones will liquefy.

3 tablespoons extra virgin olive oil, or more as needed

2 or 3 large green, reddish green, or greenish red tomatoes, cored and cut crosswise into $^1/_2$-inch-thick slices

Plain bread crumbs, preferably fresh (page 876), cornmeal, or all-purpose flour for dredging

Salt and freshly ground black pepper

1 Put the olive oil in a large deep skillet over medium-high heat. When hot, dredge the tomato slices, one at a time, in the bread crumbs and add them to the skillet.

2 Cook, adding a little more olive oil if needed to keep the slices sizzling and seasoning with salt and pepper as they cook. Turn when the first side is golden brown, then cook the other side; total cooking time will be less than 10 minutes. Handle gently and serve hot or at room temperature.

Tropical Tubers

Taro, Cassava (Yuca, Manioc); Boniato (Batata); Malanga (Yautia, Tannia)

A group of tubers that's popular predominantly in Caribbean, South American, Polynesian, and West African cuisines, these are quite starchy and are generally handled the way you do potatoes.

Taro, the main ingredient in the equally loved and loathed Hawaiian dish poi, has brownish gray fiber-covered striped skin and gray-white flesh with purple stippling. It's more flavorful than potatoes, whether boiled or fried, but becomes very dry if overcooked.

Cassava has an elongated, tapered oval shape with a dark brown, woody, and often waxed and shiny skin; the flesh is white, crisp, and loaded with starch (it's what tapioca is made from, which gives you an indication of just how much starch it contains). It must be cooked (it's poisonous when raw). You can bake it, roast it, fry it, or stew it, but it needs sauce to balance the starchiness.

Boniato looks similar to sweet potato, with smooth, thin skin, but ranges in color from brownish orange to garnet to purple; it's oval with tapered ends and can be short and squat or skinny and lean. Its flavor is like a cross between white and sweet potatoes but with a fluffier texture, and it's lovely baked or boiled.

Malanga (yautia) looks like a cross between a sweet potato and taro; the shape is similar to a sweet potato, but the skin is brown, coarse, and striated, with a rough, fibrous coat. The flesh is off-white and has the texture of jícama when raw. It is best boiled, fried, or included in stews—in short, treated exactly like a potato.

Buying and storing: All of these tubers can be found at Latin and some other markets. They should be firm and unshriveled; avoid any with sprouts or soft spots. Store taro and cassava in the refrigerator and boniato and malanga in a cool, dry, dark spot. Note that unlike other tubers, taro, boniato, and malanga do not store well; use them within a few days.

Preparing: Peel with a vegetable peeler or, for the tougher cassava, a paring knife; note that some may be waxed, so they must be peeled, but otherwise peeling isn't necessary when you're baking one of these. You can chop, slice, or grate the flesh as you like. Raw boniato flesh discolors very quickly when peeled or cut and darkens quite a bit when cooked; immediately immerse in cold water after cutting and be sure to keep it covered with liquid while cooking to minimize darkening.

Best cooking methods: Taro and malanga: boiling (see Just-Tender Boiled or Steamed Root Vegetables, pages 239–240) and frying (see Breaded Fried Eggplant (or Any Other Vegetable), page 245). Cassava: baking (see Whole Winter Squash, Cooked Three Ways, page 366), frying (see French Fries, page 346), and braising (see Braised Potatoes, page 343). Boniato: boiling (see Just-Tender Boiled or Steamed Root Vegetables, pages 239–240) and baking (see Sweet Potatoes, Simply Cooked, page 358).

When is it done? When a skewer or sharp knife inserted into one meets almost no resistance.

Other vegetables to substitute: Potatoes or sweet potatoes.

Turnips and Rutabagas

Swedes, Yellow Turnips

Most turnips are white and purple on the exterior and solid white inside. Their flavor is mildly cabbagelike, sweet, and lovely braised. Rutabagas look similar to turnips but have a dark yellow and purple exterior and bright to pale yellow flesh; they can be as large as a cantaloupe and have a more assertive flavor that's sometimes said to be coarser, though I don't buy that.

Buying and storing: Look for small (there are no really small rutabagas, but smallish), firm specimens that are heavy for their size. If greens are attached to the turnips (see page 315), they should be fresh looking with no yellowing. Rutabagas are often coated with a thick wax to keep them from drying out. Large turnips and rutabagas are often woody and have a stronger flavor than small ones. Store loosely wrapped in plastic in the refrigerator; they will keep for weeks.

Preparing: Peel and leave whole (if small enough) or slice or chop as you like; rutabagas must be peeled with a paring knife because of their wax coating.

Best cooking methods: Boiling and braising and glazing. They make good purées.

When is it done? When tender or very soft.

Other vegetables to substitute: Turnips and rutabagas are interchangeable; otherwise, parsnips, carrots, or kohlrabi.

Turnips in Mustard Sauce

MAKES: 4 servings
TIME: 20 minutes

Cooked this way, turnips develop a tangy sweet flavor that goes brilliantly with roast chicken or beef. Substitute whole mustard seeds for the prepared mustard if you want some crunch and a subtle spiciness.

Other vegetables you can use: carrots, radishes, onions, beets, parsnips, or other root vegetables.

 Fast   Make Ahead   **V** Vegetarian

2 tablespoons butter or extra virgin olive oil

1½ pounds turnips, carrots, radishes, onions, or other vegetable, peeled and cut into pieces about the size of radishes

Salt and freshly ground black pepper

1 teaspoon sugar

About 1 cup chicken, beef, or vegetable stock (to make your own, see pages 157–159)

2 tablespoons Dijon mustard, or more to taste

Chopped fresh parsley leaves for garnish

❶ Put the butter or oil in a medium saucepan, one that will hold the vegetable in one layer, over medium heat. Add the vegetable and sprinkle it with salt and pepper. Cook, stirring once in a while, until the vegetable begins to brown, about 10 minutes.

❷ Add the sugar and enough stock to cover; bring to a boil and cook, more or less undisturbed, until the liquid has mostly evaporated and the vegetable is tender and brown, 20 to 30 minutes. When done, the shiny vegetable should be sitting in a small puddle of syrupy liquid. Reduce the heat a bit and add the mustard, stirring until it's dissolved in the sauce.

❸ Taste and add more salt, pepper, or mustard if you like, then garnish and serve hot or warm.

Turnips in Creamy Mustard Sauce. Replace all or part of the stock with cream, but don't let it boil vigorously; just bubble gently.

Water Chestnuts

Not a chestnut at all, though it vaguely resembles one, the water chestnut is the tuber of a water plant indigenous to Asia. It's mildly sweet and crunchy; you've probably eaten them plenty of times in stir-fries and fried rice dishes. When fresh, they have a dark brown skin that covers the off-white, crisp flesh.

Buying and storing: If you can find fresh water chestnuts (which you will if you look in Asian markets), they should be plump, crisp, and heavy for their size.

Store wrapped tightly in plastic in the refrigerator. Otherwise, buy canned, which are a decent and readily available substitute, if nearly tasteless.

Preparing: Peel (if fresh) and slice or chop as necessary.

Best cooking method: Stir-frying, added at the last minute.

When is it done? When just heated through and still crunchy.

Winter Squash

Technically speaking a fruit and in season in fall through spring, these are marked by their tough skins, unwieldy shapes and sizes, hard and vibrantly colored flesh, edible seeds, and creamy texture when cooked. There are many varieties in this class of vegetables, but the most noteworthy and accessible are the butternut, acorn, pumpkin, spaghetti, delicata, kabocha, Hubbard, crookneck, and calabaza.

The butternut is by far the most convenient, since it's easy to peel and cut, and its flavor and texture are wonderful. Other squash can be daunting to prepare, but winter squash are cheap, so if you have to hack off huge chunks and toss them to get usable flesh, that's not so horrible (and far better than cutting yourself trying to peel all the ridges, bumps, and curves). Or don't peel them; you can roast or steam whole squash and simply scoop out the soft flesh (see the recipes that follow).

Buying and storing: Winter squash should be firm and heavy; avoid any with soft spots, cracks, or punctures. Store in a cool, dry place (not in the fridge) and use within a month.

Preparing: To peel, use a sturdy vegetable peeler or a paring knife for butternut if you're more comfortable; but for tougher, ridged squashes set the squash on its flat end or cut off an end to create a flat, stable bottom. Use a sharp knife (the larger the squash, the larger the knife) and cut off slices of the skin starting from the top where the vegetable starts to curve and slicing down to the cutting board; cut off strips around the entire vegetable and then chop off the unpeeled ends.

Spaghetti squash is a slightly different animal because its flesh is super-stringy. Though you can peel and prepare it as you would other winter squashes, it's best—and easiest—to simply cook it whole (see the first recipe that follows), then remove the seeds and scoop out the flesh.

Use a cleaver or very large, heavy knife to split the squash in half. Scoop out the seeds and stringy fiber and discard or roast the seeds (see page 317).

Best cooking methods: Steaming, braising, braising and glazing, and roasting. Makes wonderful purées.

When is it done? When very tender and nicely browned (if panfrying or roasting) but not waterlogged (if boiling).

Other vegetables to substitute: Sweet potatoes, yams, carrots, or waxy potatoes.

PEELING WINTER SQUASH

With winter squash, a little waste is inevitable, so just hack away at the skin with a knife. Most squash are simply too tough (and oddly shaped) for a vegetable peeler.

Whole Winter Squash, Cooked Three Ways

MAKES: 4 to 10 servings, depending on the size of the squash

TIME: 1 to 2 hours, depending on size, completely unattended

Ⓜ Ⓥ

These are the easiest ways to cook and extract the flesh from any winter squash, even the large, thick-skinned varieties like Hubbard and pumpkin. If the process of cutting apart a raw squash has ever seemed daunting (or scary, given the knife or cleaver required), then the first two techniques—oven roasting and steaming whole squash—will spare you that chore. The second variation describes the more traditional cut-seed-and-roast method. Each method will give you a squash that is soft and silky, perfect for purées, soups, or desserts.

Other vegetables you can use: eggplant, but it will take a lot less time.

1 or more whole winter squash (1 to 8 pounds)

❶ Heat the oven to 375°F. Rinse off the squash (or squashes). Use a thin sharp knife, an ice pick, or a long-tined fork to poke several holes in the top of the squash around the stem.

❷ Put the squash on a rimmed baking sheet or shallow roasting pan. Roast the squash, undisturbed, for at least 30 minutes. When the sides start to soften and collapse, move it around or turn it over to promote even cooking. Continue roasting until deeply colored and quite soft. Small squashes will take 45 minutes or so, large ones up to $1^1/2$ hours.

❸ Remove the squash from the oven and set it aside to cool almost completely before handling. Cut in half and scoop out the seeds and stringy fiber. Then scoop out the flesh. Use immediately or store, tightly covered, in the refrigerator for several days or in the freezer for several months.

Whole Winter Squash, Steamed. Best for soups or other dishes where the added moisture can be beneficial: Prepare the squash(es) as described in Step 1. Rig a steamer (see page 20). Pour in enough water to cover the bottom of the pot, but leave the insert dry and put the squash on top, stem side up. Cover the pot and bring to a boil, then lower the heat so the water bubbles vigorously. Check the pot every so often to make sure there's still water in the bottom; after a half hour or so, turn the squash over (unless it's too big to do so, in which case don't bother). Cooking time will be about the same as for

 Fast   Make Ahead   Ⓥ Vegetarian

roasting. When the squash is done, put the squash on a plate to cook and proceed with the recipe from Step 3.

Roasted Squash Pieces in the Shell. Slightly faster, with most of your time spent preparing the squash: Heat the oven to 400°F. Cover a rimmed baking sheet or shallow roasting pan with foil. Cut and seed the squash(es) as directed on page 366. You should be left with squash halves or large pieces. Put the squash in the pan, cut side down, and roast until starting to get tender, 20 to 30 minutes, depending on the variety. Turn the pieces over and roast until done, another 20 minutes or so. Cool a bit, then scoop out the flesh.

Braised and Glazed Butternut Squash

MAKES: 4 servings
TIME: 30 minutes

The go-to recipe for everyday winter squash; it will work with any variety, but favor butternut because it's so much easier to deal with than the others.

Other vegetables you can use: any winter squash (except spaghetti) will work here, though they will all be more difficult to cut and peel than butternut.

2 tablespoons extra virgin olive oil

1 tablespoon minced garlic

1½ pounds butternut or other winter squash, peeled and cut into ½- to 1-inch cubes

¼ cup stock (to make your own, see pages 157–159) or water

Salt and freshly ground black pepper

Chopped fresh parsley leaves for garnish

❶ Put the oil and garlic in a large deep skillet with a tight-fitting lid over medium heat. When the garlic begins to color, after about 2 minutes, add the squash and stock and sprinkle with salt and pepper. Bring to a boil, cover, and turn the heat down to low. Cook, stirring once or twice, until the squash is tender, about 15 minutes.

❷ Uncover the pan and turn the heat up to medium-high. Cook, shaking the pan occasionally and stirring somewhat less often, until all the liquid is evaporated and the squash has begun to brown, 5 to 10 minutes. Turn the heat to low and cook until the squash is as browned and crisp as you like. Taste and adjust the seasoning, garnish with parsley, and serve.

Butternut Squash with Soy. Rich tasting and deeply colored: For the liquid, use 2 tablespoons soy sauce and 2 tablespoons water. Use ginger instead of garlic or along with it. Proceed with the recipe, garnishing with sliced scallion and sesame seeds instead of the parsley if you like.

Butternut Squash with Tomato Sauce. Add ½ to 1 cup Fresh Tomato Sauce (page 503); stir it in during the last 10 minutes or so. Cook it to the consistency and sauciness that you like. Sprinkle with grated Parmesan if you like.

Butternut Squash with Pesto. Add ½ cup Traditional Pesto (page 27) thinned with a tablespoon or two of water; stir it in during the last few minutes of cooking until the pesto coats the squash.

Butternut Squash with Yogurt. Add ½ cup yogurt in Step 2, after you've browned, reduced the heat, and let it become tender. Cook and stir long enough to warm through without boiling. Dust with paprika, chopped fresh chives, or finely chopped pistachios as a final garnish if you like.

Sweet and Sour Butternut Squash. Mix together ¼ cup cider or rice vinegar, 2 tablespoons water, and 3 tablespoons brown sugar. Pour this on the squash in Step 2 after the liquid has evaporated.

Roasted Winter Squash Slices

MAKES: 4 servings
TIME: 30 to 40 minutes

This is easiest and most attractive when you use just the top half of butternut squash, the nice, seedless cylinder. But as long as you can cut ¼-inch slices, this will work with any winter squash or root vegetable.

Sprinkling the squash with a tablespoon or so chopped fresh sage, thyme, or rosemary leaves during roasting is an excellent and simple way to add more flavor.

Other vegetables you can use: sweet potatoes or any root vegetable.

> 4 to 6 tablespoons extra virgin olive oil or melted butter
>
> 1½ pounds winter squash, peeled and cut into ¼-inch-thick slices
>
> Salt and freshly ground black pepper

❶ Heat the oven to 400°F. Put half the oil or butter on the bottom of a roasting pan and arrange the squash slices in one layer on top. Sprinkle with salt and pepper and drizzle on the remaining oil or butter.

❷ Roast without turning for 20 to 30 minutes, or until the squash is tender. Serve hot or warm.

Roasted Winter Squash Slices with Whole Garlic. Add up to 8 cloves garlic, peeled, to the roasting pan along with the squash; keep the cloves away from the outer edges of the pan to prevent them from burning.

Roasted Acorn Squash Halves. This works with any squash that has a cavity to hold the other ingredients: If the acorn squash are small, figure half a squash per person, a quarter or less per person if large. Split them into halves through the stem (even if you're planning to serve smaller portions). Put the halves in the roasting pan using rings of crumpled foil to help them stay upright; sprinkle the cavities with salt and pepper, then fill each with orange juice and a good pinch of grated orange zest. Top each with ¼ teaspoon chopped garlic or a tablespoon of brown sugar if you like. Smear the rim of the squash with the oil or butter and roast as in Step 2. Divide the halves as you like after roasting.

Winter Squash Curry

MAKES: 4 servings
TIME: About 30 minutes

Peeling and chopping the squash is probably the hardest part of this recipe. All sorts of vegetables work in addition to or instead of squash; use this recipe as a base and improvise from there.

Other vegetables you can use: any winter squash, potatoes, sweet potatoes, any root vegetable, eggplant, cauliflower, mushrooms, okra, peas, any summer squash, or green or wax beans.

> 2 tablespoons neutral oil, like grapeseed or corn
>
> 1 onion, chopped
>
> 1 tablespoon curry powder (to make your own, see pages 66–67)
>
> 1 tablespoon minced fresh ginger
>
> 1½ pounds butternut or other winter squash, peeled and roughly chopped
>
> 1 cup coconut milk, stock (to make your own, see page 389 or pages 157–159), or water
>
> Salt and freshly ground black pepper
>
> Chopped fresh cilantro leaves for garnish

❶ Put the oil in a pot or deep skillet with a tight-fitting lid over medium-high heat. When hot, add the onion and cook until softened, about 5 minutes. Add the curry and ginger and cook until the onion just starts to brown, about 2 minutes.

❷ Add the squash and coconut milk and sprinkle with salt and pepper. Bring to a boil, cover, and turn the

 Fast   Make Ahead   **V** Vegetarian

heat down to low. Cook, stirring once or twice, until the squash is tender, about 20 minutes. Check the squash periodically to make sure there is adequate liquid; if the squash is done and there is still a lot of liquid, remove the lid and turn the heat to medium-high until it's thicker than stew. Taste and adjust the seasoning, garnish with cilantro, and serve hot or warm.

Winter Squash, Thai Style. Serve over Steamed Sticky Rice, Thai Style (page 459) or wide rice noodles: In Step 1, when you put the ginger in the oil, add 1 minced fresh chile (like jalapeño or Thai), or to taste, or hot red pepper flakes or cayenne to taste. Add 2 tablespoons peanut butter along with the coconut milk.

Winter Squash, Afghan Style. Best with butternut; don't skip the yogurt sauce here: Cook the onion until browned in Step 1. Substitute 1 teaspoon ground turmeric for the curry and garlic for the ginger; use stock or water. Proceed with the recipe. Serve drizzled with Herbed Yogurt Sauce (page 24; with fresh or dried mint).

Winter Squash with Mirin. Omit the curry and use a mixture of $^1/_2$ cup water, 3 tablespoons soy sauce, and 3 tablespoons mirin (or half honey and half rice wine or white wine vinegar) instead of the coconut milk. Proceed with the recipe. Garnish with chopped scallion.

The Basics of Stuffed Vegetables

The dishes in this section combine the best of two worlds: fresh produce with an interesting filling based on meat, grains, or vegetables. Different vegetables require slightly different stuffing techniques, and some of the most common are given here. But one general piece of advice: Resist the urge to overstuff.

You can easily improvise stuffed vegetables: Choose something that has a natural cavity, like peppers or winter squash; that can be hollowed out, like tomatoes, eggplant, and onions; or that has a leaf that can be rolled or folded (cabbage and similar greens). The stuffings can be as simple or as elaborate as you like, but keep in mind that moist stuffings work in any vegetable, while dry ones are best reserved for moist vegetables.

Most vegetables require a bit of cooking (boiling, steaming, and roasting work well) before stuffing to ensure that the vegetable will be tender and fully cooked, to decrease the final cooking time, and to keep the stuffing from getting too dry. You want the precooked vegetable to be just tender—not quite fully cooked—before stuffing it. The only exception is when your stuffing includes raw meat or fish, in which case you want everything to cook thoroughly together.

I usually finish cooking stuffed vegetables in a fairly hot oven, which adds a bit of depth and richness to the dish. But steaming, braising, frying, grilling, and broiling also work well. Whatever cooking technique you use, be sure to cook the dish until the vegetable or fruit is tender and the stuffing is hot.

Tomatoes Stuffed with Sausage and Rice

MAKES: 4 or more servings
TIME: 50 minutes with cooked rice

Here tomatoes are stuffed and then roasted in a hot oven to maximize caramelization. This technique works for all sorts of vegetables; see the variations and the list of other vegetables to use that follows.

You can ready the tomatoes for stuffing in two ways: by slicing off a lid and creating a container out of the whole tomato or by halving the tomato, scraping out the insides, and stuffing each half (this is best suited for

When stuffing an eggplant—or any other vegetable—don't put in so much stuffing that it spills out.

You can cut the top off the tomato, and hollow out the inside. After filling, put the top back on, like a lid.

Stuffing a cabbage or other leaf is much like making a burrito: Put a not-too-large amount of filling on the third closest to you and fold over that end. Fold in the sides, then roll it up.

Or you can halve the tomato—lengthwise or on the equator—and scoop and fill that way.

F Fast   **M** Make Ahead   **V** Vegetarian

7 VEGETABLES AND STUFFINGS TO MIX AND MATCH

VEGETABLE	PREPARATION	STUFFING	HOW TO COOK
Mushrooms	Use large white or cremini mushrooms—you want mushrooms with good-size caps to hold the stuffing. Remove the stems and scrape out any of the gills to increase the cavity space.	Mix finely chopped shrimp, a bit of chopped garlic and minced scallion, a dash of soy sauce, and a sprinkle of dark sesame oil. Fill the mushrooms, mounding the stuffing.	Bake in a 350°F oven, steam, or grill until the shrimp stuffing is cooked through, about 10 minutes. Serve with Soy Dipping Sauce and Marinade (page 25).
Eggplant	Peeling is optional; halve lengthwise or—for large, thick eggplant—cut crosswise into 3-inch-thick cylinders; drizzle with olive oil and roast in a 350°F oven until tender. Scoop out the insides or use a spoon to mold a cavity.	Cook chopped onion, celery or fennel, and minced garlic in olive oil until tender; add pine nuts and raisins; sprinkle with a bit of balsamic vinegar and salt and pepper; fill the cavities and sprinkle with grated Parmesan or bread crumbs.	Bake in a 375°F oven until the eggplant is very tender. Sprinkle with chopped fresh parsley or basil leaves.
Zucchini	Use fat and straight zucchini or yellow squash; halve lengthwise and use a spoon to scrape out the seeds.	Mix cooked couscous, chopped tomato, olives, Harissa (page 75), and some salt and pepper. Stuff the zucchini, mounding the couscous about an inch or so high.	Bake in a 375°F oven until the zucchini is tender and the stuffing is hot, about 20 minutes. Sprinkle with chopped fresh cilantro or parsley leaves.
Acorn Squash	Halve the squash, scrape out the seeds, and rub the inside with some olive oil or butter; roast, cut side down, in a 375°F oven for 25 minutes.	Mix cooked wild rice, caramelized or sautéed onions (see page 325), dried cranberries, some orange zest, a bit of orange juice, and chopped pecans; sprinkle with salt and pepper. Flip the squash over and fill with the stuffing.	Bake in a 375°F oven until the flesh is tender, another 20 minutes or so. Sprinkle with more chopped pecans.
Cabbage or Kale Leaves	Use large untorn leaves and put in a steamer above a couple inches of salted water. Cover and cook until the leaves are just flexible enough to bend. Make a "V" cut in each leaf to remove the tough central stem.	Mix cooked lentils (see page 412) with cooked basmati rice and sprinkle with salt and pepper. Put a mound, about ¼ cup or so, in the middle of the leaf; fold the edges over the stuffing to create a package; skewer the rolls with a toothpick or two to hold them together or just put them seam side down.	Put the packages in the steamer (check that there is enough water) and cook until the leaves are tender, 10 to 15 minutes. Drizzle with olive oil or melt a pat of butter on top. Sprinkle with chopped fresh herbs.
Chayote	Peel, halve, remove the pit, drizzle with extra virgin olive oil or dot with butter, and bake, covered, in a 350°F oven until tender, about 20 minutes. Scoop out a spoonful of the flesh to make a larger cavity for stuffing; mix the flesh with the filling.	Mix crumbled corn bread or tortilla chips, crumbled chorizo or other sausage (optional), and any salsa with some crumbled queso fresco or grated Monterey Jack; season with salt and pepper; fill cavities of chayote halves.	Bake in a 375°F oven until the chayote is tender. Sprinkle with chopped cilantro leaves.

VEGETABLE	PREPARATION	STUFFING	HOW TO COOK
Onions	Halve the onions around their equator and put in a greased pan, cut sides down. Drizzle with some melted butter and pour ¼ cup white wine or water over all. Bake until they're just tender, 15 to 20 minutes. Then remove the inner layers of onion, leaving the outside 3 layers intact. Slice a very thin layer off the rounded bottom to help the onion stay upright if necessary.	Cook, squeeze, and chop 1 pound of tender greens (see page 239). Mix with crumbled blue or feta cheese and fill the onions. Sprinkle the tops with fresh bread or panko and drizzle with more melted butter or olive oil.	Bake in a 375°F oven until the stuffing is hot and the onion is tender, about another 20 minutes. Sprinkle with crumbled cooked bacon if you like; serve hot or at room temperature.

large tomatoes or for making stuffed tomato appetizers).

Other vegetables you can use: Bell peppers, mushrooms, small eggplant, and summer squash can be stuffed raw. Chayote, onions, winter squash, cabbage, or any sturdy cooking green must be parcooked before being stuffed. (In all cases except for the peppers you will need to create a little hollow space by scraping away some of the interior flesh before filling.)

4 to 6 firm ripe tomatoes, about 6 ounces each

8 ounces fresh sausage, removed from the casings if necessary

1 cup cooked white, basmati, brown, or wild rice or other cooked grain

1 tablespoon minced garlic (optional)

Salt and freshly ground black pepper

½ cup extra virgin olive oil

Chopped fresh parsley or basil leaves for garnish

① Heat the oven to 450°F. Cut a ¼-inch slice from the smooth end of each tomato (the stem end is typically flatter and makes for a more stable base). Reserve these slices. Use a spoon to scoop out all of the insides of the tomatoes, leaving a wall about ¼ inch thick. Discard the woody core and seeds and chop the pulp; mix it with the sausage, the rice, the garlic if you're using it, and some salt and pepper.

② Sprinkle the inside of the tomatoes with salt and pepper, stuff them with the sausage mixture, and replace the top slices. Spread half the olive oil in a shallow roasting pan that will allow for a little room between the tomatoes and put them in the pan. Sprinkle all with salt and pepper and put the roasting pan in the oven.

③ Roast the tomatoes for 30 to 40 minutes, until they are shriveled and the sausage is cooked through. Take a peek into the middle of one of the tomatoes; if the sausage is still pink, continue cooking. Serve hot, warm, or at room temperature, drizzled with the remaining olive oil and garnished with the herb.

Tomatoes Stuffed with Rice and Cheese. Substitute 1 cup grated Gruyère, Asiago, manchego, Monterey Jack, or mozzarella cheese for the sausage.

Quick Stuffed Tomatoes. Halve the tomatoes, core, and scoop out the seeds. Omit the sausage and rice. Mix together ½ cup bread crumbs, preferably fresh (page 876), ½ cup freshly grated Parmesan, the garlic, salt and pepper, and just enough olive oil to make it hold together a bit. Fill the tomato halves with the bread

F Fast **M** Make Ahead **V** Vegetarian

crumb mixture. Proceed with the recipe and reduce the cooking time to 20 to 30 minutes, depending on the size of the tomato.

The Basics of Mixed Vegetable Dishes

These are among the most flexible dishes in the entire chapter, because there are very few rules, and most vegetables complement others nicely. Pay attention to size, remembering that similar-size pieces cook at similar rates, and to texture; harder vegetables take longer to cook than softer ones, of course. To compensate, either precook the hard ones a bit (see page 239) or just hold out the soft ones until near the end of the cooking time.

More is not necessarily better (too many vegetables will muddy the flavor); usually three or four vegetables per dish are sufficient. If you're looking for a "bigger" dish, remember that adding a little meat, fish, poultry, or even tofu turns these recipes into main courses. See "How to Add Meat, Fish, or Poultry to Almost Any Vegetable Dish" (page 246).

Oven-Baked Ratatouille

MAKES: 4 to 6 servings
TIME: about 1½ hours, largely unattended

The original "What do we have on hand?" recipe: You combine vegetables, herbs, and olive oil, in various proportions, and cook them on the stove or in the oven until very soft. Since it's widely considered a dish from Provence, zucchini (and/or eggplant) and tomatoes are frequently present, but there are really very few rules, except longish, slow cooking and lots of good olive oil; herbs help too. Choose herbs based on availability, but if I had my choice, I'd use a teaspoon of thyme or marjo-

ram for the cooking and garnish with a handful of basil or parsley.

Other vegetables you can use: Obviously, you can stew whatever you want, but potatoes and mushrooms are the most common additions that I haven't included here.

1½ to 2 pounds eggplant, preferably small, sliced ½ inch thick and salted if time allows (see page 293)

½ cup extra virgin olive oil, plus a little more for garnish

2 large onions, sliced

1 pound zucchini, trimmed and cut into large chunks

2 red or yellow bell peppers, cored, seeded, and sliced

4 plum tomatoes, cored and chopped, or 2 round tomatoes (drained canned are fine)

Fresh herbs such as thyme, marjoram, rosemary, savory, basil, parsley, and/or chervil, to taste, plus more for garnish

Salt and freshly ground black pepper

10 cloves garlic, halved

1 Heat the oven to 350°F. If you salted the eggplant, squeeze out excess liquid, then rinse and dry.

2 Film a casserole or heavy ovenproof skillet with a couple tablespoons of the olive oil, then make a layer of onion, followed by one of eggplant, zucchini, peppers, tomatoes, herbs, a sprinkling of salt and pepper, and half the garlic (the order doesn't matter at all). Repeat. Drizzle with the remaining olive oil and put in the oven.

3 Bake for about 1 hour, pressing down on the vegetables occasionally with a spatula, until they are all completely tender. Garnish with more herbs, drizzle with a little more olive oil, and serve hot, warm, or at room temperature.

Stovetop Mixed Vegetables with Olive Oil. This requires a little more attention: Combine all the ingredients in the largest skillet you have (a broad saucepan will work also) and cook, stirring occasionally, over medium heat, adjusting the heat so the mixture simmers in its own juices without browning. Cooking will be just a little quicker, perhaps 45 minutes or so.

Roasted Vegetables, Catalonian Style. Best served at room temperature: Reduce the olive oil to ¼ cup and omit the herbs. Toss the vegetables in the olive oil and roast. Proceed with the recipe. When the vegetables are cooled, toss with 2 tablespoons sherry or other good vinegar and sprinkle with salt and pepper.

Stir-Fried Vegetables, Vietnamese Style

MAKES: 4 servings
TIME: 30 minutes

For a simple stir-fry, this packs a lot of punch. And the keys are no more than lots of garlic and lots and lots of black pepper.

Other vegetables you can use: really, any assortment you like, provided you cook them in batches (as here) to make sure each is perfectly cooked.

¼ cup neutral oil, like grapeseed or corn

1 cup broccoli or cauliflower florets about 1 inch across

2 medium carrots, thinly sliced

½ cup snow or snap peas, trimmed

1 medium to large onion, thinly sliced

2 dried Thai chiles, or hot red pepper flakes or cayenne to taste

1 tablespoon minced garlic

2 tablespoons nam pla (Thai fish sauce) or soy sauce, or to taste

1 teaspoon freshly ground black pepper, or to taste

Salt

❶ Put 1 tablespoon of the oil in a nonstick skillet over high heat. When hot, add the broccoli and cook, stirring occasionally, for about a minute. Add 2 tablespoons water and continue to cook and stir until the vegetable is crisp-tender, about 5 minutes. Remove from the pan and repeat the process with the carrots and then the snow peas.

❷ Put a little more oil in the pan and add the onion. Cook over high heat, stirring once in a while, until it softens and begins to char, 3 to 5 minutes. Add the chiles and garlic and cook for 30 seconds.

❸ Add ¼ cup water, along with the fish sauce and pepper; return the cooked vegetables to the pan. Cook, stirring, until the mixture is combined and lightly sauced, then taste, adjust the seasoning, and serve.

Stir-Fried Vegetables and Pork, Vietnamese Style. Add 1 pound boneless pork, preferably from the shoulder, cut into thin shreds and thoroughly dried. In Step 1, make sure the skillet is very hot; add the pork, stir once or twice, and cook until it begins to brown, about a minute. Stir again and cook for another minute; remove from the pan and add more oil if necessary. Proceed with the recipe, returning the cooked pork to the pan during the last minute or so of cooking.

Mixed Spicy Vegetables, Thai Style

MAKES: 4 servings
TIME: 30 minutes

Half stir-fry, half braise, this quick, thick stew can be varied in a number of ways, all delicious. If you like Thai-style curries, this is for you.

3 tablespoons peanut or neutral oil, like grapeseed or corn

1 large white onion, sliced

2 tablespoons chopped garlic

2 dried chiles, 1 minced seeded fresh chile, or 1 teaspoon Chile Paste (page 74) or red or green curry paste (to make your own, see page 75 or 76), or to taste

1½ pounds eggplant, zucchini, summer squash, or a combination, peeled as necessary and cut into 1½-inch chunks

1½ cups coconut milk (to make your own, see page 389)

3 lime leaves, chopped, preferably fresh (dried are okay), or the zest of 1 lime

3 tablespoons soy sauce or nam pla (Thai fish sauce)

Salt and freshly ground black pepper

Lime wedges for garnish

❶ Put the oil in a 10- or 12-inch skillet over medium-high heat. When hot, add the onion and cook, stirring occasionally, until it softens a bit, 5 minutes or so. Stir in the garlic and chiles, then add the eggplant or squash. Cook, stirring occasionally and adjusting the heat as necessary so the vegetable cooks quickly without burning, until it softens (zucchini will cook faster than eggplant or squash, so give the other vegetables a head start if cooking a combination), 10 to 20 minutes.

❷ Add the coconut milk and the lime leaves and simmer until thickened, about 5 minutes. Add the soy sauce, then taste and add salt and pepper if necessary. Serve hot, with lime wedges.

Mixed Spicy Vegetables with Chicken. Substitute 1 pound boneless chicken, cut into thin shreds and thoroughly patted dry, for about ³⁄₄ pound of the mixed vegetables. In Step 1, make sure the skillet is very hot; add the chicken, stir once or twice, and cook until it begins to brown, about a minute. Stir again and add the onion; proceed with the recipe.

Mixed Spicy Vegetables, Indian Style. Add 1 tablespoon minced fresh ginger and reduce the garlic to 2 teaspoons (add them together); use 2 fresh chiles, like serrano or jalapeño, seeded and minced, instead of dried chiles. In Step 2, add the coconut milk and

1½ teaspoons garam masala (to make your own, see page 67). Omit the lime leaves, soy sauce, and lime wedges.

8 Additions to Mixed Spicy Vegetables, Thai Style

With or without eggplant, this can become a bigger, more interesting dish, one that can be made with almost any vegetable you have on hand. For example, add:

1. 1 to 2 cups tomatoes, after the eggplant begins to soften
2. 1 to 2 cups peeled and cubed potato, preferably a waxy variety, in place of or in addition to the eggplant, at the same time
3. 1 to 2 cups peas, snow peas, or snap peas, when the eggplant is about half cooked
4. ½ to 1 cup chopped carrots or celery, along with the onion
5. 1 tablespoon minced fresh ginger, along with the garlic and chile
6. ½ cup or more shredded fresh basil leaves, preferably Thai, or cilantro, mint, or a combination, at the last second
7. About 1 pound chopped boneless pork (preferably from the shoulder; Boston butt or picnic), beef (preferably sirloin, cut across the grain), or shrimp (peeled), in place of or in addition to the eggplant, at the same time
8. 1 to 2 cups firm- to extra-firm tofu (blotted dry, cut into ¼-inch cubes), just before the coconut milk

Layered Vegetable Torte

MAKES: 4 to 6 servings
TIME: At least 2 hours or a day largely unattended

A gorgeous dish, in which the sliced vegetables are layered and pressed to form the torte—you could call it a pie—so that when it's cut you can see the bands of vegetables. This dish makes a really spectacular meal centerpiece or party dish. And it can be assembled and refrigerated up to 2 days ahead; in fact, the longer it's pressed, the better it keeps its shape when sliced. You can grill the vegetables instead of roasting them if you like for even more flavor or if it's more convenient.

Other vegetables you can use: thinly sliced and parcooked butternut squash, summer squash, potato, sweet potato, leeks, onions, turnips, beets, peppers, and chiles.

2 medium eggplant

4 medium zucchini

Salt

4 red bell peppers, roasted and cleaned (see page 330)

1/2 cup extra virgin olive oil, or more as needed

Freshly ground black pepper

20 or so fresh basil leaves, some chopped or torn for garnish

Freshly grated Parmesan cheese for garnish (optional)

1 Peel the eggplant if the skin is thick or the eggplant is less than perfectly firm. Cut it and the zucchini into 1/4-inch-thick slices; salt the eggplant if time allows (see page 293). Cut each roasted pepper into thirds or fourths and set aside.

2 Heat the oven to 400°F. Smear 2 (or more) baking sheets with 2 tablespoons oil each. Lay the eggplant slices on one sheet and the zucchini on the other in a single layer. (You may need to work in batches; cooking the eggplant on the 2 baking sheets, then cooking the zucchini.) Sprinkle with some salt and pepper (if you did not salt the eggplant) and drizzle or brush another couple tablespoons oil over each sheet of vegetables. Roast until the eggplant and zucchini are soft, about 15 minutes for the zucchini, 20 or so for the eggplant.

3 Coat a deep pie dish with some oil. Layer a third of the eggplant slices into the bottom of the pan, covering the bottom (trim the eggplant pieces if necessary), then layer half the zucchini, peppers, and basil, sprinkling each layer with a bit of salt and pepper; repeat the layers, ending with eggplant.

4 Put a plate or other flat object (you want it to distribute weight evenly across the top of the pie) over the top of the pie and weight it with a large tomato can or something similar. Let it rest at room temperature for at least an hour or in the fridge for a day, then remove the weight; it can be stored in the refrigerator for 2 to 3 days before being served. (Put it on a large plate or platter, as juices might be squeezed out.)

5 Serve at room temperature or heat it in a 325°F oven until warm, about 30 minutes. Garnish with the chopped basil and Parmesan and cut into wedges to serve.

Cheesy Vegetable Torte. Mozzarella works nicely with the vegetables, but really almost any cheese (except very soft cheeses like ricotta) will work, depending on the vegetables you use in the pie: Grate or slice the cheese and add 1 or 2 layers between the vegetables. After Step 3, bake the pie in a 325°F oven until hot (you want the cheese to melt into the vegetable layers), about 40 minutes.

Autumn Vegetable Torte. Almost dessert; it's wonderful sprinkled with brown sugar or drizzled with maple syrup and served for brunch too: Substitute peeled butternut squash, peeled sweet potato, and cored apples for the eggplant, zucchini, and red peppers. Instead of the basil, use fresh sage leaves or a couple tablespoons chopped fresh rosemary.

Crisp Vegetable Pancake, Korean Style

Pajon

MAKES: 6 to 8 servings

TIME: 45 minutes

M **V**

These nearly addictive savory cakes are almost crêpelike in their crisp and chewy texture. That texture is at its best—crisp on the outside, tender and chewy on the

 Fast   Make Ahead   **V** Vegetarian

inside—if you use rice flour, which you'll find at most Asian markets. Serve the pancakes hot or at room temperature with Soy Dipping Sauce and Marinade (page 25), or a mixture of soy sauce and vinegar.

Other vegetables you can use: corn kernels, shredded cabbage, or radish.

2 cups flour, preferably half all-purpose, half rice flour

2 eggs, lightly beaten

1 tablespoon neutral oil, like grapeseed or corn, plus more as needed

5 scallions, green parts only, cut into 3-inch lengths and sliced lengthwise

20 chives, preferably Chinese ("garlic") chives, or parsley or cilantro

2 medium carrots, grated

1 small yellow squash or zucchini, grated

1 Mix the flour, eggs, and oil with $1^1/_2$ cups water until a smooth batter is formed. Let it rest while you prepare the vegetables. When you're ready to cook, stir the scallions, chives, carrots, and squash into the batter.

2 Heat a large nonstick skillet over medium-high heat and coat the bottom with oil. Ladle in a quarter of the batter and spread it out evenly into a circle. Turn the heat to medium and cook until the bottom is browned, about 5 minutes, then flip and cook for another 5 minutes (see the illustration for flipping Rösti, page 345). Repeat with the remaining batter.

3 As the pancakes finish, remove them, and, if necessary, drain on paper towels. Cut into small triangles and serve with a soy sauce dipping sauce.

Kimchi Crispy Pancake. Add about 1 cup chopped Kimchi (page 230) to the batter.

Seafood and Vegetable Pancake, Korean Style. Add up to 2 cups sliced shrimp, squid, oysters, or mussels (precooked and shelled, alone or in combination). Reduce the vegetables by half. Proceed with the recipe, making the pancakes a bit thicker to hold the seafood.

The Basics of Cooking Fruit

Once you get used to the idea of cooking fruit—and seasoning it in ways both sweet and savory—you significantly increase your recipe repertoire. And cooking makes excellent use of overripe, underripe, even slightly damaged fruit.

Fruit is slightly more forgiving than vegetables when it comes to overcooking, but even though the window from just-tender to perfect may be slightly wider, the flesh goes from there to mush much faster. That makes slow cooking like poaching, stewing, or roasting most appealing for times when you want to walk away from the stove. High-heat methods (grilling and sautéing) require more attention. And because fruit is naturally high in fructose, it will burn more easily if overheated. So cook fruit at a slightly lower temperature than you would vegetables and keep an eye on it, stirring and turning as necessary.

Firmness is the best way to predict how long a fruit will take to cook: The least fibrous fruits (bananas, strawberries, papaya, and raspberries) cook fastest, while firmer fruit (pineapple, apple, and even citrus) are far more durable. Ideally, remove fruit from the heat before it's completely tender (use a fork or a knife tip to judge tenderness).

Cooked fruit can be incorporated into all sorts of dishes, not just desserts: Think of halved fruit on the grill and compotes and chutneys; none of these, even the most complex of them, take more than a few minutes to put together. For some ideas about how to season fruit before, during, and after cooking, see page 380.

To Peel or Not to Peel?

It makes a difference: Peeled fruit will cook through and lose its shape faster than unpeeled fruit, which might make you tend to cook fruit with its skin on. But if the flesh gets even slightly overdone, it tends to separate from the skin, especially during moist cooking like poaching and sautéing. Then you're left with the worst of both textures: soft fruit and tough skin.

For every rule there's at least one exception, so try to use common sense: If the skin isn't edible—as in melons, mangoes, or papayas—you can usually peel the fruit before cooking. (There are exceptions, like bananas, where the skin is needed to protect the flesh and keep it intact.) However, leaving the edible skins on peaches, apples, plums, and pears during high-heat, fast-cook methods like grilling, broiling, or roasting helps hold the flesh together and improves color and flavor. Virtually everything else should be peeled if at all practical (to keep the skins from slipping off small fruits, just be careful not to overcook them).

Fruit-Cooking Techniques

Here's a rundown of the major options for cooking fruit.

Poaching Fruit

Good candidates for poaching are pears, apples, pineapple, cherries, grapes, peaches and nectarines, plums, and quince. (Dried fruit is also wonderful poached.) It's best to poach fruit in a liquid like seasoned juice, vinegar, or wine; water leaches out too much of the flavor.

The idea is to put the poaching fruit in just enough seasoned liquid to cover it. Keep the mixture barely bubbling and cook, turning the fruit once or twice, until a toothpick or skewer pierces to the center. A pear might take 20 minutes or so, while cherries will be done in less than 10. Let the fruit cool in the liquid so it absorbs as much flavor as possible, then remove. Serve with the poaching liquid as is (like a soup) or boil the liquid until it thickens into a syrupy sauce. Poached fruit keeps in the fridge for several days.

Stewing Fruit

Fruit compote is a fancy name for stewed fruit, about the easiest thing in the world: Put cut fruit—either one kind or an assortment—into a pan with a tight-fitting lid. Sprinkle with a little sugar or other sweetener (or try salt and freshly ground black pepper). Add a couple tablespoons of water, cover, and turn the heat to medium-low. Cook, stirring occasionally, until some of the juice is released and the fruit begins to soften, anywhere from 5 to 20 minutes depending on the fruit.

In a pinch you can microwave fruit as you would vegetables (see page 236), though it's really just as easy—and only slightly less fast—to stew it. You can also "stew" fruit without any cooking at all. See "Macerating and Seasoning Fruit" (page 379).

Sautéing Fruit

Start with a deep, broad skillet, set it over medium to medium-high heat, and swirl around a little oil or melt a pat of butter, just enough to coat the pan and the fruit; figure 1 to 2 tablespoons per pound. When the oil is hot or the butter melts, stir or toss the fruit around in the pan until it's cooked, using sweet or savory seasonings as you like.

Roasting or Baking Fruit

Roasting is one of my favorite ways to cook fruit, because, as with vegetables, it helps develop deep color and flavor. The only trick is to make sure the sugars in the fruit caramelize without burning. Start by setting the oven between 325°F and 350°F, a little lower than you would for vegetables. Grease a rimmed baking sheet or shallow roasting pan or line it with a piece of parchment and add whole or cut fruit, taking care not to overcrowd. Drizzle or brush with a little oil or melted butter and season as you like. Roast, checking occasionally and turning as necessary, until tender and golden, anywhere from 15 to 45 minutes depending on the fruit.

Oven-Drying Fruit

This make-ahead technique leaves fruit chewy, moist, and slightly crisp; you control the ultimate texture. See "Dried Fruit" (page 384) and Oven-Dried Tomatoes (page 362).

Grilling or Broiling Fruit

Broiling or grilling is among the best ways to cook fruit and may change the way you think about the backyard barbecue. And grilled fruit is more flexible than grilled vegetables because you can vary the flavors from sweet to savory.

Grilled fruit teams beautifully with a green salad, complements the smokiness of grilled meats, seafood, or chicken, and works as an ingredient; you can even use grilled fruit for making salsas. Sweet grilled fruit can be served with ice cream, sorbet, granita, rice pudding, or custard or next to cake or other drier desserts. Or use it to make grilled fruit pizza; see page 178.

Start with fruit that is ripe but still somewhat firm so it will hold together on the grill. Use a clean grill, with lower heat than you would for vegetables; since most fruits are sugar laden, they will char fairly quickly, in just a couple minutes in most cases. And give the fruit a good brushing of oil or melted butter before you put it on the grill, or else you'll be scraping it off. See "Ideas for Broiling or Grilling Fruit" on page 380.

Frying Fruit

With few exceptions, fruit should be breaded or battered before being deep-fried; coating the fruit not only protects it from overcooking but also helps control splattering. Flour and cornmeal (or a mixture of the two) are easy enough, though a batter creates wonderful fruit fritters. You can either panfry in shallow oil ($^{1}/_{2}$ inch deep or so) or deep-fry in enough oil to submerge them (2 or 3 inches of oil in a deep pot).

To panfry: Set a deep skillet over medium to medium-high heat and pour in the oil. It should be hot but not smoking before you add the fruit (test a small piece first; it should sizzle immediately and energetically).

To deep-fry: The oil should reach a temperature between 350°F and 375°F. (See "Deep Frying," page 19.) Be careful to allow enough room at the top of the pot for the fruit to displace the oil and cause it to rise. And be careful not to crowd.

Macerating and Seasoning Fruit

Macerating fruit—both fresh and dried—is similar to marinating; you soak it in liquid. Juicy fresh fruits like berries, citrus, and peaches often need only a sprinkle of sugar or salt to draw out their juices and create the macerating liquid, while other fruits benefit from added liquid like simple syrup, fruit juice, wine or brandy, or even water. The end result is softened fruit (and plumped if you're using dried) flavored with the soaking liquid. It's a versatile way to add a kick to less-than-perfect fruit.

To macerate and season fruit: Chop or slice large or medium fruit (small fruit can be left whole) and peel it if the skin is tough or if you prefer it peeled. Mix together the fruit, the liquid, and whatever seasonings you're using. Fresh fruit needs only about $^{1}/_{2}$ cup of liquid per pound of fruit, but dried fruit absorbs a good amount of liquid, so it should cover the fruit by an inch or even a little more. Cover and set aside at room temperature (or in the refrigerator if the kitchen is warm), stirring every few hours.

Soft and juicy fresh fruit can take as little as 15 to 20 minutes to macerate; denser ones, like apple and pineapple, can take 3 or 4 hours; dried fruit requires 12 to 24 hours to soften fully. You want the fruit to be tender but not mushy.

Eat as is or with some cream, yogurt, or sour cream or use macerated and seasoned fruit as a topping for pancakes, waffles, yogurt, or ice cream; as a filler for crêpes or blintzes; added to sauces and dressings; and as a garnish for simply cooked meat, fish, seafood, or chicken. It's also a tasty addition to beverages, like iced tea.

IDEAS FOR BROILING OR GRILLING FRUIT

This chart provides some tips and suggestions for flavoring, seasoning, saucing, and serving any fruit you can grill.

FRUIT	PREPARATION	HOW TO BROIL OR GRILL	HOW TO SAUCE, SEASON, OR SERVE
Citrus	Cut in half along their equator or into 1-inch-thick slices; brush with oil or melted butter.	Cook over direct heat, turning occasionally, until browned, 3 to 5 minutes.	Top with Chile Paste (page 74) or sprinkle with minced fresh ginger.
Figs	Cut in half through the stem or grill whole; brush with oil or melted butter.	Cook, cut side down, over direct heat until browned, 2 to 3 minutes.	Spread with Pesto with Butter (page 27), Port Wine Mustard (page 45), Balsamic Syrup (page 51), or Brown Butter (page 56).
Mangoes	Peel and cut large slices or wedges off the pit; brush with oil.	Cook over direct heat, turning occasionally, until browned, 3 to 5 minutes.	Spoon on some Fresh Tomatillo Salsa (page 33), Cilantro "Pesto" with Ginger and Chile (page 28), Cilantro-Mint Chutney (page 37), or Chile and Coconut Sauce (page 54).
Melons	Cut into wedges—peeled or not—or 1½-inch cubes; skewer cubes; oil is optional.	Cook over direct heat, turning occasionally, until browned, 3 to 5 minutes.	Top with Fresh Tomato or Fruit Salsa (page 23) or Mint Purée (page 28), or sprinkle with lemon or lime juice.
Peaches and Nectarines	Halve or quarter; brush with oil or melted butter.	Cook, cut side down, over direct heat until browned, 2 to 3 minutes. Flip and cook the other side for a minute or two if you like.	Smear with Basil Purée (page 28), Ginger Yogurt Sauce (page 24), Compound Butter (page 32), or Chipotle Paste (page 74). Off the grill, crumble blue or feta cheese on top.
Pineapple	Peel and cut into slices, wedges, or 1½-inch cubes; skewer cubes; brush with oil.	Cook over direct heat, turning occasionally, until browned, 3 to 5 minutes.	Drizzle with Ponzu Sauce (page 40) or Basil-Soy Dipping Sauce (page 38).
Plantains	Use plantains that are yellow with some black; cut off each end; slice in half lengthwise or peel and cut into 1-inch-thick slices; brush with oil.	Cook over direct heat, turning occasionally, until browned, 3 to 7 minutes depending on ripeness.	Top with Coconut Chutney (page 37), Cilantro "Pesto" with Ginger and Chile (page 28), or Simpler Peanut Sauce (page 55).
Plums	Halve or quarter (skewer if you like); brush with oil or melted butter.	Cook, cut side down, over direct heat until browned, 2 to 3 minutes.	Top with Herbed Five-Minute Drizzle Sauce (page 22), Sweet Yogurt Sauce (page 25), or Honey Mustard (page 44).

The Fruit Lexicon

Here is an alphabetical rundown of common fruits and what to do with them.

Apples

More than 10 billion pounds of apples are harvested each year in the United States, making it our primary fruit. There are thousands of varieties of apples in every shade of yellow, gold, red, and green, ranging from sweet to tart and mealy to crisp. Unfortunately, growers have concentrated on just a few types, and these are among the least interesting; probably the best of the widely grown varieties are McIntosh (even that's become increasingly hard to find) and Golden Delicious. You'll find the most variety and most interesting apples at local orchards in the fall, especially if you are in the Northeast.

In general, apples are divided into three categories: eating, cooking, and all-purpose (that is, eating, cooking, and whatever else you might think of). On the previous page is a list of some of the most common and some not-so-common apples, with notes on flavor, texture, and use.

Buying and storing: All apples should be firm and heavy for their size; avoid any with soft spots. Use those that are less than perfectly firm for cooking. Store in a cool, dry place or in the refrigerator for weeks.

Almost all apples in this country are harvested in the late summer and fall, but wholesalers keep the fruit in reduced-oxygen storage, where they remain in reasonably decent shape for months. But they deteriorate quickly when removed from these special storage conditions, so in winter and spring, use apples quickly. Of course, increasingly we see apples imported from the southern hemisphere, in every season but fall.

Preparing: Rinse and take a bite or peel and cut (see illustrations, right). For peeling, start at the stem or flower end and work in latitudinal strips or around the circumference; a U-shaped peeler is best.

For coring, you have several options. You can remove the core and leave the apple whole by digging into the stem end with a sturdy melon baller and removing it; this

You can core an apple in two ways. For baked apples, use a melon baller and dig into the flower (nonstem) end, taking out a little at a time until the core has been removed.

For other uses, simply cut the apple into quarters and remove the core with a paring knife or melon baller.

leaves the blossom end intact, a nice presentation for baked apples. Or you can buy a slicer-corer, which will cut the apple into six or eight slices around the core in one swift motion. Or you can quarter the apple and dig out each piece of the core with a paring knife. Finally, you can just cut chunks of apple from around the core with a paring knife.

Apples brown quickly once peeled or cut; to prevent this, drop them into acidulated water (one part lemon juice to about ten parts water) or white wine or toss with lemon or lime juice.

Other fruits to substitute: Pears.

EVERYDAY APPLES

APPLE VARIETY	DESCRIPTION	FLAVOR AND TEXTURE	CATEGORY
Braeburn	Red with lighter flecks and a green tinge around the stem; yellow flesh	Sweet, slightly tangy, juicy, and crisp	All-purpose
Cortland	Red with bright green patches; white flesh that doesn't turn brown quickly	Sweet, juicy, and tender	All-purpose
Empire	Red with lighter flecks and yellowish green patches; cream-colored flesh	Sweet-tart, juicy, and very crisp but can also be mushy	All-purpose
Fuji	Red with yellow and green mottling; cream-colored flesh; nothing special	Sweet, juicy, and fairly crisp	Eating
Gala	Red with gold mottling; light yellow flesh	Mild, sweet, and crisp	Eating
Golden Delicious	Greenish gold skin, sometimes with a blush of pink; light yellow flesh	Full-flavored, sweet-tart, juicy, and crisp	All-purpose
Granny Smith	Green with light flecks; white flesh	Tart to sweet-tart, juicy, and very crisp; holds shape well when cooked	All-purpose
Ida Red	Large and brilliant red; light green flesh with a touch of pink	Sweet, juicy, and firm; holds shape well when cooked	Cooking
Jonagold	Red with golden-yellow flecks and streaks of green; light yellow flesh	Very sweet, juicy, and crisp; better than Golden Delicious but harder to find	All-purpose
Jonathan	Red with some bright yellow streaks; off-white flesh	Sweet-tart with a bit of spice, juicy, and crisp; does not bake whole well	All-purpose
Macoun	A New England favorite; red with green patches and mottling; white flesh; available late fall only	Very sweet, juicy, and tender	Eating
McIntosh	Bright red with green patches; off-white flesh	Sweet and crisp when very fresh; becomes mushy quickly	All-purpose
Pink Lady	Rosy pink and golden yellow; white flesh that doesn't turn brown quickly	Sweet-tart, juicy, and very crisp; lots of flavor	All-purpose
Red Delicious	The most common, but most often mealy; dark red; off-white flesh	Sweet but not complex, often mealy	Eating
Rome	Bright red and round; greenish-hued flesh	Mildly tart and tender	Cooking

F Fast   **M** Make Ahead   **V** Vegetarian

Applesauce

MAKES: About 2 quarts
TIME: About 1 hour, largely unattended

Most people think of applesauce as a sweet, almost dessertlike condiment. And it can be. But I prefer a neutral approach that allows for savory seasonings. See the list that follows for some ideas.

A food mill is the easiest way to go and produces the best applesauce, because the skins lend both their flavor and color and there's no need to do the up-front work. If you don't have one, you must core and peel the apples before cooking. Make as much as your time and the size of your pot allows by doubling or tripling the quantity. Applesauce freezes well and is handy when packed in small containers.

Other fruits you can use: pears or cantaloupe.

5 pounds apples, preferably a mixture of varieties
Salt

① Cut the apples in half or, if they're very large, into quarters. If you don't have a food mill, peel and core. Put about ½ inch of water and a pinch of salt in the bottom of a large pot and add the apples. Cover and turn the heat to medium.

② When the water begins to boil, uncover the pot. Cook, stirring occasionally and lowering the heat if the mixture threatens to burn on the bottom, until the apples break down and become mushy, at least 30 minutes. Let sit until cool enough to handle.

③ If you have a food mill, pass the mixture through it, discarding the solids that stay behind. If not, mash if you like with a fork or potato masher. Freeze or refrigerate.

10 Great Seasonings for Applesauce

Just put any of the following ingredients into the pot or pan along with the apples. Start with a teaspoon or less, then taste after cooking and add more as needed.

1. Freshly ground black pepper
2. Ground cumin, coriander, caraway, or cardamom seeds
3. Minced fresh chile (like jalapeño or Thai) or hot red pepper flakes or cayenne
4. Chipotle chiles, dried or canned (with a little of their adobo sauce)
5. Minced fresh ginger (good with savory or sweet)
6. Granulated or brown sugar
7. A grating of nutmeg
8. Ground cloves or allspice
9. Any spice blend (to make your own, see pages 65–69)
10. Roasted Garlic (page 303)

Sautéed Apples or Other Fruit

MAKES: 4 servings
TIME: 30 minutes

Think of this as a universal recipe for sautéing nearly any fruit. You can cook the apples with no sugar at all (in fact, they're wonderful with onions) and serve them as a side dish, or you can make them into this dessert, which is sort of a tarte Tatin without the crust. Serve as is or with a scoop of vanilla ice cream or a dollop of Whipped Cream (page 882) or crème fraîche.

Other fruits you can use: Pears, apricots, peaches, nectarines, plums, banana, cherries, or pineapple.

4 tablespoons (½ stick) unsalted butter
About 1½ pounds firm crisp apples, like Golden Delicious, peeled, cored, and cut into 8 or 10 pieces each
½ cup granulated or brown sugar
½ teaspoon ground cinnamon

① Put the butter in a large deep skillet over medium heat. When the butter is melted, add the apples and stir; turn the heat to low, cover, and cook for 10 minutes.

② Add the sugar and cinnamon and raise the heat to medium. Cook, stirring frequently, until the apples are tender and glazed, another 10 minutes or so. Serve hot or warm.

Baked Apples

MAKES: 4 servings

TIME: About 1 hour

A simple and healthy side dish or dessert, especially if you keep the cream to a minimum. Here's the basic recipe; note that suggestions for making it more complicated follow.

Other fruits you can use: any ripe firm pears, like Bosc.

4 large round apples, preferably Cortland or Ida Red

About 1 cup water, sweet white wine, or apple juice

Sugar as needed (optional)

① Heat the oven to 350°F.

② Core the apples (see illustrations on page 380) and peel the top half of each, leaving the stem end intact. Put in a baking dish with about ½ inch of liquid on the bottom. If you're using sugar, put about 1 teaspoon in the cavity of each apple and sprinkle another teaspoon or so on top.

③ Bake open end up, uncovered, until the apples are very tender, about an hour. Cool and serve warm or at room temperature or refrigerate (it's best to bring the apples back to room temperature before serving). Best served with sweet or sour cream or yogurt.

5 Simple Ideas for Baked Apples

1. Cream the sugar or spices with 2 tablespoons unsalted butter before adding it.
2. Substitute maple syrup, honey, or brown sugar for the granulated sugar.
3. Add about ½ cup chopped nuts, shredded coconut, raisins, and/or chopped figs or dates to the sugar for filling.
4. Fill the apple cavities with jam about 10 minutes before the end of baking.
5. Fill the apple cavities with grated cheddar or crumbled blue cheese before baking.

Apricots

An ancient stone fruit practically worshiped by the ancient Greeks and cultivated in China—its likely birthplace—for thousands of years. Good apricots are luxuriously sweet and tart with silky skin and a fleshy and succulent interior. But a perfectly ripe, juicy, and flavorful apricot is hard to find, even if you live where they're grown (now mostly California).

Ripe apricots are delicate and extremely perishable, so they're usually picked well before they're ripe. Although they will ripen some after picking, they'll rarely develop into the unbelievably delicious fruit that they are when tree ripened. You can find them that way in some summer farmers' markets, though again not easily. Fortunately, dried apricots are spectacular.

Buying and storing: Fresh summertime apricots should be deeply colored (some even with a speckling of dark orange, almost brown), heavy, fragrant, and yielding to gentle pressure. Once you've tasted a good one, you'll never want anything less. Leave unripe specimens at room temperature (and in a paper bag to hasten ripening). Store ripe fruit in the refrigerator for a day or two, but eat as soon as possible.

Dried apricots should not be too leathery. When you find ones you like (check Middle Eastern and Asian markets), buy them in bulk, as they'll keep for a year or more in a cool, dry place, though they do dry out eventually.

Preparing: Not much to it—tear or cut it in half and remove the pit or just bite into it. Peel apricots by plunging them into boiling water for about 10 seconds and then slipping off the skin. Dried apricots can be soaked

Dried Fruit

Fruit was originally dried to preserve it, but drying also intensifies flavor, sometimes making dried fruit superior to fresh specimens; think of dried apricots and prunes, for example.

Several methods can be used to dry fruit, starting with the most basic and primitive: sun-drying. Here the fruit is often cut in half or into pieces and just left out in the sun for several days.

More common drying methods include air-drying, a combination of air circulation and low heat that can be done in an oven, though it's best with a dehydrator; sugar-drying (soaking or simmering the fruit in a sugar syrup, followed by air-drying—think crystallized ginger); and frying (best for high-starch, low-moisture foods like bananas).

Regardless of the method, many commercially dried fruits are treated with sulfur dioxide before processing, a preservative that helps the fruit hold its color, flavor, and shape. If you're sensitive to sulfites—or can taste them—look for nonsulfured dried fruits.

Drying Fruit at Home

Unless you have a dehydrator, oven-drying is your best option; it adds no extra sugar or fat, takes a few hours, and gives you plenty of control over the final product, which may be plump and chewy or shriveled and completely dry, depending on the size of the pieces and how long you dry them.

There's nothing complicated here. Small items like grapes, berries, and cherry tomatoes can be left whole; medium-size, halved or sliced; and large and/or very hard fruit, like papaya, pineapple, and coconut, must be sliced. Put the prepared fruit on a rack over a baking sheet—cut side down where applicable—and put in a 225°F oven for anywhere from 2 to 12 hours. Rotate the baking sheet every couple hours and check; the fruit is done when it's as shriveled and dried as you like. Completely dried and brittle fruit can be stored almost indefinitely in an airtight container in your pantry; fruit that's still moist should be wrapped in plastic or put in a container and refrigerated; it will keep for at least a few days, probably much longer.

In a dehydrator, the water is evaporated from fruit very slowly, with only a little heat. Most machines have a small electrical element in the base, with a tower of racks and a vent on top. Depending on the fruit and how packed the dehydrator is, it could take up to 24 hours to dry fully, though as with oven-drying, you can stop the process at any point. Dehydrators are handy, especially if you intend to dry a lot of fruit or vegetables.

You can also make fruit chips, using the same technique in the oven or a dehydrator; apples, pineapples, coconut, and thin-skinned lemons and oranges are best: Use a mandoline for even slices (squeeze lemon juice over apple slices to prevent discoloring). Put the slices on a lightly oiled baking sheet, and set your oven to the lowest setting (turning it on and off if the slices begin to brown), and dry the fruit until completely crisp, 2 to 3 hours; or use a dehydrator. Brush the slices with some Sugar Syrup (page 921) before drying for a sweeter result. Use fruit chips as a garnish on desserts or salads or just as a crunchy snack.

in liquid to soften or cooked. Either way, even a little can add a lot to sweet and savory dishes. Try sautéing them along with the aromatics and let them melt away into the dish or add at the last minute.

Other fruits to substitute: Peaches or nectarines.

Bananas

A tropical plant with hundreds of varieties (including plantain; see page 334), the most familiar being yellow—sometimes called *sweet* or *dessert*—banana. But there are also tiny finger bananas and red and even blue varieties, all with varying flavors and sweetness. Yellow and even green bananas are also wonderful cooked, as long as they're not too ripe; they become luxuriously sweet and soft.

Buying and storing: Bananas ripen nicely off the plant, and they are often sold green. Leave at room temperature for anywhere from a day to a week; the longer they ripen, the softer and sweeter they become. How ripe is really a matter of personal preference, and you undoubtedly know yours already. Any banana can be stored in the refrigerator to retard further ripening; the skins may turn black, but the flesh remains the same for weeks.

Preparing: Peel and eat or chop or slice as needed. Squeeze some lemon or lime juice over the freshly cut banana to prevent discoloring.

Other fruits to substitute: There is no substitute for raw bananas. Substitute plantains for bananas when cooking.

Sautéed, Roasted, or Broiled Bananas

MAKES: 4 servings
TIME: 15 minutes

 F **V**

A fast and easy dessert or side dish—serve with pork chops and roasts or grilled fish—and one for which you will almost always have the ingredients on hand.

Other vegetables you can use: ripe plantains.

4 bananas, ripe but not too soft
3 tablespoons unsalted butter
2 tablespoons sugar, or to taste (optional)
Freshly squeezed lemon juice

To sauté: Put the butter in a large deep skillet over medium-high heat. When the butter is melted, add the banana pieces and cook until golden and beginning to brown on both sides, about 10 minutes. Sprinkle with the sugar if you're using it and cook for another minute. Squeeze a bit of lemon juice over the top just before serving.

To roast: Heat the oven to 400°F. Put the bananas in a roasting pan, dot with the butter, and sprinkle with the sugar if you're using it. Cook the bananas until they are golden brown, about 10 minutes. Squeeze a bit of lemon juice over the top just before serving.

To broil: Heat a broiler and put the rack 4 to 6 inches from the heat source. Put the bananas on a baking sheet, dot with the butter, and sprinkle with the sugar if you're using it. Cook the bananas until they are golden brown, about 5 minutes; watch them carefully. Squeeze a bit of lemon juice over the top just before serving.

Berries

There are hundreds of types of berries, from all over the world. They all grow on vines or bushes, and they range in color from white to blue to red, orange, yellow, or black. They can be sweet or tart and everything in between and, with the exception of the blueberry, cranberry, and a couple of less common varieties, they're very perishable.

Almost all are now cultivated, and most are picked well before their prime, which is a problem because they don't ripen once picked, so they sometimes wind up

 Fast   **M** Make Ahead   Vegetarian

tasting like cardboard (sweetened cardboard if we're lucky). For the best or even good berries, you've got to go local (a farmstand, your garden, or even wild) and in season.

Of all the berries, strawberries are perhaps the ones that have been most mistreated by industrialized agriculture. Most are grown more for their hardiness and disease resistance than for their flavor, and that's a real shame because a truly ripe strawberry is heavenly. But as good as they are raw—even better with cream—or used in shortcake or jam, that's about the extent of their talent; they just don't work their way into many other dishes.

Blueberries can be considered the all-purpose berry: hardy (for a berry), fairly inexpensive in season, beautifully colored, delicious, and excellent for eating out of hand and cooking. The blueberry's closest relatives, huckleberry and juneberry, are too fragile ever to make it even to a farmers' market.

Blackberries and raspberries, along with all their cousins (boysenberries, loganberries, and dewberries to name a few), are varying degrees of sweet-and-tart and equally lovely for out-of-hand eating or cooking.

See the cranberry listing on page 389.

Buying and storing: All berries should be fragrant (especially strawberries), deeply colored, and soft but not mushy. Eat them ASAP; they are too perishable (and expensive) to store.

Strawberries: Taste one. If it's crunchy and flavorless, move on. If it's sweet and flavorful, buy only as many as you'll use in the next 24 hours. Don't refrigerate. Peak season is typically May and June. Out of season, they're just not that good.
Blueberries: Look for plump and unshriveled berries without any green. Inspect prepacked cartons carefully for mushy and/or moldy berries. Size is irrelevant. Taste one or two to be sure. Peak season is July and August.
Blackberries and raspberries: If you live in the northern half of the United States, you should know that these berries grow wild and in abundance; keep

your eyes peeled for low-lying bushes on your next walk through the woods. When buying in plastic containers, inspect the pad of paper underneath the berries; if it's heavily stained with juices, keep looking. Peak season is summer.

Preparing:

Strawberries: See the illustration below. Wash and dry. Pull or cut off the leaves and use a paring knife to dig out the stem and core.
Blueberries: Pick over, remove any stems, and wash.
Blackberries and raspberries: Wash and dry very gently. I do not wash wild berries as long as I'm sure of the source.

Other fruits to substitute: Berries are fairly interchangeable when used raw, or use grapes; blueberries, blackberries, and raspberries can substitute for one another in cooked dishes.

PREPARING STRAWBERRIES

To prepare strawberries, first remove the leaves, then cut a cone-shaped wedge with a paring knife to remove the top of the core. A small melon baller also does the job nicely.

Cherimoyas
Custard Apples

A medium-size tropical fruit (related to the soursop or guanabana) with green, leathery, scaled-looking skin and—at its best—a white, creamy, dreamy, custardlike interior with a pineapple-banana flavor. Although some are grown in California and Florida, they are not common, good ones even less so. The best come from Central America and Mexico.

Buying and storing: Look for plump, firm fruit, heavy for its size, with no brown patches; they will ripen if left at room temperature and are ready when they yield slightly to gentle pressure; at that point, store wrapped loosely in plastic in the refrigerator.

Preparing: Cut in half, remove the large seeds, and scoop out the flesh with a spoon. Eat raw.

Cherries

When cherries are good, they are succulent, juicy, fleshy, and even crisp, with a completely lovable flavor. We don't get the good ones as often as we like, but it's still worth a shot.

There are two types of cherries: sweet and sour (or tart). The former is best for eating out of hand, the latter for pie making and cooking. Most of the cherries we find at supermarkets are the sweet, deep red, and heart-shaped Bing cherries. Sour cherries are more often sold at farmers' markets and farmstands; they are typically smaller, brighter red, and rounder in shape than the sweet varieties and are too tart to eat raw.

Buying and storing: If you're going to pick them one by one (taste one), look for shiny, plump, and firm specimens with fresh-looking green stems. Otherwise, if the majority look sound, grab by the handful. Store wrapped loosely in plastic in the refrigerator; use as soon as possible; they won't last long.

Preparing: Wash and dry for eating out of hand; additionally stem and pit for cooking. A cherry pitter (which also works for olives) is handy if you're going to pit a large number.

Other fruits to substitute: Fresh currants or dried cherries; for cooking, cranberries or blueberries.

Stewed Cherries, Sweet or Savory

MAKES: 4 to 6 servings
TIME: About 30 minutes

When it's sweet, it's a simple treat, not unlike cherry pie without the crust. When it's savory, it's a lovely sauce for any kind of game bird (duck especially), pork, or juicy and rich steak. Either way, it's best made with sour cherries. Use fresh if you can find them, though frozen are good, too.

To make it savory, use the stock or wine and add sugar to taste if you're using sour cherries; to make it sweet, use the wine or water and add as much sugar as you like.

Other fruits you can use: apricots, cranberries, currants, grapes, or blueberries.

2 pounds cherries, preferably sour

1 cup water, red wine, or stock (see headnote)

Sugar to taste

Salt and freshly ground black pepper (for savory)

1/4 teaspoon ground cinnamon (optional for sweet), or 1 sprig fresh thyme (optional for savory)

1 tablespoon freshly squeezed lemon juice if using sweet cherries, or to taste

1 teaspoon minced lemon zest (optional for sweet)

1 Pit the cherries and combine them with the liquid in a medium saucepan over medium-high heat and cook, stirring occasionally, until the cherries are very tender, about 20 minutes.

2 Stir in the sugar, salt, pepper, and cinnamon if you're using them; taste and add more seasoning, including the lemon juice and zest if you like. Serve the cherries warm, at room temperature, or cold.

Cherries in Port, Sweet or Savory. Make either the sweet or savory version, but substitute port (wine) for the water, wine, or stock. Port is sweet, so be sure to taste the cherries before adding the sugar.

Cherries Jubilee. Omit the cinnamon, lemon juice, and lemon zest. Proceed with the recipe, making the stew quite sweet. Dole out 4 to 6 servings of vanilla or other ice cream. Add ¼ cup brandy (it must be at least 80 proof) to the cherries while still warm; carefully touch with a match, then spoon the flaming mixture over the ice cream and serve.

Coconuts

Here's a cool factoid: The average coconut palm lives for about 70 years and can produce thousands of coconuts. A whole fresh coconut is a large oval-shaped pod with pointed ends and a hard leathery green or brown exterior; this outer husk is usually removed before export to reveal the brown furry fruit we know as a coconut. Beyond this layer is a thin brown skin, then the white coconut meat and the translucent coconut juice (not to be confused with coconut milk; see page 389). Although fresh whole coconut is wonderful, store-bought shredded fresh and dried coconut is awfully convenient and tastes good too.

Buying and storing: Whole coconuts should be uniformly very hard—check the three eyes especially—and you should be able to hear the juice inside when you shake one. Store in a cool, dry spot for weeks or even months. Sometimes you can find shelled fresh coconut at Asian markets; make sure it looks fresh and moist, then keep in the fridge and use within a few days. Store shredded coconut in a similar spot or in the freezer for up to 6 months.

Preparing: Use an ice pick, scissors blade, or corkscrew to find the soft eye, then drive the point into the eye and drain out the juice. Put the coconut inside a double layer of plastic grocery or trash bags. Go outside or wherever there is a concrete step or floor; slam the coconut into the concrete as many times as it takes to break it open. Remove the brown skin and chop, slice, or shred the white meat as you like.

Best cooking method: Toast for 5 to 10 minutes in a dry skillet set over medium-low heat or on a baking sheet in a 350°F oven until it darkens as much as you want. (Be sure to keep an eye on it and shake the pan occasionally; once it starts to turn it goes fast.)

When is it done? When lightly golden brown.

Coconut Milk

MAKES: About 2 cups
TIME: 20 minutes

While it's fine to use canned, homemade coconut milk is super-easy and much more pure in both flavor and ingredients. All you need is dried unsweetened coconut, which is available in natural food stores, as well as Indian, Latin, and Caribbean groceries, as well as many supermarkets.

This recipe gives you a fairly thick milk, akin to canned. Either thin it with water or repeat the process on the coconut again; the second pressing will be thinner.

1 cup unsweetened dried coconut meat

❶ Combine the coconut with 2 cups very hot water in a blender. Pulse on and off quickly, then turn on the blender and let it work for 15 seconds or so (take care that the top of the blender stays in place). Let sit for a few minutes.

❷ Put through a strainer, pressing to extract as much of the liquid as possible. Discard the solids and use the milk immediately or store, covered, in the refrigerator for up to a few days.

Cranberries

Cranberries are bright red, round, and too hard and astringent to be eaten out of hand, so they are always cooked or combined with other ingredients; fortunately, they make the ultimate tart condiments: Cranberry Relish with Orange and Ginger (page 36) and Traditional Cranberry Sauce (page 51). There are many species of cranberry (like the Scandinavian lingonberry) but we rarely see any other than Early Black (small and dark red) and Howes (lighter red and more oblong than the Early Black).

Buying and storing: Most are sold in plastic bags in the fall and winter. Toss those that are off-color or shriveled. Store in the refrigerator for weeks or in the freezer indefinitely.

Preparing. Nothing to it: Pick over, wash, and, if necessary, dry.

Other fruits to substitute: Dried cranberries, sour or sweet cherries, fresh currants, or blueberries.

Currants

A small berry that grows in clusters, currants can be brilliant red, purplish black, or white and are good in pies, jams, jellies, and other desserts. They're also delicious with other fruits or simply with some cream and sugar.

Buying and storing: Look for firm, plump, intact berries. They are not highly perishable but should be used within a few days. Store wrapped in plastic in the refrigerator.

Preparing: Remove the stems, pick over, wash, and—if necessary—dry.

Other fruits to substitute: Cherries, raspberries, or blueberries.

Dates

Available most often dried, dates are occasionally available fresh in late summer to the middle of fall, in Middle Eastern and farmers' markets. And what a delight—sticky-sweet, tender, and juicy.

Dried dates are even sweeter, and chewy, with a papery outer skin. The best varieties are medjool; deglet noor and bread dates (khadrawy) are more common but less sweet. The fruit grows in large clusters at the top of hundred-foot-tall palm trees that grow in arid desert climates like the Middle East (where they originated), California, and Arizona. They are often picked green and allowed to ripen off the tree to a yellow, brown, black, or mahogany color, depending on the variety. Because of their intense sweetness, they are often chopped and added to baked goods, granola, pilafs, and braises.

Buying and storing: Fresh dates should be unblemished and quite moist; they are often sold on the stem. Store on the counter or, for longer storage, wrapped in plastic in the refrigerator. Dried dates should be moist and tender; some varieties have a dull and dried-out-looking exterior and others a shiny and succulent appearance, but avoid any that have sugar crystals or are shriveled and hard. Newly dried dates are much better—they're moister—than stale dried dates. Store on the counter if you're going to eat them right away or for up to 6 months in a sealed container in the refrigerator.

Preparing: Remove the pits by slicing the fruit lengthwise and pulling the seed out by the tip. Or just squeeze.

Other fruits to substitute: Raisins, prunes, or dried apricots or figs.

Figs

A venerable Mediterranean staple. In the United States, most are grown in California and the Southwest, where they are abundant in mid- to late summer. (In some Mediterranean lands they are almost too plentiful to sell for several months a year, because you can pick them anywhere.) When fresh and ripe, figs are supple, sweet, and wonderful. The delicate skin is soft and delicious, the interior flesh succulent, gorgeously white and pink, and loaded with tiny edible seeds. Dried, they are even sweeter, and meaty.

There are many varieties of figs, ranging in color from deep purple to brown, reddish orange to green and yellow; the shapes can be round to pearlike. We see only a few in fresh form; the black Mission fig and the green

Calimyrna are the most common. Dried are most often black and sometimes brown.

Buying and storing: Ripe fresh figs are usually available toward the end of summer. Since they're extremely delicate and don't travel well at all, in colder areas of the country they are usually not ripe or very expensive—or both. Look for soft, undamaged fruit that's heavy for its size; oozing a bit of sugary syrup is almost a sure sign of perfect ripeness. Hard or dried-out figs will not ripen and are best macerated or poached. Fresh figs are very perishable and should be eaten as quickly as possible; store loosely wrapped in plastic or covered with a paper towel in the refrigerator for a day or two at most. Dried figs involve less guesswork; they should be moist and tender and are a better deal when purchased in bulk than prepackaged. Store in a cool, dark, dry place.

Preparing: Wash and eat fresh ones. Dried figs may be eaten, soaked, or cooked as any dried fruit.

Other fruits to substitute: There is no substitute for fresh figs; dried can be replaced by nearly any dried fruit, like raisins, prunes, or dried apricots.

Broiled Figs with Cream Cheese

MAKES: 4 servings
TIME: 15 minutes

A lovely appetizer, hors d'oeuvre, or fancy salad garnish. You can also grill these; just wrap them loosely in foil, leaving the top opened.

Other fruits you can use: dried Calimyrna figs (the tan ones, typically squashed into a saucer shape); snip off the stems and fill.

6 ounces cream cheese, at room temperature

2 tablespoons honey

2 teaspoons finely chopped fresh rosemary leaves

12 ripe figs, halved lengthwise

Mix together the cheese, honey, and rosemary. Heat the broiler and adjust the rack so it's about 4 inches from the heat source. Dollop or pipe the goat cheese on the cut side of the fig halves (cut a very thin slice off the curved bottom if the fig won't stand upright). Broil until the cheese is lightly browned and soft; serve hot or warm.

Broiled Figs with Mascarpone. Substitute mascarpone cheese for the cream cheese. Omit the honey if you like.

Broiled Figs Brûlée. Omit the cream cheese, honey, and rosemary; add $1/4$ cup or more sugar. Sprinkle the sugar on the cut side of the fig halves. Broil until the sugar is browning and bubbling; serve immediately.

Grapes

The grape is actually a smooth-skinned berry and comes in a huge variety of colors, flavors, shapes, and sizes. It's used for eating out of hand as well as making wine, raisins, juice, jams, and jellies. But grapes are also wonderful baked into the top of flatbread or pizza, cooked with pilafs and grain dishes, or tossed with salads.

Globally, there are two categories of grapes: white (also called *green*) and black (often referred to as *red*). White grapes are green to greenish yellow in color, and black grapes range in color from reddish to the deepest of purple. Americans eat mostly seedless grapes, but, in fact, breeding out the seeds also breeds out much of the flavor.

Generally, table grapes are sweet with a bit of acid and thin-skinned. Raisin-, juice-, and preserves-making grapes are typically sticky sweet with a pronounced flavor and large seeds (they are also delicious for eating out of hand but aren't commonly available). Wine grapes are usually quite acidic, tannic, and sometimes sweet—when fully ripe, some can be lovely eaten raw, but they're almost never sold for eating.

A wider variety of grapes are usually offered in the late summer to early fall at farmers' markets (especially in California, as you might imagine). Muscat (round and golden-green in color) and Concord (round and bluish purple in color) are worth seeking out, but so are many of the less common varieties.

Buying and storing: Ideally you want fresh-looking, green stems with only some brown; the grapes should be plump, sweet, and flavorful—taste one.

Preparing: Pesticides are used heavily on grapes, so rinse them very well.

Other fruits to substitute: Blueberries or cherries.

Grapefruit

West Indian in origin, now widely grown in Florida (which produces the best), California, and elsewhere. There are two types of grapefruit, white and red, differentiated more by the color of their flesh than their skin. Red grapefruit were once sweeter than white, but that's no longer really true. Each year, it seems, breeding techniques make grapefruit sweeter and sweeter, and seeds have become a thing of the past. Pomelo (or shaddock) and ugli (aptly if cruelly named) are similar and may be treated as grapefruit.

Buying and storing: Look for specimens that are heavy for their size—the heavier, the juicier. Store in the refrigerator after a day or two at room temperature.

Preparing: Cut the grapefruit in half through its equator, then around the sides, cutting the flesh from the skin, and then along each of the sides of the segments; eat with a spoon. Or peel and separate the segments as you would an orange; this is especially useful with smaller specimens.

Other fruits to substitute: Oranges or pomelos.

Broiled Grapefruit

MAKES: 2 to 4 servings
TIME: 15 minutes

Substitute brown sugar or honey for the sugar if you like or try sprinkling the top with shredded coconut and/or very finely minced fresh or crystallized ginger.

Other fruits you can use: oranges, pineapple slices, tangerines, or pomelos.

2 large grapefruit, cut in half and sectioned

1 tablespoon melted butter (optional)

4 teaspoons sugar, or to taste

❶ Heat the broiler and set the rack 4 to 6 inches from the heat source.

❷ Brush the grapefruit with butter if you like and sprinkle with sugar. Put on a roasting pan and then under the broiler. Broil, rotating the pan once, until the top is hot and bubbly, 5 to 10 minutes. Serve hot.

Kiwis

Chinese Gooseberries

A native Chinese fruit named after New Zealand's national bird (oddly the fruit and the flightless bird do look somewhat similar), the kiwi has become commonplace in our supermarkets. Its oval shape and fuzzy brown exterior belie its brilliant green and white flesh, which is stippled with tiny black and completely edible seeds. Kiwis are soft, juicy, and sweet-tart when ripe, and more on the tart side (though not entirely bad) when not quite ripe enough. There is also a yellow-fleshed variety that is sweeter and has less fuzz. Both green and yellow kiwis make nice additions to fruit salads or a pretty garnish, especially for desserts.

Buying and storing: Most will be fairly hard at supermarkets. Look for unshriveled and unblemished specimens without soft spots. They will ripen if left at room temperature. When ripe, store in the refrigerator.

Preparing: Peel and slice or cut in half and scoop out the flesh with a spoon.

Other fruits to substitute: Carambola (another pretty fruit), grapes, or honeydew.

Kumquats

Kumquats look like tiny oranges. Though the entire fruit is edible, it's the skin that's the best part, believe it or not: It's thin and sweet, while the flesh is heavily seeded and very tart. You can peel them (which is easy) and just eat the skin or slice them thinly, chop them, or poach them whole in sugar syrup. Kumquats are most often available in the winter, sometimes still attached to the branch; look for them at specialty or Asian markets.

Buying and storing: Buy firm, unblemished fruits; store in the refrigerator.

Preparing: Wash, dry, and slice, chop, or quarter, removing the seeds, or use whole.

Other fruits to substitute: Oranges or tangerines.

Lemons and Limes

The most useful kitchen fruits; a squirt of their juice or a sprinkle of zest can add just the right amount of acid and flavor to perfectly balance a dish, sauce, or beverage. The lemon is the essential fruit in European cooking, while the lime takes center stage in Asian and tropical cooking; it pays to keep some of each in your kitchen. Be sure not to neglect the zest as it brings the wonderful flavor of the fruit but without the acid (the zest is only the yellow or green portion of the outer skin; the white pith underneath is bitter).

There is a common lemon and common lime variety that you will see everywhere; there are also two less common but prized varieties of both the lemon and the lime: Meyer lemons and key limes. Meyer lemons have a unique floral and piney fragrance; they are a bit less acidic than regular lemons and are not easy to find outside of California. Key limes (mostly from Florida) are tiny and round and, like the Meyer, have a more floral and less acidic flavor than regular limes. Both Meyer lemons and key limes work nicely in desserts.

Buying and storing: Buy plump specimens that are heavy for their size and yield to gentle pressure; very hard or lightweight fruit will be dry. Store in the refrigerator.

Preparing: Cut into halves, quarters, wedges, or slices and remove the pits with the point of a knife. Or cut into halves (or thirds through the axis for limes) and juice.

There are a few ways to zest citrus; how you choose to do it should partly depend on how you'll use it. A zester is a nifty tool with small sharp-edged holes that cuts off long, thin strips of zest, which can then be minced; they are wonderful for garnishing when whole. Another method is to use a vegetable peeler or paring knife to remove the peel in long ribbons. Unless you're really skilled with the knife or peeler, this technique inevitably brings part of the bitter white pith with it; to do a perfect job you should then lay the strips down on a cutting board and scrape the white part off with a paring knife, then slice or mince as you like. The third method is to use a sharp grater (like a Microplane grater), which results in tiny flecks of zest that are nearly undetectable in dishes except for their flavor.

Other fruits to substitute: Lemons and limes are more or less interchangeable, though they are of course different from one another.

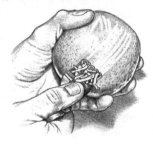

Pull the zester across the skin of the citrus as you would a vegetable peeler.

Preserved Lemons

MAKES: 1 quart
TIME: 20 minutes plus 2 weeks to cure

There are a couple of recipes in this book that call specifically for preserved lemons—a staple ingredient in North African cooking. But don't let geography come between you and this quick pickle: Chopped up, you can add them to all sorts of pilafs and braised vegetable dishes. Or make a refreshing drink by muddling a couple in the bottom of a glass, then topping it off with ice and sparkling water. I'm sure you'll find even more ways to use them before your first batch runs out; they keep in the fridge for months.

About 3 pounds lemons, preferably unwaxed, quartered lengthwise

About ¾ cup kosher salt

Half 3-inch cinnamon stick

2 or 3 cloves

1 star anise

2 or 3 black peppercorns

2 cardamom pods

1 bay leaf

❶ Fill a clean quart-sized jar with a tight-fitting lid with boiling water and soak its lid in boiling water too. Let the water sit while you cut the lemons, then dump the water out.

❷ Sprinkle a ¼-inch-deep layer of salt across the bottom of the jar. Nestle a layer of quartered lemons into the bottom of the jar, sprinkle liberally with salt, then repeat, adding the spices and bay leaf as you go. Stop when the jar is about three-quarters full and squeeze the remaining lemons into the jar—seeds and all—so that the fruit is completely submerged in the lemon juice–and–salt brine. (If you don't have enough lemons on hand, top lemons off with freshly squeezed juice no later than the following day.)

❸ Set the jar out on a counter and vigorously shake it once a day for 7 to 10 days—during this time it will start to bubble a little and the dried spices will swell back to their original size. (You'll be surprised at the size of the cloves!)

❹ Put the jar in the refrigerator and let the lemons continue to cure for another week before using. (The lemons will keep for at least 2 months in the refrigerator, though you'll probably want to get into them sooner.)

When they have cured, unscrew the lid. After a moment, they should smell sweet and citrusy—an ammonia smell means they've gone wrong somewhere along the line.

❺ To use in stews, blanch the quartered lemons in unsalted boiling water for 10 seconds, just long enough to leach out a little of the salt. For salads or quick-cooked dishes, scrape the flesh away from the peel, discard the flesh, and blanch the peel in unsalted boiling water as above.

Lychees

Litchis

Natives of southern China, lychees are 1½-inch oval fruits with brilliant red to pinkish tan scaly—sometimes prickly—inedible skin that protects the juicy white flesh, which in turn surrounds a shiny brown inedible seed. The texture of lychees is like that of a fleshy grape, and the flavor is sweet and one-of-a-kind, though akin to that of cherries. (Canned lychees are mostly just sugary sweet and not worth eating.) They are also dried and sometimes called *lychee nuts,* though they aren't nuts and the seeds are no more edible than when fresh. Summer is peak lychee season; look for them at Asian and farmers' markets.

Buying and storing: Summer is peak lychee season, when you'll find them at Asian and farmers' markets. Look for fragrant, brightly colored fruit with flexible—not dried-out or brittle—skins; they should be heavy for their size. Store wrapped loosely in plastic in the refrigerator; use as soon as possible.

Preparing: Use the stem to break open the skin and gently peel it off; eat the fruit and spit out the seed.

Other fruits to substitute: Grapes, or kiwi or carambola for a tropical flavor.

Mangoes

There are dozens of shapes, sizes, and colors of mango, from orange size to melon size; green to yellow, orange,

 Fast Make Ahead Ⓥ Vegetarian

SKINNING AND SEEDING MANGO, VERSION I

1

2

3

SKINNING AND SEEDING MANGO, VERSION II

1

2

3

(STEP 1) There are two ways to get the meat out of a mango. The first way begins with peeling, using a normal vegetable peeler. (STEP 2) Then cut the mango in half, doing the best you can to cut around the pit. (STEP 3) Finally, chop the mango with a knife.

(STEP 1) Begin by cutting the mango in half, doing the best you can to cut around the pit. (STEP 2) Score the flesh with a paring knife. (STEP 3) Turn the mango half "inside out," and the flesh is easily removed.

or red; exceedingly tart to syrupy sweet. Both ripe and unripe mangos are useful: unripe for chutney, pickling, and making amchoor (see page 64) and ripe for eating straight, making salsas, fruit salads, and cooking (especially on the grill). Supermarkets carry the most common yellow and red mango year-round, but you'll find a wider selection in Latin, Asian, and Indian markets; the small yellow mangoes are, for my money, the best. In the United States mangoes are grown in California, Florida, and Hawaii, but the majority are imported from Mexico and farther south.

Buying and storing: Color isn't as important as texture; the softer it is, the riper. Some varieties of mango will start to wrinkle a bit at the stem when they are perfectly ripe. Bought at any stage, however, the mango will ripen if left at room temperature. Once ripe, store in the refrigerator or it will rot.

Preparing: There are a few different ways to go about preparing a mango; how you do it will depend on your knife skills and your patience. (See the illustrations on page 394.) The quick and messy way is to just peel off the skin—a small knife makes quick work of it—and attack. For a neater presentation, trim a piece off the bottom end. Stand the fruit on a cutting board, trim off the skin with a sharp paring knife, then slice fruit from around the pit.

Other fruits to substitute: Papaya, cantaloupe or other fleshy orange melons, or oranges.

Melons

Melons are divided into two types: the muskmelon and watermelon. Muskmelons have either a netted skin (like the cantaloupe) or a smooth skin (like the honeydew) and a hollow cavity with seeds; their flesh ranges in color from pinkish orange to lime green to nearly white. Watermelons are pretty much what you think they are: They have a smooth skin in varying shades of green, solid or striated, and watery, sugary sweet flesh with (until recently) seeds embedded throughout.

Melons are summer fruit, and you'll find the widest variety and most flavorful at farmstands and farmers' markets. Selecting the right melon is part skill and part luck. If you're at a farmstand or farmers' market, ask for help. Otherwise, start by smelling it; if it smells sweet and like a melon, that's a good start. Then try shaking it; loose seeds are a sign of ripeness for muskmelons. Last, for muskmelons, gently squeeze the end opposite the stem—it should yield slightly; for watermelons, slap the side and listen for a hollow sound.

Buying and storing: Eat a ripe melon right away or store it in the refrigerator. Underripe melons can be left out at room temperature for a couple days to sweeten, but they won't ripen to perfection.

Preparing: Cut the melon in half and scrape out the seeds of muskmelons with a spoon; continue cutting it into quarters or slices. Use a paring knife to slice off the rinds if you like. Watermelons can be served casually in wedges with seeds. But if you want to seed them, cut into wedges and slice off the top or "heart" to reveal the row of seeds. Remove them with the tines of a fork. Then cut to the desired size.

A melon baller easily lets you scoop out circles of melon. Or you can simply cut the flesh into pieces. Grated melon is good for yogurt sauces and raw salsas; just be sure to do it over a bowl to save the juices.

MELON BALLING

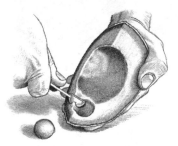

Using a melon baller is intuitive, easy, and fun—just scoop out the balls from any cut and seeded melon.

F Fast   **M** Make Ahead   **V** Vegetarian

Allow a chilled melon to come to room temperature before serving; when it's chilled, the flavors are muted. Try a squeeze of lemon or lime juice on the melon—it adds flavor to an underripe melon and complements a ripe one. A sprinkle of salt is an interesting change of pace (as is a dash of ground chile).

Other fruits to substitute: Melons are interchangeable with one another and with papaya, mango, and (sometimes) cucumber.

Grilled Watermelon Steak

MAKES: 4 to 6 servings

TIME: 30 minutes

I know it sounds gimmicky, but grilled watermelon treated like a vegetable with savory seasoning is delicious. Most of the water cooks out of it, leaving behind a tasty little "steak" with great texture. Plus, it looks terrific. You can broil it too; just make sure the juices can drain free so it doesn't steam.

Serve this as part of any barbecue meal with grilled meats, seafood, or vegetables and Beer-Glazed Black Beans (page 420).

Other fruits or vegetables you can use: any melon, but you'll get smaller slices; and any winter squash.

1 small watermelon

¼ cup extra virgin olive oil

1 tablespoon minced fresh rosemary leaves

Salt and freshly ground black pepper

Lemon wedges for serving

❶ Heat a charcoal or gas grill or a broiler to moderately high heat and put the rack about 4 inches from the heat source. Cut the watermelon lengthwise, into halves or quarters, depending on the size of the melon. From each length, cut 2-inch-thick slices, with the rind intact. Use a fork to remove as many seeds from the heart as you can without beating the flesh up too much.

❷ Mix the olive oil with the rosemary and sprinkle with salt and pepper. Brush or rub the mixture all over the watermelon slices. Grill or broil for about 5 minutes on each side. The flesh should be lightly caramelized and dried out a bit. Serve with lemon wedges.

Chile-Rubbed Grilled Watermelon Steak. Great as part of any Mexican-style meal: Instead of the rosemary, use 2 tablespoons chili powder (to make your own, see page 66). Serve with lime wedges instead of the lemon if you like.

Oranges and Tangerines

The orange tree is a bushy evergreen that simultaneously produces leaves, flowers, and fruit; it's grown in warm areas across the globe.

There are three types: sweet (like the Valencia, navel, or temple), loose skinned (any Mandarin or tangerine), and bitter (Seville). Sweet and loose-skinned oranges are used for eating and juicing, while bitter ones are used only for making marmalades and other cooked products (we don't see them fresh too often in this country). The outer, orange-colored skin (zest) and interior flesh are edible, while the white pith on the skin is bitter.

Mandarin oranges are simply a smaller and looser-skinned type of orange. Clementines, Satsumas, and tangerines are all varieties of Mandarins; they are sweet-tart in flavor and are perfect for eating out of hand, but spectacular juiced too.

Buying and storing: Oranges are available all year long; tangerines enjoy a brief season in late fall and winter. Sweet and bitter oranges should be heavy for their size and yield to gentle pressure but have no soft spots. The color of the skin varies by type, but some "russeting" (brown flecks) or "regreening" (green patches) is perfectly fine. Mandarin oranges should be heavy for their size and without any unusually soft spots, though in general they feel softer than sweet oranges.

Preparing: See the illustrations on page 398. Oranges are easiest to eat when cut into quarters or eighths. To

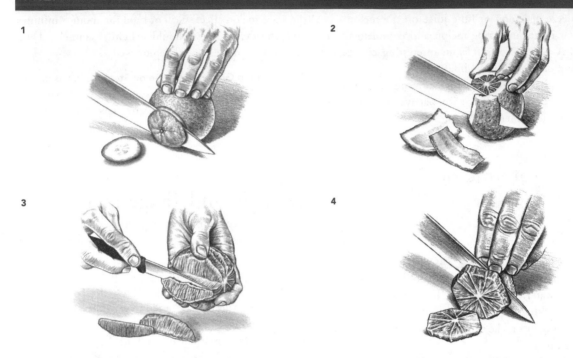

(STEP 1) Before beginning to peel and segment citrus, cut a slice off both ends of the fruit so that it stands straight. (STEP 2) Cut as close to the pulp as possible, removing the skin in long strips. (STEP 3) Cut between the membranes to separate segments. (STEP 4) Or cut across any peeled citrus fruit to make "wheels."

peel, cut four or eight longitudinal slits from pole to pole, through the skin but not into the flesh. Peel each of these off. Mandarin oranges can be peeled using your fingers without any difficulty.

Other fruits to substitute: Sweet and Mandarin oranges are interchangeable; lemon or lime juice can replace the acidic flavor of bitter oranges.

Papayas

Native to tropical regions of the Americas—the exact place of origin is debated—this tree fruit grows as large as 20 pounds. It's eaten both green (see Green Papaya Salad, page 213) and ripe, ideally with a sprinkle of lime. When ripe, papaya skin is golden yellow to deep orange; the flesh is soft, melonlike, a deep orange, and the edible seeds a shiny greenish gray.

Buying and storing: Often available—and good—year-round, especially in Asian and Latin markets. Green, tart, unripe papayas are hard and solid green. Ripe ones have yellow and orange-colored skin, yield to gentle pressure, and are aromatic; harder specimens will ripen at room temperature. Once ripe, store in the refrigerator.

Preparing: Wash, peel, cut in half, and scoop out the seeds. Then slice or chop.

F Fast   **M** Make Ahead   **V** Vegetarian

Other fruits to substitute: Mango, cantaloupe or other fleshy orange melons.

Passionfruit

Egg shaped, with purplish brown skin, this tropical fruit has a brightly colored yellow-orange pulp filled with dozens of edible seeds. The flavor is quite tart—almost too tart to eat straight—but sensational, and the fragrance is wonderful too. I like to strain the pulp and blend it into juices, smoothies, and ice cream and sorbet bases.

Buying and storing: Look for deeply colored fruit that's firm and heavy for its size. Ripe passion fruit will have a dimpled or slightly shriveled exterior. When ripe, store in the refrigerator.

Preparing: Cut in half and scoop out the flesh with a spoon. For just the juice, use a strainer to separate the seeds; press the flesh to extract as much of the juice as possible.

Other fruits to substitute: The juice can be replaced with orange, guava, or mango juice.

Peaches and Nectarines

Among the best summer eating fruit, peaches and nectarines are closely related stone fruits that originated in China and came to Europe via the Persian Empire. They are nearly identical in shape and color, but peach skin has a soft fuzz and nectarine skin is smooth. (And no, nectarines are not a hybrid of peaches and plums, as is so often said.) The flesh is succulent, juicy, and sweet-tart.

Variations in color don't matter much, but there are two broad categories of peaches and nectarines based on how much the flesh clings to the pit: freestone and clingstone. Both are good; freestones are certainly easier to cut up.

Buying and storing: Tree-ripened fruit is best, but peaches and nectarines do ripen at room temperature

(and quickly, so keep your eye on them). Put hard fruit in a paper bag to hasten ripening or just ripen it on the counter. Look for plump, gently yielding, and fragrant specimens without any bruises. Don't buy too many at once unless you're planning to cook with them; they usually all ripen at the same time.

Preparing: Wash, peel if you like, and eat. To pit, cut in half from pole to pole; twist the halves, which will either come completely free of the pit (freestone) or leave a fair amount of flesh on the pit (clingstone). To peel, drop into boiling water for 10 to 30 seconds, just until the skin loosens; plunge into a bowl of ice water; remove the peel with your fingers and/or a paring knife.

Other fruits to substitute: Peaches and nectarines are interchangeable; otherwise, substitute apricots, plums, or mangoes.

Mary Willoughby's Broiled Peaches

MAKES: 4 servings
TIME: 20 minutes or less

In the words of John—Mary's son—"These are good when you cook them so long that the edges are black." I like them a little less done than that, but use your judgment. Best, for obvious reasons, with freestone peaches. Serve them as a dessert with whipped or ice cream or savory (see the variations) with salad or as a side dish with, for example, Skillet Pork Chops, Eight Ways (page 720).

Other fruits you can use: nectarines, apricots, plums, ripe pears, or pineapple.

4 peaches

About 2 tablespoons unsalted butter

About 2 tablespoons honey

❶ Heat the broiler and put the rack about 4 inches from the heat source.

2 Cut the peaches in half and remove the pits. Set each one on its "back" and fill the cavities with about a teaspoon each butter and honey. Broil until the edges just begin to brown, or a little longer, 3 to 5 minutes. Serve hot or warm.

Broiled Peaches with Honey Mustard. Use mustard instead of the butter. Proceed with the recipe.

Broiled Peaches with Herbs. Omit the honey. Sprinkle the halves with a tiny bit of salt, freshly ground black pepper, and some chopped fresh herbs; thyme, rosemary, tarragon, and basil are good.

Grilled Peaches. Heat a charcoal or gas grill to moderately high heat and put the rack about 4 inches from the heat source. Melt the butter or use extra virgin olive oil instead. Brush the peaches on both sides with butter or oil and, starting with the cut side down, grill over direct heat until softened and marked as done as you like, anywhere from 3 to 5 minutes. Turn and grill on the skin side the same way. Remove from the grill, turn the cut sides up, and immediately drizzle with honey. Crumble blue cheese on top if you like.

Pears

Pears are one of the few fruits that actually improve after being picked; their flesh sweetens and softens to an almost buttery texture. In fact, they are known as *butter fruit* in several European languages. But finding a perfectly ripe pear can be tricky: Their peak is fleeting, so we often end up with either a crunchy fruit with little flavor or a mushy one with unappealing texture.

Related to apples—they are both technically members of the rose family—pears are grown throughout the world in moderate climates. There are over five thousand varieties, many produced regionally. You're likely to find dozens of varieties beyond the usual Anjou and Bartlett at local farmers' markets and orchards; different varieties of pears have different seasons, though they are most abundant in the fall.

Here are short descriptions of the most common pears:

Anjou: One of the most common varieties; green and red types with a broad oval shape; the flesh is firm (they're good for poaching) and sweet but not spectacular.

Asian: Round, apple shaped with a yellow to russeted-gold color; the flesh is crisp (and is best that way, which is unusual for a pear) and juicy, with a delicate apple-pear flavor.

Bartlett: The most common variety and the only one used for commercial canning and drying. Bell shaped and green when unripe, yellow with a red blush when ripe, with soft, sweet, and juicy flesh; rarely impressive.

Bosc: Somewhat tear shaped with an elongated neck; golden brown russet color with a juicy flesh similar to Anjou but more aromatic. At its best, spectacular.

Comice: Squat pear shape with a stubby neck and stem; green with a bronze blush and very sweet, juicy, soft flesh. Wonderful fragrance and probably the best widely available pear.

Packham: Imported in winter from the southern hemisphere; fat, round, and a bit irregular in shape; green to greenish yellow in color, fairly sweet flesh; rarely great.

Seckel: Miniature and precious looking (lovely for poaching whole); green with a deep red blush and spicy flavor. The skin can be tough, but these are worth trying.

Buying and storing: Pears ripen best off the tree, so don't be discouraged if all you can find are hard, green fruit. Leave them at room temperature until the flesh yields gently when squeezed and you can smell a nice pear aroma; some varieties will also change color, from green to yellow. Asian pears are meant to be firm and crunchy. Store ripe fruit in the refrigerator.

Preparing: Peeling is not necessary, but it's easy with a vegetable peeler. Core it by slicing the pear into quarters and then cutting out the core; or halve it and dig out

F Fast   **M** Make Ahead   **V** Vegetarian

the core with a melon baller (see page 396); or to keep the fruit whole, dig out the core from the blossom (large) end with a small melon baller.

Other fruits to substitute: Apples.

Poached Pears with Vanilla

MAKES: 4 servings

TIME: about 20 minutes, plus time to cool

Pears can be poached at any stage of ripeness, with sugar added to the cooking water making up for any lack of fully developed natural sugars. So even with an unripe pear, this becomes an impressive, light dessert.

Other fruits you can use: apples, apricots, peaches, nectarines, kumquats, or pineapple.

2¹/₂ cups sugar

¹/₂ vanilla bean, split lengthwise, or one 3-inch
    cinnamon stick

4 pears

❶ Combine the sugar and vanilla or cinnamon with 5 cups water in a medium saucepan (large enough to accommodate the pears) over high heat. Peel the pears, leaving their stems on. Core them by digging into the blossom end with a melon baller, spoon, or paring knife.

❷ Lower the pears into the boiling water and adjust the heat so that it simmers gently. Cook, turning the pears every 5 minutes or so, until they meet little resistance when prodded with a thin-bladed knife, usually from 10 to 20 minutes. Turn off the heat and allow to cool in the liquid.

❸ Transfer the pears to serving plates. (At this point, you may cover and refrigerate the pears for up to a day; bring to room temperature before serving.) Reduce the poaching liquid to a cup or less (this can also be stored for a day), then spoon a little over each pear before serving.

Poached Pears with Asian Spices. Add 3 star anise, 5 slices fresh ginger, and 2 cloves to the poaching mix.

Pears Poached in Red Wine. Substitute 1¹/₂ cups water, 1¹/₂ cups red wine, ³/₄ cup sugar, one 3-inch cinnamon stick, and 1 lemon, sliced, for the poaching liquid.

Persimmons

A vibrant orange fruit with either a juicy, jellylike interior or a crisp, applelike quality, depending on the variety. The heart-shaped and traditional Hachiya persimmon—that's the mushy one—is by far the most common, but the squat Fuyu variety is gaining ground.

Hachiyas are oblong with a pointed end and are extraordinarily tart—mouth-puckeringly so—when unripe, but gradually ripen, becoming soft, mushy, and almost translucent, like a way overripe tomato; the flesh at this point is somewhat gelatinous and deliciously sweet. Newcomers almost always eat persimmons before they're fully ripe, because it's hard to believe just how soft they must be to be good; but we all learn with practice—and the ultimate experience is definitely worth it.

The Fuyu, on the other hand, is smaller, tomato shaped, and firm. Unlike the Hachiya, it's deliciously crunchy and sweet with a subtle cinnamon flavor when hard; treat it like an apple and take a bite or slice it into wedges (peeling is optional).

Buying and storing: Look for deeply colored fruit; the softer the better for Hachiya, and hard like an apple for the Fuyu, if that's how you like it. Bought at any stage, however, the Hachiya will ripen at room temperature, which can take up to a month (hasten ripening by putting the fruit in a paper bag). Once ripe, store in the refrigerator.

Preparing: Ripe Hachiyas can be eaten out of hand (over a sink—it's messy), or cut off the top and scoop out the flesh with a spoon. Remove the stem from a hard Fuyu and bite in or slice like an apple.

Other fruits to substitute: There is no replacement for a raw, ripe Hachiya; apple or pear can replace a firm Fuyu, but only in terms of texture.

Pineapples

One of the glories of nature, the pineapple is native to Central and South America, and its prickly, diamond-patterned scaly skin ranges from yellow to green to brownish red when ripe. The flesh is juicy, sweet-tart, and acidic. At its best, it's among the best-tasting fruits there is, especially when roasted, broiled, or grilled.

Things have gotten better in the last ten years, too. Before then, pineapples were picked green and, since they didn't sweeten much after they were picked, were often disappointing. (If they were picked ripe and shipped by air, they were expensive.) But the new "gold" hybrids, which now represent nearly 100 percent of many Hawaiian producers' crops, are almost always sweet and juicy, with lovely golden flesh. Which makes the pineapple among the most reliable fruit you can buy.

Buying and storing: Look for fruit that has a good pineapple aroma, deep yellow or golden color, and yields only slightly to gentle pressure. Underripe pineapples will decrease in acidity if left at room temperature but will not ripen or sweeten. Once ripe, eat immediately or store in the refrigerator and use as quickly as possible.

Preparing: There are a few ways to dismember a pineapple; I favor two. For either, first cut off the spiky top. Then, with a chef's knife, peel around the perimeter and remove all the spiny skin; use a paring knife to dig out any eyes. At that point, cut the pineapple crosswise into round slices or top to bottom into halves

PREPARING PINEAPPLE

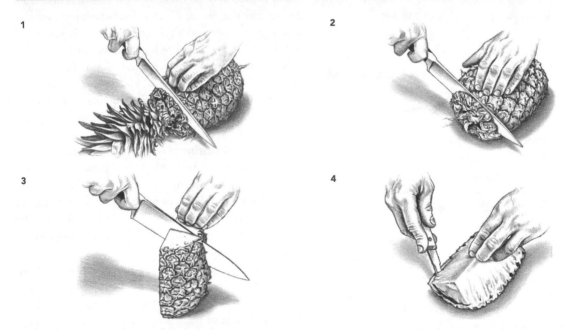

(STEP 1) Cut off the top of the pineapple about an inch below the flower. (STEP 2) Slice off the stem end as well. (STEP 3) Cut the pineapple into quarters. (STEP 4) Use a grapefruit knife to separate the fruit from the rind and a paring knife to dig out any eyes. Remove the core (the hard edge where the fruit comes to a point), slice, and serve.

or quarters and cut out the woody core. Alternatively, after trimming, cut straight down from top to bottom with a chef's knife to cut the pineapple in half (see the illustration on the previous page); then cut each half in half again to make quarters. Use a smaller knife to cut off the woody core portion from each quarter (at the peak of your triangles) and then use a grapefruit or paring knife to separate the flesh from the skin by cutting between the two; cut the quarter into slices and serve.

Other fruits to substitute: Oranges, grapefruit, kiwis, or carambola.

Plums

Purple, black, red, orange, or green, there are hundreds of varieties of plums, ranging in size, shape, and flavor in addition to color. They can be syrupy sweet, sweet-tart, or mouth-puckeringly tart. My favorite are the dark red–fleshed sweet ones, though I recommend trying as many different varieties as you can. They're now even crossbred with apricots or other plums for some very interesting combinations, like pluots, all of which can be treated like plums.

Buying and storing: Although plums are often available at supermarkets year-round, the best are the local varieties you buy in season, between May and October.

Ripe plums are quite soft, even oozing a sugary syrup—eat these right away—but avoid those that are mushy, split, or smell fermented. Underripe fruit is hard and sour; leave out at room temperature to ripen. You can also refrigerate plums; it will slow down the ripening process but not stop it. Prunes, like other dried fruit, are best bought in bulk at a natural food store.

Preparing: Rinse and eat. You can peel them before cooking: drop into boiling water for about 10 seconds, or until the skins loosen, then peel with a paring knife.

Other fruits to substitute: Apricots, peaches, or nectarines.

Pomegranates
Chinese Apples

An odd fruit—and a real pain in the neck to handle—but the rewards in flavor, texture, and even nutrition make it worth it. The pomegranate is round and ranges in size from orange to grapefruit size; its exterior skin is speckled dark red and leathery, and the edible (and potassium-rich) seeds are covered with a crisp and snappy ruby-red flesh contained in inedible white pith. The seeds can be eaten whole or the juicy flesh sucked off and the seeds discarded; it's a matter of personal taste. They're also nice as a final garnish to salads or braised dishes. When fresh fruit isn't available, pomegranate molasses or unsweetened juice is perfect for bringing the flavor to cooking.

Buying and storing: Pomegranate season is very short—October to November—but the fruit keeps fairly well. Look for unblemished specimens that are heavy for their size and with no soft spots. The will keep in a cool dark spot for a couple weeks at least, or in the fridge for several weeks.

Preparing: Either cut in half or cut an inch or so into the top and pry open into segments. Breaking the segments apart can be done underwater; the bad seeds and inedible pieces float to the top, the good seeds at the bottom, and the staining juice doesn't squirt all over. Or you can seed pomegranates in a plastic bag to contain the mess.

Other fruits to substitute: Cherries, currants, or raspberries.

Quince

Quince, which is related to the apple, has been cultivated and cherished for its fragrance and fruity flavor since the time of Ancient Rome. But it's almost always cooked, because it's astringent when raw. Its high pectin content makes it a natural for making preserves; in fact, the word *marmalade* is derived from the Portuguese word for quince *marmelo*.

The fruit is somewhat pear shaped with smooth golden skin and a lovely floral fragrance; the flesh is firm, light yellow, and similar to that of a pear. When cooked, it turns a dark orange color. The quince season is short, from October to December, and it's tough to find them at other times.

Buying and storing: Look for firm, unshriveled specimens that are golden yellow in color and fragrant. Store wrapped loosely in plastic in the refrigerator; they will keep for weeks.

Preparing: Peel and remove the core (the seeds are mildly poisonous—not enough to worry about, but don't eat them); chop or slice as needed.

Other fruits to substitute: Apples or pears.

Rhubarb

Rhubarb looks like red celery, but don't let that fool you; beyond that and the strings that run its length, the two have little else in common. Usually used as a fruit in sweet preparations (though not always; see Dal with Rhubarb, page 433), rhubarb alone is actually extremely tart. You can take advantages of its tartness, or cook it with sugar or other sweet fruits, which is why we see it most often made into pies, preserves, and compotes, often paired with strawberries.

Buying and storing: Look for firm and crisp stalks. Store in the refrigerator and use it as quickly as possible.

Preparing: See the illustrations on page 283. Although it's not entirely necessary, rhubarb is best if you string it; grab one end between a paring knife and your thumb and pull straight down to remove the celerylike strings that run lengthwise through each stalk. (Be aware that rhubarb leaves and roots are poisonous, though only mildly so.)

Best cooking methods: Braising and stewing.

When is it done? When very tender and easily pierced with a skewer or thin-bladed knife.

Other fruits to substitute: Cranberries, tart cherries, or fresh currants.

Star Fruit

Carambola

The now-familiar yellow, semitranslucent tropical fruit with five pointed ridges that—when sliced crosswise—creates a pretty star shape. They're fragrant, juicy, and sweet-tart when perfectly ripe, but often the ones we get here fall short of that. The skin is edible, and they are best eaten raw and are lovely sliced into salads or used as a garnish for cold meat or seafood or ice cream and simple cakes.

Buying and storing: Look for fragrant, yellow, plump fruit that's unblemished and unshriveled. They will ripen some if left at room temperature. When ripe, store wrapped loosely in plastic in the refrigerator.

Preparing: Rinse, dry, and slice crosswise.

Other fruits to substitute: Kiwi (another pretty fruit), orange segments, or table grapes.

Beans

WE HAVE COME FULL CIRCLE AND ONCE

again are beginning to appreciate beans (a generic

term used for beans, peas, split peas, lentils, and other

legumes). In fact they are even becoming chic. I adore

beans; they're among my favorite staples, and I cook

them several times a week, for both side dishes and

main courses.

Beans are low in fat and calories and a source of

high-quality protein, fiber, and complex carbohy-

drates. They're easily stored and almost never go bad.

They're environmentally friendly and inexpensive; even

precious heirloom varieties are no more than seven bucks a pound, but common beans—white beans you buy in a supermarket, for example—can be as cheap as fifty cents. So it would seem to me that the only question is "How can I cook them more often?"

Fortunately, there are thousands of ways to serve beans (and tofu, which is soybean "cheese" and to which I've devoted a section at the end of the chapter). As a simple side dish, with olive oil, lemon juice, butter, or herbs, beans bring variety to the winter table. As part of a stew, with or without meat, they offer heartiness that no vegetable imparts. And cooked quickly and simply with fresh vegetables, they add body and earthy flavor.

Although there are literally hundreds of varieties of dried beans, virtually all of them can be treated in the same way. Since there are some misconceptions about storing and cooking beans, I'll cover the basics and offer some essential recipes before looking at the individual types and categories.

The Basics of Beans

All beans, lentils, peas, and peanuts—and some grasses—belong to the Leguminosae family; we call them all *beans*, or *legumes* (they're also called *pulses*). These plants produce their seeds in a pod, and it's these seeds we eat. (When both pods and seeds are eaten—think green beans or snow peas—the legumes are usually categorized as vegetables.)

Legumes are easily dried and preserved for storage and future use and have been for eons. Though you can sometimes (and happily) find other forms of beans—see "Fresh and Frozen Shell Beans" on page 426—most legumes are sold dried and must be cooked for a relatively long period of time to rehydrate and become edible. This incredibly simple task has generated as much controversy as anything in cooking. The ironclad rules people have come up with are enough to put you off from cooking beans, and they may well have done so for you. I'll make things easy, because it's just not that complicated, and there's plenty of flexibility.

How Much Beans to Make?

Because beans are so convenient to cook in large batches to eat now or store for later, many recipes in this chapter call for 1 pound of beans, which yields 6 to 8 servings. The majority of those are side dishes, though the heartier ones with seafood, meat, or other substantial ingredients are designed to be main dishes. For more about freezing leftover beans, see the sidebar on page 420.

Buying and Storing Beans

Dried beans rarely go "bad," but they *do* get old. Stale beans might taste musty, but more often old beans just require more water and longer cooking time to soften up. Unfortunately, you have little way of knowing when beans were dried, though there are some visual clues: Avoid packages with a large percentage of broken beans, imperfect skins, or discoloration. Ideally, you'd buy beans at a place where they're sold and restocked frequently.

Store them in a cool, dry place, making sure they are tightly sealed, either in their original packaging or (better) a plastic container or glass jar. Since freezing dehydrates beans, it's not a great idea.

I try to finish all the beans I've accumulated during the course of the year each summer so I know I'm not keeping any for longer than a year. Most beans are harvested late in summer, so the new crop is available in stores in the fall. Since newer beans taste better, cook faster, and contain more nutrients, it's worth updating.

From everyday to heirlooms to hybrids, the world of beans is endless. Fortunately you can find some of the best beans at international groceries and natural food stores, and many specialty varieties are now sold on-line, though often at a steep premium.

Beans look different, and there are subtle differences in flavor and texture, but most are truly interchangeable. To help you along, most recipes in this chapter include a listing of "Other beans you can use."

EVERYDAY BEANS

LEGUME	DESCRIPTION	FORMS AND VARIETIES	COOKING TIMES (VARIES DEPENDING ON THE AGE OF THE BEAN AND WHETHER YOU SOAK THEM FIRST)
Adzuki Beans *Aduki*	Small, oval, and maroon with a streak of white. Earthy and slightly sweet; dense and creamy. Most often used in sweet dishes in East Asia.	Dried, canned, fresh, and as sweet red bean paste (used in Asian cuisines)	Short (under 40 minutes)
Black Beans *Turtle Beans, Frijoles Negros*	Medium size, oval, and deep black. Rich and earthy, almost mushroomlike. (Don't confuse them with Chinese fermented black beans, which are actually soybeans.)	Dried, frozen, and canned	Medium (40 to 90 minutes)
Black-Eyed Peas *Cowpeas*	Small and plump, ivory-colored beans with a black spot. They are quicker cooking, absorb flavors well, and are most popular in the South.	Dried, fresh, frozen, and canned	Medium (40 to 90 minutes)
Cannellini Beans *White Kidney Beans*	Large, kidney-shaped, off-white, with nutty flavor and a creamy consistency. One of the best white beans.	Dried and canned	Medium (40 to 90 minutes)
Chickpeas *Garbanzo Beans, Ceci, Channa Dal*	Among the best. Acorn-shaped tan beans with robust and nutty flavor. They take a long time to cook, but the cooking liquid is very flavorful.	Mostly tan, but sometimes red or black. They may be dried, fresh, frozen, canned, or ground into flour (called *besan*; see page 441).	Long (1 to 2 hours)
Cranberry Beans *Borlotti, Crab Eye, Roman, Romano, Rosecoco, Saluggia Beans*	Beautiful dried or fresh; creamy, with bright to deep red dappling; similar in flavor and texture to pinto beans. Delicious fresh.	Dried, fresh, and sometimes frozen	Medium (40 to 90 minutes)
Fava Beans *Broad, Faba, Haba, Fève, Horse, Windsor Beans*	Large, flattened, wide oval beans, light brown when dried and green when fresh. Tedious to peel, but delicious. Nutty and creamy when dried, sweet when fresh. Delicious, but tedious to peel, since you must remove both the outer pod when fresh, as well as the thin skin around each bean. But you can find them already peeled in both dried and fresh (usually frozen) forms.	Dried (buy the split favas, which are already peeled), fresh (still in the pod, usually, in spring and fall), and frozen	Long (1 to 2 hours)

LEGUME	DESCRIPTION	FORMS AND VARIETIES	COOKING TIMES (VARIES DEPENDING ON THE AGE OF THE BEAN AND WHETHER YOU SOAK THEM FIRST)
Flageolet Beans	Immature kidney beans, small, kidney shaped, and pale green. A favorite in France; quick-cooking for their size with an herbal, fresh taste.	Dried, fresh, and canned	Medium (40 to 90 minutes)
Gigante Beans *Great White Beans, Gigande, Hija*	Huge, off-white, and sweet, with potatolike texture; fun to cook and eat. Popular in Greek, Spanish, and Japanese dishes.	Dried and canned (sometimes with tomato sauce)	Long (1 to 2 hours)
Great Northern Beans	All-purpose white beans; large, oval, and widely available.	Dried, frozen, and canned	Medium (40 to 90 minutes)
Kidney Beans	Shiny, reddish brown, up to an inch long; kidney-shaped (duh!), keep their shape when cooked, and absorb flavors well.	Red, light red or pink, or white (see cannellini beans). Dried, frozen, and canned.	Medium (40 to 90 minutes)
Lentils	Tiny, thin skinned, disk shaped, and quick cooking.	There are hundreds of varieties of lentils. Available mostly dried, sometimes split and peeled, and less often canned.	Short (under 40 minutes)
Lima Beans *Butter Beans, Butter Peas, Fordhook, Baby Lima; Christmas, Chestnut, or Speckled Lima*	Generally pale green when fresh and white when dried, both large and small limas are flat, kidney shaped, and have a hearty texture and nice buttery flavor. Large lima beans are a good substitute for gigantes.	Fresh, frozen, and canned, with several varieties that vary in color and size. The most common are large; Christmas limas have pretty reddish purple markings.	Medium (40 to 90 minutes)
Mung Beans *Mung Dal, Green Grams*	Tiny, pellet shaped, and usually green (when whole) or yellow (when peeled); tender and slightly sweet when cooked. Used in dals; ground and used to make bean thread noodles in China; they also make the most familiar sprouts.	Green, black or yellow; dried or peeled and split. For dal, see page 434.	Short (under 40 minutes)

EVERYDAY BEANS (CONTINUED)

LEGUME	DESCRIPTION	FORMS AND VARIETIES	COOKING TIMES (VARIES DEPENDING ON THE AGE OF THE BEAN AND WHETHER YOU SOAK THEM FIRST)
Navy Beans *Pea, Boston, Yankee Beans*	Small, round, plump, white, common, and very useful. Dense and mild flavored with a creamy consistency that makes wonderful purées and baked beans.	Dried, frozen, and canned	Medium (40 to 90 minutes)
Peanuts *Goober, Groundnut, Ground Pea*	A legume, eaten like a nut but really bridges the gap. See page 316.	Whole and shelled in jars, cans, and bags and as peanut butter; usually sold dry roasted	Medium (40 to 90 minutes) for raw peanuts
Peas, Dried *Split peas, Maquis peas*	Small and round; specifically grown for drying. When cooked, they're starchy and earthy. Best for soup and dal (see page 433).	Green and yellow are nearly the same in all ways but color. They are most commonly sold split, either dried or canned.	Short (under 40 minutes)
Pigeon Peas *Gandules,* *Congo, Goongoo, Gungo* *Pea, Toovar Dal*	Tan and nearly round, with one side flattened; sweet and a bit mealy. Usually dried, but sometimes sold fresh. Popular worldwide.	Many different colors: tan to black, brown, red, yellow, and spotted. Usually dried, sometimes split and peeled; also fresh, frozen, and canned.	Short (under 40 minutes)
Pink Beans *Chili Beans*	Virtually interchangeable with pintos. Slightly kidney shaped, rounder, and solidly pinkish tan. Common in the Caribbean.	Dried and canned	Medium (40 to 90 minutes)
Pinto	Medium size, oval, with a reddish tan and brown speckled exterior (*pinto* means "painted" in Spanish). Earthy and creamy. Commonly refried.	Dried, frozen, and canned	Medium (40 to 90 minutes)
Soybeans **When young and green:** *Edamame*	Round, small, and either yellow or black and nutty; the most widely grown bean in the world. Edamame are immature soybeans: large, shiny, and usually green, a good substitute for fresh lima or fava beans; see page 424. (Soybeans are the basis of tofu and many other products; see "The Basics of Tofu," page 443).	There are hundreds of varieties of soybeans, available dried, canned, and sometimes fresh or frozen. Edamame are available fresh or in their pods or already shucked. Fermented black beans are made from black soybeans; see page 407.	Medium (40 to 90 minutes)

The Basics of Preparing and Cooking Beans

Most beans are cleaned by machines, which do a good job. But it's still worth spending a minute sorting through them before soaking or cooking: Put them in a pot and fill it with water, then swish the whole thing around. Remove any beans that are discolored, shriveled, or broken and, obviously, remove any pebbles or other stray matter. Then dump the beans into a colander and rinse for a minute or so.

Dried beans require water and heat to become edible. How much water they absorb and how long it takes to cook them varies, which makes exact cooking times literally impossible to pinpoint; but in any case the amount of water beans absorb is finite, so if you soak them first, you'll need less water during cooking.

This is important to remember because legumes are best cooked when they bubble gently, covered by an inch or two of water, but not much more than that. You don't want to cook beans as you would pasta—in a lot of water, at a vigorous boil—then drain the water off. For one thing, the skins will break and tear too soon. For another, a more concentrated cooking liquid is both flavorful and nutritious. And that's what creates the wonderfully creamy texture that makes many bean dishes so appealing.

Cooking Beans

When it comes to cooking beans, myths proliferate. The three big ones, all untrue:

1. You must soak beans before cooking.
2. You must not add salt during cooking.
3. You must not add acid during cooking.

To elaborate:

1. You can soak beans or not, as you like; there are advantages to soaking, but that doesn't make it essential. Soaking speeds cooking, so if you have time, do it. But don't let the fact that you didn't plan to cook beans until the last minute stop you from cooking them at all. With a pressure cooker (see page 11), you can move beans from pantry to table in a half hour or so. Even without pressure cooking, many beans can simmer away on a back burner, with only an occasional stir, and soften completely in as little as an hour (far less for lentils and split peas).

2. At some point during cooking (more on this later), you should in fact salt the beans; just not at the beginning, though some people would debate even that. It's often said that salting during cooking prevents beans from softening. *But it's not true.* See "Tips for Determining the Texture of Beans," (page 412).

3. Similarly, acid is said to slow bean cooking (and, conversely, alkaline substances such as baking soda are said to speed it). In fact, baking soda helps to break down the skin of beans, and acid helps to keep skins intact. If you're looking for a mushy bean dish, in which the individual beans begin to lose definition, you might indeed add a pinch or two of baking soda to the pot. If, however, you like well-defined, individual beans, include a teaspoonful of vinegar or lemon juice in the water. I don't include acid unless I want its flavor.

Over the years I've tried all sorts of formulas for cooking beans in all different styles. Generally, I prefer beans that are creamy (these take a little longer, until their skins burst and the insides begin melting into the cooking liquid), but there are times you might want firm beans for a salad or skillet dish, or just because you like them more that way. There's no big mystery here: Just taste them as they cook and take the pot off the heat when they're done the way you want them.

If this all sounds imprecise, it is, and that's a good thing: *For many bean dishes, you don't even need a recipe,* because few kitchen chores are simpler than cooking beans. You put the cleaned—and probably soaked—beans in a pot, cover them with cold water, and turn the heat on. It takes just a couple of minutes to bring the pot to a boil, at which

F Fast   **M** Make Ahead   **V** Vegetarian

point you lower the temperature so the beans bubble gently. Then you walk away for a while, coming back to add water as necessary. The timing varies, but little else changes except for ingredients you might add.

Serving Beans

Sometimes you drain beans before serving them or using them in other recipes (even then you might save the cooking liquid to cover leftover beans or to enrich soups or stocks; chickpea-cooking liquid is especially good for this). More often, though, you want to end up with about an inch of cooking liquid when the beans are done to your liking. This is easy enough: Check the pot every half hour or so while the beans cook and add about a cup of water if they threaten to dry out.

This liquid makes beans and rice a natural combination, but of course beans are fine with grains like barley, couscous, or millet as well. You can also serve beans on top of toasted bread; when the slices are thick and hearty, you've practically got a meal, but you can take the subtle approach and smear a dollop on top of thinly sliced Crostini (page 83).

Stir-fried or sautéed bean dishes are delicious tossed with all kinds of noodles. Purées, once you thin them a bit, make excellent sauces, especially on pasta, or you can add a spoonful to enrich soup. Beans also make excellent impromptu fillings for burritos, tacos, and enchiladas. And if you keep some firm-cooked beans handy, you'll always have a nice add-in for salads.

ESSENTIAL RECIPES

Since I almost always cook dried beans from scratch, I'm starting this section with the easiest way to prepare them plain. Beyond that are super-fast recipes that work well with either cooked-from-scratch or canned beans.

✪ Cooked Beans, the Quick-Soak Way

MAKES: 6 to 8 servings
TIME: 2 hours to soak plus 30 minutes to 2 hours to cook, depending on the bean, largely unattended

My favorite method and the easiest way to cook beans because most of the time they aren't cooking at all; they're soaking. Incredibly, if you start a pot of dried beans from scratch without soaking and start a pot with this method, both will be ready at about the same time, with no difference in taste or texture. What changes is that you don't have to check as much or add water as often if you soak them.

If you're cooking lentils or split peas—which take no more than 30 minutes to get tender—always follow the no-soak variation.

1 pound dried beans (any kind but lentils, split peas, or peeled and split beans), washed and picked over

Salt and freshly ground black pepper

1 Put the beans in a large pot with a tightly fitting lid and cover with cold water by 2 to 3 inches. Bring the pot to a boil and let it boil, uncovered, for about 2 minutes. Cover the pot and turn the heat off. Let the beans soak for about 2 hours.

2 Taste a bean. If it's tender (it won't be done), add a large pinch of salt and several grinds of black pepper. Make sure the beans are covered with about an inch of water; add a little if necessary. If the beans are still hard, don't add salt yet, and cover with about 2 inches of water.

3 Bring the pot to a boil, then adjust the heat so that the beans bubble gently. Partially cover and cook, stirring infrequently, checking the beans for doneness every 10 or 15 minutes, and adding a little more water if necessary. If you haven't added salt and pepper yet, add them when the beans are just turning tender. Stop cooking when the beans are done the way you like them, taste and adjust the seasoning, and use immediately or store.

Cooked Beans, the No-Soak Way. This is the only way to cook lentils, split peas, and other very small legumes, but it's fine for other beans too; they'll go from raw to mushy very slowly: Put the beans in a large pot with a tightly fitting lid and cover with cold water by 2 or 3 inches. Bring the pot to a boil, then reduce the heat so that the beans bubble gently. Partially cover and cook, stirring infrequently, checking the beans for doneness every 10 or 15 minutes, and adding a little more water if necessary. When the beans start to get tender, add a large pinch of salt and several grinds of black pepper; stop cooking when the beans are done the way you like them, taste and adjust the seasoning, and use immediately or store.

Cooked Beans, the Long-Soak Way. No more than 12 hours of soaking, please, or your beans will become mushy and bland: Put the beans in a large pot with a tightly fitting lid and cover with cold water by several inches. Leave them to soak for 6 to 12 hours, then drain and return them to the pot. Cover with about 2 inches of water, bring to a boil, and reduce the heat so that the beans bubble gently. Partially cover and cook, stirring infrequently, checking the beans for doneness every 10 minutes or so, and adding a little more water if necessary (frequent checking is important: long-soaked beans turn from tender to mushy rather fast). When the beans start to get tender, add a large pinch of salt and several grinds of black pepper; stop cooking when the beans are done the way you like them, taste and adjust the seasoning, and use immediately or store.

5 Ways to Flavor Beans as They Cook

Add any of the following ingredients to the pot, alone or in combination, when you start cooking the beans.

1. Herbs or spices: A bay leaf, a couple of cloves, some peppercorns, thyme sprigs, parsley leaves and/or stems, chili powder (to make your own, see page 66), or other herbs and spices
2. Aromatics: An unpeeled onion, a carrot, a celery stalk, and/or 3 or 4 cloves of garlic

Tips for Determining the Texture of Cooked Beans

You can control the texture of any beans you cook by using a few simple techniques:

To keep beans from breaking apart and becoming gritty: Don't salt beans during soaking or the early stages of cooking. Salt breaks down their skins and changes the way the beans absorb water. (You should, however, add salt when the beans begin to become tender; salted beans cook slightly faster and develop better flavor.)

For beans that are firm but tender, with intact skins: This is what you want for salads, garnishing, or sautés: Add up to 2 tablespoons white (distilled) vinegar or lemon juice to the cooking water when you add the salt. The beans will taste a little more acidic, but that's not necessarily a bad thing, especially if you plan to use them in salads or add other strong-flavored ingredients.

For richer, creamier beans: Add a cup or two of any milk—dairy or nondairy—to the cooking water. Cow's and goat's milk, as well as coconut, oat, soy, nut, and rice milks, are all fair game. And, of course, butter or flavorful oil, like extra virgin olive or nut oils, will also make beans rich and creamy.

For thicker, creamier bean dishes: Before adding cooked beans to any recipe, put 1/2 cup or so on a small plate and mash them with a fork. Then just add them with the rest of the beans as directed. This works for soupy bean stews as well as sautés, whenever you want a little more body. (You can also simply put an immersion blender into the pot and whir briefly.)

3. Stock: Chicken, beef, or vegetable stock (to make your own, see pages 157–159), in place of all or part of the water
4. Other beverages: A cup or so of beer, wine, coffee, tea, or juice
5. Smoked meat: Ham hock, pork chop, beef bone, or

 Fast   Make Ahead   **V** Vegetarian

sausage, fished out after cooking, the meat chopped and stirred back into the beans

13 Simple Additions to Cooked Beans

Talk about making a good thing better; few things are easier than this. Add any of the following ingredients to cooked beans (the amounts assume around 3 cups of cooked beans, or 4 servings) or follow the procedures as described.

1. 2 tablespoons butter, extra virgin olive oil, or dark sesame oil
2. $^1/_2$ cup chopped fresh parsley, cilantro, mint, or any basil leaves
3. 2 tablespoons chopped fresh rosemary, tarragon, oregano, epazote, thyme, marjoram, or sage leaves
4. 1 cup any cooked sauce, chutney, raw sauce, or Ginger-Scallion Sauce (page 39)
5. With room-temperature beans: Up to $^1/_2$ cup any vinaigrette (page 199), mayonnaise (page 41), or yogurt sauce (page 24)
6. A tablespoon or so of any curry powder or spice blend (to make your own, see pages 65–69)
7. Stock (to make your own, see pages 157–159) or other flavored liquid for reheating the beans
8. Soy, Worcestershire, or Tabasco sauce to taste
9. 1 or 2 tablespoons miso thinned with hot bean-cooking liquid and warmed gently with the beans
10. Chopped onion or other aromatic vegetables added during reheating
11. Chopped leafy greens, like kale or collards, added during reheating
12. Peeled, seeded, and chopped tomato added during reheating
13. A few slices diced bacon (or pancetta), cooked until crisp, the beans reheated in the rendered bacon fat, and the cooked bacon used as a garnish

✪ White Bean Purée

MAKES: 4 servings

TIME: 10 minutes with cooked beans

One of the most useful bean preparations there is, as a side dish, sauce, spread, or dip. Serve it with bread or pita chips or carrot and celery sticks; use it as a spread for Crostini (pages 83–84); or pool under any grilled seafood, poultry, meat, or vegetables. For a smoother, richer, more luxurious purée, add $^1/_4$ cup or so cream to the main recipe or to any of the first four variations.

Other beans you can use: nearly any—cannellini, Great Northern, dried favas and limas, chickpeas, pinto, kidney, most heirlooms, soybeans, or black beans and lightly cooked fresh beans like fava, edamame, or lima.

> 3 cups cooked or canned navy or other white beans, drained but still moist, liquid reserved
>
> About 1 cup bean-cooking liquid, stock (to make your own, see pages 157–159), or water
>
> 3 tablespoons butter or extra virgin olive oil
>
> Salt and freshly ground black pepper
>
> Chopped fresh parsley leaves for garnish

1 Purée the beans by putting them through a food mill or using an upright or immersion blender; add as much liquid as you need to make a smooth but not watery purée.

2 Put in a microwave-safe dish or medium saucepan along with the butter or olive oil. Heat gently until the butter melts and the beans are hot; sprinkle with salt and pepper.

5 Beans to Always Keep on Hand

1. Northern, navy, cannellini, or other white beans
2. Chickpeas
3. Pinto or kidney beans
4. Lentils
5. Black beans

✪ Essential Recipe

3 Garnish with parsley and serve hot (as a side dish) or warm or at room temperature as a dip or spread.

Bean Purée with Roasted Garlic. Many kinds of beans work beautifully with roasted garlic; white beans of any kind, favas, chickpeas, pintos, black-eyed peas, and soybeans are all fine: Add 15 to 20 cloves of Roasted Garlic (page 303) and 1 teaspoon fresh thyme leaves in Step 1. Proceed with the recipe.

Garlicky Puréed Beans. A little lemon zest is good here too: Add 1 teaspoon or more minced garlic and a few fresh rosemary leaves or $^1/_2$ teaspoon dried in Step 1.

Cheesy Puréed Beans. Stir in $^1/_4$ cup finely grated Parmesan, pecorino, fontina, or Gouda in Step 2. Heat until the cheese is melted, stirring frequently.

White Bean and Celery Root or Parsnip Purée. Even more substantial and a terrific substitute for mashed potatoes: Add 1 cup cooked chopped celery root (see page 283) or parsnips (see page 328) in Step 1.

Black Bean Purée with Chipotles. Spicy and smoky; perfect with "Naked" Tamales (page 490) or Chiles Rellenos (page 333): Add 1 or 2 tablespoons chopped canned chipotle chiles in adobo sauce in Step 1. Garnish with cilantro.

✪ Beans and Tomatoes

MAKES: 4 servings

TIME: 20 minutes with cooked beans

F **M** **V**

An elegant, absolutely delicious side dish that's even better if you use chicken stock to cook the dried beans. This will make converts of self-professed bean-haters.

Other beans you can use: any white beans at all; large limas or gigantes are gorgeous.

2 tablespoons butter or extra virgin olive oil

$^1/_4$ cup chopped shallot or scallion

1 teaspoon fresh thyme leaves or $^1/_2$ teaspoon dried thyme

2 cups peeled, seeded, and diced tomato (drained canned is fine)

4 cups cooked or canned navy or pea beans, drained

$^1/_2$ cup chicken, beef, or vegetable stock (to make your own, see pages 157–159), juice from canned tomatoes, or water

Salt and freshly ground black pepper

Freshly grated Parmesan cheese (optional)

1 Put the butter or oil in a large, deep skillet over medium heat. When the butter is melted or the oil is hot, add the shallot and cook, stirring, until it softens, 3 to 5 minutes. Add the thyme and cook for about 30 seconds.

2 Add the tomato and cook, stirring occasionally, until it breaks up and becomes "saucy," about 10 minutes. Then add the beans and stock and turn the heat up to medium-high. Cook, stirring, until the mixture is hot and creamy, about 5 minutes. Season and serve, topped with the Parmesan if you like.

Bean and Tomato Casserole. More substantial and a good light main course; use any kind of cooked beans or a mixture: Slice 4 tomatoes. Add 2 large chopped onions; $1^1/_2$ cups grated cheddar, Jack, or Asiago cheese; and 2 tablespoons chopped fresh oregano or marjoram leaves. Heat the oven to 400°F; grease the bottom and sides of a 2-quart baking dish or casserole. Put about half the beans in the bottom (sprinkle with salt and pepper if they need it), followed by a layer of tomatoes, then the onions, and a sprinkling of the herbs and cheese. Repeat. Bake until the casserole is hot and the cheese is bubbly, 20 to 30 minutes depending on the size of the baking dish.

Bean Casserole with Hominy and Tortillas. In the preceding variation, substitute 2 cups cooked hominy (use canned or see Cooking Grains, the Easy Way, page 451) for 2 cups of the beans. Put a layer of corn tortillas (3 or 4, depending on the size of your dish) on top of the bean-hominy mixture before topping with the tomatoes, onions, and cheese. Bake as directed.

Chicken, Tomatillo, and Bean Casserole. Follow the first variation, only use a large white bean, like cannellini, lima, or gigante. Add 2 cups shredded cooked chicken and substitute 2 cups sliced tomatillo (about 20; canned are fine) for the tomato. Use Monterey Jack, Chihuahua, or cotija for the cheese. Layer the ingredients, beginning with the beans and ending with the cheese, then repeat. Bake as directed. Garnish with chopped fresh cilantro and lime wedges if you like.

✪ Lentils and Potatoes with Curry

MAKES: 4 servings
TIME: About 1 hour

This is a classic Indian-style dal—a spicy, somewhat soupy bean dish. You may want to double the recipe so you have some handy in the fridge or freezer, because it reheats beautifully. Don't worry if the potatoes crumble a bit on the second go-around; they will only add body to the dish. Eat as a thick soup or serve with rice as a side dish. (For more about dals, see pages 433–434.)

Other beans you can use: yellow or green split peas or red lentils; just reduce the cooking time by 15 minutes or so.

1 cup dried brown lentils, washed and picked over

3½ cups water, coconut milk (to make your own, see page 389), or stock (to make your own, see pages 157–159), plus more if needed

1 tablespoon curry powder (to make your own, see pages 66–67)

2 medium starchy potatoes, peeled and cut into large chunks

Salt and freshly ground black pepper

Yogurt for garnish

Chopped fresh cilantro leaves for garnish

① Combine the lentils, liquid, and curry powder in a medium saucepan over medium-high heat and bring to a boil. Turn the heat down to medium-low so that the mixture bubbles gently, cover partially, and cook, stirring occasionally, until the lentils start to absorb the water a bit, about 15 minutes.

② Add the potatoes and cover the pan completely. Cook undisturbed for 10 minutes or so, then stir gently and check to make sure the lentils aren't too dry. If they are, add a little more liquid. Add salt as the lentils become tender.

③ Cover and continue cooking until the lentils are soft and beginning to turn to mush and the potatoes are tender at the center, another 5 to 10 minutes; add liquid if necessary. The mixture should be moist but not soupy. Add lots of black pepper, stir, then taste and adjust the seasoning and serve, garnished with yogurt and cilantro.

Buttery Lentils and Potatoes with Curry. A little smoother and more flavorful: When you stir and check the mixture in Step 2, stir in 2 tablespoons cold butter.

Plain Talk About Beans and Gas

You don't hear about this issue as much as you once did, even a decade ago. I suspect it's because beans have become more prevalent in our diets. I never have been a fan of additives that minimize flatulence, and, in fact, I often don't bother to drain off the water after quick-soaking legumes, which is supposed to be one of the ways to minimize beans' negative effects. If you eat a lot of high-fiber plant foods, then your system is probably efficient at digesting them; it's as simple as that. However, some people are allergic to beans, and constant gastric distress is one signal. So if you're truly uncomfortable after eating legumes, see your doctor.

✪ Essential Recipe

✪ Roasted Chickpeas

MAKES: 4 servings

TIME: Less than 30 minutes with cooked chickpeas

F **M** **V**

When you cook chickpeas long enough, whether on the stovetop or in the oven, their exterior becomes crisp. These are equally good as a side dish or finger food.

3 tablespoons olive or neutral oil, like grapeseed or corn

2 cups well-drained cooked or canned chickpeas

1 tablespoon minced garlic

Salt and freshly ground black pepper

1 tablespoon curry powder or other spice blend (optional; to make your own, see pages 65–69), or to taste

Freshly squeezed lemon juice, to taste (optional)

1 Heat the oven to 400°F. Put the oil in a large oven-proof skillet or a roasting pan large enough to hold the chickpeas in one layer and turn the heat to medium. When hot, add the chickpeas, garlic, and some salt and pepper. Shake the pan so that all the chickpeas are well coated with oil and are sitting in one layer. Put the skillet or pan in the oven.

2 Roast, shaking the pan occasionally, until the chickpeas begin to brown, 15 or 20 minutes. Remove from the oven and cool slightly. If you like, sprinkle with the spice blend or more salt and pepper or simply with a little more oil and some freshly squeezed lemon juice. Serve hot or at room temperature.

✪ Baked Beans

MAKES: 6 to 8 servings

TIME: At least 4 hours, largely unattended

M

These are traditional baked beans and as such are fairly straightforward. But you can make changes pretty easily; see "7 Ideas for Baked Beans," which follows.

Other beans you can use: red beans or lima beans.

1 pound dried navy, pea, or other white beans, washed and picked over

8 ounces salt pork or slab bacon

$1/2$ cup molasses, or to taste

2 teaspoons ground mustard or 2 tablespoons prepared mustard, or to taste

Salt and freshly ground black pepper

1 Cook the beans as in Cooked Beans, the Quick-Soak Way, or one of its variations (page 411), but only until they begin to become tender, 15 to 30 minutes, depending on the bean and the technique. Heat the oven to 300°F. Cube or slice the salt pork or bacon and put it in the bottom of a bean pot or other deep ovenproof pot with a lid, like a Dutch oven. Drain the beans (reserve the cooking water if you like), then mix them with the molasses and mustard. Pour them over the meat. Add enough boiling water (or bean-cooking water or both) to cover the beans by about an inch.

2 Bake, uncovered, checking and stirring every half hour or so (you can ignore them for the first hour) and adding more water if necessary. After about 3 hours, taste and adjust the seasoning; you may add more salt, sweetener, or mustard.

3 When the beans are very tender, scoop the meat up from the bottom and lay it on top of the beans; raise the heat to 400°F. Cook until the pork browns a bit and the beans are very bubbly, about 10 minutes. (You may repeat this process several times, scooping the meat to the top and browning it; each repetition darkens the color of the dish and adds flavor.) Serve hot.

Vegetarian Baked Beans. No smokiness, less fat, but still real good: Substitute 2 tablespoons butter or neutral oil and 1 large or 2 medium onions, quartered, for the meat. Add 2 cups peeled, seeded, and chopped tomato (canned is fine; include the juices) along with the molasses and mustard.

Baked Beans with Cracker Crumb Crust. Works with the main recipe or the vegetarian version: After uncover-

 Fast   Make Ahead   **V** Vegetarian

ing the beans and raising the oven temperature at the end of Step 3, sprinkle the top of the beans with about $1\frac{1}{2}$ cups crumbled saltines or bread crumbs. Return the pot to the oven and bake until the crust is golden (20 to 30 minutes).

Tomato-Baked Beans. Inching toward a one-pot meal: In Step 1, when you mix the beans with the molasses and mustard, add $1\frac{1}{2}$ cups chopped tomato (canned is fine; don't bother to drain) and $\frac{1}{4}$ cup tomato paste. Proceed with the recipe.

7 Ideas for Baked Beans

1. Add ketchup to taste or substitute sugar or maple syrup (or a combination) for the molasses.
2. Add Worcestershire, soy, or Tabasco sauce to taste.
3. Add an onion or two, quartered, and/or a few chunks of peeled carrots.
4. Substitute sausage, cut into chunks, for the salt pork or bacon.
5. Add 2 cups coconut milk (to make your own, see page 389) along with the water.
6. Add 1 or 2 tablespoons curry powder, chili powder, or any other spice mix you like (to make your own, see pages 65–69).
7. Add 4 cups beef, chicken, or vegetable stock (to make your own, see pages 157–159) after baking to make soup.

Stir-Fried Tofu with Scallions

MAKES: 4 servings
TIME: 20 minutes

Master this and you master the world, at least the world of stir-frying tofu, which is not insignificant. Start with firm or extra-firm tofu or use any of the prepared tofu methods on pages 444–446.

> $1\frac{1}{2}$ to 2 pounds firm to extra-firm tofu, prepared by any of the methods on pages 444–446 or simply blotted dry

3 tablespoons peanut or neutral oil, like grapeseed or corn

1 tablespoon chopped garlic

1 tablespoon chopped fresh ginger (optional)

2 small dried chiles (optional)

1 or 2 bunches scallions, trimmed and cut into 2-inch lengths, white and green parts separated (about 2 cups total)

$\frac{1}{3}$ cup vegetable stock (to make your own, see page 157) or water

2 tablespoons soy sauce, or to taste

1 tablespoon toasted sesame seeds (optional; see page 317)

❶ Cut the tofu into $\frac{1}{2}$-inch or slightly larger cubes. Put the oil in a large skillet over high heat. When hot, add the garlic, ginger, and chiles and cook, stirring, for about 10 seconds. Add the tofu and the white parts of the scallions; cook, stirring occasionally, until the tofu begins to brown, a couple of minutes. Add the stock and cook, stirring, until about half of it evaporates, less than a minute; add the green parts of the scallions and stir for about 30 seconds.

❷ Add the soy sauce and stir. Taste and adjust the seasoning, garnish with the sesame seeds if you like, and serve.

Stir-Fried Tofu with Scallions and Walnuts. You can use cashews, peanuts, or other nuts here if you like: In Step 1, before cooking the tofu, use an additional tablespoon of oil to stir-fry 1 cup shelled nuts (they may be whole or broken) until glossy and just beginning to brown, just a minute or two. Remove with a slotted spoon and set aside, then proceed with the recipe.

Stir-Fried Tofu with Scallions and Black Beans. Fermented black beans are a simple but huge flavor booster for any stir-fry: Before cooking, soak 2 tablespoons fermented black beans in $\frac{1}{4}$ cup rice wine, sherry, or water for about 10 minutes. In Step 1, reduce the stock to $1/4$ cup and add the black bean mixture along with the green parts of the scallions. Proceed with the recipe.

Stir-Fried Tofu with Scallions, Orange Zest, and Chiles. Use an exhaust fan or the chile smoke may get to you: In Step 1, before cooking the tofu, use an additional tablespoon of oil to stir-fry the zest of a navel orange, cut into large pieces, and 3 to 50 small dried red chiles (traditionally a handful, but you can use less) until glossy and just beginning to brown, about a minute. Remove with a slotted spoon and set aside, then proceed with the recipe. Do not eat the chiles; they'll just lend a pleasant heat and smokiness to the dish.

7 Additions to Any Stir-Fried Tofu

You can build on this recipe by moving on to Stir-Fried Tofu with Bell Peppers or Other Vegetables (page 447), but here are some even quicker ideas:

1. Add up to 1 cup any cooked fish, seafood, poultry, or meat—shredded, sliced, chopped, or crumbled—along with the tofu. (You might need a little more liquid or oil.)

2. Add 2 teaspoons five-spice powder (to make your own, see page 68) and/or a few star anise, added with the tofu (this is good with hoisin sauce; see number 6).

3. Add 1 medium to large tomato, halved, seeded (page 361), and chopped, along with the white parts of the scallions.

4. Add 1 cup bean sprouts, along with (or instead of) the scallion greens.

5. Add 1 tablespoon sugar (or to taste), honey, or other sweetener, along with the green parts of the scallions.

6. Add 1 tablespoon (or to taste) Chile Paste (page 74) or hoisin sauce, along with the soy sauce.

7. Add 1 tablespoon (or to taste) dark sesame oil, along with the garnish.

Recipes That Start with Cooked (or Canned) Beans

Once you have plain cooked beans, all that's left is seasoning. You can go the stovetop or oven route here, with recipes and variations that span a range of side-dish and main-course possibilities. Some add more than a couple ingredients, but none is anything but dead simple. Start with cooked beans from the fridge or freezer (or from a can in a pinch), and dinner will be on the table in 45 minutes or less.

Real Refried Beans

MAKES: 4 servings

TIME: 20 minutes with cooked beans

You don't have to use lard here, but it's traditional and really delicious. (It's also not even bad for you, but I won't tackle that argument here.) What's not traditional—but *is* good—is butter. If you're going to cook these in advance and reheat them, do so with a little more fat.

Other beans you can use: any red or pink beans.

$1/2$ cup lard, bacon fat, or drippings from Mexican chorizo, butter, or $1/4$ cup neutral oil, like grapeseed or corn

3 to 4 cups drained cooked or canned pinto, pink, or black beans, liquid reserved

1 cup chopped onion

1 tablespoon ground cumin, plus more to taste

$1/4$ teaspoon cayenne, plus more to taste

Salt and freshly ground black pepper

Chopped fresh cilantro leaves for garnish (optional)

1 Put the fat in a large skillet, preferably nonstick, over medium heat. When hot, add the beans and mash with a large fork or potato masher until they're the texture you like.

2 Add the onion, cumin, and cayenne, sprinkle with salt and pepper, and continue to cook and mash, stirring, until the beans are more or less broken up (some remaining chunks are fine) and the onion is lightly cooked, about 5 minutes more. Thin with a little of the bean liquid until you get the consistency you want. Taste and adjust the seasoning if necessary. Garnish with cilantro if you like.

8 Additions to Refried Beans
1. Minced fresh or pickled chile to taste
2. Chopped scallion or white onion
3. Minced fresh ginger or garlic
4. Chopped seeded tomato
5. Grated cheddar, Monterey Jack, or Chihuahua cheese or crumbled queso fresco
6. Cooked rice
7. Crumbled chorizo
8. Sour cream or crema

Black Beans with Orange

MAKES: 4 servings

TIME: 30 minutes with cooked beans

The combination of black beans and orange, popular in Latin America, is a terrific one and produces a dish that is equally fine with or without meat and with or without added heat. Like most black bean dishes, it's striking in appearance. Serve this with lots of rice or warm tortillas.

Other beans you can use: red beans in a pinch.

3 cups cooked or canned black beans, with about 1 cup of their liquid

1 tablespoon ground cumin

Salt and freshly ground black pepper

1 navel orange, well washed

2 tablespoons extra virgin olive oil

1 onion, chopped

1 bell pepper, preferably red or yellow, cored, seeded, and chopped

1 or 2 fresh chiles, like New Mexico or habanero, seeded and chopped, or 1 or 2 dried chiles, like chile de arbol or piquin, soaked (see page 70), cleaned, and chopped (optional)

1 tablespoon minced garlic

1/2 cup dry red wine or freshly squeezed orange juice

Chopped fresh cilantro or parsley leaves for garnish

1 Put the beans and their liquid in a large pot over medium heat; add the cumin and a good pinch of salt and pepper, bring to a boil, and adjust the heat so the mixture simmers.

2 Halve the orange. Peel one half and add the peel to the beans, then divide the segments and set aside. Squeeze the juice from the other half and set aside.

3 Put the olive oil in a skillet over medium heat. Add the onion, the bell pepper, and the chiles if you're using them and cook, stirring occasionally, until the peppers soften, 8 to 10 minutes. Add the garlic and cook, stirring, for 1 minute more. Add this mixture to the beans.

4 Turn the heat under the skillet up to high and add the wine. Cook for about 5 minutes, then add to the beans along with the reserved orange juice. Taste and adjust the seasoning if necessary. Serve with rice, garnished with the reserved orange sections and cilantro, or store in the refrigerator for up to 2 days and reheat before serving, garnishing at the last minute.

Black Beans with Crisp Pork and Orange. Even better if you render some good bacon or salt pork first, use the fat to cook the meat and vegetables, and add the meat to the simmering beans: In Step 3, start by browning 8 ounces Italian sausage cut into 1-inch pieces. Remove with a slotted spoon and add to the simmering beans. Brown 8 ounces or more pork shoulder cut into chunks. Remove and add to the beans; cook the onion and pepper in the remaining fat, then proceed with the recipe, adding the onion and pepper to the pot too.

Freezing Home-Cooked Beans Versus Buying Canned Beans

There's no denying that cooking beans takes a while. There are two ways of getting around this. One is to buy canned beans, which are cooked. But they have disadvantages:

- They give you no control over texture. Although many people like the extremely soft texture of canned beans, they come that way and that way only.
- You'll never get the same beany flavor as you do from dried, and the canning liquid is never as delicious as your own cooking liquid.
- Only the most common types of beans are available in cans.
- They are relatively expensive.
- They range wildly in quality (some are pretty bad).

You're much better off freezing cooked beans. Most of the recipes here start with 1 pound of beans, which makes 6 to 8 servings. This is my general practice, so I can refrigerate or freeze what I don't immediately need (usually about half). It takes literally seconds of extra work. You can, of course, make half a recipe if you prefer. But if you get in the habit of cooking a pound of dried beans at a time, you'll find that canned beans become an afterthought, a staple of last resort.

To freeze, let the cooked beans cool in their liquid, then put beans and liquid into plastic containers with tight-fitting lids or zipper bags. Put in a splash of white vinegar or lemon juice if you want to help keep the beans intact, then cover and refrigerate for up to 5 days or freeze for up to 6 months. (As with all frozen foods, you're better off using them sooner.) Thaw for a day or so in the fridge, thaw in the microwave, or put the block of beans and liquid in a covered pan with a little water over medium-low heat (check occasionally to make sure they have enough water, but don't overstir or try to break up the ice block or the beans will break into bits). Generally beans can go from frozen to hot in less than 30 minutes.

---

5 More Ideas for Black Beans with Orange

This hearty, rich dish, with its mild acidity, cries out for more elaborate treatments. Try these:

1. Add a tablespoon or so of minced fresh ginger along with the garlic.
2. Cook a cup or two of chopped fresh or canned tomatoes along with the beans in Step 1.
3. Add 1 or 2 ripe plantains, peeled and cut into chunks (see page 334), along with the beans in Step 1.
4. Add a tablespoon of curry powder (to make your own, see pages 66–67) or Spanish pimentón along with the beans in Step 4.

5. Garnish with a tablespoon of mixed grated fresh orange and lemon or lime zest.

Beer-Glazed Black Beans

MAKES: 4 servings

TIME: 20 minutes with cooked beans

It's amazing how much flavor you can get from adding beer to black beans. Lagers and wheat beers will produce a lighter, fruitier dish; porters will add richness and stouts deep, caramelized flavors.

 Fast   Make Ahead   Vegetarian

Other beans you can use: pinto, pink, or black-eyed peas.

2 tablespoons extra virgin olive oil

1 onion, chopped

1 tablespoon minced garlic

1 cup beer

3 cups cooked or canned black beans, drained but still moist

1 tablespoon chili powder (to make your own, see page 66) or ground cumin

1 tablespoon honey

Salt and freshly ground black pepper

1 Put the oil in a skillet over medium-high heat. Add the onion and cook, stirring occasionally, until soft, about 5 minutes. Add the garlic, cook for about a minute, then add the remaining ingredients with a good sprinkling of salt and pepper.

2 Bring to a steady bubble and cook until the liquid is slightly reduced and thickened, about 15 minutes. Taste and adjust the seasoning if necessary. Serve hot or refrigerate for up to 3 days and then reheat.

Beer-Glazed Black Beans and Tomatoes. Add 1 cup chopped tomato, fresh or canned, or 1 to 2 tablespoons tomato paste in Step 1.

Beer-Glazed Black Beans with Bacon. This is good with tomatoes too: Cook 4 to 8 ounces bacon, cut into cubes or small pieces, over medium heat until crisp. Scoop out the bacon with a slotted spoon and use the bacon fat to cook the onion. Proceed with the recipe, stirring in the cooked bacon at the last minute.

Beer-Glazed Black Beans with Chipotle Paste. The sweet heat of this paste melts into the beans: Stir in a dollop of Chipotle Paste (page 74), in Step 1, along with the beans.

White Beans with Cabbage, Pasta, and Ham

MAKES: 4 servings
TIME: 30 minutes

Made with good chicken stock, this is a sensational cold-weather dish that can be made with a variety of greens (try spinach, for example), pasta shapes, or meats, like cooked bacon or sausage. See the chart on page 422 for ideas.

Other beans you can use: chickpeas or pink beans.

Salt

3 cups chopped cabbage, preferably Savoy

8 ounces small pasta, like cavatelli or orecchiette

2 tablespoons extra virgin olive oil

2 cups chopped leek or onion

1 celery stalk, chopped

2 sprigs fresh thyme

1/4 cup chopped prosciutto or 1/2 cup chopped ham

1 cup chicken or other stock (to make your own, see pages 157–159), or more as needed

3 cups cooked or canned cannellini or other white beans, drained but still moist

Freshly ground black pepper

Freshly grated Parmesan or pecorino Romano cheese for garnish

1 Bring a large pot of water to a boil over high heat and salt it. Add the cabbage and cook until just tender, about 3 minutes; use a slotted spoon or small strainer to fish it out, drain (shock if you like; see page 240), and set aside. When the pot returns to a boil, add the pasta and cook until tender but firm, about 7 minutes or so, and drain it.

2 Meanwhile, put the oil in a large skillet over medium heat. when hot, add the leek and celery and cook until softened, about 5 minutes. Add the thyme, prosciutto, stock, beans, and cabbage and sprinkle with salt and pepper; cook until the flavors blend and everything is well heated, about 5 minutes more. If the mixture dries out, add a little more stock; it should be moist but not soupy.

BEAN, GREEN, AND PASTA COMBOS

You can follow the recipe for White Beans with Cabbage, Pasta, and Ham (pages 421–422) and change the greens, beans, and pasta as you like. Some of the ideas here have meat or seafood added; some don't. All (except the fish combos) benefit from a grating of cheese.

BEAN	GREEN	PASTA	BONUS INGREDIENT
Chickpeas or Fava Beans	Spinach	Rigatoni or radiatore	Cooked ground lamb, seasoned with cumin, cayenne, and cinnamon
Chickpeas	Chard	Linguine	Clams or mussels (a couple dozen or so; add them in place of the ham in Step 2, cover, and cook until they open, about 10 minutes)
Cranberry Beans	Radicchio (use about half as much) or chicory	Farfalle	A splash of balsamic vinegar or a drizzle of Balsamic Syrup (page 51)
Flageolets	Kale or collards	Penne or ziti	Bits of roasted duck, chicken, or pork
Lentils	Endive	Small shells	Cooked and crumbled Italian sausage
Lima Beans (any kind, but fresh are fantastic)	Napa or Savoy cabbage	Large shells	Shrimp or other seafood, chopped if necessary into pieces about the size of the beans (uncooked is fine; it will cook as you heat and stir in Step 3)

3 Combine the bean mixture and pasta in the large pot and stir gently. Taste and adjust the seasoning, sprinkle with Parmesan, and serve.

Bean and Potato Gratin

MAKES: 4 servings

TIME: 1½ hours with cooked beans, largely unattended

This dish is based on boulangerie potatoes, a French classic that was traditionally baked at the local baker's until the potatoes became meltingly soft and the stock reduced to a rich glaze. With beans, it could easily be a main course or remain a side dish.

Other beans you can use: pink or red beans.

2 tablespoons fresh thyme leaves

3 cups cooked or canned white beans, drained but still moist

Salt and freshly ground black pepper

3 medium starchy or all-purpose potatoes, peeled

1 cup chicken, beef, or vegetable stock (to make your own, see pages 157–159) or water

3 tablespoons butter

 Fast   Make Ahead   Vegetarian

1 Heat the oven to 325°F. Stir a tablespoon of the thyme into the beans, taste, and adjust the seasoning. Spread the beans into the bottom of a large baking dish and set aside.

2 Halve the potatoes lengthwise and slice thinly into half-circles. Lay the potatoes in overlapping rows to cover the beans. Pour the stock over the top, dot with pieces of butter, and sprinkle with salt, pepper, and the remaining thyme.

3 Cover with foil and bake for 45 minutes. Remove the foil and continue baking until the top is browned and glazed, another 45 minutes or so. Serve immediately or let rest for up to an hour and serve at room temperature.

Creamy Bean and Potato Gratin. Add $1/2$ cup cream to the beans.

Bean, Potato, and Leek Gratin. Cook 2 cups chopped leek in butter until very soft—almost melting—about 20 minutes. Top the beans with the leek and then the potato slices.

Stewed Chickpeas with Chicken

MAKES: 4 servings

TIME: About 45 minutes with cooked chickpeas

With its Spanish/North African seasonings, this is an exotic but simple stew. It also can be made, and quite flavorfully, without the chicken—see the first variation.

Other beans you can use: fava or lima beans.

4 cups cooked or canned chickpeas, drained

2 cups bean-cooking liquid, stock (to make your own, see pages 157–159), or water

Salt and freshly ground black pepper

1 tablespoon neutral oil, like grapeseed or corn

2 to 3 pounds chicken parts, preferably leg-thigh pieces separated at the joint, skin removed if desired

1 large onion, chopped

1 celery stalk, chopped

1 carrot, chopped

1 tablespoon minced garlic

1 teaspoon minced fresh ginger

1 teaspoon ground coriander

2 teaspoons ground cumin

2 cups peeled, seeded, and chopped tomato (canned is fine; include the juices)

Chopped fresh cilantro or parsley leaves for garnish

1 Heat the oven to 400°F. Warm the beans in a large pot with the liquid; add salt and pepper. Adjust the heat so the mixture bubbles very slowly.

2 Put the oil in a large, deep skillet over medium-high heat. Brown the chicken well on all sides, about 15 minutes; season with salt and pepper, transfer the chicken to a roasting pan, and put in the oven.

3 Pour off all but 3 tablespoons of the fat remaining in the skillet. Turn the heat down to medium and add the onion, celery, and carrot. Cook, stirring occasionally, until the vegetables are softened, about 10 minutes. Add the garlic, ginger, coriander, cumin, and tomato and cook for 5 minutes more, stirring occasionally and scraping the bottom of the pan to loosen any brown bits. Add the mixture to the simmering beans.

4 When the chicken has cooked for about 15 minutes, check for doneness (the juices will run clear if you make a small cut in the meat near the bone). When it is ready, remove it from the oven. When the vegetables are tender, put the chickpeas and the vegetables on a large, deep platter; top with the chicken, garnish, and serve.

Stewed Chickpeas with Vegetables. Omit the chicken. In Step 2, sauté 3 cups cubed, salted eggplant (see page 293) or zucchini in $1/4$ cup olive oil until tender,

15 to 30 minutes. Remove and proceed to Step 3. Combine the chickpeas and their seasonings with the eggplant and/or zucchini and roast for about 10 minutes, or until the mixture is bubbly and the top begins to brown. Garnish and serve.

Chickpea and Chicken Tagine. Ideal with cooked couscous, barley, or bulgur: Omit the celery and carrot. In Step 2, do not bother to put the chicken in a roasting pan; instead add the browned pieces to the simmering beans. In Step 3, add ¹/₂ teaspoon ground cinnamon, ¹/₂ vanilla bean (see page 63), and ¹/₂ cup raisins or chopped dates along with the other spices in the skillet; stir and cook for a minute before adding the tomato. Proceed with the recipe, only

cover the pot and make sure the mixture in the pot bubbles along gently until the chicken is very tender, 45 to 60 minutes.

Edamame

Not long ago, you saw edamame—green soybeans—only in Japanese restaurants. Now they're everywhere, including the freezer case of most supermarkets. Colorful, plump, and sweet, with a buttery texture and super-high protein content, they can be used in virtually anything you'd make with fresh or frozen limas or favas.

Buying and storing: Edamame are immature soybeans, harvested at about 80 percent of their growth cycle. They're available both in the pod and shelled, usually frozen, though fresh beans are now showing up in supermarkets. Store fresh edamame in plastic bags in the fridge for up to a week or so. Frozen and well wrapped, the beans will keep for months.

Preparing: Wash before cooking; use a brush to scrub some of the fuzz off the pods if you like.

How to cook: Because they are immature and not dried, edamame cook much faster than mature fresh or frozen shell beans (See page 83 for a simple recipe for boiled, salted edamame.)

Edamame with Stock or Soy Sauce

MAKES: 4 servings

TIME: 15 minutes

This super-easy little dish cooks up in no time. It's delicious—even served cold—on top of soba noodles or rice. If you don't have dashi or stock, use soy sauce as directed; it's even quicker and easier and nearly as good.

Other fresh beans you can use: lima, fava, or cranberry.

- 1 tablespoon neutral oil, like grapeseed or corn
- 1 tablespoon minced fresh ginger
- ¹/₄ cup chopped scallion
- 1 cup Dashi (page 160), stock (to make your own, see pages 157–159), bean-cooking liquid, or ¹/₄ cup soy sauce mixed with ³/₄ cup water
- 1 small carrot, julienned or finely chopped
- ¹/₂ cup snow peas, trimmed and julienned or finely chopped
- 2 cups shelled edamame, fresh or frozen (and thawed if you have time)
- Salt and freshly ground black pepper

❶ Put the oil in a skillet over medium heat. When hot, add the ginger and scallion and cook, stirring occasionally, until the scallion is soft, about 3 minutes. Add the dashi and bring to a steady bubble. Add the carrot, snow peas, and edamame and sprinkle with salt and pepper.

2 Cook until the beans are tender, 5 to 15 minutes. Taste, adjust the seasoning, and serve.

Edamame with Ponzu. The zing of the yuzu juice is fantastic, but you can also use a combination of citrus when none is available: Add roughly the same amount of julienned daikon as carrot and omit the snow peas. Substitute ³/₄ cup Ponzu Sauce (page 40) for the dashi.

Edamame with Tofu. With either the main recipe or the ponzu variation, in Step 2, during the last 5 minutes of cooking, stir in 1 cup (or more) cubed firm tofu or add 8 ounces or so of silken tofu and gently break it up with a spoon. (You may need to add a little more liquid.)

Edamame with Shrimp. With either the main recipe or the ponzu variation, in Step 1, stir in about 8 ounces peeled shrimp, along with the edamame. Cook until the shrimp are pink and opaque. Proceed with the recipe.

Edamame with Tomatoes and Cilantro

MAKES: 4 servings
TIME: 25 minutes

Easy but high powered, this changes form easily: Cook the tomatoes with their juices for a saucy dish (as directed here) or add them at the last minute for a fresher, more saladlike dish. Other cooked vegetables can be tossed in as well; try corn kernels, cubed eggplant, summer squash, chopped cauliflower, or broccoli.

Other fresh beans you can use: any.

2 tablespoons extra virgin olive oil
1 small onion or 3 scallions, chopped

1 tablespoon minced garlic
1 teaspoon ground cumin
1¹/₂ cups chopped ripe tomato (canned is fine, drained or not)
2 cups shelled edamame, fresh or thawed frozen
Salt and freshly ground black pepper
¹/₄ cup chopped fresh cilantro leaves

1 Put the oil in a skillet over medium-high heat. When hot, add the onion and garlic and cook, stirring occasionally, until soft, about 3 minutes.

2 Add the cumin and tomato and cook at a gentle bubble until the tomato begins to break apart, about 10 minutes.

3 Stir in the edamame and sprinkle with salt and pepper. Cook until the edamame are tender, about 5 to 7 minutes. Taste and adjust the seasoning, sprinkle with cilantro, and serve.

Edamame with Tomatoes and Olives. Substitute 8 pitted and sliced black olives for the cumin and basil leaves for the cilantro.

Edamame with Dijon and Wax Beans. Omit the garlic, cumin, tomato, and cilantro. Add a couple tablespoons water along with the edamame, cook for a couple minutes, then add 2 teaspoons chopped fresh tarragon or thyme leaves, 3 tablespoons Dijon mustard, and 1 cup trimmed and cooked wax beans.

Edamame with Ground Pork. Before starting the recipe, put the olive oil in the skillet over medium-high heat. When hot, add 8 ounces ground pork. Stir and cook, crumbling the meat as it browns; when it's nice and crisp and cooked through, after about 10 minutes, remove it with a slotted spoon and pour off all but 2 tablespoons of the fat. Follow the recipe from the beginning. In Step 3, stir the cooked pork in with the edamame and proceed with the recipe.

Fresh and Frozen Shell Beans

Some shell beans—like limas, black-eyed peas, pigeon peas, cranberry beans, favas, and edamame—are sold fresh in season, and some are sold frozen year-round. Frozen are pretty good, but fresh—which take some work, if you have to shell them—can be fantastic. You'll find them at farmers' markets, international groceries, and some supermarkets.

To prepare fresh beans, shell, wash, and pick through them, discarding any that are discolored, misshapen, or broken. (Favas also require peeling, see page 407). Put them in a pot with a tight-fitting lid and enough water to cover by no more than 2 inches. Bring to a boil, then lower the heat so they bubble gently, partially cover, and cook for 20 minutes or so before you start testing for doneness; don't add salt until they start getting tender. (You can also steam them over an inch or so of water or microwave in a covered container with a little water.) Frozen beans can be cooked without thawing; they'll take about the same amount of time.

Fresh Favas with Croutons

MAKES: 4 servings
TIME: 30 minutes

Fresh fava beans are a springtime treat. Though the shucking and peeling are time-consuming, the fresh, verdant flavors you get in the end make the time worthwhile. Substitute frozen beans out of season or when time is an issue.

Other beans you can use: Just about any fresh or frozen bean you can find will be delicious—limas, edamame, black-eyed peas, or cranberry beans.

¼ cup extra virgin olive oil

8 ounces bread (about 4 thick slices), preferably day-old, cubed

3 cups fresh fava beans (about 3 pounds in pods), shelled, blanched, and peeled (see page 426), or frozen

Salt and freshly ground black pepper

2 tablespoons freshly squeezed lemon juice

Chopped fresh parsley leaves for garnish

1 Put half the oil in a skillet over medium heat. When hot, add the croutons and cook, stirring frequently, until golden brown, about 5 minutes.

2 Add the remaining olive oil and the favas and sprinkle with salt and pepper; cook for about 2 minutes. Stir in the lemon juice, then taste and adjust the seasoning. Garnish with parsley and serve immediately.

Herbed Fresh Favas with Croutons. Use whatever fresh herb you have on hand: Add 2 to 3 tablespoons chopped fresh herbs, like dill, basil, mint, chives, or chervil; or add a dollop of any of the pestos or herb pastes on pages 27–31.

Fresh Favas with Feta and Croutons. Perfect over orzo: In Step 2, add ½ cup or more crumbled feta cheese along with the lemon juice and sprinkle with chopped fresh marjoram or oregano leaves.

Beans in a Pot

Here's how to cook dried beans from scratch so that they absorb the flavor of their cooking liquid. From simple but killer preparations like Chickpeas in Their Own Broth (page 430) to Red Beans with Meat (page 434), these satisfying dishes can be adjusted so that they're vegetarian or contain so much meat that the beans become the backdrop.

Most are simmered on the stove, though some are oven braised. None require much attention once they get going; all can be made ahead and reheat beautifully, though garnishes should be reserved for right before serving.

 Fast   Make Ahead   Vegetarian

White Beans, Tuscan Style

MAKES: 6 to 8 servings

TIME: 1 to 2 hours, largely unattended

There are two approaches here: Let the beans keep their shape or cook them almost to death so they become creamy. I prefer the latter but can appreciate both. Serve these hot, warm, or at room temperature and toss with a bit of cooked small pasta (like orecchiette) or greens (like cabbage) for lunch or dinner. These reheat perfectly too; just add a bit of water if the beans are too dry and add some fresh garlic and olive oil at the end if you can.

1 pound dried cannellini or other white beans, washed, picked over, and soaked if you like

20 fresh sage leaves or 1 tablespoon dried sage

10 cloves garlic, peeled

Salt and freshly ground black pepper

2 tablespoons extra virgin olive oil, or more to taste

Chopped fresh parsley leaves for garnish (optional)

1 Put the beans in a large pot with water to cover and bring to a boil. Add the sage and 6 cloves of the garlic and lower the heat so the beans bubble steadily but not violently. Cover loosely. Cook, stirring occasionally, until the beans begin to soften; add a good sprinkling of salt and pepper. Continue to cook until the beans are very tender, anywhere from 30 minutes to an hour, depending on the type of bean and whether you soaked the beans, adding water if the beans dry out.

2 Drain the cooking liquid if necessary. Mince the remaining garlic and add it; cook for about 10 minutes, until the minced garlic has mellowed a bit. Taste and adjust the seasoning, stir in the olive oil, garnish with parsley if you like, and serve.

White Beans and Sausage. You might call this franks and beans; in any case, it's good with a cup or so of finely chopped cabbage or kale added at the same time as the sausage: While the beans cook, cut into 1-inch pieces from ½ to 1 pound good Italian sausage, sweet or hot. Brown well in a skillet, with no added fat. As the beans become tender, add the sausage pieces and proceed with the recipe.

White Beans and Tomatoes. With or without sausages: Add 2 cups chopped tomato (canned is fine; don't bother to drain) after the beans begin to become tender. Proceed with the recipe. If you have good fresh tomatoes, dice about a cup and stir them in with the minced garlic.

White Beans and Shrimp. An excellent combination and no more difficult than the basic recipe; also good with tomatoes, as in the preceding variation, and with a couple cups of cooked small pasta added at the last minute: Add about 1 pound small peeled shrimp (or use larger shrimp, cut up) to the beans along with the minced garlic.

Beans and Greens

MAKES: 4 servings

TIME: 1 to 2½ hours, depending on the bean

I never tire of this combination, especially since there are so many possible variations (be sure to see "Bean, Green, and Pasta Combos," page 422, too). Add the greens after the beans are almost done so the beans are creamy and the greens silky without disintegrating.

Start with cooked or canned beans here if you prefer; cook them with the greens, chop the onion, and omit the bay leaf and clove.

Other beans you can use: any white or ivory bean, including soybeans.

Other greens you can use: escarole, romaine, any cabbage, mustard or turnip greens, kale or collards, spinach, bok choy, arugula, watercress.

8 ounces dried white beans or chickpeas, washed, picked over, and soaked if you have time

1 medium onion, unpeeled

1 bay leaf

1 clove

Salt and freshly ground black pepper

1 bunch (about 1 1/2 pounds) broccoli raab or other greens, with no stem over 1/4 inch thick, well washed and roughly chopped

1 tablespoon minced garlic, or more to taste

2 tablespoons extra virgin olive oil, or more to taste

1/2 cup freshly grated Parmesan cheese or Fried Bread Crumbs (page 876) or both for garnish

❶ Put the beans in a large pot with water to cover and bring to a boil over high heat. Cut a slit in the onion and insert the bay leaf; insert the clove and put the onion in the pot. Adjust the heat so that the mixture bubbles gently; cover partially and cook, stirring occasionally.

❷ When the beans begin to soften (anywhere from 30 minutes to an hour, depending on the bean and whether or not you soaked them), sprinkle with salt and pepper. Continue to cook, stirring occasionally and adding water if necessary, until the beans are tender but still intact (about as long as it took for them to begin to soften).

❸ Add the greens and cook until they are tender, 10 to 30 minutes, depending on the thickness of the stems. If you want a soupy mixture, add more water.

❹ Remove the onion. Taste and adjust the seasoning. About 3 minutes before serving, add the garlic and olive oil and stir. Spoon the beans and greens into individual bowls and garnish with the cheese and/or bread crumbs. Serve immediately.

Beans and Mushrooms

MAKES: 4 servings

TIME: 1 to 2 1/2 hours, depending on the bean

Ⓜ **Ⓥ**

The earthy flavors of beans and mushrooms complement each other perfectly; use dried or fresh mushrooms, in virtually any combination. You might also garnish the dish with Sautéed Mushrooms (page 313), using shiitakes if you can and getting 'em nice and crisp.

Other beans you can use: any white or pink beans or green or brown lentils.

8 ounces dried pink or cranberry beans, washed, picked over, and soaked if you have time

2 ounces dried porcini mushrooms, or more if you like

1 medium onion, unpeeled

1 bay leaf

Salt and freshly ground black pepper

1 tablespoon minced garlic, or more to taste

1 tablespoon chopped fresh sage leaves, or dried sage

1/4 cup extra virgin olive oil or melted butter

❶ Put the beans in a large pot with water to cover and bring to a boil over high heat. Meanwhile, soak the mushrooms in hot water to cover. Cut a slit in the onion, insert the bay leaf, and put the onion in the pot. Adjust the heat so that the mixture bubbles gently; cover partially and cook, stirring occasionally.

❷ When the mushrooms are soft, drain them, reserving the liquid. Squeeze them dry, trim away any hard spots, and chop them. When the beans begin to soften (anywhere from 30 minutes to an hour, depending on the type of bean and whether you soaked the beans), sprinkle with lots of salt and pepper and stir in the reserved mushroom-soaking liquid. Continue to cook, stirring occasionally, until the beans are tender but still intact (about as long as it took them to begin to soften). Add the mushrooms and cook for 10 to 15 minutes more.

❸ Remove the onion. Taste and adjust the seasoning. About 3 minutes before serving, add the garlic, sage, and olive oil or butter, stir, and serve.

Beans with Shiitakes. The shiitakes add complexity: Replace the dried porcini with about 8 ounces fresh shiitakes, stems removed. Substitute rosemary or thyme for the sage.

Ⓕ Fast   **Ⓜ** Make Ahead   **Ⓥ** Vegetarian

Flageolets with Morels. Quite fancy and nice; dried or fresh morels are good here, as is a touch of cream added at the end: Use flageolets and morels instead of the cranberry beans and porcini. If you're using fresh morels, use about 8 ounces, cleaned and halved, skip Step 2, and use Mushroom Stock (page 157) to replace the mushroom-soaking liquid in Step 2. Replace the sage with tarragon or chervil and use the melted butter instead of the olive oil.

Chili non Carne

MAKES: 6 to 8 servings

TIME: About 2 hours, largely unattended

Chili means different things to different people; I think of it as slow-cooked red beans seasoned with cumin and chiles, though some insist that chili should be made with meat and few or even no beans. To me, at that point you've entered the realm of cassoulet (see page 186), though the second variation includes meat.

Other beans you can use: red or pink beans are traditional, but you can also use cannellini or other white beans alone or in combination.

1 pound dried pinto beans, washed, picked over, and soaked if you like

1 whole onion, unpeeled, plus 1 small onion, minced

Salt and freshly ground black pepper

1 cup bean-cooking liquid, vegetable stock (to make your own, see pages 157–159), or water

1 fresh or dried hot chile, seeded and minced, or to taste (optional)

1 teaspoon ground cumin, or to taste (optional)

1 teaspoon minced fresh oregano leaves or ½ teaspoon dried oregano (optional)

1 tablespoon minced garlic

Chopped fresh cilantro for garnish

❶ Put the beans in a large pot with water to cover and bring to a boil over high heat, skimming the foam if necessary. Add the whole onion. Adjust the heat so the beans bubble steadily but not violently and cover loosely.

❷ When the beans begin to soften (30 minutes to an hour, depending on the type of bean and whether or not you soaked the beans), season with salt and pepper. Continue to cook, stirring occasionally and adding water if necessary, until the beans are quite tender but still intact (about as long as it took them to begin to soften).

❸ Drain the beans, reserving the cooking liquid if you choose to use it. Discard the onion and add all the remaining ingredients except the cilantro. Turn the heat to medium and bring to a boil. Cover and turn the heat down to low.

❹ Cook, stirring occasionally and adding more liquid if necessary, until the beans are very tender and the flavors have mellowed, about 15 minutes. Taste, adjust the seasoning, and garnish with cilantro. Serve with rice, crackers, or tortilla chips and bottled hot sauce.

Chili with Tomatoes. This simple addition makes a big difference; you might also add ¼ teaspoon or so of ground cinnamon: Substitute 2 cups peeled, seeded, and chopped tomato (canned is fine; don't bother to drain) for the bean or other liquid. Cook carefully, adding a little more liquid if needed. Top with freshly grated cheddar or other semihard cheese if you like.

Chili con Carne. Try this with the preceding variation: While the beans are cooking, put 1 tablespoon neutral oil, like grapeseed or corn, in a large skillet over medium heat. Add 1 pound hand-chopped or ground beef, pork, turkey, or chicken and cook, stirring, until the meat has lost its color, about 10 minutes. Season the meat with salt, pepper, and about 2 teaspoons chili powder (to make your own, see page 66), or to taste. Stir it into the beans along with the other ingredients.

White Chili. Substitute any kind of white beans for the pinto beans. In Step 3, when you discard the onion, stir in 2 cups shredded or chopped cooked chicken (grilled is terrific).

Chickpeas in Their Own Broth

MAKES: 4 servings
TIME: Up to about 2 hours
Ⓜ Ⓥ

This is just about the easiest thing you can make with chickpeas, though it's important to start with dried chickpeas (or those you've already cooked) versus canned, because they generate delicious broth (which is even better with the addition of a cup or two of chicken stock). Add bits of cooked sausage or cured salami to the simmering chickpeas if you like or add crumbled cooked sausage to the garnish. Or see the variations.

1½ cups dried chickpeas, washed, picked over, and soaked if you have time

Salt and freshly ground black pepper

One 6-inch piece French or Italian bread, a day or two old

½ cup extra virgin olive oil

1 tablespoon minced garlic

Chopped fresh parsley leaves for garnish

❶ Put the chickpeas in a large pot with their soaking liquid (or just cover with water) and bring to a boil over high heat, skimming the foam if necessary. Adjust the heat so the beans bubble steadily but not violently and cover loosely. Cook, adding water as necessary to keep them covered. When the chickpeas are nearly tender (anywhere from 30 minutes to an hour, depending on the beans and whether you soaked them), add a large pinch of salt and several grinds of black pepper and continue to cook, stirring occasionally and checking the beans for doneness every 10 or 15 minutes; keep them nice and wet. Stop the cooking when the beans are quite tender but still intact (about as long as it took to get nearly tender). (At this point, you may cover and refrig-erate the beans until you're ready to eat or up to a day in advance.)

❷ Meanwhile, roughly chop the bread and put it in a food processor; pulse until you have chunks no larger than a pea but not much smaller. Put all but 2 table-spoons of the olive oil in a large skillet over medium heat. Add the bread and a sprinkling of salt and cook, shak-ing the pan occasionally, until the crumbs are nicely browned, 5 to 10 minutes. Use a slotted spoon to remove the bread crumbs from the skillet and drain them on paper towels.

❸ Warm the chickpeas in their broth if necessary; add the garlic and add a good sprinkling of salt and pep-per. Top with the bread crumbs, garnish with parsley, and serve.

Chickpeas in Their Own Broth with Chorizo. Before serv-ing, top with ½ cup cooked and crumbled chorizo (either Mexican or Spanish) along with the bread crumbs.

Chickpeas in Their Own Broth, Catalonian Style. After Step 1, cook a chopped onion and the garlic in 3 or 4 tablespoons extra virgin olive oil until soft. Add a splash of white wine and a tablespoon tomato paste, then cook for a minute or two. Add the vegetables and a bay leaf along with the salt and continue with Step 2.

Flageolets, French Style

MAKES: 4 servings
TIME: 1 to 2 hours, largely unattended
Ⓜ Ⓥ

This is an elegant preparation for a luxury bean (flageo-lets are actually immature kidney beans, adopted by the French even though they're native to the New World). Use crème fraîche or sour cream for even more richness.

Other beans you can use: any white beans, from lima beans to gigantes.

8 ounces dried flageolets, washed, picked over, and soaked if you like

1 medium onion

1 bay leaf

1 clove

1 carrot, cut into chunks

4 sprigs fresh thyme or $^1/_2$ teaspoon dried thyme

Salt and freshly ground black pepper

2 tablespoons butter

1 tablespoon chopped shallot

1 cup cream, preferably not ultra-pasteurized

Minced fresh parsley leaves for garnish

① Put the beans in a large pot with water to cover and bring to a boil over high heat. Cut a slit in the onion and insert the bay leaf; insert the clove into the onion as well and put the onion in the pot. Add the carrot and thyme. Turn the heat down so the beans simmer. Cover loosely.

② When the beans begin to soften, after about 30 minutes, season with salt and pepper. Continue to cook, stirring occasionally and adding water if necessary, until the beans are tender but still intact, about 45 minutes.

③ Drain the beans and discard the onion and carrot. Put the butter and shallot in a deep skillet large enough to hold the beans. Turn the heat to medium and cook, stirring occasionally, until the shallot softens, about 5 minutes. Add the cream and the beans and continue to cook, stirring, until the beans are hot and have absorbed some of the cream, about 10 minutes. Check the seasoning, garnish with parsley, and serve.

Lentils, Six Ways

MAKES: 4 servings

TIME: 45 minutes

Ⓜ **Ⓥ**

Classic braised lentil preparations. Double the recipe if you like, because the leftovers will keep in the fridge for a couple of days and reheat perfectly for lunch or a super-quick dinner.

Other beans you can use: lentils de Puy or black Beluga lentils if you can find them.

2 tablespoons extra virgin olive oil

$^1/_2$ onion, chopped

4 celery stalks, leaves included, chopped

1 carrot, chopped

2 teaspoons minced garlic

1 bay leaf

$^1/_2$ cup dry white wine

2 cups chicken, beef, or vegetable stock (to make your own, see pages 157–159) or water

1 cup dried brown lentils, washed and picked over

Salt and freshly ground black pepper

Chopped fresh parsley for garnish

① Put the oil in a medium pot over medium-high heat. A minute later, add the onion, celery, and carrot; cook, stirring occasionally, until the onion is soft, 5 to 7 minutes. Add the garlic and cook for another minute.

② Add the bay leaf, wine, stock, and lentils and bring to a boil. Adjust the heat so the mixture bubbles gently, cover partially, and cook, stirring occasionally and adding water if necessary, until the lentils are tender, 25 to 30 minutes. Sprinkle with salt and pepper and keep cooking to the desired tenderness. The lentils should be saucy but not soupy. Taste, adjust the seasoning, and remove the bay leaf. Sprinkle with parsley and serve or store, covered, in the refrigerator for up to 3 days.

Lentils, Spanish Style. Reduce the celery to 1 stalk. When you stir in the garlic in Step 1, add $^1/_2$ teaspoon crumbled saffron threads and 1 tablespoon smoked Spanish paprika (pimentón). Use red wine or sherry instead of white wine.

Lentils, Moroccan Style. A more heavily spiced dish: Double the onion and omit the celery, carrot, and wine. In Step 1, with the garlic, add 1 teaspoon each ground turmeric, ground cinnamon, and ground cumin. Replace 1 cup of the stock with $1^1/_2$ cups chopped ripe tomato with its juices. Proceed with the recipe and garnish with chopped fresh cilantro leaves.

Lentils with Roasted Winter Squash. Omit the celery and carrot. Add any medium winter squash, like acorn, butternut, kabocha, or turban, peeled, seeded, and cut into 1- to 2-inch cubes (about 2 cups); toss it in olive oil to coat and roast it on a baking sheet in a 375°F oven until tender and caramelized. (See page 367 for more details on roasting squash.) Add the squash to the lentils in the last 10 minutes or so of cooking.

Lentils

Lentils, along with barley and wheat, were among the first cultivated foods, probably about ten thousand years ago around what is now Iraq. Today lentils are staples in the Middle East and India, where they are a vital protein source. In general, Americans aren't lentil lovers, which is a shame—they're delicious, cheap, incredibly nutritious, and easy to cook.

Lentils are classified into three groups, each of which contains a number of varieties; I'm describing only the most popular and widely available here:

Brown Lentils are most commonly available (check any supermarket), have darker seed coats—ranging from brown to black—and generally hold their shape during cooking.

* Spanish Brown. Spanish Pardina, Continental, Indian Brown, Egyptian, German: Your basic lentil, found in every supermarket. Dull, light brownish green in color, flat, with an earthy, slightly peppery flavor; will fall apart if overcooked.
* Black Beluga. Beluga, Petite Beluga: Small, rounded, and jet black—they look a little like caviar—they take on a shiny green-black color when cooked. They hold their shape well and have a rich earthy flavor and a soft texture. Not unlike lentilles du Puy, right.
* Marrone: A flat tan lentil with an earthy and nutty flavor.

Green Lentils (mostly French Green and Lentilles du Puy) have glossy dark green to green-brown seed coats and hold up well to cooking but generally take the longest to cook. You're more likely to find these lentils at specialty markets.

* Lentilles du Puy. Le Puy Lentils, French Green du Puy: The most revered lentil for its robust earthy flavor and ability to hold its shape in cooking. True lentilles du Puy are grown only in Puy, France.
* French Green: A (usually) U.S.–grown version of lentilles du Puy, at about half the price. They vary in color from slate to dark green, are rounded in shape, and have an earthy and peppery flavor.

Red Lentils—usually orange—are most often peeled and split and found by their Indian names: masoor (or masar) or just plain dal. These are super quick cooking (like 15 minutes), and tend to fall apart when tender. Despite their being the world's most popular lentil, you may have to go to an Indian or Middle Eastern market to find them (they may be whole or split). They are used in many dals—see Simplest Dal, page 433.

* Red Chief: Peeled and varying from red to salmon colored. Quick cooking, with a mild, earthy flavor.
* Crimson, Petite Crimson: Small, extremely quick-cooking. They fall apart completely, making them good for thickening soups and stews.
* Petite Golden: Small, peeled, and golden-yellow in color; they're rounder in shape and don't fall apart as easily as other red lentils.
* Canary, Sutter's Gold: A hard-to-find peachy-yellow peeled lentil; quick cooking and, if not overcooked, can hold their shape.

 Fast   Make Ahead   V Vegetarian

Lentils with Parsnips. A super fall or winter dish; add a bit of cream for extra richness: Replace the celery and carrot with about 2 cups peeled and chopped parsnips and eliminate the garlic. Proceed with the recipe, stirring in ¼ cup cream during the last couple minutes of cooking if you like; sprinkle with nutmeg just before serving.

Lentils with Bacon. Reduce the celery to 1 stalk; reduce the olive oil to 1 tablespoon. Cut 4 ounces of slab bacon into small cubes. In Step 1, put the oil and bacon in the pot over medium heat. Cook, stirring occasionally, until nicely browned, about 10 minutes. Remove the bacon with a slotted spoon, leaving the fat behind. Turn the heat to medium-high and proceed with the recipe. When the lentils are done, uncover the pot and boil off any excess liquid, stirring occasionally. When the lentils start to stick, stir in the reserved bacon and heat through. Remove from the heat and stir in a teaspoon of sherry vinegar or red wine vinegar, or to taste. Adjust the seasoning, garnish, and serve.

Simplest Dal

MAKES: 4 servings

TIME: 40 minutes, largely unattended

The most basic dal, the staple dish of India. It's almost always nicely spiced and becomes creamy if you add butter or oil. Dal is usually eaten hot, but you can also serve it at room temperature or even cold, to spread on toasted wedges of pita or Flaky Indian-Style Flatbread (page 849); see the sidebar on page 434 for more specifics.

Other beans you can use: brown lentils, yellow split peas, split mung beans without skins (moong dal).

1 cup dried red lentils, washed and picked over

2 tablespoons minced fresh ginger

1 tablespoon minced garlic

4 cardamom pods

1 tablespoon mustard seeds

2 cloves

1 teaspoon cracked black pepper

1 dried ancho or other mild dried chile (optional)

Salt

2 tablespoons cold butter or peanut oil (optional)

Chopped fresh cilantro leaves for garnish

1 Combine all the ingredients except the salt, butter or oil, and cilantro in a saucepan, add water to cover by about 1 inch, and bring to a boil. Adjust the heat so the mixture bubbles gently, cover partially, and cook, stirring occasionally and adding water if necessary, until the lentils are tender, 25 to 30 minutes. Sprinkle with salt and pepper and keep cooking to the desired tenderness. The lentils should be saucy but not soupy.

2 Remove the cloves and, if you like, the cardamom pods (they're kind of fun to eat, though). Stir in the butter or oil if you're using it. Taste and adjust the seasoning, then garnish with cilantro and serve.

Dal with Rhubarb. The rhubarb almost dissolves into this, leaving behind its trademark flavor: To the pot along with the other ingredients, add 3 or 4 stalks rhubarb, strings removed (see page 404) and chopped.

Dal with Radish. Crunchy: Peel and cut 1 large daikon radish into large chunks (about 2 cups). You can also use smaller white or red radishes. Add it to the pot along with the other ingredients.

Dal with Celery Root. Peel, chop, and add 1 medium celery root (or ⅔ of a large one). Add it to the pot along with the other ingredients.

Dal with Fresh Tomatoes. Tomatoes add really nice color and a little acidity: Core 4 ripe medium tomatoes and cut them into wedges; stir them in during the last 5 minutes or so of cooking.

Dal with Chaat Masala. In the main recipe or any of the variations, omit the ginger, garlic, cardamom, mustard seeds, chile, and cloves (essentially all the other seasonings besides salt and freshly ground black pepper) and use a teaspoon or more of chaat masala (to make your own, see page 68).

Red Beans with Meat

MAKES: 6 to 8 servings

TIME: About 2 hours, largely unattended

A pot of beans flavored with meat—sometimes just what you want.

Other beans you can use: any white or pink beans.

1 pound dried kidney, pinto, or other red beans, washed, picked over, and soaked if you like (see page 411)

1 or 2 meaty smoked ham hocks, a chunk of bacon or salt pork, a meaty ham bone, or a piece of smoked turkey like a neck or wing

8 ounces sweet or hot Italian sausage

1 large onion, chopped

1 red bell pepper, cored, seeded, and chopped

1 tablespoon minced garlic

4 or 5 sprigs fresh thyme or 1 teaspoon dried thyme

2 bay leaves

1/4 teaspoon ground allspice

1 1/2 cups chopped tomato (canned is fine; include the juices)

Salt and freshly ground black pepper

Chopped fresh parsley or cilantro leaves for garnish

Tabasco or other hot sauce (optional)

1 Put the beans in a large pot with water to cover and bring to a boil over high heat, skimming the foam if necessary. Add the ham hock(s) and turn the heat down so the beans simmer. Cover loosely and stir very occasionally, adding water if necessary.

2 Meanwhile, put the sausage in a large skillet over medium heat. Cook, turning occasionally and pricking the sausage a few times to release its fat. When the sausage is nicely browned, after about 10 minutes, remove it; don't worry about whether it is done. Cut it into small chunks.

3 Cook the onion, bell pepper, and garlic in the sausage fat, stirring frequently, until the pepper is softened, about 10 minutes. Remove with a slotted spoon. Return the sausage to the skillet and cook, turning occasionally, until the chunks are browned all over, about 5 minutes. Return the vegetables to the pan, along with the thyme, bay leaves, allspice, and tomato. Turn the heat down to medium-low and cook, stirring, until the tomato breaks up, 10 to 15 minutes.

4 When the meat in the beans is very soft, remove it. When it is cool enough to handle, chop all the meat and return it to the pot, along with the sausage and vegetable mixture. Cook, until the beans are very tender; this could

F Fast   **M** Make Ahead   **V** Vegetarian

take anywhere from 30 minutes to almost 2 hours, depending on whether you soaked them. Remove and discard the bay leaves. Taste and add salt and pepper if necessary. Garnish with parsley and serve, passing Tabasco at the table.

Vegetarian Red Beans. Obviously, omit the meat. Start the beans as directed. Double the amounts of onion and pepper and add 2 chopped celery stalks. Cook the garlic and vegetables over medium heat in 2 tablespoons olive or other oil until softened, about 10 minutes. Add the thyme, bay leaves, and allspice or use 1 tablespoon chili powder (to make your own, see page 66), or to taste. Then add 2 cups chopped tomato and cook as directed. Pour this mixture into the beans and adjust the seasoning as necessary. Garnish and serve, passing Tabasco at the table.

Black-Eyed Peas, Southern Style

MAKES: 6 to 8 servings
TIME: At least 2 hours, largely unattended

Traditionally served on New Year's Day, along with a pile of collard greens. You might add some chopped collards to the pot, right from the start, and cook them until very soft—"to death," as some of my southern friends say.

Black-eyed peas are often sold frozen, and they're good, but the dried ones don't take long to cook.

1 pound dried black-eyed peas, washed, picked over, and soaked if you like

3 or 4 meaty smoked ham hocks or a meaty ham bone

2 large onions, chopped

About ½ teaspoon freshly ground black pepper

Salt and freshly ground black pepper

Red or white wine vinegar, to taste

Tabasco sauce (optional)

❶ Put the peas in a large pot with water to cover and bring to a boil over high heat, skimming the foam if necessary. Add the ham hocks, onions, and pepper. Turn the heat down so the beans simmer. Cover loosely and stir very occasionally, adding water if necessary.

❷ When the meat in the beans is very soft—at least an hour and a half later—remove it. When it is cool enough to handle, chop all the meat and return it to the pot, along with some salt if necessary.

❸ Continue to cook until the beans are very tender, 10 to 20 minutes longer. Drain if necessary and season with salt, pepper, vinegar, and Tabasco or other hot sauce if you like. Serve hot or at room temperature.

Rice and Beans

Rice and beans are among the most important culinary marriages. The combination is cheap, provides good protein, and doesn't take a lot of work. And you don't even really need a recipe: Take any well-seasoned bean dish, even leftovers, and serve it with any well-prepared rice.

Nevertheless, it's worth knowing some of the wonderful traditional preparations that are slightly more elaborate. These are my favorites.

Black Beans and White Rice, Spanish Style

Moros y Cristianos

MAKES: 4 to 6 servings
TIME: About 2 hours, largely unattended

One of the best rice-and-bean dishes. The technique of semipuréeing the half-cooked beans and adding the rice allows the bean flavor to really penetrate the rice. Throw it in the oven and an hour later you have a one-pot meal with an appealingly crisp crust.

2 tablespoons extra virgin olive oil

1 medium onion, finely chopped

1 red or yellow bell pepper, cored, seeded, and chopped

1 tablespoon minced garlic

3/4 cup dried black beans, washed, picked over, and soaked if you have time

1 1/2 cups long-grain rice

1 cup chopped tomato (canned is fine; include the juices)

Salt and freshly ground black pepper

1/2 cup chopped fresh parsley or fresh cilantro leaves

❶ Put the oil in a large ovenproof pot over medium heat. When hot, add the onion, bell pepper, and garlic and cook, stirring occasionally, until the onion is soft, about 5 minutes. Add the beans and cover with water. Bring to a boil, then turn the heat down to low so that the mixture bubbles gently. Cover loosely and cook, stirring occasionally and adding water if necessary, until the beans are about half-done—softening but still tough in the middle—about 40 minutes (an hour or more if you didn't soak the beans at all). Heat the oven to 350°F.

❷ Use an immersion blender or a potato masher to semipurée the beans in the pot (leave at least half unpuréed).

❸ Stir in the rice, tomato, and a good amount of salt and pepper. (If you don't want a crust to develop, cover the pot.) Bake in the oven until the rice and beans are tender, about an hour, adding a little water if needed. Taste and season with salt and pepper. Sprinkle with parsley and serve or store, covered, in the refrigerator for up to 2 days (reheat and stir in a little water and olive oil just before serving).

Baked Rice and White Beans, Tuscan Style. Omit the onion and tomato; the bell pepper is optional: Substitute white beans (like cannellini, navy, or Great Northern) for the black and add 2 to 3 tablespoons chopped fresh sage leaves (or just under 1 tablespoon dried) in Step 1. Proceed with the recipe and drizzle with good extra virgin olive oil just before serving.

Baked Rice and Red Kidney Beans, Jamaican Style. With coconut milk, irresistible: Replace the bell pepper with a fresh hot chile, the black beans with red kidney beans, and a 14-ounce can unsweetened coconut milk for the tomato. In Step 3, add about 2 teaspoons chopped fresh thyme leaves or 1/2 to 1 teaspoon dried thyme, to taste.

Hoppin' John

MAKES: 4 to 6 servings
TIME: 1 1/2 to 2 hours, largely unattended

The southern staples of bacon, black-eyed peas, and rice combine to make undoubtedly our best indigenous rice and bean dish. Even northerners will like it.

1 cup black-eyed or other dried peas, washed, picked over, and soaked

4 ounces slab bacon or 1 smoked ham hock

1 large onion, chopped

One 4-inch sprig fresh rosemary, 2 sprigs fresh thyme, or 1/2 teaspoon dried rosemary or thyme

Salt and freshly ground black pepper

1 1/2 cups long-grain rice

❶ Put the peas in a medium pot with the bacon or ham hock, onion, herb, and water to cover by at least 2 inches. Bring to a boil over medium-high heat.

❷ Turn the heat down to medium and cook, skimming any foam that arises, until the peas are tender, 1 to 1 1/2 hours. Remove the meat and reduce the liquid to about 3 cups; as the liquid is reducing, cut the meat into chunks, removing extremely fatty pieces if you like. Return the lean meat to the pot.

❸ Taste the cooking liquid and add salt and pepper if needed. Remove the rosemary or thyme sprigs if you used fresh herbs. Stir in the rice and cook, covered, until the rice is done and the liquid is absorbed, 15 to 20 minutes. At this point, you may let the dish sit for 15 to 20 minutes before serving.

F Fast **M** Make Ahead **V** Vegetarian

Red Beans and Rice

MAKES: 4 to 6 servings

TIME: About 30 minutes with cooked beans

(F) (V)

You can make this with or without meat, but the coconut milk really makes a difference.

> 3 cups Red Beans with Meat or Vegetarian Red Beans (page 434 or 435)
>
> 1½ cups long-grain rice
>
> 3 cups coconut milk (to make your own, see page 389), warmed
>
> Salt and freshly ground black pepper
>
> Minced fresh parsley leaves for garnish

❶ Put the beans in a saucepan that can hold at least double their bulk comfortably. Turn the heat to medium-low and warm gently. If there is a great deal of liquid in the beans, cook them, stirring frequently, until they are moist but not swimming in liquid.

❷ Add the rice and the coconut milk to the beans. Cover and turn the heat to low. Cook for about 20 minutes, or until the rice is tender and the liquid is absorbed. If necessary, uncover and raise the heat to medium-high; cook, stirring, until the liquid is absorbed. Season with salt and pepper, garnish with parsley, and serve.

Curried Red Beans with Rice. Best with Vegetarian Red Beans (page 435) or even plain cooked red beans (see page 411). Before beginning, chop 1 small red onion and mince 1 tablespoon fresh ginger. Put 1 tablespoon of butter or neutral oil in a small skillet over medium heat., When hot, add the onion and garlic and cook, stirring occasionally, until softened, about a minute. Add 2 tablespoons curry powder (to make your own, see pages 66–67). Proceed with the recipe, adding the mixture in the skillet to the pot in Step 2 when you add the rice and coconut milk. Garnish with minced fresh cilantro if you like.

Lentils and Rice with Caramelized Onions

MAKES: 4 servings

TIME: About 45 minutes

(M) (V)

This Middle Eastern staple is a vegetarian one-pot meal, easy, highly seasoned, and filling. Omit the caramelized onions if you're pressed for time, but they're really sensational.

> 3 tablespoons olive oil
>
> 1 medium onion, chopped, plus 1 large or 2 medium onions, halved and sliced
>
> 1 teaspoon minced garlic
>
> 1 teaspoon ground cumin
>
> Salt and freshly ground black pepper
>
> 2 cups lentils, washed and picked over
>
> About 6 cups chicken, beef, or vegetable stock (to make your own, see pages 157–159) or water, warmed
>
> 1 cup long- or short-grain rice
>
> Chopped fresh parsley leaves for garnish

❶ Put 1 tablespoon of the oil in a large, deep saucepan over medium heat. When hot, add the chopped onion and cook until it begins to become tender, about 5 minutes. Add the garlic, cumin, and some salt and pepper and cook for 3 minutes more. Add the lentils, stir, and add about 4 cups liquid.

❷ Cook, stirring occasionally, until the lentils begin to soften, about 20 minutes. Add enough of the stock or water so that the lentils are covered by about an inch of liquid. Stir in the rice. Cover and turn the heat to low.

❸ Meanwhile, put the remaining 2 tablespoons oil in a medium skillet over medium-high heat. When hot, cook the onion slices, stirring frequently, until they are dark brown but not burned, about 15 minutes. Scoop out the onions and let them drain on paper towels while you finish cooking the lentils and rice.

❹ Check the rice and lentils after 20 minutes. When both are tender and the liquid is absorbed, the dish is ready. If the lentils and rice are not tender, add more liquid, cover, and cook for a few more minutes. If the rice and lentils are soft and there is much liquid remaining, raise the heat a bit and cook, uncovered, stirring, until it evaporates. Taste and adjust the seasoning if necessary and serve, garnished with the caramelized onions and parsley.

Bean Fritters, Croquettes, and Cakes

All of these turn ordinary legumes into unique snacks, accompaniments, and main dishes, and it's amazing how crisp you can make mashed beans if you cook them right. They take seasonings and spices beautifully, and the transformation is so complete that you might not even recognize them as beans when you're done.

If you don't want to panfry, there's an alternative: Heat the oven to 400°F. Shape the croquettes as in the following recipes and put them on a lightly oiled, non-stick baking sheet. Roast until lightly browned and cooked through, turning once, for a total of about 20 minutes. They will be lighter in flavor, more delicate than the panfried variety, and quite good.

The Simplest Bean Burgers

MAKES: 4 to 6 servings
TIME: 20 minutes with cooked beans

This is the easiest and most versatile vegetarian burger to make. Use chickpeas, and the patties are golden brown and lovely; with black beans, much darker; with red, somewhere in between. Lentils give you a slightly grainy texture.

Like almost all veggie burger mixtures, these will hold together a little better if you refrigerate them first (ideally you'd refrigerate both before and after shaping, but that's only if you have the time).

2 cups well-cooked white, black, or red beans or chickpeas or lentils, or one 14-ounce can, drained

1 medium onion, quartered

1/2 cup rolled oats (preferably not instant)

1 tablespoon chili powder or spice mix of your choice (to make your own, see pages 65–69)

Salt and freshly ground black pepper

1 egg

Bean-cooking liquid, stock (to make your own, see pages 157–159), or other liquid (wine, cream, milk, water, ketchup, etc.) if necessary

Extra virgin olive oil or neutral oil, like grapeseed or corn, as needed

❶ Combine the beans, onion, oats, chili powder, some salt and pepper, and the egg in a food processor and pulse until chunky but not puréed, adding a little liquid if necessary (this is unlikely but not impossible) to produce a moist but not wet mixture. Let the mixture rest for a few minutes if time allows.

❷ With wet hands, shape into whatever size patties you want and again let rest for a few minutes if time allows. (At this point, you may cover the mixture or the patties tightly and refrigerate for a day or so, then bring everything back to room temperature before cooking.) Film the bottom of a large nonstick or well-seasoned cast-iron skillet with oil and turn the heat to medium. When hot, add the patties. Cook until nicely browned on one side, about 5 minutes; turn carefully and cook on the other side until firm and browned, about another 5 minutes.

❸ Serve on plates with the same sorts of side dishes you'd use for simply prepared meats or on buns with the usual burger fixings. Or cool and refrigerate for up to a day or two or freeze for up to 3 months.

Bean-and-Cheese Burgers. You don't have to mess with melting cheese on top of the burger, and—for the most part—it acts as a binder: Add 1/2 to 1 cup grated Parmesan, cheddar, Swiss, Jack, mozzarella, or other cheese to the mix (you can omit the egg if you like).

Bean-and-Spinach Burgers. You can leave it uncooked and just shred it if you prefer (figure about 2 cups), but this gives better results; it's great with a little garlic added: Squeeze dry and chop about 1 cup cooked spinach (you'll need about 8 ounces of raw spinach to start, or you can use frozen spinach); add it to the mix and proceed with the recipe.

Bean-and-Veggie Burgers. Many options, but don't overdo it or the burger will fall apart: Add up to ½ cup carrots, bell peppers, shallots, leeks, celery, potato, sweet potato, winter squash, zucchini, or a combination. Cut into chunks as you do the onion and grind with the beans or shred or mince and add afterward.

SHAPING VEGGIE BURGERS

1

2

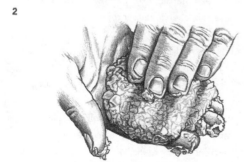

(**STEP 1**) Gently form the mixture into a ball (it helps if your hands are wet), then (**STEP 2**) press—again, gently—into a patty.

Falafel

MAKES: 6 servings

TIME: 1 hour plus 24 hours to soak the beans

Most bean fritters are made from cooked beans, but for falafel they're just soaked. Leaving the beans in plenty of water for a full day softens them enough to be minced. The spices and aromatics only add to the fabulous bean flavors, and it wouldn't be unheard of to double or even triple the amount of garlic. Serve the falafel in pita with lettuce, tomatoes, cucumbers, and other raw vegetables; with a green salad; or on their own, with Tahini Sauce (page 35) or any yogurt sauce (page 24); some Harissa (page 75) or other Chile Paste (pages 74–75) is great too.

Other beans you can use: dried lima beans; also see the variations.

1¾ cups dried chickpeas or 1 cup dried chickpeas plus ¾ cup dried split fava beans

2 cloves garlic, lightly crushed

1 small onion, quartered

1 teaspoon ground coriander

1 tablespoon ground cumin

Scant teaspoon cayenne, or to taste, or mild chili powder (to make your own, see page 66), to taste

1 cup chopped fresh parsley or cilantro leaves

1 teaspoon salt

½ teaspoon freshly ground black pepper, or to taste

½ teaspoon baking soda

1 tablespoon freshly squeezed lemon juice, or more to taste

Neutral oil, like grapeseed or corn, for deep-frying

1 Put the beans in a large bowl and cover with water by 3 or 4 inches—they will triple in volume as they soak. Soak for 24 hours, checking once or twice to see if you need to add more water to keep the beans submerged.

2 Drain the beans well and transfer them to a food processor with all the remaining ingredients except the oil; pulse until minced but not puréed, scraping down the sides of the bowl as necessary; add water tablespoon by tablespoon if necessary to allow the machine to do its work, but keep the mixture as dry as possible. Taste and adjust the seasoning, adding more salt, pepper, cayenne, or a little more lemon juice as needed.

3 Put at least 2 inches (more is better) of oil in a large, deep saucepan; the narrower the saucepan, the less oil you need, but the more oil you use, the more patties you can cook at the same time. Turn the heat to medium-high, and heat the oil to about 350°F (a pinch of the batter will sizzle immediately).

4 Scoop out heaping tablespoons of the mixture and shape them into balls or small patties. Fry in batches, without crowding, until nicely browned, turning as necessary; total cooking time will be less than 5 minutes. Serve hot or at room temperature.

Nutty Falafel. Lots of good texture from the chopped nuts: Replace $^1/_2$ cup of the beans with walnuts, almonds, peanuts, or hazelnuts (don't soak the nuts). Omit the garlic, cumin, and cayenne and use the parsley instead of the cilantro or a tablespoon or so thyme leaves. Proceed with the recipe.

Black-Eyed Pea Fritters. Street food in West Africa and totally addictive: Replace the chickpeas or favas with black-eyed peas, the onion with $^1/_2$ cup chopped scallion, the coriander with hot red pepper flakes, and the cumin with minced fresh ginger.

Mashed Beans

These are an excellent substitute for mashed potatoes. (In fact, you can vary and season them the same way; see the box on page 340.) Throughout the Mediterranean, mashed fava and chickpeas are classic (for Hummus and similar dips, see pages 93–96). In Italy, large creamy white beans are a favorite. But really, any bean is fair game, provided it's cooked until tender.

Mashed beans are easier and faster than purées (they're also not as smooth), since all you need is a potato masher or ricer or just a sturdy fork. Start with about 3 cups of cooked beans and a cup of their cooking liquid—or milk, cream, stock, wine, or water. Put the beans in a medium pot with about $^1/_2$ cup of liquid, a pat of butter or a tablespoon of extra virgin olive oil, and a sprinkle of salt and freshly ground black pepper, and turn the heat to medium. As the beans heat, roughly mash and stir them. If they begin to stick to the pan, add more liquid to loosen them up to the consistency you like; see the following list for seasoning ideas.

10 Additions to Any Mashed Beans

Just stir any of these in and heat through, then taste, adjust the seasoning, and serve. You can use most in combination: For example, add lemon zest, shallots, and lemon juice to the beans, then garnish with a drizzle of olive oil and chopped fresh parsley.

1. Chopped fresh herbs, like parsley, basil, cilantro, chives, tarragon, chervil, dill, or mint
2. Grated lemon zest
3. Sautéed or Roasted Garlic (page 303)
4. Chopped fresh tomatoes
5. Feta, Parmesan, or blue cheese (crumbled or grated)
6. Roasted or boiled potatoes
7. Chopped steamed or roasted broccoli or cauliflower
8. Cooked and crumbled bacon or sausage
9. Cooked and chopped greens, like dandelion, escarole, collards, kale, spinach, or mustard or broccoli raab
10. Chopped shallots, scallions, or sweet onion

F Fast   **M** Make Ahead   **V** Vegetarian

Bean Griddlecakes

MAKES: 4 servings

TIME: About 30 minutes

Ⓕ Ⓜ Ⓥ

Use virtually any cooked beans here. All you really need is a sprinkle of cheese, a dollop of sour cream or any pesto, a drizzle of vinaigrette, or a small bowl of salsa for dipping. As you can see from the list here, there are plenty of possibilities.

> 2 cups cooked or canned beans, drained
>
> 1 cup half-and-half or whole milk, plus more if needed
>
> 1 egg
>
> 2 tablespoons melted butter, extra virgin olive oil, or neutral oil, like grapeseed or corn, plus more for cooking the griddlecakes
>
> 1 cup all-purpose flour
>
> Salt and freshly ground black pepper

❶ Put a skillet over medium-high heat or heat an electric griddle to 375°F. Put the beans in a large bowl and mash them roughly with a fork. Use the fork to stir in the half-and-half, the egg, and the 2 tablespoons melted butter or oil. Stir until the mixture is thoroughly combined.

❷ Add the flour and sprinkle with salt and pepper (keeping in mind how well seasoned the beans were to begin with). Stir with the fork just enough to fold in the flour, adding more half-and-half if necessary to produce the consistency of thick pancake batter.

❸ Start cooking when a drop of water dances on the surface of the skillet or griddle. Working in batches, use a little more butter or oil to grease the cooking surface. Spoon on the batter to form 3- or 4-inch pancakes. Cook until bubbles form on the surface, then turn and cook the other side until golden, about 4 minutes per side. Keep finished griddlecakes in a warm oven if you like while you finish the others. Serve hot or at room temperature.

Bean Sprout Griddlecakes. Serve with soy sauce or one of the Asian sauces on pages 38–41: Instead of whole cooked beans, use 3 cups washed and drained mung or soybean sprouts. Use 2 tablespoons dark sesame oil instead of the butter or other oil in the batter, then use a neutral oil, like grapeseed or corn, to grease the pan. Add $1/2$ cup sliced scallion to the batter if you like.

11 Tasty Additions to Bean Griddlecakes

1. 2 tablespoons minced mild fresh herbs like parsley, mint, basil, chives, chervil, or cilantro
2. 2 teaspoons minced potent fresh herbs like rosemary, thyme, tarragon, oregano, or epazote
3. 2 teaspoons minced fresh or crystallized ginger
4. 1 teaspoon minced fresh garlic
5. Up to $1/4$ cup chopped or sliced scallion or minced red onion
6. Minced fresh chile (like jalapeño or Thai), hot red pepper flakes, or cayenne to taste
7. 1 tablespoon any spice blend, like curry powder or chaat masala (to make your own, see pages 66–68)
8. Up to $1/4$ cup chopped nuts, like almonds, walnuts, pecans, peanuts, or hazelnuts
9. Up to 1 cup corn kernels (frozen are fine; fresh are also fantastic added raw)
10. Crumbled cooked bacon or sausage
11. Minced anchovies

5 Sauces for Bean Griddlecakes

1. Fast Tomato Sauce (page 502)
2. Basil-Soy Dipping Sauce (page 38)
3. Simple Miso Dipping Sauce (page 39)
4. Harissa (page 75)
5. Fresh Tomato or Fruit Salsa (page 23), Fresh Tomatillo Salsa (page 33)

The Basics of Chickpea Flour

Chickpea flour, which is nothing more than ground dried chickpeas (and is also called *besan* or *gram flour*), can be found in Indian, Middle Eastern, some Asian and health food markets, and often in Italian markets as well. It's used around the world—from Europe to the Middle East and throughout Asia—and it'll become a regular in your kitchen too once you've tried it. Like chickpeas, it has a nutty, robust flavor and is instantly likable.

The large chickpea pancake known as *socca* or *farinata* (page 116) is commonly eaten as an appetizer; both it and Chickpea Fries are wonderful as they are or dressed up with herbs, spices, or cheeses.

Chickpea Fries

Panelle or Panisse

MAKES: 4 to 6 appetizer servings
TIME: 45 minutes

As good as, maybe better than, French fries: Even though they require two steps—making the chickpea porridge, then shaping and frying—they're not much more difficult and are far more reliable. You can produce them ahead of time and flavor them in at least a dozen different ways, serving them with just about any sauce you like.

Neutral oil, like grapeseed or corn, for greasing and frying

1 cup chickpea flour, sifted

Salt and freshly ground black pepper

2 tablespoons extra virgin olive oil

Finely grated Parmesan cheese for garnish (optional)

❶ Grease a baking sheet or pizza pan with a rim and set aside. Bring 2 cups of water to a boil in a medium pot. Gradually add the chickpea flour, with a large pinch of salt and pepper, whisking constantly to prevent lumps from forming. Reduce to a gentle bubble, stir in the olive oil, and cook for just a minute.

❷ Scoop the chickpea mixture onto the prepared pan and spread into an even layer. Let cool for a few minutes and then cover loosely with parchment or plastic. Refrigerate until chilled through, about 30 minutes (but up to a day, covered tightly, after it's completely cool).

❸ Put ⅛ to ¼ inch oil in a large skillet over medium heat. Meanwhile, cut the chickpea mixture into 3 × ½-inch fries (or into triangles or into rounds using a cookie cutter). Gently put batches of the fries into the hot oil, rotating them gently for even cooking and browning on all sides, about 3 to 4 minutes.

❹ Drain the fries on paper towels and immediately sprinkle with salt, lots of pepper, and a good dusting of Parmesan if you like. Serve hot or at room temperature with lemon wedges.

CUTTING CHICKPEA FRIES

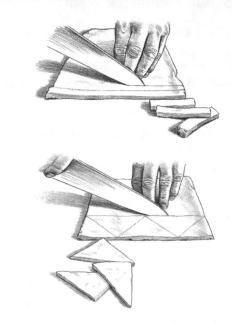

Spread the chickpea mixture on a rectangular sheet and let it firm up. Then you can cut it into fries (batons) or triangles before deep-frying.

❶ Fast　　Ⓜ Make Ahead　　Ⓥ Vegetarian

Peanut and Chickpea Fries. The peanut flour adds a wonderfully nutty flavor—serve savory or sweet, sprinkled with confectioners' sugar: Replace half of the chickpea flour with peanut flour.

21 Main-Course Bean Dishes

With corn bread (or any bread) and salad, almost any bean dish can serve as a main course. But the following are especially satisfying:

1. Bean and Tomato Casserole (page 414)
2. Bean Casserole with Hominy and Tortillas (page 414)
3. Baked Beans (page 416)
4. Stir-Fried Tofu with Scallions (page 417)
5. Black Beans with Crisp Pork and Orange (page 419)
6. White Beans with Cabbage, Pasta, and Ham (page 421)
7. Bean and Potato Gratin or any of its variations (page 422)
8. Stewed Chickpeas with Chicken or any of its variations (page 423)
9. Edamame with Tofu or Edamame with Shrimp (page 425)
10. Edamame with Ground Pork (page 425)
11. Fresh Favas with Croutons or any of its variations (page 426)
12. White Beans and Sausage or White Beans and Shrimp (page 427)
13. Beans and Greens (page 427)
14. Chili non Carne or its variations (page 429)
15. Red Beans with Meat or its variations (page 434)
16. Black-Eyed Peas, Southern Style (page 435)
17. Red Beans and Rice (page 437)
18. Lentils and Rice with Caramelized Onions (page 437)
19. Falafel and its variations (page 439)
20. Bean Griddlecakes (page 441)
21. Braised Tofu with Spicy Ground Pork (page 448)

The Basics of Tofu

Tofu has gone mainstream; you see it in every supermarket and it's on restaurant menus all over the country. And it's about time: Tofu (or bean curd) is among the most valuable foods on the planet, a nutritional powerhouse, and almost as versatile as the egg.

Tofu is nothing but coagulated soy milk, made as you would fresh cheese. It comes in myriad forms and shapes and can be fried, stir-fried, baked, grilled, boiled, braised, broiled, whipped, blended, even served cold right out of the package, included in smoothies, or used in sauces.

Types of Tofu

Your local Asian market may stock tofu in many forms. In supermarkets, you'll at least find "brick"-formed regular and silken tofu.

"Regular" Tofu
Brick, Momen, or Chinese Tofu

The most familiar tofu, shaped like bricks and sold sealed in plastic tubs with water or in an open tub. The texture is dense and crumbly; its firmness—determined by water content—may be soft, medium, firm, or extra-firm. The firm and extra-firm varieties hold their shape and are suitable for just about any cooking technique: stir-frying, baking, braising, grilling, or frying. Soft and medium tofu hold their shape when cut but not necessarily when cooked, so they're best served raw or used as thickeners or blended to replace eggs or dairy.

Silken Tofu
Kinugoshi or Japanese Tofu

Also brick shaped and usually sold in aseptic boxes, silken tofu can be as soft as custard, though it's sold in soft, firm, and extra-firm varieties. It's an excellent thickener or replacement for eggs or dairy, and firm and extra-firm versions can be diced and added to broths and soups, crumbled, deep-fried, or even gently stir-fried.

Pressed or Extra-Firm Tofu

Not to be confused with tofu you press yourself (below), this is subjected to high pressure to form a very firm tofu that has the density of Swiss cheese and comes plain or seasoned. It's labeled a number of ways but is always brown and dense and sold whole or cut into thin strips used like noodles. Whole, it's ideal for stir-frying, marinating, grilling, and in salads; cut, it makes a delicious addition to soups. Smoked tofu is similar in texture with a stronger flavor. You'll also find various types of Chinese and Japanese styles of fried tofu, sold in different packaging.

SQUEEZING TOFU

Put cut tofu between four layers of paper towels, weight evenly (about a pound, no more than two, is right), and let sit for a few minutes, up to a half hour or so.

Buying and Storing Tofu

Like all perishable products, tofu is best when fresh. Supermarket tofu (typically the kind sold in plastic tubs) has an expiration date; once opened it can be stored (refrigerated) in fresh water, which should be changed daily, for a few days. (The same thing goes for bulk tofu you might buy from a tub of water in an Asian market or aseptic boxed tofu once you open it.) Tofu has spoiled when it smells and/or tastes sour and the storing water is cloudy (though cloudy water alone does not mean the tofu is off). For longer storage, tofu can be frozen; see below.

Preparing Tofu

Though it's perfectly fine to drain tofu, pat it dry, and use it right away, you can easily vary the texture of tofu before cooking. The most important ways to prepare tofu before you use it are freezing, squeezing, baking, grilling, and deep frying. Here are details of the first two, and recipes for the remainder:

Freezing: The best way to store tofu for long periods, freezing also changes the texture completely, creating a darker, firmer, chewier, and meatier brick with a dry and spongy texture that's perfect for grilling, stir-fries, and braised dishes. To freeze, drain the tofu and pat it dry; wrap it in plastic (or put in a container) and freeze for several hours or up to 3 months. For extra chew, cut the tofu into cubes and dry them well before freezing. Allow enough time to defrost tofu before slicing and cooking.

Squeezing: Here you just press some of the liquid from a brick of regular tofu to give it a drier and firmer texture that makes it denser and easier to handle and cook. Cut the tofu in half through its equator; put the halves on four sheets of paper towels, then cover with another four sheets. Cover with a heavy cutting board or similar weight so the tofu bulges at the sides slightly but doesn't crack. Wait 20 to 30 minutes, or as time allows (even the few minutes it takes you to prepare other ingredients will help); change the towels if they become saturated. Of course, the longer you squeeze the tofu, the more liquid it will release and the drier it will become. (Drier tofu absorbs more flavors, which is especially important for marinating.)

Baked Tofu

MAKES: 4 or more servings
TIME: About 1 hour
Ⓜ Ⓥ

Good as this technique is—it's easier, less messy, and less fatty than the more common deep frying—it's relatively unknown. But treated this way, tofu becomes crusty, with an almost egglike interior. Cool, then slice or cube it, and you're ready for anything: sandwiches, salads, stir-fries, you name it, virtually anywhere you'd use Deep-Fried Tofu (page 446). (See "16 Sauces for Any Simply Cooked Tofu," page 446.)

1 to 2 pounds firm tofu, frozen or squeezed (see previous page) or simply patted dry

Salt

1 Heat the oven to 350°F. Dry the tofu with paper towels—you don't have to be too compulsive about this; just blot off excess water—and sprinkle it with salt. Put in a nonstick skillet or baking pan.

2 Bake for about 1 hour, undisturbed. The tofu is done when the crust is lightly browned and firm. Remove and use immediately or cool, wrap, and refrigerate for up to 3 days.

Soy-Baked Tofu. About 10 seconds' more work, and—for many uses—a significant improvement. After blotting off water, brush liberally with soy sauce. You may still want to sprinkle with salt, but very lightly.

Miso-Baked Tofu. Now you're adding serious flavor, but still quite easily: Thin a couple tablespoons of any miso with sake, white wine, vegetable stock (to make your own, see page 157), or water, just to brushable consistency. After blotting off water, brush the tofu liberally with this mixture.

Barbecue-, Teriyaki-, or Ponzu-Baked Tofu. Perhaps better suited to Grilled or Broiled Tofu (below), but easier, more leisurely, and not at all bad: After blotting off water, brush the tofu liberally with any barbecue sauce (see page 52), Teriyaki Sauce (page 55), or Ponzu Sauce (page 40).

Grilled or Broiled Tofu

MAKES: 4 to 6 servings
TIME: 30 minutes

It's almost essential to freeze or press the tofu (see page 444) before grilling or broiling, adding a step. But once that's done, the process is easy enough, especially if you use the broiler. (Of course if you have a grill going already, so much the better.)

Like baking, frying, and braising, this can be used to prepare tofu for other dishes, like stir-fries, but it's also good on its own. To season it more assertively before cooking, try rubbing it the same way you would meat or poultry, with chili powder, jerk seasoning, curry powder, or five-spice powder (to make your own, see pages 66–68).

1½ to 2 pounds any tofu, frozen or squeezed (see page 444) or simply patted dry, cut in half horizontally

Salt

Soy sauce as needed

Mirin (or honey mixed with an equal amount of water), as needed (optional)

1 Heat a charcoal or gas grill to moderately high heat or heat the broiler and put the rack about 4 inches from the heat source. Sprinkle the tofu lightly with salt.

2 Cut the tofu into large cubes and skewer or simply put the whole pieces on the grill or under the broiler. Carefully cook until lightly browned, then brush with soy sauce or soy sauce mixed with an equal quantity of mirin. Continue to grill or broil until nicely browned; total cooking time will be less than 10 minutes.

3 Serve immediately (whole or sliced), with a little more soy sauce drizzled on top or with any of the sauces in the list on page 446, or cool, wrap, and refrigerate for another use.

Miso Grilled or Broiled Tofu. Use any miso you like here, but any dark (red or brown) miso is best, I think: Warm together ½ cup red miso with 2 tablespoons sake or white wine and 2 tablespoons mirin (or 1 tablespoon honey mixed with 1 tablespoon water); taste and add a little more mirin if you like. In Step 2, brush the tofu liberally with this mixture and continue to cook, turning and basting, until the tofu is dark brown. Serve immediately.

Barbecue-, Teriyaki-, or Ponzu-Glazed Tofu. In Step 2, brush the tofu liberally with any barbecue sauce (see page 52), Teriyaki Sauce (page 55), or Ponzu Sauce (page 40) and continue to cook, turning and basting, until nicely browned. Serve immediately.

Deep-Fried Tofu

MAKES: 4 or more servings

TIME: 20 minutes

Deep frying is used throughout Asia to produce tofu with a nice crust and tender interior. It's faster than baked tofu, but—needless to say—a little bit messier. Fried tofu can be simply sauced and served, or used later in stir-fries, sandwiches, salads, or whatever you like.

There are two ways to prepare the tofu for frying. One is to cut it in half horizontally; this is easy and fast, but it exposes less of the surface area to frying, so you have fewer crisp edges. The other is to cube, slice, or cut it into rectangles, triangles (traditional), or circles; this takes a little more effort initially, but it reduces cooking time and gives slightly better results. Either way, pat the tofu dry before frying to reduce spattering.

> Neutral oil, like grapeseed or corn
>
> 1 to 2 pounds any tofu, squeezed (see page 444) or simply patted dry and cut in half horizontally, cubed, or sliced
>
> Salt (optional)

1 Heat 2 inches or more oil in a deep, heavy skillet or saucepan (see "Deep Frying," page 19) over medium heat to 350°F.

2 When the oil is hot, slide in the tofu—in batches if necessary—and fry, turning occasionally, until golden brown and puffy, just a few minutes; do not overcook or the tofu will toughen. Remove with a slotted spoon, drain on paper towels, and sprinkle with salt if you like.

Use immediately or cool, wrap, and refrigerate for up to 3 days.

Slightly More Refined Deep-Fried Tofu. Many Japanese prefer to rinse the tofu after frying to remove traces of oil; this practice does yield a cleaner (and obviously less oily) taste, and it's not much more work. There are two ways you can proceed: Bring a pot of water to a boil; after the tofu has drained for a minute, poach it in the water for 30 seconds or so; you can repeat if you like. Or simply put the fried tofu in a colander and rinse it for a minute or so with hot water (as hot as you can make it), straight from the tap. Drain, pat dry, and use immediately or cool, wrap, and store.

16 Sauces for Any Simply Cooked Tofu

1. Sesame-Soy or Miso Five-Minute Drizzle Sauce (page 22)
2. Fresh Tomato or Fruit Salsa or its variations (page 23)
3. Soy Dipping Sauce and Marinade or its variations (page 25)
4. Cilantro "Pesto" with Ginger and Chile (page 28)
5. Basil-Soy Dipping Sauce (page 38)
6. Thai Chile Sauce (page 39)
7. Ginger Scallion Sauce or its variations (page 39)
8. Simple Miso Dipping Sauce (page 39)
9. Miso Carrot Sauce with Ginger (page 40)
10. Ponzu Sauce or its variation (page 40)
11. Basic, Curry, or Asian Barbecue Sauce (page 53)
12. Peanut Sauce (page 55)
13. Teriyaki Sauce or its variations (page 55)
14. Dashi Dipping Sauce or its variations (page 56)
15. Chile Paste, Eight Ways (page 74)
16. Any Vinaigrette (page 199), especially the Asian-style variations

 Fast   Make Ahead   Vegetarian

Stir-Fried Tofu with Bell Peppers or Other Vegetables

MAKES: 4 servings

TIME: 30 minutes

As with any stir-fry, this one is infinitely variable: You pull what you have out of the refrigerator, get to work, and not long afterward you're ready to eat. If you make the main recipe, then the variations, you'll soon be combining at will without much more than a glance at the recipe.

- 1¹/₂ to 2 pounds firm to extra-firm tofu, frozen or squeezed (see page 444) or simply patted dry
- 3 tablespoons peanut or neutral oil, like grapeseed or corn
- 1 large onion, cut in half and sliced
- 3 bell peppers, 1 green, 1 yellow, and 1 red or any combination, cored, seeded, and sliced
- 1 tablespoon chopped garlic
- 1 tablespoon chopped fresh ginger
- ¹/₄ cup rice wine, sherry, sake, white wine, or water
- ¹/₃ cup chicken, beef, or vegetable stock (to make your own, see pages 157–159) or water
- 2 tablespoons soy sauce
- ¹/₂ cup roughly chopped scallion

1 Cut the tofu into ¹/₂-inch or slightly larger cubes. Put 2 tablespoons of the oil in a large skillet, preferably nonstick, over high heat. When hot, add the onion and cook, stirring occasionally, until it begins to soften, a couple of minutes. Add the peppers and continue to cook, stirring occasionally, until both onions and peppers are crisp-tender and a little charred at the edges, around 5 minutes. Remove with a slotted spoon and set aside for a moment.

2 Add the remaining tablespoon of oil, then the garlic and ginger, and cook, stirring, for about 10 seconds. Add the tofu and cook, stirring occasionally, until it begins to brown, a couple of minutes. Add the wine and stock and cook, stirring, until about half of it evaporates;

return the pepper-onion mixture to the pan and cook, stirring, for a minute or so to reheat.

3 Add the soy sauce and scallion and cook, stirring, until the scallion becomes glossy, about 30 seconds. Serve immediately.

Stir-Fried Tofu with Peas, Snow Peas, or Snap Peas. Use these singly or in combination: In Step 1, the onion is optional. In place of the peppers, add 2 cups peas (frozen are fine, but they should be defrosted first if at all possible) and cook until bright green and just beginning to brown; snow peas and snap peas should not soften too much. Remove and proceed with the recipe.

Stir-Fried Tofu with Broccoli or Cauliflower. Parboiling isn't absolutely necessary, but it actually saves time and effort: In Step 1, cook the onion; in place of the peppers, use 2 cups broccoli or cauliflower (or both) that has been cut into bite-sized pieces and parboiled for just a minute or two. Cook, stirring occasionally, until tender but not soft. Remove and proceed with the recipe.

Stir-Fried Tofu with Cabbage, Kale, Collards, or Other Greens. If you use no stems thicker than ¹/₈ inch or so, no parboiling is necessary: In Step 1, the onion is optional. Add 3 cups shredded or chopped cabbage, kale, collard, or other greens (mustard, turnip, cress—whatever you like); cook, stirring occasionally, until wilted and tender, about 5 minutes. Remove and proceed with the recipe.

Braised Tofu with Eggplant and Shiitakes

MAKES: 4 servings

TIME: 30 minutes

A more-or-less traditional Sichuan preparation, creamy and delicious with soft-cooked eggplant, made crisp by the addition of sautéed shiitakes. Substitute green beans for the eggplant if you like.

- ¼ cup peanut or neutral oil, like grapeseed or corn
- 1 cup sliced shiitake caps (reserve stems for stock or discard)
- Salt and freshly ground black pepper
- 1 tablespoon chopped garlic
- 1 tablespoon minced fresh ginger (optional)
- 1½ pounds eggplant, trimmed, cut into 1½-inch chunks, and salted, rinsed, and dried if you like (see page 293)
- 1 tablespoon Chile Paste (page 74), or to taste (optional)
- ½ cup stock (to make your own, see pages 157–159) or water
- 2 tablespoons soy sauce
- 1 pound tofu, prepared by any of the methods on pages 444–445 or simply blotted dry, cut into ¼-inch cubes
- 1 tablespoon dark sesame oil (optional)
- Chopped fresh cilantro leaves for garnish (optional)
- 1 tablespoon toasted sesame seeds (see page 317) for garnish (optional)
- 2 tablespoons minced scallion for garnish (optional)

❶ Put half the oil in a deep skillet or shallow saucepan over medium-high heat. Add the shiitakes and some salt and pepper and cook, stirring occasionally, until the mushrooms are crisp, 5 to 10 minutes. Remove with a slotted spoon and set aside.

❷ Add the remaining oil and, a few seconds later, the garlic and the ginger if you're using it. As soon as it sizzles, after about a minute, add the eggplant. Cook, stirring every minute or so, until it browns, 5 to 10 minutes. Add the chile paste if you're using it, along with the stock. Stir, scraping the bottom of the pan if necessary to release any stuck bits of eggplant. Cook until the eggplant is really tender, 10 to 15 minutes more, adding a little more liquid if necessary (unlikely but not impossible).

❸ Stir in the soy sauce and tofu and cook, stirring occasionally, until the tofu is heated through, about 5 minutes; stir in the reserved shiitakes and turn off the heat. Taste and adjust the seasoning, then add the sesame oil if you like, garnish as desired, and serve.

Braised Tofu with Chicken or Shrimp and Eggplant. Omit the shiitakes. Use 8 ounces sliced boneless, skinless chicken breast or thighs or peeled shrimp.

Braised Tofu with Spicy Ground Pork. Omit the shiitakes and the eggplant. Use 1 pound ground pork and be sure to use the chile paste. Reduce the oil to 2 tablespoons and skip Step 1. In Step 2, sauté the pork with the garlic as is described for the eggplant, breaking it into chunks as it cooks. Keep cooking and stirring until well browned, then drain off any excess fat and add the liquid. Proceed with the recipe.

F Fast   **M** Make Ahead   **V** Vegetarian

Grains

AT ONE TIME THE WORD "GRAINS" RARELY meant anything but a breakfast cereal or white rice; everything else was exotic or "weird." That's changed dramatically. Almost everyone has tried whole grains such as brown rice, kasha, bulgur, even quinoa, all of which are stocked in supermarkets and offered even in chain restaurants and employee cafeterias. And I'm sure you'll find—if you haven't already—that if you keep whole grains in your pantry, you use them. The more I stock them, the more I cook them, and the more I cook them, the more I like them.

449

It helps, of course, that you can eat your fill of whole grains and actually feel virtuous. (How many foods can you say *that* about?) Eating a variety of grains is the most enjoyable way not only to add lots of daily fiber to your diet but also to steer away from overrefined carbohydrates.

There is a type of grain to fit every cooking situation. Some—like couscous and bulgur—require only steeping in boiling water for a few minutes, while others simmer without any attention for anywhere from 10 minutes to more than an hour. And none of this should be intimidating. To make cooking grains even easier I've developed the closest thing imaginable to an all-purpose recipe, one that works with almost every grain: Cooking Grains, the Easy Way (page 451). Many grains are interchangeable, but most of the recipes in this chapter tell you which other grains you can use anyway.

A word about the organization of this chapter: Since most people still find rice the most enjoyable grain, all the rice information and recipes immediately follow the Essential Grain Recipes. After rice come the other grains, and at the end of the chapter are multigrain recipes.

The Basics of Grains

Almost all grains are grasses and therefore have the same basic composition: If you were to look at a single grain and work from the outside in, you would first see the bran, very thin but tough layers that protect the interior. Next comes the germ, which is the embryo at the base of the grain, and the endosperm, which makes up the bulk of the grain and provides food for the germ.

We sometimes eat the bran and germ, which contain the most nutrients and fiber, as well as the oil that makes grains perishable, but all parts of most grains are edible, though rice, barley, and oats have an additional protective outer layer, an inedible husk or hull that must be removed before being eaten.

Milling

The process of removing parts of grains to make them edible or (by some standards) more palatable is called *milling.* When only the hull is removed from a grain kernel, it retains its bran and germ and is called *brown,* as in brown rice, or *whole,* as in whole oats (or, for that matter, whole wheat, which can be eaten with no milling at all).

The less grains are milled, the higher they are in both nutrients and flavor, and the longer they take to cook. This is a trade-off and a choice. (You can precook and have the best of all worlds—convenience, flavor, and nutrition; see page 451.) Highly milled grains, like white rice, pearled barley, and rolled oats, contain just the endosperm, the white or light tan interior of the grain, containing little more than starch and protein. They're not as nutritious as whole grains, like wheat, oats, barley, quinoa, and rye—which have more fiber, micronutrients, and protein—but they're faster cooking, a characteristic that's easy to like.

Buying and Storing Grains

Though whole grains are increasingly available in supermarkets, your best shopping bets remain specialty supermarkets, natural food stores, and places that sell a lot of foods in bulk. International markets may be the only sources in your area for grains like farro, millet, and hominy. Mail-order and on-line shopping also offer a wide selection; see page 982.

Stored in a cool, dry place, white rice, for example, will keep almost indefinitely. Brown rice and other whole grains are more sensitive; the natural oils in the bran and germ can turn rancid. Since you never know how long they've already been sitting on the store shelf, brown rice and other whole grains are best stored in the refrigerator, or even your freezer if possible. (No need to defrost before use.) I try to buy relatively small amounts (a pound or so) of many, many grains and use them within a year or so.

F Fast   **M** Make Ahead   **V** Vegetarian

Rinsing and Draining Grains

Grains are cleaned in the milling process, so you don't need to pick through them as you do beans. But because rice may have been coated with talc, quinoa may retain a bit of its natural saponin (a slightly bitter compound), and any grain may be gritty, I like to rinse them before cooking.

Swish them in a strainer under cold running water or put them in the pot you're going to use, fill it with water, swirl the grains around, then pour off the water; repeat until the water is clear. You need not drain the grains well if you're just going to boil them, but you should if you're making pilaf, risotto, or similar dishes.

ESSENTIAL RECIPES

Cooking Grains, the Easy Way, the first recipe here, is *almost* all you need to know about cooking grains. Although you can find detailed instructions for cooking different grains in lots of sources, the fact is that timing is really the only significant variable.

Of course you want to add some flavor to your cooked grains; you can start with the variations and with Cooked Grains in Butter or Oil and then move on to the selected classics here, including a super-easy pilaf alternative, couscous, and fried rice (for polenta, see page 485; for risotto, page 466).

✪ Cooking Grains, the Easy Way

MAKES: 4 servings (3 to 4 cups)

TIME: 10 minutes to more than 1 hour, depending on the grain

Ⓜ Ⓥ

This process will allow you to cook almost any grain perfectly every time. (The most notable exceptions are bulgur, white or whole wheat couscous, and wild rice, which all have their own basic recipes in this chapter.) You really don't even have to measure anything. I'm providing a recipe for the method, but you don't need it: Put the grains in a pot with water and cook them until they're done the way you like them. Period.

> 1 cup white or brown rice, pearl couscous, quinoa, barley (any type), oat groats, buckwheat groats, cracked wheat, hominy, whole rye, farro, or kamut or 1¹/₂ cups wheat berries
>
> Salt
>
> Extra virgin olive oil, other oil, or butter

❶ Combine the grain with a large pinch of salt and water to cover by about an inch in a small to medium saucepan. (Use 3 cups water for pearled barley, which predictably absorbs a more precise amount of water.) Bring to a boil, then adjust the heat so the mixture bubbles gently.

❷ Cook, stirring occasionally, until the grain is tender. This will take as little as 7 or 8 minutes with pearl couscous (for "regular" or whole wheat couscous, see page 477) and as long as 1 hour or more for some brown rice, unpearled or hulled barley, wheat berries, and other unhulled grains. Hominy can take 2 hours or longer. Add boiling water as necessary to keep the grains covered, but—especially as the grain swells and begins to get tender—keep just enough water in the pot to keep the grain from drying out.

❸ The grain is done when it tastes done; whole grains will always have some bite to them, but milled or cut grains will become mushy if overcooked, so be careful. Ideally, you'll have cooked out all of the water at about the same time the grain is tender, but if any water remains, strain the grain.

❹ Toss the grain with olive or other oil or butter to taste if you're serving right away or see "7 Ways to Enhance Cooked Grains" (page 452). If you're storing it, toss it with a couple of tablespoons of olive or other oil to keep the grains from sticking together too much, then cover and refrigerate or freeze.

7 Ways to Enhance Cooked Grains

In Step 4, use a large fork to toss any of the following ingredients in with the grains and butter or oil:

1. Just-tender cooked vegetables, like peas, chopped greens, broccoli or cauliflower florets, or chopped root vegetables
2. A couple spoonfuls of a simple sauce, like any Flavored Oil (page 26) or Compound Butter (page 32) or Vinaigrette (page 199); Traditional Pesto (page 27); Five-Minute Drizzle Sauce (page 22); any Chile Paste (page 74); or Simple Miso Dipping Sauce (page 39)
3. $1/4$ to $1/2$ cup finely grated or crumbled cheese, like Parmesan, feta, any blue cheese, or goat cheese
4. 2 or 3 tablespoons minced fresh herbs, like chives, parsley, rosemary, or mint
5. 1 to 2 cups any cooked beans
6. $1/2$ to 1 cup of dried fruit, like raisins, cranberries, cherries, or chopped dates or apricots, with or without chopped nuts or seeds
7. Cooked chopped sausage, bacon, ham, or any cooked meat or fish

Making Grains Sophisticated

You can refine Cooking Grains, the Easy Way in different ways. You can toast or sauté the grain first, cooking it in a dry pan or with some fat just till aromatic, which will enhance its flavor, or you can also add spices, herbs, or bits of just about any food you can think of. Perhaps the easiest way to make grains more flavorful and nutritious is to use liquid other than water: stock, juice, wine, any dairy or nondairy milk, or a combination. And when the grain is tender, you may serve it immediately or set it aside for later; you can serve it plain, cook further in some new way, or toss it with other ingredients.

✪ Cooked Grains with Butter or Oil

MAKES: 4 servings
TIME: About 10 minutes

I urge you to cook extra grains so you can store them in the refrigerator and reheat them with flavorings in a snap. Even if you do nothing more than warm them in olive oil, maybe with a little garlic, they'll be delicious. And, as you can see from the variations, you can take this in plenty of directions.

> 3 tablespoons olive oil, butter, or a combination
>
> 1 teaspoon minced garlic (optional)
>
> 3 to 4 cups any cooked grain
>
> Salt and freshly ground black pepper

1 Put the oil and/or butter in a large skillet over medium heat. When the oil is hot or the butter is melted, add the garlic if you're using it and cook, stirring, for about 30 seconds.

2 Add the grain and cook, stirring occasionally, until hot, 10 minutes at the most. Sprinkle with salt and pepper; taste, adjust the seasoning, and serve.

Cooked Grains with Toasted Spice. To the heating oil or butter, add 1 tablespoon (or to taste) curry powder, chili powder, or virtually any spice mixture (to make your own, see pages 65–69). Proceed (you can use either of the preceding variations if you like), making sure to taste and adjust the seasoning before serving.

Cooked Grains with Onion. You can add minced fresh chile (like jalapeño or Thai), hot red pepper flakes, or cayenne to taste if you like here too: In Step 1, use the garlic or not, as you like. Add about 1 cup chopped onion and cook, stirring occasionally, until just beginning to brown, about 10 minutes.

F Fast   **M** Make Ahead   **V** Vegetarian

Cooked Grains with Onion and Mushrooms. Reduce the onion in the preceding variation to about ¹/₂ cup and add ¹/₂ cup sliced shiitake mushroom caps or other mushrooms. Cook, stirring occasionally, until both onion and mushrooms brown at the edges, about 10 minutes.

Simpler-than-Pilaf Baked Rice

MAKES: 4 servings

TIME: 30 minutes

This basic, valuable technique is a combination of pilaf and paella but simpler than either, especially if you omit the spices and go with just salt and pepper. See "15 Ingredients to Stir Into Rice Pilaf or Simpler-than-Pilaf Baked Rice" (page 461) for ideas too.

2 tablespoons butter or 1 tablespoon neutral oil, like grapeseed or corn

One 3-inch cinnamon stick

2 cloves

1 teaspoon cumin seeds or 5 white cardamom pods (optional)

1¹/₂ cups long-grain rice, preferably basmati

Salt and freshly ground black pepper

❶ Heat the oven to 350°F. Put half the butter or all of the oil in an ovenproof pot with a lid over medium heat. When the butter is melted or the oil is hot, add the spices and cook for about a minute. Add the rice and some salt and pepper and cook, stirring, for about a minute.

❷ Add 2¹/₂ cups water, bring to a boil, cover, put in the oven, and bake for 10 minutes. Remove the rice from the oven, but do not uncover; let it rest in a warm place for another 10 minutes. Remove the cinnamon and cloves (the cardamom pods are good to eat); taste

and adjust the seasoning if necessary, stir in the remaining butter if you're using it, and serve immediately.

Simpler Baked Rice with Tomato. Omit the cinnamon, cloves, and cumin. To the hot oil in Step 1, add 1 medium to large chopped tomato or about ³/₄ cup drained canned tomato, ¹/₄ teaspoon cayenne (or to taste), and, if you have it, a large pinch of saffron threads. Reduce the water to 1 cup and stir in ¹/₄ cup roughly chopped parsley or fresh basil at the end of the resting time.

Simpler Baked Brown Rice. The main recipe and the preceding variation can be made with brown rice: Increase the liquid to 3 cups, the baking time to 30 minutes, and the resting time to 15 minutes.

Simplest Fried Rice

MAKES: 4 servings

TIME: 20 minutes with cooked rice

The easiest fried rice dish, very fast, very easy, and very good. It's also an excellent way to use leftover rice. See the recipe on page 468 if you're looking for something more complex or exciting.

¹/₄ cup peanut or neutral oil, like grapeseed or corn

2 medium bell peppers, preferably 1 red and 1 yellow, cored, seeded, and cut into strips

Salt and freshly ground black pepper

3 to 4 cups cooked white or brown long-grain rice (start with about 1¹/₂ cups raw), chilled for at least a few hours

2 tablespoons soy sauce, or to taste

1 tablespoon dark sesame oil

❶ Put the oil in a large skillet over medium-high heat. When hot, add the peppers, sprinkle on some salt and pepper, and raise the heat to high. Cook, stirring occasionally, until they begin to brown, about 10 minutes.

2 Add the rice, separating it with your hands as you do so. Cook, stirring and breaking up the rice lumps, until the rice is hot and begins to brown, about 10 minutes. Stir in the soy sauce and sesame oil, taste and adjust the seasoning, and serve.

Simplest Fried Rice with Onion. Substitute 2 cups thinly sliced onion for the peppers or use half peppers and half onion, but cook the onion on their own for a few minutes first.

Simplest Fried Rice with Frozen Vegetables. Substitute a mixture of peas and carrots or peas, carrots, and corn for the bell peppers. You can even use frozen bell pepper strips if you like and probably never notice.

Simplest Fried Rice, Thai Style. In Thailand, they call this Chinese food: In Step 2, after adding the rice, stir in 1 or 2 teaspoons (or to taste) red curry paste (to make your own, see page 75). Garnish with cilantro and scallion.

Simplest Fried Rice with Lettuce. In Step 2 after stirring in the rice, stir in 2 cups thinly sliced iceberg or romaine lettuce.

Simplest Fried Rice with Fish, Poultry, or Meat. In Step 2 after stirring in the rice, stir in 1 cup chopped cooked fish, poultry, or meat and cook until just heated through.

✪ Simple White or Whole Wheat Couscous

MAKES: 4 servings

TIME: 5 to 15 minutes, depending on the type of couscous

Here's the go-to recipe for both white and whole wheat couscous. For pearl (or Israeli) couscous, which is larger,

use Cooking Grains, the Easy Way (page 451). Like bulgur, couscous is best steeped rather than cooked. From there you can use it in soup, salad, or grain recipes, top it with stewed meats, seafood, or vegetables, or dress it simply as you would any plain-cooked grain.

1 cup white or whole wheat couscous

Salt

Put the couscous in a medium pot with a tight-fitting lid and add 1 1/2 cups of water and a generous pinch of salt. Bring the water to a boil, then cover and remove from the heat. Let white couscous steep for about 5 minutes, whole wheat for about 10. (Or you can let them sit for up to 30 minutes or so, depending on how hot you want them.) Fluff with a fork and serve.

16 Dishes to Serve over Couscous

Like polenta, couscous is best served with savory stews, whether meat or vegetable. Some ideas:

1. Sautéed Eggplant with Basil (page 295)
2. Winter Squash Curry (page 368)
3. Chickpeas in Their Own Broth (page 430)
4. Lentils, Six Ways (page 431)
5. Poached Fish Steaks or Fillets with Vegetables (page 569)
6. The Simplest and Best Shrimp Dish (page 573)
7. Pan-Cooked Salmon Fillets with Lentils (page 582)
8. Braised Chicken and Lentils or Chickpeas (page 650)
9. Chicken and Fruit in Curry Sauce (page 683)
10. Chicken and Lentils in a Pot or Saffron Chicken in a Pot (page 689)
11. Pheasant Stewed with Dried Fruits and Vinegar (page 711)
12. Beef Stew with Bacon or Beef Stew with Prunes (page 725)
13. Braised Pork Curry (page 757)
14. Lamb Stew with Mushrooms (page 773)

  Fast   Make Ahead   **V** Vegetarian

15. Lamb Curry (page 775)

16. Veal Stew with Tomatoes (page 783)

The Basics of Cooking Rice and Other Grains

Cooking grains is straightforward; see Cooking Grains, the Easy Way (page 451), which covers most bases. Although any grain may be toasted (in a dry skillet) or sautéed (in a skillet with a little oil or other fat) before further cooking, there's rarely much more to it than that.

Microwaves, pressure cookers, rice cookers, and slow cookers might all seem like logical tools to turn to in the quest for faster-cooking whole grains, but simple techniques are your best choice. (Rice cookers work well for white rice because it is highly processed and consistent; but don't bother trying it for other grains.)

Grains and Liquid

Grains are dried plant foods, like most beans, which means they must be rehydrated while they're cooking. As grains rehydrate, they swell, gaining volume by absorbing liquid. The amount of time this process and the accompanying cooking takes and the amount of liquid the grain needs to become fully cooked depend on five factors:

1. The nature of the grain: Larger takes longer, and some are just tougher than others.

2. How dry the grain is: Older grains are drier than newer ones.

3. How many of its outer layers have been removed: Brown rice has a hull; white rice does not.

4. How much it has been milled: "Rolling" or "cutting" oats exposes more surface area.

5. Whether it has been precooked to some extent: Kasha is toasted buckwheat, bulgur is precooked cracked wheat, and some rice is sold "converted" or parboiled. (You can also precook grains yourself; see page 451.)

Making Extra Grains

Whole grains can take some time to cook, but they will keep in the fridge for days (and the freezer for months). So I encourage you to cook 2 or 3 cups (raw) of any grain at once. With a batch in the fridge, you can more quickly make virtually all the recipes in this chapter or use them in any number of soups, salads, and vegetable dishes.

Forms of Rice

Though long- and short- (or medium-) grain is the basic distinction, it's not the only one. Here's a handful of other potentially confusing rice terms.

Brown Rice

Any rice can be "brown," a term that describes rice that has had only its inedible hull removed, leaving the bran and germ. All the fancy specialty colored rices—red, black, purple, etc.—are just brown rice with a different-color bran.

White Rice

When you mill off the bran and the germ—of any colored rice—it goes from being brown to white.

Converted and Instant Rice

Converted (or parboiled) rice is typically long-grain rice that's been soaked and steamed before drying and milling. During this process many of the natural vitamins and minerals found in the bran are absorbed by the endosperm, resulting in a slightly more nutrient-rich white rice. Generally it's more expensive and not worth the cost.

Instant rice is white or brown rice that's partially or fully cooked and dried. Cooking time is reduced to 5 or 10 minutes, but the flavor and texture (and your wallet!) really suffer.

Broken Rice

These are rice kernels that have been busted up into pieces, which helps them release more starch during cooking. See the descriptions of sticky rice (page 456).

The Rice Lexicon

There are thousands of varieties of rice; throw in the regional names for each variety and you've got a mass of confusion. In an effort to clear things up and make this information useful, I'll stick with the varieties that you're most likely to find in the United States, which is still a lot.

Unlike other grains, rice is best grown in standing water in flooded flats of land or on terraced hillsides. China and India are the top producers (and consumers) of rice, though the United States is a major exporter.

There are two main groups of rices. Indica—long-grain rices—which produce fluffy and separated grains when cooked, are grown in more tropical regions, like Southeast Asia, India, Pakistan, and the southern United States. Japonica, the other main group, are medium- and short-grain rices (there's not much of a difference between "medium" and "short" in this case), sticky and moist when cooked. They're grown in more northern climates, like northern China, Japan, Korea, Europe, and California.

Long-Grain Rices

Generally, slender grains that are at least three times longer than they are wide. When cooked, they're fluffy and separated.

Southern Long-Grain

Varieties and Forms: White, brown, converted, instant.

Description: The most common long-grain rice in the world and the most widely grown rice in the United States. If rice is labeled just *long-grain,* it's most likely this.

Basmati

Varieties and Forms: White, brown.

Description: The best-known and most aromatic rice of South Asia and relatively (though not absolutely) expensive. The grains elongate and separate when cooked and have a nutty aroma and complex flavor. Great stuff, worth keeping on hand all the time.

Jasmine

Varieties and Forms: White, brown, broken.

Description: An aromatic rice with a sweet aroma, this Thai specialty is white, smooth, and slightly stickier than basmati, with a milder flavor.

American Aromatics

Varieties and Forms: Texmati, Kasmati, Calmati, Jasmati, Della, Wild Pecan, Louisiana Pecan, and Popcorn; white or brown.

Description: Knockoffs of either basmati or jasmine, usually without the same intensity as their role models.

Long-Grain Sticky Rices

Varieties and Forms: Thai, Sticky Jasmine, Glutinous, Sweet, or Kao Niow; white or unmilled (called *Thai black* or *purple, black sticky rice*).

Description: This is the stuff you know from Thai restaurants (in Thailand and elsewhere, it's formed into small balls and eaten like bread) and much different from plain long-grain white rice. To be sure you're getting real sticky rice, look for broken jasmine or a Thai brand, with long grains that may or may not be broken. (The black variety is black or dark purple in color.) They're aromatic, with a sweet flavor and very sticky but firm texture.

Red Rices

Varieties and Forms: California Red, Wehani, Himalayan Red, and more; brown.

Description: Brown rices that, through breeding or accident, have red bran. They're usually more expensive than standard brown rice but not much different in flavor. Like all brown rice, these have a nuttier flavor, chewier texture, and longer cooking times than white rices.

Short- and Medium-Grain Rices

These Japonica rices are fat, round grains with a neutral flavor; they're sticky and moist when cooked. They're listed here from most commonly used and easiest to find to the more specialized.

Common Short- and Medium-Grain Rices

Varieties and Forms: There are many, from Calrose to Koshihikari; they are either white or brown.

Description: Often grown in California, the grains are glossy, sticky but firm, moist, and neutral in flavor. They are good, inexpensive substitutes for Arborio, Valencia, and other short- and medium-grain rices. This is the rice associated with Southeast Asia and Japan and used for stuffings, mixed rice, and sushi.

Risotto Rices

Varieties and Forms: Most commonly Arborio, but also Carnaroli, Vialone Nano, and more; white and (occasionally) brown.

Description: These are traditionally Italian-grown rices that are now also grown in California. They have a stark white center that remains firm as long as it's not overcooked and starchy outer layers that absorb liquid and create that creamy risotto texture. Use common short- or medium-grain rice (see preceding description) as a substitute if you like.

Top 5 Rices to Keep on Hand

If you're like most people, you've got some rice in the pantry; more practiced cooks might have a couple of varieties. But since rice keeps almost forever, why not have a few? These are my essentials:

1. White basmati. The best by itself.
2. Arborio or other short-grain white. For risotto, sushi rice, and paella. Also great by itself.
3. Long-grain brown (usually brown basmati). Makes lovely pilafs.
4. Short-grain brown. For fuller, healthier risotto or to accompany stir-fries.
5. Thai sticky (broken jasmine). Not easy to find, so worth stocking. When you want it, you've got it.

Paella Rices
Spanish Rice

Varieties and Forms: Valencia, Bomba, Bahia, Granza; almost always white.

Description: A medium-grain rice that produces a creamy texture, similar to risotto, though the grains remain more separate. It has a neutral flavor that perfectly absorbs the flavors of the other ingredients in the dish.

American Black, Red, and Mahogany Rices
Japonica

Varieties and Forms: Available in various colors and often blended into mixtures.

Description: American-grown specialty aromatic rices that have a nutty and somewhat spicy flavor. The colors are deeply hued and quite beautiful.

Short-Grain Sticky Rices
Glutinous, Sweet, Waxy

Varieties and Forms: Chinese, Japanese, Korean, mochi; white and brown (unmilled).

Description: Short-grain sticky rices are opaque and plump with a slightly sweet flavor and sticky but firm texture. Often used in desserts and sweet dishes.

Bhutanese Rice
Description: A pretty, medium-grain red rice grown in the tiny, high-altitude Himalayan country of Bhutan. It has a nutty and earthy flavor and cooks more quickly than other brown rices.

Availability: Specialty stores, mail order.

Forbidden Rice
China Black

Description: Said to have been grown originally only for the Chinese emperor, this rice is prized for its black color, soft texture, and earthy taste. Lovely stuff and increasingly easy to find.

As you can imagine, many of these can be combined; use your judgment.

1. Stir in a tablespoon or more butter.
2. Stir in a tablespoon or more extra virgin olive oil.
3. Drizzle with soy sauce.
4. Add lots of freshly ground black pepper.
5. Stir in a couple tablespoons minced fresh herbs.
6. Stir in a tablespoon or two minced garlic or chopped onion lightly cooked in olive oil or butter.
7. Top with shredded or minced scallion or shallot.
8. Stir in a teaspoon or more—just a suspicion—vinegar.
9. Add lemon juice to taste (great with butter and black pepper).
10. Mix in 1/2 cup or so grated or crumbled cheese, from mild to strong.
11. Mix in 1/2 to 1 cup cooked beans, with some of their liquid.
12. Top with a bit of Fast Tomato Sauce (page 502).
13. Stir in a tiny bit of ground cinnamon, allspice, nutmeg, and/or cloves—exercise restraint and be sure to taste.
14. Season with any spice mixture (to make your own, see pages 65–69).
15. Stir in 1 cup fresh or defrosted frozen peas.
16. Add up to 1/2 cup crumbled cooked bacon, sausage, or chorizo or chopped ham.
17. Stir in up to 1/4 cup dried shrimp or a couple of mashed anchovies.
18. Instead of some or all of the water, use any stock (to make your own, see pages 157–159).
19. Instead of some or all of the water, use coconut milk (to make your own, see page 389).

White Rice

MAKES: 4 servings
TIME: 20 to 30 minutes

The method described here will work well for any kind of white rice. It's almost as easy to make pilafs (see pages 460–462) and other slightly more sophisticated rice dishes as it is to make basic rice, but sometimes this plain staple is what you're looking for. Even so, it is, like all grains, vastly better when made with stock or other liquid; see "19 Thirty-Second Ways to Jazz up Plain Rice" at left.

You can cook rice ahead, but only 30 minutes or so; Keep it warm over the lowest heat possible, or wrap the pot in a towel.

1 1/2 cups white rice
Large pinch salt

❶ Put the rice in a small saucepan with water to cover by about 1 inch. Add the salt and bring to a boil over medium-high heat, then adjust the heat so the mixture boils steadily but not violently. When small craters appear, lower the heat a bit more and, when all visible moisture disappears, turn off the heat entirely—this will be 10 to 15 minutes after you started.

❷ At this point you can serve the rice (it will be moist but fine) or cover it, with the heat off or at an absolute minimum, and let it sit for 15 or even 30 minutes, during which time it will become a bit drier.

White Rice in the Microwave. Easy enough, especially for two servings: Put 1 cup white rice in a 1-quart measure or bowl and add a large pinch of salt and 1 1/2 cups water. Cover tightly with plastic wrap and cut a slit in the top of the wrap. Microwave for 12 1/2 minutes, or until done, then let sit for 5 minutes or so before serving.

 Fast   Make Ahead   Vegetarian

Coconut Rice. Best with short-grain rice: Instead of the water, use 3 cups coconut milk (to make your own, see page 389). Add a bay leaf or a teaspoon of minced fresh ginger if you like. Proceed with the recipe, adding water if needed toward the end of cooking.

Brown Rice

MAKES: 4 servings
TIME: About 45 minutes

Brown rice can substitute for white rice in a vast number of recipes; nutritionally, of course, it's far superior; (taste-wise, it's neither better nor worse, only different). It takes longer to cook than white rice but as long as this is the first thing you tackle when you get into the kitchen, you can still prepare a meal involving brown rice in under an hour.

1½ cup brown rice

Large pinch salt

❶ Put the rice in a small saucepan with water to cover by about 1 inch. Add the salt and bring to a boil over medium-high heat, then adjust the heat so the mixture simmers gently. Cover and cook for 30 to 40 minutes, checking occasionally to make sure the water is not evaporating too quickly (you can add a little more liquid if necessary). When the liquid has been absorbed, taste and see if the rice is tender or nearly so. If not, add about ½ cup more liquid and continue to cook, covered.

❷ When the rice is tender, you can serve it or turn the heat off—or keep it at an absolute minimum—and let it sit for 15 or even 30 minutes, during which time it will become a bit drier. See "19 Thirty-Second Ways to Jazz Up Plain Rice" (page 458).

The Easy Way to Substitute Brown Rice for White

Substituting brown rice for white in pilaf, paella, and even risotto is incredibly easy: Just precook the exact same quantity of brown rice, then substitute that for the raw white rice in any recipe. The techniques after that remain exactly the same. You get the nutty, rich, toasted, satisfying taste of brown rice and a terrific texture.

Start by bringing a large pot of salted water to a boil. Stir in the brown rice and adjust the heat so that the water bubbles along nicely. Don't stir the rice again; just let it cook for 10 to 15 minutes. Drain the rice, then proceed with whatever recipe you choose. You can even parboil the brown rice up to an hour or so beforehand.

Steamed Sticky Rice, Thai Style

MAKES: 4 servings
TIME: About 2 hours, largely unattended

In Thailand, among other places, sticky rice is eaten at just about every meal, like bread. It has substance, flavor, and chew, and almost everyone who tries it loves it. And it's easy to make, though it takes some planning. You'll find the right rice in Asian markets (and make sure you have some cheesecloth in the house).

1½ cups sticky rice (broken jasmine is most common; see page 456)

Salt and freshly ground black pepper or soy sauce

Rinse the rice, then soak it in water to cover for 1 to 24 hours. Drain, then wrap in cheesecloth and put in a steamer above boiling water (to rig a steamer, see page 20). Steam for about 30 minutes, until tender. It's almost impossible to overcook sticky rice, so you can keep it warm over low heat for an hour longer or even more. (You can even cook the rice in advance: Keep it tightly wrapped and refrigerated and resteam just before serving.) Sprinkle with salt and pepper or soy sauce before serving.

Sticky Rice with Soy Sauce and Coconut Milk. Toss the cooked rice with 1 cup coconut milk (to make your own, see page 389) and 1 tablespoon soy sauce. Rewrap and steam (or microwave) for a few minutes to reheat.

Sticky Rice with Shallots and Peanuts or Coconut. While it's cooking, toast about $1/2$ cup peanuts or shredded unsweetened coconut in a dry skillet over medium heat until fragrant, about 2 minutes. Chop the peanuts (you don't have to chop the coconut), then toss with $1/4$ cup chopped shallot or scallion, $1/4$ cup chopped fresh cilantro leaves, 1 tablespoon soy sauce, and 2 teaspoons freshly squeezed lime juice. Toss with the cooked rice and rewrap and steam (or microwave) for a few minutes to reheat.

Rice with Cheese

MAKES: 4 servings
TIME: 30 minutes

The rice-based version of macaroni and cheese, equally luxurious.

 Salt

 1 cup Arborio or other short-grain rice

 3 tablespoons butter

 $1/2$ cup grated fontina or other semisoft cheese

 Freshly grated Parmesan cheese

 Freshly ground black pepper

❶ Bring a medium pot of water to a boil and salt it. Add the rice in a steady steam and stir. When the water returns to a boil, lower the heat and simmer the rice until tender but not mushy, about 15 minutes. Drain.

❷ Put the butter in a saucepan large enough to hold the rice over medium heat. When the butter is melted and just beginning to turn brown, add the rice and toss together. Stir in the fontina, then a handful of Parmesan, along with a bit of salt and some pepper. Serve, passing more Parmesan at the table.

Rice with Cheese and Ham. Add $1/2$ cup chopped ham and $1/2$ cup defrosted frozen green peas if you like along with the cheese.

Rice Pilafs

To make pilaf, you sauté rice in butter or oil before adding other ingredients, at the very least a flavorful liquid like stock. Yellow rice is a form of pilaf, as is biryani (see Chicken Biryani, page 654), as, one could argue, is paella. The technique is universal, and I try to cover many of the bases here.

Much is up for grabs: You can use long- or short-grain rice (even brown rice is fair game, but the technique is slightly different; see page 459); stock, wine, water, yogurt, or anything else you like as the liquid; and the herbs, spices, and solid ingredients can all be varied as you like.

One other thing that is really great about pilaf: Within limits, it can be reheated successfully, either in the microwave or on the stove. Just add a little water first, cover it, and reheat gently.

Rice Pilaf, Seven Ways

MAKES: 4 servings
TIME: About 30 minutes, plus a little time to rest

Easy, fast, and reliable, pilaf has another bonus: Cooking it in advance (slightly) is not just possible but desirable.

2 to 4 tablespoons butter or extra virgin olive oil

1 cup chopped onion

1½ cups rice, preferably basmati

Salt and freshly ground black pepper

2½ cups stock (to make your own, see pages 157–159)

Chopped fresh parsley leaves for garnish

❶ Put 2 tablespoons of the butter or oil in a large, deep skillet with a lid over medium-high heat. When the butter is melted or the oil is hot, add the onion. Cook, stirring, until the onion softens, about 5 minutes.

❷ Add the rice all at once, turn the heat down to medium, and stir until the rice is glossy, completely coated with butter or oil, and starting to color lightly, about 5 minutes. Season well with salt and pepper, then turn the heat down to low and add the stock all at once. Stir once or twice, then cover the pan.

❸ Cook until most of the liquid is absorbed, about 15 minutes. Turn the heat to the absolute minimum (if you have an electric stove, turn the heat off and let the pan sit on the burner) and let rest for another 15 to 30 minutes. Add the remaining butter or oil if you like and fluff with a fork. Taste and adjust the seasoning, fluff again, garnish, and serve.

Red or Green Rice Pilaf. Better known as arroz rojo or verde, these are Mexican versions: Use olive or neutral oil, like grapeseed or corn, and add 1 teaspoon minced garlic just after you stir in the rice. For arroz rojo, add about 1 cup chopped tomato (canned is fine; don't bother to drain) just before you add the stock; reduce the stock to 1¾ cups. For arroz verde, add about 1 cup roasted poblano (see page 330). Finish with parsley or cilantro and a squeeze of lemon or lime juice.

Pilaf with Currants and Pine Nuts. Classic: Use butter. Along with the rice, add ¼ cup currants or raisins (or other dried fruit), 2 tablespoons pine nuts (or other nuts), 1 teaspoon ground cumin, and ½ teaspoon ground cinnamon.

Vermicelli Pilaf. Break enough vermicelli or angel hair pasta into 1-inch lengths to make about a cup. Use oil or butter and cook this along with the rice until nicely browned. Proceed with the recipe, increasing the stock to about 3 cups.

Mexican Rice with Vegetables. In Step 2, just after adding the rice, stir in ⅓ cup each minced carrot, celery, red or other bell pepper, and minced green beans or whole peas. Proceed with the recipe, garnishing with parsley or fresh cilantro.

Kimchi Rice. Use dark sesame oil instead of butter. Don't salt the rice in Step 2. Just after adding the rice, stir in ½ cup chopped Kimchi (page 230). Proceed with the recipe, seasoning with soy sauce as needed and garnishing with sliced scallion.

Pilaf with Meat. A main course for sure: Before cooking the onion, put 1 tablespoon of the butter or oil in the pan over medium heat. Crumble 8 ounces ground meat (lamb, pork, turkey, chicken, beef, or a combination) and add it to the pan, along with a large pinch of salt; cook, stirring occasionally to break up the lumps, until the meat loses its color. Remove with a slotted spoon. When you add the liquid in Step 2, return the meat to the pan, along with a couple of bay leaves if you like, and finish the dish.

15 Ingredients to Stir into Rice Pilaf or Simpler-than-Pilaf Baked Rice

Stir in any of the following, alone in combination, just after adding the rice in either the Rice Pilaf, Seven Ways, or Simpler-than-Pilaf Baked Rice (page 453).

1. 1 cup seeded and chopped tomato (drained canned is fine)

2. ½ to 1 cup sliced fresh mushrooms, like button or shiitake caps, or reconstituted dried porcini or shiitake mushrooms

3. 1 to 2 tablespoons minced fresh strong herbs, like rosemary, thyme, oregano, or sage, or up to 1 cup chopped fresh mild herbs, like parsley, basil, mint,

dill, or chervil (these are best stirred in just before serving the pilaf)

4. 1 cup fresh or frozen lima beans, edamame, or chopped green beans or peas

5. 1 cup drained cooked or canned legumes, like chickpeas, black-eyed peas, lentils, or pigeon peas

6. 2 tablespoons or more mashed Roasted Garlic (page 303) or 1 tablespoon minced raw garlic

7. $^1/_4$ cup Caramelized Onions (page 325)

8. Up to 1 cup cooked and crumbled bacon or sausage or chopped ham or up to $^1/_2$ cup other chopped cured meat like prosciutto, coppa, salami, or bresaola

9. Up to 1 cup (about 4 ounces) cleaned chopped squid, shrimp, or firm-fleshed fish like cod, snapper, or monkfish

10. Up to $^1/_2$ cup (about 2 ounces) flaked smoked fish, like salmon, trout, or mackerel

11. $^1/_2$ cup or so white or red wine (let it boil a bit before adding the stock)

12. $^1/_2$ cup chopped toasted nuts, like almonds, pecans, walnuts, pine nuts, cashews, pistachios, peanuts, or hazelnuts

13. $^1/_4$ to $^1/_2$ cup chopped dried fruit (especially good with nuts)

14. 1 tablespoon or so minced or grated lemon, lime, or orange zest

15. 1 tablespoon cumin, coriander, mustard, or fennel seeds or 1 tablespoon ground spice mixture, like curry powder, garam masala, five-spice, or any others (to make your own, see pages 65–69)

Rice Cooked in Onions

Soubise

MAKES: 4 to 6 servings
TIME: 1 hour, largely unattended

An impressive and easy dish for entertaining, this will stay warm for a long time or can be kept hot over very low heat (and if it browns on the bottom, so much the better). The most difficult part of the preparation is slicing the onions, but the food processor's slicing disk was created for tasks exactly like this one.

> Salt
>
> 3 to 6 tablespoons butter
>
> 4 or 5 large onions, sliced (6 to 8 cups)
>
> Freshly ground black pepper
>
> 1 cup basmati rice
>
> Large pinch saffron threads (optional)
>
> $^1/_2$ cup cream (optional)
>
> Chopped fresh parsley leaves for garnish

❶ Bring a saucepan of water to a boil and salt it. Meanwhile, put 3 tablespoons of the butter in a broad, deep skillet or ovenproof pot with a lid over medium heat. When the butter is melted, add the onions along with a large pinch of salt and some pepper and cook, stirring occasionally, just until the onions begin to soften, about 5 minutes. Turn the heat to low and stir occasionally to prevent sticking.

 Fast   Make Ahead   V Vegetarian

❷ Add the rice to the boiling water and cook, stirring occasionally, until it loses its translucence, about 5 minutes. Drain the rice (leave it wet) and add it to the onion along with the saffron if you're using it. Stir, turn the heat to minimum, and cover.

❸ Cook, stirring occasionally, for about 45 minutes, or until the onions are very soft and the rice is cooked through; don't stir at all during the last 10 or 15 minutes, so that the bottom browns a bit. Taste and adjust the seasoning, then stir in the cream and/or remaining butter if you like. Heat through once more, turn off the heat, and let sit for 10 minutes or so (or longer; this will retain its heat for at least 30 minutes, and it can be reheated gently if you like). Garnish with the parsley and serve.

Yellow Rice, the Best Way

MAKES: 4 servings
TIME: 40 minutes

There is the right way to make this, and then there are a number of easier ways. Even the easy ways are good (see the variations), but this right here—with saffron and other spices and a couple of vegetables—is the ultimate.

2½ cups chicken, beef, or vegetable stock (to make your own, see pages 157–159) or water

Large pinch saffron threads

2 to 4 tablespoons butter or extra virgin olive oil

1 cup chopped onion

1 red bell pepper, cored, seeded, and chopped

1 tablespoon minced garlic

1½ cups long- or medium-grain white rice

Salt and freshly ground black pepper

1 ripe tomato, cored, seeded, and chopped

⅛ teaspoon ground allspice

2 bay leaves

1 cup fresh or frozen peas

Chopped fresh parsley leaves for garnish

Lemon wedges

❶ Warm the stock with the saffron. Put the butter or oil in a large, deep skillet over medium-high heat. When the butter is melted or the oil is hot, add the onion and bell pepper and cook, stirring occasionally, until the onion turns translucent, about 5 minutes.

❷ Stir in the garlic and the rice, sprinkle everything with salt and pepper, turn the heat down to medium, and stir until the rice is glossy, completely coated with oil or butter, and starting to color lightly, about 5 minutes. Add the tomato, allspice, bay leaves, peas, and stock. Stir, adjust the heat so that the liquid boils steadily but not violently, and cover.

❸ Cook for about 15 minutes, or until most of the liquid is absorbed. Turn the heat to the absolute minimum (if you have an electric stove, turn the heat off and let the pan sit on the burner) and let rest for another 15 to 30 minutes. Check the seasoning, garnish with parsley, and serve with lemon wedges.

Yellow Rice, the Fast Way. Omit the bell pepper, tomato, allspice, bay leaves, and peas: Bring 3 cups of stock or water to a boil. Put 2 tablespoons olive oil in the skillet over medium-high heat. When hot, add the onion and a sprinkling of salt and pepper. Cook, stirring occasionally, until the onion softens and turns translucent, about 5 minutes. Add the rice to the onion and cook, stirring occasionally, until glossy. Add the saffron if you're using it (or use 1 teaspoon ground turmeric), then the boiling stock. Adjust the heat and finish cooking as directed.

Yellow Rice with Chorizo. Add ½ to 1 pound sliced Spanish chorizo or other cooked or smoked sausage (like linguiça, kielbasa, or Italian sausage). Omit the bell pepper, allspice, and bay leaves and add 2 teaspoons ground mild chile powder or Spanish paprika. In Step 1, cook the chorizo before the onion until it browns; then add the onion and bell pepper. Add the chile powder or paprika with the tomato.

Shrimp Jambalaya

MAKES: 8 servings
TIME: About 1 hour

In Louisiana jargon, this often improvised rice dish would be called a red jambalaya because of the tomatoes. For a brown interpretation, see the variation. Use medium-grain rice for a stickier dish, long-grain for fluffier.

3 tablespoons extra virgin olive oil

2 cups diced onion

2 cups diced bell pepper, preferably red or yellow

$^1/_2$ cup chopped ham (optional)

Salt and freshly ground black pepper

2 cups white rice

2 tablespoons minced garlic

$^1/_2$ teaspoon cayenne, or to taste

2 teaspoons fresh thyme leaves, several sprigs fresh thyme, or 1 teaspoon dried thyme

2 cups peeled, seeded, and chopped tomato (drained canned is fine)

4 cups shrimp or vegetable stock (to make your own, see page 159 or 157) or water

2 pounds shrimp, peeled and cut into pieces if very large

$^1/_2$ cup chopped fresh parsley leaves, sliced scallion, or a combination for garnish

1 Put the olive oil in a medium to large ovenproof pot over medium-high heat. When hot, add the onion, bell pepper, and ham if you're using it; sprinkle with salt and pepper and cook, stirring occasionally, until the onion softens and everything begins to brown, about 10 minutes.

2 Stir in the rice, garlic, cayenne, and thyme and stir for about a minute. Add the tomato and cook, stirring, until the tomato begins to break up, about 5 minutes.

3 Stir in the stock. Bring to a boil, turn the heat down to medium, and cook, uncovered, stirring occasionally, until the rice is tender and the liquid just about absorbed, 20 to 30 minutes.

19 Grain Dishes That Are Good Cold or Reheated

Some grain dishes must be eaten the minute they're done. Others are not bad eaten standing in front of the refrigerator the next day. Still others reheat well (just cook gently in a little oil or butter). Here's a list of those that retain much of their quality for a day or two. (I include risotto in this list even though few people will admit to eating risotto cold just like pasta because it's heresy to do so.) You can serve many of these as cold salads: moisten with a little oil, vinegar, stock, or whatever seems appropriate.

1. Black Beans and White Rice, Spanish Style (page 435)
2. Any Rice Pilaf (page 460)
3. Shrimp Jambalaya or its variation (pages 464–465)
4. Brown Rice Pilaf with Two Mushrooms (page 465)
5. Any Risotto (pages 466–468)
6. Any Fried Rice (pages 468–469)
7. Paella with Chicken and Chorizo (page 471)
8. Couscous with Cauliflower and Almonds (page 479)
9. Pearl Couscous Pilaf with Dried Tomatoes (page 481)
10. Bulgur with Spinach (page 482)
11. Barley and Beef Stew (page 484)
12. Polenta (page 485)
13. Quinoa with Roasted Corn (page 485)
14. Kasha with Golden Brown Onions (page 491)
15. Cracked Wheat with Mustard (page 492)
16. Wild Rice Pilaf (especially the variations; page 494–495)
17. Wheat Berries with Walnuts (page 495)
18. Pozole with Pork and Chipotle (page 496)
19. Four-Grain Pilaf (page 497)

F Fast   **M** Make Ahead   **V** Vegetarian

4 Add the shrimp and stir with a fork. Cook for another 2 or 3 minutes, then cover and let rest for at least 10 and up to 20 minutes. Garnish as you like and serve.

Chicken and Sausage Jambalaya. This is called brown jambalaya: Omit the ham, tomatoes, and shrimp. Use chicken stock or water and increase the quantity to 6 cups. In Step 1, add 8 ounces coarsely chopped sausage (preferably spicy) to the vegetables, breaking it up into chunks as it cooks. When everything starts to sizzle, turn the heat down a bit, and cook, stirring occasionally, until the sausage is crisp and the onion is golden, about 15 minutes. Stir in 2 cups roughly chopped boneless, skinless chicken (white or dark meat, or a combo). When it starts to cook, add the stock and proceed with the recipe, cooking for about 30 minutes before setting aside to rest.

Brown Rice Pilaf with Two Mushrooms

MAKES: 4 servings
TIME: About 1 hour, largely unattended

You can substitute brown rice for white in any pilaf (see "The Easy Way to Substitute Brown Rice for White," page 459). But this technique yields incredible flavor, decreases the overall cooking time somewhat, and is suited to any of the variations or suggestions for the previous rice pilafs, with a bit more liquid and time.

Brown basmati is the way to go here; its aroma, sautéing in olive oil, will just knock you out. If you want to use white basmati, use 1½ cups with the same amount of liquid and decrease the cooking time in Step 2 to 20 minutes.

½ cup dried porcini or other mushrooms

2½ cups mushroom or other stock (to make your own, see pages 157–159) or water, plus more if needed

6 tablespoons extra virgin olive oil (or half oil and half butter)

1¼ cups brown basmati rice

1 cup sliced onion

Salt and freshly ground black pepper

1½ cups sliced shiitake mushroom caps (reserve the stems for stock if you like)

1 Combine the dried porcini with the stock in a small saucepan and warm it while you begin cooking the rice. Put half the oil into a deep skillet with a lid over medium-high heat. When hot, add the rice and cook, stirring occasionally, until it is extremely aromatic and beginning to brown, about 10 minutes.

2 Toss in the onion and the softened porcini (hold off on the stock) and continue to cook, sprinkling with salt and pepper and stirring occasionally, until the onion begins to soften, about 5 minutes. Add the liquid all at once, adjust the heat so that the mixture bubbles very gently, and cover. From this point, the rice will take about 40 minutes to become tender; check after 20 and 30 minutes to make sure there's enough liquid and, if not, add about ½ cup more.

3 About 15 minutes before the pilaf is done, put the remaining oil in a skillet over medium-high heat. When hot, add the shiitakes, along with a large pinch of salt and some pepper, and cook, stirring occasionally, until the mushrooms brown on the edges, about 10 minutes.

4 When the rice is tender, uncover and cook over medium heat until almost all the liquid is gone. Stir in the browned shiitakes, taste and adjust the seasoning, and serve immediately.

Brown Rice Pilaf with Two Mushrooms and Chicken or Meat. Chop 2 cups grilled, roasted, or otherwise cooked chicken, turkey, beef, or pork. In Step 3, stir it into the pan with the mushrooms when they are finished cooking.

Brown Rice Pilaf with Two Mushrooms and Tofu. Cut 8 ounces tofu into small dice. In Step 3, add the tofu to the shiitakes in the pan during the last 5 minutes of cooking. You will need to increase the cooking time by a few minutes to get everything browned lightly.

Risotto

The creamy Italian rice dish known as *risotto* is about three things: short-grain rice, good-tasting liquid, and a few seasonings and other ingredients. Few dishes are simpler once you learn them, and few can be varied with quite the freedom. Or use leftovers more readily, since what often distinguishes one risotto from the next is what you stir in toward the end of cooking.

According to the canon, you must use Arborio or one of its relatives (see page 457) to make "real" risotto. (Of course according to the canon, you must use rich chicken stock too. And stir nonstop. So much for the canon.) But I've long had success with most short-grain rice, especially the common short-grain varieties, which cost about a fifth of Arborio; try them. Many people have been scared off risotto by the claim that it must be stirred constantly. You do have to pay attention, but that doesn't mean constant stirring.

Let's just stay once you start the process you shouldn't leave the stove for more than a minute or so at a time. Because the heat is relatively high and there's a delicate balance between rice and liquid, there's a danger of scorching (nonstick skillets are helpful but not essential). Just be careful not to overcook. Handle risotto as you would pasta: Remove the rice from heat when there is still a tiny bit of crunch in the center of the rice kernels.

Simple Risotto

MAKES: 4 to 6 servings
TIME: 45 minutes

Ⓥ

If you don't have homemade stock on hand, I suggest just simmering a carrot, an onion, a celery stalk, and a garlic clove in water for 20 minutes and using that. If you must use straight water, up the other flavorings a bit.

> 2 tablespoons butter or extra virgin olive oil, to taste
>
> 1 medium onion, chopped
>
> Large pinch saffron threads (optional)
>
> 1 1/2 cups Arborio or other short- or medium-grain rice
>
> Salt and freshly ground black pepper
>
> 1/2 cup dry white wine or water
>
> 4 to 6 cups chicken, beef, or vegetable stock (to make your own, see pages 157–159)
>
> 2 to 4 tablespoons softened butter or extra virgin olive oil
>
> Freshly grated Parmesan cheese (optional)

❶ Put the 2 tablespoons butter or oil in a large, deep nonstick skillet over medium heat. (Allow the remaining butter to soften while you cook.) When the butter is melted or the oil is hot, add the onion and saffron and cook, stirring occasionally, until the onion softens, 3 to 5 minutes.

❷ Add the rice and cook, stirring occasionally, until it is glossy and coated with butter or oil, 2 to 3 minutes. Add a little salt and pepper, then the white wine. Stir and let the liquid bubble away.

❸ Use a ladle to begin adding the stock, 1/2 cup or so at a time, stirring after each addition. When the stock is just about evaporated, add more. The mixture should be neither soupy nor dry. Keep the heat at medium to medium-high and stir frequently.

❹ Begin tasting the rice 20 minutes after you add it; you want it to be tender but still with a tiny bit of crunch; it could take as long as 30 minutes to reach this stage. When it does, stir in the softened butter or oil (more is better, at least from the perspective of taste!) and at least 1/2 cup of Parmesan if you're using it. Taste, adjust the seasoning, and serve immediately, passing additional Parmesan at the table if you like.

Risotto alla Milanese. The classic: Use the saffron and add 1/4 cup chopped prosciutto (or bone marrow when you can find it) along with the onion.

Risotto with Herbs or Pesto. Along with the cheese, stir in ¼ to ½ cup chopped fresh parsley, basil, dill, mint, chervil, oregano, marjoram, or a combination or Traditional Pesto (page 27) or other herb paste.

Risotto with Lemon. Follow the preceding variation, but when the rice is almost done (Step 4), stir in the grated zest of a lemon. Stir in the juice of the lemon along with the butter at the very end. Add the Parmesan and serve as directed.

Risotto with Three Cheeses. Over the top: When you would ordinarily stir in the Parmesan, add equal amounts (¼ to ⅓ cup each) of grated Parmesan or pecorino Romano, crumbled Gorgonzola or other creamy blue cheese, and shredded or chopped fontina or other semisoft but not-too-mild cheese. Other cheeses that will do nicely: cubed or shredded mozzarella; shredded mild cheese, like Jack; any hard cheese, like Grana Padano.

Risotto with Seafood. Omit the porcini and other mushrooms. Use fish, shrimp, or lobster stock (to make your own, see page 159–160) according to the fish you choose; fish stock if using a combination. Omit the cheese. In Step 4, when the rice is almost done, stir in 1 pound of the following, alone or in combination: cleaned or shelled shrimp or squid; shucked mussels; thick firm fish fillets, cut into 1-inch chunks; scallops; shelled lobster pieces; or lump crabmeat. In Step 4, when you would stir in the cheese, add a little extra butter or olive oil if you like.

Risotto with Dried and Fresh Mushrooms

MAKES: 4 to 6 servings
TIME: 45 minutes

If you have dried mushrooms on hand (the addition of fresh mushrooms is a bonus), you can make this tasty risotto anytime. But note that any vegetable—artichoke hearts, green beans, snow peas, and so on—can be cooked on the side and stirred into the risotto at the last minute, as the fresh mushrooms are here (see the list that follows).

½ cup dried porcini mushrooms

4 to 6 tablespoons butter or extra virgin olive oil, to taste

1 medium onion, chopped

1½ cups Arborio or other short- or medium-grain rice

Salt and freshly ground black pepper

½ cup dry white wine or water

4 to 5 cups chicken, beef, or vegetable stock (to make your own, see pages 157–159) or water

1 cup sliced shiitake or portobello mushroom caps

Freshly grated Parmesan cheese (optional)

❶ Rinse the dried mushrooms once or twice, then soak them in hot water to cover. Put 2 tablespoons of the butter or oil in a large, deep nonstick skillet over medium heat. When the butter is melted or the oil is hot, add the onion and cook, stirring occasionally, until it softens, 3 to 5 minutes.

❷ Add the rice and cook, stirring occasionally, until it is glossy and coated with butter or oil, 2 to 3 minutes. Add a little salt and pepper, then the white wine. Stir and let the liquid bubble away. Drain the porcini and chop them, then stir them in, along with about half of their soaking liquid.

❸ Use a ladle to begin adding the stock, ½ cup or so at a time, stirring after each addition. When the stock is just about evaporated, add more. The mixture should be neither soupy nor dry. Stir frequently, keeping the heat at medium to medium-high. Meanwhile, put the remaining butter or oil (more will make a creamier risotto) in a small skillet over medium-high heat. When the butter is melted or the oil is hot, add the fresh mushrooms and cook, stirring occasionally, until lightly browned and almost crisp, about 10 minutes, then remove from the heat.

4 Begin tasting the rice 20 minutes after you add it; you want it to be tender but still with a tiny bit of crunch; it could take as long as 30 minutes to reach this stage. When it does, stir in the cooked mushrooms, with their butter, and at least $^1/_2$ cup of Parmesan if you're using it. Taste, adjust the seasoning, and serve immediately, passing additional Parmesan at the table.

Risotto with Meat. Omit the porcini and other mushrooms. Add 2 to 4 ounces of any of the following, alone or in combination: ground meat (beef, pork, veal, or poultry); sausage, removed from its casings; or diced prosciutto, pancetta, or country ham. Add the meat with the onion, stirring and breaking up any lumps that form. Proceed with the recipe, omitting the finishing butter.

Risotto with Vegetables and Herbs. Omit the porcini. In Step 1, add 1 celery stalk and 1 medium carrot, chopped, as well as 1 sprig fresh rosemary or thyme (or $^1/_2$ teaspoon dried), along with the onion. Cook until the vegetables are glossy and the onion softens, then proceed with the recipe.

The Basics of Fried Rice

Fried rice has many attributes, not the least of which is that it can be made with leftover rice. In fact it *should* be made with leftover rice—or at least rice that's been cooked ahead. Warm, just-made rice inevitably clumps together, which is why so many novice cooks (I remember this vividly) believe that fried rice is impossible to make well at home. But when cooked long-grain rice is chilled—even for a few hours, though a day or so is even better—it dries out, separates into individual grains, and can be stir-fried with a minimum of oil. (The rice that is delivered with Chinese take-out meals is nearly perfect for this purpose.)

Making fried rice is akin to making other stir-fries (see page 18). The choices of vegetables and other major ingredients are unlimited, but if you follow the proportions in this prototypical recipe you will never go far wrong. There are some other points to make, however.

5 Tips for Making Great Fried Rice

1. Peanut oil is ideal here, but neutral oil like or grapeseed or corn is fine.
2. If you're adding raw or cooked meat, poultry, or seafood, dice it into small pieces ($^1/_2$ inch or less) or use ground meat; add it to the hot oil just before adding the rice and cook it or heat it through.
3. No matter how much or how little garlic and ginger you use, they should be cooked in the oil for no more than 30 seconds before you add the rice, or their flavor will become too mild.
4. You can scramble the eggs separately and cut them into the mix to keep them at their most distinctive; or (this is what I do) make a well in the rice and scramble them in that, which retains their identity at least somewhat; or simply stir them into the rice mix, in which case they will act as a pleasing thickening and bonding agent.
5. Some liquid in addition to soy sauce is needed here. The most authentic choice is rice wine (which is sold at most Asian stores and keeps nearly forever), but sherry and white wine make decent substitutes. Stock is also good, and water works too, since there are already plenty of flavors in fried rice.

Fried Rice with Shrimp and Pork

MAKES: 4 servings
TIME: 30 minutes

Adding both meat and seafood to fried rice is common in restaurants and not really that difficult. If you have neither Roast Pork nor Chinese sausage, ham is a fine substitute. No meat at all is fine too, of course. For bare-bones fried rice based on vegetables, see the recipe on page 469.

1 cup fresh or frozen peas

3 tablespoons peanut or neutral oil, like grapeseed or corn

1 medium onion, roughly chopped

1 red bell pepper, cored, seeded, and roughly chopped

8 ounces small shrimp, peeled (optional)

8 ounces diced roast pork (see page 754–755), Chinese sausage, or other meat (optional)

1 tablespoon minced garlic, or to taste

1 tablespoon minced fresh ginger, or to taste

3 to 4 cups cooked any long-grain rice (start with about 1 1/2 cups raw), preferably basmati or jasmine and preferably chilled

2 eggs, lightly beaten (optional)

1/4 cup rice wine, sherry, dry white wine, stock (to make your own, see pages 157–159), or water

2 tablespoons soy sauce

1 tablespoon dark sesame oil

Salt and freshly ground black pepper

1/4 cup chopped scallion or fresh cilantro

❶ If the peas are frozen, soak them in cold water to defrost while you begin cooking. Put 1 tablespoon of the oil in a large skillet over high heat. When hot, add the onion and bell pepper and cook, stirring occasionally, until they soften and begin to brown, 5 to 10 minutes. Lower the heat if the mixture threatens to scorch. Use a slotted spoon to transfer them to a bowl.

❷ Add the shrimp and cook over high heat until they turn pink. Add the pork and brown lightly, 2 to 3 minutes. Add to the bowl with the vegetables. Drain the peas if necessary and add them to the skillet; cook, shaking the skillet, for about a minute, or until hot. Add them to the bowl.

❸ Put the remaining oil in the skillet, followed by the garlic and ginger. About 15 seconds later, begin to add the rice, a bit at a time, breaking up any clumps with your fingers and stirring it into the oil. When all the rice is added, make a well in its center and break the eggs into it if you're using them; scramble them a bit, then incorporate them into the rice.

❹ Return the meat and vegetables to the pan and stir to integrate. Add the rice wine and cook, stirring, for about a minute. Add the soy sauce and sesame oil, then taste and add salt and pepper if necessary. Turn off the heat, stir in the scallion, and serve.

14 Super Additions or Substitutions for Fried Rice

The list of things you can add to fried rice is longer than the list of things you cannot. But they basically fall into three categories: vegetables, protein, and seasonings.

Vegetables:

1. Very tender vegetables and those that can be eaten raw can be stirred in at the last minute.
2. Those that will cook in about the same amount of time as the onion or pepper (scallion, shredded zucchini, corn kernels, etc.) should be cooked with or instead of the onion.
3. Harder vegetables—broccoli, cauliflower, eggplant, potato, winter squash—should either be cut into very tiny bits, so they will cook in just about the same amount of time as the onion, or quickly parboiled (or deep-fried if you prefer) before being incorporated as any other vegetable.
4. Tomatoes are a special case: Cut them into small wedges and add just after the rice, or you will have tomato sauce. (Not that there's anything wrong with that, and if that's what you want, add the tomatoes when the onion is about half cooked.)
5. You can also garnish with raw vegetables, like cucumbers made according to the Quick-Pickled Vegetables recipe (page 229), chopped cabbage, or tomato wedges.

Protein:

6. Diced or ground meat (pork, beef, poultry, etc.), raw or cooked. Add as you would the shrimp (if raw meat) or roast pork (if cooked) in the main recipe.

7. Small or chopped peeled shrimp, cleaned and chopped squid, small or halved scallops. Add with or instead of the whole shrimp in the main recipe.

8. Any tofu—smoked, pressed, flavored, defrosted frozen; you name it—is great here. Add as you would the shrimp in the main recipe.

9. Hard-Boiled Egg (page 791) is another good option, either chopped or sliced and added right after the rice.

Seasonings:

10. Hoisin sauce or ketchup (to make your own, see page 51), stirred in just after the rice.

11. Basil (preferably Thai), 10 or 15 big leaves, torn up and added at the last moment, instead of or in addition to cilantro.

12. Curry powder or almost any other spice mix (to make your own, see pages 65–69), stirred in just before you add the rice.

13. Seaweed "Shake" (page 69) is good, as are toasted sesame seeds (see page 317).

14. Fresh chiles, minced, at the beginning, or Chile Paste of any kind (pages 74–75) at the end, always to taste.

The Basics of Paella

Not to put too fine a point on it, but paella is rice with stuff in it, often leftovers. There's no reason to get too fussy about it, any more than you would any other rice dish. First you make a *sofrito*—usually an aromatic vegetable like onion or garlic with herbs and sometimes tomato paste, fried in olive oil until it becomes a thick paste in which the rice is cooked. Saffron is the traditional seasoning, but I think smoked paprika is a great addition (or substitution) and adds deep flavors. Add a bit of chicken here, some sausage there, top with a bit of seafood, and cook it all together—on a stove, over a live fire, or in an oven—in an open pan that concentrates their flavors.

A great trick is to season paella again at the end of cooking or with a condiment like Garlic Mayonnaise (page 42).

The real deal, however, is the pan: It need not be a *paellera* (a traditional two-handled paella pan), but it should be wide enough to hold the grains of rice in a thin layer (a large skillet is usually fine). This will help develop the crusty bits of rice that can form at the bottom of the pan (called *socarat*), which are many people's favorite part.

The Simplest Paella

MAKES: 4 servings

TIME: 30 minutes

Far from a major production, basic paella is a simple combination of rice and shrimp, a terrific weeknight dish, as it has been in coastal Spain for centuries.

3½ cups stock (to make your own, see pages 157–159) or water

Pinch saffron threads

3 tablespoons extra virgin olive oil

1 medium onion, chopped

Salt and freshly ground black pepper

2 cups short- or medium-grain rice, preferably paella rice (see page 457) or Arborio

2 cups peeled shrimp (about 1 pound), cut into ½-inch chunks

Chopped fresh parsley leaves for garnish

❶ Heat the oven to 450°F. Warm the stock with the saffron in a small saucepan. Put the oil in a 10- or 12-inch ovenproof skillet over medium-high heat. When hot, add the onion, sprinkle with salt and pepper, and cook, stirring occasionally, until it softens, 3 to 5 minutes.

2 Add the rice and cook, stirring occasionally, until it's shiny, another minute or two. Carefully add the warm stock and stir until just combined, then stir in the shrimp.

3 Put the pan in the oven and bake, undisturbed, for 15 minutes. Check to see if the rice is dry and just tender. If not, return the pan to the oven for 5 minutes. If the rice looks too dry at this point, but still isn't quite done, add a small amount of stock or water. When the rice is ready, turn off the oven and let it sit for at least 5 and up to 15 minutes.

4 Remove the pan from the oven and sprinkle with parsley. If you like, put the pan over high heat for a few minutes to develop a bit of a bottom crust before serving.

Paella with Chicken and Chorizo. Omit the shrimp if you like and add 2 bone-in, skin-on chicken thighs, 2 tablespoons chopped garlic, 8 ounces Spanish chorizo or other cooked or smoked sausage, 2 teaspoons paprika (preferably smoked; see page 62), ¹/₂ cup dry white wine, and ¹/₂ cup tomato purée, In Step 1, cook the chicken in the oil until deeply browned on both sides, then add the onion and garlic and cook until soft. Add the chorizo, paprika, wine, and tomato purée; bring to a boil and cook for 5 minutes, stirring occasionally. Add the rice, scattering it in the pan as evenly as possible, and proceed from Step 2, tucking the shrimp (if using) into the top before putting in the oven.

Vegetarian Paella. Omit the shrimp and saffron and use vegetable stock (to make your own, see page 157) or water. Add 1¹/₂ pounds ripe tomatoes, cored and cut into thick wedges, 1 tablespoon minced garlic, 1 tablespoon tomato paste, and 2 teaspoons smoked or other paprika. Toss the tomatoes with 1 tablespoon oil and a sprinkle of salt and pepper and set aside. In Step 1, add the garlic along with the onion, then add the tomato paste and paprika; cook for a minute. Proceed with Step 2, putting the tomato wedges on top of the rice and drizzling with the accumulated tomato juice.

Paella with Eggs. Use the main recipe or the vegetarian variation. In Step 3, use a large spoon to make 4 indentations in the rice mixture and carefully crack an egg into each before putting in the oven.

Stuck-Pot Rice with Potato Crust

MAKES: 4 to 6 servings
TIME: 1¹/₂ hours, largely unattended

Visualize a stovetop paella served upside down, the gorgeous crust sitting on top. Made with rice, potatoes, or anything else that browns and sticks to the bottom of a pot—and given the fact that the recipe actually directs that you simply walk away (you'll ruin it if you don't)—stuck-pot rice is one of the easiest ways to get an impressive rice dish on the table.

Use brown basmati rice here if you like. The kernels will be slightly less starchy than with white basmati rice, but the flavor will be deep and delicious.

Take the time to line the pot lid with a clean towel. This absorbs water so the condensation from the lid doesn't drip back into the rice.

Salt

1¹/₂ cups white or brown basmati rice

Freshly ground black pepper

4 tablespoons butter or extra virgin olive oil

Large pinch saffron threads (optional)

1 large or 2 small waxy potatoes, like red or other thin-skinned variety

1 medium fennel bulb, trimmed and thinly sliced

1 Fill a large, heavy pot with a tight-fitting lid with water, bring to a boil, and salt it. Stir in the rice and return to a boil, then lower the heat so the water bubbles along nicely. Cook undisturbed until partially done—

white rice for about 5 minutes, brown rice for about 15 minutes. Drain and set aside. Taste, add salt if necessary, and sprinkle with pepper. Wipe out the pot.

❷ Melt 2 tablespoons of the butter in a small bowl or pot (or just put in 2 tablespoons oil), stir in the saffron if you're using it, and set aside. Peel the potato and cut crosswise into thin slices.

❸ Put the remaining butter or oil back into the large pot over medium-high heat. Add the fennel, sprinkle with salt and pepper, and cook, stirring occasionally, until soft, about 2 minutes. Remove from the heat.

❹ Add ¼ cup water and the butter-saffron mixture (or the plain melted butter or oil) to the pot. Carefully cover the bottom of the pan with a layer of potato slices. Add half the rice, then the fennel, and finally the other half of the rice. Wrap a clean kitchen towel around the lid of the pot so that the corners are on top and don't fall anywhere near the stove and cover the pot. Turn the heat to medium-high. When you hear the water spattering—about 5 minutes—turn the heat down to very low. Cook, completely undisturbed, for about 45 minutes, or until the potatoes start to smell toasty—you will know—but not burned. Remove from the heat and let sit for another 5 minutes.

❺ Carefully remove the lid and the cloth and turn the pot upside down over a large plate. If the potatoes come out in a single crust, terrific. If not, use a spatula to scrape the pieces out of the pan and put them on top of the rice. Serve immediately, sprinkled with a bit of salt and pepper if you like.

Stuck-Pot Rice with Lima Beans. Replace the saffron with 2 tablespoons chopped fresh dill or 1 tablespoon dried. Instead of the fennel, use 1½ cups fresh or frozen lima beans.

Stuck-Pot Rice with Lemon and Herbs. Instead of saffron, use ½ cup minced mild fresh herbs—like parsley, mint, or a combination—or 1 teaspoon strong herbs, like tarragon, thyme, or rosemary, or a couple teaspoons of oregano or marjoram. Use 2 thinly sliced lemons (peels and all) instead of the fennel.

Stuck-Pot Rice with Pita Crust. Like buttered toast: Omit the potato and skip the fennel layer; keep the saffron if you like. Instead of the potatoes, use 1 large or 2 small pita breads with pockets, split and halved, so they are divided into thin pieces. Use the pita pieces to line the bottom of the pot in Step 4.

Stuck-Pot Rice with Lentils and Potato or Pita Crust. Omit the fennel and saffron. In Step 1, don't salt the water. When it comes to a boil, add 1 cup of any lentils. When it comes to a boil again, add the rice and cook and drain as directed. When cooled a bit, sprinkle with salt and pepper and stir; taste and adjust the seasoning (the lentils and rice will not be cooked all the way through yet). Proceed with the recipe or the pita variation.

Stuck-Pot Rice with Chicken and Potato Crust. Add 1½ to 2 pounds bone-in, skin-on chicken parts. Brown the meat in hot oil until golden brown on all sides; you don't want to cook it through, but it shouldn't be raw either, so expect to spend about 15 minutes. In Step 4, nestle the chicken parts into the first layer of parcooked rice and then top with the fennel and the second half of the rice. Cook the dish as directed. To serve, check a piece of chicken for doneness without disturbing the crust. When ready, turn the whole thing onto the plate, leaving the chicken partially hidden in the rice.

The Basics of Sushi

The ingredients for making excellent sushi at home are simple, easy to find, and inexpensive: short-grain rice, rice vinegar, a few sheets of nori, and any filling you want (including leftovers). This can be cooked shrimp, raw tuna, smoked salmon, cucumbers, avocado, or something more elaborate.

Sushi comes in many forms. The simplest are sushi bowls (*chirashi*), a mound of seasoned sushi rice with the other ingredients scattered on top. Rolled sushi (*maki*)

❶ Fast   ❶ Make Ahead   ❶ Vegetarian

involves using a bamboo mat to wrap sheets of nori around the rice and filling. Finger sushi (*nigiri*) is sushi rice formed into a small rectangular brick and topped with whatever you choose; once you make Sushi Rice (page 474), you simply shape and improvise the toppings. And then there are *onigiri*, the super-easy rice balls everyone loves.

With practice, you can master all forms of sushi

SUSHI BOWLS (CHIRASHI SUSHI)

Chirashi means "scattered," and that's exactly what this is: various ingredients scattered over sushi rice. Here's a handy little chart to get you going on making your own:

Pick any "Centerpiece," add an item or two from the "Vegetable(s)" column, and finish with as much or as little "Sauce and/or Garnish" as you like. Slice the food into pieces as you like (in some cases I've offered suggestions).

The only advice I have is to match plain things—like pork cutlet—with more complicated sauces or marinades and vice versa; you don't want too many complicated components competing with one another. Once you get the hang of it, you'll be rifling through the book to make up your own combinations (or just improvising from your refrigerator).

CENTERPIECE	VEGETABLE(S)	SAUCE AND/OR GARNISH
Broiled or Grilled Chicken Thighs, Japanese Style (page 662)	Shredded or grated raw daikon, cucumber, or carrots, or marinated in any of the sauces listed at right	Soy sauce or Soy Dipping Sauce and Marinade (page 25)
Pan-Roasted Tuna Steaks (page 606)	Sliced avocado	Mayonnaise (to make your own, see page 41) flavored with wasabi; thinly sliced scallion
Grilled or Broiled Pork Chops (page 747)	Japanese pickles, any kind found in a Japanese market, or Spicy Pickles, Asian Style (page 229)	Toasted sesame seeds (see page 317)
Chicken or Steak Teriyaki (page 671 or 731)	Sushi-Style Spinach (page 353)	Sake, mirin (or equal parts honey mixed with water), or rice vinegar
Oven-"Fried" Sesame Chicken (page 657) or Extra-Crisp Chicken Cutlets (page 678)	Quick-Cooked Bok Choy (page 265)	Pickled Ginger (page 304)
Marinated and Grilled or Broiled Flank Steak (page 729)	Sautéed Mushrooms or Sautéed Mushrooms with Asian Flavors (pages 313–314)	Wasabi paste
Pan-Cooked Salmon (page 580)	Roasted Scallions, Asian Style (page 328)	Ponzu Sauce (page 40)
Stir-Fried Vegetables (page 241)	Broiled Jícama with Ponzu Glaze (page 307)	Dashi Dipping Sauce (page 56)
Grilled or Broiled or Deep-Fried Tofu (page 445 or 446)	Quick-Braised Burdock and Carrots (page 273)	Simple Miso Dipping Sauce (page 39) or Miso Carrot Sauce with Ginger (page 40)
Sliced raw sushi-grade tuna or other fish	Sea Green and Celery Stir-Fry (page 349)	Nori Chips (page 350)
Medium-Boiled Egg (page 791)	Stir-Fried Asparagus (page 259) or Dry-Pan Eggplant (page 294)	Crumbled Toasted Nori (page 350) or Seaweed "Shake" (page 69)

enough so that you'll be confident serving guests a platter of simply cut sushi rolls and finger pieces, an impressive and fairly easy party dish. But sushi need not be special-occasion food: A sushi bowl is one of the best ways ever to use small bits of leftover meat, seafood, vegetables, beans, and sauces. The chart on page 473 will help you get started with possible ingredient combinations.

Sushi Rice

MAKES: 4 servings (about 4 cups)

TIME: 40 minutes

Sushi rice can be served warm or at room temperature, but it cannot be made more than a couple of hours ahead or it will lose its great texture.

1 recipe White Rice or Brown Rice (page 458 or 459), made with short-grain or sushi rice

¹/₄ cup rice vinegar

2 tablespoons sugar

1 teaspoon salt

❶ While the rice is cooking, combine the vinegar, sugar, and salt in a small saucepan over medium heat and cook, stirring, until the sugar dissolves, less than 5 minutes. Put the saucepan in a bowl filled with ice and stir the vinegar mixture until cool.

❷ When the rice is done, put it in a bowl more than twice the size needed to hold the rice—probably the largest bowl you have. Begin to toss the hot rice with a flat wooden paddle or spoon or a rubber spatula—as if you were folding egg whites into a batter, but much faster and not quite as gently. While you're tossing, sprinkle the rice with the vinegar mixture (if the paddle becomes encrusted with rice, dip it in some water, then shake the water off and proceed). The idea is to cool the rice quickly as it absorbs the vinegar.

❸ Sushi rice will not keep for long, but if you cover it with a damp cloth, you can wait a couple of hours to pro-

ceed. Or eat it right away: see "Sushi Bowls" (page 473) and "Sushi Rolls" (page 475).

Sushi Rolls

Maki Sushi

MAKES: 6 rolls

TIME: 40 minutes with prepared rice and filling

Use the items listed in the "Sushi Bowls" chart on page 473 or your own ideas, but keep these points in mind: Sushi roll filling works best when it's cut into thin strips (julienned; see page 13) so you can set the slices down the length of the roll. And overstuffing will get you in trouble; think of the filling as a seasoning and the rice as the main component.

It's not ideal, but you can make sushi rolls a couple of hours ahead: Wrap the rolls in damp paper towels and plastic and store them in a cool place (do not refrigerate, which will harden the rice).

6 square sheets nori

2 tablespoons rice or other mild vinegar

1 recipe Sushi Rice (previous recipe), about 4 cups

Wasabi paste as needed

1 cup filling (see "10 Fillings for Sushi Rolls," which follows)

Pickled Ginger (optional; page 304)

Soy sauce (optional)

❶ Begin by toasting 6 sheets of nori: Use tongs to hold them, one at a time, over a medium-high flame for a few seconds, until they change color. If you have an electric stove, run them under the broiler for 15 seconds to a minute on each side. Mix 1 cup water with the vinegar in a bowl (this is called "hand water").

❷ Put a square of nori, shiny side down, on a bamboo mat. Using your hands, spread it evenly with a

$^1/_2$-inch layer of sushi rice, leaving a 1-inch border on all sides; rinse your hands in the hand water as needed. (Although rolling is easy, you won't do it perfectly at first, so you might start with a slightly thinner layer of rice.) Smear the rice with a finger full of wasabi (careful; it's hot), then put some filling (not too much) along one edge.

3 Use the mat to tightly roll the nori around the rice, forming it into a log; you can unroll the mat at any time and check to see how things are going. This takes a little bit of practice but is not at all difficult; you'll quickly get the hang of it. To roll, follow the illustrations below.

Slice the rolls into 1-inch sections and serve with pickled ginger and soy sauce if you like.

10 Fillings for Sushi Rolls

Remember, keep the filling at a minimum; using one filling is usually helpful; chop or slice it thinly—julienne cut (page 13) is always best but not essential. Here are both traditional and nontraditional possibilities:

1. Carrots, daikon, cucumber (peeled and seeded, page 293), or scallions, julienned
2. Avocado slices
3. Ceviche, chopped

ROLLING AND CUTTING SUSHI ROLLS

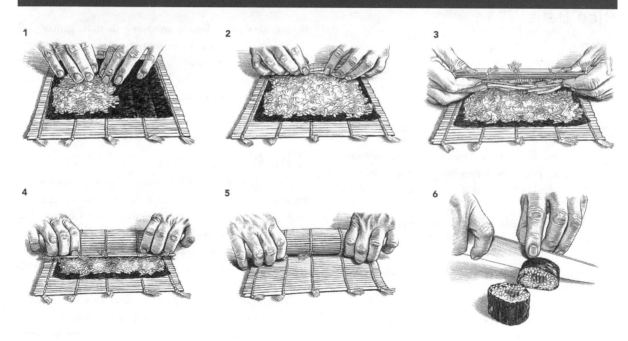

(STEP 1) First put a square of toasted nori on to a bamboo sushi-rolling mat; then press a bed of sushi rice onto it, $^1/_2$ inch thick. (STEP 2) Put any filling you like about $^1/_2$ inch from the edge nearest you. Do not overfill! (You will at first, but you'll stop soon enough.) (STEP 3) Start rolling, tucking in the edge of the nori as you do so. (STEPS 4–5) Keep rolling, as tightly as you can; you will soon get the hang of it. (STEP 6) Cut the roll into 1-inch lengths.

4. Pickled vegetables, like Spicy Pickles, Asian Style (page 229)
5. Kimchi (page 230), chopped
6. Cooked, squeezed, and chopped spinach, especially Sushi-Style Spinach (page 353)
7. Sautéed Mushrooms with Asian Flavors, preferably with sliced shiitakes (page 314)
8. Sushi-grade tuna, salmon, or other spanking-fresh raw fish, sliced or chopped
9. Pan-Roasted Tuna Steaks page 606), cut into strips
10. Simply cooked fish or seafood, like poached and chilled shrimp or crabmeat, grilled fish, or even fried items like soft-shell crabs, clams, or oysters

Rice Balls

Onigiri

MAKES: 4 to 8 servings
TIME: 30 minutes

Rice balls are a fast snack, and there's almost nothing to them: cooked short-grain rice, gently pressed together, sometimes stuffed with a piece of food, sometimes wrapped with nori, sometimes both, and sometimes neither. They can also be grilled after shaping, which is a nice touch.

Serve these as a side dish with any Japanese dish.

Salt

1 recipe White Rice or Brown Rice (page 458 or 459), made with short-grain or sushi rice, about 4 cups, still warm

Lightly salted cucumber chunks and/or pieces of daikon (optional)

Soy sauce

4 square sheets nori, lightly toasted (see page 350)

❶ Work with wet hands; sprinkle a little salt on your hands, then grab about ¹/₂ cup rice and gently shape it into a ball; the rice should hold together easily. If you want to stuff the rice balls, poke a hole in each and put in a bit of either of the vegetables (or any other filling you like). Reclose the hole.

❷ Brush each ball lightly with soy sauce.

❸ Brush the rough side of each nori sheet with a little soy sauce, then cut each sheet in half (done most easily with scissors). Wrap each ball with a piece of nori, shiny side out. Serve within a few hours.

Rice Balls with Sesame. Sprinkle the balls with toasted sesame seeds (see page 476) before wrapping.

Rice Balls with Fish. Stuff the balls with small bits of cooked fish, like Crispy Skin Salmon, Grilled or Broiled with Gingered Greens (page 583; omit the greens or serve them alongside).

Grilled Rice Balls. Before wrapping in nori, gently grill the rice balls over a medium-low flame, turning and basting with soy sauce as they're grilling, for a total of 5 to 10 minutes. Serve hot or warm, wrapped in nori or not, as you choose.

The Grain Lexicon

Grains—even rice, really—have a lot in common, so though they have distinctly different flavors, textures, and colors, most are interchangeable to an extent that may surprise you. To help you experiment and make the best use of whatever you have on hand, I've included the line "Other grains you can use" in recipes that work with other options.

These grains are organized first around cooking times, from shortest to longest, and second around what's most common and versatile (and my personal favorites). Cooking time varies up to 10 minutes, depending on the age of the grain and how it was milled, the heat of your stove, and whether you like your grains chewy or fluffy. Use visual cues and taste to confirm desired doneness.

 Fast   Make Ahead   Ⓥ Vegetarian

EVERYDAY GRAINS

GRAIN	COOKING TIME	DESCRIPTION	FORMS AND VARIETIES
Couscous	5 to 10 minutes for white; 10 to 15 minutes for whole wheat	Traditionally tiny, yellow, hand-rolled semolina dough. Now bits of rough-looking pasta, and the national "grain" (it isn't) of Morocco, served with almost every stew. Pearl couscous is also made from semolina dough, but extruded through a round mold and toasted, giving it a more uniform and larger, pearllike shape, a nuttier flavor, and a chewier texture; it's also more forgiving during cooking.	Usually made from semolina flour, sometimes in varying colors. Whole wheat couscous is also available and very good (it takes a little longer to cook). Pearl couscous, also called *Israeli couscous, super couscous, maftoul, pearl couscous,* or *Israeli toasted pasta,* takes even longer still to cook.
Bulgur *Bulghur, Burghul, Bulger* (often confused with cracked wheat, which it is not; see below)	10 to 20 minutes, depending on the grind	Finely ground wheat kernels, first steamed, then hulled, dried, and ground to varying degrees. Fine grind is quick and convenient, usually edible after soaking. Its nutty, mild flavor and fluffy, dry texture make it perfect for soaking up liquids and turning into salads. A good rice alternative.	Available in fine, medium, coarse, and sometimes very coarse grinds, which are sometimes identified by numbers, from #1 for fine to #3 or even #4 for the coarsest.
Rolled Oats *Old-Fashioned Oats*	15 to 20 minutes	Whole oats are toasted, hulled, steamed, and flattened with giant rollers to make these familiar flakes. The quick-cooking variety is cut before being steamed and flattened; instant is cut, precooked, dried, steamed, and then flattened. Stay away from these if you want any flavor at all.	Raw or quick-cooking (steamed) rolled oats, instant oats. Some are more heavily processed than others.
Barley: Pearled *Peeled Barley, Polished Barley*	About 20 minutes	Pearled barley has been hulled, steamed, and polished (the bran removed, see Hulled Barley, next page). Creased, oval, dull white and tan grains that cook fairly quickly and have a creamy, chewy texture when cooked.	Pearled is the familiar barley, sold everywhere and cooked much like rice, for which it can almost always be substituted. You may occasionally see barley flakes, which can be treated like rolled oats.
Quinoa (pronounced keen-wa) *Mother Grain, Supergrain*	About 20 minutes	Originally from the Andes, the most common quinoa is light tan, disk shaped and pinhead size. Nutty and grassy in flavor, with a slightly crunchy but soft texture. Even plain, it's as good as grains get.	Three main cultivated varieties, generally differentiated by color: white, red, and black; you can find whole grains of each. Also made into flakes, which can be used like rolled oats.
Cornmeal *Grits (usually from white corn; sometimes from hominy), Polenta*	20 to 30 minutes	Yellow or white (occasionally blue or red) dried corn kernels, ground to varying degrees. Fine grind is usually used in baking; medium grind is best for polenta; coarse makes a grittier polenta or grits (see page 477).	Fine, medium, and coarse grinds; water, stone, or steel ground. Water or stone grinding is a more traditional method and arguably superior to steel ground, because the bran and germ remain intact. (This makes cornmeal perishable, however, so be sure to store it in the fridge or freezer.)
Kasha *Roasted Buckwheat*	20 to 30 minutes	Hulled and roasted buckwheat kernels, brown, triangular, and distinctively nutty. Usually toasted in a skillet, sometimes with egg (see page 317), before adding liquid.	Whole grains

GRAIN	COOKING TIME	DESCRIPTION	FORMS AND VARIETIES
Buckwheat Groats *Peeled Buckwheat*	20 to 30 minutes	Essentially raw kasha, buckwheat groats are hulled and crushed; they're greenish tan, triangular, and fresher tasting than kasha—almost grassy in fact.	Whole grains; also rolled into flakes
Cracked Wheat	20 to 30 minutes	Often confused with bulgur (see previous page), cracked wheat is raw. It offers the same nutty wheat flavor as bulgur and wheat berries, but with a chewier, heartier texture than bulgur and quicker cooking times than wheat berries.	Fine, medium, and coarse grains (see bulgur, above), but most commonly available in medium grind
Millet	20 to 30 minutes	Small, yellow, and beadlike, with a tiny spot at one end. Pleasant tasting, mildly nutty and cornlike; cooks up fluffy. Said to be one of the first grains used by humans, it remains a staple in Africa and South Asia.	Whole grains are most common. Occasionally you may find puffed millet, but it's rare.
Farro *Often confused with spelt (which it's not)*	20 to 30 minutes	An ancient wheat-related grain, popular in early Rome, recently "rediscovered" in Tuscany. Tan and oval, not unlike peeled wheat in appearance, farro has a nutty, wheaty flavor and retains a chewy texture when cooked. With a starch similar to short-grain rice, it's a nice whole grain substitute in risotto.	Whole and crushed or "cracked" grains
Hulled Barley *Whole Barley, Pot Barley, Scotch Barley*	45 to 60 minutes	"Hulled" is the least-processed form of barley, with just the outer hull removed. It looks like a darker pearled barley, but takes longer to cook and has a chewier texture and a higher nutritional value.	Hulled barley comes in both whole grain and the slightly more processed Scotch barley (aka "pot barley"), which has more of the outer layers of the grain removed and is quicker cooking, less chewy, and somewhat less nutritious.
Steel-Cut Oats *Oat Groats, Whole Oats, Scotch Oats, Irish Oats, Porridge Oats*	45 to 60 minutes	Like rolled oats, oat groats (with only the outer hull removed) have a nutty, sweet flavor. But they're slow-cooking and quite chewy. Cut grains cook faster and are often used for breakfast cereal.	Whole grains or cut grains
Wild Rice *Indian Rice, Manomin, Water Oats*	45 to 60 minutes	A marsh grass native to the Great Lakes region, once a staple for many Native Americans. Long, narrow, deep brown cylinder-shaped grains that crack open to reveal a white interior when cooked.	Whole grains. There is both farm-raised "wild" rice and truly wild rice, which tends to be less uniform in color, better tasting, and more expensive.

F Fast   **M** Make Ahead   **V** Vegetarian

GRAIN	COOKING TIME	DESCRIPTION	FORMS AND VARIETIES
Whole Wheat *Wheat Berries* **Kamut®** *QK-77*	60 to 90 minutes	The second-largest grain crop in the world (after corn), whole wheat is unmilled kernels with the bran and germ still intact. Light brown, rounded, oval grain with a nutty flavor and very chewy texture. A modern breed of an ancient variety of wheat, kamut (pronounced KAH-moot) is tan, with kernels two to three times larger than common wheat. It's also more nutritious, with a sweeter, more buttery flavor.	Wheat varieties are named for the seasons they are grown in and the traits of their hulls: hard red winter, hard white winter, soft white spring, etc. Both types of grain come whole and in flakes, which cook in about half the time. Wheat also comes cracked (see above) and "peeled," which is slightly faster cooking.
Whole Rye *Rye Berries*	60 to 90 minutes	Rye plays an integral role in the cuisines of northern Europe and Russia but isn't as widely popular in the United States—a shame, since it's delicious. The berries are unmilled kernels with bran and germ still intact. The flavor is nutty, the texture firm.	Whole grains and flakes. (Flakes cook in about half the time.)
Hominy *Pozole, Posole*	Anywhere from 2 to 4 hours; less if you soaked it first	A native American ingredient, hominy is corn that has been processed—usually with lime or lye—to remove the germ and bran. In appearance, hominy looks like giant sweet corn kernels only lighter; the flavor is uniquely corny.	Dried whole kernels, partially cooked whole kernels (*nixtamal*), canned, broken, or ground; there are yellow, white, red, and blue varieties.

Couscous with Cauliflower and Almonds

MAKES: 4 servings

TIME: About 20 minutes

When cauliflower is finely chopped and fried as in this recipe, its crumbly texture mimics cracked grains. I like this best with the nutty flavor of whole wheat couscous.

Other grains you can use: bulgur.

1/2 cup almonds

3 tablespoons extra virgin olive oil

1 large shallot or small red onion, chopped

1 small cauliflower, chopped (about 3 cups)

Salt and freshly ground black pepper

1 cup whole wheat or regular couscous

1 teaspoon smoked or hot paprika

1 1/2 cups chicken or vegetable stock (to make your own, see page 157), white or rosé wine, water, or a combination

1/2 cup chopped fresh parsley leaves

Freshly grated manchego or other semihard sheep's milk cheese for garnish (optional)

❶ Put the almonds in a deep skillet with a lid over medium-high heat. Cook, stirring constantly, until toasted and fragrant, just a couple of minutes. Remove them from the pan and set aside to cool.

❷ Return the pan to the heat and add the olive oil. When hot, add the shallot and cook, stirring occasionally, until soft and beginning to color, about 2 minutes. Add the cauliflower and sprinkle with salt and pepper. Cook, stirring occasionally, until it is coated with the oil and starts to soften and turn golden, 5 to 10 minutes.

Stir in the couscous and keep stirring until it too is coated with oil and begins to toast, 3 to 5 minutes.

❸ Sprinkle the mixture with paprika and stir to combine. Stir in the stock and bring to a boil. Cover and turn the heat off. Let rest, undisturbed, for 15 minutes. Chop the almonds as finely as you can. Add them along with the parsley and fluff gently with a fork. Return the lid and again let the couscous rest for another minute or two, then taste and adjust the seasoning. Serve immediately, garnished with grated cheese if you like, or let cool and serve at room temperature, up to an hour or so later.

Couscous with Broccoli and Walnuts. Toast $^1/_2$ cup walnuts instead of the almonds. Instead of cauliflower, use a few stalks of broccoli. Omit the paprika. Instead of cheese, garnish with bread crumbs, preferably fresh (page 876), if you like.

Top 5 Grains to Keep on Hand

You can often substitute one grain for another, but not always—nor would you always want to. Grains are different enough that it's worth keeping a few of them around. These are my favorites:

1. **Bulgur:** Fast, convenient, versatile; wonderful in summer.
2. **Cornmeal:** Great flavor, easy to cook in a variety of ways, eminently lovable. A must-have because of both polenta and corn bread.
3. **Wheat berries:** Slow to cook, but delicious, satisfying, and healthful. Good for breakfast too.
4. **Quinoa:** Quick cooking, convenient, delicious, and healthful. No wonder it's called the supergrain.
5. **Hominy:** Hard to find, so I buy it when I see it. The heartiest grain.

Couscous Casserole

MAKES: 4 servings
TIME: 30 minutes

Like many casseroles, this one is a fine example of how to use leftovers to create a fast, easy, good-tasting dish. It's also perfect to make in advance: Assemble, cover, and store it in the fridge for up to a day, then bake it. If you like, sprinkle some grated Parmesan or other hard cheese on the top before baking.

Other grains you can use: fine bulgur.

$^1/_4$ cup extra virgin olive oil, plus oil for the dish

1 pound ground or chopped cooked beef, pork, lamb, turkey, or chicken

2 medium zucchini, summer squash, or eggplant, thinly sliced

Salt and freshly ground black pepper

$^1/_4$ cup chicken or vegetable stock (to make your own, see page 157) or water

1 recipe Fast Tomato Sauce (page 502) or 4 cups any tomato sauce

1 Roasted Red (or yellow) Pepper (page 330), and chopped (optional)

$^1/_2$ cup whole wheat or regular couscous

❶ Grease a $1^1/_2$- to 2-quart soufflé or gratin dish or an oblong baking pan. Heat the oven to 400°F.

❷ Put 2 tablespoons of the oil in a skillet over medium-high heat. When hot, add the meat and stir to break it up; cook until it begins to color, about 5 minutes. Put the zucchini slices on a baking sheet, drizzle with the remaining oil, and sprinkle with salt and pepper. Roast in the oven until just tender, 5 to 8 minutes.

❸ Put the stock and tomato sauce in a medium saucepan over medium heat and bring to a gentle bubble. Toss in the roasted pepper if using, then stir in the couscous and turn off the heat.

❹ Spoon a thin layer of the tomato sauce mixture into the bottom of the prepared pan and top with zucchini slices and then a portion of the meat. Repeat the layers,

 Fast   Make Ahead   ⓥ Vegetarian

finishing with the tomato sauce. Reduce the oven temperature to 350°F; bake the casserole until it's bubbling along the edges, about 25 minutes. Serve hot or store, covered, in the refrigerator for up to a day or two before reheating.

Couscous Casserole with Ricotta. A vegetarian version: Replace the ground meat with 1 cup or more ricotta, using it when you assemble the dish in Step 4.

Couscous Casserole with Chard. Especially good with ground lamb: Use Garlicky Tomato Sauce (page 503) and replace the zucchini with about a cup of chopped cooked chard.

Couscous Casserole with Cauliflower. Use Spicy Tomato Sauce (page 503) and replace the zucchini with about ½ head coarsely chopped cauliflower.

Couscous Casserole, North African Style. Add a tablespoon or so Harissa (page 75) and ½ teaspoon each ground cumin and caraway to the tomato sauce. Use just eggplant and in Step 3 add 1 cup cooked and drained chickpeas. Proceed with the recipe and make the last layer eggplant. Leave uncovered during baking for a crispier eggplant crust or cover for a soft layer.

Pearl Couscous Pilaf with Dried Tomatoes

MAKES: 4 servings
TIME: 20 minutes

Pearl couscous—often called *Israeli couscous*—is so forgiving: It won't turn to mush with too much liquid, it can be served hot or at room temperature, it reheats well, and it's delicious in a number of different guises (note the variations). Highly recommended.

2 tablespoons extra virgin olive oil

½ onion, chopped

1 cup pearl couscous

4 dried tomatoes, reconstituted as you would mushrooms (see page 314) and chopped

1 clove garlic, minced

3 tablespoons chopped pitted black olives

1¼ cups chicken or vegetable stock (to make your own, see pages 157) or water

Salt and freshly ground black pepper

Chopped fresh basil, mint, or oregano leaves for garnish

1 Put the oil in a pot with a lid over medium-high heat. When hot, add the onion and pearl couscous and cook until the couscous is lightly browned and the onion is soft, about 5 minutes. Add the dried tomatoes, garlic, and olives and cook for another 2 minutes.

2 Stir in the stock, sprinkle with a bit of salt (remember, the olives will add salt) and a good amount of pepper, and bring to a boil. Turn the heat to low so that the mixture bubbles gently, cover, and cook until the liquid is absorbed and the couscous is al dente, about 10 minutes. Taste, adjust the seasoning, sprinkle with chopped herbs, and serve hot or at room temperature. Or store, covered, in the refrigerator for up to 2 days (reheat or bring back to room temperature and stir in a little olive oil just before serving).

Pearl Couscous Pilaf with Shrimp. Add 8 ounces peeled and deveined shrimp, cut into pieces if large, in the last 5 minutes of cooking.

Pearl Couscous Pilaf with Spinach. Omit the onions, dried tomatoes, and olives. Double the garlic and add about a cup of cooked chopped spinach, squeezed almost dry, and ¼ cup each pine nuts and raisins.

Basic Bulgur

MAKES: 4 servings
TIME: Less than 30 minutes

Because bulgur is partially cooked, it's easier to prepare than other grains. It's also light and fluffy, with a dry texture that's perfect for soaking up butter or oil, pan juices, dressings, and sauces.

1 cup bulgur (any grind)

2¹/₂ cups boiling water

❶ Put the bulgur in a bowl and pour the boiling water over it. Stir once and let sit.

❷ Fine bulgur will be tender in 10 to 15 minutes, medium in 15 to 20 minutes, and coarse in 20 to 25. If any water remains when the bulgur is done, squeeze the bulgur in a cloth or put it in a fine-meshed strainer and press down on it. Season and serve as you like.

Bulgur with Spinach

MAKES: 4 servings

TIME: 45 minutes

A good use for leftover spinach if you have it.

Other grains you can use: couscous; quinoa, cracked wheat, or millet, cooked until tender in Step 3; precooked wheat berries or hominy.

About 8 ounces (1 pound before trimming) spinach or chard leaves, well washed

2 tablespoons butter or extra virgin olive oil

1 small onion, minced

Pinch ground cloves

1 cup medium- or coarse-grind bulgur

Salt and freshly ground black pepper

1³/₄ cups chicken, beef, or vegetable stock (to make your own, see pages 157–159) or water, heated

❶ Steam or simmer the spinach (see page 239) just until wilted, 1 to 3 minutes; plunge into ice water to stop the cooking. Drain, squeeze dry, and coarsely chop.

❷ Put the butter or oil in a large saucepan or skillet, preferably nonstick, over medium heat. When the butter is melted or the oil is hot, add the onion and cook,

stirring, until it softens, about 5 minutes. Stir in the cloves.

❸ Add the bulgur and stir until it is coated with butter or oil. Add the spinach and a little salt and pepper; stir until all the ingredients are blended, then add the liquid all at once. Turn the heat as low as possible, stir, and cover. Cook for 10 minutes, then turn off the heat and let sit for 15 minutes more. Adjust the seasoning and serve.

Creamed Bulgur with Spinach. This can be used with either of the following variations as well: Substitute freshly grated nutmeg for the cloves. Heat 1 cup cream, half-and-half, or whole milk until it's steaming and add to the bulgur along with the stock. It should be very soft but not soupy.

Bulgur with Fennel or Leeks. Substitute a thinly sliced fennel bulb or 1 large or 2 small leeks with some green parts remaining, cleaned and thinly sliced (about 2 cups), for the spinach. Omit the onion. Lightly brown the fennel in the butter or oil and proceed with the recipe.

Bulgur with Brussels Sprouts. Substitute 8 ounces trimmed and halved Brussels sprouts for the spinach. Proceed with Step 1 (no need to squeeze dry and chop). Add the sprouts along with the onions and proceed with the recipe.

Bulgur Pilaf with Vermicelli

MAKES: 4 servings

TIME: 30 minutes

I love this simple pilaf, which contains browned or small pasta (or broken larger pasta).

Other grains you can use: whole wheat or regular couscous.

4 tablespoons butter or extra virgin olive oil

1 large or 2 medium onions, chopped

¹/₂ cup vermicelli, broken into 2-inch-long or shorter lengths, or other, smaller pasta

1 cup fine- or medium-grind bulgur

Salt and freshly ground black pepper

1 tablespoon tomato paste (optional)

2¹/₄ cups chicken, beef, or vegetable stock (to make your own, see pages 157–159) or water, heated to the boiling point

❶ Put the butter or oil in a medium skillet or saucepan with a lid over medium heat. When the butter is melted or the oil is hot, add the onion and cook, stirring, until soft, about 5 minutes.

❷ Add the vermicelli and the bulgur and cook, stirring, until the pasta is lightly browned, less than 5 minutes. Sprinkle with salt and pepper and add the tomato paste if you're using it and the boiling stock. Turn the heat to low, cover, and cook for 10 minutes, then turn off the heat and let sit until the bulgur is tender, about 15 minutes. Adjust the seasoning and serve.

Bulgur Pilaf with Vermicelli and Sausage. Add about 6 ounces sausage, removed from its casings and crumbled. Cook in the oil, stirring to break the clumps, until it loses its pink color, then add the onion. Proceed with the recipe.

Bulgur Pilaf with Lentils. Add the tomato paste, 1 cup cooked lentils, and 1 teaspoon each minced garlic, hot red pepper flakes, and ground cumin or curry powder (to make your own, see page 66).

Barley Pilaf

MAKES: 4 servings
TIME: 45 minutes

In typical pilaf fashion, here you sauté barley before cooking it with stock or water. Vary it in any way you would Rice Pilaf, Seven Ways (page 460).

Other grains you can use: millet, quinoa.

2 tablespoons butter or extra virgin olive oil

¹/₂ cup chopped scallion or onion

1 cup pearled barley

1 teaspoon chopped fresh tarragon leaves, ¹/₂ teaspoon dried, or 1 tablespoon chopped fresh chervil, mint, dill, or parsley leaves

3 cups chicken, beef, or vegetable stock (to make your own, see pages 157–159) or water

Salt and freshly ground black pepper

Chopped fresh parsley leaves for garnish

❶ Put the butter or oil in a medium to large skillet over medium-high heat. When the butter is melted or the oil is hot, add the scallion and cook, stirring, until softened, about 5 minutes.

❷ Add the barley and cook, stirring, for a minute or so, until glossy; add the herb, stock, and salt and pepper. Bring to a boil.

❸ Turn the heat down to low, cover, and cook for 30 minutes. Check the barley's progress: It's done when tender and all the liquid is absorbed. Continue to cook if necessary, adding a tablespoon or two more liquid if all the liquid has been absorbed and the barley is not quite done. If the barley is tender but a little liquid remains, cover, remove from the heat, and let rest for 10 minutes. If ¹/₄ cup or more of liquid remains (unlikely), uncover, raise the heat a bit, and cook, stirring, until the barley is fluffy and the liquid evaporated. Fluff with a fork, garnish with parsley, and serve.

Slow-Cooked Pearled Barley with Onions and Mushrooms

MAKES: 4 servings
TIME: Several hours, largely unattended

This is a recipe you can throw together in 5 minutes and then walk away, and it'll be fine anytime after 4 hours or so. Assuming your slow cooker has a "keep warm" setting, I wouldn't hesitate to start it 6 or even 8 hours before eating.

You can add more flavor to this by stirring in a tablespoon or so of any curry powder or other spice mix (to make your own, see pages 65–69), along with a tablespoon or so of minced garlic.

Other grains you can use: kasha, buckwheat groats, millet, or cracked wheat.

1 cup pearled barley

2¹/₂ cups chicken, beef, or vegetable stock (to make your own, see pages 157–159) or water

Salt and freshly ground black pepper

1 cup chopped onion

¹/₄ cup dried porcini or other mushrooms, rinsed (optional)

¹/₂ cup sliced shiitake, portobello, or button mushroom caps (save the stems for stock if you like)

1 tablespoon extra virgin olive oil or butter

Chopped fresh parsley leaves for garnish

❶ Combine all the ingredients except the oil and parsley in a slow cooker and stir once; cover the machine and turn it on high.

❷ Check for doneness after about 4 hours. The liquid should be absorbed and the barley tender. If liquid remains, re-cover and cook for another hour or two; if the barley is dry but not tender, add ¹/₂ or so more liquid and cook for another hour or two.

❸ When the barley is done, stir in the oil, garnish with parsley, and serve.

Stovetop Pearled Barley with Onions and Mushrooms. Increase the liquid to 3 cups and proceed as in Step 1, using a large pot with a tight-fitting cover instead of the slow cooker. Bring to a boil, cover, and simmer very slowly until done, about 1 hour.

Slow-Cooked Pearled Barley with Onions and Ham. Use this with the main recipe or the first variation: Substitute (or add) 1 smoked ham hock, a ham bone, or ¹/₂ cup or so chopped prosciutto, Serrano, or other ham for the dried and fresh mushrooms.

Barley and Beef Stew

MAKES: 4 servings
TIME: About 1¹/₂ hours

Here barley almost plays a supporting role, in a hearty meat-and-vegetable stew. Use any root vegetables you like here and serve with crusty bread.

Other grains you can use: kasha, buckwheat groats, millet, or cracked wheat.

2 tablespoons extra virgin olive oil

1 pound beef chuck or round, trimmed of surface fat and cut into ¹/₂-inch cubes

Salt and freshly ground black pepper

1 large onion, chopped

3 cups chicken or beef stock (to make your own, see page 157 or 158) or water

2 medium carrots, cut into chunks

2 celery stalks, roughly chopped

2 medium potatoes, preferably waxy, peeled and quartered

8 garlic cloves, peeled (optional)

2 cups sliced mushrooms, preferably an assortment, or 1 cup sliced button mushrooms and ¹/₂ cup dried porcini or other dried mushrooms, reconstituted in hot water to cover (optional)

¹/₃ cup pearled barley

1 teaspoon fresh thyme leaves or ¹/₂ teaspoon dried

Chopped fresh parsley or celery leaves for garnish

❶ Put the oil in a deep saucepan over medium-high heat. When hot, add the meat, sprinkle with salt and pepper, and cook until browned on all sides, about 10 minutes. Add the onion and cook until softened, about 5 minutes. Pour in the stock (if you used dried mushrooms, include their strained liquid and reduce the amount of stock or water accordingly). Bring to a boil, then turn the heat down so the mixture barely bubbles. Cover and cook for 30 minutes, stirring a couple times.

F Fast   **M** Make Ahead   **V** Vegetarian

2 Add the remaining ingredients except the parsley. Bring to a boil over medium-high heat, then lower the heat so the mixture barely bubbles. Cover and cook for about 30 minutes, stirring once or twice.

3 The stew is done when everything is tender. Taste, adjust the seasoning, garnish, and serve.

Barley and Vegetable Stew. Use vegetable stock to make a vegetarian dish if you like: Omit the meat and skip Step 1. In Step 2, put all the ingredients except the parsley in the pot and proceed with the recipe.

Quinoa with Roasted Corn

MAKES: 4 servings

TIME: About 1 hour, largely unattended

This dish makes an unbeatable bed for grilled meat, poultry, seafood, or vegetables. Both the quinoa and corn have a pleasant subtle crunch. (Always remember to rinse quinoa before cooking.)

Other grains you can use: cracked wheat or steel-cut oats.

> 2 tablespoons extra virgin olive oil
>
> 1 1/2 cups corn kernels (preferably freshly shucked), defrosted if frozen
>
> Salt and freshly ground black pepper
>
> 3/4 cup quinoa, well rinsed and drained very well
>
> 1 1/2 cups chicken, beef, or vegetable stock (to make your own, see pages 157–159) or water
>
> Chopped fresh chives, chervil, parsley, or cilantro leaves for garnish

1 Put the oil in a skillet with a lid over medium-high heat. When hot, add the corn, sprinkle with salt and pepper, and cook, stirring occasionally, until the corn begins to brown, about 10 minutes.

2 Add the quinoa and stir; when the grains start popping and toasting, a couple minutes later, add the stock

and bring to a boil. Stir one last time, cover, and reduce the heat to low. Cook, undisturbed, for 15 minutes.

3 Uncover and test the quinoa for doneness. If the kernels are still sort of hard, make sure there's enough liquid to keep the bottom of the pan moist, cover, and cook for another 5 minutes or so. When ready, taste, adjust the seasoning, and garnish with the herbs, adding a few extra grinds of pepper. Serve immediately or let cool to room temperature.

Quinoa with Shallots or Leeks. Replace the corn with 2 shallots, minced, or 1 leek, trimmed until just a little green remains, carefully rinsed, and thinly sliced. Cook over medium heat until soft, about 3 minutes for the shallots, 7 minutes for the leeks. Proceed with the recipe.

Quinoa with Caramelized Onions. Omit the corn. Add 2 large onions, thinly sliced. Cook over medium heat until dry and sticking, about 15 minutes. Add the oil and continue to cook the onions until brown, another 10 to 15 minutes. Proceed with the recipe.

Quinoa with Ground Meat and Soy Sauce. Instead of the corn, use about 8 ounces of any meat. Instead of the olive oil, use 2 tablespoons peanut oil and 1 tablespoon dark sesame oil. Cut a few coins of fresh ginger to add with the stock. In Step 1, keep cooking and stirring until the meat is well browned; drain excess fat if you like. Season with soy sauce instead of some of the salt and garnish with 1/2 cup sliced scallion.

Polenta

MAKES: 4 servings

TIME: 20 minutes

As with risotto, a big deal was made of the difficulty of preparing polenta when it first became popular in the United States. But you can make polenta easily, in about the time it takes to clean and pan-cook some spinach or make a quick tomato sauce to put on top of it. If you want to make grilled polenta (see the variation), reduce the amount of water slightly (or cook it a little longer) so the polenta is thick rather than creamy and soft.

You can make polenta with water only, but it's a little richer and creamier with some milk in there. And polenta sets as it cools, which means you can slice it into squares for grilling or frying (see the variations).

Other grains you can use: grits.

1/2 cup milk, preferably whole

Salt

1 cup coarse cornmeal

1 tablespoon butter or extra virgin olive oil, or more (optional)

Freshly grated Parmesan cheese (optional)

Freshly ground black pepper

❶ Combine the milk with 2 cups water and a large pinch of salt in a medium saucepan over medium heat. Bring just about to a boil, then add the cornmeal in a steady stream, whisking all the while to prevent lumps from forming. Turn the heat down to low and simmer, whisking frequently, until thick, 10 or 15 minutes. If the mixture becomes too thick, simply whisk in a bit more water. For soft polenta, you want a consistency about as thick as sour cream; for Grilled or Fried Polenta (see the variation), you want something approaching thick oatmeal.

❷ Add the butter and/or cheese if you're using them, then taste, add salt if necessary and lots of pepper, and serve (or prepare it for Grilled or Fried Polenta or Polenta Gratin).

Polenta with Herbs. This is also good for Grilled or Fried Polenta: Add 1 teaspoon each chopped fresh sage and fresh rosemary (or 1/2 teaspoon each dried), along with the cornmeal. When the polenta is done, stir in 1/2 teaspoon minced garlic if you like, along with the butter or oil. Cheese remains optional.

Polenta with Fresh Corn. When the polenta is almost ready, stir in the kernels stripped from 2 ears of corn and cook for 1 minute more.

Polenta Gratin. Immediately after cooking, spoon or pour the polenta into a buttered baking dish of a size that will give you a layer about 1 inch thick. Top with about 1 cup freshly grated Parmesan cheese and broil until the cheese melts and browns slightly. Serve (with a spoon) hot or at room temperature.

Grilled or Fried Polenta. Make sure the polenta is fairly thick when cooked and omit the butter and cheese. Pour the cooked polenta out onto a cutting board or into a loaf pan. Let cool for at least 10 minutes (it can really sit there all day), then cut into 1/2-inch-thick slices. When you're ready, brush with olive oil and grill with a little salt and pepper or brown the slices in hot olive oil in a pan.

Microwave Polenta. Frankly, I find this more trouble than it's worth, but some people swear by it, and it is a little faster: Combine the milk, water, salt, and cornmeal in a bowl and whisk until smooth. Cover and microwave for about 2 minutes; whisk. Re-cover and repeat the process, microwaving for 1 minute at a time, until the mixture is creamy and smooth. (Total time will be around 5 minutes or a little longer.) Again, if it thickens too fast, whisk in a little more water. Finish as directed.

14 Dishes to Serve on Top of Polenta

You can top a mound of soft polenta (or squares of Grilled or Fried Polenta) with almost any savory, liquid dish just as you would rice. Here are some ideas:

1. Sautéed Eggplant with Tomatoes (page 295)
2. Braised Endive, Escarole, or Radicchio with Prosciutto (page 298)
3. Sautéed Mushrooms (page 313)
4. Roasted Winter Squash Slices (add butter and Parmesan; see page 368)
5. Beans and Tomatoes (page 414)
6. Fast Tomato Sauce (page 502)

Ⓕ Fast   Ⓜ Make Ahead   Ⓥ Vegetarian

The Many Forms of Dried Corn

Fresh corn is pretty easy to understand: It's a grain we eat like a vegetable. But when it's dried, things get downright confusing. Understanding the differences among pozole, hominy, polenta, grits, and cornmeal is complicated by foreign languages, outdated names, and misinformation.

The first thing to know is that these products are either simply dried corn or dried corn that's been processed with something alkaline to easily remove the hull and germ. This technique, which gives the kernels that distinctive flavor associated with good corn tortillas, has been around for thousands of years. The earliest American inhabitants discovered that soaking corn along with wood ashes (which contain lime—not the fruit but the agricultural product, calcium hydroxide) made the corn more digestible and therefore more beneficial.

- **Hominy:** Whole dried corn kernels are soaked in lime (calcium hydroxide) before removing the hull and germ. See details in "The Grain Lexicon" (page 476). Cook as you would other grains. (It will cook faster if you soak it as you would beans; see page 411.) Canned hominy is precooked. Hominy recipes are given later in this chapter (starting on page 496) since this grain takes the longest to cook of all.
- **Pozole or Posole:** The Aztec name for hominy; also the name of any stew that features hominy and, usually, pork (see page 496).
- **Masa:** The "dough" or paste made from grinding corn cooked with lime, or nixtamal. When coarsely ground, it's used for tamales; when finely ground, it is the base for tortillas. You might be able to get a tortilla bakery to sell you some.
- **Masa Harina:** This is masa dried into a convenient mix for making dough for tortillas, tamales, and other Mexican dishes. Its texture is somewhere between flour and fine cornmeal. Most supermarkets now carry masa harina; store for up to 6 months, preferably in the refrigerator.
- **Dried Corn:** Dried without lime, not very common, and not nearly as tasty as hominy. Cook like any other whole grain.
- **Cornmeal:** Ground dried corn without the lime. See "The Grain Lexicon" (page 476) for details. When cooked, most Americans call it "cornmeal mush." But raw cornmeal also goes by two other names that are the same as finished dishes: polenta, an Italian specialty best made from medium-ground yellow cornmeal (or a combination of fine and coarse), and grits, which in the American South today are simply coarsely ground white cornmeal, though true hominy grits are indeed ground from hominy.
- **Corn Flour:** Finely ground dried corn (more finely ground than cornmeal) used for baking, usually in combination with wheat flour since it has no gluten and can be heavy.
- **Popcorn:** There are two explanations for why popcorn pops. One is that it contains spirits, which escape when exposed to heat, leaving their exploded shell behind. I like this story, but it's more believable that the starch and water content in popcorn is relatively high, which makes the hull explode under high heat. When heated in oil (see the recipe on page 81), popcorn is the classic snack. (Boiled popcorn is edible, but not as good as either dried corn or hominy.)

Polenta "Pizza"

MAKES: 4 servings
TIME: About 40 minutes

This is a fun way to eat polenta, especially if you've got kids eager to get into the kitchen. Pizza toppings beyond sauce and mozzarella will work here, but you'll need a fork. (For a handheld corn-flavored pie, start with Crunchier Pizza Dough, page 179.)

You can prepare this crust in advance. Make a batch of polenta (make extra, so you can eat some warm), add a little oil, then spread it on a pan or even a plate, cover, and refrigerate for up to a day or so.

Other grains you can use: grits, cooked as you would Polenta (page 485).

3 tablespoons extra virgin olive oil, plus oil for the pan

1 recipe Polenta (page 485), made with 2¹/₂ cups water and without butter or cheese

Salt and freshly ground black pepper

1¹/₂ cups Fast Tomato Sauce (page 502)

1¹/₂ to 2 cups grated mozzarella, Parmesan, or fontina cheese, crumbled Gorgonzola, or a combination

Chopped fresh herbs, like basil, parsley, oregano, or marjoram, or a mixture

1 Heat the oven to 400°F. Brush a thin layer of olive oil on a pizza pan or cookie sheet. Stir 1 tablespoon of the oil into the cooked polenta and pour and spoon it onto the prepared pan. Work quickly so the polenta doesn't stiffen and spread it evenly.

2 When the polenta is cool enough to handle, cover it with a sheet of plastic wrap or wax paper and press it to a thickness of about ¹/₂ inch all over, then remove the wrap and sprinkle with salt and pepper. Spread the tomato sauce over the polenta, then sprinkle with the cheese and the herbs. Drizzle with another tablespoon or so of olive oil and put in the oven.

3 Bake until the cheese is melted and the pizza is hot, 12 to 15 minutes. Cut into slices and serve hot or at room temperature.

Mexican-Style Cornmeal Pizza. Use either grits or polenta. Substitute Salsa Roja (page 48) for the tomato sauce. Instead of the Italian cheeses, use cotija, Chihuahua, or Monterey Jack. Omit the herbs before baking and garnish with chopped fresh cilantro and scallion.

Breakfast Polenta Pizza. Omit the tomato sauce. Make 4 indents in the polenta and crack an egg into each. Top with a grating of cheese (cheddar is fine here), some snipped fresh herbs (I like sage), and crumbled crisp cooked bacon or cooked sausage if you like. Bake until the eggs are set, 10 to 15 minutes.

Tamales

MAKES: 24 tamales
TIME: At least 2 hours

Tamales are work, usually a group effort, but worth the labor (check out the "Naked" Tamales variation for a quicker version).

Lard is traditional and wonderful, but if you want an alternative, try this: Freeze 1 cup extra virgin olive oil until it solidifies (it will need at least an hour; the thinner it's spread out, the more quickly it will freeze). Substitute this for the lard and work quickly to beat the baking powder and masa into it; it will not fluff up like lard, but the results are good.

24 dried corn husks

2 pounds ground fresh masa or 3¹/₂ cups dry masa harina

2¹/₄ cups chicken stock (to make your own, see page 157), plus more as needed

1 cup lard, cubed

1 teaspoon salt

1 teaspoon baking powder

1¹/₂ cups Shredded Pork (page 759), shredded cooked chicken, or Real Refried Beans (page 418)

 Fast   Make Ahead   Vegetarian

① Sort through the corn husks and make sure they're all clean; soak in warm water for at least 3 hours or overnight. Drain, then separate the husks. Continue to soak until ready to use.

② If you're using dry masa harina, add the stock a little at a time just until combined. Stop when the mixture is crumbly.

③ In a mixer, beat the lard with the salt and baking powder until fluffy. If you're using fresh masa, alternatively add the masa and stock, continuously beating. If you're using the masa harina, add the masa harina mix-

ture. Beat until the dough is light and fluffy, adding more stock if needed. The mixture is ready when a small ball of the dough floats in water.

④ Drain a husk and pat dry with paper towels. Spread 2 tablespoons of the masa dough in the center of the husk, then wet your fingers and pat into a 4 × 3-inch rectangle along the right edge of the husk, leaving at least 2 inches on each side. Spoon 1 tablespoon of filling lengthwise down the center of the dough rectangle. To wrap the tamales, fold the dough rectangle in half, bringing the right side of the dough over the filled center.

FORMING TAMALES

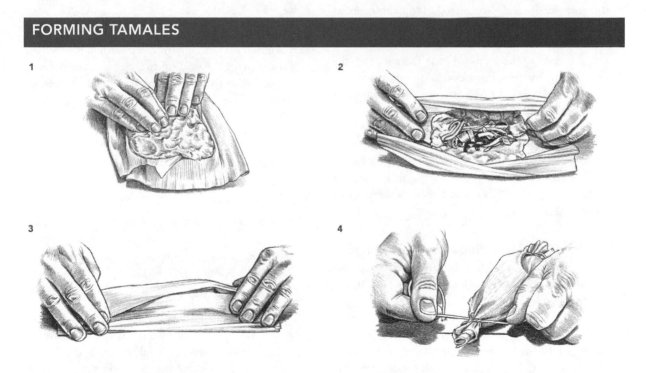

(STEP 1) For each tamale, drain a husk and pat dry with paper towels. Spread 2 tablespoons of the masa dough in the center of the husk, then wet your fingers and pat into a 4 x 3-inch rectangle along the right edge of the husk, leaving at least 2 inches on each side. (STEP 2) Spoon 1 tablespoon of filling lengthwise down the center of the dough rectangle. To wrap the tamales, fold the dough rectangle in half, bringing the right side of the dough over the filled center. (STEP 3) Continue rolling tightly to the end of the husk. (STEP 4) Then secure the open ends with kitchen string. Repeat with the remaining ingredients.

Continue rolling tightly to the end of the husk, then secure the open ends with kitchen string. Repeat with the remaining ingredients.

5 Prepare a large steamer by setting a steamer rack about 2 inches above gently boiling water. Stack the tamales, seam down, on the rack. Cover and steam until done, about 45 minutes. To test for doneness, remove one tamale and open the husk—the filling should be firm and come away easily. Serve warm or at room temperature.

"Naked" Tamales. Use ramekins if you have them and reduce the cooking time by about half, but unless you have 24, you'll have to work in batches. Omit the corn husks and skip Step 1. Heat the oven to 400°F. Grease a standard loaf pan or a 10-inch springform cake pan. Follow Steps 2 and Step 3. Put half the masa in the prepared pan. Top with the filling and put the remaining dough on top. Cover the pan with foil and put in a large roasting pan; carefully pour boiling water into the roasting pan to come halfway up the tamale pan. Put the whole thing in the oven and bake for about an hour, or until the masa is pulling away from the sides of the pan. Let cool a bit, then turn the tamale out onto a platter. Cut the loaf or cake into slices or wedges and serve.

10 Dishes That Make Super Tamale Fillings

Debone if necessary and chop or shred the ingredients into small pieces; be careful not to overfill the tamales.

1. Turkey Thighs in Almond Mole (page 702)
2. Broiled or Grilled Boneless Chicken Thighs, whole or in kebabs, spicy (page 642–643)
3. Braised Beef Brisket (page 743)
4. West Indian Crispy Pork Bits with Mexican Flavors (page 749)
5. Shredded Pork (page 759)
6. Beer-Glazed Black Beans (page 420)
7. Chili non Carne (page 429)
8. Chopped grilled vegetables, like eggplant, zucchini, tomatoes, chiles or bell peppers, or squash (see "Grilling or Broiling Vegetables," page 238)
9. Raw fresh corn kernels, with or without a little crumbled queso fresco
10. Grated Jack, cheddar, or cotija cheese

Grits Gratin with Arugula and Garlic

MAKES: 4 to 6 servings
TIME: 45 minutes with prepared grits

A light one-dish meal; as the garlicky arugula wilts, the slices of grits form a yummy golden crust akin to croutons.

You can make the grits up to a day in advance, pour into a loaf pan or rimmed baking sheet, and let them set before proceeding.

Other grains you can use: coarse cornmeal.

¼ cup extra virgin olive oil, plus oil for the pan

3 or 4 cloves garlic, crushed

½ teaspoon sugar

4 cups arugula leaves

Salt and freshly ground black pepper

2 tablespoons balsamic or sherry vinegar

1 recipe Polenta (page 485), made with grits and molded according to Grilled or Fried Polenta

½ cup freshly grated Parmesan cheese

1 Heat the oven to 400°F. Grease a shallow 2-quart gratin dish or 9 × 13-inch baking pan with a little olive oil.

2 Put 2 tablespoons of the oil in a large, deep skillet over medium-low heat. When hot, add the garlic and sugar and cook, stirring occasionally, until the garlic is soft, plump, and starting to color, about 10 minutes. Turn off the heat and add the arugula. Sprinkle with salt and pepper, toss gently once or twice, and spread the leaves in the bottom of the prepared dish. Drizzle with the vinegar.

3 Turn the grits out of the pan and cut into $^{1}/_{2}$-inch-thick slices; sprinkle with salt and pepper. Carefully spread them out on top of the arugula, overlapping them a little if necessary. Drizzle with the remaining oil and sprinkle with the cheese. Bake until the topping is golden and bubbling, 20 to 25 minutes. Serve, topped with lots of black pepper.

Grits Gratin with Escarole, Garlic, and Lemon. Instead of the arugula, use torn escarole leaves. Substitute lemon juice for the vinegar.

Grits Gratin with Arugula and Bacon. Add a few slices of chopped bacon and reduce the oil to 2 tablespoons. Cook the bacon in the oil (with or without the garlic) until lightly crisp.

Grits Gratin with Arugula, White Beans, and Garlic. When you toss the arugula with the garlic and olive oil in Step 2, add 1 cup cooked white beans.

Kasha with Golden Brown Onions

MAKES: 4 servings
TIME: 30 minutes

The classic Eastern European kasha dish and, with its deeply browned onions, warm tasting and wonderful. Many people toss their kasha with an egg before cooking, because it keeps the grains separate. But toasting it in oil accomplishes the same goal—take your pick. (Without either, the kasha will become mushier, which is fine too.)

3 cups chopped onion

3 tablespoons neutral oil, like grapeseed or corn

1 egg or 2 more tablespoons neutral oil, like grapeseed or corn

1 cup kasha

Salt and freshly ground black pepper

2 cups chicken, beef, or vegetable stock (to make your own, see pages 157–159) or water, warmed

1 to 2 tablespoons butter (optional)

1 Put the onion in a large skillet with a lid over medium heat. Cover the skillet and cook for about 15 minutes, until the onion is dry and almost sticking to the pan. Add the 3 tablespoons oil, raise the heat to medium-high, and cook, stirring, until the onion is nicely browned, another 15 minutes or so.

2 Meanwhile, if you're using the egg, beat it, then toss it in a bowl with the kasha. (If not, proceed to Step 3.) Put the mixture along with some salt and pepper in a heavy, large, deep skillet over medium-high heat. Cook, stirring, until the mixture smells toasty, about 3 minutes. Proceed to Step 4.

3 If you're using the 2 tablespoons oil instead of egg, put it in a heavy, deep skillet over medium-high heat. When hot, add the kasha, along with some salt and pepper, and cook, stirring, until the mixture smells toasty, about 3 minutes.

4 Turn the heat to a minimum, carefully add the stock, and stir once. Cover and cook until the liquid is absorbed, about 15 minutes. Turn off the heat. Stir in the onion, taste, and adjust the seasoning. Serve or let the kasha sit for up to 30 minutes before serving.

5 When you're ready to serve, fluff with a fork, adding the butter if you like at the same time.

Kasha with Bacon and Golden Brown Onions. Add 4 to 6 ounces bacon, chopped, to the onion after it's cooked for 15 minutes. Cook until the bacon is crisp and the fat rendered and the onions are browned, about 10 minutes. Proceed with the recipe. Garnish with chopped fresh parsley if you like.

Kasha with Carrots or Parsnips. Replace the onion with 2 cups or so (about 1 pound) chopped carrots or parsnips. In Step 1, put the oil in the pan first, then add the carrots or parsnips; cook until they are golden brown and tender, only about 15 minutes total.

Kasha with Mushrooms. Replace the onion with 2 cups or so (about 8 ounces) chopped or sliced mushrooms of any variety. In Step 1, put the oil in the pan first, then add the mushrooms; cook until the mushrooms are golden brown and soft, about 5 minutes.

Kasha Varnishkas. These quantities will make enough to serve 6 to 8; halve the recipe if you want less: When you begin the onions, bring a large pot of water to a boil and salt it. When the kasha is just about done (or is already resting), cook 1 pound of farfalle (bowtie) pasta until it's tender but not mushy and drain it, reserving some of the cooking water. Use a fork to toss the pasta with the kasha and onions, definitely adding some butter and enough of the reserved cooking water to make the dish a little creamy.

Cracked Wheat with Mustard

MAKES: 4 servings
TIME: About 20 minutes

The difference between savory, fluffy cracked wheat and breakfast porridge is basically a lot less water and a fork. Don't confuse cracked wheat (which is raw) with bulgur (which is precooked and dried). If you use bulgur here, you'll end up with mush.

Other grains you can use: steel-cut oats, Israeli (pearl) couscous.

2 tablespoons extra virgin olive oil

1 cup cracked wheat

Salt and freshly ground black pepper

1/4 cup dry white wine (optional)

2 teaspoons Dijon mustard

1 tablespoon minced fresh tarragon or 2 tablespoons minced fresh chives, chervil, or parsley leaves

1 pat butter (optional)

❶ Put the oil in a medium pan with a lid over medium-high heat. When hot, add the cracked wheat and sprinkle with salt and pepper. Cook, stirring frequently with a fork, until it smells like fresh toast, 3 to 5 minutes. Add the wine if you're using it, stir briefly to combine, and cook until it almost boils off, a minute or two.

❷ If you didn't add wine, add a cup of water. If you did add wine, add 3/4 cup water. Either way, stir again briefly with the fork, bring to a boil, cover, and reduce the heat to low. Cook, undisturbed, for about 15 minutes.

❸ Lift the lid and use the fork to stir in the mustard, the tarragon, and the butter if you like. Cover again, turn the heat off, and let sit for at least 5 and up to 15 minutes. Taste and adjust the seasoning, then fluff one last time with your fork and serve.

6 Ways to Spin Cracked Wheat with Mustard
Instead of mustard, add these combos, mixing in with a fork, all in Step 3 except for the last two, either with or without the butter:

1. 3 finely chopped scallions and 2 tablespoons sunflower seeds
2. 2 tablespoons of your favorite Chile Paste (page 74)
3. 2 tablespoons maple syrup (or less, to taste) and a pinch of cayenne
4. 1/2 cup fresh or frozen peas and 1/4 cup minced fresh mint leaves (A dollop of plain yogurt goes great with this.)
5. 6 ounces or so sausage, removed from its casing, crumbled, and cooked in the oil until browned before the wheat is added
6. Use dark sesame or peanut oil instead of extra virgin olive oil and finish by stirring in 1 tablespoon or so

of soy sauce, $^1/_2$ cup chopped roasted peanuts, and $^1/_2$ cup chopped fresh cilantro.

Millet-Cauliflower Mash

MAKES: 4 servings
TIME: 45 minutes, largely unattended

With the protein from the millet, these will stick to your ribs longer than mashed potatoes, and virtually all the variations and additions you find there (page 340) will work with this too.

2 tablespoons neutral oil, like grapeseed or corn

1 cup millet

Salt and freshly ground black pepper

$^1/_2$ head cauliflower, coarsely chopped (about $1^1/_2$ cups)

3 cups chicken, beef, or vegetable stock (to make your own, see pages 157–159), or water

1 head Roasted Garlic (page 303), squeezed from the skin (optional)

❶ Put the oil in a large pot with a lid over medium heat. When hot, add the millet and stir constantly until it toasts and turns golden, about 3 minutes.

❷ Sprinkle with salt and pepper and add the cauliflower and $2^1/_2$ cups of the stock. Bring to a boil, then lower the heat so the mixture bubbles gently, cover, and cook, stirring occasionally, until the millet bursts, about 30 minutes. Add a little stock anytime the mixture gets too dry.

❸ Remove from the heat and use an immersion blender to purée the millet and cauliflower in the pan. Or cool the mixture slightly, pour into a food processor or food mill (which will make the mash very fluffy), and purée carefully. Return the mash to the pot, add the roasted garlic if you're using it, and reheat gently, stirring in the remaining stock if needed. Taste, adjust the seasoning, and serve.

Cheesy Millet Mash. After puréeing, in Step 3, add 1 cup grated cheddar, manchego, or Gruyère cheese to the mash, along with $^1/_4$ cup or so of milk and a pat of butter if you like.

Autumn Millet Bake

MAKES: 4 to 6 servings
TIME: About $1^1/_2$ hours, largely unattended

Perfect for Thanksgiving, though you'll probably want to eat it more than once a year. The slightly sweet flavor of the squash is nicely balanced with tart fresh cranberries and the nutty flavor of millet.

Other grains you can use: quinoa, cracked wheat.

$^1/_4$ cup extra virgin olive oil, plus oil for the dish

$^3/_4$ cup millet

1 medium butternut or other winter squash or 1 small pumpkin, peeled, seeded, and cut into 1-inch cubes

1 cup fresh cranberries

Salt and freshly ground black pepper

1 tablespoon chopped fresh sage leaves or 1 teaspoon dried sage

2 tablespoons maple syrup or honey

1 cup chicken or vegetable stock (to make your own, see page 157) or water, warmed

$^1/_4$ cup pumpkin seeds or coarsely chopped hazelnuts

❶ Heat the oven to 375°F and grease a 2-quart ovenproof dish, a large gratin dish, or a 9 × 13-inch baking dish with olive oil.

❷ Put 2 tablespoons of the oil in a small skillet over medium-high heat. When hot, add the millet and cook, stirring frequently, until fragrant and golden, about 3 minutes. Set aside.

❸ Spread the squash cubes in the bottom of the prepared baking dish. Scatter the cranberries around and spoon the millet mixture on top. Sprinkle with salt and pepper and the sage and drizzle with syrup. Carefully pour the warmed stock over all. Cover tightly with foil and bake, undisturbed, for about 45 minutes. Carefully taste to see if the millet is done. If not, add a little warm water if it looks dry, re-cover, and return to the oven for 10 minutes or so.

❹ Uncover and turn the oven up to 400°F. As discreetly as possible, sneak a taste and adjust the seasoning. Sprinkle the seeds on top (a good way to camouflage your taste) and return the dish to the oven. Bake until the mixture bubbles and the top is browned, another 10 minutes or so. Serve piping hot or at room temperature.

Autumn Millet Bake with Cream. Reduce the stock to $^1/_2$ cup and add 1 cup warmed cream.

Wild Rice Pilaf

MAKES: 4 servings
TIME: 40 minutes

You can cook wild rice in equal quantities with brown rice, white rice, or pearled barley (I like this combo very much) and integrate its flavor into almost any other rice dish. But beware that it takes almost as long as brown rice to cook, so plan ahead a bit (or parboil it according to the instructions on page 20 before combining it with white rice). The easiest way to cook it by itself is with the recipe for Cooking Grains, the Easy Way (page 451), but this recipe is a little more sophisticated. In fact, the main recipe and its variations all make excellent poultry stuffing; double the quantities if roasting a turkey.

2 tablespoons butter or extra virgin olive oil

1 cup wild rice

3 cups chicken, beef, or vegetable stock (to make your own, see pages 157–159) or water

1 bay leaf

Salt and freshly ground black pepper

Chopped fresh parsley leaves for garnish

❶ Put the butter or oil in a deep skillet or saucepan with a lid over medium heat. When the butter is melted or the oil is hot, add the wild rice and cook, stirring frequently, until fragrant and glossy, just a couple minutes. Stir in the stock, bay leaf, and some salt and pepper and bring to a boil.

❷ Cover, turn the heat to low, and cook, undisturbed, for 30 minutes. Check the progress: The rice is done when the grains have puffed up and are quite tender, regardless of whether the liquid has been absorbed. If the rice is not done, continue to cook, adding more liquid if necessary. If it is done, drain if necessary (this is unlikely). Taste and adjust the seasoning and fluff with a fork; garnish with parsley and serve.

Wild Rice with Dried Fruit. When you fluff the wild rice in Step 2, stir in $^1/_2$ cup chopped dried fruit, like apri-

Is Wild Rice Wild?

Wild rice is a water grass indigenous to North America that has been harvested since prehistoric times. For Native Americans in the Great Lakes region it was a main source of protein and other nutrients. Now there is cultivated wild rice, which usually comes from California, and wild wild rice, which still comes mostly from Minnesota and neighboring states and provinces. The cultivated kind is less expensive and actually quite a different experience, though both can be quite good and both can taste like pine needles. Bottom line: Wild rice is a nice change, but there are other, more interesting grains that don't cost five or six bucks a pound. Whatever you do, don't buy the little boxes you find in the supermarket, which are inferior; rice by mail order or from a good specialty market is better (see page 982).

cots, cherries, cranberries, mangoes, or apples. Put the lid back on for a minute or two to warm through and plump.

Wild Rice with Curried Nuts. Use butter, peanut oil, or neutral oil, like grapeseed or corn. In Step 1, before you cook the rice, add 1 tablespoon curry powder or any other spice mix (to make your own, see pages 65–69) to the hot oil and cook, stirring, for a few seconds. Stir in $^1/_2$ to 1 cup roughly chopped cashews, almonds, pecans, or walnuts. Cook, stirring, until they begin to brown. Remove with a slotted spoon, add the rice, and proceed with the recipe. When the rice is done, drain if necessary, then return to the pot and stir in the nut-butter mixture. Cook over medium-low heat, stirring, until hot.

Wild Rice with Brussels Sprouts. Reduce the butter or oil to 1 tablespoon. While the rice is cooking, prepare 8 ounces Brussels sprouts according to the recipe for Roasted Brussels Sprouts with Garlic (page 271). Stir them into the rice just as it is finishing cooking and serve.

Wild Rice with Chestnuts. Also fall-like and good combined with the Brussels sprouts (above) or mushrooms (below): Roast about 12 chestnuts (see page 287). Peel, roughly chop, stir into the rice just as it finishes cooking, and serve.

Wild Rice with Mushrooms. Reduce the butter or oil to 1 tablespoon. While the rice is cooking, cook about 1 cup sliced mushrooms (shiitakes are best) in 2 tablespoons butter or extra virgin olive oil until crisp, about 10 minutes. Or add 1 recipe Sautéed Mushrooms (page 313). Stir into the rice just as it finishes cooking and serve.

Wild Rice with Roasted Winter Squash. Reduce the butter or oil to 1 tablespoon. Roast about 1 cup butternut or other winter squash (see page 367) with butter or olive oil; stir into the rice just as it finishes cooking and serve.

Wheat Berries with Walnuts

MAKES: 4 servings
TIME: 45 minutes

This starter recipe for wheat berries is open to variation and will work with about a dozen other grains. Even better, you can serve it at room temperature.

Other grains you can use (reduce the quantity to 1 cup): couscous, pearl couscous, bulgur, quinoa, buckwheat groats, cracked wheat, wild rice, farro, hulled barley, spelt, rye berries, or kamut.

> $1^1/_2$ cups wheat berries
>
> 2 tablespoons extra virgin olive oil or butter
>
> 1 shallot or $^1/_2$ medium onion, minced
>
> $^3/_4$ cup chopped walnuts
>
> 2 teaspoons chopped fresh thyme leaves (optional)
>
> Salt and freshly ground black pepper

❶ Put the wheat berries in a pot with water to cover by at least an inch. Bring a boil and cook until the grains are tender, about 40 minutes. (If you're using other grains, check the chart on page 477 for cooking times.) Check periodically to make sure the water hasn't boiled off; add more water as needed.

❷ Meanwhile, put the oil in a skillet over medium heat. When hot, add the shallot and cook until tender, about 5 minutes. Add the walnuts and thyme if you're using it and cook for another minute, stirring often. When the wheat berries are done, drain them and add to the skillet along with a good sprinkling of salt and pepper. Serve immediately or cool to room temperature.

Wheat Berries with Walnuts and Apples. Core and dice (peeling is optional) 1 all-purpose apple, like Golden Delicious; add to the pan with the shallot.

Wheat Berries with Walnuts and Butternut Squash. Add 1 cup peeled and diced butternut squash. In Step 2, cook the squash in the oil along with about $^1/_2$ cup water until it's tender and the pan is almost dry, about

15 minutes. Add the shallot and another tablespoon of oil. Proceed with the recipe. Use sage or rosemary instead of the thyme if you like.

Wheat Berries with Walnuts and Beets. Add 1 cup diced cooked beets (page 263) along with the walnuts in Step 2. Garnish with crumbled goat cheese if you like.

Creamed Hominy

MAKES: 4 servings

TIME: About 20 minutes with cooked or canned hominy

This is good, old-fashioned creamed corn, only with more flavor. Serve as a side dish with roasted, grilled, or simply pan-cooked meat or poultry.

3 cups cooked (see Cooking Grains, the Easy Way, page 451) or canned hominy, well drained

1 cup cream, half-and-half, or whole milk

2 tablespoons butter

Salt and freshly ground black pepper

1 Roughly chop about half the kernels of hominy. Combine the chopped and whole kernels and cream in a medium saucepan over medium-high heat. Bring to a boil, stirring occasionally, then turn the heat to medium-low.

2 Simmer, stirring occasionally, until most of the cream is absorbed, 5 to 10 minutes. Stir in the butter, sprinkle with salt and pepper, and serve.

Pozole with Pork and Chipotle

MAKES: At least 8 servings

TIME: 3 to 4 hours, largely unattended; 1 hour with cooked hominy

M

This Mexican dish is perfect for parties; since the ingredients are reasonable, it can feed a crew. Though the recipe takes some planning, it's easy. Serve it with a stack of warm tortillas, Red or Green Rice Pilaf (page 461) or Mexican Rice with Vegetables (page 461), a full spread of assorted cooked vegetables (like cubed potatoes, carrots, or chayote; sliced chard or kale; or green beans), and loads of garnishes (see the list that follows).

The pozole can be made ahead through Step 2; just cool, cover, and store the stew in the fridge for up to 2 days. Reheat before serving; the flavor will be better than if you served it immediately after making. If you want to speed things up a tad, presoak the hominy as you would beans (see page 411).

1½ cups dried hominy, or 4 cups precooked or canned hominy, liquid reserved

1 pound pork shoulder, trimmed of excess fat and cut into chunks

Salt and freshly ground black pepper

1 tablespoon fresh oregano or marjoram leaves or 1 teaspoon dried

1 dried chipotle or 1 chile in adobo, or to taste

1 tablespoon ground cumin, or to taste

1 large onion, chopped

1 tablespoon minced garlic

1 If you're using precooked or canned hominy, proceed to Step 2. Put uncooked hominy in a large pot with water to cover. Bring to a boil, then reduce the heat so the hominy bubbles gently. Cover and cook, stirring occasionally and adding water as necessary to keep the mixture covered, until the hominy has burst and is tender, 3 to 4 hours. Drain and reserve the liquid.

2 Combine the hominy, pork, some salt and pepper, the oregano, chile, cumin, and onion in a large saucepan over medium-high heat. Add water or some of the hominy-cooking liquid to cover by about an inch. Bring to a boil, then adjust the heat so the mixture simmers steadily but not violently. Cook, stirring occasionally, until the pork is tender, about an hour; add more liquid if necessary.

3 Stir in the garlic and cook for a few minutes more. Taste and adjust the seasoning, then serve in bowls—the

 Fast   **M** Make Ahead   **V** Vegetarian

mixture should be soupy—garnished with any or all of the suggestions from the list that follows.

Pozole with Pork, Chipotle, and Pumpkin Seeds. Toast 1 cup pepitas (pumpkin seeds) in a small dry skillet over medium heat, shaking the pan frequently until the seeds pop and color slightly. Combine them with a bit of the broth in a blender and process until smooth. Stir them into the stew and heat through.

Corn with Pork and Chipotle. Use 6 cups freshly shucked corn kernels instead of the hominy (or pan-roast or grill the corn first if you like; see page 289). Add it in Step 3.

10 Garnishes for Pozole with Pork and Chipotle

1. Chopped cilantro leaves
2. Crumbled queso fresco or farmer's cheese or goat cheese
3. Diced avocado
4. Crumbled cooked bacon or pork rinds
5. Sliced scallion, radishes, and cabbage
6. Lime wedges
7. Minced jalapeño or other fresh chile
8. Crumbled guajillo or other dried chile
9. Any fresh or cooked salsa or hot sauce
10. Mexican crema or sour cream

Four-Grain Pilaf

MAKES: 4 servings
TIME: 30 minutes

The assortment of flavors, textures, and colors makes this simple grain dish exciting.

Other grains you can use: any combination of four grains that require similar cooking times (see the chart on page 477).

3 tablespoons extra virgin olive oil or butter

1 small red onion, chopped

Salt and freshly ground black pepper

1/4 cup quinoa

1/4 cup millet

1/4 cup whole wheat or regular couscous

1/4 cup fine-grind bulgur

2 1/2 to 3 cups chicken, beef, or vegetable stock (to make your own, see pages 157–159) or water

1/2 cup chopped fresh parsley leaves

❶ Put the oil or butter in a medium ovenproof pot or deep skillet with a lid over medium-high heat. When the oil is hot or the butter is melted, add the onion, sprinkle with salt and pepper, and cook, stirring frequently, until the onion softens, about 3 minutes.

❷ Stir in the quinoa and coat with the oil. When the kernels start to toast and get fragrant, repeat first with the millet, then with the couscous, and then with the bulgur, leaving the previous grains in the pot. This whole process of toasting the grains in the oil should take no more than 5 minutes.

❸ Stir in 2 1/2 cups of the stock, bring the mixture to a boil, then cover and turn the heat to medium-low. Cook, undisturbed, for 10 minutes or so, then lift the lid and taste for doneness. If the grains are almost done but a lot of water remains, raise the heat and let the pilaf boil until it starts to dry out, then cover and turn the heat off. If the grains are almost done but the mixture is almost dry, cover and cook for another couple of minutes, then turn the heat off. If the grains are not almost done and the mixture is almost dry, add another 1/2 cup stock, cover, and cook for 5 to 10 more minutes. Let rest for 3 to 5 minutes. Use a fork to stir in the parsley and fluff the grains. Taste, adjust the seasoning, and serve.

Grain Griddlecakes

Adding a little binder (usually egg), filler (usually flour), and leavening (baking powder) to cooked grains is one of the best uses for leftovers. The result is a savory main dish or accompaniment. And it doesn't take much leftover grain—a cup or so will suffice—to jump-start a batch of griddlecakes.

Griddlecakes are always best eaten immediately, but you can keep them warm while you continue cooking large batches: Just put a wire rack set on a cookie sheet, a heatproof plate, or a pan in a 200°F oven and set the finished griddlecakes in there for a few minutes.

Parmesan Rice Cakes

MAKES: 4 servings

TIME: About 20 minutes

Cheese ensures these griddlecakes are crisp, well browned, and rich. Feel free to substitute aged cheddar, Gruyère, a semidry or dry pecorino, or even crumbled feta cheese for the Parmesan. Serve these plain or with any tomato sauce (pages 502–504).

Other grains you can use: pearled or hulled barley, farro, kamut, rye, spelt, or wheat berries.

2 eggs

$1/_2$ cup milk, half-and-half, or cream, plus more as needed

$1^1/_2$ cups cooked White Rice or Brown Rice (page 458 or 459)

$1/_2$ cup freshly grated Parmesan cheese

$1/_2$ cup all-purpose flour

$1/_2$ teaspoon baking powder

Salt and cayenne

$1/_4$ cup neutral oil, like grapeseed or corn, or 4 tablespoons ($1/_2$ stick) butter

$1/_4$ cup chopped fresh parsley for garnish (optional)

❶ Heat a heavy skillet or griddle to about 375°F.
❷ Whisk the eggs and milk together in a medium bowl until well combined. Whisk in the rice and cheese. Switch to a spoon, add the flour and baking powder, and

sprinkle with just a little salt and as much cayenne as you like. Add enough extra milk to make a smooth, medium-thick batter.

❸ When a drop of water skips across the skillet or griddle before evaporating, it's ready. Put a little oil or butter in the pan and let it bubble. Using a large spoon, scoop up a bit of the batter and put it in the pan. It should spread to about 3 inches. Cook as many griddlecakes at once as will fit comfortably, turning them after a couple of minutes, when they are brown. Total cooking time will run between 5 and 8 minutes. Serve immediately, ideally straight from the pan, sprinkled with parsley if you like.

Parmesan Rice Cakes with Ham or Bacon. Add $1/_2$ cup chopped cured ham, like prosciutto, Serrano, or country ham, or pancetta or bacon, cooked crisp; mix in with the rice and cheese.

Oat Griddlecakes

MAKES: 4 servings

TIME: 30 minutes with cooked oatmeal

Porridge—any grain that cooks up soft and creamy—is naturally "wetter" than whole-kernel cooked grains and therefore easier to make into cakes. In fact, when you take a bowl of leftover porridge out of the fridge, it's a solid mass that can be cut up and panfried or grilled like Polenta (pages 485–486). These griddlecakes are delicious with herb sauces like Mint Purée, Chimichurri, and Arugula "Pesto" (pages 27–28).

Other cooked grains you can use: grits, polenta, sticky rice, cracked wheat, any rolled grains.

About $1/_4$ cup neutral oil, like grapeseed or corn, or 4 tablespoons ($1/_2$ stick) butter

$1/_2$ cup minced onion

Salt and freshly ground black pepper

1 egg

 Fast   Make Ahead   Vegetarian

$^{1}/_{4}$ cup milk, half-and-half, or cream

2 cups cooked oatmeal (see page 820)

$^{1}/_{4}$ cup all-purpose flour

$^{1}/_{2}$ teaspoon baking powder

1 Put 2 tablespoons of the oil or butter in a small skillet over medium-high heat. When the oil is hot or the butter is melted, add the onion, sprinkle with salt and pepper, and cook, stirring frequently, until the onion is soft and starting to brown, about 2 minutes. Turn the heat down to medium-low and continue cooking, stirring occasionally, until well caramelized, 5 to 7 minutes more. Remove from the heat and set aside.

2 Heat a heavy skillet or griddle to about 375°F.

3 Whisk the egg and milk together. Add the oatmeal and keep whisking until smooth. Switch to a spoon and add the flour, $^{1}/_{2}$ teaspoon salt, and the baking powder. Stir until just combined, then stir in the cooked onion.

4 When a drop of water skips across the skillet or griddle before evaporating, it's ready. Put a little oil or butter in the pan and let it bubble. Using a tablespoon, scoop up a bit of the batter and put it in the pan. Cook as many griddlecakes at once as will fit comfortably, turning them after a couple of minutes, when they are brown; add a little more oil or butter between batches if necessary. Total cooking time will run between 5 and 8 minutes. Serve immediately, ideally straight from the pan.

Savory Oatcakes with Bacon. Cook about 4 ounces bacon, chopped, until crisp and the fat is rendered. Drain and reserve the excess fat from the pan and cook the onion as directed in Step 1. Proceed with the recipe, adding the bacon to the batter along with the onion.

Savory Oatcakes with Peas and Carrots. In Step 1, when you turn down the heat, add $^{1}/_{4}$ cup peas (frozen are fine) and $^{1}/_{4}$ cup chopped carrot to the pan.

13 Additions to Oat Griddlecakes

Whisk these into the main recipe, either alone or in combination, with the egg before adding the oatmeal.

1. A minced shallot
2. A couple cloves Roasted Garlic (page 303), squeezed from their skins
3. A tablespoon or so of soy sauce (reduce the salt)
4. Horseradish (freshly grated or prepared), to taste
5. A tablespoon of chopped fresh chives
6. $^{1}/_{4}$ cup finely chopped nuts, like almonds, walnuts, hazelnuts, or pecans
7. $^{1}/_{4}$ cup peanut or any nut butter
8. $^{1}/_{4}$ cup minced scallion
9. $^{1}/_{4}$ cup chopped dried fruit, like apricots, cherries, cranberries, or apple
10. $^{1}/_{2}$ cup chopped cooked greens, like kale, spinach, or chard, squeezed dry
11. $^{1}/_{2}$ cup corn kernels (thawed frozen are fine)
12. $^{1}/_{4}$ cup or so crisp cooked chopped or crumbled bacon or pancetta
13. 1 tablespoon any curry powder (to make your own, see pages 66–67), or more to taste

Lamb and Bulgur Patties

Kofte

MAKES: 4 to 6 servings

TIME: 25 minutes with cooked bulgur

A Middle Eastern style–burger that can be an appetizer, a side dish, or a light main dish. Serve with a dipping or drizzling sauce like Lighter Cilantro (or Other Herb) "Pesto" (page 28), Yogurt Tahini Sauce (page 35), or Creamy Cilantro-Mint Chutney (page 37), or sprinkle with lemon juice and za'atar before serving.

Other grains you can use: cooked cracked wheat.

1 pound boneless lamb, preferably from the shoulder, excess fat removed

1 medium onion, quartered

Salt and freshly ground black pepper

2 cloves garlic, peeled

Pinch cayenne

1 teaspoon ground cumin

1 egg

1½ cups soaked bulgur (page 481), drained until dry

½ cup chopped fresh parsley leaves

2 tablespoons neutral oil, like grapeseed or corn, if panfrying

❶ Cut the lamb into large chunks and put in a food processor with the onion, a large pinch of salt, some pepper, the garlic, cayenne, cumin, and egg. Process until smooth, stopping the machine and scraping down the sides if necessary. Mix in the bulgur and parsley by hand.

❷ To broil: Heat the broiler—the rack should be about 4 inches from the heat source—and shape the kofte into 4 or 6 elongated (small football-shaped) meatballs. Broil, turning once, until nice and brown, about 10 minutes total.

To panfry: Shape the kofte into 8 small patties. Put the oil in a large skillet, preferably nonstick, over medium heat. When hot, add the patties, rotating as necessary and turning once or twice, until crisp and golden on each side, about 10 minutes. Serve hot or at room temperature.

Pasta, Noodles, and Dumplings

THE SIMPLEST AND TRUEST GENERALIZATION

one can make about pasta, noodles, and dumplings—

there really is no single term embracing them all—is

that people love them. With the exception of saying

that they contain flour and water (and sometimes even

that's not always true, especially with Asian noodles),

everything else is up for grabs.

Dried pasta—the kind you buy in a box—is a

reliable and beloved staple. It's cheap, convenient,

and can be prepared in thousands of different

ways. Add dried Asian noodles to your pantry, and

you've virtually doubled your repertoire of fast-cooking meals.

But fresh pasta is not all that difficult to make (though in truth it's usually not a weekday dish), and it's really quite special, richer and more flavorful than dried, as the water is usually replaced by egg. Special, too, are dumplings, ravioli, and other stuffed doughs, which can be time-consuming but also can be made in advance and frozen. Lots of saucing ideas are included in this chapter, including a list of recipes that work with either fresh or dried pasta. (In fact, almost every recipe made with fresh pasta can be made with dried, and vice versa.)

Finally, there are things that are a cross between noodles and dumplings, like gnocchi, spaetzle, and passatelli which are quite easy to make (requiring neither machine nor rolling pin) and are most certainly fair game for weeknights.

ESSENTIAL RECIPES

This is irresistible weeknight food that's easy to vary (the first recipe, for example, has 20 variations). All the recipes start with dried pasta combined with simple sauces. With the exception of Macaroni and Cheese, they're all fast, some so fast you'll be amazed. (By the way, if you're in a hurry and craving mac 'n' cheese, make Spaghetti with Butter and Parmesan, page 506, instead.)

✪ Fast Tomato Sauce, with or without Pasta

MAKES: 4 servings
TIME: 20 minutes
F **M** **V**

This tomato sauce is among the most basic and useful all-purpose sauces and one that's too easy not to make yourself. The main recipe uses basic pantry ingredients and is familiar to just about everyone, and the variations show you a range of possible directions to take it. Add

cooked dried—or fresh—pasta and you have a simple meal.

I suggest making double or triple batches of this sauce and freezing some. Prepare the recipe through Step 2 (omitting the spaghetti, obviously, and the cheese), then let the sauce cool, pack it away in freezer bags or tightly sealed containers (small quantities are most useful), freeze, and use within 6 months or so. You can defrost it slowly in the fridge, faster in the microwave, or heat gently in a covered pan, stirring occasionally to prevent sticking.

Salt

3 tablespoons extra virgin olive oil or butter

1 medium onion, chopped

1½ to 2 pounds canned tomatoes, drained and chopped

Freshly ground black pepper

1 pound any dried pasta (spaghetti is the classic)

Freshly grated Parmesan or other cheese, to taste (optional)

Chopped fresh parsley or basil leaves for garnish (optional)

1 Bring a large pot of water to a boil and salt it. Put the olive oil or butter in a 10- or 12-inch skillet over medium-high heat. When the oil is hot or the butter is melted, add the onion and cook, stirring occasionally, until soft, 2 or 3 minutes. Add the tomatoes and a sprinkling of salt and pepper.

2 Cook, stirring occasionally, until the tomatoes break down and the mixture comes together and thickens, 10 to 15 minutes. Taste, adjust the seasonings, and keep warm. (Or let cool, cover, and refrigerate for up to several days; reheat gently before serving.)

3 Cook the pasta in the boiling water until tender but not mushy. When it is done, drain it, reserving a bit of the cooking water. Reheat the sauce briefly if necessary. Toss the pasta with the sauce, adding a little more oil or some of the cooking water if it seems dry. Taste and adjust the seasoning, then toss with some cheese and parsley if you're using it.

20 Quick and Easy Ways to Spin Fast Tomato Sauce

Generally, if you're adding ingredients that need to cook—like vegetables—you should toss them in the oil before the tomatoes and cook for a few minutes. If not, just add them along with the tomatoes or after the tomatoes begin to break down. Some additions might increase the cooking time a bit, though none will take you longer than 45 minutes total. You'll know when tomato sauce is ready because it suddenly goes from looking rather watery to having that familiar saucy look.

1. Fresh Tomato Sauce: A superb option and useful for all the variations here, but only for a couple of months a year (I like this very much with butter): Substitute chopped fresh ripe tomatoes (preferably peeled and seeded, about 2 cups) for the canned. Cooking time will be about the same. Garnish with lots of Parmesan or chopped parsley or basil.

2. Garlicky Tomato Sauce: Omit the onion. Lightly crush and peel 2 to 10 (or even more) cloves garlic; cook in the oil or butter over medium-low heat, turning occasionally, until golden brown about 5 minutes. Raise the heat, add the tomatoes, and cook as directed. Garnish with parsley or basil.

3. Spicy Tomato Sauce: Known as *arrabbiata,* this is one of those rare dishes in which garlic is actually browned intentionally; still, don't overcook it. Omit the onion; put about 1 tablespoon chopped garlic in the oil along with 3 to 5 (to 10, for that matter) small dried red chiles. Cook, stirring, until the garlic is brown, then turn off the heat for a minute, add the tomatoes, and resume cooking. Remove the chiles before serving if you like. Garnish with parsley or basil.

4. Tomato Sauce with Aromatic Vegetables: With the onion, add $1/2$ cup each minced carrot and peeled and minced celery; cook until tender, about 10 minutes, before adding the tomatoes. Especially good puréed (see variation number 19). Garnish with cheese or parsley or basil.

5. Tomato Sauce with Wine: Add $1/4$ cup dry white or red wine just before the tomatoes; let it bubble away for a moment before proceeding. Garnish with parsley or basil.

6. Tomato Sauce with Bay Leaves: Add 5 to 10 bay leaves and a small pinch (about $1/8$ teaspoon) ground cinnamon before adding the tomatoes. Remove and discard the bay leaves before serving; garnish with parsley or basil.

7. Mushroom Sauce: Cook 1 cup trimmed and sliced mushrooms (or, even better, start with Sautéed Mushrooms, Dry Style, page 314), adding the onion along with the mushrooms and the tomatoes after the mushrooms are cooked. Garnish with parsley or basil.

8. Tomato Sauce with Fresh Herbs: Really delightful, especially in summer. At the last minute, add $1/4$ to $1/2$ cup chopped fresh basil, parsley, dill, mint, or a combination. Or add smaller amounts of stronger herbs (fresh at the last minute, dried along with the tomatoes): sage (maybe 10 leaves), rosemary (a teaspoon dried or a tablespoon fresh), thyme ($1/2$ teaspoon dried or 1 teaspoon fresh), oregano or marjoram (the latter is better, a teaspoon dried or a tablespoon fresh), or tarragon ($1/2$ teaspoon fresh or $1/4$ teaspoon dried). Garnish with cheese or a little more herb.

9. Cheesy Tomato Sauce: Parmesan, of course, is standard but hardly essential, and cheeses can be combined. In a warmed bowl, just before adding pasta and sauce, put in $1/2$ cup or more ricotta, goat cheese, or mascarpone for a creamy sauce; a couple tablespoons of grated Parmesan, Grana Padano, manchego, or other hard cheese for a stronger-tasting one; or up to a cup of grated fresh mozzarella for a gooey, pizzalike pasta dish. Garnish with more cheese or some parsley or basil.

10. Vegetable Tomato Sauce: The vegetables must be tender before you add the tomatoes; this is nice puréed (see variation number 19). After the tomatoes are cooked, add a cup of almost any cooked vegetable, chopped or sliced (like eggplant, zucchini, squash, fennel, celery, carrots, peppers, artichoke hearts,

mushrooms, or cauliflower; grilled vegetables are ideal). Heat through. Garnish with cheese and chopped parsley or basil.

11. Dried Tomato Sauce: Add ¼ cup chopped reconstituted dried tomatoes to the oil before adding the tomatoes. Garnish with cheese or chopped parsley or basil.

12. Tomato Pesto Sauce: Use as much or as little pesto as you like. After the sauce has finished cooking, stir in some Traditional Pesto or one of its variations (page 27) or, after tossing the pasta, top each serving with a spoonful of pesto; the fragrance at the table is awesome.

13. Red Pepper and Tomato Sauce: With homemade Roasted Red Peppers (page 330), just amazing. Add 1 or more chopped roasted red peppers along with the tomatoes. Garnish with chopped parsley or basil.

14. Puttanesca Sauce: A Roman classic. When you add the garlic to the olive oil, stir in a few oil-packed anchovies (and omit or at least reduce the salt); mash them up a bit as you stir. Then add 2 tablespoons drained capers, some hot red pepper flakes if you like, and ½ cup pitted black olives (the wrinkled, oil-cured type, like Moroccan, works best). Then add the tomatoes. Garnish with chopped parsley or basil.

15. Creamy Vodka Sauce: Spicy in an odd way. About 2 minutes before the sauce is done, stir in ¼ cup or so of vodka and ¼ cup cream, or to taste.

16. Thicker, More Intense Tomato Sauce: Blend in about ¼ cup tomato paste just before adding the tomatoes. Garnish with cheese or parsley or basil.

17. Oven-Roasted Tomato Sauce: Also great thinned with a little vegetable stock (to make your own, see page 157), wine, or water. Use Oven-Roasted Plum Tomatoes or the canned variation (page 361) instead of canned or fresh tomatoes.

18. Grilled Tomato Sauce: Especially if you've already got the grill going, cut the tomatoes into thick slices and grill quickly on both sides until browned, about 5 minutes total. Grill a red bell pepper and a jalapeño or two, then peel, seed, and chop. Add 1 teaspoon minced fresh oregano leaves and 1 tablespoon or so red wine vinegar after Step 1. Garnish with parsley.

19. Puréed Tomato Sauce: Smooth and creamy. You can finish any sauce by passing it through a food mill or whizzing it in a blender or food processor (for safety's sake, cool it slightly first); add a little cream or ricotta cheese if you like. Reheat it briefly before saucing the pasta. Garnish with cheese or parsley or basil.

20. Tuna Sauce: Add a 6-ounce can tuna, preferably the Italian kind packed in olive oil, to the sauce after adding tomatoes. This is especially good with the additions given for Puttanesca.

✪ Linguine with Garlic and Oil

Pasta Aglio e Olio

MAKES: 4 servings
TIME: 30 minutes

One of my all-time favorites, the quintessential late-night Roman dish uses olive oil as a primary flavor, so use the best you have. Any shape of pasta will do here, though linguine is traditional. Be careful not to overcook the garlic.

There are times when an oil-based sauce is not thin enough to coat your pasta. In this case, add more oil or a bit of pasta-cooking water.

Salt

⅓ cup extra virgin olive oil, or more as needed

2 tablespoons minced garlic

1 or 2 small dried red chiles, or to taste, or hot red pepper flakes to taste (optional)

1 pound long, thin pasta, like linguine or spaghetti, or any other pasta

½ cup chopped fresh parsley leaves (optional)

❶ Bring a large pot of water to a boil and salt it. Put the oil, garlic, the chiles if you're using them, and a pinch

 Fast   Make Ahead   **V** Vegetarian

of salt in a small skillet or saucepan over medium-low heat. Let the garlic sizzle a bit, shaking the pan occasionally, just until it turns golden, about 3 minutes. Turn off the heat if the pasta isn't ready.

2 Cook the pasta until it is tender but not mushy. When it is done, drain it, reserving a bit of the cooking water. Reheat the garlic and oil mixture briefly if necessary. Dress the pasta with the sauce, adding a little more oil or some of the cooking water if it seems dry. Taste and adjust the seasoning, then toss with the parsley if you're using it.

Linguine with Garlic, Oil, and Anchovies. In Step 1, add 4 to 6 anchovy fillets (with their oil, if any; rinsed and picked over if salted) to the oil along with the garlic; mash the anchovies until they break down and virtually dissolve into the oil.

Linguine with Garlic, Oil, and Fresh Herbs. When the garlic is done, toss in a mixture of 1 cup or more fresh herbs, whatever you have on hand; try, for example, ¼ cup minced parsley leaves; ¼ cup minced basil or chervil leaves; 1 sprig tarragon, minced; several sprigs of dill, minced; a sprig or two of thyme, leaves stripped from the stem and minced; and 1 tablespoon or more of minced chives (this is merely a suggestion; substitute freely). The mixture will absorb all the oil, so, in Step 3, when you toss it with the pasta, be sure to add more oil or some of the pasta-cooking water. Garnish with more chopped herbs.

Linguine with Garlic, Oil, and Bread Crumbs. Use a large skillet over medium heat and start by putting in only the oil. When hot, add ½ cup bread crumbs, preferably fresh (page 876), and cook, stirring frequently, until golden and fragrant, 2 to 3 minutes; remove with a slotted spoon. Add a little more oil, turn the heat down to medium-low, and stir in the chiles if you're using them, the garlic, and a large pinch of salt. Proceed with the recipe, stirring in the crunchy bread crumbs as a garnish at the last moment.

Linguine with Garlic, Oil, and Chickpeas. Good with cut pasta, like ziti, penne, or shells: While you're cooking the pasta, toss about 1 cup cooked chickpeas (drained canned are fine) into the cooked garlic-oil mixture and warm gently.

Linguine with Garlic, Oil, and Nuts. Use walnuts, almonds, hazelnuts, pecans, or pine nuts and add anchovies if you like (see the first variation): Chop about ½ cup nuts in a food processor or by hand. Use a large skillet over medium heat and start by putting in only the oil. When hot, add the nuts and cook, stirring frequently, until they start to toast and become fragrant, just a minute or two. Then turn the heat down to medium-low and stir in the chiles, garlic, and a large pinch of salt. Proceed with the recipe from Step 1.

✪ Pasta with Pancetta and Pecorino

Pasta alla Gricia

MAKES: 3 to 6 servings
TIME: 30 minutes

This wonderful little group of recipes shows you how to glean a lot of flavor from bits of crisp-cooked meat, grated cheese, and freshly ground black pepper, the variations building in complexity from there.

The most common meat for these pastas is pancetta—salted, cured, and rolled pork belly—which is available at almost any decent Italian deli and many supermarkets, but you can also use bacon (or even better, if you can find it, guanciale, which is cured pig's jowl; see page 982 for mail-order sources). Pecorino Romano is the cheese of choice here, but Parmesan is also good.

Salt

2 tablespoons extra virgin olive oil, or more as needed

¹/₂ cup (about 4 ounces) chopped pancetta, guanciale, or bacon

1 pound linguine or other long pasta

¹/₂ cup grated pecorino Romano cheese, or more to taste

Freshly ground black pepper

❶ Bring a large pot of water to a boil and salt it. Put the oil and pancetta in a medium skillet over medium heat. Cook, stirring occasionally, until nicely browned, about 10 minutes. Turn off the heat.

❷ Cook the pasta in the boiling water until tender but not mushy. Drain it, reserving a bit of the cooking water.

❸ Toss the pasta with the pancetta and its juices; stir in the cheese. If the mixture is dry, add a little of the pasta-cooking water (or a little olive oil). Taste and adjust the seasoning, then add black pepper (you want a lot) and serve.

Pasta Carbonara. Basically pasta with bacon and eggs: While the pasta is cooking, warm a large bowl and beat 3 eggs in it. Stir in about ¹/₂ cup freshly grated Parmesan and the pancetta and its juices. When the pasta is done, drain it and immediately toss with the egg mixture. If the mixture is dry (unlikely), add a little pasta-cooking water. Add plenty of black pepper and some more Parmesan to taste and serve.

Pasta all'Amatriciana. The balance of sweet onion, salty bacon, and acid tomatoes is incredible: After Step, remove the pancetta with a slotted spoon and, in the juices left behind, sauté 1 medium onion, sliced, over medium heat, stirring occasionally, until well softened, about 10 minutes. Turn off the heat and let the mixture cool a bit (this will prevent spattering). Stir in 2 cups chopped tomato (drained canned are fine) and turn the heat back to medium. Cook the sauce, stirring occasionally, while you cook the pasta. When the pasta is done, drain it and toss it with the tomato sauce, the reserved pancetta, and at least ¹/₂ cup freshly grated pecorino Romano or Parmesan.

Pasta with Bacon and Dried Tomatoes. After Step 1, remove the pancetta with a slotted spoon and, in the juices left behind, gently cook ¹/₂ cup sliced or chopped dried tomatoes over medium-low heat. Keep the heat on, and when the pasta is done, add a couple tablespoons of the pasta-cooking water to the tomatoes and stir until they absorb the water and plump a bit. Add the reserved pancetta and the pasta and at least ¹/₂ cup freshly grated pecorino Romano or Parmesan.

✪ Spaghetti with Butter and Parmesan

MAKES: About 4 servings
TIME: 30 minutes

A jumping-off point for many creamy sauces—including the beloved fettuccine Alfredo—and one of the recipes that demonstrates the value of water in pasta sauces: You can use as little as ¹/₂ stick of butter here and still make a credible sauce, as long as you thin it slightly with the pasta-cooking water. Of course, within limits, more butter is better.

Salt

4 to 6 tablespoons (¹/₂ to ³/₄ stick) butter

1 pound long pasta, like spaghetti or linguine, or any other pasta

1 cup freshly grated Parmesan cheese, or more to taste

Freshly ground black pepper

❶ Bring a large pot of water to a boil and salt it. Meanwhile, bring the butter to room temperature (you can soften it in a microwave, but don't melt it). Put it in a warm bowl.

❷ Cook the pasta until tender but not mushy; drain it, reserving some of the cooking water. Toss the pasta

F Fast   **M** Make Ahead   **V** Vegetarian

with the butter, adding a little of the cooking water if necessary to thin the sauce. Toss with the Parmesan, sprinkle with salt and pepper, and serve immediately, passing additional Parmesan at the table.

Pasta with Butter, Sage, and Parmesan. A classic when made with browned butter, almost as good with olive oil: Heat 4 or more tablespoons butter with 20 or 30 fresh sage leaves over medium heat for about 3 minutes; the butter should brown and the sage sizzle. Toss the cooked pasta with the butter, sage, and Parmesan, thinning the sauce with pasta-cooking liquid if necessary.

Pasta with Butter, Parmesan, Cream, and Vegetables. With just enough cream to lightly coat the pasta: Use 4 tablespoons ($^1/_2$ stick) butter. In Step 1, when the butter has reached room temperature, whisk in $^1/_2$ cup heavy cream. Proceed with the recipe, adding up to 1 cup peas (fresh or thawed frozen) or cooked and chopped spinach, asparagus, or other tender cooked vegetables at the last moment.

Pasta with Butter, Parmesan, and Italian Ham. Cut about 6 ounces pancetta, coppa, or prosciutto into $^1/_4$-inch dice. Put 2 tablespoons of the butter and the meat in a skillet over medium-high heat and cook until the meat is lightly crisped, about 5 minutes. Add this to the warm bowl with the remaining 2 tablespoons butter and proceed with the recipe.

Fettuccine Alfredo. Reduce the butter to 2 tablespoons and melt it gently. Use fettuccine. While the pasta cooks, whisk 2 eggs with $^1/_2$ cup heavy cream and 1 cup grated Parmesan in a warmed bowl. Sprinkle with pepper. When the pasta is cooked, toss it with the cheese-egg-cream mixture, adding a little of the cooking water if necessary to keep the mixture moist. Drizzle with the butter, toss well, and serve immediately.

10 Additions to Spaghetti with Butter and Parmesan

Add one or a combination to the basic recipe or any of the variations.

1. Any chopped fresh herb of your choice or a mixture of herbs (see Linguine with Garlic, Oil, and Fresh Herbs, page 505); mint is especially nice, about $^1/_2$ cup or so
2. About 1 cup cooked peas
3. $^1/_4$ cup chopped toasted almonds or pistachios
4. Up to 2 cups cooked and drained broccoli florets
5. 2 or 3 large cooked artichoke hearts, sliced
6. A tablespoon or so grated lemon or orange zest
7. A tablespoon or so salted or brined capers
8. Ground dried or dried and smoked chiles, like ancho, chipotle, or guajillo, to taste
9. 2 to 4 sunny-side-up fried eggs, roughly chopped, or poached eggs (toss with the pasta)
10. 10 to 20 mashed Roasted Garlic cloves (page 303)

Spaghetti with Pesto

MAKES: About 4 servings
TIME: 20 minutes

F **V**

One of the fastest and easiest pasta sauces, assuming you have ready-made pesto on hand. Or you can make a simple and lovely pesto or purée with any single or mixed mild herb (see pages 27–28 for ideas).

Salt

1 pound spaghetti or other long pasta (or use a fancy-shaped pasta)

2 tablespoons extra virgin olive oil

1 cup Traditional Pesto (page 27)

Freshly grated Parmesan cheese for garnish

1 Bring a large pot of water to a boil and salt it. Cook the pasta until tender but not mushy.

2 Meanwhile, stir the olive oil into the pesto to thin it a little. When the pasta is almost done, thin the pesto further with pasta-cooking water, (a couple tablespoons at a time) until it has the consistency of heavy cream.

❸ Drain the pasta and toss it with the pesto. Taste and adjust the seasoning. Top with grated cheese and serve, passing additional grated cheese at the table.

Baked Macaroni and Cheese

MAKES: 4 to 6 servings

TIME: About 45 minutes

Ⓜ **Ⓥ**

One of the most popular recipes in the original *How to Cook Everything*, which I attribute to too many people growing up with what the Canadians call "Kraft dinner." The real thing is rich, filling, delicious, and dead easy. You can change the type of cheese you use: Try blue cheese, goat cheese, smoked Gouda, or even mascarpone. Or mix in some crisp-cooked chunks of thick-cut bacon or pancetta, about $^1/_2$ cup.

Salt

2$^1/_2$ cups milk (low-fat is fine)

2 bay leaves

1 pound elbow, shell, ziti, or other cut pasta

4 tablespoons ($^1/_2$ stick) butter

3 tablespoons all-purpose flour

1$^1/_2$ cups grated cheese, like sharp cheddar or Emmental

$^1/_2$ cup freshly grated Parmesan cheese

Freshly ground black pepper

$^1/_2$ cup or more bread crumbs, preferably fresh (page 876)

❶ Heat the oven to 400°F. Bring a large pot of water to a boil and salt it.

❷ Heat the milk with the bay leaves in a small saucepan over medium-low heat. When small bubbles appear along the sides, about 5 minutes later, turn off the heat and let stand. Cook the pasta in the boiling water to the point where you would still think it needed another minute or two to become tender. Drain it, rinse it quickly to stop the cooking, and put it in a large bowl.

❸ In a small saucepan over medium-low heat, melt 3 tablespoons of the butter; when it is foamy, add the flour and cook, stirring, until the mixture browns, about 5 minutes. Remove the bay leaves from the milk and add about $^1/_4$ cup of the milk to the hot flour mixture, stirring with a wire whisk all the while. As soon as the mixture becomes smooth, add a little more milk, and continue to do so until all the milk is used up and the mixture is thick and smooth. Add the cheddar or Emmental and stir.

❹ Pour the sauce over the pasta, toss in the Parmesan, and sprinkle with salt and pepper. Use the remaining 1 tablespoon butter to grease a 9 × 13-inch or like-size baking pan and turn the pasta mixture into it. (You can make the dish to this point, cover, and refrigerate for up to a day; return to room temperature before proceeding.) Top liberally with bread crumbs and bake until bubbling and the crumbs turn brown, 15 to 20 minutes. Serve piping hot.

Simpler Macaroni and Cheese. The ingredients are layered and cooked together so it's less creamy: For Step 3, butter the baking pan with an extra 1 or 2 tablespoons butter. Layer in one-third of the pasta, sprinkle with half of the flour, fleck with half of the butter, cover with about $^1/_2$ cup of the grated cheeses, pour half of the heated milk over the top, and sprinkle with salt and pepper. Repeat the layers, using the remaining flour, butter, and milk, and top with the remaining pasta, cheeses, and bread crumbs. Bake until bubbling and browned on top, about 30 minutes.

Rich Macaroni and Cheese. Reduce the milk to $^3/_4$ cup. Omit the bay leaves, the first 3 tablespoons butter, and all of the flour. Substitute mascarpone for the grated cheddar. Add about a cup or so sautéed wild mushrooms (see page 313), if you like, and 1 tablespoon chopped fresh sage leaves (or 1$^1/_2$ teaspoons dried sage). Cook the pasta as directed. Mix together the milk, mascarpone, and Parmesan in a large bowl.

 Fast   Make Ahead   **Ⓥ** Vegetarian

Add the cooked pasta and the sage, sprinkle with salt and pepper, and combine. Proceed with Step 4.

Macaroni and Goat Cheese with Roasted Red Peppers. Add 2 Roasted Red Peppers (page 330), chopped, and $1/2$ cup each chopped fresh basil leaves and toasted pine nuts. Substitute 1 cup soft goat cheese for the Parmesan and reduce the grated cheese by $1/2$ cup. Omit the bay leaves. Proceed with the recipe, stirring in the peppers, basil, and pine nuts in Step 4 with the pasta.

Macaroni and Chile Cheese. For a spicy dish, use a hotter chile or add a tablespoon chopped chipotle chile with adobo sauce: Use grated Jack or cheddar for all 2 cups of the cheese. Add 2 medium poblano or other mild green fresh chiles, roasted, cleaned, and chopped (see page 330); $1/4$ cup or so chopped fresh cilantro leaves, and 1 medium tomato, sliced. Proceed with the recipe, stirring in the chiles and cilantro in Step 4 with the pasta, then top with the tomato slices and bread crumbs.

6 Great Mac-and-Cheese Combos

Any pasta will work with any of the cheeses, so mix these up as you like. Some drier hard cheeses, like Parmesan, Asiago, manchego, and some pecorinos, are best when combined with softer cheeses; similarly, very strong cheeses are best paired with mild cheeses. Try:

1. Pasta shells with $1/2$ cup cream cheese and $1^{1}/2$ cups pecorino
2. Fusilli or corkscrews with $1^{1}/2$ cups smoked Gouda or mozzarella and $1/2$ cup Parmesan
3. Wagon wheels with $1^{1}/2$ cups goat cheese and $1/2$ cup Romano or Parmesan
4. Rotini or spirals with 1 cup Gorgonzola and 1 cup Bel Paese or fontina
5. Tube pastas, like penne, rigatoni, and ziti, with 1 cup manchego and 1 cup Jack
6. Orecchiette with 1 cup ricotta and 1 cup Parmesan or pecorino

✪ Cold Noodles with Sesame or Peanut Sauce

MAKES: 2 main-course or 4 side-dish or appetizer servings
TIME: 30 minutes

A crowd-pleaser and an easy starter or side—or a main course on a hot day. To make it more substantial, add $1/2$ cup or so of small tofu cubes or cooked soybeans. Or top each serving with a few slices of grilled, roasted, or poached chicken. The cucumber adds nice crunch and freshness to what is otherwise a pretty dense dish.

Salt

1 medium or 2 small cucumbers (optional)

12 ounces fresh Chinese egg noodles or long pasta, like linguine

2 tablespoons dark sesame oil

$1/2$ cup tahini, peanut butter, or a combination

2 tablespoons sugar

3 tablespoons soy sauce, or to taste

1 teaspoon minced fresh ginger (optional)

1 tablespoon rice or white wine or other vinegar

Hot sesame oil or Tabasco sauce to taste

$1/2$ teaspoon freshly ground black pepper, or more to taste

At least $1/2$ cup chopped scallion for garnish

❶ Bring a large pot of water to a boil and salt it. Peel the cucumbers if you're using them, cut them in half lengthwise, and, using a spoon, scoop out the seeds (see page 293). Cut the cucumber into shreds (you can use a grater for this) and set aside.

❷ Cook the noodles in the boiling water until tender but not mushy. Meanwhile, whisk together the sesame oil and tahini, sugar, soy, ginger, vinegar, hot oil, and pepper in a large bowl. Thin the sauce with hot water until it's about the consistency of heavy cream; you will need $1/4$ to $1/2$ cup. Stir in the cucumber. When the pasta is done, drain it and run the pasta under cold water. Drain.

③ Toss the noodles with the sauce and cucumbers. Taste and adjust the seasoning (the dish may need salt), then garnish with the scallion and serve.

Spicy Cold Noodles with Pork. In Step 2, omit the tahini and hot oil from the dressing, adding 2 teaspoons Chile Paste (page 74) or chile oil, or more to taste, 2 tablespoons dark sesame oil, and an extra tablespoon of rice vinegar. In Step 3, toss about 8 ounces thinly sliced roasted or grilled pork or smoked ham with the noodles and sauce. Garnish with bean sprouts, chopped cilantro, sliced scallion, and/or chopped radishes as you like.

✪ Pad Thai

MAKES: 4 servings
TIME: 30 Minutes

Easy to make at home—easier than you thought, I'm sure—and better than most pad Thai you've had in restaurants. Just make sure you have everything on hand and prepared before you start stir-frying, because it goes pretty fast once the heat is on.

    12 ounces dried flat rice noodles, ¼ inch thick

    5 tablespoons peanut or neutral oil, like grapeseed or corn

    3 eggs, lightly beaten

    4 garlic cloves, minced

    4 ounces small shrimp, peeled

    4 ounces pressed tofu (see page 444), or extra-firm tofu, prepared by any of the methods on pages 444–446 or simply blotted dry, sliced

    2 scallions, cut into 1-inch lengths

    1 cup bean sprouts, rinsed and trimmed

    2 tablespoons nam pla (Thai fish sauce)

    2 teaspoons tamarind paste or ketchup

    2 teaspoons sugar

    ¼ cup chopped peanuts

    ¼ cup chopped fresh cilantro leaves

    2 small fresh green chiles, preferably Thai, seeded and sliced (optional)

    1 lime, cut into wedges

① Put the noodles in a bowl and pour boiling water over them to cover. Soak until softened, at least 15 minutes; if you want to hold them a little longer, drain them, fill the bowl with cold water, and return the noodles to the bowl.

② Put 2 tablespoons of the oil in large skillet over medium heat. When hot, add the eggs and scramble quickly for the first minute or so with a fork almost flat against the bottom of the pan; you're aiming for a thin egg crêpe of sorts, one with the smallest curd you can achieve. Cook just until set and transfer the crêpe to a cutting board. Cut into ¼-inch strips and set aside.

③ Raise the heat to high and add the remaining oil. When hot, add the garlic and shrimp and cook, stirring occasionally, until the shrimp lose their raw gray color, about 2 minutes. Remove from the pan with a slotted spoon and transfer to a plate next to the stove. Add the tofu, scallions, and half of the bean sprouts to the pan and cook, stirring occasionally, for 3 minutes. Transfer with a slotted spoon to the plate with the shrimp.

④ Put the drained noodles, eggs, nam pla, tamarind, and sugar in the pan and cook, stirring occasionally, until the noodles are heated through, then add the stir-fried tofu mixture. Toss once or twice and transfer the contents of the pan to a serving platter. Top with the peanuts, cilantro, chiles, and remaining bean sprouts. Serve with the lime wedges.

Vegetarian Pad Thai. Omit the shrimp and increase the tofu to 8 ounces. Substitute soy sauce for the fish sauce.

The Basics of Dried Pasta

You can make your own pasta (see pages 537–539), but even the most devoted and skilled home cooks I know do

F Fast   **M** Make Ahead   **V** Vegetarian

so just a few times a year. (There are exceptions; you might make Spaetzle, page 552, more often, because it's so easy).

So for the most part you're going to buy pasta. You can buy fresh, which is available in several levels of "freshness": At good Italian or Asian markets, fresh noodles are made regularly and are usually very good. Supermarkets also sell "fresh" pasta that falls somewhere in between fresh and dried; it varies in quality but is usually too expensive and not all that terrific.

Almost everyone buys dried pasta routinely. For most occasions, you want to buy pasta that is 100 percent durum wheat. Ironically, though the flour comes from the States or Canada, the best pasta comes from Italy. Good pasta is easier to avoid overcooking and has a deeper, more appealing color and a texture that grabs the sauce better. For more information about pastas made from other flours, see "What to Expect from Whole Wheat Pasta" (page 522).

Cooking Pasta

With a few exceptions, you must cook pasta in abundant water; figure a gallon or so per pound (even a little more is better, and you can, of course, use less water and a small pot if you're not cooking a whole pound). You should salt the water well too—a fistful is about right, but if your hands are small you need more than that (a couple of tablespoons). It doesn't matter much when you add the salt. While the pasta cooks, adjust the heat to keep the water boiling and stir frequently.

If you have problems with sticking, it's because you either don't use enough water, don't salt enough, or don't stir enough. (And without enough salt, your pasta will be both sticky and bland.) No matter what you learned in college, adding oil to the water will not cure the problem. In fact it's counterproductive, because it keeps the sauce from grabbing properly.

If your pot is not deep enough for spaghetti or other long pasta, either break the pasta in half or hold the noodles by one end and dunk the other. As the bunch soft-ens, swirl the strands around until they bend enough for you to submerge the whole thing. Or get a bigger pot.

Don't undercook or overcook. Easy enough to say and easy enough to do: When the pasta starts to soften, taste it; it's done when it retains a little bite but is no longer chalky. If you cut a piece in half, you'd still see a little hard white bit in the center. At that point, get ready to drain; it will cook a little more on the way to the table and be al dente—literally "to the teeth" or what I call "tender but not mushy"—when you eat it. It doesn't take much practice to get this right.

Don't trust anyone's pasta-cooking times. It varies from box to box and even day to day. Cook by taste and you'll never go wrong. This holds true for every noodle you make, from fresh egg pasta made in your own kitchen to dried rice noodles from Thailand.

How Much Pasta to Cook?

Good question, really. When I was young (and so was my metabolism), I'd consider it suitable to split a pound of pasta with an equally hungry friend; this, however, is a large amount of food. Generally, I think a pound of pasta serves three (fairly generously) to four (with plenty of side dishes) as a main course and four to six, no problem, as an appetizer or side dish.

Draining, Saucing, and Tossing Pasta

Have a heated bowl ready; pasta cools quickly, and you want to eat it hot. A bowl from your cool cupboard is going to rob your pasta of heat immediately. It's best to warm a heatproof bowl with hot water (you can often put it under the colander so that the draining cooking water heats it) or put it in a warm oven while you're cooking. Then drain, quickly but not thoroughly: in most cases, the pasta should remain quite moist. (Before draining, dip out a cup or so of pasta-cooking water and reserve in case you need to thin out your sauce. See below for more on this.)

It was once true—in fact ten years ago it was true—that Americans ate more sauce on their pasta than Italians. But as scarcity has decreased in Italy, and all but the most traditional Italians have become "modernized," you see what was once considered oversauced pasta all over the place. So sauce as you like, but for crying out loud don't drown the pasta.

The real problem is that if a sauce is too thick we overcompensate by drowning the pasta with it, in an attempt to make the dish moist enough. If you have a thick sauce, one that is clumping up on the pasta instead of nicely coating it (or if you don't have enough sauce), thin it out with a little pasta-cooking water, a tablespoon or so at a time, until you achieve the desired consistency. This technique is used by most home cooks in Italy, and pasta-cooking water can be replaced by stock or water you used for cooking vegetables.

Toss quickly; pasta is best when it's very hot. Don't worry about solids collecting at the bottom of the bowl; you can scoop them over the pasta after it's served. Garnish at the last minute. Serve and eat immediately.

The Pasta Lexicon

Dried pasta comes in countless shapes. Sometimes the shape matters: When you have a chunky sauce, for example, it's nice to use a shape that will catch the chunks, like shells. For soup, you want small pasta that will fit on a spoon; angel hair or spaghetti is often good in broth. Smooth—or almost smooth—sauces are luxurious twirled with long strands or wide ribbons, but so are sauces made from big pieces of seafood, meat, or vegetables.

These conventions are flexible (at least outside of Italy); using an "inappropriate" shape is, after all, not the same as using salt instead of sugar. So I (a confessed non-Italian) would argue that it's a rare case where you should change the type of sauce you're making because you don't have the "correct" pasta shape. Most recipes here offer a couple of suggestions in the ingredient list, whether the title indicates "pasta" in a general way or calls for something specific, like linguine. But by all means, eat the shape of pasta that you like, even if it's not the exact kind called for in the recipe.

Following is a very abbreviated list of pasta shapes; these are the ones you're likely to find without much trouble.

Long Pasta

Capelli d'angelo (angel hair): Very thin strands
Spaghetti/spaghettini: Round strands of varying thickness
Bucatini: Fat, round strands with a hole through the center
Linguine: Narrow, flat strands
Fettuccine: Wide, flat strands
Tagliatelle: Wide ribbons, between fettuccine and pappardelle
Pappardelle: Very wide ribbons
Lasagne: Sheets or extra-wide ribbons—sometimes curled at the edges

Cut Pasta

Ditalini: Short, pencil-width tubes
Chifferi (gomiti): The classic bent-elbows
Penne and ziti: Smallish tubes cut at an angle
Rigatoni: Large (often ribbed) tubes, cut straight
Conchigliette and conchiglie: Seashells, small and large (good for stuffing)
Cannelloni (manicotti): Very large tubes for stuffing; sometimes ribbed

Fancy Pasta

Orecchiette: Literally "little ears," small saucer-shaped disks
Cavatelli: Small, folded disks that look like tiny taco shells
Gemelli: Cut pieces of two thick strands of pasta twisted together
Trenette: Small, three-sided tubes

F Fast   M Make Ahead   V Vegetarian

32 Pasta Dishes You Can Make in the Time It Takes to Boil Water and Cook Pasta

Figure it takes about 10 minutes to boil a gallon of water and 10 minutes to cook most dried pasta. So all of these are on the table in 20 to 30 minutes, depending on how much chopping is involved:

1. Pasta with Fast Tomato Sauce (page 502)
2. Pasta with Fresh Tomato Sauce (page 503)
3. Pasta with Garlicky Tomato Sauce (page 503)
4. Pasta with Spicy Tomato Sauce (page 503)
5. Pasta with Tomato Sauce with Wine (page 503)
6. Pasta with Tomato Sauce with Bay Leaves (page 503)
7. Pasta with Tomato Sauce with Fresh Herbs (page 503)
8. Pasta with Cheesy Tomato Sauce (page 503)
9. Pasta with Vegetable Tomato Sauce (page 503)
10. Pasta with Creamy Vodka Sauce (page 504)
11. Pasta with Thicker, More Intense Tomato Sauce (page 504)
12. Pasta with Puttanesca Sauce (page 504)
13. Pasta with Puréed Tomato Sauce (page 504)
14. Pasta with Tuna Sauce (page 504)
15. Linguine with Garlic and Oil and its variations (page 504)
16. Pasta with Pancetta and Pecorino (page 505)
17. Spaghetti with Butter and Parmesan (page 506)
18. Pasta Carbonara (page 506)
19. Spaghetti with Pesto (page 507), assuming you have pesto (see page 127) on hand
20. Linguine with Raw Tomato Sauce (page 514)
21. Macaroni with Prosciutto, Tomatoes, and Whole Garlic Cloves (page 514)
22. Pasta with Mushrooms (page 518)
23. Pasta with Leeks and Parsley (page 520)
24. Penne with Pumpkin or Winter Squash (page 521)
25. Pasta with Corn, Zucchini, and Tomatoes (page 521)
26. Ziti with Creamy Gorgonzola Sauce (page 525)
27. Pasta with Walnuts (page 526)
28. Linguine with Clams (page 527)
29. Pasta with Spicy Crab (page 528)
30. Squid and White Beans with Broken Noodles (page 530)
31. Thirty-Minute Ragù (page 532)
32. Pasta with White Sausage Sauce (page 533)

Farfalle: What we call butterflies or bowties
Fusilli, rotini, and spiralini: Curlicues, corkscrews, and spirals with subtle differences
Radiatore: Short tube shapes with lots of deep grooves for collecting sauce
Tortellini: Squares, stuffed and folded into ringlike knots
Ravioli: Stuffed squares, small to medium

Miscellaneous

Couscous: Teeny granules of pasta cooked like grains (see page 454)
Orzo: Shaped like grains of rice, only bigger

Pasta with Tomato-Based Sauces

Pasta and tomatoes seem to have been made for each other, and the combinations are close to infinite in number, which makes tomato-based sauces the most popular for pasta. Add spices, cheese, butter, or more vegetables and they gain complexity, depth, and flavor.

The first choice is in your tomato. Canned are by far the most convenient, and they're reliable as well. But in the summer, turn to fresh tomatoes first; the flavor, texture, and color are all superior. If you want to make fresh tomato sauce regularly (or if you want to make large batches and freeze or can the sauce, as many people do), invest in a food mill (see page 10), which streamlines the process. Or make Linguine with Raw Tomato Sauce; it's super easy and really wonderful.

See Fast Tomato Sauce, with or Without Pasta (page 502), for the most basic tomato sauces.

Linguine with Raw Tomato Sauce

Linguine con Salsa Cruda

MAKES: About 4 servings
TIME: About 30 minutes

With good tomatoes and good basil, this uncooked sauce is unbeatable and absurdly easy to make. This sauce is also good with fried foods (or chips, for that matter), on top of Polenta (page 485), or anywhere you'd use raw salsa or relish.

You can use good-quality canned plum tomatoes; it won't be the same, but it won't be bad (do not, however, use dried basil, here or anywhere else). And don't smash the garlic too thoroughly or you'll have trouble removing it before serving.

Salt

2 cups roughly chopped ripe tomatoes or chopped canned plum tomatoes, well drained

2 tablespoons extra virgin olive oil

Freshly ground black pepper

2 cloves garlic, lightly smashed

$1/4$ to $1/2$ cup chopped fresh basil leaves

1 pound linguine or other long pasta

Freshly grated Parmesan cheese (optional)

❶ Bring a large pot of water to a boil and salt it. Put the tomatoes, oil, some salt and pepper, the garlic, and half the basil in a broad-bottomed bowl. Mash together well, using a fork or potato masher, but do not purée. (At this point, you can let the sauce rest at room temperature for an hour or two.)

❷ Cook the pasta in the boiling water until tender but not mushy. Ladle some of the cooking water into the sauce to thin it out a bit and warm it up. Remove the garlic. Toss the pasta with the sauce; taste and adjust the seasoning. Top with the remaining basil and serve, passing the grated Parmesan at the table if you like.

7 Things to Add to Linguine with Raw Tomato Sauce

Stir any of these in with the tomatoes. You can also add any of these to Fast Tomato Sauce (page 502).

1. 2 to 4 tablespoons Traditional Pesto or any herb purée (pages 27–29)
2. 1 or 2 chopped Roasted Red Peppers (page 330)
3. Up to 12 cloves Roasted Garlic (page 303)
4. $1/4$ cup reconstituted and chopped Oven-Dried Tomatoes (page 362) or store-bought dried tomatoes
5. 2 tablespoons or more Tapenade (page 96) or chopped pitted black olives
6. 2 tablespoons smashed or roughly chopped capers
7. 2 to 4 roughly chopped anchovy fillets

Macaroni with Prosciutto, Tomatoes, and Whole Garlic Cloves

Maccheroni alla San Giovanniello

MAKES: About 4 servings
TIME: About 30 minutes

A rougher, heartier version of Pasta with Pancetta and Pecorino (page 505). Not for the timid, but beloved by many, including me.

 Fast   Make Ahead   Vegetarian

Salt

1/3 cup extra virgin olive oil or butter

10 cloves garlic, lightly crushed

1/2 cup prosciutto or other salted ham or slab bacon, cut into cubes or strips

6 plum tomatoes, cored and roughly chopped, or 1 1/2 cups chopped drained canned tomato

Freshly ground black pepper

1 pound cut pasta, like ziti or penne

1 cup roughly chopped fresh basil leaves

1 cup freshly grated pecorino Romano or Parmesan cheese or a combination

1 Bring a large pot of water to a boil and salt it. Put the oil, garlic, and prosciutto in a medium to large skillet over medium-low heat. Cook slowly, stirring occasionally, until the garlic is deep gold, nearly brown, all over, 10 to 15 minutes.

2 Add the tomatoes, along with a sprinkling of salt and pepper; stir and cook while you cook the pasta. Spoon some of the pasta-cooking water into the sauce to thin it out a bit if it looks dry.

3 Drain the pasta when tender but not mushy, reserving some of the cooking water. Toss the pasta with the sauce and most of the basil, along with the cheese, adding a little of the reserved water if necessary to thin the sauce. Taste and adjust the seasoning. Chop the remaining basil more finely, garnish the pasta with it, and serve.

Pasta with Eggplant, Tomatoes, and Bread Crumbs

MAKES: About 4 servings

TIME: 40 minutes

V

The trick here is incorporating crisp-cooked bread crumbs at the last minute. You *must* use fresh bread crumbs, most pieces about the size of a pea.

Salt

1/4 cup extra virgin olive oil (1/2 cup if you're omitting the pancetta)

1/4 cup chopped pancetta or bacon (optional)

1 cup coarse Fresh Bread Crumbs (page 876)

Freshly ground black pepper

2 small to medium eggplant (about 12 ounces), cut into 1/2- to 1-inch chunks

6 small or 3 medium tomatoes (about 12 ounces), cored, seeded, and cut into 1/2- to 1-inch chunks

1 to 2 teaspoons thinly sliced garlic, to taste

1 pound spaghetti, linguine, or other long pasta

Chopped fresh basil or parsley leaves for garnish

1 Bring a large pot of water to a boil and salt it. Put half the oil in a large skillet over medium-high heat. When hot, add the meat if you're using it, stirring occasionally, until just about crisp, about 5 minutes. Remove with a slotted spoon. Add the bread crumbs and cook, stirring almost constantly, until nicely browned, 3 to 5 minutes; sprinkle with a bit of salt and pepper as they cook. Remove with a slotted spoon and add the remaining oil.

2 Add the eggplant, stirring occasionally and sprinkling with salt and pepper, until browned and tender, about 15 minutes. When it's done, begin cooking the pasta in the boiling water until tender but not mushy. Add the tomatoes and garlic to the eggplant; cook, stirring occasionally, until softened, about 10 minutes.

3 When the pasta is done, drain it and toss with the eggplant mixture, the bread crumbs, and the meat if you used it. Taste and adjust the seasoning, garnish with basil, and serve.

Pasta with Eggplant, Anchovies, Olives, and Capers. Stir in 4 to 6 anchovy fillets (rinsed if salted), 1/2 cup halved pitted black olives, and 1 tablespoon drained capers along with the tomatoes in Step 2. Go easy on the salt.

Pasta with Eggplant, Onion, and Ricotta. Omit the meat, bread crumbs, tomatoes, and garlic. Cook 1 large onion, chopped, with the eggplant. Stir in $^1/_2$ cup each ricotta and grated Parmesan cheese, along with $^1/_2$ cup pasta-cooking water, with the eggplant just before you toss with the pasta. Proceed with the recipe. Garnish with chopped fresh basil or parsley leaves.

12 Alternative Toppings for Pasta

The most common garnishes for pasta in Italy are grated cheese (most notably Parmesan and pecorino Romano) and chopped parsley. But fried bread crumbs, for example, are a venerable substitute (cheap, readily available, and crunchy); nuts are used, especially in the South; a variety of herbs will work; and so on. Some ideas:

1. Roughly chopped olives
2. Sour cream, crème fraîche, or mascarpone
3. Dried tomatoes or dried porcini mushrooms (or both), roughly ground in a spice or coffee mill
4. Fried garlic slivers (slow-cook a couple of cloves of garlic, slivered, in a couple of tablespoons of olive oil, until lightly browned)
5. Fried shallots (see Crisp Sautéed Leeks, page 312)
6. Fried capers (flash-cook a tablespoon or two of capers in a tablespoon of olive oil for 30 to 60 seconds)
7. Chopped or grated hard-cooked egg or a poached egg
8. Toasted nuts or seeds (page 317), ground if you like, and flavored with woody herbs, like walnuts with rosemary or thyme
9. Flash-cooked fresh chile slices, like jalapeño, Thai, or serrano
10. A sprinkling of a spice blend, like garam masala, chili powder, or za'atar (to make your own, see pages 66–67)
11. Bread crumbs, preferably fresh (page 876), lightly fried, and seasoned
12. Crumbled fresh cheese or farmer cheese, ricotta salata, feta, blue, goat, or queso fresco

Pasta with Vegetables or Beans

You can toss pasta with many different vegetable dishes, which means you can turn just about any vegetable into a pasta sauce. To make the results as flavorful as possible, cook the aromatics (like onions) in oil or butter, then add the vegetable, then cook until soft. You can toss it with the pasta at that point or purée the sauce first, then add cheese and garnishes. That covers almost all the options, but there are other techniques scattered among the recipes in this section.

The possibilities are literally endless; take a look at "27 Vegetable and Legume Dishes to Toss with Pasta" (page 520) for more ideas.

Pasta with Broccoli, Cauliflower, or Broccoli Raab

MAKES: About 4 servings
TIME: About 40 minutes

Use the same water for the broccoli as you do for the pasta to save cleaning a pot and to make things go a bit faster. Olive oil is not just a cooking medium here but also one of the main flavors. So, in addition to the $^1/_4$ cup used to cook the garlic, I add some to taste at the end, usually a teaspoon or so per serving.

Salt

About 1 pound broccoli, cauliflower, or broccoli raab, trimmed and cut into pieces

$^1/_4$ cup extra virgin olive oil, or more as needed

 Fast   Make Ahead   **V** Vegetarian

1 tablespoon chopped garlic, or more to taste

1 pound penne, ziti, or other cut pasta

Freshly ground black pepper

1 Bring a large pot of water to a boil and salt it. Boil the broccoli until it's fairly tender, 5 to 10 minutes, depending on the type (broccoli raab is fastest, cauliflower slowest) and the size of your pieces. Meanwhile, put the oil in a large skillet over medium-low heat. When hot, add the garlic and cook until it begins to sizzle, about a minute; keep warm.

2 Scoop the broccoli out of the water with a slotted spoon or small strainer and transfer it to the skillet (keep the pot of water boiling). Cook over medium-high heat, stirring and mashing the broccoli, until it is hot and quite soft, adding some of the pasta water as needed to help soften the broccoli.

3 Meanwhile, cook the pasta. When the pasta is just about but not quite done, drain it, reserving about a cup of the cooking water. Add the pasta to the skillet with the broccoli and a couple of tablespoons of the reserved cooking water; toss with a large spoon until well combined. Sprinkle with salt and pepper, along with some of the pasta water to keep the mixture from drying out. Serve immediately.

Pasta with Greens. Here, if your judgment is good, you can cook the greens along with the pasta; usually you add them to the boiling water during the last minutes of cooking, but the thick stems of kale or collards may take just about as long as the pasta to get tender. Until you're confident, follow the basic recipe: Use 1 to 1 1/2 pounds spinach, kale, collards, chard, mustard, or other greens instead of the broccoli. If the stems are thick, separate them from the leaves (see page 308) and chop roughly into 1-inch lengths; roughly chop the leaves. Cook the stems or whole greens until tender and proceed with the recipe.

Pasta with Broccoli, Cauliflower, or Broccoli Raab and Sausage. Cut 2 or 3 (about 8 ounces) hot or sweet Italian sausages into thin slices and cook them along with the garlic (and hot pepper flakes to taste if you like) until nicely browned. Proceed with the recipe.

13 Ways to Boost Pasta with Broccoli, Cauliflower, or Broccoli Raab

Just a few of the ideas to make this dish more flavorful; many can be combined with each other.

1. Cook 3 or 4 dried chiles along with the garlic or stir in hot red pepper flakes when you toss the pasta.
2. Add a teaspoon or so of minced garlic to the mixture about 30 seconds before you turn off the heat.
3. Cook several saffron threads in the oil along with the garlic.
4. Add 1/2 cup or so of Traditional Pesto (page 27) when you toss the pasta.
5. Stir in a couple of tablespoons of tomato paste—or a cup of chopped cherry or regular tomatoes—when you combine the pasta and vegetable.
6. Add a couple of tablespoons of Tapenade (page 96) just when you toss the pasta.
7. Add 1 cup sliced mushrooms to the oil once the garlic sizzles and continue to cook, stirring occasionally, until you add the vegetable, then proceed.
8. Toss in a cup or so of quick-cooking, fragile vegetables, during the last 30 to 60 seconds of cooking: think pea shoots, shelled fresh peas, chopped spinach, or arugula.
9. Stir in 1/2 cup of so of Roasted Red Pepper purée (page 330) when you toss the pasta.
10. Serve with a generous sprinkling of freshly grated Parmesan cheese or Toasted Bread Crumbs (page 876).
11. Add 1/4 cup or so chopped pancetta or bacon to the pan before adding the garlic; add the garlic when the pancetta is starting to crisp. (You won't need as much olive oil.)
12. Toss in 2 to 4 anchovy fillets along with the garlic.
13. When you toss the pasta, add 8 ounces or so of sliced grilled or roasted chicken (see page 340 or 341, hot or at room temperature, not straight from the fridge).

Pasta with Mushrooms

MAKES: 4 servings
TIME: 30 minutes

In many parts of Europe, you would make these with fresh porcini, at least seasonally. Almost needless to say, it is an amazing dish when made this way, but it's still a very good one when made with shiitakes or even ordinary button mushrooms.

Salt

1 pound shiitakes or other fresh mushrooms

1/3 cup plus 1 tablespoon olive oil

Freshly ground black pepper

2 tablespoons minced shallot or 1 tablespoon minced garlic

1 pound dried pasta

1/2 cup chicken, beef, or vegetable stock (to make your own, see pages 157–159) or pasta-cooking water

About 1/2 cup chopped fresh parsley leaves, plus more for garnish

1 Bring a large pot of water to a boil and salt it. Remove the stems from the shiitakes (discard them or use them for stock). If you're using wild mushrooms, wipe them clean or rinse them quickly if they are very dirty. Trim off any hard, tough spots. Cut the mushrooms into small chunks or slices.

2 Put 1/3 cup of the oil in a medium to large skillet over medium heat. When hot, add the mushrooms and sprinkle with salt and pepper. Raise the heat to medium-high and cook, stirring occasionally, until the mushrooms begin to brown, at least 10 minutes. Add the shallot, stir, and cook until the mushrooms are tender, another minute or two. Turn off the heat.

3 Cook the pasta until tender but not mushy. When it is almost done, add the stock to the mushrooms, turn the heat to low, and reheat gently. Drain the pasta, reserving a little of the cooking water. Toss the pasta and the mushrooms together with the remaining tablespoon of olive oil; add a little of the pasta-cooking water if the dish seems dry. Taste and adjust the seasoning. Stir in the parsley and serve garnished with more parsley.

Pasta with Fresh and Dried Mushrooms. As in any mushroom recipe, you can enhance the taste of ordinary button mushrooms by adding a portion of dried porcini: Soak 1/4 to 1/2 cup dried porcini in hot water to cover for about 10 minutes, or until softened. Drain the porcini, squeeze out excess moisture (reserve the soaking liquid), cut into bits, and add in Step 2 along with the fresh mushrooms. In Step 3, use the mushroom-soaking liquid to augment or replace the stock or pasta-cooking water.

Pasta with Zucchini and Ricotta. Set 1 cup of ricotta on the counter to come to room temperature while you prepare the pasta. Substitute diced zucchini for the mushrooms and chopped fresh basil for the parsley;

 **F** Fast   **M** Make Ahead   **V** Vegetarian

begin the recipe at Step 2. When the pasta is done, toss it with the zucchini, ricotta, and basil until creamy.

Pasta with Eggplant and Balsamic Vinegar

MAKES: About 4 servings

TIME: 30 minutes

We usually think of balsamic vinegar as a salad ingredient—and indeed this dish is terrific served at room temperature as a pasta salad—but its complex flavor goes a long way toward seasoning a simple pasta sauce and balancing the meatiness of eggplant. Use grated Parmesan or pecorino Romano here if you prefer.

2 or 3 small eggplant (about 1 pound)

Salt

$1/4$ cup extra virgin olive oil, plus more as needed

Freshly ground black pepper

1 tablespoon chopped garlic

2 tablespoons balsamic vinegar

$1/2$ teaspoon hot red pepper flakes, or to taste

1 pound bucatini or cut pasta, like penne or farfalle

$1/2$ cup crumbled feta or grated ricotta salata cheese, plus more as needed

$1/2$ cup chopped fresh basil leaves

❶ Peel the eggplant if the skin is thick or the eggplant is less than perfectly firm; cut them into $1/2$-inch cubes and salt them if the eggplant are large and time allows (see page 293). Bring a large pot of water to a boil and salt it.

❷ Put the oil in a large skillet over medium heat. When hot, add the eggplant, sprinkle with salt and pepper, and cook, stirring occasionally until tender, golden, and slightly crisp on all sides, 5 to 10 minutes. Add the garlic and cook, stirring constantly, until soft and turning golden, less than a minute. Add the vinegar; give a good stir and let it bubble until it thickens slightly but doesn't

evaporate, just a few seconds. Add the red pepper and remove from the heat.

❸ Cook the pasta in the boiling water until tender but not mushy. When it's done, drain it, reserving about $1/2$ cup of the cooking water. Toss the pasta and eggplant together with a drizzle of olive oil, a few sprinklings of black pepper, and $1/2$ cup of cheese, adding a bit of the pasta water if the mixture seems dry. Taste and adjust the seasoning. Garnish with the basil and serve, passing more cheese at the table if you like.

Pasta with Red Peppers and Balsamic Vinegar. You can start with Roasted Red Peppers (page 330) for a more refined dish, but it's not necessary: Instead of the eggplant, use 3 medium red peppers, cored and cut into slices. Reduce the cooking time in Step 2 to about 5 minutes.

Linguine with Slow-Cooked Onions

MAKES: About 4 servings

TIME: About 1 hour

When cooked slowly, onions turn so sweet that they need plenty of salt, pepper, and Parmesan, or this preparation ends up one-dimensional. But with those simple additions, the dish is perfectly balanced. If you like, add a few anchovies, capers, olives, or a little vinegar near the end of cooking.

5 or 6 medium to large onions (about 2 pounds)

$1/3$ cup plus 2 tablespoons extra virgin olive oil

Salt and freshly ground black pepper

1 pound linguine or other long pasta

Freshly grated Parmesan cheese

❶ Slice the onions thinly; this is a good job for the food processor's slicing disk. Put them in a large dry skillet over medium-low heat, cover, and cook, checking and stirring every 5 minutes. The onions will first give up lots

27 Vegetable and Legume Dishes to Toss with Pasta

This is just the beginning of a list that could grow and grow. In all cases if, after saucing, you think the dish needs more moisture, while tossing just add a little of the pasta-cooking water or extra oil or butter—or both.

of liquid, then dry out; after 20 to 30 minutes, when they begin to brown and stick to the pan, remove the cover. Add ¹/₃ cup of the olive oil, along with a healthy sprinkling of salt and pepper. (You can make the sauce up to this point; cover and refrigerate for up to 2 days.) Turn the heat up to medium.

② Bring a large pot of water to a boil and salt it. Continue to cook the onions until they are uniformly brown and soft, almost pasty, 10 to 20 minutes more.

③ Cook the pasta in the boiling water until tender but not mushy. When it's done, drain it, reserving about ¹/₂ cup of the cooking water. Taste the onions and adjust the seasoning as necessary; add the remaining 2 tablespoons olive oil and a little of the reserved water. Drain the pasta and toss it with the onions and some Parmesan, adding a bit of the reserved water if the mixture seems dry. Serve, passing additional Parmesan at the table.

Pasta with Leeks and Parsley

MAKES: About 4 servings
TIME: 30 minutes

F **V**

Leeks become tender quickly enough to make a distinctive sauce for pasta in little more time than it takes to boil the water and cook the pasta. And teamed with the classic southern Italian quartet of garlic, chile, parsley, and olive oil (butter's good, too), the sauce is delicious.

Salt
4 tablespoons extra virgin olive oil or butter
2 cloves garlic, lightly crushed
2 or 3 dried red chiles or hot red pepper flakes to taste
3 large or 4 medium leeks (at least 1 pound), trimmed, washed, and chopped
¹/₂ red bell pepper or 1 tomato, chopped (optional)
1 pound spaghetti, linguine, or other long pasta
Freshly ground black pepper
³/₄ cup chopped fresh parsley leaves

① Bring a large pot of water to a boil and salt it. Meanwhile, put half the oil or butter in a large skillet over medium-high heat. When the oil is hot or the butter is melted, add the garlic and chiles and cook, stirring occasionally, until the garlic browns, about 2 minutes; remove the chiles (and the garlic if you prefer).

② Add the leeks and cook, stirring occasionally, until softened, about 10 minutes. Add the bell pepper, if you're using it, and lower the heat; continue to cook, stirring once in a while, until the leeks begin to caramelize, about 5 minutes.

③ Cook the pasta in the boiling water until tender but not mushy. When it's done, drain it, reserving about $^{1}/_{2}$ cup of the cooking water. Toss the pasta and leeks together with the remaining oil or butter, a few sprinklings of black pepper, and all but a little of the parsley, adding a bit of the cooking water if the mixture seems dry. Taste and adjust the seasoning. Garnish with the remaining parsley and serve.

Pasta with Cabbage and Parsley. Substitute 1 small or $^{1}/_{2}$ large head green or Savoy cabbage (about 1 pound) for the leeks; core and thinly shred it. Proceed with the recipe. Add about $^{1}/_{2}$ cup freshly grated pecorino Romano or Parmesan for garnish.

Penne with Pumpkin or Winter Squash

MAKES: About 4 servings
TIME: 30 minutes

Zucca—the Italian equivalent of pumpkin or butternut squash—forms the basis for a slightly sweet, hot, spicy (the nutmeg is lovely) pasta sauce.

Salt

1 medium pumpkin or butternut squash (about 1$^{1}/_{2}$ pounds), peeled and seeded

2 tablespoons butter or extra virgin olive oil

Freshly ground black pepper

$^{1}/_{2}$ teaspoon hot red pepper flakes, or to taste

1 pound penne or other cut pasta

$^{1}/_{8}$ teaspoon freshly grated nutmeg, or to taste

Pinch sugar (optional)

$^{1}/_{2}$ cup freshly grated Parmesan cheese

① Bring a large pot of water to a boil and salt it. Cut the pumpkin into chunks and put it in a food processor fitted with a metal blade. Pulse the machine on and off until it appears grated. Alternatively, grate or chop the squash by hand.

② Put the butter or oil in a large skillet over medium heat. When the butter is melted or the oil is hot, add the pumpkin, a good sprinkle of salt and pepper, the red pepper, and about $^{1}/_{2}$ cup water. Cook at a steady bubble, stirring occasionally. Add more water, about $^{1}/_{4}$ cup at a time, as the mixture dries out, taking care not to make it soupy. When the pumpkin begins to disintegrate, after 10 or 15 minutes, add the pasta to the boiling water. While it cooks, season the pumpkin with the nutmeg, sugar if you like, and additional salt and pepper if needed.

③ When the pasta is tender but not mushy, drain it, reserving about $^{1}/_{2}$ cup of the cooking water. Add the pasta to the pumpkin and a bit of the reserved cooking water if the mixture seems dry; toss with a large spoon until well combined. Taste and add more of any seasonings you like, then toss with the Parmesan and serve.

Penne with Carrots or Parsnips. Substitute peeled carrots or parsnips for the pumpkin; pulse or grate as directed. If you like, omit the nutmeg and toss in a teaspoon of chopped tarragon or chervil at the very end.

Pasta with Corn, Zucchini, and Tomatoes

MAKES: About 4 servings
TIME: 30 minutes

A summer mélange of whatever is on hand, tossed with pasta. Like ratatouille, this is flexible not only in its seasonings but also in its main ingredients: You can use onions, garlic, or shallots, singly or in combination; add green beans (or fresh limas) to the mix; substitute eggplant for the zucchini.

Salt

3 tablespoons extra virgin olive oil or 2 tablespoons oil and 1 tablespoon butter

1 cup corn kernels (from 2 or 3 ears of corn)

1 cup diced zucchini or summer squash (about 5 ounces)

Freshly ground black pepper

1 medium onion or 3 or 4 shallots, finely chopped

1/4 teaspoon minced garlic (optional)

1 tablespoon chopped fresh tarragon leaves

4 plum or 2 large ripe tomatoes, diced

1 pound cut pasta, like penne, rigatoni, or fusilli

1 Bring a large pot of water to a boil and salt it. Put 2 tablespoons of the oil in a large skillet over medium-high heat. When hot, add the corn and cook, stirring only occasionally, until the corn is dry and really beginning to brown, about 5 minutes. Add the zucchini and some salt and pepper. Cook, stirring occasionally, until the zucchini begins to brown.

2 Add the onion and the garlic if you're using it. Cook, stirring occasionally, until the onion softens, about 5 minutes. Add the tarragon and cook for 30 seconds, then add the tomatoes and continue cooking while you cook the pasta.

3 Cook the pasta in the boiling water until tender but not mushy. If the sauce dries out (with plum tomatoes, this is likely), add some of the pasta-cooking water, about 1/4 cup at a time, to thin it somewhat but not make it a soup. When the pasta is done, drain it and toss with the sauce and the remaining oil or the butter. Taste and adjust the seasoning and serve immediately.

Pasta with Edamame, Mint, and Pecorino. Or use fresh or frozen fava or lima beans if you have them: Substitute 3 cups edamame (frozen are fine) for the corn, zucchini, and tomatoes; and 1/4 cup chopped fresh

mint for the tarragon. Add 1/2 cup freshly grated or shaved pecorino Romano. Cook the onion in the oil until softened first, then add the edamame; cook for 3 or 4 minutes. Just before tossing with the pasta, stir in the mint and pecorino.

What to Expect from Whole Wheat Pasta

Now that many more people are eating whole grains, whole wheat pasta has become a supermarket staple. And while I'm not exactly a convert, there are times when I like its hearty, satisfying flavor and texture. Ideally whole wheat pasta should be flecked with bits of bran, have a pleasantly nutty flavor, and cook from brittle to tender without instantly turning to mush; and, as with regular pasta, the Italian brands deliver more of what I want.

Whole wheat pasta may take a minute or two longer to cook, and you'll never get quite the same creaminess after saucing because the starch doesn't release the same way. But what you will get is a near-ideal vehicle for assertive sauces (especially nut sauces) or sauces that include big chunks of vegetables.

8 Wonderful Recipes for Whole Wheat Pastas
Sauce and toss just as you would traditional pasta (pages 511–512). Remember to save some cooking water while draining to help thin the sauce if necessary.

1. Traditional Pesto or its variations (page 27)
2. Spaghetti and Fast Tomato Sauce or its variations (pages 502–504)
3. Linguine with Garlic and Oil or its variations (page 504)
4. Linguine with Raw Tomato Sauce (page 514)
5. Any of the pastas with vegetables or legumes (pages 514–524)
6. Ziti with Creamy Gorgonzola Sauce (page 525)
7. Pasta with Walnuts (page 526)
8. Creamy Baked Noodles with Eggplant and Cheese (page 536)

 Fast   Make Ahead   Vegetarian

Pasta with Lentils or Other Legumes

MAKES: 6 to 8 servings
TIME: About 1 hour

Lentils are ideal here, because they cook so quickly, but you can use almost any legume as long as it's soft enough. For last-minute cooking, start with precooked (see page 411), canned, or frozen beans. (If you do that, simply cook them with the vegetables until the vegetables are tender.)

You can turn this into a more-beans-than-pasta-type dish, like White Beans with Cabbage, Pasta, and Ham (page 421), or even a soup, like Pasta e Fagioli (page 124), simply by adjusting the ingredients and liquid.

³⁄₄ cup dried lentils, washed and picked over, or
    1¹⁄₂ to 2 cups cooked or canned small beans

2 carrots, chopped

1 large or 2 medium onions, chopped

2 cups chopped tomato (drained canned is fine)

Salt and freshly ground black pepper

1 tablespoon chopped fresh marjoram or oregano or
    1 teaspoon dried

3 tablespoons extra virgin olive oil

1 pound elbows, shells, or other cut pasta

1 teaspoon minced garlic

1 Combine the lentils, carrots, half the onion, and water to cover in a large pot over medium heat. Simmer until the lentils are tender but not mushy, 20 to 30 minutes (some lentils may take even longer, but check frequently to avoid overcooking). Add the tomato, sprinkle with some salt and pepper and half the herb, stir, and cook for another 10 minutes or so; keep warm over low heat. (At this point, you may refrigerate the sauce, tightly covered, for a day or two or freeze it for several weeks.)

2 Bring a large pot of water to a boil and salt it. Heat 2 tablespoons of the olive oil in a medium skillet over medium-high heat. When hot, add the remaining onion and cook, stirring, until it begins to brown and become crisp, about 10 minutes.

3 Cook the pasta in the boiling water until still fairly firm and a bit chalky in the center. Drain it, reserving a cup or so of the cooking water. Stir the pasta into the lentils along with the garlic, the cooked onion, and the remaining herb and olive oil. Add enough of the pasta-cooking water to moisten the mixture. Cook for 2 or 3 minutes, or until the pasta is just tender. Taste and adjust the seasoning, and serve in a warm bowl.

Whole Wheat Farfalle with Roasted Potatoes

MAKES: About 4 servings
TIME: About 45 minutes

Whole wheat pasta isn't a must here, but its bold, nutty flavor complements the tender browned potatoes. Pass freshly grated Parmesan cheese along with the dish at the table.

¹⁄₄ cup extra virgin olive oil, plus more for greasing the
    pan

3 or 4 medium waxy potatoes, peeled and cut into
    1-inch cubes

Salt and freshly ground black pepper

1 pound whole wheat farfalle or other cut pasta

1 tablespoon chopped garlic

2 teaspoons hot red pepper flakes, or to taste

¹⁄₄ cup chopped fresh parsley leaves or chives

1 Heat the oven to 400°F. Smear a large roasting pan or rimmed baking sheet with a little of the oil. It should be large enough to hold all the potatoes in a single layer without overcrowding.

2 Put the potatoes in the pan, sprinkle with a good amount of salt and pepper, and drizzle with 2 tablespoons of the oil; toss to coat. Roast the potatoes until they brown on the bottom sides, about 20 minutes;

stir, and continue roasting until tender, another 20 to 30 minutes.

❸ Meanwhile, bring a large pot of water to a boil and salt it. Cook the pasta until tender but not mushy and drain it. Toss the potatoes with the garlic and red pepper flakes, then toss with the pasta and remaining oil. Taste and adjust the seasoning. Sprinkle with the herb and serve immediately.

Whole Wheat Pasta with Browned Chicken. Substitute 1^1/$_2$ pounds boneless chicken (any parts, skinless or not), cut into chunks, for the potatoes. Skip Steps 1 and 2. Put 2 tablespoons of the oil in a large skillet over medium-high heat. When hot, add the chicken, sprinkle with salt and pepper, and cook until browned and cooked through, stirring occasionally, about 8 minutes. Proceed with Step 3.

Whole Wheat Pasta with Roasted Butternut Squash or Sweet Potatoes. Substitute butternut squash, peeled, seeded, and cubed, or peeled and cubed sweet potatoes, for the white potatoes. Add 1 tablespoon minced fresh rosemary or sage leaves if you like.

Pasta with Dairy-Based Sauces

One of the best and simplest combinations for pasta sauces is butter and cheese. The simplest of these, butter and Parmesan, can be found as an essential recipe on page 506, but there are as many combinations as there are cheeses, including those based on Gorgonzola (or another creamy blue cheese), ricotta (especially the creamy fresh

---

25 Pasta Sauces You Can Make in Advance

These are fresh and fresh-tasting sauces that can be made several hours or even a day in advance (most can be frozen as well), as long as they are not overcooked and are reheated gently. Always make the pasta at the last minute. If possible, add some fresh herbs during reheating; a drizzle of olive oil, if used in the basic sauce, is another good last-minute addition.

1. Fast Tomato Sauce, with or Without Pasta (page 502)
2. Garlicky Tomato Sauce (page 503)
3. Spicy Tomato Sauce (page 503)
4. Tomato Sauce with Aromatic Vegetables (page 503)
5. Tomato Sauce with Wine (page 503)
6. Tomato Sauce with Bay Leaves (page 503)
7. Mushroom Sauce (page 503)
8. Vegetable Tomato Sauce (page 503)
9. Puttanesca Sauce (page 504)
10. Creamy Vodka Sauce (page 504)
11. Thicker, More Intense Tomato Sauce (page 504)
12. Oven-Roasted Tomato Sauce (page 504)
13. Grilled Tomato Sauce (page 504)
14. Puréed Tomato Sauce (page 504)
15. Tuna Sauce (page 504)
16. The sauce for Pasta with Eggplant, Tomato, and Bread Crumbs (page 515; add the bread crumbs until just before serving)
17. The sauce for Pasta with Lentils or Other Legumes (page 523)
18. The sauce for Ziti with Creamy Gorgonzola Sauce (page 525)
19. The sauce for Penne with Tomato-Shrimp Sauce (page 528)
20. The sauce for Penne with Tomato-Seafood Sauce (page 529)
21. The sauce for Penne with Tomato-Squid Sauce (page 529)
22. Meat Sauce, Bolognese Style (page 531)
23. Thirty-Minute Ragù (page 532)
24. The sauce for Andrea's Pasta with Pork Ribs (page 532)
25. The sauce for Pasta with White Sausage Sauce (page 533)

 Fast   Make Ahead   Vegetarian

ricotta sold at Italian and specialty food stores), and strong-tasting cheeses like fontina and Taleggio.

While butter, cheese, and cream are rich ingredients, they are delicious and strong, so you don't need to use much to make a good pasta sauce. To make the thicker dairy products into a sauce, you simply need to add enough pasta-cooking water to thin them. When the pasta is nearly done cooking, scoop out a cup or so of the water. After you drain the pasta and add the sauce ingredients, stir in the cooking water a little at a time. Stop adding water when the sauce has reached the right consistency.

Orzo, Risotto Style

MAKES: 4 servings
TIME: 25 minutes

This isn't really risotto, of course, but it mimics it nicely. Use any dried small pasta here (like orecchiette or shells) or break long strands into 1-inch pieces. The cooking time and absorption rate might vary a bit, so be sure to add the stock a little at a time and check frequently for doneness.

2 tablespoons extra virgin olive oil

1 large shallot, minced

2 cups orzo (about a pound)

Salt and freshly ground black pepper

$^1/_2$ cup dry white wine or water

4 to 5 cups chicken, beef, or vegetable stock (to make your own, see pages 157–159) or water

2 tablespoons butter, softened

$^1/_2$ cup freshly grated Parmesan cheese, plus more for serving

1 Put the olive oil in a large, deep nonstick skillet over medium heat. When hot, add the shallot and cook, stirring occasionally, until it softens, 2 to 3 minutes.

2 Add the orzo and cook, stirring occasionally, until glossy and coated with oil, 2 to 3 minutes. Add a little salt and pepper, then the wine. Stir and let the liquid bubble away.

3 Use a ladle to begin to add the stock, $^1/_2$ cup or so at a time, stirring after each addition. When the stock is just about evaporated, add more. The mixture should be neither soupy nor dry. Keep the heat at medium to medium-high and stir frequently.

4 Begin tasting the orzo 10 minutes after you add it; you want it to be tender but still with a tiny bit of crunch; it could take as long as 20 minutes to reach this stage. When it does, stir in the softened butter and at least $^1/_2$ cup of Parmesan. Taste and adjust the seasoning and serve immediately, passing additional Parmesan at the table if you like.

Saffron Orzo, Risotto Style. Sprinkle a pinch saffron threads into the orzo just before adding the wine in Step 2.

Lemon Orzo, Risotto Style. Grate the zest of 2 lemons and squeeze their juice. In Step 2, when you add the orzo, add the zest. Add the lemon juice along with the wine and a lot of black pepper.

Ziti with Creamy Gorgonzola Sauce

MAKES: About 4 servings
TIME: 30 minutes

The best Gorgonzola (it must be Italian) is soft and creamy; combine it with butter and cream and you have luxury combined with intense flavor. Other top-notch blue cheeses—think Stilton and Roquefort—work well here too.

Salt

2 tablespoons butter

1 cup crumbled Gorgonzola or other good blue cheese

1/2 cup milk, half-and-half, or cream

1 pound ziti, penne, or other cut pasta

1/2 cup freshly grated Parmesan cheese, plus more for serving

1 Bring a large pot of water to a boil and salt it. Melt the butter in a 1- or 2-quart saucepan over low heat. Meanwhile, put the Gorgonzola in a small bowl and mash it with a fork or potato masher, gradually adding the milk. Don't worry about making it smooth; just make sure it is well combined.

2 When the butter is melted, add the cheese-milk mixture and continue to cook, stirring and mashing occasionally.

3 Meanwhile, cook the pasta in the boiling water until tender but not mushy. Drain it and mix with the Gorgonzola sauce in a large, warm bowl; stir in the Parmesan, then taste and adjust the seasoning. Serve, passing additional Parmesan at the table if you like.

Farfalle with Gorgonzola, Arugula, and Cherry Tomatoes. When you toss the cheese sauce with the pasta in Step 3, add 2 cups arugula (trimmed of very thick stems if necessary and washed and dried) and 1 cup cherry or grape tomatoes, halved.

Pasta with Walnuts

MAKES: 4 servings

TIME: 20 minutes

A delicious and absolutely authentic midwinter pasta dish, with a sauce that's usually served—in Piedmont at least—with pansotti (see page 544); but store-bought pasta is a good short-cut.

Salt

1 thick slice Italian bread

1/2 cup milk

1 cup walnut or pecan halves

2 cloves garlic, peeled

1/2 cup freshly grated Parmesan, plus more for serving

2 teaspoons fresh marjoram leaves or 1/2 teaspoon dried marjoram

1/2 cup extra virgin olive oil

1 pound linguine, spaghetti, or other long pasta

1 Bring a large pot of water to a boil and salt it. Soak the bread in the milk. Combine the nuts, garlic, cheese, and marjoram in a food processor and turn the machine on. With the machine running, gradually add the oil, using just enough so that the mixture forms a very thick paste.

2 Squeeze out the bread and add it to the mixture, which will be very thick. Add the milk the bread soaked in, a good sprinkling of salt and pepper, and enough water to make a saucy mixture.

3 Cook the pasta in the boiling water, stirring occasionally, until tender but not mushy; drain it, reserving 1/2 cup of the pasta-cooking water. Toss the pasta with the sauce, adding a little of the cooking water (or more olive oil) if necessary to thin the sauce. Taste and adjust the seasoning, then serve with more Parmesan.

Pasta with Seafood

Some types of seafood—shrimp and mussels are terrific examples—exude delicious liquid when cooked, making them ideal components of pasta sauce. Others just taste so good that they augment other ingredients perfectly. You'll find both here. In any case, fish should almost always be cooked (or added to the sauce) at the last minute.

Few pasta sauces with fish need added cheese. This is a matter of personal preference, of course, but chopped fresh parsley or lightly toasted bread crumbs—or a combination—make better complements.

14 Seafood, Meat, and Poultry Dishes That Work as Pasta Sauces

Make sure these dishes are piping hot before adding them to pasta. And if they seem soupy rather than saucy, drain (and reserve) some of the liquid before tossing, then use the reserved liquid to moisten the pasta if you need to.

1. Bouillabaisse (page 146)
2. Steamed Clams, Mussels, or Other Shellfish (page 570)
3. Braised Scallops or Braised Squid in Tomato Sauce (page 570)
4. Steamed Clams or Mussels, Unleashed (page 619)
5. Squid in Red Wine Sauce (page 626)
6. Octopus with Tomatoes and Red Wine (page 628)
7. Herb-Roasted Chicken Cutlets (page 672); cut them into strips or chunks first
8. Chicken Cutlets Roasted with Tomatoes (page 672); cut them into chunks first
9. Sautéed Chicken Cutlets with Wine Sauce (page 679); cut them into strips or chunks first
10. Beef Daube (page 738)
11. Braised Pork with Red Wine (page 757)
12. Italian Sausage with Peppers and Onions (page 763); cut the sausage up if you like
13. Lamb Stew with Mushrooms (page 773)
14. Veal Stew with Tomatoes (page 783)

Linguine with Clams

MAKES: About 4 servings
TIME: 30 minutes

F

You can make clam sauce with canned clams, but once you try it with fresh you may never go back; this dish is amazing. To read more about clams, see page 616.

Salt

¼ cup extra virgin olive oil

3 pounds littleneck or other tiny hard-shell clams or cockles, scrubbed

1 tablespoon minced garlic

1 teaspoon hot red pepper flakes, or to taste (optional)

1 pound linguine or other long pasta

Salt and freshly ground black pepper

Chopped fresh parsley leaves

1 Bring a large pot of water to a boil and salt it. Put half the olive oil in a large, deep skillet over high heat. When hot, add the clams and cook, gently shaking the skillet or stirring the clams occasionally, until the first few of them open, after about 5 minutes.

2 Add the garlic and, if you're using them, the hot red pepper flakes and cover for a minute. Uncover, then continue to cook, stirring occasionally, until almost all of the clams are open (any that are not open at this point may be opened at the table with an ordinary butter knife), about 3 more minutes. Turn off the heat and leave the clams covered.

3 Meanwhile, cook the pasta in the boiling water, stirring occasionally, until it is just becoming tender but is still underdone; drain it, reserving 1 cup of the cooking water. Sprinkle the clams with salt and pepper and drizzle with the remaining olive oil. Turn the heat to medium; add the pasta to the clams and cook, stirring, until the pasta is tender, just a minute or so, adding the reserved cooking water if the mixture seems dry. Stir in the parsley, taste and adjust the seasoning, and serve.

Pasta with Red Clam Sauce. Just before adding the pasta to the clams, add about 1½ cups chopped fresh or canned tomato (you can peel and seed them first if you have the time and energy).

Pasta with Clams and Pesto. Prepare the clams as instructed. In Step 2 when the clams begin to open, uncover and stir in 1 cup Traditional Pesto (page 27).

Pasta with Spicy Crab

MAKES: About 4 servings
TIME: 20 minutes

Texture, heat, and simplicity are the big selling points here. Go for fresh crabmeat if you can get it, frozen crabmeat if you cannot; it doesn't matter much whether it's "lump" or other meat in this case.

Salt

⅓ cup extra virgin olive oil

2 tablespoons slivered or minced garlic

2 dried red chiles, or to taste

1 pound any long, cut, or fancy pasta

8 ounces crabmeat, or more to taste

¼ cup chopped fresh parsley leaves

❶ Bring a large pot of water to a boil and salt it. Put the oil, garlic, chiles, and a large pinch of salt in a broad, deep saucepan over medium-low heat. Cook, shaking the pan now and then, until the garlic colors and just begins to darken, 3 to 5 minutes; turn off the heat.

❷ Cook the pasta in the boiling water. When it is just about done, turn the heat under the oil back to low and add the crab; stir once or twice. Drain the pasta (reserve a bit of the cooking water) and toss it in the crab sauce to coat. If the mixture seems a bit dry, add some of the reserved cooking water or more olive oil. Stir in the parsley, adjust the seasoning, and serve.

Pasta with Spicy Shrimp. Substitute 12 ounces large (21–30) peeled shrimp for the crabmeat. Put 2 tablespoons oil in the pan over medium-high heat; when hot, add the shrimp and chiles and cook, stirring occasionally, until the shrimp is just pink, about a minute. Stir in the garlic and cook until the shrimp is cooked, 1 to 2 minutes.

Penne with Tomato-Shrimp Sauce

MAKES: At least 4 servings
TIME: 40 minutes

This is an all-purpose recipe, useful for almost any finfish or shellfish you have in the house; see the variations for a couple of suggestions.

Salt

3 tablespoons extra virgin olive oil

1 small dried hot red chile or hot red pepper flakes, to taste

2 cloves garlic, lightly crushed

2 cups chopped fresh tomatoes, seeded (or drained canned)

1 teaspoon minced fresh rosemary or ½ teaspoon dried rosemary

Freshly ground black pepper

1 pound penne or other cut pasta

¾ to 1 pound large (21–30) shrimp, peeled, cut up if very large

½ cup chopped fresh parsley leaves

❶ Bring a large pot of water to a boil and salt it. Put the oil in a large skillet over medium-high heat. When hot, add the chiles and garlic and cook, stirring, until the garlic turns brown (this is a somewhat strong-tasting sauce), about a minute.

❷ Remove and discard the chiles and garlic and add the tomatoes. Cook, stirring, until the tomatoes begin to liquefy, about 5 minutes; add the rosemary and a good sprinkling of salt and pepper. Cook for another 5 minutes, then turn off the heat. (At this point, you may refrigerate the sauce, covered, for a day or two or freeze for several weeks. Reheat before adding the shrimp.)

❸ Cook the pasta in the boiling water; when the pasta just begins to soften, stir the shrimp into the sauce—they need cook for only 3 or 4 minutes—along with most of the parsley. Drain the pasta when it is tender but not mushy, then toss it with the sauce and remaining parsley. Serve immediately.

Penne with Tomato-Squid Sauce. Substitute squid for shrimp. Clean and rinse the squid, then cut it up (see the illustrations on page 625). Proceed with the recipe, adding the squid only when the sauce is done, in Step 3. Cook for 2 minutes, then taste for doneness. Be careful not to overcook.

Penne with Tomato-Tuna Sauce. Add one 6- or 7-ounce can tuna (packed in olive oil) and 2 tablespoons capers. Stir the tuna, breaking it into flakes, and the capers into the cooked sauce just before tossing with the pasta.

Penne with Tomato-Seafood Sauce. Use any variety of seafood, always ending with those that will cook the most quickly. If you choose to add clams and/or mussels near the end of cooking, cover the skillet until they open. Remember, too, that as you add more seafood you will be adding more liquid indirectly (since most fish give up water as they cook) and, of course, more solids, so you will be able to sauce more pasta and serve more people.

Penne with Shrimp and Roasted Red Peppers. Omit the chiles if you like. Substitute 3 or 4 Roasted Red Peppers (page 330), chopped, for the tomatoes and 2 tablespoons capers or ¼ cup halved pitted black olives for the rosemary. In Step 2, cook the peppers and capers or olives for just 5 minutes. Proceed with the recipe, adding more olive oil if necessary to enrich the sauce.

Penne with Shrimp in Creamy Vodka Sauce. Add ¼ cup vodka and ¼ cup cream just before the tomatoes are done; omit the rosemary.

Mussels over Linguine, Portuguese Style

MAKES: 6 servings
TIME: 45 minutes

You can serve any of the steamed mussel preparations on pages 618–620 over pasta, but this one really begs for it. Be sure to serve this with plenty of crusty bread.

Salt

½ to 1 pound linguiça, Spanish chorizo, or kielbasa

1 tablespoon extra virgin olive oil

2 cloves garlic, chopped

4 or 5 plum tomatoes, cored and roughly chopped (canned are fine; include the juices)

¼ cup chopped fresh basil or parsley leaves, plus more for garnish

About 3 pounds mussels, cleaned (see page 617)

1½ pounds linguine, spaghetti, or other long pasta

❶ Bring a large pot of water to a boil and salt it. Remove the skin from the sausage and chop into ¼- to ½-inch pieces. Combine the olive oil and sausage in a large, deep pot over medium heat and cook, stirring, for about 5 minutes.

❷ When the sausage begins to brown, add the garlic. Cook for 1 or 2 minutes longer, stirring occasionally, then add the tomatoes and ¼ cup basil. Cook for a minute or two, stirring, until the tomatoes soften, a few minutes. Add ½ cup water if you're not using canned tomatoes, stir, add the mussels, cover, and raise the heat to high.

❸ Cook the pasta in the boiling water until tender but not mushy. Continue to cook the mussels, shaking the pot occasionally, until all of them are open, about 10 minutes. Drain the pasta, put it in a very large serving bowl, and pour the mussels and sauce over it. Garnish with basil and serve.

Squid and White Beans with Broken Noodles

MAKES: 4 servings
TIME: 30 minutes with cooked beans

Squid generates much of its own liquid—and with it a distinctive and delicious briny flavor—so you usually don't need stock, wine, or anything else. To break the egg noodles, bang them with a rolling pin in their bag until broken into random but not-too-small bits.

Salt

¼ cup extra virgin olive oil

4 cups cooked or canned white beans with about a cup of their liquid

¾ to 1 pound cleaned squid, cut up

Freshly ground black pepper

Fish or chicken stock (to make your own, see page 159 or 157) or water, if needed

2 cups broken egg noodles (about 8 ounces)

1 tablespoon minced garlic

Chopped fresh parsley leaves for garnish (optional)

1 Bring a medium pot of water to a boil and salt it. Put half the olive oil in a medium saucepan over medium heat. When hot, add the beans and their liquid and bring to a boil, stirring. Add the squid, along with a sprinkling of salt and pepper; reduce the heat so the mixture bubbles steadily and cook, stirring occasionally, while you cook the noodles.

2 Cook the noodles in the boiling water until barely tender, about 5 minutes. Drain and add them to the sim-

mering beans. Cook, stirring occasionally, until the squid and noodles are both tender, adding a little liquid if necessary, about 3 minutes. (Do not add the liquid prematurely; the squid will produce a lot of liquid on its own.)

3 When the dish is just about done, add the garlic; cook it just long enough to take the edge off its rawness—it should still be quite strong. Taste and adjust the seasoning. Garnish with the parsley, drizzle with the remaining olive oil, and serve.

Pasta with Sardines

MAKES: 4 servings
TIME: 30 minutes with canned sardines

By all means, if you have the time and energy to grill or broil fresh sardines—and then remove the bones—go for it (see the variation). But good-quality canned sardines, packed in olive oil, are fine here.

Salt

¼ cup currants

¼ cup pine nuts

¼ cup extra virgin olive oil

1 large onion, chopped

Freshly ground black pepper

1 pound bucatini or cut pasta, like penne or farfalle

4 cans sardines, packed in extra virgin olive oil (about 1 pound)

1 teaspoon grated lemon zest (optional)

½ cup chopped fresh parsley leaves, plus parsley for garnish

1 Bring a large pot of water to a boil and salt it. Soak the currants in warm water to cover. Toast the pine nuts in a large dry skillet over medium heat, shaking the pan occasionally, until lightly browned, just a few minutes; then remove them.

F Fast   **M** Make Ahead   **V** Vegetarian

2 Put the olive oil in a medium skillet or saucepan over medium heat. When hot, add the onion. Cook, stirring occasionally, until softened, 5 to 10 minutes; sprinkle with salt and pepper. Start cooking the pasta.

3 Drain the currants and add them to the onion, along with all but a tablespoon of the pine nuts, the sardines (with their oil), and the zest if you're using it. Cook, stirring gently, until heated through, just a couple minutes. Cover and keep warm until the pasta is ready.

4 When the pasta is tender but not mushy, drain it, reserving a little of the cooking water. Put it in a bowl and add the sardine sauce and the parsley; add some of the reserved cooking water if necessary. Taste and adjust the seasoning, then garnish with the remaining parsley and pine nuts.

Pasta with Fresh Sardines. Start with about 1½ pounds of fresh sardines and grill or broil according to the directions on page 563 or 564. When cooled enough to handle, remove the bones, trying to leave the flesh in big pieces. Then substitute the fresh sardines for the canned.

Pasta with Radicchio, Pine Nuts, and Raisins. Substitute 2 or 3 heads radicchio (about 1 pound), trimmed and shredded, for the sardines. Substitute 1 tablespoon tomato paste for the optional lemon zest. In Step 3, add the radicchio to the onions, then stir in the tomato paste. Proceed with the recipe. Reserve 1 cup of the pasta water and use it as needed.

Pasta with Meat Sauce

These sauces are big and heavy enough that you can usually do without a second course, unless you serve very small amounts, which is not a bad idea.

For the most part, too, they are long-cooking sauces, not what you'd whip up while the water is coming to a boil (the Thirty-Minute Ragù variation is a fine exception). They need slow simmering to tenderize the meat and transfer its flavor to the sauce.

Spaghetti and Meatballs

The recipe for this Italian-American classic is simply a matter of assembling other dishes, two of which can be made well in advance. The sauce can be either Fast Tomato Sauce (page 502) or Meat Sauce, Bolognese Style (page 531). Then make Meatballs, Three Ways (page 114; use the main recipe). Thirty minutes to an hour before you're ready to serve, put the sauce over medium heat and slip the meatballs into the pot. Lower the heat if necessary and let the pot bubble along gently, stirring occasionally, until everything is heated through. Meanwhile, start the spaghetti.

When everything is ready, taste and adjust the seasoning of the sauce and drain the spaghetti, reserving a cup of the cooking water. Toss some of the sauce and a little of the reserved water with the pasta and serve with the meatballs, passing the remaining sauce and lots of Parmesan cheese at the table.

Meat Sauce, Bolognese Style

Ragù

MAKES: A little more than 4 cups (enough for about 3 pounds pasta)
TIME: At least 3 hours, largely unattended

Ragù doesn't require much in the way of work, but it does require occasional attention over the course of a morning or afternoon (the variation, however, is pretty fast). Double or triple the recipe if you like (it freezes well).

2 tablespoons extra virgin olive oil

1 small onion, chopped

1 carrot, chopped

1 celery stalk, chopped

¼ cup chopped bacon or pancetta

8 ounces lean ground beef

8 ounces lean ground pork (or use all beef)

¾ cup dry white wine or juice from the tomatoes

One 28- or 35-ounce can whole plum tomatoes, drained (reserve the juice if you're using it instead of wine)

1 cup beef or chicken stock (to make your own, see page 158 or 157)

Salt and freshly ground black pepper

1 cup cream, half-and-half, or milk

Freshly grated Parmesan cheese (optional)

1 Put the olive oil in a large, deep skillet or saucepan over medium-low heat. When hot, add the onion, carrot, celery, and bacon. Cook, stirring occasionally, until the vegetables are tender, about 10 minutes.

2 Add the ground meat and cook, stirring and breaking up any clumps, until all traces of red are gone, about 5 minutes. Add the wine, raise the heat a bit, and cook, stirring occasionally, until most of the liquid is evaporated, about 5 minutes.

3 Crush the tomatoes with a fork or your hands and add them to the pot; stir, then add the stock. Turn the heat to low and cook at a slow simmer, stirring occasionally and breaking up the tomatoes and any clumps of meat that remain. After an hour or so, sprinkle with salt and pepper. Cook for at least another hour, until much of the liquid has evaporated and the sauce is very thick. (At this point, you may refrigerate the sauce for a day or two or freeze it for several weeks. Reheat before proceeding.)

4 Add the cream and cook for another 15 to 30 minutes, stirring occasionally. Taste and adjust the seasoning. Serve immediately with any cooked pasta, passing grated Parmesan, if you like, at the table.

Thirty-Minute Ragù. Here I like ground lamb best for its bold flavor, but beef, veal, pork, turkey, or chicken will also work: Omit the carrot, celery, bacon, white wine, and stock. Substitute 8 to 12 ounces ground lamb (or other meat) for the pork and beef. Use a 28-ounce can tomatoes with the juice and reduce the

cream to ½ cup. In Step 1, cook the onion until tender, about 5 minutes. Proceed with Steps 2 and 3, but cook the tomatoes just until they start to break down, about 15 minutes; add the cream and cook for another 10 minutes. Meanwhile, cook 1 pound linguine or other pasta, drain, and then toss with the ragù. Garnish with freshly grated pecorino Romano and serve.

Andrea's Pasta with Pork Ribs

MAKES: 4 servings

TIME: 1½ hours

M

One of my favorite pasta recipes, a Neapolitan specialty—taught to me by my old friend Andrea—that can make just a few ribs go a long way.

2 tablespoons extra virgin olive oil

2 small dried hot red chiles (optional)

3 cloves garlic, chopped

6 to 8 meaty spareribs, separated

Salt and freshly ground black pepper

One 28-ounce can whole plum tomatoes with the juice

1 pound ziti, penne, or other cut pasta

Freshly grated pecorino Romano cheese (optional)

1 Put the oil in a deep, broad saucepan over medium heat. When hot, add the chiles if you're using them and the garlic and cook, stirring, for about 30 seconds. Add the ribs and raise the heat to medium-high; cook, stirring occasionally, until the ribs have browned and given off some of their fat, 10 to 15 minutes. Sprinkle with salt and pepper, crush the tomatoes with a fork or your hands, and add them to the pot.

2 Turn the heat to medium or medium-low—enough to maintain a nice steady bubbling, but nothing violent. Cook, stirring occasionally, until the ribs are very tender, nearly falling off the bone, about 1 hour. Remove the chiles from the sauce if you used them. (You can

F Fast   **M** Make Ahead   **V** Vegetarian

make the dish ahead to this point; cover and refrigerate for up to 2 days. Gently reheat before proceeding.)

3 Bring a large pot of water to a boil and salt it. Cook the pasta until tender but not mushy. Drain it and sauce it; serve a rib or two to each diner along with the pasta. Pass the grated cheese at the table if you like.

Pasta with White Sausage Sauce

MAKES: About 4 servings

TIME: 30 minutes

A simply made sauce, unusual and delicious.

Salt

2 tablespoons butter

8 ounces sweet or hot Italian sausage, removed from the casing

Freshly ground black pepper

1 pound ziti or other cut pasta

Freshly grated Parmesan cheese, to taste

1 Bring a large pot of water to a boil and salt it. Put the butter in a medium skillet over medium heat. As it melts, crumble the sausage meat into it, making the bits quite small, $^1/_2$ inch or less. Add $^1/_4$ cup water and adjust the heat so that the mixture bubbles gently, adding a little more water if necessary, until the sausage is cooked through and tender, about 5 minutes. (You can make the sauce in advance to this point; cover and refrigerate for up to a day. Reheat gently.)

2 Meanwhile, cook the pasta until tender but not mushy. Drain it, reserving about a cup of the cooking water. Toss the pasta with the sauce, adding some of the reserved cooking water if necessary. Taste and adjust the seasoning, then toss with the Parmesan and serve.

Pasta with White Sausage Sauce and Greens. Use escarole, broccoli raab, arugula, spinach, kale, or chic-

ory: Fill a large bowl with ice water. Once the pasta water comes to a boil, put a pound of washed greens into the pot and blanch for no more than a minute (only 20 seconds for spinach or arugula). Fish them out with a slotted spoon, spider, or strainer and immediately plunge in into the bowl of ice water. When cool, squeeze dry and roughly chop. Return the water to a boil and proceed with the recipe, adding the cooked greens to the sauce along with the water in Step 1.

Baked Pasta

Some of these dishes are made with fresh pasta, others with dried, partially cooked pasta; all are substantial and also quite flexible: You can include almost anything you like in the layers of lasagne or the sauce for baked ziti. For one more, see Baked Macaroni and Cheese (page 508).

Lasagne is kind of a special case, one that—in one form at least—has become an American classic. "Lasagne," however, refers to the noodles, not a particular style of preparing them, so there are dozens of types, and many can be improvised. If you can get (or make; see page 537) fresh noodles, they're far better than dried here. Either will absorb lots of liquid, so you need plenty of sauce or the lasagne will be dry. Generally, you want about equal weights of pasta and sauce (including solids), which translates to 1 pound of raw pasta to about 4 cups of sauce.

Classic Lasagne, Bolognese Style

MAKES: About 6 servings

TIME: 45 minutes with prepared sauce

Spinach pasta is traditional, but you can use any pasta you like here. If you're making fresh pasta, use a little more flour than called for in the recipe—about 3 cups. This makes a stiffer dough that's easier to handle.

If you're baking a frozen uncooked lasagne, start it in the cold oven, covered with foil, and figure at least an hour before it is heated through and ready to uncover and finish cooking (for as much as another 30 minutes). Bake precooked frozen lasagna the same way; only it will take just a few minutes after uncovering to get bubbly.

Salt

1 recipe Fresh Spinach Pasta (page 542) or other fresh pasta or dried lasagne noodles (about 1 pound)

1 recipe Béchamel Sauce (page 57), about 1$^1/_2$ cups

2 tablespoons butter, softened, or extra virgin olive oil

3 cups, more or less, Meat Sauce, Bolognese Style (page 531)

1$^1/_2$ cups freshly grated Parmesan cheese

Freshly ground black pepper

❶ Bring at least 5 quarts of water to a boil in a large pot and salt it. If you're using homemade fresh pasta, roll it out. Assuming your baking pan is 9 × 13 inches, make your pasta ribbons 26 inches long, then cut them in half. You will still need to cut the noodles so that they fit reasonably snugly into your pan.

❷ Cook the noodles a few at a time; keep them underdone (if they're fresh, this means little more than a minute of cooking time; a few minutes for dried). Drain carefully in a colander, then lay flat on towels. (At this point, prepare the béchamel sauce if you have not done so already.) Heat the oven to 400°F.

❸ Smear the bottom of your baking pan with the butter or oil, then put in a layer of noodles, touching but not overlapping. Trim any overhanging edges. Cover the noodles with about one-quarter each of the béchamel, meat sauce, and Parmesan, then with a light sprinkling of black pepper (between the meat sauce and the Parmesan, there should be enough salt, but if you feel it is underseasoned, add a little salt to each layer also). Make 3 more layers, ending with a sprinkling of Parmesan. (At this

point, you may refrigerate the dish, well wrapped, for a day or freeze it for a month; defrost in the refrigerator for a day before cooking if possible.)

❹ Bake for about 20 to 30 minutes, until the lasagne is bubbly. Remove from the oven and let rest for 5 minutes before cutting and serving. Or let cool completely, cover well, and refrigerate for up to 2 days or freeze for up to a month.

Vegetarian Lasagne. Substitute 3 cups Mushroom Sauce (page 503) or any vegetarian tomato sauce for the Meat Sauce, Bolognese Style.

Classic Lasagne, Italian-American Style. Omit the béchamel. On each layer of the first 3 layers of noodles, spread about 1 cup ricotta (thinned, if necessary, with some of the sauce). Top the ricotta with meat sauce, the meat sauce with about a cup of grated mozzarella, the mozzarella with a sprinkling of Parmesan. On the top layer, omit the ricotta.

White Lasagne. Omit the meat sauce and double the béchamel. Proceed with the recipe. Especially good with some ham and sautéed mushrooms and/or spinach (cooked and squeezed; see page 239) nestled among the layers.

Pesto Lasagne. Substitute Traditional Pesto (page 27) for all or half of the sauce; if you're using any tomato sauce, use Fast Tomato Sauce (page 502) instead of the meat sauce. Additionally, substitute 2 cups ricotta for the béchamel. Alternate layers of pesto and tomato sauce if you're not using all pesto.

15 Simple Ideas for Lasagne

Layer any of these dishes, alone or in combination, between your lasagne noodles, with tomato sauce, béchamel, cheese, or nothing.

1. Meatballs, Three Ways (page 114)

2. Cooked spinach or any other green, squeezed dry and chopped (see page 239)

3. Sautéed Artichoke Hearts (page 254)

F Fast   **M** Make Ahead   **V** Vegetarian

4. Grilled or Broiled Eggplant (page 294) or Eggplant Slices with Garlic and Parsley (page 297)
5. Sautéed Mushrooms (page 313)
6. Caramelized Onions (page 325)
7. Roasted Red Peppers (page 330)
8. Sautéed Zucchini (page 355)
9. Oven-Roasted Plum Tomatoes (page 361) or Grilled or Broiled Tomatoes with Basil (page 362)
10. Roasted Winter Squash Slices (page 368)
11. Oven-Baked Ratatouille (page 373)
12. Strong cheese, like Gorgonzola
13. Fresh herbs, especially basil (whole leaves are nice) or chopped parsley
14. Slices of Italian sausage
15. Veal Stew with Tomatoes (page 783) or other stewed meat

Baked Ziti

MAKES: 4 to 6 servings
TIME: About 1 hour

A lasagne shortcut, with none of the layering hassle. Be sure not to overcook the pasta; it should be too tough to actually eat when you mix it with the sauce, which will make it perfect after baking.

Salt

3 tablespoons extra virgin olive oil or butter, plus more as needed

1 pound any mushrooms, preferably mixed with about 1 cup reconstituted dried porcini (see page 314)

1 large onion, diced

1 tablespoon minced garlic (optional)

Freshly ground black pepper

One 28-ounce can plum tomatoes with the juice, chopped

1 pound ziti or other large cut pasta

1 pound mozzarella, preferably fresh, grated or chopped

About ½ cup freshly grated Parmesan (optional)

1. Bring a large pot of water to a boil and salt it. Heat the oven to 400°F.

2. Put the olive oil or butter in a large skillet over medium-high heat. When the oil is hot or the butter is melted, add the mushrooms and cook, stirring occasionally, until they soften, release their water, and then begin to dry again, about 5 minutes. Add the onion and, if you're using it, the garlic; sprinkle with salt and pepper. Lower the heat to medium and continue to cook, stirring occasionally, until the vegetables are soft, about 2 minutes.

3. Add the tomatoes and bring to a boil. Turn the heat down so that the mixture bubbles gently and cook, stirring occasionally, while you cook the pasta; don't let the sauce get too thick.

4. Cook the pasta in the boiling water until it is just starting to soften but is still too hard to eat. Drain it (don't shake the colander; allow some water to cling to the noodles) and toss it with the sauce and about half the mozzarella. Grease a large baking dish (9 × 13 inches or the like) and pour or spoon the mixture into it. Top with the remaining mozzarella and the Parmesan if you're using it and bake until the top is browned and the cheese is bubbly, 20 to 30 minutes.

Baked Ziti with Ricotta. Stir up to 1 cup of ricotta cheese into the sauce right before using and proceed with the recipe. Or nestle dollops of ricotta in the baking dish as you add the pasta.

Baked Ziti with Meat Sauce. Omit the mushrooms, onion, garlic, and tomatoes and use 1 recipe Meat Sauce, Bolognese Style (page 531), or its faster variation. Skip Steps 2 and 3 and gently heat the sauce before proceeding.

Baked Ziti with Goat Cheese and Olives. Instead of the mushrooms, use 1 cup pitted olives (try to keep them in large pieces). Use bits of goat cheese instead of the mozzarella. Proceed with the recipe, being careful not to oversalt the sauce.

Creamy Baked Noodles with Eggplant and Cheese

MAKES: 4 servings

TIME: About 1½ hours, largely unattended

This dish is a streamlined version of the classic Greek casserole known as *pastitsio*, which combines the concepts of lasagne and macaroni and cheese by baking a layer of vegetables between two layers of creamy noodles. Simply double the recipe to make a batch that will fit into a 9 × 13-inch baking pan or deep gratin dish.

Salt

2 tablespoons extra virgin olive oil, plus more as needed

1 pound eggplant, peeled if you like and cut into 1-inch cubes

Freshly ground black pepper

1 small red onion, chopped

1 tablespoon minced garlic

¼ teaspoon ground cinnamon

¼ teaspoon ground cloves

Cayenne or hot red pepper flakes, to taste

2 cups chopped tomato (canned is fine; use a little of the juice)

4 tablespoons (½ stick) butter

8 ounces ziti, penne, elbows, or other cut pasta

2 tablespoons bread crumbs, preferably fresh (page 876)

1½ cups milk

2 tablespoons all-purpose flour

Pinch of freshly grated nutmeg

2 eggs, beaten

1 cup freshly grated Parmesan or kefalotyri cheese if you can find it

1 Bring a large pot of water to a boil and salt it. Heat the oven to 350°F. Put the olive oil in a large, deep skillet over medium-high heat. When hot, add the eggplant, sprinkle with salt and pepper, and cook, stirring occasionally and adding a little more oil if necessary, until the eggplant is softened and browned all over, about 5 minutes. Remove with a slotted spoon.

2 Add more oil to the pan if needed to coat the bottom and return it to the heat. Add the onion and garlic and cook, stirring occasionally, until soft, about 2 minutes. Stir in the cinnamon, cloves, and cayenne, then the tomato. Turn the heat down to medium-low and cook, stirring occasionally, until the sauce thickens, about 10 minutes. Return the eggplant to the pan, taste and adjust the seasoning, then set aside.

3 Melt the butter in a medium saucepan over low heat. Add the pasta to the boiling water and cook until barely tender, not quite done enough to eat. Drain well; put the pasta in a large bowl and toss with 1 tablespoon of the melted butter and 1 tablespoon of the bread crumbs. Set aside. Use 1 tablespoon of the melted butter to grease an 8- or 9-inch square baking pan or small ovenproof dish.

4 In a small saucepan or microwave, heat the milk until small bubbles appear. Reheat the remaining 2 tablespoons butter over medium-low heat in its saucepan. Add the flour to the melted butter and stir almost constantly with a wire whisk until the mixture turns golden, about 5 minutes. Slowly add the milk, whisking constantly; cook, whisking, until the mixture thickens, 3 to 5 minutes. Add the nutmeg and sprinkle with salt and pepper.

5 Stir a couple tablespoons of the hot milk mixture into the beaten eggs, then a little more. Pour this mixture back into the remaining milk mixture and stir in about half of the Parmesan (reserve some for sprinkling later).

6 Put half the pasta in the baking dish; cover with half the tomato-eggplant sauce. Cover with the remaining pasta, then the remaining tomato sauce and all the cheese sauce. Sprinkle with the remaining Parmesan and the remaining bread crumbs (another little grating of nutmeg here won't hurt either). Bake for about 45 minutes, or until the top turns golden brown. Let rest for a few minutes before cutting and serving. (You can assemble the dish up to several hours before baking; let the components cool a bit, cover well, and refrigerate. Transfer it directly to the oven from the fridge, adding about 10 minutes to the baking time.)

Creamy Baked Noodles with Mushrooms and Cheese. For a meatier texture, replace the eggplant with any fresh mushrooms.

The Basics of Fresh Pasta

It's likely that noodles were first cooked in China, Italy, or both; at the end of the day it doesn't matter much. A paste (English for "pasta") made of flour and liquid—whether water, oil, eggs, or a combination—was a simple enough step in the development of cuisine, and cutting the paste into strands . . . well, we all know how much fun making clay ropes is. It's a bit of work—at least the first time you do it—but you will be stunned at what a lovely thing you've produced. Making pasta elicits a sense of accomplishment, as if you've created something terrific. And you have.

Two basic doughs—one flour and water, the other flour and egg—form the backbone of all fresh noodles: pasta, ravioli, gnocchi, dumplings, even spaetzle. The differences among these boil down to the shape or use of dough and the filling, if any. This first section focuses on Italian-style pastas but includes variations to make fresh Asian-style noodles too, with recipes that range from rich and eggy to eggless to bright and herby; they're all pretty much classic in both noodle-making traditions.

Basic Pasta-Making Techniques

You can make fresh pasta by kneading it to a firm, smooth dough, but it's far easier to start the dough in a food processor, then finish it with a pasta-rolling machine.

For literally handmade pasta, pile your flour on a smooth, clean work surface (for Fresh Egg Pasta) or in a large bowl (for Eggless Pasta) and create a hollow in the

To make the pasta by hand, first make a well in the mound of flour and break the eggs into it.

To knead the dough, use the heel of your hand to push into the middle of the dough, fold the dough over, rotate it 90 degrees, and push into it again.

middle of the flour. Put your eggs or liquids into this well, then use a fork or wooden spoon to incorporate the flour. Once a dough begins to form, use your hands to fully incorporate the remaining flour. It'll be messy at first but should start to come together within a couple of minutes. It's at this point, when the dough is still shaggy, that you want to add more liquid (water or olive oil) or flour in small amounts. You'll know which to add by the look and feel of the dough; if it's mushy and sticking to your hands, you need more flour; if it's not coming together and separated into dried-out-looking pieces, you need more liquid.

From this point it's a matter of kneading, and although it takes some energy, it's much faster and easier than kneading bread dough. Form the dough into a ball, then sprinkle it and your work surface with flour. Use the heel of your hand to push into the middle of the dough, fold the dough over, rotate it 90 degrees, and push into it again. Continue kneading until the dough is completely smooth, somewhat skinlike, with some elasticity (if you pull off a piece, it should stretch a bit before breaking; if it breaks off immediately, keep kneading). If the dough is sticking to your hands or the work surface, sprinkle it with flour; it doesn't need to be drowning in flour—just enough to keep it from sticking.

The food processor is not for purists, but I like it, and the end result is the same—or nearly the same—as hand-made. Put the flour and salt in the processor's container and pulse it a couple times; add the egg and a bit of the liquid you're using and turn the machine on. Gradually add the rest of the liquid(s) until the dough forms a ball.

With either method, you must let the dough rest for at least 30 minutes before rolling it out. Then knead the dough by hand (see above) or sprinkle it with a good amount of flour and use the pasta-rolling machine to knead it. To knead using a pasta roller, set the rollers at the thickest setting and work the dough through several times, folding it over after each roll. Slowly work your way down to about the middle roller setting and then let the dough rest.

Using a Manual Pasta-Rolling Machine

If fresh pasta is something you make or intend to make regularly, a good pasta-rolling machine is essential. (You can roll pasta without one; just use a rolling pin; roll from the center out and keep flouring and turning the dough.) It will cut your rolling time by at least half, and most come with a cutter attachment, which will also save you time and give you beautifully cut pasta. These machines are simple to use, easy to maintain, and worth the investment, which is only about $40.

1. For starters, secure the machine on a sturdy counter or tabletop, making sure the crank handle has clearance and there is surface area on both sides of the machine.

2. Sprinkle the machine and surrounding surfaces with some flour and set the rollers at their thickest setting (most machines use sequential numbers to indicate settings, but some use letters or just tick marks).

3. Dust the portion of dough with some flour and then pass it through the machine. Add more flour if the dough sticks.

4. Decrease the width of the rollers by one notch and pass the dough through; continue decreasing the width one notch at a time and rolling the dough. If the dough tears or sticks, ball up the dough and start over.

5. When you get to the thinnest setting, cut the sheet of pasta in half so it's a more manageable length. Roll the

1

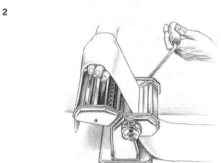

2

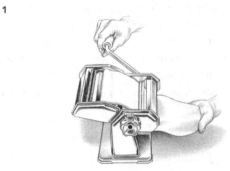

(STEP 1) Begin by putting a piece of dough through the widest setting, usually #1. (STEP 2) Decrease the distance between the two rollers, making the strip of dough progressively thinner. Note that as the dough becomes longer, it will become more fragile. Dust with flour between rollings if necessary.

sheet through twice more; it's now ready for cutting, stuffing, or freezing.

6. To clean the machine, use a clean, dry brush (a pastry or painting brush) and brush off the flour. Use a dinner knife to scrape off any bits of dough stuck to the rollers and wipe off the exterior with a damp cloth or paper towel. Do not wash; the flour in it will gum up and the gears may rust.

Cutting Pasta

Cutting the pasta into shapes is really fun, and these can be just about anything (even maltagliati, "badly cut," is traditional; cook the scraps as you would any fresh pasta or add them to a soup or broth). Use your machine cutting attachment for the long, flat fettuccine or tagliatelle or your knife or pasta or pizza cutter (basically the same thing; one is just bigger than the other) for other shapes and sizes (see "Free-Form Pasta," page 541).

To hand-cut fettuccine, pappardelle, lasagne, or similar ribbonlike pasta, dust the sheet of pasta with some flour, loosely roll it lengthwise, and cut it crosswise as wide or narrow as you like. Toss the cut pasta so it doesn't stick together, adding in a bit more flour (or fine cornmeal) if necessary. Pull the noodles apart if they do stick together.

(STEP 1) To make any broad noodle, roll up the pasta sheet, sprinkle it with cornmeal or flour, and cut across the roll at the desired width. **(STEP 2)** Sprinkle with more cornmeal and leave the noodles in a tangle (short term) or hang individually to dry if not using right away.

Using Other Flours in Fresh Pasta

This chart is a quick reference for using alternative flours in any of the fresh pasta recipes.

FLOUR	EFFECT ON FLAVOR AND TEXTURE	QUANTITY TO USE IN RECIPES
Semolina	Pleasant grittiness, but trickier to handle	2 cups semolina
Whole wheat	Nuttier flavor and more fiber, but dough will be stiffer and less elastic	1 cup whole wheat and 1 cup all-purpose flour
Buckwheat (fine ground)	Delicate texture and flavor, but dough tears more easily	1 1/2 cups buckwheat and 1/2 cup all-purpose flour
Whole durum wheat	Excellent taste and handling results but tough to find	2 cups whole durum wheat

There are a couple of rules to keep in mind when replacing all-purpose flour with another flour in fresh pasta dough. The first—and most crucial—is to consider the gluten content of the replacement flour. Flours that contain little or no gluten, like buckwheat, simply cannot make the same kind of chewy, tender pasta that all-purpose flour does. (It's the gluten in flour that enables the dough to be rolled thin and hold its shape when boiled.) The other factor to consider when using alternative flours is flavor. Buckwheat and whole wheat must be combined with all-purpose flour to mellow them.

What to Do with Fresh Pasta

Keep it simple and toss it with a sauce or pesto or—even simpler—just butter and Parmesan (see "Saucing and Tossing Fresh Pasta," page 543). More time-consuming—but rewarding—is making ravioli or other stuffed pastas (see page 544). Baked pasta, like lasagne, is another good option; see page 533. Finally, try adding fresh pasta—especially the odd pasta scraps left over after cutting—to soups.

Fresh Egg Pasta

MAKES: 4 servings (about 1 pound)

TIME: At least 1 hour, somewhat unattended

Egg pasta at its best; this Emilia-Romagna-style pasta is rich and golden in color from the egg yolks. Because this recipe contains a good amount of egg, the dough is moist and forgiving—a benefit if you're a beginner.

> About 2 cups all-purpose flour, plus more if needed
>
> 1 teaspoon salt
>
> 2 whole eggs
>
> 3 egg yolks

❶ With a food processor: Combine the flour and salt in the container and pulse once or twice. Add the eggs and yolks all at once and turn the machine on. Process just until a ball begins to form, about 30 seconds. Add a few drops of water if the dough is dry and grainy; add a tablespoon of flour if the dough sticks to the side of the bowl.

By hand: Combine $1^1/_2$ cups of the flour and the salt on a counter or large board. Make a well in the middle.

Put the eggs and yolks into this well. Beat the eggs with a fork, slowly and gradually incorporating the flour, a little at a time. When it becomes too hard to stir with the fork, use your hands. When all the flour on the surface has been mixed in, knead the dough, pushing it against the board and folding it repeatedly, until it is not at all sticky and has become quite stiff. Add only small amounts of flour during kneading if you absolutely need it.

Sprinkle the dough with a little of the reserved flour and cover with plastic or a cloth; let it rest for about 30 minutes. (At this point, you may refrigerate the dough, wrapped in plastic, until you're ready to roll it out, for up to 24 hours.)

❷ Clean your hands and clamp a pasta machine to the counter; sprinkle your work surface lightly with flour. Cut off about one-third of the dough; wrap the rest in plastic or cloth while you work. Roll the dough lightly in the flour and use your hands to flatten it into a rectangle about the width of the machine. Set the machine to its highest (that is, thickest) setting and crank the dough through. If it sticks, dust it with a little more flour. Repeat. Set the machine to its next-thinnest setting and repeat. Each time, if the pasta sticks, sprinkle it with a little more flour, and each time put the dough through the machine twice.

❸ Continue to work your way down (or up, as the case may be—each machine is numbered differently) through the numbers. If at any point the dough tears badly, bunch it together and start again (you will quickly get the hang of it). Use as much flour as you need to, but in small amounts each time.

❹ Pass the dough through the machine's thinnest setting; (if this fails, pass it through the next-thinnest once). Repeat two more times (by this time it will be going quickly), then flour the dough lightly, cover it, and set it aside. Repeat the process with the remaining dough.

❺ Cut each sheet into rectangles roughly 16 inches long; trim the ends to make it neat. At this point the dough is ready to be used. You can leave it as sheets to make lasagne or stuffed pasta or cut the sheets to make noodles. Cut by hand or pass the dough through the

 Fast   Make Ahead   Vegetarian

machine once more, this time using the broadest (tagliatelle) cutter. Or cut by hand into broad strips (pappardelle). Cook right away or hang the strands to dry for up to a couple of hours.

6 To cook the noodles, drop them into boiling salted water; they'll be done when tender, in less than 3 (and probably less than 2) minutes. Sauce them immediately and serve.

Pizzocheri. The robust buckwheat pasta of northeastern Italy: Use $1^1/_2$ cups fine buckwheat flour and $^1/_2$ cup all-purpose flour.

Chinese-Style Egg Noodles. The recipe remains the same, but roll the dough as thin as possible. Then cut the noodles up to an inch wide or very narrow, in shorter strands than you would Italian pasta.

Fresh Eggless Pasta

MAKES: 4 servings (about 1 pound)
TIME: At least 1 hour, somewhat unattended

Just as simple and almost as easy to work with as the egg pasta, though less rich.

2 cups all-purpose flour, plus more as needed

1 teaspoon salt

2 tablespoons butter, softened, or extra virgin olive oil

With a food processor: Combine the flour and salt in the container and pulse once or twice. Turn the machine on and add $^1/_2$ cup hot water and the butter or olive oil through the feed tube. Process just until a ball begins to form, about 30 seconds. Add a few drops of water if the dough is dry and grainy; add a tablespoon of flour if dough sticks to the side of the bowl.

By hand: Whisk together the flour and salt on a counter or large board. Make a well in the middle. Put the butter or olive oil into this well, along with about $^1/_2$ cup hot water. Beat the water with a fork, slowly and

---

Free-Form Pasta

Nicely cut pasta is gorgeous, but free-form pasta, which ranges in shape and size from small pinches of dough to fat ribbons or whatever you like, is also appealing and equally traditional. To avoid rolling dough altogether, check out Spaetzle (page 552).

- Pasta grattata: Literally grated pasta dough, the simplest fresh pasta, usually served in the broth in which it's cooked. Use either Fresh Egg Pasta or Eggless Pasta dough, letting it rest in the refrigerator for at least 30 minutes. Grate the dough while still very cold (using the large holes on a standard cheese grater), straight into a pot of simmering stock or over a piece of wax paper, keeping the pasta as separate as possible so it doesn't stick. Or pinch off small pieces of the dough and cook as you would any fresh pasta.
- Pasta handkerchiefs: Roll either Fresh Egg Pasta or Eggless Pasta dough to less than $^1/_4$ inch thick and cut it into squares no larger than 4 inches across; cook as you would any fresh pasta.
- Wide pasta ribbons: Think lasagne but narrower. Roll either Fresh Egg Pasta or Eggless Pasta dough to less than $^1/_4$ inch thick and cut it into ribbons as wide as you like with a knife; cook as you would any fresh pasta.

---

gradually incorporating a little of the flour at a time. When it becomes too hard to stir with the fork, use your hands. When all the flour has been mixed in, knead the dough, pushing it against the board and folding it repeatedly until it is not at all sticky and is quite stiff. Add water $^1/_2$ teaspoon at a time if the mixture is dry and not coming together; add flour if it is sticky.

Sprinkle the dough with a little of the reserved flour and cover with plastic or a cloth; let it rest for about 30 minutes. (At this point, you may refrigerate the dough, wrapped in plastic, until you're ready to roll it out, for up to 24 hours.)

Clean your hands, then follow Steps 2 through 6 in the Fresh Egg Pasta recipe (page 540) for rolling, cutting, and cooking.

Asian-Style Dumpling Wrappers. Omit the butter and add more water—a little at a time—to reach the consistency described. Rest the dough as directed. Knead the ball for a minute, then cut it into 4 pieces. On a lightly floured surface, roll each piece into a 1-inch log, then cut into 1-inch pieces and roll each one out from the center to form a 4-inch round or square, adding a bit more flour if necessary. (You can also roll sheets of dough with a pasta machine, then cut it into the desired shapes; see page 538.) Use immediately or dust with flour, stack, wrap tightly, and refrigerate (up to a couple of days) or freeze (up to 2 weeks). For filling ideas, see page 548.

Herbed Fresh Pasta

MAKES: 4 servings (about 1 pound)
TIME: At least 1 hour, largely unattended

Fresh herbs are a must in this recipe; they create a pretty, green-tinged pasta that's full of bright flavor.

1 tablespoon minced fresh sage leaves, 1 teaspoon minced fresh rosemary or thyme leaves, or ¼ cup minced fresh basil, chervil, or parsley leaves

2 cups all-purpose flour, plus more as needed

1 teaspoon salt

3 eggs

With a food processor: Combine the herb with the flour and salt in the container and pulse once or twice. Add the eggs all at once and turn the machine on. Process just until a ball begins to form, about 30 seconds. Add a few drops of water if the dough is dry and grainy; add a tablespoon of flour if dough sticks to the side of the bowl. (The amount of flour you need depends on the amount of herb you use and its moisture content; ¼ cup of parsley, for example, will take considerably more flour than 1 teaspoon of rosemary.)

By hand: Combine 1½ cups of the flour, the herb, and the salt on a counter or large board. Make a well in the middle. Put the eggs into this well. Beat the eggs with a fork, slowly and gradually incorporating a little of the flour at a time. When it becomes too hard to stir with the fork, use your hands. When all the flour on the board has been mixed in, knead the dough, pushing it against the board and folding it repeatedly until it is not at all sticky and is quite stiff. Add only small amounts of flour during kneading if you absolutely need it.

Sprinkle the dough with a little of the reserved flour and cover with plastic or a cloth; let it rest for about 30 minutes. (At this point, you may refrigerate the dough, wrapped in plastic, until you're ready to roll it out, for up to 24 hours.)

Clean your hands and follow Steps 2 through 6 in the Fresh Egg Pasta recipe (page 540) for rolling, cutting, and cooking.

Fresh Spinach Pasta. Lots of color in this pasta; the spinach flavor is subtle: Add 8 ounces fresh spinach or 4 ounces frozen spinach and about ½ cup flour. Stem and wash the fresh spinach; steam it (see page 239), then drain, squeeze (get as much water out as possible), and chop it very fine. Add the spinach with the eggs, making sure to break up any clumps of spinach.

Fresh Red Pasta. Again, the color is more pronounced than the flavor. Use red bell pepper or beets; the beets will color the pasta more vibrantly: Add ½ cup well-drained puréed cooked beets (see page 542) or puréed cooked red bell pepper (page 543) and about another

$^1/_2$ cup flour. Add the purée with the eggs. Proceed with the recipe.

Whole-Leaf Herbed Fresh Pasta. This takes a bit more effort but looks spectacular. Roll out the dough to the thinnest setting, put whole or roughly chopped stemmed herb leaves (parsley, chervil, tarragon, or small basil or sage leaves work best) randomly on one sheet of pasta, sprinkle with a tiny bit of water, and put another sheet of pasta on top; roll the sheets together (essentially pressing the leaves between the layers of dough).

5 Other Flavored Pastas

There are many add-ins that will add a touch of flavor and color to fresh pasta dough. Serve black pepper pasta with Spicy Tomato Sauce (page 503); saffron, mushroom, and herb pastas are lovely with a rich, creamy sauce, like Beurre Blanc (page 59) or Brown Butter (page 56); the tomato and roasted garlic simply with extra virgin olive oil and lots of Parmesan or pecorino.

1. Black Pepper Pasta: Freshly grind about a tablespoon of black pepper into the flour.
2. Saffron Pasta: Steep a large pinch of crumbled saffron threads in a couple of tablespoons hot water; add along with the eggs or with the hot water. You may need a little more flour to compensate for the extra liquid.
3. Mushroom Pasta: Grind dried mushrooms to a fine powder in a clean coffee or spice grinder and add to the flour; you want a tablespoon or two of powder. Porcini are excellent.
4. Tomato Pasta: Use completely dried tomatoes (see Oven-Dried Tomatoes, page 362). Grind them to a fine powder in a clean coffee or spice grinder and add to the flour; you want a tablespoon or two of powder.
5. Roasted Garlic Pasta: Mash several cloves Roasted Garlic (page 303) to a smooth paste; add along with the eggs or hot water, making sure to mix the garlic in very well. You may need to add more flour to compensate for the extra liquid in the garlic.

Saucing and Tossing Fresh Pasta

Fresh pasta—including stuffed pasta and gnocchi—is versatile, and it can be substituted for dried pasta in some recipes. But you always need to keep in mind three things: Fresh pasta cooks in under 5 minutes; its simple and delicious flavor is easily overwhelmed by sauce and garnishes; and oversaucing and tossing will quickly turn fresh to mush.

When saucing, add just enough to coat the pasta; if your sauce is too thick and clumping, thin it with some of the pasta-cooking water rather than adding more sauce to compensate. Adding some pasta water also helps to keep the pasta loose to make tossing quick and easy; if it's too dry, you'll wind up breaking the pasta when you toss it.

Simplest Sauces for Fresh Pasta

All of these recipes call for dried pasta but can also be made using any fresh pasta and finished in 30 minutes or less. But remember: Fresh pasta takes less than 2 minutes to cook, so adjust the boiling time accordingly.

1. Traditional Pesto (page 27)
2. Fast Tomato Sauce and its variations (page 502)
3. Garlic and Oil (page 504)
4. Pancetta and Pecorino (page 505)
5. Butter and Parmesan (page 506)
6. Mushroom (page 518)
7. Leeks and Parsley (page 520)
8. Creamy Gorgonzola Sauce (page 525)
9. Spicy Crab (page 528)
10. Thirty-Minute Ragù (page 532)
11. White Sausage (page 533)

The Basics of Stuffed Pasta

Ravioli or tortellini differ from many Asian dumplings (see the appetizer chapter) only in the nature and flavor of the stuffings. But in Italy alone there are literally dozens of different types of stuffed pasta, from simple rolls to complex folds. I'm focusing on a few basics: ravioli (squares), tortellini (folded loops), and cannelloni (large open-ended tubes), which can all be stuffed with any of the fillings that appear in the following recipes.

Though it's not ideal, you can freeze stuffed pasta to use at a later date. Once they're made, dust with cornmeal and seal in zippered bags, then freeze; use as soon as you can.

Stuffing Pasta

How you fill your pasta is a matter of taste. If you like a moist, gooey stuffing, stuff it with a soft cheese like ricotta (adding a sharper-tasting cheese, like goat's or sheep's milk cheese, gives more character). For contrasting texture, mix in chopped herbs, vegetables, or nuts. For drier filling, start with bread crumbs or chopped or puréed vegetables.

Serving Stuffed Pasta

While stuffed pastas take some time to make, cooking and saucing them is fast. Generally, if the stuffing is well contained, as with ravioli or tortellini, you boil and sauce it like any other pasta; if you like, you can boil, then sauté in a butter or oil sauce (like herbed Brown Butter) to develop a crust on one side, then finish the sauce with some pasta-cooking water and grated cheese.

If pasta is loosely stuffed, as with cannelloni, it's best baked directly in the sauce (see Spinach-Cheese Cannelloni, page 546). Finally, small stuffed pasta, like tortellini, can be dropped into brothy soups.

Butternut Squash Pansotti

MAKES: 4 servings (about 60 pansotti)
TIME: 1¹⁄₂ hours with prepared pasta sheets

If you're going to make one stuffed pasta, this should be it: It takes only one fold to create these triangular packages. Serve in Brown Butter (page 56) with sage or rosemary leaves, the sauce from Linguine with Garlic and Oil and any of the variations (page 504), or the sauce from Spaghetti with Butter and Parmesan (page 506) or Fettuccine Alfredo (page 507).

2 cups cooked (preferably baked) butternut squash (see page 366)

2 eggs

¹⁄₂ teaspoon freshly grated nutmeg

Salt and freshly ground black pepper

1 teaspoon sugar, or to taste

¹⁄₂ cup freshly grated Parmesan cheese

Cornmeal or all-purpose flour for dusting

1 recipe Fresh Egg Pasta or Eggless Pasta (page 540 or 541), rolled into sheets and kept moist under a towel or plastic wrap

❶ Purée the squash, preferably by passing it through a food mill or ricer. Combine it in a bowl with the eggs, nutmeg, and some salt and pepper. Taste; if the mixture is not sweet, add a little sugar. Stir in the Parmesan and taste again; add more of any seasoning you like.

❷ Lightly dust a flat work surface with some cornmeal or flour. Working with a few sheets at a time, cut any length of fresh pasta dough so that it is 4 or 5 inches wide. Cut into 2- to 2¹⁄₂-inch squares. Brush the dough very lightly with water so it will stick together when you shape the pansotti. Put a rounded teaspoon of stuffing on each square and fold in half to make a triangle, pressing tightly to seal the edges. Put the pansotti on cookie sheets, dusting them with cornmeal and keeping them separate, until you're ready to cook. (At this point, you

 F Fast   **M** Make Ahead   **V** Vegetarian

can refrigerate the pansotti on the cookie sheets for up to a day or freeze them for up to 3 months.)

❸ Bring a large pot of water to a boil and salt it. Cook the pansotti, 30 or so at a time, for just a few minutes, until they rise to the surface. Drain, sauce, and serve immediately.

Sweet Potato Pansotti. Wonderful boiled and sautéed with extra virgin olive oil and pecans or walnuts (for the technique, see Linguine with Garlic, Oil, and Nuts, page 505): Substitute cooked sweet potato for the butternut squash and omit the sugar.

Chestnut Pansotti. Perfect with the sauce from Spaghetti with Butter and Parmesan (page 506): Substitute cooked, peeled, and crumbled chestnuts (see page 287) for the butternut squash. Add 3 tablespoons minced shallot or onion, if you like, and mix in with the eggs.

Ravioli Nudi

MAKES: About 4 servings
TIME: 30 minutes

Nudi means "naked" and refers to ravioli filling without the case: "unwrapped" dumplings that you can serve with or without pasta—as you like.

8 ounces each ground veal and pork or any combination of ground meats you prefer

1 egg

$^{1}/_{4}$ cup freshly grated Parmesan cheese, plus cheese for serving

$^{1}/_{4}$ cup chopped fresh parsley leaves

$^{1}/_{4}$ cup chopped onion

Salt and freshly ground black pepper

1 pound any pasta, fresh or dried (optional)

4 tablespoons ($^{1}/_{2}$ stick) butter

20 fresh sage leaves

❶ Combine the meat in a bowl with the egg, cheese, parsley, onion, and a sprinkling of salt and pepper. Mix well but do not knead. Form into tiny balls, about $^{1}/_{2}$ inch in diameter, and put on cookie sheets. Refrigerate until you're ready to cook, or up to several hours. Bring a large pot of water to a boil and salt it.

❷ Cook the meatballs in the boiling water for about 5 minutes; remove with a slotted spoon and keep warm.

❸ Cook the pasta, if you're using it, in the same water until tender but not mushy. Meanwhile, cook the butter and sage together in a small pan over medium-low heat until the butter is light brown, about 5 minutes.

❹ Drain the pasta, reserving a bit of the cooking water, then toss it with the butter-sage mixture and enough of the reserved water to make the mixture saucy. Top with the meatballs and serve, passing grated Parmesan at the table.

Vegetarian Ravioli Nudi. Substitute 1 cup bread crumbs, preferably fresh (page 876), for the meat. Add another egg and increase the Parmesan to $^{3}/_{4}$ cup and the parsley to $^{1}/_{2}$ cup. Allow the bread crumb mixture to rest for at least 10 minutes before shaping into balls. Proceed with the recipe, cooking the dumplings until they rise to the surface, about 3 minutes.

Spinach-Ricotta Ravioli

MAKES: 4 to 6 servings (30 to 60 ravioli)
TIME: About 1 hour with prepared pasta sheets

A standby stuffed pasta. Serve it with Fast Tomato Sauce, with or Without Pasta (page 502), Traditional Pesto (page 27), or the sauce from Fettuccine Alfredo (page 507).

1 egg

1 cup cooked spinach (about 8 ounces raw), squeezed dry and chopped

1 1/2 cups ricotta cheese, drained in a strainer for a few minutes

1/4 cup chopped fresh parsley leaves

1 teaspoon minced garlic

A small grating of nutmeg

1 cup freshly grated Parmesan cheese

Salt

Cornmeal or all-purpose flour for dusting

1 recipe Fresh Egg Pasta or Eggless Pasta (pages 540 or 541), rolled into sheets and kept moist under a towel or plastic wrap

1 Combine the egg, spinach, ricotta, parsley, garlic, nutmeg, and Parmesan in a bowl and mix well. (At this point, you may refrigerate the stuffing, covered, for up to a day.)

2 Bring a large pot of water to a boil and salt it. Put a little water in a small bowl and lightly dust a flat work surface with some cornmeal or flour. Cut each pasta sheet into 2 or more 4-inch-wide strips. Drop heaping teaspoons of the stuffing at about 1 1/2-inch intervals about 1 inch from one long edge of the strip (that is, about 3 inches from the other edge). Dampen the edges with a little water (the tip of your finger is a fine tool for this), then fold the dough over onto itself, pressing with your fingers to seal. Trim the dough with a sharp knife or fluted pastry wheel, then cut into individual ravioli. (You can prepare the ravioli up to this point in advance; dust with cornmeal and refrigerate for up to a day or freeze.)

3 Cook the ravioli, 20 or 30 at a time, for just a few minutes, until they rise to the surface. Drain, sauce, and serve immediately.

Ricotta and Herb Ravioli. Substitute 1 cup chopped mild fresh herbs, like basil, parsley, chives, chervil, mint, or dill, for the spinach.

Cheese Ravioli. Herbed Fresh Pasta (page 542) is really nice here; substitute bread crumbs, preferably fresh (page 876), for the spinach. For stronger flavor, use sharper cheese, like aged pecorino, to replace some of the Parmesan.

Spinach Ravioli. Or use chard, kale, or dandelion greens: Increase the cooked chopped spinach to 2 cups and add 1/4 cup chopped fresh herbs, like sage, chervil, basil, fresh fennel fronds, or a mixture. Omit the egg and ricotta.

Mushroom-Cheese Ravioli. Use any kind of mushrooms you like: Substitute 3/4 cup Sautéed Mushrooms (pages 313–314) for the spinach and reduce the ricotta to 1 1/4 cups. Drain the mushrooms and finely chop.

Spinach-Cheese Cannelloni. Make a simple sauce, like Fast Tomato Sauce, with or Without Pasta (page 502), or the one with Spaghetti with Butter and Parmesan (page 506). Heat the oven to 375°F. Cut the pasta sheets into rectangles (about 4 × 6 inches), boil them for 2 minutes, then drain. Use a tablespoon to dollop out a line of the filling along the short edge of a piece of pasta, about an inch or so from the edge; roll the pasta into a tube shape. Spread a small spoonful of sauce in the bottom of an ovenproof baking dish and

MAKING CANNELLONI

To make cannelloni, put a small amount of filling about an inch up from the end nearest you, spreading it almost but not quite to the sides; then simply roll up.

F Fast   **M** Make Ahead   **V** Vegetarian

28 Dishes for Stuffing Pasta

From caramelized onions to mashed favas. Drain off excess liquids and mash, crumble, or finely chop large pieces as you like. Then use as filling for any of the recipes in this section.

1. Puréed Vegetables (page 242)
2. Sautéed Artichoke Hearts (page 254)
3. Sautéed Cabbage with Balsamic Vinegar (page 275)
4. Cauliflower with Garlic and Anchovies (page 280)
5. Glazed Chestnuts (page 287)
6. Sautéed Eggplant with Basil (page 295)
7. Braised Endive, Escarole, or Radicchio with Prosciutto (page 298)
8. Roasted Garlic, peeled and roughly mashed (page 303)
9. Sautéed Mushrooms (page 313)
10. Caramelized Onions (page 325)
11. Anything-Scented Peas (page 329)
12. Spinach with Currants and Nuts (page 352)
13. Sweet Potatoes, Simply Cooked (page 358)
14. Oven-Roasted Plum Tomatoes (page 361)
15. Whole Winter Squash, Cooked Three Ways (page 366)
16. White Beans, Tuscan Style (page 427)
17. Beans and Mushrooms (page 428)
18. Broiled Fish Fillets (and a Lot Else) (page 563)
19. Roasted Shrimp with Herb Sauce (pages 577–578)
20. Salmon Roasted in Butter (page 583)
21. Boiled or Steamed Crab or Lobster (pages 614–615)
22. Herb-Roasted Chicken Cutlets (page 672)
23. Sautéed Chicken Cutlets with Wine Sauce (page 679)
24. Beef Daube (page 738)
25. Braised Beef Brisket (page 743)
26. Veal Stew with Tomatoes (page 783)
27. Braised Pork with Red Wine (page 757)
28. Lamb Stew with Mushrooms (page 773)

add the cannelloni, putting them side by side and in a single layer; cover with the remaining sauce, sprinkle with grated Parmesan, and bake until bubbling, about 20 minutes.

Meat Tortellini

MAKES: 4 to 6 servings (50 to 60 tortellini)
TIME: About 1 hour

Tortellini are tricky because of their small size, but you can make them bigger if you like (and call them *tortelloni*) or make ravioli, which are easier still. Serve in a flavorful broth or with Fast Tomato Sauce (page 502), the sauces from Spaghetti with Butter and Parmesan (page 506), or any tomato sauce.

2 tablespoons extra virgin olive oil

1 pound ground meat, preferably a mixture of beef, veal, and pork or pork sausage

1 cup red wine or beef or chicken stock (to make your own, see pages 157–159), or more as needed

Salt and freshly ground black pepper

1 teaspoon minced garlic

¼ cup chopped prosciutto or other ham (optional)

½ cup chopped fresh parsley leaves

½ cup freshly grated Parmesan cheese

1 egg

Bread crumbs, preferably fresh (page 876), if needed

Cornmeal or all-purpose flour for dusting

1 recipe Fresh Egg Pasta or Eggless Pasta (page 540 or 541), rolled into sheets and kept moist under a towel or plastic wrap

❶ Put the olive oil in a large, deep skillet over medium heat. When hot, add the meat and cook, stirring and breaking up any lumps, until it loses its color, about 10 minutes. Add the wine and a sprinkling of salt and pepper, then turn the heat down to very low. Cook, stirring occasionally and adding more liquid if necessary, until the meat is tender and the sauce thickened, about 45 minutes.

❷ Add the garlic and the ham if you're using it and cook for another 5 minutes. Cool thoroughly, then stir in the parsley, Parmesan, and egg. If the mixture is still liquidy, stir in some bread crumbs. (At this point, you may refrigerate the filling, covered, for up to a day.)

❸ Lightly dust a work surface with some cornmeal or flour. Cut any length of fresh pasta dough so that it is 4 or 5 inches wide. Cut into 2- to 2$^1/_2$-inch squares.

❹ Brush the dough very lightly with water so it will stick together when you shape the tortellini. Put a rounded teaspoon of stuffing on each square and fold into a triangle, pressing tightly to seal the edges. Fold the widest point toward the stuffing, then pick up the triangle and press the two bottom points together. Put your finger inside the newly formed ring and fold over the top of the dough inside the circle. Press to seal. Keep the tortellini separate on cornmeal- or flour-dusted cookie sheets until you're ready to cook. (At this point, you may

MAKING TORTELLINI

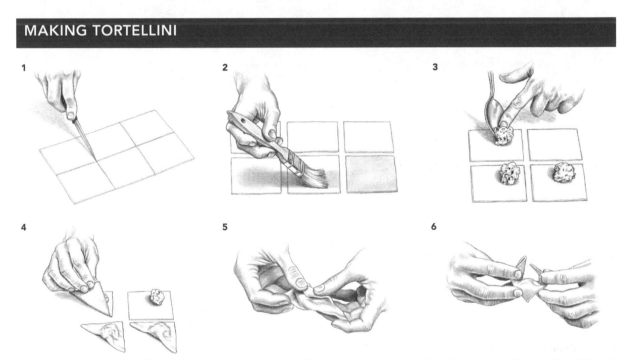

(STEP 1) One a counter dusted lightly with flour, cut any length of fresh pasta dough so it is 4 or 5 inches wide. Cut into 2- to 2$^1/_2$-inch squares. (STEP 2) Brush the dough very lightly with water so it will stick together when you shape the tortellini. (STEP 3) Place a small mound of filling on each square. (STEP 4) Fold into a triangle, pressing tightly to seal the edges. (STEP 5) Fold the widest point toward the filling. (STEP 6) Pick up the triangle and press the two bottom points together. Place your finger inside the newly formed ring and fold over the top of the dough inside the circle. Press to seal. Keep the tortellini separate until you are ready to cook.

Ⓕ Fast   Ⓜ Make Ahead   Ⓥ Vegetarian

dust the tortellini with flour and refrigerate for up to a day or freeze for up to 3 months.)

⑤ Bring a pot of water to a boil and salt it. Cook the tortellini, 30 or so at a time, for just a few minutes, until they rise to the surface. Drain, sauce, and serve immediately.

Cheese Tortellini. Omit the olive oil, ground meat, wine, garlic, and ham. Skip Steps 1 and 2. Instead, combine 1 pound ricotta cheese with the parsley, Parmesan, and egg and add a pinch of nutmeg; sprinkle with a little salt and pepper. Use this mixture to fill the tortellini. Proceed with the recipe.

Seafood Tortellini. Substitute filleted and skinned white fish, like flounder or cod, peeled and cleaned shrimp, or lobster or crabmeat, for the ground meat. Omit the wine or stock, garlic, prosciutto, and Parmesan. Cook the seafood by steaming (see page 570), poaching or boiling (see page 569), or sautéing (see page 564). Add 3 tablespoons minced shallot or onion. Chop or flake the seafood and mix it with the shallot, parsley, egg, a sprinkling of salt, and a pinch of cayenne instead of black pepper. Add bread crumbs only if absolutely necessary. Proceed with the recipe from Step 3.

The Basics of Gnocchi and Other (Mostly) Italian Dumplings

Gnocchi (pronounced, kind of, nyo-kee) are easy-to-make Italian dumplings incorporating cooked potatoes, flour, and sometimes an egg; they're then boiled and sauced. Starchy potatoes are a must here, as it's the potatoes' starch—along with the flour's gluten—that holds the dough together.

Other ingredients may be substituted for and added to the potatoes, from spinach to sweet potatoes, cheese, semolina, or cornmeal. Most of the following are indeed Italian, but Spaetzle (page 552) hails from Alsace, and some of the others are modern variations that have no

MAKING GNOCCHI

1

2

3

(STEP 1) Start by rolling a piece of the dough into a log. Use flour as needed to prevent sticking, but try to keep it to a minimum. **(STEP 2)** Cut the dough into approximately 1-inch lengths. **(STEP 3)** Roll each of the sections off the back of a fork to give it the characteristic ridges.

specific European provenance. Other dumplings in this section use day-old bread, bread crumbs, flour, and egg to bind the dough.

Gnocchi Technique

Getting the dough just right for gnocchi takes a delicate balance of potato, flour, and gentle mixing. The first time you make it you'll probably use a bit too much flour and overmix the dough, but don't be discouraged if your gnocchi aren't delicate and fluffy. You'll improve with each batch and get to the point where it's easy enough to make a batch of gnocchi for lunch.

Tips for Making Great Gnocchi

- Use freshly cooked potatoes (leftover baked or mashed potatoes are better for croquettes).
- Add the flour in small amounts so you don't add too much.
- Mix and then knead the dough gently; you're trying not to overdevelop the gluten.
- Keep your work surface well floured so the gnocchi don't stick.
- Roll the logs out quickly and don't worry too much about getting them perfectly even, which may overwork your dough. They're supposed to look handmade!
- Test-cook a piece of the dough just as it comes together; it may be closer to ready than you think.
- Indenting the gnocchi with your finger or rolling them over a fork, cheese grater, or gnocchi board is optional, but it helps the gnocchi grab the sauce. To indent the dumplings, just flour your thumb and roll it over the gnocchi. Using the fork, grater, or board takes some practice; use your thumb to roll the gnocchi over the tines or ridges—your thumb will simultaneously indent the opposite side.

Potato Gnocchi

MAKES: 4 servings

TIME: 1½ hours

The classic recipe, with variations. Whenever you add ingredients to gnocchi dough, they won't be quite as ethereal, but will be fluffy and flavorful.

1 pound starchy potatoes, washed

Salt and freshly ground black pepper

About 1 cup all-purpose flour, plus more as needed

1 Put the potatoes in a pot with salted water to cover over high heat; bring to a boil, adjust the heat so the water simmers, and cook until the potatoes are quite tender, about 45 minutes. Drain and peel (use a pot holder or towel to hold the potatoes and peel with a small knife; it will be easy). Rinse the pot, fill it again with salted water, and bring to a boil.

2 Use a fork, potato masher, or ricer to mash or rice the potatoes in a bowl along with some salt and pepper. Add about ½ cup of flour and stir; add more flour until the mixture forms a dough you can handle. Knead on a lightly floured surface for a minute or so. Pinch off a piece of the dough and boil it to make sure it will hold its shape; if it does not, knead in a bit more flour. The idea is to get a dough with as little additional flour and kneading as possible.

3 Roll a piece of the dough into a rope about ½ inch thick, then cut the rope into 1-inch lengths; traditionally, you would spin each of these pieces off the tines of a fork to score it lightly. As each one is ready, put it on a sheet of wax paper dusted with flour; do not allow them to touch.

4 Add the gnocchi to the boiling water a few at a time; stir. (You will need to work in a couple of batches so they aren't too crowded in the pot.) A minute after they rise to the surface, the gnocchi are done; remove with a slotted spoon. Put in a bowl and sauce or reheat in butter within a few minutes; these do not keep well.

Herb Gnocchi. Add ½ cup chopped fresh herbs, like basil, parsley, mint, dill, chives, or chervil, and mix in with the mashed or riced potatoes.

Spinach Gnocchi. Add 10 ounces fresh spinach or 5 ounces frozen spinach and a pinch of nutmeg if you like. Stem and wash the fresh spinach; steam it (see page 239), then drain, squeeze (get as much water out as possible), and chop it very fine. Add it to the potatoes along with the nutmeg.

Sweet Potato or Butternut Squash Gnocchi. Substitute sweet potatoes or butternut squash for the potatoes. It's best to roast or steam the sweet potatoes or squash, because they will absorb too much water if boiled. You can microwave the sweet potatoes too. If you're using butternut squash, add an egg and mix it in with the mashed squash; you will likely need more flour too.

Porcini Dumplings

MAKES: 4 servings

TIME: About 1 hour

If you have a source for fresh porcini mushrooms, this is a good way to use them; fresh shiitakes are a good substitute, and dried porcini will improve their flavor. Serve the dumplings in a flavorful broth, add them to Wheat, Whole Barley, or Farro Soup (page 140), top with a creamy sauce like Béchamel (page 57), or toss with pasta with Fast Tomato Sauce (page 502) as a twist on spaghetti and meatballs.

2 cups torn or chopped day-old bread or 1 cup bread crumbs, preferably fresh (page 876)

1/2 cup milk or cream

3 eggs

1 cup freshly grated Parmesan cheese

2 tablespoons extra virgin olive oil or butter

2 ounces dried porcini, reconstituted (see page 314), drained, and chopped

1 pound any fresh mushrooms, trimmed and chopped

Salt and freshly ground black pepper

2 teaspoons minced garlic

1 teaspoon minced fresh rosemary leaves

❶ Combine the bread, milk, eggs, and Parmesan in a large bowl, mix well, and set aside.

❷ Put the oil or butter in a large skillet over medium heat. When the oil is hot or the butter is melted, add the mushrooms, then sprinkle with salt and pepper. Cook for a few minutes, then add the garlic and rosemary; continue cooking, stirring occasionally, until tender and with some liquid in the pan, another couple minutes or so.

❸ Add the mushrooms to the bread mixture, stir well, and let sit for at least 15 minutes or up to a day, covered and refrigerated.

❹ Bring a large pot of salted water (or mushroom or other stock; to make your own, see pages 157–159) to a boil, then reduce the heat so it bubbles steadily. Form the mixture into balls (no more than 1 1/2 inches in diameter). If the batter is too soft, add bread crumbs; if it's too stiff, add milk or cream. Drop the dumplings into the pot as you roll them. When they come to the surface, they are done; remove with a slotted spoon.

"Twice-Cooked" Gnocchi

Pan-cooking or roasting cooked gnocchi or baking them with a premade sauce adds color, richness, and flavor.

To roast: Put a couple of tablespoons extra virgin olive oil or butter in a skillet over high heat; when the oil is hot or the butter is melted, add the boiled and drained gnocchi (don't overcrowd the pan; cook in batches if necessary) and cook, stirring as they brown, 5 to 10 minutes. Or roast in a 450°F oven: Toss the gnocchi in olive oil or butter and put on a baking sheet; cook, shaking the tray to roll the gnocchi every couple minutes, until all the sides are golden brown, another 5 to 10 minutes.

To bake them in a sauce: Heat the oven to 425°F. Grease a gratin or other baking dish and add the gnocchi; spoon on a sauce like Fast Tomato Sauce (page 502) or Meat Sauce, Bolognese Style (page 531) or simply toss them in melted butter, sprinkle with cheese (or other topping, see "12 Alternative Toppings for Pasta," page 516), and bake until the sauce is bubbling and hot, about 10 minutes, depending on the size of the dish.

Spaetzle

MAKES: 4 servings

TIME: 30 minutes

Hailing from Alsace, spaetzle (spay-tzul) are between dumpling and pasta, made from a pancakelike batter that's dropped into gently boiling water and cooked. They can then be seasoned and served, sautéed, tossed with sauce, or added to a broth or soup. They're fabulous mixed with Mornay (Cheese) Sauce (page 58), put in a gratin dish, topped with grated cheese and/or bread crumbs, and baked until bubbling—an Alsatian mac and cheese.

You can use many techniques for dropping the batter into the water—a spaetzle maker (it looks like a grater without sharp edges, with an attachment that slides across the top), a colander, or simply a spoon: Just load the spoon with about a tablespoon of the batter and let the batter drop into the water; size isn't that important here, and you need not worry if the pieces break up.

Salt

2 cups all-purpose flour

1/2 teaspoon or more freshly ground black pepper

3 eggs

1 cup milk, more or less

2 to 4 tablespoons butter or extra virgin olive oil

Chopped fresh parsley leaves or chives for garnish

1 Bring a large pot of water to a boil and salt it. Combine the flour with the pepper and a large pinch of salt in a bowl. Lightly beat the eggs and milk together in a separate bowl and then stir it into the flour. If necessary, add a little more milk to make a batter about the consistency of pancake batter. Have a large bowl of ice water ready.

2 Scoop a tablespoon or so of the batter and drop it into the boiling water; small pieces may break off, but the batter should remain largely intact and form an uneven disk. Spoon in about one-third to one-fourth of the batter, depending on the size of your pot. When the spaetzle rise to the top, a couple minutes later (you may have to loosen them from the bottom, but they'll float right up), cook for another minute or so, then transfer with a slotted spoon or strainer into the bowl of ice water. Repeat until all the batter is used up.

3 Drain the spaetzle. (At this point, you may toss them with a bit of oil and refrigerate, covered, for up to a day.) Put the butter or oil in a large skillet, preferably nonstick, over medium-high heat. When the butter is melted or the oil is hot, add the spaetzle, working in batches, and quickly brown on both sides. Serve hot, garnished with the parsley or chives.

Herb Spaetzle. A mix of parsley, chervil, chives, and tarragon is lovely: Add about 1 cup chopped fresh herbs; stir into the batter.

The Basics of Asian Noodles

Some Asian noodles are practically identical to their European counterparts. Others are radically different in handling, taste, texture, and cooking. A familiarity with Asian noodles will expand your culinary repertoire significantly and happily.

The assortment of Asian noodles now widely available is absolutely thrilling. To the novice, though, it can be overwhelming. To help you make sense of it all, here's a rundown of the varieties you're likely to encounter, along with preparation tips and cooking times.

Chinese Egg Noodles

Long, thin, golden noodles made with wheat flour; round or flat, fresh or dried. The fresh noodles cook quickly, in 3 minutes or so, or you can add them to hot soup to cook. Dried take a little longer, about 5 minutes (timing depends on the thickness of the noodle, of course); leave them slightly undercooked if you are adding them to soup or stir-frying them.

Chinese Wheat Noodles
Long and thin and either round or flat; fresh or dried. They are typically white or light yellow and are made of wheat, water, and salt. Boil the dried noodles for about 5 minutes and the fresh for half that time, roughly. Again, cooking time depends on the thickness of the noodle.

Rice Sticks, Rice Vermicelli
White, translucent rice noodles, most often from Southeast Asia, ranging from angel hair thin (vermicelli) to spaghetti thickness to greater than $1/4$ inch. Soak in hot water for 5 to 30 minutes, until softened, then drain and boil or stir-fry for an additional minute or two. (See Pad Thai, page 510.) For soups, add them directly to the broth or soak them for 5 to 10 minutes and then drop them into the soup.

Udon
Round, square, or flat wheat noodles from Japan, available in a range of thicknesses and lengths; usually dried but may be fresh. Most typically served in soups and stews, though you can also use them in braised dishes or serve them cold. Boil fresh or dried noodles for a few minutes, until just tender (dried take a bit longer, of course).

Soba
Long, thin, flat Japanese noodles made from a combination of buckwheat and wheat flour, distinctively nutty and light beige to brownish gray (sometimes green tea is added, so they're green). Most often dried, but you may see fresh. Boil dried noodles for 5 to 7 minutes, fresh for 2 to 4.

Somen
White, round, ultra-thin all-wheat noodles from Japan that cook in just a couple minutes. Best in soups.

Ramen and Saimin
Long, slender, off-white wheat Japanese noodles that appear either crinkled in brick form or as rods; fresh, dried, frozen, or instant. The instant variety is typically deep-fried to remove moisture before being dried and packaged. (Saimin is similar but made with egg.) When fresh, boil ramen for just a couple of minutes; dried takes around 5.

Bean Threads
Mung Bean Threads, Cellophane Noodles, Glass Noodles, Spring Rain Noodles

Long, slender, translucent noodles made from mung bean starch, usually sold in 2-ounce bundles. To prepare, soak the noodles in hot or boiling water until tender, 5 to 15 minutes; use kitchen scissors to cut them into manageable pieces if necessary. (If you're adding them to soup or deep-frying them, don't bother to soak.) You can also cook the noodles by boiling them for a couple minutes.

Tofu Noodles
These are narrow, flat, beige noodles, made from pressed tofu and fabulous in salads and stir-fries. They are available fresh, frozen, and dried. To use the fresh noodles, simply rinse and pat dry; defrost frozen noodles in the fridge, then treat as fresh. Soak dried noodles in warm water for about 15 minutes, then rinse and drain.

Cold Soba Noodles with Dipping Sauce

MAKES: 4 small servings
TIME: 30 minutes

Even in the States, we now have restaurants specializing in the classic Japanese cold soba noodles, served with a dashi-based dipping sauce. They make a perfect light meal.

Salt

1 cup Dashi (page 160) or chicken stock (to make your own, see page 157)

¼ cup soy sauce

2 tablespoons mirin or 1 tablespoon honey mixed with 1 tablespoon water

12 ounces dried soba noodles

1 teaspoon finely grated or minced fresh ginger for garnish

2 tablespoons minced scallion for garnish

Toasted sesame seeds (see page 317) for garnish

1 Bring a large pot of water to a boil and salt it. Meanwhile, combine the dashi or stock, soy, and mirin; taste and add a little more soy if it's not strong flavored enough.

2 Cook the noodles until tender but not mushy, just as you would Italian pasta. Drain and rinse quickly under cold running water until cold. Drain well. Serve the noodles with the garnishes, with the sauce on the side for dipping (or spooning over).

Cold Soba Noodles with Mushrooms. Add 4 dried shiitake mushrooms, stems removed and reconstituted in very hot water (change the water once if necessary) until soft, about 20 minutes. Or use 4 to 6 fresh shiitakes (stems removed), steamed over the noodles or sautéed (see page 313). Slice the mushrooms very thinly and toss with the cooked noodles, then garnish.

Stir-Fried Asian Noodles

Most cooked Asian noodle dishes are stir-fried (like Pad Thai, page 510), not boiled and sauced like European ones, a preparation that gives them a completely different character. When you get used to the pattern, they're easy, fun, habit-forming, and better than most restaurant noodle dishes.

Stir-Fried Noodles with Meat and Vegetables

Lo Mein

MAKES: 4 servings
TIME: 30 minutes

The model for stir-fried noodle dishes, which can be made with just about anything, and a valuable addition to any cook's repertoire.

The best cuts of meat to use are sirloin strip (beef), pork shoulder (Boston butt or picnic), and chicken breast or thigh. The meat will be easier to slice thinly if you freeze it for 30 to 60 minutes first. (This is always the case with boneless meat or poultry.) Tofu is also good, especially store-bought spiced and pressed tofu or tofu that you've frozen.

Salt

12 ounces fresh Chinese egg noodles or about 8 ounces dried Chinese wheat noodles or spaghetti

3 tablespoons peanut or neutral oil, like grapeseed or corn

8 ounces beef, chicken, pork, shrimp, tofu, or what-have-you, very thinly sliced and cut into 2-inch-long strips

2 tablespoons soy sauce

1 large onion, thinly sliced

1 pound chopped broccoli florets or chopped asparagus

1 red bell pepper, cored, seeded, and cut into thin strips

1 tablespoon minced garlic

2 teaspoons minced or grated fresh ginger

½ cup chicken stock (to make your own, see page 157) or water

½ cup unsalted cashews, roughly chopped, or shelled whole peanuts (optional)

1 Bring a large pot of water to a boil and salt it. Cook the noodles until tender but not mushy, about 4 minutes for fresh noodles, longer for dried, then drain and quickly rinse under cold running water. Toss with 1 tablespoon of the oil to prevent sticking and set aside. Soak the meat in the soy sauce.

❷ Put another tablespoon of the oil in a deep skillet over high heat. When hot, add the onion and cook, stirring occasionally, until it begins to brown, about 5 minutes. Add the broccoli and red pepper and cook, stirring occasionally, until the broccoli is crisp-tender, 5 to 8 minutes. Add the garlic and ginger and cook for 1 minute, stirring almost constantly. Remove this mixture from the pan.

❸ Add the remaining oil to the pan and turn the heat to high. Drain the meat (reserve the soy sauce), add to the pan, and cook, stirring occasionally, for about 1 minute. Add the reserved soy sauce, along with the chicken stock, and stir. Add the drained noodles, vegetables, and nuts. Toss to mix and reheat, then serve.

Stir-Fried Udon Noodles. Great with pork and shiitake mushrooms but, here, too, any meat or vegetables can be used: Substitute udon noodles for the egg noodles and $1/2$ cup chopped scallion for the onion. Omit the garlic, ginger, and cashews. Add $1/4$ cup bonito flakes as a garnish if you like.

18 Dishes to Toss with Asian Noodles

1. Stir-Fried Vegetables (page 241)
2. Stir-Fried Asparagus (page 259)
3. Stir-Fried Bean Sprouts (page 261)
4. Quick-Cooked Bok Choy (page 265)
5. Asian Greens, Chinese Restaurant Style (page 266)
6. Stir-Fried Vegetables, Vietnamese Style (page 374)
7. Mixed Spicy Vegetables, Thai Style (page 374)
8. Shrimp and Scallion Stir-Fry (page 575)
9. Stir-Fried Shrimp with Black Beans (page 576)
10. Squid with Chiles and Greens (page 626)
11. Stir-Fried Chicken with Cabbage (page 643)
12. Stir-Fried Chicken with Broccoli or Cauliflower (page 674)
13. Stir-Fried Chicken with Ketchup (page 677)
14. Stir-Fried Spicy Beef with Basil (page 719)
15. Stir-Fried Beef with Onions (page 731)
16. Stir-Fried Pork with Spinach (page 748)
17. Braised Pork with Spicy Soy Sauce (page 758)
18. Stir-Fried Lamb with Green Peppers (page 769)

Broad Rice Noodles with Chiles, Pork, and Basil

MAKES: About 4 servings

TIME: About 45 minutes, including time to soak the noodles

I have been making this dish for about 20 years and still love it—it's hot, sweet, and herbaceous. I keep it short of

Improvising Stir-Fried Noodles

Think of assembling Asian noodle dishes in the same way you do Italian pasta dishes. The only difference is that you almost always cook an ingredient, then remove it from the pan before cooking the next ingredient, as with most types of stir-fries. (You can put everything in a single bowl to avoid doing extra dishes.) When the noodles are ready, everything goes back in the pan.

That said, here's a basic, infinitely expandable stir-fried noodle "recipe": Cook udon, soba, somen, or any rice noodles (see "The Basics of Asian Noodles," page 552) until tender but not mushy. Follow the cooking technique in Stir-Fried Noodles with Meat and Vegetables (previous page): Cook the vegetables first, then the meat, and then add the noodles; toss until heated through. For more moisture, add a little of the noodle-cooking water or stock, a splash of soy sauce, or a drizzle of peanut, neutral, or dark sesame oil.

fiery, then pass hot red pepper flakes at the table for those with cast-iron palates. If you're sure everyone you're eating with likes heat, increase the dried chiles to a handful or more.

12 ounces wide rice noodles (fettuccine width)

2 tablespoons peanut or neutral oil, like grapeseed or corn

1 tablespoon minced garlic

5 small dried hot red chiles, or to taste

5 to 8 ounces ground pork or other ground meat, like beef or turkey

1 tablespoon soy sauce and 2 tablespoons Thai fish sauce (nam pla, available at Asian markets) or 3 tablespoons either or any combination

1 tablespoon sugar

2 tablespoons rice or other vinegar

1 cup shredded fresh basil leaves

Salt if necessary

Hot red pepper flakes (optional)

❶ Soak the noodles in warm water to cover until soft, 15 to 30 minutes. You can change the water once or twice to hasten the process slightly, or you can simply cook the noodles as you would any other, taking care not to overcook. Drain thoroughly, then toss with half the oil.

❷ Put the remaining oil in a large, deep nonstick skillet over medium-high heat for a minute or so, until the first wisp of smoke appears. Add the garlic and chiles and cook, stirring, for a minute. Add the meat and reduce the heat to medium. Cook, stirring and mashing with a wooden spoon to break up clumps, until almost all traces of red or pink disappear, 3 to 5 minutes.

❸ Add the soy and/or fish sauces and the sugar; stir to mix. Add the drained noodles and toss and stir to combine. Add the vinegar and most of the basil. Stir and taste; add salt if necessary. Serve garnished with the remaining basil, passing the hot red pepper flakes on the side if you like.

Rice Noodles with Coconut Milk. In Step 2, add ¹/₂ cup sliced onion and ¹/₂ cup roughly chopped red bell pepper after the initial cooking of the garlic and chiles. Increase the sugar to 2 tablespoons. In Step 3, use 1 cup coconut milk (to make your own, see page 389) instead of the vinegar.

Vegetarian Broad Rice Noodles. In Step 2, add 1 teaspoon minced fresh ginger along with the garlic and chiles. Cook ¹/₂ cup scallion, cut into 1-inch lengths, and ¹/₂ cup roughly chopped red bell pepper after the initial cooking of the garlic and chiles. Substitute 1 cup pressed or frozen tofu, diced (see page 444) or 1 cup chopped seitan for the meat. You can also successfully combine this variation with the coconut milk variation.

Curried Rice Noodles with Pork or Chicken and Shrimp

MAKES: 4 servings
TIME: 30 minutes

These curried noodles are a specialty of Singapore and can be prepared much more simply: Stir-fry the noodles with onions and curry powder, for example, or with a bit of egg. This is a relatively elaborate version and can be made more so with the addition of bean sprouts (with the basil), sliced Chinese sausage (with the pork or chicken), egg (as in the noodle stir-fry on page 510), or vegetables like broccoli (parboil it first, as in the stir-fry on page 259) or tomato.

12 ounces thin rice noodles ("vermicelli" or "rice stick")

¹/₄ cup peanut or neutral oil, like grapeseed or corn

4 ounces boneless pork or chicken, diced

4 ounces peeled shrimp, diced

1 onion, diced

 Fast   Make Ahead   **V** Vegetarian

1 red or yellow bell pepper, cored, seeded, and chopped

1 tablespoon minced garlic

1 tablespoon minced fresh ginger

1 or 2 small hot red dried chiles, chopped, or 1 teaspoon hot red pepper flakes, or to taste

1 tablespoon curry powder (to make your own, see pages 66–67), or more to taste

1 tablespoon sugar

2 tablespoons soy sauce

2 tablespoons nam pla (Thai fish sauce) or more soy sauce

Stock or water as needed

$^1/_2$ cup torn fresh basil leaves, preferably Thai basil

Salt if necessary

$^1/_2$ cup minced scallion

$^1/_4$ cup chopped peanuts

1 Put the noodles in a large bowl and cover them with boiling water. Prepare the other ingredients while the noodles sit.

2 Put half the oil in a large nonstick skillet over high heat. When hot, add the meat and cook, stirring constantly, until the meat loses its color, 3 or 4 minutes. Remove with a slotted spoon and set aside. Add the shrimp and repeat the process; remove.

3 Add the remaining oil, wait a few seconds for it to get hot, and add the onion and bell pepper; cook, stirring occasionally, until the onion begins to brown, 3 to 5 minutes. Add the garlic, ginger, and chiles and cook, stirring, for 30 seconds. Drain and add the noodles; add the curry powder and sugar and stir for a few seconds. Cook, stirring occasionally, for about a minute. Stir in the soy sauce and nam pla; return the meat and shrimp to the pan.

4 Add about $^1/_2$ cup of liquid to allow the noodles to separate and continue to cook, stirring occasionally, until the noodles begin to brown. Turn off the heat and stir in the basil; taste and adjust the seasoning, adding more

salt, curry, chile, soy sauce, or nam pla to taste. Garnish with the scallion and peanuts and serve.

Curried Rice Noodles with Vegetables and Tofu. Substitute 1 pound (or brick) firm tofu for the meat and shrimp; drain and cut it into $^1/_2$- to 1-inch cubes. Use snow peas, sliced mushrooms, shredded cabbage or bok choy, or trimmed green beans in addition to or instead of the onion and/or bell pepper.

Glass Noodles with Vegetables and Meat

Chop Chae

MAKES: 8 servings
TIME: 1 hour

Classic Korean, seen more often in restaurants than homes, but easily done. Since chop chae is best at room temperature, you can make it a couple of hours in advance. Substitute shrimp or fish for the meat (or omit it entirely) if you like.

Salt

2 tablespoons dark sesame oil, plus more as needed

4 ounces boneless beef sirloin, cut into bits

2 medium carrots, julienned or minced

1 large onion, thinly sliced and separated into rings

12 scallions, roughly chopped

2 cups chopped cooked spinach (see page 239)

1 cup trimmed mushrooms, preferably a mixture of oyster, shiitake, and enoki

1 tablespoon minced garlic

8 ounces Korean sweet potato vermicelli or bean threads

2 tablespoons soy sauce, or more to taste

Freshly ground black pepper

$^1/_4$ cup pine nuts, lightly toasted (see page 317)

$^1/_4$ cup sesame seeds, lightly toasted (see page 317)

1 Bring a large pot of water to a boil and salt it. Put 1 tablespoon of the sesame oil in a large nonstick skillet over medium-high heat. When hot, add the meat and cook, stirring occasionally, until browned, about 5 minutes. Remove with a slotted spoon and put in a large bowl. Cook the carrots in the same skillet, stirring occasionally, just until they lose their crunch, about 5 minutes. Add to the meat.

2 Put the remaining sesame oil in the skillet and add the onion; cook, stirring occasionally, until it begins to brown, about 5 minutes. Remove with a slotted spoon and add to the meat. Raise the heat to high and add the scallions. Cook, stirring, until they wilt, just 2 or 3 minutes. Add to the meat mixture.

3 Add a little more oil if necessary and stir-fry the spinach over medium heat until hot, about a minute. Add to the meat mixture. Add the mushrooms and the garlic and cook, stirring occasionally, until they soften, about 5 minutes. Add to the meat.

4 Add the noodles to the boiling water and turn off the heat. The noodles will be tender in about 5 minutes; drain. Add the noodles and soy sauce to the skillet and cook, stirring occasionally, for about 5 minutes. Add to the meat mixture.

5 Toss the noodles and vegetable mixture well, adding salt, pepper, and more sesame oil or soy sauce to taste. Garnish with the pine nuts and sesame seeds and serve at room temperature.

 Fast   Make Ahead   Vegetarian

Fish and Shellfish

WHEN IT COMES TO FISH, THE GOAL IS PURE:

Buy it right, cook it simply. The cooking could hardly be easier; the buying is not as easy as it sounds. Though globalization has affected fish no less than anything else—you're as likely to be offered fish from New Zealand as you are from New England—fish remains different from other animals we eat for one main reason: A bewildering variety of fifty or sixty species makes appearances in the supermarket, mostly on a rotating basis. This makes fish more confusing than it might be otherwise, and the fact that almost nothing is local anymore doesn't help matters. Younger people have never known a time when green-lipped mussels or orange roughy wasn't common; but those of us who are older remember when they first appeared, as if they were invented.

There have been other changes. Twenty years ago, aquaculture (farming) of finfish was considered revolutionary (though mollusks have been farmed for centuries). Now it's harder to find wild salmon, shrimp, catfish, and sometimes even striped bass than it is to find farmed varieties. This is a good thing in some respects—it preserves the increasingly scarce wild stocks of these fish, and it's kept prices relatively low. But the farmed stuff never—I repeat, never—tastes as good as that from the wild. (And there are environmental questions about it.)

Despite these and the obvious other major difficulties with fish—it's best when super-fresh (sometimes when alive), it spoils more quickly than most other foods, and, confoundingly, sometimes frozen is better than fresh (more on this shortly)—there are four features of fish that make them an absolute joy in the kitchen. First of all, the variety of flavors is fantastic; second, many fish are so similar that they can be grouped (as I do here for many of the fish) and readily substituted for one another; third, their cooking time is ridiculously fast, usually from 0 to 10 minutes; and fourth, they're the healthiest animal product you can eat, hands down.

In fact, buying is the only challenging part of working with fish, and even that isn't that big a deal once you understand the basics. At any market there will always be some fish that are in good shape and meet your current needs. You just have to be flexible. Toward that end, I've included suggestions for other fish (and even other meat or poultry) that you can substitute in many of the recipes. In sections covering a particular type of fish, such as thick fillets, the opening text names the varieties you can use. So the next time you go to the store looking for swordfish that isn't there, you'll know what you can buy instead—without needing to change the recipe.

In fact, it's easier to cook fish than it is to buy it: Once you get into the right category—mollusks, shellfish, fish

steaks, and so on—the techniques are pretty much consistent from one variety to the next. That's why after the Essential Recipes, I've organized the chapter to start with the most common, most available, most accessible seafood (which is shrimp) and proceeded to the types of fish that might be less familiar.

The Basics of Buying Fish

Here's the quick, no-nonsense course in supermarket fish shopping; there are more details in the discussions of individual fish, but this will get you started.

Sustainable Seafood

Like so many other foods, fish now comes from all over the globe, but some of it is in short supply; dozens of species have been overfished or polluted out of existence, or nearly so. In an attempt to allow these species to reach commercial quantities again—or, in some cases, just to survive—their consumption is either forbidden or restricted, by government mandate or by the recommendation of concerned third parties.

For consumers, it's easy enough to keep track of what fish should be avoided, even when they do make it to market. And in an effort to be sensitive to this issue, I've limited the number of recipes that call for the most unsustainable species and always offer other alternatives. But since the endangered list changes all the time—swordfish, for example, goes on and off the lists—I'm passing along what I think are the best resources to help you make confident purchasing decisions. Here are the websites:

The Monterey Bay Aquarium: mbayaq.org/cr/
    seafoodwatch.asp

Audubon's Living Oceans Guide:
    http://seafood.audubon.org

Blue Ocean Institute's Seafood Guide:
    blueocean.org/Seafood

Needless to say, or almost needless to say, you should avoid fish counters that smell or look dirty. I'd like to think that at this stage of the game you wouldn't encounter such a disgrace, but if you do, run, don't walk. (It might not be a bad idea to stop long enough to complain to the management, which might encourage them to clean up their act.)

Generally, steer clear of prewrapped fish. It might be good, and there's nothing intrinsically wrong with it, but it's difficult to evaluate. (Though you could poke a hole in the plastic and smell it; I've done that plenty of times, and it works. If it's bad, don't put it back—hand it to someone and tell them to get the rest of it off the shelves.)

Purchasing shellfish is usually pretty straightforward: Lobster, crab, whole clams, oysters, mussels, and certain other mollusks must be alive when sold. Lobsters and crabs should be quite lively; if they seem tired, move on. The muscles of live mollusks make it difficult to pry their shells apart, and this is a good test. If, however, mollusks are shucked and separated from their guts, as scallops routinely are (and oysters frequently are), the shelf life is extended considerably. In this case, smell them if possible.

Shrimp are almost always shipped frozen and defrosted before sale. It's better, though, to buy them still frozen; you may get a more favorable price, and you can control how and when they are defrosted. The best way to defrost shrimp is in the refrigerator (which takes a while) or under cold running water (which is quite rapid).

These days most finfish is sold in the form of fillets and steaks, and most of these are shipped after cutting; few fish counters butcher whole fish anymore. The surface of fillets and steaks should be bright, clear, and reflective—almost translucent. The color should be consistent with the type of fish. For example, pearly white fish should not have spots of pink, which are usually bruises, or browning, which indicates spoilage. Creamy or ivory-colored fish should have no areas of deep red or brown. It's easy enough to get to know the ideal appearance of your favorite fish and reject any that doesn't meet your standard, but it's just as important to know the warning signs for fish in general.

Whole fish gives you more signals than fillets or steaks. Look for red gills (located right behind the head), bright reflective skin, firm flesh, an undamaged layer of scales, and no browning anywhere; the fish should smell sweet or salty—not "fishy." The best whole fish look alive, as if they just came out of the water.

In general, trust your instincts. Good fish looks good, has firm, unmarred flesh, and smells like fresh seawater. If your supermarket fishmonger won't let you smell the fish, and it passes the appearance tests, try buying it, opening the package right on the spot, and, if the smell is at all off, handing it right back. If you're reluctant to do that, take any fish that doesn't meet your expectations when you cook it back to the supermarket for an exchange or a refund. Demand quality.

The Basics of Cooking Fish

Contrary to reigning wisdom, seafood is the easiest kind of animal protein to cook: It's fast, because the flesh responds to heat almost instantly; in fact, dozens of varieties cook in 5 minutes or less. You expose fish to heat (usually relatively high heat), sprinkle it with salt and pepper (or other seasonings), give it a turn (or not, if it's fragile), garnish (lemon wedges will do the trick), and a few minutes later, you're eating.

And, in the many years I've been cooking and writing about fish, my approach has changed and I've come to think that—within limits—the exact species of fish isn't as important as the shape and the cut of the fish. The thickness of a fillet, for example, is of critical importance when cooking—far more important, really, then whether the fillet is of red snapper or cod.

Of course, other factors come into play: Oily fish is completely different from lean fish and demands some acidity and assertive seasoning and saucing; lean, delicate fish are easily overpowered. The sweetness of shellfish is nicely balanced with a little heat. Steely salmon has an affinity for the floral flavors of aromatics and herbs.

I'm streamlining to the bare bones here, and that's the point of the Essential Recipes that follow. Let me say this one more time, with feeling: Cooking fish is not complicated. Almost every fish can be prepared using any of these ten essential techniques (and in the few cases where they can't, I'll say so). When you build confidence in basic techniques—rather than trying to master an entire fish vocabulary and repertoire of recipes—cooking seafood at home is suddenly far more accessible, spontaneous, and flexible. So if you're the least bit intimidated by cooking seafood, please start here.

Of course there are times—plenty of them, I hope—when you'll want something a little more involved than lightly seasoned, simply cooked fish with a squeeze of lemon. Those sorts of recipes follow this section and are arranged according to type of fish—beginning with shrimp, the most popular—through mixed seafood dishes and finally burgers and cakes. And none of them is difficult or time-consuming.

The Basics of Preparing Fish

A fillet is a boneless piece of fish cut lengthwise from either side. See page 586 for details.

A steak is a cross-section piece of fish that includes both sides, whatever bones there are in the crosscut, and (usually) the skin. See page 601 for details.

Fillets and steaks should be rinsed and patted dry. You can leave the skin on (to skin fish, see page 579) and, if it's been scaled, the skin is usually good to eat; if not, it can still stay on, but you'll leave it on the plate.

The surest way to keep the skin from sticking during cooking is to use a nonstick skillet. Otherwise, be sure there's at least a film of fat in the pan (or that the grill is clean, hot, and oiled) and that both the fat and the pan are hot before adding the fish. Another foolproof way is to dredge the fish in flour first.

To help keep thin, delicate fillets from flaking apart after cooking, again be sure your pan is hot and use the broadest spatula you have to pick them up in one assertive, smooth motion. If you cook a lot of fish, consider investing in a flexible fish spatula.

You can leave the shells on shrimp (and deveining is optional), but squid and octopus must be cleaned before cooking.

Clams, mussels, and oysters must be scrubbed clean.

Whole fish should be scaled, then gutted and cleaned; usually a fishmonger will do that for you, but you can do it yourself if you like or must; see pages 595–597.

You can cook fish to varying degrees of doneness, though the window between the stages is obviously shorter with fish than with meats and is virtually nonexistent with thin fish fillets. With few exceptions—most notably octopus, striped bass, and monkfish—you don't want to cook fish to complete doneness (these three, and a few others, are best when cooked through). In other rare cases—like sushi-grade tuna or good salmon—you might even eat it quite rare. But for the most part, you want to pull it from the heat when the flesh just starts to turn opaque and flakes easily without being dry. I give a range of time and visual cues in each recipe.

How Much Fish to Make?

In general, figure about 1½ pounds of any cleaned boneless seafood—fish fillets, scallops, squid, whatever—will serve four people. Whole fish is a little trickier: Small whole fish should weigh about a pound per person, but as they grow in size there's more meat per bone, so a 2-pounder will feed two or three people, and a 4-pounder will feed about six. For mollusks and shellfish where the shells are significant—mussels, clams, lobster, crab—count on a pound per person.

You can cook fillets whole and serve them family style or divide among individual plates, or just cut them into portions before cooking.

 Fast   Make Ahead   **V** Vegetarian

There are more detailed instructions and specifics in the "Basics of . . ." section for each group of fish, beginning on page 572.

ning on page 572.

ESSENTIAL RECIPES

Here are the 10 basic techniques for cooking virtually any kind of fish, mollusk, or shellfish. For ideas about how to season fish before, during, and after cooking, see the sidebar on page 566.

✪ Broiled Fish Fillets (and a Lot Else)

MAKES: 4 servings

TIME: No more than 2 minutes

Hands down, broiling is the easiest way to cook all kinds of seafood, even mussels and clams; see the variations. (Only super-thick or uneven steaks and roasts are off-limits.) The key is to preheat the broiler and the pan. I like a large cast-iron skillet, but you can use a heavy rimmed baking sheet, a roasting pan, or the base of your broiler pan (the part that's left after you remove the insert).

3 tablespoons extra virgin olive oil or melted butter

About 1½ pounds thin fish fillets, like flounder or sole

Salt and freshly ground black pepper or a pinch cayenne

Chopped fresh parsley leaves for garnish (optional)

Lemon wedges for serving

1 Heat the broiler until quite hot. Move the rack as close to the heat source as possible (3 or 4 inches is good and 2 inches is not too close). Put a sturdy pan on the rack and heat it for about 5 minutes.

2 When it's hot, remove the pan and pour in the olive oil, then put the fillets in the oil and sprinkle with salt and pepper. (If your pan won't hold all the fish comfortably, work in batches, transferring the first fillets to warmed plates or a heated platter before proceeding.) Time under the broiler will be 90 seconds to 2 minutes, rarely more. Do not turn; the fillets are so thin it's not necessary. The fish is ready when it becomes opaque and the tip of a knife flakes the thickest part easily.

3 To serve, carefully remove the fillets with a spatula, sprinkle with parsley if you like, and pour the pan juices over all. Garnish with lemon wedges.

Broiled Thick Fillets or Steaks. Broiling is ideal for 1-inch-thick pieces of fish like salmon, halibut, tuna, snapper, swordfish, cod, striped bass, catfish, and so on. If it's a fillet, and you're planning to eat the skin (make sure it's scaled), broil skin side up. While the pan is heating, brush the fish lightly with the olive oil (saving whatever remains) and sprinkle with salt and pepper. When the pan is ready, put the fish in the pan and drizzle the remaining oil around all. Broil, carefully turning sturdier, thicker fillets or steaks once about halfway through the cooking, for no more than 10 minutes for medium to medium well; use your judgment.

Broiled Scallops or Shrimp. While the pan is heating, turn the fish in the olive oil and a sprinkle of salt and pepper. Broil for about 3 minutes, shaking the pan occasionally and turning once.

Broiled Clams, Mussels, or Oysters. Put clams or mussels directly into the preheated skillet. They're done when they open, within 10 minutes. If the shells start to crack, remove the open mollusks and return the pan to the oven. (Any that do not open are safe to eat, as long as they were alive when you bought them; open them with a dull knife or broil for a few minutes longer.) Sprinkle with salt and pepper, and parsley if you like, before serving.

Broiled Whole Fish. Works best with fish under 3 pounds: While the pan is heating, turn the fish in the olive oil and a sprinkle of salt and pepper; get some inside the cavity too. Depending on the thickness, broil each side for 5 to 8 minutes; it's okay if the skin blisters and chars a bit.

Broiled Squid. While the pan is heating, toss the cleaned squid (whole or cut up) in the olive oil and sprinkle with salt and pepper. Put it in the hot pan and cook, shaking the pan as necessary until opaque, anywhere from 1 to 3 minutes depending on how big the pieces are, but no longer or they'll become rubbery.

Broiled Octopus. Boil the octopus in seasoned water until quite tender. The amount of time is unpredictable (see page 624), but this can be done up to a day in advance. Then broil until nicely browned on most sides, anywhere from 5 to 10 minutes.

✪ Grilled Fish Fillets or Steaks

MAKES: 4 servings
TIME: 40 minutes

Most fillets, regardless of their thickness, are simply too delicate to grill. But some sturdy, large-flake varieties of fish are exceptions, most notably salmon, striped bass, halibut, blackfish, and grouper—all with the skin left on, which adds stability—as well as monkfish.

Fish steaks are relatively foolproof—they're practically designed for grilling. And whole grilled fish, regardless of their size, are also good, though a grilling basket—which is nice but not absolutely necessary—helps keep them from starting to fall apart.

It always helps to make sure the grill is clean and well oiled just before you put the fish on. Just hold some paper towels in tongs and dip them in a small bowl of oil, then rub on the grates.

About 1½ pounds thick, sturdy fish fillets or steaks

2 tablespoons extra virgin olive oil

Salt and freshly ground black pepper

1 teaspoon minced garlic (optional)

Lemon wedges for serving

① Heat a charcoal or gas grill until quite hot and put the rack 3 or 4 inches from the heat source. Drizzle the flesh of the fish with olive oil and sprinkle it with salt and pepper. Rub the flesh with the garlic if you like.

② When the fire is ready, grill the fish for about 5 minutes, or until it's firm enough to turn. Turn and grill until done, usually another 3 to 5 minutes. When done, the fish will still be firm and juicy but opaque, and a thin-bladed knife will pass through it fairly easily. Serve with lemon.

Grilled Shrimp or Scallops. Shrimp are indestructible, but skewer scallops through their equators rather than their axes, or they may break (or put them in a basket). Grill until brown—just a couple minutes—then turn and brown again. Total cooking time should be just about 5 minutes; stop cooking before the interior of the shrimp or scallop becomes opaque.

Grilled Whole Fish, Large or Small. Good for carp, catfish, red snapper, sea bass, mackerel, or sardines; 2 to 3 pounds total will serve 4. Make sure all are gilled, gutted, and scaled. If grilling one large fish, make 3 or 4 diagonal, parallel slashes on each side of the fish, just about down to the bone. Rub with oil and sprinkle with salt and pepper. Small fish will take just a couple minutes per side; one large fish will take 5 to 8 minutes. Brush with additional oil if you like. To check for doneness, peek down to the bottom of the gashes, where the meat should be white.

✪ Pan-Cooked Thin Fish Fillets

MAKES: 4 servings
TIME: 20 minutes
🄵

You can call this sautéing or panfrying; the differences are subtle enough not to matter much. Both depend on a fair amount of fat and usually a coating of some kind—it's optional, but a light coating of flour or cornmeal, for example, promotes browning and helps keep the fish

 Fast   Make Ahead   **V** Vegetarian

moist. For a thicker, more flavorful coating, see the list of options on page 569.

The main recipe is the classic preparation for fillets of sole (*meunière*), which works equally well for any thin fillets. Note that you must work in two batches, because you can't crowd or fit this many fillets in the pan at once. Put the first two on plates and serve piping hot while the second batch cooks. It takes only a few minutes.

Four 6-ounce fillets of flounder, sole, or any other 1/4-inch-thick fish

Salt and freshly ground black pepper

2 tablespoons extra virgin olive oil

4 tablespoons butter or more oil

All-purpose flour or cornmeal for dredging

1/4 cup freshly squeezed lemon juice

Chopped fresh parsley leaves for garnish

Lemon wedges for serving

1 Warm 4 dinner plates in a 200°F oven. Sprinkle the fillets with salt and pepper.

2 Heat a large skillet over medium-high heat for 2 or 3 minutes. Add 1 tablespoon of the oil and 1 tablespoon of the butter. When the butter foam subsides, dredge two of the fillets, one by one, in the flour, shaking off any excess, and add them to the pan. Raise the heat to high and cook the fillets until golden on each side, 4 to 5 minutes total. Transfer to the warm serving plates and return to the oven if you like. Wipe the pan and repeat with the remaining fillets.

3 Turn the heat down to medium and add the remaining butter to the pan. Cook until the butter foams, a minute or two. Add the lemon juice and cook, stirring and scraping the bottom of the pan, for about 15 seconds. Pour the sauce over the fillets. Garnish with parsley and serve immediately with the lemon wedges.

Pan-Cooked Thick Fish Fillets. Here you might fit all the fillets in one large skillet: Cook the fillets for about 5 minutes per side, turning once. Any thick fillet will still be firm and juicy when done but will have turned

opaque inside; a thin-bladed knife will pass through it fairly easily.

Pan-Cooked Whole Fish. This works best with small fish, those that weigh 12 ounces or less: Remove the heads from the fish if you like (or if necessary to get them in the pan) and make sure they're gutted and scaled. Put the fish in the pan, one at a time, taking care not to overcrowd, and cook, turning only once, for a total of 8 to 12 minutes, depending on the thickness of the fish. When done the fish will have turned opaque inside; a thin-bladed knife will pass through it fairly easily.

Pan-Cooked Shrimp, Scallops, or Squid. Shrimp can be peeled or not, as you like; squid can be left whole or cut into rings. Proceed with the recipe, shaking the skillet or stirring with a spoon or spatula to brown the seafood on all sides. Total cooking time won't be more than 3 minutes or so. Shrimp are ready when they turn pink but are still a little translucent inside; scallops are ready when they're firm but not tough; and get the squid out of the pan the second it starts to shrink and turn opaque.

Roasted Thick Fish Fillets or Steaks

MAKES: 4 servings

TIME: 30 to 45 minutes, depending on thickness

F

Some fish steaks and fillets—especially the triangular fillets from large round fish—are so thick they almost qualify as roasts, which makes them too big to cook by direct heat. Fortunately, the same sear-and-roast technique that works so well on other animals is perfect for large pieces of fish, and it's faster. Provided you don't overcook, results are crisp on the outside and juicy inside. And as a bonus, you get a quick little sauce out of the deal.

The best tool for this job is an ovenproof skillet—you start on the stove and transfer the whole thing to the

How to Season Simply Cooked Fish

The Essential Recipes in this chapter need little more than salt, pepper, and lemon wedges. But flavoring concoctions—to rub, dip, or drizzle before or after cooking—can turn even the simplest seafood dishes into something grand.

Seasoning Seafood Before Cooking

Let me start by bashing two myths: Rubs aren't just for grilling; you can season food with a spice blend before any cooking method. (Except, of course, for boiling; but here you can just dump the equivalent of a rub in the water, and it'll season the fish—that's what a fish boil is.)

The other myth is that you can't season seafood with anything too flavorful. Yes, many fish are so splendid with a minimum of seasoning that you don't have to do much. But most fish are often complemented by salty, sweet, sour, and even bitter ingredients, and they stand up just fine. The trick is to use a light hand with the flavoring and rely on complexity rather than intensity. Letting the fish sit in seasoning or marinade will help develop some flavor, but don't go beyond 30 minutes or so—plenty of time to prepare other elements of the meal.

13 Flavorings I Like for Seasoning Fish

1. Ground spices, like cumin, coriander, or mustard
2. Whole herb or spice seeds, like dill or fennel (or any of the spices above)
3. Crumbled saffron threads
4. Rub with any kind of oil and roll in chopped fresh herbs
5. Vinegar, citrus juice, mustard, or even mayonnaise, brushed lightly on the fish
6. Miso, especially white or yellow, thinned with a little water or sake
7. Flavored Oil, including nut or seed oils like walnut or sesame (page 26)
8. Herb purées (pages 27–28)
9. Chili powder (to make your own, see page 66)
10. Curry powder (to make your own, see pages 66–67)
11. Jerk seasoning (to make your own, see page 68)
12. Five-spice powder (to make your own, see page 68)
13. Chile pastes (see pages 74–75)

21 Sauces, Seasonings, and Condiments for Simply Cooked Fish

In general, any of these ideas work for fish cooked by any technique, though fried and sautéed seafood usually works best with something acidic to balance the richness. And if there's already a pan sauce or some braising or steaming liquid you won't need much else.

1. Virtually any Five-Minute Drizzle Sauce (page 22)
2. Virtually any fresh or cooked salsa (see pages 23, 33–35, and 48–50)
3. Any Yogurt Sauce (page 24)
4. Compound Butter (page 32)
5. Any chutney (see pages 36–38)
6. Basil-Soy Dipping Sauce (page 38)
7. Thai Chile Sauce (page 39)
8. Ginger-Scallion Sauce (page 39)
9. Simple Miso Dipping Sauce (page 39)
10. Ponzu Sauce (page 40)
11. Mayonnaise (page 41), especially the flavored ones
12. Corn and Tomato Relish (page 50)
13. Balsamic Syrup (page 51)
14. Barbecue sauce (to make your own, see page 52), especially with shrimp
15. Teriyaki Sauce (page 55)
16. Brown Butter (page 56)
17. Velouté (White) Sauce (page 57)
18. Beurre Blanc (page 59)
19. Seaweed "Shake" (page 69)
20. Any Vinaigrette (pages 199–202)
21. Fast Tomato Sauce and most of its variations (page 502)

F Fast   **M** Make Ahead   **V** Vegetarian

oven. And if you don't have herbs handy, just salt and pepper is fine; or try one of the ideas for rubs in the list at left.

$^{1}/_{2}$ to 1 cup chopped mixed fresh herbs: parsley, basil, chervil, tarragon, rosemary, chives, marjoram, sage, or whatever you have on hand (use the smaller amount if you're using stronger herbs)

Salt and freshly ground black pepper

2 tablespoons extra virgin olive oil

About 1$^{1}/_{2}$ pounds large fish fillets (like monkfish, halibut, or tuna) or steaks of any size

1 cup chicken, fish, or vegetable stock (to make your own, see pages 157–159), red or white wine, or water, plus a little more if needed

❶ Heat the oven to 450°F. Mix the herbs with some salt and pepper. Heat a large ovenproof skillet over medium-high heat for about 2 minutes; add the olive oil. When it's good and hot, dredge the fish in the herb mixture. Brown for a couple of minutes on both sides (or all sides if the roast is triangular). Add the liquid to the pan and put it, uncovered, in the oven.

❷ Roast until the fish is tender, 20 to 30 minutes, turning once or twice (1-inch-thick steaks of most other fish will take 5 or 10 minutes less). Regardless of the thickness, the fillet will still be firm and juicy when done but will have turned opaque inside; a thin-bladed knife will pass through it fairly easily.

❸ Transfer the fish to a warm platter. If the pan juices are a little thin, reduce a bit; if they're too thick, add a little more stock or water and cook over medium heat for a minute or two. Serve the fish with the sauce spooned over.

Roasted Whole Fish. Works for small and large fish; the size is limited only by the size of your pan: Grease a roasting pan with a little olive oil and lay the fish in the bottom. Cut 3 or 4 parallel diagonal gashes in both sides of the fish, almost down to the bone. Rub the fish with some more oil (you'll need more than 2 tablespoons for all this) and sprinkle the inside with salt and pepper and half the herbs; sprinkle the outside with more salt and pepper. Roast the fish until it releases easily from the pan and the skin is crisp, 15 to 20 minutes or more for larger fish. Lift the fish out of the pan and add the liquid, scraping up any browned bits. Return the fish to the pan and roast until opaque but still juicy, another 15 minutes or so, again depending on the size. Add more liquid to the pan if it looks too dry. Serve with the pan juices, sprinkled with the remaining herbs.

Roasted Clams, Oysters, or Mussels. Put the mollusks in a pan large enough to hold them comfortably. Sprinkle with salt and pepper, drizzle with the olive oil, and pour the liquid over all. Put in the oven and roast, shaking the pan as needed, until the shells start to open, 10 to 20 minutes, depending on the size of the mollusks. Transfer those that have opened to serving bowls and return the pan to the oven, along with a splash more liquid if necessary. When all are opened, sprinkle with the herbs, pour the pan juices over all, and serve.

Oven-"Fried" Fish Fillets

MAKES: 4 servings
TIME: 25 minutes

This is a retro recipe that lives on because it's both easy and tasty. You can also use thin flatfish fillets here; just be careful handling them (they'll cook in about half the time.) For more ideas about how to vary this recipe, see the list that follows and "How to Season Simply Cooked Fish" (page 566).

> About 1¹/₂ pounds thick fish fillets (any of the fish listed on pages 585–586)
>
> 1¹/₂ cups milk, buttermilk, or yogurt
>
> Bread crumbs, preferably fresh (page 876), for dredging
>
> Salt and freshly ground black pepper
>
> 3 tablespoons melted butter or extra virgin olive oil
>
> Lemon wedges for serving

❶ Soak the fillets in the milk while you heat the oven to 450°F. Put the bread crumbs on a plate and sprinkle with salt and pepper.

❷ When the oven is hot, pull the fish from the milk and let it drain a bit. Dredge the still-wet fish in the bread crumbs, patting them to make sure they adhere. Drizzle a little of the butter or oil over the bottom of a 9 × 13-inch baking pan or large rimmed baking sheet, then lay the fillets in the pan. Drizzle with the remaining butter or oil.

❸ Bake near the top of the oven for 8 to 15 minutes, depending on the thickness; the fish will be crisp on the outside and tender and opaque when done. Serve immediately, with lemon wedges.

Oven-"Fried" Fish Sticks or Nuggets. Cut the fillets into finger-length rectangles or squares of relatively equal size. Proceed with the recipe, reducing the cooking time by about half.

5 Ways to Vary Oven-"Fried" Fish Fillets, Sticks, or Nuggets

1. Use cornmeal—or a mixture of flour and cornmeal—instead of the bread crumbs.
2. Skip the soak, rubbing the fillets with freshly squeezed lime juice and dredging them in flour spiked with a little chili powder (to make your own, see page 66).
3. Skip the soak, smearing the fillets with miso thinned with a little white wine or sake and dredging the fish in panko.
4. Instead of the bread crumbs, use finely ground nuts—hazelnuts, pecans, almonds, or coconut, for example—for dredging.
5. Use crushed cereals like Rice Krispies or corn flakes.

✪ Deep-Fried Seafood

MAKES: 4 servings
TIME: 30 minutes

This recipe works for shrimp, clams, oysters, squid, very small fish, and sturdy fillets (catfish is classic)—in short, just about everything. As with all deep frying, make sure the oil is hot. I like a light dusting on most fried seafood, and the cornstarch-flour combination ensures a crisp, thin exterior. But if a thicker coating is what you're after, see the variation and list that follow.

Just a word about preparing the fish: Make sure everything is patted dry before dredging. Cut the squid bodies into rings if you like and remove the shellfish and mollusks from their shells (obviously).

> Neutral oil, like grapeseed or corn, as needed
>
> About 1¹/₂ pounds cleaned fish fillets (whole or cut into chunks), shrimp, oysters, or clams
>
> Salt and freshly ground black pepper
>
> 1 cup all-purpose flour
>
> 1 cup cornstarch
>
> Lemon wedges for serving

 Fast   Make Ahead   **V** Vegetarian

❶ Put at least 2 inches of oil in a deep pan over medium-high heat; bring to 350°F (see "Deep Frying," page 19). Meanwhile, season the seafood with salt and pepper and combine the flour and cornstarch in a bowl.

❷ When the oil is hot, dredge the seafood lightly in the cornstarch-flour mixture, tapping to remove excess, and add the pieces slowly to the oil without crowding (cook in batches if necessary), adjusting the heat as necessary so the temperature remains nearly constant. Fry, turning once or twice, until the seafood is lightly browned and cooked through (a skewer or thin-bladed knife will pass through each piece with little resistance). This will take no longer than 5 minutes, unless your pieces are large or extra-thick. Remove with a slotted spoon and drain on paper towels. Sprinkle with additional salt if you like and serve with lemon wedges.

Deep-Fried Seafood with a Thicker Crust. While the oil is heating, soak the fish in milk or buttermilk as described in Oven-"Fried" Fish Fillets (previous page). Dredge as directed in Step 2, only press the flour mixture into the milk adhering to the fish to create a thick coating; you will probably need another ¹/₂ cup or so to do the job. Then shake off the excess and proceed with the recipe. Cooking times might increase by a minute or two.

Spicy Deep-Fried Seafood. Spike the cornmeal with 2 tablespoons of black pepper or a pinch of cayenne or any spice blend (to make your own, see pages 65–69) or chopped fresh herbs.

6 Other Coatings for Oven-"Fried" or Deep-Fried Seafood
1. A mix of half cornmeal and half flour (or all cornmeal or all flour)
2. Finely ground cracker crumbs
3. Shredded coconut (best mixed with a little flour or stirred into a batter)
4. Tempura batter (page 101)
5. Beer batter (see page 247)
6. Bread crumbs, preferably fresh (page 876), or panko

❂ Poached Fish Steaks or Fillets with Vegetables

MAKES: 4 servings
TIME: 30 minutes

The vegetables here provide a bed for cooking the fish, leaving you with a built-in garnish. Serve this hot in a shallow bowl with lots of good bread, boiled potatoes, or plain rice to soak up the cooking liquid. Or cool in the liquid and serve just the fish, chilled, with Herbed Mayonnaise (page 42) or Lemon Vinaigrette (page 201). This is also an excellent way to cook fish for salads.

Any fish steaks will work for poaching (as will sturdy fillets, for that matter) but I think it's best with mild-flavored ones like halibut, cod, grouper, monkfish, and tilefish. That said, poaching is also one of the best ways to cook salmon.

3 tablespoons butter, more or less as you like

2 carrots, diced

2 onions, diced

2 celery stalks, diced

1 clove garlic, minced

Salt and freshly ground black pepper

2 fish steaks or sturdy fillets, ³/₄ to 1 pound each

About 2 cups fish, chicken, or mild vegetable stock (to make your own, see pages 157–159)

❶ Melt the butter over medium heat in the smallest skillet with a lid or Dutch oven that will later hold the fish. Turn the heat down to low, add the vegetables and garlic, sprinkle with some salt and pepper, and cook, stirring, until the vegetables soften, 5 to 10 minutes.

❷ Put the fish on top of the vegetables and add enough stock to come just up to the top, not over it. Bring to a boil, then cover and remove from the heat. The fish will be done in about 10 minutes (a thin-bladed knife inserted between bone and flesh should reveal little or no translucence). Remove the fish with a slotted spoon and serve, topped with vegetables and a little of the broth.

Poached Whole Fish. You will need a large, deep skillet or a roasting pan set over 2 burners, depending on the size of your fish: Double or triple the recipe ingredients as necessary, in proportion to the size of the fish. Follow the recipe through Step 1, cooking the vegetables just until soft. Put the fish on top, cover with the stock, and bring to a boil. If the pan you're using doesn't have a lid, cover with aluminum foil. Large whole fish will take up to 30 minutes to cook; smaller ones will take 15 to 20 minutes. Remove the fish from the liquid and serve as directed.

4 Other Liquids for Poaching Fish

Water will work too, but all of these are more flavorful:
1. Red or white wine or sake
2. A mixture of $^1/_2$ cup soy sauce and $1^1/_2$ cups water
3. Half orange juice and half water
4. Half coconut milk (to make your own, see page 389) and half water

✪ Steamed Clams, Mussels, or Other Shellfish

MAKES: 4 servings
TIME: 15 minutes

F

We always think of clams and mussels being cooked this way, but the same idea also works for shrimp and crab (see the variations). In all cases, steaming leaves you with rendered juices that are excellent as they are or easily enhanced with spice pastes, herbs, condiments, or other flavorings; see "How to Season Simply Cooked Fish" (page 566).

> 4 pounds clams or mussels, well scrubbed
> 1 cup white wine, water, or a mixture
> Salt and freshly ground black pepper
> Lemon wedges for serving
> Melted butter for dipping (optional)

❶ Put the clams or mussels in a large pot with a lid. Pour the wine over all and sprinkle with salt and pepper. Cover, bring to a boil, then reduce the heat to maintain a steady bubble (you'll hear it and see some steam escaping).

❷ Cook, undisturbed, for 5 minutes, then lift the lid to check the progress. If the majority of shells haven't opened, cover again and give them a couple more minutes. When they're all open, remove and serve with the cooking liquid and lemon wedges and little bowls of melted butter if you like.

Peel-and-Eat Steamed Shrimp. Use 2 pounds of shrimp. Check after 3 minutes of steaming. When they're just turning pink, but still slightly translucent inside, remove from the heat. Give it a couple good stirs and serve.

Steamed Crabs or King Crab Legs. You can cook king crab legs while they're still frozen; just allow a minute or two more time: Use a bigger pot and make sure there's enough liquid to fill about an inch in the bottom. Rig a steamer (see page 20) to keep the crab out of the water. Put the crabs or legs in the steamer, cover, and bring to a boil. Check in 5 minutes; they're done when reddish pink and hot throughout, with flaky but still juicy flesh inside. If not, keep cooking for another couple minutes.

✪ Quick-Braised Fish Fillets or Steaks in Tomato Sauce

MAKES: 4 servings
TIME: 30 minutes

F

Fish takes beautifully to simmering with other ingredients and yields a stewlike sauce, and it's fast. Any firm-fleshed, thick steaks or fillets will work here, but you want to be careful not to overcook the fish; even with all this moisture, the fish will turn out dry. Serve this over rice or toss the sauce with pasta and top with the fish.

 Fast   Make Ahead   **V** Vegetarian

Extra virgin olive oil as needed

About 1½ pounds thick fish fillets or steaks

Salt and freshly ground black pepper

All-purpose flour for dredging

1 tablespoon minced garlic

1 large onion, sliced

¼ cup dry white or red wine or water

2 cups chopped tomato (drained canned is fine)

½ cup fresh chopped basil for garnish (optional)

① Put about ⅛ inch oil in a large, deep skillet over medium-high heat. Sprinkle the fish with salt and pepper.

② When the oil is hot—it will shimmer, and a pinch of flour tossed into it will sizzle—dredge the fish in flour and brown quickly, about 2 minutes per side. Do not crowd the fish; you may have to work in batches. As you finish browning, transfer the fish to a plate. Pour off all but 2 tablespoons of the oil and lower the heat to medium.

③ Stir in the garlic and onion, sprinkle with salt and pepper, and cook, stirring, until they begin to soften, about 2 minutes. Stir in the wine and let most of it bubble away, then add the tomato and cook, stirring occasionally, for about 5 minutes, just until the tomato releases some juice.

④ Return the fish to the pan (now it's okay to crowd) and continue to cook until done, about 5 minutes more (a thin-bladed knife inserted into the center will meet little resistance). Taste and adjust the seasoning; serve garnished with the basil if you like.

Quick-Braised Scallops in Tomato Sauce. Substitute sea scallops for the fish fillets or steaks.

Braised Whole Fish in Tomato Sauce. You'll need a big pan (a roasting pan with a foil cover works well) unless you braise several smaller fish. Use 3 to 5 pounds of fish. Double the other ingredients. The fish will take 10 to 20 minutes to cook, depending on the size.

Braised Squid in Tomato Sauce. Takes much longer but demands no attention: Use 2 to 3 pounds cleaned squid, cut into rings or left whole as you like. Double the other ingredients. Proceed with the recipe, but cook the squid, stirring occasionally, until very tender but not yet completely dry, about 45 minutes. Serve with pasta or toasted bread.

Fish Baked in Foil

MAKES: 4 servings
TIME: 40 minutes

Ⓜ

You can cook the fish in individual packages or toss it all together in a covered casserole. But the individual portions are lovely. And you can assemble the packages well in advance and refrigerate them, which makes this an excellent dish for entertaining.

You can use parchment paper if you like, though it's a little more difficult to seal (see the illustration with the summer squash recipe, page 356).

Four 6-ounce thick fish fillets or steaks

¼ cup extra virgin olive oil

Salt and freshly ground black pepper

1 teaspoon minced garlic

¼ cup chopped fresh parsley or basil leaves

Lemon wedges for serving

① Put a baking pan in the oven and heat it to 400°F. Take 4 sheets of aluminum foil (or parchment), each about 18 inches long, and put one piece on top of the other (you will make 4 packages). Rub a piece of fish with some of the olive oil, then season it with salt and pepper and center it on a piece of the foil. Sprinkle with garlic and parsley and fold the foil over the fish, crimping the edges as tightly as possible. (To be sure there's no leakage, use double thickness to wrap fillets if you like.) Repeat the process. (You can refrigerate the packages until you're ready to cook, no more than 6 hours later.)

❷ Put the packages in the baking pan and bake for about 15 minutes (or about 8 minutes from the time it starts sizzling). Let sit for a couple of minutes before carefully cutting open the package—remove the fish with a spatula, pour the juices over all, and serve with lemon wedges.

Fish Baked in Foil with Vegetables. Add any or all of the following to each package: 1 seeded and diced plum tomato; a few black olives; some capers; some very thinly sliced potato, lemon, fennel, or onion.

Whole Fish Baked in Foil. A 3- to 4-pound fish is ideal, or use 2 or 4 smaller fish and share: Cut the foil or parchment big enough to entirely wrap the whole fish (you may need a piece for the bottom and one for the top). Follow the recipe; you might need to add more oil, garlic, or herbs, depending on the size of your fish. Bake for 15 minutes for small individual fish; 20 to 25 minutes for larger fish.

The Basics of Shrimp (and Crawfish)

Shrimp, the most popular noncanned seafood in America, can be domestic or imported, wild or farmed. I generally prefer wild shrimp from the Pacific or the Gulf of Mexico, but it's not often you'll have a choice beyond farmed. Best of all is fresh local shrimp, that's quite rare unless you live on the Gulf Coast (or where there's a seasonal resource, as there is in Maine, the Carolinas, and elsewhere).

The reality is that almost all shrimp is frozen before sale, and I recommend buying shrimp frozen rather than thawed. Since the shelf life of previously frozen shrimp is not much more than a couple of days, buying thawed shrimp gives you neither the flavor of fresh nor the flexi-bility of frozen. Stored in a home freezer, shrimp retain their quality for a month or more.

Some frozen shrimp is sold in blocks of 5 pounds (or 2 kilos, slightly less than that); usually it's packed in IQF (individually quick frozen) bags of 2 pounds or 1 kilo. These are super-convenient, because you can take six shrimp out of the freezer and defrost them, leaving the rest frozen. If you have time, defrost shrimp in the refrigerator for about 24 hours; if you're in a hurry, in cold water. Partial defrosting to cut a block in half to refreeze some for later use, while not ideal, is still preferable to buying thawed shrimp.

Despite the popularity of shrimp, there are few rules governing its sale. Small, medium, large, extra-large, jumbo, and other size classifications are subjective and relative. Small shrimp of seventy or so to the pound are frequently labeled *medium,* as are those twice that size and even larger. It helps to learn to judge shrimp size by the number per pound, as retailers do. Shrimp labeled *16/20,* for example, require sixteen to twenty to make a pound. *U-20* means under twenty will make a pound. I look for shrimp sized between fifteen and thirty per pound, which give the best combination of flavor, ease (peeling tiny shrimp is a nuisance), and value. Smaller shrimp are less expensive.

If your palate is sensitive to iodine—not everyone's is—you might want to steer clear of brown shrimp, especially large ones, which are most likely to taste of this naturally occurring mineral. The iodine is found in a type of plankton that makes up a large part of the diet of brown shrimp; traditionally, this distinctive flavor is preferred along the Gulf Coast.

Shrimp is among the easiest shellfish to cook. It isn't always done when it turns pink—some of the larger shrimp take a little longer to cook through—but it usually is. And it's easy enough to cut one open to be sure.

Brining shrimp before cooking, or even just salting it, can enhance its flavor and texture, but only in simple grilled, broiled, or panfried recipes. Here's how: Dissolve 1 cup salt and ¹/₂ cup sugar in a large bowl of water. Add

Ⓕ Fast   Ⓜ Make Ahead   Ⓥ Vegetarian

PEELING SHRIMP

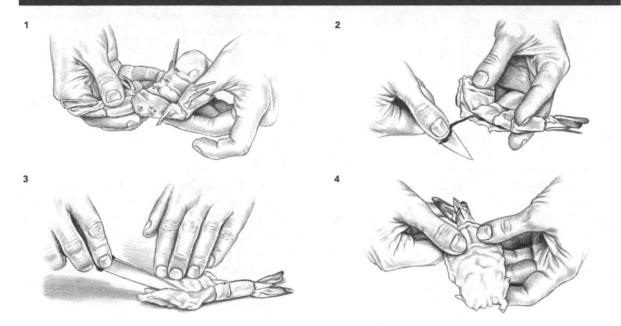

(STEP 1) To peel shrimp, grasp the feelers on the underside and pull the shell away from the meat. **(STEP 2)** Deveining is optional. Should you choose to devein, make a shallow cut on the back side of each shrimp, then pull out the long, black threadlike vein. **(STEPS 3–4)** To butterfly shrimp, cut most of the way through the back of the shrimp and open it up.

whole or peeled shrimp and fill with ice. Put in the fridge for 2 hours or so. (Or sprinkle the shrimp liberally with coarse salt, toss well, and refrigerate.) Either way, rinse the shrimp well and drain before using.

One last note: If you buy shell-on shrimp and peel them yourself, you can make a quick stock by simmering the shells—in just enough water to cover—for about 10 minutes.

I include crawfish (also called *crayfish*) in this section. Although many devotees of that shellfish believe them to be not only different from shrimp but superior to them, I find the two generally interchangeable (in all ways except peeling, which is more tedious for crawfish). You can also use small scallops in virtually all of these recipes.

The Simplest and Best Shrimp Dish

MAKES: 4 servings
TIME: About 30 minutes

Excuse the superlatives; this spin on a Spanish tapa is my favorite, and everyone I serve it to loves it. The shrimp juices infuse the oil, and the sum is beyond delicious. It's good with bread, over rice, tossed with pasta, or stuffed into tacos.

Other seafood you can use: similar-sized scallops (or larger, though they'll take longer to cook).

$^{1}/_{3}$ cup extra virgin olive oil, or more as needed

3 or 4 big cloves garlic, cut into slivers

About 1$^{1}/_{2}$ pounds shrimp, 20 to 30 per pound, peeled, rinsed, and dried

Salt and freshly ground black pepper

1 teaspoon ground cumin

1$^{1}/_{2}$ teaspoons hot paprika

Chopped fresh parsley leaves for garnish

1 Warm the olive oil in a large, broad ovenproof skillet or heatproof baking pan over low heat. There should be enough olive oil to cover the bottom of the pan; don't skimp. Add the garlic and cook until it turns golden, a few minutes.

2 Raise the heat to medium-high and add the shrimp, some salt and pepper, the cumin, and the paprika. Stir to blend and continue to cook, shaking the pan once or twice and turning the shrimp once or twice, until they are pink all over and the mixture is bubbly, 5 to 10 minutes. Garnish and serve immediately.

Shrimp Scampi. In Step 2, omit the cumin and paprika; sprinkle with salt and pepper. When the shrimp turn pink on one side, turn them over and add $^{1}/_{4}$ cup chopped fresh parsley leaves. Raise the heat slightly and cook until the shrimp are done, about 2 minutes more. Stir in 1 tablespoon freshly squeezed lemon juice, dry sherry, vinegar, or white wine if you like and cook for another 30 seconds before garnishing with more parsley and serving.

Shrimp with Spicy Orange Flavor. Using the Shrimp Scampi variation, add 2 or more small dried hot red chiles and the roughly chopped zest of 1 orange along with the garlic. Add the juice of the orange along with the shrimp and spices. Substitute cilantro for the parsley if you like.

Garlic Shrimp with Tomatoes and Cilantro. Omit the cumin and paprika and double the amount of garlic; slice it thinly if you like. Dice 4 plum tomatoes; sub-stitute fresh cilantro for the parsley. In Step 2, scatter the tomatoes into the pan along with the shrimp; cooking time will be increased by a couple minutes. Garnish with cilantro.

Spicy Grilled or Broiled Shrimp

MAKES: 4 servings
TIME: 20 minutes

Keep the grill heat high and the cooking time short and you'll get slightly charred, juicy shrimp every time. A squeeze of lemon finishes them nicely, but they're also good as is, drizzled with Vinaigrette (page 199) or served with a dipping sauce.

Other protein you can use: similar-sized scallops (or larger, though they'll take longer to cook); cut-up boneless chicken thighs; thinly sliced beef sirloin.

1 large clove garlic, peeled

1 tablespoon coarse salt

$^{1}/_{2}$ teaspoon cayenne

1 teaspoon paprika

2 tablespoons extra virgin olive oil

2 teaspoons freshly squeezed lemon juice

About 1$^{1}/_{2}$ pounds shrimp, 20 to 30 per pound, peeled, rinsed, and dried

Lemon wedges for serving

1 Heat a charcoal or gas grill or the broiler until hot and put the rack as close to the heat source as possible.

2 On a cutting board, using a chef's knife, mince and mash the garlic with the salt until it forms a paste; transfer to a small bowl. Mix in the cayenne and paprika, then the olive oil and lemon juice. Smear the paste all over the shrimp. Grill or broil the shrimp, turning once, for 2 to 3 minutes per side. Serve immediately or at room temperature, with lemon wedges.

F Fast   **M** Make Ahead   **V** Vegetarian

6 WAYS TO FLAVOR GRILLED OR BROILED SHRIMP

FLAVOR	SEASONING	LIQUID	GARNISH
Rosemary and Orange	Garlic, salt, 1 teaspoon minced fresh rosemary, 2 teaspoons grated orange zest	Olive oil, lemon juice or white wine	Toasted bread crumbs or chopped fresh parsley
Chipotle	Garlic, salt, 1 or 2 canned chipotle chiles (with a little adobo)	Olive oil, lime juice	Chopped fresh cilantro
Pesto	1/4 cup Traditional Pesto (page 27)	None needed	None needed
Miso	2 tablespoons white or yellow miso	Dark sesame oil and sake	Minced fresh chives
Curry Paste	Red or green curry paste (to make your own, see pages 75–76)	About 3 tablespoons coconut milk (to make your own, see page 389)	Chopped fresh mint or Thai basil
Lemongrass	2 inches lemongrass, minced; 1 teaspoon minced fresh ginger; 1 small fresh Thai chile, minced; salt	Neutral oil, like grapeseed or corn; nam pla (Thai fish sauce)	Chopped scallion

Shrimp and Scallion Stir-Fry

MAKES: 4 servings

TIME: 30 minutes

Super-simple and one of the best shrimp dishes I know, this is vibrant green and infused with a fresh onion flavor. For a more straightforward approach to shrimp stir-fry, see the variations.

Other protein you can use: similar-sized scallops (or larger, though they'll take longer to cook); thinly sliced boneless beef sirloin or pork or lamb shoulder; cut-up boneless chicken thighs; or firm tofu cubes.

Salt

4 bunches scallions, trimmed

1 clove garlic, peeled

3 tablespoons peanut or neutral oil, like grapeseed or corn

About 1 1/2 pounds shrimp, 20 to 30 per pound, peeled, rinsed, and dried

1/2 cup chopped fresh cilantro leaves

❶ Bring a medium pot of water to a boil and salt it. Meanwhile, cut 3 bunches of the scallions into 3- or 4-inch lengths; chop the remaining bunch and set it aside. Add the long scallion pieces to the boiling water and cook until bright green, about 1 minute, then drain, reserving about 1/2 cup of the cooking water. Plunge the scallions into a bowl of ice water, then drain again and purée in a blender with the garlic, using a little of the reserved cooking water to make the mixture smooth.

❷ Put the oil in a large skillet over high heat. When hot, add the shrimp and a large pinch of salt and cook, stirring only occasionally, until the shrimp are uniformly pink, 3 to 5 minutes. Turn the heat down to low and add the chopped scallion and the cilantro. Stir, then stir in the scallion purée. Taste and adjust the seasoning and serve immediately.

Simpler Shrimp and Scallion Stir-Fry. Reduce the scallions to 2 bunches. Cut the white parts into 1-inch pieces and chop the green tops; keep them separate. Skip Step 1. In Step 2, when the shrimp are just starting to turn pink, add the white parts and stir until the shrimp are uniformly pink and the scallions have begun to sear and wilt. Turn the heat down to low and proceed with the recipe.

Simpler Shrimp and Any Vegetable Stir-Fry. The vegetables will be super-crisp, almost raw. Try this with bell pepper, cabbage, bok choy, fennel, spinach, snow or snap peas, asparagus, green beans, edamame, or other fresh or frozen shell beans: Omit the scallions. Wash and trim 8 ounces vegetables; if large, cut into 2-inch strips or pieces (leave peas or shell beans whole). Skip Step 1. In Step 2, add the vegetables when the shrimp just start to turn pink, then cook and stir until the shrimp are uniformly pink. Turn the heat down to low, add the cilantro, and stir. Taste and adjust the seasoning and serve immediately.

Stir-Fried Shrimp with Black Beans

MAKES: 4 servings

TIME: 30 minutes

Chinese black beans give this stir-fry deep flavor. It's slightly more involved than the previous recipe, only because you make a quick flavorful stock with the shrimp shells. If you don't want to go that route, or you're substituting a protein other than shrimp, simply skip making the stock and use 1 cup water, white wine, or sake in its place.

Other protein you can use: similar-sized scallops (or larger, though they'll take longer to cook); shucked or unshucked clams or mussels; shelled lobster; peeled crawfish; thinly sliced beef sirloin or pork or lamb shoulder; cut-up boneless chicken thighs; or tofu cubes.

About 1½ pounds shrimp, 20 to 30 per pound

1 tablespoon fermented black beans

2 tablespoons dry sherry or white wine

1½ teaspoons sugar

2 tablespoons soy sauce

1 clove garlic, sliced, plus 1 tablespoon minced garlic

1 teaspoon salt

2 teaspoons dark sesame oil

1 pound bok choy or any cabbage, trimmed, washed, and dried

2 tablespoons peanut or vegetable oil

1 tablespoon minced or grated fresh ginger

¼ cup chopped scallion

1 Peel the shrimp. Put the shells in a medium saucepan with 1 cup water, turn the heat to high, and bring to a boil. Turn the heat to low, cover, and cook while you work on the rest of the recipe, about 10 minutes. Soak the black beans in the sherry.

2 Put the shrimp in a bowl with ½ teaspoon of the sugar, 1 tablespoon of the soy sauce, the sliced garlic, the salt, and 1 teaspoon of the sesame oil. Give it a good stir and let sit while you assemble the other ingredients.

3 Separate the bok choy leaves from the stems; chop the stems into ½- to 1-inch pieces and chop the leaves. Drain the shrimp shells, reserving ¾ cup of the stock.

4 Heat a large nonstick skillet over medium-high heat for 3 to 5 minutes. When hot, add 1 tablespoon of the peanut oil and raise the heat to high. When it begins to smoke, add the minced garlic and, immediately thereafter, the shrimp and its marinade. Cook the shrimp for about 2 minutes, stirring occasionally. Spoon it out of the skillet.

5 Put the remaining peanut oil in the skillet and, when it smokes, add the ginger, followed immediately by the bok choy stems. Cook, stirring, until the bok choy is lightly browned, 3 to 5 minutes, then add the greens. Cook, stirring, for 1 minute, then add the shrimp stock and let it bubble away for a minute or two. Return the shrimp to the skillet and stir; add the black beans and their liquid, the scallion, and the remaining sugar and soy sauce. Stir and cook for 1 minute. Turn off the heat, drizzle on the remaining sesame oil, and serve.

Stir-Fried Shrimp with Cashews. Omit the black beans and sherry. In Step 5, add $^1/_2$ cup cashews to the pan along with the ginger.

Stir-Fried Shrimp with Water Chestnuts. If you can't find fresh, canned are okay too: Omit the black beans and sherry. In Step 5, add $^1/_2$ cup sliced water chestnuts along with the bok choy stems.

Chile Shrimp

MAKES: 4 servings
TIME: 20 minutes

Based on a popular street snack in Singapore, this simplified version uses shrimp instead of the traditional whole crabs. Serve over plain rice or rice noodles (be sure to start them before you begin this recipe) or stuff the shrimp into a split loaf of toasted Italian bread for a cross-cultural poor boy sandwich.

Other protein you can use: similar-sized scallops (or larger, though they'll take longer to cook); shelled lobster, clams, or mussels; lump crabmeat or whole small crabs in the shells.

2 inches fresh ginger, peeled

3 cloves garlic, peeled and lightly crushed

2 shallots, roughly chopped

4 small fresh chiles, like Thai, or dried red chiles, stemmed and seeded, or to taste, or hot red pepper flakes to taste

3 tablespoons neutral oil, like grapeseed or corn

2 tablespoons tomato paste or 1 medium tomato, cored and chopped

2 tablespoons freshly squeezed lime juice

2 tablespoons nam pla (Thai fish sauce)

2 teaspoons soy sauce

1 tablespoon sugar

About 1$^1/_2$ pounds shrimp, 20 to 30 per pound, peeled, rinsed, and dried

1 Put the ginger, garlic, shallots, and chiles in a food processor and process until minced. Put the oil in a large skillet over medium-high heat. When hot, add the minced chile mixture and cook, stirring constantly, for about 30 seconds.

2 Stir in the tomato paste, lime juice, nam pla, soy sauce, sugar, and 2 tablespoons water. Add the shrimp and stir to coat with the sauce. Cook just until the sauce is bubbling and the shrimp turns pink, about 5 minutes. Serve immediately.

Roasted Shrimp with Herb Sauce

MAKES: 4 servings
TIME: 30 minutes

Try making this on a weeknight; it's perfect with rice, pasta, or good chewy bread since the sauce is so addictive. It also makes a hard-to-beat party recipe, with the shrimp served on toothpicks for dipping.

Other seafood you can use: similar-sized scallops (or larger, though they'll take longer to cook); crawfish, peeled or not; mussels or clams.

2 cloves garlic, peeled

$^1/_3$ cup extra virgin olive oil

6 scallions, roughly chopped

1 small bunch fresh parsley (thin stems are okay; discard thick ones)

2 pounds shrimp, 20 to 30 per pound, peeled

Salt and freshly ground black pepper

$^1/_3$ cup shrimp, fish, or chicken stock (to make your own, see pages 157–159), white wine, or water

1 Heat the oven to 500°F. Combine the garlic and oil in a food processor and pulse until smooth, scraping down the sides as necessary. Add the scallions and parsley and pulse until the mixture is minced. Toss this mixture with the shrimp and sprinkle with salt and pepper.

2 Put the shrimp in a roasting pan that will hold them comfortably in one layer. Add the liquid and put the pan in the oven. Roast, stirring once, until the mixture is bubbly and hot and the shrimp are all pink, 10 to 15 minutes. Serve immediately.

Roasted Shrimp with Mint Sauce. Use all mint or half mint and half parsley.

Spicy and Garlicky Roasted Shrimp. Triple the amount of garlic and add it, along with 4 small dried chiles (like Thai) or a few pinches of hot red pepper flakes, or to taste, to the mixture in the food processor in Step 1.

Roasted Shrimp in Herb Sauce, Indian Style. Substitute cilantro for the parsley. Add 1 tablespoon curry powder (to make your own, see pages 66–67) to the mixture in the food processor in Step 1.

Crawfish or Shrimp Boil, Louisiana Style

MAKES: 4 to 6 servings
TIME: 30 minutes, plus time to cool

It's traditional to serve the seafood (and vegetables; see the variation) in the center of a newspaper-covered table with some French bread and a bowl of the cooking water—which will taste pretty good after having all this cooked in it—handy for dipping.

About 6 quarts water, fish stock, or shrimp stock (to make your own, see page 159)

4 bay leaves

2 teaspoons dried thyme or several sprigs fresh thyme

1 tablespoon black peppercorns

4 cloves garlic, crushed

1 tablespoon coriander seeds

3 cloves

4 small dried hot red chiles

Salt

4 pounds whole crawfish or shrimp

Tabasco or other hot red pepper sauce for serving

Lemon wedges for serving

Freshly ground black pepper

1 recipe Garlic Mayonnaise (page 42), Celery Rémoulade (page 210), or Tartar Sauce (page 42) for dipping (optional)

1 Bring the liquid to a boil in a medium to large saucepan and add the bay leaves, thyme, peppercorns, garlic, coriander, cloves, chiles, and plenty of salt. Turn the heat down to medium and cook for 10 minutes.

2 Add the crawfish or shrimp. Cook for 5 minutes, then turn off the heat and let the seafood cool down for a few minutes in the liquid.

3 Remove the crawfish or shrimp with a slotted spoon, sprinkle with more salt, and serve, passing hot sauce, lemon wedges, black pepper, and sauce at the table.

Crawfish or Shrimp Boil with Vegetables. More of a meal: In Step 1, add 1 1/2 pounds waxy potatoes and 1 pound onions (all cut into large chunks if they're bigger than eggs). Boil with the seasonings until just beginning to get tender, about 10 minutes. When you add the seafood in Step 2, add 4 to 6 ears of shucked corn (cut in half if you like). Proceed with the recipe.

The Basics of Salmon and Trout

Salmon and trout—close cousins and different from other fish—are distinctively rich, oily, and sometimes downright fatty, full of flavor but almost never "fishy."

At this point in time, all Atlantic salmon—regardless of which ocean it comes from—is farmed. It's not bad stuff, eating wise—it has a lot of fat, so it's easy to cook—but there are questions about what it eats and how raising it affects the environment, as there is with almost all aquaculture (and agriculture) these days. Pacific salmon, on the other hand, is always wild and is preferable—though the season for fresh fish is limited to mostly spring and summer, and some species are better than others. Sockeye (my favorite) and king (the most popular) are the best; coho is also good, chum is not bad, and pink is usually canned.

But unless you live in the Pacific Northwest, buying fresh wild salmon (most of which comes from Alaska) is occasional and expensive; deceptive or well-intentioned but ignorant purveyors will often tell you that their Alaskan salmon—or even farmed salmon—is "king." In a supermarket, you'll rarely be offered anything fresh but chum and farmed Atlantic salmon. Top-quality fish markets offer real king and sockeye, and label it so, but usually only for a few weeks each summer. Frozen king, sockeye, and coho can be good, but it's still not common.

The chances are good, then, that you'll be buying farmed salmon fillets or steaks. Full-service fish markets and good supermarket counters scale their fish before cutting it up; since salmon skin is delicious, especially when it's crisp, this is a bonus. If you buy some that still has scales, you have three choices: Scale the fish yourself (see page 595), which, for whole fish or fillets, is not difficult (it's nearly impossible to scale steaks once they've been cut); skin the fish, also quite easy to do; or, easiest of all, cook the fish with the scales on and discard the skin. In a way, this last is a nice solution, because the scales give added protection against overcooking, and the skin peels right off afterward, taking the scales with it.

You can use any cooking technique you like for salmon, as long as you don't overcook it. The time varies according to your taste. Many people—myself included—prefer salmon cooked to what might be called medium-rare to medium, with a well-cooked exterior and a fairly red center. (This is essential for wild salmon, which is usually

SKINNING A FILLET

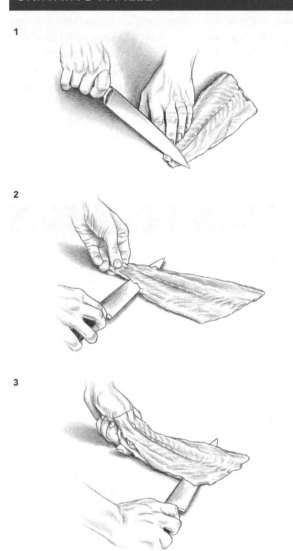

1

2

3

Skinning a fillet is much easier than it looks; use any sharp knife. (STEP 1) Cut a small piece from the tail end, at an angle, to expose the skin. (STEP 2) Grasp the exposed piece of skin (use a towel to get a grip if necessary) and insert the knife between skin and flesh, angled slightly toward the skin. (STEP 3) Run the knife up the entire length of the fillet.

quite lean.) I use a knife to peek at the center of a piece of salmon to judge its doneness. Remember that fish retains enough heat to continue cooking after it has been removed from the heat source, so stop cooking just before the salmon reaches the point you'd consider it done.

The trout you'll find in stores is almost always farmed. In fact, unless you're a fisherman, or know one, you may never eat wild trout. Until recently, most farmed trout was almost tasteless, and overrated compared to salmon. But there are now some farmed varieties of trout—steelheads, Arctic char, and orange-fleshed rainbow trout—that look and eat a little like salmon. These are best

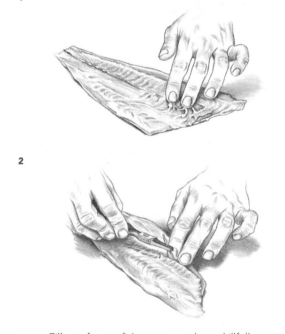

REMOVING PIN BONES

1

2

(STEP 1) Fillets of many fish, no matter how skillfully removed, may contain long bones along their center that must be removed by hand. Feel with your fingers to see if your fillet contains pin bones. (STEP 2) Remove them with a needle-nose pliers or similar tool.

treated as salmon, and can be used in any salmon recipe. The trout recipes I offer here are designed for wild trout or store-bought—that is, farmed—trout.

Pan-Cooked Salmon

MAKES: 4 servings

TIME: 20 minutes

The simplest way to cook any salmon and the best way to cook wild (Pacific) salmon. If you use farmed (Atlantic) salmon here, it's so fatty you can cut the amount of oil in half or eliminate it altogether, as long as you use a cast-iron skillet. Salt and pepper is the only seasoning in the recipe, but feel free to lightly sprinkle on any spice mixture from the section beginning on page 65. And for sauce ideas, see the list that follows.

Other seafood you can use: trout fillets (though you won't be able to cut them in half and they'll cook more quickly).

    2 tablespoons neutral oil, like grapeseed or corn

    Four 6-ounce salmon fillets

    Salt and freshly ground black pepper

    Lemon or lime wedges for serving

❶ Put a heavy skillet, preferably cast-iron, over medium heat for about a minute; add the oil. Sprinkle the fish with salt and pepper. When the skillet is hot, add the fish and raise the heat to medium-high.

❷ After 4 minutes, turn the salmon over and cook to reach your desired stage of doneness, another 2 to 5 minutes. Serve browned side up with the lemon on the side.

Flash-Cooked Salmon. Cut the salmon fillets in half horizontally to make 8 thin pieces. Start with very cold salmon (freeze it for 30 minutes if you have time), hold your knife parallel to the cutting board, and use the palm of your other hand to apply pressure on the fillet so the knife glides through evenly. Sprinkle each

❻ Fast   **Ⓜ** Make Ahead   **Ⓥ** Vegetarian

piece with salt and pepper on both sides. Put 4 plates in a 200°F oven. In Step 1, cook the salmon for 45 seconds to 1 minute on each side. You'll see the opaque pink color that salmon turns as it cooks climbing up the sides of the fillets almost as soon as it hits the pan, and the idea is to serve it just a touch rare in the middle. You'll need to cook the fish in batches, but given the quick cooking time, that shouldn't be much of a problem. Put the salmon on the warmed plates as it finishes.

10 Sauces for Pan-Cooked Salmon

Spoon this over the fillets just before serving.

1. Any Five-Minute Drizzle Sauce (page 22)
2. Fresh Tomato or Fruit Salsa (page 23) or Fresh Tomatillo Salsa (page 33)
3. The Simplest Yogurt Sauce (page 24)
4. Soy Dipping Sauce and Marinade (page 25)
5. Compound Butter (page 32)
6. Tahini Sauce (page 35)
7. Cilantro-Mint Chutney (page 37)
8. Miso Carrot Sauce with Ginger (page 40)
9. Balsamic Syrup (page 51)
10. Virtually any Vinaigrette (pages 199–202)

Panfried Trout with Bacon and Red Onions

MAKES: 2 servings
TIME: 45 minutes

Think of this as campfire food, made at home.

Other seafood you can use: salmon or any thick fillets or steaks (see page 601) or whole sardines.

4 thick slices bacon

1 large red onion, thinly sliced

2 whole trout, about 12 ounces each, gutted and split or filleted

Salt and freshly ground black pepper

1 cup cornmeal

1/2 cup beer (a strong ale is good) or water

Chopped fresh parsley leaves for garnish

1 Put the bacon in a large skillet, preferably cast-iron, over medium heat. Cook, turning several times, until it just begins to get crisp, about 5 minutes. Remove and drain. Immediately put the onion in the hot bacon fat and cook, stirring occasionally, until softened and starting to turn golden, about 5 minutes, then remove from the pan with a slotted spoon. Roughly chop the bacon.

2 Rinse and dry the fish and sprinkle it with salt and pepper. Dredge the fish in the cornmeal, put in the pan, and raise the heat to high. Cook on both sides until nicely browned and the interior turns white, 8 to 12 minutes total. Transfer to a platter.

3 Turn the heat under the skillet down to medium-low and add the beer, scraping up any browned bits that have stuck to the pan. Let the beer bubble and thicken a bit, then return the onion and bacon to the pan. Spoon the bacon and onions and pan sauce over the fish, garnish with parsley, and serve.

Panfried Trout without Bacon and Onions. Simpler and faster: Omit the bacon, onions, and beer. Omit Step 1. Instead, melt 4 tablespoons (1/2 stick) butter or extra virgin olive oil in the skillet. When it starts to foam, dredge the fish in cornmeal and proceed with Step 2. Omit Step 3; instead of making the pan sauce, serve the trout with Tartar Sauce (page 42) and lots of lemon wedges.

Salmon with Beurre Rouge

MAKES: 4 servings
TIME: 20 minutes

French butter sauces have a reputation for being difficult and time-consuming. But beurre rouge, a pink variation

on light-colored beurre blanc, is foolproof and fast, guaranteed to yield an impressive sauce that's silken smooth. Just be patient: Don't stir in the butter all at once, and let the sauce develop and reduce a bit into a syrup. You will be successful making it the first time. If you'd rather not multitask, make the sauce first and keep it warm over minimum heat—stirring now and then—for the brief time it takes to cook the fish.

Other seafood you can use: trout or shrimp (both of which will probably cook more quickly, depending on their size, so make the sauce first), or scallops.

2 tablespoons minced shallot

2 cups fruity, not-too-tannic red wine

2 tablespoons red wine or balsamic vinegar

About 1 1/2 pounds salmon fillets

Salt and freshly ground black pepper

8 tablespoons (1 stick) cold butter, cut into 6 or 8 pieces

Chopped fresh parsley or chervil for garnish

❶ Combine the shallot, wine, and vinegar in a small saucepan over high heat. Cook until reduced to about 1/4 cup, 10 minutes or so, then turn the heat as low as possible.

❷ Meanwhile, put a large skillet over medium heat; sprinkle the salmon with salt and pepper and put it in the skillet skin side up. Raise the heat to medium-high and cook until nicely browned, about 5 minutes, then turn.

❸ When the red wine mixture is reduced to about 1/4 cup (again over low heat), add the butter a piece at a time, stirring after each addition until it is incorporated. When all the butter has been added, taste and adjust the seasoning.

❹ When the salmon is done to your liking, about 3 to 5 minutes after you turn it (use a sharp knife to peek inside its thickest part to judge doneness), transfer it to a platter or serving plates. Spoon the sauce over the fish, garnish with parsley, and serve.

Pan-Cooked Salmon Fillets with Lentils

MAKES: 4 servings
TIME: About 1 hour

Salmon and green lentils are an excellent combination. Err on the side of undercooking the lentils. You want them to have an almost nutty texture.

Other seafood you can use: trout, shrimp (both of which will cook more quickly, so make the sauce first), or scallops.

2 to 3 cups dried green lentils, washed and picked over

2 medium carrots, cut into 1/4-inch cubes

1 small potato, peeled and cut into 1/4-inch cubes

1 medium onion, chopped

2 cloves garlic, minced

A few sprigs each fresh parsley and thyme, a bay leaf, and a few chives, tied in cheesecloth for easy removal, or about 1 1/2 teaspoons mixed dried herbs

Salt and freshly ground black pepper

2 tablespoons extra virgin olive oil

Four 6-ounce salmon fillets

Chopped fresh parsley leaves or chives for garnish

❶ Put the lentils in a large, deep saucepan with water to cover. Cook over medium heat, stirring occasionally, until they begin to soften, 15 to 20 minutes, then add the carrots, potato, onion, garlic, and herbs.

❷ Continue to cook, adding just enough water if necessary to keep the beans moist, until the lentils and vegetables are tender, 35 to 45 minutes total. Remove the fresh herbs, sprinkle with salt and pepper, add the olive oil, and keep warm.

❸ Heat a large skillet, preferably cast-iron, over high heat for about 5 minutes. Sprinkle the bottom of the skillet with salt, then add the salmon, skin side down. Cook over high heat until well browned on the bottom, about 5 minutes. Flip the salmon and cook for 1 minute longer (more if you like your salmon well done). Put about 1 cup of lentils in the center of each of 4 serving plates and top with a salmon fillet. Garnish with parsley and serve.

Salmon Roasted in Butter

MAKES: 6 to 8 servings
TIME: 15 minutes

This is one of those salmon dishes that change dramatically when you use really fresh fish, since there are really only two ingredients.

Other seafood you can use: trout or scallops (adjust the cooking time depending on their size).

4 tablespoons (1/2 stick) butter

One 2- to 3-pound salmon fillet (skin-on is nice)

Salt and freshly ground black pepper

Chopped fresh parsley leaves for garnish

❶ Heat the oven to 475°F. Melt the butter in a medium roasting pan—either on top of the stove or in the oven as it heats—until the foam subsides. Sprinkle the salmon with salt and pepper.

❷ Put the salmon in the butter, flesh side down, and put the pan in the oven. Roast for about 5 minutes, then flip and roast for 3 to 6 minutes longer, until the salmon is done (peek between the flakes with a thin-bladed knife). Sprinkle with a little more salt if you like, garnish with parsley, and serve.

Salmon Roasted with Herbs. In Step 1, use 2 tablespoons olive oil or half oil and half butter. In Step 2, add a handful (2 to 4 tablespoons, depending on their strength) chopped fresh herbs—tarragon, parsley, chervil, basil, dill, thyme, or a combination—and 2 tablespoons minced shallot, then roast as directed.

Salmon Roasted with Buttered Hazelnuts. In Step 1, use only 1 tablespoon of olive oil or butter. Before cooking the fish, melt 3 tablespoons of butter in a small saucepan over medium-low heat. When the butter foam subsides, add 1 cup roughly chopped hazelnuts and cook, stirring, just until they begin to brown. Place the fish in the pan, season with salt and pepper, and spoon the browned nuts on top. Roast as in Step 2 but without turning.

Salmon Roasted with Olives. Pit and chop 1 cup of black olives, like kalamata or Moroccan. Sprinkle the salmon with pepper, but omit the salt if the olives are very salty. Follow the preceding variation, substituting the olives for the nuts.

Crispy-Skin Salmon, Grilled or Broiled, with Gingery Greens

MAKES: 4 servings
TIME: 40 to 60 minutes

Still one of my all-time favorite recipes, with the rich flavor of salmon cut by sharp greens and bright ginger. You have some choices when it comes to the vegetable: Substitute green beans, asparagus, any kind of peas, or even grated sweet potato for the greens if you like; add a minute or two to the cooking time as necessary.

One 2-pound salmon fillet, skin on (but scaled)

1 pound kale, collards, or other greens

5 tablespoons extra virgin olive oil

1 teaspoon minced garlic

2 teaspoons minced or grated fresh ginger or 1 teaspoon ground ginger

1 tablespoon soy sauce

1 teaspoon dark sesame oil

❶ Heat a charcoal or gas grill with a lid or the broiler until moderately hot and put the rack about 4 inches from the heat source. Rinse the fish well and let it rest between paper towels, refrigerated, while you prepare the greens.

② Wash the greens in several changes of water and remove any pieces of stem thicker than ¹/₄ inch in diameter. Steam or boil them in a medium saucepan, covered, over or in 1 inch of water until good and soft, 10 minutes or more depending on the green (older collards will require 30 minutes). Drain them, rinse in cool water, squeeze dry, and chop.

③ Heat 2 tablespoons of the olive oil in a large skillet. When hot, add the garlic and cook for 1 minute; do not brown. Add the greens and cook, stirring occasionally, for about 3 minutes; add the ginger and cook for another minute, then add the soy sauce and sesame oil and turn off the heat. Transfer to a platter and keep warm.

④ With a sharp knife, score the skin of the salmon in a crosshatch pattern. Oil the fish well with the remaining olive oil. Put the fillet on the preheated grill, skin side down, and cover. Or put the fish under the broiler, skin side up. In either case, cook undisturbed until done, 5 to 10 minutes.

⑤ Remove the fish carefully with a large spatula (or two) and put it on top of the greens. Serve immediately, making sure everyone gets a piece of skin.

SCORING THE SKIN ON FISH

Cut hatch marks through just the skin of the fish, first in one direction then in the other, to form a tic-tac-toe pattern.

Cold Poached Salmon with Lime-Ginger Sauce

MAKES: 4 to 6 servings
TIME: 30 minutes, plus time to chill

I have never been disappointed by this poaching recipe, and salmon cooked this way is so versatile for salads, sandwiches, Sushi Bowls (page 473), and other quick dishes. So go ahead and make the full 3 pounds, regardless of who's coming to dinner. For poached salmon with more neutral flavorings, try the essential fish poaching recipe on page 569.

In my book, the best sauce for poached salmon is a flavored mayonnaise (see page 42). But use any of the sauces listed after Pan-Cooked Salmon on page 581.

Other seafood you can use: 1 large or up to 3 small trout or 4 to 6 trout fillets (adjust the cooking time accordingly).

1 whole salmon, 3 pounds or larger, gutted, gilled, and scaled; one 3-pound crosscut section from a larger salmon; or one 3-pound fillet, skin on (but scaled)

2 heaping tablespoons salt

1 tablespoon minced or grated fresh ginger

2 tablespoons peanut or vegetable oil

2 tablespoons soy sauce

6 tablespoons freshly squeezed lime juice

3 tablespoons minced fresh basil or chervil leaves, plus more for garnish (optional)

① Put the salmon in a pot large enough to hold it (a deep roasting pan works). Cover the salmon with cold water and use aluminum foil to make a lid for the pan if it doesn't have one. Add the salt and bring to a boil. Immediately turn off the heat and let the salmon sit in the hot water for 10 minutes for a fillet, up to 30 minutes for a large whole fish. Check for doneness by peeking near the center bone, using a thin-bladed knife; do not overcook. Remove the fish from the water, drain, and chill for up to a day before serving.

 Fast   Make Ahead   **V** Vegetarian

2 Meanwhile, whisk together the ginger, oil, soy sauce, lime juice, and 3 tablespoons minced herb. Drizzle some of this over the fish. To serve the salmon, insert the tine of a fork under the skin at the midline of each side of the fish, then run it lengthwise, splitting the skin. The skin will peel off easily. Take the salmon off the bone in the kitchen or at the table, using a spoon and following the natural contours of the fish. Garnish with more of the herb if you like.

Gravlax

Salt-and-Sugar-Cured Salmon

MAKES: 12 or more appetizer servings
TIME: 20 minutes, plus at least 2 days to cure

Cured fish is always impressive, and it's surprisingly little work to do yourself. Use king or sockeye salmon in season or Atlantic farmed salmon from a good source. In either case, the fish must be spanking fresh. Gravlax keeps for a week after curing; and, though it's not an ideal solution, you can successfully freeze gravlax for a few weeks.

> One 3- to 4-pound cleaned salmon without the head, skin on
>
> 1 cup salt
>
> 2 cups brown sugar
>
> 1 tablespoon freshly ground black pepper
>
> 1/4 cup spirits, like brandy, gin, aquavit, or lemon vodka
>
> 2 good-size bunches fresh dill, roughly chopped, stems and all
>
> Lemon wedges for serving
>
> Cold Mustard Sauce (page 42) for serving (optional)

1 Fillet the salmon (see page 586) or have the fishmonger do it; the fish need not be scaled. Lay both halves, skin side down, on a plate.

2 Toss together the salt, brown sugar, and pepper and rub this mixture all over the salmon (the skin too); splash on the spirits. Put most of the dill on the flesh side of one of the fillets, sandwich them together, tail to tail, and rub any remaining salt-sugar mixture on the outside; cover with any remaining dill, then wrap tightly in plastic wrap. Cover the sandwich with another plate and top with something that weighs a couple of pounds—some unopened cans, for example. Refrigerate.

3 Open the package every 12 to 24 hours and baste, inside and out, with the accumulated juices. When the flesh is opaque, on the second or third day (you will see it changing when you baste it), slice thinly as you would smoked salmon—on the bias and without the skin—and serve with rye bread or pumpernickel, lemon wedges, and, if you like, Cold Mustard Sauce (page 42).

The Basics of Thick White Fish Fillets and Whole Fish

Sometimes thick fillets come from the same fish found in the thin white fish section (see page 606)—they're just cut from larger fish—and some are fish that produce only thick fillets. So you'll see some species in both places. The fish listed here are all white, tender, and mild flavored (with the exception of wild catfish), at least an inch thick, and often considerably thicker—1 1/2 inches is common and 2 inches is not unheard of.

Since thick fillets don't cook in a flash, you can broil and even roast them long enough to assure browning. With the sturdiest fillets (those marked by a ✦ in the following list), it also means that they'll have plenty of time to crisp up in a skillet, yet remain sturdy enough to turn without breaking.

Atlantic pollock, also known as *Boston bluefish*
✦ Blackfish
 Sea bass
✦ Carp
 Catfish
 Cod

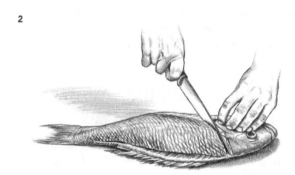

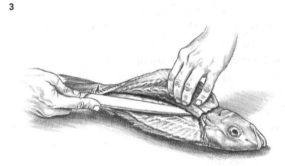

(STEP 1) Lay the fish on its side and cut all the way down its back, just to one side of the top fin. (STEP 2) Make a deep vertical incision just below the gills, from the top of the fish to the bottom. (STEP 3) Cut over the backbone and the ribs, right down through the belly flap, to release the fillet. Repeat on the other side of the fish.

◆ Grouper
◆ Monkfish (usually but not always suitable in recipes for other members of this group)
Orange roughy
Pacific pollock, also known as *Alaskan pollock*
◆ Red snapper and other snappers
Sablefish, also known as *black cod* (usually but not always suitable in recipes for other members of this group)
Sea trout, also known as *weakfish*
◆ Striped bass
◆ Sturgeon
◆ Tilefish
◆ Turbot
Whiting, also known as *hake*

Note that some of these—striped bass and cod, for example—are large enough that you can ask for a "center cut" of the fillet. This piece will be of fairly even thickness from one end to the other, minimizing the differences in doneness between portions of the fish.

Note, too, that most of these can—and should—be sold with their skin removed. But if you are roasting or pan-cooking the fish, and you'd like some crisp skin, choose red snapper, striped bass, or tilefish—even cod if you are lucky enough to see it with its skin. And you might even find some of the smaller fish on this list sold whole, which is always a treat.

These fish still cook relatively quickly, in 8 to 10 minutes per inch of thickness with most cooking methods. There is, of course, some variation based on the nature of the individual fish (striped bass, for example, needs slightly longer cooking to become tender; cod somewhat less to avoid dryness), its initial temperature, and the actual heat of your stove or oven.

To tell when the fish is done:
1. Begin checking the fish after about 7 minutes of cooking time per inch of thickness. First, insert a very thin-bladed knife or a skewer into the thickest part. If it penetrates with little or no resistance, the fish is done, or nearly so.

Ⓕ Fast   Ⓜ Make Ahead   Ⓥ Vegetarian

2. Use the same blade to gently open the fish at its thickest part and peek inside (a flashlight can be helpful here if your kitchen light is not direct). Once it is opaque throughout, the fish is completely done. You can stop cooking just before this point—when a bit of translucence remains—and the fish will finish cooking on the way to the table. This judgment will come easily with practice.

Fish and Beans

MAKES: 4 servings

TIME: 30 minutes with cooked or canned chickpeas

This is based on a lovable Spanish dish, one you can vary any number of ways simply by using different beans and fish; some ideas follow. Use beans you've cooked yourself if at all possible. But canned are fine in a pinch.

6 tablespoons extra virgin olive oil

Four 6-ounce thick white fish fillets (see page 585)

All-purpose flour for dredging

Salt and freshly ground black pepper

2 medium onions, cut into $^1/_4$-inch-thick slices

4 cups cooked or canned chickpeas or cannellini beans, cooking liquid reserved

$^3/_4$ cup dry sherry, white wine, or water

2 tablespoons minced garlic

$^1/_4$ cup chopped fresh parsley leaves

❶ Heat the oven to 300°F. Put 2 tablespoons of the oil in a skillet large enough to hold the fish in one layer over medium-high heat. Dredge the fillets lightly in the flour and, when the oil is hot, add them, one at a time, to the skillet, shiny (it won't have skin, so shiny) side up. Cook, undisturbed, until the cooked side is browned evenly, about 5 minutes. Turn the fish onto an ovenproof dish, browned side up, sprinkle with salt and pepper, and put it in the oven.

❷ Immediately add 2 more tablespoons of oil and the sliced onions to the skillet and cook, stirring, just until they start to color, a minute or two.

❸ Add the chickpeas to the skillet (along with about $^1/_2$ cup of their liquid if they were not canned) and cook, stirring, for about a minute. Add all but a tablespoon of the sherry and raise the heat to high. Cook, shaking the pan now and then, until the liquid is all but evaporated and the chickpeas are beginning to brown, about 5 minutes. Stir in the garlic along with some salt and pepper and cook for 1 minute, stirring occasionally; stir in the remaining olive oil and sherry.

❹ By this time the fish will be done. (If it is not, keep the chickpeas warm over low heat until it is.) Serve the fish on top of the chickpeas, scattered with parsley.

5 Ways to Spin Fish and Beans

1. Mash or purée the beans at the end of Step 3.

2. Mix some boiled or roasted potato cubes into the beans while they're heating.

3. Cook some roughly chopped greens—like kale, collards, spinach, or cabbage—in the pan with the beans.

4. Add some fresh ripe cherry tomato halves to the beans just before serving; give them a few quick stirs to warm and wilt them.

5. Go for Asian flavors: Use a neutral oil, like grapeseed or corn, and use scallions instead of onions. Use soybeans or adzuki beans and substitute sake for the sherry and cilantro for the parsley. Drizzle with a little soy sauce and a few drops of dark sesame oil at the very end.

Fish Steamed over Summer Vegetables

MAKES: 4 servings

TIME: 30 to 40 minutes

Versatile and foolproof, this recipe provides both fish and side dish in one preparation (it's a summer main-

5 WAYS TO VARY FISH STEAMED OVER VEGETABLES

Follow the main recipe, using the substitutions below; the total quantity of vegetables should be roughly 6 cups raw. If liquid is required to keep them moist, add it after you put the fish in the pan. Feel free to mix and match as you like.

VEGETABLE BED	FAT (FOR THE OLIVE OIL)	VEGETABLES (FOR THE ZUCCHINI, EGGPLANT, TOMATOES, AND OLIVES)	ADDED LIQUID	FINISHING FLAVORS (FOR THE BASIL)
Autumn Vegetables	Extra virgin olive oil	Butternut squash and chestnuts, apples, or pears	None needed	1/4 cup chopped hazelnuts
Spring Vegetables	Butter	Fresh or frozen peas and scallions, cut into chunks (use only about 4 cups and put the fish on immediately after the vegetables)	1/4 cup cream	1/4 cup chopped fresh mint or chives
Potatoes	Extra virgin olive oil or butter	Red potatoes, fingerlings, or other waxy potatoes	1/2 cup water or beer	1/4 cup chopped fresh chives
Greens	Extra virgin olive oil	Roughly chopped kale, collards, bok choy, cabbage, spinach, you name it (if they're tender, put the fish on immediately after the vegetables)	1/4 cup water	1/4 cup chopped black olives and hot red pepper flakes to taste (optional)
Gingered Sweet Potatoes	1 tablespoon dark sesame oil and 2 tablespoons neutral oil, like grapeseed or corn, or butter	Sweet potatoes, grated fresh ginger (omit the garlic and onion)	1/4 cup water or soy sauce	1/2 cup chopped scallion

stay for gardeners). The idea is to give the vegetables (whichever you choose) a head start in a hot skillet, then use that as a bed to steam sturdy fillets, steaks, or whole fish (which might take just a couple minutes longer).

In the main recipe, the vegetables are a summertime ratatouille-type blend. See the chart above for other ideas; you'll have to adjust the time a bit depending on the vegetables you choose. The goal is to let the vegetables soften but not fully cook. That way when you lay on the fish, everything finishes cooking together.

Other seafood you can use here: halibut, salmon, or trout; avoid fish that tend to dry out quickly, like tuna and swordfish.

F Fast   **M** Make Ahead   **V** Vegetarian

3 tablespoons extra virgin olive oil, plus more if needed

1 tablespoon minced garlic

1 large onion, chopped

Salt and freshly ground black pepper

2 medium or 1 large zucchini, trimmed and cut into 1-inch chunks

2 small or 1 medium eggplant, peeled if you like, and cut into 1-inch chunks

1 medium red bell pepper, cored, seeded, and cut into 1-inch chunks

3 small or 2 medium tomatoes, cored and roughly chopped, with their juice

1 teaspoon fresh thyme or marjoram leaves

1/2 cup black olives, pitted if you like (optional)

About 1 1/2 pounds sturdy white fish fillets, steaks, or whole fish (see page 585 or 601)

1/2 cup roughly chopped fresh basil leaves

❶ Put 2 tablespoons of the olive oil in a large skillet with a lid over medium-high heat. Immediately add the garlic and, when it sizzles, the onion and sprinkle with salt and pepper. Cook, stirring occasionally, until they begin to soften, about 5 minutes.

❷ Add the zucchini, eggplant, bell pepper, and more salt and pepper. Lower the heat a bit to keep the vegetables from burning and cook, stirring occasionally, until the eggplant is fairly soft, another 10 to 15 minutes. Add the tomatoes, thyme, and the olives if you're using them and cook, stirring occasionally, until the tomatoes begin to break up, 5 minutes or so. Taste and adjust the seasoning.

❸ Sprinkle the fish with salt and pepper and lay it on top of the vegetables. Adjust the heat so the mixture simmers. Cover and cook for 5 to 12 minutes, or until a thin-bladed knife inserted into the fish at its thickest point meets little resistance. (The thinnest fillets will be done in 5 minutes, but most will take about twice that long and a few even longer.) Transfer the fish to a plate, then stir the basil into the vegetables and spoon them around the fish; drizzle all with the remaining olive oil (use a little more if you like) and serve.

Breaded Thick Fillets, with or without Apples

MAKES: 4 servings
TIME: 30 minutes

Apples and fish are a lovely combination from northern France, but don't feel obligated to use the fruit. If you skip the apples, cut the butter in half, and start with Step 2, you end up with nicely breaded fish fillets—or fish sticks if you cut the fillets crosswise into fingers. Then all they need is some lemon wedges.

Other seafood you can use: halibut or salmon (fillets or steaks), large shrimp or scallops, or smelts.

4 crisp not-too-sweet apples, such as Granny Smith

6 tablespoons (3/4 stick) butter

All-purpose flour for dredging

Salt and freshly ground black pepper

1 egg

1 cup bread crumbs, preferably fresh (see page 876), plus more as needed

Four 6-ounce red snapper or other fillets marked with ✦ on pages 585–586

2 tablespoons freshly squeezed lemon juice

1 tablespoon white wine, Calvados, or brandy (optional)

❶ Peel and core the apples, then cut them into rings or thin wedges. Melt half the butter in a large skillet over medium heat. Add the apples, raise the heat to medium-high, and cook, tossing and stirring occasionally, until nicely browned on all sides, about 7 minutes. Transfer to a plate and keep warm in a 200°F oven while you prepare the fish.

❷ Wipe out the pan (carefully—it's hot) and return it to medium-high heat. Season the flour with salt and pepper on a plate and beat the egg in a bowl. Put the bread crumbs on a plate. Add the remaining butter to the skillet and, when the foam subsides, dredge each fillet in the flour, then dip it in the egg, dredge it in the bread crumbs, and put it in the pan.

❸ Cook until the fillets are nicely browned on both sides, 6 to 8 minutes total. The fillets will be white, opaque, and tender inside when done. Transfer the fish to a platter. Drizzle the lemon juice and wine over the apples, spoon a portion onto each fillet, and serve.

Pecan-Breaded Thick Fillets, with or without Apples. Substitute ground pecans (not a powder, but ground fairly fine—you can use other nuts as well) for half the bread crumbs.

PREPARING MONKFISH

Monkfish fillets (which are actually tails) have a thin gray membrane covering them. Remove as much of it as you can with your fingers and a sharp knife.

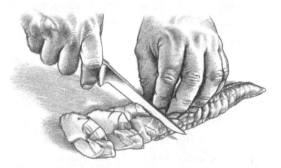

To get medallions, cut the monkfish crosswise, on the diagonal, in slices about 1¹⁄₂ inches thick.

Poached Monkfish or Thick Fillets with Artichokes

MAKES: 4 servings
TIME: 40 minutes

Artichokes are undeniably a little time-consuming to prepare, but this dish is undeniably worth it. For easier accompaniments, see the variations.

Other seafood you can use: shrimp, large scallops, halibut or salmon (steaks or fillets), or squid (shorten the cooking time by about half).

> At least 10 baby artichokes or 4 large artichokes
> 5 tablespoons extra virgin olive oil
> 1 pound waxy potatoes, peeled and, if necessary, cut into 1-inch chunks

Monkfish: A Different Kettle of Fish

I've grouped monkfish with thick white fillets, but it's a little more complicated than that. What we call a monkfish fillet is really the monkfish tail, an irregular, tapered triangle that has firm, nonflaky flesh, rich flavor, and chewy texture. In fact, it used to be called poor man's lobster (though it's not so cheap anymore!).

This makes monkfish a mixed blessing: highly desirable; sometimes tricky to cook; versatile enough to use in recipes that call for steaks, fillets, or—when you cut it crosswise into medallions—even scallops or shrimp.

If the piece of fish you're cooking is extremely uneven, you have some choices to ensure success: You can always cut it into medallions (see the illustration at left). Or butterfly it to make it more even. Or use a cooking method like grilling, where the heat source is a little uneven, too, so you can put the thick part over the hottest part of the fire. But I find that as long as you don't overcook the thickest part of the fish, the thinnest part usually comes out just fine.

 Fast   Make Ahead   Vegetarian

Salt and freshly ground black pepper

Several sprigs fresh thyme

1 cup dry white wine, stock (to make your own, see pages 157–159), or water

1 cup small black olives, like Niçoise, pitted if you like

1 tablespoon minced garlic

About 1¹/₂ pounds monkfish, cut into medallions (see previous page), or thick fillets (see page 585)

Chopped fresh parsley leaves for garnish

Lemon wedges for serving

1 If you're using baby artichokes, trim the tops and bottoms and scoop out the chokes with a small spoon. For whole artichokes, follow the directions under "Preparing Whole Artichokes" (page 254).

2 Put all but a tablespoon of the olive oil in a large skillet with a lid over medium heat. Add the baby artichokes or quarters and the potatoes and cook until they're glossy and beginning to soften, about 2 minutes; do not brown. Sprinkle with salt and pepper, add the thyme and wine, bring to a boil, cover, and adjust the heat so the mixture simmers.

3 Cook just until the potatoes are just tender, 10 to 15 minutes, then uncover and raise the heat again. Stir in the olives and garlic, then nestle the monkfish into the mixture. Cover and cook until the fish is opaque, 3 to 5 minutes. Taste and adjust the seasoning, then garnish with parsley and serve with the lemon wedges and a drizzle of the remaining olive oil.

Sautéed Monkfish or Thick Fillets with Fennel. Omit the artichokes and olives. Thinly slice 2 trimmed fennel bulbs, reserving the fronds for garnish if you like. Skip Step 1 and substitute the fennel for the artichokes. Garnish with the chopped fennel fronds.

Baked Monkfish or Thick Fillets. Works for the main recipe or the fennel variation: Heat the oven to 350°F. Spread half the oil in a ceramic casserole or baking dish and put the fish in it. Toss the remaining ingredi-ents (except the garnish) together and scatter them around the fish. Bake, uncovered, until the fish is cooked through and everything else is soft, 20 to 30 minutes.

Caramel Fish Fillets

MAKES: 4 servings
TIME: 30 minutes

Sounds crazy, I know, but it's a ubiquitous dish in Viet-nam. The fish is basically poached in melted sugar, which becomes a miraculously not-too-sweet sauce. Black pep-per is the main seasoning and also somewhat amazing in its effect. Serve the fish and sauce over simply cooked white long-grain rice or Steamed Sticky Rice, Thai Style (page 458 or 459).

Other protein you can use: shrimp or scallops; thinly sliced or cubed pork shoulder or boneless chicken thighs; beef sirloin; or tofu cubes.

1 cup sugar

¹/₂ cup nam pla (Thai fish sauce), plus more to taste

3 or 4 medium shallots, sliced (about ¹/₂ cup)

1 teaspoon freshly ground black pepper, or more to taste

Juice of 2 limes, plus more to taste

About 1¹/₂ pounds thick white fish fillets (see page 585)

Chopped fresh cilantro leaves for garnish

1 Put a large, deep skillet over medium heat and add the sugar and a tablespoon or two of water. Cook, occa-sionally shaking the pan gently, until the sugar liquefies and begins to bubble, about 5 minutes. When the sugar is all liquid, cook until it darkens, another minute or so; turn off the heat. Mix the nam pla with ¹/₂ cup water; carefully, and at arm's length, add this to the melted sugar. Turn the heat up to medium-high and cook, stir-

Serving Fish on a Bed

Unlike meat and even poultry, fish fillets fall apart with the touch of fork. So they're perfect for serving on top of something else: When you go to take a bite, whatever's underneath doesn't squish out all over the plate. (If you've ever tried to eat a sandwich on a bagel, you know the principle well.) Instead you get two delicious flavors at the same time and something approaching a fancy-restaurant presentation to boot.

Mashed potatoes, mashed sweet potatoes, and vegetable purées of all sorts are the most common beds for fish. And warm fish on a small pile of dressed greens is always a winner. But cooked beans, grains (including grain pilafs), polenta, risotto, pasta or noodles, and even grilled or roasted vegetables are all excellent candidates.

Start by putting the bed in the center of the each plate or one large platter. Then top with the fish—it's nice if it's crisp, for contrasting textures, but even steamed fish is fine. If there's a pan sauce, spoon it over all or drizzle around the sides of the plate. If there's not a sauce, consider topping the fish with a salsa or chutney or vinaigrette or simply chopped olives, tomatoes, chopped fresh herbs, or just a squeeze of fresh lemon or lime juice.

ring constantly, until the caramel melts into the liquid, 1 or 2 minutes. Add the shallots and cook, stirring occasionally, until they soften, about 5 minutes.

❷ Add the black pepper and lime juice, then lay the fish in the sauce. If the sauce does not reach at least halfway up the fish, add some water. Simmer until the fish is done (a thin-bladed knife inserted into the center will meet little resistance). Taste and add more fish sauce, lime juice, or pepper if necessary, then garnish with cilantro and serve, with the sauce poured on top of the fillets.

Grouper or Other Thick White Fillets in Yellow Curry

MAKES: 4 servings

TIME: 45 minutes

For braising you have to use one of the sturdier species; you can also use steaks or cut-up whole fish. If you're not crazy about curry, see the variations.

Other seafood you can use: halibut, cod, or tilefish steaks; or whole fish—like red snapper, sea bass, or porgy—cut into pieces, bones and all.

3 tablespoons peanut or neutral oil, like grapeseed or corn

About 1½ pounds grouper or other sturdy thick fillets (see the species marked with ✦ on pages 585–586), cut into chunks

Salt and freshly ground black pepper

All-purpose flour for dredging

2 cups sliced onion

2 tablespoons curry powder or garam masala (to make your own, see pages 66–67)

2 cups coconut milk (to make your own, see page 389)

2 tablespoons freshly squeezed lemon juice

Chopped fresh cilantro leaves for garnish

❶ Put 2 tablespoons of the oil in a large skillet over medium-high heat. Sprinkle the grouper chunks with salt and pepper and dredge lightly in flour, shaking off the excess. When the oil is not (a pinch of flour will sizzle), add the fish and cook over high heat until lightly browned, 3 to 4 minutes. Remove the fish with a slotted spoon and set aside.

❷ Pour out the oil and lower the heat to medium. Wipe out the skillet if there are black bits in it (carefully—it's hot). Add the remaining tablespoon of oil and the onion and cook, stirring, until very soft and beginning to brown, about 10 minutes. Stir in the curry powder, sprinkle with a bit more salt and pepper, and cook, stirring occasionally, for about 2 minutes.

 Fast   Make Ahead   **V** Vegetarian

③ Add the coconut milk to the onion mixture; bring to a boil over medium-high heat and cook until reduced by about one-third, about 3 minutes. Add the fish, reduce the heat to medium, and cook until the fish is tender, about 5 minutes. Add the lemon juice, taste and adjust the seasonings, garnish with cilantro, and serve.

Grouper or Other Thick White Fillets in Red or Green Curry. Substitute ¼ cup Red or Green Curry Paste (page 75 or 76) for the curry powder. Use 2 bunches scallions instead of the onion if you like. Substitute 2 tablespoons nam pla (Thai fish sauce) for the lemon juice. Proceed with the recipe, garnishing with a combination of mint and basil (Thai basil if you can find it) instead of the cilantro. Add a sprinkling of chopped peanuts if you like.

Grouper or Other Thick White Fillets in Tomato-Basil Cream. Use extra virgin olive oil instead of the peanut oil; omit the curry powder. Substitute 1 cup cream and 1 cup tomato purée for the coconut milk and 1 cup chopped or julienned basil leaves for the cilantro. Proceed with the recipe, adding half the basil in Step 2, where you would have added the curry powder.

Grouper or Other Thick White Fillets in Chipotle Cream. Rich and spicy: Use extra virgin olive oil instead of the peanut oil; omit the curry powder. Purée or mash 1 or two canned chipotle chiles in 2 tablespoons of their adobo. Substitute 2 cups cream or half-and-half for the coconut milk. Proceed with the recipe, adding the chipotle in Step 2, where you would have added the curry.

Grouper or Other Thick White Fillets in Roasted Garlic Cream. Roast 2 heads garlic (see page 303) and purée or mash with a fork. Use extra virgin olive oil instead of the peanut oil; omit the curry powder and the onion. Substitute 2 cups cream or half-and-half for the coconut milk. Proceed with the recipe, adding the mashed garlic in Step 2, where you would have added the curry. Garnish with 2 teaspoons chopped fresh rosemary.

Grouper or Other Thick White Fillets in Herb Broth. Use extra virgin olive oil instead of the peanut oil; omit the curry powder, onion, and coconut milk. Before beginning, purée 1 cup mixed mild herbs—like dill, chives, chervil, parsley, or mint—in 2 cups white wine, fish stock (to make your own, see page 159), water, or a combination. Proceed with the recipe, simmering this mixture in the pan for a few minutes in Step 3 before returning the fish to the pot.

Cod or Catfish Fillets, Roasted with Potatoes

MAKES: 4 servings
TIME: 1 hour

Crisp roasted potatoes and fish are a winning combination. But a lot of other vegetables are nice too, so check out the list that follows; cube or slice them as you like. To accommodate the different cooking times, roast until the vegetables are golden and just tender, turning as needed, before adding the fish. Increase the cooking time slightly if you use one of the sturdier fillets marked with a ✦ on the list on pages 585–586.

Other vegetables you can use here: mushrooms, carrots, beets, parsnips, celery root, ribbons of cabbage, winter squash, eggplant, tropical tubers, yams, or sweet potatoes.

Other seafood you can use here: any of the species listed on page 585, halibut or salmon (fillets or steaks), or whole fish, like sea bass, grouper, or snapper (increase the cooking time to about 20 minutes).

6 tablespoons (¾ stick) butter

2 to 3 pounds waxy red or white potatoes

Salt and freshly ground black pepper

About 1½ pounds cod or catfish fillets

2 tablespoons chopped fresh chives or
    dill (optional)

Crème fraîche, sour cream, or yogurt (optional)

1 Heat the oven to 425°F. Put 4 tablespoons ($^1/_2$ stick) of the butter in a roasting pan or baking dish large enough to hold the fish comfortably. Put the pan in the oven to melt the butter.

2 Peel the potatoes and slice them $^1/_8$ to $^1/_4$ inch thick (I use a food processor or a mandoline for this). Remove the pan from the oven when the butter is melted. When the oven is hot, stir the potatoes into the butter and sprinkle them liberally with salt and pepper. Return the dish to the oven and set a timer for 10 minutes.

3 Every 10 minutes, turn the potatoes gently with a spatula. When they are nicely browned all over—30 to 40 minutes—put the fish on top of them, dotting the top with the remaining 2 tablespoons butter. Roast for 8 to 12 minutes, depending upon the thickness of the fillets. The fish is done when it's opaque throughout and offers no resistance to a thin-bladed knife; avoid overcooking. Serve with a dollop of crème fraîche and a sprinkling of herbs if you like.

Cod or Catfish Fillets, Roasted with Potatoes, Onions, and Olive Oil. In Step 1, gently heat $^1/_4$ cup extra virgin olive oil instead of butter. In Step 2, add 2 cups sliced onion along with the potatoes. In Step 3, drizzle the cod with 1 tablespoon additional olive oil. Finish as directed.

Spicy Deep-Fried Fish, Indian Style

MAKES: 4 servings
TIME: 40 minutes

Based on a dish I've enjoyed in India, these fish are marinated, then breaded, then fried crisp for a distinctive flavor and texture that always wins people over. Serve right out of the pan, with plain basmati rice, or rolled up in freshly made Chapati (page 848), with Raw Onion, Coconut, or Cilantro-Mint Chutney (pages 36–37).

Other seafood you can use: small to medium scallops or shrimp or squid (reduce the cooking time by half).

1 inch fresh ginger, peeled

2 cloves garlic, peeled

1 fresh hot green chile like jalapeño, seeded

$^1/_2$ teaspoon salt

$^1/_2$ teaspoon freshly ground pepper

3 tablespoons freshly squeezed lemon or lime juice

About $1^1/_2$ pounds sturdy white fish fillets (see page 585), skinned and cut into 2-inch cubes or 4-inch strips about 1 inch wide (almost like fish fingers)

2 tablespoons all-purpose flour

1 teaspoon chili powder (to make your own, see page 66)

1 egg, beaten

Neutral oil, like grapeseed or corn, for deep-frying

1 lemon or lime, cut into wedges

1 Put the ginger, garlic, chile, salt, and pepper into a food processor; process until everything is finely minced. Add the lemon or lime juice and process until well combined. Pour this mixture over the fish, toss gently to coat, cover, and refrigerate for at least 20 minutes or up to an hour.

2 Meanwhile, mix together the flour, chili powder, and egg in a large bowl. Add just enough water to make a thick batter, about $^1/_2$ cup. Pour 2 inches of oil into a deep, heavy saucepan or Dutch oven; bring to 350°F over medium-high heat (see "Deep Frying," page 19). A drop of the batter will sizzle energetically but not violently when the oil reaches this temperature.

3 Remove the fish from the marinade, coat with the batter, and slide gently into the oil. Fry in batches if necessary; do not overcrowd. Fry, turning once, until the fish is crisp and golden brown on all sides, about 7 minutes

F Fast   **M** Make Ahead   **V** Vegetarian

total. Drain on paper towels and serve immediately with lemon wedges.

Deep-Fried Fish with Twice-Fried Ginger, Garlic, or Shallots

MAKES: 4 servings
TIME: 30 minutes

I learned to make this dish with ginger but have decided that garlic and shallots are equally good. The options just mean you can make it more often without repeating yourself.

Other seafood you can use here: salmon or halibut, shrimp or scallops.

Neutral oil, like grapeseed or corn, for deep-frying

8 ounces ginger, garlic, or shallots, peeled and trimmed as needed and thinly sliced or chopped

About 1½ pounds thick white fish fillets (see page 585), cut into large chunks

Salt and freshly ground black pepper

1 cup all-purpose flour

1 cup cornstarch

4 scallions, cut into 2-inch lengths

1 tablespoon soy sauce or nam pla (Thai fish sauce)

Fresh cilantro leaves for garnish

❶ Put at least 2 inches of oil in a deep pot that will hold the fish chunks in one layer; bring to 350°F over medium-high heat (see "Deep Frying," page 19).

❷ When the oil is hot, fry the ginger, garlic, or shallots until lightly browned, 3 to 10 minutes, depending on what you're using and how you cut it. Adjust the heat as needed so the temperature remains nearly constant. Meanwhile, sprinkle the fish with salt and pepper and combine the flour and cornstarch in a bowl.

❸ Remove the ginger with a slotted spoon and set aside. Dredge the fish lightly in the flour-cornstarch mixture, tapping to remove the excess and add the pieces slowly to the oil, again adjusting the heat as necessary so the temperature remains nearly constant. Fry, turning once or twice, until the fish is lightly browned and cooked through (a skewer or thin-bladed knife will pass through each chunk with little resistance), 3 to 5 minutes. Remove with a slotted spoon and drain on paper towels.

❹ Fry the scallions for 15 seconds and remove with a slotted spoon; drain. Refry the ginger for about 30 seconds, then remove and drain. Put the fish on a plate and garnish with the ginger and scallions; drizzle with the soy sauce or nam pla, top with cilantro, and serve.

Quick-Braised Whole Fish in Black Bean Sauce

MAKES: 4 servings
TIME: 30 minutes

Okay, so not everyone likes to cook whole fish—or has a pan big enough to do it, though you can easily remove the head and tail if necessary. But this is a Chinese classic and really quite easy. If you're still not convinced, try the variation for fillets. Serve this over rice, with Spicy Pickles, Asian Style (page 229). If you didn't buy the fish cleaned and scaled, see pages 595–597.

Peanut or neutral oil, like grapeseed or corn, as needed

¼ cup fermented black beans

¼ cup rice wine, dry sherry, or water

SCALING FISH

Use a spoon or dull knife to scrape the scales from the fish, and always work from the tail up.

GUTTING FISH

1

2

This may be "icky," but few culinary tasks are easier. **(STEP 1)** Cut a long slit from the end of the fish's "throat" to the rear vent. **(STEP 2)** Reach in and pull out the guts. Discard; these are not good in stock. Rinse out any remaining bits.

REMOVING GILLS

Use scissors to remove the gills, taking care not to cut yourself; gills are sharp. Cut the gills on both sides from where they attach to the body. Remove and discard—gills are too bitter to use for stock.

REMOVING FINS

Like the gills, fins are best tackled with scissors. Note that they are removed only for appearances and may be left on whole fish during cooking if you prefer.

 Fast   Make Ahead   Vegetarian

2 cups all-purpose flour

One 3-pound whole sea bass, carp, grouper, tilapia (not my favorite), snapper, or mackerel

Salt and freshly ground black pepper

1 tablespoon minced fresh ginger

1 tablespoon minced garlic

4 scallions, roughly chopped

1 large onion, sliced

2 cups chopped tomato (drained canned is fine)

Soy sauce if needed

① Put about $1/8$ inch oil in a broad, deep skillet over medium-high heat. Soak the beans in the wine. Mix the flour with enough water to make a paste the consistency of sour cream. Cut 3 or 4 parallel diagonal gashes into each side of the fish, all the way down to the bone; sprinkle the fish inside and out with salt and pepper.

② When the oil is hot—it will shimmer, and a pinch of flour tossed into it will sizzle—coat the fish with the batter, add to the pan, and brown it quickly, about 3 minutes per side, then transfer it to a plate. Turn off the heat and let the pan cool down a bit, then discard the oil and wipe out the pan.

③ Put 2 tablespoons fresh oil in the pan and turn the heat to high. When hot, add the ginger, garlic, and scallions and cook, stirring, for about 30 seconds. Add the onion and cook, stirring occasionally, for about 2 minutes, just until it begins to soften. Turn the heat down to medium and add the tomato and the black beans with their liquid; cook, stirring occasionally, for about 5 minutes, just until the tomato begins to release some juice.

④ Return the fish to the pan and continue to cook until done, 10 to 15 minutes more (a thin-bladed knife inserted into the center will meet little resistance). Taste and add soy sauce if the dish is not salty enough; serve the fillets with the sauce over rice.

Quick-Braised Thick White Fish Fillets in Black Bean Sauce. Use any of the species listed on page 585. Or

REMOVING HEADS AND TAILS

1

2

Like the tail, the head is best left on unless your pot won't hold the fish without removing it (the "cheeks" are good to eat). **(STEP 1)** To remove it, make a cut right behind the gill covers to guide the knife. **(STEP 2)** Use a mallet to pound the knife through the backbone if necessary.

I do not recommend removing the tail unless your cooking method requires it or your utensil is too short to hold the whole fish. If you must, however, simply use a sharp, heavy knife to cut right through the tail.

try large scallops or shrimp or squid: Start with about $1^1/_2$ pounds of seafood. For the fillets, cooking time in Step 2 will be about 2 minutes per side; about 5 minutes in Step 4. For scallops, shrimp, or squid, 2 minutes per side and just a minute or so for final rewarming in Step 4.

The Basics of Scallops

The creamy and almost translucent scallop is easy to cook, delicious, wonderfully textured—as long as it's not overcooked—and widely available. All of this makes it the most accessible mollusk.

This happy state comes in part from the fact that scallops are usually shucked immediately after harvest. Then, to prevent spoilage, the guts are removed and discarded. What remains is the massive muscle. (Sometimes the muscle is sold together with the reddish orange roe, which is delicious.) So they keep better and elicit none of the "yuck" reaction people sometimes have to other mollusks.

Note that all scallops are sold with their tendon, a stark white strip of gristle that attaches the muscle to the shell. It's often overlooked, and can be, especially with smaller scallops. But if you're cooking just a few scallops, or making ceviche, or have a little extra time, just strip it off with your fingers. This is an added refinement, far from essential but worthwhile since this tendon is chewy.

Sometimes scallops are soaked in phosphates, which cause them to absorb water and lose flavor. Always buy scallops from someone you trust and let him or her know that you want unsoaked (sometimes called "dry") scallops.

Types of Scallops

Sea scallop: Harvested year-round, sea scallops range from mild to quite briny. They are the biggest, at least an inch thick and twice that in diameter. They are best cooked so that their interior remains creamy. Some range to several ounces; most weigh $^1/_2$ ounce or so.

Bay scallop: Caught in the winter months in a small area between Long Island and Cape Cod, these are the most expensive (and the best) scallops. Cork shaped and about the size of pretzel nuggets, they are slightly darker in color than other scallops. If you're not paying at least $25 a pound—and probably more—you're not buying real bay scallops. The farmed version from China is much less expensive but nowhere near as good.

Calico scallop: These are the little inexpensive scallops, found off the Atlantic and Gulf coasts and also in Central and South America. They're shucked by blasting the shells with a hit of steam. Of course this semicooks them as well, further contributing to their tendency to become overcooked. Calicos run to two or even three hundred scallops per pound, although larger ones are also harvested (and passed off as bays).

Seared Scallops with Pan Sauce

MAKES: 4 servings
TIME: 15 minutes, more or less

Here's the secret to simple and perfectly cooked scallops: Brown them in a hot pan, remove, make a little sauce, then return them to the pan just long enough to heat through and coat with the sauce.

Other seafood you can use: shrimp, squid (cook them for half the time), any thick white fish fillets from the list on page 585, salmon or halibut (fillets or steaks), monkfish cut crosswise into thick medallions, swordfish or tuna steaks. (Increase the cooking time a bit for fish, depending on the thickness of the cut.)

2 tablespoons butter

2 tablespoons extra virgin olive oil

1 teaspoon minced garlic

F Fast   **M** Make Ahead   **V** Vegetarian

About 1 1/2 pounds scallops, preferably sea or bay

Salt and freshly ground black pepper

Juice of 1 lemon

1 tablespoon chopped fresh chives

① Heat a large skillet over medium-high heat for 3 or 4 minutes; add the butter and olive oil, garlic, and, 30 seconds later, the scallops, a few at a time if they're big. Turn them as they brown, allowing about 2 minutes per side (less for scallops under an inch across, somewhat more for those well over an inch). Sprinkle them with salt and pepper as they cook; transfer them to a bowl as they finish.

② Add the lemon juice to the pan, scraping to remove any brown bits, and cook until the liquid is reduced to a glaze, 1 to 2 minutes. Return the scallops to the skillet, along with the chives, and stir to coat with the sauce and heat through, 1 to 2 minutes. Serve immediately.

Butter-Poached Scallops. In Step 1, heat the skillet over medium heat for just 2 minutes; use all butter and add the scallops all at once. Don't brown the scallops; keep the heat at medium and cook them on both sides until opaque, 5 to 8 minutes total, depending on their size. In Step 2, add 1 teaspoon minced fresh tarragon leaves or 1/2 teaspoon dried tarragon along with the lemon juice. Finish as directed, stirring in another teaspoon or two of butter with the scallops (omit the chives) and garnishing with chopped fresh chervil, tarragon (just a little), or parsley leaves.

Seared Scallops with Cherry Tomatoes. Omit the lemon juice. Halve about 8 ounces cherry tomatoes. In Step 2, add the tomatoes to the pan and cook just long enough for them to wrinkle a bit and release their juice. Garnish with the chives or chopped fresh basil or mint leaves.

Seared Scallops with Ginger. In Step 1, use peanut or neutral oil, like grapeseed or corn. Add 1 tablespoon minced or grated fresh ginger with the garlic. Add 3 chopped scallions to the skillet with the scallops. In Step 2, use a mixture of 1 tablespoon soy sauce, 1 tablespoon dry sherry or white wine, and 2 tablespoons water or chicken, fish, or vegetable stock (to make your own, see pages 157–159) in place of the lemon juice. Finish with chives or some minced scallion and add salt and pepper if necessary.

Seared Scallops with White Wine. Transfer the cooked scallops to a warm platter and turn the heat to high. Add 1 cup dry white wine to the pan (a really good one will not be wasted here) and cook, stirring and scraping the pan with a wooden spoon, until the wine is reduced by more than half and is syrupy and thick, about 3 minutes. Pour this over the scallops, garnish, and serve.

Seared Coconut Curry Scallops. Use all butter or substitute neutral oil, like grapeseed or corn, for the olive oil. As the scallops sear in Step 1, sprinkle them lightly with curry powder (to make your own, see pages 66–67). In Step 2, before adding the lemon juice to the pan, stir in 1 teaspoon more of the curry and keep stirring for 15 seconds or so. Then add the lemon juice along with 1/2 cup coconut milk (to make your own, see page 389). Proceed with the recipe, garnishing with chopped fresh cilantro (or some toasted coconut) instead of the chives.

Sesame-Crusted Seared Scallops. Use all butter or substitute neutral oil, like grapeseed or corn, for the olive oil. Omit the lemon juice. Before cooking, put about 1/2 cup sesame seeds on a plate and coat both flat sides of the scallops in the seeds, pressing to make them stick. Proceed with the recipe, going easy on the salt as the scallops cook. In Step 2, add 1/4 cup soy sauce and 1/4 cup water to the pan instead of the lemon juice and cook until reduced to a glaze, a minute or two. Garnish with chopped scallion instead of the chives.

Roasted Sea Scallops

MAKES: 4 servings

TIME: 30 minutes

You must use sea scallops for this dish; even bay scallops are likely to overcook.

Other seafood you can use: shucked oysters (especially for the variation); any thick or thin white fish fillets on page 585 or 607; monkfish cut crosswise into thick medallions. (If you're using fish, you might have to cook a little bit more or less, depending on the thickness.)

    1 medium tomato, peeled if you have time, cored, and
        roughly chopped

    1 medium onion, chopped

    2 tablespoons minced fresh parsley leaves, plus
        parsley for garnish

    1 teaspoon paprika

    1 tablespoon extra virgin olive oil, plus more for drizzling

    Salt and freshly ground black pepper

    About 1¹/₂ pounds sea scallops

    ¹/₂ cup bread crumbs, preferably fresh (optional;
        page 876)

❶ Heat the oven to 450°F. Mix the tomato, onion, parsley, paprika, oil, and some salt and pepper together in a baking dish just large enough to hold the scallops in one layer.

❷ Bake until the juices begin to bubble, about 10 minutes. Nestle the scallops into the tomato mixture, sprinkle the top with bread crumbs if you like, and drizzle with a little more oil. Return to the oven and roast just until the scallops are opaque about halfway through, about 10 minutes, depending on their size. Serve, spooning some of the pan mixture on the side.

Roasted Scallops with Creamed Spinach. Omit the tomato, onion, parsley, and paprika. In Step 1, put a pound of fresh spinach in the bottom of the dish, sprinkle with salt, pepper, and a pinch of nutmeg, and pour 1 cup cream over all. Cover with foil and bake as directed in Step 2. Remove the foil, give the spinach mixture a good stir, then proceed with the recipe.

Grilled or Broiled Scallops with Basil Stuffing

MAKES: 4 servings

TIME: 30 minutes

One of my all-time favorite recipes. Even though it's super-easy to split and fill scallops, the results are guaranteed to impress.

Other seafood you can use: shrimp (split lengthwise for stuffing); monkfish cut crosswise into thick medallions.

    ¹/₂ cup fresh basil leaves

    1 clove garlic, peeled

    1 teaspoon salt

    ¹/₄ teaspoon freshly ground black pepper

    ¹/₃ cup plus 1 tablespoon extra virgin olive oil

    About 1¹/₂ pounds large sea scallops

    Lemon wedges for serving

❶ Mince the basil, garlic, salt, and pepper together until very fine, almost a purée (a food processor won't really help you much here). Mix in a small bowl or cup with 1 tablespoon of the olive oil.

❷ Make a deep horizontal slit in the side of each scallop, but don't cut all the way through. Fill each scallop with about ¹/₂ teaspoon of the basil mixture; close. Pour the remaining oil onto a plate or pan and turn the scallops in it. Let them sit while you heat a charcoal or gas grill or the broiler until very hot and put the rack about 4 inches from the heat source.

❸ Put the scallops on the grill or under the broiler (don't pour the remaining oil over them, as it will catch fire), and grill or broil for 2 to 3 minutes per side, no more. Serve immediately, with lemon wedges.

Grilled or Broiled Scallops with Thai Basil Stuffing. Substitute Thai basil for the basil and use 2 teaspoons nam pla (Thai fish sauce) instead of the salt. Substitute peanut or neutral oil, like grapeseed or corn, for the olive oil. While you're making the paste in Step 1, stir in a tablespoon or so of minced fresh chile (like jalapeño or Thai) or hot red pepper flakes and a pinch of sugar. Use this mixture to fill the scallops and then grill or broil, garnishing with lime wedges instead of the lemon.

Grilled or Broiled Scallops with Miso Stuffing. Omit the basil and garlic and substitute peanut or neutral oil, like grapeseed or corn, for the olive oil. Make a paste by combining 1/2 cup white or yellow miso with 2 tablespoons mirin (or 1 tablespoon each honey and water), a light sprinkling of salt, a pinch of cayenne, and the oil. Use this to fill the scallops, and smear around the outsides with the remaining oil.

Bacon-Wrapped Grilled or Broiled Scallops. Omit the basil. Make a marinade with all the olive oil, garlic, and a sprinkle of salt and pepper; roll the scallops around in this mixture and let them sit. Cook 8 slices of bacon until done. Cut the bacon into pieces that will wrap around the scallops and secure them with soaked toothpicks, stuck horizontally through the sides of the scallops.

Kombu-Wrapped Grilled or Broiled Scallops. Omit the basil and substitute dark sesame oil for the olive oil. Make a marinade with the oil, garlic, and a sprinkle of salt and pepper; roll the scallops around in this mixture and let them sit. Put about 1/2 ounce of kombu (seaweed) in a bowl and cover with cold water. Soak for about an hour, until soft and dark green. Drain and pat dry. Cut the kombu lengthwise into strips and wrap around the scallops, securing with a soaked toothpick stuck horizontally through the sides of the scallops. Proceed with the recipe, serving with Soy Dipping Sauce and Marinade or Ponzu Sauce (page 25 or 40) if you like instead of lemon.

The Basics of Fish for Steaks

Tuna, halibut, swordfish, and their kin—these are the big fish usually cut into steaks. (Halibut is a notable exception, which you frequently find in both steaks and fillets.) Occasionally you still see large mild-flavored fish—cod, whiting, and tilefish, for example—cut into steaks. But the days when these fish were allowed to grow so large are in the past, and the world of steak fish is now dominated by a few giants, especially swordfish and tuna. (Salmon steaks, the most popular of all, are covered in the section starting on page 578.)

All the varieties available as steaks are in the following list. Some are boneless (marked with a ★), and some have a more delicate texture (marked with a ☙). All can be grilled—and are excellent that way—though you must take extra care with delicate fish like cod, not only to prevent them from falling apart but also because they overcook and dry out easily. You want foolproof? Stick with tuna, sword, and shark, and other really sturdy fish.

Of course, you can use any other method for cooking steaks: Broiling, roasting, and pan-cooking are the easiest and the best; but when roasting, I usually plan for 2 or 3 minutes extra.

Some of these fish—most notably tuna—are sometimes served raw (or nearly so) in Sushi Rolls and Bowls (see pages 473 and 474), salads, or other, more elegant dishes. You can prepare raw fish at home as long as you buy from a reputable source known for purchasing premium fish. Some will be dubbed *sushi grade,* but that doesn't necessarily mean the fish is absolutely fresh, so no matter what, use your eyes and nose to assess its bright color and clean smell. Ask the person behind the counter to press on it; the flesh should be firm without any gaping at all. And use fish you intend to eat raw the same day you buy it.

A Dozen Fish Frequently Cut into Steaks

☙ Bluefish (strong flavored, a good sometime substitute for tuna)

- Cod (more delicate than halibut but a good substitute)

  Grouper (sturdy, firm-textured steak; close to monkfish)
- Halibut (classic white steak, mild flavored but fairly sturdy)
- Mackerel (strong flavored; in the tuna family)

  Mahi-mahi (in a class by itself; fairly sturdy, fairly strong flavored)
- ★ Mako (almost tough flesh, mild flavored)
- ★ Monkfish (not a true steak, but works well in steak recipes)
- ★ Sturgeon (tough and oily; at its best, wonderful, though farmed varieties are inferior)
- ★ Swordfish (classic)
- Tilefish (not common; mild and somewhere between cod and halibut in texture)
- ★ Tuna (all varieties are good)

When Are Steaks Done?

Because they are of uniform thickness, or nearly so, steaks usually cook evenly. Be aware, though, that some of these fish—most notably swordfish and tuna—have a much more interesting texture and flavor when they're cooked to medium or even medium-rare than when cooked to well done. Some, like halibut and cod, become downright dry if they're overcooked. And sturgeon and mako are on the tough side if they're either under- or overcooked. So the doneness level is important. And here's how you check:

1. Begin checking the fish after about 7 minutes of cooking time per inch of thickness. White-fleshed fish are done when a thin-bladed knife or skewer passes easily through the center. If you're in doubt, take a thin-bladed knife and make a small cut near the center of one of the steaks. Pry the flesh apart and peek in there to judge the level of doneness; all traces of translucence should be gone.

2. For darker fish—bluefish, mackerel, and mahi-mahi, for example—start with the cut-and-peek technique.

When they are white throughout, or very nearly so, remove them from the heat.

3. For mako, monkfish, and sturgeon, judge doneness not only by appearance but also by tenderness; sometimes they are tender just before the translucence disappears, other times just after. It will be a matter of just a minute or two.

4. Swordfish is at its most moist if you stop cooking when just a little translucence remains in the center; cook it to the well-done stage if you prefer, but get it off the heat quickly or it will be dry.

5. Tuna is best when still red to pink in the center. Fully cooked tuna is almost inevitably dry.

CUTTING FISH STEAKS

1

2

(STEP 1) Mark the fish by scoring it lightly with a knife to ensure you'll cut even steaks. (STEP 2) With most fish, the backbone is so thick that you'll need a little help to get the knife through; use a meat mallet or an ordinary rubber or wooden mallet.

 Fast   Make Ahead   Vegetarian

Grilled Marinated Swordfish, Tuna, or Other Fish Steaks

MAKES: 4 servings
TIME: 45 minutes

This simple marinade promotes both flavor and browning, but you can use straight olive oil, salt, pepper, and nothing else if you like. Be sure to check out the lists on page 566 for more ideas about seasoning and serving simply cooked fish; all can be applied here.

Other seafood you can use: any of the steaks listed on pages 601–602 marked with a star, shrimp or squid (reduce the cooking time by about half), scallops, monkfish medallions.

Two 1-inch-thick swordfish or tuna steaks, about 1½ pounds

Juice of 1 lime

2 tablespoons soy sauce

Lime or lemon wedges for serving

1 Heat a charcoal or gas grill or the broiler until quite hot and put the rack fairly close to the heat, 3 or 4 inches at most.

2 Soak the steaks in a mixture of the lime juice and soy sauce for 15 to 30 minutes if desired.

3 Grill the fish, brushing once or twice with the soy-lime mixture. After 4 minutes, the fish should be nicely browned; turn it. Three minutes later, check the fish for doneness by peeking between the layers of flesh with a thin-bladed knife; when the knife meets little resistance and just a touch of translucence remains, the swordfish is done. Serve immediately, with lime or lemon wedges.

Grilled Swordfish, Tuna, or Other Fish Steaks with Mustard Sauce. Excellent with boiled potatoes. In Step 2, omit the marinade. Instead, brush the fish with 1 tablespoon olive or other oil, then sprinkle it with salt and pepper. Grill as in Step 3. Combine ¼ cup olive oil, 3 tablespoons Dijon mustard, ¼ cup minced shallot, 2 tablespoons chopped fresh parsley leaves, 2 tablespoons freshly squeezed lemon juice, and salt and pepper to taste. Drizzle the steak with a bit of this mixture, then pass the rest at the table. Omit the lemon or lime wedges.

Herb-Rubbed Grilled Swordfish, Tuna, or Other Fish Steaks. Step 1 remains the same. In Step 2, omit the marinade and, before grilling, rub the fish with a mixture of 1 tablespoon grated or minced lemon peel, 1 teaspoon coarse salt, 1 large minced clove garlic, and 2 tablespoons minced mixed fresh herbs, such as parsley, chives, basil, sage, thyme, and/or rosemary. Grill as in Step 3 and serve with lemon wedges.

Olive-Rubbed Grilled Swordfish, Tuna, or Other Fish Steaks. In Step 2, omit the marinade. Instead, finely chop ½ cup pitted green or black olives. Put them in a bowl with a tablespoon of lemon juice, a tablespoon of minced garlic, a small pinch of salt (unless the olives are already very salty), and lots of black pepper. Use a fork to mash this mixture into a rough paste. Rub it all over the steaks, let them rest as described in Step 2, then proceed with the recipe. Garnish with chopped fresh parsley leaves.

Grilled or Broiled Fish Skewers, Basted with Herbs

MAKES: 4 servings
TIME: 45 minutes

The master recipe for fish kebabs, brushed after grilling, with a quick herb paste. Grill some vegetables at the same time and you have a full meal without dirtying a pot.

Other seafood you can use: scallops or shrimp; lobster chunks; or squid (cut the cooking time in half).

About 1½ pounds fish steaks (see page 601), cut into large chunks with the skin

⅓ cup extra virgin olive oil, plus more for brushing on the fish

Salt and freshly ground black pepper

2 cloves garlic, peeled

1 tablespoon chopped fresh oregano, rosemary, lavender, or thyme leaves

¼ cup chopped fresh parsley leaves, plus parsley for garnish

Juice of 1 lemon

1 If you're using wooden skewers, soak them in water for at least 15 minutes. Heat a charcoal or gas grill or the broiler until quite hot and put the rack 3 or 4 inches from the heat source. Thread the fish onto skewers to make 4 kebabs (the fish will be easier to turn if you use 2 skewers per kebab). Brush the fish with a little olive oil and sprinkle with salt and pepper.

2 Chop the garlic and herbs as fine as possible and combine them with the ⅓ cup oil and some salt and pepper, mashing and stirring with a fork into a rough purée. (A mortar and pestle or a small food processor is ideal for this, but you can easily do it by hand). Stir in the lemon juice and set aside.

3 Grill the fish, turning as each side browns, a bit more than 2 minutes per side or about 5 minutes total, until tender but not dry; when a thin-bladed knife inserted into the center meets only a little resistance, it's done. Right before removing from the fire, brush or drizzle with the herb sauce. Serve garnished with a little more parsley.

Crisp Cod or Other Fish Steaks with Orange Sauce

MAKES: 4 servings
TIME: 20 minutes

F

An updated take on fish steaks with pan sauce. For other flavor ideas, see the variations. If this feels like too much fat for you, decrease the butter by a tablespoon or so,

especially if you're using one of the sturdier fish from pages 601–602.

Other seafood you can use: any of the thick white fillets on pages 585–586.

About 1 cup all-purpose flour

Salt and freshly ground black pepper

½ teaspoon cayenne, or to taste (optional)

2 tablespoons butter or more oil

2 tablespoons extra virgin olive oil

4 small cod steaks or any of the fish steaks listed on pages 601–602, 4 to 6 ounces each, ¾ to 1 inch thick

1 large shallot or small red onion, thinly sliced

1 tablespoon grated orange zest

1 cup freshly squeezed orange juice

Chopped fresh basil or mint leaves for garnish

1 Heat the oven to 200°F. Heat a large skillet over medium heat for 2 or 3 minutes. Season the flour with the salt, lots of black pepper, and the cayenne if you like.

2 When the skillet is hot, add the butter and olive oil. When the butter foam subsides, dredge each steak in the flour, shaking off the excess. Put them in the skillet and turn the heat up to medium-high. Cook, rotating the steaks so they brown evenly and turning after about 4 minutes. Cook for another 3 minutes or so, then check: The fish is done when a thin-bladed knife meets little resistance and little or no translucence appears in the center. Cook it for a minute or two longer if necessary, then transfer to a plate and transfer to the oven.

3 Add the shallot to the pan and cook, stirring and scraping the bottom of the pan until the shallot begins to crisp, just a minute or so. Add the zest and juice, raise the heat until the mixture bubbles, and cook, stirring occasionally, until it reduces and becomes syrupy, about 3 minutes. Taste and adjust the seasoning. Serve each steak with a spoonful of sauce and garnish with fresh basil or mint.

Crisp Cod or Other Fish Steaks in Green Sauce. Use all olive oil if you like. Instead of the shallot, zest, and juice, use 2 tablespoons minced garlic, 1 cup chopped parsley, and 1 cup dry white wine. Proceed with the recipe and serve with lemon wedges.

Crisp Cod or Other Fish Steaks with Capers and Lemon. Omit the shallot, zest, and juice. Trim the ends off 2 lemons and cut them into rounds as thinly as you can. In Step 3, add the lemon slices, 2 tablespoons drained capers, and ¼ cup dry white wine or water to the pan. Cook, scraping up the browned bits at the bottom of the pan. When the sauce has thickened a bit, pour it over the fish and serve.

Crisp Cod or Other Fish Steaks with Dill and Scallions. Omit the shallot, zest, and juice. Use cornmeal in place of flour for dredging. In Step 2, use all the olive oil to cook the fish; remove the fish. In Step 3, add 3 tablespoons chopped fresh dill and 3 tablespoons chopped scallion to the pan. Cook, stirring, over medium heat, for about 1 minute. Add ¾ cup wine, fish, vegetable, or chicken stock (to make your own, see pages 157–159), cream, or water and stir while you let most of it bubble away. Pour the sauce over the fish and serve immediately, with lemon wedges.

Halibut Steaks with Creamy Saffron Sauce

MAKES: 4 servings
TIME: 30 minutes

You can use the stand-alone sauce in this recipe with any simply cooked fish (steak or fillet), though I especially like it here, with the gentle butter-poaching technique and a delicate-tasting fish like halibut.

Other seafood you can use: any fish steaks listed on pages 601–602, any of the thick fillets on pages 585–586, or scallops or shrimp.

1 cup yogurt, preferably whole-milk

Salt and freshly ground black pepper

Small pinch cayenne

1 shallot, minced

½ teaspoon saffron threads

Juice of ½ lemon, or more to taste

About 1½ pounds halibut steaks or fillets in 2 or 4 pieces

2 tablespoons butter

1 In a small bowl, whisk the yogurt with some salt and pepper, the cayenne, and the shallot. Rub the saffron between your fingers to crush it, then stir it into the yogurt mixture. Let sit for about 20 minutes (or refrigerate for up to 2 hours). Just before serving, add the lemon juice, then taste and adjust the seasoning.

2 Sprinkle the halibut with salt and pepper. Put the butter in a large skillet over medium heat. When the butter melts, add the fish and cook gently, turning once or twice, until a thin-bladed knife meets little resistance when inserted into the thickest part; this will generally be less than 10 minutes. Serve the fish hot, warm, or at room temperature, with the sauce spooned over it.

Pan-Roasted Swordfish with Gingered Pea Purée

MAKES: 4 servings
TIME: 30 minutes

Mint and peas are a springtime cliché, and you can go that route here, but I think ginger is a more interesting counterpoint. Pan roasting begins with searing the steaks on the stovetop, then transferring them to the oven. For other ideas about what to put under pan-roasted fish, see "Serving Fish on a Bed" (page 592).

Other seafood you can use: salmon, tuna, or halibut (steaks or fillets).

2 cups fresh or frozen peas

Salt

2 tablespoons extra virgin olive oil

2 tablespoons chopped pancetta, guanciale, or bacon (optional)

About 1½ pounds swordfish steaks

Freshly ground black pepper

1 tablespoon minced fresh ginger

2 tablespoons butter

1 Heat the oven to 500°F. Cook the peas in boiling salted water until tender, just a couple of minutes. Drain them, then plunge into a bowl of ice water to stop the cooking. Drain well while you cook the fish.

2 Put the olive oil in a large ovenproof skillet over medium-high heat. If you're using the pancetta, add it now and cook for a few minutes, stirring occasionally, until it has rendered some of its fat. Raise the heat to high and add the fish; sprinkle it with salt and pepper. Cook until browned on one side, 3 to 5 minutes, then turn and transfer to the oven.

3 Mash the peas—you can use a potato masher, an immersion blender (add a tiny bit of cream or water if necessary), or a food processor—along with the ginger. Reheat with the butter, adding some salt and pepper if necessary.

4 When the fish is done—after 5 to 10 minutes of roasting (a thin-bladed knife will meet little resistance when inserted into the center)—transfer it to a plate, along with the pan juices. Spoon a bit of the pea purée onto each of 4 plates and top with a piece of the fish. Serve immediately.

Pan-Roasted Tuna Steaks

MAKES: 4 servings

TIME: 20 minutes

F

Restaurant-style seared tuna with a crisp exterior and a juicy interior. If you like, cook the fish to rare or medium-rare and slice thinly for Sushi Rolls and Bowls

(see pages 473 and 474), salads, or a sashimi-style appetizer. But you've got to use very fresh sushi-grade tuna from a reliable source.

Other protein you can use: salmon, tuna, or halibut (steaks or fillets), or even lamb.

2 tuna steaks, about 1½ pounds

Salt and freshly ground black pepper

2 tablespoons extra virgin olive oil

1 Heat the oven to 500°F. Sprinkle the fish with salt and pepper. Put a large ovenproof skillet over high heat and add the olive oil. When hot, add the fish. Cook until browned on one side, 3 to 5 minutes, then turn and transfer to the oven.

2 When the fish is done as you want it—anywhere from 3 minutes for rare to 10 minutes for cooked through (a thin-bladed knife will meet little resistance when inserted into the center)—transfer it to a plate, along with any pan juices. Serve whole, cut in half, or thinly slice and serve fanned out on a platter or individual plates so the interior is face up.

Sesame-Crusted Pan-Roasted Tuna Steaks. Use dark sesame oil instead of the olive oil. Press sesame seeds into all sides of the tuna and proceed with the recipe.

Miso-Chile Pan-Roasted Tuna Steaks. Use peanut oil instead of the olive oil and omit the salt and pepper. Make a paste of 1 cup red miso, 1 tablespoon minced fresh ginger, 1 teaspoon minced garlic, and ½ teaspoon cayenne, or to taste. Thin with a little mirin, sake, or white wine as needed, then spread the mixture all over the tuna steaks. Cover and refrigerate for up to 4 hours (up to 24 hours for lamb). Proceed with the recipe.

The Basics of Thin White Fish Fillets

What the fillets in this group have in common is the way they cook—quickly. And they have much in common

F Fast   **M** Make Ahead   **V** Vegetarian

with thick white fillets, too; sometimes, in fact, they're the same species! They are all stark white, or nearly so, and mild flavored. They are all under an inch thick, ranging from the very thin flounder and the other flatfish, which are often a $1/4$ inch or so thick, up to an inch for red snapper. They differ primarily in their texture, which ranges from extremely tender to somewhat sturdy. All of the sturdier ones (marked in the following list with a ✦) can be substituted in the recipes for the more tender ones; not vice versa, though. See the Essential Recipe on page 564 for the most basic way to prepare thin white fish fillets.

- ✦ Catfish
- ✦ Dogfish, also known as *Cape shark*

    Flatfish of any type: flounder, fluke, sole, dab, plaice

    Haddock (likely to have skin on, but it's edible)

    Large- or small-mouthed bass (freshwater)

    Pickerel (freshwater)

    Pike (freshwater)

    Ocean perch
- ✦ Red snapper or other snappers
- ✦ Rockfish of any type
- ✦ Sea bass

    Tilapia (see the sidebar at right)

    Sea trout, also known as *weakfish*
- ✦ Wolffish, also known as *ocean catfish*

    Whiting, also known as *hake*

All of these fish cook very quickly and overcook almost as fast. A $1/4$-inch-thick flounder fillet can, under the right circumstances, cook through in 2 minutes. Even a relatively thick piece of red snapper will be done in less than 10 minutes in almost every instance. How do you know when they're done?

1. For thinner fillets, less than $1/2$ thick: By the time the outside of these fillets is opaque, the inside is nearly done. This is absolutely true if you turn the fish over, as you do in a pan. But even in a broiler or oven, external opacity is a sign of internal doneness.

2. With thicker fillets, between $1/2$ and 1 inch thick: You can roughly estimate doneness by timing. About 8

minutes is the longest you want to cook any fillet under 1 inch thick. In addition, take a peek between the flakes of the fish; if most of the translucence is gone, and the fish is tender, it's done.

3. For mixed fillets, with thick and thin parts: When the thinnest part flakes, the thicker part is done. When the thicker part flakes, it's overcooked.

Remember, all food continues to cook between stovetop or oven and table, and fish is so delicate that fish that is fully cooked in the kitchen will likely be slightly overcooked in the dining room.

Crisp Sesame Fish Fillets

MAKES: 4 servings
TIME: 20 minutes

Here's an easy variation on Pan-Cooked Thin Fish Fillets (page 564) that spawns simple variations of its own. As is often the case with thin fish fillets, you're going to need to cook the fish in batches since the fillets take up so much room in the pan. Serve with Steamed Sticky Rice,

Thai Style (page 459) and Basil-Soy Dipping Sauce (page 38) for drizzling.

Other seafood you can use: skate (which may take a little longer to cook).

Four 6-ounce thin fish fillets (see page 607)

Salt and freshly ground black pepper

1 cup sesame seeds

1 tablespoon dark sesame oil

2 tablespoons butter or peanut or neutral oil like grapeseed or corn, plus more as needed

Chopped fresh parsley, cilantro, or mint leaves for garnish

Lemon or lime wedges for serving

1 Heat 4 dinner plates in a 200°F oven. Season the fillets with salt and pepper. Put the sesame seeds on a plate.

2 Put a large skillet over medium-high heat for 2 or 3 minutes. Add the sesame oil and the butter. When the butter foam subsides, dredge the fillets, one by one, in the sesame seeds, pressing them gently into the fish, then shaking off any excess, and add them to the pan. Raise the heat to high and cook the fillets until golden on each side, 4 to 5 minutes total. Transfer to the warm serving plates, garnish with herbs, and serve with lemon or lime wedges.

Crisp Sesame Fish with Soy Glaze. Add another tablespoon of sesame oil. When you remove the fish from the pan in Step 2, add it, along with $^1/_4$ cup soy sauce, $^1/_4$ cup water, and 2 tablespoons sugar. Cook, stirring and scraping up the browned bits from the pan, until the sugar dissolves, about a minute. Pour the sauce over the fish and garnish with sliced scallion and minced fresh hot chile and lime wedges if you like.

Crisp Pistachio- or Almond-Crusted Fish. Substitute extra virgin olive oil for the sesame oil and use the butter instead of peanut or neutral oil. Omit the sesame seeds and grind 1 cup pistachios or almonds into a fine powder (a food processor or blender will do the

trick). Proceed with the recipe, using the nuts to dredge the fish. Garnish with parsley and serve with Citrus Mayonnaise made with lemon zest (optional; page 42), along with lemon wedges.

Crisp Fish with Anchovy Sauce. Substitute extra virgin olive oil for the sesame oil and use the butter instead of peanut or neutral oil. Use flour to dredge the fish instead of sesame seeds. After removing the fish from the pan in Step 2, add the remaining 2 tablespoons butter, 2 or 3 anchovy fillets (packed in oil), $^1/_2$ cup dry white wine or water, and the juice of 1 lemon. Cook, stirring and mashing, until the sauce becomes smooth and fragrant. Pour the sauce over the fillets, garnish with parsley, and serve with lemon wedges.

Garlicky Lime-Cooked Fish

MAKES: 4 servings
TIME: 30 minutes

A typical Mexican beach dish, perfect with rice, beans, tortillas, and salsa. Use minced fresh chiles—like jalapeño or serrano—if you like, adding them to the pan when you add the fish or as a last-minute garnish.

Other seafood you can use: skate, thick white fillets (see page 585), shrimp, or scallops (which may take a little longer to cook).

$^1/_4$ cup neutral oil, like grapeseed or corn

5 cloves garlic, thinly sliced

Salt

Four 6-ounce thin fish fillets (see page 607)

Pinch cayenne

$^1/_2$ cup freshly squeezed lime juice (from 4 to 6 limes)

1 avocado, pitted, peeled, and cut into small dice

$^1/_2$ cup chopped fresh cilantro leaves

1 Combine 2 tablespoons of the oil with the garlic in a small, heavy saucepan over medium-low heat. Cook,

F Fast **M** Make Ahead **V** Vegetarian

Many recipes for thick fillets—and, to a lesser degree, steaks—will work for thin fillets too. All you need to do is reduce the cooking time in direct proportion to thickness; usually it will be half or even less. Since thin fillets—especially the very thin ones—are delicate, remember to use recipes that don't involve turning more than once. This makes broiling (without turning) ideal; panfrying, baking, and even short roasting or gentle poaching will also work. But save grilling, steaming, and braising for sturdy, thick fillets and whole fish.

Here are 10 recipes elsewhere in the chapter that are fine for thin, delicate fillets. Some may require less cooking time. Their variations work too.

1. Broiled Fish Fillets (and a Lot Else) (page 563)
2. Pan-Cooked Thin Fish Fillets (page 564)
3. Oven-"Fried" Fish Fillets (page 568)
4. Fish and Beans (page 587)
5. Breaded Thick Fillets, with or Without Apples (page 589)
6. Sautéed Monkfish or Thick Fillets with Fennel (page 591)
7. Seared Scallops with Pan Sauce (page 598)
8. Crisp Cod or Other Fish Steaks with Orange Sauce (page 604)
9. Halibut Steaks with Creamy Saffron Sauce (page 605)
10. Skate with Brown Butter, Honey, and Capers (page 629)

shaking the pan occasionally, until the garlic browns, 5 to 10 minutes; sprinkle with a little salt and turn off the heat.

❷ Meanwhile, put the remaining oil in a large skillet over medium-high heat. When hot, add the fish, sprinkle with salt and cayenne, and cook, undisturbed, for about 2 minutes. Reduce the heat to medium and add all but a tablespoon or two of the lime juice. Cook until the fish is cooked through, another 2 minutes or so. (Don't bother to turn thin fish fillets, but do turn a thick fillet or scallop; if you're using shrimp, stir occasionally.)

❸ Carefully transfer the fish to a platter. Stir the avocado and cilantro into the pan juices and pour the mixture over the fish, along with the garlic and its oil and the remaining lime juice. Serve immediately.

The Basics of Crab and Lobster

Crabs and lobster are delicious and treasured crustaceans, with sweet, delicious, chewy meat that is best left pretty much alone.

Crab

All crabs must be sold either live, cooked, or frozen. They can all be cooked by simple boiling: For live crabs, you need only put them in a large pot of boiling water; if they have been cooked before freezing submerge them in boiling water just long enough to heat through. Crabs also taste good cold. So you can even defrost cooked frozen king crab legs slowly in the refrigerator and serve them with any mayonnaise (see page 41) or Mustard Sauce (page 42) and have an eating experience you couldn't duplicate if you worked for two hours.

Here are the most common types:

Dungeness crab: There's nothing better than this Pacific crab, which runs from 3 to 4 pounds and tastes more like lobster than the other crabs. It's almost always cooked and refrigerated (for local sales) or frozen (for shipping) immediately after the catch. It's sold whole and is easy to eat.

Blue crab: The familiar 4- to 6-inch blue crustacean, often with red claw tips. Often sold live, it's also picked from the shell wherever it grows, to be sold throughout the country, already cooked and then refrigerated or frozen. When sold this way as picked meat, *claw* is best, *lump* means large pieces from the body, and *flake* means smaller pieces. Fresh blue crabmeat is expensive but incredibly convenient and wonderfully flavorful; with a squirt of lemon, it's celestial. Or toss it with some mild mayonnaise (to make your own, see page 41) to make a simple crab salad. Frozen, canned, and pasteurized "fresh" crabmeat are all inferior—but worth eating.

Rock crab: Similar in size and shape to blue crab, with a harder shell. Good eating; treat it like blue crab.

Soft-shell crab: Spring brings one of the best treats of all to fish counters: the live soft-shell crab. This strange delight is nothing more than a plain old blue crab, caught just after it has molted—shed—its hard outer shell. Once out of the water the crabs will not form new shells. But they live for only a couple of days and are therefore either shipped immediately, by air, or cleaned and frozen. When you get a live soft crab home, you have three choices: Clean it (your fishmonger may do this for you) and eat it, clean it and refrigerate it (which will give you a day or two to think about it, but no longer than that), or clean it and freeze it. Though soft-shells freeze fairly well, this last option is a bit wasteful since frozen soft crabs are available year-round.

Cleaning soft-shelled crab is a messy job, not for the squeamish: Use a sharp knife or scissors to cut off their faces, then scrape underneath both sides of the shell flap to remove the gills. And finally, if you want to remove the last bit of tough shell, pull off the "apron," which looks like a "T" on the male and a bell on the female; lift the "tab" on the underside and clean underneath their leathery coat of armor.

King crab: The largest crab, which may weigh 25 pounds and measure 6 feet from tip to tip. This northwestern (mostly Alaskan) delicacy is not available fresh elsewhere in the country; the crabs are cooked, dismembered, and frozen. Sometimes the legs are split, which is nice because it makes eating them so easy. But they're not difficult in any case. Two or three legs make a good serving.

Stone crab: The recyclable crab of Florida; claws are broken off by fishermen, and the crab is returned to the water, where it generates another limb (it's illegal to be in possession of whole crabs). It has a very hard shell, which is usually cracked with a small wooden mallet. Serve cold (they're usually sold cooked), with Mustard Sauce (page 42).

Note: Surimi, a processed blend of fish, sugar, and other ingredients, is sometimes made to look like crab (it's sold as *crabstick* or *imitation crab*). Unless the label says *crabmeat*—and unless it's expensive—it probably isn't.

Lobster

Almost everything you do to a lobster beyond steaming or boiling is overkill; a good, fresh, big one, not overcooked, makes butter and everything else superfluous.

Buying can be the hard part; as a friend who sells lobster for a living says, "Just because it's alive doesn't mean it's fresh." When you're buying lobster, lift each one (make sure its claws are pegged or banded); if it doesn't flip its tail and kick its legs, look for another. Tired lobsters are not fresh.

In the summer lobsters—like crabs—grow by discarding their old shells and growing new ones. But soft-shell lobsters ("shedders") have a smaller meat-to-shell ratio than hard-shells, and they fill with water as you cook them. Some people believe that soft-shells have sweeter meat, and, indeed, some are terrific, but I look for hard-shells; you can tell the difference with a little squeeze—soft shells yield to pressure.

Then there's size to consider. Lobsters grow slowly and have been overfished for decades. Consequently, there are more "chickens" (1-pounders), eighths ($1\frac{1}{8}$ pounds), and quarters ($1\frac{1}{4}$ pounds) than there are larger lobsters. But, in my experience, two people sharing a

F Fast   **M** Make Ahead   **V** Vegetarian

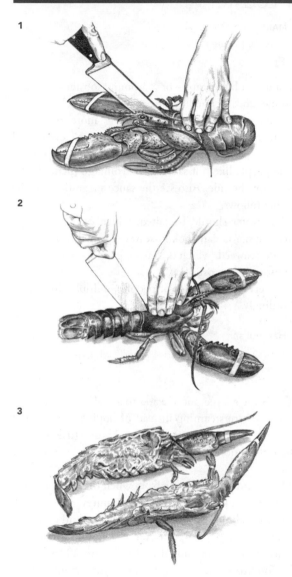

(STEP 1) Before grilling or stir-frying, you can kill a lobster by parboiling it for a couple of minutes (see page 612), or you can simply plunge a heavy knife right into the "crosshairs" behind the head. (STEP 2) Cut up through the head and down through the tail. (STEP 3) Your final product will look like this.

3-pound lobster will get more meat of equally high quality than if each has his or her own 1½-pound lobster. There's less work, less waste, and more meat hidden in those out-of-the-way places.

Should you boil or steam? It doesn't matter much. If you're cooking one batch of lobsters—whatever fits in your pot—steam them; it's easier and, because the lobster absorbs less water, far less messy. But lobsters flavor the cooking water (you should consider saving it as broth), which in turn flavors the lobsters. So if you're cooking a bunch, boil them. And eat the last of the batch yourself—or be generous, as you like. As for other cooking methods, grilling, stir-frying, roasting, and broiling are all good options (but you have to be bored with steaming or boiling to bother).

To kill a lobster before cooking, as you do for any method other than steaming or boiling, use a thin, sturdy, pointed knife to poke a hole behind the lobster's eyes, right at the "crosshairs." It's also good to do this after boiling, then to drain out the water that's accumulated in the beast. As an added refinement, you might also crack the claws (with a nutcracker, small hammer, or the back of a chef's knife) and split the tail before taking the lobster to the table. All of this, along with eating instructions, is illustrated on page 613.

There are few parts of a lobster that you can't eat. If you split the lobster for grilling, you can remove and discard the head sac before cooking. You can also remove the tomalley (the green, liverlike organ) and—in female lobsters—the coral (the very dark red eggs, which turn bright red after cooking) to use raw in sauces. Otherwise, just remove the head sac after boiling.

Finally, there is the spiny lobster, also called *Florida lobster, rock lobster,* or, in Florida, *crawfish.* These lobsters and their related species are available worldwide, and it is their tails that are frozen to become the ubiquitous "lobster tails." With no claws, these babies are far simpler to eat than northern lobsters. They're not bad at all and can be used in any recipe for lobster, shrimp, or crawfish.

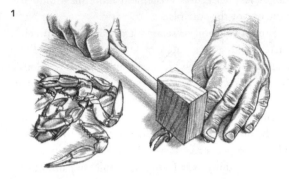

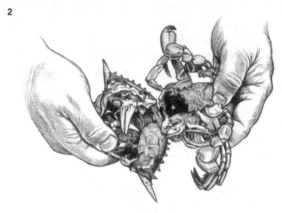

(STEP 1) Twist off the claws and break them open with a mallet or nutcracker to pick and suck out the meat. (STEP 2) Break off the apron, then pull off the top shell. Rub off the feather gills. (STEP 3) Break the body in two; then break it in two again. Go to work, picking and sucking that meat out.

Boiled or Steamed Crab or Lobster

MAKES: 1 or 2 servings
TIME: 10 minutes

Put a dozen blue crabs—or a 3-pound lobster—in front of someone, and you'll be amazed at how much one person can eat. Crabs require nothing more than salt, lemon, or melted butter, and lobsters don't even need that—but see the variation if you want something jazzier. Some people like hot sauce or mayonnaise (plain or flavored) on the side. Also see the sauce suggestions in the list that follows.

The water should be salted, which can be done in three ways: You can cook in seawater, which is nice; you can add seaweed, which is charming (and works); or you can use salt, as most of us do.

To serve any number of people, multiply this recipe accordingly.

Handful salt

6 to 12 blue or rock crabs or 1 or 2 lobsters, about 3 pounds total

1 Bring a large pot of water to a boil (or just an inch or so if you're steaming instead of boiling); salt it. Put the crabs or lobster in the pot one by one (use tongs—when they don't try to pinch you, they're probably dead).

2 Count cooking time from when the water returns to a boil: Cook crabs for about 5 minutes, or until red; lobster for about 8 minutes for its first pound and then an additional 3 or 4 minutes per pound thereafter. (Thus a 3-pounder should boil for 15 to 20 minutes.) The foolproof way to check doneness (essential with larger lobsters) is to insert an instant-read thermometer into the tail meat by sliding it in between the underside of the body and the tail joint; lobster is done at 140°F. Drain in a colander for a few minutes and eat, cool and eat later, or remove the meat from the shells to use for

 Fast   Make Ahead   Vegetarian

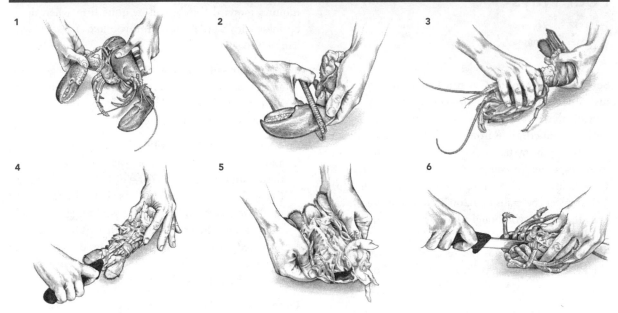

(STEP 1) Twist the claws to remove them; they will come off easily. (STEP 2) Use a nutcracker to split their shells and a pick to pull out the meat. (STEP 3) Twist the lobster in half to separate the tail from the body. (STEPS 4–5) Cut through the soft side of the tail and crack it open like a shrimp to remove the tail meat. (STEP 6) Cut through the underside of the front part of the body to extract the meat there.

something else. (If you'd like to drain the water accumulated in the lobster shell, poke a hole in the crosshairs right behind the eyes and drain out the water.)

❸ To eat crabs and lobster, see the illustrations above and on the previous page.

Spicy Crab or Lobster Boil. To 1 gallon of well-salted water, add 2 roughly chopped onions; 2 roughly chopped celery stalks; the juice of 2 limes or $1/4$ cup white wine vinegar; 1 tablespoon fresh thyme leaves or 1 teaspoon dried thyme; 1 teaspoon ground allspice; 2 dried or fresh hot chiles or 1 teaspoon cayenne; 1 tablespoon paprika; and 1 teaspoon freshly ground black pepper. Bring to a boil and let bubble for 15 minutes before adding the shellfish and finishing as directed.

6 Unusual Dipping Sauces for Any Simply Cooked Crab or Lobster

1. Soy Dipping Sauce and Marinade (page 25)
2. Cilantro (or Other Herb) Sauce (page 28)
3. Basil-Soy Dipping Sauce (page 38)
4. Thai Chile Sauce (page 39)
5. Simple Miso Dipping Sauce (page 39)
6. Any of the flavored mayonnaises on page 42 (best with cold crab or lobster)

Sautéed Soft-Shell Crabs, Four Ways

MAKES: 4 servings
TIME: 30 minutes

Soft-shell crabs contain so much moisture that they're just about impossible to overcook, and they cook so quickly they're difficult to undercook. Plus, they have both built-in crispness from the shell (which is delicious) and a sweet, briny flavor. So they need no further adornment, especially if you make the buttery variation. But you can always make a Five-Minute Drizzle Sauce (page 22); transfer the crabs to a 200°F oven and use the same pan. If the crab you bought hasn't been cleaned, see the directions on page 610.

Other protein you can use: shrimp or boneless chicken breasts or thighs (just cook them about twice as long).

Neutral oil, like grapeseed or corn, as needed

2 eggs

2 cups milk

1 cup cornmeal

1 cup all-purpose flour

$^1/_2$ teaspoon cayenne, or more to taste

Salt

4 large soft-shell crabs, cleaned

Lemon wedges for serving

1 Put about $^1/_4$ inch of oil in a deep skillet broad enough to accommodate the crabs over medium heat. Beat the eggs and milk together in a bowl. Combine the cornmeal, flour, cayenne, and a large pinch of salt on a plate.

2 When the oil is hot—a pinch of flour will sizzle—dip the crabs in the egg mixture, then dredge in the cornmeal mixture, shaking to remove the excess. Put in the skillet; adjust the heat so the crabs bubble gently but not furiously in the oil.

3 When the bottoms are nicely browned, 3 to 5 minutes, turn the crabs and brown the other side, about 3 minutes more; the crabs will be quite firm when done. Sprinkle with a little more salt if you like and serve with lemon wedges.

Simplest Sautéed Soft-Shell Crabs. Omit the egg, milk, and cornmeal. In Step 2, when the oil is hot, dredge the crabs in the seasoned flour, shake a bit to remove the excess, and cook as directed.

Breaded Sautéed Soft-Shell Crabs. Omit the cornmeal and use 1 cup bread crumbs—panko are nice, or use fresh crumbs (see page 876)—or fine cracker crumbs (try graham crackers for a fun switch): In Step 1, set up the seasoned flour in one bowl, the egg mixture in another, and the crumbs in another. When the oil is hot, dredge the crabs first in the flour, then in the egg mixture, then in the crumbs, patting them to make them adhere. Proceed with the recipe.

Buttery Sautéed Soft-Shell Crabs. Use butter to cook the crabs; just let it melt in the pan in Step 2. You could use as much as a stick. Be sure to pour the pan juices over the crabs when you serve them. Garnish with chopped fresh parsley if you like.

Grilled or Broiled Soft-Shell Crab or Lobster

MAKES: 4 servings
TIME: 30 minutes

Soft-shell crabs are among the easiest things in the world to grill or broil; they don't even need brushing with oil. But since grilling whole lobsters is far from foolproof, I always split them and remove the inedible parts. See the instructions on page 611.

4 large soft-shell crabs, about 1 pound each (or more smaller ones) or 4 lobsters, about $1^1/_2$ pounds each

F Fast   **M** Make Ahead   **V** Vegetarian

Salt and freshly ground black pepper

Lemon quarters and/or melted butter for serving

1 Heat a charcoal or gas grill or the broiler until moderately hot and put the rack at least 4 inches from the heat source.

2 Kill the crabs as described on page 610 or lobsters as illustrated on page 611. If you're using lobster, cut them in half and remove the head sac. You can leave the coral and tomalley (see page 611) in the body or remove and reserve them for sauces.

3 Grill or broil the crab for 3 to 4 minutes per side; lobster for about 5 minutes on each side, starting with the cut side up, sprinkling them with salt and pepper before turning. Crabs should be firm to the touch, and lobster meat is done when firm and opaque. Serve with lemon quarters and/or melted butter.

Broiled Stuffed Lobster

MAKES: 4 servings
TIME: 30 minutes

F

No "baked stuffed lobster" you've ever had in a restaurant can match this, the crisp, seasoned bread crumbs providing a nice foil for the sweet lobster meat.

4 lobsters, about 1¼ pounds each

1 clove garlic, peeled

1 cup fresh parsley leaves

Salt and freshly ground black pepper

¾ cup extra virgin olive oil, plus more if needed

2 tablespoons freshly squeezed lemon juice, plus more if needed

2 cups bread crumbs, preferably fresh (page 876)

1 Kill the lobsters as illustrated on page 611; cut them in half, then remove the head sac. Remove and reserve the tomalley and coral if any (see page 611). Heat the broiler and put the rack about 6 to 8 inches from the heat source.

2 Combine the garlic, parsley, some salt and pepper, the olive oil, lemon juice, and any tomalley and coral in a food processor and process until smooth. Add the bread crumbs and pulse a couple times to combine. Add a little more olive oil or lemon juice if the mixture seems dry. Stuff the lobsters' body cavities with this mixture and broil until the tail meat is white and firm and the stuffing nicely browned, 5 to 10 minutes. (If the lobster is browning too quickly, either move it farther from the heat source or turn off the broiler and turn the oven heat to 500°F to finish the cooking.) Serve.

Broiled Lobster with Vanilla Stuffing. A surprising combination: Omit the garlic, parsley, and lemon juice. Substitute softened butter for the oil. Scrape the seeds from a vanilla bean (see page 961) and, in Step 2, combine it in the food processor along with the butter, salt, pepper, tomalley, and coral.

Steamed Dungeness Crab with Tomatoes and Basil

MAKES: 4 servings
TIME: 40 minutes

Even though virtually all Dungeness crab—outside of Alaska or the Pacific Northwest—is already cooked, it's okay to cook it lightly again. (If you can find raw crab, cook it the same way.) This dish puts a fresh spin on the Italian and Italian-American slow-cooked fish stew known as *cioppino*. Serve this with lots of sourdough bread for sopping up the sauce.

2 tablespoons extra virgin olive oil

1 white or red onion, halved and thinly sliced

1 tablespoon minced garlic

Salt

Cayenne, to taste

1 cup dry white wine

6 cups chopped tomato (drained canned is fine)

2 to 4 Dungeness crabs, depending on their size, broken or hacked into large pieces

1 cup chopped or julienned fresh basil leaves

Freshly ground black pepper

❶ Put the oil in a large pot with a tight-fitting lid or a Dutch oven over medium-high heat. When hot, add the onion and garlic, sprinkle with salt and cayenne, and cook, stirring frequently, until soft and turning golden, about 3 minutes. Add the wine and let half of it bubble off, a couple minutes more.

❷ Add the tomato and give the mixture a good stir, mashing the tomato down a bit. Put the crabs on top, cover, and reduce the heat to medium-low, so the mixture bubbles steadily. Cook until the crabs are hot all the way through and the tomato is saucy, about 15 minutes.

❸ Remove the lid, stir in the basil and a good grinding of black pepper, taste and adjust the seasoning, and serve.

The Basics of Clams, Mussels, and Oysters

Mollusks, they're called, and they're among the tastiest sea creatures that exist. Clams and oysters, of course, are often eaten raw (mussels are not), though clams are equally good cooked. (I think oysters are at their best raw, but I'm not against cooking them.)

Buying fresh mollusks is easy, since those in the shell must be alive. When hard-shell clams, mussels, or oysters die, you can easily move their shells apart; otherwise, they're shut up pretty tight, and usually you cannot even slide their shells from side to side. If they are open a little, then they should close quickly when tapped lightly. Live soft-shell clams ("steamers") react visibly to your touch, retracting their necks and closing slightly (they are never closed all the way—hence their nickname,

"gapers"). Dead mollusks smell pretty bad, so it's unlikely you'll be fooled.

Never store clams, mussels, or oysters in sealed plastic (or plastic bags) or under water; they'll die. Just keep them in a bowl in the refrigerator, where they will remain alive for several days (in the old days, oysters were kept alive for months in barrels).

Though they have different flavor, texture, and appearance, clams, mussels, and oysters can all be prepared the same way: You cook them until their shells open, or you shuck them to remove their shells and cook them as you would other fish.

Clams

Clams range from little ("littlenecks") to sea clams that weigh hundreds of pounds; they may be hard (littlenecks, cherrystones, or quahogs), or soft (steamers, razor clams, and other clams with fragile shells). The biggest and toughest are chopped into bits to be made into chowder. The choicest—essentially the smallest—are sold live and are great raw or briefly cooked.

Clams may be dug at any time of year, but since it's easier to dig in the summer months, they may be more plentiful and less expensive at that time. Commercially harvested clams are shipped with a certification tag, which you can ask to see when you buy—and you should if you don't know the dealer. Eating raw clams may be risky; see the general discussion on food safety on page 3.

Steamers and other soft-shell clams (which are hard to find any distance from their source) usually contain large quantities of sand, and you must wash them well before cooking (soft-shells are never eaten raw). Hard-shells require little more than scrubbing their shells with a stiff brush under running water. To shuck them for serving raw or cooking out of the shell, see the illustrated steps that follow. Hard-shells are also nice lightly steamed, like mussels, especially the smaller ones. The freshest clams need only lemon; sauces are superfluous.

SHUCKING CLAMS

To open a clam, you must use a blunt, fairly thick knife; there is a knife made specifically for this purpose (called, not surprisingly, a *clam knife*), and it's worth having for this chore. Hold the clam in your cupped hand and wedge the edge of the knife into the clam's shell opposite the hinge. Once you get it in there, the clam will give up all resistance.

Run the knife along the shell and open up the clam. Try to keep as much juice inside the shell as you can. Detach the meat from the shell and serve.

Mussels

Mussels are usually less expensive than clams and can be heavenly. They come from everywhere, from Maine to New Zealand. I prefer wild to cultivated mussels, but definite strides have been made in farm-raising mussels, so I don't fuss much about it. And farmed mussels are cleaner and require only thorough rinsing.

In fact, the only disadvantage to wild mussels lies in cleaning them. If you have the time, let them sit in a pot under slowly running cold water for 30 minutes or so. Then scrub the mussels carefully, discarding any with broken shells, those whose shells remain open after being tapped lightly, and those that seem unusually heavy (chances are they're filled with mud). As you clean them, pull or scrape off the "beard"—the weedy growth attached to the bottom of shell—from each one. Rinse thoroughly.

REMOVING A MUSSEL BEARD

Most mussels have a "beard," a small amount of vegetative growth extending from their flat side. Pull or cut it off before cooking.

Oysters

The best oysters should be eaten raw; they can be cooked, of course, but they lose something in the translation. Nevertheless some—especially huge ones from warm water—are better cooked.

Oysters are perfectly safe year-round, but they really *are* best in months whose names contain an *r* and, if you want to eat only the best oysters, in winter. At that time, few species are spawning, and the water in the best beds—the northernmost beds—is as cold as it gets before icy waters make harvesting difficult or impossible. And cold water means peak flavor.

There are five major species of oysters seen in the United States: the familiar Atlantic (*Crassostrea virginica*), known for its brininess and grown all along the Atlantic and Gulf coasts; the Pacific (*Crassostrea gigas*), known for its wildly scalloped shell and fruity flavors; the Belon or European (*Ostrea edulis*), a round, metallic-tasting, flat-shelled oyster grown in Western Europe and sometimes here; the Olympia (*Ostrea lurida*), the half-dollar-sized oyster that is indigenous to the Northwest and grown only there; and the kumamoto, a Japanese variety (a subvariety of the Pacific) that's become popular on the West Coast.

Within each species, there are nicknames: The Atlantic is not only called the *Eastern* but is casually referred to by many of its places of harvesting, especially Bluepoint, Wellfleet, and Apalachicola; the European is known as the *flat* (*plat* in French); and the Pacific, which is also grown in Europe, is sometimes called a *Portuguese* (*Portugaise*), from a now-extinct species that once made up the majority of oysters grown in Europe.

Nomenclature is confusing but important, because each of the species is markedly different from the others. Even within a species the differences between a northern and a southern oyster can be profound, because much of the distinctive flavor of a given oyster comes from its habitat. If you're eating oysters on the half-shell, learn to recognize your favorite; I strongly believe that the best oysters come from the coldest waters, so I look for those. If you're cooking oysters, the differences are not as important.

Buying and Serving Raw Oysters

Buying oysters for cooking is easy; you can use those that have been shucked, packaged, and marked with a sell-by date. But for oysters on the half-shell, you first have to determine which oyster you like and then make sure the shells are undamaged and shut tight. To clean them, just scrub the shells thoroughly with a not-too-stiff brush. There's never any sand inside.

Shucking is the truly difficult part; illustrations follow, but also ask your fishmonger if he can do it for you. Keep them on a bed of crushed ice and eat them within a couple of hours.

1

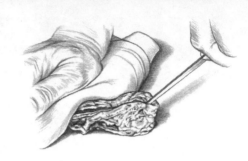

2

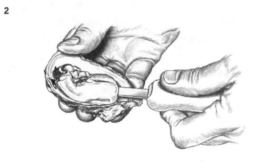

You can use an oyster knife, a can opener, or any sturdy (but preferably not too sharp) knife to open an oyster. The danger is in slipping, so protect your hand with a towel or glove. (**STEP 1**) Place the oyster, cupped side down, on a flat surface and insert the knife into the hinge. Press and wiggle and twist that knife in there until the oyster pops. Twist off the top shell, trying to keep as much juice inside as possible. (**STEP 2**) Detach the meat from the shell and serve.

To serve oysters on the half-shell, use any condiment you like. I prefer nothing at all, or at most a squeeze of lemon. But many people prefer freshly ground black pepper, Tabasco sauce, or shrimp cocktail sauce (see Shrimp Cocktail, page 87). Another possibility is a flavored vinegar called *mignonette*: Make this by combining a teaspoon of coarsely ground black pepper, a tablespoon of minced shallot, and ¹/₂ cup good-quality champagne or white wine vinegar.

F Fast   **M** Make Ahead   **V** Vegetarian

Steamed Clams or Mussels, Unleashed

MAKES: 4 servings
TIME: 30 minutes

The simplest way to steam clams and mussels is to put them in a pot with some water. But it's not that much harder to build in added flavors; you can vary the aromatic vegetables, the liquid, and even the last-minute stir-ins (see the chart on page 620).

When you're done, there's almost a whole meal in the pot. All you need is some bread or simply cooked rice, grain, or potatoes to sop up the broth. Or you can ladle spoonfuls over a bowl of pasta. Serve leftover clams or mussels cold in salads or spreads.

Other seafood you can use: in-shell scallops or oysters.

2 tablespoons extra virgin olive oil

1 large shallot or small red onion, chopped

$1/2$ cup white wine, beer (ale is nice), or water

4 to 6 pounds clams or mussels, well washed

Fresh parsley leaves or sprigs for garnish

Lemon wedges for serving

1 Put the oil in a saucepan large enough to hold all the clams or mussels over medium heat. When hot, add the shallot and cook, stirring occasionally, until it begins to soften, 5 minutes.

2 Add the liquid along with the clams or mussels, turn the heat up to high, and cover the pot. Cook, shaking the pot occasionally, until they all (or nearly all) open, about 10 minutes. Turn off the heat.

3 Scoop the clams into a serving bowl. Remove as many shallots as you can with a slotted spoon and scatter them on top. Pour or ladle off the accumulated liquid, leaving any sediment in the bottom of the pan, and pour it over the clams. Garnish with parsley and serve with the lemon wedges.

Grilled Clams, Mussels, or Oysters

MAKES: 4 appetizer servings
TIME: 30 minutes

Use all one type of seafood or a mixture. This can also be made in a very hot oven, in which case it's called a pan-roast. Long tongs are a must here so you can move the hot shells around.

Other seafood you can use: shell-on or peeled shrimp, in-shell scallops.

30 to 40 clams or mussels or 24 oysters, well washed

4 tablespoons ($1/2$ stick) butter

Tabasco or other hot sauce, to taste (optional)

Freshly squeezed lemon juice, to taste

1 Heat a charcoal or gas grill until quite hot or heat the oven to 500°F. When the fire is hot, put the seafood on the grill or put them in a basket and put the basket on the grill. (If you're using the oven, put them in a roasting pan and slide it into the oven.)

2 Melt the butter in a small saucepan over low heat, add the hot sauce and the lemon juice, and let it sizzle for a couple of minutes over low heat.

3 As the clams open—some will take a minute or two, others several—transfer them to a platter and move the more stubborn members to hotter parts of the fire. Try to keep the liquor in the shells of those that open, but don't be a fanatic about it; you're bound to lose some. When they're all cooked, drizzle the seasoned butter over them and take to the table. Be careful: The hot shells can be damaging to careless lips. Use a small knife to open any clams that may have remained closed; as long as they were alive to begin with, they are perfectly safe.

Grilled Oysters, California Style. Shuck the oysters, saving as much liquid in the bottom shells as possible, along with the oysters. Discard the top shells. Melt the but-

6 WAYS TO VARY STEAMED CLAMS OR MUSSELS

The timing and procedure remain the same as in the main recipe. What changes are the flavors, and obviously there are far more possibilities than those outlined here.

VARIATION	FAT (INSTEAD OF THE OLIVE OIL)	AROMATICS (INSTEAD OF THE SHALLOT)	LIQUID	STIR-IN (WITH CLAMS OR MUSSELS)	GARNISH
Steamed Clams or Mussels with Tomatoes	Use the olive oil.	Lots of chopped garlic: 6 cloves	1 cup chopped tomato (partially drained canned is fine)	A sprig of fresh thyme or a couple of bay leaves	Chopped fresh parsley or basil and Fried Bread Crumbs (page 876; optional)
Steamed Clams or Mussels, French Style	Butter	2 or 3 shallots, 2 or 3 cloves garlic (optional)	Dry white or fruity red wine	½ cup cream	Chopped fresh chervil or parsley
Soy-Steamed Clams or Mussels	Peanut or neutral oil, like grapeseed or corn	¼ cup chopped scallion, 1 tablespoon minced fresh ginger	2 tablespoons soy sauce plus ½ cup sake or water	Minced fresh chiles (like Thai or serrano) or hot red pepper flakes, to taste	Chopped shiso leaves (optional)
Steamed Clams or Mussels, Thai Style	Peanut or neutral oil, like grapeseed or corn	2 stalks lemongrass, trimmed, smashed, and roughly chopped; 1 fresh or dried chile	Juice of 1 lime plus ½ cup water	1 tablespoon nam pla (Thai fish sauce), ½ cup chopped fresh Thai basil	More Thai basil and lime wedges
Steamed Clams or Mussels with Something Meaty	Some chopped bacon, ham, prosciutto, or spicy sausage, cooked in olive oil until crisp (drain off some fat afterward if you like)	1 small yellow or ½ sweet onion, chopped	½ cup white wine, ale, or water	Nothing	Chopped fresh parsley or chives
Steamed Clams or Mussels in Curry Broth	Butter or neutral oil, like grapeseed or corn	Lots of fresh ginger: a 2-inch piece, minced; 2 tablespoons curry powder (to make your own, see pages 66–67)	1 cup coconut milk (to make your own, see page 389)	Diced carrot, or peas, or parboiled potato (optional)	Chopped fresh cilantro

 F Fast   **M** Make Ahead   **V** Vegetarian

ter with 1 cup barbecue sauce (to make your own, see page 52) and add hot sauce—or a little horseradish or lemon juice—if you like. Put the oysters, face up, on the grill. When the liquid starts to bubble and the oysters begin to cook, put a spoonful of sauce on top of each. They're done when the sauce dries out a bit and the oysters start to turn opaque—just a few minutes. Serve with oyster crackers or crusty bread.

Baked Clams with Wasabi Bread Crumbs

MAKES: 4 main-dish or 6 to 8 appetizer servings
TIME: About 1 hour

Clams Casino are ubiquitous—and often mediocre—baked stuffed clams. These are far more interesting and just as easy. Serve with Cold Soba Noodles with Dipping Sauce (page 553) and thick tomato slices and you have a meal. Or they make relatively fancy appetizers or party food.

Other seafood you can use: shucked mussels or oysters (cut the recipe in half if you like).

24 clams, well washed

2 tablespoons dark sesame oil

2 cups panko

2 teaspoons wasabi powder, or to taste

2 tablespoons chopped fresh chives

1/4 cup soy sauce, or to taste

Salt and freshly ground black pepper

Lemon wedges for serving

① Heat the oven to 450°F. Shuck the clams, reserving half the shells and as much of the liquor as possible. (If you're not confident about shucking, steam the clams lightly, removing them the second their shells begin to open and preserving as much of their liquid as possible. You can also microwave, again removing them the second they begin opening.) Chop the clams (I suggest by hand, but you can use a mini food processor if you are careful not to overprocess).

② Heat the sesame oil in a medium skillet over medium heat. Add the panko and cook, stirring, just until the crumbs begin to brown a bit. Add the wasabi and cook, stirring, until fragrant, just a minute or two. Off the heat, stir in the chives. Add the reserved liquor and the soy sauce, a little at a time, to moisten the mixture. Fold in the chopped clam meat and taste, adding more wasabi, soy, or a sprinkle of salt and pepper as needed.

③ Stuff the shells with this mixture, put them on a baking sheet or roasting pan, and bake until lightly browned, about 10 minutes. Serve hot or warm, with lemon wedges.

Oysters and Potatoes, Stewed in Cream

MAKES: 4 servings
TIME: 30 minutes

Perhaps the most luxurious dish in the chapter; adding cream to oysters is gilding the lily, but hey—once in a while? Many stewed oyster recipes start with cooked flour for thickening, but I like the potatoes as both a companion for the oysters and a subtle thickener.

Other seafood you can use: cod or other thick white fillets or steaks.

1 pound small waxy potatoes, halved

Salt

3 tablespoons butter

2 or 3 shallots, sliced

Freshly ground black pepper

1/2 cup white wine or sherry

2 cups cream

16 to 24 shucked oysters, liquid reserved

1 tablespoon chopped fresh tarragon leaves or 2 tablespoons chopped fresh chives or chervil

1 Put the potatoes in a pot with a tight-fitting lid. Add enough water to cover and a pinch of salt; bring to a boil. Reduce the heat so the water bubbles vigorously and cook, stirring once or twice, until just barely tender at the center; a small knife will still meet some resistance when inserted. Drain, reserving the liquid. When it settles a bit, pour off the top so that about 2 cups of the starchiest liquid remains.

2 Return the pot to medium heat (no need to wipe it out) and add the butter. When it foams, add the shallots, sprinkle with salt and pepper, and cook, stirring, until soft and golden, about 3 minutes. Raise the heat a bit and add the wine, stir until it almost all bubbles away, about a minute, then add the cream, the reserved oyster and potato liquids, and the potatoes. Bring the mixture just to a boil, stirring occasionally to prevent sticking, then lower the heat so it barely bubbles.

3 Slip the oysters into the pot, cover, and turn off the heat. After 5 minutes, take a peek; the oysters should be turning opaque; if not, put the lid on for another minute or two. Sprinkle the tarragon on top and give the mixture a good stir. Taste and adjust the seasoning and serve.

The Basics of Mackerel, Bluefish, and Like Fish

These fish are a special case, because their flesh is dark, oily, and quite flavorful—they're not unlike tuna (and some, like mackerel, are closely related), but they haven't become as popular. Some prejudice against these fish stems from the fact that their high fat content allows them to spoil quickly. But this also gives them great flavor (and means they're high in beneficial omega-3 fatty acids). Other fish that fall into this category and can be used in these recipes are shad, bonito, mullet, king or Spanish mackerel, and pompano. Tuna is also similar as is, to some extent, mahi-mahi. Sardines and oysters have the same characteristics but must for the most part must be cooked differently since they're so small.

25 Seafood Recipes Elsewhere in This Book

F Fast   **M** Make Ahead   **V** Vegetarian

Mackerel is one of the prettiest fish there is and one of the tastiest, cheapest, and still most plentiful. Make sure, though, that it's in good shape: Even more than most fish, mackerel is best eaten when it is super-fresh. It does not freeze well, and its quality deteriorates rapidly once the fish is out of water. Newcomers should try it in the first recipe here, a classic Japanese teriyaki-style dish that is perfectly suited to mackerel and other dark-fleshed fish, whose rich flavor is nicely cut by the sharp taste of soy, vinegar, and ginger.

Mackerel Fillets Simmered in Soy Sauce

MAKES: 4 servings
TIME: 20 minutes

What you're doing here is poaching in a flavorful soy sauce broth. Oily, dark-fleshed fish are perfect for this treatment, though I've had surprisingly good results with sturdy mild fish and even shrimp. You really must serve this Japanese-style dish over white or brown rice.

Other seafood you can use: bluefish, shark, sardines, any sturdy thick or thin fillet (see the lists on pages 585 and 607), salmon or halibut (fillets or steaks), shrimp, or octopus (let the octopus simmer until it's done, which could be up to 45 minutes or more).

3/4 cup soy sauce

1/2 cup sake, dry sherry, or water

1 tablespoon sugar, plus more to taste

3 tablespoons rice or white wine vinegar

6 or 7 thin slices fresh ginger

5 or 6 cloves garlic, crushed

About 1 1/2 pounds mackerel fillets, skin on

Finely grated fresh ginger or lemon zest for garnish

❶ Mix the soy sauce, sake, sugar, vinegar, ginger, garlic, and 3/4 cup water together in a large skillet. Bring to a boil and simmer over medium heat for about 5 minutes.

❷ Add the fish skin side down and simmer until the fish is cooked through, 7 to 10 minutes. (You can hasten the cooking a bit by covering the pan, but it isn't necessary.) The fish is done when the flesh turns opaque and the tip of a sharp knife inserted into the thickest part meets little resistance. Spoon a serving of fish and some sauce onto a mound of white rice; garnish and serve.

Sake-Simmered Fish. Lighter and perfect for delicate-flavored fish: Reduce the soy sauce to just 2 tablespoons. Increase the sake to 1 1/4 cups. Proceed with the recipe, adding a sprinkle of salt and pepper to the simmering liquid if you like.

Simmered Fish, Vietnamese Style. Omit all the ingredients for the simmering liquid except the garlic. In Step 1, combine 1/4 cup each sugar, nam pla (Thai fish sauce), and water in the skillet. When the sugar dissolves and the mixture bubbles, add 1/4 cup minced lemongrass, along with the garlic and a generous sprinkle of black pepper. Bring to a boil and then simmer for 3 minutes. Add the fish and 1/2 cup chopped scallion and proceed with the recipe. Taste and sprinkle with salt if necessary. Garnish with chopped fresh cilantro and peanuts.

Marinated Mackerel

Escabeche

MAKES: 4 servings
TIME: 45 minutes, plus time to cool

Like pickling, only the fish is breaded and lightly fried before marinating. The results are flavorful, unusual, and excellent for parties or picnics since it's one of the rare fish dishes that you can—and should—make well in advance.

Other seafood you can use: bluefish, shark, sardines, any sturdy thick or thin fillet (see the lists on pages 585 and 607), or salmon or halibut (fillets or steaks).

³/₄ cup extra virgin olive oil

About 1¹/₂ pounds mackerel fillets, skin on or off

All-purpose flour for dredging

Salt and freshly ground black pepper

10 cloves garlic, lightly crushed

2 bay leaves

5 sprigs fresh thyme or 1 teaspoon dried thyme

¹/₂ teaspoon cayenne, or to taste

1 cup red wine vinegar or other vinegar

1 cup dry red wine

❶ Put about ¹/₂ cup of the oil in a large nonreactive skillet over medium-high heat. When hot, dredge the fillets lightly in the flour and add them, one at a time, to the skillet. Do not crowd; it's likely you'll have to cook in batches. Sprinkle the fillets with salt and pepper as they cook. As the fillets brown, turn them and brown the other side. The total cooking time for each fillet will be about 6 minutes. Once the fish turns opaque, poke the thickest part of the fillet with the point of a small, sharp knife. When that point meets little resistance, the fish is done. Transfer the fillets as they finish to a platter or gratin dish; they may overlap slightly.

❷ Let the pan cool and wipe it out. Add the remaining oil and turn the heat down to medium. When hot, add the garlic and cook, stirring occasionally, until it begins to turn color. Add the bay leaves, thyme, and cayenne and stir; add the vinegar, bring to a boil, and simmer for a minute. Add the wine, bring back to a boil, and simmer for about 5 minutes. Add 1 cup water, bring back to a boil, and cook quickly to reduce the mixture to about half its volume, about 15 minutes.

❸ Pour the liquid over the fish. Let cool to room temperature and serve or cover and refrigerate (the escabeche will remain good for at least a couple of days; bring back to room temperature before serving).

The Basics of Squid and Octopus

Both of these cephalopods (the word essentially means that their feet grow out of their heads) are increasingly popular, but mostly in restaurants. It's a shame; they're not hard to cook, they're relatively inexpensive, and they're among the best-flavored kinds of seafood.

Squid, in the form of fried calamari, is ubiquitous in restaurants. But you can easily cook it at home. Like shrimp, squid freezes well and can be defrosted and refrozen with little loss of flavor or texture. Frozen squid, typically cleaned before freezing, is available in supermarkets all over the country, frequently for a few dollars a pound. Fresh squid should be purple to white, not brown, with a clean, sweet smell (spoiled squid smells particularly foul). Increasingly you can buy cleaned fresh squid; if you need to clean it yourself, see the next page.

Cooking squid is all about speed; like scallops and shrimp, it's almost impossible to undercook. When I was learning about squid, the old-timers would say, "Cook it for 2 minutes or 2 hours," and that advice is just about right. From hitting the heat to turning opaque—a sign that it's done—squid usually takes no more than a couple of minutes.

After that, it becomes tough, and it takes long cooking with liquid for it to become tender again. In braised dishes, after 30 to 60 minutes of cooking, toughness is no longer a concern. But take care not to cook longer than necessary because, when the squid has lost all of its water (about two-thirds of its total weight), it can become quite dry.

Most octopus is cleaned and frozen at sea; defrost it in the refrigerator or in cold water.

Nearly everyone will tell you that octopus must be "tenderized" before cooking, and nearly everyone has some odd method of doing so—dipping it into boiling water three times, kneading it with grated radish, or hurling it against a stand of rocks (or, more likely, the kitchen sink). The reality is that some octopus is more tender than others (generally, smaller ones are more tender than larger, but not always), so I don't pretenderize; instead, I

❺ Fast   Ⓜ Make Ahead   Ⓥ Vegetarian

CLEANING SQUID

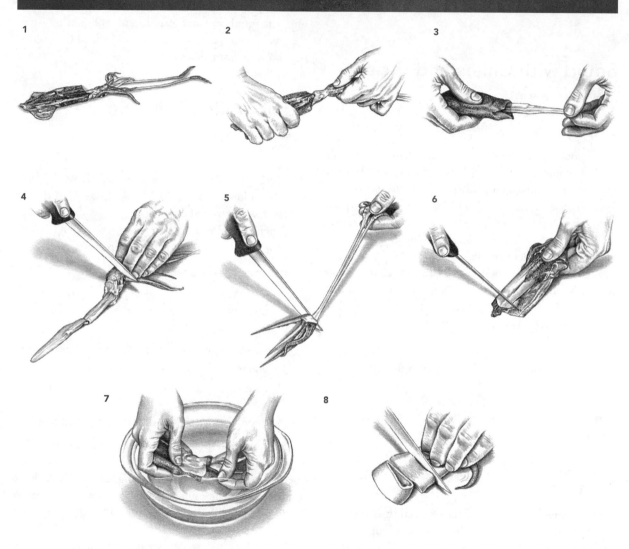

(STEPS 1-2) Pull off the tentacles and head; they'll come out in one piece. (STEP 3) Reach inside the body, pull out the hard, plasti-clike quill, and discard. (STEP 4) Cut the tentacles from the head and discard the head and the hard, ball-shaped beak inside it. (STEP 5) You may remove any longish tentacles if you find them offensive, although they're perfectly edible. (STEP 6) Peel off the skin, using a knife if necessary (your fingernails will likely be enough). (STEP 7) Alternatively, submerge the squid in a bowl of water, which may make skinning it easier. (STEP 8) To make squid rings, simply cut across the cleaned body.

cook it until it's tender (revolutionary!), which sometimes takes quite a while.

Squid with Chiles and Greens

MAKES: 4 servings
TIME: 20 minutes

Squid cooks so fast and freezes so well that this dish can easily become a pantry staple for weeknights. As with most stir-fries, just about all the ingredients can be varied. Serve with Steamed Sticky Rice, Thai Style (page 459), or over rice noodles.

Other seafood you can use: shrimp or scallops.

Other vegetables you can use: any cooking green, like pea shoots, cabbage, watercress, or spinach; chopped carrots or parsnips (for a nice all-white dish); chopped bell peppers. (You can add a little chopped fresh Thai basil or mint at the end if you're not using greens.)

About 1¹/₂ pounds cleaned squid

8 to 12 ounces bitter greens, like collards, kale, arugula, or dandelion

3 tablespoons peanut or neutral oil, like grapeseed or corn

1 chopped jalapeño or other fresh chile, or to taste, or several dried hot chiles

1 tablespoon chopped garlic

Salt

❶ Separate the squids' tentacles from their bodies if that has not been done; slice the bodies into rings; cut the tentacles in half if they're large (see the illustrations on page 625). Rinse well and drain while you prepare the other ingredients. Strip the greens' leaves from the stems and discard any stems thicker than ¹/₈ inch. Chop, rinse, and dry; you want 2 to 3 cups.

❷ Put the oil in a large skillet over high heat. When hot, add the chile and the garlic and stir for about 15 seconds. Add the greens and cook, stirring almost constantly, until they wilt, about 2 minutes. Add the squid and a large pinch of salt and cook, stirring occasionally, until the squid becomes opaque and its liquid moistens the greens, about 2 minutes. Taste and adjust the seasoning and serve immediately.

Squid in Red Wine Sauce

MAKES: 4 servings
TIME: 1 hour

An ideal winter dish, served over thick toasted bread, pasta, or folded into Simple Risotto (page 466) during the last few minutes of cooking.

Other seafood you can use: octopus or conch (though either will probably take a little longer to get tender).

3 tablespoons extra virgin olive oil

5 cloves garlic, crushed

2 pounds cleaned squid, the bodies cut up if large

1¹/₂ cups fruity red wine

Several sprigs fresh thyme or 1 teaspoon dried thyme

Salt and freshly ground black pepper

4 large Real Croutons (page 877) or plain Crostini (page 83; optional)

Chopped fresh parsley leaves for garnish (optional)

❶ Put 2 tablespoons of the olive oil in a large skillet or Dutch oven with a lid over medium-high heat. Add the garlic and cook, stirring, until lightly browned, about a minute. Add the squid and stir, then lower the heat to medium and add the wine. Stir, add the thyme, and cover.

❷ Cook at a slow simmer until the squid is tender, about 45 minutes. (At this point, you may let the dish sit for an hour or two, covered, before proceeding.) Uncover, sprinkle with salt and pepper, raise the heat, and cook until most but not all of the liquid has evaporated, about 5 minutes. Stir in the remaining olive oil, spoon the mixture over the croutons if you're using them, and garnish with the parsley if you like.

❶ Fast   ⓜ Make Ahead   ⓥ Vegetarian

Almond-Stuffed Braised Squid

MAKES: 4 servings

TIME: 1 hour

Squid seem to have been created for stuffing. So, over the years, I have devised this simple, sensible procedure, which produces a stuffed squid much like the one I've eaten in northern Spain. Squid shrinks significantly during cooking, so be careful to stuff it very loosely; overstuffing may result in burst squid.

1/4 cup extra virgin olive oil, or more as needed

1/4 cup bread crumbs, preferably fresh (page 876)

1/2 cup chopped almonds

8 large whole squid (bodies at least 6 inches long), cleaned, washed, and dried (about 1 1/2 pounds)

2 ounces dry-cured ham, like prosciutto (optional)

1 small onion, quartered

4 cloves garlic, peeled

6 anchovy fillets or 1 teaspoon drained capers (optional)

Salt and freshly ground black pepper

1 or 2 small dried chiles, like Thai, or hot red pepper flakes, or to taste

1 cup dry white wine

Chopped fresh parsley leaves for garnish

1 Put 2 tablespoons of the oil in a large skillet over medium heat; add the bread crumbs and almonds and cook, stirring occasionally, until lightly browned, about 5 minutes. Put the squid tentacles in a food processor, along with the ham if you're using it, the onion, 2 cloves of the garlic, and half the anchovies or capers if you're using them. Process until fairly fine but not puréed. Combine with the bread crumb mixture and a bit of salt and pepper. If the mixture seems dry, add a little olive oil.

2 Use a small spoon to stuff the squid bodies about half full of this mixture. Close the openings with 1 or 2 toothpicks (round ones are less likely to break than flat ones).

3 Chop the remaining garlic and anchovies or capers. Put 2 tablespoons olive oil in a large skillet over medium heat; add the garlic, anchovies, and chiles and cook until the garlic begins to gain color. Carefully add the squid (it will spatter) and partially cover the pan. Brown the squid on both sides, adjusting the heat as necessary; this will take only a couple of minutes.

4 Add the wine, bring to a boil, reduce the heat so the mixture simmers, and cover. Cook until the squid is tender (a toothpick will penetrate it fairly easily, but it will be tender like shrimp, not tender like cod), about 30 minutes. Remove the cover and, if the sauce is very thin, raise the heat and let it reduce a bit. (At this point, you may refrigerate for up to a day, then reheat gently before proceeding.) Serve the squid whole or sliced, garnished with parsley and a spoonful or two of the pan juices.

Herb-Stuffed Braised Squid. Omit the almonds and increase the bread crumbs to 1/2 cup. In Step 1, add 2 cups packed mixed fresh herbs to the food processor and proceed with the recipe.

Grilled Octopus

MAKES: 4 servings

TIME: 1 1/2 hours or more, largely unattended

Octopus requires simmering before grilling, a step that doesn't require much attention and can be done up to a day or two in advance. Be sure to cool the octopus, wrap it well, and refrigerate it.

Grilled octopus is excellent on a bed of White Beans, Tuscan Style (page 427) or Skordalia (page 94), or with grilled bread, a salad and Garlic Mayonnaise (page 42) for dipping.

One 2- to 3-pound octopus, cleaned and rinsed

3 cloves garlic, lightly crushed

1 bay leaf

1/2 cup extra virgin olive oil

2 tablespoons freshly squeezed lemon juice

1 tablespoon minced fresh oregano or marjoram leaves or 1 teaspoon dried

1 In a large saucepan, combine the octopus, garlic, bay leaf, and water to cover. Bring to a boil over high heat, turn the heat down to medium, and simmer until the octopus is nearly tender, 1 hour or more (poke it with a sharp, thin-bladed knife; when the knife enters fairly easily, the octopus is ready). Drain the octopus in a colander; discard the liquid or reserve it for stock (it makes great risotto).

2 Cut the octopus into large pieces. Heat a charcoal or gas grill until quite hot and put the rack no more than 4 inches from the heat source. Whisk together the olive oil, lemon juice, and herb. Brush the octopus pieces with this mixture and grill them quickly on all sides until they become slightly crisp, about 10 minutes total. As they come off the grill, brush them with a little more of the oil and lemon juice mixture. Serve immediately, passing the remaining mixture at the table.

Octopus with Tomatoes and Red Wine

MAKES: 4 servings

TIME: 2 to 3 hours, largely unattended

Don't let the prep time scare you away from this dish. Once you get things rolling, you really can walk away. Better still, cook the whole thing a few hours before you plan to serve it since timing octopus can be unpredictable. To prepare it even further in advance, work through Step 1; be sure to let the octopus cool, wrap it well, and refrigerate it. For a bigger dish, stir in Crisp Panfried Potatoes (page 341) at the last moment.

Other seafood you can use: conch.

One 2- to 3-pound octopus, cleaned and rinsed

3 cloves garlic, lightly crushed, plus 1 tablespoon minced garlic

1 bay leaf

3 tablespoons extra virgin olive oil

1 large onion, coarsely chopped

1 teaspoon fresh thyme leaves or 1/2 teaspoon dried thyme

10 fennel seeds

3 medium tomatoes, cored and cut into chunks (6 or 8 drained canned plum tomatoes are fine)

2 cups dry red wine

Salt and freshly ground black pepper

1/2 cup chopped fennel, parsley, or basil leaves

1 In a large saucepan, combine the octopus, crushed garlic, bay leaf, and water to cover. Bring to a boil over high heat, turn the heat down to medium, and simmer until the octopus is nearly tender, 1 hour or more (poke it with a sharp, thin-bladed knife; when the knife enters fairly easily, the octopus is ready). Drain the octopus in a colander, reserving the liquid.

2 Raise the heat to high and reduce the liquid until just about 1 cup remains, about 20 minutes.

3 Cut the octopus into bite-sized pieces. Put the oil in a large, deep skillet over medium-high heat. When hot, add the octopus and cook, stirring, until it begins to brown, about 5 minutes. Add the onion and lower the heat to medium. Cook and stir until the onion softens a bit, 2 or 3 minutes.

4 Add the thyme, fennel seeds, and tomatoes and stir. Cook for 1 minute, then add the wine. Raise the heat to high and boil for 2 minutes. Add the reduced octopus stock; bring to a boil, then turn the heat to low. Sprinkle with salt and pepper.

5 Cook until the liquid is reduced to a sauce (raise the heat if the octopus becomes very tender but too much liquid remains), about 20 minutes. Add the minced garlic, stir, and cook for another 5 minutes. Add half the chopped fennel leaves and stir. Garnish with the remaining herbs and serve.

Octopus with Rice. In Step 2, reduce the octopus-cooking liquid to 3 cups rather than 1 (add water in the unlikely

F Fast   **M** Make Ahead   **V** Vegetarian

event that you don't have 3 cups). Use 2 cups of the liquid to cook 1 cup rice (see White Rice, page 458). When the octopus is cooked, serve it over the rice.

Miscellaneous Fish and Shellfish

There are a number of fish and shellfish that don't readily fit into any of the categories in this chapter. It's difficult to make generalizations about them, but the ones I've chosen here are some of the most popular, even though they're far from common. When buying unusual fish, take extra care to make certain of freshness.

Slow-Grilled Sardines

MAKES: 2 servings
TIME: 15 minutes

Fresh sardines are widely beloved in Europe and easily broiled. But since you don't see them too often, this slightly special treatment (which works with only oily, skin-on fish) is a real treat, leaving them dried and crisp, with a smoky flavor.

Sardines are often sold gutted, with their heads on. If they are not gutted, follow the instructions on page 597 to gut them. Rinse and dry well. Serve as directed with lemon wedges or with Compound Butter flavored with mustard (page 32).

Other seafood you can use: whole mackerel (it will take longer to cook), bluefish fillets.

6 to 12 large sardines, a total of about 1 pound, gutted, with heads on

Melted butter or extra virgin olive oil for brushing

Salt and freshly ground black pepper

Chopped fresh parsley leaves for garnish

Lemon wedges for serving

❶ Heat a charcoal or gas grill until moderately hot and set it up for indirect cooking, putting the rack about 4 inches from the heat source. Brush the fish inside and out with butter or oil; sprinkle with salt and pepper.

❷ Put the sardines on the cool side of the grill, side by side, without crowding; cover, and cook for about 10 minutes before checking. If the sardines are opaque and firmed up a bit, carefully move them directly over the heat to crisp the skin on both sides, about a minute on each side. If they're not quite ready, cover and cook for a few more minutes. Garnish with parsley and serve with lemon wedges.

Skate with Brown Butter, Honey, and Capers

MAKES: 4 servings
TIME: 20 minutes

Skate used to be a royal pain in the neck—it's nearly impossible for home cooks to get the skin off—but now that almost all skate is filleted before it comes to market, we can simply sauté it just like any other fillets. Skate browns beautifully, which sets up this impressive pan sauce based on the classic *beurre noisette,* or "brown butter." The honey helps balance the acidity of the capers and lends complexity.

Other seafood you can use: halibut (steaks or fillets), sea bass, red snapper, grouper, or other sturdy, white-fleshed fish, thick or thin (see pages 585 and 607); adjust the cooking time accordingly.

All-purpose flour for dredging

Salt and freshly ground black pepper

3 tablespoons extra virgin olive oil

2 skate wing fillets, about 1½ pounds total

4 tablespoons (½ stick) butter

¼ cup honey

2 tablespoons drained capers, or to taste

2 tablespoons white or red wine vinegar

Chopped fresh parsley leaves for garnish

1 Put a large skillet over medium-high heat. While it is heating, sprinkle the flour with salt and pepper and put it on a plate. Put the oil in the skillet—it should coat the bottom well—and turn the heat up to high. When the oil shimmers, dredge the skate lightly in the flour, shaking to remove the excess, and add it to the pan.

2 Cook until the skate is nicely browned on the first side, about 5 minutes, then turn. Cook on the second side, adjusting the heat so the fish does not burn, until it is firm to the touch, another 3 minutes or so. Reduce the heat to medium and transfer the skate to a warm platter.

3 Add the butter and honey to the pan and cook, stirring occasionally, until bubbly and brown, about 2 more minutes. Add the capers and swirl them around, then pour the sauce over the fish. Immediately add the vinegar to the pan that the butter was in, swirl it around, and pour it over the fish. Garnish with parsley and serve immediately.

Salt Cod in Tomato Sauce

MAKES: 4 servings, 6 over pasta

TIME: About 24 hours, largely unattended; 30 minutes with prepared salt cod

M

Salting fish is one of the oldest ways to preserve it, and salt cod—variously known as baccalà, bacalao, and stockfish (slightly different, but not much) is a wonderful example of an old technique that lives on not because it's needed but because it's loved—like prosciutto and pickles. Mild, with a firm flake, it's versatile enough for any number of dishes—once you reconstitute and desalinate it, that is. But salt cod is worth the work.

1 pound boneless salt cod

2 tablespoons extra virgin olive oil

3 cloves garlic, lightly smashed

3 anchovies, or to taste

One 28-ounce can whole plum tomatoes, drained and chopped

Salt and freshly ground black pepper

2 tablespoons drained capers

1/2 cup pitted black or green olives

Hot red pepper flakes, to taste

Chopped fresh parsley leaves for garnish

1 Soak the cod for 12 to 24 hours in cold water to cover; change the water routinely, every hour or so (except when you're sleeping) being ideal. You can hasten this process by simmering the cod in water for 5 minutes, then rinsing it and changing the water and repeating this process until most of the saltiness has abated (taste a bit to find out). This sometimes takes four or five changes of water, however.

2 Put the desalinated fish in a large pot with water to cover. Bring to a boil, then reduce the heat so the water simmers gently and cook for about 15 minutes, or until reasonably tender—salt cod never gets soft—and not too salty. (Sometimes so much salt is removed during the soaking and cooking process that you must add salt to the dish in which you're using the fish.) At this point, you may store the salt cod, wrapped and refrigerated, for a couple of days.

3 Combine the oil and garlic in a large skillet over medium heat. Add the anchovies and cook, stirring occasionally, until the garlic is lightly golden and the anchovies are broken up, less than 5 minutes. Raise the heat to medium-high and add the tomatoes, along with a little salt and pepper. Cook for a few minutes, stirring occasionally, until the tomatoes become saucy.

4 Add the capers, olives, red pepper flakes, and cod. Cook for about 10 minutes, stirring occasionally and gently, until the cod is hot. Taste and adjust the seasoning, then garnish with parsley and serve.

F Fast   **M** Make Ahead   **V** Vegetarian

Salt Cod Mousse

Brandade de Morue

MAKES: 8 to 12 appetizer servings

TIME: 45 minutes with prepared salt cod

A luxury, and a delicious one, best served on toast as an appetizer in fairly small quantities because it's so rich. Traditionally the cooked salt cod is pounded to death in a big mortar and pestle so that it achieves a very creamy consistency; a food processor works pretty well, but the texture is not quite the same.

1 pound boneless salt cod, soaked, drained, and cooked (see Steps 1 and 2 of preceding recipe)

2 cloves garlic, or to taste, peeled

²/₃ cup extra virgin olive oil

²/₃ cup cream, half-and-half, or milk

Freshly ground black pepper

Juice of 1 lemon, or to taste

¹/₈ teaspoon freshly grated nutmeg

Salt if necessary

❶ Put half the cod in a food processor with the garlic and a couple tablespoons of the olive oil. Process, stopping the machine to stir down the sides once or twice, until as smooth as possible. Add the remaining cod and repeat.

❷ Through the feed tube, add small amounts of olive oil alternating with small amounts of cream. Continue processing until the mixture becomes smooth, creamy, and light. (You may not need all of the oil and cream.) Add some pepper, some of the lemon juice, and the nutmeg. Blend and taste; the mixture may need a bit of salt and more lemon juice. (At this point, you may refrigerate the dish for several hours or even a day, until you're ready to eat.)

❸ Just before serving, heat the brandade in a 300°F oven, covered, until hot and bubbly. Serve with bread, toast, or crackers.

Fresh Sea Snails with Garlic Butter

MAKES: 4 appetizer servings

TIME: About 1¹/₂ hours, largely unattended

Sea snails—periwinkles—are infinitely tastier than garden snails, though they're tiny, which makes cleaning and eating them a bit of a hassle. (You can buy garden snails canned if you like.) You could substitute minced ginger or shallots for the garlic or chill and serve the finished snails over a bed of greens, drizzled with Vinaigrette (page 199). If you have canned snails (*escargots*), just heat them in the garlic butter over low heat and serve. Slices of baguette are the usual accompaniment, for dipping in the juices.

2 pounds fresh snails (periwinkles)

1 cup cornmeal

2 tablespoons white or red wine vinegar or rice vinegar

8 tablespoons (1 stick) butter

1 tablespoon minced garlic

Salt and freshly ground black pepper

¹/₂ cup roughly chopped fresh parsley leaves

❶ Put the snails in water to cover and mix in the cornmeal; soak for at least 30 minutes (1 hour is better), stirring occasionally. During this time, pour off the water once or twice and refill (leave as much of the cornmeal in the bowl as you can), mixing with your hands and rinsing as you do so.

❷ Drain the snails and put them in a medium saucepan. Cover with fresh water and the vinegar and bring to a boil. Turn the heat to medium and cook for about 15 minutes.

❸ After the snails have cooked for about 10 minutes, cut the butter into pieces and melt it over medium-low heat in a small saucepan. Add the garlic and cook, stirring occasionally, for about 5 minutes, or just until the garlic loses its rawness. Season with salt and pepper and keep warm.

④ Remove a snail from the pot and, using a pin or toothpick, try to pull the snail from its shell; if the operculum (the hard disk at the opening of the shell) falls off and the snail meat comes out easily, the snails are done. If not, continue cooking until the snails are ready. Drain the snails, then return them to the pot with a couple tablespoons of the butter. Garnish with parsley and serve with pins or toothpicks to remove the snails, along with the rest of the garlic butter.

Conch with Tomatoes

MAKES: 4 servings
TIME: 45 minutes or more

Since conch is a little tougher than squid, shrimp, or clams, it requires longer cooking to become tender. But once you get the pot going, you can walk away for a while. Like snails, in-shell conch have a hard disk (the operculum) that covers their opening, though these days it's quite common to find shelled meat frozen. Just let it thaw in the fridge before using.

Serve this over plain rice or toss with pasta. Or just serve in a shallow bowl with lots of bread alongside.

½ cup extra virgin olive oil

2 cloves garlic, slivered

4 or 5 small dried hot red chiles, or to taste

3 cups chopped tomato (drained canned is fine)

Salt and freshly ground black pepper

½ pound conch meat, operculums removed, ground or chopped

½ cup chopped fresh parsley

① Put the olive oil in a large skillet over medium heat. When hot, add the garlic and chiles. Cook, stirring, until the garlic browns, about a minute. Turn off the heat and wait a minute before adding the tomato. Sprinkle with salt and pepper.

② Cook over medium heat until the tomato gets saucy, about 5 minutes, then add some more salt and pepper and the conch. Simmer, stirring occasionally, until the conch is fairly tender, at least 30 minutes. Taste and adjust the seasoning, stir in the parsley, and serve.

Shad Roe

MAKES: 2 servings
TIME: 10 minutes

Shad is an indigenous American fish that spawns in eastern rivers every spring. The roe, its eggs, is considered a seasonal delicacy, especially for people on the East Coast (shad fillets are also a seasonal treat; cook as you would any thick white fish fillet, taking special care not to overcook). As with any fish, there are two keys to a great dish: Buy it fresh and don't overcook it; rare to medium is right, because overcooked roe is gritty. This can be served as an appetizer or as a part of a larger meal; it's wonderful on a bed of lightly dressed greens. It's good fried with bacon too.

4 tablespoons (½ stick) butter (or 2 tablespoons if you prefer), cut into chunks

1 pair shad roe, about 6 ounces total

Salt and freshly ground black pepper

Lemon wedges for serving

① Heat a medium to large skillet over medium heat for 3 or 4 minutes.

② Add the butter and let it melt. When the foam subsides, turn the heat to medium-high, add the roe, and cook until lightly browned, 3 to 4 minutes. Turn and brown the other side. Do not overcook; the roe should remain quite tender, not firm and springy. Sprinkle with salt and pepper and serve immediately, with lemon wedges.

Seafood Burgers, Cakes, and Other Dishes

Often the best way to introduce the uninitiated (or the skeptical) to seafood is to cook it as an ingredient in familiar preparations like burgers, cakes, croquettes, and stews—as opposed to showcasing the fish as the main event. Indeed these are some of my favorite ways to eat seafood since they tend to be more forgiving. They may not be any faster (in some cases they're somewhat involved), but the results are immensely appealing for seafood novices, while adding variety to an experienced cook's fish repertoire. A few of such dishes start with already-cooked fish, which makes them excellent vehicles for leftovers.

Shrimp Burgers

MAKES: 4 servings
TIME: 30 minutes

The most successful alternative burgers deliver both superior flavor and interesting texture: These burgers easily exceed those requirements. Since shrimp contains natural gelatin, you can incorporate a considerable amount of flavorings without the burgers' falling apart. Grill these over a well-oiled rack, broil, or pan-cook in a little oil or butter.

I took an Asian flavoring route here, but that's easy enough to change: Omit and substitute what you like (just don't increase the quantity of vegetables or your burger might indeed fall apart). Try small amounts of herbs—tarragon, mint, basil, chives, or chervil—or Chile Paste (page 74) or curry powder (to make your own, see pages 66 or 67).

Other seafood you can use: scallops, salmon, or mackerel (handle either gently or mix with some shrimp as "glue").

1 large clove garlic, peeled

1 dried or fresh chile, seeded, or more to taste

1 inch fresh ginger, more or less, roughly chopped

About 1½ pounds shrimp, peeled

¼ cup roughly chopped shallot, scallion, or red onion

¼ cup roughly chopped red or yellow bell pepper (optional)

Salt and freshly ground black pepper

½ cup fresh cilantro leaves, or to taste

Neutral oil, like grapeseed or corn, as needed

Toasted buns (optional)

Lime wedges or ketchup for serving

1 Heat a charcoal or gas grill or the broiler until moderately hot and put the rack about 4 inches from the heat source. (If pan-cooking, wait until the burgers are formed to proceed.)

2 Combine the garlic, chile, ginger, and a third of the shrimp in a food processor and process to a purée, stopping the machine to scrape down the sides of the container as necessary. Add the remaining shrimp along with the shallot, bell pepper, some salt and pepper, and the cilantro and pulse as many times as is necessary to chop the shrimp, but not too finely. Shape the mixture into 4 burgerlike patties.

3 Brush the grill or the patties lightly with oil and place them on the grill or under the broiler. (Now is the time to heat the pan for stovetop cooking, add the oil, and, when it's hot, add the burgers.) Cook undisturbed until a dark crust appears on the bottom and the burgers release fairly easily with a spatula, about 5 minutes. Turn and cook until opaque throughout, 3 to 4 minutes on the other side. Serve on buns or not, as you like, with lime or ketchup.

Crab Cakes, Curried or Plain

MAKES: 4 servings
TIME: 15 minutes, plus time to chill

I expect crab cakes to be mostly crab, don't you? That's why just about every addition here is for flavor or is optional—there's not a lot of bread.

Other seafood you can use: lobster.

1 pound fresh lump crabmeat, picked over for cartilage

1 egg

1/4 cup chopped red bell pepper (optional)

1/2 cup chopped scallion (optional)

1/4 cup mayonnaise (to make your own, see page 41)

1 tablespoon Dijon mustard

Salt and freshly ground black pepper

2 tablespoons bread crumbs, preferably fresh (page 876), or cracker crumbs, or as needed

About 1 cup all-purpose flour for dredging

Curry powder (optional; to make your own, see pages 66–67)

2 tablespoons peanut, extra virgin olive, or vegetable oil

2 tablespoons butter or more oil

Lemon wedges and/or Tartar Sauce (page 42)

❶ Mix together the crabmeat, egg, bell pepper, scallion, mayonnaise, mustard, and some salt and pepper. Add enough bread crumbs to bind the mixture just enough to form into cakes; start with 2 tablespoons and use more if you need it.

❷ Refrigerate the mixture until you're ready to cook (it will be easier to shape if you refrigerate it for 30 minutes or more, but it's ready to go when you finish mixing).

❸ Season the flour with salt and pepper and add some curry powder if you like. Heat a large skillet, preferably cast-iron, over medium-high heat for 2 or 3 minutes. Add the oil and butter and heat until the butter foam subsides. Shape the crabmeat mixture into 1-inch-thick cakes, dredge each in the flour, and cook, adjusting the heat as necessary and turning once (very gently), until golden brown on both sides, about 5 minutes per side. Serve with lemon wedges and/or tartar sauce.

Fish Fritters

MAKES: 6 to 8 appetizer or 4 main-dish servings
TIME: 30 minutes

Few dishes are as versatile as fritters, and few fritters are as wonderful as those made with fish. It doesn't matter whether the seafood is raw or cooked, as long as you finely chop or flake it and combine it thoroughly with the other ingredients.

Other seafood you can use: shrimp, crawfish, scallops, clams, mussels, oysters, crab, lobster, or cooked conch.

1 pound thick or thin fish fillets or steaks without skin or bones (see pages 585 and 607), raw or cooked

1 onion, chopped

2 garlic cloves, minced

Salt and freshly ground black pepper or cayenne

1 cup all-purpose flour

2 eggs

1/2 cup chopped fresh parsley or cilantro

Neutral oil, like grapeseed or corn, for deep frying

Lime wedges for serving

❶ Chop the fish with a knife, then, if it's cooked, shred it with your fingers; if it's raw, keep chopping until it's finely chopped. Combine it with the onion and garlic, sprinkle with salt and pepper or a little cayenne, and mix well with a wooden spoon. Add the flour and stir a few times, then beat in the eggs one at a time. Add about 1/2 cup water and stir, then continue to add water (about another 1/4 cup) until a batter forms—it should be a bit thicker than pancake batter, but not much. Stir in the herb.

❷ Let the mixture rest while you put at least 2 inches oil in a deep pan on the stove and bring to 350°F over medium-high heat. (A drop of the batter will sizzle energetically but not violently when the oil reaches this temperature. See "Deep Frying," page 19.) Using a tablespoon, gently drop spoonfuls of the cod mixture into the oil and fry, turning once, until golden brown, about 5 minutes total. Work in batches, taking care not to crowd the fritters.

❸ Drain on paper towels. Sprinkle with more salt if you like and serve with lime wedges or keep in a warm oven until ready to serve.

Indian Shrimp Fritters. Substitute 1 pound shrimp, peeled and ground, for the fish. Add 1 teaspoon ground cumin and 1 teaspoon ground turmeric to the shrimp, onion, garlic, and pepper mixture. Substitute 2 fresh hot green chiles, seeded and minced, for the parsley.

Salmon Croquettes

MAKES: 4 servings
TIME: 20 minutes

A perfect use for leftover salmon or really any fish. You can broil or even grill these croquettes if you're careful. Keep them 6 to 8 inches away from the heat source to avoid burning.

Other seafood you can use: trout, halibut, or any cooked thick or thin white fish (see pages 585 and 607).

> 1 to 2 cups leftover cooked salmon
>
> 1 to 2 cups leftover Mashed Potatoes (page 339)
>
> $1/2$ to 1 cup chopped onion or scallion
>
> $1/4$ cup chopped fresh parsley leaves
>
> 1 teaspoon minced or grated fresh ginger or garlic (optional)
>
> 1 egg
>
> 1 teaspoon Dijon mustard
>
> Salt and freshly ground black pepper
>
> About 1 cup bread crumbs, preferably fresh (page 876), or as needed
>
> $1/4$ to $1/2$ cup extra virgin olive oil
>
> Lemon wedges for serving

❶ Combine the salmon, mashed potatoes, onion, parsley, ginger, egg, mustard, and some salt and pepper in a bowl. Add just enough bread crumbs to stiffen the mixture without making it too dry.

❷ Shape into thumb-sized cylinders or silver-dollar-sized cakes; dredge in additional bread crumbs, then dry on a rack, refrigerated, for 15 to 30 minutes. Heat a large, deep skillet over medium heat for 2 or 3 minutes. Add a film of the olive oil, add the croquettes, taking care not to crowd them in the pan, and cook until they are nicely browned on all sides, about 10 minutes total. If you need to cook the croquettes in batches, add more olive oil. Serve with lemon wedges.

Mixed Seafood and Rice, Japanese Style

Kayaku gohan

MAKES: 4 servings
TIME: 40 minutes

This might remind you of paella, and it's just as good, especially if you start by making dashi, which literally takes 10 minutes.

Other protein you can use: virtually any combination of seafood, as well as chicken.

> 2 tablespoons neutral oil, like corn or canola
>
> 5 fresh or dried shiitake mushroom caps, soaked in hot water until soft if dried, sliced
>
> 1 medium onion, chopped
>
> 8 ounces cleaned squid, tentacles halved, bodies sliced into rings, or more shrimp, peeled
>
> $1^3/4$ cups short-grain white rice
>
> 1 cup peas, fresh or thawed frozen
>
> 4 cups Dashi (page 160) or water, or more as needed
>
> 2 tablespoons soy sauce
>
> 1 tablespoon mirin (or $1^1/2$ teaspoons honey mixed with $1^1/2$ teaspoons water)

8 ounces shrimp, peeled and cut into small pieces

Salt if necessary

1 Put the oil in a large pot with a lid or a Dutch oven over medium-high heat. When hot, add the sliced mushroom caps, onion, and squid (if you're using all shrimp, don't add the shrimp until Step 3) and cook, stirring occasionally, until the edges of all three are brown, about 10 minutes.

2 Reduce the heat to medium and add the rice; cook, stirring until combined. Add the peas and the dashi, along with the soy sauce and mirin. Stir, reduce the heat to medium-low, and cover. A minute later, check that the mixture is simmering and adjust the heat if necessary; cook for 15 minutes.

3 When you remove the cover, the mixture should still be a little soupy (add a little dashi or water if it's dried out); add the shrimp and stir, then raise the heat a bit and cook until the rice is tender and the mixture is still moist but not soupy. Taste and adjust the seasoning, then serve.

Fish Stew with Sauerkraut

Choucroute de Poisson

MAKES: 4 servings

TIME: 1 hour

Sauerkraut provides just the right acidity for the fish, smoked fish, and—optional—smoked meat. Be sure to use a mixture of fish that includes some white-fleshed fish fillet, like cod, snapper, or halibut; some smoked fish, like trout or haddock; and a piece of skinned salmon. Serve with boiled potatoes.

1 pound sauerkraut, preferably fresh (or stored in glass or plastic, not cans), rinsed and drained

4 ounces smoked ham or sausage, chopped (optional)

1 teaspoon dried juniper berries, lightly crushed with the side of a knife

1 teaspoon fresh thyme leaves or $^1/_2$ teaspoon dried thyme

1 bay leaf

1 cup dry white wine

About 1$^1/_2$ pounds mixed fish (see headnote)

Salt and freshly ground black pepper

1 shallot, minced

$^1/_4$ cup cream

8 tablespoons (1 stick) butter, slightly softened

Juice of 1 lemon

Chopped fresh parsley leaves for garnish

1 Put the sauerkraut, the ham if you're using it, the juniper, thyme, bay, and all but 2 tablespoons of the white wine in a deep skillet with a lid or a Dutch oven over medium-high heat. When the mixture begins to bubble, lower the heat and cover, adjusting the heat so the mixture simmers. Cook for about 40 minutes, stirring occasionally. Lay the fish fillets on top of the sauerkraut, sprinkle with salt and pepper, and cover the pan once again.

2 Cook the remaining white wine with the shallot in a small saucepan over medium-high heat until the liquid has almost evaporated, about 5 minutes. Turn the heat to low, add the cream, and stir. Add the butter, a little bit at a time, stirring all the while. When the mixture is creamy, stir in the lemon juice along with some salt and pepper. Keep warm.

3 When the fish is tender, about 10 minutes after adding it, spoon the sauerkraut and fish onto a platter; drizzle the sauce over all. Garnish with parsley and serve, preferably with boiled potatoes.

 F Fast   **M** Make Ahead   **V** Vegetarian

Poultry

THE CHAPTER AT A GLANCE

WE STILL LOVE OUR BEEF, BUT STATISTICALLY speaking, chicken is king: Americans eat more of it than any other meat. Not surprising, since chicken—and other birds, like turkey—is low in fat, cooks quickly, and has mild flavor and tender texture, all factors that people consider when they're thinking about what to buy for dinner.

It's also cheap (far cheaper than it should be, really; see "What Ingredients Should I Buy," page 2). Better-tasting chicken—which is often chicken that's raised in a more conscientious fashion—costs more money but is much more widely available than it was ten years ago.

Chicken's mild taste begs you to add flavor, by adding other ingredients or browning it. That's easy enough, and basic seasonings do wonderful things for chicken, so dishes can remain uncomplicated and still be quite delicious, and you have unlimited flavor options. Even plain old good technique will help enormously: Roast chicken, with no more than olive oil or butter and salt and pepper (see page 640), is a near-universal favorite.

After some basic poultry information and the Essential Recipes, the chapter is organized around the way most Americans purchase chickens for home cooking: parts first—both bone-in and boneless—followed by techniques and recipes for preparing whole birds, turkey, duck, and other poultry.

The Basics of Buying Chicken

No matter what recipe you use, the results will be better if you start with a high-quality bird. Fortunately, many supermarkets now offer a choice: one or two brands of what should rightly be called industrially produced chicken; one kosher or premium label (like Bell & Evans); and something approaching free range. If you're really lucky, you'll find a chicken that's truly local and free range, but you'll probably have to go to a farmers' market and spend five bucks a pound for this. (It's worth noting that no one is getting rich selling you a chicken for fifteen dollars, and that this—not the three-dollar chicken you so often see in supermarkets—represents something like the true cost of raising, transporting, and selling a real chicken.)

Types of Chicken

Store brand and national brand: These are almost always the same thing. The birds are raised on the same large-scale farms by the same methods, just packaged with different labels. They're the least expensive chickens, but they also have the least flavor and the mushiest texture. For those reasons alone, you're better off moving up the ladder to another option. If you cannot, for whatever reason—availability, budget, you're the cook but someone else did the shopping—try to undercook the white meat a little bit while fully cooking the thigh (see "Chicken Doneness and Safety," next page). Further, use a cooking method—broiling, grilling, sautéing, or frying—that will get that skin browned and crisp, and cook with plenty of added flavor in the form of herbs, spices, aromatic vegetables, seasonings like oil, butter, and vinegar, and so on.

So-called natural: Even these chickens—and just about every other chicken you will ever see—are entitled, through some egregious error on the part of the federal government (lobbyist-induced, no doubt), to be labeled *natural*—even though most are raised with a heavy dose of antibiotics—rendering that term just about meaningless. In fact, anything you read on a label other than the government's green organic seal is assumed to be truthful but is in fact not certified by anyone other than the producer. The USDA actually calls this honor system "truthfulness in labeling."

Kosher: Mostly, you're going to have to live in or near a big city to have this option, but it is a better one. Kosher chickens start with a slightly better breed, which is then fed and handled more honorably. In addition, kosher chickens are salted before sale (that's part of the koshering process, which can be simulated with brining or salting; see page 656), which gives them tighter, meatier texture and more flavor. (Kosher chicken wins almost every "taste test" in which it's included.) It's often sold frozen, which is not ideal, but it's still better than store-brand chicken. It's more expensive, of course, about the same price as premium chicken. But it's good to cook with and to eat.

Premium: Though the laws behind kosher chicken don't mean much to anyone who doesn't keep kosher, at least the laws exist; "premium" may mean "better" or it may just mean "more expensive." Some premium brands walk the line between traditionally and industrially raised chickens; their products are good. But the term is vague, so you're going to have to let experience guide you; fortunately, it's not like you're risking a lot.

Free range: A hodgepodge that depends as much on the good will of the producer as anything else. Again, using this term alone to judge quality is iffy, but it's an arena in which you're most likely to find really good chickens, ones that truly taste like something. In my experience, some are tough but flavorful (making them excellent candidates for recipes like Chicken in a Pot, page 688); others are virtually indistinguishable from more mass-produced chickens; still others are wonderful.

Organic: To be certified organic and receive the USDA's green seal, chickens must be produced under specific conditions that assure the birds have at least some mobility, do not receive antibiotics or other drugs, and eat only organic, non-GMO (genetically modified organism) feed. Being organic doesn't guarantee the chicken will taste better (or be free of salmonella), though it is the only way you can know for sure that it was raised decently and fed well.

Specialty or locally raised: Usually the most expensive and highest-quality chickens: In this category I count imported chickens and locally raised or American "heritage" birds, those breeds that are not generally suited to the demands of large-scale farming but are valued by small farmers for both flavor and texture. Specialty birds may or may not be organic. You'll find imports only at high-end markets and grocers, usually frozen. If you want to explore this option, a far better choice is to seek out locally raised chickens (which are often heritage breeds) at farmers' markets, some natural food stores, or directly from the producer.

Fresh versus Frozen Chickens

For years, much of the chicken that was sold as "fresh" had actually been shipped frozen. Although this practice has been discontinued, it served to point out one thing: Chicken freezes well. This means that you can usually buy frozen birds with confidence (and in some areas that's the only way premium, kosher, and free-range chickens are sold) and also that you can buy as much chicken as you can store when it's on sale and freeze it yourself. It's even less expensive, of course, to buy whole birds and cut them up yourself. And leaving them whole gives you the option of cooking them in any form you want once they're defrosted. Cutting up a chicken, illustrated in detail on page 648, is simple and takes less than 5 minutes once you've had some practice.

To freeze, just remove the chicken from the package, wrap it tightly in two layers of plastic, and put it in the freezer. The quality will deteriorate—as will that of anything else you freeze—but as long as you use the chicken within a month or two, you probably won't notice any difference.

Chicken Size (and Age)

Years ago chickens were labeled *fryers, broilers, pullets, hens,* and *fowl* according to size, sex, and age. Now, you rarely see anything other than frying/broiling chickens (anything under 4 pounds or so) and roasting chickens (anything larger). Fowl (sometimes labeled *stewing chicken*) is a large bird that is likely to be tough unless cooked in liquid; it should be quite flavorful in a simmered dish like Chicken in a Pot (page 688) and is good for stock. So are capons (neutered male birds), which are also good for roasting, though you rarely see them anymore.

Chicken Doneness and Safety

The absolute safety of food can never be assured, and mass production and wide distribution makes undercooking any food somewhat risky. But among animal products chicken is a special case, because sampling estimates that up to 25 percent—maybe even more—of supermarket birds contain the potentially harmful bacteria salmonella.

Salmonella is killed by cooking chicken until it is fully done. You can reliably judge this in two ways: The easiest and surest is to use an instant-read thermometer; poke it into the breast in two or three places (don't touch the bone), then into the thigh (again, avoiding the bone), and, finally—if you're cooking a whole bird—into the joint between the thigh and lower leg. The government currently recommends an internal temperature of 165°F in all these places.

Like all meat, though, chicken continues to cook after you take it off the heat. And from a flavor standpoint, you don't want to overcook; it's unusual for overcooked chicken to be anything but dry and chewy. On the other hand, of course you want to make your chicken safe.

So here's my compromise: To avoid overcooking, I remove chicken when the temperature is below the "safe" level and let the chicken rest for 5 or 10 minutes before serving—basically the time it takes to serve it. And I've never had a problem.

If you want chicken that tastes its best, pull it off the heat at 155°F; if you care about chicken that's absolutely safe, take it off the heat at 165°F. If you want some sort of balance between the two, remove the bird at around 160°F. (This is less of an issue with chicken parts, which cook quickly and almost inevitably to 165°F, than it is with whole chicken, where some parts cook faster than others.)

You can also check for doneness visually by making a small cut in any section, right down to the bone; a tinge of pink is acceptable (again, because the meat will finish cooking completely by the time you get it to the table), but you should see no red whatsoever. Again, if you want to be really sure, wait until the meat is white at the bone.

When the chicken is done, don't let it touch marinades or anything else that came into contact with it before cooking (unless, in the case of marinades, you boil them while you're cooking the chicken). See page 3 for a discussion of food safety in general.

ESSENTIAL RECIPES

There was a day when whole roast chicken was the go-to recipe for chicken dinner, but with poultry parts and boneless cutlets and pieces far outselling whole birds in this country, other preparations are actually more accessible. Butchering a raw bird—or even cutting up a cooked one—is a little intimidating for a lot of new cooks (though I urge you to overcome any fears in the section beginning on page 684).

✪ Roast Chicken Parts with Olive Oil or Butter

MAKES: 4 to 6 servings
TIME: 40 minutes

The simplest chicken recipe there is and perhaps the easiest as well. Add the herb here if you like or see the flavoring ideas that follow. This is the kind of dish you'll never get tired of, because you can change the flavoring every time you make it.

4 tablespoons extra virgin olive oil or butter

1 whole chicken, 3 to 4 pounds, trimmed of excess fat and cut into 8 pieces, or any combination of parts

Salt and freshly ground black pepper

1/2 cup any chopped mild green herb—like parsley, dill, or basil—or a combination of herbs (optional)

❶ Heat the oven to 450°F. Put the oil or butter in a roasting pan and put it in the oven for a couple of minutes, until the oil is hot or the butter melts. Add the chicken and turn it a couple of times in the fat, leaving it skin side up. Sprinkle with salt and pepper and return the pan to the oven.

❷ After the chicken has cooked for 15 minutes, sprinkle on one-quarter of the herb, if you're using any, and turn the pieces. Sprinkle on another quarter of the herb and roast for another 10 minutes.

❸ Turn the chicken over (now skin side up again), add another quarter of the herb, and cook until the chicken is done (you'll see clear juices if you make a small cut in the meat near the bone), another 5 to 15 minutes at most. Garnish with the remaining herb and skim excess fat from the pan juices if necessary; serve, with some of the juices spooned over it.

Roast Chicken Parts with Black Beans. First, soak 2 tablespoons fermented black beans in water, sherry, or wine to cover. In place of the butter or olive oil, use peanut oil or a neutral oil, like grapeseed or corn. Mix together 1 tablespoon minced garlic, 2 minced scallions, 1 tea-

 Fast   Make Ahead   Vegetarian

spoon minced fresh ginger, 2 tablespoons soy sauce, and 1 teaspoon sugar or honey. Drain the black beans and add them to this mixture; thin it to a paste, if necessary, with a little more soy sauce. In Step 1, spread a little of this mixture all over the raw chicken and put the chicken in the roasting pan; return the pan to the oven. Proceed with Steps 2 and 3, using the soy-based mixture for basting in place of the herb mixture.

14 Ideas for Roast Chicken Parts with Olive Oil or Butter

You can combine these ideas at will; it's hard to go wrong here. Add with the chicken at the beginning of cooking unless otherwise specified.

1. Add a few sprigs of a stronger herb like thyme, sage, oregano, or rosemary.
2. Add several cloves of garlic (20 wouldn't be too many).
3. Add a cup or so of chopped onion, shallot, or leek.
4. Add a cup or so of sliced fresh mushrooms, after the first 15 minutes of roasting.
5. Add a lot of hot dried chiles, a couple of roasted, soaked, and chopped milder chiles, or both.
6. Add 2 or 3 lemons (oranges and limes are good too), cut in half; when the chicken is done, squeeze the hot lemon juice over it.
7. Use peanut oil instead of olive oil and add several slices of ginger and garlic after turning the chicken skin side up again. When chicken is done, drizzle with soy sauce and dark sesame oil, then garnish with scallions and/or cilantro.
8. Use Compound Butter (page 32), Flavored Oil (page 26), or Vinaigrette (page 199) from the beginning of the cooking or as a basting sauce during cooking.
9. Rub the chicken with $1/2$ cup or so of Traditional Pesto (page 27) or any other herb purée (see pages 27–29) from the beginning of the cooking.
10. Stir in a dollop of grainy French-style mustard when the chicken is done.
11. Add a couple handfuls of cherry tomatoes and some black olives after turning the chicken skin side up again.

12. Stir in a cup of any salsa (pages 23, 33–35, and 48–50) in the last 10 minutes of cooking or spoon on top of the cooked chicken before serving.
13. Add a cup or so of Tomato Sauce with Fresh Herbs (use dill; page 503) in the last few minutes of cooking or spoon on top of the cooked chicken before serving.
14. Stir a couple tablespoons of any curry powder into a cup of yogurt or coconut milk and spoon or brush it on as a basting sauce during cooking.

✪ Grilled or Broiled Boneless Chicken

MAKES: 4 servings
TIME: 20 minutes

Olive oil and lemon: It doesn't get any simpler or much better. Parsley and garlic complete the picture, but they're optional. This is the kind of basic dish (the variations are not much more difficult) that new cooks can't believe, because it shows how good home cooking can be with so little effort. Although boneless chicken is fine grilled, I think boneless cuts are actually slightly better broiled, because the seasonings stay with the meat instead of dripping onto the fire. It's also easier, of course. Your choice. For more about the different cuts available, see "The Basics of Boneless Chicken," page 666.

> About 1$1/2$ pounds boneless, skinless white-meat chicken (breasts, cutlets, or tenders), pounded to uniform thickness if necessary and blotted dry
>
> 3 tablespoons extra virgin olive oil
>
> 3 or 4 cloves garlic, slivered (optional)
>
> Salt and freshly ground black pepper
>
> Lemon wedges
>
> Chopped parsley leaves for garnish (optional)

❶ Heat a charcoal or gas grill or a broiler to medium heat and put the rack 4 inches from the heat source.

❷ If you're broiling, put the chicken in the pan in

11 MORE WAYS TO VARY GRILLED OR BROILED BONELESS CHICKEN

Each of the following flavoring and serving ideas uses the cooking method described in the main recipe for Grilled or Broiled Boneless Chicken. Replace the olive oil and garlic with the fats and seasonings listed; instead of the parsley, garnish and serve as suggested.

VARIATION	FAT	SEASONING	GARNISH AND SERVING SUGGESTIONS
Mediterranean Grilled or Broiled Boneless Chicken	Extra virgin olive oil	2 tablespoons cracked or ground pepper (or use half pepper and half ground coriander seeds); 1 tablespoon minced garlic	Garnish with chopped fresh oregano if you like. Serve with Sweet Potatoes, Simply Cooked (page 358) or Socca (page 116).
Herbed Grilled or Broiled Boneless Chicken	Extra virgin olive oil	2 to 4 tablespoons mixed chopped fresh herbs—parsley and either chervil, basil, dill, tarragon, mint, or whatever you have on hand—and the garlic	Serve with Sautéed Mushrooms (page 313) and Mashed Potatoes (page 339).
Spiced Grilled or Broiled Boneless Chicken	Extra virgin olive oil	1 tablespoon ground cumin, 1 teaspoon ground allspice, 1 teaspoon ground ginger, 1/2 teaspoon ground cinnamon, 1/4 teaspoon cayenne, and 1/8 teaspoon freshly grated nutmeg or 2 tablespoons curry powder, five-spice powder, or any other spice mixture (to make your own, see pages 65-69)	Serve with Dry-Pan Eggplant (page 294), drizzled with any Yogurt Sauce (page 24) or Tahini Sauce (page 35). Serve plain basmati rice or other grain and garnish with chopped fresh parsley or cilantro leaves.
Grilled or Broiled Boneless Chicken, North African Style	Extra virgin olive oil (just 2 tablespoons)	2 tablespoons honey, 1 tablespoon dry sherry (or use dry white wine, freshly squeezed orange juice, or water), 1 tablespoon ground cumin, and the garlic	Collards or Kale with Tahini (page 309) or Simple White or Whole Wheat Couscous (page 454)
Grilled or Broiled Boneless Chicken with Tarragon Mustard	Melted butter	2 teaspoons chopped fresh tarragon and 1 tablespoon Dijon mustard	Potato Gratin (page 346) and Slow-Cooked Green Beans (page 305)
Curried Grilled or Broiled Boneless Chicken	Yogurt	1 tablespoon curry powder (to make your own, see pages 66–67)	Cooked basmati rice (see page 458) and any Yogurt Sauce (page 294)
Parmesan Grilled or Broiled Boneless Chicken	Mayonnaise	2 tablespoons lemon juice, 1 tablespoon grated lemon zest, and 2 tablespoons grated Parmesan cheese (go easy on the salt)	Any pasta with Fast Tomato Sauce (page 502), or on top of a big bowl of mixed greens with a drizzle of Balsamic Syrup (page 51) or Vinaigrette (page 199)
Grilled or Broiled Boneless Chicken with Thai Flavors	Coconut milk (to make your own, see page 389)	1 tablespoon peanut butter and a pinch of hot red pepper flakes or cayenne	Reconstituted and drained bean thread or rice vermicelli, tossed with Thai Chile Sauce (page 39), garnished with slices of raw carrot, bell pepper, and scallion

 Fast   Make Ahead   Ⓥ Vegetarian

VARIATION	FAT	SEASONING	GARNISH AND SERVING SUGGESTIONS
Grilled or Broiled Boneless Chicken with Garam Masala	Coconut milk, (to make your own, see page 389)	1 tablespoon garam masala (to make your own, see page 67) or a pinch of saffron threads	Grilled or Broiled Eggplant (page 294)
Miso Grilled or Broiled Boneless Chicken	1 tablespoon dark sesame oil and 2 tablespoons neutral oil, like grapeseed or corn	2 tablespoons any miso paste, plus 2 tablespoons finely chopped walnuts (easy on the salt)	Cold Soba Noodles with Dipping Sauce (page 553), along with sliced cucumber and tomato
Sesame Grilled or Broiled Boneless Chicken	1 tablespoon dark sesame oil and 2 tablespoons neutral oil, like grapeseed or corn	2 tablespoons soy sauce; the garlic remains optional (you can add some grated or minced fresh ginger if you like, too)	Steamed Sticky Rice, Thai Style (page 459) or Sushi Rice (page 474) and Stir-Fried Asparagus (page 259)

which you'll cook it and toss with the oil, the garlic if you're using it, and some salt and pepper. If you're grilling, do the same in a pan or on a plate. If you like, cover and set aside for an hour or so to develop the flavor.

3 Grill or broil the chicken very quickly, turning once, no more than 3 or 4 minutes per side (to check for doneness, cut into a piece with a thin-bladed knife; the center should be white or slightly pink). Sprinkle with lemon juice and, if you like, parsley; serve immediately or at room temperature.

Grilled or Broiled Boneless Chicken Thighs. Works with the main recipe or the other variation: Substitute boneless chicken thighs for the breasts. Adjust the cooking time to 7 to 10 minutes per side, depending on their thickness.

Grilled or Broiled Boneless Chicken with Soy and Lime. You may not need any salt here: Use 1 tablespoon dark sesame oil in place of the olive oil; add 2 tablespoons soy sauce; the garlic remains optional (you can add some grated or minced fresh ginger, too, if you like). Proceed with the main recipe or the preceding variation; serve with lime and garnish, if you like, with cilantro.

Stir-Fried Chicken with Cabbage

MAKES: 4 servings
TIME: 30 minutes
F

The simplest chicken-and-vegetable stir-fry since it requires no parboiling. Napa cabbage shreds nicely and cooks quickly, but you can use gai lan (the best option if you can find it), bok choy, ordinary green head cabbage, Savoy cabbage, or other members of the cabbage family like turnip greens or broccoli raab. This also works well for snow peas, sliced celery, or bell pepper, where you still want some crunch. And as long as you dice them into small ($^1/_2$ inch or less) pieces, you can even use long-cooking vegetables like carrots, beets, or rutabaga.

Other protein you can use: shrimp, cut-up pork shoulder or loin (or beef steak), or cubes of firm tofu.

2 tablespoons peanut or neutral oil, like grapeseed or corn

2 tablespoons minced garlic

1 tablespoon grated or minced fresh ginger

1/4 cup chopped scallion, plus more for garnish

1 pound Napa or other cabbage, cored and shredded

1 pound boneless, skinless chicken breast or thighs, cut into 1/2- to 3/4-inch chunks or thin slices and blotted dry

1 teaspoon sugar (optional)

2 tablespoons soy sauce

Salt and freshly ground black pepper

1/2 cup chicken or vegetable stock (to make your own, see page 157), white wine, or water

1 Put a large, deep skillet over medium-high heat. Add half the oil, swirl it around, and immediately add half the garlic and ginger. Cook for 15 seconds, stirring, then add the scallion and cabbage. Raise the heat to high and cook, stirring occasionally, until the cabbage scorches a little in places and becomes soft, 5 to 8 minutes, then transfer everything to a plate.

2 Turn the heat down to medium, add the remaining oil, let it get hot, and add the remaining garlic and ginger. Stir, then add the chicken. Raise the heat to high, stir the chicken once, then let it sit for 1 minute to brown. Cook, stirring occasionally, until the chicken has lost its pink color, 3 to 5 minutes. Don't worry about the chicken cooking through; it will. And don't worry about the chicken bits that stick to the bottom; you'll get them later.

3 Turn the heat down to medium, return the cabbage to the pan, and toss once or twice. Add the sugar if you're using it, along with the soy sauce, and toss again. Sprinkle with salt and pepper and add the liquid. Raise the heat to high and cook, stirring and scraping the bottom of the pan, until the liquid is reduced slightly and you've scraped up all the bits of chicken. Garnish with chopped scallion and serve.

Stir-Fried Chicken with Orange Flavor, Sichuan Style. You don't eat these chiles, but they add a beguiling smokiness: Omit the cabbage and increase the chicken to about 1 1/2 pounds. In Step 1, add 20 or more small whole dried red chiles and the zest of 2 oranges left in strips, along with the garlic and ginger; hold off on adding the scallion. Remove the chile mixture and proceed with Step 2. In Step 3, add the scallion when you return the orange and vegetables. Add 2 tablespoons freshly squeezed orange juice along with the soy sauce; reduce the amount of stock or water to 2 tablespoons. Garnish, if you like, with orange sections and more chopped scallion.

✪ Simplest Whole Roast Chicken, Six Ways

MAKES: 4 servings
TIME: About 1 hour

We justifiably associate roast chicken with elegance, but it can also be super weeknight food, cooked in just about an hour. This method works because the high heat provided by the heated skillet cooks the thighs faster than the breasts, which are exposed only to the heat of the oven. It gives you nice browning without drying out the breast meat, and it's easily varied.

If at any point during the cooking the pan juices begin to smoke, just add a little water or wine (white or red, your choice) to the pan. This will reduce browning, however, so don't do it unless you must.

I suggest serving the pan juices with the chicken (you can call it *sauce naturel* if you like), but if you prefer to make a more complicated pan sauce, see pages 45–48.

1 whole chicken, 3 to 4 pounds, trimmed of excess fat

3 tablespoons extra virgin olive oil

Salt and freshly ground black pepper

A few sprigs fresh tarragon, rosemary, or thyme (optional)

5 or 6 cloves garlic, peeled (optional)

Chopped fresh herbs for garnish

❶ Heat the oven to 450°F. Five minutes after turning on the oven, put a cast-iron or other heavy ovenproof skillet on a rack set low in the oven. Rub the chicken with the olive oil, sprinkle it with salt and pepper, and put the herb sprigs on it if you're using them.

❷ When both oven and pan are hot, 10 or 15 minutes later, carefully put the chicken, breast side up, in the hot skillet; if you're using garlic, scatter it around the bird. Roast, undisturbed, for 40 to 50 minutes or until an instant-read thermometer inserted in the meaty part of the thigh registers 155–165°F.

❸ Tip the pan to let the juices from the bird's cavity flow into the pan (if they are red, cook for another 5 minutes). Transfer the bird to a platter and let it rest; if you like, pour the pan juices into a clear measuring cup, then pour or spoon off some of the fat. Reheat the juices if necessary, quarter the bird (see the illustrations on page 685), garnish, and serve with the pan juices.

Herb-Roasted Chicken. A little more elegant: Start the cooking without the olive oil. About halfway through, spoon a mixture of ¹/₄ cup olive oil and 2 tablespoons chopped fresh parsley, chervil, basil, or dill over the chicken. Garnish with more chopped herbs.

Lemon-Roasted Chicken. Brush the chicken with olive oil before roasting; cut a lemon in half and put it in the chicken's cavity. Roast, more or less undisturbed, until done; squeeze the juice from the cooked lemon over the chicken and carve.

Roast Chicken with Paprika. With good paprika (see page 62), quite delicious: Combine the olive oil with about 1 tablespoon sweet paprika or smoked pimentón.

Roast Chicken with Soy Sauce. Chinese-style roast chicken, made easy: Replace the olive oil with peanut or neutral oil, like grapeseed or corn. Halfway through the cooking, spoon or brush over the chicken a mixture of ¹/₄ cup soy sauce, 2 tablespoons honey, 1 teaspoon minced garlic, 1 teaspoon grated or minced fresh ginger (or 1 teaspoon ground ginger), and ¹/₄ cup minced scallion.

Roast Chicken with Cumin, Honey, and Orange Juice. Sweet and exotic: Halfway through the cooking, spoon or brush over the chicken a mixture of 2 tablespoons freshly squeezed orange juice, 2 tablespoons honey, 1 teaspoon minced garlic, 2 teaspoons ground cumin, and salt and pepper to taste.

5 More Ways to Flavor Simplest Whole Roast Chicken

There are many ways to flavor a roast chicken; here are some simple ideas to get you started:

1. Lemon: Use 3 tablespoons freshly squeezed lemon juice in addition to or in place of olive oil.

2. Lime: Use 3 tablespoons freshly squeezed lime juice in a soy sauce mix (as in the Roast Chicken with Soy Sauce variation) or with some minced jalapeño or serrano chiles or hot red pepper flakes, chopped fresh cilantro leaves to taste, and a tablespoon or two of peanut oil.

3. Honey-Mustard: Combine 2 tablespoons to ¹/₃ cup mustard with 2 tablespoons honey and rub the chicken with this mixture during the final stages of roasting.

4. Wine: Put ¹/₂ cup white wine and 2 cloves crushed garlic in the bottom of the roasting pan; baste with this in addition to or in place of the olive oil mixture.

5. Curry: In place of the olive oil, use neutral oil, like grapeseed or corn—or butter. Combine ¹/₂ cup coconut milk (to make your own, see page 389) and 2 tablespoons curry powder (to make your own, see pages 66–67) and baste the chicken with this mixture during the final stages of roasting.

✪ Chicken Braised in Soy Sauce and Lemon

MAKES: 4 servings

TIME: 30 to 40 minutes

Ⓜ

This is a quick and easy chicken braise, a kind of simplified teriyaki (for the "real" thing, see page 671) that makes plenty of light sauce for plain white rice. The lemon really pulls it all together.

1/4 cup peanut or neutral oil, like grapeseed or corn

1 whole chicken, 3 to 4 pounds, trimmed of excess fat and cut into 8 pieces, or any combination of parts

1 teaspoon minced garlic

1 tablespoon minced or grated lemon zest

1/4 teaspoon cayenne, or to taste

2 tablespoons soy sauce

1 teaspoon sugar

Juice of 1 lemon

❶ Put the oil in a deep skillet with a lid or a Dutch oven over medium-high heat. When the oil is hot, add the chicken, skin side down, and brown it well, rotating and turning the pieces as necessary; the process will take 10 to 15 minutes. (You can skip this step if you like, as noted in "Braised Chicken Parts," page 649; heat a tablespoon of oil and go directly to cooking the garlic.)

❷ When the chicken is nicely browned, remove it from the skillet and turn the heat down to low. Pour or spoon off all but a tablespoon of the oil. Add the garlic and cook, stirring, until it softens, a minute or two. Stir in the zest, cayenne, soy sauce, sugar, and 1/3 cup water. Add the chicken and turn it once or twice in the broth. Adjust the heat so that the liquid bubbles gently but steadily. Cover and cook, turning once or twice, until the chicken is cooked through, 10 to 20 minutes (longer if you skipped the browning step); the bird is done when an instant-read thermometer inserted into the thickest part of the thigh reads 155–165°F.

❸ Transfer the chicken to a serving platter and stir the lemon juice into the broth. Pour some of the broth over the chicken and pass the rest at the table.

✪ Chicken MarkNuggets

MAKES: 4 servings

TIME: About 30 minutes

Ⓜ

Dumb name, huh? Well, I don't want to get sued. And these are better, anyway. To make sure of that, start with quality ingredients.

Other protein you can use: shrimp, clams, squid, or oysters.

About 1 1/2 pounds boneless white-meat chicken (breasts, cutlets, or tenders), pounded to uniform thickness if necessary, blotted dry

1 cup all-purpose flour for dredging

2 eggs, beaten

2 cups bread crumbs, preferably fresh (page 876), or panko for dredging

Salt and freshly ground black pepper

1/2 teaspoon cayenne

Peanut or neutral oil, like grapeseed or corn, for deep frying

Any of the sauces in "12 Sauces for Fried Chicken" (page 666)

❶ Heat the oven to 200°F. Cut the chicken into 2-inch pieces. Set out the flour, beaten eggs, and bread crumbs on plates or shallow bowls next to each other. Sprinkle the eggs with salt and pepper, and the cayenne.

❷ Dredge the chicken, a few pieces at a time, in the flour, then dip in the egg, then dredge in the bread crumbs. Put the breaded chicken pieces on a baking sheet and, when it's all breaded, transfer to the refrigerator to chill for at least 10 minutes and up to 3 hours. (At this point, you may freeze the MarkNuggets in zipper bags or wrapped in plastic wrap for up to a month.)

Ⓕ Fast   Ⓜ Make Ahead   Ⓥ Vegetarian

3 Put at least 2 inches oil in a deep pan on the stove over medium-high heat; bring to 350°F (see "Deep Frying," page 19). When hot, turn the heat up a bit and add a few chicken pieces, regulating the heat so that there is a good constant sizzle but no burning. Cook in batches as necessary, making sure not to crowd the pan.

4 Turn the chicken pieces as they brown. The total cooking time should be 4 minutes or less. As each piece is done, transfer it to an ovenproof platter and put the platter in the oven. Serve as soon as all the pieces are cooked with sauce for dipping.

Cornmeal Chicken MarkNuggets. Substitute cornmeal for the bread crumbs.

Coconut Chicken MarkNuggets. Excellent with Cilantro-Mint Chutney (page 37): Substitute 1 cup shredded coconut for half the bread crumbs.

Super-Crunchy Pan-Fried Chicken Breasts with Curry. Omit the eggs and bread crumbs; instead of the cayenne, use 1 tablespoon of any curry powder or other spice mixture. Rub the chicken all over with a tablespoon of rice or cider vinegar; sprinkle with salt, pepper, and the spice mixture; and rub again. Whisk the flour with about 1/2 cup warm water to make a paste about as thick as yogurt. Heat about 1/4 inch of the oil in a skillet over medium-high heat. Dredge the chicken in the batter and pan-fry in batches as described above.

✪ Basic Roast Turkey Breast, on the Bone

MAKES: 6 to 12 servings or more
TIME: About 1 hour
Ⓜ

At 3 to 6 pounds, a turkey breast is a fine choice for a small party and produces plenty of leftovers for sandwiches. The roasting itself is a breeze, and you can also use any of the variations for whole roast chicken on pages 686–687, adjusting the cooking time accordingly.

One 3- to 6-pound turkey breast

About 3 tablespoons extra virgin olive oil or melted butter for basting

Salt and freshly ground black pepper

1 Heat the oven to 450°F. Put the turkey on a rack in a roasting pan. Brush the turkey with oil, season it with salt and pepper, and put it in the oven.

2 Roast for about 45 minutes, basting every 15 minutes or so, then begin checking every few minutes with an instant-read thermometer. The turkey is ready when the thermometer reads 15–165°F. Let the turkey rest for 5 to 10 minutes before carving and serving.

The Basics of Chicken Parts

This, of course, is the way almost everyone buys bone-in chicken these days. Whether cut into eight pieces—two legs, two thighs, two breast halves, and two wings—or packaged as individual parts, it's undeniably convenient. But you can save money and have a few trimmings for the stockpot if you cut up whole birds yourself (see page 648).

In these recipes, I usually specify cut-up whole chickens. But if it's guaranteed juicy tenderness you're after, use all dark meat; breasts easily become overcooked. Bone-in breasts tolerate a wider range of cooking times without drying than boneless breasts. But when you cook white and dark meat together you must not overcook the white meat (or undercook the dark). You can improve the odds of everything finishing at the same time by starting the legs a little before the breasts and by keeping them in the hottest part of the pan. And to help parts cook more quickly, cut the legs in two, right through the joint between the thigh and the drumstick (see the illustrations on page 648).

In any case, remove the breasts as soon as they're done, even if the legs have a few minutes more to go. When measured with an instant-read thermometer, the range for both breasts and thighs is 155–165°F (see "Chicken Doneness and Safety," page 639).

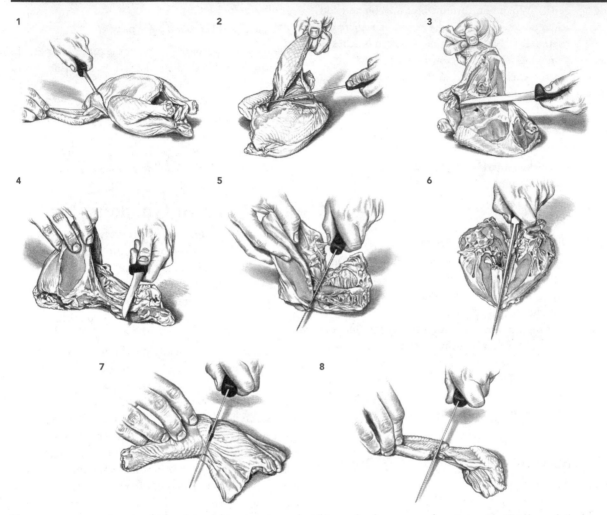

There are many ways to cut a chicken into eight or ten pieces, but this one has become my favorite. **(STEP 1)** Cut through the breast near, rather than through, the wing joint. This serves two purposes: It's easier (you don't have to locate the exact spot of the joint), and it gives you a much meatier wing at little sacrifice to the breast. **(STEP 2)** Hold up one of the legs by its end and slice the skin between the breast and leg; it's easy to see. **(STEP 3)** Find the joint where the thigh meets the carcass and cut through it. **(STEP 4)** Pop the back off the breast; the carcass will break in half quite easily. **(STEP 5)** Cut the back away from the breast. (Make sure you save the back, wing tips, and any other scraps for stock.) **(STEP 6)** Cut the breast in half; what's illustrated here is cutting lengthwise, but you can cut across the breast as well. You can also cut it into three or four pieces instead of two. **(STEP 7)** Find the joint connecting the leg and thigh and cut through it if you like. **(STEP 8)** Find the joint connecting the wing sections and cut through it if you like. Cut off the wing tips (they have virtually no meat) and reserve for stock.

Braised Chicken Parts

Most of these are fast, flavorful, one-pot chicken dinners, often including vegetables and/or rice that cook along with the chicken. Recipes like these develop more flavor and texture when they begin with browning the chicken, but it's a step you can consider optional. It takes time and energy to create a crisp skin (it also messes up the stove), but when you add liquid and cover the pan to finish the cooking, the skin softens again (and many people remove the skin anyway). The initial browning adds flavor; but if you're in a hurry or you're going to do away with the skin, skip it.

For these recipes you need a very large (at least 12 inches), deep skillet or a Dutch oven so all the chicken will fit comfortably in one layer.

Chicken in Red Wine Sauce

Coq au Vin

MAKES: 4 servings
TIME: About 40 minutes

The French home-style standard, very dark and rich. If you use a typical chicken, it's actually a pretty quick recipe to prepare; traditionally, the bird would be old and tough (if you've come across such a bird, cook it this way, but for a while longer). Use a decent but not necessarily expensive red wine and serve with hearty bread or Mashed Potatoes (page 339).

1 ounce dried porcini mushrooms

4 ounces slab bacon, cut into ¼-inch dice

20 pearl onions, peeled, or 1 large onion, sliced

8 ounces button mushrooms, trimmed and roughly chopped

1 whole chicken, 3 to 4 pounds, trimmed of excess fat and cut into 8 pieces, or any combination of parts

6 cloves garlic, peeled

Salt and freshly ground black pepper

2 cups chicken stock (to make your own, see page 157)

2 cups Burgundy (Pinot Noir) or other fruity red wine

2 bay leaves

Several sprigs fresh thyme

Several sprigs fresh parsley

2 tablespoons butter

Chopped fresh parsley leaves for garnish

1 Soak the porcini mushrooms in hot water to cover while you proceed with the recipe. Put the bacon in a large, deep skillet with a lid that will hold all the chicken. Cook over medium-high heat, stirring occasionally, until the bacon gives up its fat and becomes brown and crisp, about 10 minutes. Add the onions, button mushrooms, and chicken, skin side down, and brown the chicken well, rotating and turning the pieces as necessary; the process will take 10 to 15 minutes. About halfway through this time, add the garlic and sprinkle the chicken with salt and pepper.

2 Pour or spoon off any excess fat and add the stock, wine, and herbs. Adjust the heat so that the mixture bubbles gently but steadily. Cover and cook for about 20 minutes, or until the chicken is tender and cooked through; the bird is done when an instant-read thermometer inserted into the thickest part of the thigh reads 155–165°F. (If you like, you can remove the breast pieces, which will finish cooking first, and keep them warm while the leg pieces finish.) Transfer the chicken to a platter and keep warm.

3 Drain the porcini, add them to the skillet, and turn the heat to high (if you like, strain the mushroom-soaking liquid and add that too). Boil until the mixture is reduced by about three-quarters and becomes fairly thick and saucy. Lower the heat, stir in the butter, and return the chicken to the pan, just to reheat a bit and coat with the sauce. (You can make the dish ahead to this point and refrigerate for up to a day; reheat gently.) Taste and adjust the seasoning, garnish with parsley, and serve.

Chicken and Lentils

MAKES: 4 servings
TIME: 1 hour, largely unattended

A simple, spicy, North African–style dish made in one pot. Using chickpeas (see the variation) is a little more work but worth the effort when you have some extra time. Serve this with rice, warmed pitas, or any crusty loaf.

¼ cup extra virgin olive oil

1 whole chicken, 3 to 4 pounds, trimmed of excess fat and cut into 8 pieces, or any combination of parts

1 large or 2 medium onions, sliced

1 tablespoon chopped garlic

1 tablespoon chopped or grated fresh ginger or 1 teaspoon ground ginger

1 cup chopped tomato (canned is fine; include the juices)

1 teaspoon ground coriander

Salt and freshly ground black pepper

1 large bunch fresh cilantro or parsley sprigs, tied together with kitchen string

Two 3-inch cinnamon sticks

1 cup dried brown or green lentils, washed and picked over

❶ Put the oil in a deep skillet with a lid or a Dutch oven over medium-high heat. When hot, add the chicken, skin side down, and brown it well, rotating and turning the pieces as necessary; the process will take 10 to 15 minutes. (You can skip this step if you like, as noted on page 649; heat a tablespoon of oil and go directly to cooking the onions.)

❷ When the chicken is nicely browned, remove it from the skillet and turn the heat down to medium. Pour or spoon off all but a tablespoon of the oil. Stir in the onions, garlic, ginger, tomato, coriander, and some salt and pepper. Add 4 cups water, along with the cilantro or parsley bundle, cinnamon sticks, and lentils. Adjust the heat so the mixture bubbles gently but steadily, cover, and cook for about 30 minutes, or until the lentils are almost tender.

❸ Discard the herb bundle and cinnamon sticks and return the return the chicken to the pan, skin side up. Cover and continue to let the mixture bubble gently until the chicken is cooked through, another 10 to 20 minutes; the chicken is done when an instant-read thermometer inserted into the thickest part of the thigh reads 155–165°F. Taste and adjust the seasoning and serve. (At this point, you may let the dish sit for a few hours or cover and refrigerate for up to a day before reheating and serving; you may have to add a little water to thin the sauce a bit.)

Braised Chicken and Chickpeas. If you must, use canned, though it's so much better (and not that much work) to start with dried: Follow the method for cooking beans on page 411, cooking the chickpeas to the point where they would be ready to salt—just barely tender. Use about 2 cups cooked chickpeas (and a little of their cooking liquid) instead of the lentils in this recipe; save the rest (and their liquid) for another use.

Chicken with Yogurt and Indian Spices

MAKES: 4 servings
TIME: About 45 minutes

Sweet, saucy, and warming. Wonderful over the main recipe for Rice Pilaf, Seven Ways (page 460), or white or brown basmati rice. For extra flavor, start with whole cumin, coriander, cardamom, and cinnamon and toast and grind them yourself (see page 60).

¼ cup peanut or neutral oil, like grapeseed or corn

1 whole chicken, 3 to 4 pounds, trimmed of excess fat and cut into 8 pieces, or any combination of parts

1 large or 2 medium onions, sliced

Salt and freshly ground black pepper

1 tablespoon chopped garlic

1 tablespoon chopped or grated fresh ginger or
   1 teaspoon ground ginger

$1/2$ teaspoon cayenne, or to taste

1 teaspoon ground cumin

1 teaspoon ground coriander

1 teaspoon ground cardamom

$1/2$ teaspoon ground turmeric

$1/2$ teaspoon ground cinnamon

2 cups yogurt

Chopped fresh cilantro leaves for garnish

❶ Put the oil in a deep skillet with a lid or a Dutch oven over medium-high heat. When hot, add the chicken, skin side down, and brown it well, rotating and turning the pieces as necessary; the process will take 10 to 15 minutes. (You can skip this step if you like, as noted on page 649; heat a tablespoon of oil and go directly to cooking the onions.)

❷ When the chicken is nicely browned, remove it from the skillet and turn the heat down to medium. Pour or spoon off all but a tablespoon of the oil. Stir in the onions, along with some salt and pepper. Cook, stirring, until the onions soften, about 5 minutes. Add the garlic, ginger, and spices, along with $1/2$ teaspoon freshly ground black pepper. Cook with the onions, stirring, until very aromatic, 2 or 3 minutes. Stir in the yogurt, then return the chicken pieces to the pan.

❸ Cover and cook over medium-low heat so that the mixture doesn't boil, turning the pieces every 5 minutes or so, until the chicken is cooked through, 10 to 20 minutes (longer if you skipped the browning step); it's okay if the mixture curdles a bit. The bird is done when an instant-read thermometer inserted into the thickest part of the thigh reads 155–165°F. Taste and adjust the seasoning, garnish with cilantro, and serve.

How to Render Chicken (or Any Other) Fat

Rendering fat takes time but almost no effort. To render a pound of fat—whether chicken, duck, pork, or a combination—cut it into roughly $1/2$-inch pieces and put it in a medium skillet over low heat. Add any leftover trimmings you might have saved. Cook, stirring only occasionally, until there is nothing left but clear fat in which pieces of browned skin are sitting; this will take at least 30 minutes. (About $1/2$ cup of minced onion, added during the second half of the rendering process—with or without 3 or 4 bay leaves—is a nice touch, but you have to know you're not going to use the fat for anything with which these flavors will clash.) After the fat has cooled slightly, strain it. Refrigerate and use for cooking. The bits of crispy skin (and onion if you used it) may be salted and eaten as a snack or combined with other dishes. The fat itself will keep, refrigerated, for weeks.

Chicken with Clams

MAKES: 4 servings
TIME: About 1 hour

Pork with clams is a Portuguese standard, but this is an odd East-West variation that has become an American classic in its own way. I first ate it nearly 30 years ago and have been slowly tinkering with the recipe (and improving it, I hope) ever since. I've never tired of it; the clams add a delicious brininess to the braised chicken (take it easy on the salt).

$1/4$ cup extra virgin olive oil

About 1 cup all-purpose flour for dredging

Salt and freshly ground black pepper

1 whole chicken, 3 to 4 pounds, trimmed of excess fat
   and cut into 8 pieces, or any combination of parts,
   blotted dry

1 tablespoon minced garlic

Pinch cayenne

1 medium carrot, diced

$1/2$ cup dry white wine or water

1 tablespoon minced or grated fresh ginger, plus a little more for garnish

2 dozen littleneck clams, scrubbed and rinsed (see page 616)

1 teaspoon dark sesame oil

$1/2$ cup roughly chopped scallion for garnish

Chopped fresh cilantro leaves for garnish (optional)

1 Put the oil in a deep skillet with a lid or a Dutch oven over medium-high heat. Put the flour on a plate or in a shallow bowl and sprinkle it with salt and pepper. When the oil is hot (a pinch of flour will sizzle), dredge the chicken pieces in the flour (thighs first, followed by drumsticks, then finally breasts and wings), shaking off any excess. As you coat the pieces, add them to the oil and brown on all sides. Regulate the heat so that the oil bubbles but is not so hot that it will burn the chicken. Rotate and turn the chicken as necessary until the chicken is nicely browned; the process will take 10 to 15 minutes.

2 Remove the chicken from the skillet and turn the heat down to medium. Pour or spoon off all but a couple of tablespoons of the oil. Add the garlic, cayenne, and carrot and cook, stirring, for about 5 minutes. Add the wine, ginger, and chicken. Sprinkle all with pepper, but hold off on additional salt.

3 Adjust the heat so that the mixture bubbles gently but steadily. Cover and cook, turning the pieces every 5 minutes or so, until the chicken is almost cooked through, 10 to 15 minutes (longer if you skipped the browning step). When the chicken is almost cooked through (an instant-read thermometer inserted into the thickest part of the thigh will read about 150°F), add the clams. Re-cover and raise the heat to medium.

4 Cook until the clams open and the chicken temperature is 155–165°F, about 10 minutes. Stir in the sesame oil, taste and adjust the seasoning, then garnish with the scallion, remaining ginger, and the cilantro if you're using it, and serve.

Chicken and Garlic Stew

MAKES: 4 servings

TIME: About $1^{1}/_{4}$ hours, largely unattended

A now-classic braised dish, sometimes called "chicken with forty cloves of garlic." When it first became popular in the United States, back in the sixties (which is when I first made it), it was a radical notion; now it seems tame. But it's still delicious, with its soft, mild-flavored garlic, which is wonderful spread on good bread.

It's not necessary to peel the garlic; in fact, the skins keep the cloves intact. They are easily peeled with a knife and fork (or fingers) at the table.

2 tablespoons extra virgin olive oil

1 whole chicken, 3 to 4 pounds, trimmed of excess fat and cut into 8 pieces, or any combination of parts

At least 2 heads garlic, separated into cloves but not peeled

$1/2$ cup chopped fresh parsley leaves, plus more for garnish

$1/2$ teaspoon ground cinnamon or $1/4$ teaspoon ground allspice

Salt and freshly ground black pepper

$1/2$ cup dry white wine, chicken, meat, or vegetable stock (to make your own, see pages 157–159), or water

1 Put the oil in a deep skillet with a lid or a Dutch oven over medium-high heat. When hot, add the chicken, skin side down, and brown it well, rotating and turning the pieces as necessary; the process will take 10 to 15 minutes. (You can skip this step if you like, as noted on page 649; just use 1 tablespoon of oil and proceed to Step 2.)

2 Add the garlic, parsley, and cinnamon, sprinkle with salt and pepper, and pour the liquid over all. Bring to a boil, then adjust the heat so the mixture bubbles gently but steadily.

3 Cover and cook, undisturbed, for about an hour, until the chicken and garlic are very tender. (You can

 F Fast   **M** Make Ahead   **V** Vegetarian

make the dish ahead to this point and refrigerate for up to a day; reheat gently.) Transfer to a deep platter, garnish with parsley, and serve, spreading the softened garlic cloves onto good crusty bread.

Cooking Rabbit

Because rabbit is so lean and muscular, it doesn't work well with dry-heat cooking methods like broiling, grilling, or roasting. But you can substitute rabbit—which really does taste like chicken—for virtually any recipe for braised chicken.

Some supermarkets and specialty food stores regularly carry rabbit frozen or even fresh, or you can order it from the same sorts of places where you'll find quail or other game birds. If it's not cut up, split the rabbit along the backbone, then separate the loin (akin to chicken breast) from the hindquarters. You can then cut it into eighths, just as you would chicken (see the illustrations on page 648).

Chicken and Rice Dishes

It's amazing how many wonderful dishes are made with little more than chicken and rice. From fragrant, beguiling Chicken Biryani to the more austere but no less enjoyable Arroz con Pollo, you can't go wrong. These are like braised dishes in their technique, but the results are moist rather than stewy; with a salad or vegetable, they make a complete meal.

I suggest using the rice that's closest to traditional, but in general use long-grain, like basmati, if you want separate, super-fragrant grains and short-grain if you want a clumpier, more substantial-feeling dish. Both are appropriate, and it's fine to swap, but just know what you're getting into. (If you want the real rundown, see pages 455–457.)

Arroz con Pollo

MAKES: 4 servings
TIME: About 1 hour

There are as many ways to make this as there are to make fried chicken, and they're all pretty good. This version is stripped to its bare essentials: onion, chicken, and rice. You can add peas, red pepper, tomato, seasonings like bay leaves and allspice—well, see the variation for a more complex version. Stock makes the best cooking liquid, but the commonly used water works well, because as it simmers with the chicken they combine to produce a flavorful broth, which is in turn absorbed by the rice.

Saffron is not essential here, though it is welcome. More often than not, though, people make arroz con pollo with turmeric or annatto oil, which are more about color than flavor; the dish is customarily yellow. Take your pick.

3 cups chicken or other stock (to make your own, see pages 157–159) or water

3 tablespoons extra virgin olive oil

1 large or 2 medium onions, sliced

Salt and freshly ground black pepper

1 1/2 cups short-grain white rice

Pinch saffron threads (optional)

1 whole chicken, 3 to 4 pounds, trimmed of excess fat and cut into 8 pieces, or any combination of parts

Chopped fresh parsley leaves for garnish

Lemon or lime wedges for serving

❶ Warm the stock while you cook the onions. Put the olive oil in a large skillet with a lid over medium-high heat. Add the onions and a sprinkling of salt and pepper. Cook, stirring occasionally, until the onions soften and become translucent, 5 to 10 minutes.

❷ Add the rice to the onions and stir until it's coated with oil, a minute or two; sprinkle with the saffron if you like and stir again. Nestle the chicken pieces in the rice, add a little more salt and pepper, and pour in the warmed stock. Bring the mixture to a boil; adjust the heat so that the mixture bubbles gently but steadily.

3 Cover and cook for about 20 minutes, until all the liquid is absorbed and the chicken is cooked through; the bird is done when an instant-read thermometer inserted into the thickest part of the thigh reads 155–165°F. (At this point, you may keep the dish warm over very low heat for another 15 minutes, and it will retain its heat for 15 minutes beyond that and still be good warm rather than hot.) Garnish with parsley and serve with lemon or lime wedges.

Grand Arroz con Pollo. It's all about additions. While the stock warms, render about 4 ounces bacon, cut into small cubes, in the skillet in 1 tablespoon oil. Remove it with a slotted spoon and cook the onions and rice as directed. When the rice is ready, add 1 tablespoon chopped garlic, 1 chopped red bell pepper (or a mixture of red and green), 1 chopped tomato (preferably peeled and seeded; you can use canned), a pinch of ground allspice, a bay leaf, and the saffron. Proceed with the recipe; if you like, add 1 cup peas, fresh or thawed frozen, to the dish about 10 minutes before the dish is finished.'

Chicken Biryani

MAKES: 4 servings
TIME: About 1 hour

The prince of chicken-and-rice dishes, simply magnificent but easy enough for a weeknight. (The chicken isn't browned, which actually makes it easier than many similar preparations.) You must use butter, and a fair amount of it, and preferably good spices: cardamom in the pod (which is delicious to eat), whole cloves (which are not!), a cinnamon stick, and real saffron.

4 tablespoons (½ stick) butter

1 large or 2 medium onions, sliced

Salt and freshly ground black pepper

1 large pinch saffron threads

10 cardamom pods

5 cloves

One 3-inch cinnamon stick

1 tablespoon minced or grated fresh ginger

1½ cups basmati rice

3 cups chicken stock, preferably homemade (see page 157)

1 whole chicken, 3 to 4 pounds, trimmed of excess fat and cut into 8 pieces, or any combination of parts

¼ cup slivered blanched almonds (optional)

1 Put 2 tablespoons of the butter in a deep skillet with a lid or a Dutch oven over medium-high heat. When melted, add the onions and some salt and pepper and cook, stirring occasionally, until the onions soften but are not browned, 5 to 10 minutes. Add the spices and stir for another minute.

2 Add the rice and cook, stirring occasionally, until it is glossy and all the ingredients are well combined, 2 or 3 minutes. Add the stock, chicken, and some more salt and pepper and bring to a boil; adjust the heat so that the mixture bubbles gently but steadily.

3 Cover and cook, undisturbed, until the chicken and rice are both tender and the liquid is absorbed, about 25 minutes. The bird is done when an instant-read thermometer inserted into the thickest part of the thigh reads 155–165°F. If either chicken or rice is not quite done, add a little—no more than ½ cup—boiling water, re-cover, and cook for another 5 minutes before checking again. When the chicken and rice are done, turn the heat off and re-cover.

4 Meanwhile, melt the remaining butter in a small skillet over medium heat. Add the almonds if you're using them (if you're not, simply melt the butter) and brown them very lightly, for just 3 minutes or so. Pour this mixture over the biryani, sprinkle with a bit more salt, and re-cover; let rest for another 2 or 3 minutes. (You can keep the dish hot at this point in a 200°F oven for up to 30 minutes without sacrificing its quality.) Take the pot to the table, uncover, and serve.

Chicken with Rice, Hainan Style

MAKES: 4 servings

TIME: 1½ hours, plus time to rest

In this Chinese classic, you poach the chicken, then the rice in the resulting stock and serve them together, with garnishes and a flavorful sauce. Not to put too fine a point on it, the dish itself is kind of bland; but with sauce, it's delicious, because the rice has that nice chickeny fattiness.

1 whole chicken, 3 to 4 pounds, trimmed of excess fat and cut into 8 pieces, or any combination of parts

Salt

3 tablespoons roughly chopped garlic

5 slices fresh ginger, smashed

¼ cup peanut or neutral oil, like grapeseed or corn

2 cups any rice

2 tablespoons dark sesame oil

Ginger-Scallion Sauce (page 39)

About 2 cups peeled, seeded (see page 293), and diced cucumber

2 tomatoes, sliced

Chopped fresh scallion and/or cilantro leaves for garnish

1 Put about 4 inches of water in a large pot over high heat. Rub the inside and outside of the chicken with salt and about half the garlic and ginger. When the water boils, put the chicken in the pot; it should be just submerged (add more water if necessary and return to boiling, or remove some if you have to). Cover, reduce the heat to medium, and cook for 10 minutes. Turn off the heat and let the bird remain in the water for 1 hour, covered. The meat should be opaque all the way to the bone; if not, return the pot to a boil and cover again for another 5 minutes.

2 Remove the chicken from the pot (leave the stock in there) and set aside. (At this point, you may refrigerate the chicken and cooking water if you want to make the rice later or even the next day.) Put the oil in a skillet over medium heat. When hot, add the remaining garlic and ginger; cook, stirring occasionally, until the garlic begins to brown, about 3 minutes. Add the rice and stir, then add 4 cups of the stock; bring to a boil again, adjust the heat so that the mixture bubbles gently but steadily, and cover. Cook until the rice has absorbed all the liquid, about 20 minutes. Taste and adjust the seasoning.

3 Rub the chicken with sesame oil and cut it into bite-sized pieces (you decide whether to include the bones). Drizzle some of the sauce over it and serve over the rice, decorated with the cucumber and tomatoes and sprinkled with the scallion and/or cilantro over all. Serve with more of one or both of the sauces. You can also heat the remaining stock and serve it in small bowls, sprinkled with the scallion, on the side.

Roast Chicken Parts

I've come to appreciate the beauty of roasting chicken parts. They may not make for the same striking presentation as a whole roast chicken, but they do cook considerably faster, and there's not as much judgment involved. *And* there's no carving. For the easiest example, see the Essential Recipe Roast Chicken Parts with Olive Oil or Butter, page 640.

Since the first edition of this book was published, there's been a lot of talk about brining—a technique used most frequently for poultry but also for shrimp (see page 572) and, to a lesser degree, pork. The thinking behind brining makes sense: Submerge the flesh in a saltwater solution for minutes, hours, or days, depending on its size, to promote an exchange of moisture via the process of osmosis. The seasoned water is absorbed, resulting in a tastier, moister, and more tender meat.

For chickens, Cornish game hens, and other small birds, the process isn't too onerous. You've probably got a nonreactive container (like a stainless-steel pot, ceramic crock, or covered plastic tub) big enough to handle the task and enough refrigerator space to borrow for a couple hours. Whole turkeys are another matter entirely, often requiring a couple days in a sterile bucket and several cubic feet of prime fridge shelf space or a carefully monitored setup in an ice chest (or, if you're lucky, outside temperatures consistently in the thirties).

It's a hassle, but brining is sometimes worth it. If you're going to slow-smoke something like a pork butt or ribs (and subject it to hours next to a wood or charcoal fire), or roast a turkey, then, yes, brining can make a big difference. I also occasionally brine-soak whole chickens (though it's easier to buy a kosher chicken, which is essentially prebrined) or pork chops destined for the grill.

In almost all other cases (again, except for shrimp; see page 572), simple salting produces almost the same result. Here's how: Liberally sprinkle both sides of the poultry or pork with a coarse, pure salt, like kosher or sea salt, and rub it in. (Adding a few herbs at the same time isn't bad either—try a couple tablespoons of chopped thyme and garlic mixed with the salt.) Cover and let it rest on a plate—in the fridge if it will sit for more than an hour or so. Then rinse the meat well, dry, and proceed with the recipe, omitting additional salt until you taste before serving.

There are other advantages too: More of the seasoning comes into direct contact with the chicken, so it has more impact. You can pretty much count on nice browning and crisp skin, as long as you use high enough heat. You don't have to worry about burning as much as you do with broiling or grilling, and the cleanup is pretty easy.

I often use all leg-thigh—or even all thigh—pieces in these recipes; they remain moist even if you overcook them slightly, and give you the crunchiest skin. (If you separate leg from thigh at the joint, a simple cut—illustrated on page 648—you'll also reduce cooking time by about 10 minutes.) But you can use a cut-up whole chicken if you prefer; just make sure to cut the leg-thigh pieces in two so they'll cook almost as quickly as the breast pieces; even then, you may want to remove the breasts a little early to keep them from drying out.

Roast Chicken Parts with Fennel, Celery, or Carrots

MAKES: 4 servings
TIME: 40 minutes

Fennel and other crunchy vegetables, like celery and carrots, are delicious when cooked to full tenderness and make a good base for roast chicken parts. (You can even use parsnips, turnips, rutabagas, or kohlrabi.) This dish has an elegant look. Sprinkle with lightly chopped fennel fronds instead of parsley if you like.

1/3 cup extra virgin olive oil, or as needed

About 1 1/2 pounds vegetables: 2 or 3 bulbs fennel, trimmed and cut into 1/4-inch-thick slices; 2 bunches celery, trimmed and roughly chopped; carrots, trimmed and cut into 1/4-inch-thick coins; or a combination

Salt and freshly ground black pepper

 Fast   Make Ahead   **V** Vegetarian

1 whole chicken, 3 to 4 pounds, trimmed of excess fat and cut into 8 pieces, or any combination of parts

Chopped fresh parsley leaves for garnish

Lemon wedges for serving

❶ Heat the oven to 450°F. Drizzle the bottom of a shallow roasting pan or rimmed baking sheet with about half the olive oil and cover it with a layer of the fennel or other vegetable, allowing the pieces to overlap if necessary but using the whole sheet. Drizzle the remaining olive oil over the fennel and sprinkle with salt and pepper. Roast for about 10 minutes.

❷ Top the fennel with the chicken parts, sprinkled with salt and pepper, all skin side up. Ideally, you'll have a layer of fennel pretty much covered by a layer of chicken, but don't go nuts over it. Spoon some of the olive oil from the bottom of the pan over the chicken. Roast for about 15 minutes, then baste the chicken with the pan drippings and rotate the pan. If necessary, adjust the oven temperature so the chicken browns but does not burn.

❸ The chicken will be done in about 30 minutes. Serve each piece with a portion of the fennel and a little of the pan juices spooned over, garnished with the parsley and with a lemon wedge.

Oven-"Fried" Chicken

MAKES: 4 servings
TIME: 50 minutes

The idea here is to get the crunch of traditional fried chicken without the fat and mess of deep frying. Remove the skin for a lower-fat version or use boneless, skinless breasts or thighs; they won't take quite as long to cook. If you don't have buttermilk on hand, substitute an egg beaten with a tablespoon of water.

Other protein you can use: pork chops (bone-in or boneless).

1 cup buttermilk

1 teaspoon paprika (optional)

$^1/_2$ teaspoon cayenne, or less to taste, or freshly ground black pepper

$1^1/_2$ teaspoons salt

1 whole chicken, 3 to 4 pounds, trimmed of excess fat and cut into 8 pieces, or any combination of parts

2 cups panko or bread crumbs, preferably fresh (page 876)

Neutral oil, like grapeseed or corn, as needed

❶ Heat the oven to 400°F. Mix the buttermilk, paprika, cayenne, and salt in a large bowl. Add the chicken and let it soak for a few minutes. Meanwhile, put the bread crumbs on a plate or in a shallow dish and brush a baking sheet with the oil.

❷ Remove the chicken parts from the bowl a piece at a time and coat in the bread crumbs; press the chicken into the bread crumbs to help them stick. Put the coated chicken on the oiled baking sheet, leaving at least an inch between pieces. Bake the chicken until the exterior is golden brown and the chicken is done (you'll see clear juices if you make a small cut in the meat near the bone), 30 to 40 minutes. Serve immediately.

Oven-"Fried" Herb Chicken. A mixture of chopped herbs is best, but a single herb is good too: Add $^1/_2$ cup chopped mixed fresh herbs, like parsley, chives, basil, and/or dill, with a smaller portion of thyme, rosemary, marjoram, and/or sage, and $^1/_2$ cup freshly grated Parmesan; mix in with 1 cup of the bread crumbs.

Oven-"Fried" Peanut or Other Nut Chicken. Finely chopped nuts add flavor and texture: Substitute 1 cup finely chopped peanuts or other nuts for half the bread crumbs.

Oven-"Fried" Sesame Chicken. Serve these with Soy Dipping Sauce and Marinade (page 25) or any soy-based sauce: Substitute sesame seeds for half the bread crumbs.

Chicken Adobo

MAKES: 4 servings

TIME: About 1¼ hours

This Philippine classic has been called the best chicken dish in the world by a number of my friends and readers. It is cooked in liquid first, then roasted, grilled, or broiled. Here, however, the initial poaching liquid is reduced to make a sauce to pass at the table for both the chicken and white rice, the natural accompaniment.

The coconut milk isn't mandatory, though it does enrich the sauce considerably.

Other protein you can use: pork chops (bone-in or boneless).

1 cup soy sauce

½ cup white or rice vinegar

1 tablespoon chopped garlic

2 bay leaves

½ teaspoon freshly ground black pepper

1½ cups coconut milk (optional; to make your own, see page 389)

1 whole chicken, 3 to 4 pounds, trimmed of excess fat and cut into 8 pieces, or any combination of parts

1 Combine the soy sauce, vinegar, garlic, bay leaves, pepper, 1 cup water, and half the coconut milk, if you're using it, in a covered skillet or saucepan large enough to hold the chicken in one layer. Bring to a boil over high heat. Add the chicken; reduce the heat to medium-low and cook, covered, turning once or twice, until the chicken is almost done, about 20 minutes. (At this point, you may refrigerate the chicken in the liquid for up to a day before proceeding; skim the fat before reheating.)

2 Heat the oven to 450°F or heat a charcoal or gas grill or the broiler to moderate heat and put the rack about 4 inches from the heat source. Remove the chicken pieces from the liquid and dry them gently with paper towels. Boil the sauce, along with the remaining coconut milk if you're using it, over high heat until it is reduced to about 1 cup; discard the bay leaves and keep the sauce warm. Meanwhile, grill, broil, or roast the chicken until brown and crisp and hot, turning as necessary, 10 to 15 minutes total (roasting will take a little longer). Serve the chicken with the sauce.

The Basics of Grilled or Broiled Chicken Parts

Broiling chicken is pretty much the same as broiling anything else (see "Broiling," page 17, and "Grilling," page 17), but grilling chicken parts is best with a two-step approach and two-heat fire (see right). Although I love grilling as much as anyone, with chicken broiling makes a lot of sense. It's just plain easier to adjust the distance from heat source to food with a broiler, which means it's easier to limit flare-ups. And because bone-in chicken takes a while to cook, it's easy to brown chicken in a home broiler.

Note that most grilled and broiled chicken dishes are as good at room temperature as they are hot, which means you can cook them at your leisure.

Grilling Chicken Parts

The key to grilling chicken parts is to render the solid fats without letting them fall onto a heat source so intense they flare up and set the chicken itself on fire. Therefore, it's essential to begin grilling over low and indirect heat. A covered gas grill with one side set on low (or even, in some cases, off) and the other on medium to high, with the chicken on the cool side, works well, as does a low to medium charcoal fire, with the coals banked to one side of the grill and the chicken set off the heat and the cover on. (For general instructions about grilling, see page 17.)

F Fast   **M** Make Ahead   **V** Vegetarian

To do this, start a charcoal fire or get the gas grill going as described above. When the grill is ready, start the chicken skin side up—again, on the cool side of the cooking area. After some of the fat has been rendered, turn it, still over the cool side of the fire; if it flares up, move it to an even cooler part of the fire or turn it so the skin side is up again. When the skin has lost its raw look and most of the fat has been rendered, usually after 20 minutes or so,

it's safe to move the chicken directly over the fire (still, the fire should not be blazing hot). By now the chicken is mostly cooked through; all you are doing is browning it nicely on both sides and finishing the cooking.

Grilled chicken parts are done when firm and browned; if you have any doubts about doneness, cut into it, right alongside the bone. The juices should run clear. This will not make for the most attractive presenta-

The Special Case of Chicken Wings

There are literally dozens of recipes in this chapter that can be adapted for chicken wings, which are a unique combination of white meat and dark. If you cut up your own chickens, you can cut a little into the breast when removing the wings, giving them an extra hunk of white meat (this is how chickens are routinely cut up in France). And for quicker cooking and neater eating, cut the wing in three before you start cooking (see page 648). Freeze the wing tips for making chicken stock. Now you have a two-boned middle section (all dark meat) and the drumsticklike upper wing—with at least some white meat on it and maybe more if you cut up the chicken yourself. They both take about the same amount of time to cook, though the dark-meat section usually remains moister. You'll probably find that everyone at your table prefers one or the other, even if they don't yet know it.

I like broiling, grilling, and stir-frying for chicken wings, and here's why: Broiling and grilling are fast and easy and give consistently good results. Stir-frying, while a bit trickier, is by far the easiest way to cook wings on top of the stove. Roasting saves you neither time nor much effort over broiling, and the results are usually not quite as good. Browning and braising, simmering, or any other method of cooking wings with liquid is not especially satisfying because the wings have a relatively large amount of skin and both the wings and cooking liquid become gummy.

There's an appetizer recipe for Chicken Wings, Six Ways, on page 115, and be sure to see "Infinite Ways to Season or Serve Any Grilled or Broiled Chicken Dish" on page 661. But here is a list of other chicken recipes that also work well with wings. Just note that, largely because of their size, chicken wings cook up to twice as fast as bone-in breasts or legs.

11 of the Best Recipes for Chicken Wings

1. Grilled or Broiled Boneless Chicken with Thai Flavors (page 642)
2. Super-Crunchy Pan-Fried Chicken Breasts with Curry (page 647).
3. Grilled or Broiled Chicken with Provençal Flavors or any of its variations (page 660)
4. Grilled or Broiled Chicken, Japanese Style, or its variation (page 662)
5. Chili-Spiced Fried Chicken (page 665)
6. Grilled or Broiled Boneless Chicken Escabeche or its variation (page 669)
7. Chicken Teriyaki (page 671)
8. Stir-Fried Chicken with Basil and Chiles, Thai Style (page 675)
9. Stir-Fried Chicken with Black Beans (page 676)
10. Stir-Fried Chicken with Ketchup (page 677)
11. Grilled or Broiled Split Chicken or any of its variations (page 693)

tion, but it's more attractive than bloody chicken. With experience, you'll be able to judge doneness by appearance and feel alone.

If you really want to—and you're willing to keep an eye on things—you *can* grill chicken over direct heat in an uncovered grill, whether wood, hardwood charcoal, briquettes, or gas. Don't build too hot a fire and keep part of the grill cool—don't put any fuel under it at all—so you can move the pieces over to it should any of them cause flare-ups. Take your time and don't leave the grill unattended for more than a minute.

Broiling Chicken Parts

Start with a roasting pan; you can line it with aluminum foil to ease cleanup if you like. Because broiling is upside-down grilling, start with the skin side *down* and broil, making sure the pieces do not burn, until they're nearly done, about 15 minutes, then turn and cook until the skin is nicely browned (another 5 minutes or so). If a lot of fat starts to collect in the pan, spoon or pour some of it off.

If, in your judgment, the pieces need a few more minutes, turn skin side down again and cook until done and the juices by the bone run clear. But to make sure the skin is crisp, flip the pieces one more time and broil them skin side *up* for a minute or so.

Simply Grilled or Broiled Chicken Parts

MAKES: 4 servings
TIME: 20 minutes

 F M

This basic recipe begins with chicken, salt, pepper, and . . . whatever you want to put on it. Lemon, and maybe a drizzle of olive oil, is the classic and a good place to start. The other recipes are not much more complicated, but as you can see from the variations and the list, you have plenty of options.

1 whole chicken, 3 to 4 pounds, trimmed of excess fat and cut into 8 pieces, or any combination of parts
Salt and freshly ground black pepper
Extra virgin olive oil
Lemon wedges

1 Heat a charcoal or gas grill or the broiler to moderate heat and put the rack about 6 inches from the heat source. If grilling, keep part of the grill cool for indirect cooking. Sprinkle the chicken with salt and pepper and brush with some olive oil.

2 To grill: When the fire is ready, start the chicken skin side up on the cool side of the grill. After some of the fat has been rendered, turn the chicken; if it flares up, move it to an even cooler part of the fire or turn it so the skin side is up again. When the skin has lost its raw look and most of the fat has been rendered, usually after 20 minutes or so, it's safe to move the chicken directly over the fire. Cook, turning now and then, until both sides are nicely browned and the flesh is firm and cooked through, 5 to 10 minutes longer.

To broil: Start with the skin side *down* and broil, making sure the bird does not burn, until it's nearly done, about 15 minutes, then turn and cook until the skin is brown (to check for doneness, cut into a piece close to the bone; the juices should run clear), 5 to 10 minutes longer.

3 Serve hot, warm, or at room temperature, with the lemon wedges.

Grilled or Broiled Chicken with Provençal Flavors

MAKES: 4 servings
TIME: 45 minutes

 M

A more exotic combination and, with fresh, flavorful herbs, really a joy, a dish that is best eaten outdoors. See the variations for more simple flavoring ideas.

 Fast   Make Ahead   V Vegetarian

1 teaspoon fresh thyme leaves

1 teaspoon chopped fresh rosemary leaves

½ teaspoon chopped fresh lavender leaves (optional)

¼ cup roughly chopped fresh parsley leaves

Salt and freshly ground black pepper

Extra virgin olive oil

8 bay leaves

1 whole chicken, 3 to 4 pounds, trimmed of excess fat and cut into 8 pieces, or any combination of parts

Lemon wedges

❶ Heat a charcoal or gas grill or the broiler to moderate heat and put the rack about 6 inches from the heat source. If grilling, keep part of the grill cool for indirect cooking.

❷ Combine the herbs in a small bowl, sprinkle with salt and pepper, and add enough olive oil to make a paste. Loosen the skin of the chicken and slide a bay leaf between the skin and the meat of each piece, then insert a portion of the herb paste. Re-form the skin over the flesh and sprinkle with a little more salt and pepper.

❸ To grill: Brush the chicken with olive oil and put the pieces skin side up on the cooler side of the grill. After some of the fat has been rendered, turn the chicken; if it flares up, move it farther away from the fire, or turn it skin side up again. When the skin has lost its raw look and most of the fat has been rendered, after about 20 minutes, move the chicken directly over the fire. Cook, turning as needed, until both sides are nicely browned and the flesh is firm and cooked through (to check for doneness, cut into a piece close to the bone; the juices should run clear), 5 to 10 minutes longer.

To broil: Start with the skin side down and broil, making sure the pieces do not burn, until it's nearly done, about 15 minutes, then turn and cook until done, 5 to 10 minutes longer.

4 Serve hot, warm, or at room temperature, with the lemon wedges. (The bay leaf is not edible.)

Grilled or Broiled Chicken with Mustard. Call this deviled if you like: Combine ¹/₂ cup Dijon or coarse mustard, 1 tablespoon freshly squeezed lemon juice, and some salt and pepper. Set aside ¹/₄ cup or so of the mustard mixture. If you're grilling, spread some of the mixture all over the chicken. If you're broiling, spread a little of the mixture on a foil-lined pan; put the chicken pieces on top. Spread a little more of the mixture on the chicken. Grill or broil as directed, basting occasionally with the mustard mixture. Brush once more with the reserved mustard when the chicken is done; serve hot or at room temperature.

Grilled or Broiled Chicken with Lemon and Herbs. Loosen the skin of each piece of chicken (use a paring knife if necessary to separate skin from meat) and insert a bit of fresh herb—a leaf of sage, tarragon, or basil or a few pieces of rosemary, chervil, or thyme—between the skin and the meat. Rub the chicken all over with freshly squeezed lemon juice and sprinkle it liberally with salt and pepper. Grill or broil as directed, brushing with more lemon juice from time to time. Garnish with chopped fresh herbs and serve with lemon wedges.

Grilled or Broiled Chicken with Cilantro and Lime. Much beloved: Combine 3 tablespoons peanut or other oil, 2 tablespoons chopped fresh cilantro, 1 tablespoon freshly squeezed lime juice, 1 tablespoon chopped shallot or onion, ¹/₄ teaspoon cayenne (or to taste), and some salt and pepper. If you're grilling, spread some of the mixture all over the chicken. If you're broiling, spread a little of the mixture on a foil-lined pan; put the chicken pieces on top and sprinkle them with salt and pepper. Spread a little more of the mixture on the chicken. Grill or broil as directed, basting occasionally

with the mixture. When the chicken is done, drizzle it with the remaining mixture and garnish with additional chopped cilantro; serve with lime wedges.

Grilled or Broiled Chicken with Citrus Sauce. Combine the zest and juice of a lemon with the sections of another lemon, the sections of an orange, and the sections of a grapefruit. Add ¹/₄ cup olive oil, 1 teaspoon fresh thyme (or ¹/₂ teaspoon dried), ¹/₂ teaspoon minced garlic, 1 small onion, chopped, and some salt and pepper; warm gently. Grill or broil the chicken, using just a little olive oil to lubricate the pan and/or chicken as it cooks. Serve the chicken with the Citrus Sauce.

Grilled or Broiled Chicken with Spicy Maple Syrup Glaze. Combine ¹/₄ cup maple syrup with a sprinkle of salt, pepper, and about ¹/₂ teaspoon smoked paprika or cayenne if you like. After the chicken has lost its raw look, brush it with the maple syrup mixture as it cooks.

Grilled or Broiled Chicken with Soy Glaze. Brush the chicken with Soy Dipping Sauce and Marinade (page 25); continue basting the chicken with the sauce as it cooks.

Grilled or Broiled Chicken, Japanese Style

MAKES: 4 servings
TIME: 45 minutes, plus time to marinate

If you like that slightly sweet, soy-saucy crunch of grilled Japanese food, this recipe is for you.

¹/₄ cup soy sauce

2 tablespoons sake or dry white wine

2 tablespoons mirin (or 1 tablespoon honey mixed with 1 tablespoon water)

3 scallions, roughly chopped

1 tablespoon minced garlic

F Fast   **M** Make Ahead   **V** Vegetarian

1 tablespoon minced fresh ginger

1 whole chicken, 3 to 4 pounds, trimmed of excess fat and cut into 8 pieces, or any combination of parts

Neutral oil, like grapeseed or corn, for brushing

Lemon wedges for garnish

1 Mix everything together except the oil and lemon wedges in a large baking dish or heavy plastic bag. Cover and refrigerate for at least 2 hours and as long as overnight, turning occasionally. When you're ready to cook, heat a charcoal or gas grill or the broiler to moderate heat and put the rack about 6 inches from the heat source. If grilling, keep part of the grill cool for indirect cooking.

2 To grill: Start the chicken skin side up on the cool side of the grill, brushing it with some oil. After some of the fat has been rendered, turn the chicken; if it flares up, move it to an even cooler part of the fire or turn it so the skin side is up again. When the skin has lost its raw look and most of the fat has been rendered, after about 20 minutes, it's safe to move the chicken directly over the fire. Cook until both sides are nicely browned and the flesh is firm and cooked through (to check for doneness, cut into a piece close to the bone; the juices should run clear), 5 to 10 minutes longer.

To broil: Start with the skin side down and broil, making sure the bird does not burn, until it's nearly done, about 15 minutes, then turn and cook until done, 5 to 10 minutes longer.

3 Serve hot, warm, or at room temperature, with the lemon wedges.

Grilled or Broiled Chicken, Southeast Asian Style. Minor adjustments make a huge difference in flavor: Use nam pla (Thai fish sauce) in place of the soy sauce; omit the sake, scallions, and ginger. Add to the marinade 2 tablespoons chopped lemongrass (the tender core only), 1 tablespoon coriander seeds, and a full teaspoon of ground black pepper. Garnish with lime instead of lemon.

The Basics of Fried Chicken

Fried chicken isn't particularly difficult, but it presents some challenges, addressed in the order in which you'll need to during cooking.

Choose an oil: A neutral-flavored oil, like grapeseed or corn, works well for frying pretty much anything (corn is usually much cheaper and is adequate), though I like to use peanut oil for Asian-style fried chicken and olive oil if I want that flavor. (There is a myth that olive oil is not good for frying; on the contrary, it adds a delicious flavor to many savory fried foods.) A mixture of lard and butter makes the best-tasting frying fat, if you can find good lard—not an easy task—but it's difficult to convince people that they won't drop dead after one bite. (You won't, and you'll thank me if you try it.)

Choose a skillet (or other vessel): Think broad, deep, and heavy. Broader vessels do use up a lot of oil, but they enable you to fry a lot at once, which reduces the need to cook in batches. For chicken, I usually use the biggest, deepest skillet I have and sacrifice the oil; it's not that expensive anyway. Whatever vessel you choose should be of fairly heavy metal so that it will hold heat well (cast iron is excellent).

Get the temperature right: Allow some time to bring the oil up to temperature (around 350°F), and try not to let it get too much above that. A deep-frying or candy thermometer is helpful, but there are some sensory clues: Oil thins and shimmers as it warms, and it becomes fragrant. And you can always test-fry something when you think the oil is ready: When the oil is the right temperature, a small cube of bread or chicken will first sink, then quickly rise to the surface. If it sinks and stays there, the oil is too cold; if it doesn't sink at all, the oil is too hot, and it's probably smoking or about to (in which case, reduce the heat and wait a while). As with frying any food, the temperature will plunge as soon as you begin to add the chicken, so turn the heat to high when you do to recover; lower it again when necessary.

Control spattering: It's the water in foods that spatters. Drying the chicken with paper towels helps, as does a dry coating. But some spattering is inevitable, and if you want to avoid the risk of getting hit by a pop or two of oil (usually not so bad, but never pleasant), and you want to reduce the cleanup, cover the pan while you're frying (with a pot lid, not a splatter screen, which never works anyway), at least for the first half, when spattering is usually worst. See Fried Chicken Made Easy (next page), which uses this technique.

Cook in batches: If you crowd your food, it won't fry right; *the pieces cannot touch one another* if you want a real crust to form (and if you don't want a real crust, you don't need to be frying). Sometimes this means you must cook in batches. So be it. Keep the cooked pieces warm on a paper-lined tray (or on wire racks) in a very low oven, serve it less than piping hot, or serve it in batches. The chicken will be fine no matter which of these you choose. But it won't be fine if you put too much in the pan at once.

Drain: Paper bags or paper towels are both fine. If you fry well, and you will—it's simply not that difficult—there won't be a lot of grease to drain anyway.

Dispose of the oil: If you live in the country, you probably have your own method already. If you live in the city or suburbs, the best method is this: Let the oil cool. If you're going to save it (once-used oil is still fine to fry with again or to use for stir-frying, but oil is so cheap that many people don't bother), strain it, pour it into a jar, and refrigerate. If you're not going to save it, pour it into a jar, cover the jar, and throw it in the trash. Or use a plastic container, like a used yogurt container, but tape the top on (I use duct tape for this, because I don't want to take any chances).

 Fast   Make Ahead   **V** Vegetarian

See "Deep Frying" (page 19) for more detail. But unless you deep-fry daily, the answer to the question "Should I buy a deep fryer?" is no. You don't need it. A cast-iron skillet will do a better job than a fancy plug-in model; save your money for higher-quality chicken.

Fried Chicken Made Easy

MAKES: 4 to 6 servings
TIME: About 30 minutes

You can skip the pepper and cinnamon here, but American fried chicken should have some punch, so I include them. Like all good fried chicken, this one is great hot or at room temperature.

> 1 whole chicken, 3 to 4 pounds, trimmed of excess fat and cut into 8 pieces, or any combination of parts
>
> Neutral oil, like grapeseed or corn, olive oil, or a combination of lard and butter, as needed
>
> 2 cups all-purpose flour
>
> 1 tablespoon salt
>
> 1 tablespoon freshly ground black pepper, or more to taste
>
> 2 tablespoons ground cinnamon
>
> Lemon wedges (optional)

❶ Dry the chicken well with paper towels. Heat at least ¹/₂ inch of the fat over medium-high heat in a large, deep skillet, broad saucepan, or similar vessel with a lid. While it is heating, mix together the flour and seasonings in a plastic bag. Toss the chicken in the bag, 2 or 3 pieces at a time, until they are well coated with flour. Put them on a rack as you finish. (Or wait until the oil is hot, then toss the chicken with the flour one piece at a time and add the pieces directly to the fat one at a time.)

❷ When the fat reaches 350°F, raise the heat to high and slowly but steadily add the chicken pieces, skin side down. When they have all been added (or, if you're working in batches, one batch), cover the skillet, reduce the heat to medium-high, and set a timer for 7 minutes. After 7 minutes, uncover the skillet, turn the chicken, and continue to cook, uncovered, for 7 minutes.

❸ Turn the chicken skin side down again and cook for about 5 minutes more, turning as necessary to ensure that both sides are golden brown. As the chicken pieces finish cooking (to check for doneness, remove one piece and cut into it close to the bone; the juices should run clear), remove them from the skillet and drain them on paper bags or towels. Serve hot, warm (keep warm in a low oven if you like), or at room temperature, with lemon wedges if desired.

Chili-Spiced Fried Chicken. Even more punch: Use neutral or peanut oil. Sprinkle the flour with 2 tablespoons each chili powder (to make your own, see page 66) and ground cumin, 2 teaspoons ground coriander, ¹/₂ teaspoon cayenne (optional), and some salt and pepper; omit the cinnamon. Serve with lime wedges.

Fried Chicken with Bay Leaves. Use olive oil and heat it with 10 bay leaves. When the bay leaves begin to sizzle, add 4 or 5 garlic cloves. Cook, moving the bay leaves and garlic around in the oil, for 3 to 5 minutes, until the garlic begins to brown, then remove the garlic and the bay leaves. Omit the cinnamon and add 1 tablespoon fresh (or 2 teaspoons dried) thyme leaves to the flour mixture.

4 Spice Rubs for Fried Chicken

Rub the spice mixture onto the chicken or simply add it to the flour.

1. Chili powder (to make your own, see page 66)
2. Curry powder (to make your own, see pages 66–67)
3. Garam masala (to make your own, see page 67)
4. Jerk seasoning (to make your own, see page 68)

12 Sauces for Fried Chicken

1. Any raw or cooked salsa (pages 23, 33–35, and 48–50)
2. Soy Dipping Sauce and Marinade (page 25)
3. Blue Cheese Dressing (page 25)
4. Cilantro (or Other Herb Sauce) and its variation (page 28)
5. Any chutney (pages 36–38)
6. Ponzu Sauce (page 40)
7. Herbed Mayonnaise (page 42)
8. Real Ranch Dressing (page 42)
9. Molasses Mustard (page 44)
10. Lemon-Caper Sauce (page 46)
11. Ketchup (to make your own, see page 51)
12. Barbecue sauce (to make your own, see page 52)

Spicy Batter-Fried Chicken

MAKES: 4 to 6 servings
TIME: 30 minutes

Crunchier and spicier than the previous recipe.

Neutral oil, like grapeseed or corn, or peanut oil, as needed

Salt and freshly ground black pepper

2 tablespoons curry powder (to make your own, see pages 66–67)

1 teaspoon ground allspice

2 tablespoons chopped garlic

1 teaspoon minced fresh chile, like serrano, or to taste, or hot red pepper flakes or cayenne, to taste

1 cup all-purpose flour

1 egg

1 whole chicken, 3 to 4 pounds, trimmed of excess fat and cut into 8 pieces, or any combination of parts

Lemon or lime wedges

1 Heat at least ¹/₂ inch of the fat over medium-high heat in a large, deep skillet, broad saucepan, or similar vessel that can later be covered. While it is heating, combine the seasonings with the flour; beat the egg with ¹/₂ cup water and stir into the flour. The mixture will be thick.

2 When the fat reaches 350°F, raise the heat to high and begin to dip the chicken pieces in the batter and then add them, one at a time, to the skillet. When they have all been added, cover the skillet if you prefer, reduce the heat to medium-high, and set a timer for 7 minutes. After 7 minutes, uncover the skillet, turn the chicken, and continue to cook, uncovered, for another 7 minutes. Continue to fry, turning a couple more times, until nicely browned all over, about 5 minutes longer.

3 As the chicken pieces finish cooking (to check for doneness, cut into a piece close to the bone; the juices should run clear), remove them from the skillet and drain them on paper bags or towels. Serve hot, warm (keep warm in a low oven if you like), or at room temperature, with the lemon or lime.

Buttermilk-Fried Chicken. Requires a little planning, but the results are tender and flavorful: Omit the curry, allspice, garlic, chile, egg, and water. Put the chicken pieces in a zipper bag or a deep bowl, sprinkle them generously with salt and pepper, and coat thoroughly with 1 to 2 cups of buttermilk. Let the chicken marinate for several hours (or overnight) in the fridge. When you're ready to cook, combine the flour with ¹/₂ cup cornmeal in a shallow bowl and heat the fat. When the fat is hot, take the chicken pieces out of the buttermilk, roll them around in the flour mixture, and add them to the pan one at a time as described in Step 2. Proceed with the recipe.

The Basics of Boneless Chicken

Boneless chicken breasts are standard weeknight fare for many Americans—just think how often you visit a friend and see a package defrosting in the fridge. And no wonder: They can be cooked in minutes using a number of

 Fast   Make Ahead   Vegetarian

techniques: on top of the stove in a skillet, on a grill, under a broiler, or in the oven. They can be cooked with little or no added fat and take well to almost any seasoning. Their main problem is that overcooking leaves them tough and dry.

Boneless thighs have different advantages: They are more flavorful, since dark meat contains more fat—and they're more tolerant of slight overcooking, for the same reason. They're now almost as widely available as boneless breasts and are ideal for stir-frying and especially grilling, either whole or as kebabs. (Breasts are better for sautéing and for serving with richer sauces.)

I take the extra step of blotting boneless chicken pieces dry before grilling, broiling, roasting, or sautéing.

Reducing the amount of moisture on the surface of the pieces will ensure they sear rather than steam. (You can also dry skin-on chicken, though I don't think it's necessary.)

With either, use bold flavorings and keep the cooking time short, as little as 6 minutes for thin boneless breasts and tenderloins, never more than 15 or so even for thick whole boneless thighs. Generally, I remove them from the heat when the inside is still a little underdone, rather than completely opaque. (It's not easy to use an instant-read thermometer on thin boneless breasts, but you can get an accurate reading by sliding the probe in from the end, rather than the top, and inserting it into the middle. Breasts or thighs are ready to come off the heat at

SECTIONING AND BONING CHICKEN LEGS

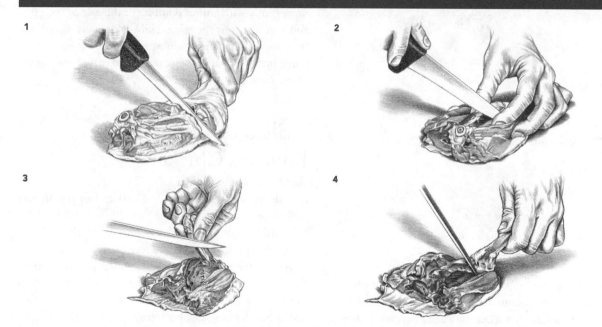

(STEP 1) To cut the leg-thigh piece in two, simply find the joint where they meet and cut through it with a sharp knife. You'll know when you've found it because the knife will not hit bone. (STEP 2) To bone the thigh, cut the meat away from the thick center bone on the meat (nonskin) side. (STEP 3) Continue to cut until the bone is nearly free. (STEP 4) Cut the bone from the remaining meat and remove the skin.

1

2

3

(STEP 1) Use a sharp, thin-bladed knife (usually called a *boning knife*) and cut as close to the bone as you can on the breast-bone (not rib) side. (STEP 2) Continue to cut the meat away from the bone, keeping the knife blade just about parallel to the bone. (STEP 3) When the meat is almost detached, make the final cut. Trim the boneless breast of any pieces of tendon and, if you like, remove the skin.

155–165°F (see page 639); they will continue cooking for several minutes more as you serve them.)

Note that you can easily make your own boneless chicken breasts by buying whole breasts (skin and bone attached) or whole chicken, and removing the meat (see the illustrations that follow). It doesn't take long, especially once you get good at it, it leaves you with terrific bones for stock, and it's considerably cheaper. Boning a thigh isn't much more difficult. (What's hard is boning a whole leg, but you'll sometimes see these sold in super-markets now also; when you do, grab 'em.) Of course none of this is as convenient as buying the meat already boned, which is often the whole idea.

A word about terms: A "chicken breast" is the whole breast, two sides joined by a breastbone. Thus a whole breast, boned and cut in half, produces two "fillets," which can be made even thinner by slicing the piece in half again (so you'd have four "cutlets") or by pounding them gently with a meat pounder or the side of your fist. You can also buy boneless chicken tenders (short for "tenderloins"), a long, thin strip of white meat with a tough little piece of tendon on one end that is best cut off before cooking.

Grilled or Broiled Boneless Chicken

You don't have to build a killer fire or heat your broiler for half an hour to cook chicken cutlets. But you should grill or broil them fairly close to the heat source, which will enable you to brown the outside of the chicken before the inside dries out and toughens.

Any of these recipes (or the Essential Recipe on page 641) can be used for turkey cutlets (or veal or pork) as well as for chicken. Most of them (especially those that add strong flavors) are also terrific with boneless thighs. (Even though they're largely interchangeable, I tell you which is preferred in the recipes where it matters at all.) You'll have to increase the cooking time somewhat, to around 6 to 8 minutes per side.

F Fast   **M** Make Ahead   **V** Vegetarian

Grilled or Broiled Boneless Chicken Escabeche

MAKES: 4 servings

TIME: 20 minutes if eaten immediately or up to 6 hours if marinated

Escabeche means that the meat is first cooked, then marinated, though not necessarily for any length of time. Breast and thigh meat both work perfectly here; if you mix them, remember the thighs take longer. And you can use any Vinaigrette (page 199) in place of the garlicky variation listed here; you can also use other herbs instead of parsley.

Other protein you can use: boneless pork or veal loin.

About 1¹/₂ pounds boneless chicken (breasts, cutlets, tenders, or thighs), pounded to uniform thickness if necessary

2 tablespoons extra virgin olive oil

¹/₂ cup Roasted Garlic Vinaigrette (page 201)

Chopped fresh parsley leaves for garnish

① Heat a charcoal or gas grill or the broiler to moderate heat and put the rack 4 inches (or less) from the heat source. Rub the chicken with the oil and grill or broil quickly, 3 to 4 minutes per side (to check for doneness, cut into a piece with a thin-bladed knife; the center should be white or slightly pink). Meanwhile, gently warm the vinaigrette.

② Remove the chicken and put it on a serving platter; pour the vinaigrette over it. Serve immediately, garnished with the parsley, or refrigerate for 1 to 6 hours to develop the flavors, then serve cold or at room temperature, garnished with parsley.

Grilled or Broiled Boneless Chicken with Wasabi Sauce. No more difficult, a little more exotic: In place of the vinaigrette, combine 1 halved clove garlic, ¹/₂ cup rice or other mild vinegar, 2 tablespoons mirin or 1 tablespoon honey mixed with 1 tablespoon water, 2 tablespoons soy sauce, 1 tablespoon minced fresh ginger, ¹/₂ to 1 teaspoon wasabi powder or 1 tablespoon prepared horseradish, and some salt and pepper. Warm this mixture as for the vinaigrette and proceed with the recipe. Garnish with chopped scallion and/or cilantro.

Grilled or Broiled Chicken Kebabs

MAKES: 4 servings

TIME: About 30 minutes, plus time to marinate

Well-seasoned grilled or broiled kebabs will make anyone a convert to dark-meat chicken. You can use chicken breasts here too, but watch them closely so they don't overcook and dry out.

Other protein you can use: turkey thighs; pork or veal shoulder, steak, or loin; sturdy fish like swordfish or salmon.

About 1¹/₂ pounds boneless chicken thighs or legs, cut into 1¹/₂-inch chunks

2 large onions

2 tablespoons extra virgin olive oil

Juice of 1 lemon

1 tablespoon minced garlic

Salt and freshly ground black pepper

3 bay leaves, crumbled

1 tablespoon fresh marjoram or oregano leaves or 1 teaspoon dried oregano

Lemon wedges or ground sumac (available in Middle Eastern stores)

① If you're using wooden skewers (you'll need at least 8), soak them in warm water while you prepare the chicken. When you're ready to cook—if you choose not to marinate the meat—heat a charcoal or gas grill or the broiler to moderate heat and put the rack about 4 inches from the heat source.

② For the marinade, chop one of the onions and combine it in a large bowl with the oil, lemon juice, gar-

7 WAYS TO VARY GRILLED OR BROILED CHICKEN KEBABS

These variations follow the same technique as the main recipe. Remember the salt and pepper!

VARIATION	MARINADE	OTHER INGREDIENTS TO SKEWER (OPTIONAL)	GARNISH(ES)	COOKING INSTRUCTIONS
Spicy	1 tablespoon chopped garlic; 1 tablespoon chopped fresh ginger; the juice and zest of 1 lime; 1 teaspoon minced fresh chile, hot red pepper flakes, or cayenne, or to taste; 1 teaspoon ground cumin; 1 teaspoon coriander seeds or ground coriander; 2 tablespoons tomato paste; 1 medium onion, chopped	Large chunks of zucchini	Sprinkle with chopped cilantro and serve with lime wedges.	Marinate the chicken as in Step 1 and proceed with the recipe.
Gently Spiced	1 teaspoon ground cardamom; 1 tablespoon minced garlic; 1 teaspoon ground allspice; 1/4 teaspoon freshly grated nutmeg; 1 teaspoon ground turmeric; 1 teaspoon chopped fresh thyme leaves or 1/2 teaspoon dried thyme; peanut oil, as needed	Eggplant cubes tossed in peanut oil	Sprinkle with chopped parsley and serve with lemon wedges.	Add enough peanut oil to the marinade to make a paste; add the chicken; proceed with the recipe.
With Spicy Peanut Sauce	Grated zest and juice of 1 lime; 1 tablespoon peanut oil or other oil; 1 tablespoon soy sauce; 2 tablespoons minced garlic; 2 tablespoons chopped fresh cilantro; 1/4 teaspoon cayenne, or to taste; 2 tablespoons natural peanut butter; 1 medium onion, chopped	1-inch pieces of scallion	Sprinkle with chopped fresh cilantro and serve with lime wedges.	Marinate the chicken as in Step 1 and proceed with the recipe.
With Yogurt-Cumin Sauce	1 cup yogurt; 1 medium onion, chopped; 1 tablespoon chopped garlic; minced zest and juice of 1 lime; 1 tablespoon ground cumin; 1/4 teaspoon cayenne, or to taste; 1 teaspoon ground coriander; 1 teaspoon paprika	Pieces of red bell pepper	Sprinkle with chopped fresh cilantro.	Marinate the chicken as in Step 1 and proceed with the recipe.
With Cherry Tomatoes	3 tablespoons extra virgin olive oil; 1 teaspoon balsamic or sherry vinegar; 1/2 cup chopped fresh basil leaves	A handful of asparagus (peeled and parboiled if it's thick); 15 to 20 cherry tomatoes	Sprinkle with chopped fresh basil.	Don't marinate the chicken for longer than 30 minutes. Proceed as in Step 2, skewering the asparagus and 15 to 20 cherry tomatoes in place of the onion; cook the chicken on separate skewers or broil it all together.
Citrusy	2 tablespoons soy sauce; 1 tablespoon peanut or other oil; grated zest and juice of 1 medium orange, 1 lemon, and 1 lime; 1 tablespoon minced fresh ginger; 1 tablespoon honey; 1 small onion, minced	Chunks of jícama	Sprinkle with chopped fresh parsley, cilantro, or chives (optional).	Marinate the chicken as in Step 1 and proceed with the recipe.

 **F** Fast   **M** Make Ahead   **V** Vegetarian

7 WAYS TO VARY GRILLED OR BROILED CHICKEN KEBABS
(CONTINUED)

VARIATION	MARINADE	OTHER INGREDIENTS TO SKEWER (OPTIONAL)	GARNISH(ES)	COOKING INSTRUCTIONS
Japanese-Style (Yakitori)	¹/₂ cup sake, ¹/₄ cup mirin or 2 tablespoons honey mixed with 2 tablespoons water, ¹/₂ cup soy sauce, and 2 tablespoons sugar	Whole mushrooms	Sprinkle with a little shichimi pepper if you have it and serve with lemon wedges.	Build a slightly less hot fire than normal and watch carefully during cooking, as the sugar will burn more readily.

lic, some salt and pepper, the bay leaves, and the marjoram; taste and adjust the seasoning. Marinate the chicken in this mixture for at least a few minutes or an hour or so at room temperature or longer—even overnight—in the refrigerator.

❸ Cut the remaining onion into quarters, then separate it into large pieces. Thread the chicken and onion alternately onto skewers, leaving a little space between pieces.

❹ Broil or grill, turning once or twice, until the chicken is cooked through, 12 to 15 minutes (to check for doneness, cut into a piece with a thin-bladed knife; the center should be white or slightly pink). Serve with the lemon wedges or sprinkle with a bit of sumac.

Chicken Teriyaki

MAKES: 4 servings
TIME: About 20 minutes

A little sweet; no wonder many Americans love it. Serve with plain short-grain brown or white rice.

Other protein you can use: boneless turkey breasts or thighs, pork chops, or tuna or sirloin steaks.

¹/₃ cup soy sauce

¹/₃ cup sake or slightly sweet white wine, like a German Kabinett or Spätlese (use water if necessary)

¹/₃ cup mirin (or 3 tablespoons honey mixed with 3 tablespoons water)

2 tablespoons sugar

About 1¹/₂ pounds boneless chicken thighs, legs, breasts, or tenders

2 teaspoons grated lemon zest (optional)

❶ Combine the soy sauce, sake, mirin, and sugar in a bowl. If time allows, marinate the chicken in this mixture in a covered dish for 2 hours at room temperature or overnight, refrigerated, turning the meat occasionally. If you're cooking right away, don't bother combining the meat with the sauce.

❷ Heat a charcoal or gas grill or the broiler to moderate heat and put the rack about 4 inches from the heat source. Meanwhile, soak the skewers (you'll need at least 8) in warm water if you're using wood. Remove the meat from the marinade and thread it onto the skewers. Boil the sauce for a couple of minutes in a small saucepan, until it produces lively bubbles and begins to get thick.

❸ Grill or broil the skewers until browned all over and cooked through, basting frequently with the sauce and turning the chicken every 2 or 3 minutes, 10 to 15 minutes (to check for doneness, cut into a piece with a thin-bladed knife; the center should be opaque or slightly pink). Give the meat one final baste and serve hot or at room temperature.

Chicken Teriyaki on the Stove. Heat a large skillet over medium-high heat for about 2 minutes, then add the chicken. Brown quickly on both sides, no more than 2 minutes per side. Transfer it to a plate and turn the heat to medium. Add 2 tablespoons water, followed by the sake, mirin, sugar, and finally soy sauce. Stir to blend and, when the sauce produces lively bubbles and starts to thicken, add the chicken. Cook, turning the chicken in the sauce, until it becomes more of a glaze than a liquid, a couple of minutes tops. By that time the chicken should be cooked; if not, keep cooking, adding a tablespoon or so of water if necessary to keep the glaze from burning.

Roasted Boneless Chicken

The best oven-cooked boneless chicken is easy, but more akin to braising than roasting. The result is tender, moist chicken. It's not browned but it is delicious.

Herb-Roasted Chicken Cutlets

MAKES: 4 servings
TIME: 30 minutes

Here the chicken combines with stock and the meat's juices to produce a simple sauce. Nice over rice.

Other protein you can use: any cutlets—pork, veal, or turkey.

> 1 tablespoon minced fresh tarragon (optional)
> ¼ cup chopped fresh dill or chervil leaves
> ½ cup chopped fresh parsley leaves

Salt and freshly ground black pepper

3 tablespoons butter, extra virgin olive oil, or a combination

About 1½ pounds boneless chicken (breasts, cutlets, tenders, thighs, or legs), pounded to uniform thickness if necessary

1 cup chicken or vegetable stock (to make your own, see page 157) or water, plus a little more if needed, warmed

❶ Heat the oven to 325°F. Mix the herbs with some salt and pepper; set aside about a tablespoon of this mixture and put the rest on a plate. Put the butter and/or olive oil in a baking dish and put in the oven; roll the chicken in the herb mixture. When the butter melts or the oil is hot, add the chicken and stock and return the pan to the oven.

❷ Roast the chicken, turning once or twice, until it is cooked through, about 15 minutes, perhaps longer for thighs (to check for doneness, cut into a piece with a thin-bladed knife; the center should be white or slightly pink). Remove the pan from the oven and transfer the chicken to a warmed plate. If the juices remaining in the pan are thin, return the pan to the stove and cook over high heat for a minute or two to thicken them. Garnish the chicken with the remaining herb mixture and serve with some of the sauce spooned over it.

Chicken Cutlets Roasted with Tomatoes

MAKES: 4 servings
TIME: 40 minutes

Scented with spice, this has a Moroccan feel to it but is no more difficult than putting together a tomato sauce.

Other protein you can use: any cutlets—pork, veal, or turkey.

  F Fast　**M** Make Ahead　**V** Vegetarian

1/4 cup chopped fresh parsley or cilantro leaves, plus more for garnish

1 teaspoon chopped garlic

Pinch cayenne

1 tablespoon ground cumin

1/2 teaspoon ground coriander

Salt and freshly ground black pepper

About 1 1/2 pounds boneless chicken (breasts, cutlets, tenders, thighs, or legs), pounded to uniform thickness if necessary

2 tablespoons extra virgin olive oil

2 cups chopped tomato (drained canned is fine)

1 Heat the oven to 400°F. Mix together the parsley, garlic, cayenne, half of the cumin, the coriander, and some salt and pepper; rub this mixture all over the chicken.

2 Mix the remaining cumin with the olive oil, tomato, and some more salt and pepper; spread half of this mixture on the bottom of a roasting pan. Put the chicken on top and spread the remaining tomato mixture over it. Roast until the chicken is tender and cooked through, 20 minutes or more, basting once or twice with pan juices (to check for doneness, cut into a piece with a thin-bladed knife; the center should be white or slightly pink). Garnish with parsley or cilantro and serve hot or warm.

Roasted Chicken Cutlets with Bread Crumbs

MAKES: 4 servings
TIME: 40 minutes

This is the easiest way to give boneless, skinless chicken a tasty crunch. If you like, mix a handful of chopped nuts in with the bread crumbs; almonds, walnuts, hazelnuts, and pistachios are all good, as are peanuts, especially with Soy Dipping Sauce and Marinade (page 25).

Other protein you can use: any cutlets—pork, veal, or turkey.

2 tablespoons neutral oil, like grapeseed or corn, or melted butter, plus more for greasing the pan

1 cup coarse bread crumbs, preferably fresh (page 876), or panko

1/2 cup chopped fresh parsley or finely chopped nuts (see the headnote)

Salt and freshly ground black pepper

About 1 1/2 pounds boneless white-meat chicken (breasts, cutlets, or tenders), pounded to uniform thickness if necessary

1 egg white, lightly beaten

1 Heat the oven to 400°F. Grease a baking sheet with a little oil or butter. Combine the bread crumbs, 2 tablespoons oil, and 1/4 cup of the parsley in a shallow bowl and sprinkle with salt and pepper. Toss until well coated.

2 Dip one side of each chicken breast first in egg white, then in the bread crumb mixture, pressing down to make it adhere. Put each breast, crumb side up, on the baking sheet. If there's any leftover topping, sprinkle it on top of the breasts and press down a bit.

3 Roast until the chicken is tender and cooked through, 20 minutes or more, basting once or twice with pan juices (to check for doneness, cut into a piece with a thin-bladed knife; the center should be white or slightly pink). Garnish with the remaining parsley and serve.

Cheesy Roasted Chicken Cutlets with Bread Crumbs. Use other hard cheeses if you like; just make sure they're finely grated: Omit the parsley and reduce the oil or butter to 1 tablespoon. Mix 1/4 cup finely grated Parmesan cheese in with the bread crumbs and oil. Proceed with the recipe. Garnish with chopped fresh basil if you like.

Roasted Chicken Cutlets with Olives and Bread Crumbs. Instead of mixing chopped parsley into the bread crumbs, use 1/4 cup minced olives (and use less salt) in the bread crumb mix. Proceed with the recipe, garnishing with parsley or toasted almonds if you like.

Roasted Chicken Cutlets with Miso and Bread Crumbs.
Perfect on top of a bowl of Sushi Rice (page 474), drizzled with Ponzu Sauce (page 40): Omit the egg. In Step 1, when you toss the bread crumbs in oil, skip the salt. Smear each chicken breast with $1/2$ teaspoon of any miso instead of dipping in the egg white. Proceed with the recipe.

The Basics of Stir-Fried Chicken

Stir-fried chicken dishes offer so much in the way of flavor, versatility, nutrition, and ease that they should be among the first things that anyone—weeknight cooks, chicken lovers, those in a hurry, those of you who like to improvise—learns to cook. Boneless breasts and thighs are both fine here (you can also stir-fry chicken wings, though they're not boneless, of course; see page 659).

Don't expect to stir-fry the way you see chefs do in restaurants or on TV; some adjustments must be made for the relative lack of power generated by home stoves. (See "Stir-Frying," page 18.) In restaurants, huge flames under deep woks allow meat and vegetables to sear together. If you try that at home, the amount of food will overwhelm the heat your stove generates, and you'll end up braising rather than browning. To compensate, you must sometimes parboil the vegetables, though usually stir-frying in batches does the trick: you cook vegetables and meat or other protein separately, with some seasonings added during each batch. It's a little slower, but it still usually amounts to less than 15 minutes in front of the stove.

In general, stir-frying is more about technique than recipe. All the parts are interchangeable—protein, vegetables, and seasonings—so once you get the hang of it you can improvise more freely than with any other type of cooking.

All this is a long way of saying "substitute at will." For the chicken, use any meat or meat substitute (conversely, if you see other stir-fry recipes in the book that are appealing, and you want to use chicken, go right ahead); same with the vegetables, as long as you take two things into account: One, starchy or root vegetables—potatoes, for example, or beets—do not work well in stir-fries (turnips and other cabbagey root vegetables are sometimes an exception). Two, you'll need to make adjustments in cooking times. Turnips, even cut small, take far more time to cook than broccoli, and spinach leaves far less than kale.

You can also vary the proportions in stir-fries. I specify a pound of meat for four servings, which makes these light on meat, at least relative to the traditional American diet. But if you're looking to cut back on meat intake even more, they'll taste just as good with 8 ounces (increase the amount of vegetables, however); if you want more chewiness, increase the meat as you like. (If you do this, increase the seasonings slightly instead of cutting back on the vegetables.)

To stir-fry Chinese restaurant style, you can thicken the pan juices with a little cornstarch to make a glossy sauce. It's a step I rarely take, but it's described in more detail on page 47.

Stir-Fried Chicken with Broccoli or Cauliflower

MAKES: 4 servings, with rice
TIME: 20 to 30 minutes

This is the model recipe for making stir-fried chicken with firm vegetables, those that must be parboiled before stir-frying, like asparagus pieces, carrot chunks, and eggplant cubes. The extra step actually saves time—rather than stir-frying everything, it's much faster to soften broccoli and like vegetables with a quick parboiling (as here, or see page 243). But if you want to cook everything in one pan, just cut the broccoli into small dice—

$^1/_2$ inch or so—and cook it as you would the cabbage in the recipe that follows.

2 cups broccoli or cauliflower florets and stems, cut into bite-sized pieces

$^1/_4$ cup peanut or neutral oil, like grapeseed or corn

2 tablespoons minced garlic

1 tablespoon grated or minced fresh ginger

1 medium to large onion, sliced

$^1/_2$ cup chopped scallion, plus more for garnish

1 pound boneless, skinless chicken breast or thighs, cut into $^1/_2$- to $^3/_4$-inch chunks or thin slices and blotted dry

1 teaspoon sugar (optional)

2 tablespoons soy sauce

Salt and freshly ground black pepper

$^1/_2$ cup chicken or vegetable stock (to make your own, see page 157), white wine, or water

❶ Parboil the broccoli or cauliflower for 2 minutes in a pot of boiling water, then drain.

❷ Put a large, deep skillet over high heat. Add half the oil, swirl it around, and immediately add half the garlic and ginger. Cook for 15 seconds, stirring, then add the onion and cook, stirring, for 2 minutes. Add the broccoli or cauliflower and the scallion and cook over high heat until the broccoli or cauliflower becomes tender but not at all mushy, about 5 minutes.

❸ Turn the heat down to medium and remove the vegetables. Add the remaining oil to the pan, then the remaining garlic and ginger. Stir, then add the chicken. Raise the heat to high, stir the chicken once, then let it sit for 1 minute before stirring again. Cook, stirring occasionally, until the chicken has lost its pink color, 3 to 5 minutes.

❹ Return the vegetables to the pan and toss once or twice. Add the sugar if you like, then the soy sauce; toss again. Sprinkle with salt and pepper, then add the liquid. Raise the heat to high and cook, stirring and scraping the bottom of the pan, until the liquid is reduced slightly and you've scraped up all the bits of chicken, about 30 seconds. Garnish with scallion and serve.

Stir-Fried Chicken with Kale or Collards. If you're just using leaves, you can follow the recipe for Stir-Fried Chicken with Cabbage (page 643). If you want to include stems, substitute 2 cups kale or collard leaves and stems for the broccoli. Simmer the greens for about 2 minutes. Rinse under cold water, squeeze dry, and chop.

Stir-Fried Chicken with Basil and Chiles, Thai Style. Fairly fiery, but perfumed too. If you want the latter without the former, reduce or omit the chiles: Omit the broccoli and Step 1. In Step 2, add 2 or 3 minced fresh or dried chiles (like jalapeño or serrano), or to taste, or hot red pepper flakes or cayenne to taste, along with the garlic and ginger. Double the onion and cook it until soft, about 5 minutes; hold off on adding the scallion. Remove the onion and proceed with Step 3. In Step 4, add the scallion when you return the onion, along with 1 cup shredded fresh basil leaves, preferably Thai. Substitute nam pla (Thai fish sauce) for the soy sauce (or use half-and-half) if you like. Garnish with minced fresh basil or scallion.

Stir-Fried Chicken with Chinese Mushrooms. You can use fresh or dried mushrooms here or add $^1/_4$ cup tree ears, lily buds, or other dried fungi you might find in a Chinese market; soak them along with the mushrooms: If you're using dried mushrooms, soak about $^1/_2$ cup dried shiitake ("black") mushrooms in several changes of hot water until soft, about 20 minutes; if you're using fresh shiitakes, just trim and slice a cup, discarding the stems or reserving them for stock. Drain and reserve the liquid from the soaked mushrooms, then trim off any hard parts and cut into bits. Cook them with the broccoli or cauliflower in Step 2, then proceed with the recipe. Use the reserved liquid to replace some or all of the stock or water.

Stir-Fried Chicken with Black Beans

MAKES: 4 servings, with rice
TIME: 20 to 30 minutes

Of all the easy additions to stir-fries, fermented black beans are among the best. They give a special flavor and look, and the technique is effortless. Furthermore, a year's supply of black beans will set you back about a buck at a Chinese market.

You can use black beans in either of the preceding chicken stir-fries too (or any other stir-fry for that matter). Just soak them as you would here and add them in the last step.

Other protein you can use: shrimp, sliced pork tenderloin, or big cubes of firm tofu.

2 tablespoons fermented black beans

2 tablespoons rice wine, dry sherry, or white wine

¼ cup peanut or neutral oil, like grapeseed or corn

2 tablespoons minced garlic

1 tablespoon grated fresh ginger

1 cup sliced onion

1 pound boneless, skinless chicken breast or thighs, cut into ½- to ¾-inch chunks or thin slices and blotted dry

¼ cup chopped scallion, plus more for garnish

1 teaspoon sugar (optional)

2 tablespoons soy sauce

Salt and freshly ground black pepper

¼ cup chicken or vegetable stock (to make your own, see page 157), white wine, or water

1 tablespoon dark sesame oil

① Soak the black beans in the wine. Meanwhile, put a large, deep skillet over high heat. Add half the oil, swirl it around, and immediately add half the garlic and ginger. Cook for 15 seconds, stirring, then add the onion.

12 Simple Additions to Stir-Fried Chicken

You can throw almost anything you like into a stir-fry, but these are some of my favorites; some require a trip to an Asian market, but many will be in your pantry.

1. Add 1 tablespoon or more of bottled hoisin, plum, oyster, or ground bean sauce with the soy sauce.

2. Add ¼ teaspoon or more Vietnamese-Style Chile Paste, Chile and Black Bean Paste, or Chile-Garlic Paste (page 75) with the liquid.

3. Add 1 teaspoon dark sesame oil with the soy sauce. A tablespoon or so of toasted sesame seeds (see page 317) is also good, alone or with the oil.

4. Toss the chicken chunks with 1 tablespoon curry powder or five-spice powder (to make your own, see pages 66–68).

5. Toss in ½ to 1 cup raw or roasted cashews or peanuts when you return the vegetables to the pan.

6. Omit the stock or water and add ½ to 1 cup coconut milk (to make your own, see page 389) along with the soy sauce.

7. Add 1 cup chopped fresh tomato when you return the vegetable to the pan.

8. Replace half the soy sauce with nam pla (Thai fish sauce) or freshly squeezed lime juice or vinegar.

9. Add 1 cup mung bean sprouts when you return the vegetable to the pan.

10. Add ½ cup chopped shallot with the chicken.

11. Use snow peas, mushrooms, or other quick-cooking vegetables, alone or in combination, in addition to or in place of other vegetables.

12. Stir in ¼ cup cooked grains (like barley, wheat berries, buckwheat, or quinoa) when you return the vegetables to the pan.

Raise the heat to high and cook, stirring occasionally, until the onion becomes soft, about 5 minutes. Remove the onion.

 Fast   Make Ahead   Vegetarian

❷ Still over high heat, add the remaining oil to the pan, then the remaining garlic and ginger. Stir, add the chicken, stir again, then let it sit for 1 minute before stirring again. Cook, stirring occasionally, until the chicken has lost its pink color, 3 to 5 minutes.

❸ Turn the heat down to medium, add the scallion, and toss. Return the onion to the pan and add the sugar if you're using it and the soy sauce. Toss again, sprinkle with salt and pepper, then add the beans with their liquid and the stock. Raise the heat to high and cook, stirring and scraping the bottom of the pan, until the liquid is reduced slightly and you've scraped up all the bits of chicken, about a minute. Turn off the heat, drizzle on the sesame oil, garnish with scallion, and serve.

Stir-Fried Chicken with Ketchup

MAKES: 4 servings
TIME: 20 minutes

Before you turn your nose up at the name of this dish, think of all the other condiments you cook with—hoisin sauce, oyster sauce, mayonnaise, Worcestershire sauce, salsa—and then think how good ketchup can taste. And if you like this dish—which I'm betting you will—you'll want to play with it: Cook some peanuts with the chicken, toss some slivered scallions in at the end (the color is brilliant), or substitute soy sauce for the salt.

Other protein you can use: squid, shrimp, or sliced firm tofu.

1¹/₂ pound boneless, skinless chicken breasts or thighs, cut into ³/₄- to 1-inch chunks and blotted dry

¹/₂ cup cornstarch, rice flour, or all-purpose flour, or more as needed

¹/₄ cup neutral oil, like grapeseed or corn

Salt and freshly ground black pepper

2 tablespoons slivered garlic

¹/₂ teaspoon cayenne, or to taste

1 cup ketchup (to make your own, see page 51)

Chopped fresh cilantro leaves for garnish

❶ Toss the chicken with flour so that it is lightly dusted. Put 2 tablespoons of the oil in a large skillet, preferably nonstick, over high heat. When the oil smokes, add the chicken in one layer and sprinkle with salt and pepper.

❷ When the chicken browns on one side, toss it and cook until just about done: Smaller pieces will take 5 minutes total, larger pieces about 10. Transfer to a plate, then turn off the heat and let the pan cool for a moment.

❸ Add the remaining oil to the pan and turn the heat to medium-high. Add the garlic and cayenne and cook, stirring, for about 2 minutes. Add the ketchup and stir; cook until it bubbles, then darkens slightly, about a minute. Return the chicken to the pan and stir to coat with the sauce. Taste and adjust the seasoning, then serve, garnished with the cilantro.

Stir-Fried Tofu with Ketchup. Instead of the chicken, use 1¹/₂ pounds firm or extra-firm tofu, cut into 8 slices and lightly squeezed (see page 444). Proceed with the recipe. (It will need to cook for only 5 minutes or so in Step 2.)

The Basics of Sautéed Chicken Cutlets

Yet another chicken preparation that can rescue you on any given weeknight. Typically, classically, and best prepared with chicken breasts; thighs are a good substitute, but they're a little fatty for this approach, which itself contains more fat than most of the other techniques in this chapter. (Better substitutes are cutlets of lean turkey, veal, pork, or fish.)

Bear in mind that you must use a large enough skillet; this may mean using a little more fat, but it will prevent overcrowding and make it easier to turn the meat. (For more general information about sautéing, see page 18.) Make sure, too, that the skillet is good and hot—not smoking—before you add the fat and that the fat is hot before you add the meat (oil will shimmer and sizzle when you add a pinch of flour; the foam of butter will subside and begin to turn brown). This is intended not just to prevent sticking but to brown the meat properly. Too-cool temperatures, which can also result from adding too much meat to the pan too quickly or from overcrowding, result in a soggy coating.

Note that if you want a nice crust, you must use sufficient fat. If you want to follow these recipes using less fat, by all means do so. The chicken will still be moist and tender, but the cooking will probably be a little uneven, and you can forget about the crunchy crust.

Finally, sautéing requires near-constant attention. Yes, you can answer the doorbell, but your station is the stove. For even browning, which means even crispness, you must tend to the food. The payoff is meat that is crisp on the outside and moist and tender on the inside.

Set the oven at about 200°F when you begin this cooking process. If you choose to make a sauce, a warm oven will hold the chicken perfectly as you do so. But even if you do not, it gives you the option of moving those pieces that finish cooking a little more quickly than others, whether because they are thinner or closer to the center of the pan, to a place where they will stay hot and crisp until you need them. Don't abuse this procedure, though; the cooked cutlets will not hold in the oven for more than 10 minutes or so.

Sautéed Chicken Cutlets

Chicken Meunière

MAKES: About 4 servings
TIME: 20 minutes

🅕

Here are detailed instructions for the simplest sauté. Given good chicken, accurate cooking, and lemon wedges or something akin to them, it's brilliant.

Other protein you can use: any cutlets—pork, veal, or turkey.

About 1½ pounds boneless white-meat chicken (breasts, cutlets, or tenders), pounded to uniform thickness if necessary and blotted dry

Salt and freshly ground black pepper

1 cup all-purpose flour, bread crumbs, preferably fresh (page 876), or cornmeal

2 tablespoons extra virgin olive oil

2 tablespoons butter or more olive oil

Lemon wedges for serving

Chopped fresh parsley leaves for garnish (optional)

❶ Put a large skillet over medium-high heat for 2 or 3 minutes. Meanwhile, sprinkle the chicken with salt and pepper and put the flour on a plate.

❷ Add the oil and butter to the skillet and swirl it around. When it is hot—a pinch of flour will sizzle— dredge a piece of the chicken in the coating, pressing to coat evenly. Shake it a little so that excess coating falls off. Add the chicken piece to the pan, then move on to the next one. (Don't be tempted to dredge in advance and add all the pieces at once; the coating will become soggy, and the heat in the pan will drop too quickly.)

❸ Cook the chicken, regulating the heat if necessary so that there is a constant sizzle but no burning. After 2 minutes, rotate the chicken (do not flip) so that the outside edges are moved toward the center and vice versa. When the pieces are brown, after 3 to 4 minutes (a minute or two more for dark meat), turn them over.

❹ Cook on the second side until the chicken breasts are firm to the touch, 3 to 4 minutes (a minute or two more for dark meat), lowering the heat if necessary to avoid burning the coating. (To check for doneness, cut into a piece with a thin-bladed knife; the center should be white or slightly pink.) Serve with lemon wedges; garnish with parsley if you like.

Extra-Crisp Chicken Cutlets. Use seasoned bread crumbs (see "7 More Ways to Vary Sautéed Chicken Cut-

🅕 Fast   Ⓜ Make Ahead   🅥 Vegetarian

lets," which follows) if possible. In Step 1, set up 3 bowls: one with all-purpose flour, one with a beaten egg, and one with the bread crumbs. In Step 2, when the oil is hot, dredge each piece of chicken first in the flour, then in the egg, and finally in the bread crumbs, pressing to help them adhere. Proceed with the recipe.

Chicken Parmigiana. Make Extra-Crisp Chicken Cutlets, cooking the chicken just enough to brown it (don't worry about cooking it fully). Heat the oven to 400°F. Spread about ½ cup of Fast Tomato Sauce (page 502) on the bottom of a 9-inch square baking dish. Put the cutlets on top of the sauce and top with another cup of sauce. Sprinkle 1½ cups coarsely grated Parmesan or mozzarella (or a combination) over the sauce. Bake until the cheese melts and the sauce is hot, 10 to 15 minutes. Top with a tablespoon or two of minced fresh parsley or oregano leaves and serve.

7 More Ways to Vary Sautéed Chicken Cutlets

1. Use Seasoned Bread Crumbs: Whir 3 or 4 slices of not-too-fresh bread (it can be quite stale) in a food processor with 1 clove of garlic and ½ cup fresh parsley leaves until fairly fine.

2. Add spices to the flour or cornmeal: Combine the flour or cornmeal with 1 tablespoon chili powder, curry powder, five-spice powder (to make your own, see pages 66–68), or ground cumin. Use all oil—preferably peanut or vegetable oil—and garnish with lime wedges.

3. Coat with sesame seeds or ground nuts instead of flour, pressing well to help them adhere. Use all oil (peanut or vegetable oil is best in this case) and cook over slightly lower heat to avoid burning; increase the cooking time by 1 to 2 minutes.

4. Marinate the chicken breasts in buttermilk or yogurt, any Vinaigrette (page 199), or coconut milk (to make your own, see page 389) for up to a few hours before cooking. Be sure to scrape all the liquid off

before proceeding. Use any of the coating techniques described in this section.

5. Rub some spices into the chicken before cooking. See "4 Spice Rubs for Fried Chicken" (page 665) for ideas, but a single spice, like smoked paprika, ground turmeric, or crumbled saffron, will do.

6. Serve any simply sautéed chicken cutlets—breaded or not—with a dipping sauce or salsa. Any of those listed in "Infinite Ways to Season or Serve Any Grilled or Broiled Chicken Dish" (page 661) and "12 Sauces for Fried Chicken" (page 666) will work fine here too.

7. Don't dredge the chicken in anything at all. Simply rub with salt and pepper or a little of any spice blend (to make your own, see pages 65–69) and cook directly in the hot butter or oil. If you crank up the heat a little bit, you'll get a nice brown crust with tender, juicy insides; reduce the cooking time accordingly.

Sautéed Chicken Cutlets with Wine Sauce

MAKES: 4 servings
TIME: 25 minutes

Spend an additional 5 minutes in front of the stove and you can make a flavorful sauce—technically called a *reduction sauce*—to pour over the chicken breasts and any rice, potatoes, or pasta you might serve with them. Almost any liquid will do: wine, stock, water, cream, fruit juice (almost; see "The Basics of Reduction Sauces," page 45).

Other protein you can use: any cutlets—pork, veal, or turkey.

About 1½ pounds boneless chicken (breasts, cutlets, tenders, thighs, or legs), pounded to uniform thickness if necessary and blotted dry

Salt and freshly ground black pepper

1 cup all-purpose flour, bread crumbs, preferably fresh (page 876), or cornmeal

2 tablespoons extra virgin olive oil

3 tablespoons butter or more olive oil

1/2 cup dry white wine or more stock

1/2 cup chicken or vegetable stock (to make your own, see page 157) or water

1/4 cup chopped fresh parsley leaves, plus more for garnish

❶ Heat the oven to 200°F. Put a large skillet over medium-high heat for 2 or 3 minutes. Meanwhile, sprinkle the chicken with salt and pepper and put the flour on a plate or in a shallow bowl.

❷ Add the oil and 2 tablespoons of the butter (or more oil) to the skillet and swirl it around. When it is hot—a pinch of flour will sizzle—dredge a piece of the chicken in the coating, pressing to coat evenly. Shake it a little so that excess coating falls off. Add the chicken piece to the pan, then move on to the next one. (Don't be tempted to dredge in advance and add all the pieces at once; the coating will become soggy, and the heat in the pan will drop too quickly.)

❸ Cook the chicken, regulating the heat if necessary so that there is a constant sizzle but no burning. After 2 minutes, rotate the chicken (do not flip) so that the outside edges are moved toward the center and vice versa. When the pieces are brown, after 3 to 4 minutes, turn them over.

❹ Cook on the second side until the chicken is firm to the touch, 3 to 4 minutes. (Cut into one with a thin-bladed knife; the center should be white or slightly pink.) Since they will sit in the oven for 5 minutes, marginal undercooking is preferable to marginal overcooking. Transfer the chicken to a platter and put it in the oven.

❺ With the heat still on medium-high, add the wine to the skillet. Let it bubble away, stirring and scraping the bottom of the pan, until it is reduced by about half, about 2 minutes. Add the stock and cook,

stirring, until the mixture is slightly thickened and a bit syrupy, another 2 or 3 minutes. (If you want just a little bit of sauce, cook longer; if you want more, cook a little less.)

❻ Add the remaining butter (or oil, if you're not using butter) and swirl the pan around until the butter melts (if you're using olive oil, stir vigorously with the back of a spoon). Add any juices that have accumulated around the cooked chicken, along with the 1/4 cup parsley. Stir, taste, and adjust the seasoning. Spoon the sauce over the chicken, garnish with parsley, and serve.

Sautéed Chicken Cutlets with Cream Sauce. Classic and rich: In Step 1, use flour for dredging. In Step 4, after removing the chicken, cook 1/4 cup chopped shallot in the remaining fat over medium heat, stirring, until soft, about 5 minutes. Sprinkle with 1 teaspoon paprika as they cook. Raise the heat to medium-high and continue with the recipe. After you add the wine and stock and reduce the sauce, turn off the heat, wait 30 seconds, then stir in 1 cup heavy cream, sour cream, or yogurt. Turn the heat to low; reheat, stirring, but do not boil (be especially careful if you use yogurt). Spoon some of this sauce over the chicken and garnish with minced parsley or a sprinkling of paprika. Pass the remaining sauce at the table.

Sautéed Chicken Cutlets with Ginger and Warm Spices. More modern and sharper: In Step 1, use flour, rice flour, semolina, or cornmeal for dredging; combine with 1/2 teaspoon or more cayenne. In Step 2, use peanut oil if possible. In Step 4, after removing the chicken, cook 1/2 cup chopped onion in the remaining fat over medium heat, stirring, until softened, 3 to 4 minutes. Stir in 1 tablespoon minced fresh ginger, 1/8 teaspoon freshly grated nutmeg, 1 teaspoon paprika, and 1/4 teaspoon ground cinnamon. Omit the wine and increase the stock to 1 cup. Omit the butter and parsley; instead, stir 1/4 cup chopped fresh cilantro leaves and 1 tablespoon freshly squeezed lime juice

F Fast   **M** Make Ahead   **V** Vegetarian

into the sauce before spooning it over the chicken. Garnish with a little more cilantro and serve with lime wedges.

Sautéed Chicken Cutlets with Lime Sauce. Another nontraditional but very nice sauté: In Step 1, use cornmeal for dredging. In Step 2, use peanut oil if possible. In Step 4, after removing the chicken, top each piece with some thinly sliced lime and put in the oven. With the heat on medium, add a little more oil to the pan, along with 2 teaspoons chopped garlic and 1 tablespoon chopped shallot or onion. Cook for a minute, then add $1/2$ cup white wine, stock (to make your own, see pages 157–159), or water; let it bubble away for a minute, then add 1 tablespoon soy sauce and 1 tablespoon freshly squeezed lime juice. Serve with lime wedges and garnish with fresh cilantro or mint leaves.

13 Simple Additions to Sautéed Chicken Cutlets with Wine Sauce

Combine these as you like.

1. Add 1 to 2 tablespoons capers along with the stock.
2. Add 1 teaspoon to 2 tablespoons any chopped fresh herb in place of the parsley; use chives, dill, basil, chervil, or cilantro for garnish.
3. Stir in 1 tablespoon balsamic or other vinegar just before adding the butter or oil at the end.
4. Cook 2 tablespoons minced shallot, scallion, or onion or 1 teaspoon minced garlic in the fat remaining in the pan for 1 minute, stirring, just before adding the wine. Add 1 tablespoon chopped anchovy if you like.
5. Add 1 tablespoon freshly squeezed lemon or orange juice after swirling in the butter or oil at the end. Add 1 teaspoon to 1 tablespoon grated lemon or orange zest at the same time if you like. (Or if you like grapefruit, zest that.)
6. Add 1 cup chopped fresh tomato (peeled and seeded if possible) just after reducing the stock.

7. Cook $1/2$ cup chopped mushrooms in the fat remaining in the pan for 1 minute, stirring, just before adding the wine. Or use reconstituted dried mushrooms.
8. Stir in 1 teaspoon to 1 tablespoon Dijon or other mustard after swirling in the butter or oil at the end.
9. Replace the wine with $1/4$ cup cream sherry or Madeira.
10. Use butter and increase the amount in the final addition to as much as 4 tablespoons ($1/2$ stick). The butter should be cold and cut into small bits, then incorporated a little at a time.
11. Add 2 or 3 tablespoons pitted and chopped olives along with the stock.
12. Add $1/2$ cup or more peeled, seeded, and diced tomato along with the stock.
13. Right after you remove the chicken breasts, add a handful of chopped almonds or pistachios to the pan and toast, stirring constantly, for a few seconds. Then add the wine and proceed.

Double-Coconut Sautéed Chicken Breasts

MAKES: 4 servings
TIME: About 40 minutes

Ground coconut makes a flavorful and crunchy crust, but it burns easily, so be careful. There are alternatives too: sesame seeds (mix white and black for a very cool look) or finely chopped peanuts, cashews, or almonds.

Other protein you can use: any cutlets—pork, veal, or turkey.

1 cup coconut milk (to make your own, see page 389)

A few threads saffron or $1/2$ teaspoon ground turmeric

About $1^1/2$ cups shredded coconut

3 tablespoons peanut or neutral oil, like grapeseed or corn

About 1½ pounds white-meat boneless chicken (breasts, cutlets, or tenders), cut into 1-inch chunks and blotted dry

Salt and freshly ground black pepper

1 tablespoon minced shallot

Chopped fresh parsley or cilantro leaves for garnish

1 Warm the coconut milk (it will be warm already if you prepared it yourself) and add the saffron or turmeric to it. Let it sit, stirring once or twice, as the mixture cools. Put the coconut on a plate.

2 Heat a large skillet over medium heat for 2 or 3 minutes. Add 2 tablespoons of the oil to the skillet; dredge the chicken in the coconut and add a piece at a time to the skillet. Cook the chicken, turning frequently, sprinkling it with salt and pepper and adjusting the heat so it becomes nicely browned on all sides; total cooking time should be no more than 6 to 8 minutes. As the pieces finish, transfer them to a plate.

3 When all the chicken is cooked, wipe out the skillet and return it to the stove over medium heat. Heat the remaining tablespoon of oil and add the minced shallot. Cook, stirring occasionally, until the shallot softens, 3 or 4 minutes. Add the coconut milk, raise the heat to medium-high, and bring the mixture to a boil, stirring frequently. Reduce the heat to medium and cook, stirring, until the mixture thickens slightly, 3 or 4 minutes. Add the chicken pieces to the sauce and heat for a minute or so. Taste, adjust the seasoning, garnish with parsley or cilantro, and serve.

Poached Chicken Cutlets

Of all the techniques given for boneless chicken breasts, this is probably the most forgiving, somewhere between braising and sautéing, without browning. Since the chicken is cooked in liquid from start to finish, you have a little more latitude in timing, although severe overcooking will result in dry chicken in a wet sauce, so it's still best to strive for precision. All of these dishes create enough sauce to moisten a side dish of rice, noodles, polenta, potatoes, or bread.

Poached Chicken with Lemon Sauce

MAKES: 4 servings
TIME: 30 minutes

A more-or-less traditional Provençal preparation, one that must be served with good bread, or at least a spoon for the sauce.

Other protein to use: any cutlets—pork, veal, or turkey.

4 tablespoons butter or extra virgin olive oil

2 leeks, washed well and diced, including some of the green part, or 2 small onions, diced

½ cup dry white wine or water

½ cup chicken or vegetable stock (to make your own, see page 157) or water

½ teaspoon chopped fresh thyme or tarragon leaves or a good pinch dried

About 1½ pounds boneless white-meat chicken (breasts, cutlets, or tenders), cut into 1- to 1½-inch chunks if you like

2 tablespoons freshly squeezed lemon juice

Salt and freshly ground black pepper

Chopped fresh parsley leaves for garnish

1 Put half of the butter or oil in a large skillet over medium heat. When the butter is melted or the oil is hot, add the leeks and cook, stirring, until softened, about 5 minutes. Add the wine, stock, and herb; bring to a boil and let bubble for a minute or two.

❷ Add the chicken, turn the heat down to medium-low, cover, and simmer until the meat is barely cooked through, 5 or 6 minutes. Remove the chicken with a slotted spoon and keep warm.

❸ Turn the heat up to high and cook the sauce rapidly, stirring occasionally, until just about $^3/_4$ cup remains; this will take 5 to 10 minutes. Lower the heat to medium-low, add the lemon juice, then stir in the remaining butter or oil, a bit at a time. If you're using oil, add it gradually, stirring vigorously with the back of a spoon as you do so.

❹ Sprinkle with salt and pepper and return the chicken chunks to the sauce to heat through. Garnish with parsley and serve immediately.

Simplest Poached Chicken. If you don't have any fresh herbs handy, use a couple of bay leaves; omit the lemon. Complete the recipe after Step 2; you'll have plenty of chicken for salads or sandwiches.

Chicken in Ginger Sauce. Best over rice, white or brown. In Step 1, use peanut or neutral oil, like grapeseed or corn. Substitute 1 teaspoon chopped garlic and 3 tablespoons minced or grated fresh ginger for the leeks and cook for only 2 or 3 minutes. Reduce the wine to $^1/_4$ cup and omit the herb; add $^1/_4$ cup soy sauce after you have reduced the wine and stock. Steps 2 and 3 remain the same, but you need not reduce this sauce; simply adjust the seasoning after the chicken is cooked through and serve. Omit the lemon juice and garnish with minced cilantro instead of parsley.

Chicken and Fruit in Curry Sauce. Also best over white rice: In Step 1, use peanut or neutral oil. Substitute 1 cup sliced onion for the leeks. When they're soft, add 2 tablespoons spice blend, like curry powder or garam masala (to make your own, see pages 66–67) and stir for 1 minute; omit the wine, stock, and herb. In Step 2, add 2 cups peeled and chunked apples, bananas, papayas, or a mixture, along with 1 cup peeled and chopped tomato, with the chicken. Cook, covered, for 5 minutes, then remove the cover and raise the heat to medium-high; cook until the mixture thickens slightly, just another minute or two. Omit the lemon juice. Garnish with minced cilantro instead of parsley, then serve.

Chicken Cutlets and Tomatoes in Packages

MAKES: 4 servings
TIME: 1 hour

You can steam chicken directly over water, but better, in my opinion, is to steam the chicken, along with the flavorful juices of wine, tomato, oil, or stock, in a wrapped package in the oven. This method—traditionally called cooking *en papillote*—is simple and foolproof. It's also impressive to serve individual packages at the table, using either parchment paper or aluminum foil to wrap the chicken and its seasonings. Easier still, if not quite as attractive, is to combine everything in a covered glass or ceramic baking dish.

Other protein you can use in this recipe: any cutlets—pork, veal, or turkey.

4 boneless, skinless chicken breast pieces (3 whole breasts), about 1$^1/_2$ pounds

4 thick slices ripe tomato

Salt and freshly ground black pepper

12 fresh tarragon leaves or about $^1/_2$ teaspoon dried tarragon, or use basil, chervil, or dill

About 2 tablespoons extra virgin olive oil

Freshly squeezed lime juice

❶ Heat the oven to 450°F. Tear off two 1-foot-square pieces of aluminum foil and put one on top of the other (the more traditional parchment paper is, of course, also acceptable). Put a chicken cutlet on the foil; top with a slice of a tomato, sprinkle with salt, pepper, and tarragon, and add a drizzle of oil and lime juice. Seal the package and repeat the process. Alternatively, layer all the ingredients neatly in a Dutch oven or covered baking dish. (At this point, you may refrigerate the packages or dish for up to 4 hours before proceeding.)

② Put the packages in a large baking dish and bake for about 20 minutes; the chicken will be white and tender when finished. If you're cooking in a baking dish, check after 15 minutes. Serve closed packages, allowing each diner to open his or her own at the table.

Chicken Cutlets with Broccoli and Sun-Dried Tomatoes in Packages. Substitute a small piece of oil-cured sun-dried tomato and 2 or 3 small broccoli florets for the ripe tomato. Use marjoram, thyme, or oregano for the herb and substitute freshly squeezed lemon juice for lime juice.

Chicken Cutlets with Grated Vegetables in Packages. Mix together about 1/2 cup each (3 cups total) of mixed grated vegetables, such as carrots, zucchini or summer squash, onion, potatoes, turnips, sweet potatoes, or winter squash and use this as the first layer. Use the tomato if in season. Sprinkle a few drops of balsamic or other vinegar over the top; omit the lime juice.

Chicken Cutlets with Peas in Packages. Best with shelled fresh peas, though frozen are fine too; don't bother to thaw: Omit the tomato; use any of the herbs listed or substitute mint. Instead of the olive oil, use butter and substitute lemon or orange juice for the lime. In Step 1, start each package with 1/2 cup peas; sprinkle with salt and pepper. Then top with the chicken, a piece of butter, a squeeze of lemon or orange, and another sprinkle of salt and pepper.

The Basics of Whole Chicken

There is no secret to making near-perfect whole roast chicken: If you start with a good bird, time the cooking properly, and serve it promptly—the crisp skin and moist interior for which roast chicken is justly renowned are fleeting qualities—you'll meet with success, probably on your first try. For the simplest take on whole roast chicken, see the Essential Recipe on page 644.

Take a few moments to trim the bird of excess fat, which means cutting off the flap that covers the inside cavity. Refrigerate or freeze it for rendering (see page 651) if you like. If they're still attached, you can also cut off the little pointed wing ends (they're good for stock). You can use a knife for these tasks, but kitchen scissors are easiest.

Trussing: I don't bother anymore. I guess because it keeps the wings and legs in place, trussing makes the bird slightly easier to handle, and supposedly it makes the presentation somewhat more attractive, though both of these points are arguable. Trussing does help keep any stuffing in place, but it also reduces the surface area of the bird, meaning there's less browning and less of that wonderful crispy skin. So to me trussing adds a somewhat tricky step to a simple process without providing much benefit.

Roasting racks and pans: You don't *need* a rack to roast chicken, though elevating the bird above the floor of the roasting pan helps to keep its skin crisp and prevents it from sticking. But note that for the most basic recipe, my cast-iron skillet method (see page 687) needs no rack at all, and it works just fine. Or you can use an ordinary roasting pan; try the smallest roasting pan that will comfortably hold your bird, so you can concentrate the juices and keep them from burning. (You'll need a larger pan if you want to add roast vegetables to the mix.)

Stuffing: I don't usually stuff chickens, but this doesn't mean you cannot: Use any of the stuffings on pages 698–700, or see the list "5 Other Recipes You Can Use to Stuff Poultry" on page 699. Plan to increase the cooking time by about 25 percent and use your instant-read thermometer; see "Stuffing for Turkey and Other Poultry" (page 698). Put any extra stuffing in a separate baking dish and add to the oven halfway through cooking.

F Fast   **M** Make Ahead   **V** Vegetarian

QUARTERING ROAST CHICKEN

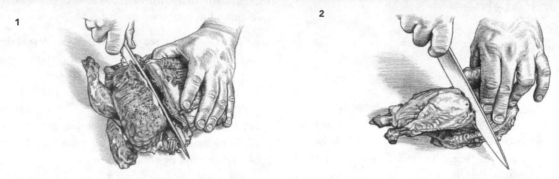

(STEP 1) Cut straight down on each side of the breastbone, following the shape of the carcass. Continue to cut down toward the back until you reach the joints holding the thigh and wing to the carcass. Remove the backbone from one half if you like. **(STEP 2)** With each half, cut between the breast and thigh to easily separate them.

CARVING ROAST CHICKEN

(STEP 1) Cut straight down on each side of the breastbone, following the shape of the carcass. **(STEP 2)** Continue to cut down toward the back until you reach the joints holding the thigh and wing to the carcass. **(STEP 3)** Cut through those joints to free the entire half of the bird. **(STEP 4)** Separate the leg and breast sections by cutting through the skin that holds them together; hold the knife almost parallel to the cutting board, cut from the breast toward the leg, and you will easily find the right spot. **(STEP 5)** Separate the wing from the breast if you like. **(STEP 6)** Separate leg and thigh; the joint will offer little resistance once you find it.

Roast Chicken with New Potatoes

MAKES: 4 servings
TIME: About 1 hour

The key here is to cut the potatoes or other vegetables small enough so they cook in the time allotted for the bird. The skillet or roasting pan you use should be large enough to accommodate both bird and vegetables in one layer. Larger and your vegetables will dry out; smaller and they won't brown. Peel the potatoes or not, as you prefer.

> 6 tablespoons extra virgin olive oil or butter
>
> 1 tablespoon chopped fresh thyme, rosemary, marjoram, oregano, or sage leaves or a combination, plus more for garnish
>
> Salt and freshly ground black pepper
>
> 1 whole chicken, 3 to 4 pounds, trimmed of excess fat
>
> 1½ to 2 pounds red or white waxy potatoes, the smaller the better, or larger potatoes cut into ½- to 1-inch chunks

1 Heat the oven to 450°F. Mix together the olive oil, herb(s), and some salt and pepper. Put the chicken, breast side up, in a roasting pan (on a rack if you prefer). Toss half of the herb mixture with the potatoes and scatter them in the pan, then put the pan in the oven. After the chicken has roasted for about 20 minutes, spoon some of the herb mixture over it and the potatoes. Shake the pan so the potatoes turn and cook evenly.

2 Shake the pan and baste the chicken again after another 10 minutes; at this point the breast should be beginning to brown (if it isn't, roast for a few more minutes). Turn the heat down to 325°F, baste again with the remaining herb mixture, and roast until an instant-read thermometer inserted into the thickest part of the thigh reads 155–165°F. Total roasting time will be 50 to 70 minutes.

3 Remove the chicken and taste a potato; if it isn't quite done, raise the heat to 425°F and roast while you rest and carve the chicken; it won't be long. Serve the chicken, garnished with herbs, with the potatoes scattered around it, hot or warm.

Roast Chicken with Root or Other Winter Vegetables. Instead of all potatoes, use about 2 pounds of one or a mix of carrots, celery, celery root, parsnips, turnips, kohlrabi, white or sweet potatoes, any winter squash, garlic, shallots, onions, and so on. Peel them (you need not peel individual garlic cloves) and chop into pieces no more than 1 inch in diameter (so the vegetables finish cooking with the chicken).

Roast Chicken with Herb Butter

MAKES: 4 servings
TIME: About 1 hour

A slightly simplified version of a classic that preserves the most important elements: a crisp-skinned chicken smacking of butter and herbs. This recipe is one of the

Flavor Under the Skin

Here's a terrific way to flavor the meat—rather than the skin—of any skin-on poultry, especially when grilling or roasting. Simply loosen the skin with your fingers, slip a pinch of the seasonings under the skin, and rub a little bit. Flavored butters, chopped fresh herbs or aromatics, or any of the spice rubs on pages 65–69 will work well. Here are three recipes that specifically call for this technique:

1. Roast Chicken with Herb Butter (above)
2. Grilled or Broiled Chicken with Provençal Flavors (page 660)
3. Grilled or Broiled Chicken with Lemon and Herbs (page 662)

 Fast   Make Ahead   **V** Vegetarian

few in which substituting olive oil simply won't do; if you will not or cannot cook with butter, stick with Simplest Whole Roast Chicken, Six Ways (page 644).

8 tablespoons (1 stick) butter

2 tablespoons chopped fresh dill, tarragon, parsley, or chervil leaves, or a combination

Salt and freshly ground black pepper

1 whole chicken, 3 to 4 pounds, trimmed of excess fat

1/2 cup dry white wine or water, plus more if needed

1 clove garlic, lightly smashed (optional)

Chopped fresh parsley or other herb leaves for garnish

1 Heat the oven to 450°F. Use a fork or mini food processor to combine half the butter with the herb(s) and some salt and pepper. With your fingers, loosen the skin of the chicken wherever you can without tearing it and spread some of this mixture between skin and meat. Put a little in the chicken cavity and spread the remainder on top of the breast. Sprinkle the outside of the bird with salt and pepper.

2 Put the remaining butter in a cast-iron skillet or roasting pan and put the pan in the oven. When the butter has melted and its foam subsided, add the wine and the garlic if you're using it. Put the chicken, breast side down, on a rack in the pan and return to the oven. Roast for 20 minutes, spoon some of the butter mixture over it, then turn the bird breast side up. (If, at any point, the pan juices are beginning to stick to the pan, add a little more liquid.) Baste again, then again after 10 minutes; at this point the breast should be beginning to brown (if it hasn't, roast for a few more minutes). Turn the heat down to 325°F, baste again, and roast until an instant-read thermometer inserted into the thickest part of the thigh reads at least 155–165°F. Total roasting time will be under 1 hour.

3 Before removing the chicken from the pan, tip the pan to let the juices from the bird's cavity flow into the pan (if they are red, cook for another 5 minutes). Transfer the bird to a platter and let it rest for about 5 minutes before carving. Garnish with minced herbs and serve with the pan juices.

Roast Chicken with Herb Butter and Wine Sauce. Steps 1 and 2 remain the same. In Step 3, while the bird is resting, place the roasting pan on a burner over high heat. Add 1 cup dry white wine and cook, stirring and scraping the bottom of the pan to loosen any solids that have stuck there, until the liquid is reduced by about half. Add 1 tablespoon of the minced fresh herb you have been using (2 teaspoons if you used tarragon), stir again, and serve with the chicken.

Other Methods for Cooking Whole Chicken

There is more than one way to cook a whole bird. In addition to roasting chickens, you can poach them in stock or other flavorful liquid (and cook them again afterward, to crisp them up a bit), grill them, and even smoke them. All of these methods give wonderful results.

I like poaching (you can call it *boiling* or *simmering*) whole chicken because it's just about foolproof, it creates some stock that you can use in the final dish or elsewhere, and it can be done in advance. Since you're usually not looking for crisp skin (if you are, you just run the cooked bird under the broiler or put it on the grill for a few minutes), you can cook it with much less attention than you need for other methods. And, as long as you don't overcook, the bird is always tender and moist when it's done.

Braising is a little more complicated, since it involves two cooking techniques: searing, then simmering in liquid. But it also is easier and more reliable than roasting and gives you an opportunity to really flavor the bird well. Plus you end up with a terrific sauce.

Grilling a whole bird is a little tricky, but with today's larger, covered grills—especially gas grills—it's not as hard as you might think. And you can easily grill split and butterflied birds with excellent results (see page 692). With charcoal you need to pay only a little extra attention to maintain the heat of the fire and turn the bird. (For more about grilling in general, see page 17.)

Chicken in a Pot

MAKES: 4 servings
TIME: About 1½ hours

One of the classic and best one-pot dinners. Serve this as a stew, with everything in the bowl, or as a plain broth with Yogurt or Buttermilk Biscuits (page 845) or Spaetzle (page 552), followed by the chicken and vegetables on a platter.

Canned stock is a decent option here, as is water, because the cooking liquid gains flavor from the chicken and vegetables during the simmering. Of course, real stock is the best option.

1 whole chicken, 3 to 4 pounds, trimmed of excess fat

8 cups chicken stock (to make your own, see page 157) or water

3 onions, quartered

2 large or 4 small to medium carrots, cut into chunks

2 leeks, split, trimmed, washed, and cut into 2-inch lengths

1 bay leaf

4 allspice berries

10 whole black peppercorns

4 sprigs fresh thyme or 1 teaspoon dried thyme

Salt and freshly ground black pepper

Minced fresh parsley or dill for garnish

❶ Put the chicken in a large pot with the stock, onions, carrots, and leeks. Bring to a boil over medium-high heat, then immediately reduce the heat to medium-low. Skim any foam that rises to the surface. Add the bay leaf, allspice, peppercorns, and thyme to the pot along with some salt and pepper. Simmer until the chicken and vegetables are nearly tender and the chicken is cooked through, about 45 minutes; the bird is done when an instant-read thermometer inserted into the thickest part of the thigh reads 155–165°F. With 15 minutes of cooking time remaining, heat the oven to 200°F.

❷ When the chicken is done, use a slotted spoon to transfer it and the vegetables to an ovenproof platter and put the platter in the oven. Raise the heat to high and boil the stock until it reduces by about 25 percent, 10 to 15 minutes.

❸ Strain the stock into a large bowl or another large pot; taste and adjust the seasoning. Serve the soup as a first course, garnished with parsley or dill, followed by the chicken and vegetables, or cut the chicken up and serve everything in deep bowls, garnished with parsley or dill.

Sour Chicken in a Pot with Cabbage. If you like egg-lemon sauce, you'll love this: In Step 1, add 4 cups chopped green, Savoy, or Napa cabbage to the pot 15 minutes after you add the herbs. After reducing and straining the liquid in Steps 2 and 3, beat together 1 cup cream, 1 egg, and 2 tablespoons red or white wine vinegar or freshly squeezed lemon juice. Add 1 cup of the hot stock to the cream mixture and stir. Return this mixture to the pot and heat through; do not boil. Taste and adjust the seasoning. You can also make this variation without the cream and egg—simply stir vinegar to taste into the stock.

Chicken and Dumplings, the Easy Way. Follow the recipe through Step 1. While the chicken is cooking, make the dough for Buttermilk Biscuits (page 845) or any of its variations (cheese dumplings are a treat). Once the chicken and vegetables are in the oven, strain the stock, return it to the pot, and adjust the heat so it bubbles vigorously but isn't at a rolling boil. Drop heaping tablespoons of the biscuit dough into the hot stock and cover the pan. Cook, undisturbed, until the dumplings are cooked through (a toothpick will come out clean), 10 to 15 minutes. Serve the dumplings and a little broth if you like with the chicken and vegetables.

Ⓕ Fast   Ⓜ Make Ahead   Ⓥ Vegetarian

Chicken and Lentils in a Pot. Indian spices give this dish an exotic flair: Use 1¹/₂ tablespoons Hot Curry Powder or garam masala (to make your own, see page 66 or 67) instead of the bay leaf, allspice, peppercorns, and thyme. Add about 5 quarter-size slices fresh ginger and 2 large cloves garlic. In Step 3, strain the stock, return it to the pot, and bring to a boil. Add 1 cup dried brown or green lentils and cook until tender, about 25 minutes. Proceed with the recipe; serve the lentils with the chicken and vegetables, garnished with chopped cilantro.

Saffron Chicken in a Pot. The saffron gives the chicken a beautiful golden color: Substitute heavy cream for 2 cups of the chicken stock for a luxurious dish. Add a large pinch of crumbled saffron threads with the spices in Step 1.

Miso Chicken in a Pot. Any miso will do, though a white (and mild) miso is my favorite: Omit the allspice and thyme. In Step 2, after the stock is reduced, add 2 cups each shredded Napa cabbage and sliced shiitake mushrooms; cook until the cabbage is tender, about 5 minutes. Reduce the heat so the stock is barely bubbling, and stir in about ¹/₄ cup miso until dissolved. Proceed with the recipe and garnish with chopped scallion.

White Cut Chicken

MAKES: 4 servings
TIME: 40 minutes, largely unattended

The simplest, most straightforward poached chicken dish there is, popular throughout China and in some Chinese restaurants here in the States. Almost always served at room temperature, it's tender and flavorful with nothing more than soy sauce, but it's legit (and, I think, even better) with Ginger-Scallion Sauce (page 39). Save the cooking liquid for soup stock.

5 or 6 slices fresh ginger (don't bother to peel)

5 scallions, chopped

2 star anise

2 tablespoons salt

2 tablespoons sugar

1 whole chicken, 3 to 4 pounds, trimmed of excess fat

❶ Combine all the ingredients except the chicken in a large pot with 8 cups water. (Make sure you have enough room at the top to make room for the chicken.) Bring to a boil over high heat. Put the chicken in the pot, breast side up, and bring the water back to a boil. Turn the heat to low, cover, and simmer for 20 minutes. Remove from the heat and then let the chicken sit in the water for another 10 minutes or so; the bird is done when an instant-read thermometer inserted into the thickest part of the thigh reads 155–165°F.

❷ Remove the chicken from the pot, cool to room temperature, and cut into serving pieces (see page 685). Serve with soy sauce and Ginger-Scallion Sauce, page 39, or cover and refrigerate until ready to serve.

Grilled, Smoky Whole Chicken

MAKES: 4 to 6 servings
TIME: About 1¹/₄ hours

Yes, it can be done, and—especially with a gas grill—it's pretty easy. As is often the case, I recommend indirect heat (see "Grilling," page 17) and using some wood chips for extra flavor. This recipe is complete, but for a little more detail, see "The Basics of Grilled or Broiled Chicken Parts" (page 658).

1 whole chicken, 3 to 4 pounds, trimmed of excess fat

2 tablespoons extra virgin olive oil

Salt and freshly ground black pepper

Any of the seasonings from "Infinite Ways to Season or Serve Any Grilled or Broiled Chicken Dish," page 661

1 Heat a charcoal or gas grill to moderate heat, with the fire built up on one side so part of the grill is cool, and put the rack 4 to 6 inches from the heat source. If you like, soak some wood chips in water to cover for a few minutes, then sprinkle them directly on the grate over the hotter part of the fire or put them in a foil container over the flames. Rub the chicken with the oil and sprinkle it with some salt and pepper; if you're using a seasoning rub, now's the time to put it on.

2 Put the chicken on the cool side of the grill, breast up, and, once some of the fat has been rendered, after about 20 minutes, turn it onto one of its sides. If at any point the fire flares up, move it to an even cooler part of the fire. Turn every 5 to 10 minutes until most of the fat has been rendered and the bird looks pretty much cooked, usually after about 40 minutes, adding more coals if necessary to keep the fire going. At this point, move the chicken directly over the fire and brown, turning frequently. If at any point the fire flares up, return the bird to the cool part of the grill.

3 When the chicken is done (it will be firm and brown, and an instant-read thermometer inserted into the meaty part of the thigh will measure at least 155–165°F), let it rest for a few minutes, then serve hot, warm, or at room temperature, with lemon wedges or any of the suggestions from "Infinite Ways to Season or Serve Any Grilled or Broiled Chicken Dish."

Chicken Pot Pie

MAKES: 4 to 6 servings
TIME: About 2 hours

Whether you start from scratch (as in the main recipe) or with leftovers (as in one of the variations), chicken pot pie is extreme comfort food. Don't let the extra steps put you off, since each component (the piecrust, the chicken and sauce, and the vegetables) can be executed a day or two ahead and the whole assembled right before baking.

For vegetables I use carrots, peas, and pearl onions—the classics—though you can try other complementary trios, like parsnips, green beans, and shallots or rutabaga, celery, and leeks.

1 whole chicken, 3 to 4 pounds, trimmed of excess fat

2 onions, quartered

3 bay leaves

10 whole black peppercorns

Salt

1 recipe Savory Tart Crust (page 930), chilled

2 tablespoons butter or extra virgin olive oil, plus more for greasing the baking dish

1 cup pearl onions, peeled (frozen are fine; run under cold water to thaw a bit, then drain)

2 large or 4 small to medium carrots, diced

2 tablespoons all-purpose flour

1 tablespoon chopped fresh sage or 1 teaspoon dried sage

Freshly ground black pepper

1/2 cup cream

1 cup peas (frozen are fine; don't bother to thaw)

1 egg, beaten

1 Put the chicken and onions in a large pot with just enough water to cover. Bring to a boil over medium-high heat, then immediately reduce the heat to medium-low. Skim any foam that rises to the surface. Add the bay leaves, peppercorns, and a generous pinch of salt. Simmer until the chicken and vegetables are nearly tender and the chicken is cooked through, about 45 minutes; the bird is done when an instant-read thermometer inserted into the thickest part of the thigh reads 155–165°F.

2 Remove the chicken to cool and save the cooking liquid. (This is a good time to make the tart dough if you haven't already done so.)

3 Remove the chicken meat from the bones, roughly chop or pull into pieces, and reserve. Return the carcass to the pot (break the pieces up a bit so they're all submerged, but don't add any more water), and bring the liquid back to a boil. Reduce the heat so the liquid bubbles steadily and cook, stirring occasionally, for 20 minutes or so. Strain into a wide pot, bring the liquid to a boil, and reduce until you have about 1½ cups, 15 to 30 minutes, depending on how much you started with. (At this point, the chicken and cooking liquid may be stored separately in the refrigerator for up to 2 days.) If you're baking the pie now, heat the oven to 375°F and generously grease a 2-quart baking dish.

4 Put 2 tablespoons butter or oil in a deep skillet over medium heat. When the butter is melted or the oil is hot, add the onions and carrots and cook, stirring frequently, until just beginning to soften, about 5 minutes. Reduce the heat to medium-low and stir in the flour; continue cooking and stirring until it just turns tan. Add the sage and cook and stir for another minute. (At this point you can refrigerate the vegetable mixture for up to a day, then reheat just before proceeding.)

5 Add the chicken-cooking liquid and the cream to the vegetable-flour mixture and turn the heat up to medium. Cook, stirring constantly, until the mixture begins to bubble and thicken, but don't let it come to a rolling boil. Taste and adjust the seasoning, turn off the heat, and stir in the chicken pieces and the peas. Put the mixture into the prepared baking dish. (At this point, you may cover and refrigerate the filling for up to a day; bring to room temperature before proceeding.)

6 Roll out the tart crust large enough to cover the baking dish. Lay it on top of the dish and flute it as for a piecrust (see page 927) or just leave it draped over the sides a little. Use a sharp knife to cut 3 or 4 vents in the top. Brush the top with the beaten egg. Bake for 50 to 60 minutes, until the crust is deeply golden and the filling is bubbling.

Faster Chicken Pot Pie. For when you have leftovers or pick up an already-cooked bird: Skip Steps 1, 2,

and 3 and start by putting 4 cups of chicken stock (to make your own, see page 157) in a large pot and bringing it to a boil. Reduce by about half. Meanwhile, bone and chop the cooked chicken. You should have about 3 cups, but if not, simply substitute more vegetables (green beans are nice) to make up the difference. Proceed with the recipe from Step 4.

Chicken Pot Pie with Mashed Potato Crust. Replace the tart dough with 1 recipe Mashed Potatoes (page 339). Omit the egg. Proceed with the recipe through Step 5 or follow the preceding variation. In Step 6, top the filling with mashed potatoes and spread to cover. Bake as directed.

Chicken Pot Pie with Biscuit Crust. Replace the tart dough with 1 recipe Buttermilk Biscuits (page 845). Proceed with the recipe through Step 5 or follow the first variation. In Step 6, roll out the biscuit dough into one piece large enough to cover the baking dish or cut into biscuits; top the filling with the biscuit dough or the cut biscuits. Bake as directed.

The Basics of Split Chicken

Cooked faster and easier to handle than whole chicken, split or butterflied (or, to use an antiquated term, *spitchcocked*) chicken is *almost* whole: The backbone is usually (though not always) removed. It cooks nearly as quickly as cut-up chicken and retains more of its juice. Split chicken is not always readily available in the supermarket, but it's easy to split a chicken at home; follow the illustrations. (In some places, you can ask the supermarket butcher to do it for you.)

Almost any recipe can be adapted for split chicken; follow the guidelines outlined here and season the chicken any of the ways you would for sautéed, grilled, roasted, or broiled whole chicken or parts.

1

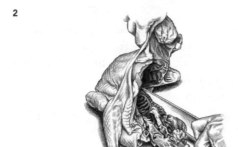

2

3

(STEPS 1–2) To split a chicken: With the breast facing up, use a heavy knife to cut on each side of the backbone, cutting from front to rear. Once the backbone is removed, you will be able to lay the chicken out flat and flatten it on both sides. (STEP 3) If you like, you can split the chicken into two halves.

Chicken Under a Brick

Pollo al Mattone

MAKES: 4 servings
TIME: 45 minutes

The wonderful dish associated with Lucca, Italy, in which split chicken is weighted to flatten it, producing an evenly cooked, crisp, and moist bird with little effort (other than some heavy lifting). *Mattone* means "tile," but I usually weight the chickens with a cast-iron pan and a couple of big rocks. The only problem is that handling the hot, heavy pan takes a steady, strong wrist, so use two hands.

I specify rosemary here, which is delicious. But most herbs are equally wonderful: Try savory or dill (in similar quantity); parsley, basil, chervil, chives (use twice as much); or tarragon, oregano, marjoram, or thyme (use half as much).

1 whole chicken, 3 to 4 pounds, trimmed of excess fat

1 tablespoon minced fresh rosemary leaves or 1 teaspoon dried rosemary, plus 2 optional sprigs fresh rosemary

2 teaspoons salt

1 tablespoon coarsely chopped garlic

2 tablespoons extra virgin olive oil

1 lemon, quartered

❶ Remove the backbone and split the chicken (see left). Heat the oven to 450°F. Mix together the rosemary leaves, salt, garlic, and 1 tablespoon of the olive oil and rub this all over the chicken. Tuck some of it under the skin as well.

❷ Heat a large ovenproof skillet over medium-high heat for about 3 minutes. Press the rosemary sprigs, if you're using them, into the skin of the chicken. Put the remaining olive oil in the pan and wait a minute for it to heat up. Put the chicken in the pan, skin side down, along with any pieces of rosemary and garlic. Weight the chicken with another skillet or a flat pot cover and a cou-

❶ Fast   ⓜ Make Ahead   ⓥ Vegetarian

ple of bricks or rocks. The basic idea is to flatten the chicken by applying a fair amount of weight evenly over its surface.

❸ Cook over medium-high to high heat for 10 minutes; transfer, still weighted, to the oven. Roast for 15 minutes more. Take the chicken from the oven and remove the weight; turn the chicken over (it will now be skin side up) and roast for 10 minutes more. To check for doneness, insert an instant-read thermometer into the thickest part of the thigh; it should read 155–165°F. Cut into pieces and serve hot or at room temperature, with lemon wedges.

Grilled or Broiled Split Chicken

MAKES: 4 servings
TIME: 45 minutes

Basically the same ingredients as in the preceding recipe, but cooked by a different technique. It's not essential to weight the bird when you grill it, although it still helps the meat to brown evenly (it's impossible to weight it for broiling, of course). A couple of bricks or rocks, wrapped in aluminum foil, will do the trick.

1 whole chicken, 3 to 4 pounds, trimmed of excess fat

1 tablespoon minced fresh rosemary leaves or
   1 teaspoon dried rosemary

2 teaspoons salt

1 tablespoon roughly chopped garlic

2 tablespoons extra virgin olive oil

1 lemon, quartered

❶ Heat a charcoal or gas grill or the broiler to moderate heat, with the fire built up on one side so part of the grill is cool, and put the rack 4 to 6 inches from the heat source. If you like, soak some wood chips in water to cover for a few minutes, then sprinkle them directly on the grate over the hotter part of the fire or put them in a foil container over the flames. Remove the backbone and

split the chicken (see previous page). Mix together the rosemary leaves, salt, garlic, and 1 tablespoon of the olive oil and rub this all over the chicken. Tuck some of it under the skin as well.

❷ To grill: Put the chicken on the cool side of the grill, skin side up, cover the grill, and cook until much of the fat has been rendered, about 20 minutes, turning after about 10 minutes (if the fire flares up after turning, reduce the fire if it's a gas grill or turn it back to the other side or move it to an even cooler part of the fire). Turn once or twice more, until most of the fat has been rendered and the bird looks pretty much cooked, about 30 minutes more, adding more coals if necessary. At this point, move the chicken directly over the fire and brown, turning frequently. If at any point the fire flares up, return the bird to the cool part of the grill.

To broil: Start with the skin side down and broil, making sure the bird does not burn, until it's nearly done, about 20 minutes, then turn and cook until the skin is brown. If it needs a few more minutes, turn skin side down again and cook until done, then just run the bird, skin side up, under the broiler one more time, for a minute or so.

❸ When the chicken is done (it will be firm and brown, and an instant-read thermometer inserted into the meaty part of the thigh will measure at least 155–165°F), let it rest for a few minutes, then drizzle with the remaining olive oil and serve hot, warm, or at room temperature, with lemon wedges or any of the suggestions from "Infinite Ways to Season or Serve Any Grilled or Broiled Chicken Dish" (page 661).

Grilled or Broiled Split Chicken with Honey and Mustard.
This is delicious, but you must watch it very carefully, because the honey makes it especially susceptible to burning. Combine $1/4$ cup Dijon or other good mustard and $1/4$ cup honey; add $1/2$ teaspoon minced fresh thyme or tarragon leaves (or $1/4$ teaspoon dried). Smear the chicken with this mixture and let it sit while you prepare the fire or heat the broiler, or refrigerate for up to a couple of hours. Steps 2 and 3 remain

the same. Serve hot or at room temperature, with lemon wedges.

Tandoori Chicken. You can marinate this for up to a day if you like: In a blender or food processor, combine 1 medium onion; 2 cloves garlic; a $1/2$-inch piece of fresh ginger (or 1 teaspoon ground ginger); 1 tablespoon ground cumin; 1 teaspoon ground coriander; $1/4$ teaspoon cayenne, or to taste; 1 teaspoon salt; and 1 cup yogurt. Blend until smooth. Marinate the chicken in this mixture, refrigerated, for 12 to 24 hours, turning occasionally. Scrape off most of the marinade before grilling. Steps 2 and 3 remain the same. Serve hot.

The Basics of Whole Turkey

You can't buck tradition: Once a year, most Americans are going to eat turkey. And properly cooked, a turkey provides not just plentiful but good eating; however, it is a tricky bird to handle, especially given its size. The good news is that turkey parts are no more difficult to deal with than other cuts of meat. But to start with the big birds:

Types of Turkey

Like chicken, there are several kinds of turkeys for sale, including standard, "wild," free range, self-basting (like Butterball), and kosher. My views on each:

Standard: This often amazingly cheap bird is versatile and, well, standard. It is raised under the same (usually deplorable) conditions as standard chicken and so has the same environmental and ethical baggage attached. For many of us, though, it is the only option, and until something better comes along—like a consistently high-quality free-range bird—this is often the best bet.

"Wild" turkey: True wild turkeys not only exist, they're thriving. But you're not going to get one to eat unless you or a friend shoot it yourself. The "wild" turkeys sold by mail-order houses and specialty stores are

domesticated. They're quite expensive, not especially flavorful, and generally pretty tough. Try one out yourself before you commit to making it your Thanksgiving bird.

Free range: In theory a better bird than standard but, in fact, wildly inconsistent and often outrageously expensive. Your best bet is to find a local source and, if it's good and reasonably priced, stick to it. But many free-range turkeys are tougher than the standard variety and no more flavorful.

Self-basting: This and other fat-injected turkeys are not terrible in concept—since turkey meat is almost inevitably dry, an internal load of fat makes some sense—but they are terrible in execution, since the ingredients used are little more than seasoned vegetable oil. If you don't overcook turkey and you baste frequently, you'll do just as well—better, maybe—with a standard bird.

Kosher: Marginally better in flavor and texture than standard birds, at about twice the price. Usually sold frozen, although increasingly seen fresh at Thanksgiving. Worth a try. You can pretty much duplicate its better qualities by brining a standard bird; see "Is Brining Worth the Effort?" on page 656.

Fresh versus Frozen Turkey

Although more and more turkey is sold fresh—you can now find it almost every day of the year—much is still frozen. Unless the turkey is of ultra-high quality, it doesn't make much difference. Frozen turkey is often put on sale at almost incomprehensibly low prices and offers the convenience (as long as you have a large freezer) of having the bird whenever you want it.

Of course, if your turkey is frozen, you must defrost it before cooking, and even small turkeys don't defrost quickly. The easiest way to defrost a turkey is to let it sit in the refrigerator for two days before you plan to cook it. If you're in a hurry, defrost it by letting it sit in a sink or bowlful of cold water, changing the water occasionally; but you should still plan for it to take a whole day or more for a large bird.

F Fast   **M** Make Ahead   **V** Vegetarian

TIMING CHART FOR DEFROSTING LARGE BIRDS

WEIGHT	DEFROSTING TIME: REFRIGERATED	DEFROSTING TIME: COLD WATER
6 to 8 pounds	18 to 24 hours	4 to 6 hours
10 to 12 pounds	24 to 36 hours	8 to 12 hours
14 to 18 pounds	36 hours+	12 to 16 hours
18 pounds+	48 hours+	18 hours+

TIMING CHART FOR ROASTING TURKEY

All these times are approximate, but in most cases—if your turkey is fully defrosted, and your oven is pretty accurate—they'll be close, though probably on the long-and-extremely-safe side. Remember, an instant-read thermometer inserted into the meatiest part of the turkey's thigh will read 155–165°F when the bird is ready to come out of the oven (though its look and clear juices running from its vent are also good indicators). Remember, too, that the bird must rest for at least 15 minutes before being carved, and the temperature will go up another 5 degrees or so during that time. (See my recommendations in "Chicken Doneness and Safety," page 639.)

WEIGHT	ROASTING TIME: UNSTUFFED	ROASTING TIME: STUFFED
8 to 12 pounds	2³/₄ to 3 hours	3 to 3¹/₂ hours
12 to 14 pounds	3 to 3³/₄ hours	3¹/₂ to 4 hours
14 to 18 pounds	3³/₄ to 4¹/₄ hours	4 to 4¹/₄ hours
18 to 20 pounds	4¹/₄ to 4¹/₂ hours	4¹/₄ to 4³/₄ hours
20 to 24 pounds	4¹/₂ to 5 hours	4³/₄ to 5¹/₄ hours
24 to 30 pounds	5 to 5¹/₄ hours	5¹/₄ to 6¹/₄ hours

Roasting Whole Turkey

Your basic Thanksgiving-sized turkey (say, twelve pounds or more? maybe twenty in your case?) is way too big to mess around with. I always get a laugh out of recipes that have you turning the birds this way and that: For many of us, just getting a pan big enough to hold the thing is an issue, and figuring how to turn something whose size is about the same as that of your nephew is not most people's idea of a good yearly activity. Myself, I'd rather be out cleaning roof gutters.

So I roast the bird breast side up the whole time. And guess what? It works well, almost perfectly, especially if you follow the high-heat method described here, which even results in moist breast meat.

Forty-Five–Minute Roast Turkey

MAKES: At least 10 servings
TOTAL TIME: 45 minutes

It's almost a given that time and oven space are at a premium on Thanksgiving Day, and this method of roasting turkey, unorthodox as it is, addresses both. Split, flattened, and roasted at 450°F (lowering the heat if the bird browns too fast), a 10-pound bird will be done in about 40 minutes. Really. It will also be more evenly browned (all of the skin is exposed to the heat), more evenly cooked (the legs are more exposed; the wings shield the breasts), and moister than birds cooked conventionally. But it works only for relatively small turkeys.

One 8- to 12-pound turkey

10 or more garlic cloves, lightly crushed

Several sprigs fresh tarragon or thyme or several pinches dried

¹/₃ cup extra virgin olive oil or melted butter

Salt and freshly ground black pepper

1 Heat the oven to 450°F. Put the turkey on a stable cutting board, breast side down, and cut out the backbone. Turn the bird over and press on it to flatten. Put it breast side up in a roasting pan that will accommodate it (a slightly snug fit is okay). The wings should partially cover the breasts, and the legs should protrude a bit.

2 Tuck the garlic and the herb under the bird and in the nooks of the wings and legs. Drizzle with the olive oil and sprinkle liberally with salt and pepper.

3 Roast for 20 minutes, undisturbed. By this time the bird should be browning; remove it from the oven, baste with the pan juices, and return it to the oven. Reduce the heat to 400°F (or 350°F if it seems to be browning very quickly).

4 Begin to check the bird's temperature about 15 minutes later (10 minutes if the bird is on the small side). It is done when the thigh meat measures 155–165°F on an instant-read meat thermometer; check it in a couple of places.

5 Let the bird rest for a few minutes before carving, then serve with the garlic cloves and pan juices. (Or make Turkey Gravy, page 698.) Or serve at room temperature.

HOW TO CARVE A TURKEY

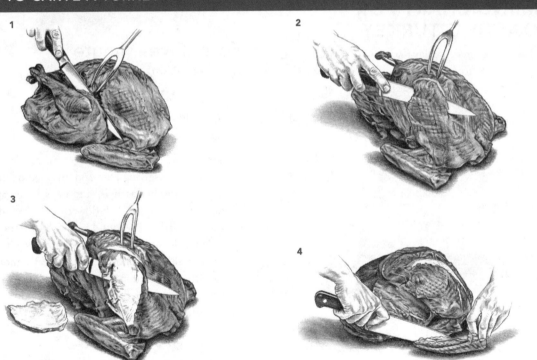

(STEP 1) First, remove the leg-thigh section by cutting straight down between the leg and carcass and through the joint holding the thigh to the carcass. Repeat on the other side and set aside for the moment. (STEPS 2–3) The easiest option is to cut thick slices of white meat from the breast. To remove the breast first, see the illustrations on the opposite page. (STEP 4) Cut the wings from the carcass and carve the meat from the leg-thigh section.

F Fast   **M** Make Ahead   **V** Vegetarian

Classic Roast Turkey, with Gravy and Stuffing

MAKES: At least 15 servings, plus leftovers

TIME: 2½ hours or more

Without the stuffing, this will roast a little faster; in fact, without the stuffing, this is a pretty simple preparation and might make you think about preparing turkey year-round. It is, after all, a classic in sandwiches.

One 12-pound turkey

1 recipe any stuffing (see pages 698–700)

8 tablespoons (1 stick) butter at room temperature or a few tablespoons extra virgin olive oil

Salt and freshly ground black pepper

1 cup roughly chopped onion

1 cup roughly chopped carrot

½ cup roughly chopped celery

Stems from 1 bunch fresh parsley, tied together (optional)

Turkey Gravy (recipe follows)

1 Heat the oven to 500°F. Rinse the turkey and remove the giblets; use them to make stuffing or stock if you like. Loosely pack the turkey cavity with the stuffing, then tie the legs together to enclose the vent. Smear the bird all over with butter or brush it with oil, then sprinkle well with salt and pepper.

2 Put the turkey on a rack in a large roasting pan. Add ½ cup water to the bottom of the pan along with the turkey neck, gizzard, any other trimmings, and the vegetables and parsley. Put in the oven, legs first if possible.

3 Roast for 20 to 30 minutes, or until the top begins to brown, then turn the heat down to 350°F. Continue to roast, checking and basting with the pan juices every 30 minutes or so; if the top threatens to brown too much, lay a piece of aluminum foil directly onto it. (If the bottom dries out, add water, about ½ cup at a time; keep at least a little liquid in the bottom of the pan at all times.) The turkey is done when an instant-read thermometer inserted into the thickest part of the thigh measures 155–165°F. If, when the turkey is nearly done, the top is not browned enough, turn the heat back up to 425°F for the last 20 to 30 minutes of cooking.

REMOVING TURKEY BREASTS

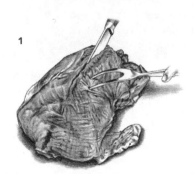

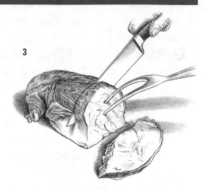

(STEP 1) For more even cuts of meat, you can choose to remove the breast from the carcass after cutting off the wings, thighs, and legs. Begin by slicing directly down the breast bone. **(STEP 2)** Keep the side of the blade pressed against the bone as you free the entire breast. **(STEP 3)** Slice the breasts crosswise as you would a boneless roast.

4 Remove the turkey from the oven. Take the bird off the rack and make the gravy while the bird rests; let it sit for about 20 minutes before carving, longer if you don't mind it at room temperature.

Turkey Gravy

MAKES: 5 to 6 cups (enough for 12 servings)
TIME: 20 minutes, after roasting a turkey

"Gravy" is little more than thickened stock—essentially a reduction sauce (see page 45)—and when that stock comes out of a roasted turkey, it's pretty good stuff. It's no wonder people love it. Double or triple (or quadruple, if it comes to that) this recipe as needed.

6 cups stock, preferably turkey but chicken (to make your own, see page 157) is fine

Salt and freshly ground black pepper

5 tablespoons butter (optional)

1/3 cup cornstarch (optional)

1 Remove any giblets from the bottom of your roasting pan and pour or spoon off excess fat (that's a judgment call, but leave at least some fat in there). Leave as many of the solids and as much of the dark liquid behind as possible. Put the roasting pan over 2 burners and turn the heat to high.

2 Add the stock and cook, stirring and scraping all the brown bits off the bottom of the pan, until the liquid has reduced by about one-quarter, 5 to 10 minutes. (If you're not using cornstarch and you want a thicker gravy, continue to reduce a little more.) Turn the heat down to medium and continue to simmer for about 5 minutes, tasting and adjusting the seasoning. Strain the liquid into a saucepan, discarding the solids.

3 Over medium heat, stir in the butter if you're using it and keep warm until ready to serve. If you're using cornstarch, mix it with 1/4 cup cold water, then add to the simmering gravy, stirring constantly. It should thicken almost immediately; serve hot.

Stuffing for Turkey and Other Poultry

I tend to be pretty conservative with almost all aspects of turkey-making for feasts (no cilantro here!), and that includes the stuffing. (When you're serving a dozen people or more, many of them kids, you don't want to slave over a fancy stuffing just to hear people say "Ick.") So I keep stuffings simple and strive to make them one of the less challenging aspects of the meal. Any stuffing you make from scratch is going to be infinitely better than the instant kind most people are used to, so you're way ahead of the game.

Two more thoughts about stuffing: Some is better cooked outside of the bird. If you want a moist, soft, juicy stuffing, pack it in there. But if you want a clean-flavored, crisp stuffing that can stand on its own as a side dish, cook it on its own. (And, although this is not really a concern if you cook your birds thoroughly—the temperature of the stuffing needs to reach 165°F, just like the meat—the chances of harmful bacteria developing in the bird are greater if you cook the stuffing inside it.)

The other thing: Don't skimp on the fat or the seasonings. Lean, underseasoned stuffing is little more than mushy bread.

My Favorite Bread Stuffing

MAKES: About 6 cups (enough for a 12-pound bird)
TIME: 20 minutes, plus time to bake

This classic dressing is based on a wonderful recipe by James Beard; it's amazing with butter, but check out the variations if you prefer olive oil. Also, feel free to use whole grain bread for more flavor.

1/2 pound (2 sticks) butter

1 cup chopped onion

1/2 cup pine nuts or chopped walnuts

6 to 8 cups fresh bread crumbs (page 876)

1 tablespoon minced fresh tarragon or sage leaves or 1 teaspoon dried

 Fast   Make Ahead   **V** Vegetarian

Salt and freshly ground black pepper

1/2 cup chopped scallion

1/2 cup chopped fresh parsley leaves

❶ Put the butter in a large, deep skillet or Dutch oven over medium heat. When melted, add the onion and cook, stirring, until it softens, about 5 minutes. Add the nuts and cook, stirring almost constantly, until they begin to brown, about 3 minutes.

❷ Add the bread crumbs and the herb and toss to mix. Turn the heat down to low. Add the salt, pepper, and scallion. Toss again; taste and adjust the seasoning. Add the parsley and stir. Turn off the heat. (At this point, you may refrigerate the stuffing, well wrapped or in a covered container, for up to a day before proceeding.)

❸ Pack into a chicken or turkey if you like before roasting or just bake in an ovenproof glass or enameled baking dish for about 45 minutes at 350–400°F. (Or you can cook it up to 3 days in advance and just warm it up right before dinner.)

Bread Stuffing with Giblets and Fruit. Finely chop the gizzard, heart, and liver. In Step 1, add the giblets to the onion after it softens. Omit the nuts. In Step 2, add 2 teaspoons fresh thyme leaves (or 1 teaspoon dried), 1 finely crumbled bay leaf, 1 1/2 cups coarsely chopped pitted prunes, and 2 cups peeled and diced tart apples. Omit the tarragon and scallion.

Bread Stuffing with Sage and Chestnuts. Start by boiling or roasting 3/4 to 1 pound chestnuts until they are tender (see Boiled, Grilled, or Roasted Chestnuts, page 287, for details). Shell, skin, and chop. Cook the onion as in Step 1. When soft, add the chestnuts and 1/2 cup dry white wine (omit the nuts). Simmer for 5 minutes. In Step 2, use sage and just 2 tablespoons minced fresh parsley.

Bread Stuffing with Sausage. In Step 1, omit the butter. Cook 1 pound sausage meat (you can squeeze the meat from links) in its own fat over medium heat until pinkish gray. Spoon off the fat, then add the onion and cook until softened, about 5 minutes. Omit the nuts. Add 1 tablespoon minced garlic, 1 teaspoon minced fresh ginger (or 1/2 teaspoon ground ginger), and 1 teaspoon ground cumin (optional). Omit the tarragon or sage.

Bread Stuffing with Mushrooms. In Step 1, use butter or olive oil and cook 1 cup sliced button mushrooms along with the onion. If you have them, add 1 ounce soaked, drained, trimmed, and minced porcini mushrooms at the same time (see page 314). Add 1 teaspoon minced garlic when the mushrooms have softened. Omit the nuts. Use sage or thyme (1 teaspoon fresh or 1/2 teaspoon dried).

Bacon-Nut Stuffing

MAKES: At least 6 servings (enough for a 6-pound bird)
TIME: About 2 hours

A nice stuffing for chicken or turkey.

8 ounces slab or sliced bacon

2 cups roughly chopped onion

1 teaspoon chopped garlic

2 cups bread crumbs, preferably fresh (page 876)

1/2 cup pine nuts or chopped walnuts

1/2 cup dry white wine, chicken or vegetable stock (to make your own, see page 157), or water

1 teaspoon fresh thyme leaves or 1/2 teaspoon dried thyme, plus several sprigs fresh thyme if available

1 bay leaf

Salt and freshly ground black pepper

❶ If you're using slab bacon, cut it into ¹/₂-inch cubes; if you're using sliced bacon, coarsely chop it. Cook the bacon in a large skillet over medium heat, stirring or turning until crisp, about 10 minutes. Drain, dry, and crumble.

❷ Remove all but 3 tablespoons of the fat from the pan and, still over medium heat, cook the chopped onion, stirring, until softened, about 5 minutes. Add the garlic, bread crumbs, nuts, wine, thyme, bay leaf, and bacon and remove from the heat. Season to taste with salt—you may not need any—and pepper.

❸ Pack into a chicken or turkey if you like before roasting or just bake in an ovenproof glass or enameled baking dish for about 45 minutes at 350–400°F. (Or you can cook it up to 3 days in advance and just warm it up right before dinner.)

Turkey Parts

Turkey is in fact raised fifty-two weeks a year. So turkey parts—legs, ground turkey, boneless breasts, even (sometimes) specialty cuts like "osso buco" (see page 702)—are common.

All for the better: Whole turkey breast is quite good roasted, either on or off the bone (see the Essential Recipe on page 647). Turkey thighs make a nice change and become reminiscent of pork when braised. And boneless turkey may in fact be slightly tastier than commercial chicken cutlets and can be treated exactly the same and used in every recipe in which you would use boneless chicken pieces (pages 666–674).

Roast Boneless Turkey Breast with Savoy Cabbage

MAKES: 6 to 12 servings or more
TIME: About 1 hour

I love this dual method of cooking cabbage, half sautéed, half roasted. Some of the cabbage becomes tender, and

 Fast   Make Ahead   Vegetarian

some remains crunchy, a nice combination that makes a fine base for any poultry, from turkey to pheasant.

1 medium head (about 2 pounds) Savoy or green cabbage

2 tablespoons extra virgin olive oil or peanut oil, plus 1 teaspoon for greasing the pan

1 tablespoon minced fresh ginger

1 teaspoon chopped garlic

Salt and freshly ground black pepper

One 3- to 6-pound turkey breast, taken off the bone (see page 668), or 2 filleted turkey breast halves, rinsed and blotted dry

1 tablespoon dark sesame oil

$1/2$ cup chopped scallion greens for garnish

❶ Heat the oven to 450°F. Core and shred the cabbage, then roughly chop. Divide in half and chop one half a little more finely.

❷ Put 2 tablespoons oil in a large skillet over medium heat. When hot, add the roughly chopped cabbage and cook, stirring occasionally, until softened, about 10 minutes. Add the ginger and garlic and continue to cook until the cabbage is slightly browned, another 5 minutes or so. Add some salt and pepper, cover, and keep warm.

❸ While the cabbage is cooking, use the remaining 1 teaspoon oil to lightly grease the bottom of a baking dish slightly larger than the turkey. Cover the bottom of the dish with the finely chopped cabbage. Sprinkle with salt, add the turkey, and sprinkle that with a little more salt. Roast for 25 to 30 minutes, until the turkey is almost done; it will be firm to the touch but not rubbery, white or very pale pink inside, and about 155–165°F on an instant-read thermometer.

❹ Scatter the sautéed cabbage around the turkey and roast for another 5 minutes. Slice the turkey and put it on a platter, surrounded by the cabbage. Sprinkle everything with sesame oil and scallion greens and serve hot or warm.

Roast Boneless Turkey Breast with Fennel. Roasted fennel's sweet and rich flavor pairs nicely with poultry: Substitute 2 large fennel bulbs, trimmed and sliced, for the cabbage. Omit the garlic and sesame oil and add 1 cup orange juice if you like. Proceed with the recipe, basting the turkey with the orange juice every so often.

Roast Boneless Turkey Breast with Pearl Onions. Cipollini onions are nice here too if you can find them: Substitute about $1^1/2$ pounds pearl onions, trimmed, for the cabbage. Omit the ginger, garlic, and sesame oil. Add a tablespoon or so chopped fresh rosemary or thyme leaves. Proceed with the recipe, adding the onions and herbs in the last 10 minutes of roasting.

Turkey Thighs Braised in Red Wine

MAKES: About 6 servings

TIME: About $1^1/2$ hours, plus time to marinate

With their dark, rich meat and somewhat coarse texture, turkey thighs are reminiscent of pork. Substitute them for chicken parts or pork in any braise.

3 tablespoons extra virgin olive oil

2 to 3 pounds (4 to 6) turkey thighs, skin removed if you like, blotted dry

1 cup roughly chopped onion

$1/2$ cup roughly chopped carrot

1 celery stalk, roughly chopped

2 teaspoons chopped garlic

2 cups fruity red wine

$1/4$ cup red wine or other vinegar

3 cloves or a pinch ground cloves

3 juniper berries

1 bay leaf

1 piece orange peel (optional)

Salt and freshly ground black pepper

1 ounce dried porcini mushrooms or ¹/₂ cup sliced shiitake mushroom caps (optional)

Stock (to make your own, see pages 157–159) or water as needed

Chopped fresh parsley leaves for garnish

❶ Put 2 tablespoons of the oil in a Dutch oven or other heavy pot with a lid over medium-high heat. When hot, brown the thighs on all sides. Remove the thighs, pour out the fat, let the pan cool a bit, and wipe it out with a few paper towels.

❷ Turn the heat down to medium and add the remaining oil. When hot, add the onion, carrot, celery, and garlic. Cook, stirring, until the vegetables soften, about 5 minutes.

❸ Add the wine and raise the heat to medium-high. Bring to a boil and cook, stirring, for 1 minute. Add the vinegar, cloves, juniper, bay leaf, orange peel if you're using it, and some salt and pepper and stir. Return the thighs to the pot, reduce the heat to low, and cover. The meat should cook slowly, with just a few bubbles rising from the liquid. If you're using porcini, soak them in hot water to cover until softened, about 10 minutes.

❹ Turn the turkey every 15 minutes or so and add a little stock or water if the pan becomes dry. When the turkey is tender—usually about 45 minutes after covering—add the mushrooms and their strained soaking liquid, if any.

❺ Remove the turkey from the pot and keep it warm. Skim the fat from the surface of the remaining liquid, raise the heat to high, and reduce the liquid by about half. Check for seasoning and spoon over the turkey. Garnish and serve.

Turkey "Osso Buco." If you can find them, use turkey thighs and legs cut crosswise or have your butcher cut them for you: Omit the garlic, vinegar, cloves, juniper, orange peel, and mushrooms. Substitute 1 cup white wine for the red and add 2 sprigs fresh thyme or ¹/₂ teaspoon dried. Proceed with the recipe. Serve with Yellow Rice, the Best Way (page 463) or Polenta (page 485).

Turkey Thighs in Almond Mole

Almendrado de Pavo

MAKES: 6 or more servings

TIME: About 1¹/₂ hours, somewhat unattended

The most exciting turkey dish I've had in the last twenty years was both completely traditional and as far from the Thanksgiving spirit as you could imagine. That's because the tradition was Oaxacan and the turkey was in a mole sauce. Many moles use dozens of ingredients and odd techniques (like burning) and take days to make. Others, like this almond-based example, are easy enough for a weeknight and, when it comes to producing a flavorful dish without too much trouble, far more reliable than the roasted holiday bird.

2 dried ancho or other mild chiles

¹/₄ cup neutral oil, like grapeseed or corn

1 teaspoon minced fresh chile, like jalapeño or serrano, or to taste, or hot red pepper flakes or cayenne, to taste

1 large white onion, chopped

1 cup almonds

Salt and freshly ground black pepper

5 large cloves garlic, peeled, or more to taste

3 or 4 tomatoes, cored and chopped (about 3 cups)

¹/₂ teaspoon ground cinnamon

Pinch ground cloves

1 tablespoon dry red wine or other vinegar, or to taste

2 cups chicken stock, preferably homemade (page 157), or as needed

4 turkey thighs, about 3 pounds

Slivered almonds for garnish (optional)

❶ Soak the anchos in hot water to cover. When they're softened, after 15 to 30 minutes, remove their stems and seeds. Put half the oil in a deep skillet with a lid or a Dutch oven over medium-high heat. Add the fresh chile and onion and cook, stirring occasionally, until the onion begins to soften, 3 to 5 minutes. Add the almonds, some salt, at least $^1/_2$ teaspoon pepper, the garlic, tomatoes, cinnamon, cloves, soaked ancho chiles,

About Ground Chicken and Turkey

Ground chicken and turkey can be used in any recipe calling for ground meat; they're different, of course, but they'll work, and sometimes just as well as ground beef, veal, or pork. Their advantage, presumably, is that they are lower in fat than their cousins, though that's probably not always the case, so if that's your concern, please read the label to make sure the fat content is 5 percent or less. If it isn't, you can always use a food processor or meat grinder to grind your own chicken or turkey, using skinned breast or thigh meat or a combination (or very lean beef).

If you do choose to use a food processor, cut the meat, which should be very cold or even partially frozen, into chunks. Pulse in the machine until it reaches the texture you like. A distinct advantage to grinding your own meat is that you can add herbs, spices, or other seasonings during the final stages of processing, making your burgers that much more flavorful. See "Do-It-Yourself-Ground Meat" on page 722.

In general, ground chicken and turkey are good substitutes for other ground meat where the meat will be cooked until well done, like Meatballs, Three Ways (page 114), Meat Loaf (page 723), Chili con Carne (page 429), Meat Sauce, Bolognese Style (page 531), Classic Lasagne, Bolognese Style (page 533), Ravioli Nudi (page 545), and Pot Stickers or Steamed Dumplings (page 104).

vinegar, and enough stock to keep moist and cook, stirring occasionally, until the tomatoes begin to break up, about 10 minutes.

❷ Cool slightly (or for several hours), then purée in a blender. Taste and add more salt, pepper, or vinegar if you like. (You can refrigerate the purée for up to a day before continuing.)

❸ Put the remaining oil in the skillet over medium-high heat. When hot, then add the turkey, skin side down. Sprinkle it with salt and pepper and, a couple of minutes later (it's not important that it brown well), pour the puréed sauce over it. Adjust the heat so the mixture simmers steadily when covered and cook, checking the heat occasionally and turning the pieces once or twice, until the thighs are very tender, about an hour.

❹ Taste the sauce and adjust the seasoning. Garnish with almonds if you like and serve hot.

The Basics of Cornish Hens, Poussins, and Guinea Hens

These birds may all be cooked using any chicken recipe, as long as you adjust for time. That's a good thing, because for the most part they're more flavorful, especially when compared to store- and name-brand chickens.

Look for small Cornish, just over 1 pound each. They serve one or two people each and are ideal for splitting before cooking. Poussins, which are essentially baby chickens, may be treated as Cornish hens but tend to be a little bigger. Both have a distinct advantage over chicken: Because they're so small, you can grill them quickly (and even over direct heat) and they're unlikely to burn or dry out.

Guinea hens are a variety of chicken, usually more flavorful. Buy them if you see them and roast them simply, as you would a good chicken.

Grilled or Broiled Cornish Hens with Vinegar

MAKES: 2 to 4 servings

TIME: About 40 minutes

This light sauce is super with any grilled poultry, from chicken to squab (it's good with rabbit too). Once you split the hens, you can cook them according to any recipe for split chicken (pages 692–694), adjusting the cooking time accordingly.

Other protein you can use: split rabbit (see page 653).

2 Cornish hens, about 1 pound each

1 cup chicken, beef, or other stock (to make your own, see pages 157–159)

2 tablespoons vinegar

Salt and freshly ground black pepper

Minced fresh parsley leaves for garnish

1 Heat a charcoal or gas grill or the broiler to moderate heat and put the grill rack about 4 inches from the heat source. Remove the backbone of the hens by cutting along their length on each side. Boil the stock and the backbones in a small saucepan until reduced by about half, about 30 minutes. Stir in the vinegar and some salt and pepper if necessary.

2 Grill or broil the hens, turning frequently so they brown but do not burn and sprinkling them with salt and pepper. Toward the end of the cooking time (which will be 20 to 30 minutes total, depending on the intensity of the heat), begin basting the hens with the vinegar sauce. When the hens are done, drizzle them with the remaining sauce. Garnish with parsley and serve hot or at room temperature.

6 Other Sauces That Are Great Basted on and Served with Grilled or Broiled Cornish Hens

1. Any Five-Minute Drizzle Sauce (page 22)

2. Soy Dipping Sauce and Marinade (page 25)

3. Compound Butter (page 32)

4. Ponzu Sauce (page 40)

5. Balsamic Syrup (page 51)

6. Any Vinaigrette (pages 199–202)

Cornish Hens and Sauerkraut

MAKES: 4 to 6 servings

TIME: About 2 hours

An elegant but straightforward dish and an excellent introduction to sauerkraut. But steer clear of the canned stuff; instead, look for a bottled brand that contains no more than cabbage, salt, and water. This preparation also works well with pheasant, chicken, and duck.

4 Cornish hens, about 1 pound each

4 slices bacon, diced, or 3 tablespoons extra virgin olive oil

2 pounds sauerkraut

2 cloves

1 teaspoon juniper berries, crushed with the side of a knife

 Fast   Make Ahead   **V** Vegetarian

1 sprig fresh thyme or a pinch dried thyme

1 bay leaf

1 cup dry white wine

Stock (to make your own, see pages 157–159) or water as needed

Salt and freshly ground black pepper

1 Remove the backbone of the hens by cutting along their length on each side. Separate breast and leg quarters. Cook the bacon over medium heat in a large, deep ovenproof skillet until crisp, about 10 minutes, or heat the oil until it shimmers. Remove the bacon with a slotted spoon and reserve. Add the hen pieces to the bacon fat or olive oil and brown them on all sides. Meanwhile, rinse the sauerkraut in a colander and heat the oven to 300°F.

2 When the bird is nicely browned, add the sauerkraut, cloves, juniper berries, thyme, bay leaf, and white wine to the skillet. Cook over medium heat until about half of the liquid has evaporated, about 10 minutes; move the skillet into the oven.

3 Bake for about 30 minutes, stirring occasionally and adding liquid as needed to keep the sauerkraut just moist, until the legs are tender and the sauerkraut is slightly browned. Remove the skillet from the oven, then remove the cloves and bay leaf. Taste the sauce, adjust the seasoning, and serve hot or warm.

The Basics of Duck and Goose

These two birds have a lot in common: They're fatty—amazingly so if you're used to chicken—which means they must be treated differently from other birds. It also means they develop a beautifully crisp, dark skin. All duck has dark meat that is far richer than that of chicken.

Both birds have dark meat that is flavorful without being at all gamy. (I'm talking about domesticated ducks and geese. Wild ones are quite gamy—but they're also hard to come by.) Finally, because they are water birds, they have a huge chest cavity and a bone structure that makes their size deceptive. If you've ever roasted a 4- or 5-pound duck and tried to serve six people, you know what I mean; there's really enough meat on the bird to serve only two or three. That's why duck is a good candidate for smoking; when it's done, you can cut it up and use it in stir-fries, where it lends its flavor to other ingredients.

"Duck," by the way, usually means Pekin duck, the kind found at every supermarket. It's usually sold "fresh" but in fact is shipped frozen and then thawed; truly fresh duck is rare.

Many cooks avoid duck because of its high fat content. But there are lots of methods that render the subcutaneous fat from duck without drying out the meat, a few of which I describe in the following recipes. But even if you simply roast the bird in an empty pan, you get a lot of nice, clean fat that you can save (it keeps for weeks in the refrigerator, months in the freezer) for cooking other dishes in which you want a flavor boost. (This is equally true of goose.)

Increasingly, supermarkets now carry duck breasts (which are a good substitute for beef) or duck legs, which are incomparably wonderful when braised (see page 709). But rarely do you see them both packaged together (i.e., a cut-up whole duck). It's a shame, because duck parts cook well together since they are all dark meat, as you'll see if you try the following recipes. Fortunately, though, duck is nearly as easy to cut up as a chicken (see page 648), so you might give it a shot. If you decide to use duck breasts alone for any of these recipes, just be careful not to overcook them.

Goose is nearly always sold frozen. The easiest way to thaw goose is to let it sit in the refrigerator for 2 days before you plan to cook it. If you're in a hurry, defrost it by letting it sit in cold water, changing the water occasionally; but you should still plan for it to take the better part of a day for a 10-pound bird.

Whole duck is the most common way to cook duck, but not the easiest; these days, I prefer to cut my duck up before cooking, just like cutting chicken; see page 648. But there is no arguing that these are the duck presentations that are the most impressive, so there are times I turn to them, and times you will also.

Roast Duck

MAKES: 2 to 4 servings
TIME: About 1¼ hours

Duck is so difficult to roast badly that all experienced cooks seem to claim their procedure is the best. Having tried many methods, I can say that the results are all about the same. So I rely on this one, which is pretty simple and probably the easiest way to guarantee a succulent but beautifully browned bird. For more a more elaborate roast duck, see the variation.

Trying to stretch a duck to serve four is not easy, but if the four are not big on meat and you provide plenty of side dishes, it can be done.

1 whole duck, 4 to 5 pounds, trimmed of excess fat

Freshly ground black pepper

¼ cup soy sauce, more or less

❶ Heat the oven to 450°F. Discard the neck and giblets or keep them for another use; remove excess fat from the duck's cavity.

❷ Put the duck breast side down (wings up) on a rack in a roasting pan; add water to just below the rack. Sprinkle with pepper and brush with a little soy sauce.

❸ Roast for 30 minutes, undisturbed. Prick the back all over with the point of a sharp knife, then flip the bird onto its back. Sprinkle with pepper and brush with soy sauce again. Add a little more water to the bottom of the pan if the juices are spattering (carefully—you don't want to get water on the duck).

❹ Roast for 20 minutes, prick the breast all over with the point of a knife, and brush with soy sauce. Roast for 10 minutes and brush with soy sauce. Roast for another 5 or 10 minutes if necessary, or until the duck is a glorious brown all over and an instant-read thermometer inserted into the thigh measures 155–165°F. Let rest for 5 minutes before carving and serving.

Duck à l'Orange. The old classic, still good; the acidity of the orange cuts through the duck's fat nicely: In Step 2, before putting the duck in the pan, stuff it with a roughly chopped onion, a couple of smashed cloves of garlic, and a quartered orange. While the duck is roasting, remove the zest from another orange, then juice it and mince half the zest; simmer the remaining zest in ½ cup stock (to make your own, see pages 157–159; duck stock would be good) for 2 minutes. Peel and section 2 more oranges. When the duck is done, remove and discard the stuffing; transfer the bird to a warm platter. Drain all the fat from the pan and put it on the stove over high heat; add ½ cup dry white wine or water and cook, stirring and scraping the bottom of the pan, until the liquid is reduced slightly. Strain the stock and add it to the pan along with the orange juice and sections; bring to a boil and cook, stirring, for 1 minute. Carve the duck, spoon the sauce over it, garnish with the reserved zest, and serve. (If you want a thicker sauce, stir 1 tablespoon cornstarch mixed with 2 tablespoons water into it and cook, stirring, until thickened.)

Steamed and Roasted Duck

MAKES: 2 to 4 servings
TIME: About 1½ hours
Ⓜ

This method produces a crisp, delicious, Chinese-style roast duck with very little fat, and half the cooking can be done a day or even two in advance.

1 whole duck, 4 to 5 pounds, excess fat removed

Salt and freshly ground black pepper

2 tablespoons soy sauce

Ⓕ Fast   Ⓜ Make Ahead   Ⓥ Vegetarian

2 tablespoons honey

1 tablespoon minced or grated fresh ginger (or 1 teaspoon ground ginger)

1 tablespoon chopped garlic

2 tablespoons dry sherry or white wine

2 tablespoons dry white wine or water

❶ Rig a steamer (see page 20). Put 1 to 2 inches of water in the bottom. Put the duck on the rack or plate, cover the pot, and turn the heat to high. Steam for about 45 minutes, adding boiling water if necessary.

❷ Remove the duck from the pot, put it on a rack, and cool for at least 15 minutes (you can also wrap it well and refrigerate for up to 2 days).

❸ Heat the oven to 375°F. Combine all the remaining ingredients in a saucepan and cook over low heat, stirring, until just shy of a boil. Put the duck, breast side down (wings up), on a rack in a roasting pan. Baste with the sauce.

❹ Roast the duck for 15 minutes, baste it, then turn it breast side up. Raise the heat to 425°F. Baste the bird again and roast it until the skin is crisp, another 15 minutes or so, until the internal temperature is 155–165°F. Let the duck rest for a few minutes, then carve and serve.

Roasted Cut-Up Duck with Turnips

MAKES: 4 servings
TIME: About 1½ hours

You won't get crisp skin here, but you'll get very tender meat. The turnips—or other root vegetable of your choice—simmer in the fabulous duck drippings.

1 whole duck, 4 to 5 pounds, excess fat removed and cut into 8 serving pieces

Salt and freshly ground black pepper

1 teaspoon fresh thyme leaves

1 bay leaf

2 cloves garlic, lightly crushed

2 pounds purple-topped turnips, peeled and cut into 1-inch chunks

Chopped fresh parsley leaves for garnish

❶ Heat the oven to 350°F. Sprinkle the duck with salt and pepper and put the pieces in a large, ovenproof skillet with a lid or a Dutch oven over medium-high heat. Brown carefully on both sides, rotating and turning as necessary; take your time to do this thoroughly, allowing up to 15 or 20 minutes total; remove the pieces as they are browned.

❷ Drain the fat, return the duck to the pan and add the thyme, bay leaf, and garlic; cover, put it in the oven, and roast for about 30 minutes.

❸ Remove the pan from the oven and carefully pour off most of the fat. Add the turnips, cover again, and return it to the oven. Stir and baste the turnips every 10 minutes or so until the duck is done, 30 minutes or so longer (the juices will run clear, the leg bone will wiggle a little in its socket, and the meat will be tender). Taste, adjust the seasoning, and serve garnished with parsley.

Braised Duck with Apples and Calvados. A wonderful fall dish: Substitute 1 pound Granny Smith or Golden Delicious apples, cored and cut into eighths, for half the turnips. Add 1 cup stock (to make your own, see pages 157–159) or water and ¼ cup Calvados or any apple brandy. In Step 2, add the stock and brandy with the herbs.

Fast "Roast" Duck, Chinese Style

MAKES: 4 servings
TIME: About 1 hour

Producing the type of roast duck you see hanging in the windows of many Chinese restaurants is nearly impossible at home; but you can get similar results in less than an hour if you just begin by cutting up the duck. And with just a little attention, the duck will gain a glorious, mahogany color that will belie the amount of work you put into it.

1 whole duck, 4 to 5 pounds, excess fat removed and cut into 8 pieces

Salt and freshly ground black pepper

2 tablespoons rice wine or dry sherry

3 tablespoons soy sauce

$\frac{1}{2}$ cup brown sugar

One 3-inch cinnamon stick

5 or 6 slices fresh ginger

4 star anise

2 cloves

1 teaspoon coriander seeds

1 Put the duck, skin side down, in a 12-inch skillet over medium-high heat and sprinkle it liberally with salt and pepper. When the duck begins to sizzle, cover the skillet and turn the heat down to medium. After 15 minutes, turn the duck and sprinkle the skin side. After 15 more minutes, uncover the skillet and turn the heat back to medium-high. Cook the duck, turning as necessary, so that it browns nicely on both sides; this will take another 15 minutes or so.

2 Transfer the duck to a plate and pour off all but a tablespoon of fat (if there are any solids, leave them in the pan). Over medium-high heat, add the rice wine and bring to a boil. Add the soy sauce and 2 tablespoons water and bring to a boil; stir in the brown sugar and spices until smooth. Once the mixture starts bubbling, return the duck to the skillet and cook, turning it frequently, until the sauce is very thick and the duck is well glazed, 5 to 10 minutes. Remove the duck, then scoop the whole spices out of the sauce. Spoon the sauce over the duck and serve.

Duck Confit

MAKES: 6 to 8 servings

TIME: About 24 hours, largely unattended

It's mildly onerous to render duck fat, though preparing the confit—a word that's come to mean long, slow cooking in fat—is straightforward. You have a couple of choices: Render your own, purchase duck fat from a specialty store or online (from a site like hudsonvalley-foiegras.com), or use extra virgin olive oil. The last solution is perfectly acceptable, though it won't leave you with the delicious leftover duck fat to use for cooking.

I like to eat duck confit with something sharp or acidic (or both), like a salad with frisée or radicchio; add a crumble of blue cheese and a handful of hazelnuts and you're all set. Confit is also excellent sautéed with cooked white beans for a fast skillet cassoulet.

1 cup coarse salt

1 tablespoon freshly ground black pepper

2 tablespoons fresh thyme leaves, chopped, or 1 tablespoon dried thyme

2 bay leaves, ground or finely crumbled

8 duck legs or 4 legs and thighs, rinsed and blotted dry

8 cups rendered duck fat (see "How to Render Chicken (or Any Other) Fat," page 651) or extra virgin olive oil

1 Combine the salt, pepper, thyme, and bay leaves. Put the duck legs on a rimmed baking sheet and sprinkle with the salt mixture. Wrap in plastic, put in the refrigerator, and cure overnight or for at least 8 hours.

2 Put the fat or oil in a wide Dutch oven or pot over medium heat. Meanwhile, rinse the salt mixture from the legs and blot the legs dry. When the fat is melted and just barely sending up a bubble, carefully add the duck legs (use tongs to prevent splattering). Adjust the heat so the oil sends up bubbles every now and then. Cook the legs, undisturbed, until the meat has pulled away from the leg bone and is very tender, about 2 hours. (At this point, the whole pot can be cooled, covered, and refrigerated for up to a couple of weeks.)

❸ To serve, heat the oven to 300°F. Remove the legs from the fat and let the excess fat drain off. Put a large skillet over medium-high heat; when it's hot, add the duck pieces, skin side down, and cook until the skin is browned and crisp, about 10 minutes; transfer to a rack in the oven and bake until completely golden brown, about 15 minutes. Serve hot, warm, or room temperature.

Crisp-Braised Duck Legs with Aromatic Vegetables

MAKES: 4 servings

TIME: About 2 hours, largely unattended

I rarely have time for duck confit, but this recipe gives you a lot of the same benefits: crisp skin, very tender meat and, as a bonus, delicious vegetables.

4 duck legs, trimmed of excess fat

1 large onion

8 ounces carrots

3 celery stalks

Salt and freshly ground black pepper

2 cups stock (to make your own, see pages 157–159) or water

❶ Heat the oven to 400°F. Put the duck legs, skin sides down, in a skillet large enough to accommodate all the ingredients comfortably; turn the heat to medium and cook, rotating (but not turning) the pieces as necessary to brown the skin thoroughly and evenly. Meanwhile, peel and dice the vegetables.

❷ When the skins are nicely browned, turn them over and sear for 1 to 2 minutes, sprinkle with salt and pepper, and transfer to a plate. Remove all but enough of the fat to moisten the vegetables (there's plenty more fat where that came from). Add the vegetables along with some salt and pepper and cook over medium-high heat, stirring occasionally, until they begin to brown, 10 to 15 minutes.

❸ Return the duck legs to the pan, skin sides up, and add the stock; it should come about halfway up the duck legs but should not cover them. Turn the heat to high, bring to a boil, and transfer to the oven.

❹ Cook for 30 minutes, then turn the heat to 350°F. Continue to cook, undisturbed, until the duck is tender and the liquid reduced, at least another 30 minutes and probably a bit longer. (When done, the duck

---

14 Poultry Dishes You Can Reheat

Prepared in advance or simply left over, most moist chicken dishes are fine reheated. Some of the best:

1. Chicken Braised in Soy Sauce and Lemon (page 646)
2. Chicken in Red Wine Sauce (page 649)
3. Chicken and Lentils (page 650)
4. Chicken with Yogurt and Indian Spices (pages 650–651)
5. Chicken and Garlic Stew (page 652)
6. Chicken Teriyaki (page 671)
7. Double-Coconut Sautéed Chicken Breasts (page 681)
8. Chicken in a Pot (page 688)
9. Turkey Thighs Braised in Red Wine (page 701)
10. Turkey Thighs in Almond Mole (page 702)
11. Cornish Hens and Sauerkraut (page 704)
12. Roasted Cut-Up Duck with Turnips (page 707)
13. Duck Confit (page 708)
14. Pheasant Stewed with Dried Fruits and Vinegar (page 711)

will hold nicely in a 200°F oven for up to another hour.) Serve hot.

Roast Goose

MAKES: 6 to 10 servings
TIME: About 3 hours

Like duck, goose does not serve many people per pound. But the rich, dense meat is enormously satisfying, and the skin makes the effort worth it. If you plan on serving lots of people, figure about six servings; you can easily stretch it, though, with a few side dishes. One way to extend the goose is to stuff it as you would a turkey, using any of the stuffings on pages 698–700; stuffings with fruit are best with goose, because the acidity balances the fat nicely.

1 whole goose, 8 to 10 pounds, excess fat removed
Salt and freshly ground black pepper

1 Heat the oven to 350°F. Prick the goose skin all over with a sharp fork, skewer, or thin-bladed knife; try not to hit the meat (the fat layer is usually about ¹/₄ inch thick). Sprinkle the goose with salt and pepper and put it, breast side down, on a rack in a roasting pan.

2 Put the roasting pan in the oven and roast the goose for 20 minutes, prick the exposed skin again, then roast until it begins to brown, about 20 minutes longer. Turn the goose breast side up, prick again, and baste with some of the accumulated pan juices (there will be plenty). Roast for another hour, pricking the skin and basting 2 or 3 times.

3 Unless the goose is already very brown, raise the heat to 400°F and continue to roast until the meat is done, about another 30 minutes. At that point, all juices, including those from the center vent, should run clear, and the leg bone should wiggle a little in its socket. When the bird is done, an instant-read thermometer inserted into the thigh will measure about 165°F. Carve as you would turkey (see page 697) and serve.

The Basics of Squab and Pheasant

Game birds like these need not be gamy to be distinctive, and in fact gaminess is becoming rare as these are farm raised more and more. Still, it's amazing how different in flavor they can be, even within species: Farm-raised pheasant are plump and mild-tasting, not unlike chickens; "free-range" birds are leaner and slightly gamy; and most truly wild specimens—which have darker skin, meat, and fat—have a powerful flavor.

Squab, pheasant, and partridge (and quail, see page 712), the most common game birds, are sometimes sold fresh, but more often they're frozen. You can cook them as you would any chicken dish, though I generally prefer them simply roasted, grilled, or broiled. Squab—in my opinion the most delicious bird there is—can be ordered by any butcher; each bird weighs about a pound and is so rich that it can legitimately serve two. Pheasant is fairly common and is often sold in rural areas where it is raised; it can also be ordered. Pheasant have tough, muscular legs that require longer cooking than their breasts. The answer, quite frequently, is to cook the legs and breasts separately. In restaurants, that may mean "cooking the breast and tossing the rest." At home it makes more sense to work with recipes that exploit the good flavors of the entire bird. Domesticated pheasant, the most common kind, are much like chickens, weighing in at 2 pounds and more and you check for doneness the same way.

Grilled or Broiled Squab, Vietnamese Style

MAKES: 4 to 8 servings
TIME: About 1 hour

This simple boning technique—in which the wing is left intact, protecting the breast against overcooking—can be used with any bird, including chicken. You can substitute quail (just split them in half) or even Cornish game hens; the results will be somewhat less flavorful but much less expensive.

4 squab, about 1 pound each, innards and excess fat removed

1 tablespoon peanut or extra virgin olive oil

1 tablespoon chopped garlic

2 tablespoons chopped shallot

2 teaspoons sugar

1/4 cup nam pla (Thai fish sauce) or soy sauce

1 teaspoon dark sesame oil

1/2 teaspoon freshly ground black pepper

❶ Bone the squab following the illustrations on page 713.

❷ Mix together all the other ingredients and marinate the squab for up to 2 hours in the refrigerator (even a 20-minute bath is effective). Heat a charcoal or gas grill or the broiler to very high heat and put the rack about 4 inches from the heat source. Grill or broil the squab for about 6 minutes per side, basting frequently and turning once. It is at its best when crisp outside and still fairly pink inside.

Pheasant Stewed with Dried Fruits and Vinegar

MAKES: 2 to 4 servings
TIME: About 1 hour

Pheasant is like an extreme version of chicken, with tough legs that must be cooked for considerably longer than tender breasts. This easy sweet-and-sour recipe takes that into account. Serve it on a bed of barley, orzo, or rice. Use any dried fruit you like here.

12 dried apricots

12 pitted prunes

2 tablespoons extra virgin olive oil

1 pheasant, 2 to 3 pounds, cut into serving pieces (see page 648)

Salt and freshly ground black pepper

1 cup sliced onion

1 tablespoon chopped garlic

2 cups chicken, beef, or pheasant stock (to make your own, see pages 157–159) or water

2 tablespoons sherry vinegar or wine vinegar

Chopped fresh parsley leaves for garnish

❶ If the fruit is especially dry, soak it in warm water to cover for 10 to 20 minutes; if it's moist enough to eat, don't bother.

❷ Put the oil in a large, deep skillet or Dutch oven over medium-high heat. When hot, begin browning the pheasant pieces. Turn them frequently and regulate the heat so that they do not burn. Sprinkle the pieces with salt and pepper as they cook. When they are nicely browned, transfer to a plate.

❸ Turn the heat down to medium and add the onion to the pan; cook, stirring occasionally, for 2 or 3 minutes. Add the garlic and cook for 30 seconds more. Add the stock, fruit (drain it first, if necessary), and vinegar. Turn the heat up to high and bring to a boil. Return the pheasant to the pan, turn the heat down to low, and cover.

❹ After 20 minutes, check the breast pieces; when they are done (cooked through but still tender), transfer them to a warm plate; cover loosely with aluminum foil. Continue to cook the legs until tender, another 20 to 30 minutes.

❺ If the sauce is watery, turn the heat to high and cook, stirring and scraping the bottom of the pan, until the liquid is reduced by about half. When done, return the breast pieces to the skillet and reheat them. Garnish with parsley and serve.

The Basics of Quail

Maybe it's the size of quail that makes them so intimidating at first. But you can roast quail or fry them, braise, grill, broil, or sauté them, and it's tough to go wrong; furthermore, if you're in a hurry, you can bring them from fridge to table in as little as 20 minutes. Largely, this is because they weigh about 4 ounces each (you need two per serving), so even though they're best cooked well done, they don't take long.

Quail has the bone structure and color of chicken (even the cooked meat looks similar), but it's got a strong flavor that minimizes the need to dress it up. Like that of chickens, quail production is centered mostly in the South, but unlike chickens the birds are raised mostly if not entirely free range. This puts their flavor squarely between that of domesticated birds and the truly wild birds like partridge, grouse, and woodcock, whose starkly gamy flavors are hard to take for people who were not raised on them.

You can cook them as is and let everyone nibble on the small bones. But I like to semibone the bird before cooking—a technique you can use with any small bird and even with chicken—cutting straight down along the breastbone to produce a bird that's really easy to eat. (See the illustrations on the next page.) The birds' skin is so delicate that you may wind up with a quartered bird—because there's nothing else holding breast and leg together—but that's easy enough to deal with also.

It's nearly impossible to find quail fresh, and they're rarely stocked at supermarkets or even butchers or specialty stores. But every major food wholesaler can supply them, so your supermarket or butcher should be able to provide them on a couple of days' notice. The Internet offers another alternative.

Grilled Quail, Tuscan Style

MAKES: 4 servings

TIME: 30 minutes, longer if you have time

This is one of the reasons people like the way Tuscans cook birds: It's straightforward, and augments the quail's intrinsic flavor with a strong herb. Nice, simple grilled food.

> 8 quail
>
> Salt and freshly ground black pepper
>
> 2 tablespoons minced garlic
>
> 20 fresh sage leaves, roughly chopped
>
> 3 tablespoons extra virgin olive oil

1 Heat a charcoal or gas grill to moderate heat and put the rack about 4 inches from the heat source.

2 Cut along each side of the breastbone of each bird, then straight down through where the thigh meets the body; you will have 2 semiboneless halves. (If the skin holding the thigh and leg together separates, don't worry about it.) Combine with all the remaining ingredients in a bowl or heavy plastic bag and stir or shake to coat. Marinate for an hour or so if time allows, or as long as you can.

3 Grill the quail, turning as needed, until nicely browned and cooked through, about 15 minutes. Serve hot, warm, or at room temperature.

Roast Quail with Honey, Cumin, and Orange Juice

MAKES: 4 servings

TIME: About 40 minutes

Crisp skin with extra-good flavor in well under an hour—this will make you a quail fan if nothing else does.

> 8 quail
>
> Salt and freshly ground black pepper to taste
>
> 2 tablespoons extra virgin olive oil
>
> 2 tablespoons freshly squeezed orange juice
>
> 2 tablespoons honey
>
> 1 teaspoon minced garlic
>
> 1 tablespoon ground cumin

F Fast   **M** Make Ahead   **V** Vegetarian

❶ Heat the oven to 500°F. Sprinkle the quail all over with salt and pepper, then put them, breast sides up, in a roasting pan just large enough to accommodate them. Combine the remaining ingredients and brush about half of this mixture over the birds; put in the oven.

❷ After about 10 minutes of roasting, baste with the remaining mixture, then continue to roast until done, about 10 minutes more. Serve the birds hot, with the pan juices, or warm or at room temperature.

SEMIBONING SQUAB AND QUAIL

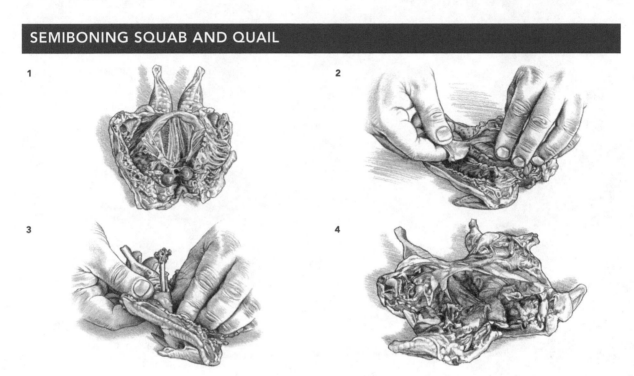

(STEP 1) Put the bird on its back on a cutting board. Using a sharp boning knife or kitchen shears, cut down the backbone on both sides and remove it as you would to butterfly chicken (see page 692). Open the bird out, skin side up, in "butterfly" position. Press down gently between the two breasts to flatten it a bit (you should hear the breastbone crack). Then turn the bird back over. (STEP 2) Use a sharp knife to cut underneath the cartilage or "flap" in the center of the bird and remove it. Use the same technique to cut through the "shoulder" joint, where the wing meets the body. Carefully cut the meat away from under the rib cage. Remove the rib cage and wishbone. (STEP 3) Using your hands, pop out the "hip" joint and separate the thigh from the body, then cut through the skin, meat, and tendons with the knife. Repeat the process for the other half of the bird. (STEP 4) You will have a whole butterflied bird. Handle it gently, since the leg and breast quarters are held together by nothing more than skin. (To cut the bird into halves, simply cut straight through the center.) Discard the bones, or reserve to make stock.

Meat

THERE'S NO DENYING WE LOVE OUR MEAT,

and many of us still put it at the center of our plate as often as we can. The reasons are the same as they always were: Meat is filling and requires little work to prepare. It's a relatively inexpensive and an excellent source of many nutrients. And most people like it.

How much meat you eat is obviously a matter of choice, but the trend toward smaller portion sizes has had an impact on the estimated number of servings for the recipes in this chapter. In most of my recipes, I assume that a pound of meat serves three to four people rather than the two to three it did not long ago. Obviously, you can change proportions to reflect your own preferences.

The fat question is also worth considering. Reigning wisdom has it that fat is "bad" for you, but this is far from clear, and even if it were, there are lots of kinds of fat, and the jury is still out even on the presumably most evil, saturated fat.

But for the last 30 years saturated fat has been considered unhealthy, and the meat industry has responded by making its products leaner than ever before. Which presents cooks with a dilemma. Since fat—good or bad—adds flavor and moisture, you have two choices: Buy meat that has some fat on it or pay a little more attention when cooking lean meat. (Most veteran cooks do a little of each, and that's how this chapter is shaped; smartly crafted—I hope—recipes featuring lean meat and wonderful—again, I hope—recipes featuring more old-fashioned, fattier cuts of meat.)

When cooking lean meat, you might want to add a bit more seasoning or take advantage of recipes using powerful seasonings (there are plenty of those here); and you might want to slightly undercook the leanest cuts so they remain juicy. When a lean pork chop or sirloin steak is cooked through, there is just no pleasure in the eating.

The Basics of Cooking Meat

Many meat cuts are interchangeable (as you'll see in this chapter, where many recipe headnotes have a substitution line), and generally meat can take a fair amount of seasoning before being overwhelmed. Once you learn the basic techniques, you can take meat in just about any direction you like, giving it a flavor spin that can originate in almost any region of the world.

Most meat tastes best when it's browned, because the process of browning creates literally hundreds of flavor compounds. You can brown by grilling, broiling, pan-grilling, roasting, or sautéing, usually with added fat. The first four of these techniques are not merely the initial process of a given recipe but the entire technique; that is, when you brown meat by grilling, broiling, pan-grilling, or roasting, you usually finish cooking it that way also.

That is sometimes the case with sautéing, too. But when you're braising or stewing meat (or poultry, for that matter), you frequently want to give it an initial sauté to heighten flavors by browning. The impact of browning is more noticeable in some final braised dishes than in others, but, given that most braised recipes have several added flavors, it isn't always essential, and it's unlikely that you'll be disappointed by the results if you skip it. Don't get me wrong: I'm all for browning, but if I have to choose between finding another recipe and proceeding without the browning step, I'll sometimes choose the latter, and I'm rarely sorry.

F Fast   **M** Make Ahead   **V** Vegetarian

When you *do* brown meat, consider doing it in the oven. It's easier to brown a large quantity of meat at high heat (450–500°F) in the oven than on top of the stove and far less messy, and uses less fat in the process.

Meat cooks best if it is at room temperature when it hits the heat. A half an hour or so out of the fridge is usually all it takes, which is frequently the time it will take you to prepare other ingredients or start a grill. You don't want it to sit out for more than an hour before cooking, however.

Finally, you definitely don't want to cook still-frozen meat. Ideally, you'll thaw it over the course of a day or two in the fridge. Second best is to put the wrapped meat in a large container of cool water and change the water every 30 minutes or so. I don't recommend defrosting meat in the microwave, because it semicooks, or on the countertop, because it's not safe.

ESSENTIAL RECIPES

The techniques represented in this section can be applied to all meats; just follow the substitution suggestions that follow the headnotes to get an idea of which meats and cuts work best in each recipe.

✪ Grilled, Pan-Grilled, or Broiled Steak, Many Ways

MAKES: 2 to 4 servings
TIME: About 10 minutes

A gas grill simply will not do the trick for the best grilled steak. If you want your steak crisp and slightly charred on the outside and rare inside, you need a blazing hot fire and no cover; use real hardwood charcoal if at all possible. If you don't have one, see the variations for non-grilling methods.

Other cuts and meats you can use: For more beef cuts, see "The Basics of Steak and Other Quick-Cooking

Beef" (page 728). Also try center-cut lamb or veal chops or shoulder steaks or pork chops no more than about an inch thick.

> 2 beef strip, rib-eye, or other steaks, 8 ounces each and about 1 inch thick, preferably at room temperature
>
> Salt and freshly ground black pepper

❶ Build a medium-hot charcoal fire; you should not be able to hold your hand 3 inches above it for more than 2 or 3 seconds. The rack should be 3 or 4 inches from the top of the coals.

❷ Dry the steaks with paper towels and sprinkle with a little salt and pepper. Grill them without turning for 3 minutes (a little more if they're over an inch thick, a little less if they're thinner or you like steaks extremely rare). Turn, then grill for 3 minutes on the other side. The steaks will be rare to medium-rare.

❸ Check for doneness; if you must, make a small slit and look. (With practice, you'll know by sight and touch.) If you would like the steaks better done, move them away from the most intense heat and grill for another minute or two per side; check again. When done, sprinkle with more salt and pepper if you like and serve.

Grilled Porterhouse or T-Bone Steak. These are best when 1½ inches thick or thicker, weighing about 2 pounds, in which case they will easily serve 4 to 6 people. In Step 2, grill for 4 to 5 minutes per side, taking care not to burn the meat; the leaner tenderloin (the smaller of the two pieces on either side of the bone) is best very rare, so keep it toward the coolest part of the fire. Check for doneness. If not done to your liking, move the steak to a cooler part of the grill and cook for another 2 to 3 minutes per side before checking again.

Pan-Grilled Steak. A terrific option for 1-inch-thick steaks (not much thicker, though), as long as you have a decent exhaust fan; otherwise, see the next option. Heat a cast-iron or other sturdy skillet just large enough to hold the steaks over medium-high heat for 4 to 5 minutes; the pan should be really hot—in fact, it should be smoking. Sprinkle its surface with salt and put in the steaks. Clouds of smoke will instantly appear; do not turn down the heat. The timing remains the same as for grilled steaks and if you want pepper, add it after you turn the steaks for the last time.

Broiled Steak. Again, good for 1-inch-thick steaks. Heat the broiler until quite hot and adjust the rack so it's 3 or 4 inches from the heat source. About 10 minutes before you're ready to cook, put a cast-iron or other sturdy, heatproof skillet on the rack. Prepare the steaks as described in Step 2 and put them into the hot pan. Timing will depend on the heat of your broiler, so check for doneness frequently. The steak will sear on both sides without turning. Serve, if you like, with the pan drippings poured on top.

Pan-Grilled/Oven-Roasted Steak. An excellent method if you don't have a first-rate exhaust system or your steak is thicker than 1 1/2 inches. Turn the oven to its maximum temperature, at least 500°F, and set a rack in the lowest possible position (if you can put a skillet directly on the oven floor, so much the better). Heat a cast-iron or other sturdy ovenproof skillet large enough to hold the steaks over medium-high

Bringing Global Flavors to Grilled Steak

Bistro Steak. After cooking, top each steak with 1 teaspoon to 1 tablespoon Compound Butter (page 32) or Flavored Oil (page 26). For example, try parsley butter mixed with a little garlic (and some minced anchovy if you like).

Tuscan Steak (Bistecca alla Fiorentina). Drizzle some flavorful extra virgin olive oil over the steak when done; top with freshly squeezed lemon juice to taste.

Miso Steak. The long marinating time especially benefits tenderloin medallions or steaks (otherwise known as *filet mignon*): Combine 1 cup dark (red) miso, 1 tablespoon minced fresh ginger, 1 teaspoon minced garlic, and 1/2 teaspoon cayenne, or to taste. Thin with enough mirin or sake to make the mixture pasty. Spread the meat with this paste, then proceed, or cover and refrigerate for up to 24 hours. Grill, broil, or pan-roast as described in the main recipe or variations.

Steak, Vietnamese Style. Serve the steak sliced on a pile of greens with the sauce on top or with large lettuce leaves for rolling up meat and sauce: Before cooking the steak, pulse the following ingredients in a food processor until finely chopped but not quite puréed: 1 tablespoon nam pla (Thai fish sauce); 1 teaspoon cracked or coarsely ground black pepper; 1 teaspoon sugar; 1 small (Thai) chile, seeded, or 1/2 teaspoon hot red pepper flakes, or to taste; 2 tablespoons fresh lime juice; 2 teaspoons chopped garlic, or to taste; 2 medium to large shallots, chopped, 1/2 cup chopped fresh mint or Thai basil; 1/2 cup chopped fresh cilantro; a sprinkle of salt.

Steak, Romanian Style (Fleica). If you have a mortar and pestle, pound 3 or 4 peeled garlic cloves together with the juice of a lemon and 1/2 teaspoon coarse salt, or more to taste. Otherwise, mince the garlic and stir it with the salt into the lemon juice, then use the back of a wooden spoon to smash the garlic as much as you can. Press freshly ground black pepper into the uncooked steaks and then spread the garlic mixture evenly on both sides. Let the steaks sit while you build and heat a charcoal fire or the broiler. Melt 3 tablespoons butter. When you're ready to cook, brush a little of the melted butter onto the steaks and then put them on the grill.

 Fast   Make Ahead   **V** Vegetarian

heat for 4 to 5 minutes; the pan should be really hot, just about smoking. Sprinkle its surface with coarse salt and put in the steaks. Immediately transfer the skillet to the oven (wearing a thick oven mitt to protect your hand). Roast the steaks, turning once and sprinkling the top with pepper; timing remains the same as for grilled steaks, unless your steak is thick.

★ Stir-Fried Spicy Beef with Basil

MAKES: 4 to 6 servings

TIME: 15 minutes, plus time to freeze or marinate the meat

Once you get this Thai-style dish set up, it's faster than cooking the rice that goes alongside it. You can use round or chuck meat here, but the best cuts are flank or sirloin, which are more tender and equally tasty. Thai basil is nice here if you can find it, but any fresh basil is fine.

Other cuts and meats you can use: pork, preferably from the shoulder or leg (fresh ham); lamb, preferably from the shoulder or leg; boneless chicken.

1¹⁄₂ pounds flank or sirloin steak

¹⁄₂ cup loosely packed fresh basil leaves

1 tablespoon peanut oil, plus 1 teaspoon for marinating

1¹⁄₂ tablespoons minced garlic

¹⁄₄ teaspoon hot red pepper flakes, or to taste

1 tablespoon soy sauce or nam pla (Thai fish sauce)

Juice of ¹⁄₂ lime

❶ Slice the beef across the grain as thinly as you can; it's easier if you freeze it for 15 to 30 minutes first. Cut the slices into bite-sized pieces.

❷ Wash and dry the basil; if the leaves are large, chop them coarsely. If time permits, mix the beef, basil, and the teaspoon of peanut oil in a bowl, cover, and refrigerate for an hour or so (this helps the flavor of the basil permeate the meat).

❸ When you're ready to cook, have all the ingredients ready (including a serving dish and rice, if you're making any). If you have not yet done so, mix together the beef and basil. Heat a large skillet over high heat until it smokes, 3 or 4 minutes.

❹ Lower the heat to medium and add the tablespoon of peanut oil. Swirl it around and add the garlic. Stir once or twice. As soon as the garlic begins to color—after about 15 seconds—return the heat to high and add the beef-basil mixture. Stir quickly and add the red pepper. Stir frequently (but not constantly), just until the meat loses its red color, a minute or two longer. Add the soy sauce and lime juice, stir, turn off the heat, and serve immediately, over rice if you wish.

Super-Spicy Beef with Orange Flavor. In Step 2, substitute the zest of 1 large orange for the basil. Mince about 1 tablespoon of the zest and leave the rest in larger pieces. Combine all of it with the meat. In Step 4, add 10 to 30 small dried hot red chiles, or to taste, along with the garlic. Continue as directed, adding some of the orange's juice along with the lime juice at the end. Serve immediately, over rice if you wish.

Stir-Fried Curry Beef. Omit the basil and pepper flakes. For Step 2, marinate the meat in 1 tablespoon soy sauce, 1 tablespoon rice wine, dry sherry, stock, or water, and 1 teaspoon sugar. In Step 4, add 1¹⁄₂ tablespoons minced fresh ginger and 1 thinly sliced onion along with the garlic and cook until the onion is softened, 5 to 10 minutes. Stir in 3 tablespoons curry powder (to make your own, see pages 66–67) and cook for 30 seconds. Add the meat and cook until browned, then add ¹⁄₄ cup water instead of the soy sauce and lime and cook until the liquid is gone, about 2 minutes. Garnish with chopped fresh cilantro leaves and serve immediately.

✪ Skillet Pork Chops, Eight Ways

MAKES: 4 servings
TIME: 30 minutes

The essential sear-and-simmer technique that leaves you with any number of excellent pan sauces (see the variations).

Other cuts and meats you can use: bone-in chicken thighs (which will require more cooking) or pork medallions cut from the tenderloin (which will cook more quickly).

4 shoulder or center-cut loin pork chops, about 1 inch thick, trimmed of excess fat

Salt and freshly ground black pepper

2 tablespoons extra virgin olive oil

$1/2$ cup dry white wine

1 teaspoon minced garlic or 2 tablespoons minced shallot, onion, or scallion

$1/2$ cup chicken, beef, or vegetable stock (to make your own, see pages 157–159) or water, plus more if needed

1 tablespoon butter or more olive oil (especially if it's flavorful)

1 tablespoon freshly squeezed lemon juice or vinegar

Chopped fresh parsley leaves for garnish

❶ Sprinkle the chops with salt and pepper. Put a large skillet over medium-high heat for 2 or 3 minutes. Add the olive oil; as soon as the first wisps of smoke rise from the oil, add the chops and turn the heat to high. Brown the chops on both sides, moving them around so they develop good color all over, no longer than 4 minutes total and preferably less.

❷ Reduce the heat to medium. Add the wine and the garlic and cook, turning the chops once or twice, until the wine is all but evaporated, about 3 minutes. Add the stock, turn the heat down to low, cover, and cook for 10 to 15 minutes, turning the chops once or twice, until the chops are tender but not dry. When done, they will be firm to the touch, their juices will run just slightly pink, and, when you cut into them (which you should do if you're at all unsure of their doneness), the color will be rosy at first glance but quickly turn pale.

❸ Transfer the chops to a platter. If the pan juices are very thin, cook, stirring and scraping the bottom of the pan, until the liquid is reduced slightly. If they are scarce (unlikely), add another $1/2$ cup stock or water; cook, stirring and scraping the bottom of the pan, until the liquid is reduced slightly. Then stir in the butter or a few drops of oil over medium heat; add the lemon juice, pour over the chops, garnish with parsley, and serve.

Pork Chops with Mustard. In Step 3, stir in 1 tablespoon or more of Dijon mustard with the lemon juice (some capers are good here, too, as is a dash or two of Worcestershire sauce). Finish as directed.

Pork Chops with Sweet Soy Sauce. Use neutral oil, like grapeseed or corn, or butter. Substitute mirin (or equal parts honey and water) for the wine, a mixture of equal parts soy sauce and water for the stock, and rice vinegar for the lemon juice. In Step 2, when you add the garlic, add 5 or 6 slices fresh ginger. Instead of the parsley, garnish with $1/2$ cup chopped scallion.

Pork Chops with Sherry-Garlic Sauce. In Step 3, after removing the chops, add $1/2$ cup not-too-dry sherry (oloroso or amontillado) and cook, stirring and scraping the bottom of the pan, until the liquid is reduced slightly. Add 1 tablespoon olive oil and 1 tablespoon minced garlic and continue to cook until the liquid becomes syrupy, about 5 minutes. Omit the butter. Stir in $1/4$ cup minced fresh parsley leaves and the juice of $1/2$ lemon. Taste and adjust the seasoning. Pour over the chops, garnish, and serve.

Pork Chops with Apples or Pears. In Step 3, after removing the chops, cook 2 cups peeled, cored, and sliced pears in the remaining liquid, stirring and scraping the bottom of the pan as the apples cook and adding about $1/2$ cup more white wine or stock if necessary.

F Fast   **M** Make Ahead   **V** Vegetarian

When the pear slices are soft, after about 5 minutes, stir in 1 tablespoon freshly squeezed lemon juice. Omit the butter. Taste and adjust the seasoning. Pour over the chops, garnish, and serve.

Pork Chops with Onions and Peppers. Steps 1 and 2 remain the same; undercook the chops slightly and heat an oven to warm. In Step 3, after removing the chops, put them in the warm oven. Stir in 2 cups thinly sliced onion and 2 cups seeded and sliced bell peppers, any color but green. Stir, re-cover the pan, and cook for 5 minutes over medium heat. Uncover and cook, stirring, until the vegetables are softened and beginning to brown, about 5 more minutes. Moisten with $1/2$ cup stock, then cook until most of the stock is absorbed, about 5 minutes. Omit the butter. Stir in 1 tablespoon freshly squeezed lemon juice or vinegar, taste and adjust the seasoning, and serve over the chops. A teaspoon of minced fresh marjoram, oregano, or thyme leaves (or $1/2$ teaspoon of dried herb) or a tablespoon or two of minced fresh basil or parsley is good stirred into the vegetables just as they finish cooking.

Pork Chops with Butter and Shallots. Do the initial browning in half oil, half butter. In Step 3, after removing the chops, pour off all the liquid and add 2 tablespoons butter and $1/4$ cup minced shallot to the skillet. Cook over medium heat until the shallot softens, 3 or 4 minutes. Add $1/2$ cup stock (to make your own, see pages 157–159) or water and cook, stirring, until syrupy, about 5 minutes. Add $1/4$ cup minced fresh chervil or basil leaves or 1 teaspoon minced fresh tarragon leaves and stir. Add 1 tablespoon more butter and the lemon juice and pour over the chops. Serve, garnished with a bit more of the minced fresh herb.

Pork Chops with Prunes and Cream. Use butter instead of olive oil in Step 1. For Step 2, add 2 sprigs fresh thyme and 2 lightly smashed (and peeled) cloves garlic and cook for a minute. Add 1 cup of the wine (or use cider if you like) and 1 cup pitted prunes or dried apricots. Reduce the heat so the liquid bubbles steadily, cover, and cook just until the chops are tender, as directed. For Step 3, reduce the liquid to about $1/2$ cup, reduce the heat to medium, and stir in $1/2$ cup heavy cream. Cook, stirring constantly, until the mixture is thick. Add more cream as you like until the sauce has the consistency you like. Taste and adjust the seasoning. Garnish with chopped fresh parsley leaves if you like and serve.

✪ My Favorite Burger

MAKES: 4 servings
TIME: 20 minutes

A burger needs good, not-too-lean meat, gentle handling, and quick cooking. For more about grinding your own meat, which is easy and allows you to use better meat, see the sidebar on page 722.

Other cuts and meats you can use: fatty pork shoulder; skinned and boned chicken, turkey, or duck thighs; boneless lamb shoulder (all but the lamb will require a few more minutes of cooking time per side to cook all the way through).

> $1 1/2$ to 2 pounds not-too-lean sirloin or chuck, cut into 1-inch chunks, or preground meat
>
> $1/2$ white onion, peeled and cut into chunks (optional)
>
> Salt and freshly ground black pepper to taste

❶ Heat a charcoal or gas grill or the broiler until hot—you should barely be able to hold your hand 3 or 4 inches over the rack—and put the rack 3 to 4 inches from the heat source. (If you're cooking on a stovetop, when you're ready to start, heat a large, heavy skillet over medium-high heat for 3 or 4 minutes; sprinkle it with coarse salt.)

❷ Put the meat and onion into a food processor (in batches if your machine is small) and pulse until coarsely ground—finer than chopped, but not much. (If you're starting with preground meat, mince the onion if you're using it and incorporate it into the meat.) Put it in a bowl

Do-It-Yourself Ground Meat

The key to excellent burgers is starting with the right meat, which is why I encourage you to grind your own. When you buy meat labeled simply *ground beef*, you have no idea what you're getting. It likely comes from anonymous cuts of several different animals, and is ground in huge quantities (not by the pound, that's for sure), often in faraway places. If the aesthetics of that don't give you pause, consider the health concerns: It's massive batches of preground meat that carry the highest risk of salmonella and *E. coli* contamination and have caused many authorities to recommend cooking burgers to the well-done stage. And to that I ask: Why bother?

Labels like *ground sirloin, 85 percent lean*, and *ground chuck, 90 percent lean*, are better, because you know what cut of beef has been ground up and how much fat the meat contains (that's important, since sufficient fat plays into getting a good burger).

Still, when you grind your own, you know exactly what you're getting. And it's not that difficult: Take a nice-looking chuck roast, some well-marbled sirloin steaks, or some pork or lamb shoulder (or even poultry), cut it into 1- to 2-inch cubes, and pulse it in the food processor until it's chopped. (If you have a 12-cup food processor, you can do a pound or a little more at a time; with a smaller machine, you'll need to work in batches.) You can do a few pounds at a time and freeze what you won't use immediately, or you can grind the meat as you need it.

A few rules: First, buy relatively fatty meat. If you start with meat that's 95 percent lean—that's hardly any fat at all—you are going to get the filet mignon of burgers: tender but not especially tasty. If you use chuck or sirloin, with 15 to 20 percent fat, you're going to get flavorful meat with the good mouthfeel that comes with fat. The same holds true with pork and lamb, though the selections are

in fact easier, because the shoulder cuts of both animals contain enough internal fat so that they'll always remain moist unless you overcook them horribly. For ground poultry, use boneless leg and thigh meat and include a little of the skin if you like (and cook to well done).

Next, don't overprocess: You want chopped meat, not a purée. The finer you grind the meat, the more likely you are to pack it together too tightly and make the burger tough. For the same reason, handle the meat gently: Make the patties (which should weigh, in my opinion, about 6 ounces each—not small, but not huge either) with a light hand, and at no time—before, during, or after cooking—should you press them down with a spatula, like a short-order cook.

Finally, season aggressively: I'd start with a large pinch of salt and work up from there. If you grind your own beef, you can make a mixture and taste it raw. (For ground pork, lamb, or poultry, or if you're queasy about eating raw beef—though there's really no difference, safety-wise, between raw beef and rare beef—cook up a spoonful in a skillet, taste, and reseason as necessary.) For some ideas about how to season and flavor ground meat, see the list on the next page.

The cooking: For grilling you want a hot fire, but not a blazing-hot one (that fat will burn), and you want the rack—which should be very clean—3 or 4 inches above it. If you're broiling, use a rack so fat can drip away. On top of the stove, make sure the pan is hot and not crowded; otherwise the burgers will steam instead of sear. In all cases, turn only after the first side releases, after a few minutes (if you don't press with the spatula, you'll get less sticking too). Cooking time depends on the size of the burger, of course, but mine take 6 to 8 minutes total for rare to medium-rare. (Pork takes a little longer, but not much.)

 Fast   Make Ahead   **V** Vegetarian

and sprinkle with salt and pepper, then taste and adjust the seasoning (if you don't want to taste it raw, cook up a spoonful in a small skillet). Handling the meat as little as possible to avoid compressing it, shape it lightly into 4 or more burgers.

❸ Grill the burgers, about 3 minutes per side for very rare and another minute per side for each increasing stage of doneness, but no more than 10 minutes total unless you like hockey pucks. (Timing on the stovetop in a pan over medium-high heat is exactly the same; the broiler may vary a bit depending on your oven.)

❹ Serve on buns, toast, or hard rolls, garnished as you like.

Cheese-Stuffed Burgers. Especially good with smoked mozzarella or cheddar; try these burgers with ground lamb. Omit the onion. Cut 4 ounces of any melting cheese into 4 pieces and form the meat into patties around each one; sprinkle with salt and pepper and proceed with the recipe.

13 Mix-and-Match Ideas for Flavoring Burgers

Burgers respond fantastically to seasonings. Try incorporating some of the following during shaping, combining them at will.

1. 2 tablespoons minced fresh parsley, basil, chives, chervil, or other herbs
2. $1/2$ teaspoon minced garlic or 1 clove roasted garlic
3. 1 tablespoon minced anchovy
4. 1 teaspoon minced or grated fresh ginger or ground ginger
5. 1 tablespoon soy, Worcestershire, steak, or other flavored sauce
6. $1/4$ cup minced shallot or scallion
7. Tabasco or other hot sauce, to taste (start with $1/2$ teaspoon)
8. 1 teaspoon curry powder, chili powder, or other spice mixtures (to make your own, see pages 65–69) to taste

9. Up to $1/2$ cup grated or crumbled cheese (like Parmesan, cheddar, blue, or feta)
10. 1 cup cooked spinach or other greens, squeezed dry and chopped
11. 1 or 2 tablespoons ground dried porcini or $1/2$ cup reconstituted porcini, chopped
12. 1 mild dried chile, like ancho, soaked until tender and minced
13. 1 tablespoon (or more) freshly grated horseradish or prepared horseradish

✪ Meat Loaf

MAKES: 6 to 8 servings
TIME: About 1 hour, largely unattended

Free-form meat loaf has several advantages over those cooked in loaf pans: It develops a lovely crust on three sides instead of just one, and the fat can run off, rather than become trapped between pan and meat. Plus it's easy to shape by hand and always turns out in the shape you wanted. You can also shape this mixture into meatballs if you like; just bake them for about half the time.

$1/2$ cup bread crumbs, preferably fresh (page 876)

$1/2$ cup milk

2 pounds mixed ground meats: beef, veal, lamb, and/or pork (you can use turkey or chicken also if you like)

1 egg, lightly beaten

$1/2$ cup freshly grated Parmesan cheese

$1/4$ cup minced fresh parsley leaves

$1/2$ teaspoon minced garlic

1 small onion, minced

1 small carrot, minced

1 teaspoon minced fresh sage leaves or 1 pinch dried sage leaves

Salt and freshly ground black pepper

3 slices bacon (optional but good, especially if the meat is very lean)

1 Heat the oven to 350°F. Soak the bread crumbs in the milk until the milk is absorbed, about 5 minutes.

2 Mix together all the ingredients except the bacon. Shape the meat into a loaf in a baking pan; top with the bacon if you like. Bake for 45 to 60 minutes, basting occasionally with the rendered pan juices. When done, the meat loaf will be browned lightly and firm and an instant-read thermometer inserted into the center will read 160°F.

Meat Loaf with Spinach. Bring a large pot of water to a boil and salt it. Trim and wash a 10-ounce package of fresh spinach; cook it in the boiling water for 30 seconds, then remove it. Drain and cool it, then chop it finely, sprinkling with salt, pepper, and a grating of nutmeg. In Step 1, increase the bread crumbs to 1 cup. In Step 2, integrate the chopped spinach into the meat loaf, substituting a grating of nutmeg for the sage.

Spiced Meat Loaf. Omit the Parmesan and substitute cilantro for the parsley and 1 tablespoon curry powder, garam masala, chili powder, or other spice mixture (to make your own, see pages 65–69) for the sage.

Meat Loaf with Dried Tomatoes. Substitute 1 cup chopped reconstituted dried tomatoes for the carrot and fresh rosemary for the sage. Spread barbecue sauce or ketchup (to make your own, see pages 51–52) over the top if you like.

★ Beef Stew, Eight Ways

MAKES: 4 to 6 servings

TIME: 1¹/₂ to 2 hours, largely unattended

Ⓜ

Braised beef—which is what beef stew is—can be spiced in many different ways; I offer several versions here, but you can also make a chililike beef stew (add the seasonings from the recipe for Chili non Carne, page 429) or a beef curry (add the seasonings from

Lamb Curry, page 775). The substitutions are easy and work perfectly.

You can skip the initial browning if you're pressed for time, or you can use the oven: Heat the oven to 500°F and roast the meat in a large roasting pan with 1 tablespoon of the oil and the garlic clove, shaking the pan to turn the cubes once or twice, until brown all over.

Other cuts and meats you can use: cubed beef brisket, pork shoulder or fresh ham (pork leg), leg of lamb or lamb shoulder.

2 tablespoons neutral oil, like grapeseed or corn, or extra virgin olive oil

1 clove garlic, lightly crushed, plus 1 tablespoon minced garlic

2 to 2¹/₂ pounds boneless beef chuck or round, trimmed of surface fat and cut into 1- to 1¹/₂-inch cubes

Salt and freshly ground black pepper

2 large or 3 medium onions, cut into eighths

3 tablespoons all-purpose flour

3 cups chicken, beef, or vegetable stock (to make your own, see pages 157–159), water, wine, or a combination, or more as needed

1 bay leaf

1 teaspoon fresh thyme leaves or ¹/₂ teaspoon dried thyme

4 medium to large waxy or all-purpose potatoes, peeled and cut into 1-inch chunks

4 large carrots, cut into 1-inch chunks

1 cup fresh or thawed frozen peas

Chopped fresh parsley leaves for garnish

1 Heat a large pot with a lid or a Dutch oven over medium-high heat for 2 or 3 minutes; add the oil and the crushed garlic clove; cook, stirring, for 1 minute, then remove and discard the garlic. Add the meat to the skillet a few pieces at a time, turning to brown well on all sides, about 10 minutes total. Do not crowd or the cubes will not brown properly; cook in batches if necessary. Sprinkle the meat with salt and pepper as it cooks.

② When the meat is brown, remove it with a slotted spoon. Pour or spoon off most of the fat and turn the heat down to medium. Add the onions. Cook, stirring, until softened, about 10 minutes. Add the flour and cook, stirring, for about 2 minutes. Add the stock, bay leaf, thyme, and meat and bring to a boil. Turn the heat down to low and cover. Cook, undisturbed, for 30 minutes.

③ Uncover the pot; the mixture should be wet (if not, add a little more liquid). Add the potatoes and carrots, turn the heat up for a minute or so to bring the liquid back to a boil, then lower the heat and cover again. Cook for 30 to 60 minutes, until the meat and vegetables are tender. Taste and adjust the seasoning. (At this point, you may remove the meat and vegetables with a slotted spoon and refrigerate them and the stock separately. Skim the fat from the stock before combining it with the meat and vegetables, reheating, and proceeding with the recipe from this point.)

④ Add the minced garlic and the peas; if you're pleased with the stew's consistency, continue to cook, covered, over low heat. If it's too soupy, remove the cover and raise the heat to high. In either case, cook for an additional 5 minutes or so, until the peas have heated through and the garlic has flavored the stew. Garnish with parsley and serve.

Belgian Beef Stew with Beer *(Carbonnade)*. In Step 2, omit the flour. Use 1¹/₂ cups good dark beer for the liquid. Omit the potatoes, carrots, peas, and minced garlic. This is good finished with a tablespoon of Dijon mustard and served over buttered noodles or with plain boiled potatoes.

Spicy Braised Beef with Lime. In Step 1, use peanut oil if you have it. In Step 2, omit the bay leaf and thyme and add 1 tablespoon minced garlic, 2 or 3 small dried hot red chiles, or to taste, and the minced zest of 1 lime; use only 1¹/₂ cups of liquid. Do not add vegetables. When the meat is tender, finish the dish by adding more minced garlic and the juice of 1 or 2 limes, to taste. Garnish with

chopped fresh cilantro leaves and serve with Steamed Sticky Rice, Thai Style (page 459), or plain white rice.

Beef Stew with Bacon. In Step 1, cut 4 ounces bacon (preferably slab) into small cubes and cook it over medium heat, stirring, until crisp. Remove with a slotted spoon and reserve. Proceed with the recipe, browning the meat in the bacon fat. Stir in the bacon cubes a minute before serving.

Beef Stew, Greek Style. In Step 2, use 2 bay leaves and omit the thyme. Add 2 cloves, ¹/₂ teaspoon ground cinnamon, and one 6-ounce can tomato paste. In Step 3, add 20 peeled pearl onions (frozen are fine), each skewered with a toothpick through its equator (this holds them together), and ¹/₄ cup red wine vinegar; in Step 4, omit the peas. Garnish with parsley and serve over rice or broad noodles.

Beef Stew with Dried Mushrooms. Add 1 ounce dried porcini mushrooms and omit the garlic, flour, thyme, potatoes, carrots, and peas. Reduce the stock to 2 cups and heat until steaming. Soak the porcini in the hot stock until soft, about 30 minutes. Proceed with Step 1. For Step 2, cook the onions as directed and meanwhile remove the porcini from the stock and trim away any hard spots. When the onions are lightly browned, add the warmed stock, porcini, and remaining ingredients (except the parsley); cook until the meat is tender, anywhere from 45 to 90 minutes. Proceed with the recipe.

Beef Stew with Prunes. Omit the garlic, flour, thyme, potatoes, carrots, and peas. Reduce the chopped onion to just one. Proceed with Step 1. For Step 2, cook the onion with 3 cored and chopped plum tomatoes (canned are fine) as directed. Add the bay leaf along with 1 teaspoon sweet paprika, or more to taste, and one 3-inch cinnamon stick, then return the meat to the pot, along with 1 cup of stock and 1 cup dry red wine. Proceed with Step 2. For Step 3, remove the cinnamon stick and bay leaf and add

2 tablespoons sugar and 1 cup pitted prunes instead of the potatoes and carrots. Proceed with the recipe, skipping the garlic, and stirring in a tablespoon or so sherry or other vinegar before adjusting the seasoning.

Sour Beef Stew with Horseradish. Omit the garlic, flour, bay leaf, thyme, and peas. Proceed with Step 1. For Step 2, cook 1 chopped onion, 1 chopped celery stalk, 2 chopped carrots, and 2 or 3 waxy potatoes as directed. Add 1 cup of stock and $1/4$ cup white or wine vinegar, bring to a boil, and cook for a minute; then return the meat to the pot. Take 1 bunch fresh dill and remove about $1/2$ cup of dill leaves and set aside; tie the remaining stems and leaves into a bunch and add to the pot. Reduce the heat to a slow bubble, cover, and cook until the meat and vegetables are tender, about an hour. Add 1 tablespoon or more prepared horseradish and the reserved dill. Taste and adjust the seasoning. Serve immediately.

5 Tips for Changing the Flavor of Any Beef Stew

1. Use wine (experiment—red, white, even slightly sweet white, are all good) or beer (same thing: porter, IPA, lager) for the cooking liquid.
2. After the flour has been cooking for about a minute in Step 2, add 1 or 2 tablespoons spice mixture, like curry powder, garam masala, chili powder, or other (to make your own, see pages 65–69).
3. Add 1 or more dried chiles, like chipotle, guajillo, ancho, or pasilla, soaked in hot water until soft and cored, seeded, and chopped.
4. Stir in chopped fresh herbs, like cilantro, chives, tarragon, dill, or smaller amounts of sage, rosemary, or thyme, just before serving; or cook a bundle of herbs with the meat.
5. Vary the vegetables or use all one vegetable. Be sure to adjust the timing for adding them so that they don't overcook.

The Basics of Beef

Cooking beef is often no more than combining the right cooking technique with the right cut. More tender cuts like sirloin, tenderloin, and rib-eye are best grilled or roasted and cooked rare. Tougher cuts like chuck, round, and brisket must be broken down with long cooking and moist heat; if you grill chuck, for example, or roast round, it will be chewy and you will be disappointed. Similarly, braising good sirloin is not only a waste of money but will give less than ideal results.

It's almost as simple as that. The problem is that there are few real butchers left, and at most supermarkets—the newer, upscale chains are a little different—meat managers fill out a form to order beef, and the meat arrives wrapped in plastic, sometimes ready for final cutting and packaging, even packed for retail sale. Where was the animal raised? What was it fed? How old was it? Was it fatty or lean? How much did it weigh? He doesn't know, and you'll never find out.

In short, buying beef in a supermarket is a crap shoot. If you can find high-quality specialty branded meat or prime meat (in theory, the highest quality grade given by the USDA), those are good options. A real butcher, if you can find one, can guide you in selecting the cut that best meets your plans; he may even age the beef, improving both its flavor and its texture, something that is never done at a supermarket. Or, if you're energetic and have a large freezer, you can probably find someone locally who is raising a few cattle the old-fashioned way and will sell you a side or a quarter.

Increasingly, too, we're seeing higher-quality organic or truly naturally raised beef or imported beef that's raised in better conditions than most beef in the States. (We lead the world in factory farming, by a long shot.)

Any thinly cut piece of beef can be called a steak; a thick piece can be called a roast or a pot roast. Unfortunately none of these terms guarantees tenderness or tastiness; we've all had "steaks" that were tough or tasteless or roasts that refused to soften even after hours of cooking.

F Fast   **M** Make Ahead   **V** Vegetarian

MAJOR PARTS OF BEEF

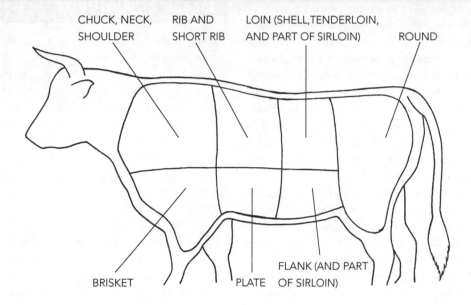

CHUCK, NECK, SHOULDER

RIB AND SHORT RIB

LOIN (SHELL, TENDERLOIN, AND PART OF SIRLOIN)

ROUND

BRISKET

PLATE

FLANK (AND PART OF SIRLOIN)

To guarantee the results you're looking for, you must start by buying the right cut.

Chuck: The neck/shoulder area is muscular and has lots of connective tissue, which means it is flavorful and best suited to long, slow cooking (or grinding). Cuts from the chuck may be called *shoulder roast (or steaks), arm roast (or steaks), blade, top blade, or underblade roast (or steaks),* and *eye roast.* The steaks have decent flavor but are tough. Boneless chuck meat is suitable for stir-frying.

Rib and Short Rib: Behind the chuck, ribs 6–12 comprise one of the most valuable parts of the steer (ribs 10–12 are best). Rib steaks (or rib-eye steaks) are as good as they come; rib roasts are the best beef to roast; and short ribs—pieces of the long rib bones cut into sections—are wonderful for braising.

Loin, or Short Loin: A highly valuable section behind the rib. Actually it's two sections: the top (shell) and the bottom (tenderloin). The tenderloin may be sold whole or cut into large lengths (which make fine roasts) or cut into small, thick steaks called *filet mignon.* It's supremely tender but not that flavorful, so much improved by sauces. The shell, which extends alongside the tenderloin to the sirloin, yields some of the best and most popular steaks, especially New York strip (also called *shell steaks, Kansas City strip, club steaks,* or *strip loin steaks*). T-bone and porterhouse steaks (nearly identical) are part tenderloin (tender but not especially tasty) and part shell (not so tender, but much more flavorful). Delmonico steaks contain no tenderloin and are often boneless. The hanging tender steak (or hanger steak) also comes from the short loin.

Sirloin: Behind the loin and the flank, the sirloin contains the rear end of the shell, which makes steaks of varying quality. They may simply be labeled *sirloin* (if there's more detail, choose pin-bone, then flat-bone, then round-bone, and finally wedge-bone; all are decent, but pin-bone is best). It also has the top and bottom butt, or rump, which may be sold as boneless sirloin or other roasts or steaks, like rump steaks or Newport steaks—none of which is superior, but all of which can be quite good.

Round: The rear end of the cow, which is best used as ground meat, is often cut into steaks (top round, also called *rump*) and roasts (top or bottom round), which are almost always tough and never especially flavorful (they're too lean). For pot-roasting, look to chuck. For oven-roasting or steaks, look to the rib, loin, or sirloin. Round meat is good, however, for stir-frying, as long as it is thinly sliced. From the rear end of the cow, too, comes "oxtail" (rarely, if ever, from ox anymore), which is cross-cut and used for soups or stews.

Flank: Under the loin is the flank, a lean cut that can be made into flank steaks, which must be thinly sliced (always across the grain) to avoid toughness. Good for stir-frying and for "London broil," which simply means broiled steak, sliced thinly across the grain.

Brisket: Directly under the chuck, the brisket has good flavor but will never become what you call tender; even if you cook the daylights out of it, it will be chewy. (This doesn't mean it's unpleasant; it's quite tasty, just chewy.) It's often used for corned beef and pastrami. In front of the brisket are the foreshank and shin, good for stew or soup meat.

Plate: Behind the brisket and under the rib, this is even tougher and harder to cook than brisket; it's often cured to make pastrami but is sometimes sold as steaks, which have good flavor but are tough. Good for braising. Skirt steak, a long, narrow strip of meat from this section of the cow (actually the diaphragm), is fantastic grilled or pan-cooked, as long as you don't overcook it.

The Basics of Steaks and Other Quick-Cooking Beef

The old adage "You can't ruin a good steak" is pretty much true. (See the Essential Recipe for steak on page

What Does *Grass-Fed* Mean?

Labeling definitions for organic and "natural" beef, pork, lamb, and veal are the same as they are for chicken (see pages 638–639). Some beef on the market, though, is "grass-fed," which means the cow was fed for its entire life on a diet of pasture grasses (as cows were "designed" to do). Almost all cattle may start life eating grass, but in this country it's typically "finished" on a diet of soy, corn, and other grains (none of which are in the cow's natural diet) to give the meat more marbling and the characteristic flavor that Americans have come to expect.

Grass-fed beef has different texture and flavor than grain-finished beef, and some argue that it's better nutritionally (and less damaging on the environment as well). In my experience grass-fed beef varies from one brand to the next and can be quite appealing when it's good.

If you want to try grass-fed beef, be sure you're getting the real deal. The government (at the time of this writing) is trying to formally define the conditions for using the grass-fed label. And until then, you don't know for sure whether the animal actually grazed in a

717.) A "good" steak means the right cut; given that, you can ruin it only by cooking it to a point of doneness that doesn't please you or by overcooking it altogether. If you're unsure of your timing, aim to undercook by a wide margin, then use a thin-bladed knife to peek inside and check for doneness; you can always cook the steak for a couple minutes more. Or use an instant-read thermometer to check for doneness. (The temperature will usually rise by about 5 degrees after you take the steak off the heat.) Rare steaks will measure 120–125°F; medium-rare to medium measures 130–150°F; I'd consider anything above that well done.

Several cuts of beef are both tender and tasty enough to be cut as steaks and grilled or broiled without much fuss. Strip steaks, usually sold boneless, make the ideal individual steak. T-bone or porterhouse steaks are best cut thick to serve two or more people. Rib-eye steaks are also very tender and very flavorful and make good individual—or even sharable—steaks.

Steaks simply labeled *sirloin* and sold bone-in or bone-out are riskier (see "Major Parts of Beef, page 727), but they're usually quite flavorful, and the worst that can happen is that they are on the chewy side. This is also the case with flank steak, which is guaranteed to be chewy but flavorful. It's a good steak to marinate and grill, then cut on a slight angle into thin slices. Like the pieces of lean top round that are often sold as steak, it is also good cut into bits and stir-fried or grilled or broiled very quickly, then sliced thin—which makes it "London broil."

Then there are the unusual cuts like flat iron, hanger, skirt, and tri-tip (cut from the sirloin roast by the same name). These are all fine alternatives if you can find them.

A word about chuck "steak": Despite the assurances of your supermarket meat manager, it's guaranteed to be very, very chewy (and fatty) if you cook it as a steak. Chuck is an ideal cut for grinding or cooking with liquid—but please don't try to grill it.

5 Unexpected Sauces for Steaks

You're probably familiar with the classic accompaniments for steak, like Béarnaise Sauce (page 58), or the more contemporary Traditional Pesto (page 27) and Chimichurri (page 28). But here are some other ideas.

1. Any Five-Minute Drizzle Sauce (page 22)
2. Any Fresh Tomato or Fruit Salsa (page 23)
3. Blue Cheese Dressing (page 25)
4. Real Ranch Dressing or any of its variations (page 42)
5. Grilled Pineapple and Onion Salsa (page 50)

Marinated and Grilled or Broiled Flank Steak

MAKES: 4 to 8 servings
TIME: About 1 hour, largely unattended

Flank steak is traditionally marinated, not for tenderness—thinly slicing it takes care of that—but for flavor. You can grill the whole piece, of course, or grill half of it and leave the rest in its marinade, refrigerated, for a day or two—it's even more flavorful then, perfect for topping a salad after cooking.

Flank steak is also good without marinating: Just coat it with curry powder, chili powder, or any other spice mixture (to make your own, see pages 65–69) before cooking.

Other cuts and meats you can use: sirloin, London broil, top round steak, or skirt steak (which will cook a minute or two more quickly per side); butterflied leg of lamb, spread out flat.

1/4 cup freshly squeezed lime juice

2 tablespoons nam pla (Thai fish sauce) or soy sauce

1 teaspoon minced garlic

1 teaspoon minced or grated fresh ginger or 1 teaspoon ground ginger

1 teaspoon sugar

Salt and freshly ground black pepper

1 flank steak, 2 to 2 1/2 pounds

1 Combine all the seasonings in a shallow bowl or platter and marinate the steak in them for at least 30 minutes (if the marinating time is longer than an hour, refrigerate). Near the end of the marinating time, heat a charcoal or gas grill or the broiler until very hot.

2 Remove the meat from the marinade and dry well with paper towels. Grill or broil the steak about 4 inches from the heat source until nicely browned, 3 to 4 minutes per side. Move the meat to a cooler part of the grill (or lower the broiling rack) and cook for another 2 minutes per side. Check for doneness by touch, use a thin-bladed knife to peek inside, or insert an instant-read thermometer—125°F is about right for rare to medium-rare. Let rest for 5 minutes before cutting across the grain into thin slices with a sharp knife.

Salad with Marinated and Grilled or Broiled Flank Steak. For 4 servings, cut half a recipe of the flank steak into chunks. Toss with 6 cups torn washed and dried mixed lettuces (a store-bought mesclun mixture is great) and top with some quartered ripe tomatoes and sliced cucumber. Mix together 6 tablespoons freshly squeezed lime juice, 1 tablespoon soy sauce, and 2 tablespoons peanut oil; add pepper, salt if necessary, and a dash of cayenne if you like. Taste and adjust the seasoning. Drizzle over the salad and serve.

Marinated Flank Steak for Stir-Fries. Reserve a quarter to half of the flank steak while you marinate the rest. Freeze the reserved piece for 30 minutes. When you remove the larger piece of steak for grilling, slice the frozen portion as thin as possible. Use the same liquid to marinate it for up to a day, then use in any stir-fry recipe (see, for example, Stir-Fried Beef with Onions and Ginger, page 731).

Steak au Poivre

Pan-Seared Steak with Black Pepper and Red Wine

MAKES: 4 servings
TIME: 15 minutes

Elegance in a hurry. For a little extra flavor, coat the steaks with the peppercorns an hour or so before cooking and let them sit at room temperature. Use a decent wine here (I like Zinfandel or something equally fruity). And make sure your skillet will hold the steaks comfortably, without either crowding them (which will cause them to steam rather than brown) or leaving too much room, which will allow the butter to burn.

This recipe is easily varied; use any spice rub or ground Sichuan peppercorns in place of the black peppercorns. And see "13 Ways to Flavor Simple Pan Sauce" (page 46).

Other cuts and meats you can use: lamb chops or veal chops.

4 tenderloin (filets mignons or tournedos), strip, or rib-eye steaks, 4 to 6 ounces each

Freshly ground black pepper or a mixture of black pepper and crushed (see Step 2) allspice berries

3 tablespoons butter or extra virgin olive oil

1 tablespoon minced shallot

¾ cup Zinfandel or other good red wine

2 sprigs fresh tarragon or ¼ teaspoon dried tarragon, plus fresh sprigs for garnish (optional)

Salt

❶ Heat a large skillet over medium heat for about 3 minutes; turn the oven to 200°F.

❷ Sprinkle the steaks liberally with pepper. If you want genuine steak au poivre, coarsely grind about 1 tablespoon of pepper and press it into the meat; about 1 part ground allspice berries to 3 parts pepper lends another interesting dimension.

❸ Put 2 tablespoons of the butter into the skillet; when the foam subsides, turn the heat up to medium-high and put in the steaks. Cook the steaks for about 3 minutes per side for medium-rare meat, a bit longer if you like it medium to well done. Undercook them a bit as they will continue to cook in the oven.

❹ Transfer the steaks to an ovenproof platter and put the platter in the oven. Over medium heat, add the remaining butter to the pan, along with the shallot. Stir until the shallot softens, about 1 minute.

❺ Add the wine and tarragon, raise the heat to high, and let most of the liquid bubble away. Pour any juices that have accumulated around the steaks into the sauce. Spoon the sauce over the steaks and serve, garnished with additional tarragon if you like.

❶ Fast   Ⓜ Make Ahead   Ⓥ Vegetarian

Chopped Steak with Wine Sauce. Use 1¹⁄₂ pounds freshly ground meat (see page 722). Shape the meat gently into 4 patties, incorporating 1 teaspoon salt and 1 teaspoon freshly ground black pepper. Omit the exterior coating of pepper.

Steak Diane. No need to heat the oven: Omit the red wine and tarragon. Flatten the filets to about 1 inch thick with the palm of your hand, the back of a skillet, or a small mallet. Cook the steaks as directed, but don't put them in the oven. Wipe out the pan before starting the sauce. In Step 5, add 1 teaspoon Dijon mustard, 1 teaspoon Worcestershire sauce (or to taste), and ¹⁄₂ cup cream or half-and-half to the shallot and sprinkle with salt and a fair amount of pepper. Cook the sauce at a steady bubble and add the seared steaks and any accumulated juices to the pan. Cook, turning 2 or 3 times, until the meat is done to your liking, just another minute or so per side for medium-rare. Transfer the meat to a plate and add lemon juice, salt, or pepper to the sauce as needed. Spoon the sauce over the meat, garnish with chopped fresh chives or parsley, and serve.

Steak Teriyaki. Use 4 strip or rib-eye steaks (or 2 larger steaks), instead of tenderloin. No need to heat the oven. Cook the steaks as directed for 2 minutes per side, omitting the pepper. To make the teriyaki sauce: Cool the pan a bit, then turn the heat to medium. Add ¹⁄₂ cup sake or slightly sweet white wine, like a German Kabinett or Spätlese, and cook, stirring, to loosen any bits of meat in the pan. Add ¹⁄₃ cup mirin (or 2 tablespoons honey mixed with 2 tablespoons water), 2 tablespoons sugar, and ¹⁄₃ cup soy sauce; stir until the mixture is at a lively bubble. Return the steaks to the pan and cook, turning the meat 2 to 3 times until the sauce reduces and becomes thick and sticky, about 5 minutes. The steaks should be medium-rare; continue to cook if necessary, adding a spoonful or two of water if the sauce threatens to burn. Serve immediately.

Stir-Fried Beef with Onions and Ginger

MAKES: 4 servings
TIME: 30 minutes, plus time to freeze the beef

Onions, beef, and ginger are an almost holy combination; the synthesis is simply delicious.

Other cuts and meats you can use: pork, preferably from the shoulder or leg (fresh ham); lamb, preferably from the shoulder or leg; boneless chicken; shrimp.

³⁄₄ to 1 pound flank or sirloin steak or other tender beef cut

Salt and freshly ground black pepper

2 tablespoons peanut or neutral oil, like grapeseed or corn

2 large or 3 medium onions, thinly sliced

1 teaspoon minced garlic

1 tablespoon plus 1 teaspoon minced or grated fresh ginger

¹⁄₂ cup beef or chicken stock (to make your own, see page 158 or 157) or water

1 tablespoon hoisin sauce or soy sauce

❶ Slice the beef as thinly as you can, across the grain. It's easier if you freeze it for 15 to 30 minutes first. Cut the slices into bite-sized pieces. Sprinkle with salt and pepper and set aside.

❷ Heat a large skillet over high heat until it smokes, 3 to 4 minutes. Add 1 tablespoon of oil and the onions. Stir immediately, then stir every 30 seconds or so until the onions soften and begin to char slightly, 4 to 5 minutes. Sprinkle the onions with salt and pepper, then remove them; keep the heat high.

❸ Add the remaining oil to the pan, then the garlic and 1 tablespoon of the ginger; stir and immediately add the beef. Stir immediately, then stir every 20 seconds or so until it loses its color, just a minute or two longer; stir in the onions. Add the stock, hoisin, and remaining teaspoon of ginger; let some of the liquid bubble away and serve immediately, over rice.

Stir-Fried Beef with Tomatoes and Black Beans. In Step 1, soak the sliced meat in 2 tablespoons soy sauce while you get everything else ready. At the same time, soak 1 tablespoon fermented black beans in 2 tablespoons dry sherry (or use stock, white wine, or water). In Step 3, add 3 or 4 scallions, including some of the green parts, cut into 1-inch lengths, along with the garlic and ginger. Add the beef and soy sauce, cook for 1 minute, then add 3 medium tomatoes, cored and roughly chopped (peel and seed the tomatoes if you like), the black beans and their liquid, and the onions. Omit the stock and hoisin sauce. Stir, taste, adjust the seasoning, and serve immediately, over rice.

Sesame Stir-Fried Beef. Omit the stock and hoisin sauce. Marinate the beef in $1/4$ cup soy sauce, 2 tablespoons rice vinegar, and 2 teaspoons sugar. Substitute dark sesame oil for the peanut oil. In Step 3, increase the garlic to a tablespoon. Cook the dish until the liquid is evaporated, garnish with chopped scallions and 2 tablespoons toasted sesame seeds (see page 317), and serve immediately.

The Basics of Beef (and Other) Kebabs

Kebabs are often made with lamb, but you can make them with any meat, poultry, or even fish. But you must choose the right cut, because no one wants a tough kebab. Here's what to look for:

Beef kebabs: Tenderloin is best—it's tender and has little flavor of its own, so it really benefits from the full-flavored treatments given here. Unfortunately, it's expensive; sirloin or ground beef pressed onto skewers (like Meatballs, Three Ways, on page 114) is a good alternative.

Lamb kebabs: Shoulder (tender but fatty) and leg (leaner, with some potential for dryness) are both good. Do not overcook leg; it should still be pink inside.

Pork kebabs: Shoulder (again, tender but fatty) is almost ideal. Tenderloin can be okay, but don't overcook; best to pull it off the heat when it's still a little pink.

Chicken kebabs: (see page 669): Thighs by a long shot. Breast meat almost inevitably overcooks.

Fish kebabs (see page 603): Sturdy chunks of tuna, swordfish, halibut, salmon, and monkfish are all good, as are shrimp and scallops.

About skewering: You have a choice between wood and metal skewers. Metal skewers require a higher initial investment but last forever (or until you lose them) and don't burn. Look for nonround ones—some are triangular, some have dual prongs; this keeps the meat from slipping. The only disadvantage to metal aside from the relative expense is that they become hot and therefore difficult to handle. Wood skewers are inexpensive but tend to burn. (Soak them for 30 minutes or longer before use to avoid this.) They're easier to handle, and you don't have to wash them since you toss them out. The choice is yours.

You also have a choice when it comes to style of skewering. Alternating pieces of meat and vegetables is undeniably attractive, but meat and vegetables may cook at different rates, and you don't want raw onions or overdone meat. So it makes more sense to make separate skewers of each.

Beef (or Other Meat or Seafood) Kebabs

MAKES: 4 to 6 servings
TIME: 45 minutes

I like to serve this with Fresh Tomato Salsa, which takes just a couple of extra minutes to prepare. See "Bringing Global Flavors to Grilled Steak" (page 718) for more ideas for seasoning your kebabs. And you can assemble them up to 4 hours in advance.

Other meats (and fish) you can use: see "The Basics of Beef (and Other) Kebabs" preceding this recipe.

F Fast   **M** Make Ahead   **V** Vegetarian

1 tablespoon extra virgin olive oil

2 tablespoons freshly squeezed lime or lemon juice or vinegar

1 tablespoon soy sauce

Salt and freshly ground black pepper

2 tablespoons minced fresh parsley or cilantro leaves, 2 teaspoons minced fresh thyme or rosemary leaves, or 1 teaspoon dried herb of your choice

1 teaspoon minced garlic

6 medium onions, quartered

2 bell peppers, any color but green, cored, seeded, and cut into 1¹/₂-inch chunks

12 medium button mushrooms, trimmed and halved

2 to 3 pounds beef tenderloin, cut into 1¹/₂- to 2-inch chunks

Chopped fresh parsley or cilantro leaves for garnish

Fresh Tomato Salsa (optional; page 23)

① Heat a charcoal or gas grill or a broiler until quite hot and put the rack about 4 inches from the heat source. If you're using charcoal, be generous—you want a large fire.

② Meanwhile, combine the oil, lime juice, soy, salt and pepper, parsley, and garlic in a small bowl. Thread the vegetables and meat on separate skewers (the vegetables need a little more time to cook), leaving a little space between pieces. Brush with most of the marinade and let sit while the fire is getting ready.

③ Start the vegetables first, cooking them on a relatively cool part of the grill. Brush them with a little of the marinade from time to time and turn them until they begin to brown and become tender, after 10 or 15 minutes. Then start the meat, on the hottest part of the fire; grill it for about 1 to 2 minutes per side, until each of the 4 sides browns. Do not overcook (cut a chunk in half after 5 minutes of cooking to judge its stage of doneness). Everything should be done at around the same time, in a total of 20 minutes or so.

④ Give everything a final baste with the marinade if any remains, put the skewers on a platter, garnish with parsley, and serve. Remove the skewers at the table and pass the platter, with the salsa following.

Spice-Rubbed Beef Kebabs. In Step 2, omit the marinade and instead make a paste of ¹/₂ cup minced onion, 1 teaspoon minced garlic, 1 teaspoon salt, 1 teaspoon freshly ground black pepper, 1 tablespoon curry powder, garam masala, chili powder, or other spice mixture (to make your own, see pages 65–69), 1 teaspoon paprika, and oil as needed. Spread this on the meat (if you would like to make vegetable skewers too, simply brush with olive oil) and grill as in Step 3. Serve with a sauce made by whisking together 1 cup plain yogurt, ¹/₄ cup minced onion or scallion, ¹/₄ cup minced fresh cilantro or mint leaves, and salt and pepper (add cayenne if you like). This dressing can be made well in advance and can also be used as a dip for cucumber and other vegetables.

The Basics of Roast Beef

Supermarkets will sell you almost anything as an oven roast, but roasting, like grilling, must start with tender meat—dry cooking does very little to tenderize meat. Which leaves you with four good choices:

Prime rib: My favorite cut of beef for roasting; like leg of lamb, it's so big that if you cook the deepest center to rare you are also going to wind up with spots that are medium and those that are well done, pleasing everyone. And good prime rib is so juicy that even well done (not overcooked, just well done) meat is tender and moist. For the best roast, ask for the small end (the twelfth through the seventh ribs) and ask the butcher—even a supermarket butcher can do this—to cut it to order for you, removing the short ribs; you want what's called a "short" roast. (You can cook those short ribs separately with any of the recipes on pages 740–741.)

If you're serving four to six people, buy three or four ribs (higher numbers are better, so look for ribs 12 through 10 or 9); if you're serving more, add another rib for every two people, unless you want to serve gargantuan portions. I usually buy a three-rib roast for up to six people and have leftovers, but I believe in serving lots of side dishes when I make a roast so no one is tempted to eat a pound of meat. For rare meat, figure *about* 15 to 20 minutes per pound of roasting for any prime rib; see the recipe for details.

Boneless prime rib: You can get the meat taken off the bones by the butcher, or do it yourself (see illustrations, next page); it will be a lot easier to carve. Be careful not to overcook; removing the bone decreases your margin of error.

Filet of beef: This is the whole tenderloin, wonderfully tender but not super-flavorful; usually sold in about 5-pound pieces. Unlike for prime rib, which requires no saucing whatsoever, you'll want a sauce with this. I don't think it's worth the expense, though it is inarguably easy and makes a beautiful presentation. You can also grill whole filet; it won't take more than 30 minutes, but don't keep it over super-hot coals the entire time or the outside will burn. Rather, sear it over the hottest part of the fire, then move it a little to the side to finish cooking; cover the grill if possible after the initial sear.

Whole strip: This is New York strip (which goes by a host of other names), so good as individual steaks, left whole. For roasts, it is boned (and called a *shell* as often as it is a *strip*). Very flavorful and very expensive, but my second-favorite roast after prime rib. A whole roast weighs about 10 pounds and will serve twenty people or more, depending on side dishes. You don't have to cook the whole strip, of course; I've roasted 3-pound pieces with great success. This can easily be grilled too, in much the same way as the filet.

A word about roasts and doneness: All beef is rare at 125°F (120°F for really rare); there are noticeable differences in meat color for each 5-degree difference in temperature. I'd never cook anything beyond 155°F, although some cooks suggest cooking roast beef to 170°F for well done. Large roasts will rise at least 5 degrees in temperature between the time you remove them from the oven and the time you carve them, so bear that in mind.

Remember, too, that cutting into a piece of meat to check its doneness is far from a sin (it's one of those things that everyone does but no one talks about). So if you're at all in doubt, cut into the middle or take a slice from the end. Your presentation will not be as beautiful, but if the meat is perfectly cooked no one will care.

Prime Rib Roast for a Small Crowd

MAKES: About 6 servings
TIME: About 1½ hours, largely unattended

This is a simple roasting technique: high heat to sear the meat, lower heat to cook it through. If you want a really crisp exterior, turn the heat back to 450°F for a few minutes right at the end of cooking; this won't affect the internal temperature too much.

Try serving prime rib with Popovers (page 847). Leftover roast beef makes great hash; see Corned Beef (or Roast Beef) Hash (page 744).

One 3-rib bone-in beef roast, about 5 pounds, trimmed of excess but not all fat

Salt and freshly ground black pepper

1 or 2 cloves garlic, peeled (optional)

1 cup red wine, stock (to make your own, see pages 157–159), or water

1 Bring the meat to room temperature by removing it from the refrigerator at least an hour before cooking, preferably two. Heat the oven to 450°F.

2 Put the meat, bone side down, in a large roasting pan. Sprinkle it liberally with salt and pepper. If you like garlic, peel the cloves and cut them into tiny slivers; use a boning or paring knife to poke small holes in the meat and insert the garlic into them.

3 Put the roast in the oven and cook, undisturbed, for 15 minutes. Turn the heat down to 350°F and continue to roast for about 1 hour; check in several places with a meat thermometer. The meat is rare when no spot

F Fast   **M** Make Ahead   **V** Vegetarian

checks in at under 125°F (120°F if you and your guests like meat really rare); cook for another 5 or 10 minutes if you like it better done, then check again, but in no case let the temperature of the meat go above 155°F.

④ Remove the meat from the oven. Pour off all but a few tablespoons of the fat and put the roasting pan on a burner over high heat. Add the liquid and cook, stirring and scraping up any brown bits, until it is reduced by half, 5 to 10 minutes. Slice the roast (page 735) and serve, splashing a little of the sauce on the meat platter and passing the rest at the table.

Prime Rib for a Big Crowd. With bigger roasts, 5 ribs or more, allow plenty of time to let the meat reach room temperature. In Step 2, use more garlic if you like. In Step 3, increase the initial browning time to 20 minutes. After that, the cooking time will be only marginally longer, but be sure to use an instant-read thermometer in several different places to check the meat. Increase the liquid in Step 4 to at least 2 cups.

Prime Rib with Roasted Vegetables. If the roast is small, cut vegetables into 1-inch chunks; if it is large, you can leave them whole as long as they are not huge. Per person, allow 1 medium peeled potato, 1 medium peeled carrot, 1 medium peeled onion, a couple of cloves of garlic (you don't have to peel these), or similar amounts of turnips, parsnips, and other root vegetables as you like (or just use potatoes). Scatter them around the roast at the beginning and drizzle them with a little bit of extra virgin olive oil. Roast with the meat; you don't need to baste. Remove the vegetables and keep warm. If you like, brown them for a minute or two longer under the broiler while the meat rests, but watch them carefully to prevent burning.

Boneless Prime Rib. Have the butcher tie it so that it is of roughly uniform thickness. Cook as directed, using a meat thermometer to gauge doneness; total weight won't matter much since there is no bone and the roast is relatively thin. A 3-pound boneless roast is almost certain to be done in less than an hour, so plan accordingly and watch it carefully; a 5- or 6-pound roast won't take a whole lot longer.

CARVING PRIME RIB

(STEP 1) Cut close to the bone, between the ribs, for the first slice. (STEP 2) Unless you want huge portions, the second slice is boneless.

Roast Tenderloin with Herbs

MAKES: At least 10 servings
TIME: At least 1½ hours, largely unattended

A large piece of beef tenderloin makes a beautiful presentation, but because the cut is relatively bland I cook it with herbs and vinegar to lend some help in the flavor department.

Other cuts and meats you can use: beef eye of round or veal loin.

1/2 cup extra virgin olive oil

1 tablespoon balsamic or sherry vinegar

1/4 cup roughly chopped fresh parsley, stems included

1 teaspoon fresh thyme leaves, several thyme sprigs, or 1/2 teaspoon dried thyme

1 bay leaf

2 cloves garlic, lightly smashed

One 5-pound beef tenderloin, trimmed of fat

Salt and freshly ground black pepper

Béarnaise Sauce (page 58), Nut Oil Vinaigrette using walnut oil (page 201), Anchovy-Caper Vinaigrette (page 200), or other sauce

❶ Combine the oil, vinegar, parsley, thyme, bay leaf, and garlic; marinate the meat in this mixture for an hour—or up to a day (refrigerated if longer than an hour). When you're ready to cook, heat the oven to 450°F.

❷ Remove the meat from the marinade and pat it dry. Roast for 20 minutes, then check with meat thermometer; when the meat measures 125°F in a couple of places, it will end up medium-rare; transfer the roast to a platter and sprinkle with salt and pepper.

❸ Let the meat rest for about 5 minutes before carving; cut into thick (at least 1/2 inch) slices and serve with the sauce of your choice.

Roast Strip Loin. You can roast anything from a 3- to a 10-pound (whole) strip; here the weight won't affect cooking time much, because there is no bone and the thickness is uniform. Cook exactly as directed, beginning to check the temperature after 45 or 50 minutes; marinating and saucing are unnecessary, but a reduction sauce (see "The Basics of Reduction Sauces," page 44) made with parsley or chervil and red wine is quite nice.

Grilling Large Cuts of Meat

Indirect heat on a grill is a lot like dry-roasting in an oven, with one added benefit—the flavor of fire and smoke. This technique works for standing rib or strip loin roasts. It will also work for leg or shoulder of lamb, pork shoulder or loin, or large cuts of veal or any other meat (including boar, venison, and so on).

Start by preparing a grill for indirect cooking: If it's gas, turn on one side only (or just the front or back burner, depending on your configuration); if wood or charcoal, build a fire on one side of the grill only. In either case (unless you're using wood or hardwood charcoal), you might want to put an aluminum tray of soaked wood chips over the flames to impart a wood flavor to the meat. If your grill has a thermometer, shoot for around 450°F when the cover is on.

Sprinkle the meat liberally with salt and pepper and rub a cut garlic clove on it if you like. (If you want a more intense garlic flavor, cut some slivers of garlic and use a sharp, thin-bladed knife to poke them into the meat.) You can also use curry or chili powder or your favorite spice rub (to make your own, see pages 65–69).

Put the roast on the cool side of the grill and set a timer for 30 minutes. From that point on, your only job is to monitor the meat's temperature and keep the fire alive (very easy with a gas grill). The target internal temperature for the meat is just over 120°F for rare or about 125°F for medium-rare (the meat's temperature will climb about 5 degrees after you take it off the grill). A 3-pound roast will take about 45 minutes, but check after 30; 5-pounders will be done in a little over an hour. But timing will depend largely on the heat of the fire and the temperature of the meat when you began cooking it. Let the meat rest for at least 5 minutes before slicing and serving.

 Fast Make Ahead **V** Vegetarian

Stuffed Flank Steak

Matambre

MAKES: 6 to 8 servings

TIME: 2 hours, plus time to marinate

One of the best-known Argentinean dishes, a flank steak stuffed with spices, vegetables, and hard-cooked eggs, then rolled. Beautiful and delicious. I like it best roasted, then pressed, chilled, and sliced. Serve with Chimichurri (page 28) or any salsa.

Other cuts and meats you can use: veal breast.

1 flank steak, 1¼ to 1½ pounds

Salt and freshly ground black pepper

1 teaspoon fresh marjoram or oregano leaves or ½ teaspoon dried

1 teaspoon ground cumin

1 tablespoon minced garlic

1 bunch fresh parsley or ½ bunch parsley and ½ bunch cilantro

3 medium carrots, cut lengthwise into quarters

2 hard-cooked eggs, chopped

1 large red or white onion, cut into chunks

1 bunch spinach, watercress, or arugula, well washed and chopped

2 tablespoons extra virgin olive oil

❶ Heat the oven to 375°F. Butterfly the flank steak: Using a long, sharp knife, cut the steak almost in half with the grain, then flip it open, like a book. Sprinkle with salt and pepper on both sides, then turn it cut side up, wide side facing you. Sprinkle with the marjoram, cumin, and garlic and cover it with a layer of the parsley. Then arrange the carrots, eggs, and onion in vertical rows, making 2 rows of each—you won't have enough to make rows across the entire steak because you need a couple inches free to make it into a neat roll. Scatter a relatively even layer of spinach over all.

❷ Roll the whole thing up like a jelly roll: Start with the narrow side; the grain of the steak should run the length of the roll. Tie in 3 or 4 places with butcher's

TO MAKE STUFFED FLANK STEAK

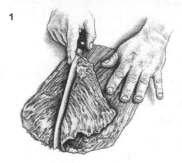  

(**STEP 1**) To butterfly the flank steak: Hold a long, sharp knife parallel to the work surface and cut through the thickness of the steak with the grain, stopping just before you divide the steak in half. Then flip it open, like a book. (**STEP 2**) Have several 12-inch pieces of string cut and handy. Put the vegetables on top of the butterflied steak as described in the recipe. Roll up the stuffed flank steak as carefully as you can. (Don't worry; it will be a little messy.) (**STEP 3**) Turn the steak seam side down to stabilize it. Then use the string to secure the stuffed roll in a few places.

twine. Put the olive oil in a Dutch oven or roasting pan large enough to accommodate the rolled steak over medium-high heat. When hot, deeply brown the steak on all sides, about 15 minutes, and then transfer the pan to the oven and roast for 1¼ to 1½ hours, until the meat is tender to the touch.

❸ Transfer to a cutting board (if you want to eat it at this point) or a clean baking dish (if you're going to chill it overnight) and let it rest for 30 minutes regardless of when you're eating it—it will be too hot out of the oven. If you're going to chill it, weight it with a plate with something heavy—a few cans, a rock, a cast-iron skillet—and chill overnight. Take the matambre from the fridge and slice it into ½- to 1-inch pieces about an hour before you want to serve it. Serve at room temperature.

Stuffed Flank Steak, Asian Style. Substitute minced fresh ginger for the marjoram and cumin, 1 recipe Sautéed Mushrooms (page 313) for the hard-cooked eggs, and ½ cup chopped scallion for the red onion; sprinkle the stuffing with a bit of soy sauce instead of salt, if you like. Use 1 tablespoon dark sesame oil and peanut or neutral oil, like grapeseed or corn, instead of the olive oil.

The Basics of Braised Beef

Meat cooked with liquid—called *braised* or *stewed*—is more popular than ever. This technique allows us to appreciate what used to be called the "lesser" cuts, beloved for their sublime flavor and, when cooked properly, fork-tenderness. Feel free to vary the cooking liquid and don't be afraid to use water; the intensity may be somewhat diminished, but the meat will make its own stock as it cooks.

Chuck, brisket, round, and rump are all good cuts for braising, as are short ribs, oxtail, and beef cheeks, and even the not-so-tough sirloin cuts benefit from it. Cooking time varies from one cut to another (and, indeed, from one animal to another). Keep the heat low and

allow plenty of time, testing every 15 minutes or so after the first hour. If the dish is done ahead of schedule, don't worry about it: Let it cool and reheat it; it will be fine. If you plan to make the dish long before serving, refrigerate it; if a thick layer of fat rises to the surface, skim some or all of it off with a spoon.

Beef Daube

MAKES: 4 servings
TIME: At least 2 hours, somewhat unattended

The classic Provençal beef braise, with bacon, vegetables, and plenty of flavor. Olives are a nice addition; check out the variations.

Other cuts and meats you can use: boneless lamb shoulder, cut into chunks.

1 tablespoon extra virgin olive oil

4 ounces good slab bacon, cut into ½-inch cubes

2 pounds boneless beef chuck or brisket, cut into 1½- to 2-inch cubes

Salt and freshly ground black pepper

2 large onions, chopped

2 celery stalks, chopped

3 carrots, chopped

5 cloves garlic, lightly smashed

3 or 4 sprigs fresh thyme

1 sprig fresh rosemary or 1 teaspoon dried rosemary

2 or 3 strips orange peel

1 cup rough red wine, preferably from the south of France, like Cahors or Côtes-du-Rhône

1 tablespoon red wine vinegar

Beef or chicken stock (to make your own, see page 158 or 157) or water, if necessary

❶ Put the olive oil in a large pot with a lid or a Dutch oven over medium heat. Add the bacon and cook, stirring occasionally, until it is crisp and has given up most of its fat, about 10 minutes. Remove with a slotted spoon and set aside, add some of the meat (working in batches if necessary so the pieces aren't crowded), and turn the heat up to medium-high. Cook, turning the cubes as they brown and sprinkling them with salt and pepper, until the meat is brown and crisp all over, at least 10 minutes. Remove with a slotted spoon.

2 Turn the heat back down to medium and add the onions, celery, carrots, garlic, thyme, rosemary, orange peel, and some more salt and pepper. Cook, stirring occasionally, until the onions soften, about 5 minutes. Add the wine and vinegar and let them bubble for a minute, then return the meat to the pan.

3 Cover and adjust the heat so the mixture simmers gently. Cook for about an hour, then add the bacon, cover, and continue to cook until tender, adding a little more liquid if the mixture threatens to dry out. Depending on the meat, the dish could be done in as little as 30 minutes more or three times as long.

4 Taste and adjust the seasoning, then serve or cover and refrigerate for up to 2 days before reheating.

Beef Daube with Olives or Dried Fruit. In Step 2, replace the rosemary with 1 teaspoon fennel seeds. When you return the bacon to the pan in Step 3, add 1 cup good green or black olives, preferably pitted, or 1 cup dried prunes or apricots.

Boeuf à la Bourguignonne. Omit 1 onion and the celery, carrot, rosemary, orange peel, and vinegar; reduce the garlic to 2 cloves. Proceed with Step 1, reserving the bacon and beef in separate bowls. For Step 2, cook the onion, thyme, and garlic, along with 3 bay leaves and 1/2 cup chopped fresh parsley leaves, as directed, then remove and add to the beef bowl. Put 12 small button mushrooms, trimmed and cut into halves or quarters, and 12 pearl onions, peeled (frozen are okay), into the pot and cook, stirring occasionally, until lightly browned, 5 to 10 minutes; remove and add to the bacon bowl. Add 1 cup good red wine, preferably Burgundy (Pinot Noir), and cook for a

minute, then add the beef and chopped onion mixtures to the pot. Proceed with Step 3; add the bacon and pearl onion mixture and proceed with the recipe.

Real Beef Stroganoff

MAKES: 4 servings
TIME: 30 minutes or less

Don't scoff; this is good stuff, despite the bad versions of it you've undoubtedly tried. Use pieces of tenderloin if you can, because the cooking is quick and the meat should be tender. Both the mushrooms and the tomatoes are optional; the dish is perfectly fine without either or with both. Serve this over buttered egg noodles or plain rice or with bread.

Other cuts and meats you can use: boneless veal or pork shoulder or veal round.

3 tablespoons butter

2 large onions, sliced

Salt and freshly ground black pepper

8 ounces mushrooms, trimmed and sliced (optional)

1 1/2 to 2 pounds beef tenderloin (filet mignon) or sirloin, cut into 1- to 1 1/2-inch chunks

1 tablespoon Dijon mustard

2 plum tomatoes (canned are fine), chopped, or 1/2 cup good tomato sauce (optional)

1 cup beef or chicken stock (to make your own, see page 158 or 157)

1/2 cup sour cream

Chopped fresh dill or parsley leaves for garnish

1 Put the butter in a large, deep skillet with a lid or a Dutch oven over medium-high heat. When the butter is melted, add the onions, along with a sprinkling of salt and pepper and the mushrooms if you're using them, and cook, stirring occasionally, until the onions are very soft but not browned, about 10 minutes. Add the beef and cook, stirring, for just a minute.

② Stir in the mustard, the tomatoes if you're using them, and the stock. Adjust the heat so the mixture bubbles steadily but not violently and cook until the meat is tender, about 5 minutes. (You can make the dish in advance up to this point; cover and refrigerate for up to a day before reheating and finishing.) Stir in the sour cream, taste and adjust the seasoning, garnish with dill, and serve.

Short Ribs Braised with Potatoes and Mustard

MAKES: 4 servings

TIME: 2 hours or more, largely unattended

The best way to cook short ribs is in liquid until they are really tender, practically mushy, with all the fat melted away; their superb flavor will intensify any liquid surrounding them. But sometimes short ribs take a *really* long time to get tender, so don't add the potatoes to this dish until the meat is just done.

Other cuts and meats you can use: beef shank, shin, cheeks, or oxtail; cooking times will probably be a little longer.

2 tablespoons neutral oil, like grapeseed or corn, or extra virgin olive oil

3 pounds meaty short ribs, more or less

Salt and freshly ground black pepper

2 cups chopped onion

1 cup chicken, beef, or vegetable stock (to make your own, see pages 157–159) or water, or more if needed

1 pound waxy red or white potatoes, peeled, halved if large

Dry red wine if needed

2 tablespoons Dijon or other good mustard

Chopped fresh parsley leaves for garnish

① Put the oil in a large pot with a lid or a Dutch oven over medium-high heat. When hot, brown the short ribs well on all sides, sprinkling them with salt and pepper as they cook and adjusting the heat so the ribs don't burn, 20 minutes or so; don't rush it. (You can also do the initial browning in the oven: Heat the oven to 500°F and roast the ribs, turning once or twice, until brown all over; the time will still be about 20 minutes.)

② Transfer the ribs to a plate, pour off all but 2 tablespoons of the fat, and turn the heat down to medium. Add the onion and cook, stirring occasionally, until soft, about 10 minutes. Stir in the stock and some salt and pepper. Return the ribs to the pot, raise the heat to medium-high, and bring to a boil. Cover, reduce the heat to low, and cook, stirring occasionally, until the meat is fairly tender, about an hour longer.

③ Add the potatoes and cook, turning the ribs in the stock every 15 minutes or so and adding a little more liquid—stock, water, or dry red wine—if the mixture seems dry. The dish is done when the meat is very tender and almost falling off the bone and the potatoes are soft, at least another 30 minutes. (At this point, you may use a slotted spoon to transfer the meat and vegetables to a platter and refrigerate them and the stock overnight. The next day, skim the fat from the stock, add the meat and vegetables back to it, and reheat.) Stir the mustard into the stew, taste and adjust the seasonings, garnish with parsley, and serve.

Short Ribs with Horseradish. When the ribs are done, transfer them and the potatoes to a platter and keep warm. Turn the heat to high and reduce the cooking liquid to about 1 cup. Add 1 tablespoon vinegar and 2 tablespoons freshly grated or prepared horseradish, or to taste. Pour the sauce over the ribs, garnish, and serve hot.

Short Ribs with Cinnamon. Omit the onions, stock, potatoes, red wine, and mustard. Proceed with Step 1, then skip Step 2. Add two 28-ounce cans whole plum tomatoes, with their juice, 3 tablespoons roughly chopped garlic, 1 teaspoon ground cinnamon, and $1/4$ teaspoon ground cloves; partially cover and cook at a gentle bubble, stirring occasionally, for least $1^1/2$ hours, until the meat falls from the bone; if the sauce begins to get too thick, add a little water and continue to cook. If you're serving this as a pasta sauce, remove the bones from the sauce and break the meat up with a spoon. Taste and adjust the seasoning, garnish, and serve.

Anise-Scented Short Ribs. Substitute ground Sichuan peppercorns for the black pepper if you like. In Step 3, cook the onion as directed, then add 5 nickel-sized slices fresh ginger and 3 cloves lightly crushed and peeled garlic and cook for another 2 minutes. Add 5 star anise, $1/4$ cup soy sauce or nam pla (Thai fish sauce), 1 tablespoon rice or white wine vinegar, 2 tablespoons sugar, and 1 cup water. Bring to a boil, add the ribs, reduce the heat to low, cover, and cook at a gentle bubble, turning the ribs occasionally, until the meat is quite tender. In Step 3, add 2 medium carrots, cut into $1/4$-inch-thick slices, cover, and continue cooking until the meat is almost falling off the bone, about 30 minutes. Transfer the ribs and carrots to a platter and set aside in a 200°F oven. Strain the cooking liquid and return to the pot; boil the liquid until it's reduced to a syrupy consistency, then spoon over the ribs and serve with rice.

Braised Oxtails with Garlic and White Wine

MAKES: 4 servings
TIME: At least 2 hours

Ⓜ

You can braise any tough cut of beef this way, though oxtail (or more often steer's tail) is traditional, and you may find it at your supermarket. The meat will become super-tender and the sauce thick and glossy.

Other cuts and meats you can use: short ribs; lamb shanks; chunks of boneless lamb or pork shoulder (which will be much faster) or beef chuck or brisket (which will be somewhat faster); bone-in chicken thighs (much quicker).

1 tablespoon extra virgin olive oil

4 ounces good slab bacon, cut into small cubes

3 to 4 pounds oxtails, cut into 2-inch lengths

Salt and freshly ground black pepper

1 large onion, chopped

2 carrots, roughly chopped

2 celery stalks, roughly chopped

1 head garlic, excess papery skin removed, halved crosswise

1 cup dry white wine

2 bay leaves

3 or 4 sprigs fresh thyme

1 medium to large tomato, roughly chopped (canned is fine; drain it first)

Beef or chicken stock (to make your own, see page 158 or 157) or water, if necessary

Chopped fresh parsley leaves for garnish

❶ Heat the oven to 300°F. Put the olive oil in a large pot with a lid or a Dutch oven over medium heat. When hot, add the bacon and cook, stirring occasionally, until it is crisp and has given up most of its fat, about 10 minutes. Remove with a slotted spoon and set aside, add the meat, and turn the heat up to medium-high. Cook, turning the chunks as they brown and sprinkling them with salt and pepper, until the meat is brown and crisp all over, at least 10 minutes. Remove with a slotted spoon.

❷ Turn the heat back down to medium and add the onion, carrots, and celery, along with some more salt and pepper, and cook, stirring occasionally, until the onion softens, about 5 minutes. Add the garlic and cook for another minute. Add the wine and let it bubble for a minute, then return the meat and the bacon to the pan, along with the bay leaves, thyme, and tomato. Stir.

③ Cover and put in the oven; cook, checking after about an hour and adding more liquid if the mixture is dry, for at least 2 hours, or until the meat is very, very tender—falling off the bone. Taste and adjust the seasoning. If the mixture is soupy, reduce the liquid over high heat until it is more like a sauce. Garnish with parsley and serve or cover and refrigerate for up to 2 days before reheating.

Braised Oxtails with Capers. Omit the bacon if you like, along with the carrots, celery, bay leaves, and thyme. Add another onion and 3 or 4 Roasted Red Peppers (page 330), chopped; use red wine instead of white. For Step 2, cook 2 chopped onions as directed, then add 1 tablespoon minced garlic. Stir and add 2 cups chopped tomato (canned are fine, with their liquid), along with the wine and 1 teaspoon ground cumin, 1 teaspoon fresh oregano leaves or $^1/_2$ teaspoon dried, $^1/_4$ teaspoon ground allspice, and at least $^1/_2$ teaspoon freshly ground black pepper. Bring to a boil and cook, stirring occasionally, until the mixture has thickened a bit, about 15 minutes. Add 1 cup capers, with a bit of their juice, and return the meat to the pot. Proceed with the recipe.

Pot Roasts

Chuck and brisket are classic and ideal cuts for braising (or stewing) whole, though you can use rump, shin, oxtails, or cheeks; cooking time will vary from one cut to another. Keep the heat very low and allow plenty of time, testing every 15 minutes or so after the first hour.

Some people believe it's impossible to overcook pot roasts, but it's not true: When the meat is tender, it is done. Hold it in the warm liquid for a while if you like (you can even slice it and let the slices rest in the gravy), but don't plan to hold it for too long. Even though the sauce is wet and rich, when all the fat is cooked out of the meat it can become dry.

Classic Pot Roast

MAKES: 6 to 8 servings
TIME: 2$^1/_2$ to 4 hours, largely unattended

Low heat is important here, as is cooking just until done; don't let it get mushy. If you have a day of advance notice, try the vinegar-marinated variation; it's absolutely delicious. If time is short, but you want more flavor, rub the meat with a tablespoon of mild chili powder (add some cayenne if you like hot food) or a few sprigs of fresh rosemary along with the bay leaf.

1 clove garlic, peeled

One 3- to 4-pound piece boneless chuck or rump roast, tied if necessary to maintain a uniform shape

1 bay leaf

Salt and freshly ground black pepper

2 tablespoons extra virgin olive or peanut oil

2 large onions, chopped

2 carrots, chopped

1 celery stalk, chopped

$^1/_2$ cup red wine or water

1 cup chicken, beef, or vegetable stock (to make your own, see pages 157–159) or water

① Cut the garlic clove into tiny slivers; insert the slivers into several spots around the roast, poking holes with a thin-bladed knife. Crumble the bay leaf as finely as you can and mix it with the salt and pepper. Rub this mixture all over the meat.

② Put the oil in a large pot with a lid or a Dutch oven over medium-high heat. When hot, add the roast and brown it on all sides, taking your time and adjusting the heat so the meat browns but the fat does not burn— 15 minutes or so. Transfer the meat to a platter. Add the vegetables to the pot, turn the heat up to medium-high, and cook, stirring frequently, until softened and somewhat browned, about 10 minutes.

③ Add the wine and cook, scraping the bottom of the pot with a wooden spoon, until the wine has just about evaporated, 5 to 10 minutes. Add about half the stock,

F Fast   **M** Make Ahead   **V** Vegetarian

return the roast to the pot, and turn the heat down to very low.

4 Turn the roast every 15 minutes, re-cover, and cook until it is tender—a fork will pierce the meat without pushing too hard and the juices will run clear—1½ to 2½ hours, but possibly longer if your roast is taller than it is long (very thick roasts may require as long as 4 hours if you keep the heat extremely low). Add more stock if the roast appears to be drying out, an unlikely possibility (and a sign that your heat is too high). Do not overcook; when the meat is tender, it is done.

5 Remove the meat from the pot and keep it warm. Skim the fat from the surface of the remaining juice. Turn the heat up to high and cook, stirring and scraping the bottom of the pan, until the liquid is thick and almost evaporated, 5 to 10 minutes. Taste and adjust the seasoning. Slice the meat and serve it with the pan juices.

Vinegar-Marinated Pot Roast (*Sauerbraten*). In a covered pot or other container (or a heavy plastic bag), marinate the meat in a mixture of 2 cups red wine or water, ½ cup red wine vinegar, 3 cloves or a pinch ground cloves, 5 juniper berries, 5 peppercorns, and half the onions, carrot, and celery. Refrigerate, turning occasionally, for 1 to 3 days. Remove from the marinade and strain out and discard the vegetables, reserving the liquid. Dry the meat well and proceed with Step 1. In Step 2, use the remaining fresh vegetables, augmenting them with more if you like. Use the reserved marinade in Step 3 in place of the red wine and stock and proceed with the recipe.

Pot Roast with Tomatoes and Rosemary. Add 2 to 4 sprigs fresh rosemary, depending on the size of the roast. Tuck a few leaves of the rosemary into the meat along with the garlic slivers. Substitute one 28-ounce can whole tomatoes (with their liquid), crushed, for the carrots and celery and add another 3 or 4 cloves garlic. Reduce the stock by about ½ cup unless you want a very saucy pot roast.

Pot Roast with Asian Spices. Omit the bay leaf. Add ½ teaspoon five-spice powder (to make your own, see page 68) and another 3 cloves garlic after cooking the onions in Step 2. Substitute ¼ cup soy sauce for the red wine (add ¼ cup water) and ¼ cup Chinese black vinegar for ¼ cup of the stock if you like.

Braised Beef Brisket

MAKES: 10 or more servings
TIME: About 3 hours, largely unattended

Brisket becomes tender only after long, slow cooking with plenty of moisture. My favorite seasonings are quite basic, and I like to serve it over broad noodles, with boiled potatoes, or in a sandwich on a crusty roll. Brisket is also nice seasoned with bolder spices or with sweet fruits and vegetables; see the variations.

Two technical points: You can skip the initial browning if you're pressed for time or don't want to bother; the difference, in the end, will be minimal. And although it's tempting to "tear" brisket along the grain, it's better to slice it against the grain; use a sharp carving knife and you will get beautiful, thin slices.

1 tablespoon neutral oil, like grapeseed or corn, or extra virgin olive oil (optional)

1 whole beef brisket, about 5 pounds

Salt and lots of freshly ground black pepper

3 tablespoons butter or more oil

2 cups chopped onion

3 tablespoons tomato paste or 1 large ripe tomato, cored and chopped (peeled and seeded if you have time)

1 teaspoon minced garlic

3 cups chicken, beef, or vegetable stock (to make your own, see pages 157–159) or water

1 Heat the oven to 325°F (you can also cook this brisket on top of the stove if you like). If you choose to brown the brisket first, heat a large pot with a lid or a Dutch oven over medium-high heat. When hot, add the oil, swirl it around, then add the beef. Sear it for about 5 minutes on each side, or until nicely browned. Sprinkle with salt and pepper and transfer to a platter.

2 Wipe out the pan with paper towels and return it to the stove; turn the heat to medium and add the butter. When it foams, add the onion and cook, stirring, until golden and soft, at least 10 minutes. Add some salt and pepper, then stir in the tomato paste and the garlic. Return the meat to the pan, add the stock, and cover.

3 Cook over low heat or in the oven, turning the meat about every 30 minutes, until tender, $2^{1}/_{2}$ to 3 hours. If the sauce seems too thin, allow the meat to rest on a platter for a few minutes while you boil the liquid down over high heat, scraping the bottom of a pan with a wooden spoon, until it thickens somewhat. Taste the sauce and adjust the seasoning. Slice the meat, return it to the sauce, and serve.

Spicy Braised Beef Brisket. Before searing, rub the meat all over with a mixture of 1 teaspoon salt, 2 teaspoons sugar, 2 teaspoons ground cumin, 1 teaspoon ground black pepper, $^{1}/_{4}$ teaspoon cayenne (more if you like), $^{1}/_{2}$ teaspoon ground coriander, and 2 teaspoons paprika. In Step 1, increase the oil to 2 tablespoons. In Step 2, use 2 tablespoons oil in place of the butter and cook the onion over medium-high heat, stirring, until it begins to brown, about 10 minutes. Proceed with the recipe.

Sweet Braised Beef Brisket with Garlic. In Step 3, when the meat is somewhat tender but not quite done—after about $1^{1}/_{2}$ to 2 hours of braising—add 1 pound peeled and chunked sweet potatoes, 2 chunked carrots, $^{1}/_{2}$ cup dried apricots, $^{1}/_{2}$ cup dried pitted prunes or other dried fruit, and 1 head garlic with most of the papery coating removed, cut in half horizontally. Continue to cook until all the fruits and vegetables are soft but not until they dissolve, 30 to 60 minutes. Serve, spreading the soft garlic on crusty bread.

Braised Beef Brisket with Sweet White Wine. Omit the butter and tomato paste. Substitute 1 cup sweet white wine, like Sauternes, Barzac, or a sweet Riesling, for the stock. Proceed with Step 1. For Step 2, add another tablespoon of oil to the pot and cook the onion, covered, until brown, 10 to 15 minutes. Add the wine and stir, then add the meat. Adjust the heat so the mixture bubbles steadily and cook until the meat is tender, anywhere from $1^{1}/_{2}$ to 3 hours.

Braised Beef Brisket with Beans and Barley. Omit the butter and tomato paste. Add 1 pound dried lima or other white beans, soaked overnight and drained. Proceed with Step 1. For Step 2, don't bother wiping out the pot; cook the onion as directed. Add 3 tablespoon roughly chopped garlic, 1 tablespoon minced fresh ginger or 1 teaspoon ground ginger, $^{1}/_{2}$ teaspoon ground cinnamon, 1 teaspoon ground cardamom, and 1 bay leaf and sprinkle with salt and pepper. Cook, stirring, for a minute. Add the meat, beans, 4 medium peeled and halved waxy potatoes, $^{1}/_{2}$ cup pearled barley, and stock or water to cover. Bring to a boil, then reduce the heat so the mixture bubbles slowly. Cover and cook as directed until the ingredients are very tender.

Corned Beef

MAKES: 6 to 12 servings
TIME: 3 hours, largely unattended
M

Corned beef is brisket (ideally) that, like wet-cured ham, has been steeped in a spicy brine. If you have a choice, buy the flat cut rather than the point cut. Cooking corned beef is literally as easy as boiling water; it's tough to overcook, so this is a good candidate for the slow cooker. With mustard, pickles, and good rye bread, this makes a fine old-fashioned meal.

1 corned beef, 3 to 5 pounds

1 bay leaf

1 head garlic

3 cloves

10 peppercorns

5 allspice berries or 1 or 2 pinches ground allspice

1 onion

① Put the corned beef in a large, heavy pot and cover with water. Add all the remaining ingredients. Bring to a boil and skim all the foam that rises to the surface.

② Lower the heat so that the water bubbles occasionally rather than constantly. Cook, turning every 30 minutes or so, for about 2 hours. Pierce with a thin-bladed knife, like a boning knife; the meat will probably still be fairly tough, but it's time to begin checking.

③ Check every 15 minutes or so; when the corned beef allows the knife to pass into the middle without much resistance, it is ready. Drain; if you like, put the meat into a 300°F oven for 10 minutes to dry out the exterior a little. (Or wrap it carefully in tin foil and refrigerate for up to 2 days; reheat at 300°F for 30 minutes in the foil; unwrap and heat for about 15 minutes more.) Slice across the grain, as you would brisket, and serve.

New England Boiled Dinner (Corned Beef and Cabbage). In Step 2, after 2 hours of cooking, add the following per person: 1 medium peeled waxy red or white potato; 1 or 2 medium carrots; 1 wedge of cabbage, pierced with a skewer or a couple of toothpicks to keep it from falling apart; and any other root vegetable you like, like whole peeled onions, peeled turnips, or parsnips. It's best to leave most vegetables whole, but if the meat appears to be nearly done, you may cut them into halves or quarters to hasten their cooking, especially if they are large. In any case, do not overcook the vegetables; when they are tender, remove them. In Step 3, put the drained meat and vegetables on a platter and let sit in a 300°F oven for 10 minutes before serving. Garnish with plenty of minced fresh parsley leaves.

Corned Beef (or Roast Beef) Hash. Toss together 2 cups cut-up leftover corned beef and 2 cups cut-up cold boiled potatoes, all in small cubes. Add 1 cup chopped onion and $1/2$ cup liquid—stock, tomato sauce, milk, cream, or gravy—enough to moisten the mixture without making it soupy. Put 3 tablespoons oil or butter in a heavy skillet, preferably nonstick,

16 Meat Dishes for the Summer Grill

If you're looking for a dish to anchor your next cookout, stop here:

1. "Grilling Large Cuts of Meat" is a good place to start (page 736)
2. Skewered and Grilled Meatballs, Three Ways (page 114)
3. Grilled, Pan-Grilled, or Broiled Steak, Many Ways (page 717)
4. My Favorite Burger (page 721)
5. Marinated and Grilled or Broiled Flank Steak and its variations (page 729)
6. Beef (or Other Meat or Seafood) Kebabs (page 732)
7. Grilled or Broiled Pork Chops (page 747)
8. Grilled or Broiled Pork Kebabs with Lemongrass (page 751)
9. Grilled or Broiled Pork Tenderloin with Mustard Curry (page 752)
10. No-Work Smoked Pork Shoulder or Spareribs (page 759)
11. Chinese Grilled Pork Shoulder or Spareribs (page 761)
12. Grilled or Broiled Lamb Chops and its variations (page 768)
13. Grilled or Broiled Butterflied Leg of Lamb and its variations (page 771)
14. Grilled or Broiled Lamb Ribs (page 778)
15. Grilled or Broiled Veal Chops (page 780)
16. Grilled or Broiled Liver (page 785)

over medium-low heat. When the oil is hot or the butter is melted, add the hash and cook, undisturbed, until a nice crust has formed, about 10 minutes. Turn the hash and brown the other side or flip half of it over onto the other or brown the top under a broiler. Serve. This can also be baked in a lightly greased baking dish at 350°F until brown on top. To make Red Flannel Hash, replace half the boiled potatoes with peeled cooked beets.

The Basics of Pork

Most pork is now so lean that with many cuts any overcooking at all results in bone-dry meat. There's evidence that this will change and once again it will be easy to grab a pork chop, broil or grill or sauté it, and enjoy it. For now, though, it's best to pay a little more and shop for "natural" pork, although even that isn't necessarily a guarantee of a nice balance of lean and fat.

There *is* an advantage to super-lean pork: It cooks a lot faster than pork used to. Most pork tastes best when still on the pink side, at around 150°F. Since trichina—which causes the dread trichinosis—is killed at 137°F, eating medium pork is widely considered safe. (Other bacteria, including salmonella, may not be killed at this temperature; if this concerns you, cook pork to 160°F—well done—but to be consistent you should be doing the same for beef and veal.)

Buying the right cut of pork is important, because only a few cuts are fatty enough to withstand prolonged cooking.

Shoulder: The front leg; the most common cuts are called *Boston butt* or *picnic ham*. Sometimes smoked, salted, or cured, like the ham (rear leg), but it's sold fresh far more often. Fatty and usually delicious, this is among the best cuts to roast or cook in liquid because it remains moist and becomes tender. Hocks and "trotters" (feet) also come from the front legs. And pork steaks are sometimes cut from the shoulder too.

Loin: Behind the shoulder, this is the area from which the ultra-lean tenderloin is taken; this is a nice tender cut, but it contains almost no fat, so it must be cooked carefully to prevent it from drying out. The loin also produces

MAJOR CUTS OF PORK

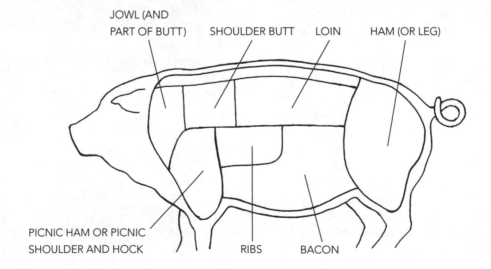

F Fast   **M** Make Ahead   **V** Vegetarian

steaks, roasts, and chops, boneless and bone in. There are several names commonly used for loin roasts: *rib end* (from the shoulder end), *loin* or *rump end* (from the rear end), and *center loin* (or *center-cut loin* or *center-cut rib*). The rear end is the leanest, the shoulder end the most flavorful. All of these roasts may be cut into chops with the same characteristics. Boneless center-cut loin is smoked to make Canadian bacon. Back ribs and country-style "ribs" (which are not ribs at all) are also cut from the loin.

Belly: The cut that contains spareribs and bacon. Salted belly is salt pork; salted and smoked belly is bacon.

Ham: The rear legs, almost always cured and/or smoked (in any number of ways), sold whole, in pieces, or in slices. Fresh ham—meaning that no further treatment has been involved—is just a regular cut of pork and can be cooked according to any recipe for shoulder, although it is leaner.

Chops and Other Quick-Cooking Pork

A good pork chop begins with the right cut. I prefer chops from the shoulder, which are not as attractive as center-cut loin chops—which have a distinct "eye" of meat (and little meat elsewhere)—but are more flavorful. No matter which you choose, it's best to make sure that chops are at least an inch thick—you'll be much happier with one thick chop than two thin ones, which invariably overcook.

Most pork is like white-meat chicken: Care must be taken when cooking smaller bits of it, as in stir-fries, or it dries out. To avoid this problem, start with pieces cut from the pork shoulder, which are the most forgiving. No matter what cut you use, cook the pork first at the highest heat possible, then remove it before cooking the remaining ingredients, adding it back only at the end of cooking to reheat briefly.

Substitute thinly cut pork for any of the meats in the other stir-fries in this and the poultry chapter or add it to any vegetable stir-fry. And for classic pork chops with pan sauce, see the essential recipe on page 720.

Grilled or Broiled Pork Chops

MAKES: 4 servings
TIME: 20 minutes

Simple, as long as you start with pork that's got some fat. For this, it's especially worth seeking out meat from a specialty purveyor, one that offers old-fashioned or heirloom pork products.

4 center-cut loin pork chops, about 1 inch thick, trimmed of excess fat

2 tablespoons extra virgin olive oil

1 tablespoon freshly squeezed lemon juice

Salt and freshly ground black pepper

Lemon wedges for serving

1 Heat a charcoal or gas grill or the broiler until moderately hot and put the rack about 4 inches from the heat source. As the fire heats, let the chops reach room temperature if you haven't already done so. If you're broiling, about 10 minutes before you're ready to cook, put a cast-iron or other sturdy, heatproof skillet on the rack. Pat the chops dry, then rub them with half the olive oil and the lemon juice. Sprinkle them liberally with salt and pepper.

2 Sear the chops over (or under) the hottest part of the fire for a minute or two per side, taking care not to let them burn. Then move them to a cooler part of the grill (or reduce the heat of the broiler or move the meat farther from the heat source) and cook, turning once or twice, until done, 10 to 20 minutes more (the timing depends on the heat of the fire, the thickness of the chops, and whether you cover the grill). The chops are done when firm to the touch, their juices run just slightly pink, and, when you cut into them (which you should do if you're at all unsure of their doneness), the color is rosy at first glance but quickly turns pale.

3 Brush the chops with a little more olive oil and serve with lemon wedges.

Herb-Marinated Grilled or Broiled Pork Chops. Start these at least 2 hours and as long as 3 days ahead. Dry the chops well. Mix together 1 teaspoon salt, 1 teaspoon dried sage or thyme or 1 tablespoon minced fresh, 1/2 teaspoon freshly ground black pepper, 1 finely crumbled bay leaf, and 1 teaspoon finely minced garlic. Rub the chops all over with this mixture. Cover or wrap the chops and let them sit at room temperature for up to 2 hours or refrigerated for up to 3 days. Proceed with the recipe but without the olive oil; serve with lemon wedges.

Pan-Grilled Pork Chops. Turn the oven to its maximum temperature, at least 500°F, and set a rack in the lowest possible position. Heat a cast-iron or other sturdy ovenproof skillet just large enough to hold the chops over medium-high heat for 4 to 5 minutes; the pan should be really hot, just about smoking. Rub the chops with olive oil only, then put in the skillet. Immediately transfer the skillet to the oven; cook for about 5 minutes per side. Season with salt, pepper, and freshly squeezed lemon juice and serve with lemon wedges.

Stir-Fried Pork with Spinach

MAKES: 4 servings
TIME: About 15 minutes

Any tender green can fill in for spinach: Arugula, cress, chard, dandelion, and even romaine lettuce all work here. Add a small handful of chopped basil or cilantro or mint at the last minute if you like. And if you want a strong garlic flavor, reserve some of the garlic and stir it in at the end of the cooking, along with the soy sauce and lime juice. Since this dish is the work of a moment, you should have all the side dishes started (or finished) before you begin.

Other cuts and meats you can use: beef, preferably sirloin; lamb, preferably from the shoulder or leg; boneless chicken.

1 pound pork, preferably shoulder, trimmed of external fat

About 1 pound spinach, trimmed of thick stems and well washed

2 tablespoons peanut or neutral oil, like grapeseed or corn

1 1/2 tablespoons minced garlic

2 tablespoons soy sauce, plus more as needed

Juice of 1/2 lime

1/4 to 1/2 cup stock (to make your own, see pages 157–159) or water (optional)

1/2 cup minced scallion or 1/4 cup minced chives for garnish

1 Slice the pork as thinly as you can (it's easier if you freeze it for 15 to 30 minutes first). Cut the slices into bite-sized pieces, about the size of a quarter. Chop or tear the spinach coarsely.

2 When you're ready to cook, have all the ingredients ready, including a serving dish and cooked rice, if you're making any. Heat a large, heavy skillet over high heat until it begins to smoke. Immediately add half the oil and all the pork. Cook, stirring occasionally (not constantly), until the pork browns and loses all traces of pinkness, about 3 minutes. Use a slotted spoon to transfer the pork to a bowl and lower the heat to medium.

3 Add the remaining oil to the skillet. Swirl it around and add the garlic. Stir once or twice. As soon as the garlic begins to color—after about 15 seconds—return the heat to high and add the spinach. Stir frequently, just until the spinach wilts, a minute or two longer.

4 Add the pork back to the skillet and stir for 1 minute. Add the soy sauce and lime juice, stir, turn off the heat, and taste, adding more soy sauce if necessary. If the mixture is drier than you like, add the stock and heat through. Garnish with the scallion and serve immediately.

Stir-Fried Pork with Asparagus. In Step 1, substitute 2 cups pencil-thin asparagus, chopped into 1-inch

F Fast   **M** Make Ahead   **V** Vegetarian

pieces, for the spinach. In Step 2, add 3 or 4 small dried hot red chiles along with the pork if you like. For Step 3, cook the asparagus until it turns bright green and begins to become tender, 3 or 4 minutes. Then add 1 tablespoon minced fresh ginger and $^1/_2$ cup chopped scallion and cook, stirring once or twice, for 30 seconds. Proceed with the recipe, substituting $^1/_4$ cup chicken stock for the lime juice and omitting the garnish.

Stir-Fried Pork with Snow Peas and Ginger. In Step 1, use 2 cups trimmed snow peas (or snap peas) instead of the spinach. In Step 3, cook 2 tablespoons minced fresh ginger with the garlic, then add the snow peas, stirring over medium-high heat until they soften and begin to brown, about 5 minutes. In Step 4, add 1 teaspoon minced fresh ginger along with the soy sauce and lime juice.

Stir-Fried Pork with Hoisin and Sesame Oil. Follow Steps 1–3 in the master recipe or any of the variations. In Step 4, stir 1 tablespoon hoisin sauce into the stir-fry along with the soy sauce; omit the lime juice. Drizzle with 1 teaspoon dark sesame oil before serving.

Stir-Fried Pork with Sweet Onions. In Step 1, substitute 3 cups thinly sliced onion (2 large) for the spinach. In Step 3, cook the onion with the garlic, stirring over medium-high heat until it softens and begin to brown, 7 to 10 minutes. Sprinkle with 1 teaspoon sugar, then proceed to Step 4.

Stir-Fried Pork in Garlic Sauce. Omit the spinach. Add 2 tablespoons minced garlic, 2 or 3 (or more) small hot dried red chiles, and 1 bunch scallions, trimmed and cut into 2-inch lengths, white and green parts separated. In Step 2, add the chiles and garlic to the hot oil first, cooking and stirring for a minute or so before adding the pork. Cook the pork, stirring once or twice, until it begins to brown and is almost cooked through, then add the scallion whites and

cook for another 30 seconds. Finish the dish as described in Step 4.

Stir-Fried Pork in Garlic Sauce, Thai Style. In Step 3 of the preceding variation, add 1 tablespoon sugar with the green parts of the scallions and substitute nam pla (Thai fish sauce) for the soy sauce.

10 Simple Additions to Pork Stir-Fries

1. Add $^1/_4$ teaspoon or more hot red pepper flakes along with the garlic.
2. Use any combination of raw vegetables, cut into small pieces, and cook with the garlic.
3. Add 1 tablespoon of sugar to the pork as it cooks for added color, crispness, and sweetness.
4. Add 2 tablespoons whole or chopped peanuts or cashews along with the vegetables.
5. Add five-spice or curry powder (to make your own, see pages 66–68) along with the pork.
6. Add $^1/_2$ cup coconut milk (to make your own, see page 389) just at the end of cooking.
7. Add 1 teaspoon ground spices, especially Sichuan peppercorns, with the garlic.
8. Marinate the pork in $^1/_4$ cup soy sauce mixed with $^1/_4$ cup water or wine and 1 teaspoon vinegar before stir-frying.
9. Use nam pla (Thai fish sauce) in place of soy sauce.
10. Add about 1 tablespoon) ground bean paste or plum sauce (you can buy either in cans in Chinese markets), or about $^1/_2$ teaspoon Chile-Garlic Paste (page 75) during the last minute of cooking.

West Indian Crispy Pork Bits

MAKES: 4 to 8 servings
TIME: About 2 hours, plus time to marinate, largely unattended

West Indian to start with, yes, but as you can see from the variations, there are many ways to season bits of pork before cooking them until they are crisp and caramelized;

I find all of them irresistible. I like them on toothpicks, but they're equally good with rice and beans.

> 1½ to 2 pounds pork, preferably shoulder, trimmed of some but not all external fat
>
> Salt and freshly ground black pepper
>
> 1 tablespoon minced garlic
>
> 1 teaspoon ground allspice
>
> ¼ teaspoon freshly grated nutmeg
>
> 1 teaspoon fresh thyme leaves or ½ teaspoon dried thyme
>
> ½ cup minced onion or scallion
>
> 1 tablespoon peanut, extra virgin olive, or neutral oil, like grapeseed or corn
>
> ¼ cup freshly squeezed lime juice
>
> ½ cup stock (to make your own, see pages 157–159) or water (optional)

1 Cut the meat into bite-sized bits. Toss with all the other ingredients except the stock. Cover and marinate, refrigerated, for up to 2 days or cook right away.

2 Heat the oven to 375°F. Put the meat in a roasting pan large enough to hold it in one layer (it will shrink considerably, so a tight fit is okay). Roast for about 1 hour, shaking and stirring the meat occasionally, until the meat is brown and crisp on all sides. Remove the meat with a slotted spoon. Serve hot or at room temperature or proceed to the next step to make a quick sauce.

3 Pour off all but a tablespoon or two of the fat, leaving any solids and as much nonfatty liquid behind as possible. Put the pan on a burner over high heat, add the stock, and cook, stirring and scraping the bottom of the pan, until the liquid is reduced by about half and all the solids are incorporated. Pour over the pork bits and serve.

Jerk Pork. Replace the thyme with 1 teaspoon ground coriander and add half (or more) of a seeded and minced Scotch bonnet chile to the marinade, or use any other chile pepper, cayenne, hot red pepper flakes, or chile sauce to taste.

Pork Bits with Iberian Flavors. Eliminate from the marinade the allspice, nutmeg, thyme, and lime juice. Add to the marinade 1 tablespoon ground cumin, 2 teaspoons paprika, 1 tablespoon grated or minced lemon zest, and ¼ cup freshly squeezed lemon juice.

Pork Bits with Asian Flavors. Eliminate from the marinade the allspice, nutmeg, thyme, and lime juice. Add to the marinade 2 tablespoons minced or grated fresh ginger or 1 tablespoon ground ginger, 2 tablespoons soy sauce or nam pla (Thai fish sauce), and 1 tablespoon sugar.

Pork Bits with Mexican Flavors. Eliminate from the marinade the allspice, nutmeg, and thyme. Add to the marinade 1 teaspoon each (or 2 teaspoons of either) ground cumin and chili powder (to make your own, see page 66) and 1 tablespoon minced fresh oregano leaves or 1 teaspoon dried oregano.

Stir-Fried "Salads"

The only downside to stir-fries is that they must be served immediately after cooking. But deconstruct the concept and add a strong Asian-style dressing and the dish is ideal as a room-temperature salad. I start by making the dressing first—Thai Chile Sauce (page 39) and Soy Vinaigrette (page 201) are both good choices. Then get the rice going.

To keep the vegetables crisp—regardless of how many you use—stir-fry each separately, adding just enough oil to prevent sticking, and transfer them to the salad bowl. Finally, stir-fry the meat or seafood and toss everything together with dressing to moisten. The salad can rest at room temperature for up to an hour before being served.

 Fast   Make Ahead   Vegetarian

Broiled or Roasted Pork with Fresh Orange Sauce

MAKES: 4 servings
TIME: 30 minutes

Fruit juice reduces into an instant sauce, in this case almost a syrup. You can use this sauce on grilled chicken, broiled fish, even steamed broccoli. But the ultimate companion is this crusty roasted pork, which was the meat it was served on when I first ate it in Spain.

2 pounds pork country-style ribs or boneless steaks
    cut from the shoulder, 3/4 to 1 inch thick

Salt and freshly ground black pepper

1 1/2 cups freshly squeezed orange juice

1/4 teaspoon cayenne, or to taste

1 teaspoon ground cumin

1 shallot, minced

A few drops vinegar or freshly squeezed lemon or lime
    juice, if necessary

1 teaspoon grated orange zest

1/4 cup chopped fresh parsley leaves

❶ Heat the oven to 450°F or heat the broiler, putting the rack about 4 inches from the heat source. Put an ovenproof skillet large enough to hold the pork in one layer over high heat. Sprinkle the meat with salt and pepper. Brown the meat quickly on both sides—about 2 minutes per side should do it—then transfer it to the oven or broiler.

❷ Meanwhile, combine the orange juice, cayenne, cumin, and shallot in a small skillet or saucepan over medium heat. Cook, stirring, until it reduces to about 1/3 cup, about 5 minutes. Taste and adjust the seasoning, adding a touch more cayenne and/or cumin if you like and some vinegar or lemon juice if the sauce lacks acidity.

❸ If broiling, turn the meat once. (If roasting, don't bother.) Cook the pork until firm but not tough and still slightly pink in the very center (the internal temperature

at the very center should be no higher than 145°F when you remove it from the heat), and transfer it to a platter. Combine the orange zest with the parsley. Spoon the sauce over the meat, then top all with the parsley–orange zest mixture and serve.

Grilled or Broiled Pork Kebabs with Lemongrass

MAKES: 4 main-dish or 8 appetizer servings
TIME: 1 hour, largely unattended, longer if you have time

Lemongrass has a citrusy flavor that is usually associated with the cuisine of Vietnam, where kebabs like these are often served on a flat bed of plain rice noodles. I like them over a salad dressed with a little Thai Chile Sauce.

Other cuts and meats you can use: beef tenderloin or sirloin or boneless chicken thighs (which will require a little longer cooking time).

1 1/2 to 2 pounds pork, preferably shoulder, trimmed of
    external fat

1 tablespoon toasted sesame seeds (see page 317)

2 stalks lemongrass, tough outer skins removed and
    tender inside finely chopped

2 large or 4 medium shallots, roughly chopped

2 large cloves garlic, roughly chopped

1 small hot red dried chile, preferably Thai, seeded
    and chopped, or hot red pepper flakes to taste

1 tablespoon freshly squeezed lime juice

1 tablespoon sugar

2 tablespoons nam pla (Thai fish sauce)

Salt if necessary

1/2 teaspoon freshly ground black pepper, or to taste

Thai Chile Sauce (page 39) for dipping

❶ Freeze the pork for 30 to 60 minutes to facilitate slicing. Meanwhile, combine all the remaining ingredients except the sauce in a small food processor and blend to a paste, stopping the machine to stir down the sides if necessary.

② When the meat is semifrozen, slice it as thinly as you can. Marinate it for as little as 20 minutes and as long as overnight in the spice paste (if the paste is too thick, thin it with a bit more nam pla; refrigerate if marinating for more than an hour).

③ Heat a charcoal or gas grill or the broiler until quite hot and put the rack about 4 inches from the heat source. If you're using wood skewers, soak them in water to cover. Skewer the pork slices, using the skewer as you would a needle to weave once or twice through the meat. Grill or broil quickly, about 2 minutes per side, until nicely browned. Serve hot, with the Thai Chile Sauce.

Sautéed Medallions of Pork with Lemon and Parsley

MAKES: 4 servings
TIME: 15 minutes

All the recipes for cutlets of veal (see pages 781–783) or chicken (see pages 672–674) work just as well with pork medallions. But here's a basic recipe to improvise as you like.

Other cuts and meats you can use: veal or chicken cutlets.

One 1- to 1¼-pound pork tenderloin

¼ cup extra virgin olive oil

All-purpose flour for dredging

Salt and freshly ground black pepper

½ cup dry white wine

2 lemons

1 or 2 tablespoons drained capers (optional)

Chopped fresh parsley leaves for garnish

① Cut the tenderloin into ¼-inch-thick slices. Pound them gently (use a flat rolling pin, the back of a skillet, or a similar object) between 2 sheets of wax paper to make them a bit thinner.

② Put the oil in a large skillet over medium heat. Season the flour liberally with salt and pepper and put the seasoned flour in a shallow bowl near the stove. When the oil is hot (a pinch of flour will sizzle), dredge the medallions, one at a time, in the flour, then put them in the skillet. Cook over heat high enough to make the oil bubble; don't crowd. Heat the oven to 200°F.

③ Turn the pieces as soon as they're browned, then cook the other side; total cooking time should be 5 minutes or less, so adjust the heat accordingly. As the meat is done, transfer it to an ovenproof platter and put it in the oven.

④ When all the pork is finished, pour off the fat from the pan. Return the skillet to the stove over medium-high heat and add the wine. Cook, stirring, until the wine is just about evaporated, 5 to 10 minutes. Squeeze in the juice of one of the lemons and add the capers if you're using them. Stir and pour this sauce (there won't be more than a few tablespoons) over the meat. Garnish with parsley and serve with the remaining lemon, quartered.

Grilled or Broiled Pork Tenderloin with Mustard Curry

MAKES: 3 to 4 servings
TIME: About 30 minutes

Pork tenderloin is lower in fat than almost any other cut of meat, though not the most flavorful, so I like to cook it with assertive spices. The cooking time is extremely short—and the leftovers make fantastic sandwiches.

2 tablespoons Dijon mustard

2 tablespoons curry powder, garam masala, or other spice mixture (to make your own, see pages 65–69), or to taste

Salt and freshly ground black pepper

1¹/₄ pounds pork tenderloin in 1 piece

Raw Onion Chutney (page 36), Corn and Tomato Relish (page 50), or bottled chutney

1 Heat a charcoal or gas grill or the broiler until quite hot and put the rack 2 to 4 inches from the heat source.

2 Blend the mustard, curry, and some salt and pepper in a small bowl, then rub this mixture all over the meat. Grill or broil, turning to brown all sides well (if it starts to burn, move the rack farther from the fire), until almost cooked through but still slightly pink in the very center, 10 to 15 minutes (the internal temperature at the center should be no higher than 145–150°F). Let the meat sit for 10 minutes before cutting it into ¹/₂-inch-thick slices and serving with chutney or relish.

Miso Grilled or Broiled Pork Tenderloin. Omit the mustard, curry, salt, and pepper. Instead, rub the tenderloin with ¹/₄ cup white, yellow, or red miso paste.

Pork Steaks and Baked Apples

MAKES: 4 servings

TIME: About 30 minutes

F

Pork and apples are a winning flavor combo but usually losers in the texture department. This Tuscan classic solves the overcooking problem with a quick-braise technique. Steaks can be cut from different parts of the pig. Try to find loin steaks or chops with some fat or steaks from the shoulder or leg.

Salt and coarsely ground black pepper

Pinch cayenne

1 teaspoon minced garlic

4 McIntosh, Cortland, Golden Delicious, or other good apples, cored and cut into eighths

¹/₂ cup semisweet white wine, like Muscatel or off-dry Riesling

3 tablespoons extra virgin olive oil

1¹/₂ to 2 pounds boneless pork steaks, cut 1 inch thick from the loin or shoulder

All-purpose flour for dredging

1 cup fruity red wine

1 Heat the oven to 400°F. Combine about a teaspoon of the salt with a pinch each of pepper and cayenne; add the garlic and sprinkle the apples with this mixture. Put in a baking dish, pour the white wine around the apples, and bake until the apples are shriveled but still moist, about 15 minutes.

2 Meanwhile, put the oil in a skillet over medium heat. When hot, dust the pork lightly with flour and sear it on both sides, for a total of just a minute or so; it need not become really brown. Add the red wine and adjust the heat so the mixture boils energetically. Cook the pork, turning occasionally, until it gains a beautiful deep color, is cooked through, and the wine reduces to a syrup—about 10 minutes. Sprinkle the meat with salt and pepper.

3 Serve the pork with the red wine sauce spooned over it, next to the apples, with a little of the white wine they cooked in.

The Basics of Pork Roasts

The preferred cut of pork for roasting is the loin, though, again, shoulder is becoming increasingly desirable—because many pieces of the loin are too lean. Still, the loin makes a nice presentation, whether bone in or out.

Many people prefer a boneless loin roast, which is certainly less work when it comes to carving, but leaving the bone in usually results in moister, more flavorful meat, and the added bulk and protection of the bone gives you more flexibility in timing. And carving isn't that difficult. The shoulder, which is larger, is another good cut for roasting, as is the whole fresh ham (which can be huge) or a piece of one. Both are available with and without bone. Lean as it is, the tenderloin also can be roasted, as long as you're quick and precise.

Finally, there is the crown roast of pork, two loin sections partially boned and tied together in the shape of a ring, or crown. Any butcher can put this together for you, and it's perhaps the most impressive roast of all. Consider it when you're planning to serve ten or more.

There is one major difference between pork roasts and those of other meat: Pork is at its best when only a trace of rosiness remains in its center. This makes an instant-read thermometer almost essential. If you remove the roast when the thermometer reads 145°F (test it in two or three places to be sure) and let it rest for a few minutes before carving, its temperature will rise to 155°F, which will leave the very center just pinkish. If you prefer it really well done, roast it to 150°F; during its rest the temperature will rise to 160°F. Any cooking beyond that is unnecessary (though the USDA recommends that you cook pork to 160°F).

Roast Pork with Garlic and Rosemary

MAKES: 6 or more servings
TIME: 1¹⁄₂ to 2 hours, largely unattended

Roast pork at its most basic. If you want even more garlicky flavor, cut a clove of garlic into tiny slivers and, using a thin-bladed knife, insert them into the meat. You can do this a day or two in advance; if you do, rub the roast all over with salt too and keep it refrigerated, covered loosely with a towel or wax paper.

> Salt and freshly ground black pepper
>
> 2 tablespoons minced fresh rosemary leaves or 1 teaspoon dried rosemary
>
> ¹⁄₄ teaspoon cayenne (optional)
>
> 1 tablespoon sugar
>
> 1 teaspoon minced garlic

> One 3- to 4-pound pork loin roast, bone in, one 2- to 3-pound boneless roast, or a similar-sized portion of shoulder or fresh ham
>
> 1¹⁄₂ cups dry white wine or stock (to make your own, see pages 157–159), plus more if necessary
>
> 1 tablespoon butter (optional)

❶ Heat the oven to 450°F. Mix a liberal amount of salt and pepper with the rosemary, cayenne if you're using it, sugar, and garlic and rub it all over the roast. Put the meat in a roasting pan (use a rack if the roast is boneless, but don't bother if the bone is still in) and put in the oven. Roast, undisturbed, for 15 minutes.

❷ Pour about ¹⁄₂ cup of the wine over the roast; lower the heat to 325°F. Continue to roast, adding about ¹⁄₄ cup of liquid every 15 minutes or so. If the liquid accumulates on the bottom of the pan, use it to baste; if not, add more.

❸ Start checking the roast after 1¹⁄₄ hours of total cooking time (it's likely to take about 1¹⁄₂ hours). When it is done—an instant-read thermometer will register 145–150°F—transfer it to a warm platter. Put the roasting pan on the stove over 1 or 2 burners over medium-high heat. If there is a great deal of liquid in it, reduce it to about ³⁄₄ cup, scraping the bottom of the pan with a wooden spoon to release any brown bits that have accumulated. If the pan is dry, add 1 cup of liquid and follow the same process. When the sauce has reduced some, stir in the butter if you like, slice the roast, and serve it with the sauce.

Roast Pork with Sage and Potatoes

MAKES: 6 or more servings
TIME: 1¹⁄₂ to 2 hours, largely unattended

This is best with firm waxy potatoes like fingerlings or red potatoes; if they're small enough, keep them whole.

 Fast   Make Ahead   Vegetarian

And of course you can skip the potatoes altogether for a more basic roast pork.

2 tablespoons minced garlic

2 tablespoons minced fresh sage leaves or 2 teaspoons dried sage

Salt and freshly ground black pepper

About 2 pounds potatoes, peeled and cut into 1-inch cubes

3 tablespoons extra virgin olive oil, plus more as needed

One 3- to 4-pound pork loin roast, bone in, one 2- to 3-pound boneless roast, or a similar-sized portion of fresh ham

1 Heat the oven to 425°F. Mix together the garlic, sage, salt, and pepper. Put the potatoes in a roasting pan that is also large enough to hold the pork and toss them with a couple tablespoons of olive oil and about 1 teaspoon of the garlic-sage mixture. Put the roasting pan in the oven while you prepare the pork.

2 Using a thin-bladed knife and your fingers, make slits all over the pork and insert most of the remaining garlic-sage mixture. Spread the rest of it all over the outside of the roast and nestle it among the potatoes. Pour a little more olive oil over the meat and put it in the oven.

3 Roast, undisturbed, for 30 minutes. Remove it from the oven, stir the potatoes (you will probably have to scrape some of them off the bottom of the pan), and baste the pork with a little of the pan juices. Lower the heat to 325°F and continue to cook, stirring the potatoes every 15 minutes or so. After 1 1/4 hours or so total cooking time, begin to check the meat (it's likely to take longer, but it's worth checking); when an instant-read thermometer registers 145–150°F, transfer the meat to a warm platter.

4 While the meat rests for 10 to 15 minutes, turn the oven heat up to 450°F to make sure the potatoes are done and crisp (use your judgment; you can simply run them under the broiler if they just need a bit of browning or keep the oven at 325°F if they're done perfectly). Carve the meat and serve with the potatoes.

Roast Pork Shoulder, Puerto Rican Style

Pernil

MAKES: 6 to 10 servings

TIME: At least 5 hours, largely unattended

I've adapted this recipe a bit, but it remains little changed from the one generously shared with me more than twenty years ago by the family of my friend Peter Blasini. It remains among my favorite treatments for pork shoulder, is a huge crowd pleaser, and is almost no work.

4 cloves garlic, peeled

1 medium onion, peeled and quartered

2 tablespoons fresh oregano leaves or 1 tablespoon dried oregano

1 mild fresh chile, seeded (optional)

1 small dried hot red chile (optional)

1 tablespoon salt

2 teaspoons freshly ground black pepper

2 tablespoons peanut or other oil

2 tablespoons wine vinegar, orange juice, or lime juice

One 4- to 7-pound pork shoulder or portion of fresh ham, trimmed of excess but not all fat

1 Mix the garlic, onion, oregano, chiles, salt, and pepper together in a food processor, adding the oil in a drizzle and scraping down the sides as necessary (or mince them together on a cutting board). Blend in the wine vinegar.

2 Rub this mixture into the pork well, getting it into every nook and cranny you can find. Put the meat on a rack in a roasting pan and let sit, uncovered, for 1 to 24 hours; refrigerate if the weather is hot or the time is greater than 1 hour or so.

3 Heat the oven to 300°F. Roast the pork for about 3 hours, turning every 30 minutes or so and basting with the pan juices, until it is well done and very tender and the skin is crisp. (The internal temperature should be at least 150°F but no more than 160°F.) Let the meat rest for 10 to 15 minutes before cutting it up; the meat should be so tender that cutting into uniform slices is almost impossible; rather, whack it up into chunks.

Roast Pork Shoulder with Cumin and Cinnamon. Ideally you want this wrapped in banana leaves (available at Asian and Latin markets), but layers of foil work too: Liberally salt and pepper the roast, then rub in 1½ teaspoons ground cumin. As you're wrapping the roast in the banana leaves or foil, put three or four 3-inch cinnamon sticks in various spots around the roast. You want a total of 3 layers of wrapping; none of the meat should be exposed. Put it in a roasting pan and proceed with Step 3.

Crown Roast of Pork

MAKES: At least 10 or 12 servings
TIME: About 2½ hours, largely unattended

Like a turkey, a crown roast can be stuffed with just about anything, including My Favorite Bread Stuffing (page 698). But since this meat is substantial, I keep the stuffing light. (I cook it separately to allow it to crisp, but you can put it in the center of the crown.)

½ cup dried tart cherries or cranberries

One 7-pound crown roast of pork, 14 to 16 ribs

Salt and freshly ground black pepper

1 carrot, chopped

1 celery stalk, chopped

1 onion, cut into quarters, plus 1 cup minced onion

3 tablespoons extra virgin olive oil

1 tablespoon minced garlic

2 teaspoons minced fresh tarragon leaves or
    ½ teaspoon dried tarragon

1½ cups water or white wine, plus more as needed

½ pound (2 sticks) butter

4 cups bread crumbs, preferably fresh (page 876)

❶ Heat the oven to 450°F. Soak the cherries in hot water to cover. Sprinkle the roast with salt and pepper and put it on a rack in a roasting pan. Toss the carrot, celery, and quartered onion with 1 tablespoon of the olive oil and some salt and pepper and scatter them on the bottom of the pan.

❷ Mix the remaining olive oil with half the garlic and tarragon. Rub this mixture all over the roast, being sure to spread a bit into all the crevices you find.

❸ Roast the meat for 20 minutes, then turn the heat down to 325°F. Moisten the vegetables with a little of the water whenever they look dry.

❹ Meanwhile, melt the butter in a deep skillet or saucepan over medium heat. Add the minced onion and cook, stirring, until soft, about 5 minutes. Drain and chop the cherries and add them, then add the bread crumbs, remaining garlic and tarragon, and some salt and pepper. Toss to combine. Put the stuffing in an 8-inch square or comparable baking dish in a 1- to 2-inch-thick layer and put in the oven. Cook the stuffing until it is crisp on top, then stir it up; repeat this process while you finish cooking the meat.

❺ Total cooking time for the roast will be about 2 hours or a little longer; its internal temperature (check it in several places), should be about 150°F. When it's ready, transfer it to a cutting board and let it rest while you make the sauce. Lower the oven temperature to keep the stuffing warm (if the stuffing looks dry, baste it with some of the juices at the bottom of the roasting pan).

❻ Pour or spoon off as much of the fat from the roasting pan as you can without losing the darker juices. Put the roasting pan on the stove on 1 or 2 burners over medium-high heat. Add about 1½ cups of water and cook, stirring and scraping, until the liquid is reduced by about half, about 10 minutes. Remove the vegetables with a slotted spoon and press them into a strainer, adding any liquid you extract to the sauce and discarding the vegetables.

❼ Pile the stuffing into the center of the roast, then present the roast whole. Carve it, then serve with a bit of the stuffing, spooning a little of the sauce over it while passing the rest.

F Fast   **M** Make Ahead   **V** Vegetarian

Pork Stews and Braises

The shoulder is the preferred cut for braising. Its adequate (usually not excessive) fat melts during the long, moist cooking process (and, if you like, can be removed easily after refrigeration).

Boneless shoulder roasts are fine for braising and easier to deal with than bone-in cuts; just make sure they are cut into evenly sized pieces or tied into a relatively uniform shape so that no part becomes overcooked at the expense of another. It is possible to overcook pork, even in liquid; the result is stringy meat (which, compared to other overcooked meat, is not altogether unpleasant).

As with other braises, if you're pressed for time, you can skip the browning step with little loss of flavor.

Braised Pork with Red Wine

MAKES: 4 servings

TIME: 2 hours or longer, largely unattended

This stew is so simple you can make it in a slow cooker since you need not brown the meat first (though there is some benefit in doing so; see the last variation). If you have stock, it will ratchet up the flavor a bit. But even with just water, the sauce is amplified by reducing and adding a little bit of butter—a classic French technique that brings everything together into a smooth, almost magical texture.

Other cuts and meats you can use: beef chuck or brisket (cooking time will be longer), bone-in or boneless chicken thighs, lamb shoulder.

2 pounds boneless pork shoulder, trimmed of excess fat and cut into large chunks

Salt and freshly ground black pepper

2 cups fruity red wine, like Beaujolais or Burgundy (Pinot Noir)

1 cup vegetable or chicken stock (to make your own, see page 157) or water

1 pound carrots, preferably fat ones, cut into large chunks

10 cloves garlic, more or less, peeled

2 tablespoons butter (optional)

Chopped fresh parsley leaves for garnish

❶ Combine all the ingredients except the butter and parsley in a saucepan, Dutch oven, or slow cooker. Bring to a boil, then adjust the heat so the mixture bubbles steadily but not vigorously. (If you're using a slow cooker, just turn it to high and walk away for a few hours.)

❷ Cook, stirring every 30 minutes or so, until the meat is very tender and just about falling apart. Use a slotted spoon to transfer the solid ingredients to a bowl and turn the heat to high. (If you're using a slow cooker, transfer the liquid to a saucepan for this step.) Reduce the liquid to about a cup or even less. Taste and adjust the seasoning, then lower the heat and, if you're using it, stir in the butter.

❸ Reheat the solids in the sauce and serve—preferably over egg noodles—garnished with the parsley.

Braised Pork with Red Wine and Coriander. Omit the carrots. For Step 1, substitute 1 head garlic, papery skins removed, halved through its equator, for the garlic cloves; add 3 tablespoons coriander seeds, cracked and wrapped in cheesecloth. Proceed with the recipe, squeezing in freshly squeezed lemon juice to taste and garnishing with chopped fresh cilantro leaves.

Braised Pork with Horseradish Sauce. In Step 1, use all stock for the liquid, and 2 cups sliced onion instead of the carrots. Add 1 teaspoon fresh thyme leaves (or 1/2 teaspoon dried) and 1 tablespoon red wine vinegar along with the other ingredients. Proceed with the recipe, stirring 1/4 cup freshly grated horseradish or 2 tablespoons prepared horseradish, or to taste, into the reduced sauce just before serving.

Braised Pork Curry. Substitute coconut milk (to make your own, see page 389) for the wine and add 2 tablespoons minced fresh ginger and 2 tablespoons curry powder or garam masala (to make your own, see pages 66–67), and cayenne to taste. Proceed with the recipe.

Seared and Braised Pork. Use this technique for any of the preceding variations or the main recipe. Start by putting 2 or 3 tablespoons oil in a large pot with a lid or a Dutch oven over medium-high heat. (Use extra virgin olive oil with Mediterranean flavor profiles, neutral oil with others.) Cook, turning when needed, to thoroughly brown all sides. When done, pour off the fat and proceed with the recipe from the beginning.

Braised Pork with Spicy Soy Sauce

MAKES: 4 to 6 servings
TIME: About 1 hour

Here's one of those high-mileage dishes that you cook once and eat many times. You can, of course, eat it hot (with lots of rice or noodles and stir-fried vegetables), but I like to make it in advance, refrigerate, and skim off the fat, then slice the meat and use it in one of three ways: reheated in the sauce, cold in sandwiches, or added to stir-fries or rice or noodle bowls.

1 fresh hot chile, seeded and minced, or 1 dried hot chile, seeded and crumbled, or to taste

2 pounds boneless pork shoulder, excess fat removed, cut into chunks

1/2 cup soy sauce or nam pla (Thai fish sauce) or half of each

1/4 cup sugar

1/2 cup chicken, beef, or vegetable stock (to make your own, see pages 157–159) or water

2 tablespoons minced garlic

2 tablespoons minced fresh ginger

1 cup thinly sliced onion

2 tablespoons freshly squeezed lime juice

Salt and lots of freshly ground black pepper

① Combine all the ingredients except for 1 tablespoon of the lime juice and the salt and pepper in a large pot with a lid. If you have the time, let the mixture sit, refrigerated, for up to a day.

② Bring to a boil over medium-high heat, turn the heat down to a minimum, and cook, covered, stirring every 10 minutes or so, until the pork is tender, less than 1 hour. (At this point, you may refrigerate the dish for a day or two before proceeding.)

③ Remove the lid, raise the heat, and boil until the liquid is reduced to less than 1 cup, about 10 minutes. Taste, add plenty of pepper and some salt if necessary, taste again, and add more pepper, chile, or soy sauce as needed. Sprinkle with the remaining lime juice and serve immediately or refrigerate and use as described above.

Braised Pork with Tofu. In Step 3, remove the roast from the pot and set aside to cool for a few minutes. As you reduce the sauce, stir in 1 pound cubed firm tofu. Slice the roast and serve it topped with the sauce and tofu, garnished with chopped scallion.

Braised Pork with Milk

MAKES: 4 to 6 servings
TIME: At least 2 hours

An easy, luxurious, and always surprising dish, where the milk reduces to curds and the pork becomes fork-tender. But you've got to use a roast from the shoulder end, either a boneless rib roast or a piece of shoulder.

Other cuts and meats you can use: To my surprise, a friend suggested I try this with bone-in chicken thighs, and it worked beautifully. Much quicker too. Also veal shoulder.

1/4 cup extra virgin olive oil

One 2- to 3-pound boneless pork rib roast or shoulder

 Fast   Make Ahead   **V** Vegetarian

Salt and freshly ground black pepper

At least 4 cups whole milk

1 Put a heavy pot with a lid or a Dutch oven that will hold the roast snugly over medium-high heat and add the oil, swirling to coat. When the oil shimmers, add the roast. Brown well on all sides, turning the meat as necessary; the process will take about 10 minutes, perhaps longer. While the meat is browning, sprinkle it with salt and pepper.

2 Add enough milk to the pan to come most of the way up the sides of the roast. Bring to a boil, then turn the heat to low so the liquid bubbles gently (adjust the heat as necessary), partly covered, for at least an hour, turning the roast once or twice.

3 Cook until the roast is quite tender and the milk is reduced to small nut-brown clumps (curds), anywhere from 1 to 2 more hours. If the milk begins to dry out before the roast is cooked, add $^1/_2$ cup milk, repeating if necessary. When the pork is done, transfer it to a warm serving platter.

4 Spoon off most of the fat from the sauce and add $^1/_4$ cup water. Turn the heat to high and reduce, scraping the bottom of the pan with a wooden spoon to dislodge the bits of pork. Carve the meat into slices, pouring half of the sauce over the roast and passing the rest at the table. Serve immediately.

Shredded Pork

MAKES: 4 or more servings

TIME: About an hour, largely unattended

The perfect filling for tacos, enhancing bean and rice dishes, or stuffing cabbage, grape leaves, empanadas, or almost anything else. You must use the shoulder here; anything else doesn't have enough fat to become tender.

2 pounds boneless pork shoulder, cut into 1-inch chunks

1 large white onion, quartered

5 cloves garlic, lightly crushed

2 bay leaves

1 tablespoon ground cumin

1 ancho or other mild dried chile (optional)

Salt and freshly ground black pepper

1 Combine all the ingredients in a large pot with a lid or a Dutch oven and add water to cover. Turn the heat to high, bring to a boil, and skim any foam that comes to the surface. Partially cover and adjust the heat so the mixture bubbles steadily. Cook until the meat is quite tender, about an hour, then cool.

2 Shred the meat with your fingers (remove the bay leaves). Taste and adjust the seasoning; use within a couple of days.

Shredded Pork with Orange Juice. Use two-thirds freshly squeezed orange juice and one-third freshly squeezed lime juice instead of water to cover in Step 1; add 1 teaspoon grated orange zest too.

Carnitas. Crisp and chewy bits of braised pork, a perfect taco filling: In Step 2, instead of shredding, break or roughly chop the meat into bite-sized pieces, return to the pan, and cook until all the liquid is evaporated. You want the meat to fry in the remaining fat until it's crisped and browned; add neutral oil, like grapeseed or corn, if needed.

No-Work Smoked Pork Shoulder or Spareribs

MAKES: 6 to 8 servings

TIME: About 4 hours, largely unattended

A gas grill works best here (though an oven will do for the first variation). You'll be amazed by the ease of this low-and-slow technique and downright shocked at the result: The meat can be served straight off the grill, with no more than a squeeze of lime and a few drops of Tabasco, or with any salsa or chutney. Or it can be shredded into a recipe of Basic Barbecue Sauce (page 52). Or your can refrigerate the whole thing, slice the shoulder or cut between the ribs, and put it back on the grill—this time over direct heat—to add a crisp steaklike char over the super-tender insides.

2 teaspoons salt

1 tablespoon sugar

2 teaspoons freshly ground black pepper

2 teaspoons ground cumin

2 teaspoons mild ground dried chile, like ancho or New Mexico

2 teaspoons good paprika

One 5- or 6-pound pork shoulder or spareribs

1 Start a gas grill, using the burners on only one side to achieve a heat of 250–300°F. Put a couple handfuls of wood chips in a tin foil pan and set it over the burners that are on. While the grill heats, mix together the dry ingredients and rub them all over the pork, including under the skin as best you can and in any crevasses you find.

2 Put the pork on the cool side of the grill, cover, and walk away. Check about 15 minutes later to make sure the chips are smoking and the heat is below 300°F. Now you can ignore the pork shoulder almost entirely; check every hour or so to make sure the heat hasn't escalated too much and the chips or charcoal do not need replenishing. If you're cooking ribs, turn them every half hour or so.

3 The pork shoulder is done when it reaches an internal temperature of about 190°F, about 4 hours later (less if you used a smaller piece of pork, more if larger). More important, the pork will be very tender. The ribs are done when they have lost much of their fat and developed an unquestionably cooked look, anywhere from 2 to 6 hours later.

4 This next step is optional for the shoulder but a must for the ribs: Just before you're ready to eat, raise the heat to high (or add a bunch more briquettes and wait a while) and brown the meat on both sides. Be very careful; they should still have enough fat on them to flare up and burn, ruining all your hard work in an instant (believe me, I've done it several times). Watch them constantly and move them frequently. Browning will take about 10 minutes. Serve immediately with any sauce you like or refrigerate overnight, slice, and grill (or pan-grill) individual slices.

15 Meat Dishes That Are as Good or Better the Next Day

Many inexpensive cuts of meat require long, slow cooking and are in fact better when refrigerated for a day before being reheated and served. This practice also makes it easy to skim excess fat before serving, since it will rise to the top and congeal as the dish chills.

Some good examples (including their variations):

1. Beef Stew, Eight Ways (page 724)
2. Beef Daube (page 738)
3. Short Ribs Braised with Potatoes and Mustard (page 740)
4. Braised Oxtails with Garlic and White Wine (page 741)
5. Classic Pot Roast (page 742)
6. Braised Beef Brisket (page 743)
7. Braised Pork with Red Wine (page 757)
8. Braised Pork with Spicy Soy Sauce (page 758)
9. Braised Spareribs with Cabbage (page 761)
10. Lamb Stew with Mushrooms (page 773)
11. Lamb Curry (page 775)
12. Lamb Shanks with Tomatoes and Olives (page 776)
13. Lamb Shanks with Lentils (page 777)
14. Forty-Minute Cassoulet (page 786)
15. Hunter's Stew (page 787)

 Fast   Make Ahead   **V** Vegetarian

Oven-"Grilled" Pork Shoulder or Spareribs. Heat the oven to 275°F. Put the rubbed meat in a roasting pan, the ribs in one layer. Bake, pouring off accumulated fat every 30 minutes or so, for at least 2 hours, or until the meat is cooked (if you're in a hurry, cover the roasting pan with foil). When you're ready to eat, roast the meat at 500°F for about 10 minutes or run them under the broiler, watching carefully, until nicely browned.

Chinese Grilled Pork Shoulder or Spareribs. Use either the oven or the grill and omit the initial rub, simply sprinkling the meat with salt and pepper. During the last half hour of slow cooking, begin basting the meat with a mixture of $^3/_4$ cup honey, $^1/_4$ cup hoisin sauce, 2 tablespoons sherry or white wine, and 1 tablespoon soy sauce. Brown as directed in Step 4, basting once or twice more and being extra careful to prevent burning.

Braised Spareribs with Cabbage

MAKES: 4 servings

TIME: About 1½ hours, largely unattended

Braised ribs give you flexibility in timing (you can braise as far in advance as you like), a no-fuss cooking process, guaranteed tenderness, and the ability to integrate vegetables into the dish. All without going outside.

Other cuts and meats you can use: baby back ribs or country-style ribs (both will become tender a little more quickly) or short ribs (which will take longer to cook).

2 tablespoons extra virgin olive oil

4 cloves garlic, peeled and crushed

2 or more dried red chiles

3 to 4 pounds spareribs, cut into individual ribs, excess fat removed

Salt and freshly ground black pepper

3 bay leaves

One 1½- to 2-pound head Savoy or green cabbage, cored and shredded

1 cup dry white wine, chicken stock (to make your own, see page 157), or water

Chopped fresh parsley leaves for garnish

1 Put the olive oil in a large, deep pot with a lid or a Dutch oven over high heat. When hot, add the garlic and chiles. When they sizzle, add the ribs, meatiest side down; sprinkle with salt and pepper and add the bay leaves. Cook, more or less undisturbed, adjusting the heat so the meat browns nicely, 5 to 10 minutes. (If the pot is crowded, you can brown the ribs in batches; or just acknowledge that your browning will be imperfect, which in this instance is okay.) Turn the ribs and brown again. Transfer the ribs to a plate.

2 Pour off any excess fat and add the cabbage and some more salt and pepper. Cook, stirring occasionally, until the cabbage browns a bit, then add the wine and stir to release any brown bits stuck to the bottom of the pan. Return the ribs to the pot; adjust the heat so the mixture bubbles steadily but not violently, and cover.

3 Cook, checking occasionally to make sure the mixture does not dry out (if it does, add a little more white wine or water). When the ribs are tender and the cabbage is very soft—this will take at least 45 minutes and possibly an hour—uncover. If the mixture is soupy, turn the heat to high and cook, stirring occasionally and carefully, until it is more of a moist stew. Garnish with parsley and serve immediately or cover and refrigerate for up to a day before reheating.

Braised Spareribs with Cabbage and Root Vegetables. Omit the chiles. Along with the cabbage, add 1 tablespoon juniper berries (or 1 teaspoon fresh thyme leaves and 1 tablespoon caraway seeds); 1 large onion, sliced; 2 medium carrots, roughly chopped; 2 celery stalks, roughly chopped; 8 ounces parsnips, roughly chopped; and 8 ounces waxy potatoes, peeled and halved or quartered. Cook as directed and garnish with parsley or chopped celery leaves.

Spareribs with Olives, Lemon, and Rosemary. For Step 1, add 3 sprigs fresh rosemary (or 1 1/2 teaspoons dried) along with the garlic. Omit the bay leaves and cabbage. Keep the ribs in the skillet; spoon out some of the fat if there's more than a couple tablespoons. Add the wine. Bring it to a boil, cook for a minute, then add 1 lemon, washed and sliced as thinly as possible, and 1 cup good oil-cured olives (pitted if you like). Proceed with Step 3.

Sesame Spareribs

MAKES: 4 servings

TIME: 45 to 60 minutes

Here you start by poaching the ribs and finish by cooking them in their own juice with a kind of dry-roasting in the fat and juices exuded by the ribs themselves, along with a dose of strong seasonings. It all results in ribs that are dark, glossy, and so tender that just a tug of the teeth will pull the meat off the bone. If possible, ask your butcher to cut the ribs into two-inch lengths, which will make them easier to cook (and to eat).

Other cuts and meats you can use: short ribs (which will take considerably longer to cook in Step 2).

3 to 4 pounds spareribs, cut into 2-inch sections

2 tablespoons chopped garlic

1/4 cup toasted sesame seeds (see page 317)

1/3 cup sugar

5 nickel-sized slices fresh ginger

1/2 cup soy sauce

2 tablespoons dark sesame oil

Salt and freshly ground black pepper

1/2 cup chopped scallion

❶ Put a large skillet that can hold the ribs in one layer over high heat and add the ribs and 1 cup water. Boil, turning the ribs occasionally, until the liquid has evaporated, about 15 minutes. Reduce the heat to medium and brown the ribs in their own fat, turning occasionally, for about 5 minutes.

❷ Add the garlic and half the sesame seeds and stir; cook for just 30 seconds. Add the sugar, ginger, soy, half the sesame oil, and another 1/2 cup water; increase the heat so the mixture bubbles steadily and cook, turning occasionally, until the liquid is thick and dark. If the ribs are tender at this point, they're ready. If not, add another 1/2 cup water and repeat the process. (You can cook in advance up to this point; cover and refrigerate before proceeding if you like.)

❸ Taste and adjust the seasoning, adding salt if necessary but sprinkling with a good amount of pepper. Add the remaining sesame seeds and sesame oil. Stir once, garnish with the scallion, and serve.

Pork Sausage and Ground Pork

Good sausage usually contains about a third as much fat as lean. Even poultry and seafood sausages must contain a bunch of fat to be good. (The best fish sausages often rely on butter or cream.) The fat allows you to make them crisp on the outside and moist on the inside. If you can't get pork fatback (plain, as opposed to salted pork fat) to mix with lean meat, just buy a fatty-looking piece of pork shoulder and don't trim the excess fat; chances are you'll get good results.

All sausages follow the same basic principle: Grind together pork, fat, and spices. You can stuff the meat into casings if you like, but it's far easier to cook patties. I use the food processor, but an old-fashioned meat grinder is just as good if not better (see "Do-It-Yourself Ground Meat," page 722).

Homemade Breakfast (or Other) Sausage

MAKES: 8 large sausages

TIME: 30 minutes

Breakfast sausages, like burgers, are far superior when you start with a whole piece of meat and season it as you like.

The variations are just a couple of possibilities. And any can be made the old-fashioned way with fatback (see below).

2½ pounds boneless pork shoulder, with its fat

1 teaspoon salt

½ teaspoon freshly ground black pepper

⅛ teaspoon freshly grated nutmeg

1 teaspoon minced fresh sage leaves or about ½ teaspoon dried sage

1 Cut the pork and fat into 1-inch cubes. Put about 2 cups of the mixture into a food processor and mince in 1-second pulses until finely chopped. Take your time and be careful not to pulverize the meat. As you finish each batch, transfer it to a bowl.

2 Season with the spices; add a little water if the mixture seems very dry. If you have time, break off a small piece, shape it into a patty, and cook it in a small skillet over medium heat until brown on both sides and cooked through. Taste it and adjust the seasonings.

3 This amount will make 8 large sausages, so you might want to freeze half if you're serving only 4 people (shape the sausage before freezing it). Shape into patties. Heat a large skillet over medium heat for 2 or 3 minutes, then add the patties. Let them cook, undisturbed, for about 5 minutes, then move them so they brown evenly. When one side is brown, turn to brown the other. Serve when nicely browned and cooked through, about 15 minutes total.

Garlic-Fennel Sausage. In Step 2, substitute 1 teaspoon or more minced garlic and 2 teaspoons fennel seeds for the nutmeg and sage; add ¼ to ½ teaspoon cayenne if you like.

Johnny Earles's Spicy Sausage. In Step 2, substitute ¼ cup minced fresh parsley leaves, 1 teaspoon minced garlic, 1 teaspoon ground coriander, 1 teaspoon ground cumin, ½ teaspoon ground dried thyme, ¼ teaspoon ground cinnamon, and ¼ teaspoon cayenne for the sage (keep the nutmeg).

Old-Fashioned Fatback Sausage. Replace ½ to ¾ pound of the shoulder (depending on how lean it is) with fresh pork fatback (not salt pork).

Italian Sausage with Peppers and Onions

MAKES: 4 servings
TIME: About 30 minutes

There are two ways to make this dish: Cook the vegetables in olive oil first, then combine them with the sausage after browning, or cook the sausages first, then use the sausage fat to cook the vegetables. The first method cuts saturated fat, the second boosts flavor; it's your choice. I detail the first method here; for the second, simply cook the sausage as directed, leave the fat in the pan, and cook the vegetables in it. Either way, when you're done, use it to fill a long bun or roll or to toss with a batch of pasta.

2 cups sliced onion

3 tablespoons extra virgin olive oil

2 bell peppers of any color, cored, peeled if desired, seeded, and cut into strips

Salt and freshly ground black pepper

1 pound fresh Italian sausage links, sweet or hot

1 Put the onion in a large skillet with a lid over medium heat, cover, and cook, undisturbed, for about 5 minutes, until the onion is dry and almost sticking to the pan. Remove the cover, add the oil, and stir. Cook for a minute or two longer, then add the peppers, salt, and pepper. Cook, stirring frequently, until the vegetables are tender and soft, about 10 more minutes. Remove the vegetables and keep warm.

2 Cook the sausage in the same pan over medium heat. Prick the sausage in a few places with a fork to allow excess fat to escape and turn the sausage frequently. Cook until nicely browned all over. Total cooking time will depend on the thickness of the sausages; the best way to determine doneness is to cut into one—when the barest trace of pink remains, they are done. Drain the sausages on a paper towel and serve with the peppers and onions.

Sautéed Sausage and Grapes. Fresh, sweet, garlicky sausage works best here. Omit the onion and bell peppers. Cook the sausage over medium-high heat until it's browned all over (it doesn't have to be cooked through). Remove it, cut it into bite-sized pieces, and return it to the pan. Continue cooking until the sausage pieces are browned, about 5 minutes. Add 2 cloves slivered garlic and cook, stirring, until the garlic is fragrant, about 2 minutes. Add 8 ounces seedless grapes and cook just enough to heat them. Sprinkle with salt and pepper, taste and adjust the seasoning, and serve immediately.

Sausage and Mashed Potatoes (Bangers and Mash). Omit Step 1. Prepare Mashed Potatoes (page 339) or use leftovers and cook the sausage as directed in Step 2. Serve the sausages with the potatoes and some good strong mustard. If you like, make a pan gravy: When the sausages have finished cooking, pour off all but 2 tablespoons of the fat. Over medium-high heat, add 1 cup stock (to make your own, see pages 155–160) or water and cook, stirring and scraping, until the liquid is reduced by half. Use this sauce for the potatoes.

Sausage and Beans. Omit Step 1. Prepare White Beans, Tuscan Style (page 427) and put in a large baking dish. Cook the sausage as directed in Step 2. Heat the oven to 350°F and, when the sausages are nearly but not quite done, nestle them in the beans. Sprinkle with bread crumbs and bake until the crumbs brown, about 15 minutes. Serve, drizzled with a little of the best olive oil you can lay your hands on.

Garlicky Pork Burger

MAKES: 4 servings
TIME: 30 minutes

F

Pork makes juicy burgers that take to all sorts of seasonings; see the list on page 723 for some ideas. Use ground pork in this recipe if you like. Simply mix all the ingredients together in a bowl until just combined, but not too much or the burgers will be tough.

1½ to 2 pounds fatty pork shoulder or three-quarters lean pork and one-quarter fat, cut into chunks

1 teaspoon salt

1 teaspoon freshly ground black pepper

1 teaspoon minced garlic

1 tablespoon fennel seeds

1 Heat a gas or charcoal grill or the broiler until moderately hot and put the rack about 4 inches from the heat source. (If you're cooking on a stovetop, when you're ready to start, heat a large, heavy skillet over medium-high heat for 3 or 4 minutes; sprinkle its surface with coarse salt.)

2 Put the meat, salt, pepper, garlic, and fennel in a food processor (in batches if your machine is small) and pulse until coarsely ground—finer than chopped, but not much. Put it in a bowl and sprinkle with salt and pepper, then taste and adjust the seasoning. (Cook a spoonful first if you like.) Handling the meat as little as possible to avoid compressing it, shape it lightly into 4 or more burgers.

3 Over a moderate fire—you should be able to hold your hand 3 or 4 inches over the rack for a few seconds—grill the burgers for about 5 minutes per side, or until medium. (Timing on the stovetop is exactly the same.) Serve on buns, toast, or hard rolls, garnished as you like.

Lemongrass Pork Burgers. To the mixture, add 3 or 4 large shallots or 1 medium red onion; another 2 garlic cloves; 2 trimmed stalks lemongrass; 1 teaspoon minced fresh chile, like jalapeño or Thai, or to taste, or hot red pepper flakes or cayenne to taste; 1 tablespoon nam pla (Thai fish sauce); and 1 teaspoon sugar. If you're using ground pork, pulse these ingredients a few times in the food processor before mixing them into the meat. If starting with chunks of pork, work all together in batches as described in the main recipe.

F Fast   **M** Make Ahead   **V** Vegetarian

The Basics of Ham

There are two basic hams: dry- and wet-cured. The first includes the world's great hams, from the Italian prosciutto to the Spanish jabugo to the best Virginia and other American country hams. In fact, most Western countries (indeed, most regions of most Western countries) have their own local ham, some smoked, some not, all cured with salt.

Wet-cured ham includes just about everything else, from the sweet, smoked, Vermont-style mail-order hams to the chemically cured hams you find at your supermarket.

Dry-cured hams keep forever (if mold appears, you just cut it away) and are best eaten in small quantities: They're too big-flavored to subdue with glazes and eat in huge slices. Cut off a sliver and make a sandwich, use a few chunks in pasta sauces, put tiny pieces on crackers, cut paper-thin slices and eat them alone or with fruit. Or cook them (see below).

Wet-cured hams are pretty much a no-brainer. You put them in the oven, heat them through, and eat them. The quality of the dish is entirely dependent on the quality of the cure. A good old-fashioned cure begins with a real brine of salt, water, and sugar and concludes with a long period of smoking. A high-tech cure begins with a chemically augmented injected brine and ends with a douse of liquid smoke. You can taste the difference. Find a brand you like—mail order is usually your best bet—and stick to it. Most supermarket hams, including canned hams, are just a step above the heavily processed ham you buy at the deli counter.

Baked Country Ham

MAKES: 15 or more servings
TIME: 36 hours, largely unattended

This soaked, glazed, and roasted ham is a rare treat worth the extra work, which is sporadic and spans out over the course of a couple days.

One 12- to 15-pound Virginia or other country ham

6 cups assorted chopped aromatic vegetables and herbs or scraps—onions, carrots, parsnips, celery, and parsley, for example

1 tablespoon black peppercorns

Several allspice berries

2 tablespoons cider or other vinegar

4 cloves, plus additional (optional) cloves for scoring ham

1 cup orange marmalade or apricot or peach preserves

1 tablespoon Dijon mustard, or more to taste

2 cups or more dry apple cider or white wine (optional)

1 If the ham is too big to fit into your biggest pot, saw off the shank. Any saw will do; just be patient. (Use the shank for soup; it will be wonderful.) Scrub the ham with a brush under running water, then soak it in cold water to cover for 24 hours, changing the water once or twice.

2 Put the ham, vegetables, peppercorns, allspice, vinegar, and 4 cloves in the pot and cover with fresh water. Bring to a boil, lower the heat, and simmer for 2 hours. Cool in its liquid for at least another 2 hours.

3 Drain the ham, discarding the cooking liquid. Skin the ham, then score the fatty layer in a diamond pattern. Insert a clove into each diamond if you like.

4 About 1 hour before you're ready to serve, heat the oven to 400°F. Put the ham on a rack in a roasting pan and, in a small saucepan, heat the marmalade or preserves over low heat until they thin slightly. Stir in 1 tablespoon or more mustard. Spoon this mixture all over the ham and bake until the outer layer is crisp and brown, about 30 minutes. If you want pan juices with which to top the ham (not necessary—it will be fine with no more than good mustard), add ½ cup of cider or wine to the bottom of the pan at the beginning of roasting and whenever it threatens to become dry.

5 Transfer the ham to a platter. To make pan juices, put the roasting pan on 1 or 2 burners over high heat. Add 1 cup of liquid to that already in the pan and cook, stirring and scraping, until the liquid has been reduced by about half and has thickened slightly. Carve the ham and serve with pan juices, mustard, or both.

Baked Wet-Cured Ham. Allow about 10 minutes of cooking time per pound. Skip steps 1 and 2. Score and stud the ham the ham with cloves as in Step 3 if you like. Heat the oven to 350°F and proceed with the recipe.

The Basics of Cooking Bacon

Bacon can be cooked almost any way you like and is incredibly useful with other ingredients. Happily, slab- and thick-cut bacon is becoming more widely available, and that—especially when naturally smoked—is the best stuff. For breakfast, figure three or four slices per serving and cook by any of the methods that follow. Doneness is a matter of taste; I like bacon cooked but still chewy, but many people prefer it crisp, almost burned. Always drain on paper towels before eating. (When you're using bacon in other dishes, draining is usually unnecessary.)

As an ingredient in other dishes, bacon is almost always better cut into chunks, big or small, than used in slices; sometimes you want to dice or mince it, in which case slices are fine as a starting place, but more often than not you'll want the chew, and you're not going to get that out of thin little pieces.

Bacon is pork belly, as is pancetta, the increasingly popular Italian form of "bacon," which isn't bacon at all, but cured, *unsmoked* pork belly. (Bacon—all bacon—is cured and smoked.) Pancetta can be used anyplace you'd use bacon, though it would make a most unusual breakfast meat.

Four Ways to Cook Bacon
Sautéing: You see what's going on, which is an advantage, and regulate the heat accordingly; but it requires

attention and invariably messes up the stove. Still, this is the most common method: Start the bacon in a large, deep skillet over medium-high heat. When it begins to sizzle, separate the slices if you haven't done so already and regulate the heat so that the slices brown evenly without burning, turning frequently. Total time will be 10 or 20 minutes, longer for large quantities.

Microwaving: The best method for three to six slices. Put the bacon on a triple layer of paper towels on a microwave-safe plate and cover with a double layer of towels. Microwave on high for 2 minutes, then check; move the pieces around a little and continue to microwave for 1-minute intervals until done. Total time will depend on the power of your microwave but will be less than 5 minutes even in a small oven.

Roasting: Slow but easy and reliable, especially for large quantities. Heat the oven to 450°F. Put the bacon in a roasting pan large enough to hold it in one layer (this may be a very large pan) and slide it into the oven. Check after 10 minutes; separate the slices if necessary. Continue to roast, turning occasionally, pouring off excess fat, and checking every 5 minutes or so; total time will be 30 minutes or so. If you like, brown under the broiler at the last minute.

Broiling: Pay close attention and this is fast and easy. Heat the broiler; set the rack about 6 inches from the heat source. Put the bacon in a roasting pan large enough to hold it in one layer (this may be a very large pan) and slide it into the oven. Check after 2 minutes; separate the slices if necessary. Continue to broil, turning occasionally, and checking every minute or two; total time will be about 10 minutes.

The Basics of Lamb

Lamb is flavorful, tender, and easy to cook, and its quality is reliable—especially compared to beef and pork. Thanks to an odd combination of factors, lamb is the closest to "natural" meat you can buy at the supermar-

F Fast   **M** Make Ahead   **V** Vegetarian

ket (sadly, there are still supermarkets that don't carry lamb), which is at least in part why it has such intense flavor.

Sheep are easy to raise and herd and can graze where other animals cannot. (Goat is similar.) Furthermore, demand for lamb has never been high, nor have prices, so producers have had little incentive to industrialize production as they have with beef and pork. As a result, I'm more comfortable buying lamb at a supermarket than any other meat.

Most lamb is best cooked rare, but not quite as rare as beef. However, it also can be quite delicious medium and even well done—this is especially true of the shoulder and chops taken from the shoulder—it has the flavor and juiciness to handle it. As for the leg, with or without the bone, its odd shape means that if the thick center is cooked to rare the thinner edges are well done. So, for once, you can satisfy everyone.

By far the smallest of the common meat animals, lamb allows us the luxury of eating whole shoulders and legs. Understanding the animal is simple:

Shoulder: Fatty and flavorful, wonderful for roasting and stewing and good cut into chops as well. Meat from this area should always be cooked medium to well done.

Shank/Breast: Inexpensive shanks are wonderful braised; the breast is usually cut into riblets, which are spectacular.

Rib: Best known for the rack of lamb, this section can also be cut into rib chops. Always good cooked rare to medium-rare.

Loin: This can be sold whole, as a saddle; it's a wonderful roast. Or it can be cut into loin chops, which are fine. It can also be boned and cut into medallions.

Leg: Sold whole or in halves, bone in or out; occasionally cut into steaks or cubed for shish kebab, for which it is wonderful.

MAJOR CUTS OF LAMB

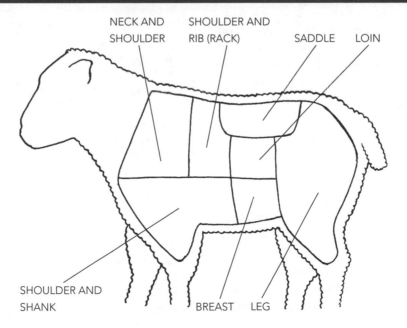

NECK AND SHOULDER

SHOULDER AND RIB (RACK)

SADDLE   LOIN

SHOULDER AND SHANK

BREAST   LEG

Chops and Stir-Fried Lamb

The cut of lamb most widely available and easiest to cook is the chop. There are several types, depending on what part of the lamb they come from. If you take a rack of lamb and cut it up, you get lamb rib chops, which are the most tender and least fatty. Loin chops, which are similar, are cut from the loin. Both rib and loin chops should be cooked rare to medium-rare. The far less expensive (and fattier) shoulder chops, however, are arguably more flavorful. They're best cooked a little longer, until just about medium.

Grilled or Broiled Lamb Chops

MAKES: 4 servings

TIME: 15 minutes

Lamb chops are a terrific convenience food, fast cooking and barely in need of seasoning—though they take to many flavors quite well. If you have a butcher or a responsive supermarket meat counter and are in the mood for a treat, you might ask for double-rib chops, which are easier to cook to medium-rare, exactly how they should be. You can also pan-grill these in a skillet; see Grilled, Pan-Grilled, or Broiled Steak, Many Ways (page 717).

4 double-rib or large shoulder lamb chops or 8 rib or loin lamb chops

Salt and freshly ground black pepper

1 clove garlic, peeled (optional)

Lemon wedges for serving

1 Heat a gas or charcoal grill or the broiler until moderately hot for double chops or very hot for single chops and put the rack about 4 inches from the heat source. Sprinkle the meat with salt and pepper. If you like, cut the clove of garlic in half and rub it over the meat. If you're broiling, about 10 minutes before you're ready to cook, put a cast-iron or other sturdy, heatproof skillet on the rack.

2 Grill or broil the chops, 3 or 4 inches from the heat source, until they are nicely browned on both sides. If they are single chops, allow no more than 2 or 3 minutes per side (even that may be too much). With double chops, there is a greater margin for error, but cooking time will most likely still be less than 10 minutes. Serve with lemon wedges.

18 Perfect Vegetable Dishes to Serve with Simply Cooked Lamb

Whether you make a bed of the vegetables and lay the lamb on top or put the lamb in the center of the plate and scatter the vegetables all around, with these simple dishes you can have a restaurant-worthy presentation in no time.

1. Sautéed Artichoke Hearts (page 254)
2. Roasted, Broiled, or Grilled Asparagus (page 258)
3. Beets Baked in Foil (page 262)
4. Beet Rösti with Rosemary (page 264)
5. Roasted Brussels Sprouts with Garlic (page 271)
6. Sautéed Cabbage with Balsamic Vinegar (page 274)
7. Roasted Carrots with Cumin (page 278)
8. Pan-Roasted Celeriac with Rosemary Butter (page 284)
9. Chard with Oranges and Shallots (page 285)
10. Pan-Roasted Corn with Cherry Tomatoes (page 290)
11. Eggplant Slices with Garlic and Parsley (page 297)
12. Fennel Baked in Stock (page 300)
13. Slow-Cooked Green Beans (page 305)
14. Leeks Braised in Oil or Butter (page 311)
15. Anything-Scented Peas (page 329)
16. Curried Stir-Fried Potatoes (page 344)
17. Stewed Tomatillos and Tomatoes (page 359)
18. Oven-Baked Ratatouille (page 373)

 Fast   Make Ahead   Vegetarian

Onion-Marinated Lamb Chops. Using the food processor or a hand grater, grate 1 medium onion. Put the onion and its juice in a bowl and toss with 1 tablespoon extra virgin olive oil, 1 teaspoon ground cumin, 1 tablespoon minced fresh cilantro leaves, and salt and pepper to taste. Spread this paste over the chops and marinate for an hour or more (refrigerate if marinating for longer than an hour). Scrape the marinade from the chops and grill or broil as directed in Step 2. Garnish with minced fresh cilantro and serve with lime wedges.

Grilled or Broiled Lamb Chops, Italian Style. Using the food processor, purée 2 or more anchovy fillets, $^1/_2$ cup fresh parsley leaves, 1 tablespoon each extra virgin olive oil and freshly squeezed lemon juice, the garlic clove, and a good sprinkling of salt and pepper. Rub the chops with half of the mixture; if you have time, marinate for an hour or so. Proceed with the recipe, basting the chops frequently with the remaining herb mixture. Serve with lemon wedges and sprinkled with chopped fresh parsley leaves.

Stir-Fried Lamb with Green Peppers

MAKES: 4 servings
TIME: 30 minutes

Green peppers are a natural with lamb because their bitterness cuts through the richness of the meat. (If bitterness isn't your thing, substitute a pound of green beans.)

Other cuts and meats you can use: beef sirloin or tenderloin; thinly sliced pork tenderloin; fresh ham, loin, or shoulder.

$^1/_4$ cup fermented black beans

$^1/_4$ cup rice wine, sherry, sake, white wine, or water

3 tablespoons neutral oil, like grapeseed or corn

3 or 4 green bell peppers, cored, seeded, and sliced

1 pound boneless lamb, preferably from the shoulder (leg is okay), cut into thin slices

1 tablespoon minced garlic

1 tablespoon minced fresh ginger

$^1/_3$ cup chicken stock (to make your own, see page 157) or water

2 tablespoons soy sauce

$^1/_2$ cup chopped scallion

1 Soak the black beans in the wine. Put 1 tablespoon of the oil in a large skillet over high heat. When the oil shimmers, add the peppers and cook, stirring only occasionally, until they brown and soften, 5 to 10 minutes. Use a slotted spoon to transfer to a bowl.

2 Add another tablespoon of the oil to the skillet. When hot, add the lamb, a couple of pieces at a time. Do not crowd; you may need to cook the lamb in 2 batches. Brown well on each side, then transfer to the bowl with the peppers.

3 Add the remaining oil, along with the garlic and ginger; cook, stirring, for 30 seconds, then add the pepper-lamb mixture, along with the soaked beans and their liquid, the stock, and the soy sauce. Cook, stirring occasionally, until the liquid is somewhat reduced (if it dries out, add a little more stock or water), 5 to 10 minutes. Stir in the scallion and serve over white rice.

Stir-Fried Lamb with Chile, Cumin, and Garlic. Use lamb shoulder and cut it into $1^1/_2$-inch cubes (freeze it until firm but not hard to make the cutting easier). Toast 1 tablespoon cumin seeds (don't use preground here) in a dry skillet over medium heat until fragrant, about 2 minutes. Toss the lamb with the cumin, $^1/_2$ teaspoon hot red pepper flakes or to taste, 1 tablespoon minced garlic, 1 tablespoon soy sauce, and salt and pepper; marinate for up to 24 hours (in the refrigerator if longer than an hour). Cook the lamb as directed in Step 2, then add 1 cup roughly chopped scallion and cook until softened and the meat is done (it's best if it's just about medium). Garnish with chopped fresh cilantro and serve immediately.

The Basics of Leg of Lamb

Leg of lamb is the near-ideal roast for six people or so—even with minimal seasoning, its flavor can power a meal. With lots of herbs and spices, it's the greatest and the ideal excuse to break out that good bottle of red wine you've been hoarding. Buy the leg without the shank, which doesn't take that well to roasting, adds expense, and necessitates a longer roasting pan.

You can also buy half-legs of lamb; the butt half is preferable. Plan on cooking times for a 3- to 4-pound half-leg to be about two-thirds of what they are for a whole leg. Consider, too, boneless leg, now sold almost as frequently as bone-in. There's no waste, and it's far easier to deal with—especially when grilling, where you can "butterfly" it (see page 772).

Roast Leg of Lamb, Four Ways

MAKES: At least 6 servings
TIME: About 1½ hours, largely unattended

The main recipe is classic and basic, but I prefer the wonderfully strong-flavored variations, all of which work perfectly with grilled leg of lamb too (see the following recipe). You can also use any of these with boned leg—just cut the cooking time by about half.

Other cuts and meats you can use: thick cuts of London broil or flank steak.

One 5- to 7-pound leg of lamb, preferably at room temperature

1 teaspoon salt

1 teaspoon freshly ground black pepper

CARVING LEG OF LAMB

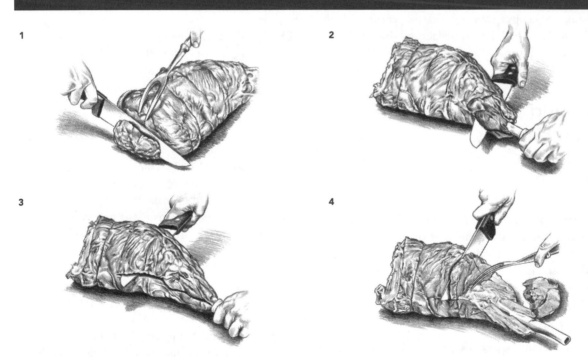

(**STEP 1**) To carve a leg of lamb, take a slice or two off the thick end and set aside. (**STEPS 2–3**) Make a long slice parallel to the cutting board as close to the bone as is possible. (**STEP 4**) Cut thin slices from the top of the leg.

     F Fast   **M** Make Ahead   **V** Vegetarian

2 pounds waxy red or white potatoes, peeled and cut into 1¹/₂-inch chunks

4 carrots, cut into 1¹/₂-inch chunks

2 onions, quartered

¹/₂ cup chicken, beef, or vegetable stock (to make your own, see pages 157–159) or water, plus more as needed

1 Heat the oven to 425°F. Remove as much of the surface fat as possible from the lamb; rub the meat all over with salt and pepper. Put it in a roasting pan and scatter the vegetables around it; moisten with ¹/₂ cup of the stock.

2 Roast the lamb for 30 minutes, then turn the heat down to 350°F. Check the vegetables; if they're dry, add another ¹/₂ cup of liquid. After about 1 hour of roasting, check the internal temperature of the lamb with an instant-read thermometer. Continue to check every 10 minutes, adding a little more liquid if necessary. When it reaches 130°F for medium-rare (125°F for very rare)—check it in several places—it is done (total cooking time will be less than 1¹/₂ hours). Let it rest for a few minutes before carving. Serve with the vegetables and pan juices.

Roast Leg of Lamb with Thyme and Orange. Omit the vegetables and stock. Mix the salt and pepper with 3 tablespoons minced fresh thyme leaves or 1¹/₂ tablespoons dried, 1 tablespoon minced garlic, and 1 tablespoon minced or grated orange zest. Use a thin-bladed knife to cut some small slits in the lamb and push a bit of the herb mixture into them; rub the lamb all over with the remaining mixture. If you have time, let the lamb sit for an hour or more (refrigerate if it will be much longer). Roast as directed in Step 2.

Roast Leg of Lamb with Garlic and Coriander Seeds. Include or omit the vegetables as you like. Mix the salt and pepper with 2 tablespoons crushed coriander seeds (put them in a plastic bag and pound gently with a rolling pin, rubber mallet, or like object)

and 1 teaspoon minced garlic. Use a thin-bladed knife to cut some small slits in the lamb and push a bit of the spices into them; rub the lamb all over with the remaining spices. If you have time, let the lamb sit for an hour or more (refrigerate if it will be much longer). Roast as directed in Step 2, omitting the liquid if you choose to omit the vegetables. This roast is better closer to medium than to rare—about 135°F.

Roast Leg of Lamb with Anchovies. Include or omit the vegetables as you like. Mix the salt and pepper with 1 tablespoon minced fresh rosemary leaves or 1 teaspoon dried, 1 tablespoon minced garlic, 3 or 4 minced anchovy fillets (optional), and 2 tablespoons olive or anchovy oil. Use a thin-bladed knife to cut some small slits in the lamb and push a bit of the spices into them; rub the lamb all over with the remaining spices. If you have time, let the lamb sit for an hour or more (refrigerate if it will be longer). Roast as directed in Step 2, omitting the liquid if you choose to omit the vegetables. When the meat is done, transfer it to a warm platter. Spoon or pour off most of the accumulated fat from the roasting pan and put it on 1 or 2 burners over medium-high heat. Add ¹/₂ cup red wine or stock and ¹/₂ cup water and cook, scraping the bottom of the pan with a wooden spoon to release any brown bits until the liquid is reduced to ¹/₂ to ³/₄ cup. Carve the lamb and serve with the sauce; garnish with sprigs of rosemary if you have them.

Grilled or Broiled Butterflied Leg of Lamb

MAKES: At least 6 servings
TIME: About 40 minutes

There's really little point in grilling a bone-in leg of lamb, especially since butterflied leg is now often sold in supermarkets. It's not cheap, but it's not that expensive either, and it's delicious, tender, and easy to cook. Even the uneven thickness is an asset: Cook the thickest parts to rare and you also get meat that is cooked to medium, which is still quite moist and tender, so everyone's happy.

The variation suggests only one of many possibilities for spicing this lamb; see the list that follows for more ideas. And if your lamb is larger than the recipe calls for, simply increase the other ingredients proportionately or cut off a chunk to freeze for later.

One to 3- to 4-pound butterflied leg of lamb

1 tablespoon extra virgin olive oil

1 teaspoon minced garlic

1 tablespoon fresh rosemary leaves or 2 teaspoons dried rosemary

2 teaspoons fresh thyme leaves or 1 teaspoon dried thyme

Salt and freshly ground black pepper

Minced fresh parsley leaves for garnish

Lemon wedges for serving

❶ Heat a charcoal or gas grill or the broiler until quite hot and put the rack at least 4 inches from the heat source. (Delay this step until you're just about ready to cook if you choose to marinate the meat.) Trim the lamb

BONING LEG OF LAMB

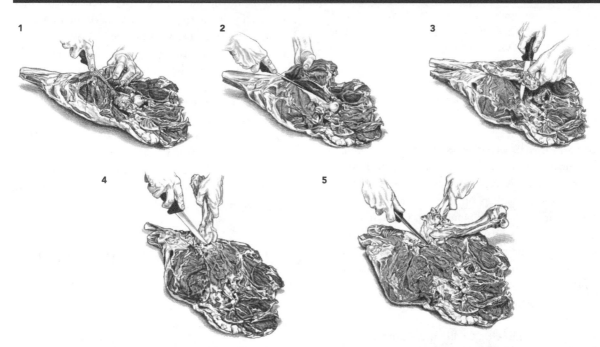

Like all boning jobs, this involves finding the bone and separating it from the meat; since the two adjoining bones in a leg of lamb are both large, it's really just a matter of patience. **(STEPS 1–2)** Turn the leg smooth side down and use a boning knife to cut on either side of the large bone, scraping off the meat. **(STEP 3)** When you can get under the bone, cut the meat away from there too. **(STEPS 4–5)** Lift the bone up and find the point at which it meets the smaller bone; cut that one away as well.

❶ Fast   Ⓜ Make Ahead   Ⓥ Vegetarian

of any excess fat. Mix together the olive oil, garlic, rosemary, thyme, and some salt and pepper; rub this mixture well into the lamb, being sure to get some into all the crevices. If you have the time, let the lamb sit for at least an hour (refrigerate if it will be much longer).

❷ Grill or broil the meat (best done in a roasting pan with a rack) until it is nicely browned, even a little charred, on both sides, about 20 to 30 minutes; the internal temperature at the thickest part will be about 125°F; this will give you some lamb that is quite rare and some that is nearly well done. Let rest for 5 minutes before slicing thinly, as you would a thick steak. Garnish and serve with lemon wedges.

Butterflied Leg of Lamb with Provençal Spices. For the herbs in Step 1, substitute 1 teaspoon chopped fresh or dried lavender, 1 teaspoon chopped fresh or dried rosemary, and ¹/₂ teaspoon fennel seeds.

6 Other Concoctions to Smear on Butterflied Leg of Lamb

1. Cumin mixed with a little honey and some minced orange peel
2. Minced ginger and scallion mixed with soy sauce
3. Traditional Pesto (page 27)
4. Curry powder or similar spice mixture (to make your own, see pages 65–69), moistened with a bit of yogurt
5. Roasted garlic pulp, mixed with olive oil and chopped fresh mint
6. A paste made by puréeing ¹/₂ cup coconut milk (to make your own, see page 389), an inch or two of fresh ginger, a bunch of scallions, an onion, a pinch of saffron or turmeric, and a large pinch of salt

Braised and Stewed Lamb

Wherever there is lamb there is lamb stew. I give many variations here, but all you have to remember if you want to experiment is to discard as much of the hard lamb fat

as you can when trimming the meat and start the vegetables after the lamb so they do not overcook and disintegrate.

The shoulder has become my favorite cut of lamb. It's lovely roasted, though it's a little too fatty for grilling, at least whole. But it's amazing when stewed or braised, and it doesn't take that long. Shoulders are usually sold in pieces (you have to ask for them whole), with the bone in or out; needless to say, boned chunks are the most convenient.

Prepare the stew a day before eating it if you like; this will allow you to skim excess fat from the surface, and the flavors will improve as well. Lamb stew freezes perfectly, so don't worry about making it as long as a week in advance or about doubling or tripling these recipes.

Lamb Stew with Mushrooms

MAKES: 4 to 6 servings
TIME: 1¹/₂ to 2 hours, largely unattended

Most of us don't have access to truly "wild" mushrooms, so try a combination of dried porcini with fresh shiitakes and button mushrooms. Serve this with buttered noodles, rice or other whole grain, or crisp bread.

Other cuts and meats you can use: boneless pork shoulder, veal shoulder, or beef chuck or brisket (which will require somewhat longer cooking time).

¹/₂ ounce dried porcini

2 tablespoons extra virgin olive oil

2 pounds boneless lamb shoulder, trimmed of excess fat and cut into 2-inch cubes, or 3 to 4 pounds bone-in lamb shoulder or neck, cut into roughly 2-inch chunks

Salt and freshly ground black pepper

8 ounces shiitake mushrooms, stems discarded (or saved for stock), sliced

8 ounces button mushrooms, trimmed and sliced

3 or 4 sprigs fresh thyme

1 tablespoon minced garlic

1 cup red wine or stock (to make your own, see pages 157–159)

Minced fresh parsley leaves for garnish

1 Soak the porcini in hot water to cover.

2 Put the olive oil in a large, deep skillet with a lid or a Dutch oven over medium-high heat. When hot, add the lamb chunks a few at a time, removing them as they brown and seasoning with salt and pepper as they cook. When they are all nicely browned, which will take 5 to 10 minutes, pour or spoon off the excess fat, then add the shiitakes, button mushrooms, drained porcini (reserve the soaking liquid), and thyme. Cook, stirring occasionally, until the mushrooms begin to brown, 5 to 10 minutes. Add the garlic and continue cooking until the mushrooms are dry and lightly browned, 5 minutes longer.

3 Add the wine, along with about $^1/_2$ cup of the porcini liquid and some salt and pepper. Bring to a boil, return the lamb to the pan, turn the heat to low, and cover. Cook at a steady bubble, checking and stirring occasionally, until the lamb is tender, about an hour (at most 90 minutes) later. (At this point, you may let the dish sit for a few hours or cover and refrigerate for up to a day before reheating and proceeding.)

4 Remove the cover; if the mixture is soupy, raise the heat a bit and cook until the sauce thickens. Taste and adjust the seasoning, then garnish with parsley and serve.

Lamb Stew with Vinegar. Use a whole head of garlic, separated into cloves, in place of the tablespoon of minced garlic. For the liquid, use $^1/_3$ cup good red wine vinegar mixed with $^1/_2$ cup stock (to make your own, see pages 157–159).

Lamb Stew with Mushrooms and Olives. As the lamb gets close to tenderness in Step 3, add 1 cup good black or green olives (or a mixture; in any case there's no need to pit as long as you warn your guests!) and finish the cooking with them in the pot.

Irish Stew. Omit all the mushrooms and skip Step 1. In Step 2, after removing the lamb from the pot, stir in 1 chopped onion. Proceed with the recipe, adding 1 pound waxy potatoes (peeled or unpeeled) to the pot during the last 30 minutes of cooking.

Lamb Stew with Eggplant or Green Beans. Omit all the mushrooms and skip Step 1. Salt 3 cups peeled and cubed eggplant (see page 293) or trim and cut in half 3 cups green beans. In Step 2, sauté the eggplant or green beans after cooking the lamb. When soft and turning color, add 1 teaspoon minced garlic and 1 cup chopped tomato (drained canned is fine). Add more liquid if the mixture is dry.

Lamb Stew with White Beans. Keep or omit the mushrooms as you like. Prepare 8 ounces of cannellini or other white beans as described in Cooked Beans, the Quick-Soak Way (page 411). (If you put raw beans in, they will take too long for the lamb.) For Step 1, brown the meat and mushrooms if you're using them. In Step 2, drain the beans (saving their liquid), then add them along with the lamb. Cook, stirring occasionally and scraping the bottom to make sure the beans do not burn; add a little of the bean liquid if necessary.

Lamb Stew with Cinnamon. Omit the porcini, button mushrooms, and thyme. In Step 2, use stock or water (not wine) and add 2 cloves, $^1/_2$ teaspoon ground cinnamon, and one 6-ounce can tomato paste. Mix well. After 30 minutes, add 20 peeled pearl onions (frozen are fine) and 1 tablespoon red wine vinegar. Remove the toothpicks, then garnish with parsley and serve over rice or broad noodles.

Lamb Stew with Orange. For Step 1, substitute 1 large chopped onion, 2 chopped carrots, and 1 chopped celery stalk for the porcini and button mushrooms; cook until the vegetables start to brown. For Step 2, add the juice of 1 orange along with the wine; push a clove into one of the orange halves and add it to the lamb.

Lamb Curry

MAKES: 4 to 6 servings

TIME: About 1½ hours, largely unattended

For this it's really worth making your own curry powder if you have 10 minutes (see pages 66–67). This simple difference is remarkable. Then, if you're really feeling ambitious, make a batch of Chapati (page 848) while the meat simmers.

  2 tablespoons peanut or other neutral oil, like grapeseed or corn

  2 pounds boneless lamb shoulder, trimmed of excess fat and cut into 2-inch cubes, or 3 to 4 pounds bone-in lamb shoulder or neck, cut into chunks

  Salt and freshly ground black pepper

  2 cups thinly sliced onion, plus 1 cup chopped onion

  1 tablespoon minced garlic

  1 tablespoon minced or grated fresh ginger or 1 teaspoon ground ginger

  2 tablespoons curry powder or garam masala (to make your own, see pages 66–67)

  ½ teaspoon cayenne (optional)

  1½ cups chicken, beef, or vegetable stock (to make your own, see pages 157–159), stock made from lamb bones, or water, plus more as needed

  ½ cup yogurt

  Minced fresh cilantro leaves for garnish

❶ Put the oil in a large, deep skillet with a lid or a Dutch oven over medium-high heat. When hot, add the lamb chunks a few at a time and brown them on all sides, removing them as they brown and sprinkling with salt and pepper as they cook. (You can also do the initial browning in the oven: Heat to 500°F and roast the lamb chunks—you may omit the oil—turning once or twice, until brown all over; time will be about the same, 20 minutes.) Drain off all but 2 tablespoons of the fat. Cook the sliced onion over medium heat, stirring occasionally, until golden brown, 10 to 15 minutes.

❷ Add the chopped onion, garlic, ginger, spice mixture, and the cayenne if you're using it. Stir and cook over medium heat for 3 or 4 minutes, until the chopped onion softens.

❸ Return the lamb to the pot along with the stock. Bring to a boil, cover, turn the heat to low, and bubble gently until the lamb is tender, at least 1 hour. Remove the cover and, if the mixture is too soupy, turn the heat to high and reduce it a bit. (If it's too dry, which is unlikely, add ½ to 1 cup more liquid and cook for 10 minutes before proceeding.) Taste and adjust the seasoning. (At this point, you may refrigerate the curry for a day or two before reheating and proceeding.) Stir in the yogurt, remove from the heat, and serve, garnished with the cilantro.

Lamb Curry with Coconut Milk. In Step 1, pour off all the fat after the lamb is browned and cook the sliced onion in 3 tablespoons butter. In Step 2, add 1 teaspoon ground turmeric (or several saffron threads, crushed between your fingers) along with the other spices. In Step 3, substitute coconut milk (to make your own, see page 389) for some or all of the stock; use more coconut milk in place of the yogurt.

Lamb Couscous

MAKES: 4 to 6 servings

TIME: About 1 hour

The couscous stretches this dish out quite a bit and absorbs all the lovely flavors of the braising liquid.

Other cuts and meats you can use: cubes of beef chuck, round, or brisket.

Other grains you can use: bulgur, precooked cracked wheat.

  2 tablespoons neutral oil, like grapeseed or corn, or extra virgin olive oil

  1½ to 2 pounds boneless lamb shoulder, cut into 1- to 2-inch chunks

Salt and freshly ground black pepper

1 large onion, chopped

3 tablespoons chopped garlic

Two 3-inch cinnamon sticks or 1 teaspoon ground cinnamon

2 teaspoons ground coriander

1 teaspoon ground cumin

2 cups lamb, beef, or chicken stock (to make your own, see pages 157–159) or water

1/2 cup raisins

Large pinch saffron threads (optional)

1/4 cup chopped fresh mint leaves or 1 tablespoon dried mint

1 cup couscous

1 Put the oil in a saucepan with a lid over medium-high heat. When hot, add the lamb, sprinkle with salt and pepper, and cook, stirring occasionally, until browned, about 10 minutes. Drain off the excess fat, add the onion, and cook until softened, about 2 minutes. Add the garlic, cinnamon, coriander, and cumin and cook for another minute.

2 Pour in the stock, add the raisins and the saffron if you're using it, add another sprinkle of salt, and bring to a boil. Turn the heat down to low so it bubbles steadily but not violently; cook, stirring once or twice, until the meat is tender, about 40 minutes. (At this point, you may refrigerate the lamb for a day or two; reheat gently before proceeding.)

3 Stir in the mint and couscous, cover, and turn off the heat; let sit for 5 to 7 minutes without disturbing. Taste and adjust the seasoning and serve.

Chicken Couscous. Substitute chicken thighs or legs for the lamb. Reduce the cooking time in Step 2 to 25 to 30 minutes.

Vegetable Couscous. Substitute peeled and cubed butternut squash, sweet or white potatoes, cauliflower, zucchini or summer squash, eggplant, cabbage, or a mixture of any of these for the lamb. Add 1 cup

cooked and drained chickpeas too if you like. Add the vegetables and chickpeas along with the stock (use chicken or vegetable stock) and cook until tender, 20 to 30 minutes.

Lamb Shanks

Lamb shanks are cheap, delicious, and soothing; simmer some on a cold winter night, open a bottle of red wine, and relax. Like most meats that take best to braising, they can be cooked in advance—up to a day or two if you refrigerate them, up to a week or two if you freeze them. Skim excess fat from the top before reheating.

You can braise lamb shanks on top of the stove or in the oven; I give examples of both methods here. Note, too, that lamb shanks take well to Asian seasonings; try them in the recipe for Anise-Scented Short Ribs (page 741).

Lamb Shanks with Tomatoes and Olives

MAKES: 4 servings

TIME: 2 hours or more, largely unattended

M

The briny flavor of olives makes this dish, so buy good ones. My favorites here are a mixture of the big green kind from southern Italy and kalamatas or the small dried olives from Morocco or Greece.

Other cuts and meats you can use: short ribs (which will also take a long time); chunks of lamb or pork shoulder (which will be faster) or beef chuck or brisket; bone-in chicken parts (which will be much quicker), preferably thighs.

1 tablespoon extra virgin olive oil

4 lamb shanks, about 1 pound each

Salt and freshly ground black pepper

2 cups sliced onion

1 tablespoon minced garlic

$^1/_2$ teaspoon fresh thyme leaves, a couple sprigs fresh thyme, or $^1/_2$ teaspoon dried thyme

$^1/_2$ cup chicken, beef, or vegetable stock (to make your own, see pages 157–159), white or red wine, water, or a combination

1 cup chopped tomato (drained canned is fine)

1$^1/_2$ cups assorted olives, pitted

Minced fresh basil or parsley leaves for garnish

1 Put the oil in a large pot with a lid or a Dutch oven over medium-high heat. When hot, add the shanks and brown on all sides, sprinkling with salt and pepper as they cook. (You can also do the initial browning in the oven: Heat to 500°F and roast the lamb shanks—you may omit the oil—turning once or twice, until brown all over; this will take a little longer but will be somewhat easier and much neater.) Remove the lamb and pour off all but 2 tablespoons of fat. Add the onion and cook over medium heat, stirring occasionally, until softened and golden, about 10 minutes.

2 Add the garlic and thyme and cook for another minute, then add the liquid, some salt and pepper, and the tomato; stir to blend. Return the lamb shanks to the pan, turn them once or twice, cover, and turn the heat to low.

3 Cook for 30 minutes, turn the shanks, and add the olives. Continue to cook for at least another hour, turning occasionally, until the shanks are very tender (a toothpick inserted into them will meet little resistance) and the meat is nearly falling from the bone. (At this point, you may refrigerate the shanks for a day or two and then reheat.) Garnish with basil or parsley and serve.

Lamb Shanks with Pasilla Chile Sauce. Soak 3 to 5 pasilla or other mild dried red chiles in hot water to cover until soft, about 30 minutes. Meanwhile, proceed with Step 1, adding 1 cup chopped tomato along with the onion. Transfer the onion mixture to a food processor. Drain the chiles, reserving the soaking liquid, and tear them into pieces while removing their

stems and seeds. Add the chiles to the processor along with 2 cloves garlic and purée, adding the chile liquid as necessary to get a smooth paste. In Step 2, substitute 1 tablespoon fresh marjoram or oregano leaves or 1 teaspoon dried for the thyme and add the chile purée with the stock or water (don't use wine). Sprinkle in salt and pepper and 1 teaspoon ground cumin. Proceed with the recipe, omitting the olives.

Lamb Shanks with Lentils

MAKES: 4 servings

TIME: At least 2 hours, largely unattended

From the countryside in the south of France, this rustic one-pot meal combines lentils, lamb, red wine, and little else. Once they simmer for a couple of hours, the lentils turn super-tender and hold all the flavors. If you like, sear the lamb first, following Step 1 of the previous recipe.

Other cuts and meats you can use: beef short ribs.

12 ounces dried lentils, preferably lentilles du Puy (see page 432), rinsed and picked over

2 medium carrots, chopped

1 onion, chopped

4 sprigs fresh thyme or 1 teaspoon dried thyme

1 tablespoon minced garlic

2 bay leaves

1 bottle dry red wine, or more as needed

4 lamb shanks, about 1 pound each

Salt and freshly ground black pepper

1 Heat the oven to 400°F. Combine the lentils, carrots, onion, thyme, garlic, bay leaves, and wine in a roasting pan or Dutch oven and stir; bring to a boil on top of the stove, then nestle the lamb shanks among the lentils, cover the pan (aluminum foil will do), and put in the oven. Lower the heat to 350°F and cook, undisturbed, for about an hour.

2 Uncover and stir the lentils gently; sprinkle with salt and pepper. Re-cover and cook for about an hour longer, until the lentils are very tender and the lamb begins to pull away from the bone; if at any point the mixture threatens to dry out, add more liquid wine or water. Don't worry about overcooking the lentils; just make sure the lamb is done. When the lamb is tender, uncover the pan, raise the heat to 400°F, and cook for another 15 minutes or so, just to brown the top a bit. Taste and adjust the seasoning and serve or refrigerate for up to a day before reheating.

Lamb Rack, Breast, and Ribs

Lamb rack is expensive and luxurious, delicious and virtually foolproof. And the traditional bread crumbs–garlic–parsley treatment has never been bettered. Boned sections of rack or saddle, sometimes called *boneless loin,* can be cut into medallions, cooked quickly, and served with a wine reduction; this is a wonderful dish to make for an intimate dinner for two.

The ribs, on the other hand, are cheap and unfortunately hard to find; sometimes you'll find them sold as "breast of lamb," and you just have to cut them up, which is easy enough. Like other ribs, these are good for grilling but must be parboiled first. After that initial treatment, which is neither time-consuming nor difficult, treat them as you would any other ribs.

Roast Rack of Lamb with Persillade

MAKES: 4 servings
TIME: 30 minutes

F

Do the math: Seven ribs per rack, with only a couple of bites per rib, means you need two racks for four people. But fourteen ribs could easily serve five or even six peo-

ple, with plenty of side dishes. Make sure the chine bone is removed (ask the butcher) so you can easily cut through the ribs to separate them at the table. But don't bother to ask to have the ribs "frenched" (the meat removed from the top of the bones); the crisp meat along the bones is one of the pleasures of a rack of lamb. You didn't want to use little frilly doilies on top of the bones anyway, did you?

> 2 racks of lamb, about 2 pounds each
>
> 2 tablespoons extra virgin olive oil
>
> Salt and freshly ground black pepper
>
> 1 cup bread crumbs, preferably fresh (page 876)
>
> ½ cup minced fresh parsley leaves
>
> 1 teaspoon minced garlic

1 Heat the oven to 500°F. Trim the lamb of excess fat, but leave a layer of fat over the meat. Cut about halfway down the bones between the chops; this allows the meat between them to become crisp.

2 Combine the remaining ingredients and rub over the meat side of the racks. Put them in a roasting pan and put in the oven; roast for 20 minutes and insert an instant-read meat thermometer straight in from one end into the meatiest part. If it reads 125°F or more, remove the lamb immediately. If it reads less, put the lamb back for 5 minutes, no more. Remove and let sit for 5 minutes. Serve, separating the ribs by cutting down straight through them.

Grilled or Broiled Lamb Ribs

MAKES: 4 servings
TIME: 1 hour

When you see lamb breast—you may have to cut it up yourself, but it isn't hard—or lamb ribs, grab 'em. These tasty bites make wonderful eating but take a two-step cooking process: They must be parboiled before grilling or broiling. If you skip the parboiling step, they'll be tough and virtually inedible.

If you start with whole breast, cut it into large sections and parboil it; then separate into ribs before grilling.

4 pounds lamb breast, whole or in riblets

Salt and freshly ground black pepper

$1/2$ cup orange marmalade or maple syrup

$1/4$ cup Dijon mustard

1 tablespoon red wine vinegar or sherry vinegar

1 teaspoon ground cumin

1 Bring a large pot of water to a boil and salt it. Add the lamb and simmer for 30 minutes if the ribs are already separate, 45 minutes if the breast is in large sections. Meanwhile, heat a charcoal or gas grill or the broiler until moderately hot and put the rack at least 4 inches from the heat source.

2 Drain the ribs and let them sit until cool enough to handle. Mix together all the remaining ingredients. If necessary, cut the sections into individual ribs (just cut between them with a boning knife) and grill or broil them, basting frequently with the sauce. These burn very easily, so turn frequently and watch carefully. When they are brown and crisp all over—no more than 10 or at the most 15 minutes—remove from the grill and serve.

5 Other Basting Sauces for Grilled or Broiled Lamb Ribs
1. Tahini Sauce (page 35)
2. Simple Miso Dipping Sauce (page 39)
3. Balsamic Syrup (page 51)
4. Basic Barbecue Sauce (page 52)
5. Coconut Curry Vinaigrette (page 202)

The Basics of Veal

Veal production spurred the original charge against inhumanely raised meat—many calves were (and still are) tightly confined. And "milk-raised" veal (raised on formula, not mother's milk) is still objectionable. But the good news is that it's easier than ever to find what the USDA calls "calf," which is also sold as "humanely raised" or "natural" veal. There is organic and free-range veal out there also, though mostly what you see in conventional supermarkets remains so-called milk-fed. With veal as with other meat, the closer you get to traditional farming practices the better.

As for cooking: Regardless of the kind of veal you buy, it will be quite lean. And even though veal is a young cow, its cuts are more similar to lamb than beef. Properly cooked, it will also be quite tender. Those cuts that are tender enough to be cooked with dry heat, primarily the chop and the rear leg, should not be overcooked. Medium—that is, with some pinkness but no redness in the interior—is how I prefer this veal, about 140°F on an instant-read thermometer. Stop cooking when the meat measures about 135°F or a little more and you'll hit it right.

Ways to Use Game in These Recipes

Whether you can get your hands on truly wild game—caught by hunters—or some of the farm-raised "game" now available, cooking with either is not any different from cooking with other meats. Just one word of caution: Game tends to be very lean. (Wild animals run around a lot.) So if you're grilling, searing, broiling, or sautéing, be extra careful not to overcook. And if you're braising, be sure to let the meat simmer long enough to get fully tender.

Here's a simple list of substitutions for cooking with game:
1. Use beef recipes for venison.
2. Use pork recipes for wild boar.
3. Use lamb recipes for goat (which is not exactly game but is still a specialty meat).
4. Use chicken recipes for rabbit (see page 753).

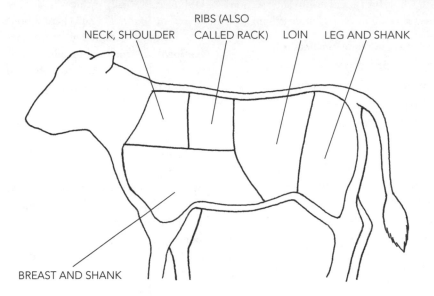

NECK, SHOULDER RIBS (ALSO CALLED RACK) LOIN LEG AND SHANK

BREAST AND SHANK

Braised veal, including osso buco, veal breast, and the cut-up shoulder, neck, and pieces from the leg that are sold as stew, must be cooked until well done and tender. However, this often takes considerably less time than corresponding cuts of beef.

Shoulder: Best for stew and roasts (blade roast, arm roast) cooked with liquid. Do not buy steaks (or chops) from this section (labeled *arm* or *shoulder steaks, blade steak*); they will be tough.

Rib: Rib chops are superb. Veal rib roasts, which are manageable in size and quite nice (and are also called *rack of veal*), may be sold bone in or out; unfortunately, they are not seen very often.

Loin: Also wonderful for chops, the loin provides good roasts, especially the boneless (and expensive) saddle roast.

Sirloin: Not that desirable in veal. Neither chops nor roasts are as good as those from the rib or loin.

Leg: Thin slices are cut for veal scallops or cutlets (or scaloppine). Rump or round roasts are neither tender nor flavorful, but roast veal leg—bone in—is a treat.

Flank: Almost always ground.

Breast: Usually sold whole (breast of veal) and can be cooked bone in or boned, in which case it is usually stuffed (you can make Matambre with it, if you like; see page 737).

Shank: Great for Osso Buco (page 784) or roasted whole.

Grilled or Broiled Veal Chops

MAKES: 4 servings
TIME: 30 minutes

Excellent veal chops are a rare occurrence, so you will want to keep things simple and savor the meat. My favorite way is to rub the meat lightly with good olive oil, then give it the perfume of rosemary and garlic.

Veal chops are best medium-rare to medium; figure 8 to 10 minutes total cooking for a 1-inch-thick chop (an

    Fast   Make Ahead   **V** Vegetarian

instant-read thermometer should read 130°F or a little more).

Other cuts and meats you can use: thick-cut, bone-in or butterflied pork loin chop.

4 veal loin or rib chops, 6 to 10 ounces each

1 clove garlic, halved

3 tablespoons extra virgin olive oil

1 tablespoon minced fresh rosemary leaves or
    1 teaspoon dried rosemary

Salt and freshly ground black pepper

1 Heat a charcoal or gas grill or the broiler until quite hot and put the rack no more than 4 inches from the heat source. As the fire heats, let the chops reach room temperature if you haven't already done so.

2 Rub the chops all over with the split garlic, then with 2 tablespoons of the olive oil. Mix most of the rosemary with some salt and pepper and rub this into the chops well.

3 Grill or broil the chops for 5 minutes. Turn, grill or broil for 4 minutes longer, and check for doneness; the center should be fairly pink. Drizzle with the remaining olive oil, sprinkle with a tiny bit more rosemary, and serve.

Veal Cutlets, 1950s Style

MAKES: 4 servings
TIME: 30 minutes

F

Back in the 1950s and 1960s, before we "discovered" boneless chicken breasts, slices of veal cut from the leg—called *cutlets, scallops,* or *scaloppine*—were the only thin, tender, boneless meat widely available. If you're lucky enough to find good veal cutlets, they are still wonderful when sautéed in olive oil and drenched in freshly squeezed lemon juice. You can make any of the following recipes with thinly pounded chicken or turkey cutlets, just as you can use most boneless chicken breast recipes for veal.

Other cuts and meats you can use: pork tenderloin, thinly sliced and pounded; also see above.

1¼ to 1½ pounds thinly sliced veal from the leg
    (scaloppine)

¼ cup extra virgin olive oil, or a little more

All-purpose flour for dredging

Bread crumbs, preferably fresh (page 876), for
    dredging

2 eggs

Salt and freshly ground black pepper

½ cup dry white wine

Juice of 1 lemon

Chopped fresh parsley leaves for garnish

1 lemon, quartered, for serving

1 Heat the oven to 200°F. The cutlets should be less than ¼ inch thick; if they're not, pound them gently (I use a flat rolling pin, but you can use the back of a skillet or a wine bottle) between 2 sheets of wax paper.

2 Put the olive oil in a large skillet over medium heat while you set out the flour and bread crumbs on plates and beat the eggs lightly in a small bowl. Sprinkle the flour liberally with salt and pepper. Set everything near the stove.

3 When the oil is hot (a pinch of flour will sizzle), dredge the cutlets, one at a time, in the flour, then dip in the egg, then dredge in the bread crumbs. Add them to the skillet as they're ready, cooking in batches if necessary to avoid crowding. Cook them over heat high enough to make the oil bubble, adding oil as needed.

4 Turn the cutlets as soon as they're browned, then cook the other side, a total of 5 minutes or less. As each piece of veal is done, transfer it to an ovenproof platter; after a few cutlets, put the platter in the oven and add to it as more cutlets cook.

5 When all the veal is finished, pour off the fat. Return the skillet to the stove and add the wine over medium-high heat. Cook, stirring, until the wine is just about evaporated, about 5 minutes. Add the lemon juice, stir, and pour this sauce (there won't be more than a few tablespoons) over the veal. Garnish and serve, passing lemon quarters at the table.

Veal Cutlets with Rosemary and Parmesan. Combine ¹/₂ cup freshly grated Parmesan cheese, ¹/₂ cup bread crumbs, 1 tablespoon minced fresh rosemary leaves or 1 teaspoon dried rosemary, and some salt and pepper in a bowl. In Step 3, dredge in flour and egg if you like or in just bread crumbs and Parmesan. Proceed with the recipe, skipping Step 5 and serving the veal with lemon quarters as soon as it's cooked.

Veal Parmigiana. Heat the oven to 450°F, then proceed with the recipe through Step 4, but undercook the cutlets slightly (less than 4 minutes per cutlet total cooking time). Put all the cutlets in a baking dish without overlapping (use 2 dishes if necessary). Top each with a spoonful or two of any tomato sauce you like (see pages 502–504) and then with a thin slice of mozzarella. Put the baking dish in the oven and cook just until the cheese melts, 5 to 10 minutes. Serve immediately.

Veal Paprikas

MAKES: 4 servings
TIME: 25 minutes

A liberal dose of paprika is the hallmark of this classic Hungarian dish, but it's balanced by the sour cream. The variations take the same cut in an Italian direction. All ways are good over buttered egg noodles, pasta, or rice, or with bread.

Other cuts and meats you can use: cutlets or chunks of pork, chicken, or turkey.

12 thin slices of veal from the leg (scaloppine), 1¹/₂ to 2 pounds

Salt and freshly ground black pepper

¹/₄ cup freshly squeezed lemon juice

1 cup sour cream

¹/₂ cup chicken stock (to make your own, see page 157)

¹/₂ cup all-purpose flour

3 tablespoons neutral oil, like grapeseed or corn

1 onion, sliced

1 tablespoon minced garlic (optional)

1 tablespoon hot paprika, plus a sprinkling for garnish

Chopped fresh parsley leaves for garnish (optional)

❶ The cutlets should be less than ¹/₄ inch thick; if they're not, pound them gently (I use a flat rolling pin, but you can use the back of a skillet or a wine bottle) between 2 sheets of wax paper. Lightly sprinkle salt, pepper, and the lemon juice over the veal. Whisk together the sour cream and stock. Put the flour on a plate.

❷ Put the oil in a large skillet over medium-high heat. When hot, dip a piece of the veal into the flour and slide into the skillet; repeat until the skillet is full but not crowded. Fry until nicely browned on both sides, just a minute or two on each, adjusting the heat so that the meat browns quickly and nicely but does not burn; remove each piece from the skillet as it finishes cooking.

❸ When all the meat is cooked, add the onion to the same skillet and cook until softened, about 5 minutes; add the garlic, if you're using it. Sprinkle with the paprika and return the meat to the pan. When the meat is warm again, pour in the sour cream–stock mixture and heat through, being careful not to let the sauce boil. Garnish and serve.

Veal Scaloppine. Use dry white wine instead of the sour cream. Use a thinly sliced lemon (skin and all) instead of the onion. Use olive oil or butter instead of the neutral oil and omit the paprika. In Step 3, add the lemons to the skillet and stir in the wine and stock. Bring the mixture to a boil until it thickens a bit, then return the veal to the pan, stir gently to coat the pieces with sauce, and heat through. Stir in a couple tablespoons of capers (rinsed) at the last minute and serve.

F Fast   **M** Make Ahead   **V** Vegetarian

Saltimbocca. Omit the lemon juice, sour cream, and chicken stock. Skip Step 1. Instead, put 1 or 2 fresh sage leaves on each piece of veal and lay 1 or 2 thin slices of prosciutto over the top; use a mallet or the bottom of a skillet to lightly pound the prosciutto into the veal. You want the meat to be about ¼ inch thick. Proceed with Step 2, transferring the meat to a serving platter in a 200°F oven. In Step 3, omit the onion, garlic, and paprika. Instead, add 1 cup dry white wine or ¾ cup Marsala to the pan and cook, scraping the bottom while stirring, until the liquid is reduced by one-third. Stir in 2 tablespoons butter. Taste and adjust the seasoning, then drizzle over the top of the veal and serve immediately.

Veal Stew with Tomatoes

MAKES: 4 servings

TIME: About 1 hour

What you see in supermarkets as "veal stew meat" is usually cut from the shoulder or leg, which makes it ideal for braising. The meat becomes tender more quickly than beef, and the possibility for variation is endless. Browning the meat first develops depth of flavor, but it's not essential; skip that step if you're pressed for time.

Other cuts and meats you can use: boneless chicken thighs.

3 tablespoons extra virgin olive oil or butter

1½ to 2 pounds lean veal stew meat, cut into 1- to 1½-inch chunks

1 cup diced onion

1 teaspoon minced garlic

Salt and freshly ground black pepper

1 cup white wine, meat or vegetable stock (to make your own, see pages 157–159), or water

2 cups chopped tomato (drained canned is fine)

1 bay leaf

1 teaspoon minced fresh thyme or rosemary leaves or ½ teaspoon dried

1 cup pitted black olives (optional)

❶ Put half the oil or butter in a large pot with a lid or a Dutch oven over medium-high heat. When the oil is hot or the butter is melted, add a few veal chunks at a time, turning them to brown all over and removing the pieces as they brown. Take your time and don't crowd the chunks or they will not brown properly.

❷ Lower the heat to medium and add the remaining oil or butter. When the oil is hot or the butter is melted, add the onion and cook, stirring occasionally, until softened, 5 to 10 minutes. Add the garlic and cook for 1 minute more. Add some salt and pepper and the liquid, bring to a boil, and cook for 1 minute.

❸ Add the tomato, bay leaf, and herb and bring to a steady boil. Return the veal to the pot, turn the heat down to very low, cover, and cook, stirring every now and then, until the veal is tender, 45 minutes or more. Add the olives if you like. Taste and adjust the seasoning, then serve. (At this point, you may let the dish sit for a few hours or cover and refrigerate for up to a day or two before reheating and serving; you may have to add a little water to thin the sauce a bit.)

Veal Stew with Caraway. In Step 2, cook 3 cups thinly sliced onion over medium-low heat until soft, about 15 minutes. Omit the garlic and proceed; in Step 3, replace the tomatoes, bay leaf, and thyme with 1 tablespoon caraway seeds and 1 tablespoon white wine vinegar or other vinegar. Cook as directed, stirring occasionally and adding liquid if needed. Omit the olives.

Veal Stew with Sage. In Step 2, use 3 or 4 chopped carrots and ½ cup chopped shallot, scallion, or onion; cook over medium heat until the vegetables begin to brown, about 5 minutes. Omit the garlic and proceed with the step. In Step 3, replace the tomato, bay leaf, and thyme with 20 fresh sage leaves, 1 teaspoon dried sage, or an equivalent amount of marjoram, rosemary, or savory. Proceed with the recipe. Omit the olives.

Veal Stew with Chinese Flavors. Serve over white rice: In Step 1, use peanut oil if you have it or the extra virgin olive oil. In Step 2, increase the garlic to 1 tablespoon and add 1 tablespoon minced fresh ginger at the same time. In Step 3, omit the tomato and herbs, but add 2 tablespoons soy sauce. Proceed with the recipe, adding a little more liquid if needed. While the stew is simmering, cook 8 ounces shiitake (or other) mushrooms, stems removed and caps roughly chopped, and 8 ounces snow peas, trimmed, in 1 tablespoon oil over medium-high heat, just until beginning to brown, 4 to 5 minutes. When the meat is tender, add the cooked vegetables to the stew along with 1 teaspoon each minced garlic and fresh ginger. Cook for 2 minutes, then drizzle 1 tablespoon dark sesame oil over all. (Do not make this variation in advance.)

Osso Buco

Braised Veal Shanks

MAKES: 4 servings
TIME: About 2 hours, largely unattended

Literally "bone with hole." And it's the creamy, delicious bone marrow that sets this dish apart, though of course the meat is good too. So be sure to check that each piece of veal shank you buy has a nice soft center (press to check).

Traditionally, osso buco is served following (or with) Risotto alla Milanese (page 466) and gremolata, a strong-flavored condiment that only takes a couple of minutes to make: Mix together 1 tablespoon minced lemon zest, 2 tablespoons minced fresh parsley leaves, and $^{1}/_{4}$ to 1 teaspoon minced garlic. Remember that this will not be cooked, so take it easy on the garlic. Sometimes gremolata seems like overkill to me, but it's worth trying.

4 large veal shanks, 8 to 12 ounces each

All-purpose flour for dredging

4 tablespoons ($^{1}/_{2}$ stick) butter, a combination of butter and extra virgin olive oil, or all olive oil

Salt and freshly ground black pepper

1 large onion, chopped

1 celery stalk, chopped

2 carrots, chopped

1 or 2 sprigs fresh thyme or $^{1}/_{2}$ teaspoon dried thyme

$^{3}/_{4}$ cup dry white wine

1 cup chicken, beef, or vegetable stock (to make your own, see pages 157–159) or water

❶ Heat the oven to 350°F. For a somewhat more elegant presentation, tie the shanks around their circumference with a piece of kitchen twine to prevent the meat from falling off the bone (you don't need to do this). Put a large pot with a lid or a Dutch oven over medium-high heat for 3 to 4 minutes.

❷ Pat the shanks dry with paper towels and dredge them in the flour. When the pot is hot, add half the butter and/or oil (a pinch of flour will sizzle when it's ready). Add the shanks and brown them well on both sides, sprinkling them with salt and pepper as they cook. This will take a total of 10 to 15 minutes.

❸ Transfer the shanks to a plate and wipe out the pot with a paper towel. Turn the heat down to medium and add the remaining butter or oil. When the oil is hot or the butter is melted, add the vegetables and thyme. Cook, stirring occasionally, until soft, about 10 minutes, sprinkling with a little more salt and pepper. Add the wine, turn up the heat a bit, and let it bubble away for a minute.

❹ Nestle the shanks among the vegetables and pour the stock over all. Cover and put in the oven. Cook for $1^{1}/_{2}$ to 2 hours, turning the shanks 3 or 4 times during the cooking, or until the meat is very tender and just about falling off the bone. (You can cook the meat in advance up to this point; cover and refrigerate before reheating.) Transfer the meat to a warm platter and sprinkle it with gremolata if you like. If the sauce is very soupy, cook it over high heat for a few minutes to reduce it somewhat, then pour it over the meat. Serve hot, with crusty bread and spoons or dull knives for extracting the marrow.

F Fast   **M** Make Ahead   **V** Vegetarian

Osso Buco with Tomatoes, Garlic, and Anchovies. In Step 3, before adding the vegetables and thyme, cook 1 tablespoon minced garlic and 3 chopped anchovy fillets in the butter and/or oil, stirring until the anchovies break up. Add the vegetables and wine as directed, then add 2 cups chopped tomato (drained canned is fine). Cook until the mixture becomes saucy. Add only 1/2 cup stock (the richer the better) and proceed with the recipe.

Sautéed Calf's Liver

MAKES: 4 servings
TIME: 15 minutes

I'm guessing the reason more people don't like liver is that they've only eaten it overcooked. But when liver is cooked medium-rare to medium, it's delicious, rich, dense, and as tender as any meat there is. Serve it with onions or sautéed apples (see the variations). If you want to serve it with bacon, cook the bacon in the pan first and use the bacon fat to cook the liver.

3 or 4 tablespoons butter, extra virgin olive oil, or a combination

1 1/2 pounds calf's liver in 3/4-inch-thick slices

All-purpose flour for dredging

Salt and freshly ground black pepper

1/2 cup white wine or chicken or beef stock (optional; to make your own, see page 157 or 158)

1 tablespoon freshly squeezed lemon juice or balsamic or sherry vinegar (optional)

Chopped fresh parsley leaves for garnish

1 lemon, quartered, for serving

① Heat the oven to 200°F. Put a large skillet over medium-high heat for 3 to 4 minutes. Add 2 tablespoons of the butter and/or oil. When the butter's foam subsides or the first wisps of smoke arise from the oil, dredge a slice of liver in the flour, shake off the excess, put it in the skillet, and sprinkle with salt and pepper. Repeat until the pan is full but not crowded; you'll probably have to do this in 2 batches.

② As soon as a slice browns on one side, after about 2 minutes, turn and brown the other side. Add more butter or oil as needed and keep the first slices warm in the oven as you finish the others.

③ When all the liver is done, you can make a quick sauce if you like: Turn the heat under the skillet to high and add the wine. Cook, stirring all the while, until it is reduced by half, about 5 minutes. Add the lemon juice and pour over the liver. Either way, garnish with parsley and serve with the lemon quarters.

Sautéed Liver with Onions. This takes a littler longer; start the onions first: Peel and slice 5 or 6 medium onions; you want at least 4 cups of rings. Put them in a dry skillet over medium-low heat, cover, and cook for about 15 minutes, stirring every 5 minutes, until the onions have given up their liquid and become dry. Uncover, add 3 tablespoons olive oil or butter, and cook over medium heat, stirring occasionally, until golden brown and tender, another 10 or 15 minutes. Cook the liver as directed and serve, garnished with the onions.

Sautéed Liver with Apples. Here the apples are cooked after the liver, so cook the liver just as you do in the master recipe and leave it in the oven. Don't make a reduction sauce, but add 2 tablespoons butter (much better than oil in this instance) to the skillet and cook 2 to 3 cups of peeled, cored, and sliced Granny Smith or other tart, crisp apples. Stir frequently until tender, about 7 or 8 minutes.

Deviled Liver. In Step 1, use a minimum of flour and spike it with 1 tablespoon dry mustard. In Step 3, stir 1 tablespoon Dijon mustard into the reduction sauce along with the lemon juice or vinegar.

Grilled or Broiled Liver. Heat a charcoal or gas grill or the broiler until moderately hot and put the rack about 4 inches from the heat source. Sprinkle the liver with salt and pepper, along with $1/2$ teaspoon ground cumin if you like. Put the liver on the grill or under the broiler and cook until brown on both sides, 6 to 8 minutes total. Grill thick onion slices along with the liver if you like and serve with lemon wedges.

Sautéed Sweetbreads

MAKES: 4 servings
TIME: 2 hours, somewhat unattended

Preparing sweetbreads—which is the general name for the thymus glands and pancreas—is a little work, but the reward is meat that is not only crisp on the outside but downright creamy inside.

Salt

1 tablespoon vinegar

2 pairs veal sweetbreads, about 2 pounds total

3 tablespoons butter or extra virgin olive oil

All-purpose flour for dredging

Freshly ground black pepper

$1/2$ cup dry white wine

Freshly squeezed lemon juice

Minced fresh parsley leaves for garnish

❶ Bring a pot of water large enough to hold the sweetbreads to a boil. Add about $1^1/2$ teaspoons salt and the vinegar. Add the sweetbreads to the boiling water and adjust the heat so that the water bubbles steadily but not furiously. Cook for 10 minutes.

❷ Drain, then plunge the sweetbreads into a bowl of ice water or run under cold water until cool. Pick off any bits of the membrane that are loose, but don't worry about it too much; they're quite tender. Dry the sweetbreads with paper towels and put them on a plate. Cover with another plate and a couple of pounds of weight—

some cans or a rock or two. Put in the refrigerator for about an hour and up to a day.

❸ When you're ready to cook, cut the sweetbreads into $1/2$-inch-thick slices. Put the butter or oil in a large skillet over medium-high heat. When the butter is melted or the oil is hot, dredge the sweetbread slices in the flour one at a time, shaking off excess flour.

❹ Sauté the slices for 2 or 3 minutes per side, or until golden brown and crisp, sprinkling well with salt and pepper as they cook. When they're done, put them on a warm platter. Add the wine to the skillet and cook, stirring, until reduced to a tablespoon or two, about 1 minute. Add a squeeze of lemon juice and pour over the sweetbreads; garnish and serve immediately.

Mixed Meat Dishes

We cook meats individually not because they're best that way but because it's easiest that way. But combining several meats in the same dish produces a variety of flavors and textures that you cannot get otherwise. Thus cassoulet is among the world's most famous stews, and meat loaf or meatballs (see page 723) made with two meats are far better than those made with one.

Forty-Minute Cassoulet

MAKES: 4 to 6 servings
TIME: 40 minutes

Cassoulet can take a lot of time and a lot of money, or you can make this version, which is fancy enough for guests, won't break the bank, and can be made well in advance, then simply reheated. It's not "real" cassoulet, but glorified beans accentuated by whatever meat is handy.

4 cups chopped tomato (canned is fine; include the juices)

1 tablespoon chopped garlic

 Fast   Make Ahead   Vegetarian

4 cups white beans, nearly fully cooked or frozen; drained if canned (save the liquid in any case)

1 cup stock, dry red wine, bean-cooking liquid, or water

Salt

$^1/_8$ teaspoon cayenne, or to taste

1 pound Italian sausage, preferably in 1 piece

1 pound pork tenderloin, cut into 1-inch cubes

1 boned duck breast

❶ Combine the tomato and garlic in a large saucepan over medium heat. Bring to a boil and add the beans; bring to a boil again, stirring occasionally, then reduce the heat so the mixture bubbles regularly but not furiously. Cook for about 20 minutes, adding the liquid when the mixture gets thick. Add the salt and cayenne when the beans are tender and flavorful.

❷ Meanwhile, put the sausage in a skillet over medium-high heat; brown on both sides, turning only once or twice. Add the sausage to the tomato-bean mixture, along with the pork. Raise the heat a bit if necessary to keep a simmer going. Stir the beans occasionally so the pork chunks cook evenly.

❸ Cut a $^1/_2$-inch crosshatch pattern in the skin side of the duck breast, right down to the fat layer. Put the breast in the same skillet you used for the sausage, skin side down, and turn the heat to medium-high. Cook until nicely browned, pouring any rendered duck fat and juices into the bean mixture. Turn the duck and brown the meat side, then crisp up the skin side again for a minute or so, once more pouring any juice into the beans. Total cooking time for the breast will be 6 to 8 minutes. Add the breast to the beans.

❹ To serve, carve the sausage and duck breast into serving pieces and put on each of 4 or 6 plates. Top with beans and pork.

4 Easy Ways to Vary Cassoulet
1. Start with dried beans, cooked with a few sprigs of fresh thyme, $^1/_2$ head of garlic, and a piece of salt pork or bacon.

2. Cook the garlic in a little duck fat—don't let it brown—before adding the tomato and beans.

3. If you can get duck confit, just brown it lightly on both sides, adding both it and its fat to the stew in place of the duck breast.

4. Finish the dish by toasting some bread crumbs, seasoned with salt and pepper, in the fat remaining from browning the duck. Sprinkle these on top of the stew, then run under the broiler to brown just before serving.

Hunter's Stew

Bigos

MAKES: 4 servings

TIME: 1$^1/_2$ hours, largely unattended

"Hunter's stew" has become a catchall name for perhaps the oldest and most popular dish of Eastern Europe. Like Cassoulet (preceding recipe) and Bouillabaisse (page 146), it is usually made with whatever is handy. It's even casual enough to accommodate leftovers and store and reheat many times.

Other cuts and meats you can use: anything—pork, veal, lamb, venison, duck, goose, or a combination. It's potluck.

4 ounces bacon or salt pork, roughly chopped

4 ounces sausage (optional)

1$^1/_2$ pounds not-too-lean beef, chuck, or brisket, cut into small cubes

1 onion, chopped

2 pounds sauerkraut, preferably fresh or stored in plastic

1 ounce dried shiitake, porcini, or black mushrooms, soaked and sliced, liquid reserved

$^1/_2$ teaspoon caraway seeds

$^1/_2$ teaspoon freshly ground black pepper

1 tablespoon sugar

$^1/_2$ cup Madeira or other sweet wine

1 Heat a large pot with a tight-fitting lid or a Dutch oven over medium-high heat. Add the bacon and cook, stirring occasionally, until most of the fat is rendered, about 10 minutes. Add the sausage and beef and brown, about 10 minutes. Remove the bacon, sausage, and beef with a slotted spoon and set aside.

2 Lower the heat to medium and cook the onion in the fat, stirring occasionally, until translucent, about 5 minutes. Add the sauerkraut, mushrooms, mushroom liquid, caraway seeds, pepper, and sugar. Stir to combine and add just enough water to barely cover. Cover, turn the heat to low, and let bubble gently for 15 minutes.

3 Return the meat to the pan and add the wine. Cover and let bubble gently until the meat is tender, about an hour (lamb, pork, and veal will probably take longer than beef). Serve hot with rye bread or cool to room temperature and refrigerate, then reheat before serving.

Hunter's Stew with Fresh Cabbage. Omit the sauerkraut from Step 2 and substitute one 2-pound head green cabbage, cored and thinly sliced; 3 tablespoons white vinegar; and 2 tart apples, peeled and sliced.

Hunter's Stew with Prunes. For a sweeter stew, substitute 8 ounces diced pitted prunes for the dried mushrooms. You don't need to soak the prunes. Add them to the bigos when you would have added the mushrooms and proceed with the recipe.

F Fast   **M** Make Ahead   **V** Vegetarian

Eggs, Breakfast, and Dairy

WE TEND TO THINK OF EGGS AS BREAKFAST food. And indeed the archetypal American breakfast almost always features them. But the standard plate of eggs, bacon, ham, what have you—a direct descendant of the typical English breakfast—now seems a bit over the top.

Many of the modern alternatives—from microwave- and toaster-cooked "treats" to overly sweetened dried cereal—are far worse, making you yearn for the days when a crust of bread left over from dinner, toasted and served with butter or jam or cheese, plus maybe a piece of fruit, was standard.

Still, there's no denying that a luxurious breakfast of eggs, pancakes, or something even more complex, along with breakfast meat, is a treat that many people look forward to all week. And preparing it is neither difficult nor time-consuming.

Breakfast is an extremely flexible concept—in many parts of the world soups and stews are the norm—so this chapter is flexible as well. In it you'll find not only what most Americans consider "normal" breakfast dishes but also a broad consideration of the egg and a variety of dairy dishes, including techniques for making your own cheese, something—like bread—all cooks should tackle at least once.

The Basics of Cooking Eggs

Here is everything you need to know about cooking eggs. Beginning cooks can use this as a primer and a reference; those with experience may find some helpful tips here. (My method of hard-cooking eggs, for example, has changed over the years.) If you do nothing else, try baking eggs (see page 798), a technique that works perfectly for a crowd and is pure luxury.

Really, boiled eggs should be called "poached," because the water should never be at a real boil; all boiling does is bounce the eggs around the pot and crack the shells. The degree of doneness is only a matter of timing, but room-temperature eggs will cook in about a minute less than those straight from the refrigerator.

If you're cooking more than one egg, make sure you use a saucepan big enough for the water to circulate freely. You'll also need to extend the cooking time to the maximum in each of the following recipes.

Slow and Low or Fast and High?

Eggs are so tolerant of a wide range of conditions that in many cases you can cook them in a hurry or quite leisurely; the only real rule is not to overcook or they will toughen. For example, for years I made my favorite scrambled eggs lovingly and leisurely, taking 40 minutes to do so (see The Best Scrambled Eggs, page 797). Then I discovered I could get just about the same texture by cooking them quickly, stirring constantly, and removing them from the heat the instant they threatened to overcook (see Everyday Scrambled Eggs, page 792). Both ways work fine; the first requires more patience, the second more attention.

It's important to be aware that eggs should never become completely hard; even "hard-boiled" eggs should have yolks that remain somewhat creamy. Often it's easier to avoid toughening when you use low heat. Fried eggs stay tender and become evenly firm over medium to low heat; boiled and poached eggs develop better texture and are less like to be damaged in water that bubbles only gently. But you can cook quickly and keep eggs tender and soft, as in real omelets (see page 802); again, it just takes attention.

ESSENTIAL RECIPES

First are all the basic egg recipes, in order of simplest to trickiest, though no cooking method is truly difficult. Even poached eggs can be conquered readily. Then comes a handful of breakfast and dairy dishes that you will turn to again and again.

⭐ Soft-Boiled Egg

MAKES: 1 serving
TIME: Less than 10 minutes

F **V**

The egg lover's way to eat eggs, barely cooked but warm and comforting. Soft-"boiled" eggs are also dreamy stirred into a bowl of reheated leftover brown rice or a cup of broth.

1 egg
Salt and freshly ground black pepper

 Fast   Make Ahead   Vegetarian

1 Fill a saucepan about two-thirds full of water and bring it to a gentle boil.

2 Use a spoon or some other handy tool to lower the egg into the gently boiling water. Adjust the heat so the water barely simmers, then cook for 3 to 4 minutes, the lower time if you want the yolk completely runny and the white still slightly liquid, the latter if you want the white very soft but set.

3 Run the egg briefly under cold water, crack the shell, and scoop out the egg into a small bowl (or eat straight from the shell). Sprinkle with salt and pepper and serve.

✪ Medium-Boiled Egg

MAKES: 1 serving
TIME: About 10 minutes

F   **V**

These are easier than poached eggs and about the same texture; when done, the white is firm and the yolk runny. You can even reheat them after shelling by dipping them in simmering water for about 30 seconds.

1 egg
Salt and freshly ground black pepper

1 Fill a saucepan about two-thirds full of water and bring it to a gentle boil.

2 Use a spoon or some other handy tool to lower the egg into the gently boiling water. Adjust the heat so the water barely simmers, then cook for 6 to 7 minutes; the shorter time guarantees a cooked but runny yolk, but there may be some undercooked white. With the longer time, the white will be fully cooked, but some of the yolk may have hardened. Try it both ways and see which you prefer.

3 To remove the shell, put the pot under cold running water for 30 to 60 seconds, then crack and peel gently, as you would a hard-cooked egg (but more carefully). Sprinkle with salt and pepper and serve.

✪ Hard-Boiled Egg

MAKES: 1 serving
TIME: About 15 minutes

F   **V**

Hard-cooked eggs are so convenient and versatile you may want to keep a few ready in the fridge at all times (they keep for a week). They're used in recipes throughout this book, from appetizers to hearty dinner dishes. I think they're best when the yolks are just slightly undercooked and still creamy, not chalky.

If the yolk has a greenish color, it's due to a small and harmless amount of sulfur present in the egg and not cooling the egg quickly enough. To prevent or minimize it, immerse the eggs in an ice water bath as soon as possible after they've finished cooking.

1 egg
Salt and freshly ground black pepper

1 Fill a saucepan about two-thirds full of water and add the egg. Bring to a boil, then turn off the heat and cover. The average large to extra-large egg will be ready 9 minutes later.

2 Plunge the egg into a bowl of ice water (or run the pot under cold water) for a minute or so, then refrigerate or crack and peel. Sprinkle with salt and pepper and serve.

✪ Fried Eggs

MAKES: 1 to 2 servings
TIME: 10 minutes

F   **V**

Correctly cooked, fried eggs are neither tough nor rubbery, but nearly as delicate as poached, with tender whites and a barely cooked yolk. Low heat is the easiest way to achieve this, but with practice you'll be able to use higher heat and get the same results. If you use the smaller amount of fat here, you'll sacrifice some flavor and will have to take more care to keep the eggs from sticking unless you use a nonstick pan.

Butter is the most luxurious medium for frying eggs. But extra virgin olive oil is also delicious (try frying eggs in it, perhaps with a few sage leaves, finishing with a grating of Parmesan), and dark sesame oil is interesting, especially if you're frying an egg to put on top of Jook or Congee (page 139).

1 teaspoon to 1 tablespoon butter or oil

2 eggs

Salt and freshly ground black pepper

1 Put a medium skillet over medium heat for about 1 minute. Add the butter or oil and swirl it around the pan. When the butter's foam subsides or the oil is hot, about a minute later, crack the eggs into the skillet. As soon as the whites lose their translucence—this takes only a minute—turn the heat to low and sprinkle the eggs with salt and pepper.

2 Cook until the whites are completely firm; the last place this happens is just around the yolk. If the egg has set up high, rather than spread out thin, there are two techniques to encourage it to finish cooking: You can cut through the uncooked parts with a knife, allowing some of the still-liquid white to fall through to the surface of the pan. Or cover the skillet and cook for a minute or two longer. When the eggs are cooked, remove them from the pan and eat immediately.

Eggs in the Nest or Eggs in the Hole. You need a little more butter here: Use a biscuit cutter or drinking glass to cut a big hole out of the middle of a slice of bread for each egg. After the butter melts in Step 1, put the bread slices and the circles in the pan and crack the eggs into the holes (you might put a little pat of butter in the holes before adding the egg). When the eggs start to firm up, carefully flip the bread slices and the circles over and cook the other side for a few more seconds, then serve.

5 Simple Ideas for Fried Eggs

1. As the butter or oil heats, season it with a few fresh herb leaves or a smashed clove of garlic.
2. Cook bacon in the skillet, then use its rendered fat to fry the eggs.
3. As the white sets, use a butter knife to fold its edges over the yolk, making a little package and further protecting the yolk from overcooking.
4. Add Worcestershire sauce or other liquid seasoning like soy or hot sauce to the white before it sets.
5. Cook $^1\!/_2$-inch-thick tomato slices—either ripe or green tomatoes—alongside the eggs (increase the amount of butter slightly).

Everyday Scrambled Eggs

MAKES: 2 servings
TIME: 10 minutes
F **V**

Very good scrambled eggs can be had in a hurry, provided you don't overcook them. Adding a little extra liquid helps prevent overcooking (and if that liquid is cream, it also lends a luxurious texture). A few drops of lemon juice will make them even more tender.

4 or 5 eggs

Salt and freshly ground black pepper

1 to 2 tablespoons milk, cream, or water (optional)

1 or 2 tablespoons butter or extra virgin olive oil

1 Beat the eggs lightly with some salt and pepper and the milk, if using. Put the butter or oil in a medium skillet, preferably nonstick, over medium-high heat. When the butter is melted or the oil is hot, add the eggs. Cook, stirring frequently and scraping the sides of the pan (a heatproof rubber spatula is a good tool here).

2 As the eggs begin to curdle, you may notice that some parts are drying out; whenever you see that, remove the pan from the heat and continue to stir until the cook-

F Fast   **M** Make Ahead   **V** Vegetarian

ing slows down a bit. Then return to the heat and continue cooking. The eggs are done when creamy, soft, and still a bit runny; do not overcook unless, of course, you intend to. Serve immediately.

Scrambled Eggs with Cheese. Use virtually any kind of cheese you like except the ones that don't melt easily, like feta or queso fresco: As the eggs begin to set, stir in $^1/_2$ cup grated cheese.

Scrambled Eggs aux Fines Herbes. Add about $^1/_2$ teaspoon chopped fresh tarragon, 1 teaspoon chopped fresh chervil, and 1 tablespoon each chopped fresh parsley and chives to the eggs before beating (or anytime during cooking).

Scrambled Eggs with Bacon or Sausage. Cook up to 8 ounces bacon or sausage in the pan before making the eggs, breaking up the pieces as they cook. Drain off all but a tablespoon or two of the fat. Proceed with the recipe, heating and using the pan with the meat and fat to cook the eggs.

12 Simple Additions to Scrambled Eggs

As in making an omelet (see page 802) or frittata (see page 804), you can add almost anything you want to the beaten uncooked eggs before scrambling. Try any of these with either the preceding recipe or The Best Scrambled Eggs (page 797), using about $^1/_2$ cup except where otherwise noted:

1. Minced pickled jalapeño to taste
2. Sautéed mushrooms, onion, spinach, or other cooked vegetables, cut into small dice
3. Diced cooked shrimp or other seafood
4. 1 teaspoon chopped fresh stronger herbs like oregano, tarragon, or thyme or 1 tablespoon milder ones like parsley, chive, chervil, basil, or mint
5. Minced smoked salmon or other fish
6. Chili (see page 429) or any cooked beans
7. Chopped salami or other smoked meats

8. Up to 1 cup peeled, seeded, and diced tomato or $^1/_4$ cup reconstituted dried tomatoes (or, even better, $^1/_2$ cup Oven-Dried Tomatoes, page 362)
9. Tabasco, Worcestershire, or other prepared sauce, to taste
10. Minced scallions
11. Chopped Roasted Red Peppers (page 330)
12. Any cooked salsa (see pages 48–50), drained if it's quite moist

✪ Poached Eggs

MAKES: 1 to 2 servings
TIME: 10 minutes

A poached egg in its natural form—with ragged edges—has its own appeal. If you really want a perfect-looking poached egg, trim away the (inevitably) ragged edges of the whites with knife or scissors.

If you want to poach more than two eggs at once, use a bigger pan to avoid crowding. To make poached eggs in multiple batches, keep a second, large pot of water warm over very low heat. Make sure the temperature hovers between 145°F and 150°F; as the eggs finish poaching, move them to the second pot of water and keep covered. Fish them all out with a slotted spoon when you're ready to serve.

1 teaspoon salt

1 teaspoon white vinegar

2 eggs

❶ Bring about an inch of water to a boil in a small deep skillet, add the salt and vinegar, and lower the heat to the point where it barely bubbles (if you were to measure it with an instant-read thermometer, the temperature would be just under 200°F). One at a time, break the eggs into a shallow bowl and slip them into the water.

❷ Cook for 3 to 5 minutes, just until the white is set and the yolk has filmed over. Remove with a slotted spoon and allow the water to drain off for a couple seconds. If you are eating the eggs right away, put them directly on the toast or what have you. If you like, drain them briefly on paper towels before serving. Poached eggs are delicate, but they can be handled as long as you're careful.

✪ Cinnamon Toast for One

MAKES: 1 serving

TIME: 5 minutes

🅕 🅥

You know how to make toast, of course, but with this old-fashioned way you can watch it and control the heat. Toast should have crunch; it's best made with slightly stale good bread—the kind you cut with a knife. White bread, the soft, packaged kind, makes lousy toast—it browns nicely but becomes soft almost immediately.

> 2 slices good bread
>
> Butter
>
> 1/2 teaspoon sugar, or to taste
>
> 1/2 teaspoon ground cinnamon, or to taste

❶ Heat a broiler or toaster oven. Toast the bread lightly on one side. Turn it over and spread liberally with butter, then sprinkle with sugar and cinnamon.

❷ Return to the broiler and toast until the butter, cinnamon, and sugar all melt together and the bread is nicely browned. Serve immediately.

8 Other Ways to Dress Up Toast

Toast the bread on one side and turn over as described in Step 1, then spread or sprinkle on the topping and return the toast to the broiler until everything is hot and bubbly.

1. Spread with butter and drizzle with honey.
2. Spread with peanut or other nut butter and top with banana slices.
3. Cover with Baked Beans (page 416).
4. Spread with any Compound Butter (page 32).
5. Smear with ricotta, cottage cheese, or goat cheese and top with chopped fresh or dried fruit.

6. Drape a piece or two of thinly sliced prosciutto over the top.
7. Welsh Rarebit: Mix Mornay (Cheese) Sauce (page 58) with a dash of Worcestershire sauce and mustard; spread a spoonful over the top. (Use it all for 4 servings or refrigerate the rest.)
8. Milk Toast: Spread with butter and sprinkle with sugar. When the toast comes out from under the broiler, put in a shallow bowl and pour hot milk over the top; let sit for just a minute.

✪ French Toast

MAKES: 4 servings

TIME: 20 minutes

🅕 🅜 🅥

Originally a way to bring new life to stale bread (it's called *pain perdu*—"lost bread"—in France), French toast can be made with virtually any fresh or stale bread, including quick breads and even tortillas. European-style loaves require a bit more soaking to soften the crust, while hearty whole grain breads make more substantial slices. My favorite are soft, thick slices of brioche or challah, which make a truly decadent French toast.

You can easily vary this basic recipe: Use soy or other nondairy milk if you like or, for richer French toast, use half-and-half or cream. Season it with ground cardamom, cloves, allspice, nutmeg, or almond extract instead of the cinnamon or vanilla.

> 2 eggs
>
> 1 cup milk
>
> Dash salt
>
> 1 tablespoon sugar (optional)
>
> 1 teaspoon vanilla extract or ground cinnamon (optional)
>
> Butter or neutral oil, like grapeseed or corn, as needed
>
> 8 slices bread

 Fast   Make Ahead   🅥 Vegetarian

1 Heat the oven to 200°F. Put a large griddle or skillet over medium-low heat while you prepare the egg mixture.

2 Beat the eggs lightly in a broad bowl and stir in the milk, the salt, and the sugar and vanilla or cinnamon if you're using them.

3 Add about 1 teaspoon of butter or oil to the griddle or skillet. When is the butter is melted or the oil is hot, dip each slice of bread in turn in the batter and put it on the griddle. Cook until nicely browned on each side, turning as necessary, for no more than 10 minutes or so total; you may find that you can raise the heat a bit. Serve immediately, or keep warm in the oven for up to 30 minutes.

Crispy French Toast. There are two ways to give French toast a bit of a crust. The first is to stir $^1/_2$ cup flour into the batter. The second is to dip the bread in the batter, then dredge it in sweetened bread crumbs or crushed corn flakes. In either case, cook as directed.

Nut-Crusted French Toast. Add another egg and decrease the milk to $^3/_4$ cup. Spread about 1 cup sliced almonds or other finely chopped nuts on a plate; after dipping the bread in the egg mixture, put the slice on the nuts and press gently to make the nuts stick; flip it over to coat the other side. Proceed with the recipe; be careful not to burn the nut coating.

Caramelized French Toast. A sugar coating melts and creates a lightly crunchy coating: Sprinkle or dredge the dipped bread with sugar. Proceed with the recipe. Serve immediately.

7 Toppings for French Toast

Aside from or in addition to the obvious maple syrup:
1. Soft Whipped Cream (page 882)
2. Sautéed apples, pears, bananas, or other fruit or any fruit compote
3. Maple Buttercream (page 918)
4. Orange Glaze (page 919)
5. Caramel Coffee Sauce (page 922)
6. Maple-Butter Sauce (page 923)
7. Any fruit purée (see page 923)

✪ Baked Goat Cheese

MAKES: 4 servings
TIME: 15 minutes

A restaurant staple that's easily made at home and seems special, especially at brunch, on top of a green salad, as an appetizer, or as a side dish.

One 6-ounce goat cheese log, cut into 8 slices or molded into 8 patties

$^1/_4$ cup extra virgin olive oil

Salt and freshly ground black pepper

$^1/_4$ cup mixed chopped fresh herbs, like basil, chives, parsley, chervil, tarragon, and thyme

$^1/_2$ cup bread crumbs, preferably fresh (page 876)

1 Heat the oven to 375°F. Brush the cheese with the olive oil and sprinkle with salt, pepper, and the mixed herbs. (At this point, you may refrigerate the cheese for up to 2 days.) Then coat with the bread crumbs.

2 Put on a baking sheet and bake the cheese until it's golden brown and soft, about 10 minutes. Let rest for just a couple minutes and serve warm.

Baked Goat Cheese with Tomato Sauce or Tomatoes. Also great with tomato-based salsas, including Salsa Cruda (page 24): Put the goat cheese slices (with or without the bread crumbs) in a gratin or baking dish and spoon about a cup or so of Fast Tomato Sauce (page 502) over the top; or top thick, seasoned tomato slices with 1 or 2 slices of goat cheese. Bake until the tomato sauce is bubbling or the goat cheese and tomato slices are soft. Sprinkle with fresh herbs and/or chopped black olives and serve.

The Basics of Eggs

The egg is a metaphor for life and possibilities and a culinary miracle that, with little effort or expertise, can become the feature of a meal, a vehicle for transforming leftovers, or a quick way to change a side dish into one that takes over the table. And eggs produce among the most satisfying, beloved (and easiest) dishes, not only for breakfast but also for convenient and super-quick lunches and dinners. (None of this even considers the egg's role in desserts and pastries, which is impossible to overstate.)

Eggs at a Glance

Eggs are a near-ideal source of protein, minerals, and vitamins and one of only a handful of foods with naturally occurring vitamin D. Although eggs have been vilified for their high cholesterol content (an egg contains around 200 mg), recent studies have questioned the link between dietary cholesterol (that found in food) and blood cholesterol (the cholesterol produced by your body). So unless your doctor advises you against high-cholesterol food, don't worry about it.

The Anatomy of an Egg

There are three main components to an egg: the shell, the white, and the yolk. The shell is made up of calcium carbonate and varies in color depending on the breed of hen. The white—or albumen—comprises about two-thirds of the egg and over half of the egg's protein and minerals. The yolk contains all of the fat and zinc, the majority of the vitamins, and the remaining protein and minerals. A small blood spot in the yolk is not harmful (nor does it mean you have a fertilized egg) but is a small vein rupture, actually indicating a fresher egg (the older the egg gets, the more diluted the blood spot becomes). If it bothers you, remove it with the tip of a knife.

The Facts About Egg Labels

If you can get eggs produced by a local farmer, do, because there are so many meaningless and misleading claims that trying to know your way around buying eggs has become more than a little bit tricky. In fact, much of the information that has always been on egg packages is standard and can often be mostly ignored; sadly, much of the new labeling is equally useless.

First of all, eggs are categorized into grades and sizes. The USDA has regulations for these categories, but often state regulations, which must be equivalent or better, override them. So egg producers using federal regulations use the USDA grade stamp on the package; but a stamp doesn't mean the eggs are of a different quality or standard from those without the stamp, making the stamp itself worthless.

The grades, AA, A, and B, are based on appearance, character, and shape of the egg. The thicker and less runny the white, the rounder and "taller" the yolks, and the less blemished and properly shaped the shell, the higher the grade. AA and A are the most commonly available grades (B grade is most often used in commercial or institutional kitchens), and there is little difference between them. Another aspect of buying you can pretty much ignore.

Grading for size is based on weight, and categories include jumbo, extra large, large, medium, small, and peewee. Extra-large and large eggs are most common, and most recipes, including mine, assume large eggs, though you can freely substitute extra large with no consequences.

Some egg labels matter. Most of these have been in use for only a few years and fall into two categories: those that are associated with specific regulated programs and those that are used but without oversight or enforcement. It's worth noting that no chickens are (legally) raised using hormones, so the label "raised without hormones" is meaningless for eggs—they all are, or are supposed to be.

Here are the labels that can be used by any egg producer with no official program or regulatory agency inspecting or guaranteeing the claims. In other words, you have to trust the word of the producer.

Free-Range (aka *Free-Roaming*): Implies that the birds are not kept in cages and sometimes have outdoor access, though it can be just a door open at some point in the day. *Free-range* as defined by the USDA applies only to chickens used for meat and not egg layers, so there are no USDA standards for so-called free-range eggs. Buyer beware.

Cage-Free: The birds are not kept in cages, but no outdoor access is guaranteed.

Natural: Probably the most abused and misunderstood label for eggs (and many other foods). In fact there are no standards for "natural" eggs. This label essentially means nothing.

Omega-3 Enriched: These have nearly six times the amount of omega-3 fatty acids in standard eggs but look, cook, and taste no different. The hen's feed is supplemented with a mix of vitamins and omega-3 fatty acids. I'd recommend getting your omega-3s elsewhere, but these are hardly harmful.

Vegetarian Fed: No animal by-products are included in the feed. If it were true, "100% Vegetarian-Fed" would be a more secure assurance of feed quality, but unfortunately it's not regulated or enforced.

There are also some labels that are associated with a specific set of voluntary rules and regulations and monitored by third-party auditors.

Organic (Certified Organic): The USDA Certified Organic stamp means the hens are raised without cages and with access to the outdoors; are fed organic, all-vegetarian diets; are raised without antibiotics, pesticides, and insecticides; and that the eggs aren't irradiated. "Certified Organic" is the only way to guarantee that your eggs were raised without antibiotics.

Certified Humane, Free Farmed, and Animal Care Certified: Technically separate, these all refer to the animals' living conditions, guaranteeing a minimum amount of space; access to fresh air, water, and food; and limited stress and/or noise, among other things. The certification is overseen by independent associations whose inspection regulations are approved by the USDA.

Buying and Storing Eggs

There are four sure signs of a fresh egg. Unfortunately, you have to crack open the egg to find out—not exactly something you can do before purchasing.

- The whites are thick and don't spread out much.
- The whites are a bit cloudy; this means that the nat-

urally occurring carbon dioxide hasn't had time to fully escape from the egg after hatching.
- The yolk is firm and stands tall.
- The chalazae (the coiled cordlike attachments to the yolk) are prominent.

Before buying, take a quick peek inside the carton to make sure all the eggs are sound. And check that the date has not passed.

Eggs should always be refrigerated (not in the door, where it's often too warm) and will keep for as long as four to five weeks beyond the pack date. Store them in their carton and away from strong-smelling foods.

Egg Dishes

These classic and modern recipes feature eggs at their most versatile. For the basic egg-cooking techniques, see the Essential Recipes, beginning on page 790.

The Best Scrambled Eggs

MAKES: 2 servings
TIME: 40 minutes

Cooked slowly for a silky texture. They're perfect for dinner or a lazy weekend brunch, because these are easily cooked while you prepare other ingredients.

4 or 5 eggs

Salt and freshly ground black pepper

2 tablespoons cream

2 tablespoons butter or extra virgin olive oil

❶ Crack the eggs into a bowl and beat them just until the yolks and whites are combined. Season with salt and pepper and beat in the cream.

❷ Put a medium skillet, preferably nonstick, over medium heat for about 1 minute. Add the butter or oil and swirl it around the pan. After the butter melts, but before it foams, turn the heat to low.

There remains widespread concern about the possibility of getting sick from salmonella—a bacterium sometimes found in chicken, eggs, and other foods—from eating raw or undercooked eggs. And yet everyone knows the perfect egg is soft and tender with a liquid yolk. Is this flirting with danger?

Not much; salmonella isn't as prevalent in eggs as it was a decade ago, and it wasn't even that bad back then. It's true, though, that the risk from eating an infected egg is not zero, so if you or the people you cook for are very old, very young, or have a compromised immune system—or if you are worried about eggs for any reason—you should use well-stored eggs (see page 797), rinse them before using (especially if you buy eggs from small farms, where the shells might not have been washed commercially), and cook them thoroughly: Salmonella is killed in eggs if their temperature is maintained at 160°F for 1 minute or 140°F for 5 minutes. At 160°F, egg yolks are firm; at 140°F, they're not.

Precooking eggs in recipes that call for raw eggs can be a little tricky, but it's useful for mayonnaise: Put the shelled eggs in a small metal or glass bowl set over a pot of bubbling water on the stove. You don't want the water to touch the bottom of the bowl. Use a whisk to stir and an instant-read thermometer to monitor their temperature. When they reach 140°F, adjust the heat on the burner to maintain that temperature and keep stirring for 15 minutes. (This completely changes the flavor and texture, of course.)

Another alternative is to hold poached eggs in a water bath: If you want to kill salmonella and still have poached eggs with runny yolks, you must keep the cooked eggs in 150°F water for 5 minutes. See the headnote with the Poached Eggs recipe (page 793) for the details.

You can also use pasteurized eggs, which are available both in and out of their shells. These have been treated with heat and pressure to kill any bacteria. Dried egg whites can also give you peace of mind, with only a little sacrifice in flavor and performance. To use, you simply mix the powder with water (the proportions are on the package) and beat as you would fresh egg whites.

3 Add the eggs to the skillet and cook over low heat, stirring occasionally with a wooden spoon. At first nothing will happen; after 10 minutes or so, the eggs will begin to form curds. Do not lose patience: Keep stirring, breaking up the curds as they form, until the mixture is a mass of soft curds. This will take 30 minutes or more. Serve immediately.

Baked (Shirred) Eggs

MAKES: 1 or 2 servings
TIME: 30 minutes

There's something about the custardy texture of baked eggs that cannot be duplicated by any other cooking method. It's also one of the best ways to cook eggs for a crowd since they all finish cooking at the same time.

Baked eggs are endlessly adaptable. You can put all sorts of raw or cooked meat or seafood, vegetables, grains, or legumes into the cup before adding the egg, which makes this an easy way to use up leftovers. You can also top the eggs right before baking with bread crumbs, grated cheese, chopped fresh herbs, or some of your favorite spice blend—either alone or in combination.

Butter or oil as needed

Cream (optional)

2 eggs

Salt and freshly ground black pepper

1 Heat the oven to 375°F. Smear a bit of butter or oil in 2 custard cups or small ramekins. If you like, put a

 Fast   Make Ahead   Vegetarian

couple of teaspoons of cream in the bottom of each (a nice touch). Break 1 egg into each cup, then put the cups on a baking sheet.

 Bake for 10 to 15 minutes, or until the eggs are just set and the whites solidified. Because of the heat retained by the cups, these will continue to cook after you remove them from the oven, so it's best to undercook them slightly (the precise time, in a good oven on a middle rack, is 12 minutes). Sprinkle with salt and pepper and serve.

Baked Eggs with Tomato. Substitute olive oil for butter if you like; omit the cream. Before adding the eggs to each cup, put a tablespoon or two of chopped fresh tomato (or a slice of tomato if your cups are broad or tomatoes small) in the bottom. Top with minced fresh parsley, chives, or cilantro. Add the eggs and bake as directed.

Baked Eggs with Spinach

Eggs Florentine

MAKES: 4 servings
TIME: About 45 minutes

Ⓥ

A perfect use for leftover cooked spinach.

2 pounds fresh spinach, washed and trimmed according to the directions on page 352

3 tablespoons butter or extra virgin olive oil

8 eggs

Salt and freshly ground black pepper

$1/2$ cup freshly grated Parmesan cheese

$1/2$ cup bread crumbs, preferably fresh (page 876)

❶ Heat the oven to 350°F. Bring a large pot of water to a boil and salt it. Put the spinach in the water and cook until it is bright green and tender, about a minute. Drain well. When it is cool enough to handle, squeeze the moisture from it and chop.

❷ Put the butter or oil in a 9 × 13-inch baking pan and put the pan in the oven. When the butter melts or the oil is hot, toss the spinach in the pan, stirring to coat with the fat. Spread the spinach out and use the back of a spoon to make 8 little nests in the spinach. Crack 1 egg into each. Top with salt, pepper, cheese, and bread crumbs.

❸ Bake for 15 to 20 minutes, or until the eggs are just set and the whites solidified. Scoop out some spinach with each egg and serve on toast or toasted English muffins.

Baked Eggs with Onions and Cheese. Substitute 4 cups sliced onion for the spinach. For Step 2, put the butter or oil in a large skillet over medium heat. Two minutes later, add the onion and cook, stirring occasionally, until very soft and tender but not browned, about 15 minutes. Skip tossing the onions in the oil in the first part of Step 3. Use cheddar or other melting cheese if you like. Proceed with the recipe.

Eggs Benedict, Unleashed

MAKES: 4 servings
TIME: 30 minutes

Ⓕ   Ⓜ

The traditional way to make the quintessential brunch classic is with English muffin, Canadian bacon, and hollandaise sauce. But the formula is easy to vary by replacing any of those three components. You can even make Benedict with scrambled or baked eggs instead of poached, which is obviously much easier for a crowd. Check the chart that follows for ideas or improvise your own combinations.

The ease or complexity of this dish depends on how involved you want the topping to be and what you make in advance. The only thing that requires last-minute attention is the eggs; everything else can be prepared ahead and kept warm.

VARIATIONS ON EGGS BENEDICT

As in the main recipe, start with a base; add some meat, fish, or vegetable; top with a poached, baked, or scrambled egg; and finish with sauce.

BASE	ON TOP OF BREAD	SAUCE	GARNISH
Yogurt or Buttermilk Biscuit (page 845), split	Sliced ham, panfried as in the main recipe	Mornay (Cheese) Sauce (page 58)	Chopped fresh chives
Any rustic bread, thickly sliced and toasted	Thinly sliced prosciutto or Serrano ham, as is or panfried as in the main recipe	Béchamel Sauce (page 57)	Grated Parmesan cheese
Corn Bread (page 831), cut into squares, split, and toasted	Crumbled or sliced chorizo, panfried as in main recipe	Salsa Roja (page 48)	A dollop of sour cream
Whole wheat sandwich bread, toasted (to make your own, see page 861)	Sautéed spinach (start with about a pound for 4 people)	Tahini Sauce (page 35)	Chopped black olives
Slices of Fried Polenta (page 485)	Broiled or grilled shrimp (see page 563 or 564)	Fast Tomato Sauce (page 502)	Chopped fresh basil or a drizzle of Traditional Pesto (page 27)
Rye or wheat toast	Thinly sliced smoked salmon or poached salmon (see page 569)	Beurre Blanc (page 59)	A sprinkling of chopped fresh chives

1 recipe Hollandaise Sauce (pages 59–60)

4 English muffins, split

2 tablespoons butter

8 slices Canadian bacon, about 8 ounces total

8 eggs

Chopped fresh parsley for garnish (optional)

Sweet or smoked paprika for garnish (optional)

1 Make or reheat the hollandaise, cover, and keep it warm over a double boiler or in a bowl set over a pot of simmering water. Toast the English muffins until golden. Keep warm.

2 Put a large skillet over medium-high heat. Add half of the butter and, when it melts and begins to bubble, add half of the bacon. Cook until lightly browned and crisped, just a minute or two, then flip and cook on the other side. Transfer to paper towels to drain and repeat with the remaining butter and bacon.

3 When you're ready to serve, poach the eggs following the directions for Poached Eggs (page 793). You may need to work in 2 batches and hold the finished eggs in warm water as described in the recipe. To assemble each Benedict, put the top and bottom of the muffin on a plate, open face. Top each with a slice of bacon, an egg, and a spoonful of hollandaise. Garnish as you like and serve.

Huevos Rancheros

MAKES: 2 servings

TIME: 35 minutes

Ⓜ Ⓥ

Huevos Rancheros are perfect for entertaining since you can prep everything ahead of time and multiply the recipe almost infinitely. You can also make it more or less

 Fast   Make Ahead   Vegetarian

complicated: If you don't want to cook beans, make the variation. If you want to go all out, serve them with sliced or crumbled chorizo or other sausage, Radish Salsa (page 34), avocado slices, chopped fresh chiles, shredded lettuce, and limes. Some crema on the side is also nice.

> 1/4 cup neutral oil, like grapeseed or corn, for frying, plus more as needed
>
> Four 5-inch corn tortillas
>
> 1/4 cup Real Refried Beans (page 418) or any soft, well-seasoned beans
>
> 1 tablespoon butter, lard, or bacon fat
>
> 4 eggs
>
> Salt and freshly ground black pepper
>
> 1/2 cup Salsa Roja or Salsa Verde (pages 48–49)
>
> 1/4 cup queso fresco or grated Monterey Jack or cheddar cheese
>
> 1/4 cup chopped fresh cilantro or parsley leaves for garnish

❶ Heat the oven to 350°F. Heat 1/4 cup of the oil in a small skillet over medium heat. When the oil is hot but not smoking, fry the tortillas one at a time until softened and heated through, about 3 seconds per side. Make sure they do not crisp. Drain on paper towels.

❷ Spread 1 tablespoon of the beans in the center of each tortilla and set aside. (At this point, you may set the tortillas aside for up to an hour or so.)

❸ Put the butter in a large skillet over medium heat. When melted and hot, add the eggs. Cook until translucent, about a minute, then turn the heat to low and sprinkle with salt and pepper. Cook until a little less done than you like them, just a few minutes. Put an egg in the center of each tortilla, then top with 2 tablespoons salsa and 1 tablespoon cheese.

❹ Carefully transfer the tortillas to a baking dish that will hold them snugly. Bake until the cheese is melted, about 5 minutes, then serve immediately, garnished with herbs.

Simplest Huevos Rancheros. Omit the tortillas and beans. Scramble the eggs in the butter; as they are beginning to set in the pan, stir in the salsa and cheese. Sprinkle with a little salt and pepper and serve.

Breakfast Burritos

MAKES: 4 servings
TIME: 20 minutes with cooked beans

Fill breakfast burritos as you would tacos: with salsa; chopped fresh tomato; cilantro; black olives; sliced scallion; chopped chiles; avocado slices; and cooked chorizo, bacon, sausage, or ground meat; and Crisp Panfried Potatoes (page 341)—alone or in combination.

You can double or triple the batch, wrap them well in plastic or foil, and tuck them away in your freezer. Reheat foil-wrapped burritos in a 350°F oven for 20 minutes or so, or remove the wrapping, drape each burrito with a paper towel, and reheat in the microwave for a couple of minutes.

> 2 cups Real Refried Beans (page 418), Chili non Carne (page 429), or plain cooked or canned pinto or black beans
>
> 4 large flour tortillas
>
> 6 eggs
>
> 2 tablespoons butter or extra virgin olive oil
>
> 1 cup crumbled fresh cheese or queso fresco or grated cheddar or Jack cheese

❶ Warm the beans or chili in a small pot. To warm the tortillas, wrap them in foil and put in a 300°F oven for about 10 minutes or stack them between 2 damp paper towels and microwave for 30 to 60 seconds.

❷ Beat the eggs lightly and combine with the butter or oil in a medium skillet over medium-high heat. Cook, stirring frequently and scraping the sides of the pan until cooked as you like, no more than a few minutes.

❸ When the eggs are nearly done, remove them from the heat and assemble the burritos. Spread the cheese on each tortilla and top with 1/2 cup or so of beans. Add the eggs and any additional fillings, sauces, or garnishes you like. Roll up (see the illustrations on page 173 if you like) and serve.

The Basics of Omelets

The classic French omelet turns the egg into an elegant centerpiece. Omelets can be thick or thin and filled with almost anything.

Though making a beautiful omelet takes practice, making a very good one is dead easy: Use a nonstick pan or a well-seasoned cast-iron pan and a plastic spatula; use hot butter or oil and keep the heat fairly high; and don't overstuff or you'll never be able to roll it up (and you might even have trouble folding). You can fold it—in half or into thirds—whichever is easier for you. Or just make a flat omelet (see pages 804–805).

Simplest Omelet

MAKES: 2 servings

TIME: 15 minutes

Omelets are ideal at breakfast, brunch, lunch, and dinner. This recipe is for a really basic omelet, cooked in one pan and shared. (For individual omelets, divide the ingredients in half and cook in batches.) But you can fill them with almost anything. The variations and list that follow range from classic (and usually simple) to a bit more complex; some are practically all-in-one meals.

4 or 5 eggs

2 tablespoons milk or cream (optional)

Salt and freshly ground black pepper

2 tablespoons plus 1 teaspoon butter or extra virgin olive oil

❶ Beat the eggs with the milk and some salt and pepper in a bowl. Put a 10-inch skillet over medium-high heat and wait a minute. Add the 2 tablespoons butter or oil; when the butter melts or the oil is hot, swirl it around the pan until the butter foam subsides or the oil coats the pan, then pour in the egg mixture. Cook, undisturbed, for about 30 seconds, then use a rubber spatula to push the edges of the eggs toward the center. As you do this, tip the pan to allow the uncooked eggs in the center to reach the perimeter.

❷ Continue until the omelet is mostly cooked but still runny in the center, a total of about 3 minutes (you can cook until the center firms up if you prefer).

❸ There are a couple of ways to proceed. You can fold the omelet into thirds, using a large spatula, or just fold the omelet in half and slide it from the pan. Rub the top of the omelet with the remaining teaspoon of butter or oil and serve.

Spanish Omelet. Before cooking the omelet, melt 1 tablespoon butter in a small saucepan over medium heat. Add 2 tablespoons chopped scallion or onion and cook for 30 seconds. Stir in 1 cup chopped tomato and cook for about 2 minutes. Sprinkle with salt and pepper and keep warm. Add the tomato mixture, with a sprinkling of smoked paprika if you like, to the eggs—in a line along the axis on which you will fold or roll—about a minute before finishing the omelet.

Denver Omelet. Before cooking the omelet, melt 2 tablespoons butter in a small saucepan over medium heat. Add 2 tablespoons each of chopped onion and red bell pepper and cook for 30 seconds. Stir in ½ cup chopped cooked ham and cook for about 2 minutes. Sprinkle with salt and pepper and keep warm. Add the ham mixture to the eggs—in a line along the axis on which you will fold or roll—about a minute before finishing the omelet.

13 Ideas for Filling Omelets

Cooked fillings, like vegetables or grains, should be warm; raw fillings, like cheese, should be grated finely so they melt or at least heat up quickly. Mix and match any of the fillings, but keep the quantity to about 1 cup.

 Fast   Make Ahead   Vegetarian

1. Grated cheese—virtually any kind that melts at least a little—about 2 tablespoons per egg
2. About ¹/₂ cup sautéed mushrooms, onion, spinach, or leftover cooked vegetables (steamed, boiled, or sautéed; rinse with boiling water if necessary to remove unwanted flavors), cut into small dice
3. Peeled, seeded, and diced ripe tomato, drained of excess moisture
4. Cottage cheese or goat cheese (mixed with fresh chopped herbs if you like)
5. Chopped ham, crisp-cooked bacon, sausage meat, or other chopped meat
6. Marmalade, jam, or jelly (sprinkle the top of the omelet with a little sugar before serving if you like)
7. 1 teaspoon chopped fresh stronger herbs like oregano, tarragon, or thyme to 1 tablespoon milder ones like parsley, chive, chervil, basil, or mint
8. Fruit, like peeled and grated apples or berries, briefly cooked with butter, sugar, and cinnamon
9. About ¹/₄ cup each cream cheese and smoked salmon, cut into bits
10. Cooked seafood, like shrimp, scallops, lobster, or crabmeat, shredded or minced
11. Minced red bell pepper, mild chiles (like New Mexican or poblano) or Roasted Red Pepper (page 330)
12. About ¹/₂ cup gently sautéed sliced or chopped onion
13. Mashed Potatoes (page 339) or any mashed vegetables, like sweet potatoes, celery root, or parsnips

FOLDING AN OMELET IN HALF

1

2

(STEP 1) First, hold the pan at a 45-degree angle so that half of the omelet slides onto the plate, then **(STEP 2)** gently increase the angle of the pan over the plate, allowing the omelet in the pan to fold over onto the first half.

FOLDING AN OMELET INTO THIRDS

1

2

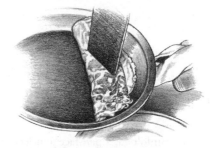

(STEP 1) Using a large spatula, loosen one edge of the omelet; lift and fold about a third of it toward the center. **(STEP 2)** Now slide the spatula under the center of the omelet; lift and fold it over the opposite edge.

Baked Sweet Omelet

MAKES: 2 servings

TIME: About 30 minutes

We don't see many sweet omelets, but they really do make sense, like other desserty breakfasts—think of it as an easy soufflé. Serve hot or at room temperature, sprinkled with powdered sugar and a selection of marmalades and jams, or macerated fruit (see page 379), and whipped cream, crème fraîche, sour cream, or yogurt.

4 eggs, separated

$^{1}/_{2}$ cup milk or cream

1 tablespoon all-purpose flour

Pinch salt

2 tablespoons sugar

2 tablespoons butter

❶ Heat the oven to 350°F. Beat the egg yolks with the milk, flour, salt, and sugar. Beat the whites until stiff but not dry.

❷ Put a large ovenproof skillet, preferably nonstick, over medium heat and add the butter. When it melts, gently fold the egg whites into the yolk mixture. Pour into the skillet and cook for 2 minutes, then transfer to the oven. Bake until puffy and browned on top, 10 to 20 minutes.

The Basics of Frittate and Other Flat Omelets

Flat omelets—the paradigm is the frittata, but the form is universal—are unfolded, open-face omelets, and completely all-purpose; I've made them for lunch, supper, brunch, and as an appetizer. They're good entertaining dishes because you can also make them in advance—they're just as good at room temperature as they are warm—and cut into wedges or squares. Furthermore, they're the easiest omelets to make; to finish cooking, you set the pan in the oven for a bit to set the top (or you can run it under the broiler, though you must be careful not to toughen the egg).

Flat omelets can be as thick or as thin as you like and can include just about any cooked meat or seafood, vegetable (fresh, frozen, or leftover), herb, cheese, pasta, or cooked grain. The Spanish version—called a *tortilla*—is most often but not exclusively made with potatoes and onions; the Italian frittata is made in countless different ways, even with ingredients that might not traditionally be thought of as Italian.

Tomato and Cheese Frittata

MAKES: 4 servings

TIME: 30 minutes

All sorts of vegetables can be used here. See the variations and the list that follows.

2 tablespoons extra virgin olive oil

$^{1}/_{2}$ onion, sliced

Salt and freshly ground black pepper

$1^{1}/_{2}$ cups peeled, seeded, and diced ripe tomato, drained of excess moisture

6 to 8 eggs

$^{1}/_{2}$ cup freshly grated Parmesan cheese

❶ Put a tablespoon of the olive oil in a large skillet over medium-high heat. When hot, add the onion and cook, sprinkling with salt and pepper, until soft, about 5 minutes. Add the tomato and turn the heat down to low. Cook, stirring occasionally until the pan is almost dry, another 5 minutes or so.

❷ Meanwhile, beat the eggs with some salt and pepper. Pour the eggs over the tomato, using a spoon if necessary to evenly distribute the vegetables. Sprinkle the cheese over top and cook, undisturbed, until the eggs are barely set, 5 to 10 minutes. (You can set them further by putting the pan in a 350°F oven for a few minutes or by running it under the broiler for a minute or two.) Serve hot, warm, or at room temperature.

Cheese Frittata. You can make this with or without the vegetables and just sprinkle grating or crumbling cheese on top at the end, then melt it in the oven or under the broiler if you prefer. Or, in Step 2, add to the beaten eggs $3/4$ cup cheese, like cottage cheese, goat cheese, ricotta, crumbled blue cheese, or grated Jack or cheddar. Proceed with the recipe.

Frittata with Crumbled Sausage. Substitute about 6 ounces crumbled sausage for the tomato; add it with the onions. Omit the Parmesan.

Pasta Frittata. Excellent for leftover pasta: Omit the tomato and increase the Parmesan to 1 cup. If you're starting with dried pasta, bring a large pot of water to a boil and salt it. Cook 4 ounces pasta until barely tender, somewhat short of where you would normally cook it. Drain and immediately toss it with 2 table-spoons softened butter or extra virgin olive oil in a wide bowl. Cool it a bit. Otherwise, use about 8 ounces of cooked pasta. (It's fine if it has some sauce sticking to it; if not, toss with the butter or oil.) In Step 2, beat the eggs with half the Parmesan, sprinkle with salt and pepper, and add some chopped fresh basil if you like. Stir in the pasta and pour into the pan. Sprinkle with the remaining Parmesan and pro-ceed with the recipe.

Frittata, Mexican Style. In Step 1, substitute 3 chopped scallions and about 1 tablespoon minced jalapeño for the onion (cook for just a minute) and, if you like, about 6 ounces chorizo for the tomato. In Step 2, add $1/2$ cup crumbled queso fresco and $1/4$ cup chopped fresh cilantro leaves to the eggs and omit the Parme-san. Proceed with the recipe. Serve with salsa and a stack of warm tortillas.

Frittata, Greek Style. Skip Step 1, use chopped cooked spinach instead of the tomato, and omit the Parmesan. In Step 2, add 1 cup or so crumbled feta cheese and 1 teaspoon chopped oregano leaves (or $1/2$ teaspoon dried) to the beaten eggs. Proceed with the recipe.

12 Additions to Flat Omelets

Just about any vegetable, herb, or cheese can be used in flat omelets, alone or in combination. Figure about 2 cups total for five eggs. If you're using leftover cooked vegetables, let them come to room temperature or give them a quick flash in the pan with some oil or butter, then add the beaten eggs and cook as directed in the frit-tata recipes.

For fresh vegetables, chop the vegetable into bite-sized pieces and cook in the pan with a tablespoon or two of oil or butter until tender (adding water as needed; see Tomato and Cheese Frittata, previous page) or boil in salted water until tender and drain very well. For frozen vegetables, defrost them either at room temperature or in the pan before adding the eggs.

1. Chopped steamed spinach or chard, mixed with a dash of lemon and nutmeg or sautéed, with minced garlic, in olive oil
2. Crisp bacon mixed with panfried apple and onion slices
3. Minced salami, cooked sausage, ham, cooked or smoked fish
4. Sautéed onion, fresh tomato, and basil
5. Asparagus (or other green vegetable), goat cheese, and basil
6. Cubed or sliced cooked eggplant and/or bell peppers (any way is good, but grilled is delicious)
7. Chopped or grated and quickly cooked zucchini (see page 239)
8. Sautéed Mushrooms (page 313)
9. Caramelized Onions (page 325) and blue cheese
10. Leftover Mashed Potatoes (page 339)
11. Peeled, seeded, and diced tomato or Oven-Dried Tomatoes (page 362)
12. Real Croutons (page 877)

Spanish Tortilla

MAKES: 4 to 6 servings

TIME: About 40 minutes

The classic Spanish omelet, served as a tapa or on sandwiches (don't laugh; it's good) that I've been making since I first visited Spain 25 years ago. Don't worry about using so much olive oil; a lot will be poured off. Save it in the fridge if you like: It's delicious and good for sautéing virtually anything.

> 1 cup extra virgin olive oil
>
> 1¼ pounds waxy potatoes, 3 to 4 medium, peeled and thinly sliced
>
> 1 medium onion, thinly sliced
>
> Salt and freshly ground black pepper
>
> Pinch smoked paprika (pimentón), optional
>
> 6 to 8 eggs

1 Put the oil in a large nonstick skillet over medium heat. About 3 minutes later, add a slice of potato; if bubbles appear, the oil is ready. Add all the potatoes and onion and sprinkle with salt and pepper along with smoked paprika if you're using it. Turn the potato mixture in the oil with a wooden spoon and adjust the heat so that the oil bubbles lazily.

2 Cook, turning the potato mixture gently every few minutes and adjusting the heat so the potatoes do not brown, until they are tender when pierced with the tip of a small knife. Meanwhile, beat the eggs with some salt and pepper in a large bowl.

3 Drain the potato mixture in a colander, reserving the oil. Wipe out the skillet, return it to medium heat, and add 2 tablespoons of the reserved oil. Combine the potato mixture with the eggs and add them to the skillet. As soon as the edges firm up—this will only take a minute or so—reduce the heat to medium-low and cook, undisturbed, for 5 minutes.

4 Insert a rubber spatula all around the edges of the cake to make sure it will slide from the pan. Carefully slide it out—the top will still be quite runny—onto a plate. Cover with another plate and, holding the plates tightly, invert them (see illustration, page 345). Add another tablespoon of oil to the skillet and use a rubber spatula to coax the cake back in. Cook for another 5 minutes, then slide the cake from the skillet to a plate. (Or you can finish the cooking by putting the tortilla in a 350°F oven for about 10 minutes.) Serve warm (not hot) or at room temperature. Do not refrigerate.

Spinach Tortilla. Omit the potatoes and onion; reduce the oil to ¼ cup. Omit the paprika. In Step 1, sauté 1 pound of fresh spinach in the oil with 1 tablespoon minced garlic and a pinch of hot red pepper flakes if you like. Stir and cook until just softened (only a few minutes). Drain and proceed with the recipe.

The Basics of Savory Soufflés

Soufflés aren't as difficult as you might think. In fact they're easy as long as you attend to a couple of key points: First, beat the egg whites correctly. It's vital to use clean metal or glass utensils; plastic can retain traces of fats and oils, which will prevent the egg whites from foaming. (For the same reason, no trace of yolk can be in the whites; their fat will keep the whites flat.) Whip them until they are shiny and can hold real peaks, but ones whose tips fold over a bit. If the whites become stiff, clumpy, and watery, they're overwhipped; you'll have to start over, but it's a mistake you are unlikely to make more than once.

Mixing the egg whites into the soufflé base is also important: You want to fully incorporate them while maintaining their airiness. (The word *soufflé* has the same root as the word for breath; this is all about air.) First, fold in about one-third of the egg whites to lighten the base. Use your hand or a rubber spatula (the new spoon-shaped ones are nice) to scoop the mixture from the bottom and fold it over the top and don't worry too

 Fast   Make Ahead   Vegetarian

much about deflating the whites at this point. Then add the rest of the egg whites, using the same folding technique, but a little more gently; incorporate well, but if light streaks of egg white remain, that's okay. If the mixture goes flat, it's overmixed and your soufflé won't rise much.

Keep in mind that soufflés with cheese and vegetable purées won't become quite as lofty as those without, but won't fall as much either; in other words, they're more stable.

SEPARATING EGGS

To separate eggs, break the egg with the back of a knife or on the side of a small bowl.

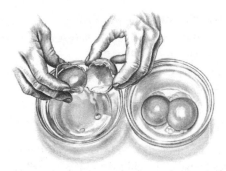

The easiest way to separate eggs is to use the shell halves, moving the yolk back or forth once or twice so that the white falls into a bowl. Be careful, however, not to allow any of the yolk to mix in with the whites or they will not rise fully during beating.

Cheese Soufflé

MAKES: 4 to 6 servings
TIME: About 1 hour

An easy, delicious, and always impressive dish. Make one large soufflé or make 4 to 6 individual soufflés in 1¹/₂ to 2 cup ramekins; the cooking time may be reduced by as much as half with the smaller dishes.

4 tablespoons (¹/₂ stick) butter, plus butter for the dish

¹/₄ cup all-purpose flour

1¹/₂ cups milk, warmed until hot to the touch (about a minute in an average microwave)

6 eggs, separated

Salt and freshly ground black pepper

Dash cayenne or ¹/₂ teaspoon dry mustard

¹/₂ cup freshly grated Parmesan cheese

¹/₂ cup grated or crumbled cheddar, Jack, Roquefort, Emmental, and/or other cheese

❶ Use a bit of the butter to grease a 2-quart soufflé or other deep baking dish. (Hold off on this step if you're not going to bake the soufflés until later.)

❷ Put the remaining 4 tablespoons of butter in a small saucepan over medium-low heat. When the foam subsides, stir in the flour and cook, stirring, until the mixture darkens, about 3 minutes. Turn the heat to low and whisk in the milk, a bit at a time, until the mixture is thick. Let cool for a few minutes, then beat in the egg yolks, sprinkle with salt and pepper, cayenne or mustard, and the cheeses. (At this point, you may cover the mixture tightly and refrigerate for a couple of hours; bring back to room temperature before continuing.)

❸ About an hour before you're ready to cook, heat the oven to 375°F. Use an electric or hand mixer or whisk to beat the egg whites until fairly stiff. Stir about a third into the sauce to lighten it, then gently—and not overly thoroughly—fold in the remaining whites, using a rubber spatula or your hand. Transfer to the prepared dish and bake until the top is brown, the sides are firm, and the center is still quite moist, about 30 minutes. Use a thin skewer to check the interior; if it is still quite wet, bake for another 5 minutes. If it is just a bit moist, the soufflé is done. Serve immediately.

Herb and Cheese Soufflé. Add chopped fresh herbs (1 teaspoon stronger herbs like marjoram, oregano, tarragon, or thyme or 2 tablespoons milder ones like parsley, chive, chervil, basil, dill, or mint); sprinkle into the yolk mixture just before folding in the egg whites.

Spinach Soufflé. You can use any cooked vegetable here, but spinach is the classic: In Step 2, add 2 tablespoons minced onion and 1 cup cooked, drained, and chopped or puréed spinach to the batter along with the Parmesan cheese; omit the other cheese.

Smoked Salmon Soufflé. Use any smoked fish you like here: Omit the cheese and the cayenne or mustard. Use a fork to roughly mash about 1 cup of flaked smoked fish; stir into the base mixture along with salt and pepper. Just before adding the egg whites, stir in a couple tablespoons of minced chives or dill if you like.

The Basics of Quiche

Egg-based pies are nearly universal, though we associate them most closely with northern France, where they are called *quiche*. Still, rich, savory custards with a flaky bottom crust are made throughout Western Europe and elsewhere in the world as well. In most, egg and cream or milk are the main components of the custard; cheese is the best-known other filling, but many vegetables and herbs play a part and vary widely. Quiche is also a terrific vehicle for leftovers.

The crust—for many the hardest part of a quiche to get right—is basically an unsweetened pie or tart crust. (Some people use puff pastry for an even richer quiche.) To achieve a perfectly flaky, crunchy crust, you must prebake it at a high oven temperature before adding the cus-

tard mix. (You can also bake most of these without any crust at all, for a savory custard; just start checking for doneness after about 20 minutes.)

Serve quiche with a salad for brunch, lunch, or dinner. It's also handy for parties, because you can make it a day before and reheat in a 350°F oven or serve at room temperature.

Cheese Quiche

MAKES: 4 to 8 servings
TIME: About 1½ hours, somewhat unattended; less if you have a premade crust

Use just about any cheese; if it's soft, like goat or cream cheese, ricotta, or cottage cheese, reduce the cream by ½ cup or so. Fresh herbs are a simple way to boost the flavor; add ¼ cup chopped fresh basil, parsley, chives, chervil, cilantro, or dill or 1 teaspoon or so chopped fresh tarragon, thyme, rosemary or about 1 tablespoon chopped fresh marjoram or oregano.

1 recipe Flaky Piecrust (page 928), made without sugar, or Savory Tart Crust (page 930), fitted into a 10-inch tart pan or 9-inch deep-dish pie pan and chilled

6 eggs at room temperature

2 cups grated Emmental, Gruyère, Cantal, cheddar, or other flavorful cheese

2 cups cream, half-and-half, milk, or a combination, heated gently just until warm

½ teaspoon salt

¼ teaspoon cayenne, or to taste

❶ Heat the oven to 425°F and set the rack in the middle. Prebake the chilled crust as described on page 928 until the crust begins to brown, 10 to 12 minutes. Remove and let cool on a rack while you prepare the filling. Reduce the oven temperature to 325°F.

❷ Combine the remaining ingredients and beat until well blended. Put the semicooked shell on a baking sheet and pour in the egg mixture. Bake for 30 to 40 minutes, or until almost firm (it should still jiggle just a little in the middle) and lightly browned on top; reduce the oven heat if the shell's edges are darkening too quickly. Cool on a rack; serve warm or at room temperature.

Pesto Quiche. Substitute ³/₄ cup Traditional Pesto (page 27) for ¹/₂ cup each of the cheese and cream.

Onion Quiche

MAKES: 4 to 8 servings

TIME: About 1¹/₂ hours, somewhat unattended; less if you have a premade crust

You can substitute nearly any vegetable you like for the onions (see "How to Use Other Ingredients in Quiche or Baked Custard"), though this is an absolute classic and—when the onions are cooked until almost creamy, as they are here—really lovely.

1 recipe Generous Pie Shell (page 929), made without sugar, or Savory Tart Crust (page 930), fitted into a 10-inch tart pan or 9-inch deep-dish pie pan and chilled

4 tablespoons butter or olive oil

6 cups thinly sliced onion

Salt and freshly ground black pepper

1 teaspoon fresh thyme leaves or ¹/₂ teaspoon dried thyme

6 eggs at room temperature

2 cups cream, half-and-half, milk, or a combination, heated gently just until warm

❶ Heat the oven to 425°F and set the rack in the middle. Prebake the chilled crust as described on page 928 until the crust begins to brown, 10 to 12 minutes. Remove and let cool on a rack while you prepare the filling. Reduce the oven temperature to 325°F.

❷ Put the butter or oil in a large, deep skillet over medium heat; when the butter melts or the oil is hot, add

How to Use Other Ingredients in Quiche or Baked Custard

There are two ways to prepare vegetables before adding them to the egg mixture for quiches and custards. The first is to cook them like the onions in the Onion Quiche. Most vegetables won't take as long as onions; use your judgment, keeping in mind that they will cook a little more as the quiche bakes. Some vegetables, however, work best after they have been cooked in boiling salted water (see "Boiling and Parboiling Vegetables," page 237), drained, then combined with the egg mixture.

In either case, cool vegetables before adding them to the eggs and limit the total quantity of extra ingredients—vegetables, cheese, nuts, whatever—to 2 cups for quiche and 1 cup for custard. Here are some specific ideas and guidelines to get you started:

- Broccoli or cauliflower: Chop into small florets and boil for a minute or two.
- Asparagus: Cook in butter or oil—or boil—until just tender. Super with goat cheese.
- Artichoke hearts: Boil for a couple minutes. Combine with ricotta and basil.
- Potatoes: Boil until you can pierce easily with a fork. Season with rosemary or dill.
- Eggplant: Peel if you like and cut into small cubes. Cook in butter or oil until browned and tender, 5 minutes or so. Good with olives, a little tomato, and Parmesan.
- Bell peppers: Cook until just tender in a little butter or olive oil.
- Tomatoes: Start with no more than 2 cups chopped fresh or drained canned tomatoes. Cook in butter or oil until quite dry.
- Greens—kale, spinach, chard, collards, watercress, and the like: Follow the directions for boiling and shocking greens (see page 239). Squeeze out as much water as possible, then coarsely chop them.

the onion and some salt and pepper. Turn the heat up to medium-high and cook, stirring frequently, until the onion is very soft and lightly browned, at least 20 minutes and probably longer; adjust the heat so it doesn't brown too much or crisp up, but just cook until the onion practically melts. Add the thyme, stir, turn off the heat, and cool slightly. Combine the remaining ingredients in a bowl and then add the onion mixture.

3 Put the semicooked shell on a baking sheet and pour in the egg mixture. Bake for 30 to 40 minutes, or until almost firm (it should still jiggle just a little in the middle) and lightly browned on top; reduce the oven heat if the shell's edges are darkening too quickly. Cool on a wire rack; serve warm or room temperature.

Onion Quiche with Bacon. Omit the butter or oil. Cook 8 to 12 slices of good bacon until nice and crisp. Remove the bacon with a slotted spoon and cook the onion in the bacon fat, stirring, until very tender, 10 to 15 minutes. Mix with the eggs. Put the bacon on the crust, pour the egg-onion mixture over it, and proceed with the recipe.

Mushroom Quiche. Fresh or dried mushrooms are equally delicious; soak dried mushrooms in hot water or some of the cream, heated, until soft (squeeze a bit if soaked in water; no need to squeeze if soaked in the cream): Substitute 4 cups sliced fresh mushrooms or 2 cups soaked and sliced dried mushrooms for the onions. In Step 2, cook the mushrooms until just tender and proceed with the recipe.

Baked Mushroom Custard

MAKES: 4 to 6 servings
TIME: 45 minutes

M **V**

This custard is pretty basic; see the first variation for an even simpler one. Toss in a bit of cheese or fresh herbs, especially chopped chives, chervil, or a bit of tarragon, to add flavor.

1 tablespoon butter

2 tablespoons finely chopped shallot or onion

2 cups chopped shiitake, cremini, or button mushrooms (about 8 ounces)

2 cups cream, half-and-half, milk, or a combination

1 sprig fresh thyme (optional)

2 eggs plus 2 yolks

Pinch cayenne

$1/2$ teaspoon salt

1 Put the butter in a medium skillet over medium-high heat. When it melts, add the shallot and cook until softened, about a minute. Add the mushrooms and cook until tender, about 5 minutes. Lower the heat a bit, pour in the cream, add the thyme if you're using it, and cook just until it begins to steam, a couple more minutes.

2 Heat the oven to 300°F and bring a kettle of water to a boil. Put the eggs, cayenne, and salt in a medium bowl and whisk or beat until blended. Remove the thyme and gradually add the cream to the egg mixture, whisking constantly. Pour the mixture into a 1-quart dish or into 4 to 6 small ramekins or custard cups.

3 Put the dish or ramekins in a baking pan and pour in hot water to within about 1 inch of the top of the dish or ramekins. Bake until the mixture is not quite set—it should jiggle a bit in the middle—30 to 40 minutes for ramekins, somewhat longer for a baking dish. Use your judgment; cream sets up faster than milk. Serve warm, at room temperature, or cold within a few hours of baking.

Baked Cheesy Custard. A cheese that melts easily is best here: Add $1/2$ cup finely grated Parmesan, Emmental, Gruyère, cheddar, Jack, or goat cheese; stir into the heated cream until melted. Omit the shallot and mushrooms if you like.

Baked Roasted Garlic Custard. Omit the shallot and mushrooms. Add 4 to 8 cloves Roasted Garlic (page 303), peeled and smashed into a paste, to the egg mixture.

The Basics of Pancakes

Pancakes are made from a simple, forgiving batter with lots of room for improvising: Beat the egg whites and/or use cottage cheese for light and airy pancakes; switch the type of flour; add fruit, peanut butter, chocolate chips, or spices. If you like thick pancakes, reduce the liquid; likewise, add more liquid for thinner pancakes.

Everyday Pancake batter whips up in no time and can be stored in the fridge for a couple of days, which makes it ideal for weekday breakfasts. You can also just mix the dry ingredients to store indefinitely (this, essentially, is Bisquick); just add the eggs and milk when you're ready to cook.

6 Tips for Making Perfect Pancakes

1. Use a nonstick griddle or skillet or one of well-seasoned cast iron to minimize butter or oil.

2. Heat until a few drops of water skid across the surface before evaporating.
3. Ladle the pancakes onto the griddle with enough room in between for flipping.
4. The edges of the pancake will set first; when bubbles appear in the center of the pancake and the bottom is golden brown, it's ready to flip.
5. Serve the pancakes immediately if possible; that's when they are best.
6. Melt the butter and gently heat the maple syrup—or whatever syrup you're using (the microwave does a good job here).

Everyday Pancakes

MAKES: 4 to 6 servings
TIME: 20 minutes

It's amazing how quickly you can whip up this batter. Store it, covered, in the refrigerator for up to 2 days. Adjust the consistency of the batter with either more milk or more flour as you like.

2 cups all-purpose flour

2 teaspoons baking powder

½ teaspoon salt

1 tablespoon sugar (optional)

2 eggs

1½ to 2 cups milk

2 optional tablespoons melted and cooled butter, plus unmelted butter for cooking, or use a neutral oil like grapeseed or corn

❶ Heat a griddle or large skillet over medium-low heat while you make the batter.

❷ Mix together the dry ingredients. Beat the eggs into 1½ cups of the milk, then stir in the 2 tablespoons cooled melted butter if you're using it. Gently stir this mixture into the dry ingredients, mixing only enough to moisten the flour; don't worry about a few lumps. If the batter seems thick, add a little more milk.

Use a little butter or oil each time you add batter, unless your skillet is truly nonstick. When the butter foam subsides or the oil shimmers, ladle batter onto the griddle or skillet, making any size pancakes you like. Adjust the heat as necessary; usually, the first batch will require higher heat than subsequent batches. The idea is to brown the bottom in 2 to 4 minutes, without burning it. Flip when bubbles appear in the center of the pancakes and the bottoms are cooked; they won't hold together well until they're ready.

④ Cook until the second side is lightly browned, a couple more minutes, and serve or hold on an ovenproof plate in a 200°F oven for up to 15 minutes.

Sourdough Pancakes. This requires a sourdough starter, but if you have one this is a good place to take advantage of your foresight: Substitute 1 cup sourdough starter (see page 858) for half the flour; reduce the milk and salt by half, the baking powder to ¹/₂ teaspoon, and the egg to 1. Mix the starter, flour, and ¹/₂ cup of the milk to a medium-thin batter; let sit for an hour. Just before cooking, stir in the salt, sugar, and baking powder; then beat in the egg.

Light and Fluffy Pancakes

MAKES: 4 servings
TIME: 20 minutes

Here the egg whites are whipped into a foam and folded into the batter, creating a cross between pancake and soufflé.

1 cup milk

4 eggs, separated

1 cup all-purpose flour

Dash salt

1 tablespoon sugar

1¹/₂ teaspoons baking powder

Butter or neutral oil, like grapeseed or corn, as needed

① Heat a griddle or large skillet over medium-low heat while you make the batter.

② Beat together the milk and egg yolks. Mix the dry ingredients. Beat the egg whites with a whisk or an electric mixer until fairly stiff but not dry.

③ Combine the dry ingredients and milk-yolk mixture, stirring to blend. Gently fold in the beaten egg whites; they should remain somewhat distinct in the batter.

④ Put about 1 teaspoon of the butter or oil on the griddle or in the skillet and, when the butter melts or the oil is hot, add the batter by the heaping tablespoon, making sure to include some of the egg whites in each spoonful. Cook until lightly browned on the bottom, 3 to 5 minutes, then turn and cook until the second side is brown, a couple more minutes. Serve or hold on an ovenproof plate in a 200°F oven for up to 15 minutes.

Cottage Cheese and Sour Cream Pancakes

MAKES: 3 to 4 servings
TIME: 20 minutes

With cottage cheese and sour cream (or yogurt) as their main ingredients, these are quite different from traditional pancakes, light, creamy, and completely delicious.

1 cup cottage cheese

1 cup sour cream or yogurt

3 eggs, separated

¹/₄ teaspoon baking soda

1 cup all-purpose flour

Dash salt

1 tablespoon sugar

Butter or neutral oil, like grapeseed or corn, as needed

Pancake Variations

These variations will work with virtually any basic pancake recipe.

Buttermilk, Yogurt, Sour Cream, or Sour Milk Pancakes. Substitute one of these for the milk in either Everyday or Light and Fluffy Pancakes (to sour your own milk, see page 823); use ½ teaspoon baking soda in place of the baking powder and proceed with the recipe. Thin the batter with a little milk if necessary.

Blueberry or Banana Pancakes. Use fresh or frozen (not defrosted) blueberries; overripe bananas are my favorite: Just before cooking, stir the blueberries into the batter. For the bananas, slice them and press into the surface of the cooking pancakes. Cook these pancakes a little more slowly than you would other pancakes, as they burn more easily.

Whole Grain Pancakes. A bit denser in texture but with distinctive grain flavor: Substitute whole wheat, quinoa, amaranth, or teff flour or cornmeal, rolled oats, or a combination for up to 1 cup of the flour.

Buckwheat Cakes. Substitute buckwheat flour for the white flour, up to the full amount, though the more you use, the flatter the pancakes will be. Double the amount of sugar if you like and increase the amount of milk or other liquid by ¼ cup if necessary (buckwheat is "thirstier" than white flour). For a hauntingly good flavor, stir in a teaspoon or so of ground coriander.

Lemon–Poppy Seed Pancakes. An especially good variation of the Light and Fluffy Pancakes: Substitute ½ teaspoon baking soda for the baking powder. Add 2 tablespoons freshly squeezed lemon juice, 2 teaspoons grated lemon zest, and 2 tablespoons poppy seeds; add with the milk.

11 Other Ideas for Pancakes

1. Add up to 1 cup peeled, grated, or finely chopped or sliced fresh fruit or chopped dried fruit (see the Blueberry or Banana Pancakes in the preceding list).

2. Add 1½ cups mashed or puréed fruit (like bananas, apricots, apples, strawberries, or pumpkin or sweet potatoes); reduce the flour by ½ cup and add another egg.

3. Stir in up to 1 cup cooked grains, like any rice, millet, wheat or rye berries, couscous, barley, quinoa, or wild rice or any rolled or flaked grains, like oats, quinoa, millet, kamut, or brown rice.

4. Add ¼ cup cocoa powder and/or a handful of chocolate chips, thinning with a little milk or buttermilk if necessary.

5. Substitute freshly squeezed orange juice for the milk and add 1 teaspoon grated orange zest if you like.

6. Substitute coconut milk (to make your own, see page 389) for the milk and/or add up to ½ cup shredded coconut.

7. Substitute ½ cup any nut flour for ½ cup of the all-purpose flour and/or use nut milk for the milk.

8. Add up to 2 teaspoons freshly minced or ground ginger or 2 tablespoons chopped crystallized ginger.

9. Add about 2 teaspoons minced or grated orange or lemon zest.

10. Add up to 1 cup chopped nuts or, even better, any Granola (page 821). Or use half chopped nuts and half nut butter (added with the milk).

11. Spoon the batter over pieces of cooked bacon.

❶ Heat a griddle or large skillet over medium-low heat while you make the batter.

❷ Beat together the cottage cheese, sour cream, and egg yolks. Combine the dry ingredients. Beat the egg whites until fairly stiff but not dry.

❸ Stir the flour mixture into the cottage cheese mixture, blending well but not beating. Gently fold in the beaten egg whites; they should remain somewhat distinct in the batter.

❹ Add about 1 teaspoon of butter or oil to the griddle or skillet and, when the butter melts or the oil is hot, add the batter by the heaping tablespoon, making sure to include some of the egg whites in each spoonful. Cook until lightly browned on the bottom, 3 to 5 minutes, then turn and cook until the second side is brown, a couple minutes more. Serve immediately; these will not hold.

Lemon-Ricotta Pancakes. Substitute ricotta cheese (you can make your own if you have time; see page 824) for the cottage cheese, increase the baking soda to $^1/_2$ teaspoon, and add 2 tablespoons freshly squeezed lemon juice and 2 teaspoons grated lemon zest.

The Basics of Waffles

Waffles, as the variations here demonstrate, can be served not only at breakfast but at lunch or even dinner (topped with a braised dish like Chicken and Garlic Stew, page 652), as well as for dessert (topped with ice cream) and as a snack.

The best waffles are super-crisp outside and creamy inside, so it's crucial to get waffles out of the iron and onto the table quickly. You can keep them warm in the oven for a little while if you absolutely must, but it sort of defeats the whole purpose: Waffles are meant to be eaten immediately.

Raised waffles, made with yeast, are absolutely unbeatable, and—as long as you remember to start a batch the night before—they're as easy as any other kind. Buttermilk waffles are almost as good and more spontaneous. Even the simplest, pancakelike waffles, which tend to be thin and crunchy, have their place. They all share a handful of guidelines:

- The iron must be hot. Almost all have lights that let you know when they're ready for baking.
- The iron should be clean and lightly oiled (even if it's nonstick). Before turning it on, brush or spray the iron lightly with grapeseed or other neutral oil (or use an oil-soaked paper towel). When it's good and hot, open the iron for a minute to let any smoke escape; close it until it reheats a bit, then start cooking.
- If you have an extra 5 minutes, separate the eggs and beat the whites by themselves until stiff, then fold them into the remaining batter right before cooking. You'll be amazed at how much fluffier this makes waffles.

Real Maple Syrup—Making the Grade

The difference between real maple syrup and the colored and flavored sugar syrup sold at most supermarkets is equivalent to the difference between butter and margarine: One is a natural, wholesome product, and the other is a nutritionally useless, not-very-good-tasting, unnatural substitute.

The label will tell you all you need to know: ingredients (it should say "pure maple syrup" and nothing else); where the syrup is from (Canada produces the bulk, while Vermont and other New England states produce some); and the grade.

Maple syrup is made by boiling and evaporating sap; it takes about 40 gallons of sap to make just 1 gallon of syrup, so it's not inexpensive. But as luck would have it, my favorite maple syrup (and, according to many aficionados, the best) is Grade B, which happens to be the cheapest. There are three levels of Grade A—Light Amber, Medium Amber, and Dark Amber—and the flavor gets stronger as the syrups get darker. But unless you prefer a milder flavor, there's no reason to buy anything but Grade B.

- Be patient and don't underbake. After pouring or spreading the batter over the bottom plate, close the top and leave it alone for at least 2 minutes. Gently pull up on the top of the iron. If the lid resists, give it another minute or two. Don't automatically trust the indicator light and don't rely on the myth about waffles being ready when there's no more steam wafting out of the iron. If you want your waffle crisp, you're probably going to have to wait an extra minute or so after the light goes on (or off, depending on your machine), then do the little tug test.
- During those couple of minutes waiting for the waffles to bake, melt the butter and warm the syrup. I use the microwave set on low.
- Serve waffles straight from the iron. If you must, hold them for a few minutes—5, tops—on a rack in a 200°F oven.

Everyday Buttermilk Waffles

MAKES: 4 to 6 servings
TIME: 10 minutes, plus time to bake

If you've got buttermilk, sour cream, or yogurt, these are the most tender, spontaneous waffles you can make. Plain milk works too; see the first variation.

2 cups all-purpose flour

1/2 teaspoon salt

2 tablespoons sugar

1 1/2 teaspoons baking soda

1 3/4 cups buttermilk or 1 1/2 cups sour cream or yogurt thinned with 1/4 cup milk

2 eggs, separated

4 tablespoons (1/2 stick) butter, melted and cooled

1/2 teaspoon vanilla extract (optional)

Neutral oil, like grapeseed or corn, for brushing the iron

❶ Combine the dry ingredients in a large bowl. In another bowl, whisk together the buttermilk and egg yolks. Stir in the butter and the vanilla if you're using it.

❷ Brush the waffle iron lightly with oil and heat it. Stir the wet ingredients into the dry. Beat the egg whites with a whisk or electric mixer until they hold soft peaks. Fold them gently into the batter.

❸ Spread enough batter onto the waffle iron to barely cover it; bake until the waffle is done, 3 to 5 minutes, depending on your iron. Serve immediately or keep warm for a few minutes on an ovenproof plate in a 200°F oven.

The Quickest, Easiest Waffles. Less air and more crisp: Instead of the baking soda, use 3 teaspoons baking powder. Use 1 1/2 cups milk instead of the buttermilk, sour cream, or yogurt. Don't bother to separate the eggs; just whisk them in whole with the milk in Step 1.

Whole Grain Waffles. This formula works for both the main recipe and the preceding variation: Substitute up to 1 cup whole wheat or other whole grain flour, cornmeal, or rolled oats (or a combination) for 1 cup of the white flour.

12 Variations on Any Waffle Batter

You can make these changes to either of the two waffle recipes.

1. Up to 2 teaspoons ground cinnamon or any curry powder (to make your own, see pages 66–67)
2. 2 or 3 strips of bacon laid over the batter after it's been spread on the waffle iron—the bacon will cook along with the waffles, and cooking time may be a minute or two longer
3. Up to 1 cup chopped (not minced) nuts, any Granola (page 821), or shredded sweetened or unsweetened coconut
4. About 2 teaspoons minced or grated orange or lemon zest
5. About 1 cup grated mild cheese, like Emmental (Swiss), cheddar, or Jack, or 1/2 cup grated Parmesan cheese
6. Whole wheat, rye, or other flour, substituted for up to half of the white flour
7. Molasses, substituted for 1/2 cup milk (excellent with cornmeal)
8. Up to 2 teaspoons freshly minced or ground ginger

9. Up to ¹/₂ cup coarsely chopped dried fruit, like apricots, cherries, cranberries, or raisins

10. Up to 1 cup fresh fruit like blueberries, raspberries, or other fruit cut into ¹/₄- to ¹/₂-inch dice

11. Up to 1 cup cooked grains, like any rice, millet, wheat or rye berries, couscous, barley, quinoa, or wild rice

12. Up to 1 cup puréed cooked potatoes, sweet potatoes, or winter squash, the last two especially nice with a sprinkling of warm spices like ground cinnamon, nutmeg, or cloves

Overnight Waffles

MAKES: 4 to 6 servings

TIME: 8 hours or more, largely unattended

Eat these traditionally with butter and syrup for breakfast or use them as a "bread" to serve with virtually any meal. With a distinctive yeasty flavor and a fluffy but chewy texture, they're that good.

¹/₂ teaspoon instant yeast

2 cups all-purpose flour

1 tablespoon sugar

¹/₂ teaspoon salt

2 cups milk

8 tablespoons (1 stick) butter, melted and cooled

¹/₂ teaspoon vanilla extract (optional)

Neutral oil, like grapeseed corn, for brushing the iron

2 eggs

❶ The night before you want to serve the waffles, combine the dry ingredients in a large bowl. Stir in the milk, then the butter and the vanilla if you're using it. The mixture will be creamy and loose. Cover with plastic wrap and set aside overnight at room temperature. (Of course you can do this in the morning if you want waffles for supper.)

❷ To start baking, brush the waffle iron lightly with oil and heat it. Separate the eggs and stir the yolks into the batter. Beat the whites until they hold soft peaks. Fold them gently into the batter.

❸ Spread enough batter onto the waffle iron to barely cover it; bake until the waffle is done, usually 3 to 5 minutes, depending on your iron. Serve immediately or keep warm for a few minutes on an ovenproof plate in a 200°F oven.

The Basics of Crêpes and Blintzes

Crêpes and blintzes are thin pancakes that can be filled with either sweet or savory fillings. Crêpes are French, have less filling, and are more about dough with flavoring than blintzes (sort of Eastern European cannelloni). In either case, making a crêpe or blintz sweet or savory is as simple as adding sugar, using a different flour, and/or using a sweet or savory filling. Savory crêpes are often made with buckwheat flour and folded; sweet ones rely on white flour and are rolled (though white ones can be filled with savory ingredients too, and the folding/rolling option is your call).

Though the sheer quantity makes them somewhat time-consuming, making crêpes and blintzes is easy: Use a nonstick or well-seasoned pan; flip by lifting the edges with a spatula and using your fingers to pull it up off the pan, then flip it to the other side. It takes just one or two tries (the first crêpes almost never work—even for professionals) and there's plenty of batter to make up for the loss.

When filling, remember that crêpes are more delicate and intended to have little filling so you can taste the crêpe. Blintzes are sturdier and can hold more filling, but still need to have space to fold nicely to make sealed packages for sautéing or baking. See the recipes and illustrations on the following pages for the specifics of rolling and folding.

 Fast   Make Ahead   **V** Vegetarian

Spoon some filling across the lower third of the crêpe.

Lift the bottom edge and roll it up.

A filled crêpe.

Crêpes, Sweet or Savory

MAKES: 12 to 16 crêpes (4 to 8 servings)
TIME: 40 minutes

 Ⓜ Ⓥ

Crêpes are perfect for breakfast, brunch, lunch, a light supper, or dessert. The batter can be made a day ahead, and even the crêpes can be made ahead, refrigerated, and then wrapped in foil and reheated in a 325°F oven.

Change the flavor of the crêpe itself by substituting cornmeal, whole wheat, rye, or rice flour—all of which lend a slightly different flavor—for half of the flour. Adding a splash of flavored brandy, amaretto, Kirsch, or rose water is a nice addition to sweet crêpe batter too.

> 1 cup all-purpose flour
>
> Pinch salt
>
> 1 tablespoon sugar (optional)
>
> 1½ cups milk, plus more if needed
>
> 2 eggs
>
> 2 tablespoons butter, melted and cooled, plus unmelted butter for cooking

❶ Whisk together all the ingredients except the unmelted butter until smooth; you can do this in a blender if you like. If the mixture isn't quite pourable, add a little more milk. If time allows, let the batter rest in the refrigerator for at least an hour and up to 24 hours.

❷ Heat the oven to 200°F. Put a nonstick or well-seasoned 8- or 10-inch skillet over medium heat and wait a couple of minutes; add a small pat of butter. Stir the batter with a large spoon or ladle; add a couple tablespoons of the batter to the skillet. Swirl it around so that it forms a thin layer on the bottom of the pan, then pour the excess batter back into that which remains.

❸ When the top of the crêpe is dry, after about a minute, turn and cook the other side for 15 to 30 seconds. (The crêpe should brown only very slightly and not become at all crisp.) Bear in mind that the first crêpe almost never works, even for professionals, so discard it if necessary; there is plenty of batter.

4 Repeat the process, adding butter to the skillet and adjusting the heat as needed, until all the batter is used up. Stack the crêpes on a plate in the oven and fill and fold them all at once. Or better still, fill and fold each crêpe while it's still in the pan and serve as they're ready; if you want your filling warmed, keep the pan over low heat for a few minutes.

5 To fill and roll or fold crêpes: Put the filling in the center of the bottom third and start rolling at the end with the filling (see the illustrations on page 817); or fold the bottom third over the filling, fold in the sides, then fold the crêpe from the bottom up. Slide it onto a plate and serve.

Lighter, Fluffier Crêpes. Separate the eggs. Add the yolks to the batter as directed, then beat the whites until stiff but not dry; gently fold them into the batter. Cook the crêpes as directed; as they finish, don't stack, but sprinkle each with about 1 teaspoon sugar (or to taste) and $1/8$ teaspoon ground cinnamon. Run under a heated broiler until the sugar melts, about 1 minute. Serve immediately, with butter or freshly squeezed lemon juice.

Buckwheat Crêpes. Resting this batter for an hour does make a difference, but if you're in a real hurry, reduce or skip this step: Substitute buckwheat flour for the white flour and add $1/4$ cup white flour. Reduce the milk to $1/2$ cup and add 1 cup water. Let the batter rest for at least an hour before cooking the crêpes.

Almond Crêpes. Substitute almond or other nut flour for half the white flour and almond milk for the regular milk, add 2 tablespoons amaretto, if you like, and use the sugar.

Chocolate Crêpes. Perfect for bananas quickly cooked with some butter and brown sugar: Add $1/4$ cup cocoa powder and use the sugar.

6 Fillings for Sweet Crêpes

As simple as sugar and lemon juice or any of these:

1. Any jam, jelly, marmalade, or macerated fruit (see page 379)

2. Nutella, any nut butter, or peanut butter
3. Any peeled, seeded (or pitted or cored) fresh fruit, cooked briefly with sugar to taste, some butter if you like, and a little rum or cinnamon (see Sautéed Apples, page 383)
4. Crème fraîche, sour cream, or yogurt (sweetened, if you like)
5. Any sweet Compound Butter (page 32) or Brown Butter (page 56), sprinkled with cinnamon, cardamom, and/or cloves
6. Creamy Caramel Sauce (page 922); not too much

6 Fillings for Savory Crêpes

Cheese and ham and cheese are the most common fillings for savory crêpes, but of course there are other possibilities:

1. Any grated or thinly sliced cheese, like Gruyère, Brie, goat, mozzarella, cheddar, or fresh cheese
2. Cooked, drained, and chopped vegetables, reheated in butter or oil per the directions on page 240 (don't bother to chop vegetables whose shape is naturally suited to crêpes, like asparagus spears)
3. Thin slice of ham and grated Gruyère or other cheese if you like
4. Any thick stew of vegetables, meat, chicken, or seafood
5. Baked Mushroom Custard (page 810), baked and then spooned into the crêpe
6. Cooked beans or lentils

Cheese Blintzes

MAKES: 4 servings
TIME: About 1 hour

M **V**

Blintzes are eggier and sturdier than crêpes, and because they are folded into little packages they can be filled more aggressively, with cottage cheese, Mashed Potatoes (page 339), or fruit. They're then sautéed or baked with butter.

FILLING AND FOLDING BLINTZES

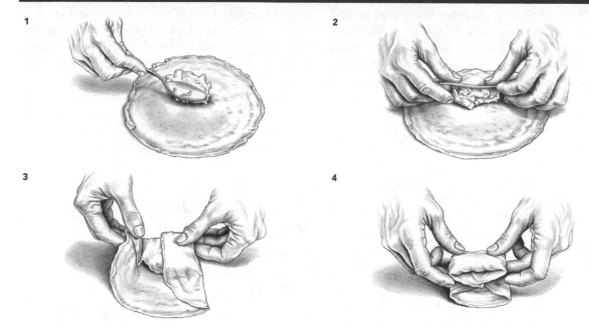

(STEP 1) Spoon some filling about a third of the way from the bottom of the blintz. (STEP 2) Fold the bottom third over the filling. (STEP 3) Fold in the sides. (STEP 4) Roll from the bottom up.

¾ cup all-purpose flour

Salt

1 cup milk

3 eggs

2 tablespoons butter, melted and cooled, plus unmelted butter for cooking, or neutral oil, like grapeseed or corn

1½ cups cottage cheese, drained if very moist

½ cup sour cream or thick yogurt

1 tablespoon sugar, or to taste

1 teaspoon ground cinnamon, or to taste

1 Whisk together the flour, a pinch of salt, and the milk until smooth; you can do this in a blender if you like. Beat in the eggs and stir in the cooled melted butter or the oil. If time allows, let rest in the refrigerator for at least an hour and up to 24 hours and beat again.

2 Put a nonstick or well-seasoned 8- or 10-inch skillet over medium heat and wait a couple minutes; add a small pat of butter. Stir the batter with a large spoon or ladle; add a couple tablespoons of the batter to the skillet. Swirl it around so that it forms a thin layer, then pour the excess back into the batter that remains.

3 When the top of the blintz is dry, after about a minute, turn and cook the other side for 15 to 30 seconds. (The blintz should brown only very slightly and not become at all crisp.) Bear in mind that the first blintz almost never works, even for professionals, so discard it if necessary; there is plenty of batter. Stack the finished blintzes on a plate; you will usually reheat them before serving.

4 Combine the cottage cheese, sour cream, another pinch of salt, the sugar, and the cinnamon. Put about 2 tablespoons of the filling in the center of the blintz about a third of the way from the bottom. Fold the bottom third over the filling, then fold in the sides, then roll from the bottom up to create a package. When they are all done, you have three choices:

To bake or broil: Arrange them on a greased (preferably buttered) ovenproof platter or baking dish. Dot with butter and sprinkle with sugar and cinnamon if you like. Bake in a 400°F oven for 10 minutes or put the dish under the broiler and watch carefully until the sugar caramelizes, about 5 minutes. Serve immediately.

To sauté: Put a tablespoon or so of butter in a large skillet over medium-high heat. When the butter melts, put several at a time into the pan and cook until brown and crisp on both sides, a total of about 5 minutes.

Mashed Potato Blintzes. Substitute well-seasoned Mashed Potatoes (page 339) or half mashed potatoes and half ground meat for the cheese filling. Proceed with the recipe, cooking longer if you added meat.

Mushroom Blintzes. Substitute Sautéed Mushrooms (page 313) for the cheese filling. Before folding, sprinkle each with a tablespoon or two of grated Parmesan or Gruyère cheese.

Fruit Blintzes. Fabulous with a dollop of crème fraîche or sour cream: Substitute any peeled, seeded (or pitted or cored) fresh fruit—apples, pears, cherries, berries, or bananas to name a few—cooked briefly with sugar to taste, some butter if you like, and a little rum or ground cinnamon for the cheese filling.

The Basics of Breakfast Cereals

Cooked cereals remain breakfast staples, as they should. Whole or partially milled grains are filling, nutritious, and flavorful—although they are almost always improved by the addition of butter and/or sweetener.

Buy your grains, if possible, in bulk at a natural food store, where they are liable to be fresher (and certainly cheaper) than the packaged stuff sold at the supermarket. And see page 451 for methods of cooking other grains, which can be readily adapted as breakfast cereals by the mere addition of sweetener.

Granola, a relatively recent addition to the American larder, is a mixture of barely cooked grains laced with nuts and sweeteners. It's easy to make at home and far better than most versions you can buy in stores.

Oatmeal or Other Creamy Breakfast Cereal

MAKES: 2 servings
TIME: 15 minutes

You can cook any kind of rolled or flaked grain this way; try wheat, rye, quinoa, millet, kamut, or brown rice flakes. And please don't bother with quick-cooking or instant oats; the old-fashioned style takes barely 5 minutes more, and the flavor and texture are far better.

This recipe gives you a fairly creamy oatmeal; if you prefer it thicker, use a bit less water.

Dash salt

1 cup rolled oats or other rolled or flaked grain

Butter to taste (optional)

Salt, sweetener (like maple syrup, sugar, or honey), and/or milk or cream as desired

1 Combine 2¼ cups water, the salt, and the oats in a small saucepan over high heat. When the water boils, turn the heat down to low and cook, stirring, until the water is just absorbed, about 5 minutes. Add butter if desired, cover the pan, and turn off the heat.

2 Five minutes later, uncover the pan and stir. Add other ingredients as desired and serve.

F Fast   **M** Make Ahead   **V** Vegetarian

10 Ideas for Oatmeal, Grits, and Other Cooked Grains

When feeding a crew, provide an array of garnishes for your guests to dress their own hot cereals.

1. Ground spices, like cinnamon, nutmeg, cloves, all-spice, cardamom, or anise
2. Chopped dried fruit
3. Chopped nuts and/or seeds
4. Fresh fruit, chopped or sliced if necessary: apples, bananas, strawberries, apricots, peaches, blueberries, cherries, or raspberries
5. Jam, jelly, marmalade, preserves, or macerated fruit (page 379)
6. Shredded coconut (great when toasted; see page 389)
7. Granola (page 821)
8. Grated cheese
9. Chopped Hard-Boiled Egg (page 791)
10. Poached Egg (page 793; or simply crack an egg into the simmering mixture during the last 3 to 5 minutes of cooking)

Grits

MAKES: 2 to 4 servings
TIME: 20 minutes

What's the difference between grits, cornmeal mush, and polenta? Not much in terms of how you cook them. But grits are made from ground dried hominy (see page 487), while cornmeal—the key ingredient in Polenta (page 485)—is ground from simply dried corn. The flavor difference is subtle. But grits are a southern favorite, mostly served at breakfast, with butter, or topped with Roasted Shrimp with Herb Sauce (page 577).

2½ cups water or half milk and half water

1 cup grits, preferably stone-ground

Salt and freshly ground black pepper

1 tablespoon butter, or more to taste

1 Put the water or milk and water in a small saucepan and bring to a boil over medium-high heat. Turn the heat down to low and slowly stir or whisk in the grits. Beat with a wire whisk to eliminate lumps.

2 Turn the heat down to a minimum and cover the saucepan. Cook, stirring occasionally, until all the water is absorbed and the grits are creamy, 10 to 15 minutes. If the mixture becomes too thick, simply whisk in a bit more water. Sprinkle with salt and pepper, stir in some butter, and serve.

Scrapple. Cook a double recipe of grits as directed (you can use cornmeal if you like). When the grits are just about done, stir in 1 to 2 cups chopped cooked bacon or sausage meat, along with 1 tablespoon minced fresh sage or 1 teaspoon dried sage. Continue to cook until the mixture is thick. Pack it into a greased small loaf pan, cover with plastic wrap, and refrigerate overnight. At breakfast time, cut into ½-inch-thick slices and panfry the slices in butter, oil, or bacon fat over medium heat until browned and crisp on both sides, about 3 minutes per side.

Granola

MAKES: About 8 cups
TIME: 30 minutes

The basic technique for making granola is always the same; it's what you put in it that makes it special. Think of this recipe as a guideline for a basic granola and then customize it in any way you like; there are lots of ideas in these pages.

Rolled oats are the most common grain, but you can use lots of other rolled and flaked grains, like wheat, rye, quinoa, millet, kamut, or brown rice flakes. Increase or decrease the other ingredients as you like and toss in other ingredients like nut butters, vanilla, or citrus zest. See the variations for some ideas.

6 cups rolled oats (not quick-cooking or instant)

2 cups mixed nuts and seeds: a combination of sunflower seeds, chopped walnuts, pecans, almonds, cashews, sesame seeds, etc.

1 cup shredded coconut (optional)

1 teaspoon ground cinnamon, or to taste

Dash salt

$1/2$ to 1 cup honey or maple syrup, or to taste

1 cup raisins or chopped dried fruit

❶ Heat the oven to 350°F. In a bowl, combine the oats, nuts and seeds, the coconut if you're using it, cinnamon, salt, and sweetener. Spread evenly on a rimmed baking sheet and bake for 30 minutes or a little longer, stirring occasionally. The mixture should brown evenly; the browner it gets without burning, the crunchier the granola will be.

❷ Remove the pan from the oven and add the raisins. Cool on a rack, stirring once in a while until the granola reaches room temperature. Transfer to a sealed container and store in the refrigerator; it will keep indefinitely.

Peanut Butter Granola. Any nut butter or tahini will work nicely here; toss in some chocolate chips if you like very sweet granola: Add $1/2$ cup peanut butter and mix with the $1/2$ cup honey or maple syrup until blended. Proceed with the recipe; stir the granola every few minutes while it's baking to prevent the peanut butter from burning.

Spiced Granola. Add another teaspoon ground cinnamon, 1 teaspoon ground ginger, $1/2$ teaspoon each ground anise and cardamom, $1/4$ teaspoon each freshly grated nutmeg and ground cloves, and 2 teaspoons vanilla extract.

Ginger-Molasses Granola. Crumbled gingersnaps (see page 897) are a great addition to this: Substitute molasses for half of the sweetener and add a 1- to 2-inch piece fresh ginger, grated into the sweetener. Add $1/4$ cup chopped crystallized ginger along with the raisins.

---

5 Important Breakfast Dishes Found Elsewhere

For some, breakfast is not complete without potatoes and sausage.

1. For fruit salad, see page 190; for macerated fruit, see page 379.
2. For home-fried potatoes, I suggest you make Crisp Panfried Potatoes (page 341), substituting butter for the olive oil if you like.
3. For hash browns, try Potato Rösti (page 345). Cook it slowly so the inside becomes tender before the outside burns.
4. For basic breakfast sausage, see page 762.
5. To cook bacon, see page 766.

The Basics of Dairy

Most dairy products should be refrigerated in their original (or clean glass) containers, ideally at 40°F or a little less. (Many cheeses can be held at room temperature for hours or even days.) Pour off what you need, then immediately return the rest to the fridge; never put unused milk or cream back in the carton or jug, or it'll cause the whole batch to spoil faster. Store cheese and butter tightly wrapped in the refrigerator. You can freeze unsalted butter for a month or so without noticeably affecting its flavor (and salted butter somewhat longer), but don't freeze milk or cream.

Milk—Whole (3.25 percent fat), Reduced-Fat (2 percent fat), Low-Fat (1 percent fat), Fat-Free, Skim, or Nonfat (0 percent fat): Unless otherwise noted, you can use any kind of reduced-fat (not fat-free) or whole milk in the recipes in this book, though I usually cook with whole milk.

Buttermilk: This tangy, thick, and sometimes lumpy liquid isn't at all what it used to be, which was the liquid that remained after churning butter. Now it's made from milk of any fat content, cultured with lactic acid–pro-

F Fast   **M** Make Ahead   **V** Vegetarian

ducing bacteria, so it's more like thin yogurt than anything else. Use it for baking, flavoring mashed potatoes, or making cold sauces, dips, and dressings.

For a quick substitute, you can "sour" regular milk: Let 1³/₄ cups of milk come to room temperature (or microwave it for 30 seconds or so). Stir in 2 tablespoons white vinegar and let the mixture sit until clabbered—thick and lumpy—about 10 minutes (you'll know). Use as a direct substitute for buttermilk.

Cream: You'll see all sorts of confusing labels for cream, but the kind you want is heavy—not whipping—cream, without any additives or emulsifiers, and not ultrapasteurized (this takes longer to whip and has a distinctive, definitely cooked, flavor). Generally 1 cup of cream whips up to about 2 cups. The fat content of whipping cream ranges from 30 percent to 36 percent; heavy cream is 36 percent fat or more.

Half-and-Half: Half milk, half cream, with a fat content that can range anywhere from 10.5 percent to 18 percent. It's nice in soups or sauces when you don't need quite the richness of heavy cream.

Sour Cream: Cream cultured with lactic acid bacteria to make it thick and produce its characteristic tangy flavor. Sour cream can be tricky to cook with because it can curdle—though not so quickly as yogurt—so add it to other ingredients over very low heat. If you want to use reduced-fat sour creams, find one without a lot of added ingredients and stabilizers.

Crème Fraîche: Like sour cream, this is thick, rich, tangy, and almost decadent. But it can be hard to find and expensive. Fortunately, you can make your own: Put a cup of cream in a small glass bowl and stir in 2 tablespoons of buttermilk or yogurt. Let the mixture sit at room temperature until thickened, anywhere from 12 to 24 hours. Cover tightly, refrigerate, and use within a week or so.

Yogurt: Cultured milk, made with bacteria that produces its unique flavor and texture. Look for "live, active cultures"—or similar terminology—on the label and avoid any with gelatins, gums, or stabilizers. Yogurt is available in whole, low-fat, and nonfat versions, as well as all sorts of crazy flavors. But you can flavor yogurt your-

self (see page 824); you can also make it yourself (see below). It can be warmed gently but not super-heated or it will curdle. In recipes, whole-milk yogurt always gives the richest results.

Butter: Butter is fat and water; the supermarket standard is 80 percent, which means 20 percent is water; higher-fat butter tends to be higher quality and better tasting. Always buy unsalted butter, also called *sweet butter;* store extra sticks in the freezer, not the fridge. Never use whipped butter in recipes, because its volume isn't the same as stick butter.

UHT Milk: Short for *ultra-high-temperature milk,* this is the nonrefrigerated stuff you see in aseptic (sterilized and vacuum-sealed) boxes on supermarket shelves. UHT milk keeps for 3 months after packaging and is always dated. It's great to have some in the pantry for emergencies.

Yogurt

MAKES: 1 quart
TIME: Overnight or longer, largely unattended

Though many excellent-quality yogurts are sold in stores, there is nothing quite like the slightly sweet flavor of homemade. And though yogurt is a little trickier to make than fresh cheese (see page 824)—mostly because the temperature must be controlled for a long time while it processes—it's easy enough to get the hang of. Whole milk makes the richest yogurt, though you can use any kind of milk you like.

1 quart milk, preferably whole

¹/₂ cup natural yogurt ("with active cultures"), ideally at room temperature

❶ Put the milk in a small to medium saucepan and bring it just to a boil; turn off the heat and cool to 110–115°F (use an instant-read thermometer).

❷ Whisk the milk and yogurt together. Put in a yogurt maker, a prewarmed thermos, or a heated bowl wrapped in a towel or blanket and set in a warm place. The idea is to keep the mixture at about 100°F.

❸ Do not disturb the mixture at all for at least 6 hours. Then carefully check by tilting the container to see whether the milk has become yogurt. If not, leave it alone for another 6 hours. When the yogurt is done, refrigerate and use within 1 week.

Yogurt Cheese. You can make this with store-bought yogurt too. There are even filters available specifically for this purpose: Instead of refrigerating the yogurt, put it in a jelly bag or several layers of cheesecloth and suspend it over the sink or a large bowl. Let drain for at least 6 hours, preferably longer, until the yogurt has a cream cheese–like consistency. Use exactly as you would cream cheese.

7 Ideas for Flavoring Plain Yogurt

Some of these—honey, maple syrup, or jam, for example—can be added to a whole batch. Some can be used in combination. Some are best used to make raitas and other sauces (see page 24). Start by adding just a little, then adjust to taste.

1. Honey
2. Maple syrup
3. Vanilla extract, with or without sugar
4. Chopped nuts
5. Preserves or jam
6. Chutneys (see pages 36–38)
7. Spice blends (see pages 65–69)

The Basics of Making Fresh Cheese

Yes, you can make cheese, and I strongly urge you to give it a try. It's almost as easy as boiling milk, and everything you need is available at the supermarket. The best thing is, this recipe requires virtually no practice; your very first batch will be better than anything you can buy.

Really.

All cheese begins by separating curds (milk solids) and whey (watery liquid). Most commercially made cheeses rely on rennet, an enzyme from the stomach of cows, to curdle milk, but there are easier ways for the home cook; buttermilk, which acts as a mild-tasting and effective coagulant, is the best. The result is tender cheese with a pure milky flavor, akin to the Indian staple paneer; true queso fresco, the fresh white cheese common in Mexico; the fromage blanc of France; or a dozen other products made worldwide. To use fresh cheese, just cut it into slices or cubes or gently crumble it by hand or with two forks (it's too soft to grate). Fresh cheese will keep for 3 or 4 days in the fridge, though you may freeze it (tightly wrapped) for up to 3 months.

Fresh Cheese, the Easy Way

MAKES: 6 to 8 servings
TIME: 2 hours, largely unattended

The recipe—and all the variations except for the cream cheese—work with 1 percent, 2 percent, or whole milk, which of course makes the richest cheeses. If you live near a farm and can find raw whole milk, you'll get the best flavor.

1/2 gallon milk

1 quart buttermilk

Salt (optional)

❶ Put the milk in a large, heavy-bottomed pot over medium-high heat. Cook, stirring occasionally to keep it from scorching, until the milk bubbles up the sides of the pot, about 10 minutes.

❷ Line a strainer with a triple layer of cheesecloth or a piece of undyed cotton muslin. Have a long piece of twine ready.

❸ Add the buttermilk to the boiling milk all at once and stir constantly until the mixture separates into curds and whey; this will take just a minute or so. It will look like cooked egg whites suspended in a slightly thick yellowish liquid. Remove from the heat and stir in a large pinch of salt if you like.

❹ Carefully pour the mixture through the cloth and strainer so that the curds collect in the bottom and the whey drains off. Gather up the corners of the cloth and twist the top to start shaping the curds into a ball. Run the bundle under cold water until you can handle it. Keep twisting and squeezing out the whey until the bundle feels firm and dry. Don't worry about handling it roughly; it can take it.

❺ Tie the string around the top to hold it tight, then tie the string around the handle of a long spoon or a stick to suspend the cheese back over the pot to drain. Let it rest, undisturbed, until cool and set, about 90 minutes. Remove the cloth and serve immediately or wrap in plastic and refrigerate for up to 3 days. Or freeze the cheese for up to 3 months.

Fresh Cottage Cheese. Incredible stuff; drain as dry or as moist as you like: Follow the recipe through Step 3. In Step 4, after you pour the curds and whey through the cheesecloth, simply leave the curds loose in the strainer until they've drained the amount of moisture you desire, anywhere from 30 to 60 minutes. Then scoop the curds into a container and store in the refrigerator.

Fresh Ricotta. Also unbelievable, especially with top-quality milk: Reduce the amount of buttermilk to 1 pint (2 cups) and proceed with the recipe through Step 3. The mixture will look like thickened buttermilk. In Step 4, after you pour it through the cheesecloth, simply leave the ricotta in the strainer until it has reached the texture you like, anywhere from 30 to 60 minutes. Then scoop the ricotta into a container and store in the refrigerator.

Fresh Cream Cheese. So rich, you won't believe it: Use 1 quart of heavy cream instead of the milk and reduce the buttermilk to 1 pint.

Pour the coagulated, lumpy mixture into a cheesecloth-lined strainer.

Twist and squeeze out excess moisture.

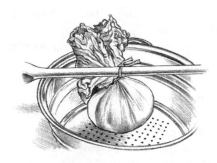

Hang from a wooden spoon or other implement over the pot, the sink, or a colander or strainer set over a bowl.

Fresh Goat Cheese. Tangy and creamy and cow's-milk free: Substitute goat's milk for the cow's milk and 1 pint goat's milk yogurt for the buttermilk.

6 Ways to Flavor Fresh Cheese

In Step 4, after pouring the curds and whey into the cloth-lined strainer, immediately stir any of the following ingredients into the curds (up to the amount indicated) and proceed with the recipe.

1. Up to ¼ cup finely chopped nuts, like walnuts, almonds, or hazelnuts
2. Up to 1 tablespoon coarsely ground black or green peppercorns
3. Up to ¼ cup Traditional Pesto (page 27) or any of the herb purées on pages 27–28
4. Up to 2 tablespoons curry powder, chaat masala, or garam masala (to make your own, see pages 66–68)
5. Up to ¼ cup Chile Paste (page 74)
6. Up to ¼ cup finely chopped Roasted Red Peppers (page 330), pimientos, piquillos, or olives

5 Simple Ways to Eat Fresh Cheese

1. Crumble as a garnish on tacos, green salads, sandwiches, or pizza.
2. Toss crumbled fresh cheese—including cottage cheese or ricotta—on hot pasta right before serving, either alone or in combination with freshly grated Parmesan cheese. With a little tomato sauce, this makes a nice "pink" pasta.
3. Use cottage cheese or ricotta as the basis for dips, spreads, or sauces by whirring a cup or so in a food processor for a few minutes with enough milk, cream, or yogurt to create the desired consistency.
4. Serve a few slices drizzled with honey and sprinkled with toasted nuts.
5. Serve a few slices drizzled with extra virgin olive oil and sprinkled with chopped fresh herbs and salt and freshly ground black pepper.

Panfried Cheese

MAKES: 4 servings
TIME: 20 minutes

Panfried cheese is universally popular, with the technique remaining pretty much the same and just the cheese changing. The Spanish version, made with paprika and manchego or other sheep's milk cheese, is my favorite. But Edam, Gouda, provolone, mozzarella, kasseri, and feta all work nicely. Softer cheeses hold their shape better during cooking if they're well chilled to begin with, so coat and refrigerate if possible.

3 tablespoons all-purpose flour

1 teaspoon paprika

½ pound mild soft sheep's milk or other cheese, cut into ½-inch slices

2 eggs, beaten

½ cup fine bread crumbs, preferably fresh (page 876)

Extra virgin olive oil for frying

1 Mix the flour and paprika together. Dredge the cheese slices in the flour, then the beaten egg, and finally the bread crumbs. If time allows, put the cheese on wax paper and refrigerate for an hour or longer.

2 Put at least ⅛ inch olive oil in a heavy skillet over medium-high heat. When the oil is hot—it will shimmer—fry the cheese slices until golden brown, about 30 seconds, then turn and brown the other side. Drain on paper towels and serve as soon as possible.

Cheese Enchiladas

MAKES: 6 to 8 servings
TIME: About 1 hour; less if you have premade sauce

Simple enough for a weeknight, especially if you have sauce already made. Use anything else you like to fill the enchiladas—in place of or along with the cheese—including simply seasoned cooked ground beef, Shredded Pork (page 759), sliced Roasted Red Peppers or chiles (page 330), or even roasted vegetables.

2 recipes Red Enchilada Sauce (page 48), about 4 cups

Neutral oil, like grapeseed or corn, for frying

24 small corn tortillas, plus more if any break

3 cups shredded Monterey Jack or cotija cheese

$^1/_2$ cup crumbled queso fresco for garnish

$^1/_2$ cup chopped red onion or scallion for garnish

$^1/_2$ cup chopped fresh cilantro for garnish

Lime wedges for garnish

❶ Prepare the sauce if you haven't already. (You may cool and refrigerate the sauce for up to 3 days; reheat gently before proceeding.)

❷ Heat the oven to 350°F. Spoon a thin layer of the sauce into the bottom of a 9 × 12-inch baking dish. Put about $^1/_2$ inch of the oil in a large, deep skillet over medium-high heat. When hot but not smoking, cook the tortillas, one at a time, until softened and pliable, about 10 seconds. Add more oil to the pan as needed. Drain on paper towels.

❸ Sprinkle a heaping tablespoon of the Monterey Jack in the center of each tortilla, roll tightly, and put the enchiladas in the prepared dish, seam side down. The rolls should be packed in snugly against one another. Cover the top with some more sauce and bake for 25 minutes. When the enchiladas come out of the oven, sprinkle them with the queso fresco, onion, and cilantro. Serve with lime wedges on the side and pass the remaining sauce at the table.

Cheese Enchiladas with Green Sauce. Also known as *Enchiladas Suisas*: Instead of making the red sauce, prepare a double recipe of Green Enchilada Salsa (page 49) as described in Step 1. Increase the amount of Monterey Jack to 5 cups. Use the remaining cheese to sprinkle on top of the enchiladas before baking.

Chicken Enchiladas. Omit the cheese if you like or reduce the quantity by half; use either red or green salsa. Prepare Grilled or Broiled Chicken with Cilantro and Lime (page 662). When cool enough to handle, pull the meat from the bone and break it into bite-sized pieces. Use the chicken, along with the cheese, to fill the tortillas, taking care not to overfill.

Bread

BREAD BAKING FILLS THE HOUSE WITH MORE welcome smells than anything. No act of cooking produces a thing that symbolizes so much love and warmth. And no food product is beloved by more people, at least in this country.

Bread *is* home cooking, though through the years it's been largely abandoned as too messy, too time-consuming, and—absurdly enough, since at its most basic it's almost literally child's play—too difficult. But although no one has found a way to make bread that doesn't require a little cleanup, it isn't that messy, it's easy, and the time it takes can be bent to your own schedule. For bread lovers, there are few reasons *not* to bake bread, if not routinely (and it is easy to work into your routine) then at least a few times a year.

Although innovations in bread baking are rare—the six-thousand-year-old process hasn't changed much since Pasteur made the commercial production of standardized yeast possible in 1859—the introduction of the gas stove, the electric mixer, and the food processor all made the process easier, faster, and more reliable. And Jim Lahey's new methods (see Jim Lahey's No-Work Bread, page 833) have made producing incredibly good bread at home even easier and more reliable. Between the food processor and Jim's style of bread there is an option for yeasted bread you will love.

But even if there were not, there are also quick breads, the unyeasted staples overlooked too often these days. These can be produced in the time it takes to make the average (real) dinner and, as long as you don't load them up with sugar, are a healthy addition to any meal, especially when you incorporate whole grains, nuts, and/or fruit. You'll use similar batters to produce muffins, biscuits, scones, and other savory baked goods, all of which are included here. And virtually all can be frozen and thawed (and warmed if you like) with great success.

ESSENTIAL RECIPES

These are the bread recipes that are simplest and remain among the best—perfect for beginners, but also for veterans who are looking for something that doesn't require a lot of thought or effort. The muffins and quick breads (do try the unusual and wonderful Olive Oil Salt Bread) are all done in less than an hour. There is one savory yeast bread here (for more on yeast breads, see page 851), but it's my favorite and probably the most talked-about recipe of 2006. And though the coffee cake is also yeasted, it is relatively easy.

✪ Olive Oil Salt Bread

MAKES: 4 to 6 servings
TIME: About 45 minutes, largely unattended

This is hands down the fastest way to get fresh warm bread on the table (the variation is actually a little faster). Rich and flaky with olive oil, this biscuitlike dough is easy to handle and takes to all sorts of additions, like cheese (especially Parmesan), chopped olives, or seasonings (see the list on page 846). Just knead them in with your hands after processing. Like most unyeasted breads, it is best eaten still warm from the oven.

$^1\!/_3$ cup extra virgin olive oil, plus more for the pan

3 cups all-purpose flour, plus more if needed

1 tablespoon baking powder

1 teaspoon salt, preferably coarse or sea salt, plus more for sprinkling

1 cup warm water

❶ Heat the oven to 375°F. Grease an 8-inch ovenproof skillet or square baking pan with about a tablespoon of olive oil. Put the flour, baking powder, and salt in a food processor and turn the machine on. Pour first the $^1\!/_3$ cup olive oil, then most of the water, through the feed tube. Process for about 30 seconds; then remove the cover. The dough should be in a well-defined, barely sticky, easy-to-handle ball. If it is too dry, add the remaining water 1 tablespoon at a time and process for 5 or 10 seconds after each addition. If it is too wet, which is unlikely, add a tablespoon or two of flour and process briefly.

❷ Put the dough into the prepared pan and press until it fits to the edges. Flip it over and press again. Cover with foil and bake for 20 minutes; then remove the foil, sprinkle the top with a little coarse salt, and bake for another 20 to 25 minutes, until the top is golden and springs back when touched gently. Cool in the pan a bit, then cut into wedges or squares and serve or store for up to a day.

 Fast   Make Ahead   Vegetarian

Griddled Olive Oil Salt Bread. On the table even faster: Instead of heating the oven, heat a griddle or put a heavy-bottomed pan over medium heat. Have the extra olive oil handy for greasing. In Step 2, divide the dough into 8 to 12 pieces and pat them into patties between your hands until they're about ¹/₂ inch thick. When the griddle or pan is hot, use enough olive oil to film the bottom and put in as many breads as will fit comfortably without crowding (you will probably have to work in batches). Cook, undisturbed, until they begin to brown around the edges and the tops bubble a bit, about 5 minutes. Then turn and cook the other side until crisp and golden, a few minutes more. Sprinkle with salt before serving.

✪ Corn Bread

MAKES: About 6 servings
TIME: About 45 minutes

Corn bread is unlike any other bread, with a deep corn flavor and slightly crunchy texture; few recipes deliver so much for so little work. The main recipe represents corn bread at its most traditional and most basic (some might call it slightly Spartan). For more intensely flavored renditions, see the variations here and the suggestions in "13 Additions to Virtually Any Quick Bread, Muffins, Biscuits, or Scones" (page 846).

1¹/₄ cups buttermilk, milk (mixed with 1 tablespoon white vinegar if you want; see Step 1), or yogurt, plus more if needed

2 tablespoons butter, extra virgin olive oil, lard, or bacon drippings

1¹/₂ cups medium-grind cornmeal

¹/₂ cup all-purpose flour

1¹/₂ teaspoons baking powder

1 teaspoon salt

1 tablespoon sugar, or more if you like sweet corn bread

1 egg

❶ Heat the oven to 375°F. If you want to make sour milk (approximating buttermilk), warm the milk gently to take the chill off—1 minute in the microwave is sufficient—and add the vinegar. Let it rest while you prepare the other ingredients.

❷ Put the fat or oil in an 8-inch ovenproof skillet or square metal baking pan over medium heat; heat until good and hot, about 2 minutes, then turn off the heat. Mix together the dry ingredients in a bowl. Mix the egg into the buttermilk. Stir the liquid into the dry ingredients just enough to combine; if it seems too dry, add another tablespoon or two of milk. Pour the batter into the prepared pan, smooth the top if necessary, and put in the oven.

❸ Bake for about 30 minutes, until the top is lightly browned and the sides have pulled away from the pan; a toothpick inserted into the center will come out clean. Serve hot or warm.

Lighter, Richer Corn Bread. Use 4 tablespoons (¹/₂ stick) of butter (do not use other fat). Increase the sugar to ¹/₄ cup. Use 2 eggs; stir their yolks into the buttermilk and beat the whites until stiff but not dry, then gently stir them into the prepared batter after the yolks and buttermilk have been incorporated. Bake as directed.

Corny Corn Bread. Add 1 cup fresh or frozen corn kernels or about 1 cup creamed corn to the liquid ingredients in Step 2.

Bacon Corn Bread. Before beginning, sauté ¹/₂ cup chopped bacon in 1 tablespoon grapeseed, corn, or other neutral oil, bacon fat, or lard until crisp. Remove the bacon with a slotted spoon, leaving the fat behind. Keep the fat hot and prepare the batter as directed; use the hot fat to prepare the pan in Step 2. Stir the bacon into the finished batter and proceed with the recipe.

Corn and Bean Bread. Use 2 eggs and 1 cup buttermilk or soured milk; omit the flour. Stir 1½ cups well-cooked white beans (canned are fine), puréed and strained, into the milk-egg mixture before adding to the dry ingredients.

Corn Muffins. To make the main recipe or any of the variations into muffins, grease a 12-cup muffin tin and put a paper cup in each if you like. Divide the dough among the cups and bake for 20 to 25 minutes.

✪ Muffins, Infinite Ways

MAKES: 12 medium or 8 large muffins
TIME: About 40 minutes

The only real difference between muffins and other quick breads is the pan you bake them in. But those little muffin cups allow for a lot more potential variation, depending on what you do at the last minute before baking.

Anything goes when it comes to varying this master recipe, including the suggestions for Fruit-and-Nut or Vegetable-and-Nut Bread on page 843. See "13 Additions to Virtually Any Quick Bread, Muffins, Biscuits, or Scones" (page 846) for more ways to spike recipe. And for a more dessertlike muffin, see the Sweet and Rich Muffins variation.

3 tablespoons melted butter or neutral oil, like grapeseed or corn, plus more for the muffin tin

2 cups all-purpose flour

¼ cup sugar, or to taste

½ teaspoon salt

3 teaspoons baking powder

1 egg

1 cup milk, plus more if needed

❶ Heat the oven to 375°F. Grease a 12-cup muffin tin and line it with paper or foil muffin cups if you like.

❷ Mix together the dry ingredients in a bowl. Beat together the egg, milk, and melted butter or oil in another bowl. Make a well in the center of the dry ingredients and pour the wet ingredients into it. Using a large spoon or rubber spatula, combine the ingredients swiftly, stirring and folding rather than beating and stopping as soon as all the dry ingredients are moistened. The batter should be lumpy, not smooth, and thick but quite moist; add a little more milk or other liquid if necessary.

❸ Spoon the batter into the muffin tins, filling them about two-thirds full and handling the batter as little as possible. (If you prefer bigger muffins, fill 8 cups almost to the top; pour ¼ cup water into the empty cups.) Bake for about 20 minutes (about 30 minutes for larger muffins) or until nicely browned and a toothpick inserted in the center of a muffin comes out clean. Remove from the oven and let rest for 5 minutes before taking them out of the tin. Serve warm.

Banana-Nut Muffins. These are good with half bran or whole wheat flour: Add ½ cup roughly chopped walnuts, pecans, or cashews to the dry ingredients. Substitute 1 cup mashed very ripe banana for ¾ cup of the milk. Use honey or maple syrup in place of sugar if possible.

Bran Muffins. Substitute 1 cup oat or wheat bran for 1 cup of the flour (you can use whole wheat flour for the remainder if you like). Use 2 eggs and honey, molasses, or maple syrup as the sweetener. Add ½ cup raisins to the prepared batter if you like.

Sour Cream or Yogurt Muffins. Reduce the baking powder to 1 teaspoon and add ½ teaspoon baking soda to the dry ingredients. Substitute 1¼ cups sour cream or yogurt for the milk and cut the butter or oil back to 1 tablespoon.

Spice Muffins. Add 1 teaspoon ground cinnamon, ½ teaspoon each ground allspice and ground ginger, and 1 pinch ground cloves and mace or nutmeg to the dry ingredients; use 1 cup whole wheat flour in place of 1 cup all-purpose flour. Add ½ cup raisins, currants, dates, or dried figs to the prepared batter if you like.

F Fast   **M** Make Ahead   **V** Vegetarian

Blueberry or Cranberry Muffins. Try substituting cornmeal for up to ¹/₂ cup of the flour: Add 1 teaspoon ground cinnamon to the dry ingredients; increase the sugar to ¹/₂ cup. Stir 1 cup fresh blueberries or cranberries into the batter at the last minute. You can also use frozen blueberries or cranberries here; do not defrost them first. Blueberry muffins are good with ¹/₂ teaspoon grated lemon zest added to the batter along with the wet ingredients. Cranberry muffins are excellent with ¹/₂ cup chopped nuts and/or 1 tablespoon minced orange zest added to the prepared batter.

Sweet and Rich Muffins. Like cake: Use butter and increase the quantity to 6 tablespoons (³/₄ stick); increase the sugar to ³/₄ cup. Use 2 eggs and decrease the milk to ¹/₂ cup, or more if needed. In Step 2, after mixing together the dry ingredients, cream the butter and sugar together with a wooden spoon or electric mixer and in a small bowl beat together the eggs with the milk. Add about a third of the dry ingredients to the butter-sugar mixture, then moisten with a little of the milk. Repeat until all the ingredients are used up, taking care not to overmix. The batter should be lumpy, not smooth, and thick but moist; add a little more milk or other liquid if necessary.

Lighter Muffins. A little more work, with noticeable results: Use 2 eggs and separate them. Add the yolks as usual; beat the whites until stiff but not dry and fold in very gently at the last moment.

Coffee Cake Muffins. Mix together ¹/₂ cup packed brown sugar; 1 teaspoon ground cinnamon; 1 cup finely chopped walnuts, pecans, or cashews; and 2 extra tablespoons melted butter. Stir half of this mixture into the original batter with the wet ingredients and sprinkle the rest on top before baking.

Savory Muffins. Cut the sugar back to 1 tablespoon. Add up to 1 cup of cooked minced onion or leek and shredded cheese to the batter just before baking.

✪ Jim Lahey's No-Work Bread

MAKES: 1 large loaf
TIME: Nearly 24 hours, almost completely unattended

This innovation—the word *recipe* does not do the technique justice—came from Jim Lahey, owner of Sullivan Street Bakery in New York City. Jim has created a way for home cooks (and not even ones who are serious bakers) to nearly duplicate an artisan bakery loaf, with a crackling crust, open-holed crumb, light texture, and fantastic flavor. All without kneading, fancy ingredients, or special equipment. A wet dough and slow fermentation are the keys to success (see "The Science Behind No-Work Bread," page 834), as is the baking method—a heated covered pot, which creates essentially an oven within an oven to trap steam as the bread bakes. This is the original, simplest version, though many people have tinkered with the formula since it was first published in 2006. I'm not kidding when I say the results will blow your mind.

The only thing required is forethought. Ideally, you will start the dough about 24 hours before you plan to eat it; you can cut that to 12 and even 9 (see the variation), but you'll be sacrificing some of the yeasty flavor and open crumb.

4 cups all-purpose or bread flour, plus flour for dusting

Scant ¹/₂ teaspoon instant yeast

2 teaspoons salt

2 cups water at about 70°F

2 tablespoons extra virgin olive oil (optional)

Cornmeal, semolina, or wheat bran as needed

① Combine the flour, yeast, and salt in a large bowl. Add the water and stir until blended; you'll have a shaggy, sticky dough (add a little more water if it seems dry). Cover the bowl with plastic wrap or put the olive oil in a second large bowl, transfer the dough to that, turn to coat with oil, and cover with plastic wrap. Let the dough rest for about 18 hours at about 70°F. The dough is ready when its surface is dotted with bubbles. Rising time will

The Science Behind No-Work Bread

This bread puts time and moisture to work so you don't have to. The dough uses very little yeast and compensates for this by fermenting very slowly, giving the yeast time to multiply on its own schedule, and this delivers a more complex flavor than simply yeasted homemade bread. The dough is extremely wet, more than 40 percent water, at the extreme high end of the range that professional bakers use to create crisp crust and large, well-structured crumb, both of which are evident in this loaf.

You couldn't knead this dough if you wanted to. And there truly is no need. The moisture in the dough—combined with the long fermentation time—gives the protein in the flour (called *gluten*; see page 835 for more on that) an environment that lets it move around and develop a distinctive elastic, weblike structure, which is necessary to trap the carbon dioxide generated by the yeast as it feeds. The resulting inflation is what we call *rising*, though in this case the texture is totally different from what you get with simply yeasted and kneaded bread.

By starting this very wet dough in a hot, covered pot, you develop a crunchy, chewy, bakery-style crust, since the moist, enclosed environment of the pot is, in effect, the oven, and that oven has plenty of steam in it, which is necessary to create that kind of surface. Once uncovered, the crust has time to harden and brown and the bread is done. (And fear not: The dough does not stick to the pot, any more than it would to a heated bread stone.)

5 Ideas for No-Work Bread

1. Replace up to half the flour with whole wheat flour.
2. Replace up to 30 percent of the flour with other whole grain flours.
3. To incorporate add-ins or seasonings (see "18 Ingredients to Add to Any Plain Yeast Bread," page 871), adding them after you've mixed the dough is best. When the ingredients are perishable, however, like bacon or cheese, you have to wait until just before the second rising.
4. To make a crustier, browner loaf, remove the lid after 20 minutes and increase the uncovered baking time to 30 minutes.
5. To change the shape of the loaf, use different pots. (A fish poacher makes a nice baguette, for example.)

be shorter at warmer temperatures, a bit longer if your kitchen is 60–65°F.

❷ Lightly flour a work surface, remove the dough, and fold once or twice; it will be soft but, once sprinkled with flour, not terribly sticky. Cover loosely with plastic wrap and let rest for about 15 minutes.

❸ Using just enough flour to keep the dough from sticking, gently and quickly shape the dough into a ball. Generously coat a cotton (not terry cloth) towel with cornmeal or wheat bran (or use a silicone baking mat); put the dough seam side down on the towel and dust with more flour or cornmeal. Cover with another cotton towel (or plastic wrap) and let rise for about 2 hours. When it's ready, the dough will be more than doubled in size and won't spring back readily when poked with your finger.

❹ At least a half hour before the dough is ready, heat the oven to 450°F. Put a 3- to 4-quart covered pot (with the cover)—it may be cast-iron, enamel, Pyrex, or ceramic—in the oven as it heats. When the dough is ready, carefully remove the pot from the oven and turn the dough over into the pot, seam side up. (Slide your hand under the towel and just turn the dough over into the pot; it's messy, and it probably won't fall in artfully, but it will straighten out as it bakes.) Cover with the lid and bake for 30 minutes, then remove the lid and bake for another 20 to 30 minutes, until the loaf is beautifully browned. (If at any point the dough starts to smell

 Fast   Make Ahead   Vegetarian

scorched, lower the heat a bit.) Remove the bread with a spatula or tongs and cool on a rack for at least 30 minutes before slicing.

No-Work Bread, Sped Up. Reduce the initial rise to 8 hours; skip the 15-minute resting period and just shape the dough as in Step 3. Proceed immediately to Step 4.

Yeasted Coffee Cake

MAKES: 2 loaves
TIME: 4 hours or more, largely unattended

Ⓜ Ⓥ

This is a classic coffee cake—slightly sweet, slightly doughy, slightly rich—with a crunchy nut topping. A springform pan is ideal here, but you can certainly bake it in a rectangular pan, a tube pan, or a large loaf pan as you like. Just shape the dough to fit whatever pan you choose as described in Step 4.

4 cups all purpose flour, plus more as needed

2 teaspoons instant yeast

2 teaspoons salt

$^1/_3$ cup sugar

6 tablespoons ($^3/_3$ stick) cold butter, plus softened butter for the bowl and pans

2 eggs

About 1 cup milk, preferably whole

$^1/_2$ cup raisins (optional)

$1^1/_2$ teaspoons ground cinnamon

$^1/_2$ cup chopped almonds, pecans, or walnuts

❶ Combine 3 cups of the flour, the yeast, salt, and 2 tablespoons of the sugar in a food processor. Process for 5 seconds. Add 2 tablespoons of the cold butter and the eggs and pulse a few times, until well combined.

❷ With the machine running, drizzle $^1/_2$ cup milk through the feed tube. Process until a dough ball forms, adding more milk a tablespoon at a time if necessary. Turn onto a lightly floured surface and knead by hand for a minute or two, adding the raisins if you like, and a little more flour if necessary to prevent sticking. The dough is ready when it is silky smooth and quite elastic.

❸ Butter a large bowl and turn the dough ball in it. Cover with plastic wrap and let rise until about doubled in bulk, at least 2 hours. Meanwhile, grease a 9- or 10-inch springform pan. Use a wooden spoon to beat the remaining butter, sugar, $^1/_2$ cup flour, cinnamon, and nuts.

❹ Heat the oven to 350°F. Punch the dough down and knead a couple times on a floured surface. Roll the dough into a ball again, then press it into the prepared pan. Sprinkle the cake with the topping, pressing down to dimple the top. Cover and let rise until puffy, another 30 minutes or so. Bake for about 45 minutes, or until a toothpick inserted in the center comes out clean. Cool on a wire rack in the pan, then remove. This keeps well for a couple of days, and is good toasted for a couple more.

The Basics of Flour

The backbone of all baking is flour, which is ground ("milled") from wheat or other grains. Though the milling determines how much of the grain is actually used and the texture of the flour, the way it bakes is ultimately a reflection of the characteristics of the original grain.

The standard baking flour in this country is all-purpose white, though as the interest in whole wheat and other whole grains increases, so does interest in flours milled from them, as well as flours made from nuts and even roots, all of which are readily available. I've included information about how to use some of these alternative flours here. They're called "flour," but they don't have the same baking qualities—I'll get into that—and they don't taste the same. Without gluten—the protein specifically found in wheat flours (and most plentiful in bread flour)—you're never going to get the same structure in either yeasted or quick breads. That's because gluten makes the dough sturdier and more elastic; low-protein flours produce the finer, tender crumb you want in desserts but not breads.

Here, then, are the primary flours you'll need for baking the breads in this chapter, plus a few more for those of you who might want to experiment further.

White Flours

These are "regular" flours, the finely ground endosperm of the wheat kernel, without the bran or germ. I use only unbleached flour; the bleaching process uses harsh chemicals and serves no purpose other than cosmetic (it's actually illegal in some European countries). Just buy good-quality unbleached flour and your baked foods will look and taste great.

All-Purpose Flour

This is the workhorse of flours. Milled from hard wheats or a combination of hard and soft, all-purpose flour, as it's often known, may be enriched with vitamins and nutrients in an attempt to compensate for those that are stripped through the removal of bran and germ. It contains 8 to 11 percent protein, which allows it to work well in a range of applications, from pastry to noodles to bread. (The protein content of every flour is listed on the label; if not specifically, just check the number of grams of protein in the nutritional information; since that's listed per 100 grams of flour, it's a percentage. So 8 grams of protein means the flour is 8 percent protein.)

Bread Flour

Milled from hard wheats, bread flour has more protein than all-purpose flour—up to 14 percent—and therefore greater gluten strength, which makes it the flour of choice for elastic, easy-to-handle bread doughs that produce chewy crumb and sturdy crust. Bread flour is sometimes "conditioned" with ascorbic acid, but even moderate quantities can make the finished dough taste slightly sour, so you're better off without it.

Cake (Pastry) Flour

Milled from soft wheat. The low-protein content of this flour (less than 9 percent) means that doughs and batters don't develop much elasticity, so it produces a tender, delicate crumb in cakes and pastries.

Self-Rising Flour

Also called *phosphated flour*. This is essentially all-purpose flour plus salt and a leavening agent like baking powder. Self-rising flour works for biscuits and quick breads but not yeast breads. In any case, it's a silly concept, since it's more expensive and cannot substitute for all-purpose flour; furthermore, it's easy enough to add those two ingredients to regular flour.

Whole Wheat Flours

Produced by milling all three components of the wheat kernel—the bran, the germ, and the endosperm. This means more fiber and nutrients than white flour (and up to 14 percent protein), as well as a pleasantly assertive flavor, especially in breads. But anything made with 100 percent whole wheat flour will be heavy and dense, so most people like to combine it with some white flour for lighter results. To incorporate whole wheat flour into a recipe without making other adjustments, just replace half of the white flour with whole wheat.

Whole Wheat Pastry Flour

Milled from soft wheat and about 10 percent protein. Like its white counterpart, it produces a delicate crumb in cakes and pastries, but with the characteristics of whole wheat, including a downside: Baked goods made with whole wheat flour are almost always heavier than those made with white pastry flour. The same rules apply here as to regular whole wheat flour: Substitute this for only 50 percent of the cake flour in any recipe and expect the results to be heavier and less delicate, with more pronounced wheat flavor.

White Whole Wheat Flour

Similar to conventional whole wheat flour in baking performance and nutritional profile, this relatively new variety is milled from white wheat instead of red wheat. It has a relatively mild flavor, so it's perfect for people who don't like the strong flavor of conventional whole wheat flour but want the nutritional advantage. It has the baking characteristics of whole wheat, which means most baked goods relying on it are on the heavy side, though a little less so than those made using dark whole wheat flour.

Flours from Grains Other than Wheat

These are the specialty flours that lack the gluten content of wheat flours. For some guidance about how to substitute them in recipes, see the chart at right.

Rye Flour

Milled from rye berries, a grass similar to but different from wheat. The flour is graded dark, medium, or light, depending on how much bran is milled out: The darker the flour, the stronger the flavor and the higher the protein and fiber, which makes this a nice substitute for a small amount of the white flour in bread recipes. Because it has a low gluten content, rye flour is almost always combined with white flour. But even if your ratio is high in wheat flour, baked goods made with rye flour tend to be moist, dense, deeply colored, and slightly (deliciously) sour tasting. Pumpernickel flour is dark whole grain rye and makes a delicious addition to many breads.

Cornmeal

Ground dried corn, available in fine, medium, and coarse grinds and in yellow, white, and blue colors, depending on the corn. Stone-ground cornmeal—which is generally what you want (see page 477)—retains the hull and germ, so it's more nutritious and flavorful than common steel-ground cornmeal, though also more perishable; store it in the freezer. In yeast breads you can generally substitute up to 10 percent cornmeal for wheat flour without adjusting the recipe.

But you will see corn bread recipes that are anywhere from 50 to 100 percent meal.

Corn flour is another name for finely ground cornmeal (but be careful; in recipes written in the UK, it means cornstarch). To make corn flour, grind medium or coarse cornmeal in a food processor for a few minutes.

SUBSTITUTING FLOURS IN BAKING

Use this chart as a quick reference for replacing a portion of the all-purpose bread flour in yeast and quick breads. (The results are usually better in quick breads, where you don't usually want a chewy texture.) You can mix and match, but don't go over the maximum percentage for any one flour.

If you're not so good at math, you might put the estimated amount of alternative flour (or flours) in the measuring cup first, then fill the remainder with all-purpose wheat flour and level it off.

FLOUR	QUANTITY TO USE IN RECIPES
Whole Wheat	Up to 50 percent
Rye	
-light	Up to 40 percent
-medium	Up to 30 percent
-dark or pumpernickle	Up to 20 percent
Cornmeal	Up to 10 percent
Buckwheat	Up to 20 percent
Rice	Up to 25–30 percent
Nut	Up to 25–30 percent
Soy	Up to 25 percent
Spelt	Up to 100 percent; then either decrease water by 25 percent or increase flour by 25 percent
Oat	Up to 25–30 percent

Buckwheat Flour

Milled buckwheat, called *groats* (see page 478), is gluten free and graded dark, medium, and light, depending on how much hull remains after milling. As with rye flour, the darker the color, the stronger the flavor. Buckwheat flour is slightly sour; it's most commonly used in pancakes, waffles, blintzes, crêpes, muffins, and noodles. In yeast breads, it must be combined with a gluten-rich flour like all-purpose or bread flour.

Rice Flour

Also called *rice powder, ground rice,* and *cream of rice,* this is ground, sifted raw white rice. In Southeast Asia it's used to make noodles, pastries, and sweets and as a thickening agent and coating. Gluten free.

Brown Rice Flour

Milled from rice that has had only the outer hull removed. Higher in protein and fiber than white rice flour, brown rice flour adds a nutty flavor and slight color to baked goods. It has a grainy, gritty texture that yields a dry, fine crumb.

Nut Flours

Made by finely grinding nuts, nut flours (also called *nut meals*) are gluten free and high in protein and fat. They work fine in quick breads or for breading vegetables or croquettes, but you must mix them with gluten-rich flours in yeast breads; generally you can substitute up to 25 percent nut flour for wheat flour in baking without making other adjustments.

Almond flour is the most widely available nut flour, with a consistency that resembles cornmeal. You'll also find hazelnut flour and chestnut flour, which has a complex, slightly sweet flavor and is sometimes used to make pasta.

Soy Flour

Made from roasted soybeans. Full-fat soy flour (sometimes called "natural") retains the oils of the soybean; defatted soy flour has had them removed. Both are high in protein, though the defatted type has a higher concentra-

tion—about 47 percent compared to 35 percent in full-fat flour. Soy flour is gluten free and must be blended with a high-gluten flour in yeast bread recipes; it also has a pronounced bean flavor that not everyone likes (I'm not wild about it myself). You can use it to replace about 15 to 25 percent of all-purpose flour to make a dense, moist loaf.

Spelt Flour

A high-protein, low-gluten flour; spelt has a pleasant nutty flavor and is a good wheat substitute for people with a low tolerance for wheat, though some people with wheat allergies are also allergic to spelt. You can find both white and whole grain spelt flour.

Oat Flour

Oat flour produces baked goods that are moist, crumbly, and nutty tasting; nice. You can grind your own coarse oat flour by giving rolled oats a whirl in the blender or food processor. For yeast breads, use no more than 30 percent oat flour and the rest high-gluten flour.

The Basics of Leavening

Leavening gives baked goods lift (the word *leaven* means "lighten"). Yeast, baking soda, baking powder, and natural starters like sourdough are all leaveners. And they all work the same way: by producing carbon dioxide bubbles that are trapped by the dough's structure and, in turn, make the dough rise.

The process of leavening is as old as baking—that is, thousands of years—but it's been understood only since the mid–nineteenth century, when Louis Pasteur discovered that yeasts are living, single-cell fungi that produce carbon dioxide through fermentation (baking and brewing have a lot in common). Before then, most breads were risen with sourdough starters, which contain wild yeasts, but shortly thereafter commercial yeast production began. Now, of course, you can buy yeast in various forms at the supermarket, including fresh, active dry, and instant, which is the most recent addition to the group and by far the most convenient.

Baking soda and baking powders are used in quick

breads, cookies, cakes, and the like; they don't add the distinctive flavor of yeast (which is not always welcome), though they do have flavor of their own.

Natural starters, like sourdough, are formed when a mixture of flour and water is left at room temperature to catch wild yeast and bacteria, always present in the air. They can take weeks or even months to develop (though you can hasten the process; see Sourdough Bread, page 858), but, once started, they can be kept active for centuries if maintained properly (I have one that is purported to have been started during the Alaska gold rush). The *Lactobacillus* bacterium is responsible for the distinctive flavor of sourdough breads.

Here are more details on leavening agents.

Yeast

Instant Yeast: Also called *fast-acting, fast-rising, rapid-rise,* and *bread machine* yeast—is the yeast I use. It's a type of dry yeast and by far the most convenient: it can be added directly to the dough at almost any point, it's fast, and it's reliable.

Instant yeast has ascorbic acid added (and sometimes traces of other ingredients too); this helps the dough stretch easily and increases loaf volumes. In most breads, you won't notice any difference in flavor. It keeps almost forever, refrigerated.

Fresh Yeast: Also known as *cake* or *compressed* yeast, fresh yeast is usually sold in foil-wrapped cakes of about $2/3$ ounce. It should be yellowish, soft, moist, and fresh smelling, with no dark or dried areas. Fresh yeast must be refrigerated (you can freeze it if you like); it has an expiration date and will die within 10 days of opening. It also must be proofed before being added to a dough. This means you must combine it with liquid; when you do, it will foam and smell yeasty (if it doesn't, it's dead). Many bakers contend that fresh yeast tastes better than dry, but I don't see it. It is kind of fun to work with, but for me instant yeast is the way to go.

Active Dry Yeast: ADY falls in between fresh and instant and was used by most home bakers until instant yeast came along. ADY is fresh yeast that has been pressed and dried until the moisture level reaches about 8 percent. Unlike instant yeast, ADY must be rehydrated in 110°F water; below 105°F it will remain inert; above 115°F it will die. So use a thermometer!

ADY is sold in $1/4$-ounce foil packets; you don't need to refrigerate them, because they are sealed for a shelf life of up to 2 years. ADY is also sold in loose bulk quantities (sometimes in jars), which you must store in the refrigerator.

Baking Soda

Baking soda (sodium bicarbonate) produces carbon dioxide only in the presence of liquid and acid or an acidic liquid, like buttermilk, yogurt, or vinegar. Every recipe that uses baking soda must have an acidic component or it will not rise. Furthermore, baking soda releases all of its gas at once, so it's best to add it with the flour, at the last minute before baking. Once it hits the acid and liquid it goes to work, and you want those bubbles formed in the oven, not on the counter.

You also must be careful not to add too much baking soda because it is quite salty. Plus, whenever you add more baking soda you must add more acid, which could make the recipe unpleasantly acidic. (The recipes here take all of this into account.)

Baking Powder

Baking powder is simply baking soda with a dry acid added to it (along with some starch, which keeps the baking powder dry and therefore inert until it is added to a recipe). Single-acting powders generally contain cream of tartar as the acid, which is activated by moisture, so the batter must be baked immediately after mixing, just like those containing baking soda. Double-acting powder, which is more common, usually contains both cream of tartar and the slower-acting sodium aluminum sulfate, so it releases gas in two phases.

When double-acting baking powder is added to a moist batter, the cream of tartar combines with the soda and produces the first leavening. The second leavening

SUBSTITUTING LEAVENERS

LEAVENING AGENT	AMOUNT	SUBSTITUTION
Baking powder, double-acting	1 teaspoon	$1/4$ teaspoon baking soda plus $1/2$ teaspoon cream of tartar plus $1/4$ teaspoon cornstarch OR $11/2$ teaspoons single-acting baking powder OR $1/4$ teaspoon baking soda plus $1/2$ cup buttermilk, sour milk, or yogurt to replace $1/2$ cup nonacidic liquid
Baking powder, single-acting	1 teaspoon	$2/3$ teaspoon double-acting baking powder OR $1/4$ teaspoon baking soda plus $1/2$ teaspoon cream of tartar plus $1/4$ teaspoon cornstarch
Baking soda	$1/2$ teaspoon	2 teaspoons double-acting baking powder (must replace acidic liquid in recipe with nonacidic liquid) OR $1/2$ teaspoon potassium bicarbonate
Yeast, active dry	1 packet ($1/4$ ounce)	1 cake fresh ($3/5$ ounce) OR 1 scant tablespoon active dry OR 2 teaspoons instant

occurs during baking. So batters using double-acting baking powder can sit at room temperature for a few minutes before being baked, but just a few; otherwise you've got to refrigerate or freeze it.

Be careful about the amount of baking powder you add: Too much can give baked goods a bitter taste and—if the air bubbles grow too big and break—even cause them to collapse.

Sourdough

Also called *levain* or *mother dough,* sourdough is a natural starter that does not rely on yeast (though I think a bit of yeast helps sourdough along and improves its flavor). Instead, you mix flour and water (adding a pinch of yeast if you like) and let it sit for a period of days; the mixture

will catch airborne wild yeast and *Lactobacillus* bacteria. This slow fermentation creates a characteristic tang and deep flavor. The day before you're ready to bake, you feed the sourdough more water and flour, let it sit for a while, then use some of it as leavening in your bread dough; see page 858. The rest you put aside for the next time, and so a good sourdough will keep for a couple of weeks or longer in the fridge without being fed. (In fact, the easiest way to make your own sourdough is to get some starter from a friend; everyone with sourdough is happy to share.)

Sponge

Sometimes called by their Italian or French name *biga* or *poolish,* a sponge—essentially a predough mixture—is made with flour, water, and yeast or sourdough. You let

 Fast   Make Ahead   **V** Vegetarian

the sponge sit for a few hours, or overnight, and then combine it with more flour and water to make the dough; this technique improves flavor and texture enormously.

The Basics of Quick Bread

Making quick bread is easy: You combine the dry ingredients, then combine the wet ingredients, combine the two, and bake. No special techniques or equipment needed. You don't even really need a loaf pan; you can bake quick breads in a square baking pan or even an ovenproof skillet.

The batter—it can't be called a dough, because it's pourable, not kneadable—is rich, usually containing eggs, butter, and milk, often with at least a little bit of sugar or other sweetener. It's usually leavened with baking powder, though you can sometimes use baking soda, and there are times when a combination is best.

In terms of their composition, quick breads and muffins are more like cakes than they are like yeasted breads (though I resist and resent the commercial tendency to make cakes in muffin form and call them muffins; muffins and quick breads should be slightly sweet and are wonderful with coffee or tea, but they're not dessert). The batter is relatively light, and the goal is a delicate, cakelike crumb, moist interior, and nicely browned but still tender crust with a little chew but no real crunch. To achieve this you need some fat, which contributes to flavor and tenderness, and minimal mixing.

Overmixing will make quick breads tough. While in yeast breads you generally want to develop gluten to get a tough crust and chewy crumb, in quick breads you want to retard gluten's development to keep the bread nice and tender. (This is why you use only all-purpose flour, not bread flour.) So heed this advice: Combine dry and wet ingredients as quickly as you can and don't beat or even stir any more than is necessary. When you see no more dry bits of flour, the job is done; don't worry about remaining lumps.

As a general rule, quick breads do not keep as well as yeasted breads, so it's best to eat them the day they're made. It's fine to bake them a few hours in advance and, once cool, keep them wrapped in wax paper or foil. If you'd like to freeze them for later or save leftovers, see "Freezing Breads and Bread Dough" (below).

Freezing Breads and Bread Dough

It's surprising how well breads freeze, provided you handle them properly. With crusty yeasted loaves, just toss them into a plastic bag and put in the freezer. Use them as soon as possible, either by defrosting (on the countertop or in the fridge) and then crisping up (unwrapped) in a 350°F oven for 10 minutes or so or by reheating them while still frozen, in a 400°F oven for about 20 minutes.

Softer, moister breads—like most quick breads—should be wrapped in plastic and then foil before freezing. Thaw in the refrigerator if time allows and remove the plastic. Rewrap in the foil if you want to warm quick breads—in a 300°F oven—though you don't need to reheat them at all.

You can also freeze yeasted doughs. After the first rising or after shaping, wrap tightly and freeze for up to 3 months. Thaw in the refrigerator, then finish any additional shaping and/or rising at room temperature. Bake as usual.

Quick Whole Wheat and Molasses Bread

MAKES: 1 loaf
TIME: About 1¼ hours, largely unattended

A super all-purpose bread that's heartier and more flavorful than most, and relatively light for a 100 percent whole grain bread. It also makes excellent sandwiches, especially when toasted.

Oil or butter for the pan

1²/₃ cups buttermilk or yogurt or 1¹/₂ cups milk and 2 tablespoons white vinegar (see Step 2)

2¹/₂ cups whole wheat flour

¹/₂ cup cornmeal

1 teaspoon salt

1 teaspoon baking soda

¹/₂ cup molasses

1 Heat the oven to 325°F. Grease an 8 × 4-inch or 9 × 5-inch loaf pan.

2 If you're using buttermilk or yogurt, ignore this step. Otherwise, make soured milk: Warm the milk gently to take the chill off—1 minute in the microwave is sufficient—and add the vinegar. Let it rest while you prepare the other ingredients.

3 Mix together the dry ingredients. Stir the molasses into the buttermilk. Stir the liquid into the dry ingredients (just enough to combine), then pour into the loaf pan. Bake until firm and a toothpick inserted in the center comes out clean, about 1 hour. Cool on a rack for 15 minutes before removing from the pan.

Lighter Whole Wheat Quick Bread. A little cakier: Use 1¹/₂ cups whole wheat and 1¹/₂ cups all-purpose flour; omit the cornmeal. Substitute honey for the molasses for lighter flavor and color. Beat 1 egg into the wet ingredients in Step 3.

Onion Pan Bread

MAKES: About 6 servings
TIME: 1 hour

Lightly caramelized onions keep this bread moist and tender, with a deep, naturally sweet flavor that's perfect with roasted meats or chicken, grilled vegetables, and sharp or smoked cheeses.

3 tablespoons butter or extra virgin olive oil

2 large onions, sliced about ¹/₄ inch thick

2 tablespoons brown sugar

2 cups all-purpose flour

1 tablespoon baking powder

1 teaspoon salt

1 teaspoon sugar

1 egg

1 cup milk

¹/₄ cup neutral oil, like grapeseed or corn

1 Heat the oven to 350°F. Put 2 tablespoons of the butter or olive oil in a medium to large skillet over medium heat. When the butter is melted or the oil is hot, add the onions and cook, stirring occasionally, until softened, about 10 minutes.

2 Use the remaining butter or olive oil to grease a 9-inch round baking dish, pie plate, or ovenproof skillet. Sprinkle with brown sugar and spread the onions around the bottom.

3 Mix together the flour, baking powder, salt, and sugar. Beat together the egg, milk, and neutral oil, add to the dry ingredients, and stir together quickly.

4 Spread the batter over the onions and bake for 35 to 40 minutes, or until a toothpick inserted in the center comes out dry. Let stand for 5 minutes before cutting into wedges (you can invert onto a plate first if you like); serve warm.

Banana Bread

MAKES: 1 loaf
TIME: About 1 hour

The best banana bread is a balancing act: It requires a fair amount of fat to keep it moist and lighten the crumb; a little whole wheat flour gives it some substance. And in my opinion the result should be sweet, but not overly so. Though coconut is my favorite secret ingredient, feel free to omit it or add more nuts, raisins, or other dried fruit instead if you like. This bread keeps better than most quick breads, though it probably won't be around too long.

8 tablespoons (1 stick) butter, softened, plus butter for the pan

$1^{1}/_{2}$ cups all-purpose flour

$^{1}/_{2}$ cup whole wheat flour

1 teaspoon salt

$1^{1}/_{2}$ teaspoons baking powder

$^{3}/_{4}$ cup sugar

2 eggs

3 very ripe bananas, mashed with a fork until smooth

1 teaspoon vanilla extract

$^{1}/_{2}$ cup chopped walnuts or pecans

$^{1}/_{2}$ cup shredded coconut

❶ Heat the oven to 350°F. Grease a 9 × 5-inch loaf pan with butter.

❷ Mix together the dry ingredients. With a hand mixer, a whisk, or in the food processor, cream the butter and beat in the eggs and bananas. Stir this mixture into the dry ingredients, just enough to combine (it's okay if there are lumps). Gently stir in the vanilla, nuts, and coconut.

❸ Pour the batter into the loaf pan and bake for 45 to 60 minutes, until nicely browned. A toothpick inserted in the center of the bread will come out fairly clean when done, but because of the bananas this bread will remain moister than most. Do not overcook. Cool on a rack for 15 minutes before removing from the pan.

Fruit-and-Nut or Vegetable-and-Nut Bread

MAKES: 1 loaf

TIME: About $1^{1}/_{4}$ hours

Ⓜ **Ⓥ**

This is the master recipe for making a whole family of breads, like Cranberry-Pecan, Zucchini-Sunflower, and Carrot-Walnut—you name it. If the fruit is really juicy (like peaches), put the pieces in a strainer and let them drain for an hour or so before proceeding. Feel free to experiment with the seasonings and see the variations for some specific combinations.

You can also bake these as muffins: Prepare the batter as directed, then divide among 12 greased muffin cups. Bake at 400°F for 20 to 30 minutes. (For more on muffins, see page 832.)

4 tablespoons ($^{1}/_{2}$ stick) cold butter, plus butter for the pan

2 cups all-purpose flour

1 cup sugar

$1^{1}/_{2}$ teaspoons baking powder

$^{1}/_{2}$ teaspoon baking soda

1 teaspoon salt

$^{3}/_{4}$ cup fruit juice, like orange or apple, or milk

1 tablespoon minced or grated orange or lemon zest

1 egg

1 cup any raw fruit or vegetable: small berries left whole, anything else peeled and grated or chopped

$^{1}/_{2}$ cup chopped walnuts or pecans

❶ Heat the oven to 350°F. Grease a 9 × 5-inch loaf pan with butter.

❷ Stir together the dry ingredients. Cut the butter into bits, then use a fork, 2 knives, or your fingers to cut or rub it into the dry ingredients until there are no pieces bigger than a small pea. (You can use a food processor for this step, which makes it quite easy, but you should not use a food processor for the remaining steps or the bread will be tough.)

❸ Beat together the juice, zest, and egg. Pour into the dry ingredients, mixing just enough to moisten; do not beat and do not mix until the batter is smooth. Fold in the fruit and the nuts, then pour and spoon the batter into the loaf pan. Bake for about an hour, or until the bread is golden brown and a toothpick inserted in the center comes out clean. Cool on a rack for 15 minutes before removing from the pan.

Dried Fruit and Nut Bread. Not as heavy as traditional holiday fruitcake: Instead of the fresh fruit, roughly chop $^{3}/_{4}$ cup any dried fruit, alone or in combination.

Before beginning the recipe, heat the fruit juice gently, then pour over the dried fruit. Let steep for 30 minutes. In Step 3, add the zest and the egg to the fruit mixture and then proceed with the recipe, folding in only the nuts before baking.

Whole Grain Fruit-and-Nut or Vegetable-and-Nut Bread. Makes a slightly denser loaf: Substitute whole wheat flour, buckwheat, cornmeal, or other flour—either alone or in combination—for up to $^1/_2$ cup of the all-purpose flour.

Pumpkin Ginger Bread with Hazelnuts. Different from the usual version because the pumpkin isn't cooked and puréed first: Grate enough pumpkin or other winter squash to yield 1 loosely packed cup. Use hazelnuts for the nuts. Instead of the zest, use minced fresh ginger or 1 teaspoon ground ginger.

Brown Sugar Carrot Bread with Almonds. Gorgeous color: Instead of granulated sugar, use dark or golden brown sugar. Grate enough carrots to yield 1 loosely packed cup. Use sliced almonds for the nuts.

7 Great Fruit or Vegetable and Nut Combinations

1. Zucchini and cashews
2. Winter squash and hazelnuts
3. Sweet potatoes and pecans
4. Cherries (pitted) and almonds
5. Cranberries and pistachios
6. Grapes (halved) and peanuts
7. Apples and walnuts

Quick Coffee Cake

MAKES: At least 8 servings
TIME: About 1 hour

A classic breakfast or brunch cake, equally good for dessert. See also Yeasted Coffee Cake (page 835).

The best ways to finish this cake: Drizzle with Mocha Glaze (page 919) or Caramel Coffee Sauce (page 922) or leave in the pan and soak in Rich Vanilla Cake Soak (page 919).

8 tablespoons (1 stick) cold butter, plus butter for the pan

2 cups plus 3 tablespoons all-purpose flour

1$^1/_4$ cups sugar

2 teaspoons ground cinnamon

1 cup chopped walnuts or pecans

2 teaspoons baking powder

$^1/_2$ teaspoon salt

1 egg

$^3/_4$ cup milk

❶ Heat the oven to 375°F. Grease a 9-inch square baking pan with butter. Combine the 3 tablespoons of flour, $^3/_4$ cup of the sugar, 1 teaspoon of the cinnamon, and 3 tablespoons of the butter with the nuts; mix with your fingers until it's just coming together. Set this streusel mixture aside.

❷ Combine the remaining 2 cups of flour, the baking powder, salt, remaining $^1/_2$ cup of sugar, remaining teaspoon of cinnamon, and remaining 5 tablespoons of butter, cut into bits, in a bowl (you can use an electric mixer for this; use low speed). Mix well with a fork until all of the flour is coated with some of the butter.

❸ Still on low speed, beat the egg into the batter, then the milk until blended. Pour half the batter into the prepared pan and sprinkle over it about half the streusel mixture. Add the remaining batter, then the remaining streusel. Bake until a toothpick inserted in the center comes out clean, about 30 minutes. Cool on a rack for at least 15 minutes before cutting. Best served warm, but not bad a day or two later, reheated.

Cinnamon-Orange Coffee Cake. Add 2 teaspoons grated or finely minced orange zest and substitute $^1/_4$ cup orange juice for the same amount of milk.

Quick Coffee Cake with Cardamom. Use almonds for the nuts if you like: Add 2 teaspoons ground cardamom;

F Fast   **M** Make Ahead   **V** Vegetarian

use 1 teaspoon in Step 1 for the streusel and 1 teaspoon in the batter, in place of the cinnamon.

Yogurt or Buttermilk Biscuits

MAKES: 10 or more biscuits, depending on size
TIME: 20 to 30 minutes

The easiest and best way to make biscuits is with yogurt, which produces tangy, tender, and flaky results. Buttermilk is my second choice, but if you have neither just make the Baking Powder Biscuits variation. For an extra-soft crumb, use cake flour. Vary these biscuits with any of the ideas listed in "13 Additions to Any Quick Bread, Muffins, Biscuits, or Scones" (page 846).

2 cups all-purpose or cake flour, plus more as needed

1 scant teaspoon salt

3 teaspoons baking powder

1 teaspoon baking soda

2 to 5 tablespoons cold butter (more is better)

³/₄ cup plus 2 tablespoons yogurt or buttermilk

❶ Heat the oven to 450°F. Mix the dry ingredients together in a bowl or food processor. Cut the butter into bits and either pulse it in the food processor (the easiest) or, if you're using a bowl, pick up a bit of the dry ingredients and rub them with the butter between your fingers and drop them again. All the butter should be thoroughly blended into the flour mixture before you proceed.

❷ Pulse a couple of times or use a large spoon to stir in the yogurt, just until the mixture forms a ball. Turn the dough out onto a lightly floured surface and knead it 10 times; no more. If it is very sticky, add a little flour, but very little; it should still stick slightly to your hands.

❸ Press the dough into a ³/₄-inch-thick rectangle and cut into 2-inch rounds with a biscuit cutter or glass. Put the rounds on an ungreased baking sheet. Gently reshape the leftover dough and cut again. Bake for 7 to 9 minutes, or until the biscuits are a beautiful golden brown. Serve within 15 minutes for them to be at their best.

Baking Powder Biscuits. Slightly different flavor, but with good texture: Increase the baking powder to 4 teaspoons and omit the soda. Use milk in place of yogurt or buttermilk.

Drop ("Emergency") Biscuits. Not quite as good, though you'll save 5 minutes: Increase the yogurt or milk to 1 cup and drop tablespoons of the dough onto a greased baking sheet. Bake as directed.

Sweet Potato Biscuits. Southern-style goodness; killer with Fried Chicken Made Easy (page 665): Grease the baking sheets. Stir 1 cup puréed cooked sweet potato or winter squash into the butter-flour mixture. Add only enough yogurt or buttermilk to form the dough into a ball, usually between ¹/₂ and ³/₄ cup (if your potatoes are very dry, you may need the whole amount). Roll the dough a little thinner—about ¹/₂ inch. Cut as directed, into biscuits (you'll get a few more), and bake for 12 to 15 minutes.

Scones

MAKES: 10 to 14 scones
TIME: 20 minutes

Scones are really just ultra-rich biscuits, with cream as the primary liquid ingredient. Sure, you can use milk, but then they won't be nearly so flaky and light.

2 cups all-purpose or cake flour, plus more as needed

1 scant teaspoon salt

4 teaspoons baking powder

2 tablespoons sugar

5 tablespoons cold butter

3 eggs

³/₄ cup cream

¹/₃ cup dried currants or raisins (or choose from the list below)

1 Heat the oven to 450°F. Mix the dry ingredients together in a bowl or food processor, reserving 1 tablespoon of the sugar. Cut the butter into bits and either pulse it in the food processor (easier) or pick up a bit of the dry ingredients, rub them with the butter between your fingers, and drop them again. All the butter should be thoroughly blended into the flour mixture before you proceed.

2 Beat 2 of the eggs with the cream in a large bowl; with a few swift strokes, combine them with the flour mixture. Fold in the currants or other ingredients if you're using any. Turn the dough out onto a lightly floured surface and knead it 10 times; no more. If it is very sticky, add a little flour, but very little; it should still stick a little to your hands.

3 Press the dough into a ³/₄-inch-thick rectangle and cut into 2-inch rounds with a biscuit cutter or glass. Put the rounds on an ungreased baking sheet. Gently reshape the leftover dough and cut again. Beat the remaining egg with 1 tablespoon water and brush the top of each scone; sprinkle each with a little of the remaining sugar.

4 Bake for 7 to 9 minutes, or until the scones are a beautiful golden brown. These keep better than biscuits but should still be eaten the same day you make them.

13 Additions to Virtually Any Quick Bread, Muffins, Biscuits, or Scones

You can adjust the recipes in this section (or the Muffins or Corn Bread in the Essential Recipes) simply by adding an ingredient (or two or three) to the liquid ingredients just before combining them with the dry ingredients. Just use a little common sense so flavors and textures don't clash.

1. Spice blends, like chili or curry powder (to make your own, see pages 65–69) or even single spices like cumin, saffron, cardamom, or caraway seeds. Generally 1 tablespoon or so, whole or ground as you like.

2. Traditional Pesto (page 27) or any other herb (pages 27–28), up to ¹/₄ cup. (Drizzle it onto the batter once it's in the pan and use a knife to swirl it in like marble cake.)

3. Minced or sliced pickled jalapeños, from a tablespoon to ¹/₄ cup, to taste.

4. Grated cheese, either soft, melting, or hard types; anywhere from ¹/₂ to 1 cup.

5. Molasses or honey, in place of the sugar (if there is any); about ¹/₄ cup.

6. Minced herbs: up to ¹/₄ cup of mild ones like mint, parsley, or cilantro; up to 2 tablespoons of strongly flavored ones like rosemary, oregano, or thyme.

7. Sautéed onions, shallots, or leeks; about ¹/₂ cup. (With this and other very savory additions, stock in place of half the milk is nice.)

8. Finely chopped nuts or seeds, like almonds, pecans, or pumpkin, poppy, or sesame seeds; up to ¹/₂ cup.

9. Dried cherries, blueberries, or cranberries or raisins (soak in a little warm water first and drain well); up to 1 cup.

10. Cooked wheat or rye berries or hulled barley; up to 1 cup.

11. Grated citrus zest; about 1 tablespoon.

12. Sprinkle the tops of unbaked quick bread or muffins with some sugar (raw sugar is particularly nice) or a mixture of cinnamon and sugar.

13. Cooked and crumbled sausage or any other cooked and minced meat or even shrimp; about a cup. Reduce the sugar to 1 teaspoon.

 Fast   Make Ahead   **V** Vegetarian

Cheese Shortbread

MAKES: 30 to 40 puffs
TIME: 30 minutes

After just one of these crisp, melt-in-your-mouth snacks you'll never want another of those bright orange cheese puffs again. The dough can be made ahead of time or the shortbreads baked a day ahead and stored in an airtight container, making them ideal for parties.

    8 tablespoons (1 stick) cold butter, cubed

    2 cups grated Emmental, Gruyère, cheddar, or other semihard cheese

    1½ cups all-purpose flour

    1 egg, lightly beaten

    ½ teaspoon salt

    ½ teaspoon cayenne

    1 tablespoon paprika or ground cumin (optional)

1 Heat the oven to 400°F. Put all the ingredients in a food processor and pulse just until the mixture resembles a coarse meal; do not overprocess. (You can also use a pastry cutter or a fork to cut the mixture to the same consistency in a bowl.) Wrap the dough in plastic and refrigerate until you're ready to bake the puffs.

2 Form the dough into 1-inch balls. Line the balls on a lightly greased or parchment-lined baking sheet, leaving 2 inches between them. Slightly flatten each ball with your fingers.

3 Bake until the pastries puff and turn golden brown, about 10 minutes. Cool completely on a wire rack, then sprinkle with additional paprika and serve.

Blue Cheese Shortbread. Substitute 1 cup crumbled blue cheese for a cup of the Emmental cheese.

Pecorino Cheese Shortbread. Substitute 1 cup each grated pecorino Romano and Parmesan cheese for the Emmental.

Herbed Cheese Shortbread. Add ¼ cup chopped mixed fresh herbs, like parsley, chives, dill, and/or basil, with a little tarragon.

Spiced Cheese Shortbread. Use 2 to 3 teaspoons garam masala or Hot Curry Powder (to make your own, see page 67 or 66) for an Indian flair, caraway for an Eastern European flavor, or toasted cumin seeds for a North African twist.

Prosciutto Shortbread. Reduce the cheese to 1 cup and use finely grated Parmesan. Chop several thin slices of prosciutto into pieces and add them to the food processor in Step 1.

Popovers

MAKES: 12 popovers
TIME: About 45 minutes

Popovers are best made at the last minute, but they're good left over as well. I think they go incredibly well with scrambled eggs, though the classic accompaniment is Prime Rib Roast (page 734).

    1 tablespoon melted butter or neutral oil, like grapeseed or corn, plus some for the muffin tin

    2 eggs

    1 cup milk

    1 teaspoon sugar

    ½ teaspoon salt

    1 cup all-purpose flour

1 Heat the oven to 425°F. Grease a 12-cup muffin tin or a popover tin and put it in the oven while you make the batter.

2 Beat together the eggs, milk, butter or oil, sugar, and salt. Beat in the flour a little bit at a time; the mixture should be smooth. Fill the muffin tins at least halfway (if your tin is large, this might make fewer than 12 popovers). Bake for 15 minutes, then reduce the heat to 350°F and continue baking for 15 minutes more, or until the popovers are puffed and browned (do not check the popovers until they have baked for a total of 30 minutes). Remove from the pan immediately and serve hot.

The Basics of Unleavened Flatbread

These easy-to-mix, easy-to-handle doughs are simply shaped by pressing or rolling. I say "simply" even though some home cooks have an innate fear of rolling pins because, like pizza (which is also a flatbread), it's not important that the resulting breads and crackers be perfectly round. Who cares? They're all delicious, and they look appealing whether they come out oval, squarish, or amoeba shaped. Once you free yourself of the stress of creating perfect circles, shaping becomes an utterly simple and fast task. (Though the fact is that if I can make near-circles, and I can, so can you.)

Unleavened breads have neither yeast nor baking powder or soda to make the dough rise. But this doesn't mean they're dense: Each has a unique texture unlike any of its leavened cousins, and some are quite light.

Crackers

MAKES: 4 servings
TIME: About 15 minutes

Homemade crackers are easy to make, with lots of room for improvising. You can blend a little cheese, nuts, garlic, or herbs into the dough before rolling or replace some of the white flour with whole wheat, rye, or cornmeal. Or, just before baking, dust the tops with coarse salt, sesame seeds, or poppy seeds. It's virtually impossible to overwork the dough since you are essentially looking for all crust.

1 cup all-purpose flour, plus more as needed

$^1/_2$ teaspoon salt

2 tablespoons butter or neutral oil, like grapeseed or corn

❶ Heat the oven to 400°F. Lightly dust 2 baking sheets with flour or put a baking stone in the oven. Put the flour, salt, and butter or oil together in a food processor. Pulse until the flour and butter are combined. Add about $^1/_4$ cup water and let the machine run for a bit; continue to add water a teaspoon at a time, until the mixture holds together but is not sticky.

❷ Roll out the dough on a lightly floured surface until $^1/_4$ inch thick or even thinner, adding flour as needed. Score lightly with a sharp knife or razor if you want to break the crackers into nice squares or rectangles later on.

❸ Use a spatula, pastry blade, or peel to transfer the dough to the prepared baking sheets or stone. Bake until lightly browned, about 10 minutes. Cool on a rack; serve warm or at room temperature or store in a tin for up to a couple days.

Cream Crackers. Rich and delicious, they really need nothing on top but a little coarse salt: Increase the butter to 4 tablespoons ($^1/_2$ stick). Substitute milk or cream for the water.

Parmesan Crackers. Perfect with salads or grilled vegetables: In Step 1, add $^1/_2$ cup grated Parmesan cheese to the mixture in the food processor, along with the flour.

Chapati

Indian-Style Flatbread

MAKES: 4 servings (8 to 12 chapati)
TIME: At least 1 hour, partially unattended

True chapati are made with a finely ground whole wheat flour (called *atta* or *chapati flour*) and then twice-cooked quickly—first on a dry griddle and then over an open flame—so that the dough traps steam and puffs up dramatically. If you have a gas stove or are able to combine the main recipe with the grilled variation, you can duplicate this technique with just a little extra work by doing the second cooking on an open flame. But fortunately, the straight recipe here still makes a bread that is unbelievably simple, nutritious, and delicious.

  Fast   Make Ahead   Vegetarian

You can mix the dough in advance, but chapati must be eaten immediately after a batch is cooked. Line a basket or plate with a cloth napkin before starting, and as the chapati come off the griddle, pile them up and wrap loosely. This will keep them warm while you cook the rest.

Eat chapati with any food, Indian or not. They're best with stews and soups, especially bean dishes and their traditional accompaniment, Simplest Dal (page 433).

2¼ cups whole wheat flour

1 cup all-purpose flour, plus more for dusting

1 teaspoon salt

1 cup warm water, plus more as needed

1 Set a fine-mesh strainer or a flour sifter over the bowl of the food processor, add the flours, and sift. Discard the coarse bran or save for another use.

2 Add the salt to the flour mixture and, with the machine running, pour in the cup of warm water. Process for about 30 seconds; then remove the cover. The dough should be in a well-defined, barely sticky, easy-to-handle ball. If it is too dry, add more water 1 tablespoon at a time and process for 5 or 10 seconds after each addition. If it is too wet, which is unlikely, add a tablespoon or two of flour and process briefly. Turn the dough out onto a lightly floured surface, cover, and let rest for at least 30 minutes and up to 2 hours. (At this point, you may wrap the dough tightly in plastic and refrigerate it for up to a day; bring to room temperature before proceeding.)

3 Divide the dough into 8 to 12 pieces. Using flour as necessary, pat or roll each piece into a 4-inch disk. Dust lightly with flour to keep them from sticking and cover them with plastic or a damp cloth while you roll out the others and set aside until you finish all the pieces. (It's okay to overlap them a bit, but don't stack them.)

4 Put a griddle or cast-iron or stainless-steel skillet over medium heat. When it's hot, roll out a disk until it's fairly thin, about ⅛ inch thick, dusting as necessary with flour; the shape doesn't matter (as long as it fits on the griddle or pan). Pat off the excess flour and put the cha-

pati on the griddle or pan, count to 15 or so, then use a spatula to flip and cook the other side until it starts to blister, char, and puff up a bit, about a minute or so. (Use this time to finish rolling out the next disk.) Turn and cook the first side again, until dark and toasty smelling. Transfer to the prepared bread basket (see the headnote) and repeat until all are cooked. Serve immediately.

Grilled Chapati. Rustic, smoky, and puffy. Perfect for when you've already got a fire going and have some room on the grill: Heat a charcoal or gas grill until moderately hot and put the rack about 4 inches from the heat source. Oil the grates well. If you have the space, take the disks outside to your grill for the final rolling. If not, roll all the chapati out, flour them well, and stack between layers of wax or parchment paper. Cook, several at a time, as described in Step 4, only directly on the grill grates instead of the griddle.

4 Ways to Vary Chapati Dough

1. Replace up to ½ cup of the whole wheat flour with cornmeal, brown rice flour, or chickpea flour (besan; see page 441).

2. Replace the all-purpose flour with whole wheat; the dough will be slightly more difficult to handle, but the results will be delicious.

3. Reduce the water to 1 cup and add ½ cup yogurt to the flour at the same time.

4. Brush the chapati with oil, coconut milk (to make your own, see page 389), or melted butter during cooking.

Paratha

Flaky Indian-Style Flatbread

MAKES: 4 servings (8 to 12 paratha)

TIME: At least an hour

Unlike chapati (preceding recipe), this dough is enriched with butter or oil, which gives it a lovely flaky texture.

Like chapati, paratha must be eaten immediately after cooking: Line a basket or plate with a cloth napkin before starting, and as they finish, pile them up and wrap loosely.

You can also grill these; follow the directions in the variation for Grilled Chapati.

1 1/2 cups whole wheat flour

1 1/2 cups all-purpose flour

1 teaspoon salt

About 4 tablespoons butter (melted) or neutral oil, like grapeseed or corn

1 Combine the flours and salt in a food processor. Turn the machine on and add 3/4 cup water through the feed tube. Process for about 30 seconds, until the mixture forms a ball and is slightly sticky to the touch. If it is dry, add another tablespoon or two of water and process for another 10 seconds. In the unlikely event that the mixture is too sticky, add flour a tablespoon at a time. Remove the dough and, using flour as necessary, shape into a ball; wrap in plastic and let rest for at least 20 minutes and up to several hours at room temperature. (At this point, you may wrap the dough tightly in plastic and refrigerate for up to a day or freeze for up to a week; bring back to room temperature before proceeding.)

2 Divide the dough into 8 to 12 pieces. Using flour as necessary, pat or roll each piece into a 4-inch disk and brush the top with butter or oil. Roll up like a cigar, then into a coil not unlike a cinnamon bun; set aside until you finish all the pieces.

3 Put a griddle or cast-iron skillet over medium heat. When it's hot, press one of the coils flat, then roll it out into as thin a disk as you can. Put on the griddle or skillet and cook until lightly browned on one side, just a minute; brush the top with butter, flip, and brown on the second side, another minute or two. Continue until all the breads are done, then serve.

Spinach Paratha. Almost as easy but with a twist: Cook 1 pound fresh spinach and squeeze well to dry (see page 239). In Step 1, add the spinach and a squeeze of lemon juice along with the water and process as directed, adding more water or flour as needed.

Aloo Paratha

Potato-Stuffed Flatbread

MAKES: 4 to 6 servings (8 to 12 paratha)

TIME: At least an hour

Ⓜ Ⓥ

I adore this bread and was fortunate enough to learn how to make it from an expert, the great Indian cook and cookbook writer Julie Sahni. This is essentially her recipe, though I've modified it over the years.

You can cook this paratha ahead and keep it at room temperature for up to 24 hours to serve without reheating or warm it briefly in a dry skillet or even a microwave. But there is nothing like one fresh from the skillet.

Ajwain comes from carom seeds, which look like celery but taste like very strong, slightly coarse thyme.

1 1/2 cups whole wheat flour

1 1/2 cups all-purpose flour, plus more for rolling out the dough

Salt

1 teaspoon ajwain, dried thyme, or ground cumin

2 tablespoons neutral oil, like grapeseed or corn, plus more for brushing the breads

1 1/2 pounds starchy potatoes, peeled and cut in half

1 jalapeño or other hot fresh chile, seeded and minced, or more to taste

2 teaspoons ground coriander

Freshly ground black pepper

Juice of 1/2 small lemon

Melted butter

1 Combine the flours with 1 teaspoon salt and the ajwain in a food processor. Turn the machine on and add the oil and 3/4 cup water through the feed tube. Process for about 30 seconds, until the mixture forms a ball and is slightly sticky to the touch. If it is dry, add another tablespoon or two of water and process for another 10 seconds. In the unlikely event that the mixture is too sticky, add flour a tablespoon at a time. Remove the dough and, using flour as necessary, shape into a ball; wrap in plastic and let rest while you make the potato mixture. (At this point, you may wrap the dough tightly in plastic and refrigerate for up to a day or freeze for up to a week; bring back to room temperature before proceeding.)

2 Put the potatoes in a large saucepan and add water to cover and a large pinch of salt. Turn the heat to high, bring to a boil, and adjust the heat so the mixture simmers steadily; cook until the potatoes are tender, 15 to 20 minutes, then drain. Mash the potatoes along with half the chile, the coriander, a large pinch of salt, some pepper, and the lemon juice; taste and adjust the seasoning (you may prefer more chile; sometimes aloo paratha are quite hot).

3 When the dough has rested, set out a bowl of all-purpose flour and a small bowl of oil, with a spoon or brush, on your work surface. Lightly flour your work surface and your rolling pin. Break off a piece of dough about the size of a golf ball. Toss it in the bowl of flour and then roll it in your hands to make a ball. Flatten it into a 2-inch disk, then use a floured rolling pin to roll it into a thin round, about 5 inches in diameter, dusting with flour as necessary.

4 Mound about 2 tablespoons of the filling into the center of one of the rounds of dough. Bring the edges of the round up over the top of the filling and press them together to make a pouch. Press down on the "neck" of the pouch with the palm of one hand to make a slightly rounded disk. Turn the disk in the bowl of flour and roll it out again into a round 6 to 7 inches in diameter. Pat it between your hands to brush off the excess flour. Put the paratha on a plate and cover with a sheet of plastic wrap. Continue to roll all of the remaining dough into parathas and stack them on the plate with a sheet of plastic wrap between them. You can keep the paratha stacked like this for an hour or two in the refrigerator before cooking them if necessary.

5 Heat a griddle or cast-iron skillet over medium-high heat for a minute or two, then put on a paratha (or two, if they'll fit) and cook until it darkens slightly, usually less than a minute. Flip the paratha with a spatula and cook for another 30 seconds on the second side. Use the back of a spoon or a brush to coat the top of the paratha with oil. Flip and coat the other side with oil. Continue cooking the paratha until the bottom of the bread has browned, flip, and repeat. Do this a few times until both sides of the paratha are golden brown and very crisp, 2 to 3 minutes total for each paratha. As the paratha finish, remove them from the pan and brush with melted butter if you're going to serve hot; otherwise wait until you've reheated them.

Cauliflower Paratha. Traditional and similar, but with that distinctive cauliflower flavor: Instead of the potatoes, use 1 small head cauliflower. Use mustard seeds instead of the ground coriander.

The Basics of Yeast Bread

You can make very good yeast bread *today*, even if you've never made it before; really. If you have a food processor, you can be pulling it from the oven 2 or 3 hours from now. You can make it even faster if you push. Or you can make it slower, with so little work that you'll be amazed. And in each of these cases it'll be good, very good, better than what is served to you in most restaurants.

Equipment

What you don't want is a bread machine. What you absolutely need is a bowl and a wooden spoon and an oven. In between, there are ranges of options. Here's what I have and what I recommend you acquire eventually, if not all at once.

A food processor: If you're going to cook regularly, you want one anyway; after the refrigerator, and maybe the dishwasher, it's the most useful kitchen appliance invented during the twentieth century. What it does for bread making is remarkable; it turns the process of making dough from a laborious chore (which has its up-sides, especially if you're a Zen type, but nevertheless discourages many people from even getting started) into a task that takes less than a minute of work. Literally. The hardest part is washing the workbowl afterward (and that's where the dishwasher comes in!).

A pizza stone: You buy one (see Sources, page 982), shove it into your oven, and forget about it. It can stay there forever, won't hurt anything else you cook in there, and is essential for pizza and a good thing to have for bread.

An instant-read thermometer: You should have one anyway (see page 9).

A small strainer: A good item for dusting flour; not essential, but nice.

That's it. You don't need bread pans, at least for European-style breads (you will for sandwich loaves, of course). And you can live without all of the preceding items, especially if you become an aficionado of Jim Lahey's No-Work Bread (page 833).

Ingredients

Pretty simple, really. All-purpose flour is good, bread flour is better; see page 836 for details. A bit of rye or whole wheat adds flavor, variety, and, of course, some fiber. You need yeast; I prefer instant (see page 839), because it's the most convenient. Water and salt: the best you have, but from the tap and the table are just fine. A bit of olive oil now and then is a nice addition. And then, of course, you can add whatever flavorings you want, but I'm talking the basics here.

Making the Dough

Dough making is the key to good bread making; starting with the wrong dough will guarantee an unsatisfactory bread no matter how perfect your baking. Starting with the right dough, however, will usually give you a good bread even if everything else is imperfect.

Eventually you will learn to mix and knead and judge dough by sight and feel alone (really); for now, just follow the recipes here, which are detailed enough. I swear a 10-year-old can make very good dough on the first try by following these directions.

Kneading—which can sometimes be skipped (time takes its place in No-Work Bread) or done entirely in the food processor—allows the flour-and-water mixture to develop gluten, the protein that gives bread structure, chewiness, and essentially the character you're looking

Dough about halfway through the mixing process—note that it's still quite shaggy.

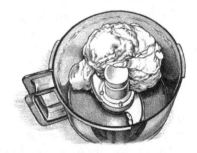

When the dough is ready, it will be ball shaped and easy to handle.

for. The No-Work method and food processor methods are ideal because they allow you to maximize the water-to-flour ratio, and good yeast dough is wet, usually too wet to handle with your hands (this is why these doughs are not only easier but better than hand-kneaded dough). Knead dough by hand once or twice if you want to get a sense of history or of how it feels when it all comes together; or don't. The doughs here should start out rough looking, what bakers call nearly shaggy. But if you flour your hands and the work surface lightly after making the dough, you'll have no trouble handling the dough from then on.

KNEADING DOUGH

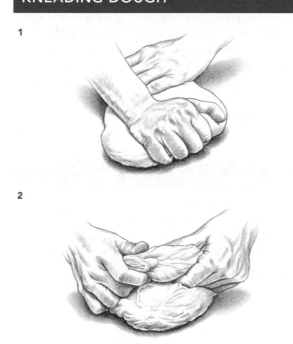

1

2

(**STEP 1**) Using as little flour as possible, press the lump of dough down with your hands. (**STEP 2**) Repeatedly fold and press until the dough becomes far less sticky and quite elastic.

Rising the Dough

Within limits, slower rising is better; it allows flavor to develop and improves the final product in subtle but noticeable ways. Some bakers rush through the rising period by increasing the amount of yeast (a practice I do not recommend because it's hard to control) or by letting the dough rise in a warm (no more than 110°F) oven, but if you have the time, consider Jim Lahey's No-Work Bread (page 833) or a schedule like this: Mix the dough in the morning, then let it rise at room temperature until noon or early afternoon. If the recipe directs, deflate the dough and allow it to rise again (usually for about half the time of the first rising); then shape it and let it rest for another hour or more before baking. Contrary to older recipe directions, there are no precise rising times; dough is really quite flexible.

Shaping the Dough

I guess this is the hard part, though it's also the most fun. And it's a matter of taste. You can use your dough to make small rolls or baguettes, which are the trickiest route; or you can make a big round, almost free-form loaf, which is the easiest. You can use loaf pans (or baguette pans, though I find them more trouble than they're worth because the dough tends to get stuck in the holes in the pan).

You can make any shape you like with basic bread dough, including pizza (see page 175). Just remember to lightly flour all your work surfaces before putting the dough on them (you can use cornmeal if you prefer, which will add a little crunch to the bread). Here are illustrations for making the most popular shapes.

A boule (ball) or free-form loaf is the simplest shape. Take the risen dough and turn it in your hands, shaping it into a round ball (you can make a long oval if you prefer) and smoothing it over so that the seams are on the bottom. (This process is different for No-Work Bread.) Pinch the seams closed. For the final rising, line a medium bowl with a clean towel and sift a bit of flour onto it. Put the dough ball, seam side up, in the towel;

sprinkle with little more flour and fold the towel over the top. Let rise for at least an hour and preferably 2 or 3. To bake, turn the dough over onto a lightly floured peel, wooden board, or flexible cutting board, slash it (see below), and slide it directly onto a pizza stone, or turn it onto a lightly oiled baking sheet, slash it, and put the sheet into the heated oven.

To make rolls, simply divide the dough into anywhere from six to twelve pieces and shape each as you would a boule. Treat them the same way from that point on, though baking time will obviously be shorter.

Baguettes are a little more complicated, but easy enough with practice. Press the dough into a rectangle; it may be any length that will fit into your oven. Fold each long side of the rectangle up into the middle, then roll into a log and use your fingers to press the resulting seam together tightly. If you'd like, you can then shape the loaf into a ring just by pinching the ends together. Spread a large, heavy piece of canvas or cotton (you can use a large tablecloth, folded into quarters to give it extra stiffness) on a table or countertop and sprinkle it lightly with flour. Or use baguette pans, sifting a little bit of flour into them, or oiling them lightly. Cover if necessary and let rise for 1 to 2 hours at room temperature;

the loaves will be about one and a half times their original size.

Slashing

To allow some of the steam built up in the dough to escape in a controlled fashion, most bakers slash the top of their dough in several places just before baking. It's not essential, but it usually results in a more attractive loaf. Use a sharp knife or razor blade; with baguettes, make three or four crosswise cuts, each about $1/4$ inch deep. With boules, make a crosshatch or similar pattern. With rolls, just make an "X."

Baking

Baking technique is important (it's easy, though), especially when you start to fine-tune your baking. (Again, it's different for Jim Lahey's No-Work Bread on page 833.) This is where the pizza stone comes in, and some rocks are handy too. Heat the oven to 400°F (higher if you want a thick, hard crust). Give it a good half hour, even more, to come to temperature, especially if you have a pizza stone in place. While the oven is heating, put on

SHAPING BOULES

(STEP 1) To make a boule, or round loaf, shape the dough into a ball. (STEP 2) Working around the ball, continually tuck the dough toward the center of the bottom, stretching the top slightly and creating surface tension. Pinch together the seam created at the bottom of the dough. (STEP 3) Just before baking, make a few shallow slashes in the surface of the dough.

1

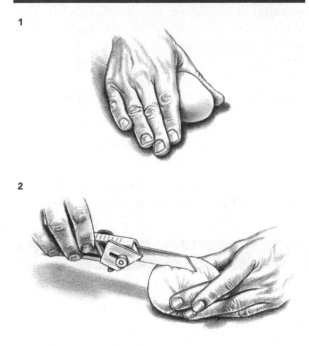

2

(STEP 1) To make dinner rolls, first roll a small lump of dough on a lightly floured surface until the seam is closed and smooth. (STEP 2) Just before baking, make a an "X" or a couple of shallow slashes in the surface of the dough.

its floor a shallow ovenproof pot (preferably cast-iron) half-filled with ordinary (but clean) rocks (you can buy some at a garden center; that's the easiest thing, though not the cheapest). This will absorb heat like mad and hold it there. Boil some water. Just before putting the bread in the oven, carefully pour boiling water to just over the top of the stones. You will get lots and lots of steam. (I always take my glasses off first.) Close the oven door. A minute later, put in the bread and start baking, turning the heat down to 375°F.

There are a zillion possible variations on this technique, but this is how I do it these days, and I'm pleased with the results. I've tried every way of getting steam into the oven—crucial for a crackling crust, but by no means essential—from using a spray bottle to dumping ice cubes on the bottom, but the rock technique (courtesy of the genius Beatrice Ojakangas, thank you!) works best.

At this point you can more or less ignore your bread until it's done, though I rotate it after 10 or 15 minutes just to make sure it bakes evenly. I do keep an eye on it, but even that isn't essential as long as the heat isn't too high (which it isn't for most of these recipes). Most bread is done when it makes a hollow sound when you thump it or when an instant-read thermometer inserted in the center of the loaf reads 210°F. If you're going to reheat it, which is often the case, underbaking is no big deal, and you can consider anything above 190°F "done." Boules usually take about 40 minutes, baguettes about 20, rolls about 15. But there are lots of variables, so keep your eyes open.

Alternatively, you can bake any loaf in an enclosed lidded pot using Jim Lahey's technique: Make the dough a little wetter than usual, but otherwise proceed with any recipe. Bake according to the directions in Jim Lahey's No-Work Bread (page 833).

Storing Bread

As I've already noted, you can store unbaked dough, well wrapped in aluminum foil or plastic, in the freezer for a couple of weeks. You can also store baked bread, wrapped in wax paper—plastic makes the crust soggy—on the counter for up to a few days (especially if you like toast); large loaves containing some whole grain flour keep better than small ones baked with just white flour, because the whole grain contains some fat (and bread baked with added fat, like those on pages 859–870, keeps even better).

Baked bread can also be frozen; in this instance aluminum foil or heavy plastic bags are fine, because you'll need to recrisp the bread anyway (see page 841).

All of this may sound like a lot, but making bread—unlike making cakes, for example, or even brownies—

offers loads of latitude. The schedule can be molded to meet your own and, as long as your yeast is alive, the chances are good you'll be far more successful than you imagine.

make at home. Containing nothing more than flour, water, yeast, and salt, they are miracles of nature, with wonderful flavor and texture and amazing crust. This dough can be made in any shape, including rolls. They are not fancy; they're just nearly perfect.

European-Style Yeast Breads

There was a time, in my overenthusiasm for things European, that I would have said these were the best breads in the world. I've since come to have a greater appreciation for Indian breads (see pages 848–851) and American-style quick breads (see page 841), so I will no longer go that far. But these are fabulous breads and ultra-rewarding to

Fast French Bread or Rolls

MAKES: 3 or 4 baguettes, 1 boule, or 12 to 16 rolls
TIME: About 2 hours, largely unattended

This bread can be made by hand or with an electric mixer (see page 863), but the food processor is the tool of

---

SHAPING BAGUETTES

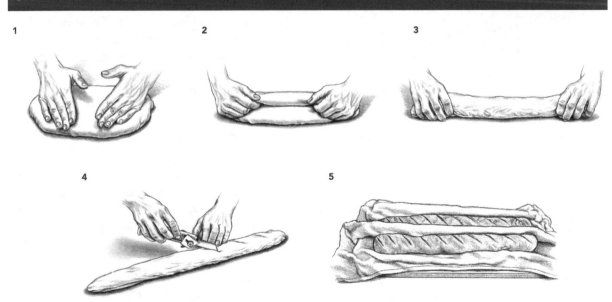

(STEP 1) Press the dough into a rectangle of any length that will fit into your oven. (STEP 2) Fold each long side of the rectangle up into the middle. (STEP 3) Roll into a log and use your fingers to press the resulting seam together tightly. (STEP 4) Just before baking, make a few shallow slashes in the surface of the dough. (STEP 5) You can create a what's called a "couche"—a bed, essentially—for your baguettes to rise with a piece of heavy canvas, a towel, or a tablecloth.

If you'd like, you can start by making a baguette (STEPS 1–3) and shape the loaf into a ring or crown.

   Fast Make Ahead **V** Vegetarian

choice and will save you tons of time. Alternatively, you can use the dough from Jim Lahey's bread (see page 833), though the shaping will be a bit more challenging because it's so soft.

3½ cups all-purpose or bread flour, plus more as needed

2 teaspoons salt

1½ teaspoons instant yeast

1 Put the flour in a food processor. Add the salt and yeast and turn the machine on; with the machine running, pour about a cup of water through the feed tube. Process until the dough forms a ball, adding a tablespoon more water at a time until it becomes smooth; if the dough begins sticking to the side of the bowl, you've added too much water. No harm done: add ¼ cup or so of flour and keep going. You're looking for a moist, slightly shaggy but well-defined ball. The whole process should take about 30 seconds, and it will once you get good at it. If the dough is too dry, add water 1 tablespoon at a time and process for 5 or 10 seconds after each addition. If it becomes too wet, add another tablespoon or two of flour and process briefly.

2 Dump the lump of dough into a large bowl or simply remove the blade from the processor bowl and leave the dough in there. Either way, cover with a plastic bag or plastic wrap and let sit for at least an hour at room temperature.

3 Use a small strainer or your fingers to dust a little flour onto a counter or tabletop. Shape the dough as you like, into small loaves, one big one, baguettes, or rolls, sprinkling with flour as necessary but keeping the flour to a minimum. Heat the oven (with a pizza stone and/or a pan filled with rocks if you have them; see page 854) to 400°F while you let the breads or rolls rise, in a cloth if you like (see page 853), covered with a towel.

4 When you are ready to bake, slash the top of each loaf once or twice with a razor blade or sharp knife. If the dough has risen on a cloth, slide or turn it onto floured baking sheets or gently move it onto a lightly floured peel, plank of wood, or flexible cutting board, then slide the bread directly onto a pizza stone. Or you can bake on lightly oiled baking sheets. Turn the heat down to 375°F.

5 Bake until the crust is golden brown and the internal temperature of the bread is at least 210°F (it can be lower if you plan to reheat the bread later) or the loaves sound hollow when tapped. Remove, spray with a bit of water if you would like a shinier crust, and cool on a wire rack.

More Leisurely and Flavorful French Bread or Rolls. All you're really doing is slowing down the process, but that also improves the quality some: In Step 2, let the dough rise for a longer period of time, which will help it develop flavor—2 or 3 hours at room temperature or up to 12 hours, refrigerated (bring it back to room temperature before proceeding). In Step 3, after shaping, let the bread(s) or rolls rise for 2 to 3 hours (or longer, refrigerated, bringing them back to room temperature before baking). Proceed as directed.

Whole Grain French Bread or Rolls. You can add color and flavor to this bread by adding whole wheat, rye, or barley flours or cornmeal, alone or in combination; or you can use a 7- or 9-grain preblended flour. Simply substitute the whole grain flour for some of the all-purpose or bread flour. If you keep the addition to ½ cup or less, you will retain the characteristic texture of this bread. You may add much more—up to a third of the total amount of flour, or just over 1 cup—and still have a very good bread with a crisp crust. Adding more than that will produce the soft crust and doughy crumb typical of breads high in whole grain; better, at that point, to make one of the other breads designed specifically for whole grain, like Black Bread (page 869).

Sourdough Bread

MAKES: 3 or 4 baguettes, 1 boule, or 12 to 16 rolls

TIME: At least 48 hours the first time, roughly 24 hours thereafter, largely unattended

You can make sourdough bread that's really sour (see the variation), but I prefer this method, which uses a bit of yeast each time; it's faster, I think it's got more complex flavor, it's easier, and it's not too sour for me. I'm including rye flour in the basic recipe because that's my favorite way to go, but you can use all white flour, or mix in whole wheat instead of or in addition to rye. (As usual, you can do pretty much whatever you want with this dough; see "18 Ingredients to Add to Any Plain Yeast Bread," page 871.)

Note that the first time you make this will take longer, because you have to create a sourdough starter (unless someone gives you some). But after that it's a straightforward and simple process. The starter must be used every few weeks, though, or it will die (I've left mine for a month and it was okay, but I felt it was risky). You can simply feed it some flour and water, but every time you make bread you're replenishing it, so as long as you make bread every now and then it will be fine.

3½ cups bread or all-purpose flour, plus more as needed

⅛ teaspoon plus ½ teaspoon instant yeast

2 teaspoons salt

1 cup rye or whole wheat flour or more white flour

❶ At least 2 days before you plan to bake the bread (3 days is better, really), mix together 1½ cups of the bread or all-purpose flour, ⅛ teaspoon yeast, and 1½ cups warm water. Stir with a wooden spoon, cover loosely, and put on top of your refrigerator or in some other out-of-the-way place. Stir every 8 to 12 hours; the mixture will become bubbly and eventually will develop a slightly sour smell. If your kitchen is very warm, this may happen in 24 hours; usually it takes a couple of days. When it's done, you've made sourdough starter!

❷ This is how you'll make the bread; begin at this step every time from now on: The night before you're ready to bake, feed the starter by combining it with the remaining 2 cups bread or all-purpose flour and about 1½ cups tepid water. You can do this in a food process or a bowl; process or mix until smooth. Cover and let rest overnight; the mixture will bubble and foam a bit. (You can shorten this process to 6 hours or so if you like.)

❸ Next, transfer half of it to a covered container and refrigerate until the next time you're going to make bread. What's left is the basis for your bread; put it in the food processor with the ½ teaspoon yeast, the salt, and the 1 cup rye, wheat, or additional white flour. Turn the machine on and add a little water at a time until a moist, slightly shaggy but well-defined ball forms (you may not need much, because the starter should be quite wet). If the dough begins sticking to the side of the bowl, you've added too much water; add a quarter cup or so of flour and keep going. If the dough is too dry, add water 1 tablespoon at a time and process for 5 or 10 seconds after each addition. If it's too wet, add another tablespoon or two of flour and process briefly.

❹ From this point on, you're making bread as you would normally: Dump the lump of dough into a large bowl or simply remove the blade from the processor bowl and leave the dough in there. Either way, cover with a plastic bag or plastic wrap and let sit for at least an hour, at room temperature.

❺ Use a small strainer or your fingers to dust a little flour onto a counter or tabletop. Shape the dough as you like, into small loaves, one big one, baguettes, or rolls, sprinkling with flour as necessary but keeping the flour to a minimum. Heat the oven (with a pizza stone and/or a pan filled with rocks if you have them; see page 854) to 400°F while you let the breads or rolls rest, in a cloth if you like (see page 853), covered with a towel, until nearly doubled in size.

❻ When you're ready to bake, slash the top of each loaf or roll once or twice with a razor blade or sharp knife. If the dough has risen on a cloth, slide or turn it onto floured baking sheets or gently move it onto a lightly floured peel, plank of wood, or flexible cutting board, then slide the bread directly onto a baking stone. Or you can bake on lightly oiled baking sheets. Turn the heat down to 375°F.

7 Bake until the crust is golden brown and the internal temperature of the bread is at least 210°F (it can be lower if you plan to reheat the bread later). Remove, spray with a bit of water if you would like a shinier crust, and cool on a wire rack.

Sandwich and Other Rich Breads

The difference between dough for European-style breads (see page 856) and American-style sandwich loaves is not only shape: it's fat. Though you can make any dough any shape you like, sandwich breads tend to have a softer crust, a finer crumb, and a more tender texture, which makes them easier to slice and easier to eat. You achieve these textural changes by adding fat, usually in the form of milk and sometimes butter as well. (Take this to an extreme and use lousy ingredients and you get store-bought white bread.)

Like that for any bread, the dough for sandwich breads can be made in a food processor pretty quickly. Because they don't depend on the interaction between yeast and flour for all of their flavor, sandwich breads generally have quicker rising times and are almost always made directly, without sponges or sourdough starter; so in some ways they're actually easier than many of the European-style loaves. Beginners may find them a tad tricky to shape, but you'll quickly get the hang of that.

Sandwich Bread, Five Ways

MAKES: 1 large loaf

TIME: At least 3 hours, largely unattended

The typical white bread is not only richer than the European-style breads on page 856 but usually baked in a loaf pan, which helps keep the crust tender. To make this bread by hand or with a standing mixer, follow the guidelines on page 863.

The Magic of Gluten

You can't talk about baking bread without mentioning gluten, the magical compound that allows yeast dough to rise and gives breads their characteristic "chew." To make gluten, it takes water and two proteins, glutenin and gliadin, both of which are abundant in wheat and present (usually in much lesser quantities) in many other grains. And since these proteins are even more accessible when the grains are ground, wheat flour is extremely high in gluten.

As you mix and knead wheat-based batters or doughs—or simply allow them to rest, as in Jim Lahey's No-Work Bread, the gluten develops into a weblike structure that supports the flour's starch and other components, which in turn traps the carbon dioxide bubbles produced by yeast during fermentation (or by other leaveners, like baking powder; see page 839). This structure becomes permanent as the bread, cake, muffin, or cookie bakes and moisture evaporates to create the nooks, crannies, and air pockets we call "the crumb."

Significant gluten development is really desirable only in making crusty, chewy breads, where you can use high-protein bread flour and work the dough vigorously. When you want a tender bread crumb, it's better to start with a relatively low-protein flour, like all-purpose or even cake flour, and take care not to knead the dough too much; if you overwork a delicate yeasted pastry dough, it becomes tough. In fact, to ensure a tender crumb in quick breads, cakes, cookies, and other nonyeasted baked foods, you usually blend in the flour briefly and as lightly as possible at the end of the recipe. That's why you often see the instruction "stir only until the flour is incorporated."

3½ cups (about 1 pound) all-purpose flour, plus more as needed

2 teaspoons salt

1½ teaspoons instant yeast

1 tablespoon sugar or honey, or more to taste

2 tablespoons neutral oil, like grapeseed or corn, or softened butter, plus more for the bowl and pan

Scant 1⅓ cups cool milk, preferably whole or 2 percent (warm the milk to at least 70°F if you're working by hand)

1 Put the flour in a food processor. Add the salt and yeast and process for 5 seconds. With the machine running, add the sweetener, oil or butter, and most of the milk through the feed tube (you will need a little less milk if you're using honey). Process for about 30 seconds,

then remove the cover. The dough should be in a well-defined, barely sticky, easy-to-handle ball. If it is too dry, add milk 1 tablespoon at a time and process for 5 or 10 seconds after each addition. If it is too wet, which is unlikely, add a tablespoon or two of flour and process briefly.

2 Use a little more of the oil or butter to grease a large bowl. Shape the dough into a rough ball, put it in the bowl, and cover with plastic wrap or a damp towel. Let rise for at least 2 hours, until nearly doubled in bulk. Deflate the ball and shape it into a ball again; let rest on a lightly floured surface for about 15 minutes, covered.

3 Using only enough flour to keep the dough from sticking to your hands or the work surface, flatten it into a rectangle, then shape it into a loaf (see the illustrations

SHAPING A SANDWICH LOAF

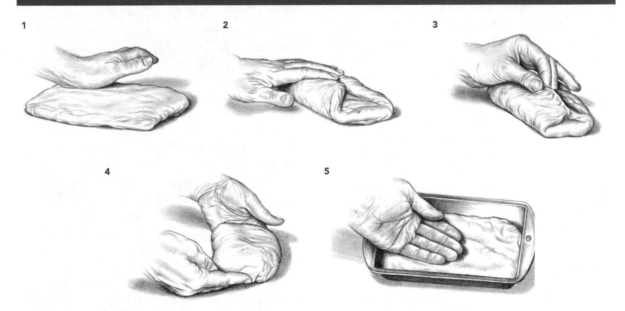

(STEP 1) If the dough has risen in an oiled bowl, you need no flour; otherwise, work on a very lightly floured surface. Use the heel of your hand to form the dough into a rectangle. **(STEP 2)** Fold the long sides of the rectangle over to the middle. **(STEP 3)** Pinch the seam closed, pressing tightly with your fingers. **(STEP 4)** Fold under the ends of the loaf. **(STEP 5)** Use the back of your hand to press the loaf firmly into the pan.

      Fast   **M** Make Ahead   **V** Vegetarian

on page 860). Use the remaining oil or butter to grease a 9 × 5-inch loaf pan. Put the loaf in the pan, flattening the top of it with the back of your hand as shown. Cover and let rise for 1 hour, or until the top of the dough is nearly level with the top of the pan.

4 Heat the oven to 350°F. Brush the top of the loaf lightly with water, then put in the oven. Bake for about 45 minutes, or until the bottom of the loaf sounds hollow when you tap it (it will fall easily from the loaf pan) or the internal temperature is about 210°F on an instant-read thermometer. Remove the loaf from the pan and cool on a wire rack before slicing.

50 Percent Whole Wheat Sandwich Bread. Substitute half whole wheat flour for half of the white flour. Use honey for the sweetener, adding 2 tablespoons or more. Increase the rising times to at least 2 hours in Step 2.

Bran and Oat Sandwich Bread. Decrease the flour to 2 cups. Add $^1/_2$ cup wheat or oat bran and $^3/_4$ cup whole wheat flour. Use about $^1/_4$ cup honey or maple syrup as the sweetener and decrease the milk to about 1 cup. Knead in $^3/_4$ cup rolled oats by hand. (If you wet your hands, it will be easier to handle.)

Anadama Bread. A New England classic. Substitute $^1/_2$ cup cornmeal for $^1/_2$ cup flour. (You may also substitute 1 cup whole wheat flour for 1 cup white flour at the same time.) Replace the sugar or honey with $^1/_2$ cup molasses and use a little less milk.

English Muffins. Much easier than you think, in some ways easier than bread, and really lovely; use the main recipe or any of the other variations. In Step 3, cut the dough into 12 roughly equal pieces (if you want perfectly sized muffins, use a scale). Using just enough flour to enable you to handle the dough, shape each into a 3- to 4-inch disk. Dust with flour and let rise for 30 to 45 minutes, or until puffy. Heat a griddle or large skillet over low heat for about 10 minutes; do not oil it. Sprinkle it with cornmeal, then pan-bake the muffins, a few at a time, on both sides, turning occasionally, until lightly browned, a total of about 15 minutes. Cool on a rack and split open with a fork before toasting.

Rich Golden Bread, Nine Ways

MAKES: 1 (huge) or 2 round loaves or 1 large sandwich loaf

TIME: At least 3 hours, largely unattended

A rich, versatile dough that you can use for almost anything: sandwich bread, coffee cake, or whenever you want a golden crumb and shiny crust. The variations and illustrations that follow outline some examples, but the possibilities are endless. For more ideas about how to flavor this, see "18 Ingredients to Add to Any Plain Yeast Bread" (page 871).

> 3$^1/_2$ cups all-purpose or bread flour, plus more as needed
>
> 2 teaspoons instant yeast
>
> 2 teaspoons salt
>
> 1 tablespoon sugar
>
> 2 tablespoons cold butter
>
> 2 eggs
>
> About 1 cup milk, preferably whole
>
> Softened butter for the pans
>
> Melted butter for brushing the loaves

1 Combine the flour, yeast, salt, sugar, and cold butter in a food processor. Pulse the machine on and off until the butter is evenly distributed in the flour, but not completely blended in. Add the eggs and pulse a few more times. With the machine running, slowly add $^3/_4$ cup of the milk through the feed tube.

2 Process for about 30 seconds, adding more milk if necessary, a little at a time, until the mixture forms a ball and is slightly sticky to the touch. If it is dry, add another tablespoon or two of milk and process for another 10 seconds. In the unlikely event that the mixture is too sticky, add flour, a tablespoon at a time.

3 Turn the dough onto a floured work surface and knead it a bit by hand. (Now's the time to add extra ingredients to the dough if you like; simply knead them in until well incorporated.) Form a smooth, round dough ball, put in a bowl, and cover with plastic wrap; let rise until the dough doubles in size, 1 to 2 hours. (You can cut this rising time short if you are in a hurry, or you can let the dough rise more slowly, for up to 6 or 8 hours, in the refrigerator. At this point, you may also wrap the dough tightly in plastic wrap and freeze for up to a month; defrost in a covered bowl in the refrigerator or at room temperature.)

4 When the dough is ready, form it into a ball and divide it into 2 pieces if you like or leave whole; roll each piece into a round ball. Put each ball on lightly floured surface, sprinkle with a little flour, and cover with plastic wrap or a towel. Let rest until the dough puffs slightly, about 20 minutes.

5 Pinch the bottom of the ball(s) to seal the seam as well as you can. Butter 1 or 2 shallow baking dishes or cake pans that will comfortably hold the loaves; they should not (yet) quite fill the pans. Cover and let rise for

an hour and preferably longer, up to 2 hours. It's okay if the dough rises over the sides of the pans a bit.

6 Heat the oven to 350°F and set a rack in the middle. Brush the top of the loaf or loaves with melted butter. Bake for about 40 minutes, until the crust is golden brown and the internal temperature of the bread is at least 210°F on an instant-read thermometer. Immediately turn the breads out of their dishes or pans and cool on a wire rack. Cut with a serrated knife—the bread will be rich and delicate.

Rich Golden Rolls. Slightly crisp on the outside, airy on the inside: In Step 4, instead of shaping the dough into a loaf or loaves, keep dividing it in half until you have 16 medium or 24 small balls. (See the illustration on page 855.) Grease a couple of baking sheets or line them with parchment. Put the rolls on the sheets, a couple inches apart, cover, and let rise for about an hour. Proceed with the recipe; reduce the baking time to 20 to 30 minutes, depending on the size of the rolls.

Rich Golden Sandwich Bread. In Step 5, instead of greasing the baking dishes or cake pans, grease a 9 × 5-inch loaf pan. Shape the dough into one large rectangle; fold it under and seal the seam as you would for sandwich bread (see the illustrations on page 860). Proceed with the recipe, adding about 5 minutes to the baking time.

Saffron Fruit-and-Nut Bread. Like a fancy holiday bread, with less work: In Step 1, add a large pinch of saffron threads to the flour mixture before running the food processor. While the dough is rising for the first time, put 1 cup dried fruit—like golden raisins, cherries, cranberries, chopped apricots, or a mix—in a small bowl; heat $1/2$ cup brandy, rum, or apple juice, pour it over the fruit, and let the fruit soak for about 30 minutes, then drain well. Coarsely chop $1/2$ cup almonds, pecans, or walnuts. In Step 3, knead in the fruit and nuts as directed.

Cocoa Swirl Bread. Not too sweet, but definitely chocolaty: Follow the directions for the Rich Golden Sandwich Bread variation. While the dough is rising for the first time, mix together $1/4$ cup cocoa powder and $1/2$ cup sugar. In Step 5, after you have shaped the dough into a rectangle, sprinkle the cocoa mixture evenly over all. Wet your hands and shake a few drops of water over all (or spray lightly with a water bottle if you have one; or use milk); use a fork to rub the cocoa and water into the dough a bit; it should be a light paste. Roll the bread over and fit into the prepared loaf pan; be sure to seal it well (see the illustrations on page 864). Proceed with the recipe.

Poppy Seed Swirl Bread. An Old World treat made easy with prepared prune (dried plum) spread, which should be available in your supermarket: Follow the variation for Cocoa Swirl Bread, only instead of a cocoa-sugar mixture, combine $3/4$ cup prune paste with $1/4$ cup poppy seeds; spread over the rectangle of dough (no need to add any water). Roll and seal the bread as directed in the preceded variation; proceed with the recipe.

Cinnamon Buns. In Step 5, butter a 9 × 13-inch baking pan or dish or a muffin tin. In a small bowl, combine 2 tablespoons ground cinnamon with $3/4$ cup sugar. Press and roll the dough into a large rectangle, about the size of the baking dish. (If the dough is very elastic, you may need to roll, then let it rest for a few minutes and roll again.) Sprinkle the cinnamon sugar evenly over all. Wet your hands and shake a few drops of water over all (or spray lightly with a water bottle if you have one); use a fork to rub the cinnamon sugar and water into the dough a bit; it should be a light paste. Roll the dough up lengthwise and seal the seam as well as you can. You'll have a long log. Slice it crosswise into 15 pieces. Put each, cut side up, into the prepared dish or pan: 3 across and 5 lengthwise (see the illustrations on page 864). Or put the pieces, swirled side up, into the muffin cups. Proceed with the recipe; reduce the baking time to about 30 minutes. If you like, when the cinnamon rolls cool down a bit, sprinkle them with powdered sugar or Vanilla Glaze (page 919). Or for sticky-bun-style decadence, smear with Caramel Frosting (page 922) and sprinkle with chopped pecans. Serve right from the pan.

Orange Date Buns. In a small bowl, combine $3/4$ cup brown sugar, $1/2$ cup chopped pitted dates, 2 tablespoons minced or grated orange zest, 2 tablespoons melted butter, and $1/2$ cup chopped pistachios or almonds if you like. Follow the directions for the Cinnamon Buns variation, sprinkling the sugar-date mixture over the rectangle instead of the cinnamon sugar. Don't bother to wet the ingredients or smear them into a paste; simply roll up, cut into slices, and proceed as described in the variation.

Making Bread Dough with a Standing Mixer

To make yeast bread (including pizza dough) with a standing mixer, the machine must be fairly powerful or it will stall. Combine half the flour with the salt, yeast, and all of the water (and butter, oil, eggs, or other liquids); blend until smooth with the machine's paddle. With the machine on slow speed, add the remaining flour a little at a time, until the mixture has become a sticky ball that pulls away from the sides of the bowl (switch to the dough hook if necessary). Knead by hand for 1 minute, adding as little flour as possible, then proceed with the recipe.

If your standing mixer is always on the counter (or you have a portable mixer), using it for quick breads might be marginally faster than by hand. Just be careful not to overmix: First stir the dry ingredients together in a separate bowl. Then using the paddle in the mixer, cream the fat and the sugar until well blended and add the milk and/or other liquid called for in the recipe. With the machine at its lowest setting, add the dry ingredients all at once and mix until just combined; stop the machine and scrape down the sides with a spoon and stir once or twice by hand. Don't worry about any lumps.

Press and roll the dough into an oblong and spread the filling mixture evenly across the top.

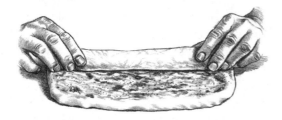

Roll it up the long way.

Slice it into swirls.

Bacon-Cheddar Buns. Cook and crumble 6 slices bacon; grate enough cheddar cheese to make $1^1/_2$ cups. Follow the directions for the Cinnamon Buns variation, sprinkling the cheese, bacon, and a pinch of cayenne if you like over the rectangle instead of the cinnamon sugar. Don't bother to wet the ingredients or smear them into a paste; simply roll up, cut into slices, and proceed as described in the variation.

Olive Oil Bread, with or Without Olives

MAKES: 1 (huge) or 2 round loaves

TIME: At least 3 hours, largely unattended

Olive oil makes this bread a better keeper than European-style breads. Yet the absence of butter and egg makes it a little lighter than the other loaves in this section.

> 3 cups all-purpose or bread flour, plus more as needed
>
> 2 teaspoons instant yeast
>
> 2 teaspoons coarse kosher or sea salt
>
> $1/_3$ cup extra virgin olive oil
>
> 1 tablespoon fresh rosemary leaves (optional)
>
> 1 cup halved and pitted black olives, preferably oil-cured but reasonably tender (optional)

❶ Combine the flour, yeast, and salt in a food processor. Turn the machine on and add the olive oil through the feed tube, followed by 1 cup water. Process for about 30 seconds, adding more water, a little at a time, until the mixture forms a ball and is slightly sticky to the touch. If it is dry, add another tablespoon or two of water and process for another 10 seconds. In the unlikely event that the mixture is too sticky, add flour, a tablespoon at a time.

F Fast   **M** Make Ahead   **V** Vegetarian

2 Turn the dough onto a floured work surface and, by hand, knead in either the rosemary or the olives or both if you like. Form a smooth, round dough ball, put in a bowl, and cover with plastic wrap; let rise until the dough doubles in size, 1 to 2 hours. (You can cut this rising time short if you are in a hurry, or you can let the dough rise more slowly, in the refrigerator, for up to 6 or 8 hours. At this point, you may also wrap the dough tightly in plastic and freeze for up to a month; defrost in a covered bowl in the refrigerator or at room temperature.)

3 When the dough is ready, form it into a ball and divide it into 2 pieces or leave it whole; roll each piece into a round ball. Put each ball on a lightly floured surface, sprinkle with a little flour, and cover with plastic wrap or a towel. Let rest until the dough puffs slightly, about 20 minutes.

4 Pinch the bottom of the ball(s) to seal the seam as best you can. Sprinkle all over with flour and put on a well-floured board or baking sheet (or dust a board with cornmeal). Let rise, covered, for at least an hour and preferably longer, up to 2 hours.

5 Heat the oven (with a pizza stone on the bottom rack and/or a pan filled with rocks if you like; see page 854) to 425°F. Slash the top several times with a razor blade (make a pattern if you like). Put a baking sheet directly into the oven or slide the dough onto the pizza stone. Bake until the bread is beginning to brown, then lower the heat to 375°F. (If the bread is browning too quickly, lower the heat a little sooner.) Bake until the crust is golden brown and the internal temperature of the bread is at least 210°F on an instant-read thermometer, about 40 to 60 minutes. Remove and cool on a wire rack.

Olive Oil Bread with Onions and Mint. A nice combo; you can make this with olives, too, but omit the rosemary: In Step 2, knead 1 large chopped onion into the dough in place of or along with the olives. Add 1 tablespoon chopped fresh mint if you like. Proceed with the recipe.

Semolina Bread. A standard in North Africa: Substitute 2 cups fine semolina flour for 2 cups of the white flour. Instead of forming into loaves, roll or press into large, flat rounds (at least 10 inches in diameter), as you would a thick pizza (see page 176). Reduce the baking time to 20 to 30 minutes, depending on the thickness.

Pancetta and Black Pepper Bread. You can use olive oil here if you'd rather not use the pancetta pan drippings: Omit the rosemary and olives. Cook 1 pound of pancetta (or bacon) until it's crisp and the fat is rendered. Coarsely chop the pancetta and set aside 1 cup (save the rest for another use). Pour off and reserve ⅓ cup of the rendered fat and discard the rest (or save it for another use); if you don't have enough, add olive oil or good-quality lard to make up the balance. Coarsely grind 2 tablespoons black pepper. Make the dough, replacing the olive oil with the reserved fat. In Step 2, knead in the pancetta pieces and the pepper. Proceed with the recipe.

Brioche

MAKES: 2 loaves
TIME: At least 3 hours, largely unattended

Brioche is the richest of all the breads in this section. Bake it as a sandwich bread (a superb use for it), as a decorative loaf (like challah, to which is it similar), or as rolls. Leftover brioche makes yummy French Toast (page 794).

4 cups all-purpose flour, plus more as needed

1 teaspoon salt

¼ cup sugar

1½ teaspoons instant yeast

8 tablespoons (1 stick) cold butter, cut into chunks, plus softened butter for the pan

3 eggs plus 1 yolk

$^1/_2$ cup plus 2 tablespoons milk

❶   Combine the flour, salt, sugar, and yeast in a food processor and process for 5 seconds. Add the cold butter and the whole eggs and process for 10 seconds. With the machine running, pour (don't drizzle) $^1/_2$ cup milk and

BREAD FLAVORING COMBOS

Here are some specific flavor combinations to get you started; as long as you don't overload the dough with too many ingredients (which will keep it from rising properly), you can mix, match, and experiment freely. See "18 Ingredients to Add to Any Plain Yeast Bread" (page 871) for the quantities and timing of the stir-ins.

BREAD DOUGH RECIPE	FLAVORINGS
Fast French Bread or Rolls (page 857)	Chopped black or green olives, plus a little olive oil; minced fresh rosemary leaves
Whole Grain French Bread or Rolls (page 857) made with some rye flour	Toasted caraway seeds and minced fresh dill (optional)
Whole Grain French Bread or Rolls (page 857) made with whole wheat or seven-grain flour	Cooked whole grain berries, like wheat or rye, and sunflower seeds
Jim Lahey's No-Work Bread (page 833)	Parmesan cheese and roasted garlic
Sourdough Bread (page 858)	Cheddar cheese and minced parsley
English Muffins (page 861)	Caramelized onions
Anadama Bread (page 861)	Golden raisins or dried apricots and chopped pecans
50 Percent Whole Wheat Sandwich Bread (page 861)	Raisins or dates and cinnamon sugar
Sandwich Bread made with all white flour (page 859)	Curry powder (to make your own, see pages 66–67) and sesame seeds

$^1/_3$ cup water through the feed tube. Process for about 30 seconds, then remove the cover. The dough should be very sticky, almost like batter. If it is too dry, add water 1 tablespoon at a time and process for 5 or 10 seconds after each addition. If it is too wet, which is almost impossible, add another tablespoon or two of flour and process briefly.

❷   Grease a large bowl with softened butter and scrape the dough into it. Cover with plastic wrap and let rise until at least doubled in bulk, 2 to 3 hours. Deflate the dough and, using just enough flour to enable you to handle it, shape it into 2 loaves, as for Sandwich Bread (page 859). Put each loaf into a buttered 8 × 4-inch or 9 × 5-inch loaf pan. Or shape the dough into rolls as illustrated on page 855. Cover and let rise for about 1 hour.

❸   Heat the oven to 400°F. Mix the egg yolk with the remaining 2 tablespoons milk and brush the top of the loaves with this mixture. Bake the brioche for about 30 minutes, or until nicely browned. When done, the bottom will sound hollow when you tap it (it will fall easily from the loaf pan) and the interior temperature will be at least 190°F on an instant-read thermometer.

Challah

MAKES: 1 large loaf

TIME: At least 3 hours, largely unattended

The traditional Sabbath bread of European Jews is rich, eggy, and very, very tender. It's not a whole lot different from Rich Golden Bread (page 861) except there is more dough to make a festive braided loaf, which is easy to make and fun to shape. However, unless you have a large food processor (one with at least an 11-cup workbowl), you will have to make this by hand or with a standing mixer (see page 863). Leftover Challah makes excellent French Toast (page 794) or can be used in Bread Pudding (page 953).

5 cups (scant 1$^1/_2$ pounds) all-purpose flour, plus more as needed

 Fast   Make Ahead   Vegetarian

2 teaspoons salt

2 teaspoons instant yeast

A few threads saffron (optional)

1 tablespoon honey or sugar

3 eggs plus 1 yolk

1⅓ cups water or milk, warmed to about 70°F if you're
working by hand

Neutral oil, like grapeseed or corn, or softened butter
for the bowl and pan

1 tablespoon poppy seeds

Coarse salt (optional)

1 Put the flour in a food processor. Add the salt, the yeast, and the saffron if you're using it and process for 5 seconds. With the machine running, add the sweetener, whole eggs, and most of the water or milk through the feed tube. Process for about 30 seconds, then remove the cover. The dough should be in a well-defined, barely sticky, easy-to-handle ball. If it is too dry, add water or milk 1 tablespoon at a time and process for 5 or 10 seconds after each addition. If it is too wet, which is unlikely, add another tablespoon or two of flour and process briefly. Knead for a minute or so by hand.

2 Grease a large bowl with oil or butter. Shape the dough into a rough ball, put it in the bowl, and cover with plastic wrap or a damp towel. Let rise for at least 1½ hours, until nearly doubled in bulk. Deflate the ball

---

How Do I Get That Shiny Crust?

It's easy: Right before the bread or rolls go into the oven, make an egg wash by beating one egg yolk with a tablespoon of water. Lightly brush the top of the loaves or rolls with a little egg wash and pop them into the oven. You can use an egg wash on any type of bread, though sweet doughs like the one for Rich Golden Bread (page 861) is the most traditional.

---

and cut it into 3 equal pieces; shape them into balls and let them rest on a lightly floured surface for about 15 minutes, covered.

3 Roll each of the balls into a rope about 14 inches long and 1 inch thick. Braid them on a lightly greased baking sheet, as illustrated on page 868. Cover and let rest for 30 minutes while you heat the oven.

4 Heat the oven to 375°F. Beat the egg yolk with 1 teaspoon water and brush the top of the loaf with this mixture; sprinkle with poppy seeds and, if you like, a little coarse salt, then put in the oven. Bake for 40 to 50 minutes, or until the bottom of the loaf sounds hollow when you tap it or the internal temperature is about 200°F on an instant-read thermometer. Cool on a wire rack before slicing. Best eaten within a day (store in wax paper if necessary).

Onion-Rye Bread

MAKES: 1 large round or oval loaf
TIME: About 4 hours, largely unattended

This is a rather easy rye bread, especially if you use a food processor. You can complete it, with little effort, in just a few hours.

1½ cups all-purpose or bread flour, plus more as
needed

1 cup rye flour, preferably stone-ground

½ cup cornmeal, plus more for dusting the baking
sheets

2 teaspoons instant yeast

1 tablespoon sugar, honey, or molasses

2 teaspoons salt

⅔ cup milk

½ cup finely chopped onion

4 teaspoons caraway seeds

2 teaspoons neutral oil, like grapeseed or corn, for the
bowl

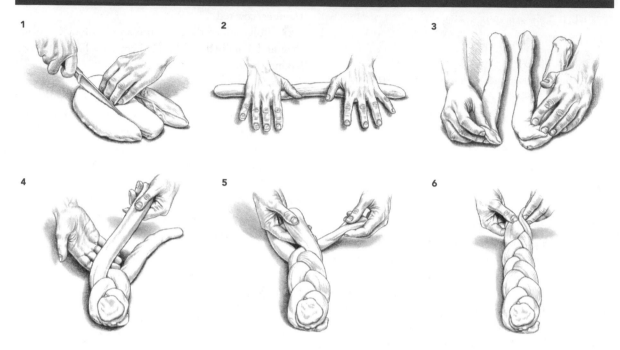

(STEP 1) Cut the dough into three equal pieces. (STEP 2) Roll each piece into a strip about 14 inches long. (STEP 3) Lay the strips next to each other and press their ends together. (STEP 4) Braid, just as you would hair. (STEPS 5–6) Finish braiding and use your fingers to tightly press the ends together.

❶ Combine the flours, cornmeal, yeast, sweetener, and salt in a food processor and process for 5 seconds. With the machine running, pour (don't drizzle) the milk and $1/4$ cup water through the feed tube. Process for about 30 seconds, then remove the cover. The dough should be in a defined but shaggy ball, still quite sticky; you would not want to knead it by hand. If the dough is too dry, add water 1 tablespoon at a time and process for 5 or 10 seconds after each addition. If it is too wet, which is unlikely, add another tablespoon or two of flour and process briefly. Turn the dough out onto a lightly floured counter and knead in the onion and 1 tablespoon of the caraway seeds by hand.

❷ Put the oil in a large bowl and turn the dough into it. Turn it all around so that it has a light covering of oil and cover with plastic wrap. Allow to double in size, at least 2 hours (you can retard the rising by refrigerating for a few hours, or hasten it by putting it in a warm place).

❸ Using only enough flour to keep the dough from sticking to your hands or the work surface, flatten it into a rectangle, then shape it into a long oval by rolling it up, pinching all the seams closed. (The process is essentially the same as for shaping a sandwich loaf, but without the pan; see page 860.) Sprinkle a baking sheet or pizza peel with cornmeal and lay the loaf on top. Cover again and let rise for about an hour.

Ⓕ Fast   Ⓜ Make Ahead   Ⓥ Vegetarian

④ Heat the oven (with a pizza stone and/or a pan filled with stones; see page 854) to 450°F; slash the top of the loaf with a sharp knife or razor blade in 4 or 5 places; brush with water, then sprinkle with the remaining teaspoon of caraway seeds. Put the baking sheet in the oven or slide the dough directly onto the pizza stone; bake for 15 to 20 minutes.

⑤ Lower the heat to 350°F and bake until the loaf is nicely browned and its bottom sounds hollow when you tap it, another 30 to 45 minutes; the internal temperature will be 210°F on an instant-read thermometer. Cool on a rack before slicing and store wrapped in wax paper after you cut it.

Black Bread

MAKES: 1 large or 2 small loaves
TIME: 3 hours, largely unattended

This bread features a one-step mixing technique that keeps the process simple, and in return you get a full-flavored, fairly dense, almost-black Russian-style loaf that's perfect with hearty soups and stews or a wedge of sharp cheddar cheese, some pickles, and a smear of grainy mustard. And it tastes like it was a lot more difficult to make than it is. I like to shape the dough into two smaller loaves and keep one in the freezer to thaw and bake later.

¹/₂ cup 100 percent bran cereal (not flakes)

2 cups all-purpose or bread flour

1 cup medium rye flour

1 cup whole wheat flour

2 tablespoons cocoa powder

2 tablespoons sugar

1 tablespoon instant yeast

2 teaspoons salt

¹/₄ cup softened butter or neutral oil, like grapeseed or corn, plus more for the bowl and pan

¹/₄ cup molasses

2 tablespoons cider vinegar or freshly squeezed lemon juice

1¹/₄ cups strong brewed coffee

① Put the cereal in a food processor and process for about 10 seconds, until it's finely ground. Add the flours, cocoa, sugar, yeast, and salt and pulse. Add the butter or oil and the molasses and vinegar and pulse a few more times. With the machine running, pour most of the coffee through the feed tube. Process for about 30 seconds, then remove the cover. The dough should be in a well-defined, barely sticky, easy-to-handle ball. If it is too dry, add coffee 1 tablespoon at a time and process for 5 or 10 seconds after each addition. If it is too wet, which is unlikely, add a tablespoon or two of flour and process briefly.

② Grease a large bowl with butter or oil. Shape the dough into a rough ball, put it in the bowl, and cover with plastic wrap or a damp towel. Let rise for at least 2 hours, until nearly doubled in bulk. Deflate the ball and shape it once again into a ball; let rest on a lightly floured surface for about 15 minutes, covered. (At this point, you may cover the dough well and refrigerate for several hours or overnight; return to room temperature before proceeding.)

③ Using only enough flour to keep the dough from sticking to your hands or the work surface, knead the dough a few times and shape the dough into a large oval loaf (or divide it in half and make 2 smaller round loaves). Grease a baking sheet with butter or oil. Put the loaf or loaves on the sheet. Cover again and let rise for 1 hour, or until the dough has plumped up again considerably.

④ Heat the oven to 325°F. Bake for 55 to 60 minutes for a large loaf or 40 to 45 minutes for smaller ones, or until the bottom sounds hollow when you tap it (it will fall easily from the loaf pan) or the internal temperature is about 210°F on an instant-read thermometer. Carefully slide the loaf from the sheet and cool on a wire rack before slicing.

Pumpernickel Raisin Bread. You can omit the raisins, of course. Soak 1 cup raisins in enough hot water or coffee to barely cover them. Drain well. In Step 3, knead the raisins into the dough along with a tablespoon of caraway seeds.

Black Bread with Chocolate. Lovely with a smear of cream cheese or sour cream: Coarsely chop a 4-ounce piece of bittersweet chocolate into chunks. In Step 3, knead the chocolate into the dough.

Bagels

MAKES: 8 to 12 bagels

TIME: 3 to 4 hours, largely unattended

These are real bagels—crisp bagels—not the puffy kind sold so often nowadays. Cooking a real bagel is a two-step process: First you boil, then you bake. (I like to make them in small quantities because the boiling step is a bit of work.) Other than that, they are as simple as any other bread. (Malt syrup, the classic sweetener, can be bought in some specialized cooking shops or wherever beer supplies are sold.)

3½ cups (about 1 pound) bread or all-purpose flour, plus more as needed

2 teaspoons salt

1 teaspoon instant yeast

2 tablespoons malt syrup, maple syrup, molasses, or sugar

Neutral oil, like grapeseed or corn, for the baking sheet (optional)

❶ Put the flour in a food processor. Add the salt, yeast, and sweetener and process for 5 seconds. With the machine running, pour (don't drizzle) 1¼ cups water through the feed tube. Process for about 30 seconds, then remove the cover. The dough should be in a well-defined ball, only slightly sticky and very easy to handle. If the dough is too dry, add water 1 tablespoon at a time and process for 5 or 10 seconds after each addition. If it is too wet, add a tablespoon or two of flour and process briefly. Turn the dough out onto a lightly floured counter or tabletop and knead for a minute or two longer by hand, adding as much flour as necessary to make a smooth, tough, very elastic dough.

❷ Dump the lump of dough into a large bowl. Cover loosely with a plastic bag, plastic wrap, or towel. Let rise for about 2 hours, at room temperature, or until the dough has roughly doubled in bulk. If you would like to let the dough rise for a longer period of time, which will help it develop flavor, refrigerate for up to 12 hours; bring it back to room temperature before proceeding.

❸ Deflate the dough ball and let it rest on a lightly floured surface, covered, for about 10 minutes. Cut it into 8 or 12 equal pieces, depending on whether you want large or small bagels. Roll each ball into a 6- to 8-inch-long rope and then shape into a circle or simply poke a hole in the middle of each ball and pull into a bagel shape. Keep all the balls covered as you work and lightly flour and cover the shaped bagels as well. When they're all done, cover and let rise for about 30 minutes.

❹ Bring a large pot of water to a boil; heat the oven (with a pizza stone and/or a pan filled with rocks; see page 854) to 400°F. Drop the bagels, one at a time, into the boiling water; don't crowd. The bagels will sink, then rise to the surface. Boil for 1 minute on each side, then remove them with a slotted spoon and put on a lightly greased rack to drain.

❺ Lightly grease a baking sheet (or use parchment paper). Alternatively, put the bagels on a floured peel and bake them directly on the pizza stone. If you're not using a pan filled with stones, spray the inside of the oven with water to create steam if you like, then put the bagels in the oven. After 5 minutes, spray again. Bake for 20 to 25 minutes, or until the bagels are nicely browned. Remove, spray with a bit of water if you would like a shinier crust, and cool on a wire rack; these keep well for a day or two.

Onion Bagels. The best, in my opinion. Two methods: The first, which is simple, is to add about ½ cup

18 Ingredients to Add to Any Plain Yeast Bread

Here are some ways to add flavor and texture to virtually any yeast bread. See the chart on page 866 for some specific ideas and combinations.

Add any of these ingredients along with the flour and yeast (before the water) if you're making a direct dough recipe; or if making a bread from a sourdough recipe, add these along with the last addition of flour and salt:

1. Spice blends: 1 to 2 tablespoons, depending on their pungency, lightly toasted first in a dry pan if you like
2. Spice seeds, like caraway or cumin: Up to 1 tablespoon, lightly toasted first in a dry pan if you like
3. Cooked whole grains: Up to ¹/₂ cup
4. Finely ground coffee or tea: Up to ¹/₄ cup
5. Wheat germ: Up to ¹/₄ cup; lightly toast first in a dry pan if you like

Knead any of these ingredients into the dough during the final shaping:

1. Chopped nuts or seeds, toasted if you like: Up to 1 cup

2. Chopped dried fruit (including dried tomatoes) or raisins: Up to ¹/₂ cup
3. Chopped bean or seed sprouts: Up to 1 cup
4. Chopped pitted olives: Up to ¹/₂ cup
5. Chopped or crumbled bits of ham, bacon, sausage, pancetta, or prosciutto, up to 1/2 cup
6. Grated hard cheese, like Parmesan, manchego, or ricotta salata: Up to 1 cup
7. Grated medium-hard cheese, like cheddar, Asiago, or pepper Jack: Up to ¹/₂ cup
8. Bits of soft cheese, like goat, blue cheese or Gorgonzola, or cream cheese: Up to ¹/₂ cup
9. Minced fresh herbs: Up to ¹/₄ cup of mild ones like parsley, mint, cilantro, dill, or chives; no more than 1 tablespoon of strong ones like rosemary, sage, or oregano
10. Minced fresh chile (like jalapeño or Thai) or hot red pepper flakes or cayenne to taste
11. Lightly mashed drained cooked beans: Up to 1 cup
12. Roasted Garlic (page 303), lightly mashed or coarsely chopped: Up to ¹/₂ cup
13. Caramelized Onions (page 325): Up to ¹/₂ cup

---

roughly chopped onion to the food processor along with the flour. The second, a little more flavorful, is to sauté ¹/₂ cup minced onion in 1 tablespoon butter or oil until very soft, stirring, for about 10 minutes. Knead these into the dough by hand after removing it from the food processor. In either case, when you're ready to bake the bagels, brush them with a little water and sprinkle each with about a teaspoon of very finely minced onion.

Raisin Bagels. Knead about ¹/₂ cup raisins into the dough by hand after removing it from the food processor.

About ¹/₂ teaspoon ground cinnamon is good here as well.

Bagels Topped with Sesame Seeds, Poppy Seeds, Coarse Salt, Etc. There are two ways to do this. As you remove the bagels from the boiling water, drain briefly and dip the top of each into a plate containing whatever topping you like. Alternatively, just before baking, brush the bagels lightly with water and sprinkle with whatever topping you like. The first method gives you a thicker topping; the second gives you more control.

Making Time to Make Bread

The fact is that you can tailor bread's rising schedule to your own. Here are a few possible scenarios:

It's easy to make dough in the morning and leave it in the fridge while you're gone for 6 or 8 or 10 hours. Before you start to prepare dinner, take the dough out and shape it, let it rise, and then bake it.

It's even easier—though it takes far longer—to make No-Work Bread. Start the night before you want to eat it, and plan on finishing it the following afternoon. Or start in the afternoon and plan to finish it midday.

Or you can mix the dough—or better still, replenish your sourdough (see page 858) or make a sponge—at night and let it rise in a cool place (or the refrigerator) overnight, then turn the sponge into dough and let it rise again throughout the day, again in a cool place or the fridge.

Since dough freezes well, you can whip up a double batch of regular dough, enough to make six dough balls. Let the dough rise all day or overnight, then divide it, wrap the balls in plastic, and toss them in the freezer. When you know you'll want bread for dinner but don't have the time or energy or foresight to make dough, remove a dough ball from the freezer when you wake up (if company is coming, better take out two). This sits on the counter if you're going to be around during the day, in the fridge if you're away. Late in the afternoon, shape the dough; while making dinner, bake it. Dough balls keep well in the freezer for a few weeks; after that the yeast begins to lose power. (Dough prepared this way is well suited to pizza or pita, where maximum rise is not that important.)

In a pinch, you can even skip rising: Make the dough, shape it, let it rest while you heat the oven, and bake it. This won't be the tastiest bread you've ever had, but it'll still beat most loaves you buy in the supermarket. There are many options, as you will see by the time you've made a few loaves; most of them are outlined in these pages.

Pita

MAKES: 6 to 12 pitas, depending on size
TIME: At least 2 hours, somewhat unattended

You can buy pita (also called *pide*), of course, though it's tough to find the real thing: the chewy, slightly puffed rounds that are the standard flatbread of the Eastern Mediterranean. Luckily baking your own is a simple enough task for bread makers, even novices. As with any bread dough, you can control the time it takes to make this by slowing the rising in the refrigerator. If you've got a pizza stone, use it for these, though a cookie sheet is okay too. If you've got time and patience, dry-bake them on top of the stove in one or two heavy skillets (see below).

You can make whole-wheat pitas by simply substituting whole wheat flour for half the white flour.

3 cups all-purpose or bread flour, plus more as needed

3 tablespoons extra virgin olive oil

2 teaspoons instant yeast

2 teaspoons coarse kosher or sea salt

1/2 teaspoon sugar

Melted butter (optional)

❶ Combine the flour, olive oil, yeast, salt, and sugar in a food processor. Turn the machine on and add 1 cup water through the feed tube.

❷ Process for about 30 seconds, adding more water, a little at a time, until the mixture forms a ball and is slightly sticky to the touch. If it is dry, add another tablespoon or two of water and process for another 10 seconds. In the unlikely event that the mixture is too sticky, add flour, a tablespoon at a time.

❸ You can simply cover the food processor bowl with plastic wrap (remove the blade first) or turn the dough onto a floured work surface and knead by hand for a few

 Fast   Make Ahead   Vegetarian

seconds to form a smooth, round dough ball. Put the dough in a bowl and cover with plastic wrap; let rise until the dough doubles in size, 1 to 2 hours. (You can cut this rising time short if you are in a hurry, or you can let the dough rise in the refrigerator for up to 6 or 8 hours.) (At this point, you may wrap the dough tightly in plastic and freeze for up to a month. Defrost in a covered bowl in the refrigerator or at room temperature before proceeding.)

➍ When the dough is ready, form it into a ball and divide it into 6 or more pieces; roll each piece into a round ball. Put each ball on a lightly floured surface, sprinkle with a little flour, and cover with plastic wrap or a towel. Let rest until the balls puff slightly, about 20 minutes.

➎ Roll each ball out to less than $1/4$ inch thickness, using flour to prevent sticking as necessary. As you work, spread the flat disks out on a floured surface and keep them covered. When all the disks are rolled out, heat the oven to 350°F (the disks should rest for at least 20 minutes after rolling). If you have a pizza stone, use it, on a rack set low in the oven; if you do not, lightly oil a baking sheet and put it in the oven on a rack set in the middle. Alternatively, lightly oil and wipe out a heavy skillet.

➏ To bake on a stone, slide the individual disks—as many as will fit comfortably—directly into the oven, using a peel or a large spatula. Or bake 2 disks at a time on a cookie sheet. Or bake over medium to medium-low heat in the skillet, turning once, until lightly browned on both sides. Baking time will be between 5 and 10 minutes, generally only 5 or 6.

➐ As the breads finish baking, remove them from the oven. If you're going to eat them fairly soon, brush with melted butter. Otherwise, cool, then store in wax paper or plastic bags; reheat gently before using.

Stuffed Pita

MAKES: 6 large pitas
TIME: 20 minutes with premade dough

🄵 🄼 🅅

This half-open bread—with the filling partially enclosed and baked right into the dough—is a street treat found throughout the eastern Mediterranean, ideal for lunch or a snack. Or cut the hearty pitas into wedges to serve at parties or picnics; they're also delicious at room temperature. Feel free to use any leftover meat, chicken, vegetable, or bean dish for the filling; you'll need no more than 3 cups total, just $1/2$ cup for each pita.

1 recipe pita dough (preceding recipe)

2 cups crumbled feta or blue cheese

4 tablespoons ($1/2$ stick) butter, softened

4 eggs

1 cup snipped fresh dill

Freshly ground black pepper

Lightly toasted sesame seeds (optional; see page 317)

➊ When you reach Step 5 in making Pita (previous recipe), put the feta, butter, eggs, and most of the dill in a bowl, along with a good sprinkling of black pepper; stir to combine. Put a portion of this filling on each of the disks and bring the sides up to seal; do not enclose entirely (the traditional filled pita is longer than it is wide, kind of boat-shaped; you can make any shape you want).

➋ Sprinkle with the remaining dill and a few sesame seeds and bake as you would pita, but for a little bit longer, perhaps 10 minutes. Eat hot or at room temperature.

Naan

MAKES: About 12 naan
TIME: 2 hours, largely unattended

🄼 🅅

Although something is lost in translation between the scorching heat of a tandoor—the clay oven of northern India—and the relatively tame 500 degrees of a home oven, you can indeed make credible, even delicious naan at home. With their slightly sour flavor and ultra-soft texture, they're the perfect accompaniment to dal (see page 433) or any Indian meat dish.

2 teaspoons instant yeast

2 tablespoons milk

2 tablespoons yogurt

1 tablespoon sugar

3¹/₂ cups unbleached all-purpose flour plus ¹/₂ cup whole wheat flour or 4 cups all-purpose flour, plus flour for rolling out the dough

1 egg

2 teaspoons salt

Neutral oil, like grapeseed or corn, for the bowl

4 tablespoons (¹/₂ stick) butter, melted and still warm

1 Stir together the yeast, milk, yogurt, and sugar in a bowl and set aside.

2 Combine the flour, egg, and salt in a food processor. Turn the machine on and add the yeast mixture through the feed tube.

3 Process for about 30 seconds, adding 1¹/₂ cups of water, a little at a time, until the mixture forms a ball and is slightly sticky to the touch. If it is dry, add another tablespoon or two of water and process for another 10 seconds. In the unlikely event that the mixture is too sticky, add flour, a tablespoon at a time.

4 Turn the dough onto a floured work surface and knead by hand for a few seconds to form a smooth, round ball. Put the dough in a lightly oiled bowl and cover with plastic wrap; let rise until the dough doubles in size, 1 to 2 hours. (You can cut this rising time short if you are in a hurry, or you can let the dough rise in the refrigerator for up to 6 or 8 hours.)

5 Put a baking sheet (or, preferably, a stone) on a rack on the lowest shelf of your oven; heat the oven to 500°F. Punch the dough down and, using as much flour as necessary to keep the dough from sticking to the board or your hands, roll it into a snake, then tear the snake into 12 equal-size balls. Let them rest for 10 minutes covered with plastic wrap or a damp towel.

6 Roll out one of the balls into an oval roughly 6 to 8 inches long and 3 or 4 inches wide. Open your oven door, grab the dough, one hand on each end of the

oval, and give it a little tug with one hand to shape it into a teardrop, then toss it onto the baking sheet or stone. Close the oven door and flip the naan after 3 minutes. The naan is ready when it's puffed, mottled, and browned around the edges, 6 to 8 minutes in total. You can cook as many naan as will comfortably fit at once.

7 Wrap the freshly baked naan in a kitchen towel to keep them warm and pliable. Serve as soon as possible, brushed on one side with melted butter.

Onion Kulcha

MAKES: 6 stuffed naan

TIME: 2 hours, largely unattended

Kulcha are like doughier, softer paratha; they're absolutely delicious. Combined with basmati rice, dal, and an Indian vegetable dish, like the Curried Coconut Eggplant with Potatoes on page 296, kulcha is a perfect centerpiece for a vegetarian meal.

1 recipe naan dough (preceding recipe)

1¹/₂ cups finely chopped red onion

¹/₄ cup minced fresh cilantro

2 teaspoons chaat masala (to make your own, see page 68)

1 teaspoon cayenne

Pinch salt

Flour for rolling out the dough

3 tablespoons melted butter

1 Punch the risen naan dough down and, using as much flour as necessary to keep the dough from sticking to your hands, roll it into a snake, then tear the snake into 6 equal-size balls. Let them rest for 10 minutes covered with plastic wrap or a damp towel.

2 Put a baking sheet (or, preferably, a stone) on a rack on the lowet shelf of your oven; heat the oven to

500°F. While the dough is resting, chop the onion and cilantro for the filling. Combine them with the chaat masala, cayenne, and salt in a small bowl and set aside.

❸ Lightly flour a work surface and rolling pin. Flatten the balls of dough into 2-inch disks with the palm of your hand, then use the rolling pin to roll them into thick rounds, about 4 inches in diameter, dusting with flour as necessary.

❹ Mound 2 heaping tablespoons of the filling into the center of one of the rounds of dough. Bring the edges of the round up over the top of the filling and press them together to make a pouch. Press down on the neck of the pouch with the palm of one hand to make a slightly rounded disk. Sprinkle the disk with flour on both sides and roll it out again into a round 4 to 6 inches in diameter. Put the kulcha on a plate and cover with plastic wrap. Stuff the remaining kulcha and stack them on the plate with a sheet of plastic wrap between each one.

❺ Cook the rolled-out and stuffed kulcha on the heated baking stone as in the naan recipe, flipping them once after 3 minutes. The kulcha are ready when they're mottled and browned around the edges, 6 to 8 minutes total. You can cook as many kulcha as will comfortably fit on your baking stone at one time.

❻ Wrap the freshly baked kulcha in a kitchen towel to keep them warm and pliable. Brush with melted butter on one side and serve.

Breadsticks

MAKES: 50 to 100 breadsticks
TIME: 1 day or so, largely unattended

In Piedmont, Italy—where breadsticks are called *grissini*—you wouldn't bother to adorn these with anything. But their slightly sweet flavor is also good with a sprinkling of poppy seeds or sea salt added right before baking. To make them rustic looking, roll the strips of dough lightly on the countertop—they'll get skinny and crooked. If you want a

more professional appearance, cut them with a pastry wheel or use a pasta machine (see Step 4).

2 teaspoons instant yeast

1 teaspoon sugar

3 cups all-purpose or bread flour

2 teaspoons salt

2 tablespoons extra virgin olive oil, plus more as needed

1/2 cup semolina or cornmeal

❶ Combine the yeast, sugar, flour, and salt in a food processor; pulse once or twice. Add the oil and, again, pulse a couple of times. With the machine running, add 1 cup water through the feed tube. Continue to add water, a tablespoon at a time, until the mixture forms a ball. The dough should be a little shaggy and quite sticky.

❷ Put the olive oil in a bowl and transfer the dough ball to it, turning to coat well. Cover with plastic wrap and let it rise for 1 hour in a warm place. Reshape the ball, put it back in the bowl, cover again, and let rise in the refrigerator for several hours or, preferably, overnight.

❸ Heat the oven to 400°F. Lightly grease 2 baking sheets with olive oil and sprinkle very lightly with the semolina.

❹ Cut the dough into 3 pieces; keep the other 2 covered while you work with the first. To roll by hand: On a well-floured surface, roll a piece of dough out as thinly as possible into a large rectangle, about a foot long. Use a sharp knife or pastry wheel to cut the dough into roughly 1/4-inch-thick strips (slightly smaller is better than slightly bigger).

To roll with a pasta machine: Roll out the dough to a 1/4-inch thickness by hand. Put it through the machine at the largest setting, then cut it using the fettuccine setting and cut the strips into 1-foot lengths.

❺ Transfer the strips to the baking sheets, spaced apart, and brush with olive oil. Bake until crisp and golden, 10 to 20 minutes, then cool completely on wire racks. Serve immediately or store in an airtight container for up to 1 week.

Herbed Breadsticks. Add 2 teaspoons fresh rosemary, thyme, or sage leaves, or a combination, to the dough mixture along with the olive oil.

Parmesan Breadsticks. Try dipping in tomato sauce: Add up to $^3/_4$ cup grated Parmesan cheese to the food processor along with the flour in Step 1.

Olive or Dried Tomato Breadsticks. Darkly colored and full flavored: Before beginning to make the dough in Step 1, use the food processor to purée $^1/_2$ cup pitted olives (green or black) or dried tomatoes along with the olive oil (instead of adding it after the flour). Then add the dry ingredients to the workbowl and proceed with the recipe.

Sesame Rice Breadsticks. Fun to serve with Asian dishes: Replace 1 cup of the flour with brown rice flour. Sprinkle the breadsticks with light or black sesame seeds before baking.

Fresh Bread Crumbs

MAKES: About 2 cups

TIME: 10 minutes

Bread crumbs instantly add texture and substance to almost anything. Sometimes they work like a seasoning or garnish. Other times, as in stuffings, they can either become the main attraction or take a subordinate role to meat, poultry, or seafood. Try to make your own whenever possible—starting with homemade bread or a good bakery loaf. The coarse texture is always preferable to finely ground store-bought.

That said, it's always a good idea to stock the pantry with a pack of panko, the Japanese-style bread crumbs that are now available everywhere and work in all types of cuisines. They're good in a pinch.

About $^1/_2$ large loaf of French or Italian bread, preferably a day or two old

1 Tear the bread into pieces and put about half in a food processor. Pulse a few times, then let the machine run for a few seconds until coarsely chopped.

2 Remove and repeat with the remaining bread. Use immediately or store in an airtight container for up to a month.

Toasted Bread Crumbs. They're less likely to become too fine if you toast the crumbs after grinding: After grinding, put the bread crumbs on a baking sheet bake in a 350°F oven, shaking the pan occasionally, until lightly browned, about 15 minutes; these may be stored as fresh (though it makes more sense to store untoasted bread crumbs and toast just before using).

Fried Bread Crumbs. These are delicious, and seasoning sticks to them better than uncoated bread crumbs; but they don't keep as well, so use them immediately after frying: Heat $^1/_4$ cup extra virgin olive oil in a large skillet and add the bread crumbs; cook, stirring occasionally, until lightly browned, about 5 minutes. Season with salt or any spice blend (to make your

---

4 Other Things to Do with (Slightly) Stale Bread

You don't want to use rock-hard bread, but dried out, day- or 3-day-old bread is perfect for:

1. Melba toast: Slice bread as thinly as possible— $^1/_8$ inch thick if possible. Put on a baking sheet and toast in a 250°F oven for about 30 minutes, turning once, or until thoroughly dry. Cool on a rack and store in a tin. (These will keep for days if not weeks.)
2. Skordalia (page 94)
3. One of the bread salads on page 222
4. Bread Pudding (page 953)

 Fast   Make Ahead   Vegetarian

own, see pages 65–69) and drain on paper towels; use immediately.

Real Croutons

MAKES: 4 servings

TIME: 15 minutes

The difference between real, homemade croutons and the packaged variety cannot be overstated; the former are delicious, reasonably healthful, and entirely addictive. (There are times I make soup or a nice big salad just as an excuse to make and eat croutons. I'm not kidding, and I'm not apologizing.) Start with good bread and good olive oil, try some of the variations, and you'll be a convert.

Remember that you can make croutons from any good bread. Corn bread, olive bread, whole grain and whole wheat breads, even raisin or other specialty breads are all excellent candidates.

1/4 cup or more extra virgin olive oil

1 clove garlic, smashed (optional)

4 (if large) to 12 (if small) 1/2-inch-thick slices good bread

Salt

Freshly ground black pepper (optional)

1 Put the oil and the garlic if you're using it in a skillet large enough to accommodate the bread in one layer and turn the heat to medium. When the oil shimmers (or the garlic sizzles), add the bread. Sprinkle it with salt and, if you like, black pepper.

2 When the bread browns lightly, turn and brown the other side. If the pan dries out (which it likely will), add more olive oil if you like. When the second side is browned, remove the croutons. Use immediately or store in a tin or wax paper for up to a day.

Cubed Croutons. Before beginning, cut the bread into 1/2-inch to 1-inch cubes. Cook them in the oil, tossing occasionally, until lightly browned all over.

Herbed Croutons. Best with cubes: As the bread browns, stir in about 1/4 cup finely minced parsley, dill, or chervil or a combination.

Highly Seasoned Croutons. Use plenty of black pepper, along with about 1 teaspoon chili powder or curry powder (to make your own, see pages 66–67) or storebought ancho chile powder.

Dry-Baked Croutons. Perfect for large batches; when kept in an airtight container, these will stay crunchy for at least a week. Plus, there's no fat: Heat the oven to 400°F. Omit the oil and garlic. Cut the bread into slices (as in the main recipe) or cubes (as in the first variation). Spread the bread out on a rimmed baking sheet. Bake the croutons, undisturbed, until they begin to turn golden, about 15 minutes. Then turn the slices or shake the pan to roll the cubes around a bit. Continue baking until they're the desired color, anywhere from 5 to 15 more minutes. Sprinkle with salt and pepper—or other seasoning—if you like.

Desserts

MANY PEOPLE WILL TURN TO THIS CHAPTER

first: To them, desserts are the most enjoyable, even most important, part of a meal. Superb, detailed books have been written not only about desserts but also about specific aspects of desserts. It's the widest and deepest topic in all of cooking, and, with its special group of ingredients and techniques, it's a field unto itself, generally speaking more technical than other aspects of cooking.

Which is not to say that you need be a wizard to make desserts. Far from it; many of them are easily accomplished by beginners. (The first recipe I ever followed was for a dessert, a chocolate pie in a meringue shell, and it worked perfectly.) The desserts here are as straightforward as the recipes in the rest of the book. If you're a newcomer I suggest you start with the Essential Recipes, which are my favorite basic desserts, a small group of classics.

But the desserts here also provide an opportunity to try your hand at restaurant-style presentations, since many complicated, fancy, and beautiful desserts are little more than two or three simpler ones combined together. If you want to put together some impressive items, take a look at "Fancy Desserts from Simple Recipes" (page 888).

ESSENTIAL RECIPES

A group of all-time favorites that are easy to make. There are dozens of other recipes scattered throughout the chapter that could qualify as essentials—Traditional Apple Pie (page 931), Shortbread (page 898), and Rice Pudding (page 954), to name a few—but for newcomers especially I think these are the best. With their variations, they could keep you busy for months if not years.

✪ Classic Chocolate Chip Cookies

MAKES: 3 to 4 dozen
TIME: About 30 minutes

These should really be called chocolate *chunk* cookies because that's what's called for in this recipe. (The chocolate chips available in every grocery store are disappointing at best and barely chocolate at worst.) For the most delicious results, buy a bar of good-quality chocolate

(any kind except unsweetened; semisweet is traditional), chop it up, and mix it into the dough.

> ½ pound (2 sticks) unsalted butter, softened
> ¾ cup granulated sugar
> ¾ cup brown sugar
> 2 eggs
> 2 cups all-purpose flour
> ½ teaspoon baking soda
> ½ teaspoon salt
> 1 teaspoon vanilla extract
> 2 cups chopped good-quality semisweet chocolate (about 8 ounces)

❶ Heat the oven to 375°F. Use an electric mixer to cream together the butter and sugars; add the eggs one at a time and beat until well blended.

❷ Mix the flour, baking soda, and salt together in a bowl. Add the dry ingredients to the dough, beat for a moment, then add the vanilla and stir in the chocolate chips.

❸ Drop tablespoon-size mounds of dough about 3 inches apart in rows and columns on ungreased baking sheets. Bake until lightly browned, about 10 minutes. Cool for about 2 minutes on the sheets before using a spatula to transfer the cookies to a rack to finish cooling. Store in a tightly covered container at room temperature for no more than a day or two.

Chocolate–Chocolate Chunk Cookies. Be sure to use good chocolate here: Melt 1 ounce each semisweet and unsweetened chocolate and add to the dough after combining wet and dry ingredients.

Toffee Chunk Cookies. Make your own toffee or use store-bought: Substitute toffee chunks for all or half of the chocolate chunks.

White Chocolate–Macadamia Cookies. Substitute 1 cup each chopped white chocolate and roughly chopped macadamia nuts for the semisweet chocolate.

F Fast   **M** Make Ahead   **V** Vegetarian

Brownies

MAKES: About 1 dozen
TIME: 30 to 40 minutes

So easy children can make them. In fact, my kids taught me two things about making brownies. One, they're better without nuts (obviously a matter of taste). Two, if you line the baking pan with lightly greased aluminum foil, you reduce cleanup time by 50 percent—not bad. These are chewy and dense, dominated by chocolate.

The best ways to finish brownies: Top with Whipped Cream (page 882); drizzle with a caramel sauce (see page 922), Butterscotch Sauce (page 922), or Vanilla Custard Sauce (page 924); or serve with a scoop of vanilla or any compatible-flavored ice cream (see pages 961–963), or combine toppings to make a brownie sundae.

> 8 tablespoons (1 stick) unsalted butter, plus a little softened butter for the pan
>
> 3 ounces unsweetened chocolate, roughly chopped
>
> 1 cup sugar
>
> 2 eggs
>
> 1/2 cup all-purpose flour
>
> Pinch salt
>
> 1/2 teaspoon vanilla extract (optional)

1 Heat the oven to 350°F. Grease an 8- or 9-inch square baking pan with butter or line it with aluminum foil and grease the foil.

2 Combine the butter and chocolate in a small saucepan over very low heat, stirring occasionally. When the chocolate is just about melted, remove from the heat and continue to stir until the mixture is smooth.

3 Transfer the mixture to a bowl and stir in the sugar. Then beat in the eggs, one at a time. Gently stir in the flour, salt, and vanilla. Pour and scrape into the prepared pan and bake until just barely set in the middle, 20 to 25 minutes. It's better to underbake brownies than to overbake them. Cool on a rack before cutting. Store, covered, at room temperature, for no more than a day.

Hazelnut Brownies. Almonds or walnuts work equally well: Substitute 1/4 cup finely ground hazelnuts for half the flour and add 1 cup lightly toasted, roughly chopped hazelnuts.

Cream Cheese Brownies. Beat together 4 ounces softened cream cheese and 1/2 cup sugar until fluffy; beat in an egg. In Step 3, put half the brownie batter into the pan and top with the cream cheese mixture; then finish with the remaining batter. Use a knife to swirl the cream cheese into the brownies if you like. Increase the baking time by 10 minutes or so.

8 Simple Ideas for Brownies

1. Add 1/4 cup peanut butter or 1/2 to 1 cup chopped toasted nuts to the batter.

2. Add 1/2 to 1 cup chocolate chunks to the batter.

3. Use 1/2 teaspoon almond or mint extract in addition to or in place of the vanilla.

4. Add 1/2 cup mashed banana to the batter.

5. Add 1/4 cup bourbon, Scotch, or other whiskey to the batter; increase the flour by 1 tablespoon.

6. Add 2 tablespoons instant espresso powder with the vanilla.

7. Stir 1/2 cup dried fruit, especially dried cherries, into the prepared batter.

8. Frost the cooled brownies with Vanilla Buttercream Frosting or Chocolate Buttercream Frosting (pages 917–918) before cutting.

Warm, Soft Chocolate Cake

MAKES: 4 individual cakes
TIME: Less than 30 minutes

Undercooked chocolate cake may or may not have originally been a mistake. Though a restaurant staple, it's only rarely made at home, which is a shame, because it's so easy. You must serve it immediately, though, so I suggest preparing the batter and pouring it into the molds well ahead of the meal so the cakes can bake as you eat and you can keep your sanity. Serve with whipped cream or softened ice cream.

8 tablespoons (1 stick) unsalted butter, plus more for the molds

2 teaspoons all-purpose flour, plus a little more for the molds

4 ounces bittersweet chocolate

2 eggs

2 egg yolks

¼ cup sugar

1 Heat the oven to 450°F. Butter and lightly flour four 4-ounce molds, custard cups, or ramekins; tap out the excess flour.

2 Use a double boiler set over hot (not boiling) water to heat the butter and chocolate together until the chocolate is almost completely melted. Meanwhile, beat the eggs, yolks, and sugar together with a whisk or an electric beater until light and thick. Beat the melted chocolate and butter together until creamy; it should be quite warm. Pour in the egg mixture, then quickly beat in the flour, just until combined.

3 Divide the batter among the molds. (At this point, you may refrigerate the desserts until you're ready to eat, for up to several hours; bring them back to room temperature before baking.) Put the molds on a baking sheet and bake until the center is still quite soft but the sides are set, 6 to 7 minutes.

4 Invert each mold onto a plate and let sit for about 10 seconds. Unmold by lifting up one corner of the mold; the cake will fall out onto the plate. Serve immediately.

✪ Whipped Cream

MAKES: 4 servings
TIME: 5 minutes

F **M** **V**

Whipping cream is so easy there's absolutely no need to buy the canned stuff. You can easily whip smaller amounts of cream with a whisk, though of course a mixer—hand-held or upright—is faster. Before you start whipping, be sure you have cold cream with no additives (if possible), a clean metal or glass bowl, and a balloon whisk or a mixer fitted with the whisk attachment. Add the sweetener or flavorings when the cream is just starting to hold its shape.

See the following list for some flavoring ideas; you can also add a tablespoon or two of sour cream, or whip crème fraîche or mascarpone, which will be tangier or thicker, respectively.

1 cup cream

Up to ¼ cup sugar (optional)

1 Use a whisk or an electric mixer to beat the cream to the desired texture. To know when to stop beating, dip the whisk or beater into the cream and pull up. You will see these, in order of time (see illustration):

Soft peaks: The cream will just make a low peak with a tip that readily folds onto itself; this is the time to slowly add the sugar if you're using it.
Stiff peaks: A fairly stiff peak with a tip that hardly bends; it should not be clumpy though (that's overwhipped).
Overwhipped: The cream will be clumpy and rough looking. Add a couple tablespoons more cream and stir it in to smooth it out. (Or keep whipping; you'll get butter.)

2 Once the whipped cream is done, fold in other flavorings if you like and serve immediately or refrigerate for up to 30 minutes or so.

8 Ways to Flavor Whipped Cream

1. Vanilla: Scrape the seeds from half a pod into the cream or use 1 teaspoon good-quality vanilla extract.
2. Honey: Use honey instead of sugar.
3. Maple: Use some maple syrup in place of sugar (add just enough to flavor the whipped cream; if you want it sweeter, add sugar so you don't liquefy the whipped cream).

 Fast   Make Ahead   **V** Vegetarian

STAGES OF WHIPPED CREAM

Soft peaks: Thickened cream that is beaten just enough so you can no longer pour it. When you dip beaters or a whisk into the bowl, the cream is not yet stiff enough to hold peaks; it just sort of flops over. But it doesn't take long from this stage to stiff peaks, so be sure to stop beating and check the consistency frequently.

Stiff peaks: Cream that stays on the spoon, slightly firm and stable, until you put a dollop next to something or use it as a filling or icing. To assess the cream in the bowl, dip the beaters or whisk into the cream and pull up; the peaks formed should stand upright with minimal drooping.

Overbeaten: If you beat whipped cream too much, it will start to look "clotted" or curdled. If this happens, try stirring in a little more cream by hand until smooth again.

4. **Sweet spice:** Sprinkle in ground cardamom, cinnamon, nutmeg, or any finely ground sweet spice.
5. **Booze:** Add 1 to 2 tablespoons bourbon, brandy, Kahlúa, Grand Marnier, framboise, amaretto, etc.
6. **Citrus:** Add $1/2$ teaspoon or so grated citrus zest.
7. **Ginger:** Add $1/2$ teaspoon finely grated or very finely minced fresh ginger.
8. **Rose or orange blossom water:** Add 1 to 2 teaspoons rose water or orange blossom water.

Blueberry Cobbler

MAKES: 6 to 8 servings
TIME: About 1 hour

Ⓥ

My friend John Willoughby found this recipe in a southern boardinghouse nearly 20 years ago. It's become my go-to cobbler recipe, because it's essentially perfect. I love this with blueberries, but you can make it with any fruit you like. Top with Buttermilk or Vanilla Ice Cream (pages 961–963) or Whipped Cream (page 882).

Cobbler dough is somewhere between a biscuit and a cookie: fluffy, a bit flaky, buttery, and at least slightly sweet. The key is not overmixing the dough; get it so that it's just combined, barely holding together, then drop it onto the filling in mounds, leaving space for steam to escape from the cooking fruit.

4 to 6 cups blueberries or other fruit, washed and well dried, peeled and sliced as necessary

1 cup sugar, or to taste

8 tablespoons (1 stick) cold unsalted butter, cut into bits, plus some for the pan

$1/2$ cup all-purpose flour

$1/2$ teaspoon baking powder

Pinch salt

1 egg

$1/2$ teaspoon vanilla extract

① Heat the oven to 375°F. Toss the fruit with half the sugar and spread it in a lightly greased 8-inch square or 9-inch round baking pan.

② Combine the flour, baking powder, salt, and remaining ¹/₂ cup sugar in a food processor and pulse once or twice. Add the butter and process for 10 seconds, until the mixture is well blended. By hand, beat in the egg and vanilla.

③ Drop this mixture onto the fruit by tablespoonfuls; do not spread it out. Bake until golden yellow and just starting to brown, 35 to 45 minutes. Serve immediately.

Apple Crisp

MAKES: 6 to 8 servings
TIME: About 1 hour

V

The hardest part of making a crisp is preparing the fruit, which doesn't take much work or time; and you can use apples, pears, stone fruits (I love tart cherries in the summer), berries, or a combination; in any case, start with 6 cups of fruit, somewhere between 2 and 3 pounds. If you use more watery fruits, like berries, toss them with a tablespoon or two of flour or cornstarch before cooking. If you use very tart fruits, like rhubarb, increase the sugar.

To vary the crust, try Streusel Topping or any of its variations (page 925). Just eliminate the ingredients called for in Step 2. Needless to say, crisps are great topped with ice cream or whipped cream.

6 cups peeled, cored, and sliced apples or other fruit

1 teaspoon ground cinnamon

Juice of ¹/₂ lemon

²/₃ cup brown sugar, or to taste

5 tablespoons cold unsalted butter, cut into bits, plus some for the pan

¹/₂ cup rolled oats (not instant)

¹/₂ cup all-purpose flour

¹/₄ cup shredded coconut (optional)

¹/₄ cup chopped nuts (optional)

Dash salt

① Heat the oven to 400°F. Toss the fruit with half the cinnamon, the lemon juice, and 1 tablespoon of the brown sugar and spread it in a lightly buttered 8-inch square or 9-inch round baking pan.

② Combine all the other ingredients—including the remaining cinnamon and brown sugar—in a food processor and pulse a few times, then process a few seconds more, until everything is well incorporated but not uniform. (To mix the ingredients by hand, soften the butter slightly, toss together the dry ingredients, then work in the butter with your fingertips, a pastry blender, or a fork.)

③ Crumble the topping over the apples and bake until the topping is browned and the apples are tender and bubbling, 30 to 40 minutes. Serve hot, warm, or at room temperature.

Free-Form Fruit Tart

MAKES: 8 servings
TIME: About 1 hour, plus time to chill the crust, largely unattended

M **V**

A simple, rustic tart, filled and baked right on a baking sheet. Among the most useful desserts in my repertoire, perfect for beginners, always impressive, really delicious. Dust with confectioners' sugar or top with any ice cream (see pages 961–963) or Whipped Cream (page 882).

1 recipe Sweet Tart Crust (pages 929–930), chilled until firm but not hard

2 pounds pitted, peeled, and sliced ripe stone fruit, like peaches, plums, or nectarines, or peeled, cored,

and very thinly sliced apples or pears, or about 3 cups berries

2 tablespoons unsalted butter, melted

① Heat the oven to 425°F. Roll the crust out until about ⅛ inch thick, either rolling it on a board sprinkled with flour or sprinkling it lightly with flour and rolling it between 2 sheets of plastic or parchment; it need not be perfectly round. Put it directly on a baking sheet.

② Cover the round with the fruit, leaving about a 1½-inch border all around. Fold up the edges of the crust around the fruit, pinching them together. Don't try to cover all of the fruit, just the outer rim of it. Brush the exposed dough with most of the butter and brush a little onto the fruit as well. Bake until the crust is golden brown and the fruit bubbly, 20 to 30 minutes.

③ Remove from the oven and cool on a rack; serve warm or at room temperature.

5 Simple Ideas for Free-Form Tarts

1. Put a layer of crushed almonds or walnuts under the fruit.
2. Brush the fruit with a combination of 2 tablespoons honey and 1 tablespoon melted butter.
3. Toss the fruit with 1 teaspoon or more ground cinnamon before placing it on the crust.
4. Sprinkle with a mixture of ½ teaspoon ground cinnamon and 2 tablespoons sugar (or just plain sugar) after brushing with butter. Don't use confectioners' sugar.
5. Toss the fruit with 1 teaspoon or more minced crystallized ginger.

FREE-FORM CRUSTS

1

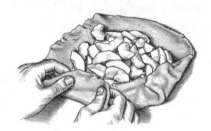

2

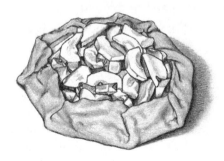

(STEP 1) To make a free-form tart, roll out the dough, then spread it with the topping, to within just an inch of two the edge. Fold the edges over, crimping them so they remain in place, (STEP 2) until you've gone around the entire circumference of the dough.

✪ Old-Fashioned Baked Custard

Pots de Crème

MAKES: 4 to 6 servings
TIME: About 45 minutes

This all-American custard is easy to make and incredibly filling. You will be sneaking leftovers at midnight and breakfast, especially if you make it with good eggs and cream. Substitute 1 teaspoon vanilla extract for the cinnamon and nutmeg if you like. Finish with Whipped Cream (page 882) and/or fresh berries.

2 cups cream, milk, or a mixture

½ teaspoon ground cinnamon

½ teaspoon freshly grated nutmeg

2 eggs plus 2 yolks

Pinch salt

$^1/_2$ cup sugar, or more if you like things very sweet

❶ Put the cream, the cinnamon, and half the nutmeg in a small saucepan over medium heat. Cook just until it begins to steam, 3 to 5 minutes.

❷ Use a whisk or an electric mixer to beat the eggs and yolks with the salt and sugar until pale yellow and fairly thick. Heat the oven to 300°F and put a kettle of water on to boil.

❸ Gradually add the cream to the egg mixture, stirring constantly. Pour the mixture into an ovenproof dish or six 4- to 6-ounce custard cups and sprinkle with the remaining nutmeg. Put the dish or cups in a baking pan and pour hot water into the pan to within about 1 inch of the top of the bowl or cups. Bake until the mixture is not quite set—it should wobble just a little in the middle—about 30 minutes for the cups, about 15 minutes longer if you're baking in a dish. Use your judgment; cream sets faster than milk. Serve warm, at room temperature, or cold, within a day.

Crème Brûlée. Substitute a vanilla bean, split lengthwise (see page 961), or 1 teaspoon vanilla extract for the cinnamon and nutmeg. Add $^1/_2$ cup more cream. Omit the whole eggs and increase the yolks to six. After baking, remove from the oven, cool, cover with plastic, and chill for up to a day or two. Put an oven rack as close to the broiler as the height of the dish or cups will allow and turn on the broiler. Sprinkle the tops of the custards evenly with $^1/_2$ cup sugar. Broil, watching carefully and turning the dish(es) as necessary. When the sugar bubbles and browns, it's ready. Let sit for a few minutes before serving. (You can also do the brûlée with a propane torch. Same concept: Heat the sugar with the flame until it bubbles and browns.)

Flan (Crème Caramel). Here a layer of caramel is put on the bottom of the custard before baking: Put 1 cup sugar and $^1/_4$ cup water in a small nonaluminum saucepan. Turn the heat to low and cook, stirring occasionally, until the sugar liquefies and turns clear, then golden brown, about 15 minutes. Remove from the heat and immediately pour the caramel into the dish or custard cups. Make the custard exactly as directed, pouring it into the prepared bowl or cups and baking. Cool on a rack, then chill or serve. To remove, dip the dish or cups in boiling water for about 15 seconds, then invert onto a plate or plates.

Chocolate Custard. A richer custard than Chocolate Pudding (page 950), but no more difficult to make: Substitute 1 teaspoon vanilla extract for the cinnamon and nutmeg. Heat 1 ounce chopped bittersweet chocolate in a double boiler or in a very small saucepan over very low heat, stirring almost constantly, until it melts; cool slightly. Proceed with the recipe, stirring the chocolate into the eggs before the cream. You can use 2 ounces of chocolate for an even more intense flavor.

Lemon Custard. You need more eggs to compensate for the added liquid and more sugar to compensate for the tartness here; as a result, this will serve 6 easily. In Step 2, increase the yolks to 4, the whole eggs to 3, and the sugar to $^3/_4$ cup. Add $^1/_2$ cup strained lemon juice and 1 tablespoon very finely minced lemon zest to the mixture and proceed with the recipe.

Pumpkin Custard. Steam or boil about 2 cups peeled and cubed pumpkin or winter squash until very tender. Cool, then purée with some of the milk after it has cooled. Increase the sugar to $^3/_4$ cup. Increase the eggs to 3 and the yolks to 3 and proceed with the recipe.

6 More Ideas for Old-Fashioned Baked Custard or Vanilla Pudding (page 950)

1. Add 1 or 2 tablespoons minced crystallized ginger just before baking.

2. Add $^1/_4$ cup or more shredded coconut just before baking.

3. Add about 1 teaspoon minced or grated orange zest just before baking.

F Fast   **M** Make Ahead   **V** Vegetarian

PLATED DESSERTS

You can make restaurant-style desserts by combining several simpler components; see "Fancy Desserts from Simple Recipes" on page 888.

CENTERPIECE(S)	ICE CREAM, SORBET, OR GRANITA	SAUCE(S)	GARNISHES
A slice of Rich Chocolate Torte (page 915)	Spice Ice Cream (page 963)	None	Chocolate Tuiles (twisted or in some interesting shape), stuck in the torte or ice cream; dollop of soft whipped cream
Blueberry Pudding Cake, warm, scooped into a bowl	Vanilla Ice Cream (page 961)	None	Lacy Oatmeal Cookies (page 895), stuck in ice cream; dollop of Whipped Cream (page 882)
Pavlova (page 901), on a cake plate or platter; or individual meringue containers (see page 902)	Strawberry (or Any Berry) Ice Cream (page 963) or coconut sorbet (optional; see page 964)	Drizzled or pooled strawberry fruit sauce (see page 924) or purée (see page 923)	Sliced fresh strawberries or other berries; dollop of Whipped Cream flavored with vanilla (page 882)
Cream Cheese Brownies with cherries (page 881)	Vanilla or Buttermilk Ice Cream (page 961 or 963)	Pooled or drizzled cherry fruit sauce (see page 924) or purée (see page 923) (optional)	Pitted fresh cherries; dollop of Whipped Cream (page 882)
Golden or Chocolate Layer Cake (page 907 or 911), made into babycakes (see page 909)	Cardamom ice cream (see page 962)	None	Chopped pistachios; dollop of Whipped Cream (page 882)
Warm, Soft Chocolate Cake (page 881)	Coffee Ice Cream (page 963)	Caramel Coffee Sauce (page 922) and/or Chocolate Sauce (page 921) dotted or drizzled on the plate	Shavings of chocolate or white chocolate (see page 911)
Angel Food Cake (page 912), split and filled with Citrus Custard Sauce (optional; page 925)	Ginger Ice Cream (page 963) and/or Orange or Orange-Cassis Sorbet (page 965)	Drizzled Orange or Creamy Orange Glaze (page 919)	Chocolate Tuiles (page 903), stuck in the cake or ice cream; or thin slices of crystallized ginger
A slice of Traditional Apple Pie (page 931)	Cinnamon ice cream (see page 962)	Pooled Creamy Caramel Sauce (page 922), Maple-Butter Sauce (page 923), or Vanilla Custard Sauce (page 924)	None
Simple Berry Tart (page 939), made into mini tarts	None	Pooled Vanilla Custard Sauce (page 924), dotted with berry fruit sauce, raw fruit method (see page 924)	Dollop of whipped cream
Cream Puffs (page 942), split and filled with ice cream and sorbet	Banana Ice Cream (page 963), strawberry sorbet (see page 964)	Drizzled Hot Fudge Sauce (page 921), Chocolate Sauce (page 921), or Berry Jam Glaze (page 923)	Sprigs of fresh mint

CENTERPIECE(S)	ICE CREAM, SORBET, OR GRANITA	SAUCE(S)	GARNISHES
Olive Oil Cake (page 914), sliced thinly or made into babycakes (see page 909)	Mascarpone Ice Cream (page 963), and/or Vanilla-Pineapple Sorbet (page 965)	Pooled or drizzled pineapple fruit sauce (see page 924) or Clear Caramel Sauce made with pineapple juice instead of water (page 922)	None
Panna Cotta (page 950) and Champagne Gelée with Berries (page 957), each layer poured into clear glasses or custard cups and allowed to set, then the next layer carefully poured on to create striped separate layers	Any Granita (optional but especially one made from berries; page 966), alongside or on top	None	Fresh berries and chocolate shavings (see page 911) on top
Vanilla or Chocolate Soufflé (page 958)	None	Vanilla Custard Sauce (page 924) and raspberry fruit sauce (see page 924) or purée (see page 923), room temperature or warm, in saucers to pour into soufflés	Dollop of whipped cream flavored with booze, orange zest, or ginger
Bread Pudding or Rum-Raisin Bread Pudding (page 953), baked in individual ramekins or muffin tins	Rum-Raisin or Vanilla Ice Cream (page 963 or 961), depending on flavor of bread pudding	Boozy Cake Soak (page 919), poured over bread pudding, or drizzled Boozy Caramel Sauce (page 922)	Dollop of whipped cream (optional); sprinkle of ground cinnamon or freshly grated nutmeg

4. Add 1 or 2 tablespoons raspberries or other fruit per serving, on the bottom underneath the custard.

5. Substitute 1 teaspoon vanilla extract for the cinnamon and nutmeg or infuse one 3-inch vanilla bean with the cream or milk (see page 961).

6. Infuse warm cream or milk with $1/2$ cup coarsely ground coffee or 1 tablespoon macha green tea (or other ingredients; see "Infusing Liquids with Flavor," page 962); let stand for 10 minutes and strain before proceeding.

Fancy Desserts from Simple Recipes

There's no denying that professional pastry chefs make desserts that are a lot more complicated than most of

us—certainly I—will ever attempt. But one way to elevate your desserts to a new level is to present them as if you were a pastry chef. That is, combine complementary or pleasantly contrasting components, then plate, sauce, and garnish to create one dramatic dish.

Of course this means more work. But if you do what the professionals do and make almost all of the components in advance (in most cases a day or two ahead), then assemble the dessert just before serving, it's not so bad. You can make individual portions or elaborate platters; pool the sauce on the bottom of the plate or drizzle and decorate the tops. My only advice is to start small—with two or three components—then build as you get more confidence.

Choose your presentation as you would any savory meal—based on balancing flavors, textures, and flavors. One approach is to create a trio around a theme (like chocolate or caramel) and offer say, a cake, a sauce, and an ice cream that revolve around that theme. Tiny individual versions of cakes, soufflés, or tarts are always popular, as are interactive desserts that require guests to dunk or sauce. If you get really ambitious, one component might be cooked (as in churros) or baked (as in a cobbler) at the last minute and served warm.

The Basics of Sugar and Other Sweeteners

Desserts are sweet; that's one of the things we like about them, and we're hot-wired to do so. Sweets provide the quickest energy of all foods, and we need energy; we just tend to overdo it.

Granulated Sweeteners

The easiest way to sweeten desserts is with white sugar: It's cheap, convenient, and effective. There are other options, of course. Sometimes you may want a sweetener that tastes different or performs differently. Or you may simply want to avoid white sugar.

White Sugar

The most common, from sugarcane or sugar beets; highly refined. White sugar comes in various granule sizes and types, each with its optimal uses, but **granulated sugar** is the equivalent of all-purpose flour: You can use it almost everywhere when recipes call for sugar. The grains are medium size and dissolve well when heated or combined with a relatively large proportion of liquid.

There are many other forms of white sugar: **Powdered sugar** (also called *confectioners', icing, 10x, 6x,* or *4x sugar*) is regular sugar ground to a fine powder, with cornstarch added to prevent caking. It's used mostly in icings (it dissolves very easily) or for sifting over desserts. **Superfine sugar** (*castor, caster,* or *baking sugar*) is somewhere between granulated and powdered sugar. It's suitable for light cakes or anything that won't be cooked but has some

liquid—like meringues—because the fine crystals dissolve quickly. (You can make your own by grinding granulated sugar in a food processor for a few seconds.) **Coarse sugar** (decorators' or pearl sugar) is processed to small, roughly shaped round grains, larger than those of granulated sugar and therefore much slower to dissolve. Use it as a garnish on cookies, cakes, or sweet breads. **Crystal sugar** is similar, though the crystals are pellet shaped, not round.

Brown Sugar

Brown sugar is simply white sugar with molasses added for a more complex taste and added moisture. It can be light or dark, depending on how much molasses has been added. (In a pinch you can make brown sugar by stirring a tablespoon or more molasses into a cup of white sugar.) Generally dark brown sugar is more intense, but the difference is subtle, and I use light and dark interchangeably. In most dessert recipes, you can substitute brown sugar for white, as long as you remember the color and flavor will be different; just be sure to pack the cups down before leveling them off as you measure. To keep brown sugar from hardening, put it in a plastic bag, put the plastic bag in a tightly sealed container, and put the container in the refrigerator.

Raw Sugar
Turbinado, Demerara, Muscovado

Made exclusively from sugarcane in a couple of different ways, these coarse-grained brown or golden sugars taste less sweet than regular sugar and have a distinctive caramel flavor. You can use raw sugar in place of white sugar in many recipes, provided the grind is fine (you can grind it finer in a spice grinder or food processor easily enough) or the cooking time is long enough to dissolve it completely; just don't expect the exact same results as with white sugar. I like it best sprinkled on top of baked goods like scones and cookies to add a mildly sweet crunch.

Other Granulated Sweeteners
Fructose, a simple sugar found in honey, fruit, berries, and some root vegetables, is often recommended to dia-

betics because it is metabolized differently than cane sugar. But it's super-concentrated and loses power when heated or mixed into liquids, so it's tricky to use; I don't mess with it.

Artificial sweeteners, like saccharin, Splenda, and stevia at best taste funny and at worst might be hazardous to your health. Use them only if you must.

Liquid Sweeteners

These dissolve faster than sugar, though they are not directly interchangeable.

Honey

Made, as you know, by bees. There are more than three hundred varieties of honey in the United States alone, including orange blossom, clover, and eucalyptus, and they all taste at least a little bit different. But most commercial honeys are blends, so they're often less exciting. All honey is about 25 percent sweeter than conventional sugar, so you use less of it to achieve the same sweetness. Start by replacing just some of the sugar in your favorite recipe (remember that the color of honey will darken food slightly). But be careful: Honey causes cookies, for example, to spread more than cookies baked with sugar.

Some guidelines for baking with honey:

1. Reduce the liquid by $1/4$ cup for each cup of honey.
2. For every cup of honey, add $1/2$ teaspoon baking soda to balance the honey's acidity.
3. When you substitute honey for sugar in quick breads, cookies, and cakes, reduce the oven temperature by 25°F to prevent overbrowning.

Molasses

A heavy brown syrup produced during the sugar-making process. The first boiling produces light molasses, which can be used like honey; the second produces dark molasses, which is thick, full flavored, and not so sweet; and the third produces blackstrap molasses, the darkest, thickest, most nutritious, and least useful of the bunch.

Vanilla Sugar

To give sugar the flavor of vanilla, put 1 vanilla bean into a jar filled with 2 cups of sugar and seal tightly. Keep a jar going all the time, adding any vanilla pods from which you have scraped the seeds, or a whole vanilla bean from time to time (you can use the vanilla bean in any recipe as you normally would). Use vanilla sugar in any pastry in which you are planning to use vanilla for a more intense flavor.

You can cook and bake with blackstrap, though it's best to blend it with light molasses or honey.

Corn Syrup

A thick, sticky sweetener processed from cornstarch. Light corn syrup is clarified; dark is flavored with caramel, which makes it sweeter and (duh) darker. It's very useful in making Caramels (page 969) and some other candies and sauces (like hot fudge; see page 921), but otherwise you can live without it. Generally, if you want sugar in a syrup form, try Sugar Syrup (page 921).

The Basics of Butter and Other Baking Fats

Butter is the most important ingredient in many desserts, especially because it combines two qualities not found in most other fats: good flavor and the ability to hold air when beaten. (Hydrogenated fats—now notoriously known as *trans fats*—like many types of vegetable shortening and margarine, are even better at holding air. But their flavor is neutral at best and foul at worst, and they're worse for your health than other fats. Don't use them.)

About salted butter: Salt is incorporated into butter largely as a preservative, which means salted butter may sit around longer than unsalted (sweet) butter before it's sold. Since butter freezes well, and since salt is an ingredient you can add anytime, I buy sweet butter. If you do buy salted butter, eliminate added salt from most sweet baked goods; there's almost always enough salt in the butter to compensate.

Some oils, like olive or nut oils, have good but overly distinctive flavor—they lack delicacy, for one thing—and add no loft to the pastry at all. Still, olive oil pastries can be quite good—and cakes even better. You can also use neutral-tasting grapeseed oil in place of butter in almost any recipe; just don't expect the same results.

Pure lard, once not only appreciated but craved, has come full circle. After falling out of favor for being perceived as unhealthy (in reality, it is no worse for you than butter, and better than shortening or margarine) and having poor quality and flavor, lard is on the rebound. But it's really best only in pie and tart crusts and some pastries. If you can get good lard, and using it appeals to you, combine one part lard with three parts butter for the best piecrust you've ever tasted.

My most basic recommendation: Use unsalted butter almost exclusively. My feeling is that if you want pastry, you must be willing to eat good-quality fat. If you're avoiding or minimizing fat and calories, pay special attention to the fruit recipes in this chapter and throughout the book (as well as the meringues here) for plenty of alternatives.

The Basics of Cookies

Cookies and brownies are desserts many people turn to regularly. Not only does everyone love them, but the first of a batch of cookies or brownies can be coming out of the oven half an hour after the inspiration hits you (by then cleanup is done too).

Cookies fall into two basic categories:

Drop cookies—you drop the dough directly onto baking sheets—are soft, buttery, sweet, and perfect for containing other ingredients; chocolate chip is the paradigm. To adjust *any* drop cookie recipe to your personal taste, remember this: Butter makes cookies tender, flour makes

them cakey, shorter cooking times (within reason) produce chewier cookies, and longer times make them crisper.

Refrigerator cookies—think cookie-cutter cookies—are made in advance. This can be an advantage, because you can make the dough days ahead and bake them whenever you get the urge. The easiest way to shape them is to refrigerate the dough in logs (round, but they can be three-sided or square if you're ambitious) and slice off cookies. Logs of dough are also convenient for freezing, and you need not defrost them before slicing and baking.

Mixing Cookie Dough

Generally, I suggest my favorite mixing method for each recipe; but you can use whatever method you like; just follow these directions:

To combine the ingredients by hand: Mix the flour, baking powder, and salt together in a bowl. Cream the softened butter with a fork, then mash in the sugar until well blended. Stir in the vanilla and the egg, then about half the flour mixture. Add the milk, then the remaining flour, then a little more milk, if necessary, to make a dough.

To combine the ingredients with an electric mixer: Combine the flour, baking powder, and salt together in a bowl. Put the softened butter and sugar in the mixing bowl and beat on low speed until creamy. Add the vanilla and egg and beat on low speed until well combined. Add about half the flour mixture, beat for a moment, then add the milk or other liquid. Beat for about 10 seconds, then add the remaining flour and a little more milk if necessary.

To make the dough in a food processor: Put all the dry ingredients in the processor and pulse once or twice to combine. Cut chilled butter into bits, add to the machine, and process for about 10 seconds, until the butter and flour are well blended. Add the vanilla, egg, and milk or other liquid and pulse just enough to blend. If more milk is needed, add it by hand.

Baking Cookies

Most ovens have hot spots, and this can make a difference: The cookies in the back of the oven or on the bottom rack, for example, may brown faster. The solution is simple: Halfway through the estimated baking time, rotate the baking sheets from back to front; if you're cooking more than one sheet at the same time, exchange them from top to bottom as well.

Storing Cookies

Cookies rarely get stale, because people eat them before they have a chance. Store them lightly covered, at room temperature, and they do fine. But they also can be frozen successfully; just make sure they're covered or wrapped very tightly to protect them from unwanted flavors. Even better (especially with refrigerator cookies) is to wrap the dough log in a couple of layers of plastic, and freeze. You can then slice directly from the freezer (30 minutes of thawing will make that job a little easier) and bake.

10 Cookies and Bars That Are Fun to Make with Kids

Kids love to eat cookies, obviously, but they like to make them too. Here are some that are easy enough to allow the single-digit set to participate. And don't forget Golden Cupcakes and Chocolate Cupcakes (pages 907–912).

1. Classic Chocolate Chip Cookies (page 880)
2. Brownies (page 881)
3. Butter Cookies and Chocolate Cookies (page 892)
4. Oatmeal Cookies (page 894)
5. Refrigerator (or Rolled) Cookies (page 895)
6. Peanut Butter Cookies (page 896)
7. Aunt Big's Gingersnaps and Gingerbread Men (page 897)
8. Molasses-Spice Cookies (page 897)
9. Butterscotch Brownies (Blondies) (page 904)
10. Magic Bars (page 904)

Butter Cookies

MAKES: 2 to 3 dozen
TIME: About 30 minutes

An ideal drop cookie for improvisation (see the list that follows for some ideas); I love them with a bit of spice and chopped walnuts. Be sure to handle this dough gently, taking care not to overwork it when mixing; good butter cookies are tender.

8 tablespoons (1 stick) unsalted butter, softened

$3/4$ cup sugar

1 teaspoon vanilla extract

1 egg

2 cups all-purpose flour

$1/2$ teaspoon baking powder

Pinch salt

$1/4$ cup milk, plus more if needed

❶ Heat the oven to 375°F. Use an electric mixer to cream together the butter and sugar; add the vanilla and egg and beat until well blended.

❷ Combine the flour, baking powder, and salt in a bowl. Add half the dry ingredients to the dough, beat for a moment, then add the milk (if you're adding any ingredients like spices, nuts, etc., now is the time). Beat for about 10 seconds, then add the remaining dry ingredients and a little more milk, if necessary, to make a soft dough that can be dropped from a spoon.

❸ Drop tablespoon-size mounds of dough about 3 inches apart in rows and columns on ungreased baking sheets. Bake until the edges are browned, about 10 minutes. Cool for about 2 minutes on the sheets before using a spatula to transfer the cookies to a rack to finish cooling. (If icing or glazing, wait until they are cool and then decorate them right on the rack for a cleaner look; let set for about 10 more minutes.) Store in a tightly covered container at room temperature for no more than a day or two.

 Fast   Make Ahead   Vegetarian

Chocolate Cookies. A combination of unsweetened and sweetened chocolate is good here, but you can use just one or the other (if you use all unsweetened, increase the sugar to 1 cup): Increase the milk very slightly, to about $^1/_3$ cup. Melt 1 ounce each semisweet and unsweetened chocolate and add to the mixture after combining the wet and dry ingredients.

Sour Cream Cookies. Sour cream not only gives the cookies a tangy taste but lets you use baking soda, whose flavor is less obtrusive than that of baking powder. They may be dropped and baked as directed or refrigerated for 1 hour, then rolled into walnut-size balls before baking: Substitute 1 teaspoon baking soda for the all of the baking powder and about $^1/_2$ cup sour cream for the milk.

Olive Oil Cookies. Substitute a good extra virgin olive oil (note that extra virgin's flavor may dominate) for the butter; increase the flour by $^1/_2$ cup.

Sweet-Savory Cookies. Rosemary, black pepper, and red wine make for an unusual but delicious cookie; make these with olive oil or butter, increasing the flour by $^1/_4$ cup if you use olive oil: Decrease the sugar to $^1/_2$ cup. Add $^1/_4$ teaspoon freshly ground black pepper and 1 teaspoon finely minced fresh rosemary leaves (or $^1/_2$ teaspoon crushed dried rosemary) with the other dry ingredients. Substitute red wine for the milk and bake as directed. When done, dust very lightly with sifted confectioners' sugar. For slightly crunchier, more flavorful cookies, substitute $^1/_2$ cup cornmeal for $^1/_2$ cup of the flour.

Maple Cornmeal Cookies. Maple and cornmeal are a natural combination: Substitute $^1/_2$ cup maple syrup and $^1/_4$ cup brown sugar for the white sugar. Use 1 cup cornmeal and $1^1/_2$ cups flour. Omit the milk.

11 Simple Ideas for Jazzing Up Butter Cookies

1. Butter Nut Cookies: Add $^1/_2$ cup chopped nuts to the finished batter.

2. Coconut Cookies: Add 1 cup shredded coconut to the finished batter.

3. Butterscotch Cookies: Use $^2/_3$ cup brown sugar in place of the white sugar.

4. Orange or Lemon Cookies: Add 1 tablespoon grated or minced orange or lemon zest to the finished batter; omit the vanilla. Add 2 tablespoons poppy seeds as well if you like.

5. Raisin Cookies: Add up to $^1/_2$ cup raisins or chopped dried fruit to the finished batter.

6. Ginger Cookies: Add 2 tablespoons or more chopped crystallized ginger to the finished batter.

7. Cinnamon Cookies: Dust the cookies with a mixture of 2 tablespoons granulated sugar and 1 teaspoon ground cinnamon just before baking.

8. Spice Cookies: Stir 1 teaspoon ground spice, especially ginger, cardamom, or cinnamon, into the finished batter.

9. Powdered Sugar Cookies: When you transfer them to a rack to cool, quickly dust them with a thick layer of confectioners' sugar. Some will melt; some won't.

10. Butter Cookies with Sea Salt: Sprinkle the tops of just-baked cookies with a few grains of coarse sea salt.

11. Drizzle with Orange Glaze or any of its variations (page 919).

Creaming: One Technique That Matters

Creaming butter (or oil) and sugar together is not just a mixing technique; it plays a role in leavening and giving structure to cakes, cookies, and pastries. The quick beating (done most easily in a standing mixer, but there are other techniques; see "Mixing Cookie Dough," page 891) breaks up the fat with the sugar crystals and forces air bubbles into the mixture, which helps add lift as desserts bake. (The eggs or egg yolks usually added at the last stage of creaming enrich and lighten the batter even further.)

8 Tips for Improvising Cookies

Improvisations are pretty easy if you start with Butter Cookies (page 892) or Shortbread (page 898). Keep in mind that the dough for Refrigerator (or Rolled) Cookies (page 895) cannot accommodate any chunky additions, like chocolate or nut chunks, as they will interfere with rolling and cutting, but you can put chunky additions on top of the cookies once they're on the baking sheet.

1. Add chocolate: Premade chocolate chips are convenient, but it's almost as easy to chop up good-quality chocolate, which tastes much better. Be careful, though: Too much, and your cookies will be a gooey mess; you're always safe with up to ¹/₂ cup or so per recipe. For drop cookies big chunks are fine. With delicate cookies like shortbread you must mince the chocolate finely or gently melt the chocolate and add it to the butter and sugar after creaming.

2. Add nuts: Chunks go into drop cookies easily. For refrigerator cookies, try whirring them in the food processor and combining the pulverized nuts with the flour. Again, adding up to ¹/₂ cup is fine. Or substitute any nut butter for up to half of the butter; substitute tahini for up to 2 tablespoons of the butter.

3. Add seeds: Poppy, sunflower, even pumpkin seeds work anywhere nuts do in cookies. Leave them whole or grind them as fine as you like in the food processor; ¹/₄ to ¹/₂ cup is usually plenty.

4. Add dried fruit: Add up to ¹/₂ cup chopped or whole small dried fruit to the finished dough.

5. Add a small pinch of spices: You can incorporate them into the dough with the dry ingredients or mix them with sugar and sprinkle on top of cookies before baking. Be careful not to overdo it, especially with strong spices like nutmeg or cloves.

6. Make Thumbprint Cookies: Roll the cookie dough into 1¹/₂-inch-diameter balls and then press the pad of your thumb into the middle, flattening the ball and making an indentation (drop cookies don't have to be rolled; just push your thumb into the dropped dough). Press a pecan, walnut, or other nut; a piece of dried fruit; an M&M or other small candy; a chunk of chocolate or any other decoration you like into the dough and bake as directed. Or bake cookies naked, then cool and fill with jam, a glaze or frosting, Chocolate Ganache (page 920), or melted chocolate.

7. Make sandwiches: Instead of frosting or glazing, smear frosting (see pages 917–918), jam, peanut butter, or other topping on the bottom of two cookies and smush them together.

8. Serve with something for dipping: Milk, of course, is the classic accompaniment, but any of the syrups, sauces, or soaks on pages 919–924 add a lot to a plate of cookies. So does a small glass of dessert wine, port, or liqueur.

Oatmeal Cookies

MAKES: 3 to 4 dozen
TIME: About 30 minutes

One of the advantages of oatmeal cookies is their flexibility; they are delicious plain or loaded with all sorts of goodies, from dried fruit to nuts. Toss in raisins, dried cranberries or cherries, chocolate chunks, or coconut—the dough can handle up to 1¹/₂ cups.

8 tablespoons (1 stick) unsalted butter, softened

¹/₂ cup granulated sugar

¹/₂ cup brown sugar

2 eggs

1¹/₂ cups all-purpose flour

 Fast   Make Ahead   Vegetarian

2 cups rolled oats (not instant)

¹/₂ teaspoon ground cinnamon

Pinch salt

2 teaspoons baking powder

¹/₂ cup milk

¹/₂ teaspoon vanilla or almond extract

❶ Heat the oven to 375°F. Use an electric mixer to cream together the butter and sugars; add the eggs one at a time and beat until well blended.

❷ Mix the flour, oats, cinnamon, salt, and baking powder together in a bowl. Alternating with the milk, add the dry ingredients to the dough a little a time, mixing on low (if you're adding ingredients like raisins, now is the time). Stir in the extract.

❸ Drop tablespoon-size mounds of dough about 3 inches apart in rows and columns on ungreased baking sheets. Bake until lightly browned, 12 to 15 minutes. Cool for about 2 minutes on the sheets before using a spatula to transfer the cookies to a rack to finish cooling. Store in a tightly covered container at room temperature for no more than a day or two.

Lacy Oatmeal Cookies. Almost tuiles, these cookies contain no flour: Melt the butter and combine it with the sugars, oats, and salt; beat in the eggs. Omit the flour, baking powder, milk, and vanilla; add the cinnamon if you like. Bake at 350°F on greased baking sheets for 8 to 10 minutes; let rest for a minute before transferring to a rack with a thin-bladed spatula to finish cooling.

Peanut Butter Oatmeal Cookies. Any nut butter works here; these cookies have a tendency to burn more quickly, so keep a careful watch over them: Substitute ¹/₄ cup peanut butter for 4 tablespoons (¹/₂ stick) of the butter.

Whole Grain Spice Cookies. Cooked whole grains (like bulgur, barley, wheat or rye berries, buckwheat, or even short-grain brown rice) replace rolled oats with tender-but-chewy results: Substitute cooked whole grains (see page 451) for the rolled oats and fluff with

a fork to separate the kernels before combining with the other ingredients. Omit the milk. In Step 2, increase the cinnamon to a teaspoon and add ¹/₂ teaspoon ground ginger and ¹/₄ teaspoon each ground allspice and freshly grated nutmeg. Proceed with the recipe, combining the dry ingredients into the egg mixture in Step 3 all at once without adding any milk.

Coconut Cookies. Shredded coconut replaces all or most of the oats: Substitute coconut milk (to make your own, see page 389) for the milk and shredded coconut for all or a portion of the oats, as you like.

Refrigerator (or Rolled) Cookies

MAKES: At least 3 dozen

TIME: 30 minutes, plus time to chill

Refrigerating this dough gives you a stiff consistency that's perfect for rolling and cutting out cookies: think Christmas cookies. Alternatively, you can roll the dough into a log and then slice off rounds to create the cookies. Make batches of dough ahead of time, freeze it, and they're cookies-on-call, ready to be sliced off the log or thawed, rolled, and cut. Generally, rolled cookies are more crumbly and less chewy than drop cookies. But if you want them on the chewy side, underbake them by a couple of minutes, removing them from the oven while the center is still a little soft.

The dough can be varied endlessly; any of the flavor ideas for Butter Cookies (page 892) work here. Top with Vanilla Glaze (page 919) and sprinkles; smear with any Buttercream Frosting (page 917) or Caramel Frosting (page 922); or drizzle with Orange Glaze (page 919), Caramel (page 922), Chocolate Ganache (page 920), or Berry Jam Glaze (page 923).

¹/₂ pound (2 sticks) unsalted butter, softened, plus some for the baking sheets

1 cup sugar

1 egg

3 cups all-purpose flour, plus more for the work
surface

Pinch salt

1 teaspoon baking powder

1 tablespoon milk, or as needed

1 teaspoon vanilla extract

1 Use an electric mixer to cream together the butter and sugar; add the egg and beat until well blended.

2 Combine the flour, salt, and baking powder in a bowl. Add the dry ingredients to the dough, adding a little milk at a time as necessary to make the dough just soft enough to handle. Stir in the vanilla.

3 Shape the dough into a disk (for rolled cookies) or a log (for sliced cookies), wrap in plastic, and refrigerate for at least 2 hours or up to 2 days (or wrap very well and freeze indefinitely).

4 Heat the oven to 400°F. Cut the dough disk in half. Lightly flour a work surface and a rolling pin and roll gently until about $^1/_8$ inch thick, adding flour as necessary and turning the dough to prevent sticking. Cut with any cookie cutter. (To slice, simply cut slices about $^1/_8$ inch thick from the chilled or frozen log.)

5 Bake on lightly greased baking sheets until the edges are lightly brown and the center set, 6 to 10 minutes. Cool for about 2 minutes on the sheets before using a spatula to transfer the cookies to a rack to finish cooling. Store in a tightly covered container at room temperature for no more than a day or two.

Lighter Rolled Cookies. Not as dense and rich as the main recipe: In Step 1, add $^1/_2$ cup more white (or brown) sugar and beat 2 eggs into the creamed butter and sugar. In Step 2, add $^1/_2$ teaspoon baking soda to the dry ingredients (including the baking powder); add $^1/_4$ cup milk to the batter along with the flour mixture.

Peanut Butter Cookies. In Step 1, cream $^1/_2$ to $^3/_4$ cup peanut butter with the butter and sugar. You can use smooth or crunchy peanut butter as you like. You can also add about $^1/_2$ cup chopped peanuts (try those with salt for an interesting change), along with the vanilla, in Step 2.

Rosemary Sugar Cookies. A sophisticated cookie that will please adults and kids: Substitute 1 teaspoon finely minced fresh rosemary (or $^1/_2$ teaspoon crushed dried) for the vanilla extract. Proceed with the recipe; sprinkle the cookies with coarse or raw sugar halfway through baking.

Brown Sugar and Salt Cookies. Use a nice sea salt or similar: Substitute brown sugar for the white sugar. Proceed with the recipe; sprinkle each cookie with just a tiny pinch of sea salt halfway through baking.

Mexican Wedding Cookies

MAKES: About 3 dozen
TIME: About 1 hour

A simple cookie whose resemblance to snowballs makes them a fun holiday cookie. They're fragile, so handle them gently when you roll them in the powdered sugar.

$^1/_2$ pound (2 sticks) unsalted butter, softened

$1^1/_2$ cups confectioners' sugar, plus more as needed

2 cups all-purpose flour

$^1/_4$ teaspoon salt

1 cup chopped walnuts, hazelnuts, pecans, or almonds

1 teaspoon vanilla extract

1 Use an electric mixer to beat the butter until light and fluffy. Add $^3/_4$ cup of the confectioners' sugar and cream together.

2 Combine the flour, salt, and chopped nuts in a bowl. Add the dry ingredients to the dough and beat until just combined. Stir in the vanilla.

3 Shape the dough into a disk, wrap in plastic, and refrigerate for at least 30 minutes or as long as 2 days (or wrap very well and freeze indefinitely).

4 Heat the oven to 350°F. Roll the dough into 1-inch balls and bake on ungreased baking sheets until the tops are just turning brown and the bottoms are golden brown, 10 to 12 minutes.

5 Put the remaining sugar in a pie plate or shallow bowl. Cool the cookies on the sheets just enough so you can handle them; use a spatula to transfer them in batches to the plate of sugar. Roll each cookie in the sugar until coated and then transfer to a rack to finish cooling. Roll them in the sugar again once cooled. Store in a tightly covered container at room temperature for no more than a day or two.

Chocolate-Filled Mexican Wedding Cookies. In Step 2, add ¹/₂ teaspoon ground cinnamon to the dry ingredients. When you roll the dough into balls in Step 4, tuck a chunk of bittersweet chocolate (about the size of a raisin) into the center of each ball. Proceed with the recipe, mixing a spoonful of cocoa powder in with the confectioners' sugar before coating if you like.

Almond Balls. Use almonds and substitute ¹/₂ teaspoon almond extract for the vanilla.

Aunt Big's Gingersnaps

MAKES: 4 to 5 dozen

TIME: About 40 minutes, plus time to chill

Not too sweet—in fact, bordering on savory—these gingersnaps are super-crisp, the kind that stick in your teeth. "The dough is also great undercooked," says my friend Sally, who is Aunt Big's niece. Try these with Vanilla or Maple Buttercream Frosting (page 917) or drizzle with Orange Glaze (page 919).

¹/₂ pound (2 sticks) unsalted butter, softened

1 cup sugar

1 cup molasses

1 heaping teaspoon baking soda

3¹/₂ cups all-purpose flour

1 heaping tablespoon ground ginger

1 tablespoon ground cinnamon

Pinch salt

1 Use an electric mixer to cream together the butter, sugar, and molasses until smooth. Mix the baking soda with 2 tablespoons hot water and beat into the dough.

2 Combine the flour, spices, and salt in a bowl. Add the dry ingredients to the dough and beat well. Shape the dough into 2 long logs, wrap in wax paper, and refrigerate for several hours or overnight (or wrap very well in plastic and freeze indefinitely; you can proceed to Step 3 with still-frozen dough).

3 Heat the oven to 350°F. Slice the cookies as thin as you can and bake on ungreased baking sheets until golden around the edges, about 10 minutes, watching carefully to prevent burning. Use a spatula to transfer the cookies to a rack to cool. Store in a tightly covered container at room temperature for up to several days.

Gingerbread Men. For softer cookies, remove the dough from the oven when the center is still puffy and soft: Shape the dough into a disk and remove from the refrigerator about 15 minutes before rolling it; heat the oven. When the dough is slightly softened, roll it out as thinly as possible; hand-cut if you're brave or use a gingerbread man cutter. Bake as directed, then cool. Decorate, if you like, with small candies and Vanilla Glaze (page 919). Store in a tightly covered container at room temperature for up to several days.

Molasses-Spice Cookies. Add ¹/₂ teaspoon freshly grated nutmeg, ¹/₈ teaspoon ground cloves, and ¹/₄ teaspoon ground allspice along with the ginger.

Espresso-Spice Cookies. Watch out for the caffeine kick if you're serving these as an after-dinner treat: Reduce the molasses to ³/₄ cup. Add 1 or 2 shots of freshly brewed espresso and mix in with the molasses in Step 1.

Shortbread

MAKES: 1½ to 2½ dozen
TIME: About 20 minutes, plus time to chill

"Short," meaning with lots of butter, makes these very tender (the cornstarch makes them even more so) and very yummy. You can cut these, put them on a baking sheet, cover them, and freeze them for days before baking, straight from the freezer. Or just chill them for half an hour or so and then slice and bake.

Try smearing these with Caramel Frosting (page 922) or drizzle with Orange Glaze (page 919), Chocolate Glaze (page 920), or Berry Jam Glaze (page 923).

½ pound (2 sticks) unsalted butter, softened

¾ cup sugar

1 egg yolk

1½ cups all-purpose flour

½ cup cornstarch

Pinch salt

1 Use an electric mixer to combine the butter and sugar; mix on low speed, just until combined, 30 seconds or so. Still on low speed, beat in the egg yolk, then the flour, cornstarch, and salt, until the mixture barely holds together; this will take a few minutes.

2 There are two ways to shape the dough, and both require chilling. If you want to make real shapes, form the dough into a rough ball or disk, wrap in plastic, and freeze or refrigerate for at least 30 minutes, until fairly firm. Roll it out on a lightly floured surface until ¼ inch thick. Cut into any shapes you like, then put the cookies on an ungreased baking sheet. They will not spread much, so you can put them pretty close together. Chill for 1 hour or freeze for as long as you want. (Once they're frozen, you can take them off the sheets and store them in a plastic bag for several days if you like.)

Alternatively, shape the dough into a round, triangular, or rectangular log and refrigerate or freeze until firm, about 30 minutes. (You can also store the log, frozen.) Slice ¼ inch thick and put on the baking sheet.

3 Heat the oven to 275°F. Bake the cookies until just firm but still quite tender and not at all brown, about 30 minutes. Cool for a minute on the sheets before using a spatula to transfer the cookies to a rack to finish cooling. Store on a plate, uncovered, for no more than a day.

Wheat Shortbread. A portion of whole wheat flour gives the shortbread a nice nutty flavor: Substitute up to ¾ cup whole wheat flour for white flour.

Pistachio or Other Nut Shortbread. Pistachios give the shortbread a beautiful green color: Substitute ½ cup pistachio or other nut flour or meal (see page 320) for ½ cup of the flour. Reduce the cornstarch to ¼ cup. Sprinkle the tops of each cookie with a pinch of ground cardamom before baking if you like.

6 Simple Ideas for Shortbread

You can combine these ideas if you like.

1. Add 2 tablespoons grated orange or lemon zest to the dough. For more flavor, decrease the butter by 2 tablespoons; replace it with 2 tablespoons freshly squeezed orange or lemon juice.
2. Add ½ cup toasted/chopped pine nuts to the dough (nice with lemon zest or rosemary).
3. Add 1 teaspoon ground cinnamon or ginger to the dough.
4. Add about 1 teaspoon minced fresh rosemary, thyme, or lavender leaves to the dough.
5. Add 1 teaspoon vanilla or almond extract to the dough (especially good with nuts).
6. Add 1 ounce melted bittersweet chocolate to the dough.

Biscotti

MAKES: 3 to 4 dozen
TIME: About 1¼ hours

The twice-baked technique makes these sliced cookies crunchy and ideal for serving with coffee.

 Fast   Make Ahead   Vegetarian

4 tablespoons (¹/₂ stick) unsalted butter, plus more for greasing the pans

³/₄ cup sugar

3 eggs

1 teaspoon vanilla or almond extract

2 cups all-purpose flour, plus more for the baking sheets

1 teaspoon baking powder

Pinch salt

1 or 2 tablespoons milk if necessary

① Heat the oven to 375°F. Use an electric mixer to cream together the butter and sugar until light and fluffy; add the eggs, one at a time, and beat until well blended, then add the extract.

② Combine the flour, baking powder, and salt in a bowl. Add the dry ingredients to the dough a little at a time, beating until just incorporated and adding a little milk if needed to bring the dough together.

③ Butter 2 baking sheets and dust them with flour; invert the sheets and tap them to remove excess flour. Divide the dough in half and shape each half into a 2-inch-wide log. Put each log on a baking sheet.

④ Bake until the loaves are golden and beginning to crack on top, about 30 minutes; cool the logs on the sheets for a few minutes. Lower the oven temperature to 250°F.

⑤ When the loaves are cool enough to handle, use a serrated knife to cut each on a diagonal into ¹/₂-inch-thick slices. Put the slices on the sheets, return them to the oven, and leave them there, turning once, until they dry out, 15 to 20 minutes. Cool on wire racks. These will keep in an airtight container for several days.

Chocolate-Hazelnut Biscotti. Put chocolate in the dough as explained here or just dip the baked biscotti in melted chocolate as directed in the following list—or both: Melt 1 ounce each semisweet and unsweetened chocolate and add to the butter mixture in Step 1, before adding the eggs. Add 1 cup blanched and lightly toasted hazelnuts at the end of Step 2.

7 Simple Ideas for Biscotti

Use these ideas alone or in combination:

1. Add 1 teaspoon ground fennel or anise seeds or 1 teaspoon ground cinnamon to the dry ingredients.
2. Stir 1 cup slivered blanched almonds, toasted and chopped hazelnuts, whole pine nuts, or other chopped nuts into the prepared dough before baking.
3. Mix 1 teaspoon minced lemon or orange zest into the dry ingredients.
4. Melt 8 ounces semisweet chocolate with 3 tablespoons unsalted butter. Spread this mixture onto one side of the biscotti when they are done. Cool on a rack until the chocolate coating is firm.
5. Stir about ¹/₄ cup minced crystallized ginger into the dry ingredients.
6. Mix about ¹/₂ cup dried fruit, like raisins, cherries, or cranberries, into the dough before baking.
7. Mix about ³/₄ cup chocolate chips into the dough before baking.

Coconut Macaroons

MAKES: About 2 dozen

TIME: About 45 minutes, plus time to chill

I know this isn't a common feeling, but these are one of my favorite cookies: moist, chewy, coconutty. Mine are made with lightly beaten whites, contain no butter, egg yolks, cream, or flour, and can be put together in one bowl in no time flat. For overkill, you can drizzle with or dip into melted chocolate or Chocolate Ganache (page 920); or see the sidebar on the next page.

1 cup sugar

3 cups shredded coconut

3 egg whites, lightly beaten

1 teaspoon vanilla extract

Pinch salt

How to Beat Egg Whites

Egg whites beaten until airy and stiff are the essential ingredient in many light and fluffy creations, like meringues, soufflés, and mousses. They're also used to lighten batters, such as for Olive Oil Cake (page 914), Angel Food Cake (page 912), and Everyday Pancakes (page 811). It's is an easy task, especially with an electric mixer. Simply put, the whipping forces air bubbles into the whites; these get caught in protein molecules that stretch out to hold the molecules together.

For equipment, at the most you'll need a mixer with a whisk attachment and a spotlessly clean metal or glass bowl; at the least, a big whisk, the bowl, and a well-rested arm. While a copper bowl will yield a sturdier foam, almost any type of metal or glass bowl will do. Avoid plastic, because its porous surface can retain fat molecules, and fat interferes with the whites' ability to foam.

There are really only a couple of potential pitfalls: The first is getting even the tiniest bit of yolk—or any fat—in the whites; even oil residue clinging to the sides of a bowl will ruin or at least seriously impede your whites' ability to whip up. If a bit of yolk does get in the whites, get it out or—much safer—start with a fresh egg.

The other mistake when whipping whites is overbeating them. As with whipped cream, there are various stages:

Soft peaks: The foam will just make a low peak with a tip that readily folds onto itself.

Medium peaks: A solid peak, still soft, with a tip that folds over but not onto itself.

Stiff peaks: A stiff peak with a tip that hardly bends; dragging your finger through the foam will leave a mark. It should not be clumpy, though.

Overbeaten: The foam will be clumpy, rough looking, and leaking water. Unlike whipped cream, once egg whites are overwhipped, there's no repairing the damage; the foam is just too unstable to use and will deflate when folding and cooking. Start over with fresh egg whites.

Often you'll see recipes calling for cream of tartar (an acid), salt, or sugar to be added to egg whites to make the foam fluffier, more stable, and better tasting. Never add more than the tiniest pinch of salt to the eggs; salt does add flavor, but it creates a less stable foam. Many people add cream of tartar with the belief that it helps stability, but I've never found it makes much difference except in angel food cake.

Whipping in sugar, on the other hand, has both positive and negative aspects: It makes the process slower and slightly less dramatic, but it also makes for a more stable foam when cooked. Sugar helps egg whites retain moisture while cooking, so it's less likely to fall and leak water; this is important for meringues and soufflés in particular. When you do add sugar, use superfine or confectioners' sugar, which dissolves more quickly than granulated sugar (undissolved grains of sugar can cause syrupy beads to form on the surface of a meringue), and add once the whites have formed medium peaks.

(1) Soft peak stage: Whites look soft, and when you remove the whisk or beaters, the tops fold over.

(2) Stiff peak stage: Whites look stiff, and when you remove the whisk or beaters, the tops make distinct peaks. Do not beat beyond this point.

 Fast   Make Ahead   **V** Vegetarian

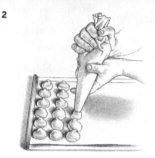

(STEP 1) If you are using a decorative tip (these illustrations do not), put it in the bottom of the pastry bag and pull from the outside until it is secure. Fold the top of the pastry bag over to fill it from the bottom. (STEP 2) Twist the top gently and hold the bag that you can apply pressure comfortably. Use the other hand to steady and support the bottom. Squeeze just enough batter or frosting out of the bag to control the shape of your work; adjust your position to maintain pressure and keep the flow steady. Pull up gently to create a decorative peak if you like. (STEP 3) The techniques are the same with a plastic zipper bag as shown here. Refill the bag as needed.

 Heat the oven to 350°F. Combine all the ingredients in a large bowl and mix well with a fork, rubber spatula, or your hands until the coconut is evenly coated.

 Use a nonstick baking sheet or line a baking sheet with parchment paper. Wet your hands and make small piles of the mixture, each 1 to 2 tablespoons, about an inch apart. Bake until light brown, about 15 minutes. Remove the baking sheet and cool on a rack for at least 30 minutes before eating. These keep well in a covered container for up to 3 days.

Walnut or Other Nut Macaroons. Super with chocolate chunks, too: Substitute finely chopped walnuts for the coconut.

Molasses Macaroons. Make these with the coconut, as in the main recipe, or nuts, as in the preceding variation: Substitute $1/4$ cup molasses for $1/2$ cup of the sugar.

Vanilla Meringues

MAKES: 4 to 5 dozen
TIME: 2 hours or more, largely unattended

Ⓜ Ⓥ

Light, sweet, and low in fat, meringues are the perfect use for leftover egg whites, as long as the weather is dry. If your oven is small, divide the recipe in half; you want to bake all the meringues at once. You can stir in all kinds of ingredients before baking if you like (nuts, toasted coconut, even bits of dried fruit); just chop them up a bit and don't use more than a cup or so. These are sort of chewy on the inside, with a crackly exterior, which is how I like them.

4 egg whites at room temperature

1 cup superfine sugar

Seeds scraped from $1/2$ vanilla bean or 1 teaspoon vanilla extract

1 teaspoon white vinegar

2 teaspoons cornstarch

Pinch salt

① Heat the oven to 300°F. Use an electric mixer or a whisk to beat the whites until foamy. Gradually add the sugar, vanilla, vinegar, cornstarch, and salt and beat until the mixture makes stiff peaks.

② Line a baking sheet with parchment or wax paper. Use a pastry bag, a zipper bag with a corner cut out, a spoon, or wet hands to form small mounds of the meringue mixture, each a couple tablespoons (larger if you like); you can space them quite closely since they won't rise (see the illustrations and sidebar, previous page).

③ Bake until hard and very lightly browned, 40 to 45 minutes. Remove the baking sheet and cool on a rack for at least 30 minutes before eating. These keep well in an airtight container for up to 3 days.

Cocoa Meringues. Substitute ¹/₄ cup cocoa powder for the vanilla.

Mocha Meringues. Add 1 more egg white. Substitute 3 tablespoons cocoa powder and 1 shot freshly brewed espresso or strong coffee for the vanilla.

Pavlova. One large meringue "cake" you can fill with whipped or ice cream and sliced fresh fruit: Dump the egg white mixture into the center of the parchment on the baking sheet and gently spread into a circle almost to the edges of the pan, so that the sides are

Meringues as Edible Containers

Meringue batter has a fluffy stiffness that holds its shape and then hardens when baked, which makes it ideal for forming cups or nests for holding purées, ice cream, or fruit.

The process looks complicated (and yields pretty spectacular results), but it's easy: Line a baking sheet with parchment or wax paper (you can secure the parchment corners with four dabs of meringue). Put the meringue in a piping bag fitted with a plain round or star-shaped tip that's at least ¹/₄ inch in diameter. To make the bottom of the container, pipe a circular spiral, leaving no space in between; circles 3 or 4 inches in diameter make a good single-serving size. Then make the "wall" by piping a ring onto the outermost bottom ring; top that with another ring if you want a deeper container. Alternatively, you can pipe little dollops of meringue along the outer ring to create a peaked wall.

If you don't have a piping bag, put the meringue batter in a plastic zipper bag and cut the corner off. It won't be as perfect in shape as the piping bag, but it will still look good. For a really rustic look, make the containers by

scooping out the center of a large dollop, leaving a "floor" of meringue.

Bake the meringue containers a bit longer than the meringue cookies to get them hard instead of chewy; 60 to 70 minutes at 300°F should do it. Let them cool on a rack before filling or store in an airtight container for up to a day.

8 Fillings for Meringue Containers

1. Fresh or cooked fruit, like berries, peaches, nectarines, apricots, plums, mangoes, cherries, cranberries (cooked), banana, or figs, whole or sliced as needed. Add them alone or on top of any of the fillings that follow.
2. Whipped Cream, plain or with any flavorings (page 882)
3. Chocolate Ganache (page 920)
4. Caramel Sauce (page 922)
5. Any fruit purée or sauce (see pages 923–924)
6. Vanilla or Chocolate Custard Sauce (page 924)
7. Citrus Curd (page 924)
8. Any ice cream (see pages 961–964)

 Fast   Make Ahead   Vegetarian

higher than the center and it looks like a shallow bowl. Proceed with the recipe.

Chocolate Tuiles

MAKES: 3 to 4 dozen

TIME: About 30 minutes

Thin, light, and crisp, tuiles are spread directly onto the baking sheets. Just after baking, when the cookies are still warm, they can be molded into cones or other shapes or simply draped over glasses, rolling pins, or the like. As the cookies cool, they become crisp (and harder to manipulate; so work quickly).

4 egg whites

1 cup confectioners' sugar

3/4 cup all-purpose flour

1/4 cup cocoa powder

8 tablespoons (1 stick) unsalted butter, melted, plus a little more if needed, plus softened butter for the baking sheets

❶ Heat the oven to 375°F. Grease 2 baking sheets or cover them with parchment or a silicone mat.

❷ Whisk the egg whites until foamy. Mix in the confectioners' sugar, flour, and cocoa, scraping down the sides as necessary. Add the melted butter and stir until just incorporated. The dough will be more like a very thick batter than a cookie dough. If it's not spreadable, add more melted butter, a teaspoon at a time.

❸ Spoon the batter by the tablespoonful onto the prepared sheets and use the back of the spoon to spread the batter into thin (less than 1/4 inch thick) 2- to 3-inch circles. Bake until firm and slightly darkened around the edges, 8 to 10 minutes. While still hot, use a metal spatula or butter knife to transfer the cookies to a rack to cool flat or drape over a rolling pin to form the traditional curved tuile shape (see page 904).

Chocolate Dessert Cups. Great for holding berries, pudding, ice cream, or flavored whipped cream. When the cookies come out of the oven, drape them over small ramekins or coffee cups to cool, pressing gently to form a "cup" on the inside. Fill just before serving so they don't get soggy.

Brownies and Bars

Brownies (and other bars) start with cookielike batter, but they're baked in a single batch, which makes them cakelike or fudgy. You want to take them out of the oven when the edges are starting to firm up and the middle is still a bit soft, because they will continue to cook as they cool. For classic chocolate brownies, see the Essential Recipe on page 881.

To obtain the classic tuile shape, lay the baked but still-soft cookies over a rolling pin, dowel, or similar object.

Butterscotch Brownies

Blondies

MAKES: About 1 dozen
TIME: 30 to 40 minutes

Basically brownies without chocolate and nearly as well loved because the butter flavor is so distinct. Any of the "8 Simple Ideas for Brownies" listed on page 881 will work here too.

8 tablespoons (1 stick) unsalted butter, plus a little for the pan

1 cup brown sugar

1 egg

1 teaspoon vanilla extract or $1/2$ teaspoon almond extract

Pinch salt

1 cup all-purpose flour

❶ Heat the oven to 350°F. Grease an 8- or 9-inch square baking pan or line it with aluminum foil and grease the foil.

❷ Melt the butter over low heat. Transfer to a bowl and use an electric mixer or whisk to beat in the sugar until very smooth, then beat in the egg and vanilla, stirring down the sides of the bowl every now and then.

❸ Add the salt, then gently stir in the flour. Pour into the prepared pan and bake until just barely set in the middle, 20 to 25 minutes. Cool on a rack before cutting. Store, covered, at room temperature for no more than a day.

Magic Bars. So named because you can put almost anything in them: Add up to $1^{1}/_{2}$ cups of anything from shredded coconut to any kind of chocolate chunks, toffee or caramel chunks, roughly chopped nuts, and/or dried fruit. Stir the additions into the batter just before pouring into the pan.

Apricot-Almond Bars. A bit more sophisticated: Use the almond extract. Add 1 cup chopped dried apricots, $1/4$ cup apricot jam, and $1/2$ cup finely chopped almonds to the batter along with the eggs. Reduce the sugar to $1/4$ cup and the flour to $3/4$ cup.

Gabrielle's Lemon Squares

MAKES: About 1 dozen
TIME: About 1 hour

These two-step squares are sweet-tart and moist. Be sure not to overbake them; they're done when the edges are firming up and the middle is still a bit soft. Rotate the pan if they appear to be baking unevenly.

8 tablespoons (1 stick) unsalted butter, softened, plus a little for the pan

$1^{3}/_{4}$ cups granulated sugar

Pinch salt

1 cup plus 3 tablespoons all-purpose flour

3 eggs

$1/4$ cup freshly squeezed lemon juice

$1/2$ teaspoon baking soda

 Fast   Make Ahead   Vegetarian

Grated or minced zest of 1 lemon

Confectioners' sugar for dusting

1 Heat the oven to 350°F. Grease an 8- or 9-inch square baking pan.

2 Use an electric mixer to cream the butter with ¼ cup of the sugar and the salt. Stir in the cup of flour. This mixture will be quite dry; press into the greased pan and bake for 20 minutes, no longer; it should just be turning golden. Remove from the oven and cool slightly.

3 Beat together the eggs, lemon juice, and remaining sugar until lightened and thick; add the remaining flour, the baking soda, and the lemon zest. Pour over the crust and bake until firm on the edges but still a little soft in the middle, 25 to 30 minutes. Cool, then dust with sifted confectioners' sugar. Cut into squares and serve. Store, covered and refrigerated, for up to 2 days.

Coconut-Lime Bars. Substitute lime juice and zest for the lemon juice and zest. Omit the confectioners' sugar. Sprinkle 1 cup shredded coconut over the filling just before baking.

Mango Bars. Follow the preceding variation, only add ¼ cup mango purée (see page 923) and reduce the lime juice to 2 teaspoons. Omit or keep the shredded coconut as you prefer.

Quick Jam Bars. Reduce the sugar to 1 cup and the flour to 1 cup. Substitute ¼ cup of your favorite jam for the lemon juice and zest. Omit the baking soda. In Step 3, combine the eggs and jam.

No-Bake Granola Bars

MAKES: About 1 dozen
TIME: 15 minutes

Better (and less junk-food-y) than store-bought and super-quick to make. They're a lot of fun to fool around with too—see the variations.

¾ cup honey

½ cup brown sugar

¼ cup neutral oil, like grapeseed or corn

3 cups Granola (page 821)

1 Put the honey, brown sugar, and oil in a small pot and bring to a boil; turn off the heat. Put the granola in a large bowl and pour the sugar mixture over the top while mixing; stir until the granola is well coated.

2 Press into an 8- or 9-inch square pan and let cool in the fridge. Cut into squares or rectangles and serve. Store in an airtight container for up to 4 days.

Dried Fruit Bars. Dates or figs are good, as are apricots, raisins, plums, pears, and more: Substitute 1½ cups dried fruit for the honey and brown sugar. Put the dried fruit and oil in a food processor and purée until smooth, stopping the machine to scrape down the sides if necessary. (Add small amounts of water if the fruit is dried out and not processing.) Proceed with the recipe.

Nutty Granola Bars. Use a variety of nuts and seeds: Substitute 1 cup mixed or single toasted roughly chopped nuts and whole seeds for 1 cup of granola.

Peanut (or Other Nut) Butter Granola Bars. Your own power bar: Substitute peanut or any other nut butter for the brown sugar.

The Basics of Cakes

The most basic cakes are essentially extra-sweet, extra-eggy quick breads, but they can become the most complex creations in cooking, with several different preparations needed before assembly; in fact some cakes are so elaborate that they take all day to make. I leave those to the pros.

The other end of the spectrum—cake mix—is barely worth eating, at least compared to the real thing. Homemade cake is meltingly tender, tasting of butter, eggs, and simple seasonings like chocolate, vanilla, or lemon, sweet but not overly so, good looking in its simplicity and regal stature. The cakes here meet those standards.

It's difficult to argue that there's a single ingredient in a cake that is of paramount importance, but cakes have a way of showcasing off-flavors: If an ingredient is stale or even second-rate, that flavor will somehow pop to the fore. Use high-quality butter, eggs, chocolate, nuts, and extracts for the best cakes.

Use the right bakeware too: If my high school math is serving me correctly, the difference between an 8-inch and a 9-inch cake pan is around 12 square inches—that's a large extra space over which to spread a batter and will change the cooking time.

To grease and flour pans: Smear the butter all over, dust with flour, then tap out the excess flour (often, butter alone suffices). To be doubly sure you don't leave part of the delicate cake behind, you might line the pan with parchment or wax paper before greasing.

As with cookies, when you're baking cakes, rotate the pan(s) about halfway through baking so that different sections cook in different parts of the oven for equal times.

On Sifting Dry Ingredients

Flour, once an inconsistent product, is now so fine that sifting is usually unnecessary. Nor is it necessary when mixing flour with other dry ingredients, like sugar, salt, or baking powder, although it's worth whisking those ingredients together with a fork or whisk just to eliminate any lumps. When you do need to sift—to put a layer of flour on the bottom of a pan or in delicate recipes like Angel Food Cake (page 912)—put the flour through an old-fashioned sifter or simply pass through a not-too-fine sieve.

Note that cakes with icing can hold for a day, if covered, but no cake—iced or not—is ever as tender and moist as it is the day you make it.

Pound Cake

MAKES: At least 8 servings
TIME: About 1½ hours

A classic cake whose name derives from its basic ingredients: a pound each of butter, flour, sugar, and eggs. Here the formula is roughly cut in half to make one nice-size loaf, and a few extra ingredients are added to increase flavor and lighten the texture. It remains a delight, especially toasted with butter or varied as suggested. It's worth using cake flour here for extra tenderness (if you don't have it, see the sidebar or just use all-purpose flour).

Pound Cake is wonderful finished with Orange Glaze (page 919), Ginger-Marmalade Glaze (page 919), or served with Fruit Sauce, Two Ways (page 924). Or leave in the pan and pour in Rich Vanilla Cake Soak or any of its variations (page 919).

½ pound (2 sticks) unsalted butter, softened, plus some for the pan

2 cups all-purpose or cake flour

1½ teaspoons baking powder

Pinch salt

½ teaspoon freshly grated nutmeg (optional but very nice)

1 cup sugar

5 eggs, separated

2 teaspoons vanilla extract

❶ Heat the oven to 325°F. Grease a 9 × 5-inch loaf pan. Mix together the flour, baking powder, salt, and nutmeg if you're using it in a bowl and set aside.

 Fast   Make Ahead   Vegetarian

2 Use an electric mixer to cream the butter until it's smooth. Add ³/₄ cup of the sugar and beat until it's well blended, then add the remaining sugar. Beat until the mixture is light in color and fluffy, scraping down the sides of the mixing bowl if necessary. Beat in the egg yolks, one at a time. Add the vanilla and beat until blended.

3 Mix in the dry ingredients by hand just until smooth; do not overmix and do not beat. Wash the beaters thoroughly, then beat the egg whites until they hold soft peaks; fold them in gently but thoroughly (the base batter is very thick).

4 Turn into the prepared pan and bake until a toothpick inserted into the top comes out clean, about 1¹/₄ hours. Let the cake rest in the pan for 5 minutes before inverting onto a rack. Remove the pan, then turn the cake right side up. Cool before slicing. Store at room temperature, covered with wax paper, for a day or two; you can gain a couple more days by wrapping in plastic, but at some loss of texture.

Marble Cake. Before adding the egg whites in Step 3, combine 3 tablespoons cocoa powder with 5 tablespoons sugar and blend this mixture with about 1 cup of the batter. Fold the beaten egg whites into the remaining batter. Put half the batter in the bottom of the loaf pan; top with the chocolate mixture, then with the remaining batter. Use a knife or spatula to swirl the mixtures together and bake as directed.

Polenta Pound Cake. Substitute 1 cup cornmeal for a cup of the flour.

Yogurt Pound Cake. Lighter (in terms of calories and fat) and even more moist: Substitute ³/₄ cup yogurt for half of the butter.

6 Ways to Vary Pound Cake

Combine any of these ideas. One of my favorites is almond flour with orange zest; lemon with poppy seeds is classic.

1. **Real vanilla:** Use a vanilla bean in place of the vanilla extract (see "Using a Vanilla Bean," page 961).
2. **Lemon, orange, lime, or grapefruit:** Add 1 teaspoon grated or minced citrus zest and 1 tablespoon citrus juice. Omit the vanilla extract.
3. **Spices:** Add a teaspoon of ground spices, like cinnamon, ginger, cardamom, nutmeg, allspice, or cloves.
4. **Nut meal:** Substitute 1 cup any nut meal or flour for half of the flour; use all-purpose flour for the remaining cup.
5. **Crystallized ginger:** Add 1 to 2 tablespoons minced crystallized ginger.
6. **Poppy and other seeds:** Add ¹/₄ cup poppy or sesame seeds.

Do-It-Yourself Cake Flour

Cakes have a more tender crumb when made with cake flour, although all-purpose flour is often a good substitute. But when the recipe calls for only cake flour—and you don't have it—try this: For every cup of flour needed, mix ⁷/₈ cup of all-purpose flour with ¹/₈ cup of cornstarch. (An easy way is to fill and level a cup of flour, then measure and replace 2 tablespoons of the flour with cornstarch.) After you try cake flour, or the cornstarch solution, you will notice the difference and stick with it.

Golden Layer Cake

MAKES: At least 10 servings
TIME: About 1 hour

This tender, delicate cake takes either white or chocolate frosting beautifully (see pages 917–918) and can be given the subtle flavor of vanilla or the bolder flavor of orange. Make it even more golden and rich by using all egg yolks. It also makes wonderful cupcakes—see "Making Baby-cakes and Cupcakes," next page.

10 tablespoons (1¼ sticks) unsalted butter, softened, plus some for the pans and the paper

2 cups cake or all-purpose flour, plus some for the pans

1¼ cups sugar

4 eggs or 8 yolks

1 teaspoon vanilla extract or 1 tablespoon grated or minced orange zest

¼ teaspoon almond extract

2½ teaspoons baking powder

¼ teaspoon salt

¾ cup milk

1 Heat the oven to 350°F. Grease the bottom and sides of two 9-inch or three 8-inch layer cake pans; cover the bottom with a circle of wax or parchment paper, butter the paper, and sift flour over the pans; invert and tap to remove the excess flour.

2 Use an electric mixer to cream the butter until smooth, then gradually add the sugar. Beat until light in color and fluffy, 3 or 4 minutes. Beat in the eggs or yolks, one at a time, then the vanilla or orange zest and the almond extract. Combine the flour, baking powder, and salt; add to the egg mixture by hand, a little at a time, alternating with the milk. Stir just until smooth.

3 Turn the batter into the pans and bake until a toothpick inserted into the center of the cakes comes out clean, about 25 minutes. Let the cake cool in the pan for 5 minutes, then invert onto a rack to finish cooling.

4 Frost or glaze if you like (see pages 917–919). Store at room temperature, covered with wax paper, for up to a day or two; use plastic wrap and it will keep for an extra day or so.

Pistachio-Saffron Cake. Try it with Creamy Orange Glaze (page 919) or Whipped Cream with rose water (page 882): Heat the milk to steaming and steep ½

FROSTING A LAYER CAKE

1

2

3

(**STEP 1**) Put the first layer, top side down, on a plate or cake stand. Spread about a third of the frosting on top, all the way to the edges. Use a knife if you don't have a frosting spreader or long spatula. It's okay if it's a little messy. You'll smooth things out at the end. (**STEP 2**) Put the other layer on top, flat side down. Spread another third of the frosting on top. (**STEP 3**) Use the remaining frosting to cover the sides of the cake, scooping up extra to add to the top. Smooth if you like, or wiggle your hand a little bit to make little peaks and swirls.

F Fast   **M** Make Ahead   **V** Vegetarian

teaspoon crumbled saffron threads in it until it's cool. Substitute 1 cup finely ground pistachios for half the flour; use all-purpose flour for the remaining cup.

Coconut Layer Cake. Spread or pipe a layer of cooled Vanilla Pudding (page 950) between the layers for a luxurious cake: Stir $^1/_2$ cup shredded coconut into the batter along with the dry ingredients and the milk. Use Vanilla Buttercream Frosting (page 917). After frosting the bottom layer, sprinkle the frosting with $^1/_2$ cup shredded coconut. After frosting the assembled cake, press another 2 cups or more of shredded coconut onto the top and sides.

The Basics of Chocolate

Like cheese, coffee, and wine, chocolate has become the food of serious connoisseurs, complete with highbrow terminology and potential snobbery. But I approach chocolate the same way I do cheese or wine: You basically want to start with a delicious ingredient, the best quality that you can afford and find without hassle. If the chocolate is inviting when you bite into it, it's certainly good enough for cooking. This is why I avoid chocolate chips and premade sauces; they're usually not delicious when eaten straight, and it's simple enough to chunk, chop, or melt a good eating chocolate. Your desserts will be much better for that bit of extra work.

Good chocolate is available everywhere, even in supermarkets. You can even use good candy-bar chocolate for cooking; you're not limited to whatever happens to be on the shelf next to the flour. Go by quality first, then by type of chocolate. For most desserts—and for eating, actually—I turn to bittersweet or semisweet chocolate. To help you make the best decisions, here are the basics.

How Chocolate Is Made

Chocolate starts with cacao beans, the seeds of the tropical cacao tree. Twenty to fifty of them grow in an oblong pod; it takes about four hundred seeds to make a pound of chocolate. Once the seeds and the pulp are collected, they're fermented, a process that changes their chemistry and develops flavor; from here out they're called *cocoa beans*. The beans are dried (by machine or, preferably, in the sun; you can begin to see how it's possible to become as obsessive about chocolate as it is about wine). They're then sorted, roasted, and shelled. All this produces the nib, which is ground and refined into chocolate liquor (which contains no alcohol but can be thought of as a straight shot of chocolate). Separating the solids from the fat in chocolate liquor results in two products: cocoa powder and cocoa butter.

To get to edible chocolate, the liquor is mixed with other ingredients—sugar, vanilla, additional cocoa butter, milk, or (usually less desirable) vegetable oils or other additives—then gently stirred or "conched." Before chocolate can be molded and sold, it is tempered, a heating and cooling process that keeps it from crystallizing and makes the chocolate hard, smooth, and glossy. It's a complicated procedure, and here's the bottom line: The

Making Babycakes and Cupcakes

The major difference between cupcakes and babycakes is those little paper accordion cups, which you set into muffin tins and fill. (This also makes them a little smaller than babycakes, which are usually baked individually, in ramekins.) In both cases, the individual servings ratchet up the fancy factor. Add a bit of frosting or just a dollop of soft whipped cream and you're suddenly a pastry chef.

Because they're smaller, these cook more quickly, so check them frequently after the first 10 minutes. Allow the cakes to cool in their ramekins and serve as is or turn them out as directed. Glaze, soak, coat, or frost and garnish as you would a large cake.

quality of the ingredients, the number of additives, and the level of attention during the production process are what distinguishes good chocolate from bad.

How to Buy Chocolate

The types of chocolate are determined by the percentage of cocoa solids (essentially the chocolate liquor content) and how they are processed. Some names are used interchangeably, so it's best to read the label to know exactly what you're getting. A general rule of thumb: The higher the percentage of solids, the less sweet the chocolate, because there's less sugar in the formula. (Generally, higher percentages of chocolate solids mean not much else to muck up the flavor.)

Here's a quick rundown of the lingo:

Unsweetened Chocolate
Baking Chocolate, Chocolate Liquor

A combination of cocoa solids and cocoa butter and nothing else; 100 percent cocoa. Unsweetened chocolate is too bitter to eat but is useful for home chocolate making, cooking, and baking.

Bittersweet Chocolate
Semisweet, Dark, Extra Dark, Extra Bittersweet

This is the type of chocolate I use most often. The solid cocoa content ranges from 35 to 99 percent, with less than 12 percent milk solids. That's a big range, so look for an exact number, and if none is mentioned, check out the ingredient list to see what else is included. Just having a high percentage of solids doesn't guarantee good quality, but it does mean there isn't a lot of room for fillers. Try a few brands before settling on your favorites for cooking. First listen to the snap when you break a piece in two; it should sound crisp. Many good-quality bittersweet chocolates taste almost chalky if you're not used to them, but they coat your mouth evenly without any waxiness or grittiness (that's the cocoa butter at work).

Dark Chocolate
Sweet

With 15 to 34 percent cocoa solids and no more than 12 percent milk solids. Sweet chocolate is the "official" name, though it's commonly called *dark chocolate*. The good stuff is fine for eating, though not really for cooking, because it doesn't allow you to control the sweetness of your desserts as well as unsweetened and bittersweet chocolates.

Milk Chocolate

If you like sweet, melt-in-your-mouth chocolate, this is it; it must contain a minimum of 10 percent cocoa solids, 12 percent milk solids, and 3.39 percent milk fat. But don't skimp. Make sure it includes real ingredients and tastes rich and almost buttery. Milk chocolate should be as complex as bittersweet or dark chocolate, with the flavors muted against a backdrop of creaminess.

German (or German's) Sweet Chocolate

This is not from Germany; the name comes from its inventor, Samuel German, who in 1852 invented a sweetened baking bar for the Baker's Chocolate Company. It is sweeter than bittersweet chocolate. (And yes, the famous cake comes from this brand of chocolate, not the country.) Not super-high quality.

Cocoa Powder

After cocoa butter is pressed out of the nibs—or separated from the chocolate liquor—the solids are finely ground into a powder. "Dutched," "Dutch process," or "alkalized" cocoa is the most common; it's been treated with an alkaline ingredient to reduce acidity and darken the color. "Natural" cocoa powder is harder to find but worth the hunt and extra expense. It's light brown, with more chocolate flavor. But they're interchangeable in the recipes here. (If you use natural cocoa and there's no baking soda in the recipe, add a pinch to balance the acidity and improve leavening.)

 Fast   Make Ahead   **V** Vegetarian

White Chocolate

White chocolate is technically not chocolate but a confection made from cocoa butter. It must contain at least 20 percent cocoa butter, 14 percent milk solids, and 3.39 percent milk fat. It's a completely different ingredient, though you can always substitute white chocolate for dark or milk.

There's a chasm between good white chocolate and the cheap stuff. First, scan the label for strange-sounding ingredients; cocoa butter should be the first ingredient. Always taste it before you cook with it. Good white chocolate has a subtle flavor and isn't waxy, gritty, or bland. At its best, it melts very slowly in your mouth and is something like what you might imagine eating straight vanilla would be like. It doesn't keep nearly as long as dark chocolate; only a few weeks.

Storing Chocolate

There's no need to refrigerate chocolate, but you should keep it in a cool, dry place (the fridge is as good as any, as long as it's well wrapped). Stored properly, chocolate can last for at least a year; bittersweet chocolate can even improve as it ages.

Sometimes chocolate develops a white or gray sheen or thin coating: don't panic. The chocolate hasn't gone bad; it's "bloomed," a condition caused by too much moisture or humidity or fluctuating temperatures, which cause the fat or sugar to come to the surface of the chocolate and crystallize. In either case the chocolate is still perfectly fine for cooking as long as you're not making coated candy. It's also okay to eat bloomed chocolate out of hand, though it may be grainy.

Cooking with Chocolate

Good-quality chocolate bars are fine for melting or finely chopping, but if you want big chunks or decorative shavings, buy a piece from a larger brick; specialty and many natural food stores sell chocolate like this. Chop with a chef's knife on a cutting board. To make chocolate shavings, put the chocolate on a clean cloth and carefully pull the knife toward you. It might take a couple passes to get the hang of it, but they're surprisingly easy.

Be careful when you melt chocolate, because it scorches easily. First, chop the chocolate (pieces melt faster than big chunks). Then use a double boiler with your chocolate in the top layer and stir until melted. Or melt the chocolate directly over the lowest possible heat, keeping a *very* close eye on it. Or microwave the chocolate for a minute or two at the lowest setting; watch it like a hawk and interrupt to stir once or twice. Melting chocolate with liquids is trickier, so I always melt the chocolate alone, then work with it.

Chocolate Layer Cake

MAKES: At least 10 servings
TIME: About 1 hour

The real deal. Frost with Chocolate, Mocha, or Peanut Buttercream (page 918), or Caramel Frosting (page 922).

8 tablespoons (1 stick) unsalted butter, softened, plus some for the pans and the paper

2 cups cake or all-purpose flour, plus some for the pans

3 ounces unsweetened chocolate, roughly chopped

1 cup sugar

2 eggs, separated

1 teaspoon vanilla extract

2 teaspoons baking powder

1/2 teaspoon baking soda

1/2 teaspoon salt

1 1/4 cups milk

❶ Heat the oven to 350°F. Grease the bottom and sides of two 9-inch or three 8-inch layer cake pans; cover the bottom with a circle of wax or parchment paper, grease the paper, and sift flour over the pans; invert and tap to remove the excess flour.

❷ Melt the chocolate in a small saucepan over very low heat or in a double boiler over hot—not boiling—water, stirring occasionally. When the chocolate is just about melted, remove from the heat and continue to stir until smooth.

❸ Use an electric mixer to cream the butter until smooth, then gradually add the sugar. Beat until light in color and fluffy, 3 or 4 minutes. Beat in the egg yolks, one at a time, then the vanilla, and finally the chocolate. Combine the flour, baking powder, baking soda, and salt; stir into the chocolate mixture, a little at a time, alternating with the milk. Stir just until smooth.

❹ Wash the beaters thoroughly, then beat the egg whites until they hold soft peaks. Use your hand or a rubber spatula to fold them gently but thoroughly into the batter. Turn it into the pans and bake until a toothpick inserted into the center of the cakes comes out clean, about 30 minutes. Let the cake cool in the pan for 5 minutes, then invert onto a rack to finish cooling.

❺ Frost or glaze if you like (see pages 917–919). Store at room temperature, covered with wax paper, for up to a day or two; use plastic wrap and it will keep for an extra day or so.

Chocolate Cinnamon Cake. Grind a cinnamon stick for the best results: Substitute 2 teaspoons ground cinnamon for the vanilla extract.

Devil's Food Cake. Substitute 1 cup sour cream or buttermilk for the regular milk; omit the baking powder and increase the baking soda to 1¹/₂ teaspoons. Baking time will be a few minutes less.

Angel Food Cake

MAKES: At least 10 servings
TIME: About 1¹/₂ hours, plus time to cool

Spongy, light, and wonderful, with virtually no fat and a delicate sweet flavor. The tube shape of the cake makes it ideal for drizzling with a glaze (see page 919) or Chocolate Sauce (page 920). Or slice and serve with any fruit sauce (see pages 924) or simply with some sliced fruit tossed with a little sugar.

1 cup cake (*not* all-purpose) flour, sifted
1¹/₂ cups sugar
9 egg whites
¹/₄ teaspoon salt
1 teaspoon cream of tartar
1 teaspoon vanilla extract
¹/₂ teaspoon almond extract

❶ Heat the oven to 325°F.

❷ Sift the flour and ¹/₂ cup of the sugar together. Repeat.

❸ Beat the egg whites until foamy. Add the salt and cream of tartar and continue to beat until they hold soft peaks. Beat in the remaining sugar and the extracts and continue to beat until the peaks become a little stiffer.

❹ Gradually and gently fold in the flour mixture, using a rubber spatula or your hand. Turn the batter into an ungreased 9- or 10-inch tube pan (not one with ridged sides) and bake for 45 to 60 minutes, until the cake is firm, resilient, and nicely browned.

❺ Invert the cake onto a rack and let cool for about an hour. Run a dull knife carefully around the sides of the cake and remove. Cool completely before slicing with a serrated knife or pulling apart with two forks. Angel Food Cake is best the day it's made; it becomes stale quickly (although it is wonderful toasted).

Chocolate Angel Food Cake. In Step 2, substitute ¹/₄ cup cocoa powder for ¹/₄ cup of the flour. (To marble the cake, make two batters, one with all flour and one with ¹/₈ cup cocoa substituted for ¹/₈ cup flour. Add the batters alternately to the tube pan and swirl together with a knife or spatula before baking.)

Butter-Almond Cake

MAKES: At least 8 servings

TIME: About 1 hour

Ground almonds (you can use hazelnuts or walnuts instead if you like) serve as the flour in this rich cake. Use blanched almonds for a mild taste and ivory color or skin-on almonds for a nuttier flavor and look. This cake can be served plain, with a little confectioners' sugar, or with some fruit salad. Or you can split, fill, and top it with Whipped Cream (page 882), jam, or any frosting (see pages 917–918).

12 tablespoons (1¹/₂ sticks) unsalted butter, softened, plus some for the pan and the paper

All-purpose flour for the pan

1¹/₄ cups sugar

6 eggs

8 ounces almonds

Grated or minced zest of 1 lemon or orange, or more if you like

❶ Heat the oven to 350°F. Butter the bottom and sides of a 2-inch-deep 10-inch layer cake or springform pan; cover the bottom with a circle of wax or parchment paper, butter the paper, and sift flour over the whole pan; invert and tap to remove the excess flour.

❷ Use an electric mixer to cream together the butter and ¹/₄ cup of the sugar. Separate 3 of the eggs and reserve the whites. Beat in the yolks one at a time, until the mixture is light in color.

❸ Grind the nuts in a food processor until they are the consistency of meal. Turn them into a bowl and mix them with ³/₄ cup of the remaining sugar and the citrus zest. Beat in 3 whole eggs, one at a time, blending well.

❹ Wash the beaters thoroughly and beat the egg whites; when they are foamy, gradually beat in the remaining ¹/₄ cup sugar, until the whites hold soft peaks. Combine the butter and nut mixtures and stir. Gently fold in the beaten egg whites and pour into the pan.

❺ Bake until a toothpick inserted into the center of the cake comes out clean, about 30 minutes. Let cool for 10 minutes, then unmold. Store at room temperature, covered with wax paper, for up to a day or two; use plastic wrap and it will keep for an extra day or so.

Strawberry (or Other Fruit) Shortcakes

MAKES: 12 shortcakes (12 servings)

TIME: About 40 minutes from scratch, less with premade biscuits

Of course, strawberries are the classic filling, but use any ripe and flavorful fruit, like blueberries, blackberries or raspberries, peaches, apricots, or cherries. In winter, try apple slices sautéed in butter (see page 383) or poached pear slices (see page 400), along with a touch of cinnamon or cardamom in the biscuit dough.

1 recipe Yogurt or Buttermilk Biscuits (page 845; with 2 tablespoons sugar added to the dry ingredients) or Scones (page 845)

4 to 5 cups ripe berries or sliced fruit

2 tablespoons sugar, or to taste

2 cups cream, preferably not ultra-pasteurized

¹/₂ teaspoon vanilla extract

❶ Make the biscuits or scones and bake them. Let them cool on a rack; you don't want to eat them hot.

❷ Meanwhile, wash and prepare the fruit as needed. Toss with 1 tablespoon of the sugar, or more or less to taste, and let sit while you whip the cream. Whip the cream until it holds soft peaks, then slowly add the remaining sugar and the vanilla and whip for 1 minute more.

❸ Split the biscuits and fill them with cream and fruit. Serve immediately.

Olive Oil Cake

MAKES: 1 rectangular cake or 2 layers (at least 12 servings)
TIME: About 1 hour, plus time to cool

You'll probably be surprised at how delicious, fluffy, and moist this cake is; use a fruity olive oil for best results and finish with Lemon or Lime Glaze (page 919), Ginger-Marmalade Glaze (page 919), or Fruit Sauce, Two Ways (page 924).

Butter for the pan

$^1/_2$ cup extra virgin olive oil

1 cup sugar

4 eggs, separated

2 cups all-purpose flour

1$^1/_2$ teaspoons baking powder

$^1/_4$ teaspoon salt

$^1/_3$ cup freshly squeezed orange juice

2 teaspoons grated or finely minced orange or lemon zest

❶ Heat the oven to 350°F. Grease two 8- or 9-inch layer cake pans or one 9 × 13-inch pan with butter.

❷ Use an electric mixer to beat the oil and $^3/_4$ cup of the sugar together, then add the egg yolks and beat until thick and fluffy, scraping down the sides of the mixing bowl as necessary, 5 to 7 minutes. Meanwhile, combine the flour, baking powder, and salt in a bowl and set aside.

❸ Mix in the dry ingredients until smooth. Add the orange juice and zest and stir until blended. In a separate bowl, beat the egg whites until they foam, sprinkle in the remaining sugar while beating until the whites hold soft peaks; stir them in thoroughly, but as gently as possible (the base batter is very thick).

❹ Turn into the prepared pan and bake until a toothpick inserted into the center comes out clean, about 35 minutes. Let the cake cool in the pan for 15 minutes before removing it from the pan if you're using the layer cake pans; leave the cake in the 9 × 13-inch pan.

❺ Frost or glaze if you like. Store at room temperature, covered with wax paper, for up to a day or two.

Blueberry Pudding Cake

MAKES: At least 6 servings
TIME: About 1$^1/_4$ hours, plus time to cool

This is just how it sounds: soft and gooey, with a cakey crust. It's homey and comforting, especially with whipped cream. Try making it with other fruit, too.

4 tablespoons ($^1/_2$ stick) unsalted butter, melted, plus some for the pan

1 cup buttermilk

$^3/_4$ cup sugar

3 eggs, separated

$^1/_3$ cup all-purpose flour

Pinch salt

1$^1/_2$ cup blueberries

1 tablespoon grated lemon zest

❶ Heat the oven to 325°F. Grease an 8- or 9-inch ceramic or glass baking dish or a deep dish pie plate with unmelted butter.

❷ Put the butter, buttermilk, $^1/_2$ cup of the sugar, the egg yolks, flour, and salt in a blender or food processor and purée until smooth. Pour the batter into a bowl. Stir in the blueberries and zest and set aside.

❸ In a separate bowl, beat the egg whites until they hold soft peaks, sprinkle in the remaining $^1/_4$ cup sugar while beating until the whites hold stiff peaks; fold them into the batter gently but thoroughly.

❹ Turn the batter into the prepared dish and put the dish in a baking pan large enough to hold it comfortably. Add enough warm water to the baking pan to come to within an inch or so of the top of the dish (for more information about water baths, see page 949). Transfer carefully to the oven and bake until the top is golden brown and the center is just set but slightly jiggly, about 50 minutes.

5 Remove the cake from the oven and cool the dish completely on a rack, cover with plastic wrap, then refrigerate until chilled, at least 3 hours, before serving. This will keep in the refrigerator for 2 or 3 days.

Pineapple Upside-Down Cake

MAKES: One 9-inch cake (at least 8 servings)
TIME: About 1 hour

A sweet and juicy pineapple is a must here so the fruit's sugary juices seep out and caramelize to create a rich, almost crunchy topping when the cake is inverted. Use a skillet if you want to maximize this browning effect.

8 tablespoons (1 stick) unsalted butter, melted

$^1/_2$ cup brown sugar

Six $^1/_2$-inch-thick slices peeled and cored fresh pineapple or as many as will fit in the pan

1 cup buttermilk

2 eggs

$^1/_2$ cup granulated sugar

2 cups all-purpose flour

1 teaspoon baking soda

$^1/_4$ teaspoon salt

1 Heat the oven to 350°F. Liberally grease a 9-inch round cake pan or cast-iron skillet with 4 tablespoons of the butter. Sprinkle the brown sugar evenly over the bottom of the pan and arrange the pineapple slices in a single layer in the pan; set aside.

2 Whisk the remaining melted butter, buttermilk, eggs, and granulated sugar together until foamy. In a separate bowl, combine the flour, baking soda, and salt; gradually add the egg mixture to the flour mixture and stir until well incorporated.

3 Carefully spread the batter over the pineapple, using a spatula to make sure it's evenly distributed. Bake until the top of the cake is golden brown and a toothpick inserted into the center comes out clean, about 50 to 60 minutes. Let the cake cool in the pan for just 5 minutes.

4 Run a knife around the edge of the pan. Put a serving plate on top of the cake pan and flip so that the serving plate is on the bottom and the cake pan is on top. The cake should fall out onto the serving plate. If the cake sticks, turn it back right side up and run the knife along the edge again, then use a spatula to gently lift around the edge. Invert the cake again onto the plate and tap on the bottom of the pan. If any of the fruit sticks to the pan, don't worry; simply use a knife to remove the pieces and fill in any gaps on the top of the cake. Serve warm with ice cream.

Plum Upside-Down Cake. Add some rosemary for an unusual twist: For the pineapple, substitute 4 or 5 ripe, sweet plums, pitted and cut into slices or chunks, and add 1$^1/_2$ tablespoons finely chopped fresh rosemary leaves if you like. Sprinkle on the rosemary with the brown sugar in Step 1.

Apple Upside-Down Cake. For the pineapple, substitute 3 or 4 medium apples, peeled, cored, and sliced, and add 1 teaspoon ground cinnamon if you like. Add the cinnamon along with the flour in Step 2.

Berry Upside-Down Cake. For the pineapple, use 3 to 4 cups fresh berries, like blackberries, blueberries, raspberries, or gooseberries. If you use strawberries, quarter them first.

Rich Chocolate Torte

MAKES: At least 10 servings
TIME: About 3 hours, largely unattended

This is the kind of thing that restaurants would have you believe is magic. On the contrary, there are only

two challenges here: assembling the ingredients and freeing up enough time to make the cake, filling, and glaze.

The best ways to finish this cake: Top with Whipped Cream (page 882) or serve with a raspberry purée (see page 923) and/or Vanilla Custard Sauce (page 924).

8 tablespoons (1 stick) unsalted butter, softened, plus some for the pan and the paper

1 cup all-purpose flour, plus some for the pan

3 ounces unsweetened chocolate

5 whole eggs

1 cup plus 2 tablespoons sugar

2 teaspoons vanilla extract

Pinch salt

2 egg yolks

2 tablespoons cocoa powder

1 recipe Chocolate Glaze (page 921)

1 Heat the oven to 350°F. Grease the bottom and sides of a 9-inch round cake pan; cover the bottom with a circle of wax or parchment paper, butter the paper, and sift a little flour over the whole pan; invert and tap to remove the excess flour.

2 Melt the chocolate with $\frac{1}{2}$ cup water over low heat; cool. Use an electric mixer to beat the whole eggs until light; gradually add 1 cup of the sugar, continuing to beat until the mixture is very thick. Gently stir in half the flour, then the melted chocolate, then the remaining flour, and finally half of the vanilla and the salt. Turn into the prepared cake pan and bake until the cake is firm and a toothpick inserted in the center comes out dry, or nearly so, 40 to 50 minutes. Cool for 5 minutes before turning out onto a rack to finish cooling.

3 To make the filling, put the egg yolks in a blender. (If you're worried about using raw eggs, see page 798 for some alternatives.) Add the remaining sugar, the remaining vanilla, and the cocoa. Turn on the blender and add the butter, a little at a time. After the butter is blended in, refrigerate until the filling is spreadable, at least an hour.

4 When the cake is completely cool, use a serrated knife to carefully split it in half horizontally. Spread the bottom layer with chilled filling, then put the top layer in place. Chill for an hour or so, then make the glaze. Use a lightly oiled spatula to spread the glaze over the top and sides of the torte. Serve small slices, with Whipped Cream (page 882) if you like. Because of its dense texture, this cake keeps better than most; you can cover and refrigerate it for up to a couple of days—it will remain a treat.

Chocolate Hazelnut Torte. Substitute $\frac{1}{4}$ cup finely ground hazelnuts for $\frac{1}{4}$ cup of the flour. Stir $\frac{1}{2}$ cup lightly toasted hazelnuts (see page 317) into the batter just before turning into the pan.

Lemon Cheesecake with Sour Cream Topping

MAKES: At least 12 servings
TIME: About $1\frac{1}{2}$ hours

Most veteran cooks have their favorite cheesecake, and this is mine. It's relatively low in sugar, and the lemon provides balance. You can skip the sour cream topping if you feel that enough is enough.

Unsalted butter for greasing the pan

Double recipe Graham Cracker Crust (page 930)

4 eggs, separated

Three 8-ounce packages cream cheese, softened

Grated zest and juice of 1 lemon

1 cup sugar, plus 1 optional tablespoon

1 tablespoon all-purpose flour

2 cups sour cream (optional)

1 teaspoon vanilla extract (optional)

1 Liberally butter a 9-inch springform pan, then press the crust into the bottom. Heat the oven to 325°F.

2 Use an electric mixer to beat the egg yolks until light; add the cream cheese, lemon zest and juice, and 1 cup of the sugar and beat until smooth. Stir in the flour.

3 Beat the egg whites until they hold soft peaks; use a rubber spatula or your hand to fold them into the yolk-cheese mixture gently but thoroughly. Turn the batter into the prepared pan and put the pan in a baking pan large enough to hold it comfortably. Add enough warm water to the baking pan to come to within an inch of the top of the springform pan. Transfer carefully to the oven and bake until the cake is just set and very lightly browned, about 1 hour.

4 the topping, turn the oven up to 450°F and combine the sour cream with the vanilla and the remaining 1 tablespoon sugar if you're using it; spread on the top of the cake. Return it to the oven for 10 minutes, without the water bath; turn off the oven and let the cake cool for 30 minutes before removing it. With or without the topping, cool the cake completely on a rack, cover with plastic wrap, then refrigerate until well chilled before slicing and serving. This will keep in good shape, refrigerated, for several days.

Ricotta Cheesecake. This is somewhat lighter (and far lower in calories, especially if you use part-skim ricotta): Substitute 1½ pounds fresh ricotta for the cream cheese. Beat it in an electric mixer until lightened, then add the yolks. Increase the sugar to 1¼ cups. Substitute 1 tablespoon grated orange zest for the lemon zest and use 1 additional teaspoon vanilla in place of the lemon juice. You can omit or include the sour cream topping, as you like.

Cheesecake with Chocolate Topping. Definitely richer and two colors are nice too: Substitute the teaspoon of vanilla for the lemon zest and juice. Omit the optional tablespoon of sugar and the sour cream.

Make Chocolate Glaze (page 921). After the cake cools a bit, pour the glaze over the top and then let it finish cooling as directed.

Frostings, Glazes, Soaks, and Sauces

These add richness, flavor, moisture, and sometimes sweetness to cakes. You can mix and match any of these recipes with others in the chapter. It's all fair game. And when you feel a little more ambitious, try some of the more elaborate combinations in "Fancy Desserts from Simple Recipes" (page 888). But don't go overboard: Finish your dessert as you would any other dish, with components that complement, contrast, or enhance both flavor and texture, and you won't overdo it.

Vanilla Buttercream Frosting

MAKES: Enough frosting and filling for one 9-inch layer cake or 2 dozen cupcakes

TIME: 10 minutes

There is no easier frosting, and it's flexible enough (see the variations) to pair well with just about any cake, cupcake, or cookie. Cream is best here, but you can use milk if you prefer.

8 tablespoons (1 stick) unsalted butter, softened

4 cups confectioners' sugar

6 tablespoons cream or milk, plus a little more if needed

2 teaspoons vanilla extract

Pinch salt

① Use a fork or an electric mixer to cream the butter. Gradually work in the sugar, alternating with the cream and beating well after each addition.

② Stir in the vanilla and salt. If the frosting is too thick to spread, add a little more cream, a teaspoon at a time. If it's too thin (unlikely, but possible, especially after the addition of lemon or orange juice as in the variation that follows), refrigerate; it will thicken as the butter hardens.

Chocolate Buttercream Frosting. Add 2 ounces unsweetened chocolate, melted over very low heat in a double boiler and cooled, to the mixture after adding about half of the sugar.

Mocha Buttercream Frosting. An adult frosting: Add 1 ounce unsweetened chocolate, melted and cooled as in the preceding variation, to the mixture after adding about half the sugar. Substitute 2 tablespoons very strong coffee (espresso is best) for 2 tablespoons of the cream or milk.

Lemon or Orange Frosting. This is very good made with half butter and half cream cheese, but it can also be made with all butter: Omit the cream. Reduce the vanilla to 1 teaspoon. Thin the mixture with 1 large egg yolk (if you're worried about using raw eggs, see page 798) and 1 teaspoon freshly squeezed lemon juice or 1 tablespoon freshly squeezed orange juice or undiluted orange juice concentrate. Stir in 1 teaspoon grated or minced lemon zest or 1 tablespoon grated or minced orange zest.

Maple Buttercream Frosting. Thinner than the usual buttercream; use for cakes or spread on pancakes, waffles, and French toast: Substitute $^{1}/_{2}$ cup maple syrup for half the confectioners' sugar. Omit the vanilla. Proceed with the recipe, then refrigerate the frosting to solidify it somewhat before using.

Peanut Buttercream Frosting. Perfect with chocolate cupcakes or sandwiched between oatmeal cookies: Substitute $^{1}/_{4}$ cup smooth peanut butter for half the

butter. Proceed with the recipe; this may require more cream to get it to the right consistency.

Seven-Minute Frosting

MAKES: Enough frosting and filling for one 9-inch layer cake or 2 dozen cupcakes

TIME: 10 minutes

Pure white and fluffy, this meringuelike frosting is a classic. It looks beautiful on a Coconut Layer Cake (page 909) or on any kind of cupcake in big dollops.

1$^{1}/_{4}$ cups sugar

2 egg whites

2 tablespoons light corn syrup

$^{1}/_{2}$ teaspoon vanilla extract (optional)

Pinch salt

① Put all the ingredients in the top of a double boiler or in a large metal bowl that fits at least halfway into a pot. Bring about 2 inches of water to a boil in the pot.

② Use a hand-held electric mixer to combine the sugar, egg whites, corn syrup, and $^{1}/_{3}$ cup water; then put the bowl or double boiler over the boiling water while mixing on high speed. Continue mixing the egg mixture using a stirring motion with the beaters until it's fluffy and white, about 7 minutes. Remove from the heat, add the vanilla if you're using it and the salt, and continue beating until the frosting is cooled and holds stiff peaks. Use immediately.

Coconut Frosting. Use with the Coconut Layer Cake (page 909) or on cupcakes: Stir a cup or so shredded coconut into the finished frosting and/or sprinkle the finished frosted item with shredded coconut.

Raspberry Frosting. Pretty pink; perfect for a celebration: Substitute $^{1}/_{4}$ cup seedless raspberry jam for the corn syrup and 2 tablespoon of the sugar. Proceed with the recipe.

Orange Glaze

MAKES: Enough for any cake
TIME: 10 minutes

This is so simple and uncomplicated, it's barely a recipe: Put some confectioners' sugar in a bowl and stir in liquid until it's the consistency of maple syrup (thicker if you want to spread it on or sandwich it between cookies).

Use any nearly any citrus in place of the orange; tangerine, grapefruit, and blood orange all work well.

    1/2 cup freshly squeezed orange juice

    1 tablespoon grated orange zest

    1/2 teaspoon vanilla extract (optional)

    3 cups confectioners' sugar, plus more as needed

    Pinch salt

Combine all the ingredients and beat until combined and smooth; it should be about the consistency of thick maple syrup—just pourable. Use immediately or store, covered, in the refrigerator for up to 2 weeks.

Creamy Orange Glaze. Substitute 1/4 cup cream for half of the orange juice and add 3 tablespoons very soft butter if you like.

Vanilla Glaze. Substitute cream, milk, or a combination for the orange juice. Omit the zest and use the vanilla extract, increasing it to 1 teaspoon if you like.

Lemon or Lime Glaze. Substitute 1/4 cup lemon or lime juice and 1/4 cup water for the orange juice. Omit the vanilla.

Mocha Glaze. Substitute 1/2 cup freshly brewed coffee for the orange juice and add 1 ounce melted semisweet or bittersweet chocolate or 3 tablespoons cocoa powder. Omit the zest.

Coconut Glaze. Omit the shredded coconut if you want a smooth glaze: Substitute coconut milk for the orange juice and 1/4 cup shredded coconut for the zest. Omit the vanilla extract.

Rich Vanilla Cake Soak

MAKES: Enough for any single-layer square or round cake
TIME: 10 minutes

Soaking a cake yields a real treat, turning it into something else entirely, like a pudding with more structure. And depending on the soak you choose, the flavor can run from subtle to pronounced. Using real vanilla beans here is key (vanilla extract will work, but it's just not the same).

For oblong or other large cakes baked in bundt or ring pans, double this recipe.

    1 cup cream, half-and-half, or milk

    1/4 cup sugar

    Pinch salt

    2 tablespoons unsalted butter (optional)

    1 vanilla bean or 1 tablespoon vanilla extract

❶ Put the cream, sugar, salt, and butter if you're using it in a small pot. Split the vanilla bean in half lengthwise and use a small sharp knife to scrape the seeds into the cream mixture; add the pod too. Cook over low heat (do not boil), whisking frequently, until the sugar is dissolved and the vanilla is fragrant, about 10 minutes. Let cool to room temperature, then remove and discard the pod (or whisk in the extract if using).

❷ To use, leave the cake to cool in the pan (or return it if you took it out to cool it); pour the soak over the cooled cake and let it sit for at least an hour. Or put the soak in a jar and refrigerate for a day or two; bring to room temperature before using.

Boozy Cake Soak. For adults only unless you cook off the alcohol: Substitute 1/2 cup bourbon or Calvados, whiskey, brandy, cognac, limoncello, or any compatible liquor for half the cream; substitute water for the remaining 1/2 cup cream if you like. For Step 1, either proceed as directed (cooking off the alcohol) or combine the water, sugar, butter, and vanilla; cook and let sit, then add the alcohol.

4 More Uses for Chocolate Ganache

Few dessert sauces have as many uses as ganache; here are my favorites.

1. **Ganache Cake Coating:** Put your cake on a wire rack over a baking sheet with sides. Warm the ganache; it should be slightly thicker than heavy cream so it can spread over the cake. Pour or ladle the ganache onto the cake from the middle outward, letting it flow down the sides of the cake as well. Do not spread the ganache as it will pick up cake crumbs and ruin the smooth coating. Transfer the cake, rack, pan, and all, to the fridge until the ganache sets, about 30 minutes. Transfer the cake to a serving plate and scrape up the leftover ganache in the pan; use it for filling or truffles (it will have crumbs in it so it's not suitable as a coating or sauce). Lovely with Butter-Almond Cake (page 913), Golden Layer Cake (page 907), or Chocolate Layer Cake (page 911).

2. **Ganache Cake Frosting or Filling:** Starting with a sturdy cake that doesn't crumb much, warm the ganache so it's spreadable; use a warm metal spatula to spread a layer of ganache 1/4 inch or so thick over the surface of the cake. (For a fragile cake that crumbles easily, follow the directions in "Ganache Cake Coating" above.)

3. **Ganache Sauce:** Thin the ganache with additional cream; it should be easily pourable and not harden too much when cooled to room temperature. To test the consistency, spread a small spoonful on a plate; it should thicken but remain very soft if not saucy. Pair it with Banana Strudel (page 947), Bread Pudding (page 953), or Cream Puffs (page 942).

4. **Quick Ganache Truffles:** Chill the ganache in the fridge until it's solid all the way through, 1 to 2 hours depending on quantity. Scoop out a tablespoonful, quickly roll it into a 1-inch ball (wearing latex gloves helps to prevent melting); repeat, lining the truffles on a plate or baking sheet. If the truffles become too soft to handle, stick them in the fridge or freezer for a few minutes. Roll them in cocoa powder, powdered sugar, or a sugar and ground cinnamon mixture. Serve immediately or store, wrapped in plastic, in the fridge for a day or so.

Vanilla–Brown Sugar Cake Soak. Substitute 1 cup water for the cream and use 1/2 cup brown sugar for the white sugar. Proceed as directed.

Chocolate Ganache

MAKES: About 1 1/2 cups
TIME: 15 minutes

Ganache—a simple mixture of chocolate and cream with a fancy French name—is one of the most useful of all dessert sauces (see "4 More Uses for Chocolate Ganache"). You can use milk or white chocolate in place of bittersweet chocolate; just decrease the cream to 3/4 cup.

1 cup cream

8 ounces bittersweet chocolate, chopped

❶ Put the cream in a pot and heat it until it's steaming. Put the chocolate in a bowl, pour on the hot cream, and stir until the chocolate is melted and fully incorporated.

❷ Use immediately as a sauce or let cool to room temperature and whip to a smooth frosting or filling.

      Fast   Make Ahead   Vegetarian

Chocolate Glaze. Reduce the cream to ³/₄ cup. Add 6 tablespoons (³/₄ stick) unsalted butter; ¹/₂ cup confectioners' sugar (or a little more to taste); ¹/₂ teaspoon vanilla extract, and a tiny pinch of salt. Proceed with the recipe, melting the butter in the cream and stirring in the other ingredients with the chocolate. Use immediately or store, covered, in the fridge and melt over very low heat (or in a double boiler) before using.

Chocolate Sauce

MAKES: About 1¹/₂ cups
TIME: 15 minutes

This is a rich chocolate sauce, more substantial than syrup. Note the Hot Fudge Sauce variation.

4 ounces semisweet or bittersweet chocolate, chopped

4 tablespoons (¹/₂ stick) unsalted butter

¹/₄ cup sugar

Pinch salt

1 teaspoon vanilla extract

❶ Combine the chocolate, butter, sugar, salt and ¹/₄ cup water in a small saucepan over very low heat. Cook, stirring, until the chocolate melts and the mixture is smooth.

❷ Add the vanilla and serve immediately, keep warm over hot water until ready to serve, or refrigerate for up to a week and rewarm before using.

Hot Fudge Sauce. This is chewy and fudgy when you put it on top of ice cream: After the ingredients are combined, add ¹/₃ cup corn syrup to the mixture. Bring to a boil, turn the heat to low, and cook for 5 to 10 minutes, until thick and shiny. Add vanilla and serve hot. Or store for up to a week and re-

heat very gently (a double boiler is best) before serving.

Sugar Syrup

MAKES: 2 cups
TIME: 10 minutes

Also called *simple syrup,* this is perfect for adding sweetness to something without worrying about the sugar dissolving. It comes in handy when making sorbets and granitas and for sweetening iced drinks, including tea, coffee, and cocktails.

Make this syrup in any quantity you need; the ratio—equal parts water and sugar—is always the same.

2 cups sugar

Combine the sugar and 2 cups water in a small pot; bring to a boil and cook until the sugar is dissolved, stirring occasionally. Set aside and cool to room temperature. Use immediately or store in a clean container or jar, covered, in the fridge for up to 6 months.

Coffee Syrup. Use as you would any dessert sauce: Replace some or all of the water with strong coffee or espresso.

7 Ways to Flavor Sugar Syrup
Steep the flavoring in the hot syrup for 5 to 10 minutes, then strain out or leave in (for larger items, like vanilla pods).
1. Seeds from a vanilla bean, with the scraped pod if you like
2. Cinnamon sticks, whole cloves, allspice, or crushed cardamom pods
3. Citrus zest, any kind, grated, minced, or in strips
4. Tea leaves (green tea is especially nice)
5. Ginger, grated or minced
6. Lavender buds (just a bit or it'll taste soapy)
7. Fresh herbs, whole stems, especially mint, peppermint, verbena, and basil

Caramel

MAKES: About 1½ cups
TIME: 20 minutes

The most elementary candy or candy coating (it hardens when it cools), the base for a range sauces . . . the uses are many.

Beware: This mixture gets extremely hot and can cause bad burns; so resist any temptation to stick your finger into the hot sauce or lick the coated spoon until you're absolutely sure it's cooled.

2 cups sugar

Pinch salt

1 Combine the sugar and salt with 1 cup water in a broad saucepan or deep skillet over medium-low heat.

Cook until the sugar dissolves, without stirring, but swirling the pan gently, 3 to 5 minutes.

2 The mixture will bubble and gradually darken; cook until it's caramel colored and the temperature measures 245°F (a small piece of it will form a firm ball when dropped into a glass of cold water, but the thermometer is an easier and surer test), about 15 minutes.

3 Carefully pour or drizzle over whatever you like for a crunchy candy coating, drizzle onto wax paper to make decorative garnishes, or make one of the sauces that follow.

Clear Caramel Sauce. After Step 2, carefully add ¼ cup water (it will bubble up) and stir until it's incorporated. Add more water to reach the desired consistency.

Creamy Caramel Sauce. Substitute cream (preferably not ultra-pasteurized) for the water and add 2 tablespoons unsalted butter and 1 teaspoon vanilla extract if you like. Proceed with the recipe, adding the vanilla after Step 2 and adding more cream if it's too thick.

Boozy Caramel Sauce. Use the Creamy Caramel Sauce variation and add 2 or 3 tablespoons liqueur after Step 2.

Caramel Coffee Sauce. Substitute freshly brewed coffee or half coffee and half cream for the water.

Caramel Frosting. Make the Clear Caramel Sauce variation; after it cools completely, add 1 pound cream cheese, softened. Whip the cream cheese until fluffy and drizzle in the caramel until it's thoroughly mixed; thin with a little milk or cream as needed.

Butterscotch Sauce

MAKES: About 1½ cups
TIME: 10 minutes

Good butterscotch is like a good butter cookie—easy to make, simple tasting, and very rich.

 Fast   Make Ahead   Vegetarian

³/₄ cup cream

6 tablespoons (³/₄ stick) unsalted butter, cut into pieces

³/₄ cup brown sugar

Pinch salt

1 Combine the cream and butter in a small saucepan and cook over medium-low heat, stirring occasionally, until the butter melts.

2 Stir in the sugar and salt and cook, stirring frequently, until the mixture is thick and shiny, 5 to 10 minutes. Taste and add more sugar if you like. Use right away or refrigerate, well covered, for up to 1 week and rewarm before using.

Maple-Butter Sauce. Serve this with Bread Pudding (page 953) or French Toast (page 794) for a deluxe breakfast: Reduce the cream to ¹/₂ cup and substitute maple syrup for the brown sugar. In Step 2, add an egg yolk along with the maple syrup. Proceed with the recipe. Keeps for up to 3 days.

Berry Jam Glaze or Sauce

MAKES: Enough for any cake
TIME: 15 minutes

F **M** **V**

There is no glaze easier than this one; it's just jam thinned with water and makes virtually anything look terrific. Since it's pretty sticky, use a pastry brush or drizzle it.

1 cup berry jam or preserves

1 tablespoon freshly squeezed lemon juice (optional)

Put the jam in a small pot, add 1 cup water, and turn the heat to medium. Bring to a low bubble and cook to a syrupy consistency, about 10 minutes. Set aside to cool and mix in the lemon juice if you like; use immediately or store, covered, in the refrigerator for up to 2 weeks.

Apricot Jam Glaze. Add a pinch of cardamom and this glaze becomes exotic: Substitute apricot jam for the berry and add 1 teaspoon ground cardamom if you like.

Ginger-Marmalade Glaze. I love this with pound cake: Substitute orange marmalade for the berry jam and add 2 teaspoons finely minced ginger or 2 tablespoons chopped crystallized ginger.

The Basics of Fruit Purées

The most efficient method to purée fruit is with a blender; it's quick and makes a purée that's smooth if not velvety. The food processor is equally fast; it won't produce a super-smooth purée with hard fruit—like raw apples—but soft or cooked fruit becomes uniformly smooth. The third option is the hand method; use a fork or potato masher, either of which will leave some lumps.

For truly smooth purées, press the puréed fruit through a fine-mesh strainer set over a bowl. This works well only for cooked or very soft fruit, and it's time-consuming, but the results are creamy.

Occasionally you'll want to add liquid to the purée—for flavoring, sweetness, or simply if the fruit is hard and needs some liquid to get the purée going. Fruit juice, water, cream, and lemon or lime juice are good options, depending on the fruit and the purée's final use. Usually you'll add the liquid by the tablespoonful so you don't dilute the fruit flavor any more than you must.

Purées made from raw apples, pears, and bananas will brown quickly, so don't make them much in advance, though a good squeeze or two of lemon or lime juice—and coat your cutting board and knife in some for good measure—will minimize browning.

Strawberries, raspberries, blackberries, seeded grapes, and other fruit with tiny seeds may be strained after puréeing, as may fibrous fruit, like mangoes. Otherwise, strain as you think it's necessary to remove unwanted bits of flesh or skin. You will probably need to use a wooden spoon or the back of a ladle to push the pulp through a strainer; scrape the underside to remove every bit of fruit.

Fruit Sauce, Two Ways

MAKES: About 2 cups

TIME: 5 to 10 minutes

There are two ways I like to make fruit sauces: The first, which is no work at all, gives you pure, straightforward flavor and a very saucy consistency; it works well with soft fruits and berries. The second, which is thicker, is more luxurious, and wonderful with apples and pears. Take your pick.

Raw Fruit Method:

2 cups berries or other soft ripe fruit—peaches, cherries, nectarines, mangoes, etc.—picked over, pitted, peeled, washed, and/or dried as necessary

Confectioners' sugar, to taste

A little freshly squeezed orange or lemon juice or fruity white wine (optional)

❶ Purée the fruit in a blender; if you're using raspberries or blackberries, put the purée through a sieve to remove the seeds.

❷ Combine with confectioners' sugar to taste. If necessary, thin with a little water, or use orange juice, lemon juice, or fruity white wine. Use immediately or refrigerate for a day or two.

Cooked Fruit Method:

1/2 cup sugar

3 tablespoons unsalted butter

2 cups berries or other ripe fruit—apples, pears, bananas, peaches, cherries, nectarines, berries, mangoes, melons, etc.—picked over, pitted, peeled, washed, and/or dried as necessary

❶ Combine 1/2 cup water with the sugar and butter in a heavy-bottomed medium saucepan over medium-high heat and cook, shaking and stirring, until the mixture is thick and syrupy but not browned.

❷ Toss in the fruit and cook over low heat until the fruit begins to break up and release its juices, about 2 minutes for berries, longer for other fruit (some fruits, like apples, may also require the addition of a little more water). Press the fruit through a fine-mesh strainer or run it through a food mill to purée and remove any skins or seeds. Serve warm or at room temperature. This sauce keeps well, refrigerated, for up to a week.

Vanilla Custard Sauce

Crème Anglaise

MAKES: About 2 cups

TIME: 15 to 30 minutes

An excellent classic sauce for cakes, poached fruit, and more. This one-pot method is simple and yields fine results. You can change the flavor easily; see "Infusing Liquids with Flavor" (page 962).

1 vanilla bean, split, or 1 teaspoon vanilla extract

2 cups milk

4 egg yolks

1/2 cup sugar

❶ If you're using the vanilla bean, heat the milk and the bean together in a small saucepan until the milk steams. Remove from heat, cover and let sit for 15 minutes. Remove the bean and scrape the seeds into the milk. If you're not using the bean, just heat the milk.

❷ Once the milk has cooled back down to almost room temperature, add the remaining ingredients and whisk well to combine. Cook over medium heat, whisking almost constantly, until the mixture thickens and reaches 175–180°F. Don't let it boil. (There will be a thick coating on the back of a spoon; see the illustration on page 949.)

❸ While still hot, strain the sauce through a strainer and let cool a bit; stir in the vanilla extract if you're using it. You can serve the sauce warm or chilled. It keeps, tightly covered, in the refrigerator for up to 3 days.

 Fast   Make Ahead   **V** Vegetarian

Chocolate Custard Sauce. In Step 2, add ¹/₂ cup (about 3 ounces) chopped semisweet or bittersweet chocolate to the pot and let it melt as the mixture heats.

Citrus Custard Sauce. Lemon is traditional, but lime is delicious too: Omit the vanilla. Add the zest and juice of 3 lemons (or 4 limes) and 8 tablespoons (1 stick) unsalted butter. Double the sugar. Skip Step 1. In Step 2, combine the lemon juice and zest, butter, milk, yolks, and sugar all together in a medium saucepan and proceed with the recipe.

Streusel Topping

MAKES: About 2 cups

TIME: 10 minutes

This topping is like a delicate, crumbled nut cookie, lovely on any crisp or sprinkled on quick breads, muffins, tarts, or pies before baking. Use whole wheat flour for an earthy flavor; vary nuts and spices to complement a particular flavor in the food it's topping; or add 3 tablespoons cocoa powder for a chocolate-crumble topping.

8 tablespoons (1 stick) unsalted butter, softened

1 cup brown sugar

¹/₂ cup chopped walnuts, pecans, other nuts, or shredded coconut

1 tablespoon freshly squeezed lemon juice

¹/₂ teaspoon ground cinnamon, or to taste

1 cup all-purpose flour, plus more as needed

Pinch salt

1 Cream the butter and brown sugar using an electric mixer, food processor, or fork. Stir or pulse in the remaining ingredients until combined and crumbly; it won't hold together like a dough. (You can refrigerate or freeze until about 30 minutes before you're ready to use it. Defrost if necessary, then use.)

2 Crumble the mixture over a crisp, a fruit pie, quick bread, or muffins. Or bake on a sheet in a 350°F oven until golden brown, 15 to 20 minutes, and use as a filling for crêpes.

Oat Streusel Topping. The classic for crisps: If you like, substitute maple syrup or corn syrup for the brown sugar and ¹/₂ cup rolled oats (or other rolled grain) for half of the flour.

The Basics of Pies and Tarts

These fundamental American desserts were once made daily in many households, and no wonder: They combine common ingredients with easily mastered techniques for often dramatic and always satisfying results. All have some form of crust, a universally loved treat that almost always depends on a fair amount of fat—usually butter—to make it light, flaky, and delicious. What distinguishes pies and tarts from cobblers and crisps (see pages 883–884) is the composition of the crust, how it is formed, and whether it's on the top or bottom.

Though the technique for making pie and tart crusts must be learned, it is literally child's play. If you can roll out a Play-Doh pie, you can make a real one. If you don't feel up to the challenge, start with cobblers and crisps (in the Essential Recipes section on pages 880–888) and work your way up.

Though dedicated pie makers do get better and better at producing flaky, flavorful, nicely shaped, and beautifully colored crusts, it need not take years of trial and error to get the technique tight; in fact, you can make good crusts for pies, tarts, cheesecakes, crisps, and more your first time out, and quickly.

There are so few ingredients in the basic crust that good quality is absolutely vital for each one. The best crusts start with butter, although there are people who use a high percentage of shortening (I don't). Lard and butter, as it happens, complement each other well in crusts, but I usually use all butter: It gives the crust a rich, delicious flavor and good color (good lard and, admittedly, shortening do help with texture, but the former is sadly hard to find, and the latter—health issues aside—has a negative impact on flavor).

Technique and flour turn that butter into something magical. It isn't difficult; I routinely use my food processor to mix the dough for piecrusts, and I recommend you do too—it's quick, easy, efficient, and nearly foolproof. You can mix the dough by hand, of course, pinching the butter with flour between your fingers or using various utensils like a pastry blender or two forks. However you do it, the idea is to get small bits of butter coated in flour, which will make for a flaky and light crust. When the dough is formed you will be able to see bits of butter in it; this is a good thing—don't think it needs to be mixed more. In fact, the dough for pies and tarts should be handled minimally, because you don't want the gluten to develop as it does in bread dough; in these crusts you want tenderness, not chew.

Once you make a dough, let it rest in the refrigerator or freezer so the gluten relaxes. This also hardens the butter a bit, which makes rolling easier. Equally important, it helps the crust hold its shape in baking and form a flaky crust. Once the dough is frozen, it can be stored in the freezer for weeks or even months (be sure to wrap it well to prevent freezer burn).

Rolling the Dough

Transforming dough from a ball or disk to a fairly uniform round crust, less than $1/4$ inch thick, involves a combination of patience and practice. Ideally you'll roll

ROLLING PIE DOUGH

(STEP 1) Roll with firm, steady, but not overly hard pressure, from the inside out, sprinkling with tiny amounts of flour if necessary. (STEP 2) You can also roll between two sheets of parchment or plastic wrap, which is sometimes easier. If at any point during rolling the dough becomes sticky, refrigerate if for 15 minutes or so. (STEP 3) You can patch any holes with pieces of dough from the edges. (STEP 4) When the dough is ready, pick it up using the rolling pin (flour the dough and pin very lightly first) and then (STEP 5) drape it over your pie plate.

the dough out only once, because rerolling will toughen it. At first, though, you may need more than one try. Although rolling tart dough makes a more even and flat crust, it can just be pressed into the pan.

These tips that will make rolling dough easier:

- Start with dough that is firm and slightly chilled but not hard or frozen. It should yield a bit to pressure, but your fingers shouldn't sink in (if they do, refrigerate or freeze for a while longer).
- Flour the work surface and the top of the dough to prevent sticking to the counter and the rolling pin. Beginners should use flour liberally; as you get the hang of it, you'll use less and less flour. Alternatively, put the dough between two sheets of plastic wrap, parchment, or wax paper and roll it in there; as long as the dough is not too sticky, this will work just fine.
- Roll from the middle of the disk outward, rotating the rolling pin and the dough to make sure it's evenly rolled. Apply even and firm but gentle pressure to the rolling pin.
- Fix any holes with pieces that break off at the edges; add a dab of water to help seal your patches in place. Don't try to pinch the hole closed.
- If the dough becomes sticky, slide it onto a baking sheet and stick it in the freezer for a few minutes.
- When the dough is rolled out, move it to the pie plate or tart pan by draping it over the rolling pin and moving it into the plate; or transfer it by picking up your plastic wrap, removing one side, laying it in place, then removing the other side.
- Press the dough firmly into the plate all over. Refrigerate for about an hour before filling (if you're in a hurry, freeze for a half hour or so).

Once the dough is in the pan, you can trim it and make the edge more attractive. Tarts typically have a simple edge; just use a knife to cut away the excess dough. Fluted tart pans make a pretty, ruffled-looking edge without any extra work on your part.

Piecrusts, on the other hand, have more elaborate edges. Different pie makers prefer different techniques, some more complicated than others.

Baking the Crust

There's not much mystery behind baking crust. There are a couple ways to go about it: either baking the whole pie,

CRIMPING THE PIE SHELL

Pinching Method: Pinch the edges of the dough between the side of your forefinger and your thumb.

Knuckle Method: Use the thumb and forefinger of one hand (usually your left) to hold the dough in place from the inside. Then press a knuckle from your other hand against the crust, pushing it into the space made by your thumb and forefinger.

Fork Method: Simply press down with the tines of a fork along the edges of the dough.

Prebaking minimizes shrinking and helps produce a nicely shaped crust. It also ensures that the crust cooks through to the point of browning, giving it ideal flavor and color (browned crusts look and taste better than pale ones). And a prebaked crust is less likely to become soggy when the filling is particularly moist. Finally, when the filling is precooked or served raw (as in Fresh Strawberry Tart, for example), you have no other choice than to prebake.

To prebake, you need butter, foil, and a cup or two of raw rice or dried beans (or pie weights if you prefer). The weight helps prevent the crust from shrinking and bubbling with air pockets while it's baking. They aren't absolutely essential (you can prick the bubbles with a fork as they appear throughout the baking), but they make things easier, and your crust will look better.

Heat the oven to 425°F. Be sure the crust is pressed firmly into the pan, adequately pricked with a fork, and well chilled before baking; hard butter and the fork pricks will help the crust keep its shape.

Butter one side of a piece of foil large enough to cover the crust; press the foil onto the crust, butter side down. Weight the foil with a pile of dried beans or rice (they can be reused for the same purpose) or pie weights. Bake for 12 minutes; remove from the oven and remove the weights and foil. Reduce the oven temperature to 350°F and continue baking the crust until it has a golden brown color, another 10 minutes or so. Continue baking until the crust is completely golden brown if the pie's filling requires no additional baking (cool the pan on a wire rack before filling), or cool, fill, and finish baking per the individual recipe.

filling and all, or prebaking ("blind baking") the crust alone first. Though it adds a step, in many if not most cases prebaking the crust gives better results.

When you're baking a filled pie, always put it on a cookie sheet; it encourages bottom browning and prevents spillovers from cooking onto your oven floor. If your crust edges start to get too dark, loosely wrap a ring of foil around them.

Flaky Piecrust

MAKES: Enough for an 8- to 10-inch single-crust pie
TIME: 20 minutes, plus time to rest

I've used this recipe and technique for years and always been pleased with the results; it may be basic, but piecrusts don't get any better. The crust is flaky and flavorful—delicious in its own right, no matter what the filling.

If you're using a very moist filling, like a custard or juicy fruit filling, or when using a precooked or raw filling, prebake the crust before filling (See "Prebaking Pie and Tart Crusts," left).

1 cup plus 2 tablespoons all-purpose flour, plus more for rolling

$1/2$ teaspoon salt

1 teaspoon sugar

8 tablespoons (1 stick) cold unsalted butter, cut into about 8 pieces

3 tablespoons ice water, plus more if necessary

❶ Combine the flour, salt, and sugar in a food processor and pulse once or twice. Add the butter and turn on the machine; process until the butter and flour are blended and the mixture looks like cornmeal, about 10 seconds.

❷ Put the mixture in a bowl and add the ice water; mix with your hands until you can form the dough into a ball, adding another tablespoon or two of ice water if necessary (if you overdo it and the mixture becomes sodden, add a little more flour). Form into a ball, wrap in plastic, and freeze for 10 minutes or refrigerate for at least 30 minutes. (You can refrigerate the dough for up to a couple of days or freeze, tightly wrapped, for up to a couple of weeks.)

❸ Sprinkle a clean countertop with flour, put the dough on it, and sprinkle the top with flour. Use a rolling pin to roll with light pressure from the center out. If the dough is hard, let it rest for a few minutes. If the dough is sticky, add a little flour (if it continues to become sticky, and it's taking you more than a few minutes to roll it out, refrigerate or freeze again). Roll, adding flour and rotating and turning the dough as needed; use ragged edges of dough to repair any tears, adding a drop of water while you press the patch into place. (See the illustrations on page 926.)

❹ When the diameter of the dough is about 2 inches greater than that of your pie plate, drape the dough over the rolling pin to transfer it into the pie plate. Press the dough firmly into the plate all over. Refrigerate for about an hour before filling (if you're in a hurry, freeze for a half hour or so).

❺ Trim the excess dough to about ¹/₂ inch all around, then tuck it under itself around the edge of the plate. Decorate the edges with a fork or your fingers, using any of the methods illustrated on page 927. Freeze the dough for 10 minutes (or refrigerate it for 30 minutes).

❻ When you're ready to bake, either fill it or prick it all over with a fork for prebaking (see page 928).

Savory Piecrust. What you want for savory quiches, tarts, and so forth: Simply omit the sugar from any of the other variations.

Wheat Piecrust. Slightly nutty flavor, a deeper, golden brown color; there's some sacrifice in texture, but it's a worthwhile trade-off: Substitute ¹/₂ cup whole wheat for ¹/₂ cup of the all-purpose flour. A bit more ice water may be necessary.

Nut Piecrust. Rich and delicious, especially with macadamias or pine nuts: Substitute ¹/₄ cup finely chopped or ground nuts for ¹/₄ cup of the all-purpose flour. Pulse a few extra times in the food processor before adding the butter in Step 1. Proceed with the recipe.

Generous Pie Shell for a 10-Inch or Larger Pie or a Deep-Dish Pie. Increase the flour to 1¹/₂ cups, salt to ³/₄ teaspoon, sugar to 1¹/₂ teaspoons, butter to 10 tablespoons, water to ¹/₄ cup.

Sweet Tart Crust

MAKES: Enough for an 8- to 10-inch tart
TIME: 20 minutes, plus time to rest

Tart crust contains more butter than the piecrust, plus an egg yolk, which makes it extra-rich and almost like short-bread, so think of it as a large cookie. Like a cookie, it has many possible variations.

1¹/₄ cups all-purpose flour, plus more for rolling

¹/₂ teaspoon salt

2 tablespoons sugar

10 tablespoons (1¹/₄ sticks) frozen or cold unsalted butter, cut into chunks

1 egg yolk

3 tablespoons ice water, plus more if necessary

❶ Combine the flour, salt, and sugar in a food processor and pulse once or twice. Add the butter all at once; process until the mixture is uniform, about 10 seconds (do not overprocess). Add the egg yolk and process for another few seconds.

❷ Put the mixture in a bowl and add 3 tablespoons ice water; mix with your hands until you can form the dough into a ball, adding another tablespoon or two of ice water if necessary (if you overdo it and the mixture becomes sodden, add a little more flour). Form into a ball, wrap in plastic, and freeze for 10 minutes or refrigerate for at least 30 minutes. (You can refrigerate for up to a couple of days or freeze, tightly wrapped, for up to a couple of weeks.)

❸ Sprinkle a countertop with flour and put the dough on it; sprinkle the top with a little flour. Use a rolling pin to roll with light pressure from the center out.

If the dough is sticky, add a little flour (if it continues to become sticky, and it's taking you more than a few minutes to roll it out, refrigerate or freeze again). Roll, adding flour and rotating and turning the dough as needed; use ragged edges of dough to repair any tears, adding a drop of water while you press the patch into place.

4 When the diameter of the dough is about 2 inches greater than that of your tart pan, move the dough into the tart pan by draping it over the rolling pin and moving it into the pan. Press the dough into all the nooks and crannies in the pan, being careful not to overwork it, and use a knife to cut the edges flush with the rim of the pan. Refrigerate for about an hour before filling (if you're in a hurry, freeze for a half hour or so).

Savory Tart Crust. What you want for savory tarts or for any type of sugarless tart crust; most of the other variations can also be made savory by omitting the sugar: Simply omit the sugar.

Nut Tart Crust. Substitute 1/2 cup ground nuts, like almonds, hazelnuts, walnuts, pecans, macadamias, or peanuts, for 1/2 cup of the all-purpose flour.

Chocolate Tart Crust. An even richer-flavored crust; be sure it doesn't overwhelm the filling: Add 1/4 cup cocoa powder along with the flour.

Pistachio-Spice Tart Crust. Any nuts will work, as will any spice combination, but use the spices as subtle flavor enhancers: Substitute 1/2 cup ground unsalted pistachios for 1/2 cup of the all-purpose flour. Add 1/4 teaspoon ground cardamom and a pinch each of ground cinnamon and black pepper.

Graham Cracker Crust

MAKES: Enough for an 8- to 10-inch single-crust pie
TIME: 20 minutes

F **M** **V**

Graham cracker crusts, traditional for cheesecakes and good for cream or meringue pies, are often prebaked. You can use roughly the same proportions and techniques for any cookie crumb crust; see the variation. If you need a larger crust—or like a thick crust—just increase the ingredients proportionally. To crumble the cookies, put them in a plastic bag, seal, then roll over the bag as necessary with a rolling pin. Or just break the crackers into the container of a food processor and process until crumbly. (Or buy graham cracker crumbs!)

  3 tablespoons sugar

  6 ounces broken graham crackers, about 1 1/2 cups

  4 tablespoons (1/2 stick) unsalted butter, melted, plus more as needed

1 Combine the sugar with the graham cracker crumbs in a bowl or food processor. Slowly add the butter, stirring or processing until well blended. If the crumbs aren't all moistened, add a little bit more. Press the crumbs into the bottom and sides of a 9-inch pie plate.

2 To prebake, heat the oven to 350°F. Bake the crust for 8 to 10 minutes, just until it begins to brown. Cool on a rack before filling; the crust will harden as it cools.

Gingersnap or Other Cookie Crumb Crust. Nearly any cookies work here: Reduce the butter by 1 or 2 table-

10 Great Additions to Any Pie or Tart Crust

1. Nut flour or nut butter
2. Chopped or whole seeds, like sesame, poppy, sunflower, or pumpkin seeds
3. Shredded coconut
4. Crumbled or ground cookies, like gingersnaps, vanilla wafers, graham crackers, amaretti cookies, and more
5. Almond or hazelnut paste (omit the sugar)
6. Finely chopped dried fruit
7. Ground spices, like cinnamon, nutmeg, allspice, star anise, anise, cardamom, or coriander
8. Grated or finely minced fresh ginger, minced crystallized ginger, or ground ginger
9. Grated or finely minced citrus zest
10. Granola (page 821)

 Fast   Make Ahead   Vegetarian

spoons, depending on how buttery the cookies are, and likewise reduce the sugar a bit if they're sweet. Substitute gingersnaps, vanilla or chocolate wafers, or any crisp cookies for the graham crackers.

Fruit Pies

Fruit pies are a joy of summer and autumn, and to sully their flavor with huge amounts of sugar or their texture by overthickening is a sin. Keep thickener to a minimum and taste as you sweeten to use just the right amount of sugar. Some blueberries, which can be quite tart, will take relatively large amounts of sugar, but perfectly ripe peaches or pears need very little.

Frozen fruit has improved greatly in recent years, although it tends to become watery as it thaws. If you increase both sugar and thickener a little when using it, frozen fruit can make your winter desserts a reminder of the past summer. Usually it's not wise to thaw or wash frozen fruit before baking, though if the pieces are large—like peach halves—they should be defrosted enough to slice.

Traditional Apple Pie

MAKES: One 9-inch pie (about 8 servings)
TIME: About 1¹/₂ hours, plus time to cool

I usually don't thicken the filling for a simple apple pie, but if you don't want the juices to run, you can add the optional thickener. I also keep spices to a minimum since I'd rather taste the apples; you could safely double their quantity if you like a spicy pie and add a pinch of allspice and/or cloves if you like.

Vanilla ice cream or whipped cream is the classic accompaniment, though some enthusiasts swear by a slice of melted cheddar on top.

¹/₄ cup brown sugar

¹/₄ cup granulated sugar, or more if you would like a very sweet pie, plus a little for the top of the pie

¹/₂ teaspoon ground cinnamon

¹/₈ teaspoon freshly grated nutmeg

Pinch salt

5 or 6 Cortland, McIntosh, or other good cooking apples

1 tablespoon freshly squeezed lemon juice

1¹/₂ tablespoons cornstarch or 2 tablespoons instant tapioca (optional)

2 recipes Flaky Piecrust (page 928), bottom crust fitted into a 9-inch pie pan, top crust transferred to a rimless baking sheet, both chilled

2 tablespoons unsalted butter, cut into bits

Milk as needed

❶ Heat the oven to 450°F. Toss together the sugars, spices, and salt. Peel and core the apples and cut them into ¹/₂- to ³/₄-inch-thick slices. Toss the apples and lemon juice with the sugar-spice mixture, adding the cornstarch or tapioca if you want a less runny pie.

❷ Pile the apples into the bottom crust, making the pile a little higher in the center than at the sides. Dot with butter. Cover with the top crust. Crimp the edges with a fork or your fingers, using any of the methods illustrated on page 927.

❸ Put the pie on a baking sheet and brush the top lightly with milk; sprinkle with sugar. Use a sharp paring knife to cut two or three 2-inch-long slits in the top crust to allow steam to escape. Bake for 10 minutes; reduce the heat to 350°F and bake for another 40 to 50 minutes, or until the pie is golden brown. Do not underbake. Cool on a rack before serving warm or at room temperature.

Apple-Pear Pie. The essence of autumn: Add 1 tablespoon minced fresh ginger or 1 teaspoon ground ginger with the other spices. Use half apples and half pears. Add 2 tablespoons cornstarch or 3 tablespoons instant tapioca if you're using it.

Dutch Apple Pie. Cream poured into the pie—does it get any better? Add 2 tablespoons cornstarch or 3 tablespoons instant tapioca to the mixture. Proceed as directed, making sure to cut a large vent hole in the center of the top crust. About 30 minutes into the baking time, pour ¹/₂ cup cream into the vent hole and finish baking as directed.

Deep-Dish Apple Pie with Streusel Topping. Use a Generous Pie Shell (page 929). Increase all filling ingredients by a third. Prepare and fill a deep-dish pie plate as directed. Make Streusel Topping (page 925) and strew over the top of the apples. Bake at 375°F for 45 to 60 minutes, or until the center of the pie is bubbly and the streusel mixture and bottom crust are nicely browned.

7 Easy Additions to Apple Pie

1. ¹/₂ to 1 cup chopped nuts
2. Any appealing spice, generally in small amounts, like minced fresh or crystallized ginger, cardamom, allspice, or cloves
3. About 2 tablespoons bourbon or rum sprinkled over the top
4. About 1 cup whole cranberries, the amount of sugar increased slightly
5. 1 cup or more pitted stone fruit, like plums or cherries, cut up, or whole raspberries, blueberries, or blackberries, the amount of apples reduced accordingly
6. ¹/₂ to 1 cup dried fruit, like raisins, dried cherries, cranberries, pineapple, mango, or blueberries, or some dried apple slices to intensify the apple flavor
7. Grated lemon or orange zest

Blueberry and Other Berry Pies

MAKES: One 9-inch pie (about 8 servings)
TIME: About 1¹/₂ hours, plus time to cool

Ⓜ Ⓥ

There are variations on this standard, but it is the model for all berry pies. Again, I like to minimize the spices and other flavorings, emphasizing the flavor of the berries. Like apple pie, berry pies can be made with a Streusel Topping (page 925).

> 5 cups blueberries, picked over, briefly rinsed, and lightly dried (see "Fruit Pies," page 931, to use frozen fruit)
>
> ¹/₂ to 1 cup sugar, depending on your taste and the sweetness of the berries, plus a little for the top
>
> 2 tablespoons cornstarch or 3 tablespoons instant tapioca
>
> Pinch salt
>
> ¹/₄ teaspoon ground cinnamon
>
> Pinch ground allspice or freshly grated nutmeg
>
> 1 tablespoon freshly squeezed lemon juice
>
> 1 teaspoon minced lemon zest (optional)
>
> 2 recipes Flaky Piecrust (page 928), bottom crust fitted into a 9-inch pie pan, top crust transferred to a rimless baking sheet, both chilled
>
> 2 tablespoons unsalted butter, cut into bits
>
> Milk as needed

❶ Heat the oven to 450°F. Gently toss the blueberries with the sugar, thickener, salt, and spices. Stir in the lemon juice and the zest if you're using it and pile into the rolled-out shell, making the pile a little higher in the center than at the sides. Dot with butter. Cover with the top crust. Decorate the edges with a fork or your fingers, using any of the methods illustrated on page 927.

❷ Put the pie on a baking sheet and brush the top lightly with milk; sprinkle with sugar. Use a sharp paring knife to cut two or three 2-inch-long slits in the top crust to allow steam to escape. Bake for 10 minutes; reduce the heat to 350°F and bake for another 40 to 50 minutes, or until the pie is golden brown. Do not underbake. Cool on a rack before serving warm or at room temperature.

 Fast   Make Ahead   Vegetarian

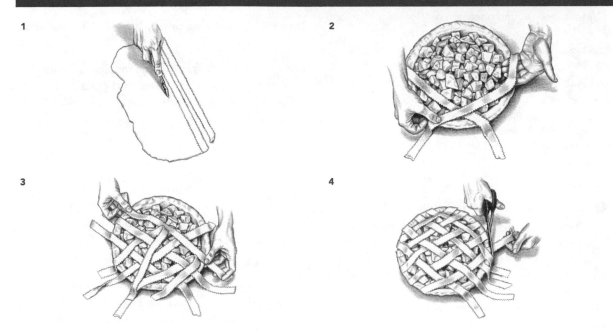

(STEP 1) Begin by rolling out a piece of dough a couple of inches longer than the pie plate and 5 or 6 inches wide. Cut ten
1/2-inch-wide strips. (STEP 2) Weave the strips over the top of the pie. (STEP 3) Continue to weave, bending back the strips laid in
one direction so you can add strips in the other. (STEP 4) When the weaving is completed, press the edges into the crust and trim.

Blackberry or Raspberry Pie. Combine these berries with each other or with blueberries: Be gentle in washing and drying the fragile berries and increase the amount of either thickener by 1 tablespoon.

Strawberry, Rhubarb, or Strawberry-Rhubarb Pie. Use a total of 5 cups of fruit, in any combination you like. String rhubarb (see page 283), then cut it into 1-inch pieces. Hull strawberries; slice in half or leave whole. If you're using rhubarb, use at least 1 cup sugar. Use 3 tablespoons cornstarch or 1/4 cup instant tapioca as thickener. Omit the lemon juice and zest.

Peach or Other Stone Fruit Pie

MAKES: One 9 inch pie (about 8 servings)
TIME: About 1 1/2 hours

Ⓜ Ⓥ

The classic two-crust peach (or nectarine, cherry, apricot, plum, what-have-you) pie. Please use perfectly ripe fruit if at all possible. Ginger Ice Cream (page 963) is fantastic with this.

About 2 pounds peaches, or a little more (6 to 10 peaches, depending on size)

1 tablespoon freshly squeezed lemon juice

About ½ cup sugar, more if the peaches are not quite ripe, plus a little for the top

¼ teaspoon ground cinnamon or ½ teaspoon almond extract

⅛ teaspoon freshly grated nutmeg or ground allspice, if you use cinnamon

1½ tablespoons cornstarch or 2 tablespoons instant tapioca

2 recipes Flaky Piecrust (page 928), bottom crust fitted into a 9-inch pie pan, top crust transferred to a rimless baking sheet, both chilled

2 tablespoons unsalted butter, cut into bits

Milk as needed

1 Heat the oven to 450°F. Peel the peaches: Bring a pot of water to a boil and drop the peaches into it, a couple at a time, for 10 to 30 seconds, until the skins loosen. Plunge into a bowl of ice water. Slip the skins off, using a paring knife to ease the process. Pit, slice, and toss with the lemon juice.

2 Mix together the dry ingredients (including the almond extract if you're using it) and toss the peaches with this mixture. Pile into the rolled-out shell, making the pile a little higher in the center than at the sides. Dot with butter. Cover with the top crust. Decorate the edges with a fork or your fingers, using any of the methods illustrated on page 927.

3 Put the pie on a baking sheet and brush the top lightly with milk; sprinkle with sugar. Use a sharp paring knife to cut two or three 2-inch-long slits in the top crust; this will allow steam to escape. Bake for 10 minutes; reduce the heat to 350°F and bake for another 40 to 50 minutes, or until the pie is golden brown. Do not underbake. Cool on a rack before serving warm or at room temperature.

Peach and Berry Pie. Blueberries are the classic choice: Add 1 cup berries to the mixture of peaches or other fruit.

Peach and Ginger Pie. Add 1 tablespoon minced fresh ginger or 1 teaspoon ground ginger to the mixture (do not combine with almond extract; use cinnamon and nutmeg).

Plum Pie. Use the small prune (Italian) plums that come into season in early autumn.

Cherry Pie. Sour cherries are best for pie: Substitute 4 to 5 cups pitted sour cherries for the peaches; omit the lemon juice unless you're using sweet cherries. If you use canned cherries, drain them well and increase the thickener by 1 tablespoon.

Cream Pie

MAKES: One 9-inch pie (about 8 servings)
TIME: About 1½ hours

Master this one basic recipe and you can make all the cream pies you've dreamed of. Egg yolks, used without their whites, are traditional and wonderful when making cream filling, and that's led to topping cream pies with meringue. But cream pies are also wonderful topped with whipped cream. If this is what you'd prefer to do, see the whole-egg variation for Cream-Topped Cream Pie.

Note that though they're called cream pies, milk is the best liquid; with cream, the mouthfeel becomes overly thick. Use whole milk, though, for best results.

1 Flaky Piecrust (page 928) or Graham Cracker Crust (page 930), fitted into a 9-inch pie pan and chilled

¾ cup granulated sugar

2 tablespoons cornstarch

Salt

4 eggs, separated

2½ cups whole milk or 2¼ cups low-fat milk mixed with ¼ cup cream

1 vanilla bean or 2 teaspoons vanilla extract

2 tablespoons unsalted butter, softened

¼ cup confectioners' sugar

❶ Prebake the crust (see "Prebaking Pie and Tart Crusts," page 928), and start the filling while the crust is in the oven. When the crust is done, leave the oven at 350°F and cool the crust slightly on a rack.

❷ In a small saucepan, combine the granulated sugar with the cornstarch and a pinch of salt. Mix the egg yolks and milk together. If you're using a vanilla bean, split it and scrape out the seeds; stir them into the milk mixture. Stir the milk-egg mixture into the sugar-cornstarch mixture over medium heat; at first, whisk occasionally to eliminate lumps. Then whisk almost constantly until the mixture boils and thickens, about 10 minutes. Stir in the butter (and vanilla extract if you're using it) and set aside.

❸ Make the meringue: Beat the egg whites with a pinch of salt, until foamy. Keep beating, gradually adding the confectioners' sugar, until the mixture is shiny and holds fairly stiff peaks.

❹ Put the pie plate on a baking sheet. Pour the warm filling into the warm crust. Cover with the meringue, making sure the meringue comes into contact with the edges of the crust. Note that the meringue will hold its shape, so you can make peaks and swirls if you like. Bake until the meringue is lightly browned, 10 to 15 minutes. Cool on a rack, then refrigerate; serve cool.

Coconut Cream Pie. Toast 1 cup shredded coconut by placing it in a dry skillet over very low heat and cooking, shaking almost constantly, until it begins to brown, 3 to 5 minutes. Remove from the pan immediately. Stir this coconut into the thickened cream filling. Top the meringue with another ½ cup untoasted coconut.

Banana Cream Pie. Use the vanilla cream or the chocolate cream in the next variation: Stir 1 cup thinly sliced banana into the thickened cream filling before pouring it into the pie shell.

Chocolate Cream Pie. I like bittersweet best: Add 2 ounces chopped or grated bittersweet or semisweet chocolate to the milk mixture as it cooks.

Vanilla-Orange Cream Pie. Aka Creamsicle pie: Substitute ½ cup freshly squeezed orange juice for ½ cup of the milk and add 1 tablespoon grated or finely minced orange zest; add both to the milk mixture in Step 2. Proceed with the recipe.

Cream-Topped Cream Pie. This cream-topped version works for the main recipe or any of the other variations: Prebake the crust until it is nice and brown, a total of about 35 minutes. Substitute 2 whole eggs for the yolks and proceed as directed. After pouring the filling into the prebaked shell, cover directly with plastic wrap (this will prevent a skin from forming) and refrigerate until cool. Just before serving, beat 1 cup cream (preferably not ultra-pasteurized) with 2 tablespoons confectioners' sugar and ½ teaspoon vanilla or almond extract, or brandy or rum, until the cream holds stiff peaks. Spoon over the pie and serve.

Lemon Meringue Pie

MAKES: One 9-inch pie (about 8 servings)
TIME: About 1½ hours

Not quite a cream pie, lemon meringue is little more than lemon flavor made solid, topped by a light cloud of sweet meringue.

1 Flaky Piecrust (page 928) or Graham Cracker Crust (page 930), fitted into a 9-inch pie pan and chilled

1 cup granulated sugar

Salt

2 cups boiling water

4 eggs, separated

$^1/_3$ cup cornstarch

2 tablespoons unsalted butter, softened

2 teaspoons grated or minced lemon zest

6 tablespoons freshly squeezed lemon juice

$^1/_4$ cup confectioners' sugar

1 Prebake the crust (see "Prebaking Pie and Tart Crusts," page 928) and start the filling while the crust is in the oven. When the crust is done, leave the oven at 350°F and cool the crust slightly on a rack.

2 In a small saucepan, combine the granulated sugar, a pinch of salt, and the boiling water and cook, stirring frequently, until the sugar dissolves, just a minute or two; keep warm. Beat the egg yolks and cornstarch until smooth. Whisk about $^1/_2$ cup of the water mixture into the egg yolks. Immediately stir the egg yolk mixture back into the water mixture and bring to a boil, whisking constantly. Keep whisking and let it boil for less than a minute, then turn off the heat and add the butter. Stir in the lemon zest and juice. Let the filling cool a bit before pouring it into the prepared crust.

3 Make the meringue: Beat the egg whites with a pinch of salt until foamy. Keep beating, gradually adding the confectioners' sugar, until the mixture is shiny and holds stiff peaks.

4 Put the pie plate on a baking sheet. Pour the filling into the crust. Cover with the meringue, making sure the meringue comes into contact with the edges of the crust. Note that the meringue will hold its shape, so you can make peaks and swirls if you like. Bake at 350°F until the meringue is lightly browned, 10 to 15 minutes. Cool on a rack, then refrigerate; serve cool.

Lemon Meringue Pie with Creamy Filling. Instead of water, use 2 cups warmed cream, half-and-half, or milk.

Lemon-Berry Pie. Top with fresh berries instead of meringue: Add 1$^1/_2$ cups mixed whole berries, like raspberries, blueberries, and blackberries; omit the meringue (Step 3). Proceed with the recipe, serving with a dollop of Whipped Cream (page 882).

Key Lime Pie

MAKES: One 9-inch pie (about 8 servings)
TIME: About 1$^1/_2$ hours, plus time to cool

Key Lime Pie may be topped with meringue (as it is here) or with whipped cream. If you'd prefer the latter, make adaptations according to the variation on page 935 for Cream-Topped Cream Pie. If you have key limes—chances are you will not—by all means use them; but normal limes are fine.

1 Flaky Piecrust (page 928) or Graham Cracker Crust (page 930), fitted into a 9-inch pie pan and chilled

4 eggs, separated

One 14-ounce can sweetened condensed milk

$^1/_3$ cup freshly squeezed lime juice

Pinch salt

$^1/_4$ cup confectioners' sugar

1 Prebake the crust (see "Prebaking Pie and Tart Crusts," page 928) and start the filling while the crust is in the oven. When the crust is done, leave the oven at 350°F and cool the crust slightly on a rack.

2 Beat the egg yolks just until combined. Beat in the condensed milk, then the lime juice, a little at a time; the mixture will thicken. Put the pie plate on a baking sheet. Pour the filling into the warm crust and bake until the filling is just firm, 10 to 15 minutes. Remove and cool on a rack for about 10 minutes.

3 Make the meringue: Beat the egg whites with salt until foamy. Keep beating, gradually adding the confectioners' sugar, until the mixture is shiny and holds fairly stiff peaks.

4 Cover the pie with the meringue, making sure the meringue comes into contact with the edges of the crust. Note that the meringue will hold its shape, so you can make peaks and swirls if you like. Bake until the meringue is lightly browned, 10 to 15 minutes. Cool on a rack, then refrigerate; serve cool.

F Fast   **M** Make Ahead   **V** Vegetarian

Pecan Pie

MAKES: One 9-inch pie (about 8 servings)
TIME: About 1½ hours

There are two types of pecan pies, one of which contains not only sugar but also corn syrup. I like this no-corn-syrup version better—it's a custard pie, loaded with pecans. Toast the pecans first for best flavor. Top with Vanilla or Coffee Ice Cream (pages 961 or 963) and/or Whipped Cream (page 882).

> 1 Flaky Piecrust (page 928), fitted into a 9-inch pie pan and chilled
>
> 2 cups pecans or walnuts
>
> 5 eggs
>
> 1 cup granulated sugar
>
> ½ cup brown sugar
>
> Pinch salt
>
> 6 tablespoons (¾ stick) unsalted butter, melted
>
> 1 tablespoon vanilla extract

❶ Prebake the crust (see "Prebaking Pie and Tart Crusts," page 928) and put the pecans on a baking sheet and bake (you can do this before the oven reaches 425°F), shaking and stirring, for about 5 minutes, or until the pecans are hot. Cool the pecans; coarsely chop half of them and leave the other half intact.

❷ Start the filling while the crust is in the oven. When the crust is done, turn the oven to 375°F.

❸ Beat the eggs well, until foamy. Beat in the sugars, salt, and butter. While the crust is baking, warm this mixture in a medium saucepan over medium-low heat, stirring occasionally, until hot to the touch; do not boil. Stir in the vanilla extract and the pecans.

❹ Put the pie plate on a baking sheet. Pour this mixture into the still-hot crust and bake for 30 to 40 minutes, until the mixture shakes like Jell-O but is still quite moist. Cool on a rack and serve warm or at room temperature.

Chocolate Pecan Pie. Before beginning Step 3, melt 2 ounces semisweet chocolate with 3 tablespoons of butter until smooth. Let cool while you beat the eggs, sugars, and salt (omit the remaining butter). Combine the chocolate and egg mixtures and warm gently as in Step 3, then proceed as directed.

Butterscotch Pecan Pie. Use 4 eggs, 1 cup brown sugar, and add ¾ cup cream. Omit the granulated sugar. Add the cream with the eggs in Step 3 and proceed as directed.

Pumpkin Pie

MAKES: One 9-inch pie (about 8 servings)
TIME: About 1½ hours

Essentially a custard pie with lots of added spice and, of course, pumpkin. Precooking the crust and filling makes the bottom of the pie nice and crisp. Substitute cooked, puréed, and strained winter squash, sweet potatoes, or white beans for the pumpkin if you like.

The best ways to finish this pie: Top with Whipped Cream flavored with cinnamon, nutmeg, or ginger if you like (page 882).

> 1 Flaky Piecrust (page 928), fitted into a 9-inch pie pan and chilled
>
> 3 eggs
>
> ¾ cup sugar
>
> ½ teaspoon ground cinnamon
>
> ⅛ teaspoon freshly grated nutmeg
>
> ½ teaspoon ground ginger
>
> Pinch ground cloves
>
> Pinch salt
>
> 2 cups canned or fresh pumpkin purée
>
> 2 cups half-and-half, cream, or whole milk

❶ Prebake the crust (see "Prebaking Pie and Tart Crusts," page 928) and start the filling while the crust is in the oven. When the crust is done, turn the oven to 375°F.

❷ Beat the eggs with the sugar, then add the spices and salt. Stir in the pumpkin purée and then the half-and-half. While the crust is baking, warm this mixture in a medium saucepan over medium-low heat, stirring occasionally, until it is hot to the touch; do not boil.

❸ Put the pie plate on a baking sheet. Pour the pumpkin mixture into the still-hot crust and bake for 30 to 40 minutes, until the mixture shakes like Jell-O but is still quite moist. Cool on a rack and serve warm or at room temperature.

Sweet Potato Pie. A touch of orange makes it stand out: Substitute puréed sweet potato for the pumpkin and add 2 teaspoons grated or finely minced orange zest.

Pumpkin Pie with Gingersnap Crust. Instead of Flaky Piecrust, prepare and prebake a Gingersnap Crust (page 930).

Pumpkin-Tofu Pie. Tofu takes the place of the eggs and half-and-half with good results; try it: Substitute a pound of silken or other soft tofu for the eggs and half-and-half. Drain the tofu, then purée it with the other ingredients, then pour it into the crust and proceed with the recipe.

Simplest Apple Tart

MAKES: One 8- to 10-inch tart (about 8 servings)
TIME: About 1½ hours

Ⓜ **Ⓥ**

A quick, crisp tart in which delicious shell and straightforward filling share center stage. You can make the same tart with pears (make sure they're ripe), peaches, or nectarines (peel stone fruits first; see Step 1 in Peach or Other Stone Fruit Pie, page 933). Top with Spice Ice Cream made with all cinnamon (page 963), Vanilla Ice Cream (page 961), or Whipped Cream (page 882).

1 recipe Sweet Tart Crust (page 929), fitted into a tart pan and chilled

2 to 3 pounds tart apples, like McIntosh

1 tablespoon freshly squeezed lemon juice

2 tablespoons sugar

½ teaspoon ground cinnamon

1 tablespoon unsalted butter

⅓ cup strained raspberry, apricot, or currant preserves (optional)

1 tablespoon water or liqueur (optional)

❶ Prebake the crust (see "Prebaking Pie and Tart Crusts," page 928) and start the apples while the crust is in the oven. When the crust is done, turn the oven to 375°F. Set the shell aside to cool.

❷ Peel and core the apples, then cut them into thin slices (about ⅛ inch thick); use a mandoline if you have one. Toss them with the lemon juice so they don't brown. Arrange the apple slices in concentric circles in the tart shell, with the circles overlapping. Sprinkle with sugar and cinnamon, then dot with butter.

❸ Put the tart pan on a baking sheet and bake until the apples are quite soft (a thin-bladed knife will pierce them easily) but still hold their shape, about 40 minutes. Cool on a rack for about 20 minutes.

❹ To glaze: While the tart is cooling, warm the strained preserves with the water or liqueur in a very small saucepan over medium-low heat until thinned. Brush this over the top of the tart. Serve the tart at room temperature.

Apple-Almond Tart. Toast ¾ cup blanched almonds while you heat the oven for the tart shell: Put them on a baking sheet and bake (you can do this before the oven reaches 425°F), shaking, for 5 to 10 minutes, or just until they begin to brown. Cool, then put them in a food processor and finely grind them (stop processing before they turn into a paste). Toss with ¼ teaspoon ground cinnamon and 1 tablespoon sugar, then spread them on the bottom of the prebaked tart shell before topping with the apples and proceeding with the recipe.

Ⓕ Fast   **Ⓜ** Make Ahead   **Ⓥ** Vegetarian

Two-Apple Tart. You'll need about twice as many apples for this tart. Prepare half of them as directed. Peel, core, and coarsely chop the other half, then cook them over low heat, partially covered and stirring occasionally, with 1 tablespoon freshly squeezed lemon juice, 1 teaspoon grated or minced lemon zest, and ¼ cup water, until soft but still holding their shape, about 15 minutes. Add sugar to taste, about ½ cup. Cool, then spread this on the bottom of the prebaked tart shell before topping with the uncooked apples and proceeding with the recipe.

Simple Berry Tart

MAKES: One 8- to 10-inch tart (about 8 servings)
TIME: About 1½ hours, largely unattended

This is half the work of, and contains far less fat than, Fresh Strawberry Tart with Pastry Cream (page 939). Use any berries you like and top with Whipped Cream (page 882) or ice cream (to make your own, see pages 961–963).

1 recipe Sweet Tart Crust (page 929), fitted into a tart pan and chilled

½ cup sugar

¼ cup cornstarch

3 cups strawberries, raspberries, blackberries, and/or blueberries, picked over, stemmed, and hulled if necessary

❶ Prebake the crust (see "Prebaking Pie and Tart Crusts," page 928) and start the berries while the crust is in the oven. When the crust is done, leave the oven at 350°F.

❷ Rub the sugar and cornstarch together with your fingers until well combined. Toss with about 2 cups of the berries; crush some of the berries with a fork or potato masher to help dissolve the sugar. Pile the berries into the tart crust, then top with the remaining berries, left whole (or halved if they are large strawberries, for example).

❸ Put the tart pan on a baking sheet and bake until the fruit mixture is bubbly, about 30 minutes. Cool, then serve warm or at room temperature.

Simple Berry Tart with Chocolate. Use milk, dark, or white chocolate: Spread a thin layer of melted chocolate, about 3 ounces, in the empty prebaked tart shell before adding the berries.

Fresh Strawberry Tart with Pastry Cream

MAKES: One 8- to 10-inch tart (about 8 servings)
TIME: About 1½ hours

Classic pastry cream makes a delicious base for any fruit, but especially fresh berries. These elegant tarts are easier to make than many pies, because everything is prepared separately and then assembled: You bake the crust, fill it with cream, top with berries, glaze if you like, and serve. Use any berries or other peeled and sliced soft fruit.

1 recipe Sweet Tart Crust (page 929), fitted into a tart pan and chilled

1 recipe Vanilla Pastry Cream (page 943), chilled

2 to 3 cups strawberries, hulled, lightly washed, and well dried

½ cup strained raspberry, apricot, or currant preserves (optional)

1 tablespoon water or liqueur (optional)

❶ After prebaking the crust (see "Prebaking Pie and Tart Crusts," page 928) and removing the weights and foil, turn the oven to 350°F and bake until the crust is a beautiful shade of brown, another 10 to 15 minutes. Cool on a rack. You can start the filling while the crust is baking or wait a few hours.

❷ Spread a layer of pastry cream on the bottom of the shell (you may not need all of it). Arrange the strawberries, hulled side down, on the cream, packing in as many as you can. If you'd like to glaze the tart, warm the strained preserves with the water or liqueur in a very small saucepan over medium-low heat until thinned. Brush the top of the strawberries with this mixture and serve.

Banana-Strawberry Cream Tart. Peel and thinly slice 2 or 3 bananas; toss them with 1 tablespoon freshly squeezed lemon juice and 1 tablespoon brown sugar. Arrange them on the cooled tart shell, then top with the pastry cream, then the strawberries.

Mixed Fruit Tarts. Use slices of kiwi, halved red grapes, various berries, and any other ripe fruit you like.

Strawberry Tart with Citrus Curd. Any type of berries will work; make lemon, lime, or a mixed citrus curd: Substitute 1 recipe Citrus Custard Sauce (page 925) for the pastry cream and proceed with the recipe.

6 Simple Ideas for Fresh Fruit Tarts

1. Put a layer of about 1 cup toasted, coarsely chopped nuts (see page 317), like almonds or pecans, beneath the pastry cream.
2. Flavor the pastry cream with about 1 teaspoon ground cinnamon.
3. Stir about 1 tablespoon of brandy, liqueur like Grand Marnier, or flavored brandy like Poire William into the pastry cream.
4. Mix berries or other fruit at will—half strawberries and half blueberries, for example, is very nice.
5. Use pitted, peeled, and thinly sliced peaches, nectarines, or apricots in place of the berries.
6. Top with Whipped Cream (page 882).

Chocolate Tart

MAKES: One 8- to 10-inch tart (about 8 servings)
TIME: 30 minutes with all components prepared

This recipe is all about assembling other recipes to make a killer, super-chocolaty tart. When they're in season, use fresh raspberries to garnish the top—and hide imperfections; other times of the year you can decorate with chocolate shavings (page 911). Top with Whipped Cream flavored with vanilla, chocolate, or mint (page 882).

> 1 recipe Chocolate Tart Crust (page 930), prebaked (see page 928) and cooled
>
> 1 recipe Vanilla Pastry Cream flavored with chocolate (page 943), chilled
>
> $^1/_2$ recipe Chocolate Glaze (page 921)

Fill the tart with the pastry cream to $^1/_4$ inch from the top of the edge; smooth the surface as much as you can. Put it in the freezer until the surface of the cream chills and stiffens a bit. Use an oiled spatula to spread the glaze over the surface of the whole tart. Chill until set. Serve chilled or room temperature.

Chocolate-Caramel Tart. Always a hit: Add a layer of Creamy Caramel Sauce (page 922) and let it cool and set up a bit before adding the pastry cream and proceeding with the recipe.

Tarte Tatin

Caramelized Apple Tart

MAKES: One 10-inch tart (about 8 servings)
TIME: About 1 hour

There is nothing better than tarte tatin, but, to be at its best, it should be made almost at the last minute. The ideal is to prepare it just before serving the meal and bake it while you're eating. Top with Whipped Cream (page 882), Vanilla Ice Cream (page 961), or Vanilla Custard Sauce (page 924).

> 6 Granny Smith or other tart, hard apples
>
> Juice of $^1/_2$ lemon
>
> 8 tablespoons (1 stick) unsalted butter, cut into pieces
>
> $^3/_4$ cup sugar

 Fast   Make Ahead   Vegetarian

1 recipe Sweet Tart Crust (page 929), chilled but not rolled out

① Heat the oven to 400°F.

② Peel, core, and quarter the apples; toss with the lemon juice. Press the butter into the bottom and sides of a heavy ovenproof (cast-iron is good) 10-inch skillet. Sprinkle the butter with the sugar. Press the apple quarters into the sugar, arranging them in concentric circles and making certain to pack them in tightly; they will shrink considerably during cooking.

③ Put the pan over medium-high heat. Cook until the butter-sugar mixture has turned a very deep, dark brown, 15 to 20 minutes. While it's cooking, roll out the pastry just a little bigger than the pan. When the apples are ready, remove the pan from the heat. Lay the pastry on top of the apples, bringing the dough to the edges of the pan to seal it. Prick the dough with a fork and bake until the pastry is golden brown, about 20 minutes.

④ Remove the tart from the oven and let it sit for 5 minutes. Shake the hot pan to loosen the apples stuck to the bottom of the skillet. Invert the whole tart onto a large serving dish, taking care not to burn yourself (the juices are hot). Serve immediately or at room temperature.

Caramelized Pineapple Tart. You have to use fresh pineapple for this; canned won't do: Substitute slices of pineapple (roughly the size of apple slices) for the apple.

Caramelized Peach or Plum Tart. Do this in the summer, when stone fruit are at their best: Substitute slightly soft peaches or plums for the apples.

The Basics of Choux and Puff Pastries

Choux, or cream puff pastry, is a miraculous dough that can be prepared by a child. There are no secrets here, just a few minutes of hard work resulting in a pastry shell that can be filled with anything creamy.

But of all pastries, puff pastry is the ultimate, a literally countless number of thin, crisp layers of pastry, each separated by a film of butter. The butter keeps the layers from sticking together, and the steam escaping from the dough during baking causes them to rise, just enough to make each distinct. Not many people make it, but those who do are devoted to it, and you may become one of them, especially after making your first batch of croissants.

Nor is it that difficult. There are really only three rules to follow:

1. Take your time (this is a long, drawn-out process).
2. If at any step in the process the butter feels oily to you, refrigerate the dough for 30 minutes.
3. Don't try it on a hot day unless your kitchen is air-conditioned; you'll never keep the butter cold enough.

The dough should always be "doughy," never oily or so hard it will be difficult to roll. Remember the goal—layers of flour separated by butter—and take it slow. I succeeded in making puff pastry on my first try, and so will you. When you're done, you'll have the best dough ever for apple turnovers, or Napoleons, and crusts for tarts, pies—including pot pies—or quiches.

It's worth mentioning that some frozen puff pastry is not at all bad (check the ingredients: they should be mostly flour and butter). And you can get decent results with layers of phyllo.

Cream Puff Pastry

Pâte à Choux

> **MAKES:** Enough for at least 2 dozen pastries
> **TIME:** 15 minutes
> **F** **M** **V**

One of the miracles of cooking, cream puff pastry expands to at least double its size, leaving a hole in the middle that is perfect for filling. So it is the base for cream puffs, éclairs, and a number of savory foods like Gougères (page 99). It takes almost no time to make, and the same dough can be either baked or deep-fried. Try it once and it'll become a part of your repertoire forever.

  8 tablespoons (1 stick) unsalted butter

  Pinch salt

  1 cup all-purpose flour

  4 eggs

❶ Combine the butter and salt with 1 cup water in a saucepan over high heat and bring to a boil. Turn the heat to low and add the flour all at once. Stir constantly until the mixture pulls away from the pan and forms a ball, about 30 seconds. Remove from the heat and beat the eggs into the mixture one at a time (this is a little bit of work; feel free to use an electric mixer). Stop beating when the mixture is glossy and try to handle the batter minimally from here on out.

❷ Bake immediately according to one of the following recipes, deep-fry as described in the variations here, or cover and refrigerate for up to 2 days before using.

To deep-fry the pastry: Put at least 2 inches peanut or neutral oil, like grapeseed or corn, in a deep pan on the stove and turn the heat to medium-high; bring to 350°F. Carefully drop spoonfuls of the dough into the hot oil, only as many as will fit comfortably at once. Cook, turning them as they brown, for a total of 5 to 10 minutes. Use a slotted spoon to remove the pastries from the oil when browned evenly and drain on paper towels. Dust or sprinkle with seasonings (confectioners' sugar, granulated sugar, ground cinnamon or other spices, salt and pepper, grated Parmesan, etc.) as you like. Serve hot, or at least warm.

Churros. Deep-fried treats from Spain and Mexico: Combine ¹/₂ cup sugar with 1 teaspoon cinnamon on a plate. To fry the pastries, either drop spoonfuls into hot oil (the easy way) or make signature churro sticks by spooning the batter into a pastry bag with a large star tip and piping strips of dough about 4 inches long into the hot oil. Either way, deep-fry as above, drain

on paper towels, then roll the hot churros around in the cinnamon-sugar mixture before serving.

Cream Puffs

MAKES: 2 dozen large or 3 to 4 dozen small
TIME: About 1 hour

You can bake this pastry up to several hours ahead, but don't fill until the last minute.

  Butter for the baking sheet

  1 recipe Cream Puff Pastry (previous recipe)

  1 recipe Vanilla Pastry Cream (page 943) or 2 cups sweetened Whipped Cream (page 882)

❶ Heat the oven to 400°F. Grease a baking sheet with butter.

❷ Pipe mounds of the cream puff pastry onto the baking sheet using a ¹/₂-inch star tip or the equivalent or use 2 spoons to form mounds about 1 inch wide and a little bit higher than that. Bake until very puffy, golden brown, and hollow sounding when tapped, about 40 minutes. Prick each with a skewer once or twice to allow steam to escape, then move to a rack and cool to room temperature.

❸ Use a pastry bag with a small pointed tip to pipe the filling directly into each cream puff or simply cut off a top cap from each, load it up with pastry cream or whipped cream with a spoon, and replace the cap. Serve immediately, as the puffs will become soggy.

Éclairs. Use a pastry bag with a large tip or opening to pipe 4- to 6-inch-long fingers of cream puff pastry onto lightly greased sheets or shape with spoons, handling as little as possible. Bake as directed. When the puffs are cool, poke a hole in one end of each éclair and pipe in the filling or simply cut a slit along the top and spoon in the filling. Top with a sauce made by melting together 1 cup milk and 1 cup chopped semisweet chocolate.

Vanilla Pastry Cream

MAKES: About 2½ cups
TIME: 20 minutes

A wonderful filling for Cream Puffs (previous recipe) or tarts (including but not limited to Fresh Strawberry Tart with Pastry Cream, page 939), it's thicker and lighter than a pudding or custard but with the same creamy texture and flavor.

⅔ cup sugar

2 tablespoons all-purpose flour

2 tablespoons cornstarch

Pinch salt

2 eggs or 4 yolks

2 cups cream, half-and-half, or whole milk

2 tablespoons unsalted butter, softened

2 teaspoons vanilla extract

❶ In a small saucepan, combine the sugar with the flour, cornstarch, and salt. Mix together the eggs or yolks and the cream. Whisk the cream-egg mixture into the sugar-cornstarch mixture over medium heat; at first, whisk occasionally to minimize the lumps. Then whisk almost constantly until the mixture just begins to boil and thickens, about 10 minutes.

❷ Adjust the heat so the mixture bubbles gently and continue to cook until the mixture coats the back of a spoon; when you draw your finger through this coating, the resulting line will hold its shape. Stir in the butter and vanilla extract, strain through a fine-mesh sieve, and set aside. Cool the pastry cream to room temperature before using (you can refrigerate it for a few hours, topped directly with plastic wrap to prevent a skin from forming).

5 Ways to Flavor Pastry Cream

1. **Chocolate:** Add 2 ounces chopped semisweet chocolate to the cream mixture as it cooks.

2. **Coffee:** Add 2 shots freshly brewed espresso or 1 tablespoon instant espresso powder to the cream mixture as it cooks.

3. **Tea:** Use a good-quality Earl Grey or other fragrant black tea or try green tea for a brighter alternative. Omit the vanilla. Before beginning, heat the cream separately and steep 2 teaspoons tea in the hot cream for 5 minutes, and then strain and proceed with the recipe.

4. **Booze:** Omit the vanilla. Add 2 tablespoons bourbon, rum, Scotch, or port wine to the finished hot cream mixture.

5. **Almond:** Use almond extract instead of vanilla extract.

Puff Pastry

MAKES: Enough for about 4 dozen small pastries
TIME: All day, largely unattended

This makes a lot, but the dough freezes perfectly for weeks as long as it's well wrapped.

4 cups all-purpose flour, plus some for the work surface

2 teaspoons salt

1 pound (4 sticks) cold unsalted butter

About ½ cup ice water

❶ Put 3 cups of the flour in a food processor with the salt. Cut about ½ stick of the butter into cubes and add to the flour. Pulse several times until the butter and flour are combined. (Alternatively, rub the butter into the flour with your fingers.) Put the mixture in a bowl and add about ⅓ cup of the ice water; use a wooden spoon or a rubber spatula to gradually gather the mixture into a ball, adding more water if necessary. Knead on a lightly floured surface until smooth, about 2 minutes; then wrap in plastic wrap and chill.

(STEP 1) Once you remove the dough from the refrigerator, put it on a lightly floured surface and roll out to a rectangle about 8 × 16 inches; it should be about ¼ inch thick. Remove the butter from the refrigerator, put it on a lightly floured surface, and roll it out to a rectangle about 4 × 8 inches. Brush excess flour from the butter and put it in the center of the dough. (STEP 2) Fold over all four corners of the dough, in a hexagon shape, to completely enclose the butter. Sprinkle the dough with flour, wrap, and refrigerate for at least 15 minutes, possibly longer. Again, you want the butter to be firm but not hard, the dough to be pliable. Remove the dough from the refrigerator, put it on a lightly floured surface, and gently roll it out again, to a rectangle about 8 × 16 inches. Be careful not to roll the edges thinner than the rest of the dough. Use flour as necessary and take your time. (STEP 3) Brush off excess flour, then bring each of the short ends of the rectangle together in the middle; roll lightly, then fold in thirds—as if folding a letter. Dust with a little flour, then wrap and refrigerate for about 30 minutes. Repeat the rolling and folding step at least two and preferably four more times; the more you do it, the lighter and finer your pastry. Chill for at least 1 hour before proceeding.

❷ Meanwhile, use an electric mixer (one with a paddle or dough hook works best) to cream the remaining butter with the remaining flour. When it is well combined, soft and smooth, shape into a disk, wrap in plastic, and refrigerate for about 30 minutes, or until cold but still malleable.

❸ Remove the dough from the refrigerator, put it on a lightly floured surface, and roll out to a rectangle about 8 × 16 inches; it should be about ¼ inch thick. Remove the butter from the refrigerator, put it on a lightly floured surface, and roll it out to a rectangle about 4 × 8 inches. Brush excess flour from the butter and put it in the center of the dough; fold over all 4 corners of the dough, in a hexagon shape, to completely

enclose the butter and pat gently to form a thick rectangle (see illustrations). Sprinkle the dough with flour, wrap, and refrigerate for at least 15 minutes, possibly longer. You want the butter to be firm but not hard, the dough to be pliable.

❹ Remove the dough from the refrigerator, put it on a lightly floured surface, and gently roll it out again, to a rectangle about 8 × 16 inches. Be careful not to roll the edges thinner than the rest of the dough. Use flour as necessary and take your time. Brush off excess flour, then bring each of the short ends of the rectangle together in the middle (see illustration); roll lightly, then fold in thirds—as if folding a letter. Dust with a little flour, then wrap and refrigerate for about 30 minutes.

 F Fast   **M** Make Ahead   **V** Vegetarian

5 Repeat Step 4 at least two and preferably four more times; the more you do it, the lighter and finer your pastry. Chill for at least 1 hour before proceeding with the following recipes.

Croissants. Makes 32 small or 16 large pastries: Heat the oven to 350°F. Beat an egg with a little water to make an egg wash. Roll the puff pastry out to a square about $1/8$ inch thick. Cut the dough into large or small squares; then cut each square in half diagonally to form a triangle. Beginning with the tip, roll each into a crescent shape and put on ungreased baking sheets, at least an inch apart. Brush with egg wash and bake until browned, 15 to 25 minutes,

depending on the size. Cool on racks and resist the urge to eat until they've cooled to barely warm.

Palmiers, Arcs, or Other Puff Pastry Cookies

MAKES: About 50
TIME: About 1 hour

Here are two ways to turn puff pastry into cookies; they're fast and easy, as long as you have the pastry. Be liberal with the sugar, since the pastry itself is not sweet-

---

MAKING PALMIERS

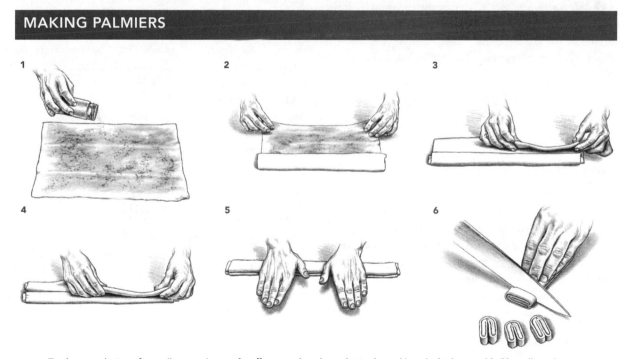

(STEP 1) To shape palmiers, first roll out a sheet of puff pastry dough until it is about $1/4$ inch thick; sprinkle liberally with sugar as you work. (STEP 2) Fold each short end of the dough to the middle. (STEP 3) Fold the dough into the middle again. (STEP 4) Now fold it in half. (STEP 5) Press gently to seal, but do not press too hard. (STEP 6) Cut $1/4$-inch slices from the roll and bake, cut side up.

ened. Use half of a puff pastry recipe if you prefer; the remainder will freeze well and the cookies don't stay crisp for more than a couple of days.

Sugar as needed

1 recipe Puff Pastry (page 943)

1 Use sugar to coat a work surface. Cut the pastry in half and roll out each half, sprinkling with sugar as you work, until it is less than $1/4$ inch thick. To make arcs, roll up the dough as you would a carpet. To make palmiers, fold each of the short ends 2 or 3 times inward to reach the middle. Then fold the dough in half along the center fold and press gently to seal (see illustrations). Wrap in plastic wrap and refrigerate for about 30 minutes.

2 Heat the oven to 350°F. Slice the rolls into $1/4$-inch-thick slices, sprinkle with a little more sugar, and put on an ungreased baking sheet. Bake until golden brown, about 30 minutes, turning the cookies once after about 20 minutes.

Apple Turnovers

MAKES: About 12 small turnovers

TIME: About 1 hour

If you've never had an apple turnover made with puff pastry, you are in for a treat. The shattering, buttery crust contrasted with the sweet, soft apple filling is nothing short of a revelation. You can also fill these with $1 1/2$ cups of berries or sliced peaches, plums, or pears.

4 tart apples, peeled and cored

1 tablespoon freshly squeezed lemon juice

1 tablespoon cornstarch

1 teaspoon minced or grated lemon zest, or more to taste

1 teaspoon ground cinnamon, or more to taste

$1/2$ cup sugar, or more to taste, plus more for the work surface and for sprinkling

$1/2$ recipe Puff Pastry (page 943)

1 Grate the apples in a food processor or on the coarse side of a box grater. Immediately toss them with the lemon juice. Add the cornstarch, lemon zest, cinnamon, and sugar. Taste and add more lemon zest or cinnamon if you like.

2 Use sugar to coat a work surface. Cut the pastry in half and roll it out, sprinkling with sugar as you work, until the dough is less than $1/4$ inch thick. Cut 4-inch squares of pastry (there will be leftovers and ragged ends; use the trimmings to make cookies). Sprinkle lightly with sugar.

3 Put 2 tablespoons of the apple filling in the center of each square; brush the edges of the pastry very lightly with water, then fold over the corners to form a triangle. Seal gently with your fingers, then slash the top of the turnover with a razor blade or sharp paring knife once or twice so steam can escape. Put the turnovers on ungreased baking sheets, about an inch apart, and chill while you heat the oven or for up to several hours.

4 Heat the oven to 350°F. Brush the tops of the turnovers with a little water and sprinkle with sugar. Bake until the turnovers are golden brown, about 40 minutes. Serve warm or at room temperature.

The Basics of Phyllo

Phyllo desserts—baklava is the model—are pretty easy to make, because the phyllo itself is premade; you just buy it, usually frozen. (You can make it, but it takes expertise and a lot of patience.) You may find fresh phyllo in Greek, Turkish, or other Mediterranean markets. If you do, grab it; use it immediately or wrap well and freeze for later.

There are just a few tips you need to know to use phyllo successfully:

1. Refrigerate phyllo for up to a week or freeze for up to a year.

 Fast   Make Ahead   **V** Vegetarian

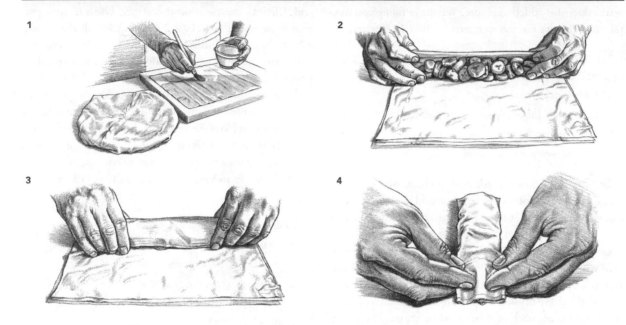

(STEP 1) Brush the layers of phyllo with butter. Keep the remaining sheets covered with a damp towel (on a plate if you like) until you use them. (STEP 2) Fill, just about to the edges. (STEP 3) Roll carefully, but not too tightly. (STEP 4) Fold the ends over.

2. Defrost frozen phyllo in the refrigerator, ideally at least 24 hours before you plan to use it. Thawing at room temperature makes the sheets stick together.

3. Phyllo dries out quickly, so when you begin working with it, keep all but the sheet you are currently using covered with plastic wrap topped with a damp towel.

4. Phyllo sheets are large; allow plenty of work space, and use a pizza wheel to cut them if you have one.

5. Patch any holes with phyllo scraps brushed lightly with butter or oil.

6. Always cook until deep golden brown and crisp.

To get that unbelievably crisp crust with phyllo it's essential to brush each sheet with melted butter (or oil, but butter is far superior); this allows the sheets to separate during baking and become crisp and flaky. Taking shortcuts with the butter or trying to reduce fat here will yield a flat, raw-looking pastry with little or no flavor.

Use fillings that are flavorful—almost overseasoned, because the pastry itself is bland—but not too moist, or the phyllo will become soggy. And of course you can make savory pies and strudel by simply substituting the filling.

Banana Strudel

MAKES: 4 to 6 servings
TIME: 45 minutes

Just like phyllo, traditional strudel dough is paper-thin and flaky when baked, so phyllo makes a good ready-made substitute. All sorts of fruits will work here, including chopped dried fruit, which can be lightly rehydrated in warm water for added moisture. Whatever filling you use, take care that it's not too wet; strain it first if necessary.

1/3 cup melted unsalted butter

2 ripe bananas, peeled and sliced

3 tablespoons brown sugar

6 to 8 sheets (about 4 ounces) phyllo dough, thawed

1/2 cup chopped macadamia nuts (optional)

1/2 cup shredded coconut (optional)

1 Put a skillet over medium-high heat; when it's hot, add 2 tablespoons of the butter, then add the bananas and brown sugar. Cook, stirring frequently, until the bananas are just softened, about 2 minutes. Set aside to cool.

2 Heat the oven to 350°F. Keep the phyllo sheets covered with a piece of plastic wrap and a damp towel over the top to keep them from drying out. Remove one sheet at a time and quickly brush it with the melted butter, repeating until you have a stack of 8 buttered sheets (it's best to do this on the parchment-lined baking sheet you'll cook it on).

3 Put the banana mixture in a line along the long edge of the phyllo. Sprinkle with the macadamias and coconut, if you're using them, and roll it into a log, putting the seam side down; tuck in the ends of the log.

4 Brush the strudel with more butter and score the top a few times with a sharp knife; wrap very well with plastic wrap and store in the fridge for up to a day, or immediately bake until golden brown, about 25 minutes. Let rest for just a couple minutes, then cut into 2- to 3-inch-thick slices.

Baklava

MAKES: 4 dozen pieces
TIME: At least 2 hours, plus time to rest

If you ask me, baklava is a two-person job, and even then it's time-consuming. But there's no way to make such a huge quantity of dessert in such a reliable manner, and it's among the most wonderful, foolproof, impressive, and delicious creations on the planet. Use a lasagne pan measuring about 16 × 10 × 2 inches. You will also need a 1-inch brush (paintbrushes, bought at the hardware store, are cheaper than and identical to most so-called pastry brushes).

Two possible variations (there are dozens, but these are the simplest): Substitute hazelnuts, almonds, or unsalted pistachios (the best, but the most expensive) for the walnuts and add about 2 tablespoons orange blossom water or rose water to the syrup after cooking it.

With thanks to Virginia Christy and her brother, Sem.

1 cup honey

3 cups plus 7 tablespoons sugar

2 teaspoons freshly squeezed lemon juice

6 cups (about 1 1/2 pounds) walnuts

2 teaspoons ground cinnamon

2 pounds phyllo dough, thawed if frozen

1 pound (4 sticks) butter, melted

1 Combine the honey, 3 cups of the sugar, and the lemon juice with 2 1/2 cups water and bring to a boil. Stir to dissolve the sugar and chill. (This can be done hours, days, even weeks in advance.)

2 Chop the nuts (the food processor makes quick work of this; be sure to pulse, not blend—you don't want ground nuts). Combine with the 7 tablespoons sugar and the cinnamon. Keep the phyllo sheets covered with a piece of plastic wrap and a damp towel to keep them from drying out.

3 Brush the bottom of your pan with butter; lay 7 sheets of phyllo on it, the narrow way, overlapping slightly and with alternating ends hanging over the edges. Brush the phyllo with butter and sprinkle with about 1/4 cup of the nut mixture. Fold the ends over, brush with butter and sprinkle with nuts, then repeat with 7 more sheets. Repeat until only 10 or 11 sheets remain. Do these sheets in the same manner, but only buttering them (you will have used up the nuts by now).

4 Refrigerate for about an hour, longer if you prefer. Heat the oven to 300°F. Score the top of the sheets, first lengthwise into 4 sections, then widthwise into 6 sections, and finally diagonally, to make about 48 triangles. Bake until golden brown, about 1 hour.

5 Cool slightly, then cut through your score marks, using a sharp, thin-bladed knife. Pour the cold syrup over all, tilting the pan so it spreads all over. Cool to room temperature, then serve. Baklava keeps well, covered, at room temperature for several days.

Walnut Phyllo "Cigars." Far easier and faster: Cut the recipe in half, or even just a quarter will do. Proceed with Steps 1 and 2. Take one sheet of phyllo at a time and quickly brush it with the melted butter. Repeat until you have a stack of 4 to 6 buttered sheets. Put $1/2$ cup of the nut mixture in a line along the narrow edge of the phyllo; sprinkle the phyllo with a couple extra tablespoons of the sugar and roll it into a long "cigar." Repeat using all the phyllo, nuts, and sugar as needed. Bake in a 325°F oven until golden brown and then cut into 3-inch "cigars." Put in a dish and drizzle with the sugar syrup; let sit for 30 minutes or longer before serving.

The Basics of Puddings, Custards, Mousses, and Gelées

There are several different ways to thicken liquids. Gently cooked eggs lend a silken texture unmatched by anything else, though cornstarch, grains, bread, gelatin, and even fruit can also create luxurious desserts.

There's no trick to cooking eggs in the recipes that use them here, except to remember that overcooked eggs are essentially scrambled eggs, which is *not* what you want. You must cook eggs at relatively low heat, and just until they thicken, to make them smooth and uniform. When you're cooking on top of the stove—as you will with most soft custards—this isn't much of a problem. But

removing custards and other egg-thickened desserts from the oven is trickier: By the time a custard appears to be set, it's almost always overcooked. You must make a leap of faith and remove it from the oven while the center is still wobbly. When you get the timing down, you'll be making brilliant custards.

Although it's not always essential, it also helps to cook your custards in a water bath: Just put the baking dish or individual custard cups in a larger baking pan (a roasting pan often works well) and pour hot water at least halfway up the height of the custard. By moderating the temperature around the custard, the water bath (also called a *bain-marie*) makes for more even cooking. (For the classic custard recipe, see Old-Fashioned Baked Custard on page 885.)

Gelled desserts (*gelées* in French) are what Jell-O imitates. Gelatin works best because it gels clear, but you can use granulated agar or arrowroot.

COATING THE BACK OF A SPOON

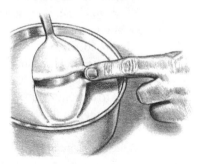

The easiest way to know when stovetop egg-based custards are done is to dip a tablespoon into the liquid and drag the tip of your finger across the back. If there is a good layer of the liquid clinging to the back of the spoon and a distinct trail from where your fingertip was, it's properly thickened. If the liquid just slides right off the spoon, or your finger trail is covered quickly by runny liquid, keep cooking.

Vanilla Pudding

MAKES: 4 to 6 servings

TIME: About 20 minutes, plus time to chill

F **M** **V**

This is a soft stovetop pudding, not much more difficult to produce than the packaged "instant" variety. Top with Whipped Cream flavored with booze, maple, or nutmeg if you like (page 882).

2^1/$_2$ cups half-and-half or whole milk

^{2}/$_3$ cup sugar

Pinch salt

1 vanilla bean or 1 teaspoon vanilla extract

3 tablespoons cornstarch

2 tablespoons unsalted butter, softened (optional)

1 Put 2 cups of the half-and-half, the sugar, and the salt in a small to medium saucepan over medium-low heat. If you're using a vanilla bean, split it in half lengthwise and use a small sharp knife to scrape the seeds into the half-and-half; add the pod. Cook just until it begins to steam.

2 Combine the cornstarch and the remaining half-and-half in a bowl and stir to blend; there should be no lumps. Fish the pod out of the steaming milk and add the cornstarch mixture to the pan. Cook, stirring occasionally, until the mixture thickens and just starts to boil, about 5 minutes. Reduce the heat to very low and continue to cook, stirring, another 5 minutes or so. Stir in the butter and the vanilla extract if you're using them.

3 Pour the mixture into a 1-quart dish or into 4 to 6 small ramekins or bowls. Put plastic wrap directly on top of the pudding to prevent the formation of a "skin," or do not cover if you like skin. Refrigerate until chilled and serve within a day.

Traditional Vanilla Pudding. Sometimes nothing beats a traditional egg-enriched pudding: Substitute 2 eggs and 4 yolks for the cornstarch. In Step 1, heat all of the half-and-half. In Step 2, whisk or beat the eggs with the sugar and salt; add one-third of the heated half-and-half gradually while whisking constantly, then whisk the egg mixture into the remaining half-and-half. Cook, whisking constantly, until the mixture is thick enough to coat the back of a spoon, about 10 minutes, then stir in the butter and vanilla extract. Proceed with the recipe.

Chocolate Pudding. In Step 2, add 2 ounces chopped bittersweet chocolate to the thickened pudding.

Butterscotch Pudding. This also can be made with the Vanilla Pudding recipe: Just substitute brown sugar for the white sugar.

Real Banana Pudding. Use whole milk, reduce the sugar to ^{1}/$_4$ cup, and add 3 very ripe bananas, peeled and cut into ^{1}/$_2$-inch pieces. In Step 1, add the bananas and steep in the warm milk for about 20 minutes. Strain out the bananas and vanilla pod; discard them and return the milk mixture to the pot. Proceed with the recipe.

Green Tea or Earl Grey Pudding. Omit the vanilla bean and steep a couple tablespoons green or Earl Grey tea in the half-and-half after it steams in Step 1. Strain the liquid and return it to the pot before proceeding with the recipe.

Ultra-Rich Pudding. Substitute cream for the half-and-half in the main recipe or any of the variations.

Panna Cotta

MAKES: 4 to 6 servings

TOTAL TIME: 30 minutes or less, plus time to chill

F **M**

The Italian custard, thickened with gelatin and flavored with vanilla. Pure silk; I like the buttermilk variation best. Lovely with a fruit purée (see page 923).

 Fast   Make Ahead   Vegetarian

3 cups cream or 1¹/₂ cups cream and 1¹/₂ cups half-and-half, preferably not ultra-pasteurized

One ¹/₄-ounce package unflavored gelatin

1 vanilla bean or 1 teaspoon vanilla extract, or to taste

¹/₂ cup sugar

❶ Put 1 cup of the cream in a medium saucepan and sprinkle the gelatin over it; let sit for 5 minutes. Turn the heat to low and cook, stirring, until the gelatin dissolves completely, 3 to 5 minutes.

❷ Cut the vanilla bean in half lengthwise. Scrape out the seeds with a sharp knife; add both seeds and pod to the pot, along with the sugar and the remaining cream. Cook over medium heat, stirring, just until steam rises from the pot, 3 to 5 minutes. Turn off the heat, cover, and let steep for 15 to 30 minutes. (If you're using vanilla extract, add the cream and sugar to the gelatin mixture and heat gently, stirring, just until the sugar dissolves; add the vanilla and proceed.)

❸ Remove the vanilla pod and pour the mixture into 4 large or 6 small custard cups. Chill until set, about 4 hours. Serve in the cups or dip the cups in hot water for about 10 seconds each, then invert onto plates. Serve within 24 hours.

Buttermilk Panna Cotta. Substitute 1¹/₂ cups buttermilk for half the cream. Use all the buttermilk in Step 1. Proceed with the recipe.

Almond "Panna" Cotta. Almond milk replaces the cream: Substitute almond milk for the cream, almond extract for the vanilla, and 2 teaspoons agar for the gelatin if you like. In Step 2, use the directions for the vanilla extract. Proceed with the recipe.

Tembleque. A Caribbean dessert made with coconut milk: Substitute coconut milk for the cream. Dissolve the gelatin in ¹/₂ cup coconut milk (to make your own, see page 389), as directed in Step 1, combine it with the remainder of the coconut milk, and skip to Step 3. Garnish the unmolded custards with a dusting of ground cinnamon just before serving.

Raspberry Fool

MAKES: 4 to 6 servings
TIME: 20 minutes

The easiest mousse you can make. A perfect treatment for raspberries, which require no cooking at all to be tender. But a fool can be made with any soft, ripe fruit (most you won't even need to strain after puréeing): Just toss with Whipped Cream (page 882) and sugar to taste.

2 to 3 cups raspberries

¹/₂ cup superfine or confectioners' sugar, plus 1 tablespoon sugar, plus more if needed

1 cup cream, preferably not ultra-pasteurized

❶ Purée about one-third of the raspberries in a blender with ¹/₄ cup of the sugar. Force the purée through a sieve to remove the seeds. Taste; the purée should be quite sweet. If not, add a little more sugar.

❷ Toss the remaining berries (saving a few for garnish) with the remaining ¹/₄ cup sugar. Beat the cream with 1 tablespoon sugar until it holds soft peaks. Beat in the raspberry purée, then fold in the sugared berries. Taste and add more sugar if necessary. Garnish and serve immediately or refrigerate for up to an hour.

Chocolate Mousse

MAKES: 6 servings
TIME: 20 minutes, plus time to chill

Once thought of as the most elegant of desserts, this ultra-rich chocolate pudding is still a real winner. It's blazing quick to make—I've prepared it after dinner and still served it before my guests left. Once the chocolate is

melted, the cooking is over; the mousse just sits until it sets up. You can spike it with rum, coffee, or other flavorings, but I like it simple—it's the intensity of the chocolate that makes it special.

Top with Whipped Cream (page 882) and shaved chocolate if you like.

2 tablespoons unsalted butter

4 ounces bittersweet or semisweet chocolate, chopped

3 eggs, separated

¼ cup sugar

½ cup cream

½ teaspoon vanilla extract

① Use a double boiler or a small saucepan over low heat to melt the butter and chocolate together. Just before the chocolate finishes melting, remove it from the stove and beat with a wooden spoon until smooth.

② Transfer the chocolate mixture to a bowl and beat in the egg yolks with a whisk. Refrigerate.

③ Beat the egg whites with half the sugar until they hold stiff peaks but are not dry (see the illustrations on page 900). Set aside. Beat the cream with the remaining sugar and the vanilla until it holds soft peaks (see the illustrations on page 883).

④ Stir a couple of spoonfuls of the whites into the chocolate mixture to lighten it a bit, then fold in the remaining whites thoroughly but gently. Fold in the cream and refrigerate until chilled. If you are in a hurry, divide the mousse among 6 cups; it will chill much faster. Serve within a day or two.

Mocha Mousse. Substitute 1 shot freshly brewed espresso for 2 tablespoons of the cream and add it to the chocolate mixture. Or add 2 teaspoons instant espresso powder to the chocolate mixture.

White Chocolate Mousse. Substitute white chocolate for the dark chocolate.

Lemon Mousse

MAKES: At least 6 servings
TIME: About 30 minutes, plus time to chill

A refreshing cold mousse that contains cream and eggs but is stabilized by gelatin, which makes it virtually foolproof. Use any citrus you like in place of the lemon, adjusting the amount of sugar accordingly. Top with Whipped Cream (page 882), mint or lemon verbena leaves, berries, or toasted almonds (see page 317).

One ¼-ounce package unflavored gelatin

½ cup freshly squeezed lemon juice

4 eggs

1 tablespoon grated or minced lemon zest

½ cup sugar

1 cup cream

① In a small saucepan, sprinkle the gelatin over the lemon juice. Let sit while you beat the eggs, lemon zest, and sugar with a whisk or an electric mixer until lemon colored and slightly thickened.

② Warm the gelatin mixture over low heat, stirring occasionally, until the gelatin dissolves, just a minute or two. Cool for 1 minute, then stir it into the egg mixture.

③ Working quickly (you don't want the gelatin to set prematurely), whip the cream until it holds soft peaks, then stir thoroughly into the egg mixture. Refrigerate, stirring occasionally for the first hour or two, until well chilled. Serve the same day.

Pomegranate Mousse. Pomegranate juice is in every market these days: Substitute 1 cup pomegranate juice for the lemon juice. Omit the zest. Use 2 yolks and 3 whites.

Lemony Yogurt Mousse. Light and with a touch of yogurt tang: Substitute yogurt for the cream and 3 egg whites for the 4 eggs. Omit the lemon juice. In Step 1, combine the yogurt, zest, and sugar and beat until mixed and slightly aerated. Beat the egg whites as directed and proceed with the recipe.

F Fast   **M** Make Ahead   **V** Vegetarian

Pear Clafouti

MAKES: 4 to 6 servings
TIME: 1 hour

This traditional French dessert is essentially a large, sweet pancake baked with fruit and among the best desserts you can make at the last minute. Put it in the oven when you sit down to dinner and you can eat it for dessert. Any berry will also work, as will cherries, apricots, plums, or apples.

Butter for the pan

$1/2$ cup granulated sugar, plus 1 tablespoon for the baking dish

About 1 pound pears, peeled, halved, and cored

3 eggs

1 vanilla bean or 1 teaspoon vanilla extract

$3/4$ cup all-purpose flour

$3/4$ cup cream or yogurt

$3/4$ cup milk

Pinch salt

Confectioners' sugar for the top

1 Heat the oven to 375°F. Butter a gratin or baking dish that will hold the fruit in one layer; sprinkle it with the tablespoon of sugar, then swirl the sugar around to coat all inner surfaces. Lay the fruit in the dish, cut sides down.

2 Use a whisk to beat the eggs until foamy. Add the remaining granulated sugar and beat with a whisk or electric mixer until foamy and fairly thick. Split the vanilla bean in half lengthwise and use a small sharp knife to scrape the seeds into the eggs, discarding the pod.

3 Add the flour and continue to beat until thick and smooth. Add the cream, milk, the vanilla extract if you're using it, and the salt. Pour the batter over the fruit and bake for about 20 minutes, or until the clafouti is nicely browned on top and a knife inserted into it comes out clean. Sift some confectioners' sugar over it and serve warm or at room temperature.

Fluffy Raspberry Clafouti. Lighter with whipped cream folded in: Whip the cream to medium peaks (see page 883) and fold it into the batter after the milk is added in Step 3.

Dried Fruit Clafouti. Use figs, raisins, prunes, dates, or apricots (or a combination): Use $1^1/_2$ cups sliced dried fruit instead of the pears. Soak them in a little warm water first (or rum, bourbon, or port wine), drain, and squeeze them dry. Before baking, sprinkle the top with chopped hazelnuts if you like.

Bread Pudding

MAKES: 6 servings
TIME: About 1 hour, largely unattended

There are few ways to use leftover bread that equal this. You can vary the recipe any number of ways, starting with different kinds of bread (whole wheat, challah, rye, or cinnamon raisin) or day-old pastry (Danish, cinnamon rolls, or muffins). Cut them into large cubes; you'll need about 3 heaping cups. Feel free to add chocolate chips, nuts, or chopped dried fruit. Top the finished pudding, if you like, with plain or flavored Whipped Cream (page 882) or Vanilla Custard Sauce (page 924).

3 cups milk

4 tablespoons ($1/2$ stick) unsalted butter, plus more for the pan

$1^1/_2$ teaspoons ground cinnamon

$1/2$ cup plus 1 tablespoon sugar

Pinch salt

8 slices white bread, preferably stale, crusts removed if they are very thick or dark

3 eggs

1 Heat the oven to 350°F. Over low heat in a small saucepan, warm the milk, butter, 1 teaspoon of the cinnamon, $^1/_2$ cup of the sugar, and the salt, just until the butter melts. Meanwhile, butter a 6-cup or 8-inch square baking dish (glass is nice) and cut or tear the bread into bite-sized pieces; they need not be too small.

2 Put the bread in the baking dish and pour the hot milk mixture over it. Let it sit for a few minutes, occasionally submerging any pieces of bread that rise to the top. Beat the eggs briefly and stir them into the bread mixture. Mix together the remaining sugar and cinnamon and sprinkle over the top. Set the baking dish in a larger baking pan and pour hot water in, to within about an inch of the top of the dish.

3 Bake for 45 to 60 minutes, until a thin-bladed knife inserted in the center comes out clean or nearly so; the center should be just a little wobbly. Run under the broiler for about 30 seconds to brown the top a bit if you like. Serve warm or cold. This keeps well for 2 days or more, covered and refrigerated.

Chocolate Bread Pudding. In Step 1, melt 2 ounces chopped bittersweet chocolate with the butter and milk.

Apple-Raisin Bread Pudding. In Step 2, add 1 cup peeled, cored, grated, and drained apples and $^1/_4$ cup or more raisins to the mixture along with the eggs.

Rum-Raisin Bread Pudding. Add $^1/_4$ cup dark rum and $^1/_2$ cup raisins to the mixture along with the eggs.

Rice Pudding

MAKES: At least 4 servings
TIME: About 2 hours, largely unattended

M **V**

This simple no-egg rice pudding is sweet and easy. Use coconut, hazelnut, or almond milk instead of cow's milk for a nice twist. Top with Whipped Cream, flavored with vanilla or rose water if you like (page 882).

$^1/_4$ to $^1/_3$ cup rice

$^1/_2$ cup sugar

Small pinch salt

1 quart milk

Pinch saffron threads (optional)

Cinnamon stick or other flavoring (optional)

1 Heat the oven to 300°F. Combine all the ingredients in a 3- or 4-quart casserole (an ovenproof saucepan will do), stir a couple of times, and place in the oven. Cook for 30 minutes, then stir. Cook for 30 minutes longer, then stir; at this point the milk will have developed a bubbly tan surface (you will stir this back into the liquid), and the rice will have begun to swell.

2 Cook for 30 more minutes. The surface will have redeveloped, darker this time, and the grains of rice will begin to predominate in the mixture; the pudding is almost done. Return the mixture to the oven and check every 10 minutes, stirring gently each time you check.

3 The pudding may be done 10, 20, or 30 minutes later. Invariably, it is done before you believe so. You must make a leap of faith and remove the custard from the oven when the rice kernels are very swollen and the mixture thick but still quite fluid. As it cools, it will thicken considerably. (If you overcook, the pudding will become fairly hard, though it's still quite good to eat.) Serve warm, at room temperature, or cold.

Rice Pudding Brûlée. When you're ready to serve the pudding, set up a broiler so that the top of the casserole will be no more than 3 inches from the heat source; 2 inches is better. Cover the top of the custard with a thin layer of sugar—a tablespoon or two. (You may also divide the custard into small bowls or ramekins before proceeding.) Turn on the broiler and put the casserole or ramekins under the heat; rotate it so that the heat hits all parts of the top evenly. Cook until the sugar bubbles and browns,

RICE PUDDING VARIATIONS

Use the main recipe as the base and switch out the prescribed ingredients; the rice and cooking technique remain the same.

VARIATION	SWEETENER	LIQUID	FLAVORINGS AND/OR GARNISH
Yogurt or Ricotta Rice Pudding	$1/3$ to $1/2$ cup sugar, or to taste	3 cups water	Stir in 2 cups yogurt or ricotta when the pudding has cooled for about 10 minutes.
Saffron-Rice Pudding	$1/3$ to $1/2$ cup sugar, or to taste	1 quart milk	Add a large pinch saffron threads and 1 tablespoon rose water, or to taste, in Step 1. Stir in 2 tablespoons each raisins, roughly chopped blanched almonds, and pistachios after it's cooked.
Hazelnut Rice Pudding	$1/3$ to $1/2$ cup sugar, or to taste	1 quart hazelnut milk or milk	Sprinkle with chopped toasted hazelnuts for garnish.
Butterscotch Rice Pudding	$1/2$ cup brown sugar	1 quart milk, 8 tablespoons (1 stick) unsalted butter	Stir in a couple tablespoons dark rum if you like. Sprinkle with toasted nuts.
Maple Rice Pudding	1 cup maple syrup	3 cups milk	Sprinkle with a bit of freshly grated nutmeg or cinnamon and some toasted nuts for garnish.
Mango Rice Pudding	$1/3$ to $1/2$ cup sugar, or to taste	$3^{1}/_{2}$ cups milk or coconut milk (to make your own, see page 389)	Stir in 1 cup mango purée (see page 923) when the pudding has cooled for at least 10 minutes.
Coconut Rice Pudding	$1/3$ to $1/2$ cup sugar, or to taste	4 cups coconut milk (to make your own, see page 389)	Sprinkle with toasted shredded coconut (see page 389).

about 5 minutes, then remove. Serve within an hour.

5 Simple Ideas for Rice Pudding

1. Add $1/4$ cup or more raisins or snipped dates, figs, or other dried fruit about halfway through the cooking.
2. Stir 1 cup chopped mango, papaya, or pineapple into the mix about halfway through the cooking.
3. Add 1 teaspoon vanilla extract or orange blossom or rose water at the end of cooking.
4. Add 1 teaspoon minced lemon or orange zest in place of spices.
5. Garnish with a sprinkling of toasted sliced almonds or other nuts.

Tapioca Pudding

MAKES: 4 servings

TIME: About 20 minutes, plus time to chill

Tapioca is somewhere between rice and cornstarch when it comes to pudding—it acts as a neutral thickener, like cornstarch, but it gives a distinctive texture, like rice. Some people don't like the texture, but others find it heavenly. I love it, especially topped with Whipped Cream (page 882).

$1/3$ cup quick-cooking tapioca

$1/2$ cup sugar

Pinch salt

2 cups milk

2 eggs, separated

1½ teaspoons vanilla extract

1 Combine the tapioca, sugar, salt, and milk in a small saucepan over medium heat. Cook, stirring, until the tapioca becomes transparent, about 5 minutes. Remove from the heat, cool for a minute or two, then beat in the egg yolks. Cool the mixture for a few more minutes before proceeding.

2 Beat the egg whites until they hold soft peaks; fold them gently into the yolk mixture along with the vanilla. Spoon into individual serving cups and serve or chill before serving; this keeps well for up to 2 days.

Coconut Tapioca Pudding. Substitute coconut milk (to make your own, see page 389) or use for all or part of the milk.

Mango Tapioca Pudding. Add 1 cup puréed, mashed, or chopped fresh, ripe mango. Add it along with the egg whites and proceed with the recipe.

Summer Pudding

MAKES: 4 to 6 servings

TIME: 20 minutes, plus time to chill

You can use any kind of berries or a mixture. Keep all the berries whole, except for strawberries, which should be sliced. And if you don't have homemade pound cake handy, substitute store-bought or any plain cake or thick slices of bread—crusts removed. Serve with lightly sweetened Whipped Cream (page 882), sour cream, or crème fraîche.

3 pounds raspberries, fresh or frozen

½ cup sugar, or to taste

2 pounds Pound Cake (page 906; about 1 cake)

1 Rinse the berries, then combine in a saucepan with the sugar and ¼ cup water. Cook gently, stirring occasionally, just until the berries soften and yield their liquid, 10 to 15 minutes. Cool.

2 Meanwhile, cut the pound cake into roughly ½-inch-thick slices. Line a medium bowl with just over half the slices of pound cake so they come about 4 inches up the sides of the bowl; pack the slices so they leave no (significant) gaps. When the berries are cool, drain them, reserving the liquid. Spoon the solids on top of the pound cake and drizzle with about half the liquid.

3 Cover with the remaining slices of pound cake, again packing them close together. Drizzle with all but a few tablespoons of the remaining liquid (refrigerate the rest).

4 Find a plate that will just fit into the bowl and press it down on top of the pudding. Weight it with a few cans (or whatever you can find that will do the trick) and refrigerate overnight.

5 To serve, run a knife around the edge of the pudding and invert onto a plate. Cut slices and serve.

Persimmon Pudding. Substitute 6 very soft Hachiya persimmons for the berries. In Step 1, slice off the tops of the persimmons, scoop the insides into the saucepan, add 1 teaspoon ground cinnamon and a pinch ground cloves, and cook with the sugar and water as directed.

Chocolate Tofu Pudding

MAKES: 4 to 6 servings

TIME: 10 minutes, plus time to chill

Go ahead, scoff. But this is the easiest pudding on the planet, and it's delicious. All you do is put the four ingredients in a blender and whirl until the mixture is smooth.

Top with chocolate shavings or sprinkle with chopped candied ginger.

    1 pound silken tofu

    8 ounces bittersweet or semisweet chocolate, melted

    3/4 cup Sugar Syrup (page 921)

    1 teaspoon vanilla extract

Put all the ingredients in a blender and purée until completely smooth. Divide into ramekins or fancy dishes if you like and chill for at least 30 minutes.

Mexican Chocolate Tofu Pudding. Add 1 teaspoon ground cinnamon, 1/4 teaspoon chili powder (to make your own, see page 66), and 2 tablespoons Triple Sec or other orange-flavored liqueur if you like.

Chocolate-Banana Tofu Pudding. Substitute 2 ripe bananas for half the tofu.

Gelée, Many Ways

MAKES: 4 servings
TIME: 25 minutes, plus time to chill

Not your average Jell-O, the main recipe is rich in chocolate but light on the tongue (and low in fat). To vary the flavor, try almost any liquid—from fruit juice to tea—as the base. Eat with a spoon—served with raspberries and/or a dollop of Whipped Cream (page 882)—or increase the thickener to make the gelée stiffer, then cut up and eat like candy or dice and add to anything from iced tea to dessert soup (see pages 966–968).

    5 teaspoons unflavored gelatin

    1 cup cocoa powder

    2 cups Sugar Syrup (page 921)

    8 ounces bittersweet chocolate, melted

❶ Put the gelatin, cocoa powder, and sugar syrup in a pot and stir it until it looks like chocolate syrup; let it sit for about 10 minutes and then bring to a boil. Remove from the heat, then whisk in the melted chocolate.

❷ Pour the liquid into individual ramekins, small bowls, cups, or a single larger dish (keep in mind you probably want the gelée to be at least 1 inch thick). Let the gelée set at room temperature or in the refrigerator until it's firm, at least 30 minutes.

Champagne Gelée with Berries. Serve in clear glass, even Champagne glasses: Substitute 3 cups chilled Champagne or sparkling wine for the cocoa and chocolate; reduce the gelatin to 1/4 cup and the sugar syrup to 1 cup. In Step 1, mix the gelatin with the simple syrup in the pot and bring it to a boil. Cool it only slightly, about 5 minutes, then stir in the Champagne. Transfer to the serving dish(es) and put in the fridge for about 5 minutes so it's just starting to set up; drop in the berries (they should suspend in the semiset gelée) and return to the fridge.

Berry Gelée. Substitute 3 cups mixed berry purée (see page 923) for the cocoa and chocolate and 1/2 cup sugar for the sugar syrup. Reduce the gelatin to 4 teaspoons. In Step 1, combine the purée, sugar, and gelatin in the pot. Proceed with the recipe and top with the whipped cream.

Lemon-Lime Gelées. Kids love these cubes; substitute any fruit juice or nectar for the water for all sorts of flavors: Add 1 tablespoon mixed grated lemon and lime zest and 2 1/2 cups water. Substitute 1/4 cup each lemon and lime juices for the cocoa and chocolate. Reduce the sugar syrup to 1 cup. Proceed with the recipe. Pour into a wide dish so the gelée is about 1 inch thick. Let it set up completely, then use a small cookie cutter (not larger than about 2 inches across) to cut into cubes, stars, hearts, or other shapes.

The Basics of Dessert Soufflés

There are three kinds of dessert soufflés: those that are based on a white sauce and beaten egg whites, like their savory counterparts; those that get their structure entirely from beaten egg whites, which are lighter; and those that are frozen. Here is one of each. See "Beating Egg Whites" (page 900) and "The Basics of Savory Soufflés" (page 806).

Vanilla or Chocolate Soufflé

MAKES: 4 to 6 servings

TIME: About 1 hour, largely unattended

Undercook this soufflé slightly so it remains moist in the middle and needs no sauce, then dust with confectioners'

sugar. Or cook it until it's dry and serve it with Vanilla Custard Sauce (page 924), Whipped Cream (page 882), fruit purée (see page 923), or any light sauce.

3 tablespoons unsalted butter, plus 1 teaspoon for the dish

1/3 cup sugar, plus more for the dish

1 cup milk

3 tablespoons all-purpose flour

2 ounces bittersweet or semisweet chocolate, chopped, or 1 1/2 teaspoons vanilla extract

4 eggs, separated

Pinch salt

Folding Cream or Egg Whites

(STEP 1) To fold beaten cream or egg whites into a batter, first lighten the mixture by stirring a couple of spoonfuls of whites into it.

(STEP 2) Then gently fold in the rest of the cream or egg whites, scooping under the mixture and smoothing over the top. You can use a rubber spatula or your hand, which works equally well.

Folding is a technique used to incorporate beaten cream or egg whites into mousses, meringues, soufflés, and other light and airy batters. The idea is to gently add the cream or whites that you've worked hard at making airy without deflating them.

You can use a rubber spatula for folding, but try your hand, which lets you feel the progress. Work in stages: Add a third or so of the whites or cream to the batter and scoop the batter from the bottom up over it, folding in the whites as gently as you can, incorporating pretty fully to lighten the mixture. Then add the remainder, in one or two stages, folding as gently as possible. Start your folds by scooping from the side to the bottom and folding the ingredients over the top in the middle; continue this folding technique while rotating the bowl slowly.

When the ingredients look mostly incorporated, stop. The most common mistake is overfolding and thus deflating the whipped ingredient. It's okay to have some streaks of whipped cream or egg white in the mixture; you just don't want large clumps of it.

 Fast　 Make Ahead　**V** Vegetarian

❶ Use 1 teaspoon of the butter to grease a 2-quart soufflé dish or other straight-sided deep baking dish. (If you want to make individual soufflés, use a little more butter and grease four 1¹/₂- to 2-cup ramekins.) Sprinkle the dish with sugar, invert it, and tap to remove excess sugar. Set aside and heat the oven to 350°F.

❷ Warm the milk in a small saucepan over low heat with the remaining ¹/₃ cup sugar. In a second small saucepan, heat the remaining 3 tablespoons butter over medium-low heat. When the foam begins to subside, stir in the flour. Turn the heat to low and cook, stirring almost constantly, until the flour-butter mixture darkens, about 3 minutes.

❸ Stir in the milk, a little bit at a time, using a whisk. It will be quite thick; stir in the chocolate if you're using it and remove from the heat. Let cool for 5 minutes. Beat the egg yolks and stir them in. Add the vanilla if you're using it. (At this point, you may cool the mixture, cover it tightly, and refrigerate for a few hours.)

❹ Beat the egg whites with the salt until very stiff but still glossy. Stir a good spoonful of them thoroughly into the sauce to lighten it, then fold in the remaining whites, using a rubber spatula or your hand. Transfer to the prepared soufflé dish(es) and bake until the center barely jiggles and is set, or nearly so, 30 to 40 minutes (15 to 25 minutes for individual soufflés). Serve immediately.

Lemon, Orange, or Grand Marnier Soufflé

MAKES: 4 to 6 servings
TIME: About 45 minutes

Without the basic white sauce, soufflés are extremely light and airy. They're also a lot easier to make and surprisingly reliable. You just can't make them ahead of time. Dust this with confectioners' sugar or top with Vanilla Custard Sauce (page 924), Whipped Cream (page 882), or fruit purée (see page 923).

About 1 teaspoon unsalted butter for the dish

1 cup sugar, plus more for the dish

6 eggs, separated

1 tablespoon minced or grated lemon or orange zest

¹/₄ cup freshly squeezed lemon or orange juice or Grand Marnier or other orange-flavored liqueur

Pinch salt

❶ Butter a 2-quart soufflé or other deep baking dish. (If you want to make individual soufflés, use a little more butter and grease four 1¹/₂- to 2-cup ramekins.) Sprinkle the dish with sugar, invert it, and tap to remove excess sugar. Set aside and heat the oven to 350°F.

❷ Whisk the egg yolks with ³/₄ cup of the sugar until light and very thick; the mixture will fall in a ribbon from the ends of the beaters when it is ready. Beat in the zest and liquid and set aside.

❸ Beat the egg whites with the salt until they hold soft peaks; continue to beat, gradually adding the remaining ¹/₄ cup sugar, until they are very stiff but still glossy. Stir a good spoonful of them thoroughly into the egg yolk mixture to lighten it, then fold in the remaining whites, using a rubber spatula or your hand. Transfer to the prepared soufflé dish(es) and bake until the center is nearly set, 25 to 35 minutes (15 to 25 minutes for individual soufflés). Serve immediately.

Frozen Berry Soufflé

MAKES: 6 servings
TIME: About 30 minutes, plus time to freeze

Not a true soufflé, strictly speaking, but very like one and easy. And it can be prepared as much as a day in advance. Top with berries or fruit purée (see page 923) and/or Whipped Cream (page 882).

3 cups berries, picked over, well washed, and dried

1 tablespoon freshly squeezed lemon juice

3 eggs, separated

1 cup sugar

2 cups cream

1 Purée the berries with the lemon juice and pass through a strainer to remove any seeds.

2 Whisk the egg yolks with ³/₄ cup of the sugar until light and very thick, 5 to 10 minutes (a standing mixer is worth using here if you have one); the mixture will fall in a ribbon from the ends of the beaters when ready. Combine the yolks with the berries.

3 Beat the egg whites until they hold soft peaks; continue to beat, gradually adding the remaining ¹/₄ cup sugar, until they are very stiff but still glossy. Stir a good spoonful of them thoroughly into the berry mixture to lighten it, then fold in the remaining whites, using a rubber spatula or your hand.

4 Whip the cream until it holds soft peaks. Fold it very gently into the egg mixture. Turn into a 1¹/₂- to 2-quart serving dish or smaller individual dishes and freeze for several hours before serving.

The Basics of Ice Cream, Sorbet, and Granita

Even the simplest homemade ice creams will amaze you, because—despite the fact that it is stored in the freezer—ice cream is best when it's fresh. In fact, ice cream is at its peak when it comes straight from the machine, at which point its temperature is just below freezing; once it has been stored at 0°F (the temperature of most home freezers), it is never quite as good again. To be sure, it is still wonderful stuff; but be certain to let it soften slightly before serving, about 30 minutes in the refrigerator or 15 minutes on the counter.

Custard-based ice cream is usually called *French ice cream.* Cornstarch mimics the eggs well, though, so you can make eggless ice cream too. You can also make ice "cream" from nondairy milks, like coconut or nut milk.

I'm not an appliance geek, but I do recommend that you buy an ice cream machine. (Like most kitchen appliances, they're fairly easy to find on eBay or at tag sales, because someone is always giving up on the idea.) The chances are you will not make ice cream regularly, but there will always be a few times a year when the idea becomes irresistible, and it's worth it to have a machine for those occasions. The best are the 1-quart-plus-capacity machines with built-in refrigeration units; they weigh about 50 pounds, cost a few hundred dollars when new, and do all the thinking for you. But there are lesser machines—especially those that crank while in the freezer (you run a cord out of the freezer to an outlet)—that work well also, and even the inexpensive hand-cranked machines, in which you prefreeze a sleeve that fits into a container with a crank, do a good job.

Frozen Yogurt

Frozen yogurt is best when it remains true to its origins—which is to say that it should taste slightly sour. The frozen yogurt served at most ice cream shops is soft ice cream by another name. The recipe here will give you a fresh-but-tangy yogurt that you can flavor in the same way as ice cream.

Ice Milk

Think of ice milk as either simple ice cream or sorbet made with dairy. Ice milk freezes harder and forms larger ice crystals, which makes the texture less smooth and creamy than ice cream; but what you lose in texture and richness you also lose in fat and calories. Like ice cream, you can make ice milk from any kind of milk as long as you adjust your expectations. I think of ice milk as more akin to sorbet than to ice cream and treat it that way.

Sorbet

Typically (though not always) fruit based and dairy and egg free, sorbet is at its core simple and all about the

 Fast   Make Ahead   **V** Vegetarian

Using a Vanilla Bean

Real vanilla beans can make a tremendous difference in many desserts, though they've become expensive, so you want to get as much flavor from each bean as possible.

Use a small sharp knife to split the bean lengthwise; use the tip of the blade to scrape the seeds out of each side. Put the seeds in the other ingredient(s) and give the pods another scraping.

If you're adding the seeds to a liquid, you can add the emptied pods to the liquid to extract more flavor from the pods. Otherwise, bury the pods in your sugar canister to make vanilla sugar (see page 890), cut into pieces and add to your vanilla extract, or steep with your next pot of tea or coffee. Whatever you do, don't let the pods' remnant vanilla flavor go to waste.

(STEP 1) To use a vanilla bean, split it in half the long way.

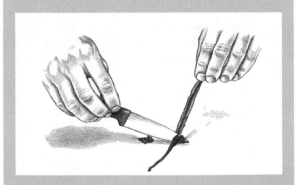

(STEP 2) Scrape out the seeds.

intensity of flavor. It can be made with just two to three ingredients at a minimum—like fruit purée (the base), sugar, and sometimes a bit of water. Any fruit, or vegetable for that matter, can serve as a sorbet base, as can chocolate, coffee, tea, and more. The range is wide—see "More Sorbet and Ice Milk Flavors" (page 965)—with a flavor for everyone and lots of room for experimentation.

The key to sorbets is to serve them fresh from the machine if at all possible. I'll even go so far as to suggest you let any uneaten sorbet thaw out in the fridge, then refreeze it in the ice cream maker the next day.

Granita

Granitas have one huge advantage over other frozen desserts: You don't need a machine to make them. And the unusual texture of granita makes it enormously appealing, at least once in a while. The crunchy flakes of intensely flavored ice are made by stirring and scraping a liquid as it freezes, which forms small ice crystals like a good snow cone. There's no special technique involved, and you can make granita with—literally—any flavored liquid you like.

Vanilla Ice Cream

MAKES: About 1 quart
TIME: About 30 minutes, plus time to chill and churn

You can reduce the number of yolks to four or even three and still produce quite a rich ice cream, even if it won't be the ultimate. The cornstarch alternative may surprise you, though; it's not as rich, but it's creamy, and added flavors stand out better without the presence of egg.

1 vanilla bean or 2 teaspoons vanilla extract

2 cups half-and-half, milk, or a combination

$^1/_2$ cup sugar

6 egg yolks or 2 tablespoons cornstarch

1 cup cream or more milk or half-and-half

❶ If you're using a vanilla bean, split it in half and scrape out the seeds; combine them with the half-and-half and ¼ cup of the sugar in a small saucepan. Heat, stirring occasionally, until steam rises from the half-and-half, 3 to 5 minutes; remove from the heat.

❷ Meanwhile, beat the yolks and the remaining sugar together until thick and slightly lightened in color (you can do this with a whisk or an electric mixer). If you're using cornstarch, mix it with 2 tablespoons or so cold water or milk to make a slurry.

❸ If you're using eggs, stir about ½ cup of the heated half-and-half into the yolk mixture and beat; then stir the warmed egg mixture back into the heated half-and-half and return it to the pan. For the cornstarch version, whisk the slurry into the heated half-and-half along with the remaining sugar. For both egg and cornstarch mixtures, heat, stirring constantly, until thick. The mixture is ready when it thickly coats the back of a spoon and a line drawn with your finger remains intact (see the illustration on page 949); this should take 3 to 5 minutes. If you're using cornstarch, strain the mixture before proceeding if you think there might be any lumps.

❹ Cool completely, then stir in the cream and freeze in an ice cream maker according to the manufacturer's directions.

10 More Simple Ideas for Ice Cream

1. Swirl in lukewarm Chocolate Sauce (page 921), any Caramel Sauce (page 922), Butterscotch Sauce (page 922), any fruit purée (see page 923), or Coffee Syrup (page 921); as soon as the ice cream is out of the machine, drizzle in the sauce, stirring slowly.

2. Add spices, like ground cinnamon, cardamom, or ginger, in place of the vanilla. Start with 1 teaspoon, taste before freezing, and add more if necessary.

3. Steep lavender, verbena, mint, or other herbs or Earl Grey tea in the hot half-and-half in place of the vanilla bean in Step 1.

4. Add any nut butter, about ¼ cup per batch, stirred in before freezing (the churning will distribute it evenly).

5. Replace the vanilla with almond extract, especially for nut ice creams.

6. Replace the vanilla with peppermint extract.

7. Add up to ¾ cup chopped toasted nuts, like almonds, walnuts, hazelnuts, pecans, peanuts, and/or macadamias, stirred in at any point.

8. Add ½ cup or more chopped, minced, or crushed candy—chocolate-covered espresso beans, Peanut Brittle (page 969), Caramels (page 969) peppermint candy, Mounds bars, Heath bars, crystallized ginger, or candied citrus peel, for example—to the mixture before freezing. Substitute almond or peppermint extract for the vanilla if appropriate.

9. Add ½ cup or more crumbled Oreos, brownies, gingersnaps, or other cookies to the mixture just before freezing.

10. Stir in up to ¾ cup chopped fresh or cooked fruit—anything from raspberries, cherries, or mango to sautéed apples or poached pears.

 Fast   Make Ahead   Vegetarian

MORE ICE CREAM FLAVORS

The base ratio always remains the same: 6 yolks—or 2 tablespoons cornstarch—with 3 cups total liquid; only the type of liquid, the flavorings (substituted for the vanilla), and the sweetener change.

VARIATION	FLAVORING(S)	LIQUID	SWEETENER
Chocolate Ice Cream	5 ounces bittersweet or semisweet chocolate, chopped (melted into the hot half-and-half)	2 cups half-and-half or milk; 1 cup cream	1/2 cup sugar
Strawberry (or Any Berry) Ice Cream	1 cup berry purée, strained (see page 923) and stirred in in Step 4	2 cups half-and-half or milk	1/2 cup sugar
Coffee Ice Cream	2 to 3 shots freshly brewed espresso or 1/2 cup ground coffee (steeped in hot half-and-half for 20 minutes; see previous page)	2 cups half-and-half or milk; 1 cup cream	1/2 cup sugar
Coconut Ice Cream	1/2 cup shredded coconut, toasted in a dry skillet until lightly browned if you like	2 cups half-and-half or nondairy or dairy milk; 1 cup coconut milk (to make your own, see page 389)	1/2 cup sugar
Spice Ice Cream	1/2 teaspoon each ground cinnamon, mace, freshly grated nutmeg, freshly ground black pepper, coriander, and 2 vanilla beans (steeped as directed); or use 1 tablespoon single spice, like cinnamon or cardamom	2 cups half-and-half or milk; 1 cup cream	1/2 cup sugar
Pumpkin Ice Cream	1 cup canned or cooked fresh pumpkin purée; 1/2 teaspoon each ground cinnamon and ginger	2 cups half-and-half or milk; 1 cup cream	1/2 cup sugar
Rum-Raisin Ice Cream	1/2 to 3/4 cup raisins; 1/4 cup dark rum (added to hot half-and-half)	2 cups half-and-half or milk; 1 cup cream	1/2 cup packed light brown sugar
Maple-Nut Ice Cream	1 cup chopped lightly toasted nuts	2 cups half-and-half or milk; 1 cup cream	3/4 cup maple syrup
Buttermilk Ice Cream	None	2 cups half-and-half or milk; 1 cup buttermilk	1/2 cup sugar
Mascarpone Ice Cream	None	2 cups half-and-half or milk; 1 cup mascarpone cheese	1/2 cup sugar
Banana Ice Cream	2 ripe bananas, peeled (steeped in hot half-and-half for 20 minutes—see previous page—then discarded)	2 cups half-and-half or milk; 1 cup cream	1/2 cup sugar
Ginger Ice Cream	2 tablespoons chopped fresh ginger (steeped in hot half-and-half; see previous page); 1/2 cup minced crystallized ginger	2 cups half-and-half or milk; 1 cup cream	1/2 cup sugar
Green Tea Ice Cream	1 tablespoon macha green tea (or infuse the liquid with leaf green tea (see previous page)	2 cups half-and-half or milk; 1 cup cream	1/2 cup sugar

12 Things to Put on Top of Ice Cream

1. Chopped Caramelized Spiced Nuts (page 81) or just toasted nuts (see page 317)
2. Whipped Cream (page 882)
3. Hot Fudge or Chocolate Sauce (page 921)
4. Coffee Syrup (page 921) or room-temperature espresso
5. Butterscotch Sauce (page 922)
6. Any Caramel Sauce (page 922)
7. Fruit Sauce, Two Ways (page 924) or fruit purée (see page 923)
8. Crushed Peanut Brittle (page 969)
9. Crumbled cookies, brownies, or cake
10. Toasted coconut
11. Fresh fruit
12. Any cooked fruit or fruit compote

Soft-Fruit Sorbet

MAKES: About 3 cups

TIME: 20 minutes, plus time to churn and chill

Berries, mangoes, peaches, apricots—you get the idea—are all excellent candidates for this simple sorbet. Use this recipe as a base for making any kind of sorbet you can think of; for more ideas, see the "More Sorbet and Ice Milk Flavors" chart that follows.

When making this, oversweeten a little, because the sweetness will be less apparent when the sorbet is frozen.

> 2½ cups ripe soft fruit, washed, stemmed, peeled, pitted, and chopped as necessary
>
> 1 cup superfine sugar or Sugar Syrup (page 921), or to taste
>
> 1 tablespoon freshly squeezed lemon juice, or to taste

1 Purée the fruit in a blender with most of the sugar or sugar syrup and the lemon juice. Taste and add more of either if necessary. If you're using mango or seedy berries, strain the purée, stirring and pressing the mixture through a sieve with a rubber spatula to leave any fibers

or seeds behind; be sure to scrape all the purée from the underside of the strainer.

2 Refrigerate until cool, then churn in an ice cream maker according to the manufacturer's directions.

Soft-Fruit Ice Milk. In terms of richness, somewhere in between sorbet and ice cream: Substitute 1 cup milk (or cream if you want it really rich) for a cup of the fruit and omit the lemon juice.

7 More Sorbet Flavors

Any of these can replace the fruit purée in Soft Fruit Sorbet.

1. Coconut milk, (to make your own, see page 389)
2. Any melon purée, mixed or alone
3. Cherry purée, fresh or frozen
4. Pomegranate juice
5. Blueberry purée (with some grated lemon zest)
6. Lychee juice
7. Kiwi purée (strained if you don't want the seeds)

10 Simple Ideas for Fruit Sorbets

1. Add 1 teaspoon or more minced citrus zest.
2. Combine fruits.
3. Add up to ¾ cup chopped or whole fresh fruit.
4. Add 1 tablespoon or more minced candied fruit or crystallized ginger.
5. Add 1 tablespoon or more flavored liqueur like amaretto, Triple Sec, and so on.
6. Add ⅛ teaspoon, or to taste, freshly ground black or pink pepper or chili powder (to make your own, see page 66).
7. Add 1 tablespoon or so fresh herb leaves, like mint, spearmint, basil, rosemary, thyme, verbena (steeped in the Sugar Syrup, page 921, or minced and added to the sorbet).
8. Use honey to sweeten instead of sugar or Sugar Syrup.
9. Add 1 teaspoon or more grated fresh ginger.
10. Add 1 teaspoon rose or orange blossom water.

 Fast   Make Ahead   Vegetarian

MORE SORBET AND ICE MILK FLAVORS

Soft-Fruit Sorbet (page 964) and its ice milk variation are the jumping-off points for these variations.

	FLAVORING(S)	LIQUID (TO REPLACE THE PURÉED FRUIT)	SWEETENER
Frozen Yogurt	³/₄ cup chopped fresh or dried fruit or 1¹/₂ teaspoons grated lemon or orange zest	1¹/₄ cups yogurt (not nonfat); ³/₄ cup milk	³/₄ cup superfine sugar or Sugar Syrup (page 921)
Orange, Tangerine, or Grapefruit Sorbet	1¹/₂ teaspoons zest; ¹/₂ teaspoon grated fresh ginger (optional)	2 cups juice	1 cup superfine sugar or Sugar Syrup (page 921)
Lemon, Lime, or Yuzu Sorbet	1¹/₂ teaspoons each grated lemon and lime zest	1 cup each freshly squeezed lemon and lime juices, or combine with yuzu juice	2 cups Sugar Syrup (page 921)
Raspberry or Strawberry-Red Wine Sorbet	1 cup raspberries or hulled strawberries	1 cup red wine (cook all ingredients for 10 minutes and strain)	1 cup Sugar Syrup (page 921)
Vanilla-Pineapple Sorbet	1 vanilla bean (steeped in hot Sugar Syrup, page 921)	2 cups pineapple purée (see page 923) or juice	1 cup superfine sugar or Sugar Syrup (page 921)
Papaya-Lime Sorbet	1¹/₂ teaspoons grated lime zest; 3 tablespoons freshly squeezed lime juice, or to taste	2 cups papaya purée (see page 923)	¹/₂ cup superfine sugar or Sugar Syrup (page 921)
Honeydew-Mint Sorbet	2 stems fresh mint (steeped in hot Sugar Syrup, page 921); 2 tablespoons finely chopped fresh mint leaves	2 cups honeydew purée (see page 923)	1 cup superfine sugar or Sugar Syrup (page 921)
Pear or Apple-Ginger Sorbet	2 tablespoons chopped fresh ginger (steeped in hot Sugar Syrup, page 921)	2 cups peeled, cored, and chopped pears or apples, puréed with lemon juice	³/₄ cup superfine sugar or Sugar Syrup (page 921)
Lime-Basil Sorbet	1 stem fresh basil (steeped in hot Sugar Syrup, page 921); 2 tablespoons finely chopped fresh basil leaves; 1¹/₂ teaspoons grated lime zest	1¹/₂ cups freshly squeezed lime juice	1¹/₂ cups Sugar Syrup (page 921)
Orange-Cassis Sorbet	2 tablespoons minced candied orange zest or 1 tablespoon orange zest	1³/₄ cups freshly squeezed orange juice; ¹/₄ cup cassis liqueur	¹/₂ cup superfine sugar or Sugar Syrup (page 921), or to taste
Chocolate or Cherry-Chocolate Sorbet	³/₄ cup unsweetened cocoa powder; 1 cup pitted and halved cherries, if you like	2 cups boiling water (mix ¹/₂ cup water with the cocoa and sugar; then add remaining ingredients)	³/₄ cup superfine sugar or Sugar Syrup (page 921)
Espresso Sorbet or Ice Milk	3 to 4 shots freshly brewed espresso; ¹/₄ crushed chocolate-covered espresso beans (optional)	2 cups water or nondairy or dairy milk or cream	1 cup superfine sugar or Sugar Syrup (page 921)

Granita

MAKES: About 3 cups
TIME: About 2 hours

Granitas are no-special-equipment-needed, minimal-effort desserts that can be made of almost any juice or other liquid imaginable. Their crunchy, icy texture makes them unusual, and they're the lightest frozen dessert you can make.

Add a splash or two of vodka or rum to this or any other granita and it becomes a frozen cocktail.

> 2 cups soft ripe fruit—cherries, berries, mangoes, melons, etc.—picked over, pitted, peeled, washed, and/or dried as necessary, or 2 cups liquid, like fruit juice, coffee, or coconut milk (to make your own, see page 389)
>
> Superfine sugar or Sugar Syrup (page 921), to taste
>
> Freshly squeezed lemon juice or grated lemon zest, to taste (optional)

1 If you're using fruit, purée it in a blender; strain if you've used mango or berries with lots of fibers or seeds. Combine all the ingredients, adding enough sugar or syrup to make a nicely sweet blend. Spike with zest if you like.

2 Pour into a shallow glass or ceramic pan and freeze for about 2 hours, stirring to break up the crystals every 30 minutes. It should be slushy and crunchy with ice crystals. If the granita becomes too hard, pulse it (do not purée) in a food processor before serving.

6 Great Granitas

Use these ingredients as your base and sweeten it as you like.

1. Pomegranate Granita: 2 cups bottled or fresh pomegranate juice, touch of lemon juice or zest (optional)
2. Orange, Tangerine, or Grapefruit Granita: $1/2$ teaspoon grated or finely minced zest, 2 cups freshly squeezed juice
3. Watermelon-Basil Granita: 2 cups chopped and seeded watermelon, $1/4$ cup fresh basil leaves; purée together and then strain
4. Green Apple–Lime Granita: 1 cored and chopped

Granny Smith apple (peeled if you like) with $1/4$ cup lime juice, $1/2$ teaspoon grated or finely minced lime zest; purée together to minimize browning
5. Red Wine Granita: $1 1/2$ cups Pinot Noir, Beaujolais, or other fruity wine, $1/2$ cup water
6. Apricot–Orange Blossom Water Granita: 2 cups pitted and chopped apricots, puréed; 1 teaspoon orange blossom water

The Basics of Dessert Soups

By no means a new concept, but one that doesn't get much attention these days. That's too bad: Dessert soups are a fantastic way to showcase ripe fruit while ending the meal on the light side. Since the fruit is the highlight, it's key to use what's in season and delicious; this is no place to compromise on quality or flavor.

Like their savory cousins, these can be either brothy, thick, or puréed; all are equally easy to make. Here are a few pointers:

- Keep the flavors simple; let the fruit or other base ingredient speak for itself.
- Make the soup no more than a day in advance, if not within a couple hours of serving; it will taste fresher.
- In most recipes, you can substitute just about any ripe and flavorful fruit for any other.
- For puréed soups, the consistency should be like that of heavy cream, neither watery nor overly thick.
- If you like, add a scoop of ice cream, sour cream, crème fraîche, yogurt, sorbet, or granita to each serving bowl; it adds another layer of flavor, texture, and temperature.

Multifruit Soup

MAKES: 4 servings
TIME: 40 minutes

This can be served as an appetizer, but most people are going to find it more appropriate at dessert. The fruit can be varied, but cherries really make the best base; leave the

 Fast   Make Ahead   Vegetarian

pits in for more flavor if you don't mind the annoyance. For wine, use Gewürztraminer or Riesling, preferably from Germany and at least slightly sweet (if the wine is *very* sweet, reduce the sugar).

    3 cups sweet cherries

    2 cups fruity white wine

    1 teaspoon minced lemon zest

    1/2 cup sugar, or to taste

    1 apple, peeled, cored, and diced

    1 pear, peeled, cored, and diced

    1 ripe peach, peeled, pitted, and diced

    2 plums, peeled, pitted, and diced

    Pinch freshly ground black pepper

    Freshly squeezed lemon juice, to taste (optional)

    Chopped fresh mint leaves for garnish (optional)

    About 1 cup sour cream for garnish (optional)

❶ Combine 2 cups of the cherries with 2 cups water in a medium saucepan; bring to a boil, then cover and adjust the heat so the mixture simmers steadily. Cook until the cherries are very soft, about 15 minutes. Cool (if you're in a hurry, put the pan in a larger pan of cold water), then force through a strainer.

❷ Return the juice to the pan and add the zest, sugar, diced fruit (including the remaining cherries), and pepper. Simmer until the diced fruit is soft, about 10 minutes, then taste and add more sugar or some lemon juice if you like. Chill and serve cold, garnished with mint and/or sour cream as desired.

Creamy Berry Soup. Good for breakfast (use yogurt), brunch, lunch, or dessert: Substitute 4 cups one or more kinds of berries, washed and hulled as needed, for the cherries and other fruits. Omit the wine, pepper, and mint. Add 1/2 teaspoon ground cinnamon and 1 cup yogurt or sour cream. Put the berries, lemon zest and juice, cinnamon, sugar, and 2 cups water in a blender; purée and then stir in the yogurt or sour cream.

Cold Cherry Soup with Mango. Whole cherries, unstrained, are used here. Serve the soup with a word of warning about the pits and a small bowl to receive them: Substi-

tute 2 cups fruity red wine, preferably Pinot Noir (Burgundy) or Gamay (Beaujolais) for the white wine, 1 peeled and diced mango for the apple, pear, peach, and plums. You may need up to a cup of sugar, depending on how sweet you like it. Omit the water, zest, and mint leaves. Combine the wine and sugar and cook until the sugar is dissolved; add the cherries and cook until tender, 8 to 10 minutes. Serve with the mango and sour cream.

Watermelon and Mint Soup

MAKES: 4 servings
TIME: 20 minutes

Light and refreshing soup, an ideal summer dessert. Cantaloupe, honeydew, and Crenshaw melons work here too, but since they aren't as watery as watermelon you'll have to press the purée more in Step 2 and may have to add a little water to the blender.

Add a splash of rum and you turn this into a cocktail you eat with a spoon.

    1/2 cup Sugar Syrup (page 921)

    4 stems fresh mint

    2 pounds ripe watermelon, rind and seeds removed
       and flesh cubed

    3 tablespoons freshly squeezed lemon or lime juice

    1 teaspoon grated lemon or lime zest

    Chopped fresh mint leaves for garnish

❶ Put the sugar syrup and mint stems in a small pot and bring to a boil; turn off the heat and steep for about 10 minutes, then discard the stems and let the mint syrup cool to room temperature.

❷ Put all but 2 cups of the cubed watermelon in a blender; add the juice and mint syrup. Purée until liquefied. Set up a fine-mesh strainer lined with a clean kitchen towel over a large bowl; strain the watermelon purée, pressing on the pulp to squeeze as much juice out as possible.

❸ Divide the watermelon soup among 4 bowls, add the watermelon cubes and zest, and garnish with the chopped mint leaves.

Sparkling Wine with Berries. Use lemon juice and zest. Substitute 3 cups mixed berries (whole or sliced as necessary) for the watermelon and add 3½ cups sparkling white wine; increase the sugar syrup to 1 cup. Skip Step 2. Proceed with the recipe. Pour the mint syrup over the fruit in the bowls, then pour on the sparkling wine.

Rhubarb-Orange Soup

MAKES: 4 servings

TIME: 15 minutes, plus time to chill

Since having this soup in England, where rhubarb is much more popular than in the United States, I can't help making this at the first sight of rhubarb in the market. Serve with Whipped Cream (page 882), sour cream, crème fraîche, or lightly sweetened yogurt if you like.

1 medium orange

2 pounds rhubarb, trimmed

1 cup sugar

1 Zest the orange and mince the zest; juice the orange. String the rhubarb (see page 283), then cut it into roughly 2-inch lengths.

2 Combine the rhubarb, sugar, 4 cups water, the orange juice, and half the zest in a saucepan and bring to a boil. (Wrap and refrigerate the remaining zest.) Turn the heat to medium and cook until the rhubarb begins to fall apart, 10 to 15 minutes.

3 Chill (if you're in a hurry, pour the mixture into a large bowl and set that bowl in an even larger bowl filled with ice water). When cool, whisk briefly to break up the rhubarb, adding the reserved zest at the same time. Serve cold, with whipped cream or any of the alternatives listed.

Cranberry-Orange Soup. Substitute 1 pound cranberries for the rhubarb. Add a whole clove and cinnamon stick if you like. Proceed with the recipe, thinning the soup with more orange juice if necessary.

The Basics of Simple Candies

Candy making can be a major challenge, but there are simple candies that are rewarding and easy. Fudge was once among the first dishes many people taught to their kids, and there are others that are equally rewarding.

If you're going to tackle candy making, even the simple kind, it's worth buying a candy thermometer, one that concentrates on the range between 230°F and 300°F, where sugar works its crystalline magic. You can judge the stage of cooked sugar by dropping a bit of it into a glass of cold water (and I've noted how to do that in individual recipes), but the thermometer is far easier and more reliable.

Bittersweet Fudge

MAKES: About 1½ pounds

TIME: About 30 minutes, plus time to rest

Like so many things, the best fudge is made with simple ingredients. Here the two that matter most are top-quality chocolate and fresh cream.

2 tablespoons unsalted butter, plus more for the pan

4 ounces unsweetened chocolate, chopped

1 cup cream

1½ cups sugar

4 tablespoons coca powder

Pinch salt

1 teaspoon vanilla extract

½ to 1 cup chopped (not minced) walnuts or pecans (optional)

1 Let the butter come to room temperature while you work; grease a 9-inch square baking pan with butter and line it with foil. Combine the chocolate and cream in a medium saucepan over low heat. Cook, stirring constantly, until well blended and smooth. Add the sugar and salt, still over low heat, and cook, stirring, until the mixture boils. Stop stirring and cook until the mixture measures 236°F

F Fast　**M** Make Ahead　**V** Vegetarian

(a small piece of it will form a soft ball when dropped into a glass of cold water, but the thermometer is an easier and surer test).

2 Immediately remove from the heat. Add the butter, but do not beat. When the mixture is just lukewarm, add the vanilla and beat vigorously with a wooden spoon until the mixture is smooth and has lost its sheen, about 5 minutes. Add the nuts if you like. Scrape into the prepared pan. When the mixture has hardened, lift the foil out of the pan, peel it off, and cut the fudge into squares. Wrap well and refrigerate; fudge keeps for weeks but is best eaten fresh.

Peanut or Other Nut Fudge. Substitute peanut or any other nut butter for the chocolate.

6 Additions to Bittersweet Fudge or Quick Ganache Truffles (page 920)

1. Any kind of roughly chopped nuts
2. Grated or finely minced orange zest
3. Chopped crystallized ginger
4. A teaspoon or two of instant espresso powder
5. Ground cinnamon or cardamom
6. Candied fruit, whole and enclosed within the truffle or minced and folded in

Caramels

MAKES: More than 1 pound
TIME: About 20 minutes, plus time to cool

Creamy and dreamy, caramels keep for weeks.

> 4 tablespoons ($^1/_2$ stick) unsalted butter, plus some for the pan
>
> $1^1/_2$ cups cream
>
> 2 cups sugar
>
> $^1/_2$ cup light corn syrup
>
> Pinch salt
>
> $1^1/_2$ teaspoons vanilla extract

1 Grease a 9-inch square baking pan. Combine all the ingredients except the vanilla in a small saucepan and turn the heat to low. Cook, stirring constantly, until the sugar dissolves, then cook, stirring only occasionally, until the mixture measures 245°F (a small piece will form a firm ball when dropped into cold water, but the thermometer is an easier and surer test).

2 Stir in the vanilla and pour into the prepared pan. When the mixture has cooled to room temperature, remove the block of caramel from the pan and use a sharp knife to cut it into small squares. Wrap each square in wax paper or plastic wrap. These keep for weeks but are best eaten fresh.

Chocolate Caramels. You can omit the butter if you like: Chop 4 ounces unsweetened chocolate. Add it along with the other ingredients and take even more care to stir almost constantly until the sugar dissolves.

Chewy Caramels. A bit of baking soda adds air bubbles that make a lighter and chewier caramel: Add 1 teaspoon baking soda; mix in thoroughly with the vanilla.

Peanut Brittle

MAKES: About 1 pound
TIME: About 20 minutes, plus time to cool

If you've never made peanut brittle, you will not believe how simple it is.

> Unsalted butter for the pan
>
> 2 cups sugar
>
> 2 cups roasted peanuts, salted or unsalted
>
> Pinch salt if you're using unsalted peanuts

1 Use the butter to grease a baking sheet, preferably one with a low rim.

2 Put the sugar and $^1/_3$ cup water in a small, deep pot over low heat. Cook, without stirring, until the sugar dissolves and starts to color. (If you like, use a brush dipped in water to wash the sugar crystals off the sides of the pot.) Keep cooking until the caramel turns golden but not dark brown, anywhere from 5 to 10 minutes.

3 Stir in the peanuts and the salt if you're using it and immediately pour the mixture onto the greased baking sheet. Cool, then break into pieces. (If you like, you can score the brittle with a knife when it has solidified slightly but not yet turned hard; that way, it will break into even squares.) Store in a covered container for as long as you like.

Popcorn Brittle. Pop about $^1/_2$ cup popcorn kernels (see page 81) and put them in a large bowl. Make the brittle and drizzle it over the popcorn while stirring to evenly coat it.

Peanut Brittle with Chocolate. Drizzle or dip the hardened brittle in any kind of melted chocolate you like.

6 Other Things to Add to Brittle

Mix and match as you like—sesame seeds with five-spice powder and macadamia with coconut are both good, for example—but keep it simple so the flavors don't muddy.

1. Any other nuts (I like salted nuts in brittle, but you can go either way): peanuts (classic, of course), almonds, walnuts, pecans, macadamia, cashews, or pistachios
2. 1 cup any seeds: white and/or black sesame seeds, pumpkin seeds, sunflower seeds, or poppy seeds
3. 2 cups shredded coconut
4. 2 cups chopped dried fruit: raisins, dates, cherries, pineapple, or apricots
5. 1 to 2 teaspoons ground or crushed spices: cinnamon, five-spice, allspice, nutmeg, cardamom, or black or pink peppercorns
6. $^1/_4$ to $^1/_2$ cup crushed espresso beans

Caramel Walnut Bars

MAKES: About a dozen squares
TIME: About 1 hour

M **V**

A baked crust topped with walnuts coated in a rich and buttery caramel; it's simultaneously crunchy, chewy, and soft—not to mention completely delicious. Any type of nuts will work here.

$^1/_2$ pound (2 sticks) unsalted butter, softened, plus some for the pan

1$^1/_4$ cups sugar

1 cup all-purpose flour

$^1/_2$ cup cream

Pinch salt

$^1/_4$ cup honey

1 cups roughly chopped walnuts

1 Heat the oven to 350°F. Grease an 8- or 9-inch square baking pan.

2 Use an electric mixer to cream 1 stick of the butter with $^1/_4$ cup of the sugar. Stir in the flour. This mixture will be quite dry; press into the greased pan and bake for 15 minutes, no longer. Remove from the oven and cool slightly.

3 Put the remaining cup of sugar and 1 tablespoon water in a saucepan over medium-high heat and cook until it melts and turns a light brown color, 5 to 8 minutes.

4 Carefully stir in the remaining butter, the cream, and the salt; stir until the mixture is combined, then add the honey and walnuts. Immediately pour the walnut mixture over the baked crust and refrigerate until set. Cut into squares or rectangles and serve. Store, covered, for up to 5 days.

Chocolate-Cherry Walnut Bars. Add 2 ounces chopped bittersweet or semisweet chocolate. Omit the honey. Add 1 cup dried cherries. Stir in the chocolate and cherries with the nuts in Step 4.

Apricot and Almond Bars. Substitute apricot jam for the honey and blanched almonds for the walnuts. Add 1 cup chopped dried apricots; add with the nuts in Step 4.

Menus

Breakfast and Brunch

Super-Fast Weekday Eggs
Eggs in the Nest or Eggs in the Hole 792
Orange or grapefruit juice
Coffee or tea

Summer Weekend Breakfast
Overnight Waffles (816) Buckwheat
    Crêpes 818
Sautéed or roasted bacon 766
Mary Willoughby's Broiled Peaches 399
Whipped Cream 882
Champagne

Winter Weekend Breakfast
Eggs Benedict, Unleashed 799
Crisp Panfried Potatoes (Home Fries)
    341
Citrus Salsa 34
Hot chocolate or coffee (spiked or not)

Make-Ahead Weekend Brunch
Tomato and Cheese Frittata 804
Rice Salad with Pesto 218
Roasted Cauliflower with Roasted Red Peppers
    and Balsamic Vinegar 280
Scones (845) with butter and jam
Bloody Marys
Coffee or tea

Blowout Brunch Buffet
Shrimp Cocktail 87

Grilled or Broiled Mushroom and Bacon Skewers
    113
Baked Eggs with Spinach 799
Cream-Braised Potatoes 343
Baked Apples 385
Fruit-and-Nut or Vegetable-and-Nut Bread
    843
Cream cheese and whipped butter
Mimosas and lemonade
Coffee or tea

Lunch

Mediterranean Lunch
Roasted Eggplant and Tomato Salad 211
The Simplest and Best Shrimp Dish 573
Crusty bread
Chocolate-Hazelnut Biscotti 899
Iced espresso

Quick Vegetarian Lunch
Simple Radish or Jícama Salad 205
Couscous with Broccoli and Walnuts 480
Chocolate Tofu Pudding 956
Salted limeade

Quick Pasta Lunch
Macaroni with Prosciutto, Tomatoes, and Whole
    Garlic Cloves 514
Balsamic Strawberries with Arugula 214
Sparkling water with orange wedges

Wrapped-in-Wax-Paper Sack Lunch
Egg Salad with Mayo on pumpernickel
    or in pita pockets 162
Asparagus Done Simply 258
Roasted Nuts with Oil or Butter 80
Canned soda or sparkling water

Packed-in-Containers Sack Lunch
Chicken Salad with Olive Oil and Fresh Herbs
    222
Puréed Vegetable Soup Without Cream (125)
    in a thermos or microwave-safe container
Quick Whole Wheat and Molasses Bread 841
Butterscotch Pudding 950
Teabags for herb tea

Last-Minute Picnic in the Park
Tuna Salad with Lemon and Olive Oil wrapped in
    lavash bread or a large tortilla 162
Carrot Salad with Cumin 188
Sour Cream or Yogurt Dip, Five Ways,
    with crackers or chips 89
Macerated Fruit 379
Ice water with a squeeze of grapefruit or a bottle of wine

Old-Fashioned Picnic Basket, Updated
Chili-Spiced Fried Chicken 665
Herb-Stuffed Eggs 85
Grilled Potato Salad 189
Spicy No-Mayo Coleslaw 206
Corn and Tomato Relish 50
Bacon Corn Bread 831
Chocolate–Chocolate Chunk Cookies 880
Pink lemonade and bottles of cold beer

Luxurious Weekend Lunch
Tomato Soup or Wintertime Tomato Soup 130
Salmon Roasted in Butter 583
Vegetable Gratin (made with spinach
    or other greens; see the chart on page 248)
Jim Lahey's No-Work Bread 833
Chocolate-Caramel Tart 940
Chilled rosé wine

All-Salad Lunch Buffet
Shaved Artichoke Salad 207
Potato Salad with Mustard Vinaigrette 189

Warm Spicy Greens with Bacon and Eggs 205
Watermelon and Tomato Salad 214
Crab Salad 225
Crackers 848
Iced peppermint tea or crisp white wine

Dinner

Weekday Mexican-Style Spread
Fish Tacos, Four Ways 163
Real Refried Beans 418
Mexican Cheese Salsa 24
Crunchy Corn Guacamole 95
Vanilla Ice Cream (961), with Chocolate Sauce (921),
    sprinkled with cinnamon

Weekday Italian Supper
Bok Choy, Mediterranean Style, served like salad, at
    room temperature 265
Penne with Tomato-Shrimp Sauce 528
Real Croutons 877
Pomegranate Granita 966
Fruity white wine

Japanese-Style Supper
Green salad with Miso Carrot Sauce with Ginger
    40
Cold Soba Noodles with Dipping Sauce 553
Cucumber slices
Miso Grilled or Broiled Boneless Chicken 643
Poached Pears with Asian Spices 401
Iced green tea, sake, or cold beer

The Fastest Soup and Salad Supper Ever
Tomato-Garlic Soup 131
Bean Salad (215), with crumbled cooked sausage added
    and served over greens if you like
Broiled Grapefruit 392
Fruity red wine

Quick Wintry Night Supper
Real Beef Stroganoff 793
Oven-Braised Celery 283
Warm, Soft Chocolate Cake 881
Hot tea or hearty ale

Weekend Chinese-Style Feast
(that's surprisingly easy)
Wonton Soup (using variation for
   Vegetarian Wontons) 127
Sesame Spareribs 762
Stir-Fried Asparagus 259
Cherry Tomato Salad with Soy Sauce over mixed salad
   greens 187
Roasted Scallions, Asian Style 327
White Rice 458 or Brown Rice 457
Butter-Almond Cake 913
Jasmine tea

Summer Indian-Style Buffet
Indian-Style Split Pea Fritters 100
Dry-Pan Eggplant 294
Tandoori Chicken 694
Chile-Rubbed Grilled Watermelon Steak 397
Curried Stir-Fried Potatoes 344
Raw Onion Chutney 36
Raita 24
Cilantro-Mint Chutney 34
Coconut Ice Cream 963
Semisweet white wine and iced mint tea

Celebrations
Holiday Brunch
Gravlax 585
The Best Scrambled Eggs 797
Potato Rösti 345
Cranberry Relish with Orange and Ginger 36
Black Bread (869), thinly sliced
Refrigerator (or Rolled) Cookies 895
Warm apple cider
Champagne
Coffee and tea

Weekday Hors d'Oeuvres
Caramelized Spiced Nuts 81
Marinated Olives 82
Cheese Straws 88
Mushroom-Egg Spread (96), on Real Croutons 877
Prosciutto and Melon 112–113
Fruity wines and sparkling water with fresh citrus

Pan-Asian Hors d'Oeuvres
Marinated Celery and Carrots, Chinese Style
   85
Edamame in Their Shells (83), sprinkled
   with toasted sesame seeds
Vietnamese Summer Rolls (107), cut into halves
   or quarters
Spicy Peanut Chicken Wings 116
Tempura 101 and Fried Rice Balls (111) with Teriyaki
   Sauce 55
Seafood and Vegetable Pancake, Korean Style (377),
   with Basil-Soy Dipping Sauce 38
Chilled sake, crisp white wine, vodka cocktails, and
   iced green tea

New Year's Eve Formal Dinner
Bruschetta (83), topped with Seafood Salad,
   Mediterranean Style 226
Lobster Bisque 146
Prime Rib Roast for a Small Crowd 734
Popovers 847
Braised and Glazed Brussels Sprouts 270
Mashed Sweet Potato Brûlée 359
Greens with Fruit, Cheese, and Nuts 203
Mocha Mousse 952
Champagne and assorted white and red wines

All-Dessert Buffet
Mexican Wedding Cookies 796
Coconut Macaroons 902
Chocolate Dessert Cups (903) filled with
   Earl Grey Pudding 950
Polenta Pound Cake (907) with Orange Glaze
   919
Chocolate Angel Food Cake 912, with Chocolate
   Glaze 921
Fresh Strawberry Tart with Pastry Cream (939)
   or Tarte Tatin 940
Baklava 948
Caramels 969
Champagne and cordials
Coffee and tea

The **102** Essential Recipes in This Book

HERE'S A LIST OF WHAT I CONSIDER ESSENTIAL RECIPES. THEY APPEAR at the beginning of each chapter, and really make up a kind of basic mini-cookbook on their own.

1. Five-Minute Drizzle Sauce 22
2. Fresh Tomato or Fruit Salsa 23
3. Simplest Yogurt Sauce 24
4. Soy Dipping Sauce and Marinade 25
5. Roasted Nuts with Oil or Butter 80
6. Caramelized Spiced Nuts 81
7. Real Popcorn 81
8. Marinated Olives 82
9. Marinated Mozzarella 83
10. Edamame in Their Shells 83
11. Bruschetta and Crostini 83
12. "Boiled Water" 123
13. Chunky Vegetable Soup 123
14. Puréed Vegetable Soup Without Cream 125
15. Noodle Soup 126
16. Chicken Soup, Many Ways 128
17. Tuna Salad with Lemon and Olive Oil 162
18. Welsh Rarebit 162
19. Fish Tacos, Four Ways 163
20. Clayuda 164
21. Rosemary Focaccia 164
22. Simple Green Salad 186
23. Tomato, Mozzarella, and Basil Salad 187
24. Cherry Tomato Salad with Soy Sauce 187
25. Carrot Salad with Cumin 188
26. Cold Cooked Greens, Greek Style 188
27. Potato Salad with Mustard Vinaigrette 189
28. Mixed Fruit Salad 190
29. Just-Tender Boiled or Steamed Vegetables 239
30. Precooked Vegetables in Butter or Oil 240
31. Roasted Vegetables (or Fruits) 241
32. Puréed Vegetables 241
33. Puréed Vegetables 242
34. Breaded Fried Eggplant (or Any Other Vegetable) 245
35. Battered and Fried Vegetables 247
36. Vegetable Gratin 248
37. Grilled Vegetables 249
38. Cooked Beans, the Quick-Soak Way 411
39. White Bean Purée 413
40. Beans and Tomatoes 414
41. Lentils and Potatoes with Curry 415
42. Roasted Chickpeas 416
43. Baked Beans 416
44. Stir-Fried Tofu with Scallions 417
45. Cooking Grains, the Easy Way 451
46. Cooked Grains with Butter or Oil 452
47. Simpler-than-Pilaf Baked Rice 453
48. Simplest Fried Rice 453

My Top **100** Fast Recipes

THERE ARE 453 RECIPES IN *HOW TO COOK EVERYTHING* THAT YOU CAN

make in 30 minutes or less. The ones on this list are key—they provide the building blocks of fast cooking. And they're good: Work your way through this list and you'll always be able to get something delicious on the table quickly.

1. Five-Minute Drizzle Sauce 22
2. Fresh Tomato or Fruit Salsa 23
3. Simplest Yogurt Sauce 24
4. Soy Dipping Sauce and Marinade 25
5. Traditional Pesto 27
6. Parsley (or Other Herb) Purée 27
7. Homemade Mayonnaise 41
8. Simple Pan Sauce 45
9. Brown Butter 56
10. Chili Powder 66
11. Fragrant Curry Powder 67
12. Roasted Nuts with Oil or Butter 80
13. Real Popcorn 81
14. Marinated Olives 82
15. Marinated Mozzarella 83
16. Edamame in Their Shells 83
17. Bruschetta and Crostini 83
18. Shrimp Cocktail 87
19. Sour Cream or Yogurt Dip, Five Ways 89
20. Hummus 93
21. Guacamole 94
22. Tapenade 96
23. Cheese Quesadillas 109
24. "Boiled Water" 123
25. Chicken Soup, Many Ways 128

26. Tomato Soup 130
27. Smoky Black Bean Soup 137
28. Fast Avocado Soup 153
29. Gazpacho, Fast and Simple 154
30. Tuna Salad with Lemon and Olive Oil 162
31. Welsh Rarebit 162
32. Simple Green Salad 186
33. Vinaigrette 199
34. Chopped Salad, Five Ways 204
35. Grilled Beef Salad with Mint 223
36. Just-Tender Boiled or Steamed Vegetables 239
37. Stir-Fried Vegetables 241
38. Breaded Sautéed Broccoli or Cauliflower 268
39. Braised and Glazed Brussels Sprouts 270
40. Quick-Glazed Carrots 277
41. Corn on the Cob, Grilled or Roasted 289
42. Grilled or Broiled Eggplant 294
43. Escarole Braised in Olive Oil 300
44. Twice-Fried Green Beans 306
45. Sautéed Mushrooms 313
46. Caramelized Onions 325
47. Anything-Scented Peas 329

My Top **100** Make-Ahead Recipes

IN MY BOOK (WHICH THIS IS, AFTER ALL) "MAKE-AHEAD" MEANS THAT

either the entire dish or the bulk of the work can be done in advance. Here's a list of some of the less-obvious examples, which can form the foundation for countless parties.

1. Simplest Yogurt Sauce 24
2. Flavored Oil 26
3. Parsley (or Other Herb) Purée 27
4. Compound Butter 32
5. Raw Onion Chutney 36
6. Ginger-Scallion Sauce 39
7. Real Ranch Dressing 42
8. Salsa Roja 48
9. Chile Paste, Eight Ways 74
10. Deviled or Stuffed Eggs 84
11. Marinated Celery and Carrots, Chinese Style 85
12. Marinated Vegetables 86
13. Flavorful Cream Cheese Spread 91
14. Grilled or Roasted Eggplant Dip 95
15. Stuffed Mushrooms 113
16. Meatballs, 3 Ways 114
17. Chicken Wings, Six Ways 115
18. Chunky Vegetable Soup 123
19. Corn Chowder 134
20. Basic Bean Soup 136
21. Simplest Split Pea Soup 138
22. Lentil Soup, Seven Ways 138
23. Vegetable Stock 157
24. Pizza Dough 178
25. Carrot Salad with Cumin 188
26. Potato Salad with Mustard Vinaigrette 189

27. Spicy No-Mayo Coleslaw 206
28. Bean Salad 215
29. Chicken Salad with Olive Oil and Fresh Herbs 222
30. Grilled Beef Salad with Mint 223
31. Grilled Vegetables 248
32. Asparagus Done Simply 258
33. Cabbage Braised with Onions 275
34. Basic Steamed Cauliflower 279
35. Eggplant Slices with Garlic and Parsley 297
36. Roasted Garlic 303
37. Grilled or Broiled Mushrooms 215
38. Roasted Onion Halves 327
39. Roasted Red Peppers 330
40. Oven-Roasted Potatoes 341
41. Oven-Roasted Plum Tomatoes 361
42. Whole Winter Squash, Cooked Three Ways 366
43. Applesauce 383
44. Preserved Lemons 393
45. Cooked Beans, The Quick-Soak Way 411
46. White Beans, Tuscan Style 427
47. Chickpeas in Their Own Broth 430
48. Lentils, Six Ways 431
49. Black Beans and White Rice, Spanish Style 435
50. Baked Tofu 444

My Top **100** Vegetarian Recipes

OF THE NEARLY 600 RECIPES IN THE BOOK MARKED WITH THE VEGETARIAN

icon, these are the most fundamental.

Sources

In most cases, your supermarket will provide all you need to cook and cook well. In the rare event that you need a specialty item, or if you want to experiment with more exotic ingredients, you'll most often turn to international markets, natural food stores, and gourmet grocers. More and more, people do this sort of shopping online (a virtually nonexistent marketplace when I wrote the first edition of this book), where there are literally thousands of options to explore. So here are some favorites (you'll know which ones they are), and some well-established food websites (I'm not endorsing everything here—just providing information), with contact numbers when available, organized by product categories.

For your own online foraging, try these two food shopping directories:
google.com/Top/Shopping/Food/
dmoz.org/Shopping/Food/

For everything from cookbooks to equipment to hard-to-find ingredients:

Amazon *(huge, but a good search engine)*
amazon.com

Earthy Delights *(everything from fresh produce to olive oil; especially good for mushrooms)*
earthy.com
800-367-4709

Specialty Meats and/or Cheeses

Zingerman's *(many other things too; reliable)*
zingermans.com
888-636-8162 or 734-477-6986

Niman Ranch *(naturally raised meats)*
nimanranch.com
866-808-0340

Artisanal Cheese *(more than 300 cheeses, with many ways to search)*
artisanalcheese.com
877-797-1200

D'Artagnan *(poultry, meat, game, truffles, and mushrooms)*
dartagnan.com
800-327-8246 ext. 0

Fresh Produce and Other Perishables

Melissa's *(also offers soy, tofu, and more)*
melissas.com
800-588-0151

Pantry Items

Barry Farm Foods *(an old-fashioned dry goods store with everything from flour and nuts to rice and grains)*
barryfarm.com
419-228-4640

Native Seeds *(American Southwest foods, herbs, and tea; you need to dig a bit into the site to get to the store, but it's worth it)*
nativeseeds.org
520-622-5561 or 866-622-5561

Rancho Gordo *(beans, chiles, corn; really good)*
ranchogordo.com
707-259-1935

Native Harvest *(wild rice, coffee, maple syrup; phone orders only)*
nativeharvest.com
888-274-8318

Maine Coast Sea Vegetables *(aka sea greens or seaweed)*
seaveg.com
207-565-2907

Whole Grains, Flour, and Baking Ingredients
Heartland Mill *(no frills, but excellent products)*
heartlandmill.com
800-232-8533 or 620-379-4472

King Arthur Flour
kingarthurflour.com
800-827-6836

Spices, Herbs, and Seasonings
Penzeys Spices *(extensive, high quality, and very reasonably priced selection)*
penzeys.com
800-741-7787

Saltworks *(all kinds of salt; pricey but comprehensive)*
saltworks.us
800-353-7258

International Foods
Kalustyan's *(for teas, grains, legumes, seasonings, dried fruit, and stuff in jars and cans; a New York fave)*
kalustyans.com
800-352-3451 or 212-685-3451

Sultan's Delight *(mostly Turkish and Middle Eastern ingredients)*
sultansdelight.com
800-852-5046

Equipment (and other stuff, too)
Williams-Sonoma
williams-sonoma.com
877-812-6235

Chefs *(the latest incarnation of Chef's Catalog)*
chefscatalog.com
800-338-3232

Sur La Table
surlatable.com
800-243-0852

Index

Page numbers in *italics* indicate illustrations.

Doneness Temperatures

Use an instant-read thermometer for the best possible accuracy; always measure with the probe in the thickest part of the meat, not touching any bone (ideally, measure in more than one place). When you gain experience in cooking, you'll be able to judge doneness by look and feel.

Beef
125°F = Rare
130–135°F = Medium-rare
135–140°F = Medium
140–150°F = Medium-well
155°F+ = Well-done

Pork
145°F = Medium-rare (and past the temperature
    at which most pathogens are killed)
150°F = Slightly pink but moist
160°F = Well-done (and probably dry)

Chicken
155°F = Breast is done
160°F = Thigh is done

Lamb
125°F = Very rare
130°F = Rare
135°F = Medium-rare
140°F = Medium
150°F = Medium-well
160°F+ = Well-done

USDA–Recommended Internal Temperatures

The recommended internal temperatures given in this book for meats and poultry are based on producing the best-tasting food and are in line with traditional levels of doneness. The United States Department of Agriculture (USDA), however, generally recommends higher temperatures, which reduces the potential danger of contracting illness caused by bacteria.

Beef, Veal, and Lamb
Ground meat (hamburger, etc.)
    160°F
Roasts, steaks, and chops
    145°F = Medium-rare
    160°F = Medium
    170°F = Well-done

Pork (all cuts, including ground)
    160°F = Medium
    170°F = Well-done

All Fish
    145°F

Poultry
    Ground chicken and turkey: 165°F
    Whole chicken and turkey: 165°F
    Stuffing: 165°F
    Poultry breasts: 165°F
    Poultry thighs: 165°F

Egg Dishes
    160°F